ROYAL COMMENTARIES
OF THE INCAS
And General History of Peru

PART TWO

THE TEXAS PAN-AMERICAN SERIES

ROYAL COMMENTARIES OF THE INCAS

And General History of Peru

PART TWO

by Garcilaso de la Vega, El Inca

Translated with an Introduction by
HAROLD V. LIVERMORE

UNIVERSITY·OF TEXAS PRESS, AUSTIN & LONDON

The Texas Pan-American Series is published with the assistance of a revolving publication fund established by the Pan-American Sulphur Company and other friends of Latin America in Texas. Also contributing to the cost of translating and publishing this book were the Pan American Union, the Rockefeller Foundation (through the Latin American translation program of the Association of American University Presses), and the Ford Foundation.

Standard Book Number 292–73358–5
Library of Congress Catalog Card Number 65–13518
Copyright © 1966 by the University of Texas Press
Manufactured in the United States of America
Second Printing, 1970

INTRODUCTION

Garcilaso's father's people and his mother's people remained in ignorance of one another's existence until about fifteen years before his birth. Although it is commonly said that Vasco Núñez de Balboa received news of a great empire to the south when he crossed the Isthmus of Panama in 1511, there is no real evidence of this. Balboa had ships dragged across the Isthmus and launched in the Southern Sea, but he was arrested and executed before his labors could bear fruit. It is likely that Pascual de Andagoya, who explored what is now the northwest coast of Colombia in 1522, heard rumors of great civilizations further south, but nothing concrete was known about them when the right to undertake further discoveries was acquired by a syndicate, or as Garcilaso says, a "triumvirate," consisting of two Extremaduran adventurers, Francisco Pizarro and Diego de Almagro, and a priest, Hernando de Luque, schoolmaster in Panama.

Pizarro's first expedition departed in November 1524 and in the course of the following three years certain news was obtained of the existence of a great empire. Its name was unknown, and Pizarro's enterprise was officially described as the "undertaking of the Levant." His soldiers were popularly known as the "men of Peru," from the name of a chieftain or perhaps a river in the Gulf of San Juan where the navel string of Central America is attached to the southern continent. This name became generalized with the conquest; and though quite without geographical or philological justification, it easily survived half-hearted attempts to impose the official titles of New Castile and New Toledo. The Incas themselves, if they called their empire anything, called it the Four Quarters of the Earth, Tahuantinsuyu, though they probably used the word rarely, for their world was limited to what they possessed and the still unsubdued tribes on their borders.

Having visited Spain to obtain royal confirmation of the privileges claimed by his syndicate, Pizarro finally sailed from Panama in December 1528. He was accompanied by 180 men and 27 horses, with which he proposed to conquer territory that stretched thousands of miles and was occupied by warlike peoples several millions strong. At the time of his journey to Europe Pizarro probably supposed that the center of the native kingdom of Peru was Tumipampa (Tomebamba), a city established by Huaina Cápac for the administration of his northern conquests: the Spaniards as yet knew nothing of the ancient capital at Cuzco. But even while Pizarro was pressing forward his exploration of the coast, the Inca empire had undergone a great upheaval. Huaina Cápac had left his legitimate son Huáscar to succeed him in Cuzco, and had established the bastard Atahuallpa in the kingdom of Quito. Atahuallpa had made war on and captured his half-brother, and the seat of Inca power had thus been suddenly brought half way to meet the Spaniards. Tumipampa, for which the rulers of Spain had thoughtfully appointed a municipality, had been destroyed.

Pizarro established his base at San Miguel (now Piura), but nearly two years elapsed before he could march inland to possess himself of the shaken throne of Tahuantinsuyu. He had realized from the example of Cortés what could be accomplished by seizing the person of an Indian emperor and using him to establish authority over his subjects. When therefore Atahuallpa sent messengers announcing that he would meet Pizarro at Cajamarca, the Spaniard staked everything on a single throw. The Inca was ambushed, his bodyguard slaughtered, and Atahuallpa himself captured. Pizarro had no difficulty in exacting an enormous ransom in silver and gold; but before it was paid Atahuallpa was "tried" and put to death, apparently because Indian armies were gathering to release him.

The prospect of wealth and power that now faced Pizarro could hardly fail to stir the cupidity of his rivals. In March 1534, while Pizarro was still at Cajamarca and Almagro was occupying the traditional capital of the Incas at Cuzco, the governor of Guatemala, Pedro de Alvarado, who had been one of Cortés' companions at the conquest of Mexico, raised a force of 500 men to march on Quito and take Atahuallpa's capital. But Pizarro's captains moved faster than Alvarado. Almagro, who had occupied Cuzco, moved north again, while Sebastián de Belalcázar, who had been left to guard San Miguel, marched inland and occupied Quito without waiting for instructions. He destroyed the remaining Inca armies, and was joined by Almagro at Riobamba.

Alvarado thus found himself anticipated. His intrusion was without any form of legality, and he was therefore satisfied to renounce any part in the conquest of Peru and to surrender his fleet, horses, and cannon in return for 100,000 pesos of gold. The bargain was approved by Pizarro, and Alvarado collected his fortune and departed, though most of his followers enlisted under Pizarro, who was in urgent need of reinforcements to occupy the vast realms that had fallen so rapidly into his hands. While he and his "first conquerors" gathered the booty of the Inca cities, these "second conquerors" were despatched to the remoter and less promising provinces.

One of the new followers acquired by Pizarro from Alvarado was the young captain Sebastián Garcilaso de la Vega Vargas, who had arrived in America a few years before. Like Pizarro and so many others, he was a native of Extremadura, but a member of a distinguished family descended on his father's side from Garci Pérez de Vargas, who served with St. Ferdinand and acquired glory at the conquest of Seville in 1248, and related through his mother to the dukes of Feria and more remotely, the dukes of the Infantado. He himself was in his middle thirties, and he had a younger brother in Guatemala, while a cousin, Gómez de Tordoya, came with him to Peru. His first task was to take 250 men and conquer the region of Buenaventura in Colombia. Far to the north of Quito, it offered no such prizes as Pizarro had won; but Captain Garcilaso was spared the prospect of a prolonged absence in a remote command by the revolt of Manco Cápac, which in 1536 threatened the Spanish hold not only on Cuzco, but on their own new city of Lima, founded as Ciudad de los Reyes in January 1535. To meet the emergency the Spanish contingents were called in; but by the time Garcilaso reached Lima the crisis was over, and Pizarro sent him and his cousin under Alonso de Alvarado to Cuzco.

Here, as in Lima, the great Indian rebellion was put down. But it was at once followed by the first outbreak of open strife between the Spaniards themselves. Cuzco was occupied by Pizarro's brothers Hernando and Gonzalo; but Almagro, who had just visited Chile and proved the absence of any new source of gold and silver, or any comparable Indian civilization, now maintained that the Inca capital fell within his sphere of influence and seized it from his partner's brothers, whom he arrested. News of these events reached Alvarado's expedition on the road. They continued their march intending to defend Pizarro's interests; but on meeting Almagro's army at the bridge of Abancay they were defeated on July 12, 1537, and many of them, including Captain Garcilaso, were taken prisoner and carried off to Cuzco. The struggle between the followers of Pizarro and those of Almagro continued until the following April, when in the battle of Las Salinas the forces of the now ailing and broken Almagro were finally defeated, and he himself was captured and strangled.

During the first part of their captivity Garcilaso and his cousin were in fact practically free, and they were placed in confinement only before the final battle. During this period of limited freedom and enforced leisure the captain came to know the Peruvian princess, Ñusta Chimpu Ocllo, a daughter of a younger son of the Inca Túpac Inca Yupanqui and second cousin of the last two Incas, Huáscar and Atahuallpa. She was baptized Isabel and known as Isabel Ocllo. Their son, born on April 12, 1539, was christened Gómez Suárez de Figueroa, which was also the name of his father's elder brother, of his father's grandfather and of the fourth count, later duke, of Feria, the husband of Jane Dormer. Despite these illustrious connections, the mestizo was to prefer his father's name, which was also that of the most distinguished writer of the family, the poet Garcilaso de la Vega, who had died in attacking the castle of Muey near Fréjus three years before the Inca's birth. Little is known of the life of his parents at this time. He speaks of a sister, who may or may not have been a half-sister, Francisca de Vargas, the fruit of an earlier union between Captain Garcilaso and Palla María Pilcosisa.

After the victory of Hernando Pizarro, the more troublesome conquerors were again sent off on errands of discovery, but Captain Garcilaso remained in Cuzco, except for a mission to the Collao in the company of Gonzalo Pizarro, with whom he was on friendly terms. He was rewarded by the grant of an allocation of Indians called Tapac-Ri in the district of Cochapampa. It was a fertile area well stocked with Peruvian sheep. The captain himself estimated his Indian serfs at six hundred, though they were later put at eight hundred; the annual income of the estate was between 13,000 and 21,000 pesos.

For about two years Captain Garcilaso divided his time between this estate and the town of Chuquisaca, now Sucre in Bolivia, where he was one of the two alcaldes. But in June 1541, the marquis Don Francisco Pizarro, governor, adelantado, and captain general of the kingdom of New Castile, as the illiterate soldier from Trujillo had become, was murdered in his palace at Lima. The deed revived the conflict between his followers and the Almagrists, which was in essence between those who had acquired wealth and Indian serfs in the conquest and those who were still poor soldiers or had personal grievances against the Pizarros. The Almagrists were led by a half-caste son of the strangled triumvir, born in Panama, who now assumed the governorship of Peru. The change caused consternation in Cuzco, where the city council, though consisting largely of prosperous "first conquerors," decided to accept it, apparently in order to gain time to organize resistance. In this Captain Garcilaso played a prominent part, and when the supporters of legality were gathered together they elected Pero Alvarez Holguín captain general, Gómez de Tordoya commander, and Garcilaso himself one of the two captains of horse. A second royalist army had been gathered by Alonso de Alvarado in Chachapoyas, and these two bodies were fused by Licentiate Cristóbal Vaca de Castro, who now arrived in Lima with royal powers to investigate and put an end to the civil strife of Peru. Under the command of Vaca de Castro the combined force defeated the younger Almagro at Chupas on September 16, 1542. The battle was a hard one and the dead included Pero Alvarez Holguín and Garcilaso's cousin.

Vaca de Castro now entered Cuzco, where he made a new distribution of the Indians. The *repartimientos,* or awards of Indian serfs in return for services, had been the main source of dissatisfaction, for, as the Inca tells us, everyone had exaggerated ideas of his deserts. Vaca de Castro now duly rewarded those who remained loyal, and in this new division Captain Garcilaso surrendered Tapac-Ri and received in exchange the properties of Cotanera and Huamanpallpa, and three small villages near Cuzco. But scarcely had these awards been carried into effect when Vaca de Castro received news of the appointment of a successor with the rank of viceroy who brought with him the new Ordinances inspired by Las Casas which abolished all forced labor of the Indians and severely curtailed the privileges of the conquerors.

The new viceroy, Blasco Núñez Vela, had none of Vaca de Castro's elasticity, and came determined to apply laws which could only precipitate a new period of civil strife. The abolition of the allocations affected not only the rich conquerors, but even the poor soldiers who had to sponge on their more successful companions until they might get land of their own: the news of the Ordinances therefore caused the utmost commotion in Peru. Captain Garcilaso was one of the *vecinos* or proprietors of Indians who wrote to Gonzalo Pizarro begging him to undertake the task of representing them in an approach to the viceroy to secure the rescission of the Ordinances. Though at first reluctant, Gonzalo Pizarro accepted the position of procurator general of the Spanish cities of Peru, and began to raise men. Although Gonzalo pretended that this was for a bodyguard, many who had at first supported him began to fear that they would be implicated in treason, and Captain Garcilaso set out with some twenty companions for Lima, where his party, representing the richer owners of Indians in Cuzco, proposed to place itself at the disposal of the viceroy.

But Blasco Núñez Vela had proved so heavy-handed in the application of the dreaded Ordinances and had so provoked the inhabitants of Lima by his refusal to accept petitions and by murdering in a fit of rage the royal factor, the leading citizen of the place, that the royal *audiencia*, the highest legal authority in Peru, itself placed him under arrest. When Garcilaso and his friends arrived the viceregal authority had thus been suspended.

Gonzalo Pizarro had meanwhile sent a representative to Lima to press the *audiencia* to appoint him governor, and in order to force their hand he seized some of the men who had fled from Cuzco and executed three of them. Captain Garcilaso only escaped this fate by the aid of a soldier who had been in the service of his family in Spain: he spent three months in hiding in the Dominican convent in Lima. The *audiencia* had sent the viceroy on a ship to Panama, and after some hesitation agreed to appoint Gonzalo Pizarro governor. He made his triumphal entry into his brother's capital on October 28, 1544, and duly pardoned many of the refugees from Cuzco, including Captain Garcilaso.

Meanwhile Chimpu Ocllo and her children had remained in Cuzco: Captain Garcilaso had acquired a handsome house commanding the main square of the city, which his enemies sacked and tried to burn. Here Chimpu Ocllo was left almost alone with the captain's children and their tutor Juan de Alcobaça and his family. They dared not venture into the street, and were brought maize secretly at night by one of Chimpu's relatives.

The "tyranny" of Gonzalo Pizarro reached its zenith in January 1546, when Viceroy Núñez Vela, who had been sent by the *audiencia* to Spain, but had disembarked at Túmbez and returned to Peru at the head of a small army, still doggedly determined to do his unpleasant duty, was killed in the battle of Añaquito. There was now no royal authority in Peru, for even the *audiencia* had split up; and Gonzalo Pizarro, procurator general of the cities of Peru and governor, was urged by his more radical supporters to make himself king. His artillery captain Bachicao, indeed, anticipated his master by calling himself count and awarding himself a fancy coat of arms. It was only with the arrival of a stunted little priest, Pedro de la Gasca, who had been appointed president of the *audiencia* of Lima by Charles V with the task of bringing peace and order to Peru, that the turbulent conquerors were gradually brought to heel. Gonzalo Pizarro had now to choose between openly defying the royal authority or acknowledging La Gasca and facing probable punishment. La Gasca tried to persuade him to adopt the latter course and offered a pardon. Some of Gonzalo Pizarro's followers promptly deserted, including many of those who had shown themselves most anxious that he should become governor. Others assured him that he could still be victorious, and that if he surrendered he would certainly be executed. Gonzalo Pizarro was an honest man, but he genuinely believed he had a right to govern Peru, and he was totally incapable of resisting the counsel of rogues and desperadoes. In these days Francisco de Carvajal, the aged "Demon of the Andes," makes his appearance as Pizarro's brilliant and brutal commander.

Gonzalo Pizarro's friends failed to persuade La Gasca to go away from Peru, and advised sending a mission to Spain. But while the rebel governor himself seems to have hoped confidently for royal favor, as time went on La Gasca's patience and persuasiveness and the awe inspired by the royal authority gradually had their effect. In Quito, Gonzalo's governor was killed, and the other towns declared in turn for the king. Diego Centeno emerged from hiding to raise the royal flag in Los Charcas and marched on Cuzco.

The crisis in the Inca capital was witnessed by the author of the *Royal Commentaries*. On hearing of Centeno's advance the vecinos formed two companies, one of horse and the other of foot, and many of them slept in the great square with their arms by their sides. Centeno forced his way in and beheaded Gonzalo's governor, but no sooner had he retired than the city was recovered by Juan de Acosta for the rebels; and when Acosta returned to Lima the Pizarrists were again overthrown.

The final crisis was now at hand. La Gasca arrived in Peru, and the royal fleet was off Lima. Gonzalo withdrew toward Arequipa. On the way Captain Garcilaso and two others left him, but returned to his side the following day, after which the captain was put in charge of Pizarro's bodyguard. Although he had hitherto shown himself as adroit as anyone at choosing the right side, his support of the rebel leader at this moment was by a turn of fate to overshadow the whole of his son's life. On October 20, 1547, the rebel forces faced Centeno's army at Huarina, southeast of Lake Titicaca, and though severely shaken at the outset, the skill of Francisco de Carvajal, the most seasoned strategist in Peru, saved them, and they finally won the day. Captain Garcilaso played his part in the rebel victory by lending his horse Salinillas to Gonzalo Pizarro.

This act did not pass unnoticed. Although Captain Garcilaso was able to show at a public inquiry (after Gonzalo's execution) that he had been made captain of the bodyguard as a sort of house arrest and was not allowed out of the rebel leader's sight and that the loan of the horse occurred after the battle was over, and this was enough to save him from being disqualified from holding office in Peru, a different version reached Spain; and when his son applied to the Spanish crown for some recompense for his father's service the suggestion of treason was sufficient to frustrate his claim.

While Garcilaso's father was thus with the king's enemies at Huarina, his mother had sheltered the Bishop of Cuzco and other royalist refugees. Once more the rebel leader made a triumphal entry into Cuzco, and the mestizo boy went out with a group of others to welcome his father. During the festivities that followed, Captain Garcilaso seems to have been still on friendly terms with Gonzalo: certainly the captain's son was in the governor's house almost every day and played with Gonzalo's son Hernando. Pizarro dined at the head of a great table at which a hundred guests sat down, and the little Garcilaso was present at these feasts and received food from the hands of the rebel leader himself.

But the royalist forces were now gathering, and the Inca describes how Gonzalo had long talks with Carvajal about the situation, and how the Demon of the Andes bustled about the city wearing his purple burnoose and plumed hat and riding a large ruddy mule, desperately putting his master's army in order. When the royalist forces crossed the Apurímac, the rebels left Cuzco and took up positions a little to the northwest. Pizarro's army was still formidable because of its skilled and well-equipped force of arquebusiers: a large body of Indians transported his six heavy bronze field pieces and their ammunition, and there were nearly 400 arquebusiers, 240 horse and 230 pikes, as well as Gonzalo's guard of 140 horse.

But when the two armies came face to face on April 8, 1548, at Sacsahuana, the rebel forces began to fall to pieces. One of the first to rejoin the royalists was Captain Garcilaso, who was followed by a host of others. Pizarro had no choice but to surrender. He and Carvajal were executed, and their heads were taken to Lima: others of the rebel leaders were slain in Cuzco and their heads exhibited in iron cages in the main square.

Now it was the turn of La Gasca to be received with music and the ringing of bells in the old Inca capital. As a mark of appreciation for Captain Garcilaso's prompt and timely desertion, the president watched the coursing of bulls and jousting in the great square from the captain's famous balcony.

There was now a brief lull before a further commotion interrupted the tranquility of life in Cuzco. The question of Indian serfdom that had touched off the previous disorders by disaffecting the recipients of the great Indian allocations was still in abeyance, and the redistribution of the land roused passions no less intense. Many of those who had been loyal at first had since been disloyal; some had had lands bestowed on them or taken away from them by the rebel leaders and had failed to keep them or recover them. Many advanced claims to be rewarded for their services in restoring Peru to the crown. There were so many and such conflicting interests that La Gasca could satisfy only a few; he attempted to divert the energies of some by giving them new discoveries or conquests, but this procedure was no longer so sure a remedy as in the past, for the main sources of wealth had now been discovered, and the right to raise an armed force for a new conquest was itself productive of disorders. The dissatisfied fed one another's discontent. One of these defrauded patriots was Francisco Hernández Girón, who had quarrelled with the corregidor of Cuzco about the enlistment of soldiers for the conquest of the Chunchus with which he had been entrusted; but on this occasion Captain Garcilaso was one of a group of prominent citizens who acted as mediators and a settlement was reached.

Rumors of the approaching suppression continued to cause unrest in Cuzco, but the appointment of a strong corregidor, Alonso de Alvarado, prevented an outbreak of violence: during this lull, the son of the new viceroy, Don Antonio de Mendoza, visited Cuzco and witnessed the festivities from Captain Garcilaso's balcony. But the viceroy himself died in July 1552, when he had been barely a year in office, and the news of the royal edict by which personal service of the Indians was at length suppressed caused a violent reaction in Peru. The young son of the count of La Gomera, Sebastián de Castilla, tried to murder Alvarado, but was betrayed and fled to Charcas, where the malcontents killed the corregidor and finally their own leader. Just over a year later, on November 15, 1553, there occurred the more serious rising of Francisco Hernández Girón, which is described at length in Part Two, Books Six and Seven. The little Inca himself was present at the strange scene in which Hernández Girón broke into a wedding feast sword in hand, and sent the guests, including the writer's father, scurrying across the roofs to safety.

Hernández Girón was finally cornered at Jauja and beheaded in Lima on December 7, 1554. Shortly before, Captain Garcilaso had been appointed corregidor and chief justice of Cuzco, a post he held for two years. Before his appointment he had contracted a regular marriage with Doña Luisa Martel de los Ríos, whose father was a native of Córdova: she herself was born in Panama and her sister married another prominent resident of Cuzco called Antonio de Quiñones. At about the same time the Inca's mother married Juan del Pedroche, who does not figure among the known citizens of Cuzco and may well have been a soldier or merchant. The Inca princess brought him a dowry of 1,500 silver pesos and a large flock of llamas, and it is possible that Garcilaso's father contributed toward this: both marriages probably took place before Francisco Hernández Girón's rising at the end of 1553. The young mestizo, who would have been about fourteen, remained in his father's household but frequently visited his mother.

Peace had brought prosperity to the captain. He was the owner of the two estates of Chinchapucyu, sixteen leagues from Cuzco, and Huamanpallpa further west, and had also a coca plantation at Hauisca, which was later made over to his son. Material gains may be inferred from the fact that on being deprived of the office of corregidor an accusation of embezzlement was brought against him. The viceroy, the marquis of Cañete, sent a very adverse report on him to Spain, and it was probably for this season that he sought and obtained leave to return to Europe for three years early in 1557. He never availed himself of this licence, but fell ill soon after and died in May 1559 after a long illness.

Under the existing laws the family estates would return to the crown on the death of his wife, Doña Luisa Martel de los Ríos. It is only possible to guess what were the young Garcilaso's relations with her. He never mentions her by name, though he does allude to her as his stepmother in his description of the wedding feast at which Francisco Hernández Girón began his revolution. He has however a bitter reference to women from Spain who came to marry the old conquerors for their fortunes and disported themselves with others after their husbands' deaths: "their sons will say how right they were, for from the hospitals in which they live they see the sons of others enjoying what their fathers won and what their mothers and their mothers' kinspeople helped them to win . . ."[1] In the same passage Garcilaso praises those conquerors who have married Indian women—"in those early days when the Indians saw some Indian woman give birth to a child by a Spaniard, her whole family gathered to serve and respect the Spaniard like an idol because he had become connected with them: and this was of great help in the conquest of the Indies." He is however thinking mainly of alliances between leading conquerors and Indians of noble origin. He never mentions his mother's husband, and says very little of her.

It seems probable that when he decided to go to Spain he intended both to continue his education and to claim some recompense from the Spanish crown for his father's services: we do not know whether he did this with the approval of his stepmother or not. In any case he turned the

[1] Part Two, Book Two. When he wrote this Garcilaso himself was in a hospital: but as mayordomo of the Limpísima Concepción in Córdova, not as a disinherited pauper.

coca farm at Hauisca over to his mother in exchange for a sum of ready money in gold: it was a mortgage rather than a sale, and there is no suggestion that he realized that he would never return to his native Peru.

One incident that occurred as he was about to leave Cuzco imprinted itself firmly in his mind. He went to take leave of the principal citizens in his native city, among them the corregidor, Licentiate Polo de Ondegardo, himself the author of interesting *Relations* on Peru. He took the young man into a chamber where lay five mummies of Inca rulers: they were said to be Viracocha, Tupac Inca Yupanqui (Garcilaso's great-grand-father), Huaina Cápac (his great-uncle) and the wives of the first two. Garcilaso describes the scene in his Part One and mentions that the mummies were carried round the streets to be shown to any Spanish gentlemen who expressed interest in them.

After putting in at the Azores, Garcilaso's ship arrived at Lisbon, a city of which he always retained fond memories. After his rebuffs in Madrid and his failure to obtain any recognition for his first book from Philip II, he offered his two principal works, the *Florida*, and the *Royal Commentaries* (Part One) to Dom Teodósio, Duke of Braganza, and his mother the Duchess Catarina. In the prefatory epistle addressed to the former he recalls that he was received in Lisbon as if he were a native of the city, and adds that his life was saved by a Portuguese: it is possible that his tutor, Juan (João) de Alcobaça, was of that nationality.

From Lisbon the young Peruvian sailed to Seville, which delighted him by its elegance and luxury: it must indeed have offered a striking contrast with the poverty of Cuzco in everything but gold and silver. He then visited his father's relatives in Extremadura, where he spent some months before departing for Montilla to visit his father's elder brother, Alonso de Vargas. This gentleman had followed a military career and, after serving Charles V and Philip II in various countries for thirty-eight years, had retired in 1555, marrying Doña Luisa Ponce de León, one of the daughters of Don Alonso Fernández de Argote, a *veinticuatro* of Córdova.

By a curious coincidence the young Inca's destinies were governed by two loans, both contracted without his knowledge. The first was the unfortunate offer of the horse Salinillas by his father to the rebel leader Gonzalo Pizarro: the second, more fruitful, was an advance of 2,800 ducats made by his uncle Alonso de Vargas in Brussels to his distant relative Alonso Fernández de Córdova, son of the count, now duke, of Feria, and his wife Doña Catalina Fernández de Córdova, marquesa of Priego and lady of Aguilar; in return the nobleman signed a document conferring on

Don Alonso an income from the properties of the marquisate, and in particular from the farmstead of Montalbán. When the old sergeant major died in 1570 his property was left to his widow for her lifetime, after that to be divided between his married sister and his nephew Garcilaso, who was thus assured of a small income.

But at the time of his arrival in Spain these few ducats would have seemed trifling in comparison with his expectations. His chief hope lay in the recognition of his father's services by the Spanish crown, and he soon left Montilla for Madrid, where he arrived late in 1561. During the time he spent in the capital he met many prominent Spaniards who had been in Peru or were connected with the New World. He saw Hernando Pizarro, now newly released from an imprisonment lasting more than twenty years. He met Bartolomé de las Casas, who gave him his ring to kiss and was disposed to be interested until he heard that Garcilaso was not a Mexican, but a Peruvian: it is not as the apostle of the Indians but as the fabricator of the detested Ordinances that the famous bishop of Chiapa appears in the *Commentaries*, and the Inca devotes two chapters to the insults that were heaped upon this great idealist in Peru. Garcilaso also met Vaca de Castro, the former Governor, now freed of the accusations that had been levelled against him and risen to become the senior member of the Royal Council. He saw Baltasar de Loaisa, the friar who had played a prominent part in putting down the revolt of Francisco Hernández Girón. There were others too, including the chess-playing pearl-fancier who lived in the Inca's lodgings.

Although Garcilaso's case at first seemed likely to prosper, his pretensions soon met with opposition. Don Lope García de Castro, a member of the Council of the Indies, who was later to be governor in Peru, brought up the ugly fact of the loan of Salinillas. Although the young Inca tried to explain the incident by saying that his father had been virtually under arrest, that the loan took place only after the battle, and that he had been the first to abandon Gonzalo at Sacsahuana, the Council was obdurate. It could point to the published *Historia General* of Gómara (1553) and possibly to the account of Diego Fernández of Palencia which circulated in manuscript, though it was only published in Seville in 1571: if Garcilaso disputed the facts, there were the historians to prove them. The young Inca convinced himself that the historians had been misled by wrong reports, and one of his reasons for writing the Second Part of the *Royal Commentaries* was to prove as much. Diego Fernández in particular, he was convinced wrote to flatter the Council of the Indies.

But having quoted López de Gómara, Zárate, and Fernández on his father's part in the battle of Huarina, adding that he himself had written what really happened, he concludes that it would be wrong for him to contradict three such grave authorities, "for neither shall I be believed, nor is it just that anyone should do so. I am satisfied to have told the truth . . . and if I am not believed, I shall do without, and accept the truth of what they say of my father, honoring myself as the son of such a brave and valorous man, who in so cruel a battle . . . alighted from his horse and gave it to his friend."

The Inca was profoundly affected by his rebuff. He had spent some eighteen months in pressing his claim when he left Madrid early in 1563. This was not a long time by the standards of the day. But Garcilaso emerged from the struggle utterly disillusioned. He was enormously proud and deeply sensitive; and he bitterly resented the frigid legalism of Madrid. So deep was the scar left by this experience that he says it deterred him from advancing claims even for his services in the war of Granada. He may indeed have staked an exorbitant claim, but it seems more probable that he found the court anxious to use any valid excuse for refusing to reward either Incas or conquerors of Peru.

In the spring of 1563 Garcilaso thought of returning to Peru: he was granted a royal license to do so on June 27 of that year and seems to have got as far as Seville, but no further. Whether the permission was withdrawn or whether he altered his mind is not known. In any case he seems to have lingered in Seville at this time and to have returned to the first object of his visit, the furtherance of his education. In Seville he began to perfect his Latin with Pedro Sánchez de Herrera, who like himself later resided in Córdova, and he may also now have embarked on the study of Italian. The probability that he had already decided not to return to Peru is suggested by the fact that he had his father's remains exhumed from the cathedral at Cuzco and buried in the church of San Isidro in Seville. His peculiar veneration for his father is shown by his pride in the exaggerated funeral oration he reproduces in the *Royal Commentaries*. Why he should at this moment have felt it necessary to bring his father's bones back to Spain is obscure: they were, it may be noted, not buried near the family home at Badajoz, but in a parish of Seville with which he had, so far as is known, no connection. Captain Garcilaso's family seems to have done little enough to help the young Inca's case, and his desire to have his father with him may have been the result of an intense feeling of loneliness and powerlessness against the dark forces of official-

dom. As if to emphasize his attachment to his father, he began in 1563
to use the name Gómez Suárez *de la Vega* instead of Figueroa, which he
had used hitherto: Garcilaso he adopted later.

He soon left Seville to reside with his uncle in Montilla, where he
stayed for more than a third of his life, covering the years from his twenties to fifty. He was twice absent on periods of military service, the first
time in 1564 and the second in 1570, when he took part in the campaign
against the moriscos of Granada. According to his own words, he received four commissions (*condutas*) as captain, two from Philip II and
two from Philip's half-brother Don John of Austria, who was given
nominal command of Granada in the morisco war in 1570. The Inca does
not appear in lists of the royal troops: he himself says that he served
without pay, but he describes himself in the title-page of the *Royal Commentaries* as "Captain of His Majesty." He may have served in the contingent provided by his kinsman the marquis of Priego. In the same year
his uncle Alonso de Vargas died, and Garcilaso came into his small inheritance. As a result, he gave up the soldiering life he had begun, and
retired, at the age of thirty-one, to the quiet town where he was to remain until he settled in Córdova, at fifty, for the last quarter of a century
of his life.

His life in Montilla, unlike his later years in Córdova, was relatively
untroubled. During his long residence in these "corners of solitude and
poverty" he passed his days in rural pursuits, in visiting his friends and
relatives, and in reading. It was here that he began to collect his excellent
library of works of Italian literature, history, Americana, and other books.
"I long ago lost faith in aspirations and despaired of hopes because of the
inconsistency of my fate," he declares in the preface to his *History of
Florida,*

examining my lot dispassionately, I ought to be very grateful to Fortune for
having treated me so ill, for had she shared her wealth and her favors with
me, perhaps I would have gone down other roads and paths that would have
led me to worse precipices or destroyed me altogether on that great sea with
its waves and storms as almost always it is accustomed to destroy those whom
it has favored and elevated to the lofty positions of the world. But since I have
experienced the disfavors and persecutions of fortune I have been forced to
retire from this world and to conceal myself in the haven and shelter of the
disillusioned, which are corners of solitude and poverty. Here, consoled and
content with the paucity of my scanty possessions, I live a quiet and peaceful
life (thanks to the King of Kings and Lord of Lords) more envied by the
rich than envious of them.

In this serene existence, to avoid idleness more wearisome than labor and to obtain greater peace of mind than wealth can bring, I have engaged in other projects and ambitions, for instance translating the three *Dialogues of Love* by León Hebreo. After publishing these translations I occupied myself with writing this present history, and with the same pleasure I am fabricating, forging, and polishing a history of Peru . . .

Even in Montilla he was not altogether without news of Peru. One of his visitors was Juan Arias Maldonado, the mestizo son of Diego de Maldonado known as "the rich" who figures prominently in the *Royal Commentaries*. He had been sent away from Peru by Garcilaso's enemy Lope García de Castro for political reasons, and the Inca twice received him at Montilla, and presented him with a horse and linen when he married in Madrid. But there were other friends conveniently near with whom he could discuss American affairs. The chief of these was Gonzalo Silvestre, who had been present at the campaign against Gonzalo Pizarro and had apparently struck the blow that wounded the rebel leader's horse and made it necessary for him to borrow the ill-starred Salinillas. As early as 1567 Garcilaso had thought of taking down Silvestre's account of the conquest of Florida, intending to serve as amanuensis and editor. But nothing was done, partly because of the distance separating the two men and partly because of Garcilaso's absences in Granada and elsewhere. His travels included visits to his father's family at Badajoz, and in 1579 he was in Seville, where he saw the great pearl brought from Panama by Diego de Témez.

He was now more than forty and had published nothing. In his retreat at Montilla, and surrounded by his library of Italian literature, he embarked on his translation of the three *Dialoghi d'amore* of León Hebreo. He had probably worked on them for several years before finally dedicating them to Philip II on January 19, 1586. He had now assumed the name by which he was to be known in future, signing his dedication Garcilaso Inca de la Vega. His desire to model himself on his distant kinsman the poet and soldier who adopted the motto of "with the sword and with the pen" is underlined in the epistle to Philip II in which the Inca says who he is, recalling the military services of his father, uncles, and himself, and states his intention of offering the first-fruits of his labors in a different field.

In addition to his wish to emulate the great poet whose name he had taken, his adoption of the career of letters permitted him to approach the crown by a different channel from the Council of the Indies. The opportunity to address Phillip II arose from an expression of interest in his

work by Don Maximilian of Austria, abbot of Alcalá la Real and a
member of the Royal Council of Castile, who had heard of him through
his chaplain, a friend of a member of the cathedral chapter in Córdova.
During the delay while Maximilian was reading the manuscript and it
was being submitted to the censorship for approval, Garcilaso addressed
a second letter to the monarch in which he underlined his desire to show
the capacities of a native of Peru, adding that anything that might be
done for him would be done on behalf of all the natives of that empire,
Indians and Spaniards alike, each of whom would take the work as his
own. However this dedication seems to have had little effect when the
work was published after long delays early in 1590.

But the tranquility Garcilaso had enjoyed in Montilla vanished in
about 1590. The cause of his departure is not certainly known, but it may
have been connected with the death of the old marquis of Priego, which
occurred in 1589 and the passage of the title to a cousin, Don Pedro Fernández de Córdova. Instead of living peaceably in the Horatian tranquility described in the dedication to the *Dialogues of Love,* Garcilaso
now found himself struggling to obtain a living. During this period also
he lost two of his close friends. In one of his two surviving letters Garcilaso describes how the venerated writer Dr. Ambrosio Morales had
taken him under his wing and treated him like a father, and had been removed by death at a time when the Inca most needed his help.

At the beginning of the following year, 1592, we find the Inca residing
in Córdova. At first he had a modest house in the Barrio de Santa María.
In June he was in the Calle de las Cabezas, and in January 1594 in another house in the Alcázar Viejo. He thought of beginning a work on the
Lamentations of Job in the summer of 1594, though he seems to have
dropped the plan because economic needs forced him to leave Córdova:
in May 1595 we find him freeing a morisco slave on payment of fifty
ducats. It was only a few years later that his material circumstances began
to improve, and he lived for a time in a pleasant house in the Calle de
los Deanes, being appointed majordomo of the Hospital of the Limpia
Concepción de Nuestra Señora, or Hospital de Antón Cabrera, where he
had a residence.

It was during these difficult years that he thought of taking orders, and
he probably did so in about 1595. He also began again to seek some kind
of recognition of his own or his father's services. In 1586, twenty-five
years after his rebuff by the Council of the Indies, he had dedicated his
translation of the *Dialogues of Love* of León Hebreo to Philip II, with

an epistle which made it clear that he was still optimistic about his chance of obtaining recognition for his literary services. He joyfully offered his *Dialogues* to Philip as the literary first-fruits of the New World, reminded him of his service in the war of Granada, recalled his princely parentage on his mother's side and the deeds of his father and uncles, promised to write a history of Florida and a work on the ancient history and conquest of Peru and asked for "divine favor and that of Your Majesty." However, it took more than three years to get the book read, approved, and licenced, and on November 1589, the Inca again addressed the monarch assuring him that he sought no other reward than that Philip should read the *Dialogues,* and again promising him works on Florida and Peru.

The *Dialogues* were published in Madrid early in 1590. If Garcilaso hoped that they would result in his receiving a royal pension he was sadly disappointed, for soon after that the doctrines of León Hebreo came under the eye of the Inquisition, and no copies were allowed to be sold. Garcilaso prepared a revised and expurgated edition, and tried apparently unsuccessfully to get a licence for this new version between 1594 and 1599. His disillusionment about assistance from the court was completed by the fate of his *Florida.* Although he gave his friend Juan de Morales, doorkeeper to the Council of the Indies, power to arrange a licence in Madrid, and this was probably granted, since he later asked Morales to seek an extension, nothing came of these approaches, and the *Florida* finally appeared in Lisbon: it was not until 1604 that licences were granted, and it was published early in 1605. By this time Garcilaso had finished Part One of the *Royal Commentaries,* which bears the date March 1604 in its last chapter: he had therefore two completed but unpublished manuscripts in his hands for about a year.

Shortly before he completed the manuscript of Part One of the *Royal Commentaries,* there had arrived in Spain Don Melchor Carlos Inca, a grandson of Inca Paullu and son of the Carlos Inca who had been Garcilaso's school fellow in Cuzco. A meeting of eleven Incas held in Cuzco on March 20, 1603, had empowered him to seek favors from Philip III for the royal blood of Peru, and he brought with him the genealogical tree "painted on a vara and a half of white China taffeta" with a list of 567 names, and a request that Garcilaso should support his approach. The Inca refused to take an active part in the application because he was fully engaged on his literary labors, but he wished the Incas well in their suit, and was able to record that Don Carlos Inca had received a pension of 7,500 ducats a year. He hoped that this was a sign of further favors for his kinsmen, and when a nephew arrived from Peru, he signed a document on June 30, 1604, transferring to this young man the right to anything the crown might bestow on him. His relative was a grandson of Chimpu Ocllo and Juan del Pedroche, the son of their daughter Luisa de Herrera and Pedro Márquez Galeote, and Garcilaso refers to him either as Alonso de Vargas or as Alonso Márquez Inca de Figueroa. However, no favors were distributed among the other Incas, perhaps because Don Carlos did not press their case. He died in 1610, leaving an infant daughter who survived him only three years. In 1611 and 1614 Garcilaso confirmed the document transferring his claims to his nephew, but the monarch did not abandon his attitude of passivity.

It was only in 1608 that the beginning of the great work on Peru was printed in Lisbon, being finally licenced for sale in September of the following year. This time there was an eloquent offer of services to Dom Teodósio's mother, the duchess of Braganza, which seems to have been as little heeded as his appeals to Madrid. However, since his appointment as majordomo to the Hospital of Antón Cabrera his financial situation had improved, and he was able to purchase for himself a chapel in the Cathedral and a few years later to shoulder half of the expense of printing Part Two of the *Commentaries*. He still kept in touch with friends and admirers from Peru. In 1611 he received the retable and watches sent him from Salamanca by Feliciano, the son of Francisco Rodríguez de Villafuerte, formerly alcalde of Cuzco, a gift which he obviously treasured: and in the following year he was visited by Fray Luis Jerónimo de Orúa, future bishop of La Imperial in Chile, who had published in Lima a book on the history of the New World and another in Naples on the martyrs of Florida.

It was in September of the same year of 1612 that Garcilaso signed an agreement with the bishop of Córdova for the purchase of the chapel in which he was to be buried in the great Cathedral Mosque: the Inca undertook to pay for the flooring of the Chapel and for an iron grille, a retable, and a crucifix. Three months later he submitted the completed manuscript of Part Two of the *Royal Commentaries* to the same bishop for his approval before placing it before the censorship in Madrid. The work was quickly read and approved with a handsome eulogy by Garcilaso's friend the Jesuit Padre Francisco de Castro, and it was duly dispatched to the capital, where on January 6, 1614, Pedro de Valencia gave it the approval of the Royal Council of Castile. However, in the royal cédula which authorizes the proprietor of the manuscript to proceed with the printing there appeared one unusual proviso: the printer was not to print the "beginning and first sheet" or to deliver more than one copy to the author before submitting it for the final appraisement.

A contract between Garcilaso and a printer and bookseller of Córdova called Francisco Romero shows that arrangements were made for the production of the book in October 1614. Romero undertook to print 1,500 copies within ten months. Half the edition was to belong to the bookseller and half to the author: the latter was to receive half the proceeds from the sale of the bookseller's share and to pay the cost of the paper for his own share. A further document signed by the Inca in the following May shows that the printing was still in progress: he then entrusted Cristóbal de Burgos y Avellano, dwelling in Madrid, with the duty of appearing in his name before His Majesty and before the Royal Council of the Indies to request some remuneration for his father's deeds in America and his own military and literary services, and with the task of approaching the Inquisition for a licence to print his emended version of the *Dialogues of Love*. After this we lose sight of the *Royal Commentaries*. In April 1616 the Inca was taken ill and drew up his testament. He gave instructions that he was to be buried without pomp in the chapel of the Souls in Purgatory which he had purchased for himself. After settling pensions on his servants, one of whom, Beatriz de Vega, was the mother of his son Diego de Vargas, he left his remaining fortune for the maintenance of his chapel.[2] During the course of the last week in his life he made frequent amendments to his dispositions, providing in great detail for the appointment of executors, rewards for his six servants, the conduct of his chapel, the disposal of the burial spaces in it, and the distribution of his household goods. He died on April 23 or 24, 1616, possibly on the same day as Shakespeare (New Style) and Cervantes (Old Style).

The inventory drawn up by his executors throws a little light on his life and interests. The contents of his extensive and varied library have been examined by Sr. J. Durand. The fact that he died with six persons in his service shows that he was no longer poor. His possessions included some silverware, a gold ring with a diamond, a small scimitar (a relic perhaps of the war of Granada), an engraved helmet, a battle axe, spurs, crossbows, two arquebusses, four moulds for making shot, some agricultural implements, and five canaries in cages and two empty cages.

There is no reference to the still unpublished *Royal Commentaries* in the will or codicils, but six months after Garcilaso's death the chapter of the cathedral commissioned Licentiate Andrés Fernández de Bonilla to

[2] The Inca never refers to Diego de Vargas as his son: his will merely states that he has brought him up. Diego de Vargas entered the church.

take up the matter and authorized him to send a trustworthy person to Madrid at the cost of the Inca's estate.[3] As a result, the work was given its *tasa* on November 17, 1616. A few copies of the book appear with the date: "In Córdova, by the widow of Andrés de Barrera, 1616," but others have: "In Córdova, by the widow of Andrés de Barrera, and at her expense, 1617." Some disagreement about the financing of the publication is probably responsible for the change.

But the most striking difference between Part Two as submitted to the censor and as finally published is the change of title. What the Inca described as *"The Second Part of the Royal Commentaries of the Incas"* finally appeared as *The General History of Peru*. That this change was imposed by Madrid seems clear from a reading of the *Aprobaciones*: as we have seen, already in 1614 the crown had issued a licence on condition that the title page was not printed. The final *tasa* bears the footnote: "This book entitled *General History of Peru* with these errata corresponds to its original. Given in Madrid, November 12, 1616."[4]

[3] Torre y del Cerro, p. 243: "que el Señor Racionero licenciado Andrés de Bonilla haga se cumplan las escrituras de la compañía de la impresión de los libros de la buena memoria de Garcilasso de la Vega."

[4] A copy of Part Two in the British Museum bears the same title as the first part with only the substitution of Second for First: even the date: "At Lisbon, in the office of Pedro de Crasbeeck, 1609" is copied. There is, of course, no question of Part Two having been printed at Lisbon, or by Crasbeeck, or in 1609, and we do not know the reason for this possibly unique title page. It seems however that the authorities in Madrid had imposed a change of title on Part Two, and it is difficult to escape the conclusion that they did not wish to see the phrase *Royal Commentaries of the Incas* in print. If this is so, Garcilaso must have felt as he lay on his death-bed, unable to sign his will because his hand trembled, that his life had been spent in vain.

CONTENTS

Book Four

BOOK FIVE

BOOK SIX

BOOK SEVEN

GENERAL HISTORY *of* PERU

which treats of its discovery and of how the Spaniards conquered it; the civil wars between the Pizarros and the Almagros about the partition of the land; the risings of various
rebels and their punishment; and other particular events
that are comprised in the history.

Written by the Inca Garcilaso de la Vega, a captain in the
service of His Majesty, etc., and dedicated to the most pure
Virgin Mary, the Mother of God and Our Lady.
Córdova, 1617.

v

BOOK
ONE *of the*
SECOND
PART

*in which is seen a triumvirate formed by three Spaniards
to conquer the empire of Peru; the advantages of this
conquest; the hardships undergone in the course of the
discovery; how Pizarro was abandoned by his followers
and only thirteen men remained with him; how they
reached Túmbez; a miracle wrought there by Our Lord
God; Francisco Pizarro comes to Spain to ask for the
right of conquest; his return to Peru; the hardships of
the journey; the embassies exchanged between the
Spaniards and the Indians; the capture of Atahuallpa;
the ransom he promised; the efforts of the Spaniards to
obtain it; the death of the two Inca kings; and
their veneration for the Spaniards.*

It contains forty-one chapters.

THE CONQUEST OF PERU

CHAPTER I

Three noble Spaniards aspire to conquer Peru.

T THE close of the Ninth Book of the First Part of our *Royal Commentaries* we left the cruel King Atahuallpa full of satisfaction and pride in the conviction that he had secured the empire for himself by his bloody usurpation, and quite oblivious of the fact that these same deeds were very soon to lead to his deprivation of it at the hands of an unknown race of new-comers, the Spaniards, who arrived at the moment when he promised himself prosperity and success, removed him from his throne, and deprived him of his life and empire.

In order to tell how this came about it will be necessary to return some years back and trace the stream of these events from its source. After their discovery of the New World, the Spaniards were filled with the desire to find other new lands and others even newer; and although many of them were rich and prosperous, they were not satisfied with what they possessed or even weary of their labors and the dangers, wounds, diseases, starvation, and hard days and worse nights they had experienced by land and sea, but always set their hands to fresh conquests and made fresh efforts to immortalize their names with even greater deeds. Thus it was in the case of the conquest of Peru. There lived in Panama one Francisco Pizarro, a native of Trujillo, a member of the very noble line of the same name from that city; and Diego de Almagro, a native of Malagón according to Agustín de Zárate, though López de Gómara says that he came from Almagro, and this seems likely from the name (his lineage is not known, but his mighty and generous deeds show that it was of the noblest, for only the scion of a noble line can perform such, and the tree is known by its fruit). Both were rich and famous as a result of their exploits on other campaigns, especially Francisco Pizarro, who had been captain and lieutenant governor in the city of Urabá in 1512: he had held this office as deputy for the governor Alonso de Hojeda, and conquered and settled it himself.

He was the first Spanish captain in that province, and the great deeds he performed and many ordeals he underwent there are described succinctly by Pedro de Cieza de León, in his ch. vi, in the following words: "And after this, Governor Hojeda founded a Christian settlement in the place called Urabá where he appointed as his captain and lieutenant Francisco Pizarro, who was later governor and marquis. And Captain Pizarro will always be remembered for the hardships he suffered at the hands of the Indians of Urabá and through hunger and sickness," etc. Thus far Pedro de Cieza. He was also present at the discovery of the Southern Sea with that outstandingly famous leader, Vasco Núñez de Balboa, and at the conquest of Nombre de Dios and Panama with Governor Pedrarias de Ávila, as López de Gómara says at the end of ch. ccxv of his *History of the Indies*.

Not content with the hardships they had already suffered Francisco Pizarro and Diego de Almagro set about an even greater undertaking; and stirred by the rumors then current about Peru, these two illustrious and famous men formed a partnership or company, together with Hernando de Luque, the schoolmaster of Panama and lord of La Taboga. All three swore in public, and made a contract not to abandon the partnership whatever expense or misfortunes might befall in the proposed conquest of Peru; and any gain they might come by, they undertook to share like brothers. It was agreed that Hernando de Luque should remain in Panama to take care of their affairs and that Francisco Pizarro should lead the expedition to discover and conquer whatever lands he might reach, while Diego de Almagro came and went between them, bringing men, arms, horses, and supplies to relieve their companions on the campaign. The schoolmaster Hernando de Luque was nicknamed Hernando el Loco [the mad], the epithet being intended for all three of them, because although they were rich men who had undergone many great travails and were no longer young—all of them were over fifty—nevertheless they now set out on new and greater adventures, and so blindly that none of them knew what country they were going to, or if it was rich or poor, or what resources would be necessary to conquer it. But the good fortune of those who now flourish there called them and even drove them to venture into the unknown, especially because God took pity on those heathen people and sent them His Gospel by this means: this we shall see from the many miracles He performed on their behalf in the course of the conquest.

CHAPTER II

*The great and excellent results of the partnership
of the three Spaniards.*

THE TRIUMVIRATE formed by these three Spaniards at Panama seems
to me comparable with that established by the three Roman emperors
at Laino near Bologna. Nevertheless the aims of the two groups were so
different that it would be ridiculous to press the comparison. Whereas
the three Romans were emperors whose purpose was to divide among
themselves the whole of the world conquered by the Romans so as
to enjoy it in peace, our three Spaniards were private persons who set
themselves the task of winning an empire in the New World without
knowing how it was to be done or what the cost would be. And when we
consider the results of the two triumvirates, we see that the Romans were
three tyrants who oppressed the world, whereas the Spaniards were three
generous leaders whose deeds were such that any of them would have
made a worthy emperor. The Roman league was intended to destroy a
world, which it did; the Spanish, to enrich one, and this it did, and still
does every day, as we shall amply prove in the following chapters. The
Romans delivered their friends, relatives, and allies to their enemies and
adversaries in a spirit of revenge; the Spaniards preferred to seek death
themselves to the advantage of their fellowmen, winning new empires at
their own expense, for the benefit of friends and foes alike, since those
who have profited by the result of their labors include Christians, gentiles,
Jews, Moors, Turks, and heretics, for all of whom these realms conquered by our triumvirate pour forth their riches every year. Finally, and
most estimable of all, is the preaching of the Holy Gospel, for these
Spaniards were the first Christians who preached it in that great empire of
Peru and opened wide the gates of the Roman Catholic Church, our
mother, through which such a multitude of Christians have entered, and
still do enter—who shall count this multitude, and who shall describe the
greatness of this deed alone?

Oh, glorious name and race of the Pizarros, how much do not all the
nations of the Old World owe to you for the great riches you have
brought from the New World! And how much more do not the empires
of Peru and Mexico owe to you in return for the labors and deeds of your

two sons Hernando Cortés and Francisco Pizarro, and his brothers, Hernando, Juan, and Gonzalo Pizarro, who brought those peoples out of the infernal darkness in which they died a living death and bestowed on them the evangelical light in which they now live! Oh generation of Pizarros, may men bless you from age to age as the parents of such sons, and may fame glorify the name of Sancho Martínez de Añasco Pizarro, the father of Diego Hernández Pizarro and ancestor of all these heroes who conferred such benefits on the peoples of two worlds, bringing temporal goods to the Old and spiritual blessings to the New, whereby our triumvirate merits as much fame, honor, and glory as the Romans deserve shame, hatred, and curses, for ours shall never be sufficiently praised by the living or by those still to come, nor the Romans sufficiently cursed for their wickedness and tyranny! Referring to this the great doctor of civil and canon law, great historian of his own times, and great gentleman of Florence, Francesco Guicciardini, a worthy son of such a mother, writes in the ninth book of his noble history: "Laino, a place famous for the memory of the meeting of Mark Antony, Lepidus, and Octavian, who, under the name of a noble triumvirate, approved and established all the oppressions that were executed in Rome, and the proscriptions and sequestrations that can never be sufficiently condemned." Such are the words of this famous gentleman about that evil triumvirate. And our own triumvirate is described at length in the histories of two ministers of the empire, the chaplain Francisco López de Gómara and the treasurer Agustín de Zárate, as well as other more modern works, which we shall quote whenever occasion offers.

CHAPTER III

The shortage of coin in Spain before the conquest of Peru.

IN ORDER to prove how greatly our triumvirate enriched the whole world it is necessary for me to embark on a long digression, recalling certain passages of history that illustrate the revenues of various countries before the conquest of Peru and comparing them with their present revenues. I shall, if I may, dilate on this point, though I shall seek to be as brief as possible. The Frenchman Jean Bodin speaks at length on this matter in his book, *Of the Commonwealth* (Book VI, ch. ii). He shows how low were the revenues of states and provinces both severally and jointly before the Spaniards won Peru, and what they are at present worth. He mentions many estates that were pledged or sold for very small sums, and records how small was the pay earned by soldiers, how little the salaries paid by princes to their attendants, and how low the prices of everything: those who wish to pursue the subject will find the facts in his book. In short, he says that one who formerly received a hundred reals now has a thousand, and that property is now worth twenty times as much as formerly. He refers to the ransom that Louis IX of France paid to the Sultan of Egypt, which he says was 500,000 francs, and compares it with what Francis I paid the emperor Charles V, which he puts at 3 million. He says too that in the time of Charles VI of France in 1449 the revenues of the French crown amounted to 400,000 francs, but that in the year of the death of Charles IX in 1564 they had reached 14 million. He gives similar information about other great potentates, all of which shows clearly how much Peru has enriched the world.

But there is no need for us to seek such information from other countries, for we can find abundance of it in our own Spain, and without going many centuries back, but no further than King Ferdinand the Saint who reconquered Córdova and Seville. The *General History of Spain* written by King Alfonso the Learned (Part IV, ch. x) says that Alfonso IX, king of León, the father of King Ferdinand, made war on his son, who sent him an embassy, with a letter to the effect that, as an obedient son, he would offer no resistance, but that he desired his father to tell him wherein he was at fault so that he might make amends. Don Alfonso replied that he had not paid 10,000 maravedis he owed him and that this was the cause of the war, whereupon King Ferdinand paid the sum and the war ended. The letter of the son to his father is too long to insert here, but we can give the reply, which summarizes the whole business. It runs word for word as follows:

Then the king of León sent this reply, but not by letter. That he intended to make war on him for 10,000 maravedis that King Henry owed him for the exchange of Santibáñez de la Mota, but if he were paid this he would not make war. And King Ferdinand did not wish to be at war with his father for 10,000 maravedis, and ordered the sum to be paid him at once.

Thus far the *Crónica General*. And in the chronicle of King Ferdinand (ch. xi) we read as follows:

A short time after this, a knight who had taken the Cross to go to the Holy Land, one Ruy Díaz de los Cameros, began to commit many misdeeds. And as many complaints reached King Ferdinand about this, he summoned him to the cortes to answer in person the accusations made against him and give satisfaction for the wrongs he had done. And Ruy Díaz came to the court at Valladolid, and was very angry when he heard about the complaints made against him. And because of his own anger and the advice he was offered by certain ill-intentioned persons, he at once left the court without awaiting the king's leave. And when King Ferdinand learned that he had left thus without leave, he was very angry and deprived him of his lands in the cortes. Ruy Díaz was at first unwilling to give up his castles, but at last had to surrender them, though only in return for the sum of 14,000 gold maravedis; and when he had been paid this sum, he delivered the fortresses to the noble King Ferdinand,

etc. In ch. xvi of the same history, when the king took possession of the kingdom of León, we read as follows:

King Ferdinand still had not possession of the kingdom, though he held the greater part of it, as our history says. He left Mansilla and went to León which is the capital of the kingdom, where he was very honorably received with much joy, and there he was raised as king of León by the bishop of the city, Don Rodrigo, and all the knights and citizens, and enthroned while all the clergy solemnly sang *Te Deum laudamus*. And they were all very merry and content with their new ruler, who thenceforward was known as king of Castile and León, which two kingdoms he had inherited legitimately from his father and his mother. And the two kingdoms, after having been divided on the death of the emperor between Don Sancho, king of Castile, and Don Ferdinand, king of León, and having remained separate for some time, were now reunited in the person of this noble Don Ferdinand III. After this, Queen Teresa, the mother of Doña Sancha and Doña Dulce, the sisters of King Ferdinand, found that he was firmly entrenched and that they could not offer resistance, and they therefore sent to him and offered to come to terms, to the annoyance of some of the Castilian grandees who for their own mischievous ends desired war and confusion between Castile and León. But when the noble Queen Berenguela had heard the envoy sent by Doña Teresa, she realized how much harm might come from the resumption of strife and zealously did her best to produce an agreement between her son the king and her sisters Doña Sancha and Doña Dulce. And she persuaded her son to remain in León while she herself went to Valencia to see Queen Teresa and the infantas, to which the king agreed. And finally it was settled that the latter should leave the king in peaceful possession of the kingdom, and should desist from any claim to the kingdom of León, delivering all they still possessed to the crown without any discussion or opposition, and that King Ferdinand should give the infantas 30,000 gold maravedis a year each during their lifetime. This having been agreed, the king came to Benavente and the princesses likewise, and the terms were set out in writing and signed by both parties, and the king paid the infantas the said 30,000 maravedis, receivable from a safe and reliable source. In this fashion he possessed the kingdom of León in peace and quiet.

And ch. xxix of the same history says:

After the marriage of King Ferdinand and Doña Juana, he visited his realms and came to Toledo. While he was there, he heard how the city of Córdoba and other towns on the frontier were sorely pressed for want of supplies: this greatly disturbed him and he took 25,000 gold maravedis and sent them to Córdoba and as much again to the other towns and fortresses,

etc. These insignificant sums are given in the chronicle of St. Ferdinand: in the next chapter we shall quote the sums mentioned in the chronicles of succeeding kings.

CHAPTER IV

The proof of the small quantity of coin in those times compared with the great quantity there is now, continued.

T HE MANUSCRIPT history of King Henry II, which was in the possession of a brother of Dr. Ambrosio de Morales (the chronicler), says that the royal revenues amounted to 30,000,000 maravedis a year, or 80,000 ducats: he, it should be recalled, was king of both Castile and León. The same chronicle has other information about the royal revenues, but I shall avoid the odium of repeating them. In the chronicle of King Henry III included at the beginning of that of his son John II who acceded in 1407, there are some remarkable statements about the small quantity of money then existing in Spain, and the low pay of soldiers and low prices of all commodities. As these events are nearer the time of the conquest of Peru, we may properly copy some of the information here, at least as far as it is relevant to our argument. The title of the second chapter of this history runs: "Chapter II. The Prince's Address to the Grandees of the Realm." The prince in question was Don Ferdinand, who won

Antequera and later became king of Aragón. His address reads as follows:

Prelates, counts, barons, procurators, knights, and squires here assembled, you know that the king my brother is ill and cannot be present at these cortes and he has therefore instructed me to inform you on his behalf of his purpose in coming to this city. It is this: because the king of Granada has broken the truce with the king and has refused to restore the castle of Ayamonte and has not paid the tribute that is due, the king proposes to make war upon him and enter the kingdom of Granada in person with a great head of war; and he seeks your counsel about this. In the first place he wishes you to understand that the proposed invasion is a just war. This understood, you will give counsel on the form it should take, both as to the number of knights and men necessary to keep up his dignity and honor, and as to the artillery, munitions, and victuals that will be required, the fleet that will be needed to guard the straits, and the money that must be found for all this and for the payment of however many men are considered to be necessary for this campaign for a period of six months.

All this is in ch. ii. Those that follow deal with the rivalry between Burgos, Toledo, León, and Seville as to which city should speak first, and the replies of the procurators to the royal demand, to the effect that they should not indicate the number of men or other requirements for the war, but that the king should stipulate them, as he does in ch. x, in the following words, which we copy literally:

10,000 men at arms, 4,000 light horse, and 50,000 crossbowmen and lancers, in addition to the forces of Andalusia itself, 30 armed galleys and 50 ships, and the following artillery: six heavy lombards and a hundred smaller pieces, two machines and twelve catapults, with picks, spades, and shovels, and twelve pairs of large blacksmith's bellows, and 6,000 large shields, and oxen and carts to carry the aforesaid, and pay for six months for the soldiers. You are to study how this shall be apportioned so that the sum shall be paid within six months without causing prejudice to my realms.

This is from ch. x; what follows comes from ch. xi. (We copy these chapters as they stand, for the details they give are very significant for the point we are seeking to prove). Ch. xi says:

When the procurators considered the king's demand it seemed a very difficult thing to execute this in so short a time. They agreed to calculate the total sum that would be required and present this to the king so that he might see how best to reconcile his needs with the welfare of his realms. This calculation showed that 10,000 lances at ten maravedis a day for six months would require twenty-seven *cuentos*. 4,000 light horse at ten maravedis a day would call for seven *cuentos,* two hundred thousand maravedis. 50,000 foot at five maravedis a day would be forty-five *cuentos.* The fleet of fifty ships and thirty galleys would cost fifteen *cuentos.* The artillery, lombards, engines, and carts, might reach six *cuentos.* This would amount to a hundred *cuentos,* two hundred thousand maravedis. Having seen this total, the procurators agreed that it could not be provided, and that the realms could not find means of raising so large a sum in so short a time. And they besought the prince to beseech the king to draw for part on his sales-tax [*alcabalas*] and consumption duties [*almoxarifazgo*] and other revenues, which would amount to over sixty *cuentos,* and for the rest on the treasure he had at Segovia, after which the kingdom would supply any difference,

etc. I do not include the whole of ch. xi as it would be too long and ir-relevant to my purpose, but the following chapter, xii, shows that the king decided that his realms should supply him with forty-five *cuentos* toward the cost of the war against Granada, and this was agreed and paid.

In the testament of the same king, Henry III, we read of various be-quests including two in particular, the first that seven chaplains should be established in the cathedral of Toledo, for which he assigns 10,500 mara-vedis rent, with 1,500 for each chaplaincy. He next bids the celebration of twelve anniversaries, one each month, in the said cathedral: for each of these he bequeaths 200 maravedis, which are to be divided among the members of the chapter who are present at each anniversary.

Further down (in ch. cviii) we read that when the infante Don Ferdi-nand was hard pressed in the siege of Antequera, he sent to his sister-in-law Queen Catherine to ask for money: she took six *cuentos* from the treasury of her son the king, with which the infante was able to complete the conquest of Antequera. Coming nearer our own times, we find that the Catholic monarchs, Ferdinand and Isabella, assessed the expense of their royal table at 12,000 ducats a year when they were rulers of Castile, León, Aragón, Navarre, Sicily, etc. And lest our chapter grow too long and wearisome, we shall here divide it into two parts, still continuing the tenor of our argument.

CHAPTER V

The cost of the New World to the kings of Castile.

COMING now to the last part of our argument, the main point of which is to establish how little money there was in Spain before the conquest of my country, we shall show the small cost not only of the great and wealthy empire of Peru but of the whole of the New World, hitherto unknown: this is in ch. xv of the *General History of the Indies* of Francisco López de Gómara which contains some notable things. For this reason I shall briefly include part of them here in summary, to avoid excessive length, but reproducing the most relevant parts word for word. Our author describes the great Christopher Columbus' unsuccessful negotiations with Henry VII of England for the discovery of the Indies, followed by those with Afonso V of Portugal; the duke of Medina Sidonia, Don Enrique de Guzmán; and the duke of Medinaceli, Don Luis de la Cerda; and tells how a Franciscan friar of La Rábida, Fray Juan Pérez de Marchena, the cosmographer and humanist, encouraged him to go to the court of Ferdinand and Isabella. Thus far we have given a summary: we now quote in full:

for they would be glad of his information, and he wrote to Fray Hernando de Talavera, the queen's confessor. In this way Christopher Columbus entered the court of Castile in 1486. He presented a petition about his desire and his business to the Catholic monarchs, Ferdinand and Isabella, but they paid little heed to it, for their minds were occupied with the expulsion of the Moors from the kingdom of Granada. He spoke with those who were said to have great influence with the king and queen in affairs, but as he was a foreigner and poorly clad, with no introduction but that of a Franciscan friar, he was neither heeded nor believed, which caused him great anguish of mind. Only Alonso de Quintanilla, the treasurer, fed him at his table and readily listened to his promises of the discovery of unknown lands, thus preventing him from losing hope of negotiating some day with the Catholic monarchs themselves. Through Alonso de Quintanilla therefore Columbus gained access to and audience of the cardinal-archbishop of Toledo, Don Pero González de Mendoza, whose prestige and authority with the king and queen were extremely great. He carefully listened to Columbus and examined him, and took him before them. Thus they heard him and read his memoranda, and though they at first considered him an impostor and his promises false, they held out hopes of satisfying him when they had concluded the war of Granada in which they were engaged. This prospect caused Columbus to raise his ambitions much beyond what he had hitherto hoped, and the courtiers who had until now mocked him to lend him an appreciative ear. He lost no opportunity to press on with his business, and advanced so far that when Granada fell he was given what he had asked for: the opportunity to discover his new lands and bring back gold, silver, stones, spices, and other precious things. Ferdinand and Isabella also awarded him a tenth of all the lands he might discover and annex, without prejudice to the claims of the king of Portugal, as he himself undertook to do. The terms of the agreement were settled at Santa Fe, and the royal grant was approved in Granada on April 30 after the conquest of the city. And as Ferdinand and Isabella had no funds to pay Columbus, their exchequer clerk, Luis de Santángel, lent them six *cuentos,* or in larger units 16,000 ducats. Two points emerge from this: one, that so small a capital sufficed to add the great revenues of the Indies to the crown of Castile; and the other, that the conclusion of the reconquest from the Moors, which had lasted more than eight hundred years, led to the opening of the conquest of the Indies, so that the Spaniards might continue their struggle against the infidels and enemies of the holy faith of Jesus Christ.

Thus far López de Gómara, who here concludes the aforementioned chapter. So that Columbus' persistence during seven or eight years, and the 16,000 ducats lent by Santángel have enriched Spain and the whole of the Old World to the extent at present seen. And as we have said enough to prove our point as regards royal wealth, we may now descend to questions of common or private wealth so that our proofs may be complete from both points of view.

CHAPTER VI

The value of common things before the conquest of Peru.

WITH REGARD to common things we shall refer to only three in particular, which shall suffice as testimony in the case we are establishing. I shall not go further so as to avoid the prolixity that would result from the innumerable instances of this kind that could be brought forward. The first testimony shall be a pasture that is now one of the best entailed properties in Extremadura. It is in the city of Trujillo and is worth more than 8,000 ducats a year. Yet the ancestors of its present owners bought it for the sum of 12,000 maravedis, a few years before the conquest of Peru.

The second testimony shall be the case of a nobleman who died in this city of Córdova a few years before the discovery of the Indies, who in his will asked *inter alia* that a certain festivity in honor of Our Lady be celebrated, that the mass be sung, and that a religious of the order of St. Francis preach a sermon: in return he left 30 maravedis as alms to provide a meal in the convent that day. The revenue of his possessions he devoted to this pious work and other bequests then amounted to 450 maravedis. The brethren who administer this bequest are the royal scribes, and considering how much the revenue has increased they have presented the convent with alms amounting to 20 or 30 ducats in each of the last fifty years, in some years reaching the higher figure and in others dropping to the lower. In some years they have given as much as forty gold *escudos,* or 16,000 maravedis, in place of the 30 maravedis offered by the testator, for the income has increased to such an extent that in the present year of 1603 the properties yield over 900 ducats in money and gifts.

The third testimony shall be the fact that in the city of Badajoz, where my father was born, there are four properties among many others, which were settled by a noblewoman, a widow, on her four children. She was the lord of a walled town with domains covering seven leagues, and a great many excellent pastures. She was deprived of this town by Henry III on the ground that a woman could not defend a place so near the frontier in time of war between Portugal and Castile, and received as a permanent rent charge the sum of 45,000 maravedis, which was then the rent produced by the town in question. Sixty years ago it was sold for 120,000 ducats, yet today it is worth above 300,000. Whoever possesses the town today as its lord can say what its rent is; I do not know. The lady left this income to her eldest son as the best portion, and left the other three 4,000 or 5,000 maravedis in pasture lands. Now these are worth as much in ducats as they were once in maravedis, and more rather than less, while the portion of the eldest has not increased by a penny, though if he had been left property, it would have improved like the rest.

The value and price of everything else that is used in the country has gone up in the same way. Whether provisions, or articles of dress, or footwear—everything has increased in the same fashion, and is still increasing. In 1560 when I arrived in Spain the first two pairs of Cordovan shoes I bought in Seville cost me a real and a half a pair, and now in 1613 a pair of the same kind, of a single sole, cost five reals in Córdova, notwithstanding that Córdova is a cheaper town than Seville. And to turn from the lowest goods, such as footwear, to the highest commodities that are bought and sold, which are rents, in 1560 property producing 1,000 maravedis was rated at 12,000, and though four years later it was raised through good management to 14,000, now no one will offer it at less than 20,000, provided it is in quantity and favorably laid out. A great many gentlemen, lords of vassals, observing the drop in property values, are taking up *censos* at 20,000 to redeem those they had at 14,000.

In addition to all this, it is public knowledge that whenever the Peru fleet puts into Seville its presence is bruited to the four corners of the Old World. For as the trade and commerce of mankind spreads from one province to another and one kingdom to another, and everything depends on the hope of gain, and the empire of Peru is an ocean of gold and silver, its rising tides bathe all the nations of the world, filling them with wealth and contentment—and these benefits are all due to our triumvirate.

CHAPTER VII

Two opinions about the wealth of Peru; the beginnings of the conquest.

HAVING SHOWN what was the revenue of Spain in former times, I should like to be able to complete the picture by stating what it is at present. But though I have sought and obtained information about large parts of it, I have been unable to get at its total, for I have no access to or dealings with the officials of the royal treasury, nor could I lawfully delve into its secrets. I do not even think that the officials themselves could tell me if they wished, for the quantity of dough is so great that even they who knead it and eat it can scarcely comprehend its total, let alone one who cannot even say what color the flour is. I can only affirm, and this is public knowledge, that in order to make up the loss suffered by the Armada sent against England, in 1589 the kingdom of Castile supplied Philip II with eight million, or 80 times a hundred thousand ducats, payable in six years, in addition to all the other royal revenues payable annually. Orders were later given for payment to be made in three years, and this was done. It is also public knowledge that soon after the accession of Philip III, the kingdom offered him a service of eighteen millions or 180 times a hundred thousand ducats, payable in six years; and these are now being paid, in addition to the other royal taxes which were already being levied. The increase in the royal income can readily be imagined from the foregoing facts, and especially when it is remembered that the royal revenues have so many more ways of increasing than private incomes, yet even many private incomes are so great that they are difficult to reckon. We might almost conclude that to be able to reckon one's wealth is a sign of poverty; and if this conclusion can be drawn from private fortunes, what shall be said of a monarch on whose empire the sun never sets, according to the cosmographers? And all these things are part of the benefits and greatness of our triumvirate.

Although it is true, as I have said, that I have no dealings with or access to the officials of the treasury, I do nevertheless enjoy the friendship of several people at court, one of whom is a gentleman called Juan de Morales, a native of Madrid, and one of his majesty's scribes and porter of the royal chamber in the Supreme Council of the Indies. I asked him very earnestly to try to find out the total of the royal revenues so as to be able to include it in this history as a proof of what we are saying; and as he delayed many days in answering me, I pressed on with my writing and completed the above remarks about the royal revenues and the difficulty I saw in calculating precisely their total. At the end of three months which Juan de Morales spent on his enquiries he answered as follows, and I give his letter word for word:

You told me that you required to know the sum of His Majesty's revenues from all sources for a certain purpose. This is a matter that has never been ascertained, either exactly or approximately, though the king has very much desired to find out, and recently gave instructions that a special ledger be opened for the purpose in a new ordinance for the Council of the Exchequer and its accounts. Yet the task has not been begun, nor is it expected that it will be begun, let alone finished, for there are such great variations in everything that there is no way of arriving at an estimate. And as it flows through such different channels, it seems impossible to bring it all together, since a total could only be arrived at after making very extensive calculations.

This evidence of Juan de Morales I was very glad to have as confirming what I had written from my own opinion and that of others. It so bears out my statement that though I had got beyond this point I have returned to include it and so to add authority to my work: I do indeed make every effort to set down the truth and to document it. As further testimony of the great difficulty of arriving at the total value of the income of the king of Spain, the emperor of the New World, I can quote the authority of Juan Botero Benes, that great chronicler of the affairs of the whole world. After giving the revenues of the king of China, and the revenues that Galicia, Asturias, and Portugal paid to the Roman empire, those of the king of France, the emperor, the kings of Poland, England, the duke of Lorraine, the king of Scotland, those of Swabia and Gothia, of the house of Austria, the king of Narsinga and the sharif and the Grand Turk, he omits giving the revenues of the king of Spain. The author or his translator probably dared not or could not bring together this vast quantity of data, or add up the enormous total which I suppose would be reached by the tribute of so many great kingdoms, including that of Peru.

In confirmation of this wealth and of the way Peru has enriched the whole world, I recall a saying of the Very Reverend Don Paulo de Laguna, who was president of His Majesty's Council of the Exchequer and later president of the Council of the Indies and monarch of the New World: he was elected bishop of Córdova in 1603, and one day in the present year 1604, in speaking of the wealth of Peru in the presence of his treasurer and confessor and one of his chaplains called Licentiate Juan de Morales, and his secretary Licentiate Pedro Cuadrado, a native of Toledo, he said: "From a single hill in Peru they have brought to Spain, up to the year 1602, 200 million registered silver pesos. Those that have come unregistered must certainly exceed another 100 million. And in a single fleet in my time they brought 25 million pesos of silver and gold from Peru."

Those present said: "If Your Lordship had not said it, it would have been impossible to believe such great figures."

The bishop replied: "I say so because they are true, to my certain knowledge. Moreover, all the kings of Spain, from Don Pelayo downwards together, have not had so much coin as King Philip II alone." The words of this great man shall stand as the final proof of our assertion.

Those who regard the wealth that Peru has sent to the Old World and scattered all over it from a different point of view than the usual one say that this flood of riches has done more harm than good, since wealth commonly produces vice rather than virtue, inclining its possessors to pride, ambition, gluttony, and voluptuousness. They maintain that men are brought up surrounded with comforts and turn out effeminate, incapable for administration in time of peace and much more so for war, and they therefore devote all their energies to inventing foods and drinks, and finery and adornments, and have already daily produced so many strange inventions that there is no longer anything left to invent, and they produce stupidities instead of adornments, which are more suitable for women to wear than men, as can readily be seen. They add that if the revenues of the rich have swollen to permit them to live in plenty and comfort, so too the miseries of the poor have multiplied, and they die of hunger and want, because of the dearth of supplies and clothing that ensues from the excess of money: today the poor cannot eat or dress, even poorly, because of this dearth, and for this reason there are so many poor in the country. They were better off when there was not so much money, and even though in those days alms were less than they now are because there was less money, they did more good because everything was so much cheaper. The conclusion is that the riches of the New World, properly understood, have not increased the volume of useful things necessary for human life, such as food and clothing, but have made them scarcer and rendered men effeminate in their power of understanding and in their bodies, dress, and customs, and that they lived more happily and were more feared by the rest of the world with what they had formerly.

The reader may choose whichever he prefers of these two points of view. I for my part dare not condemn the second, for it strengthens my case, nor can I support the first, even though it is to the honor and glory of my country. In this perplexity I may perhaps be permitted to return to where we left the thread of our history, so that we may, with divine aid, describe the origins, development, and end of that famous triumvirate.

Those three great men, having set up their association and agreed what office each should perform, first set about building two ships for their expedition, which they did with great difficulty and expense. In one of these Francisco Pizarro left Panama in 1525 with 114 men, licenced by the governor Pedrarias de Ávila. After sailing a hundred leagues they landed in a region of incredibly dense forests where it was so rainy that a clear sky was scarcely ever seen. The natives were scarcely less wild than the landscape. They appeared in large numbers and fought the Spaniards, killing several of them: Francisco Pizarro himself received seven arrow wounds in four skirmishes, but as he was well armored they were not fatal. They sorrowfully left this country, and sorrowed even more at having started the undertaking. Diego de Almagro left Panama soon after and followed them until he reached the same country, where the Indians, whose appetite for Spaniards was now roused, fell on them and knocked one of Almagro's eyes out, wounding many others and killing some, and so forcing them to abandon those parts. Such were the gains won by the Spaniards from the first land they saw in this conquest. The Spanish historians do not say what country this was. Almagro went in pursuit of Pizarro, and coming upon him at Chinchama, they agreed to continue the conquest together. Their fortune was no better in the next land they entered, for it was no less rough and rainy, and its people no less warlike. The latter appeared in great numbers and obliged them by force of arms to take ship and sail away, abusing them with shameful words, as López de Gómara says at length in his ch. cviii, as well as much else that occurred on this expedition, to which the reader is referred if he desires a fuller account.

CHAPTER VIII

Almagro twice returns to Panama for help.

DIEGO ALMAGRO returned to Panama for more men and brought eighty. But even with these the two leaders dared not begin any conquest, for they found the natives very hostile. Continuing this maritime pilgrimage they reached a country called Catámez, where there are no forests and plenty of food: here they took on supplies, and their hopes of great wealth were strongly revived by the sight of Indians with gold plugs in their faces, which were pierced to take them. They also had fine turquoises and emeralds. Because of this the Spaniards counted themselves fortunate and imagined themselves already rich. But they very soon lost their hopes of wealth, on finding a great many men approaching from the interior, very well equipped with weapons and so warlike that the Spaniards did not dare to engage them in battle, and even doubted whether they could safely remain there, despite the fact that they numbered 250. By general agreement they betook themselves to an island called El Gallo. They thus spent many days between hope and despair of success, according to the favorable or unfavorable circumstances they found. They sorely repented their undertaking. Only the two leaders remained resolute in continuing the quest and dying if need be. Thus resolved, they agreed that Francisco Pizarro should remain on the island, while Diego de Almagro returned to Panama for more men. Many of his followers were discouraged and wanted to go back with him, but Almagro refused to take them, or even their letters, to prevent them from publishing the hardships they had experienced and discrediting the enterprise: he had told incredible things of its wealth without having seen it, but by his persistence he revealed things even greater and more incredible than he had said.

Although the leaders tried to prevent the soldiers from writing to Panama, they could not stop them from doing so, for necessity sharpens the wits. A certain Saravia, a native of Trujillo, repudiated his captain Francisco Pizarro, though as he came from the same town his obligation was to follow him more loyally than the rest. He sent to Panama a ball of cotton on the pretext that they should knit him some socks with it. It contained a petition to a friend signed by many of his companions, in which they described their hardships and the death of their comrades, and their present captivity and oppression, declaring that they were deprived of the liberty of returning to Panama. The petition ended with a verse summarizing their plight as follows:

> So my lord governor
> bear this in mind:
> the scrounger's gone to Panama.
> and the butcher's stayed behind.

As a child, I often heard these lines repeated by Spaniards telling these events in the conquest of the New World. They were repeated as a sort of proverb, for they did great harm to the leaders, leading to the undoing of the undertaking, and the loss of their property and the fruits of the past hardships. I later in Spain came upon them in the chronicle of Francisco López de Gómara, and was very glad to find them for the memories they called to my mind.

CHAPTER IX

Pizarro is abandoned by his men; only thirteen remain with him.

WHEN ALMAGRO returned to Panama, he had been away more than a year on these wanderings. He found a new governor, Pedro de los Ríos, a gentleman from Córdova, who, on receiving the soldiers' petition, sent a judge, a certain Tafur, to the island of El Gallo to set free all those who wished to return to Panama. When this was known, those who had offered to accompany Almagro took their leave of him, saying that if the others were coming back there was no point in their going. Diego de Almagro was very grieved at this, for he saw all his hopes destroyed. Francisco Pizarro was no less grieved when he found all his men confused and more inclined to return than to go on, without regard for the good treatment and brotherly spirit he had shown them. To end their doubts and to see which of them would declare themselves his friends, he took his sword and traced a line on the sand with it, facing the direction of Peru, the goal of his desires, and turning to them, said:

"Gentlemen, this line stands for the labors, hunger, thirst and toil, wounds and sickness, and all other dangers and trials that must be undergone in this conquest, risking life itself. Those who have the spirit to face them and to prevail in this heroic enterprise, let them cross the line in proof of their courage and in open testimony of their loyalty to me. And let those who feel themselves unworthy of so great a task return to Panama, for I do not wish to force anyone against his will, and with those who remain, even though they are few, I trust that God will aid us to supply the want of those who have gone, to his greater glory and honor and to the perpetual fame of those who follow me."

On hearing this the Spaniards hastened to embark before anything should occur that might prevent them from returning to Panama. Thus they abandoned their captain and returned with the judge; for, like men of low condition, they were more deeply stirred by the fear of hardships than by the hope of honor and fame. Only thirteen remained with Pizarro, unwilling to abandon him despite the ill example and persuasions of the rest. They on the contrary seemed to take faith and courage as the others lost them, and crossed the line again declaring that they would die with him. Francisco Pizarro thanked them as their generosity deserved, and promised them the best of what they might conquer. They took ship to another island called La Gorgona, where they suffered great hunger. For days and months they lived entirely on what shellfish they could find, and were driven by hunger to the point of eating large snakes and other vermin which occur in great numbers on that island. It rained continuously, and the lightning and thunder were incredible. Their sufferings were beyond description.

López de Gómara mentions only two of these thirteen heroes: he was probably given no account of the other eleven, such is the usual lack of interest and negligence of the Spanish historians in naming and praising the famous men of Spain. Yet these should all be mentioned by name with their families and birthplaces, on account of the great deeds they performed in the discovery and conquest of the New World, so that their memory and fame may be perpetuated and their birthplaces and families may take pride in having bred such sons. One of the two mentioned by López de Gómara was not even a Spaniard but a Greek, Pedro de Candía, a native of Candia; the other was called Bartolomé Ruiz de Moguer, of Moguer, who was the pilot who constantly accompanied them on this voyage. The treasurer Agustín de Zárate took more pains, and names a further seven, saying: "Nicolás de Ribera of Olvera; Juan de la Torre; Alonso de Briseño, a native of Benavente; Cristóbal de Peralta of Baeza; Alonso de Trujillo of Trujillo; Francisco de Cuéllar of Cuéllar; Alonso de Molina of Ubeda." In explanation of what this gentleman writes I can add that apart from Nicolás there was another Ribera, whose Christian name I have forgotten; he may have been either Jerónimo de Ribera or Alonso de Ribera; I do remember that the two were distinguished as young Ribera and old Ribera, not because the latter was older, for in fact he was rather younger, but because he was senior in the service of Pizarro, being one of the first to leave Panama with him, while the other was one of the second or third group who came with Diego de Almagro. I heard these details in my country in the course of the conversations of eyewitnesses. Both Riberas received grants of Indians in Lima where they left sons and daughters full of bounty and virtue. Zárate's Alonso de Trujillo was Diego de Trujillo, of Trujillo: I knew him and he had Indians in Cuzco. He was still living in 1560 when I left that city. Another of the thirteen was Francisco Rodríguez de Villafuerte, a *vecino* of Cuzco, who was the first to cross the line: he also was living in 1560 and I knew him too. Only two are lacking to complete the thirteen, and their names are unknown. I have made this addition to Zárate, so as to clarify his history and in order that the children and descendants of these illustrious men may be proud of such fathers. I shall do the same in other situations which the Spanish historians have not described as fully as they might, so that the reader may have a complete account.

CHAPTER X

Francisco Pizarro presses on with his conquest.

FRANCISCO PIZARRO and his thirteen companions remained many months on Gorgona, suffering great privations with no hut or house to shelter from the perpetual rain. The best food they ate and their greatest delicacy was large snakes. They seem to have survived by a miracle; and we might say that God sustained them so as to reveal His great marvels through them and allowed the others to return to prove to the world that so great a thing was the work of God and not of man, for it was not humanly possible for thirteen men alone to dare to undertake the conquest of Peru. Even to imagine it was temerity and folly, let alone to attempt to undertake it. But the divine mercy had compassion on those poor heathens and gave the Spaniards a special courage to carry through the conquest, so as to reveal God's power in forces no stronger than Samson's hair, and bring the gift of His holy Word to those who were in such dire need of it.

After many months—since it could not be despatched earlier—the ship sent by Diego de Almagro arrived with some supplies, but no men. Such help was more apt to discourage them and convince them to return than to encourage them to press on; but God, who works in a wondrous way, so ordained that they should be as much emboldened as if the whole world was on their side. On seeing the ship, they decided to sail on and find what land and people there were south of the equator, a region hitherto scarcely seen by the Spaniards. So they embarked, and with great trouble passed through those waters, which are very difficult to navigate. They were soldiers and sailors by turns, as the need arose. They tacked out to sea and back to land, greatly hindered by the south wind and the sea currents, which latter mostly flow from south to north off that coast.

These currents are indeed a remarkable sight, and I should like to be able to describe them for the benefit of those who have not seen them. They are like raging rivers that flow with many whirlpools on all sides; and this and the great noise of the waves and the quantity of foam stirred up by the agitation of the water fills the seafarer's heart with fear and terror: it is indeed dangerous to fall into the waves, for ships sink there sucked under by the whirlpools. These currents often carry a turbid viscous water like that of a river in spate, while others are quite clear; some are broad and cover much of the sea, and others are narrow. But what most surprised me was the great difference between the water flowing in the current and the rest, which seemed like a different substance. We have mentioned the violence of the currents: on either side of them the sea was as still and calm as if there were a wall between. I have not discovered where the current begins or where it ends, or what its causes are: suffice it to say that despite the difficulties produced by these currents and an unknown sea and the ferocity of their enemies, the thirteen companions sailed on for days and even months, with courage beyond praise. They suffered greatly from hunger, for they dared not go ashore because they were so few and feared the Indians: if they came by any supplies, they were obtained through begging or theft rather than by force.

CHAPTER XI

Francisco Pizarro and his thirteen companions reach Peru.

THEY FINALLY reached the great valley of Túmbez, two years after having left Gorgona. The length of the journey alone, without knowing where they were going, was an unbearable ordeal, apart from the many other travails they underwent in the course of it. These we shall mention for the consideration of those who may read the history of this discovery; for the historians do not relate them, but rather pass over them more briefly than other episodes, when they should be told in full.

At Túmbez the Lord wrought one of His miracles in favor of His Catholic faith and of the natives, in order that they might receive it. The ship had fetched up near the town, and the Spaniards desired to know what country it was, since they saw that it was more thickly populated and had grander buildings than any they had yet seen. But they did not know how to find this out, for they dared not send one of their number lest the Indians kill him, and dared not even go in a group for the same reason. While they were thus doubting, Pedro de Candía spoke up with manly spirit and Christian faith, saying: "I am resolved to go alone and find out what there is in this valley. If I am killed, you will have lost little or nothing in being one comrade less; and if I manage to do what we wish, our victory will be the greater."

So saying he put on over his clothes a coat of mail that fell to his knees and a brave and gallant iron helmet such as they carried with them, and picked up a steel shield. He set off with his sword in his belt and a wooden cross more than a yard high in his right hand, trusting in this token of our redemption more than in his arms. Pedro de Candía was very tall, so it was said: I did not know him, but one of his sons was my fellow pupil in the primary school, and followed his father in appearance, for at eleven or twelve he was twice as big as most boys of his age.

Thus Pedro de Candía left his companions, begging them to pray for him. He advanced toward the town with a solemn and lordly expression on his face, as though he were master of the whole of that province. The Indians, who were troubled by the arrival of the ship, were even more agitated when they beheld this large man covered in iron from head to foot, and bearded, a thing they had never seen or conceived. The people he met in the fields ran away giving the alarm, and when Pedro de Candía reached the town he found the square and fortress full of armed men. They were all astonished at this strange apparition, and knew not what to say to him; they dared not do him any harm, for they thought he was divine. In order to try who he was, the *curaca* and the chief Indians decided to set on him the lion and tiger that Huaina Cápac had bidden them keep, as we have mentioned in our account of his life: they thought the animals would tear him to pieces, and having bethought themselves of the plan proceeded to put it into operation. Cieza de León, in his ch. liii where he speaks of the conquests and deeds of Huaina Cápac in the great province of Túmbez, refers briefly to this incident. I shall give his account word for word in order to have a Spanish authority for what I am saying: it will also serve to show the greatness of the beautiful valley of Túmbez. He says:

As the inhabitants of the island of Puna were in conflict with those of Túmbez, it was easy for the Inca's captains to build the fort, though without these foolish disputes they might have been in difficulties. When it was nearly finished, Huaina Cápac arrived, and ordered a temple of the Sun to be built near the fort of Túmbez and more than two hundred of the most beautiful daughters of the neighboring chiefs to be installed in it as chosen virgins. And in the fort, which is said to have been a remarkable sight before it fell to ruins, Huaina Cápac placed his captain or delegate with a number of *mitimaes* and a great store of valuables and supplies for the maintenance of the settlers and the support of the armed forces passing through. It is said that he also bade them keep a very fierce lion and tiger of which they were to take great care. They must have been the beasts that were set upon Pedro de Candía to rend him to pieces when the governor Francisco Pizarro and his thirteen companions (who were the discoverers of Peru, as we shall say in the third part of our history) reached that land. And in the fortress of Túmbez there were many silversmiths to make pitchers of silver and gold and many other kinds of precious objects, both for the service and decoration of the temple which they held sacrosanct and for the service of the Inca himself, and to make the metal plates for the walls of their temples and palaces. And the women dedicated to the service of the temple devoted themselves exclusively to spinning and weaving the finest woolen cloth, which they did with great skill. And since these matters are described at length in the second part, where I have set down what I have been able to find out about the rule of the Incas in Peru from Manco Cápac, the first, to Huáscar, who was the last authentic ruler, I shall not say more in this chapter than is necessary to explain my point.

Thus Cieza de León, on the great wealth of Túmbez and the attack on Pedro de Candía with the wild beasts. He does not go into greater detail because he reverts to the subject in its proper place, as he says, in the third part of his work, which has not yet appeared.

CHAPTER XII

The miracle God wrought at Túmbez.

To RETURN to our tale, these wild beasts, seeing the Christian and his crucifix, went toward him and, losing their native ferocity, approached like two dogs he had reared himself, and greeted him and lay down at his feet. Pedro de Candía, seeing this miracle of God and deriving courage from it, stooped to pat the beasts' heads and backs, and raised the cross over them, indicating to the heathens that its virtue had tamed and calmed the ferocity of the animals. This finally convinced the Indians that he was a child of the Sun sent from heaven. In this belief they came toward him and by common consent all adored him as the child of their god the Sun, leading him to their temple, which was lined with plates of gold, so that he might see how his father was honored in their land.

Having shown him the whole temple and the plate and other ornaments and valuables for its service, they took him to see the royal palace of his brothers the Incas, whom they also considered to be children of the Sun. He was escorted over it and shown the halls, courts, and chambers and wall coverings of gold and silver. They showed him the plate kept for the Inca's service, for even the basins and pitchers, and jars and vats for the kitchen were of gold and silver.

They went into the gardens, where Pedro de Candía saw the trees and other smaller plants, herbs, animals, and other creatures which we have already described as being made in imitation of nature and placed in their royal gardens. The Christian was just as surprised by all this as the Indians had been by his—to them—strange and marvellous appearance.

CHAPTER XIII

Pedro de Candía reports what he has seen and they all return to Panama.

PEDRO DE CANDÍA rejoined his companions with the joy that can readily be imagined and with longer and faster strides than those that took him toward the town. He told everything he had seen, to the astonishment and even incredulity of his comrades. They were satisfied with the toils they had already undergone in search of wealth and treasure, since their good fortune now offered them such abundance, if they were men enough to win it. They agreed to go back to Panama, since there was no reason to press on after they had found what they desired, and indeed more than they thought. Three Spaniards remained behind, according to Zárate, or two, according to López de Gómara, out of a desire to see the riches described by Pedro de Candía, which they may not have believed, or in the hope of obtaining part of them, if they were as copious as he had said. It is not known what happened to them, though the Spanish historians say that the Indians killed them. But the Indians deny this, saying that as they had worshipped them as children of the Sun, they would not have killed them, but rather have served them. They must have died of some disease, for that coast is unhealthy for strangers. They are probably those lacking in the total of thirteen, since as they remained behind and died among the Indians they would be less remembered than their comrades. The thirteen Spaniards spent more than three years in the discovery of Peru, as the historians bear witness. Zárate, in Book I, end of ch. ii, says:

And with this news he returned to Panama, after spending three years on the discovery, suffering great toils and dangers both from lack of food and from the resistance of hostile Indians and mutinies among his own people, for most of them lost hope of finding anything of importance. Don Francisco soothed them with great prudence and spirit, relying on Don Diego de Almagro's diligence in forwarding supplies, munitions, men, and horses. Thus though they had been among the richest men in Panama, they were now not only poor, but deeply in debt.

Thus far Zárate. López de Gómara speaks as follows at the end of his ch. cix: "Francisco Pizarro spent more than three years in the discovery of what is called Peru, suffering great labors, dangers, hunger, fear, and narrow escapes." Here this author ends his chapter.

Among the perceptive sayings of the famous Francisco Pizarro, the one they repeated oftenest, when he and his companions found themselves most exhausted in the well-nigh unbearable hardships of the discovery of Peru, and later during its conquest, was this: "Poor us, perishing in the struggle to win new kingdoms and empires, not for ourselves or our own children, but for other people's!" I heard this repeated by many of those who heard him say it and assisted him to win the empire of Peru: they used to say which were the other people's children, but I had better not repeat this, as it would be odious. The conquerors themselves used often to repeat it after the conquest during the hardships of the civil wars with Gonzalo Pizarro and Francisco Hernández Girón, in which most of them died. Each of them repeated it as his own saying, seeing how general and how true this remark of their captains had turned out to be: I myself am one of the witnesses of its truth.

CHAPTER XIV

Pizarro comes to Spain and solicits the right to conquer Peru.

FRANCISCO PIZARRO returned to Panama as rapidly as possible and informed his companions, Diego de Almagro and the schoolmaster Hernando de Luque, of the incredible riches he had discovered, to their great delight. They agreed that Francisco Pizarro should come to Spain to ask His Majesty Charles V for the right to conquer and govern what they had found. They gave him a thousand gold pesos for the journey, most of it borrowed, for they were so reduced by their previous expenses that their own resources were no longer sufficient and they had to ask the help of others. Pizarro came to Spain, presented his report to the Council of the Indies, informed His Majesty of what he had done and seen, begged to be awarded the governorship of that land in return for his past and present services, and offered to conquer it, at the risk and cost of his own life and property, and those of his friends and relatives. He offered great kingdoms and much treasure. Those who heard him thought that he was exaggerating the riches of Peru to stimulate others to go and conquer lands so rich in gold and silver; but in a few years they saw that he had fulfilled much more than he had promised. His Majesty awarded him the conquest with the title of *adelantado-mayor* of Peru, and captain general and governor of whatever he should conquer of the empire the Spaniards called Peru, which was then named New Castile, to distinguish it from the other empire called New Spain, both won in the same fashion by obstinate fools and lunatics, as foreigners say.

Francisco Pizarro, whom we shall henceforth call Don Francisco Pizarro, for the royal award added the prefix *don*, which was then less used by noblemen that it is in these days, when it has become common property—so much so that the Indians of my country, whether noble or not, supposing that Spaniards assume it as a dignity, have applied it also to themselves, and get away with it. Diego de Almagro we shall also call Don Diego, for both were companions; and it seems right that they should be so treated, as the two of them were equal. After obtaining the royal grant, Don Francisco Pizarro prepared with all diligence, and accompanied by four brothers of his and by many other noblemen from

Extremadura, he embarked in Seville, and had a prosperous voyage to Panama, where he found Don Diego de Almagro full of complaints that he had not been given a share of the titles, honors, and offices His Majesty had granted, notwithstanding his contribution to the toils, dangers, and expenses of the discovery, a contribution that even exceeded the rest, for Don Diego had given a greater quantity of money and had lost an eye.

Those who knew this did not fail to blame Pizarro for not having mentioned his companion to His Majesty, so that he might be given some honorable title. They said that this was due to his negligence or the malice of his advisers. The companions thus fell out until some mutual friends intervened, who composed their differences, with which they continued their partnership. They prepared everything necessary for the undertaking, but as friends reconciled always keep some taint of the past ill feeling, Almagro, who was entrusted with the expenses, did not provide everything as abundantly as in the past, or even a sufficient quantity of necessities for Don Francisco and his brothers. Hernando Pizarro, a rough and ill-tempered man, waxed more indignant than the rest, and insulted Don Diego de Almagro, and upbraided his brother for putting up with his meanness and cheese-paring. Don Francisco replied that it would be best to be patient with Don Diego, for he had right on his side, since he himself had been a poor friend in not bringing him any honorable office; though it was true that they would share what they won like comrades. Almagro had been told this to console him for his disappointment; nevertheless Almagro had nobly replied that what he had spent in toil and money had been to gain honor rather than wealth. This led to a perpetual hatred between Hernando Pizarro and Don Diego de Almagro, which lasted till the one killed the other, acting as judge in his own case.

The companions were finally reconciled by certain serious persons, whose intercession was requested by Don Francisco Pizarro and his other brothers, who were softer and more tractable than Hernando, for they saw that without Almagro's friendship they could not proceed. Among others who shared in this second reconciliation was Licentiate Antonio de la Gama, whom I later knew in Cuzco, where he had an allocation of Indians. Don Francisco Pizarro gave his promise and oath to renounce the title of *adelantado* in favor of Don Diego and to beg His Majesty to consent to the transfer. This pacified Don Diego, who delivered to his companion nearly a thousand ducats in gold, and all the supplies, arms, and horses he had collected, as well as two ships.

CHAPTER XV

The hardships suffered by the Spaniards between Panama and Túmbez.

D ON FRANCISCO PIZARRO put to sea with his four brothers and as many Spaniards and horses as his ships would hold. They sailed intending not to land before Túmbez, but this proved impossible on account of the south wind which is contrary on that voyage and blows constantly. They landed in another country a hundred leagues before Túmbez, and sent the ship back to Panama, meaning to continue the journey by land, which they thought would be easier than facing the south wind.

But they encountered greater hardships on the way than those caused by the contrary wind, for they suffered greatly from hunger and exhaustion owing to the roughness and barrenness of the land. They came upon great rivers that poured out into the sea, and many creeks of the sea that plunged deep into the land. These they crossed with very great toil, making rafts with whatever they could find, sometimes of wood, otherwise of rushes and osiers, or of gourds fastened together. They were built and steered under the guidance of Don Francisco, who acted as pilot and shipwright. He was experienced in such tasks, and went about them with such patience and courage that he often carried the sick over rivers and creeks on his back, to stimulate the spirits of the rest. With these difficulties they reached a province called Coaqui where they found plenty of food and fine emeralds. Most of these they broke, like inexpert lapidaries, thinking that if they were fine they should not break however hard they were struck on an anvil they used for testing. They did the same at Túmbez, where they broke a great many more of enormous value, of two, three, or four thousand ducats, more or less. These Spaniards were not the only ones who made this simple mistake, for it was also committed by those who entered the same region a little later with the *adelantado* Don Pedro de Alvarado, who also broke a great quantity of emeralds and turquoises of incalculable value, as we have mentioned above.

In addition to this loss, Pizarro's men suffered from a strange and abominable disease which broke out on their heads and faces and over the whole of their bodies. At first a sort of wart appeared, which as it developed turned into a growth as large as a black fig. It hung from a sort of stem, gave out a great deal of blood and caused great pain and nausea. The growths could not be touched and made the appearance of the sufferer most repulsive, for some hung from the forehead and others from the brow, the end of the nose, and the chin and ears. They did not know what to do about them. Many died, and many more recovered. Not all the Spaniards caught the disease, though it was general throughout Peru, and many years after I saw in Cuzco three or four Spaniards suffering from the same complaint, who afterwards recovered. This must have been due to some infection that later disappeared, for there is no record of any recurrence of this plague.

Despite all these hardships, and the sickness and death of his companions, Pizarro did not weaken, but on the contrary displayed as much anxiety to press on as to cure his friends and soldiers. He sent twenty-four or twenty-five thousand gold ducats to Panama as proof of his conquest and to supply Almagro with funds to procure help: part of this gold was obtained as ransom and part in fair fight. He went on to Túmbez, where other Spaniards came up with him after leaving Nicaragua stirred by the fame of the great wealth of Peru. Their leaders were Sebastián de Belalcázar (such was the name of this "beautiful castle," not Benalcázar as is commonly written) and Juan Fernández, whose birthplace is unknown. Pizarro was delighted at their arrival for he needed men for his conquest. Sebastián de Belalcázar was named Moyano, but took the name of his birthplace as being more dignified. He and a brother and sister were triplets. His brother was called Fabián García Moyano and his sister Anastasia Moyana: they were brave people like their elder brother, especially the sister. I had this information from a religious of the order of the Seraphic St. Francis, dwelling in the famous convent of Santa María de los Angeles in Belalcázar: he gave it to me knowing that I intended to write this history, and I was glad to have it so as to be able to mention the strange birth of this famous man.

CHAPTER XVI

The Spaniards gain the island of Puna and Túmbez.

WITH THESE reinforcements Pizarro made bold to attempt the conquest of the island called Puna, where there was said to be much wealth in gold and silver. He crossed over to it on rafts with no little danger, for it lies twelve leagues out to sea. He had battles with the natives, in which four Spaniards were killed and many others wounded, including Hernando Pizarro who received a dangerous blow on the knee. The Spaniards conquered and slew many of the Indians, winning a great quantity of loot, in gold, silver, and cloth, which was divided up at once, before the arrival of the men Hernando de Soto was bringing from Nicaragua: he had gone there with a ship on Almagro's orders to get men and arms for Pizarro, and the latter had heard from Soto to say that he was on the point of arriving, as he did just when the table had been cleared.

Pizarro, finding he had now enough men, made bold to go to Túmbez, and sought to win the good will of the inhabitants by sending forward six hundred natives of the place, whom he had found in captivity on the island of Puna, accompanied by three Spaniards as ambassadors. Through these captives he asked for peace and friendship, for they had promised to render the Spaniards great services in return for the liberty he had given them. But they behaved ungratefully and falsely, changing sides as soon as they returned to their own people. Instead of praising the Spaniards, they spoke ill of their covetousness and hunger for gold and silver, and stirred up their friends' indignation by saying the Spaniards were adulterers and fornicators. The people of Túmbez were so scandalized by this denunciation that they did not wait to hear the three Spaniards, but handed them over to the executioners to be put to death. They were thus killed and sacrificed with great savagery and cruelty. This is the account of López de Gómara and Agustín de Zárate. But Padre Blas Valera, who is worthy of great credit, says that this was only what the Spaniards imagined about the three soldiers because they failed to reappear, but that the governor later ascertained that one was drowned in a river by his own fault and the other two had died suddenly of different diseases, for the region is, as we have said, very unhealthy for strangers. It is not to be believed that the Indians would have killed and sacrificed them, in view of what happened with Pedro de Candía and the tiger and lion, which caused them to regard the Spaniards as gods.

On landing at Túmbez, Pizarro and his men had great difficulties because they did not know how to control the rafts, and they were overturned by the surf, which is very strong along the coast. They leapt ashore, went to the town, had many encounters, and were finally victorious: their enemies were so shaken by the mortality they suffered that they completely gave in. They thought this had been a punishment by the Sun, and decided to give the Spaniards a rich offering of many gold and silver jewels, supposing that this would appease them, since they were so avid for it; and the *curaca* came to offer them obedience.

When the Spaniards saw the prosperous turn of affairs, they decided to establish a town at this place, which they called San Miguel, because it was founded on St. Michael's day. It was the first Spanish town in Peru and it was founded in 1531. A few men stayed there to receive the contingent from Panama and Nicaragua, and Pizarro sent back the three ships he had to Panama to get more men. With them he sent more than thirty thousand pesos in gold and silver, as well as emeralds, to prove the wealth of his conquest. This consignment and the last showed how rich it was.

We should have mentioned that Pizarro had a commission (among other favors he received from the emperor) to be accompanied by two dozen halberdiers as a personal bodyguard and a mark of his authority. As soon as he had captured Túmbez, he wished to pick these men, so as to begin his march inland with greater circumstance. But he could find no one disposed to accept the duty, despite the fact that he made great promises. This was from their Spanish pride and individualism, which is particularly strong among those who go to Peru: however humble their origin, as soon as they get there they seem to be filled with dignity and nobility. I should not dare to make this assertion if I had not heard them in person on both sides of the ocean. Only two would accept the halberds: I knew them, and in the conquest itself and afterwards in the civil wars they proved good soldiers and held high military offices and important allocations of Indians. They both died at the hands of their enemies—we do not give their names out of respect.

Pizarro, after pacifying the province of Túmbez and the surrounding district and taking possession of its great store of wealth, wished to press on to Cajamarca to meet King Atahuallpa, of whose treasure he had had great reports—and however great these were they could readily be believed from what had been found at Túmbez. On the way they passed through a desert of more than twenty leagues of barren sand, where they suffered greatly from the drought. It was very hot and waterless, and as they were new to the country, they had not made provisions against this need. They then came to some beautiful valleys with ample supplies, where they recovered from these ordeals. On the way the governor received an ambassador from the hapless Huáscar Inca, though it is not known how he could have despatched the man, for he was then imprisoned and closely guarded by his enemies. It is suspected that the messenger was sent by one of his faithful *curacas,* out of sorrow at seeing the true Inca, the legitimate ruler of the empire, in the hands of rebels. He humbly asked for the protection and justice of the sons of his god Viracocha, since they had declared they had come to undo injustices. The message went no further, and for this reason they suspected that it came not from Huáscar but from someone who had taken compassion on the poor Inca in his captivity and suffering. The governor replied that he was already on the way to right these and any other wrongs he might find.

CHAPTER XVII

An embassy with great presents sent by the Inca to the Spaniards.

TWO DAYS later the general received another, and more splendid, embassy from King Atahuallpa. It was led by one of his full brothers called Titu Atauchi, who told him in brief that the Inca had sent him to greet the children of his god Viracocha and to offer them some of the things found in his country, in token of his desire to serve them with all his power. He begged them accept his entertainment on the way and ask for anything they might need, for everything would be amply furnished, and he desired to see them soon and serve them as children of his father the sun and his brothers, as he and all his vassals believed them to be. This the ambassador briefly declared on behalf of his king. Finally, addressing the governor, he told him on his own behalf (following the instructions he had received):

"Inca Viracocha, child of the Sun. Since I have been given the honor of this most fortunate mission, I wish to be so bold as to beg you to do me the honor of granting three favors: first that you consider my Inca and king, Atahuallpa, your friend and pledge perpetual peace and friendship with him; second, that you will pardon any offence that our people may have committed against you through ignorance or negligence, and that you may command us in everything at your pleasure and to your service, to prove our good will and see our intention to serve you and all your men from now onwards; and finally I beg you that the punishment of death you have executed on those of the island of Puna and of Túmbez and elsewhere, at the behest of our great god Viracocha, may not be repeated at Cajamàrca or against any others you may come upon henceforward, but that you may temper the wrath your father has felt on account of the offences committed against him, and that you may spare all with mercy and clemency, as you are an Inca and child of the Sun."

Having said this, he ordered the presents they had brought for the Spaniards to be placed before the governor. The captains and officials who were in charge of them then appeared, and delivered them to the Spaniards. There were many Peruvian sheep and lambs, pemmican made of the meat of wild animals—guanaco, vicuña, and deer of various kinds —together with a large number of the living creatures, in order to show of what meat the pemmican was made. They offered also many rabbits, wild and tame, many partridges, alive and dead, and waterfowl, innumerable small birds, a great quantity of maize in grain and ground into flour; much fresh and dried fruit; honey in combs and separated; the Indian pepper called *uchu*; quantities of their drink made of maize and of the seed called *mulli*. In addition they produced much of the fine clothes the king wore and of their footwear. They offered parrots, macaws, monkeys, and the other animals and creatures we have mentioned as existing in that country. In short there was nothing they might have brought that they failed to bring. They offered many gold and silver drinking bowls, plates, and dishes for use at table, emeralds and turquoises, and in particular they produced a pair of shoes like those of the Inca for the governor and two gold bracelets called *chipana,* which they wear on the left wrist. They wear only one of these bracelets, and two were sent so that there should be one to change. They were military insignia of great honor, and could only be worn by those of the royal blood and captains and soldiers who performed outstanding feats in time of war. The king had offered them from his own hand as a mark of very great honor, and had sent them to Pizarro for two reasons: first, because he was thought to be a child of the Sun and of the god Viracocha; and secondly, because he was a most famous captain, as his deeds proved.

After presenting each of these gifts, Titu Atauchi asked the governor and the other Spaniards to pardon him for having dared to bring such poor and humble gifts to the children of the Sun, for in the future they would strive to serve them better. The governor and his captains set great store by his good words and better gifts, and returned thanks first to the Inca and second to his ambassador, supposing that he was no more than an ordinary ambassador. But when they heard that he was the king's brother they showed him the greatest courtesy and honor, and after having replied briefly to his message, they sent him away very satisfied. The answer was that the Spaniards had come on behalf of the pope to undeceive them about their idolatry and teach them the true Christian religion, and on behalf of the emperor and king of ·Spain, who was the greatest prince in Christendom, to conclude perpetual peace, friendship, and brotherhood with the Inca and his whole empire, and not to make war on them or do them any other harm: later, and at leisure, they would inform the Inca of other news they brought for his ear. Neither Zárate nor López de Gómara mentions this embassy or the exchange of gifts, despite their richness and value, or the fact that the ambassador was the king's brother. They refer only to the shoes and bracelets which were brought specially for the governor, and both writers call the latter cuffs, as if they were shirt cuffs, not noticing that the Indians of Peru do not normally wear shirts.

King Atahuallpa had sent this mission and these gifts to the Spaniards to appease the Sun, thinking that the Indians of the island of Puna and those of Túmbez and others of the neighborhood had angered and offended him because they had offered resistance and had killed some of the Spaniards, as we have said; and as he and his people regarded them as children of their god Viracocha and descendants of the Sun they feared they would be severely punished for this disrespect. To this fear was added another, no less potent. This was the prophecy of their father Huaina Cápac, to the effect that after his time a people never before seen or imagined would enter his realms, depriving his children of their empire and destroying their idolatry. It seemed to King Atahuallpa that this prophecy was now being fulfilled, for he knew that very few Spaniards had entered his country, yet they had been enough to slay many Indians at Puna, Túmbez, and elsewhere, which he thought to be a punishment due to the anger of the Sun. Fearing lest the same fate should befall himself and his house and court, he sent his brother as ambassador, to beg the three favors mentioned as a return for his embassy. Atahuallpa did not want to have the request made in his own name, so as not to display openly the weakness of his cowardly spirit. The cruel Atahuallpa was hounded by these fears until his death, and because of them he neither resisted, nor used his powers against the Spaniards. They were really punishments for his idolatry and cruelty, and also the effects of divine mercy to bring these gentiles into the Roman Catholic Church.

There was no lack of differences among the Spaniards, which came to light after the embassy had left. Some said the presents were the more suspicious for their great quantity and value, and that they were intended to fill them with pleasure and satisfaction and so lull them and make them negligent, so that the Indians could take them unawares and kill them easily. They should therefore be more cautious and prepared, for so much favor was no favor, but guile and hostility. Other Spaniards, and these were the majority, took the opposite and more courageous view, saying that military practice made it necessary that they should always be on their guard, but that the generosity of the Inca, the gentleness of his words, and the magnificence of his embassy were greatly to be praised: he had after all sent his own brother, whose courtesy and discretion were obviously great, as they had observed from his speech and countenance, though they regretted that owing to the inadequacy of the interpreter, who knew little of the language of Cuzco and less Spanish, they had missed many of the ambassador's words. They realized that the long discourse delivered with due pauses and divisions had been rendered by the dragoman in very few words, ill expressed and hardly comprehensible, and some of them contradictory. The Spaniards themselves noticed this, for they could not reconcile part of the message with the rest, but found various discrepancies, to their great regret. However, they could do nothing to remedy this and had to make do with what they had. That night and for many days following they enjoyed the abundant presents Atahuallpa had sent them. They travelled on toward Cajamarca, where they expected to find the Inca, and soon entered it. They were very well received by the Indians there, for many nobles and common people had gathered on the instructions of the king to welcome those who were regarded as descendants of the Sun and children of their god Viracocha. They were therefore accommodated and offered many flowers and scented herbs which were strewn in their apartments, in addition to the great quantities of food and drink which had been made ready by the Inca's orders and was provided in particular by the *curaca* and lord of Cajamarca, called Cullqui Huaman. He, in order to demonstrate the obedience they all felt toward their king, went to all lengths to serve and regale the Spaniards. Among other services rendered by the Indians was the following: seeing that the horses had iron bits, they thought that metal was their food, and brought gold and silver in ingots and put them in the stables, telling the horses to eat it because it was better fodder than iron. The Spaniards laughed at the simplicity of the Indians and told them that they would have to give the horses a great deal of it if they wanted to appease them and make friends with them.

CHAPTER XVIII

The governor sends an embassy to King Atahuallpa.

NEXT DAY the governor held a council with his brothers and captains on the question of sending an embassy to King Atahaullpa to inform him of their approach and of their mission from the emperor and the pope, in order that they should not seem ungrateful for the presents and greeting he had sent them. It was agreed that as the Inca had sent one of his brothers, the governor should also send one of his, so that the embassy might have the same standing as the Inca's even though it was not possible to match his gifts. Hernando Pizarro and Hernando de Soto were appointed ambassadors, to go to the Inca's dwelling place at a royal palace and baths he had not far from Cajamarca, where he was celebrating certain of their heathen feasts with a great crowd of his noblemen and military leaders and seeking to restore order and reform certain matters that had gone astray in the course of the wars. Under the guise of these reforms he made new laws and statutes to cover his rebellion and secure his person, declaring that they had been revealed to him by his father the Sun, as all the Incas used to say to give authority to their acts. The truth is that although Atahuallpa slew all the members of the royal blood he could find, he never lost his fear of the few who were left. He was afraid that in the course of time the kingdom would for religious reasons set up the rightful heir as legitimate king and Inca, and sought to forestall this by saying that the Sun had given these laws, hoping that the Indians of the whole empire would be appeased by them.

The two ambassadors took with them the Indian interpreter called Felipe, a native of Puna, who was indispensable to them, though his knowledge of both languages was poor. They also took more than two hundred noble Indians in splendid array, who were sent by the *curaca* of Cajamarca to accompany the two Spaniards when he knew that they were to visit his king: they had instructions to do whatever the Spaniards asked, even to the point of laying down their lives. On leaving Cajamarca the two gentlemen from Extremadura sent a leading Indian forward to warn King Atahuallpa of their arrival and ask his leave for them to appear in his presence. The Inca replied that he would be very glad of their presence, for he had been wishing to see them for some days. He then sent one of his commanders with his regiment to receive these two children of the Sun and bring them with all reverence before him. The Inca's kindly welcome and the news that the Indians were coming to meet them caused the Spaniards to lose the fear they had felt when they knew that the Inca had thirty thousand guards in his company. They advanced toward the royal palaces and baths, and when they were half way they saw a regiment of soldiers approaching across the plain. In order to let them know that if they did not come as friends, he alone would cope with them all, Hernando de Soto spurred his horse and galloped upon them, pulling up near the commander. The Spanish historians say that this commander (as we call him) was King Atahuallpa, and Soto, according to one of them, advanced curvetting till he was close to Atahuallpa's litter. Atahuallpa himself did not stir though the horse's foam fell on his very face, but ordered many of those who had fled on the approach of the galloping horse to be killed. The author was mistaken about this matter, and his informant bore false witness against both the Inca and Hernando de Soto; for the Inca was not present, and even if he had been he would not have had anyone killed even for a grave fault, let alone for something that was not a fault but merely an expression of courtesy and respect in making way for what were thought to be children of the Sun. Any other conduct would have been sacrilege in their eyes, for apart from the discourtesy it would have been disrespectful toward those they admitted to be divine men come down from the sky. Atahuallpa was not so foolish as to have ordered Indians who had merely shown respect and honor to be killed in the presence of the ambassadors, for this would have provoked the outbreak of war with the Spaniards, when all he desired was peace and friendship with them, to assure himself against the fears with which he was filled. Nor would Hernando de Soto, having been chosen as ambassador by his companions, have been so inconsiderate and discourteous as to send the horse's foam flying into the face of one he had been sent to address on behalf of the emperor and the Holy Father. It is indeed regrettable that those who repeat in Spain reports of events that occurred so far away should see fit to invent pieces of bravado at the expense of the honor of others.

As we shall see, Inca Atahuallpa made generous and royal gestures toward the Spaniards. We may perhaps be permitted to mention his natural qualities, such as those he now displayed toward the Spaniards and many other proofs we shall find of his intelligence, ability, and prudence, since we have already spoken of his tyranny and cruelty, and it would be a great wrong to pass over the good after having dwelt on the bad. This historian is bound and obliged to write the truth, under pain of becoming a deceiver of the whole world and so set down as a rogue. What I shall say will be drawn from the reports of many Spaniards who were present at the events, and whom I myself heard in conversations in my father's house the whole year round, for these talks were their favorite pastime and the theme was usually the story of the conquests. I have also heard the version of many Indians who used to visit my mother and told her of these events, especially those referring to Atahuallpa and his end, which they used to repeat as if taking his misfortunes and death in satisfaction of the cruelty he had shown toward his own people. In addition I have reports sent me by my schoolfellows, which they have obtained from the annals and traditions of the provinces of which their mothers were natives, as I mentioned at the beginning. To these is added the account I found in the papers of the very learned and excellent writer Padre Blas Valera, who was the son of one of those present at the arrest of Atahuallpa, and who was born and brought up in the district of Cajamarca, so that he had full information of these events, derived, as he says, from the originals. He described these events more fully than the rest of the history of Peru, and his version fits in closely with the other reports I have, for they are all of the same tenor. I may also mention that I shall follow the same path as that of the Spanish histories, serving as a commentary on them where necessary and adding whatever is missing, for they omitted some points; the most likely reason for this is that they did not come to the notice of the writers.

CHAPTER XIX

The Inca's reception of the Spanish embassy.

To RETURN to the thread of our history, we must mention that the commander who advanced to receive Hernando Pizarro and Hernando
de Soto, after greeting them and worshipping them with the greatest veneration, told his captains and warriors: "These are children of our god
Viracocha." The Indians greeted them with the utmost respect and gazed
at them astonished by their appearance, dress, and speech. They then accompanied them to the Inca's presence. The Spaniards were amazed by
the wealth and splendor of the royal house and the number of people in
it. Both sides were thus full of admiration, and we cannot tell whose was
the greater. The ambassadors made a deep bow in the Spanish fashion to
the Inca, who was sitting on his golden chair. This pleased the king
greatly, and he rose to his feet and embraced them warmly and said: "Be
welcome to my realms, Cápac Viracocha." Padre Blas Valera writes these
words in the Indian language which he knew well, but I have omitted this
as superfluous. The Inca sat down, and the Spaniards were then brought
gold chairs like his, which had been made ready, for as he thought them
to be descendants of the Sun's blood, he did not want there to be any difference between himself and them, especially as one of them was the
governor's brother. When they were seated, the Inca turned his face to
his kinsmen who were around him and said: "Here you see the face,
figure and habit of our god Viracocha, just as our ancestor Inca Viracocha
left him portrayed in the stone statue, after he had appeared to him."

The king had barely said this when two very beautiful girls of the royal
blood, or *ñustas,* entered, each holding two small gold jars of the Inca's
beverage. There were four youths with them also of the royal blood,
though not of the legitimate blood, since their mothers were natives of
Atahuallpa's kingdom. The *ñustas* approached the Inca and adored him,
and the first placed one of her jars in his hand and gave the other to Hernando Pizarro, as the Inca bade her. The king's brother, Titu Atauchi,
who had been his ambassador to the Spaniards, now spoke, and told the
dragoman Felipillo to tell them that the Inca wished to drink with them,
such being the custom of the Inca kings as a token and pledge of peace,
love, and perpetual brotherhood. Hernando Pizarro, hearing the words

of the interpreter and bowing toward the Inca, took the jar and drank it. The Inca drank two or three draughts from his jar and then handed it to Titu Atauchi for him to drink what was left. He then took one of the jars the other girl was holding and had the other given to Hernando de Soto, who did the same as his companion. The Inca again drank two or three draughts, and gave the rest to another of his brothers (a son of his father's), called Choquehuaman.

After drinking the ambassadors wished to deliver their message, but the king bade them rest, for he wished to admire their figures, in which he saw his god Viracocha. At this point six pages and six girls entered, richly clad and bearing many kinds of fresh and dried fruit, the bread which they make for special occasions, and the wine made of the seed of the *mulli* tree, as well as fine cotton towels (for they had no linen). One of the girls called Pillcu Ciça Ñusta addressed the guests as follows: "Oh sons of Cápac Inca Viracocha, taste these things we bring, even though it be only for our pleasure and joy!" The Spaniards were astonished to find such courtesy and good breeding among people whom they had imagined to live in savagery and sloth. And in order not to seem to scorn what was offered with such good will and delicacy, they ate a little of the food and then said they had had enough, greatly to the satisfaction of the Indians.

CHAPTER XX

The speech of the ambassadors and the Inca's reply.

SEEING the Indians at ease, Hernando Pizarro bade Hernando de Soto speak, so as not to waste more time, bidding him deliver his message briefly, since they ought to return to their own people before nightfall rather than trust to the heathens: however great the attentions they received they could not tell if the object was not to gain their confidence and take them unawares. So Hernando de Soto rose, made a Spanish reverence by very politely uncovering his head, and then sat down again and spoke as follows:

"Most serene Inca! You will know that there are in the the world two princes more powerful than all the rest. One of them is the supreme pontiff who represents God. He administers and rules all those who keep his divine law, and teaches his holy word. The other is the emperor of the Romans, Charles V, king of Spain. These two monarchs, aware of the blindness of the inhabitants of these realms who disrespect the true God, maker of heaven and earth, and adore his creatures and the very demon who deceives them, have sent our governor and captain general Don Francisco Pizarro and his companions and some priests, who are ministers of God, to teach Your Highness and all his vassals this divine truth and His holy law, for which reason they have come to this country. And having enjoyed the liberality of your royal hand on the way, they yesterday entered Cajamarca, and have today sent us to Your Highness to lay the foundation of concord, brotherhood, and perpetual peace that should exist between us, so that you may receive us under your protection and hear the divine law from us and all your people may learn and receive it, for it will be of the greatest honor, advantage, and salvation to them all."

Here Padre Blas Valera, being a very religious man full of zeal for the salvation of the heathens, makes a great exclamation of sorrow, pointing out that words as important as those of Hernando de Soto needed an interpreter who was well versed in both languages and with enough Christian charity to render them exactly; but he would often and again bewail the misfortune of the empire of Peru that owing to the inexperience of the interpreter the first conquerors and the priests who accompanied them could blame Felipillo for all the ills caused by his ignorance, in order to clear themselves, though they had reason to place some or all of the blame on him. For he rendered the words so barbarously and badly, giving many of them the opposite meaning, that he not only upset the Inca, but angered the hearers by belittling the majesty of the embassy, as if it had come from complete barbarians. The Indians realized that many of the words passed on by the interpreter could not have been uttered by the ambassador since they did not fit in with his mission. So the Inca, troubled by this incorrect rendering, said: "What does this fellow mean, stammering from one word to another and from one mistake to the next like a dumb man?" The Inca's words were much stronger in his language than in Spanish. The captains and lords of vassals said that the errors should be attributed to the ignorance of the interpreter rather than to the indiscretion of the ambassadors, for it was hardly to be thought that they would be indiscreet since they had been chosen for the office. They thus received the embassy politely, even though it was hardly understood, and treated the ambassadors as gods, worshipping them anew. The Inca replied to them saying:

"I am very much rejoiced, divine men, that you and your companions should have come to these distant lands in my time, and that by your coming you should have fulfilled the divinations and prophecies that our ancestors have handed down to us. Yet my soul should rather be saddened, since I feel certain that all the other things prophesied by the ancients about the end of our empire must come to pass in my time, just as the prophecy of your coming has been fulfilled. However, I say that I hold these times to be fortunate ones since the god Viracocha has sent us such guests, and these times promise that the state of our affairs will change for the better, a change that is warranted by the tradition of our ancestors and the words of the testament of my father Huaina Cápac, and the great wars between my brother and myself, and now your arrival. Wherefore, although we have heard of your entry into our country and of how you have established a garrison here and caused many deaths and other calamities in Puna, Túmbez, and elsewhere, my captains and I have not tried to resist you or expel you from our kingdom, since we hold and believe that you are the sons of our great god Viracocha and messengers of Pachacámac. For this reason, and in confirmation of my father's orders that we should adore and serve you, we have made a law, and it has been published in the schools of Cuzco, that no one shall be so bold as to take up arms against you or misuse you in any way. You may therefore use us as you please and according to your will, for it will be a great glory for us to die at the hands of those we hold to be divine and messengers of God. He must have bidden you, since your past actions accord with the prophecies. I only desire to be satisfied on one point: how is it that you say on the one hand that you have come to talk of friendship and brotherhood and perpetual peace in the name of these two princes, while on the other you have caused so many deaths and such destruction in the provinces you have passed through, without speaking to any of our people to ask if our attitude is friendly or hostile? For as this was done so entirely without provocation on our part against you, I suppose that those two princes must have bidden you do it, and they must have been bidden by Pachacámac. If this is so, I repeat that you shall do whatever you will with us. I only beg you to take pity on my people, for their affliction and death will grieve me more than my own."

Here the Inca ended. His people, distressed by these last words and by the loss of the empire, which they now held to be certain, shed many tears and sighed and groaned. For the Inca had often before repeated the speech about the end of his empire. Since his father Huaina Cápac had left this prophecy in very clear terms, with the time for its realization appointed and at hand, Atahuallpa spoke of nothing else and used to say that it was the decree and decision of the great Pachacámac, which could not be frustrated. Atahuallpa's certainty of the loss of his empire caused him to be so timid and unwilling to resist the Spaniards. Among the courtiers and others who attended the Inca, there were two chroniclers or historians who recorded in their annals by means of knots, signs, and cyphers as best they could, the ill-understood message of Hernando de Soto and the Inca's reply.

The ambassadors were very surprised to see the weeping of the captains and *curacas* at what the king so calmly said. They did not know the cause of these tears, but seeing such noble people shed them, they were filled with pity and compassion. Here again the good Padre Blas Valera regrets the misfortunes of the Indians, saying that if the interpreter had given the speech of the Inca correctly, he would have moved the Spaniards to pity and charity. But he left the Spaniards as ill satisfied as the Indians, since he understood neither language properly. When the ambassadors heard speak of the death and destruction at Puna and Túmbez they suspected that the Inca wished to avenge them, for the interpreter said no more. And as they were confused by not having understood Atahuallpa's reply, they did not know what answer to make. For Felipillo was at fault not only by his ignorance of what to say in Spanish, but also because, as the Inca's speech had been rather long, he had not been able to remember all of it: he therefore failed in both ways.

The ambassadors begged the royal permission to retire. The Inca bade them go in peace, for he would soon go to Cajamarca and visit the sons of his god Viracocha and messengers of Pachacámac. The Spaniards left the palace still amazed at its riches and at the worship they were accorded. They asked for their horse, and before they mounted, two *curacas* approached with many servants, saying they begged the Spaniards not to disdain receiving a small present, though they would have desired to offer things worthy of gods. This said, they bade the servants place the gifts before them; they were like the first gift and consisted of the same things but in greater abundance, and much gold and silver, both the metals and objects made of them. The Spaniards marvelled at such courtesy, which removed their suspicions of the Inca's intentions, and they again blamed the incompetence of Felipillo in interpreting the Inca's reply, for they had fallen into this error through not understanding it; and later they were to fall into others even greater, as we shall see.

CHAPTER XXI

The two Spaniards return to the rest; they all prepare to receive the Inca.

THE TWO ambassadors rejoined the rest and told them of the wealth and splendor they had seen in the Inca's house, and the great courtesy they had received. They divided the presents among the whole band, to their great pleasure. Nevertheless as good soldiers they prepared their arms and horses for whatever might occur next day, and though they were aware of the multitude of men Atahuallpa had with him, they made ready with a good heart to fight like true Spaniards. At daybreak the horsemen ranged themselves in three bands of twenty, for there were only sixty of them all told. The section leaders or captains were Hernando Pizarro, Hernando de Soto, and Sebastián de Belalcázar. They concealed themselves behind some walls so as to be out of sight of the Indians and cause greater amazement and fear by their sudden appearance. The governor then formed a company of a hundred infantry: they were no more all told, and he wished to appear at their head. They were stationed at one end of the square of the *tambo,* which was like a field, where they awaited king Atahuallpa as he approached on a golden litter borne on the shoulders of his men with as much courtly pomp and majesty as warlike ferocity and power of arms. Many Indians walked in front of the litter, removing stones and anything that the bearers might stumble over, and even straws. Many lords were in attendance on him. His warriors were divided into four companies of eight thousand men each. The first or vanguard preceded the king like scouts, to secure the way. The main force consisting of two companies was arranged on either side of him as a bodyguard, while the fourth company came behind him. Their captain was called Rumiñaui, or "stone-eye," from the film of a cataract he had in one eye. In this order Atahuallpa travelled a league, which was the distance from his camp to the Spanish quarters. This took more than four hours. His intention was not to fight, as we shall see, but merely to hear the Spanish message from the pope and the emperor. He had been told that the Spaniards could not walk uphill, and that this was why they went up on their horses and that those who were on foot caught hold of their tails and trappings to help them climb: he was also told that Spaniards could not run as fast as Indians, or carry burdens or work as they did. In view of these reports and of the fact that he considered them to be divine, Atahuallpa approached without any suspicion of what was about to happen. He entered the square accompanied by the three squadrons of warriors, while the fourth, the rearguard, remained outside. When the king saw that the Spanish infantry were so few that they were huddled together as though they were afraid, he said to his companions: "These are messengers from God. We must not displease them, but offer them every courtesy and attention." Then a Dominican religious, called Fray Vicente de Valverde, approached the Inca with a cross in his hand, to speak to him on behalf of the emperor.

CHAPTER XXII

The discourse delivered by Fray Vicente de Valverde before Atahuallpa.

PADRE BLAS VALERA, that most scholarly student of the events of those days, who studied them with the intention of writing their history, gives the speech or discourse Fray Vicente de Valverde addressed to King Atahuallpa, which he divides into two parts. He says that he saw it in Trujillo when studying Latin: it was written in Fray Vicente's own hand and was owned by one of the conquerors called Diego de Olivares. On his death it passed to a son-in-law of his, who often read it and learnt it by heart. I have therefore thought best to include it as Padre Blas Valera writes it, for he gives it at great length and in more detail than the other historians, owing to his having seen the original. I also include it on my own authority, for it coincides in every way with the reports I have, and differs little or not at all in substance from what the Spanish historians have written. If I set it down in his Paternity's name, I shall relate it in the name of both of us, for I do not wish to appropriate another's version by putting it forward as mine, though this would do me much honor, but to assign everything to its author, and it is honor enough for me to be associated with such great men.

When Fray Vicente approached to address the Inca, the latter was very surprised at the Dominican's appearance, with his beard and shaven crown, as religious have them, his long habit, and his crucifix in his hand,

and a book, which was Silvestre's *Summa*. Others say it was his breviary and others the Bible: the reader shall choose which he wishes. In order to know how to receive this man, the king asked one of the leading Indians who had gone to offer the Spaniards everything they needed four days before.

He said: "What is the rank and degree of this Spaniard? Is he by chance higher or lower than the rest, or is he equal?"

The Indian answered: "All I could find out, Inca, was that this is the captain or leader of the word (he meant preacher), and the minister of the supreme god Pachacámac and his messenger: the rest are not like him." Then Fray Vicente came up to them and having shown his respect in the manner customary among religious, and obtaining the king's leave, he made the following speech.

First part of Fray Vicente de Valverde's speech.

"It is proper that you should know, most famous and most powerful king, that it is necessary that Your Highness and all your subjects should not only learn the true Catholic faith, but that you should hear and believe the following: First, that God, three in one, created heaven and earth and all things in the world, and He offers the prize of eternal life to the good, and punishes the wicked with perpetual suffering. In the beginning this God created man of dust, and gave it the breath of life, which we call the spirit, which God made in his own likeness. Wherefore every man consists of body and rational spirit. From this man, whom God called Adam, all the men in the world are descended, and he is the origin and beginning of our nature. This man Adam sinned by breaking the command of his creator, and with him all men hitherto born and to be born till the end of the world have sinned. No man or woman is free of this taint, nor will be, with the exception of our Lord Jesus Christ, who, being the Son of the true God, descended from heaven, was born of the Virgin Mary to redeem the whole of mankind and free it from the bondage of sin. He at last died for our salvation on a wooden cross like the one I have in my hands, for which reason we as Christians worship and revere it.

"This Jesus Christ rose by His own virtue from the dead, and after forty days He ascended into heaven and sits on the right hand of God, our Almighty Father. He left on earth His apostles and their successors so that, through words and sermons and other holy means, they might attract men to the knowledge and worship of God and the preservation of His law.

"It was His will also that Saint Peter, His apostle, should be the prince over the other apostles and all their successors and all other Christians, as the vicar of God, and that all the other pontiffs of Rome, the successors of St. Peter, whom Christians call popes, should have the same supreme authority that God gave him. And the popes, then, now, and forever, strive with great saintliness to preach to men and teach them the word of God."

Second part of Fray Vicente de Valverde's speech.

"Therefore the holy pope of Rome who now lives on earth, understanding that all the peoples and tribes of these realms have left the true God, their maker, and have sunk to worship idols and likenesses of the Devil, has conceded the conquest of these parts to Charles V, emperor of the Romans, most powerful king of Spain and monarch of all the earth, so that, having subjected these peoples and their kings and lords, and having expelled the rebels and recalcitrant from their midst, he alone may reign over and rule and govern these peoples, bringing to them the knowledge of God and obedience to His church. Our most powerful king, though greatly occupied and engaged in the government of his vast realms and provinces, accepted the pope's mission, and did not refuse it out of regard for the salvation of these peoples. He therefore sent his captains and soldiers to accomplish it as has already been done in the conquest of great islands and the lands of Mexico nearby. Having conquered them by the power of his arms, he has won them to the true religion of Jesus Christ, for God Himself said that they were to be obliged to accept it.

"Thus the great emperor Charles V has chosen as his lieutenant and ambassador Don Francisco Pizarro, who is now here, so that Your Highness' kingdoms may also receive the same benefit. He will establish a league and alliance of perpetual friendship between His Majesty and Your Highness, so that Your Highness and all your realms will become tributaries; that is to say, you will pay tribute to the emperor, and will become his vassal and deliver your kingdom wholly into his hands, renouncing the administration and government of it, as other kings and lords have done. This comes first. Secondly, after establishing this peace and friendship and having submitted willingly or by force, you shall give true obedience to the pope, the supreme pontiff, and receive and believe the faith of Jesus Christ, our God, and scorn and utterly repudiate the abominable superstition of your idols: by this act you shall learn how holy is our law and how false your own, invented by the Devil. All this, oh king, if you believe me, you should willingly grant, for it is greatly to the advantage of yourself and your people. If you refuse, know that you will be constrained with war, fire, and the sword, and all your idols shall be overthrown and we shall oblige you by the sword to abandon your false religion and to receive willy-nilly our Catholic faith and pay tribute to our emperor and deliver him your kingdom. If you seek obstinately to resist, you may rest assured that God will suffer that you and all your Indians shall be destroyed by our arms, even as Pharaoh of old and all his host perished in the Red Sea."

CHAPTER XXIII

The difficulty of interpreting Fray Vicente's speech accurately.

AFTER giving this speech, Padre Blas Valera includes some considerations relevant to our history, saying that the historians who have dealt with these events and mentioned this speech have often omitted much of both parts, and by suppressing them have left only a brief disjointed summary, which is all that has appeared in the printed histories. He says that Juan de Oliva and Cristóbal de Medina, two priests, who were great preachers and very learned in the language of the Indians, and Juan de Montalvo, a priest and a great interpreter, and Falconio Aragonés, doctor in canon and civil law, in his book *De libertate Indorum servanda* and the Franciscan Fray Marcos de Jofré and many other learned men who have written books, all refer to the speech in two parts, as given above, and that they all agree that it was short and harsh, with no touch of softness or any other concession, and that the interpretation was much worse, as we shall now see. He also mentions that the above authors speak favorably of the modesty and moderation of the speech made by Hernando de Soto and Hernando Pizarro before Atahuallpa, in comparison with that of Fray Vicente de Valverde.

With regard to the version that reached Atahuallpa, it is to be remarked that Felipe, the Indian dragoman who interpreted, was a native of the island of Puna, a man of very plebeian origin, young—for he was scarcely twenty-two—and as little versed in the general language of the Incas as in Spanish. He had in fact learned the language of the Incas, not in Cuzco, but in Túmbez, from Indians who speak barbarously and corruptly as foreigners: we have already explained that to all the Indians but the natives of Cuzco this is a foreign language. He had also learnt Spanish without a teacher, but merely by hearing the Spaniards speak, and the words he heard most often were those used by the ordinary soldiers: "by heaven," or "I swear by heaven," and others like them or worse. He also knew the words necessary for fetching anything that was asked for, for he was a servant and slave to the Spaniards, and he spoke what he knew very corruptly as newly captured Negroes do. Though baptized, he had received no instruction in the Christian religion and knew nothing about Christ our Lord, and was totally ignorant of the Apostles' creed.

Such were the merits of the first interpreter in Peru. As to his translation, he did it badly and often reversed the sense, but this was not done out of malice, but because he did not understand what he was interpreting, and spoke it like a parrot. Instead of God three in one, he said God three and one make four, adding the numbers in order to make himself understood. This is shown by the tradition of the *quipus*, or annual records in knots, kept at Cajamarca, where the event occurred. He could not express it in any other way; for there are no words or phrases in the Peruvian language for many of the concepts of the Christian religion, such as Trinity, three in one, person, Holy Spirit, faith, grace, church, sacraments, and similar words. These are totally unknown to the gentiles, and the words have never existed, and still do not exist, in their language. For this reason when the Spanish interpreters of these times wish to express these ideas adequately, they have to seek new words or phrases, or use with great care suitably dignified expressions in the old language or else lay hands on the many words the cultured and scholarly Indians have taken from Spanish and introduced into their own languages, adapting them to their own ways of speech. The Indians of today do this with great elegance, thus helping the Spaniards to find the words that are lacking, so that they can say what they want and the Indians can understand the sermons that are preached to them.

We have often referred to this difficulty in the general language of Peru when the subject has arisen, and we repeat that the inadequacy of the interpreter was literally as we have said and that the fault was not his, but the ignorance of all concerned. Even in my own times, twenty-nine years later, when the Indians had had contact with the Spaniards and were more accustomed to hearing Castilian, they still had the same difficulty as Felipillo, and never addressed Spaniards in Castilian, but always in their own tongue. In short, I may say I never knew an Indian who spoke Spanish, excepting only two boys who were my schoolfellows and went to

school as young children and learned to read and write. One was called
Don Carlos, the son of Paullu Inca. Apart from these two, all the other
Indians had so little interest in learning Spanish, and the Spaniards took
so little trouble to teach them, that no one ever thought of learning or
teaching it, but each man learned from the other whatever he needed to
know by daily intercourse and habit. The negligence on both sides was
so great that the Indian boys who were brought up with me, though they
could understand physical things I mentioned to them in Spanish, obliged
me to speak to them in their own language to convey any message of importance, for they did not know enough Spanish to put them into the Indian speech. And if this ignorance still existed after twenty-nine years of
familiarity and intercourse between Indians and Spaniards, how much
greater must have been the deficiency of the interpreter when the only
contact and concern was arms and warfare? And to show more clearly
that Felipillo's misinterpretation was not his fault, or that of Fray Vicente de Valverde, or of the Spaniards, but of the Indian language, we
may mention that even today, more than eighty years after the conquest of
the empire (and how much more so then!) there are still no words in
Indian for the matters of our holy religion, as is seen from a confessional
sent me from Peru at the beginning of 1603 by Padre Diego de Alcobaça,
printed at Lima in 1585 in three languages: Spanish, the general language of Cuzco, and the language of the province of Aymará. The parts
written in both Indian languages contain many Spanish words Indianized. At the beginning of the confessional, the second question the confessor asks is "Are you a baptized Christian?" which is translated into the
general language as *"Cristiano-batizascachucanqui?"* which contains
only one Indian word, the verb *canqui,* "are you." The first word "Christian" is pure Spanish, and the second "baptized" is also Spanish, though
Indianized. The same is done in Aymará. The fourth question, "Do you
know Christian doctrine?" is the same: only the verb "do you know" is in
Indian, and the noun and adjective are in Spanish in both Indian sections.
There are also innumerable Indianized Spanish words, from which I
quote only these few, to avoid prolixity: *God, Jesus Christ, Our Lady,
image, cross, priest, Sunday, feast, religion, church, penitence, communicate, pray, fast, married, unmarried, cohabiting,* and so. And though it is
true that some of these and other words I have not copied could be said in
Indian tongue, such as *God, Our Lady, cross, image, Sunday, feast, fast,
married, unmarried,* and others, it is a very Catholic act, and a consideration of great piety and charity in speaking to the Indians of the Christian
religion, not to use the words they used in heathen times for these and

similar things, so as not to recall the superstitions that the words convey. They should be completely forgotten.

Thus all Spaniards and Fray Vicente de Valverde and the Indian Felipillo are absolved from the blame that might be imputed to them for the badness of the interpretation, since today when there are so many priests and religious studying and toiling to learn their language so as to teach Christian doctrine to the natives, there is still so much difficulty in understanding one another, as the above-mentioned confessional shows. What would have happened then when none of this existed?

To return therefore to his attempts at translation, which rather obscured than explained the good Friar Vicente's discourse, the fact is that the Indian Felipe said many things like the one we have quoted. With regard to the seed of Adam he gave it to be understood that at one time all the men in the world, born and unborn, were together and said that they all heaped their sins on Adam, meaning that all men, born and unborn, shared in Adam's sin. He said nothing of the divinity of Christ our Lord except that he was a great man who died for men, and he said even less of the virginity, purity, and sanctity of our Lady, the Virgin Mary. And he interpreted what was said and what had been said without any order or arrangement of words, producing the opposite sense rather than the Catholic meaning.

As regards the second part of the speech, he rendered this less ill than the first, for it dealt with concrete matters of war and arms, and he so extolled the power and arms of the emperor and his diligence in sending captains and soldiers to conquer the world that the Indians understood that he was superior to all those of heaven. He said a great deal more, which he understood no better than the rest, but I shall omit them to avoid prolixity. This shall suffice; and it happened because the interpreter did not understand what he was saying and the language he was using was incapable of more. Of this defect Padre Blas Valera says one very great and noteworthy truth, that the Indians of Cuzco of the present day, who are born and bred among Spaniards and fairly well instructed in the mysteries of the faith, do not dare to explain to strange Indians what they hear in sermons by Spanish preachers for fear of making errors, such is the difficulty of the language. If this is so now that the Indians are instructed in the faith and skilled in Spanish, what would be the case when they were ignorant of both?

CHAPTER XXIV

Atahuallpa's reply to the friar's discourse.

AFTER hearing the last part of the speech in which he was asked to renounce his realms willingly or by force and become a tributary as
the pope required and the emperor desired, and on hearing the threat of
war with fire and the sword, with the destruction of himself and his
people like that of Pharaoh and his host, Atahuallpa was filled with sadness, supposing that those whom he and his Indians called Viracochas,
believing they were gods, had turned into mortal enemies since they made
such harsh demands. He gave a groan, using the word *átac*, "woe is me,"
expressing with this exclamation his great grief at hearing the last part of
the discourse. Then mastering his emotions, he replied:

"It would have caused me great satisfaction, since you deny everything
else that I requested of your messengers, that you should at least have
granted me one request, that of addressing me through a more skilled
and faithful translator. For the urbanity and social life of men is more
readily understood through speech than by customs, since even though
you may be endowed with great virtues, if you do not manifest them by
words, I shall not easily be able to perceive them by observation and experience. And if this is needful among all peoples and nations, it is much
more so between those who come from such widely distant regions as we;
if we seek to deal and talk through interpreters and messengers who are
ignorant of both languages it will be as though we were conversing
through the mouths of beasts of burden. I say this, man of God, because
I perceive that the words you have spoken must mean something different
from what the dragoman has told me. The occasion requires it; for when
we are to discuss peace, friendship, perpetual brotherhood, and even kinship, as the other messengers who came told me, all that this Indian has
said signifies the opposite; you threaten us with war and death by fire and
the sword, and with the exile and destruction of the Incas and their family, and say that I must renounce my kingdom and become the tributary
of another, either willingly or by force. Whence I deduce one of two
things: either your prince and you are tyrants who are destroying the
world, depriving others of their realms, slaying and robbing those who
have done you no harm and owe you nothing, or you are ministers of God,
whom we call Pachacámac, who has chosen you to punish and destroy us.

If this is so, I and my subjects offer ourselves to die or to suffer whatever you wish to do with us, not out of fear of your arms and threats, but to fulfil what my father Huaina Cápac left as instructions at the hour of his death, namely that we should serve and honor a bearded people like yourselves, which would come after his times, and of whose presence off the shore of his empire he had heard many years before. He told us that they would be men who had a better religion and better customs, and were wiser and braver than we. So in fulfilment of my father's decree and testament, we have called you Viracochas, believing you to be messengers of the great god Viracocha, whose will and righteous indignation, and power and arms, cannot be resisted. But he has pity and mercy too. You should therefore act like divine messengers and ministers and put a stop to the slayings and lootings and acts of cruelty that have taken place in Túmbez and the district round about.

"Moreover your mouthpiece has told me that you have mentioned five great men I should know. The first is God three and one, or four, whom you call the creator of the universe: he is perchance the same as our Pachacámac and Viracocha. The second is he whom you say is the father of all other men on whom they have all heaped their sins. The third you call Jesus Christ, the only one who did not lay his sins on the first man, but he was killed. The fourth you call pope. The fifth is Charles, whom you call most powerful and monarch of the universe and supreme above the rest, without regard for the other four. If this Charles is prince and lord of the whole world, why should he need the pope to give him a new grant and concession to make war on me and usurp these kingdoms? If he has to ask the pope's permission, is not the pope a greater lord than he, and more powerful, and prince of all the world? Also I am surprised that you should say I must pay tribute to Charles and not to the others, for you give no reason for paying the tribute, and I have certainly no obligation whatever to pay it. If there were any right or reason for paying tribute, it seems to me that it should go to the God you say created everyone and the man you say was the father of all men and to Jesus Christ who did not heap sins on him; and finally it should go to the pope who can grant my kingdoms and my person to others. But if you say I owe these nothing, I owe even less to Charles, who was never lord of these regions and has never set eyes on them. If he has any rights over me after making this concession, it is only just and reasonable that you should tell me before you threaten war, fire, blood, and death, so that I may obey the pope's will, for I am not so lacking in good sense as not to obey whoever has the right justly and lawfully to command.

"I wish also to know about the good man called Jesus Christ who never cast his sins on the other and who you say died—if he died of a sickness or at the hands of his enemies; and if he was included among the gods before his death or after it. I also desire to know of you regard these five you have mentioned to me as gods, since you honor them so. For in this case you have more gods than we, who adore only Pachacámac as the Supreme God and the Sun as the lower god, and the Moon as the Sun's wife and sister. I should therefore be very glad if you would explain these things to me through a better interpreter so that I may know them and obey your will."

CHAPTER XXV

A great fray between Indians and Spaniards.

BECAUSE of his experience of the inadequacy of the interpreter the Inca took care to adjust this reply to his abilities in two respects. Firstly, he uttered it in parts, so that the dragoman would understand better and transmit it in sections, he first said one section, then the next, and so on till the end. Secondly, he used the language of the Chinchasuyu, which the interpreter would understand better because it is commoner in those parts than the speech of Cuzco; thus Felipe would understand the Inca's meaning better and might explain it, however barbarously. After delivering the reply he ordered the annalists, who have charge of the knots, to take note of it and include it in their tradition.

By now the Spaniards, who were unable to brook the length of the discourse, had left their places and fallen on the Indians, laying hands on them to seize the many gold and silver jewels and precious stones with which the Indians had adorned their persons to solemnize the occasion of hearing the embassy of the monarch of the universe. Other Spaniards had climbed up a small tower to throw down an idol adorned with many plates of gold, silver and precious stones. This alarmed the Indians and caused a great hubbub. Seeing what was happening, the Inca shouted to his followers not to wound or harm the Spaniards even though they should seize or kill the king himself. Here Padre Blas Valera says that our Lord God, as He changed the wrath of King Ahasuerus into mildness with the presence of Queen Esther, so with the presence of the holy

cross which the good friar held in his hands, He changed the angry and
warlike spirit of King Atahuallpa, not only to gentleness and mildness,
but even to the greatest submission and humility, since he ordered his
companions not to fight even thought he were killed or captured. It is
certainly to be believed that this was a manifestation of divine mercy, for
with this and similar marvels which we shall often observe at many points
of this history, we shall see how God was disposing the spirits of those
gentiles to receive the truth of His doctrine and His Holy Gospel.

The historians bear false witness that Fray Vicente de Valverde gave
the alarm, asking the Spaniards to execute justice and vengeance for the
fact that the king had thrown on the ground the book he is said to have
asked the friar to give him. They bear false witness against the king as
well as the priest, for he neither threw the book down, nor even took it in
his hands. What happened was that Fray Vicente was alarmed by the
sudden shouting of the Indians, and feared they would harm him. He
therefore rose abruptly from the chair in which he sat talking to the king,
and in rising dropped the cross from his hands and the book from his lap.
He snatched them from the ground and hurried to his companions, shouting to them not to harm the Indians, for he was much taken by Atahuallpa, realizing his good sense and understanding from his reply and
the questions he put. The friar was on the point of satisfying these
questions when the uproar began; and because of this the Spaniards did
not hear what the priest was saying on behalf of the Indians.

The king did not say the words the historians ascribe to him: "You
believe that Christ is God and that he died: I worship the Sun and Moon,
which are immortal. And who told you that your God was the maker of
the Universe?"

They go on to say that Fray Vicente answered that the book said so,
and the king took it, turned over the leaves and put it to his ear, and when
he found it did not speak, he threw it on the ground. Then the friar
picked it up and ran to his companions saying: "Christians, the Gospels
have been dashed down! Justice and vengeance on these Indians! Come
on, cut them down: they scorn our religion and spurn our friendship!"

The reply ascribed to the Inca is also fabulous: "I am free and owe
tribute to no one; nor do I intend to pay it, for I recognize no superior
and own no king. I would gladly be the emperor's friend, since he shows
his great power by sending so many armies to such distant lands. Nevertheless when you say I should obey the pope, I disagree; for a man who
tries to give his friends other people's property and bids me give up the
kingdom I have inherited, though I do not even know him, shows he is

out of his mind. And as to the part about changing my religion when I know it is most sacred, it would be cowardly and ignorant on my part to question what pleases me so well and is approved by ancient tradition and by the witness of my ancestors."

All this is fabulous, and may be set down to the false and flattering reports given to the historians. Atahuallpa did not deny the right to ask for tribute, but insisted on being told the grounds for it, and it was at this stage that the Indians raised their outcry. The Spanish general and his captains sent the version given by the historians to the emperor, and took great trouble and pains to prohibit anyone from setting down the truth about what happened, which is what we have said. Apart from the tradition of the knots of the province of Cajamarca, I have heard this version from many conquerors who were present on the expedition, and Padre Blas Valera says that one of these was his father Alonso Valera, whom he often heard tell the story. In short, more than 5,000 Indians died that day. Of these, 3,500 died by the sword, and are rest were old men, women, and children, for great crowds of both sexes and all ages had come to see and celebrate the arrival of those they regarded as gods. More than 1,500 of them perished, trampled down by the crowd of their own people and by the rush of the horses: another great crowd of all ages had collected under the wall which the Indians knocked down with the impetus of their flight, and an incalculable number perished buried alive. The warriors numbered more than 30,000 as has been said. Two days after the rout the cross was found in the place where Fray Vicente had left it, for no one dared to touch it, and the Indians, remembering the affair of Túmbez, worshipped it in the belief that the piece of wood had some great divinity and power from God, and in their ignorance of the mysteries of our Lord Jesus Christ, they begged its pardon for having offended it. They remembered the ancient prophecy and tradition they had received from their Inca Viracocha to the effect that not only their laws, towns, and state were to be changed, but that also their ceremonies and religion were to be ended and extinguished like a fire. Not knowing when this was to be, whether then or later, the king and his subjects were filled with fear and could not bring themselves to do anything in their own defence or against the Spaniards, but rather respected them as gods, supposing them to be messengers of the god Viracocha they worshipped, and whose name they applied to the Spaniards for this reason.

The above is drawn from my own information and the pages of Padre Blas Valera, whose history I would like to be able to continue to adorn my own, for he wrote as a religious and as a scholar and sought a true account of each event, satisfying his curiosity by obtaining the versions of both Indians and Spaniards. Where I find he has any relevant material I shall always include it, because of his great authority, and indeed whenever I behold his half-destroyed papers, I weep over them afresh.

CHAPTER XXVI

The author compares what he has said with the Spanish histories.

C OMPARING the above account with what the Spanish historians have written, we see that the histories already printed give very abbreviated versions of Fray Vicente's discourse and Atahuallpa's reply and that the Spanish general and his captains in reporting the meeting suppressed whatever was unfavorable and added what seemed favorable, so as not to condemn themselves. They were writing to ask for rewards for the deeds they had done, so they obviously gilded and varnished them as best they could. Our statement that Atahuallpa bade his Indians not to fight is also found in the Spanish historians, especially López de Gómara (ch. cxiii):

There was not an Indian who fought, though they all had their arms, a remarkable fact given their warlike customs. They did not fight because they were not ordered to do so, and the signal they had to begin to fight, when necessary, was not given; and this was due to the great shock and surprise they received, for they were all paralyzed by fear on account of the noise made simultaneously by trumpets, arquebusses, artillery, and horses, the last of which wore bells on their trappings to frighten them.

Further on he says:

They died in such great numbers because they did not fight, and our men, on Fray Vicente's advice, advanced thrusting at the Indians so as not to break their swords by slashing right and left.

Such is López de Gómara's account; and the other authors say almost the same, adding that the Indians took flight when they saw that their king had been grounded and captured. All this confirms our statement that Atahuallpa told them not to fight. And this was God's mercy, so that the

Christians who were to preach His Gospel should not perish that day. If the Inca had not given these orders, the sight of him fallen on the ground and captive would have been enough to cause them all to die in defence of their prince, for they had their weapons in their hands: and they would have killed and wounded the 160 Spaniards, if only by flinging stones at them. Yet the historians say that none of them was killed or wounded, except only Don Francisco Pizarro who received a small hurt in the hand from one of his own men as he seized Atahuallpa. It is true that the Indians did not fight, for, as we have said, any order of the Inca's was a divine law and commandment, even though it cost them his and their lives, as in the present case.

When they said that Fray Vicente de Valverde gave the alarm crying for vengeance on the Indians and recommending the Spaniards to thrust and not slash with their swords so as not to break them and thus causing great loss of life among the Indians, it is obvious that this was a wrong account received by historians in Spain of events that happened three thousand leagues away. It is not to be imagined, much less believed, that a Catholic friar and theologian would utter such words, which can be believed of a Nero, but not of a priest who deserved to become a bishop for his great virtue and good doctrine, and who died at the hands of the Indians for preaching the Catholic faith. And with this we must now return to our history.

CHAPTER XXVII

The Spaniards capture King Atahuallpa.

THE SPANIARDS with horses appeared from their stations, and furiously attacked the Indian regiments, lancing everyone they could and meeting with no opposition. Pizarro and his infantry fell on King Atahuallpa full of eagerness to seize him, since they thought if they won this jewel they would have all the treasures of Peru in their power. The Indians surrounded the royal litter in great numbers to prevent his being trampled on or harmed. The Spaniards wrought cruel havoc among them, though they did not defend themselves but merely placed themselves in the way to prevent the assailants from reaching the Inca. At last they did reach him, with great mortality among the Indians; and the first

to arrive was Pizarro, who seized his garments and threw him to the
ground, though one historians says he caught him by his hair, which he
wore very long: this is a mistake, for the Indians shaved their heads.

In short, the Spaniards threw down and captured King Atahuallpa.
At this point López de Gómara says: "No Spaniard was wounded or
killed, except Francisco Pizarro, who received a blow on the hand: as he
was seizing Atahuallpa a soldier struck out with his knife to bring him
down, for which reason some say that the soldier took the king." Here
López de Gómara ends his ch. cxiii. To add what is missing to López de
Gómara's account—as we have proposed—we may add that the soldier
was called Miguel Astete: he was later a *vecino* in the city of Huamanga,
where he had an allocation of Indians. As Atahuallpa fell, this soldier
took the scarlet fringe, which he wore on his forehead instead of a crown,
and kept it. It was because of this that he and not Pizarro was said to have
captured the king. In any case, as the two reached him together the honor
should go to the captain. Miguel Astete kept the fringe until 1557, when
Inca Sairi Túpac came down from the mountains to which he had fled,
and he restored it to him, as we shall say in due course.

When the Indians saw that their king had been taken, and that the
Spaniards were still wounding and killing, they all took flight, and as
they could not get away by the way they had come, since the horsemen
had taken up their positions there, they fled toward a wall which surrounded the flat space: it was of smooth masonry and had been built in
the time of the great Inca Pachacútec who conquered Cajamarca. They
rushed at it with such force in their flight from the horses that they overturned a section more than a hundred paces long and escaped through the
breach into the country. One author says that the wall and its stones
showed more pity than the hearts of the Spaniards, since they fell down to
let the Indians escape on beholding them penned in and in terror of
death. The Spaniards were not content with seeing them flee, but pursued
them and lanced them until the night fell and covered them. They then
sacked the battlefield which was littered with many jewels of gold, silver,
and precious stones. López de Gómara speaks as follows of this in his
ch. cxiv:

They found 5,000 women in Atahuallpa's royal camp and bagnio, who received
the Christians in spite of their grief and distress: they found also many fine
tents, an infinite quantity of apparel and household utensils and beautiful
pieces and vessels of gold and silver, one of which is said to have weighed eight
arrobas of gold. Atahuallpa's plate alone was worth 100,000 ducats. The king

was much upset at finding himself in chains, and he begged Pizarro to treat him well, since fortune had brought him to this pass,

etc. This is taken literally from López de Gómara, and Zárate says almost the same. Those who wish to see the full account are referred to these writers.

CHAPTER XXVIII

Atahuallpa promises a ransom in return for his liberty; the steps taken to collect it.

T HE NOBLES who had fled the massacre at Cajamarca returned to serve their king in his confinement, on learning that he was alive. Only one commander called Rumiñaui, who had remained in the field with his regiment in the rear and had never shared the opinion that they should accept peace with the Spaniards or place confidence in them, perceived what was happening in Cajamarca, and offended that he had not been heeded, fled with all his force to the kingdom of Quito, where he intended to take the necessary measures to oppose the Spaniards. This suited his own interest, for he had the intention of leading a rebellion against Atahuallpa, following the bad example set by the latter. To this end as soon as he had reached Quito he seized some of Atahuallpa's children, giving out that he intended to guard and protect them from the Spaniards, though he soon killed them and also Atahuallpa's full brother, Quilliscacha, whom the Spanish historians call Illescas. He also slew the commander Challcuchima and many other captains and *curacas,* as we shall say in due course.

On finding himself under arrest and in chains, Inca Atahuallpa sought to escape by ransoming himself, and he promised to cover the floor of the large room in which he was imprisoned with gold and silver plate in return for his liberty: "and as he saw the Spaniards present pull a face, he thought that they did not believe him"—these are López de Gómara's words—"and undertook to give them within a certain time enough plate and other pieces of gold and silver to fill the room as high as he could reach with his hand up the wall. This was settled by the drawing of a red line right round the room. But he made the condition that the jars, pitchers, and vats which he proposed to pile up as high as the line should not be pressed down or broken," etc. This López de Gómara in his ch. cxiv. In order not to go into such detail as these historians, to whom I refer the reader for a fuller account, we shall briefly relate the events concerning the life and death of the Inca kings up to the last of them and of their descendants, which was our first intention. Later, if occasion offers, we shall set down the most notable events that occurred during the wars between the Spaniards.

Atahuallpa ordered gold and silver to be brought to pay his ransom, and it seemed impossible to fulfil what he had promised, however much was brought. The Spaniards therefore complained that as the prisoner had not carried out his promise and that the time had expired, the delay would allow the Indians to raise an army and attack and kill them, so as to free the king. These imaginings filled the Spaniards with discontent. Atahuallpa, who was very intelligent, sensed this and asked the reason. When Pizarro told him, he said that the Spaniards' suspicions about the delay arose from the fact that they did not know the distances between the chief places from which the greater part of the ransom had to be brought, Cuzco, Pachacámac, Quito, and many other provinces. He told them that the nearest place was Pachacámac, over eighty leagues away, and Cuzco was two hundred leagues and Quito three hundred, and suggested that Spaniards should be sent to inspect the treasure in these places and the whole of the rest of the kingdom, so that they could satisfy themselves as to the quantity and collect it themselves.

Seeing that the Spaniards doubted the safety of those who might volunteer to go to inspect the treasure, Atahuallpa said: "You have nothing to fear, for you have me here in iron chains." Then Hernando de Soto and Pedro del Barco, a native of Lobón, decided to go to Cuzco. Atahuallpa regretted that Soto should go, for as he was one of the first two Christians he had seen, he was attached to him and realized that he would be a friend in case of need; but he dared not oppose the idea lest the Spaniards should say that he was going back on what he had asked and they had accepted, thus increasing their suspicions. As well as these two, four other Spaniards went to visit various provinces and see the treasure that was stored there. One went to Quito, and others to Huaillas, Huamachucu, and Sicllapampa. They were instructed to watch carefully if armies were being raised anywhere in the kingdom for the purpose of freeing King Atahuallpa. But he had no idea of doing anything the Spaniards suspected him of, and his one thought was to obtain for them the quantity of gold and silver he had promised in return for his liberty, and so see himself released from the iron chains in which he was kept. He therefore ordered it to be announced throughout the kingdom that the single Spaniards were to be received and lodged with every possible attention and comfort. Because of the Inca's orders and of the marvels that had been told of the Spaniards, that they were gods and messengers of the supreme God, as they themselves had declared, and because they knew about Pedro de Candía's adventure with the lion and tiger in Túmbez, the Spaniards were received in every Indian town and village with the greatest honor and respect. They were presented with gifts of all kinds and even offered sacrifices, for the Indians adored the Spaniards as gods, in their great simplicity and superstition. And although they knew of the slaughter that had taken place at Cajamarca, from those who had escaped and fled to various places, they still held the Spaniards to be gods, though now terrible and cruel gods, and thus offered sacrifices to appease them and prevent them from doing harm, though no longer in the hope that they would do good.

Hernando de Soto, Pedro del Barco, and the other four Spaniards were carried on hammocks on the shoulders of Indians, according to the Inca's instructions, so that they should travel faster and in greater comfort. *Hamaca* is a word from the Indian language of the Windward Islands, where as the climate is very hot those of the better sort sleep in nets made of leaves of the palm or other trees. The less wealthy sleep in cotton blankets fastened by the opposite corners and slung a yard above the ground: this is cooler than sleeping on mattresses. These beds, which we might call wind-beds, are *hamacas*. In the same way the Peruvian Indians used to tie a blanket to a pole three or four yards long, and the traveller could lie in it, its other corners being knotted over the pole so that the occupant should not fall out: he was carried stretched out like a dead man. Two Indians carried him, and they changed over with others often and with great ease and dexterity. Twenty or thirty Indians would go along to take turns and thus reduce the labor. Each party would be relieved after so many leagues, so that they should not have the strain of carrying the passenger the whole way. Such was the mail-post of the Indians. The instrument was called *huantu,* "stretcher," or *rampa.* The Spaniards call it *hamaca* because it is like the beds. In this way these two brave Spaniards, Hernando de Soto and Pedro del Barco, travelled the two hundred leagues between Cajamarca and Cuzco, more safely and better attended than if they had been in their own country; the same was true of the other four, for the Inca's bidding assured their lives and secured them hospitality, with such rejoicings and celebrations that the Spaniards themselves could not find words enough for them when they told the story.

CHAPTER XXIX

Hernando Pizarro's journey to Pachacámac;
the events of the journey.

SOON AFTER the departure of Hernando de Soto and Pedro del Barco, Hernando Pizarro went to see the temple of Pachacámac, drawn by the fame of its great wealth. So as not to go alone he took a band of horse in case of emergency. One day on the journey, as the Spaniards reached the top of a hill they saw that the side of another hill facing them on the road was all of gold, for it shone dazzlingly in the sun. They pressed on full of amazement, for they could not understand what it was. When they reached it, they saw that it was jars and vats, and great and small pitchers, pots, braziers, shields, and many other objects made of gold and silver which were being brought by one of Atahuallpa's brothers, called Quilliscacha (whom we have already mentioned), as part of the ransom: it amounted to two millions, though the historians say no more than 300,000 pesos. This must have been a miscalculation, as we shall see later from the accounts. The Indians who had been carrying it had unloaded to rest, and so the hillside looked as if it were made of gold. I heard this tale in my own country from those who saw it, and it was told me in Spain by the good gentleman, Don Gabriel Pizarro, inquisitor of the Holy Inquisition of Córdova, who had heard about the hill of gold together with the anecdotes of the journey, from a gentleman called Juan Pizarro de Orellana, a companion of Hernando Pizarro's.

As to Quilliscacha, no sooner had he reached Cajamarca with the treasure than Atahuallpa sent him to the kingdom of Quito to put down and quell any rising that Rumiñaui might plan. Atahuallpa was uncertain of his intentions and therefore sent his brother after him.

Rumiñaui, who had been a good collaborator in Atahuallpa's rebellion and the acts of cruelty that followed it, knew the Inca's guile and deceit of old and suspected what was in the air. He therefore received Quilliscacha as a brother of his king, and was informed of the latter's arrest and the ransom that had been agreed. They therefore jointly ordered that all the gold and silver in the kingdom should be gathered together, although Rumiñaui did not desire the Inca's freedom, but treacherously concealed his wicked intentions and served and flattered Quilliscacha as though he were a very loyal official, until he should find an opportunity to carry out his dastardly plan, as indeed he did.

Hernando Pizarro allowed Quilliscacha to proceed, and himself continued his journey as far as the great temple of Pachacámac, whose incredible wealth, great size and large and thickly inhabited valley greatly astonished him and his companions. But the Indians were much more astonished to see the form and dress, arms and horses of their visitors. Because of this and of the Inca's commands, they worshipped them as gods and offered them such services and attentions as beggar description. As in Cajamarca, when they saw the horses with bits in their mouths they thought this was their food, and brought large quantities of gold and silver, which they begged them to eat, saying that these metals were better than iron. The Spaniards, rejoicing in the ignorance of the Indians, also as in Cajamarca, bade them bring plenty of this food and put it under the maize and hay, for the horses were great eaters and would devour it all. The Indians did so. Hernando Pizarro took as much of the gold in the temple as he could carry, and left instructions that all the remaining wealth should be conveyed to Cajamarca, telling the Indians that it was for the ransom of King Atahuallpa, so that they should bring it out willingly and not hide it.

In Pachacámac Hernando Pizarro learnt that forty leagues further on there was one of Atahuallpa's commanders called Challcuchima, with a great head of war, and he sent him a message summoning him to discuss certain matters necessary to the peace and quiet of the kingdom. The Indian would not come to the Spaniard, and Hernando Pizarro therefore went to the Indian with great danger to himself and his companions and suffering no little hardship on the way owing to the roughness of the road and the numerous large rivers they had to pass by the rope bridges we have already described, which were very strange for the horses to cross. Most of his companions disapproved of Hernando Pizarro's boldness in placing himself in the hands of a heathen, saying that they ought not to trust the Indian because of the superiority of his forces. But the Spanish leader confided in the signs, countersigns, and promises made by Atahuallpa on their taking leave of him, to be used in case they should come across one of his commanders or captains on the way. In this way Hernando Pizarro spoke to Challcuchima, and persuaded him to dismiss his army and accompany him to visit the captive king. The Indian agreed and they shortened the return road by cutting through the snowcapped mountains, where they might have perished of cold if the Indians had not come to their help and taken them to some large caves in the rocks, which are common in all the mountain ranges of Peru.

Owing to the roughness of the road the horses cast their shoes, and they were very short of these, for they had not realized how bad the roads were and had brought only a few. They were saved by the skill of the Indians, who moulded many shoes of gold and silver using a pair of iron ones, and this supplied their need. López de Gómara says the following of this incident at the end of his ch. cxiv: "Then they shod the horses with silver and some with gold, for these wore less, and they lacked iron," etc. With these difficulties Hernando Pizarro and Challcuchima reached Cajamarca. The Indian took off his shoes and pulled a garment over his shoulders as a token of submission and vassalage before appearing in the Inca's presence, and he was greatly distressed to see his king in iron chains, saying that the Spaniards had taken him because he, Challcuchima, was absent. The Inca replied that Pachacámac had ordained it so, in order to fulfil the prophecies made so many years before about the coming of these new people and the destruction of their heathen religion and loss of their empire, as his father Huaina Cápac had assured him on his death bed. He said that after his capture he had sent to Cuzco to consult his father the Sun and the other oracles in the kingdom, and especially the talking idol in the valley of Rímac. Despite its talkativeness, it had lost its voice; and what was more surprising was that the hidden oracle that spoke in the temple of Pachacámac, though it had undertaken the duty of answering questions put to it about the affairs of the kings and great lords, had also gone dumb. Though it had been told that the king was in chains and asked what would deliver him from them, it remained deaf and dumb; and the priests and wizards who used to converse so familiarly with all the other oracles in the empire advised him that they had not been able to get any reply, not even a single word, out of it, despite the sacrifices and spells they had tried on it. Atahuallpa said that he was very scandalized and alarmed at this, suspecting that his father the Sun had abandoned him, since the idols that usually spoke to the priests and other devout persons now suddenly refused to communicate with them. He said that all this was a very bad sign and a proof of his death and the loss of his empire. Atahuallpa expressed these and similar fears with heartfelt grief and anguish in talking with his commander Challcuchima in prison. He thus fully experienced the troubles and sufferings he had caused and was still causing by means of his acts of tyranny and oppression in the hearts of the unfortunate Huáscar Inca and all his friends.

CHAPTER XXX

The demons of Peru are silenced by the sacraments of the Roman Church, our holy Mother.

I T IS indeed true that as soon as the sacraments of our holy Mother, one Church, Roman, Catholic, and Apostolic, entered Peru, the demons that used to deal so familiarly with the heathen, as we have said, lost the power of speech in public. These sacraments were, first, the consecration of the body and blood of Our Lord, Jesus Christ in the masses the Christians heard on such days as they could; then the baptism given to the Indians who entered the service of the Spaniards; the sacrament of matrimony, when the Indians were married before the priest; and that of penitence, when the Spaniards confessed their sins and received the Blessed Sacrament. These four sacraments were the first to be introduced into my country; and the other three followed only later when arrangements had been made for them.

The idols lost their power of public speech, and could only speak in secret and then only rarely with great wizards who were their perpetual familiars. And though at first the partisans of Huáscar Inca—who were the first to notice this failure of their oracles—said that the Sun was angry at the tyranny and cruelty of Atahuallpa and had forbidden them to speak, they soon after discovered that the affliction was a general one. This gave rise to a universal fear and astonishment among the Indians, who could not understand the reason for the silence of their oracles, though they did not fail to suspect that it was due to the arrival of the strangers in their land. They feared and respected the Spaniards more day by day, as being a people with power to silence their oracles. They therefore confirmed the name Viracocha for a Spaniard, since he was a god they revered more highly than the huacas, of which we have already given a full description.

CHAPTER XXXI

*Huáscar Inca implores the help
of the two scouts.*

AFTER travelling more than a hundred leagues, Hernando de Soto and
Pedro del Barco reached Sausa [Juaja], where Atahuallpa's captains
held Huáscar Inca prisoner. When the Spaniards knew he was there,
they wished to see him, and the Inca, closely guarded as he was, also
tried to see them. At last they met, but what they said to one another was
not understood, as they had no interpreter, except in so far as they could
use signs. Later it was ascertained that when Huáscar Inca learned from
the Indians that the chief object of the Spaniards was to do justice and
redress wrongs—as they had always affirmed since first entering Peru—
he said that as the intention of His Majesty and of his captain general in
his name was to dispense justice both to the Spaniards and to the Indians
they conquered, and to restore to each his own property, they should be
told of his brother's usurpation, and how Atahuallpa had sought to
deprive him not only of the kingdom which was his by legitimate right of
succession, but also of his life; and that this was why he was kept closely
guarded. He begged and urged them not to go away, but to take him
with them and so assure his safety, for as soon as they went the captains
would slay him. When the captain general knew of the justice of his
claims, he would restore him to the throne; since he proclaimed that he
had come to right wrongs. Then Huáscar would give the Spaniards much
more than his brother had promised: he would not only fill the room with
gold up to the promised level, but cram it to the top of the roof, three
times as high; and he would be in a much better position than his brother
to carry out this promise because he knew where all the treasures of his
father and ancestors were, an incalculable quantity, while Atahuallpa
would have to destroy temples and altars to satisfy his promise, since he
had no other wealth. Hernando de Soto and Pedro del Barco answered
what they could understand by signs, namely the request that they should
not go on, but stay with him, saying that they had to obey their captain's
orders, who had bidden them go as far as Cuzco. They would soon return
and would do whatever they could to help him. They then took leave of
the wretched Huáscar, leaving him sadder and more disconsolate than

ever, for he had hoped for some remedy at their hands, but now quite despaired of his life, assured that his death would be hastened because he had seen and talked with them, as was indeed the case.

CHAPTER XXXII

The two Spaniards reach Cuzco and find crosses in the temples and palaces.

THE TWO companions went on to Cuzco, and as they gazed on the imperial city from the hill of Carmenca, they were filled with wonder at its beauty. They were received by a great throng with rejoicings, celebrations, and dancing. Triumphal arches of many different kinds of flowers were built at intervals over the streets, which were strewn with rushes. They were lodged in one of the palaces called Amarucancha, which had belonged to Huaina Cápac, and were told that as divine people they had been given the house of the greatest and best loved of the Incas. There was a very fine round tower, standing alone before the entrance to the house. I saw it in my time; and its walls were about four times the height of a man; but its roof, made of the excellent timber they used for their royal palaces, was so high that I might say without exaggeration that it equalled any tower I have seen in Spain in height, with the exception of the one at Seville. Its roof was rounded like the walls, and above it, in place of a weathervane—for the Indians did not observe the wind—it had a very tall and thick pole that enhanced its height and beauty. It was more than sixty feet in height inside, and was known as Sunturhuaci, "excellent house or room." There was no other building touching it. In my time it was pulled down so as to clear the square, as it now is; for the tower projected into it, though the appearance of the square was not spoiled by having the building on one side, especially as it took up very little of its space. The colossal building of the Holy Society of Jesus now stands on the site, as we have already remarked.

On the following day the Indians carried the Spaniards out in litters to see the city. They were worshipped wherever they went with all the signs of adoration the Indians had in their heathen religion. The two companions were filled with admiration at the majesty of Cuzco, and the

splendor and wealth of its temples and palaces, though these were already
much diminished owing to the recent wars between the Incas and the
arrest of Huáscar, as a result of which most of the treasures had been
hidden. They were full of praise for the construction and excellence of
the palaces and for the fact that works on such a scale had been carried
out without the aid of instruments. But they were much more impressed
by the bed of the stream passing through the city, paved with great flag-
stones with side walls of excellent masonry, which is continued outside
the city for a distance of a quarter of a league. They were amazed by the
great multitude of Indians, and the abundance of trades, through their
wares were poor and scanty. They were favorably impressed by the manners of the nobles, whom they found kind and gentle and very desirous to
please them: they would have seen much more of this had it not been
for the war between the two brothers.

Finally they were surprised to find crosses on the tops of the temples
and palaces: these were erected when the news reached Cuzco of the
incident of Pedro de Candía and the wild beasts that had been set on him
to tear him to pieces at Túmbez and of how he had tamed them with the
cross he carried in his hands. This had been told with great astonishment
by the Indians who brought the news of these wonders to Cuzco. And
when the inhabitants of the city then discovered what the symbol was,
they went to the sanctuary where the cross of jasper which we have
already mentioned was kept and worshipped it with fervent cries, begging
it that, as they had venerated it for so many centuries, though not as
highly as they should because they had not been aware of its great virtues,
it should free them from the strangers who had arrived in their land just as
it had freed that man from the wild beasts that had been set on him.
After worshipping it, they placed crosses on the temples and palaces so
as to save them and the whole kingdom from the enemies they feared.

Here it is to be remarked that even before hearing the preaching of
the Catholic faith these idolatrous heathen placed themselves and their
whole empire in the power of the cross and so of the Christian religion,
by raising the cross over their temples and palaces and adoring it and
begging it to free them from their fears. Indeed since the death of Huaina
Cápac, the Indians had been full of fears and forebodings that their
idolatry, empire, power, and state were soon to come to an end, for at the
end of his life that prince had clearly explained the signs and prophecies
they had long before received from their oracles about these events,
though the wording of these portents had been very obscure and confused. Huaina Cápac had explained them clearly and prophesied the

coming of the Spaniards and the preaching of the Holy Gospel in Peru, and assigned a time for them, which would be that of the end of his own life. The Indians therefore worshipped the Spaniards as gods with the obsequiousness and ceremony we have already mentioned, suspecting that it was they who were to fulfil their king's prophecy.

Hernando de Soto and Pedro del Barco then wrote to their captain general, describing all this and the incredible wealth they had found in Cuzco—which far exceeded what they had imagined—and the great hospitality the Indians had shown them as the result of the proclamation Atahuallpa had made throughout the kingdom on their behalf. The other four scouts who visited other parts of the country had the same experience and sent back similar reports. The Spaniards received the good news about all this wealth with great rejoicing, but they regarded the worship of their companions resulting from Huaina Cápac's prophecy as a piece of Indian witchcraft which should be ignored.

CHAPTER XXXIII

The astuteness of Atahuallpa and the death of King Huáscar Inca.

ZÁRATE relates Huáscar Inca's conversation with Hernando de Soto and Pedro del Barco as we have told it and mentions how they parted, leaving the unfortunate Inca in the plight we have mentioned. He then says in his Book II, ch. vi:

And so they continued their journey, which caused the death of Huáscar and the loss of the gold he had promised them, for the captains who held him under arrest at once sent messengers posting to Atahuallpa with news of all that had taken place. And Atahuallpa was intelligent enough to realize that if Huáscar's proposal reached Pizarro's ears, the Christians would deprive him of the throne and give it to his brother, because the latter had right on his side, and because of the great store of gold he offered, for he now understood how much the Christians loved and coveted the metal. He also thought that they might use the fact that he had arrested his brother and seized the throne to kill him and thus avoid complications. For this reason he decided to have Huáscar put to death, though he was rather afraid to do so, because he had often heard the Christians say that one of their most strictly observed laws was that whoever killed another must die for it. He therefore decided to sound out the governor to discover how he would react. This he did with great ingenuity. One day he pretended to be very sad, and wept and sobbed, refusing to eat or speak with anyone; and although the governor begged him repeatedly to tell him the cause of his sorrow, he displayed great reluctance until at last he revealed that he had been given news that one of his captains, on hearing of his arrest, had killed his brother Huáscar. This had upset him deeply, for he had looked up to Huáscar as an elder brother, and even as a father, and if he had had him arrested, this was with no intention of harming him personally or depriving him of his throne, but merely to oblige Huáscar to leave him in peaceful possession of the province of Quito, which his father had conquered and left him, and over which Huáscar had no control.

The governor comforted him, and urged him not to grieve, for death was a natural thing in the face of which men were little better than one another. When the whole country had been pacified, Pizarro would find out who had been the murderers and punish them. And as Atahuallpa saw that the marquis took the matter so lightly he decided to execute his plan. He thus sent orders to the captains who were guarding Huáscar that he was to be killed forthwith. This was done so promptly that afterwards it was difficult to ascertain whether Atahuallpa's show of grief occurred before or after the murder. The blame for this sorry affair was generally placed on Hernando de Soto and Pedro del Barco, because soldiers are not aware of the obligation on those who are given certain instructions (especially in wartime) to carry them out strictly, without the power to modify them according to circumstances, unless they have express permission to do so. The Indians say that when Huáscar saw that he was to die, he exclaimed: "My rule over my country has not been long. That of my treacherous brother, by whose hand I, his natural lord, am to die, shall be even shorter."

For this reason when Atahuallpa was killed, as we shall see in the following chapter, the Indians believed that Huáscar was a child of the Sun because he had truly prophesied his brother's death.

He likewise said that when his father had bidden him farewell, he had told him that when a bearded white race should come to their country, he was to make friends with them, for they would be lords of the kingdom,

etc. The above is from Zárate. When the Spanish historians adhere so closely to the historical truth, I am happier to quote their words literally than to write my own, so as to speak like a Spaniard and not like an Indian. I shall do this always unless there is something to add to their account.

To return to Zárate, it should be noted that he touches briefly on many points which we have treated at length in our history, such as Atahuallpa's tyranny and his cunning and shrewdness in sounding out Pizarro to see how he would take Huáscar's death. For if the Spaniard had shown the same astuteness as the Indian and answered, "You had him killed: I shall investigate and punish your crime as it deserves!" the murder would certainly not have been committed.

But as Atahuallpa saw that the governor not only suspected no ill of him, but indeed consoled rather than upbraided him, he took courage and resolved to kill the Inca, his natural lord, which was the greatest of his acts of cruelty.

Huáscar was cruelly butchered and flayed and quartered. It is not known where his body was thrown, but the Indians believe that he was eaten in a fit of rage. Padre Acosta says he was burned. Zárate also touches on the haste with which the messages were exchanged, as we have said. The news of Huáscar's death was circulated with even greater speed, for Atahuallpa ordered it to be sent to him by means of the smoke signals and beacons the *chasquis* use by day and night for such messages. It was for this reason that afterwards no one could be sure whether Atahuallpa's show of grief and sorrow had occurred before or after the death of Huáscar. This author also touches on the prophecy left by Huaina Cápac about the arrival of the Spaniards and their succeeding as lords of his kingdom.

Hernando de Soto and Pedro del Barco can hardly be blamed for not having remained with Huáscar. This was due to their not having understood his offer to give them three times as much treasure as his brother had promised. If they had understood this, they would have stayed with him, since the commission entrusted to them did not concern the conquest and pacification of the kingdom, but was limited to ascertaining whether or not Atahuallpa could fulfil his promise to raise the amount of his ransom. And as Huáscar offered to triple this, it can readily be believed that they would not have left him, so as not to lose this larger sum. They themselves made the same defence, that they had not understood, when they were accused of causing the death of Huáscar.

Such was the end of the unhappy Inca, the last ruler of that empire, who had seen all the misfortunes and calamities we have mentioned visited on his vassals, servants, kinsfolk, brothers, and children, and on his own person and all caused and executed by one of his brothers. Diego Fernández of Palencia speaks as follows of his ill treatment in prison:

"Atahuallpa's two captains returned to their master bringing Huáscar as their prisoner. They treated him very ill, giving him urine to drink and vermin and other unclean things to eat on the way. Meanwhile Don Francisco Pizarro with the other Christians entered the land, and captured

Atahuallpa at Cajamarca." These are the words of this author, who adds
later on: "They killed Huáscar at Andamarca, and Atahuallpa died at
Cajamarca." This should be written Cassamarca, "land or province of
ice": *cassa* means "ice," and *marca* the rest. Similarly Andamarca should
be written Antamarca, "province of copper," for *anta* is "copper," etc.

CHAPTER XXXIV

*Don Diego de Almagro reaches Cajamarca;
the signs and fears Atahuallpa has of
his approaching end.*

T HE DEATH of the wretched Huáscar, which occurred as we have said,
did not assure Atahuallpa of the possession of his kingdom, or of
the liberty of his person, or even of his life: rather the reverse, for within
a very few days orders were given to deprive him of it. Zárate and López
de Gómara agree about the matter of these, as on many other points in
this history. It is indeed a common punishment of heaven on those who
trust in their own cunning and oppression more than in reason and justice, and as we shall see, God permits such people to suffer these and even
greater punishments.

We should mention that Almagro was sailing from Panama in a fine
ship which he had fitted with many excellent soldiers so as to press forward with the conquest, or, as his enemies said, to steal a march over
Pizarro by landing further south, for he was aware that the limit of the
area granted to Pizarro to govern did not extend beyond two hundred
leagues south of the equator. Almagro wanted to make his own conquest
beyond this. Pizarro is said to have had news of this intention from a
secretary of Almagro's, whom his master hanged for this act of disloyalty.
Whether thus or otherwise, during his voyage Almagro heard of the
capture of Atahuallpa and of the incredible riches that were being collected for his ransom. He therefore changed his plan and went to join
his victorious companion, since half of Pizarro's gains were due to him
under the terms of their agreement. Almagro and his men reached Cajamarca and were astonished at the sight of all the gold and silver that had
been gathered together. But Pizarro's men soon disillusioned Almagro's,

by telling them that since they had not been present at the capture of the king, they were not entitled to share in the treasure so far collected, or in what remained to be collected to come up to the line that Atahuallpa had drawn and promised to reach with his ransom. The room was so large that they thought this impossible, even though all the gold and silver in the world were brought together. They therefore began to demand that the Inca should be killed so that they could share in what might be seized afterwards. In making this demand they supported their own argument with others as weak or even weaker. Nevertheless, these were sufficient to bring about the death of so great a prince as Atahuallpa. He himself was greatly in fear of being killed when he saw how the Spaniards were at odds with one another and heard them break out into violent quarrels at every touch and turn. The unhappy Inca suspected that all this would fall on his own head, and this suspicion was strengthened by the failure of the oracles to answer his questions and prayers. In addition he heard from his Indians that many shooting stars had been seen at night, both large and small; and it was on these and other lesser signs that these heathens fixed their attention in less calamitous times, to explain the superstitions and portents they fancied they could each foretell.

Finally, to his utter despair, they told him that among other signs in the skies they had seen a great greenish-black comet, a little smaller than the body of a man and longer than a pike, which appeared nightly and resembled the one that had been seen shortly before the death of his father Huaina Cápac. Atahuallpa was much scandalized by this news; and having obtained confirmation from the Spaniards, who also spoke about it, he asked permission to see it, and when he had done so he grew very sad, and ceased to speak and converse with anyone as he had done formerly. Pizarro repeatedly importuned him to tell the cause of his sadness, and in order to avoid more questioning and to prevent Pizarro from thinking there was some other cause, Atahuallpa told him:

"Apu (which is captain general), I am certain that my death will soon occur, for this comet has hold me as much: one like it was seen a few days before my father died. And I am full of grief to realize that I am to die so soon, without having enjoyed the possession of my realms, for these signs only show themselves to announce some great calamity, the death of kings or destruction of empires. I suspected all this before when I found myself in iron chains, but the appearance of this comet has now assured me of it. You will now have understood the cause of my sadness and the reason for my grief."

The governor urged him not to heed or believe these omens which there was no reason to credit. Let him wait, for very soon he would find himself freed from prison and restored to his throne. But this consolation left Atahuallpa as sad as ever, for the heathens believed very firmly in their auguries; and the king therefore took more notice of them than of Pizarro. Cieza de León in his ch. lxv, says the same as we have said about the comet, and mentions how superstitious the Indians were in this and similar respects.

As a result of these prophecies, Atahuallpa lost all hope of recovering his liberty, and his fear of death became a certainty. It occurred within fifteen days of his seeing the comet, as Cieza says in the above-mentioned chapter.

CHAPTER XXXV

Hernando Pizarro comes to Spain to report on the happenings in Peru.

WHILE Atahuallpa doubted and feared, Governor Francisco Pizarro was filled with greater hopes and ambitions, as a result of the favor his good fortune had so far shown him. And as he desired to increase his claims in the future, he thought that it would be wise to send His Majesty an account of what had happened so far. He said as much to his companion Don Diego de Almagro and his brothers, and they agreed that Hernando Pizarro should come to Spain with the mission of reporting their achievements so that His Majesty might reward them according to their deserts. Hernando Pizarro took what was necessary for the expenses of the journey from the pile of gold and silver Atahuallpa had had collected for his ransom, since his negotiations were to be on behalf of all those who had a share in it. For His Majesty he took 100,000 pesos of gold and as many again of silver, to be set against the royal fifth payable to the crown on Atahuallpa's ransom. The gold and silver were the first-fruits of what has since been brought and is still to be brought from my country for His Majesty. The silver was brought in worked objects, as Zárate says in his Book II, ch. vii:

He decided to send Hernando Pizarro to inform His Majesty of the successful result of their enterprise; and as they had no way of melting or assaying the metal in those days and it could not be ascertained for sure what part of the heap belonged to His Majesty, he brought 100,000 gold pesos and 20,000 silver marks, selecting the largest and most striking pieces so that they should be more highly valued in Spain. Thus he brought many jars, brasiers, drums, and figures of llamas, and men and women, to complete the aforesaid weight and value. With this he went off to take ship, much to the regret of Atahuallpa, who had grown very attached to him and communicated all his affairs to him. And in taking leave of him, Atahuallpa said: "Are you going, captain? I regret it, because when you have gone I know that the fat one and the one-eyed one will kill me." He referred to Almagro, who as we have said above, had only one eye, and to Alonso de Riquelme, His Majesty's treasurer, both of whom he had seen complaining against him, for reasons we shall mention later. Thus it came about that as soon as Hernando Pizarro had left, the question of the death of Atahuallpa was raised through an Indian who acted as interpreter, called Felipillo,

etc. López de Gómara, as we shall see, says that Hernando Pizarro brought the royal fifth that fell to His Majesty out of Atahuallpa's ransom.

The fact is that Hernando Pizarro did not take away from Cajamarca any more than the sum we have mentioned. But as soon as he had left, the king was killed and his ransom—which served to hasten his death rather than to save him—was shared out, whereupon sixty of the *conquistadores* came back to Spain with their respective shares, bringing thirty, forty, or fifty thousand pesos more or less, and they also brought the royal fifth for His Majesty. They caught up with Hernando Pizarro at Nombre de Dios, for he had still not taken ship, and they all came back together. This explanation confirms the accounts of these two authors, which are not contradictory.

Soon after Hernando Pizarro's departure Hernando de Soto and Pedro del Barco returned from Cuzco with news of the incredible riches they had seen there, in the temple of the Sun, in the palaces of the old kings, and in the fortress and other sanctuaries and places where the Devil spoke to the wizards and priests and his other devotees: all such places were adorned with gold and silver since they were considered to be holy places. The other four scouts brought back similar reports, and the Spaniards were delighted at the news, desiring to see and enjoy these great treasures. They therefore hastened to despatch Atahuallpa so as to relieve themselves of anxiety and remove any obstacle that might prevent or delay their laying hands on the gold and silver in the imperial city and else-

where. It was therefore decided to kill him as a way to avoid trouble and
strife. His end and death is described by both historians in almost the
same terms: I shall therefore here give López de Gómara's ch. cxix, whose
title and contents are as follows.

CHAPTER XXXVI

"The execution of Atahuallpa as a result of
deceit and false information."

THE DEATH of Atahuallpa was plotted in the most unexpected quarter, for
the interpreter Felipillo fell in love with and consorted with one of the
Inca's wives, intending to marry her if the Inca died. He told Pizarro and
others that Atahuallpa was secretly gathering forces to kill the Christians and
set him free. This rumor began to spread among the Spaniards and they began
to believe it: some said that he ought to be killed for the security of their own
lives and of the kingdom; and others that he ought to be sent to the emperor,
and that they should not kill so great a prince, whatever his guilt. The second
was the better course, but they took the first. Many say that this was due to the
pressure of Almagro's companions, who thought, and said to one another, that
as long as Atahuallpa lived they would have no claim to any gold at all until
the measure of his ransom had been filled. At last Pizarro decided to kill him in
order to save trouble, and thinking that with Atahuallpa dead, he would have
less difficulty in winning Peru.

Atahuallpa was accused of the death of Huáscar, king of the country, and it
was also shown that he had sought to kill the Spaniards; but this was due to the
knavery of Felipillo, who explained the testimony of the Indians called to give
evidence as it suited him, since there was no Spaniard who could understand or
check what he was saying. Atahuallpa always denied the charge, saying that it
was quite incomprehensible that he should have attempted anything of the sort,
since he could not have accomplished it and lived, owing to the numerous
guards and fetters about him. He threatened Felipillo and begged them not to
believe him. When he heard the sentence, he complained bitterly of Pizarro's
conduct, who was about to kill him after having promised to release him in
return for the ransom. He begged Pizarro to send him to Spain, and not to stain
his hands and his reputation with the blood of one who had done him no harm,
and who had made him rich. When they were taking him to the place of execution he asked to be baptized, on the advice of those who were consoling him,

for otherwise he would have been burnt alive. He was baptized, bound to a stake and strangled. He was buried according to Christian usage with funeral rites. Pizarro put on mourning and accorded Atahuallpa honorable obsequies.

We should not reproach those who put him to death, for time and their sins punished them later, and they all came to a bad end, as we shall see in the course of our history. Atahuallpa died bravely, and ordered his body to be taken to Quito, where his mother's ancestors, the kings of Quito, were buried. If he asked for baptism sincerely, he was indeed happy: if not, he paid for the crimes he had committed. He had many wives and left issue. He usurped much land from his brother Huáscar, but never assumed the scarlet fringe until he had taken him prisoner; and never spat on the ground, but on the hand of some noble lady, as a sign of his majesty. The Indians were astonished at his early death, and praised Huáscar as a child of the Sun when they recalled that he had prophesied how soon Atahuallpa, who had ordered his death, should himself be killed.

The above is from López de Gómara. In examining the words of this author, it is worthy of note that he mentions that Felipillo translated the words of the Indians who were called upon to give evidence according to his own caprice, since there was no Spaniard who could understand or check what he said. This seems to bear out our own statement above, to the effect that the interpreter explained the mysteries of our Catholic faith very badly to Atahuallpa, partly because he did not understand them and partly because the language lacked many of the words that were necessary for what he was supposed to say. It also lends proof to what we have said about Hernando de Soto and Pedro del Barco, who, as they did not understand what Huáscar Inca said to them, failed to remain with him and brought about his death. We might therefore say that the lack of good and faithful interpreters was the chief cause of the deaths of these two powerful kings.

Atahuallpa gave instructions that he was to be buried in Quito with his mother's ancestors, and not in Cuzco with his father's because he knew how deeply he had made himself hated throughout the empire on account of his deeds of cruelty, and feared that some insult and injury might be offered to his body. He preferred to trust his own people rather than strangers, though the burials of the Incas in Cuzco were very different from those of the chiefs of Quito in pomp and dignity. It is quite true to say that Atahuallpa did not assume the scarlet fringe until after the arrest of Huáscar, for this was the insignia of the Inca as lord of the whole empire, and while there was another legitimate ruler, such as his brother was, he could not wear it. Once he had arrested his brother, he declared himself the supreme ruler of the empire and could assume the fringe, even though he did so rebelliously, as we have seen.

We should give thanks to Our Lord God that an idolatrous Indian who had committed so many crimes as Atahuallpa should have been baptized before his death: God does not withhold his infinite mercy from sinners as great as he, or I.

He took the name of Don Juan Atahuallpa. Padre Blas Valera says that Fray Vicente de Valverde carefully instructed him in the faith for many days before he was killed, and that the Inca became quite detached from life while he was in prison, falling into a profound melancholy on finding himself alone and in chains: he would admit no Indian into his place of confinement except a young nephew of his who waited on him. The Spaniards then took him out of prison and called the chief Indians, who brought famous herbalists to treat him; they tested his fever by taking his pulse, not at the wrist as doctors in Europe do, but at the top of the nose, between the eyebrows, and they gave him a drink of herbal juices of great virtue. One of these he calls *paico*: no other is named.

Padre Valera says that the brew produced a heavy sweat followed by a very long and profound sleep, which removed the fever. When he awoke the fever was gone, and he was given no other medicine, but recovered in a few days and was then restored to his prison. Padre Valera says that when he was told of the death sentence, he was ordered to accept baptism: otherwise he would be burned alive, as Huahutimoc, the king of the other empire, was burned in Mexico. The fire was lit while he was being told of the sentence. Finally, he says, Atahuallpa was baptized, and he was strangled bound to a pole in the square, while the public crier announced the sentence. His account is entirely consistent with those of the Spanish historians. He says that Atahuallpa was three months in prison.

CHAPTER XXXVII

The evidence against Atahuallpa.

THE TRIAL of Atahuallpa was long and solemn, though López de Gómara gives it only in brief.

The governor appointed himself judge in the case and was assisted by Don Diego Almagro. Sancho de Cuéllar acted as scribe; another, as prosecutor; and another, as Atahuallpa's counsel. Two others were attorneys on either side, and yet another sought out and produced the witnesses who were to appear. Two more were named as legal advisers to give their opinion in the case. I do not give names out of respect for their families: I knew some of them. A list of twelve questions was prepared: (1) had they known Huaina Cápac and his wives, and how many wives had he? (2) was Huáscar Inca a legitimate son and heir to the kingdom, and was Atahuallpa a bastard, the son of some Indian from Quito and not of the king? (3) did the Inca have other children apart from these? (4) did Atahuallpa inherit the kingdom by his father's will or usurp it? (5) was Huáscar Inca deprived of the kingdom by his father's will or was he declared heir to it? (6) was Huáscar Inca alive or dead; did he die of an illness or was he killed on Atahuallpa's orders, and did this take place before or after the arrival of the Spaniards? (7) was Atahuallpa an idolator and did he order and compel his vassals to sacrifice men and children? (8) had Atahuallpa waged unjust wars and killed many people in the course of them? (9) did Atahuallpa have many concubines? (10) had Atahuallpa collected, spent, and wasted the tribute of the empire since the Spaniards had taken possession of it? (11) did they know that Atahuallpa had, since the arrival of the Spaniards, given his relatives and captains and many other people of all kinds, many gifts from the royal treasury and had wasted and dissipated the public and communal stores? (12) did they know if King Atahuallpa had, after his arrest, conspired with his captains to rebel and kill the Spaniards, gathering a great number of warriors and quantities of arms and supplies for the purpose?

The witnesses were examined on the basis of these questions. Ten appeared and were questioned. Seven of them were servants of the Spaniards, and three were not, so that they should not all be familiars. They stated what the interpreter Felipe wished to state, as López de Gómara says. One of the witnesses who was not a servant, called Quespe, the captain of a company, who was the last to be examined, was afraid that the interpreter might add to, or suppress from what he was saying, and replied with a single word, saying: *"i,"* "yes," and *"manam,"* "no." And so that those present should understand him and the interpreter should not substitute the negative for the affirmative, he nodded two or three times when he said yes, and shook his head and his right hand when he said no. The judges and the rest of the court were surprised at the Indian's sagacity. Nevertheless, it was decided to condemn so great and powerful a king as Atahuallpa to death, and he was informed of the sentence as we have said.

When the Spaniards heard the news many of them were greatly perturbed, including all those who were generous and compassionate minds, whether they had come with Pizarro or with Almagro. The principal of these were Francisco and Diego de Chaves, two brothers from Trujillo, Francisco de Fuentes, Pedro de Ayala, Diego de Mora, Francisco Moscoso, Hernando de Haro, Pedro de Mendoza, Juan de Herrada, Alonso de Avila, Blas de Atienza, and many more. These said that it was not permissible to kill a king who had shown them so much courtesy and done them no harm: if he were found guilty of anything it should be referred to the emperor and he should be sent back to Spain, but they should not constitute themselves judges of a king, over whom they had no jurisdiction. They ought to consider the good name of the Spanish nation, for their tyranny and cruelty in killing an imprisoned king, after giving him their word to release him in return for a ransom, the greater part of which had been paid, would be noised abroad over the whole earth. They should not sully their noble deeds with so inhuman an act. They should fear God, who would deny them the favor he had so far shown them; for after so barbarous and unjust a deed they could not expect anything to turn out well for them in the future, but should rather fear disaster and a bad end, every one of them. It was wrong to kill anyone without giving him a hearing and permitting him the opportunity to defend himself. They therefore said that they would appeal against the sentence to the Emperor Charles V, and would forthwith present their case to His Majesty, appointing Juan de Herrera to act as Atahuallpa's advocate. These and similar things were not only said, but set down in writing, and communicated to the judges with great protests against the ill effects and harm that would ensue from the execution of such a sentence. Those who stood up for Atahuallpa in this way were told by their opponents that they were traitors to the crown of Castile and to their master the emperor, since they were preventing the extension of his realms: if the tyrant Atahuallpa were killed, the empire was secured and their lives were safe, but if he lived, both would be lost. They said that they would report this argument and the remaining disputes and disorders that had occurred to His Majesty, so that he might understand who were loyal and useful servants, and who were traitors and foes to the growth of his power, thus enabling him to reward the first and punish the latter. The fire of passion flared so high that they would have quarrelled and killed one another, had not God provided a remedy, causing others, less impassioned than either of these two factions, to come between them and pacify the partisans of the Inca, urging them to consider the interests of the crown and the safety of their own lives, for it was wrong that there should be disputes and passions between Christians about infidels. They numbered barely 50, but their opponents were more than 350; and if it came to blows, they would gain nothing, but all would be lost, and they would lose a kingdom as rich as the one that lay in their hands, which they could secure by killing the king. With these threats and persuasions the defenders of Atahuallpa were placated: they agreed to his execution, and their rivals carried it out.

CHAPTER XXXVIII

A stroke of ingenuity by Atahuallpa; the amount of his ransom.

As we have said, Atahuallpa, was sharp-witted and intelligent. Among other evidences he gave of this—which expedited his death—one was as follows. On seeing the Spaniards read and write, he thought that these accomplishments were innate among them. In order to test the truth of this, he asked one of the Spaniards who guarded him or used to come in to visit him to write the name of his God on Atahuallpa's thumb-nail. The soldier did so. When another Spaniard came in, he asked: "What does it say here?" The Spaniard told him, and three or four others gave the same answer. Soon after Don Francisco Pizarro came in, and after they had spoken together for a while, Atahuallpa asked him what the letters meant. Pizarro failed to tell him, since he could not read. Thus the Inca realized that reading was not a natural gift but an acquirement. Thenceforward the governor dropped in his esteem; for the Incas, as we explained in speaking of the tests of the novices before they were armed knights, believed in their moral philosophy that superiors should excel inferiors in the arts of both war and peace, or at least with respect to everything they needed to know for the performance of their duties, since they held that it was improper that the superior should be outshone by the inferior, other things being equal. Atahuallpa's disdain and scorn for him was so pronounced that the governor became aware of it and took offence. I have heard this said by many of those who were present. From this parents, and especially noble parents, may learn not to neglect the education of their children, if it is only to the extent of learning to read and write well and having a little Latin, though the more they learn the better equipped they will be to avoid such humiliating situations as this. In these days those who neglect education are more blameworthy than their predecessors, for then there were fewer teachers of all subjects than there are today. And gentlemen should be just as proud of the nobility they acquire for themselves as of that which they inherit, for it is like a setting of precious stones in fine gold.

Another anecdote is told of Atahuallpa in proof of the quickness of his understanding. Among many other objects brought by certain Spaniards to trade with the Indians, or as the malicious would say, to deceive them, there was one of the fine glass goblets made in Venice. Its owner decided to offer it to King Atahuallpa, expecting to be well rewarded, as indeed he was, for although the Inca was in prison he issued instructions to a lord of vassals to give the Spaniard ten of his jars of gold or silver in return for it, and this was done. The Inca greatly esteemed the beauty and workmanship of the goblet, and holding it in his hands, he asked the Spaniards: "Surely no one but kings will use such beautiful vessels in Spain." One of those present, supposing that he was referring to its being made of glass rather than to its beautiful shape, answered that not only kings but also great lords and all the common people who wished could use such vessels. At this Atahuallpa dropped the goblet from his hands saying: "So common a thing does not deserve to be esteemed by anyone." This saying astonished those who heard it.

As has been seen, Atahuallpa was judicially executed without having completed the sum he had promised for his ransom for no more time was allowed him, though some say that he was killed after paying the ransom. What had been collected was divided among the Spaniards, as war booty. The historians of the times, Zárate and López de Gómara, disagree about the amount of the ransom. I believe this to be due to printing errors, and will illustrate this by quoting some of the passages. Zárate says, in his

Book II, ch. vii, literally as follows: "His Majesty received as the royal fifth 30,000 marks of pure white refined silver, and 120 million marks of gold," etc. López de Gómara, in his ch. cxviii, says: "Francisco Pizarro had the gold and silver weighed after it had been assayed: it was found to amount to 52,000 marks of good silver and 1,326,500 pesos of gold," etc.

If we seek to reconcile these two authors, we find that López de Gómara lacks 100,000 marks of silver to agree with Zárate, for in order to produce a royal share of 30,000 marks the total quantity of silver must have been 150,000. The same error, and even greater, occurs with the gold, for when Zárate says that His Majesty had 120 million marks, it is clear that there must be a printing mistake, for if we reckon the total by the value of the mark, at 72 ducats to the gold mark, the quantity in ducats is so excessive that there is no need to take it into account. If he wrote marks for maravedis, there is also obviously an error, since 120 million maravedis give 320,000 ducats, though as we shall see from the information the same authors give about the distribution of the gold, the royal fifth in gold amounted, when reduced to silver ducats, to 786,600 ducats. It therefore seems to me better to go by the sums given by these authors in their accounts of the division of the gold and silver, disregarding these totals, which are demonstrably wrong. I shall follow Zárate in these detailed accounts, for as he was accountant general to His Majesty's treasury in Peru, and heard there the account of what he wrote, he should be given more credit than one who wrote in Spain from the reports of casual travellers. What Zárate omits, the quantity of silver awarded to each of them, I shall take from López de Gómara, from whom I also get the sum given to the captains, which will be found in his history. The general's share only we have set down from the reports of those present. Both authors agree that the number of men with horses was 60. López de Gómara puts the infantry at 150, though Cieza de León, when speaking of the capture of Atahuallpa at Cajamarca in his ch. lxxvii, says he was arrested by 70 horsemen and 100 foot. I follow this author rather than López de Gómara about the number of infantry both because he was himself in Peru and wrote his account there, and also because I prefer to take the lesser number rather than the greater in everything, as I would rather be five short than five too many.

There are also differences in the shares as recorded by the same authors, for the soldiers were given six parts in gold and one in silver, while the governor, the captains and the men who came with Almagro received three in gold to one in silver. The reason why there was so much gold and

so little silver at that time—a proportion so different from that in the rest
of the world—was that the Inca kings had more gold than silver. As these
metals were not extracted as treasure or to serve as capital, but only for use
in decorating the temples and palaces, no trouble was taken to find silver
mines, for silver is only obtained with great difficulty and labor, as can be
seen today: in the mines of Potosí the miners go more than two hundred
fathoms below ground to reach the ore, as Padre Acosta says in his Book
IV, ch. viii, to which I refer anyone who wishes to know the incredible
labor necessary for the extraction of silver. The Inca kings did not therefore seek mines of silver or even of gold, since, as we have said in the
appropriate place, they did not demand these metals as tribute, but were
simply presented with them by the Indians for the service of their houses
and temples. And as gold is more easily obtained, since it is produced and
found on the surface of the earth and in streams, where it is brought down
by spates after rainfall and occurs all over Peru, though in some parts
more than in others, and it recovered by washing in the same way as silversmiths in Spain wash the sweepings of their shops, so in those days there
was more gold than silver; and when the Indians had no work to do on
their land, they would busy themselves extracting gold for presentation to
the kings.

To return therefore to our object, which is to check the quantity of
Atahuallpa's incredible ransom, we shall set down the shares recorded by
our authors. In dealing with the gold we shall give its value in silver, at
the rate of twenty to a hundred, which was current in those times in Peru
and is now in Spain: if anything, gold is worth more. For greater clarity
we shall reduce the pesos or castellanos of gold and silver to Castilian
ducats of 11 reals and one maravedi the ducat, or reckoned in maravedis
according to Castilian usage 375 maravedis. To proceed to the partition,
we shall first quote Zárate, who says: "Each horseman received more than
12,000 pesos in gold, without the silver, each of them having a quarter
more than those on foot. Even this large sum did not account for a fifth of
the quantity Atahuallpa had promised as his ransom. And as the men who
had come with Almagro, though they were numerous and of much standing, had no claim at all on this treasure, which was obtained as Atahuallpa's ransom, and they had not been present at his capture, the governor ordered them to be given a thousand pesos as a grant." This is
Zárate's version. López de Gómara says that each horseman received 360
marks of silver without the gold, and the captains 30,000 and 40,000
pesos. By combining the versions of these two authors we can arrive at

the various shares and at the sum of the royal fifth, thus verifying the various parts and the total.

The governor received 200,000 pesos as his share, 150,000 in gold and 50,000 in silver. The object he took from the pile as captain general was the Inca's litter, which weighed 25,000 gold pesos. Three captains of cavalry received 90,000 pesos in gold and 30,000 in silver. Four infantry captains received also 90,000 in gold and 30,000 in silver. The 60 horsemen had 720,000 pesos in gold and 180,000 in silver, and the 100 infantrymen, 900,000 in gold and 135,000 in silver. The 240 Spaniards who came with Almagro had 80,000 in gold and 60,000 in silver. Almagro himself was given 30,000 in gold and 10,000 in silver, not counting what Pizarro gave him from his own share, as we shall see. The royal fifth of the gold thus distributed amounts to 546,250 pesos, and the fifth on the silver is 105,750 pesos; and as all the silver was pure or what is called *cendrada,* according to the historians, and therefore worth four reals the mark more than legal currency, and all our calculations have been in legally current silver and not in refined silver, we may add 38,160 ducats on the difference between pure silver and legally current silver over the whole sum.

And so as not to weary my hearers with a long account of each of the shares, I will briefly state the total of each share in the gold reduced to ducats, allowing 20 per cent in reducing the gold marks to silver, and a further 20 per cent in turning pesos into ducats. Thus a hundred gold pesos are worth 120 silver pesos, and 120 silver pesos are 144 ducats, *i.e.,* 100 gold p. = 144 ducats. In this way we shall arrive at the total quantity in gold. And as the historians did not say if the gold was fine, as they said the silver was refined, we have reckoned the gold at 22½ carats, which is usual in Peru: if we had reckoned it at 24 carats, the standard for fine gold, we should add a total of 218,500 ducats to account for the difference of a carat and a half. But as the Spanish authors do not say that the gold was fine, I shall not add this sum, so as to avoid setting anything down without their authority. The sums in silver require no modification except the addition of 20 per cent in turning pesos into ducats. The total value was thus:

	ducats
The governor's share in the gold, and the present he chose from the heap	252,000
his silver	60,000

The 3 captains of cavalry, in gold	129,600
in silver	36,000
The 4 captains of infantry, in gold	129,600
in silver	36,000
Sixty horsemen, in gold	1,036,800
in silver	129,600
A hundred infantry, in gold	1,296,000
in silver	162,000
Almagro's 240 men, in gold	259,200
in silver	72,000
Don Diego de Almagro in gold	43,200
in silver	12,000
The royal fifth in gold	786,600
in silver	126,900
Additions for pure silver	38,170
Atahuallpa's ransom thus amounts to	4,605,670

Of this 3,933,000 ducats were in gold, and 672,670 in silver, allowing for the fact that it was pure: these two numbers give the total of 4,605,-670 ducats. This was the amount collected by the Spaniards at Cajamarca; but the quantity they obtained in Cuzco was much greater, as the same historians, López de Gómara and Zárate, state: we shall quote them in due course.

Padre Blas Valera says that Atahuallpa's ransom amounted to 4,800,000 ducats. He says that it was collected by the Indians and he ascertained the sum from them, for what was brought from each province was recorded in the knots and accounts. Our own total is taken from the Spanish historians. The difference is the sum of 194,330 ducats, by which sum our total falls short of Padre Valera's. In these days the sum of gold and silver does not cause much surprise, for it is common knowledge that for the last thirty years ten or twelve million in gold and silver has been entering the Guadalquivir annually: this sum has been sent to Spain and the rest of the Old World by my country, which proves herself a cruel stepmother to her own sons but a devoted parent to those of strangers. López de Gómara, in speaking of this ransom in his ch. cxviii, speaks as follows:

Pizarro sent the royal fifth to the emperor with a report on all that had happened by means of his brother Hernando Pizarro, who was accompanied to Spain by many soldiers with fortunes of twenty, thirty, and forty thousand ducats. In short, they brought almost all Atahuallpa's gold and filled the

Contratación at Seville with money, and the whole world with fame and the thirst for wealth.

Thus far López de Gómara. The number of conquerors who returned was sixty, and their arrival caused much comment abroad. The governor gave his partner 120,000 ducats out of his own share. The schoolmaster Hernando de Luque received nothing, since news of his death reached them at about this time: for this reason the historians do not speak of him.

CHAPTER XXXIX

The opinions expressed by the Spaniards on these events.

AFTER the deaths of the two royal brothers and enemies, Huáscar and Atahuallpa, the Spaniards remained absolute lords of both their kingdoms, for there was no one to resist them or oppose anything they tried to do thereafter. With the death of the Incas, the Indians of both parties were like sheep without a shepherd, with no one to govern them in peace or war, either for their own good or to the detriment of their foes. On the contrary, the supporters of Huáscar still remained at odds with those of Atahuallpa, and each party sought to prevail over the other by trying to serve and ingratiate itself with the Spaniards and thus get the new rulers to side with them against their enemies. Some of Atahuallpa's remaining captains resisted the Spaniards, as we shall see: others disbanded the armies under their control and tried to appoint an Inca of their own choosing, who would be more favorable to them than one appointed by strangers. They elected Paullu, a son of Huaina Cápac, one of those who escaped Atahuallpa's cruelties. The chief author of this election was the commander Quízquiz, who was at Cuntisuyu, where he received news of Atahuallpa's capture. He had hitherto been an opponent of Paullu, but necessity forces men to stoop to great depths, especially tyrants when they are falling and men of low character, even though they are elevated into high places, for they have no regard to their responsibilities, but only to their miserable pretensions. Quízquiz was one of Atahuallpa's ministers, and a brave soldier with great experience in war. Paullu was given the scarlet fringe, but he paid little attention to it, since he had no right to rule, the legitimate heir being Manco Inca. When Quízquiz saw that Paullu made no effort to govern he abandoned him and sought to rely on his own strength and skill, collecting his followers and marching to Cuzco to see what would happen to his King Atahuallpa, where we shall leave him for the present.

On seeing the honor in which the Indians generally held them and how they were adored, the Spaniards frequently conversed among themselves on the subject, especially when the six who had gone out to inspect the riches of the kingdom were present to tell of the marks of veneration and service they had been shown. Many attributed this to their own bravery. They said that the Indians had surrendered out of pure fright on seeing how strong and brave the Spaniards were, and that they could not have done anything else. They set such store by themselves and boasted without any sense of proportion because they were unaware of the superstitions of the Indians or of the prophecy the great Huaina Cápac had uttered about the coming of the Spaniards to Peru, and the destruction of their idolatry and empire.

Other Spaniards were more moderate and regardful of the honor of God and the expansion of the holy Catholic Faith. They saw things differently, and said that the great deeds the others attributed to their own strength and bravery were miracles performed by the Lord on behalf of His Gospel, so that when the faithful and infidels duly pondered them the infidels would be softened and come forward to receive His word with less resistance and greater love, and the faithful would take courage and strive to preach the Gospel with greater fervor and charity toward their neighbors and respect toward God, stirred on by the miracles He had performed through them. They truly asserted that when a single Spaniard or two could travel for two or three hundred leagues through enemy territory, borne on their enemies' shoulders and treated by them with all the honor and respect they displayed toward their gods, when it would have been a simple matter to fling them from a bridge or cast them down from one of the numerous lofty crags—this was not the work of men, but one of God's miracles. They should not therefore attribute these things to themselves, except in so far as they had acted like good Christians and preachers of Jesus Christ.

Others went further in their discussions—which sometimes took place in the presence of the governor—and said that once Atahuallpa had been baptized, it would have been better for the peace of the kingdom and the expansion of the Catholic Faith, not to have killed him, but to have kept him alive, showing him every possible honor and courtesy, and asking him, since he was now a Christian, to make another proclamation in favor of the Christian religion, like the one he had made in favor of the Spaniards, and ordering all his vassals to be baptized within a certain time. There is not the slightest doubt that they would all have been baptized, and have competed with one another to obtain baptism, for three or four considerations each would have impelled them in this direction, the more strongly when taken all together. The first was the Inca's bidding, which was regarded as a divine law even in matters of the smallest moment, and therefore much more so in a question of such importance as the adoption of the religion of those they considered to be gods. The second was the natural obedience of the Indians toward their kings. The third was that the king himself had shown them an example in accepting baptism, and they would all have done the same, for the Indians set great store by example. The fourth, and for them the strongest and most compelling consideration, which embraced all the other three reasons, was that Atahuallpa himself should ask them to follow his example in bringing about what his father Huaina Cápac had prophesied and willed, namely that they were to obey the new race who came to their country, whose religion would be better than theirs, and who would excel them in all respects. If this step had been taken, the preachers of the Holy Gospel in Peru would have had all this additional assistance. But our Lord God, in His secret wisdom, permitted things to turn out as they did.

CHAPTER XL

The results of the discord between the two brothers, the last Inca kings.

T HE WAR between the two brothers, Huáscar and Atahuallpa, brought about the total destruction of their empire, facilitating the entry of the Spaniards and making it possible for them to win Peru with such ease. Otherwise the country could have been defended by a very small force, owing to its rough and rocky character and inaccessibility. But our Lord God took pity on these gentiles and permitted the discord between the two brothers to arise so that the preachers of His Gospel and Catholic Faith might enter the more easily and with less resistance.

Padre Acosta, speaking very briefly about these two kings in his Book VI, ch. xxii, says:

Huaina Cápac was succeeded in Cuzco by one of his sons called Tito Cusi Gualpa (this should be Inti Cusi Huallpa) who was afterwards called Huáscar Inca. His body was burnt by Atahuallpa's captains. Atahuallpa was also a son of Huaina Cápac and rose up against his brother at Quito, bringing a powerful army against him. It then occurred that Atahuallpa's captains, Quízquiz and Chillcuchima, captured Huáscar Inca in Cuzco, after having recognized him as their lord and king, for he was in fact the legitimate heir. This caused great distress throughout the kingdom, and especially in the capital. And as they always had recourse to sacrifices in their hour of need and they had no power to see Huáscar free since the captains who were holding him kept him under close arrest and had a strong army sent by Atahuallpa, they therefore decided—and some say on Huáscar's orders—to celebrate a great sacrifice to Viracocha Pachayachchic (this should be Pachacámac), who is the universal creator, and ask him, since they themselves could not free their lord, to send people from heaven to get him out of his confinement. They were full of confidence in the result of this sacrifice when news came that certain people had come from over the sea and landed and arrested Atahuallpa. The Spaniards who captured Atahuallpa at Cajamarca were very few in number and the event took place soon after the Indians had made the above-mentioned sacrifice to Viracocha: it was thus that the Spaniards were called Viracochas in the belief that they were people sent by God, and this name became current and even today Spaniards are called Viracochas. And certainly if we had set the example we should have done, the Indians would have been right in calling us people sent by God. We should ponder on the high purposes of divine providence in disposing that the Spaniards should enter Peru, which would have been impossible but for the division between the two brothers and their followers and their high regard for the Christians as people sent from heaven. It certainly imposes the obligation, having won the Indians' lands, to win even more their souls for heaven.

Thus far Padre Acosta, who ends his chapter here, after giving a brief account of the war between the two brothers, the usurpation of one of them, the legality of the other's claim, the imprisonment of both of them, the smallness of the number of Spaniards at Atahuallpa's arrest, the intervention of divine providence in the conversion of the heathen, the name applied to the Christians, and the regard in which they were held, on the supposition that they had come down from heaven. All this we have described at length in its proper place.

It remains to speak of the name Viracocha, the name applied to the Spaniards as soon as they were seen in Peru because their beards and their dress recalled the phantom that appeared to Inca Viracocha, as we have mentioned in our account of his life. This phantom was thenceforward adored by the Indians as their god, the child of the Sun, as it declared itself to be. But when they shortly afterwards saw that the Spaniards arrested King Atahuallpa and killed him a few days later, condemning him to a shameful death by strangling in the public square—a fate their own laws reserved for thieves and malefactors—that the sentence was carried out while the crier announced his acts of oppression and his murder of Huáscar, then the Indians really believed that the Spaniards were the sons of this god Viracocha, the child of the Sun, and that they had been sent from heaven to avenge Huáscar and his family, and to punish Atahuallpa. This belief was much strengthened by the artillery and arquebusses the Spaniards had, for they said that the Sun had armed them with his own weapons, as a father arms his sons. These weapons are lightning, thunder, and thunderbolts, which they call *illapa*, and they therefore applied this word to the arquebus. The artillery was given the same name with the adjective *hatun illapa*, "big thunder" or "big bolt," etc.

They also gave the Spaniards the title Inca, as well as that of Viracocha, saying that as they were children of their god Viracocha, the child of the Sun, they were properly entitled to the name of Inca, as divine men who had descended from heaven. Thus all the conquerors of Peru were called Viracocha Inca, including the first who entered the country with Pizarro and the second, who came with Almagro and Alvarado; and all these were worshipped as gods. This adoration lasted until the avarice, lust, cruelty, and rigor with which many of them treated the Indians undeceived them from this false belief. They then ceased to apply the name Inca to the Spaniards, saying that they were not true children of the Sun, since their conduct did not resemble that of their predecessors, the past Incas. Although the title Inca was withdrawn, the name Viracocha was left on account of their beards and dress. This was the attitude of the Indians toward the Spaniards who proved harsh and cruel, who were given the name of *súpay*, "demon," instead of these august titles. But those who were acknowledged to be merciful, kindly, and well-disposed, and these were very numerous, were not only confirmed in the names we have mentioned, but also received the titles given to their kings, Intip Churin, "child of the Sun," Huacchacúyac, "lover of the poor." They were not even satisfied with these titles to distinguish and honor the goodness and virtue of Spaniards who treated them well, but called them sons of God, using the Spanish word for God, seeing the regard in which it was held, though as they had not the letter *d* in their language they said *Tius* for

Dios. Thus they called them Tiuspechurin, "son of *Dios*." Nowadays they have been taught and are more skilled in pronouncing Spanish. They honored and adored Spaniards who gave proof of Christianity and humane customs as we have said in those early days; and they do the same even now, and worship them inwardly and outwardly with great devotion, whether ecclesiastics or laymen, if they are known to be pious and kindly and free of avarice and lust. The Indians are indeed humble and affectionate toward their benefactors and very grateful for even the smallest benefits they receive. This gratitude was a survival of their ancient attitude toward their kings, who studied always to do them good and therefore deserved the titles they were given.

CHAPTER XLI

The loyalty of the Peruvian Indians toward the Spaniards who had defeated them in war.

THERE was another virtue displayed by the Peruvian Indians toward the Spaniards, namely that the Indian who had surrendered and been captured in war regarded himself as more subject than a slave: to him his captor was his god and idol, since he had vanquished him, and as such was to be respected, obeyed, and served faithfully unto death: the Indian must not deny him either for his country, or for his kinsmen, or for his own parents or children or wife. In this belief the Indian put the well-being of his Spanish master before that of all his own people, and would, if necessary, on the Spaniard's command, sell them and act as a scout, spy, or informer. Information acquired from such natives had a great influence on the Christian conquest of Peru. The Indians truly believed that they were bound by natural obligation to obey the particular deity that had reduced them to subjection. They were therefore incredibly loyal: they would fight against their own kind as if they were their mortal enemies and did not hesitate to kill their kith and kin in the service of their Spanish masters, regarding themselves as committed to their side and being therefore ready to die with them. When bands of Spaniards roved through the country and captured Indians the captain would divide

The loyalty of Indians to Spaniards

the prisoners among those who had no Indians to serve them, but the Indian would only go with his captor. He would say: "This one captured me: he is the one I am obliged to serve till I die." And when the captain told him that it was a military order that captives were to be divided among those who had no servants and that as his captor had them, he was assigned to another, the Indian would reply: "I will obey you on condition that when this Christian takes another Indian, I may be free to return to my master; otherwise, kill me, for I do not wish to go with anyone else." If the promise were given, he would be full of satisfaction and would himself help the Spaniard to capture other Indians in order to get back to his master. The same can be said of the Indian women in serving their masters and attending to them. I left three of these Indian prisoners in the house of my lord Garcilaso de la Vega when I left Peru. One of them was called Alli, "good." He was taken in one of the numerous battles fought in Collao after the general rising of the Indians, in which he fought like a good soldier, so engrossed in the struggle that he did not pay any attention to what was going on until he found his comrades fleeing and the Spaniards hot in pursuit of them. He thought he could save his life only by pretending to be dead, hoping to escape under cover of nightfall, which was then coming on. He took off his shirt, flung himself down among the many bodies near by and rolled himself in blood so as to resemble a corpse. After giving chase the Spaniards returned to their camp from various sides, and three or four of them happened to pass close to where the Indian was lying. As they gazed on the many dead lying on the battlefield, my lord Garcilaso de la Vega, who was one of the Spaniards, noticed this Indian and saw that he was panting. He touched him with the tip of his lance, to see if he would feel it. The Indian hastily rose to his feet and begged for mercy, fearing that they were going to kill him. Thenceforward he remained in my father's service, as loyal and submissive as we have said, and was proud to show these qualities on every occasion. He was later baptized and called Juan and his wife Isabel.

End of the First Book

BOOK TWO *of the* SECOND PART

It contains the coming of Don Pedro de Alvarado to Peru; the treachery of Rumiñaui and his cruelty to his followers; two battles between Indians and Spaniards; the treaty between the Christians and the infidels; the agreement between Almagro and Alvarado; three more battles between Indians and Spaniards, and the number of dead; the reward of Don Pedro de Alvarado and his unfortunate death; the foundation of Lima and Trujillo; the death of the Indian commander Quizquiz; Almagro's expedition to Chile and his return to Peru; the Incas' rebellion; God's miracles on behalf of the Christians; the events of the sieges of Cuzco and Lima; the number of Spaniards killed by the Indians; the voluntary exile of the Inca; differences between Almagros and Pizarros; the marquis' request for succor and his despatch of reinforcements for Cuzco; the battle of the Amáncay River and the capture of Alonso de Alvarado; new negotiations and differences between Pizarros and Almagros; the cruel battle of Las Salinas; the death of Almagro and other famous captains; the return of Diego de Alvarado to Spain and that of Hernando Pizarro and his long imprisonment.
It contains forty chapters.

CHAPTER I

Don Pedro de Alvarado joins in the conquest of Peru.

WHEN FAME noised abroad the great wealth of Peru, large numbers of Spaniards went there, as López de Gómara says in his ch. cxxvi: "So many Spaniards hastened to Peru because of the fame of its gold that Panama, Nicaragua, Guatemala, Cartagena, and other towns and islands were well-nigh emptied," etc. These Spaniards included the *adelantado* Don Pedro Alvarado, one of the most famous leaders of his day, who, not content with the deeds he had performed in the conquest of the empire of Mexico, Utlatlán, and Guatemala, wished also to undertake the conquest of Peru, obtaining permission from His Majesty the emperor Charles V to conquer, settle, and govern all the lands he might take a certain number of leagues outside the jurisdiction and government of Don Francisco Pizarro. He raised many excellent soldiers for this expedition, including distinguished gentlemen from all the Spanish provinces, though most of them were from Extremadura since Don Pedro himself came from Badajoz.

Among his many natural gifts, Don Pedro possessed that of great nimbleness and agility, by dint of which he saved his life in the retreat of Cortés from Mexico. When the Indians destroyed a bridge by means of which the Spaniards were escaping, he vaulted more than twenty-five feet over the gap they had made, using a lance he was carrying and sticking its point among a pile of dead bodies. The Indians were so astonished by this leap that they called him a son of God. López de Gómara mentions this incident in his account of the conquest of Mexico, where in speaking of Hernán Cortés in his ch. cvii he says the following:

But when he reached them he found that although some were fighting with all their might, many were already dead. The gold was lost, and with it the equipment, the cannon, and the prisoners: not a man nor a thing was in the same state as when it left the main camp. He gathered together what men he could and sent them off in front, while he himself followed and left Pedro de

Alvarado to collect and encourage those who remained. But Alvarado was unable to stand the enemy's attack. When he saw how many of his companions had died and realized that he himself would not escape if he waited, he followed Cortés, lance in hand, and crossed the bodies of dead and wounded Spaniards, with the groans of the latter in his ears. On reaching the Cobera bridge he vaulted to the other side on his lance. The Indians were astonished at this leap, and so were even the Spaniards, for the distance was great and others could not make it, though they tried and were drowned,

etc. Thus far López de Gómara.

As a child I heard Spaniards talk of the powers of this gentleman and say that after the recovery of Mexico two pieces of marble were set up on either side of the gap to show where the leap had occurred and how great it was. I can refer to these two witnesses if they have survived, unless envy has resulted in their destruction, and it would be a wonder if this were not so.

When Don Pedro de Alvarado was in Seville on his first journey to the Indies, he climbed the tower of the cathedral with some other young gentlemen in his company to enjoy the beautiful view from that splendid tower. In one of the highest windows they found a piece of scaffolding jutting out twelve or fourteen feet: it had been used to hold up a platform for a piece of work completed a few days before. One of the group, a certain Castillejo, from Córdova, aware of Don Pedro's pride in his agility and being no less proud of his own, saw the scaffolding, took off his cloak and sword, and without uttering a word, walked along the scaffolding to the very end and returned along it back to the tower. When Alvarado saw this, he felt that it had been done to dare him to do as much, and he therefore did not drop his sword or his cloak. He threw one end of his cloak over his left shoulder and the other under his left arm and then under his right, and took the sword in his left hand. In this way he stepped out to the end of the scaffolding, where he turned round and faced the tower, and stepped his way back to it.

Both men were daring to the point of rashness, and I cannot say which was the more so. On another occasion it happened that when Alvarado and some other youths were hunting they came upon some laborers who were showing off their agility by jumping over a broad pit and anyone who could leap it with his feet together was reckoned to be very nimble. Alvarado arrived at the end, and standing on the brink of the pit, said: "It's a good jump with your feet together: I don't know if I dare make it." Having said this he began his leap and pretended to fall short of the other side, striking the opposite brink with the balls of his feet and springing back with such agility that he returned to his previous position.

I heard these and similar feats told of this gentleman and many others who went to conquer the New World. It seems as if God and nature bred them with the necessary qualities of body and mind to carry out the many great labors that awaited them in the conquest of this New World, which is so vast and so inaccessible that it is even difficult to travel over it in peacetime, let alone conquer it by force of arms. But it was after all a work of God which He miraculously favored and aided, as we shall see and have already seen; otherwise human powers would not have been equal to so great an enterprise. We have spoken of the agility of Don Pedro, or Pedro de Alvarado, as others call him (which is the same thing): his deeds and feats are written in the conquest of Mexico, Nicaragua, and Peru, though not at such length as he deserves. He made a fine figure on horse or on foot. On one occasion when he returned from Mexico to Spain to free himself from certain accusations falsely laid against him by his rivals, he had to kiss the emperor's hand and give him an account of his services. He went to see the emperor at Aranjuez and His Majesty was in one of the walks in the royal gardens. On seeing Don Pedro's gallant demeanor, the emperor asked his attendants who he was, and on being told, remarked: "This man does not look as if he had done what they tell me he has done." The emperor thus freed him of the calumnies that had been brought against him and showed him much favor.

He returned to New Spain married as a result of this visit, and was accompanied by many noblewomen who were to marry the conquerors who had helped to win the empire and had acquired prosperity and great *repartimientos*. On reaching Guatemala Don Pedro was well received: the people welcomed him with much feasting and rejoicing and there was dancing in his house for many days and nights. On one occasion the conquerors were all sitting in a great hall watching an entertainment, while the ladies observed from a door looking the length of the room. They were concealed behind a curtain for decency's sake.

One said to the others: "They say that we have to marry those conquerors."

Another answered: "Are we going to marry those broken down old creatures? You can marry who you like, but I certainly don't intend to marry any of them. They can go to the devil: they are in such a state that they look as if they had escaped from hell; some are lame and some have arms missing, and some ears, and some an eye, and some half their faces, and the best-looking of them has got one or two or three scars across his face."

The first said: "We're not going to marry them for their looks, but to inherit their Indians: they're so old and worn out, they're certain to die soon, and then we can choose whatever young men we please instead of these dotards like changing an old broken pan for a new whole one."

One of these old gentlemen who was near the door and had not been noticed by the ladies, since they were looking further away, heard the whole of the conversation, and unable to bear any more interrupted them and rebuked the ladies sharply for their amicable intentions. He then turned to the gentlemen and told them what had passed, saying: "You marry these ladies, for they fully intend to repay you for the honor." So saying he returned home, called a priest and married an Indian woman of noble stock by whom he had two natural sons. He wished to legitimize them so that they should inherit his Indians, rather than some young man chosen by a Spanish wife to enjoy the fruits of his labors and turn his sons into servants or slaves.

Some in Peru have done the same and married Indian women, though not many. Most have given grounds for the words of the lady in the anecdote. Their children can testify to the wisdom of this course, for from the hospitals where they lie they can see the offspring of others enjoying what their fathers gained and their mothers and relatives helped to gain. In the early days, when an Indian woman bore a child to a Spaniard, all her relatives respected and served the Spaniard like an idol, since he had joined their family. This was of great help in pushing forward the conquest of the Indies. One of the ordinances made for the conquerors of the New World was to the effect that they should enjoy the allocations of Indians for two lives, their own and that of one son, or if they had no son, that of their wife. The wife's claim was thus put before that of the natural sons, as though she had done more than the mothers of the latter in gaining the land. It was in order to gain this inheritance that the lady in the anecdote proposed to marry the old man so as to be able to exchange him later for a young one.

CHAPTER II

*The toils undergone by Alvarado and his
companions on the way.*

M Y LORD Garcilaso de la Vega came to Peru with the good *adelantado*
Don Pedro de Alvarado. He was a captain, as Cieza de León mentions in his ch. xlii:

The *adelantado* Don Pedro de Alvarado, accompanied by Diego de Alvarado,
Gómez de Alvarado, Alonso de Alvarado, who is at present marshal in Peru,
and Captain Garcilaso de la Vega, Juan de Saavedra, Gómez de Alvarado [*sic*],
and other gentlemen of high rank whom I have named in the account I have
quoted approached the quarters of the marshal Don Diego de Alvarado, and
certain incidents occurred which caused some to believe that the two groups
would break with one another,

etc. This is according to Cieza de León, and Garcilaso is the only one of
these gentlemen he describes as captain: I knew them all except Don
Pedro de Alvarado and Diego de Alvarado.

They suffered greatly from lack of food and water on the voyage from
Nicaragua to Puerto Viejo, for they had made their preparations hastily
and had not realized the length of the journey, and had therefore neglected to load the ships with all they required. They underwent similar
hunger and thirst on landing, as we shall see from the account of the
treasurer Zárate and the priest López de Gómara, who describe Don
Pedro de Alvarado's journey from New Spain to Peru in almost the same
words: they only differ in the use of *don* and the cost of the horses which
they had to kill on the way for food. I have therefore copied literally
López de Gómara's words from his ch. cxxvii, where he touches briefly
on the many great labors suffered by Don Pedro and his companions on
the journey. Part of his account runs:

When the wealth of Peru was made known, Pedro de Alvarado obtained from
the emperor a permit to discover and settle part of the province where there
were no other Spaniards. Having got it, he sent Garci Holguín with two ships
to find out what was happening. And as Holguín returned full of praise for
the country and amazed at the amount of riches obtained by all those who had
shared in the capture of Atahuallpa, and asserted that Cuzco and Quito (which

was so close to Puerto Viejo) were also very rich, Alvarado decided to go to Peru himself. So in 1535 he fitted out five ships with more than four hundred Spaniards and many horses. He put in at Nicaragua one night and seized two good ships which were preparing to take men, arms, and horses to Pizarro. Those who were due to go in these ships were glad to accompany him rather than wait for others, and he therefore had five hundred Spaniards and many horses. They all landed at Puerto Viejo and marched toward Quito, constantly asking the way. He reached some plains covered with dense undergrowth, where his men all but died of thirst. This was prevented by the chance discovery of some canes full of water. They satisfied their hunger by killing the horses, despite the fact that they were worth 1,000 or more ducats—(Zárate says: 'though each was worth 4,000 or 5,000 Castilians,' and this is more likely to be true since he heard it in Peru). For many days they were rained on by ashes from the volcano at Quito which are scattered a distance of over eighty leagues. It throws up such flames when it erupts that it is visible for over one hundred leagues, and its noise is said to be more alarming than thunder and lightning. They had to clear a good part of the way with their own hands, so dense was the undergrowth. They also crossed some very snowy mountains, and they were astonished to find how much snow fell on the Equator. Sixty persons were frozen there, and when they found themselves free from the snowfields, they gave thanks to God for freeing them and consigned the land and its gold which had brought them starvation and death to the Devil.

These are López de Gómara's words. Zárate adds the following about the crossing of the snowcapped mountains:

They ran on without waiting to help one another, and it happened that a Spaniard who had brought his wife and two little daughters saw them sink down exhausted and was unable to help them or carry them, so he remained with them, so that all four were frozen, and though he could have saved himself he preferred to perish with them. Amid such dangers and difficulties they crossed these mountains and counted themselves greatly blessed on finding themselves on the far side.

This is from Zárate (Book II, ch. ix). It is very lamentable to find that the first Spanish woman to go to Peru should have died so miserably.

With regard to the five hundred men these authors say Alvarado took to Peru, I should add that I heard many of those who came with him say that there were eight hundred. It may be that five hundred left Nicaragua and the rest joined them after landing in Peru, so that there were eight hundred when they reached the fields of Riuecpampa, where Alvarado and Almagro made peace and came to terms, as we shall see. Another historian places these events three years earlier: the matter is not of great moment. The canes in which the water was found are called *ipa*: they are as big as the leg or thigh, and as thick at the edge as a man's finger. Wherever they grow—and they are only found in hot districts—they are used for roofing houses. The Indians told them how to get the water, for they knew the canes and their secrets. Each cane produced more than an arroba of water, for their height varied with their thickness. Zárate (in his Book II, ch. x) in describing the journey of Don Pedro de Alvarado, writes as follows:

On the way his men suffered severely from hunger and even more from thirst, and would have been quite without water if they had not found some cane-brakes, which have the special property that when they are cut at each joint, they are found to have the hollow part full of excellent sweet water. These canes are usually as thick as a man's leg, so that each hollow held more than a half a gallon [*azumbre*] of water. The canes are said to have the peculiar natural property of collecting the water from the dew which falls nightly from heaven, although the earth is very dry and absolutely springless. Don Pedro refreshed his army, both men and horses, with this water, for the plants occur over a long distance,

etc. Thus Zárate, and here we shall leave the *adelantado* Don Pedro de Alvarado to return to the Spaniards and Indians at Cajamarca.

CHAPTER III

They carry Atahuallpa's body to Quito; Rumiñaui's treachery.

A FTER burying Atahuallpa, Pizarro and Almagro went to Cuzco, visiting on the way the very wealthy temple in the valley of Pachacámac and removing the gold and silver that Hernando Pizarro had not been able to take. Thence they made for Cuzco; and though the road is extremely rough, with steep slopes, strong rivers, and deep ravines, they met with no opposition, except one incident which we shall mention.

Leaving them on this journey we may properly return to the commander Challcuchima and Atahuallpa's captains, lords of vassals, and nobles, who remained at Cajamarca, thus preserving the chronological order of events. As soon as the Spaniards left this province for Cuzco, the

Indians exhumed their king's body, since they considered it unfitting to the dignity of their Inca and contrary to the custom of his ancestors that he should remain buried in a poor grave under the ground. They also did this to fulfil his instructions: for, as we have said, he wished to be buried in Quito whither his followers bore his remains with the small pomp and solemnity that a people already subject to another empire could summon up.

When the commander Rumiñaui knew this, he made the greatest possible public demonstration for the reception and embalming of his king's body, despite the fact that it was already corrupt. Meanwhile he secretly took the steps he thought necessary for the rising and rebellion he had in mind. He displayed complete obedience to Quilliscacha, Atahuallpa's brother, and sought to discover whether he wanted to govern by persuading him to put on the royal fringe and crown, if only until such time as his brother's death should have been avenged. Rumiñaui said all this in order to allay any suspicion that Quilliscacha might have about his own hostility, and thus to take him unawares and carry out more safely what he planned. Quilliscacha replied that it was futile to seek the throne for he felt sure the Spaniards would not relinquish it, and if they did one of Huaina Cápac's surviving sons would be certain to claim it; and his claim would be better than Quilliscacha's, and all the other authorities in the empire would rally to him, partly because they were full of resentment at the result of the late wars, and partly because they regarded him as the legitimate heir, and he would not be in a position to oppose them.

Rumiñaui did not desist from his wicked design despite Quilliscacha's discreet and well-reasoned reply. On the contrary, like a savage tyrant, he was strengthened in his determination, and in his secret discussions with his friends used to say that from the examples he had witnessed he thought that the right to rule lay solely in having the courage to seize the kingdom and slay its present master, as Atahuallpa had done with his brother Huáscar Inca and the Spaniards with Atahuallpa, and that he would do the same with them, for he had no lack of courage for the deed. Having rushed into this decision he waited until the captains and chiefs reached Quito with Atahuallpa's body. Rumiñaui gave them a great reception, having collected together a multitude of people to mourn for the Inca. All wept bitterly over his body, but cut short the obsequies, which were concluded in fifteen days, though they should have lasted a year. At the end of this time Rumiñaui thought that he should not let slip the opportunity he now had to put forward his claim, since his good fortune had placed in his hands all those he needed to kill to launch his rebellion in safety. These were the sons and brother of Atahuallpa and the commander Challcuchima and all the captains and lords of vassals there present, whose removal would leave no one to oppose him in the future.

With this intention he invited them all to dine with him on the following day so as to discuss what should be done to oppose the Spaniards and to elect Quilliscacha viceroy and governor of the kingdom of Quito so long as Atahuallpa's eldest son was a minor and unable to govern in his own right. The captains and *curacas* joined Quilliscacha in council in the royal palace of the Inca and made various proposals, but arrived at no conclusion. It was then time to eat. Rumiñaui had prepared a solemn feast and invited them all to dine. After they had all eaten abundantly, they were brought the drink called *sora* or in another language *viñapu,* the use of which was, as we have said, prohibited by the Inca kings under pain of death, for it renders the drinker unconscious. It is extremely potent, and suddenly intoxicates whoever drinks it, leaving him like a dead man. Padre Acosta says it is more intoxicating than wine, and this is true, though it does not apply to the ordinary beverage they take, which only intoxicates when drunk in large quantities for a long time. When Rumiñaui saw the captains and *curacas* lying senseless on the ground, he beheaded them all, including Challcuchima, Quilliscacha, and the small sons and daughters of Atahuallpa, so that there should be no one to lead opposition to him. And in order to make his rebellion more terrifying he had Quilliscacha flayed and covered a war-drum with his skin, leaving the head hanging. By not removing it, he made it evident whose the skin was, and his cruelty was thus advertised and the memory of it renewed daily and hourly. This apt pupil and excellent minister of Atahuallpa's thus sought to have himself feared and obeyed by terrorism and not by love, a natural characteristic of tyrants, who are worse than tigers or basilisks. Zárate describes this act of cruelty and that which followed very briefly. Cieza de León says that Challcuchima was burnt by Pizarro at Sacsahuana; but this was another captain related to him and of the same name, though less distinguished. The commander Challcuchima was present at Atahuallpa's death and took his body to Quito, as we have said, and died at the hands of his own people.

CHAPTER IV

Rumiñaui buries alive all the chosen virgins of one of the convents.

THE TWO Spanish historians mention an inhuman deed much more abominable than the last, which was then committed by Rumiñaui. They say that when Rumiñaui reached Quito, he said to his wives: "Rejoice, for the Christians are coming, and you will have a good time with them." Some of them laughed, as women will, but without thinking any ill. He then executed those who had taken the remark lightly, and burned Atahuallpa's household possessions. This is the account of one of the historians, and the other uses almost the same words. What really happened was that one day the tyrant went to visit the house of the chosen virgins, intending to remove those who took his fancy among the women dedicated as wives of Atahuallpa: he intended to take them himself and then declare himself king and take possession of the kingdom. He conversed with these women about the course of the recent fighting, and described the appearance and dress of the Spaniards, extolling their courage and daring, as though to excuse himself from fleeing from such fierce and warlike people. He said that they were strange people with beards on their faces, who rode animals called horses which were so strong that a thousand or two thousand Indians could not resist one of them. Merely by the fury of its gallop a horse inspired such fear as to put the Indians to flight. He said too that the Spaniards had brought thunder with them and killed Indians at two or three hundred paces, and they were clad from head to foot in iron. And to the greater astonishment of his hearers, he finished by telling them that the Spaniards were so extraordinary that they had houses like little cabins in which they shut their private parts. He was referring to breeches-flaps or codpieces: it is difficult to see why these were invented or what they contribute to public decency.

The chosen women laughed at Rumiñaui's exaggerated description, though rather to flatter him than for any other reason. He took their laughter amiss, attributing it to impure desires, and grew furiously angry. And as his cruelty was equalled by his hatred for the Spaniards (whom he would have liked to serve in the same way), any slight occasion was enough to cause him to show both. He therefore exclaimed to the women in a towering rage: "Oh, you wicked, treacherous, adulterous women! If you derive such pleasure merely from the news I have brought, what won't you do when the Spaniards actually arrive? I promise you, you shall never set eyes upon them." So saying, he immediately had them all, young and old, taken to a stream near the city, where he had them visited with the punishment assigned by their law, burial alive, as if they had actually sinned. He had part of the hills that rose on either side of the stream heaped upon them until their bodies were covered by the pile of earth, stones, and rocks that were brought tumbling down. In this way he showed his tyrannous nature, and the deed was more grievous and abominable than the last because he had killed the strong and seasoned warriors after rendering them incapable of feeling death, whereas these poor delicate women, accustomed only to spin and weave, were buried alive under stones and rocks which the unfortunate victims saw tumbling down upon them. He witnessed this cruel scene, like a mad dog; for the greatest pleasure of men of his kind is to behold such cruelties with their own eyes from sheer pleasure in watching them, for there are no colors so agreeable to their eyes nor sauce so tasty to their palate, as to see the execution of their own wicked deeds. Oh, tyrants! How can the earth and the other elements suffer you? Such was the end of these poor virgins, brought about by so light a cause as a burst of simulated laughter inspired by the tyrant's own foolish utterance. He himself committed many other wicked deeds in his rebellion and had several encounters with Sebastián de Belalcázar, who was sent to punish his rising, as we shall see; but he at length found that he could neither resist the Spaniards nor live among the Indians, so great had been his cruelty toward them. He therefore plunged into the interior with a few members of his family, and perished miserably, like all tyrants, in the forests of the Antis.

CHAPTER V

Two skirmishes between Indians and Spaniards.

GOVERNOR Francisco de Pizarro and his companions, who with Almagro's men numbered more than 350 Spaniards, marched toward Cuzco, heedless of any danger, as if the whole kingdom was theirs and there was not a hand to be raised against them. They thus journeyed in single file, putting up at the Indian villages and travelling at their own convenience as if they were in their own country. Such is Zárate's account (Book II, ch. viii), though he attributes a bold feat to the Indian captains in the course of his journey, as we shall see. On finding his brother, King Atahuallpa, a prisoner, Inca Titu Atauchi had travelled up and down the kingdom collecting gold and silver for the ransom, to hasten his brother's release. As he was approaching Cajamarca with a great quantity of these metals, he heard on the road that his brother was dead and that the Spaniards were marching toward Cuzco in a straggling column. Having considered this report, Inca Titu Atauchi abandoned the wealth he had with him, collected what warriors he could, and followed the Spaniards to the province of Huaillas, falling suddenly upon them with a force of six thousand men at a village called Tocto. He caught eight Spaniards who had not yet left, including Sancho de Cuéllar, who had acted as scribe in drawing up the case against Atahuallpa and at the trial. This is mentioned by Zárate, who gives the name of the Indian leader as Quízquiz, but does not say that he captured anyone. This is a confusion of names.

While this was happening in Huaillas, another skirmish took place on the road between the Spaniards and the Indian commander Quízquiz, who was a famous captain of Atahuallpa's court; we have already referred to him. When he had heard in Cuzco that his king had been captured, he marched on Cajamarca with eleven or twelve thousand men from his army to see if he could rescue his Inca from prison either peacefully or by force. On the way he came up with the Spaniards, and fought a sharp engagement with them, of which the historians give a short and confused account, very favorable to the Spaniards. What really happened was that the commander Quízquiz—on learning from his scouts that the Spaniards were not far away and were strung out—disappeared from view and, retiring into some mountains, made an ambush so as to cut off their rear-guard. He attacked with great force, wounding four Spaniards and killing ten or twelve of their Indian servants. The news of this surprise attack was carried to the governor, who was in the van. He took his companions' advice, and sent two captains on horseback to the rescue, supposing that the Indians would flee for all they were worth at the sight of horses, as they had done at Cajamarca, abandoning their king. The horsemen reached Quízquiz, who received them with great astuteness, seeking to retire with his men into the moors and mountains, where the horses could not dominate the Indians. At the same time they contrived to offer battle so as to lead their enemies on. This pursuit continued for more than three hours until the horses were tired. The Indians then gave a great yell and called out their two regiments who had been lying in ambush on Quízquiz' instructions so that the Spaniards should not realize their strength. The Indians attacked very fiercely and fought with great valor. The Spaniards did the same, though the many overcame the few.

The Indians killed seventeen Spaniards, though one historian says five or six, and wounded others; some were captured, and others escaped by spurring their horses. Seventy Indians died. Those captured were Francisco de Chaves, one of the leaders; Pedro González, who was later a *vecino* of Trujillo; Alonso de Alarcón; Hernando de Haro; Alonso de Hojeda, who years later fell into a profound melancholy, lost his reason, and died at Trujillo; Cristóbal de Orozco, a native of Seville; João Dias, a Portuguese gentleman; and others of less account whose names have been forgotten. Alonso de Alarcón was caught by his horse as it fell and broke his leg at the knee, and though the Indians treated him and the other wounded Spaniards with great care he remained lame. The commander Quízquiz was too experienced a leader to wait for the arrival of the main Spanish force, but withdrew his men as soon as they had won their victory, and marched toward Cajamarca, having had news of the approach of the Inca's brother Titu Atauchi. He travelled by short cuts, crossing a wide river and breaking or burning the osier bridge so that the Spaniards could not follow him. He joined Inca Atauchi who was following the Spaniards, and they both decided to return to Cajamarca to discuss their future plans together, which they now did.

CHAPTER VI

They kill Cuéllar and come to terms with the other prisoners.

As soon as Inca Titu Atauchi and the commander Quízquiz entered Cajamarca with their Spanish prisoners they made an enquiry among the Indians about the death of King Atahuallpa. They discovered that Cuéllar had been the scribe at the trial and had announced the sentence to Atahuallpa, been present at the execution, and reported the carrying out of the sentence. They also ascertained that Francisco de

Chaves and Hernando de Haro and others of their prisoners had sided with Atahuallpa and wished to see him spared and set free, even risking their own lives to this end. When Titu Atauchi, Quízquiz, and the other captains in their council had obtained evidence and proof of all this, they decided that the scribe Cuéllar should be punished for making bold to announce the death sentence to the Inca and being present at the execution by suffering the same fate as Atahuallpa, thus expiating the crime of all those who had caused the king's death. It was also agreed that all the other Spanish prisoners should be cared for and treated with every possible attention, out of respect for Francisco de Chaves and Hernando de Haro, who were supporters of the Inca. When they were cured and restored to health they would be set free and given presents; and the virtues of the good Spaniards would thus lead to the pardon of the rest. This was decided in council and put into execution the next day. Cuéllar was removed from his prison in the place where Atahuallpa had been confined. He was taken to the public square preceded by a crier who shouted: "The Pachacámac bids this *auca* to be hanged, as well as all the rest who killed our Inca." *Auca,* as we have explained elsewhere, means "rebel, traitor, caitiff, dastard," and all the other words that can be applied to treachery. The crier was sent out to announce the sentence, not because this had been the custom in their own state, but because they heard that their king had been taken to his place of execution preceded by a crier. Cuéllar was led forth to the stake at which the Inca was strangled. This stake had hitherto been left alone by the Indians, since it was regarded as an accursed spot; but they now approached it, tied the scribe to it and strangled him, saying: "Thus shall all your companions die." His dead body was left there all day; near nightfall they dug a pit and buried his body in it. All this was done in imitation of what they had seen the Spaniards do when executing and burying Atahuallpa.

Francisco de Chaves and his companions were cured and treated with every attention; when they were well and able to walk, they were given gifts of gold, silver, and emeralds, and many Indians were sent to accompany them and carry them on their shoulders. The Indians negotiated with them, in the name of all the Spaniards, certain terms of peace and friendship requested by the former. The main points of this agreement were that all wrongs, misdeeds, and crimes committed by either side hitherto, should be wiped out and forgotten forever; that there should be peace between Indians and Spaniards, and neither side should molest the other; that the Spaniards should not oppose the claim of Manco Inca to the throne, for he was the legitimate heir; that Indians and Spaniards should behave as friends in all their dealings, and aid and succor one another as allies; that the Spaniards should free the Indians they had in chains, and not in future shackle them, but treat them freely; that the laws of the past Incas on behalf of their vassals should be inviolably observed provided they did not run counter to the Christian religion; that the governor Don Francisco Pizarro should shortly send these conditions to Spain to be confirmed by his imperial majesty. The terms were conveyed to Francisco de Chaves and his companions, partly by signs and partly by the words of the Indian servants captured with the Spaniards. Titu Atauchi, before addressing the Spaniards, told these servants what he wanted to explain to their masters, word for word, so that they should be able to interpret it properly.

When the Spaniards saw how generously Titu Atauchi and his companions had treated them while in confinement, and how attentively they had been cared for and given their freedom and gifts of gold, silver, and precious stones, and provided with a large escort of natives to accompany them back to Spanish quarters, though the Indians might easily have cut them to pieces out of rage and indignation at the death of their king, and finally how the Indians asked for negotiations on such fair and reasonable terms, they were confounded and amazed. And the Spaniards, like men who had hourly been expecting to die, were full of repentance for their remissness in teaching the Indians and preaching the holy Gospel, and resolved to make amends in future when they saw how peaceful the Indians were. They therefore made bold to reply that as the Indians were asking for concessions the Spaniards would do the same: they would like to have leave to make two requests. The Indians told them to ask whatever they wished, for it would be amply conceded. Then Francisco de Chaves said that he would like first to urge and beg in the name of the governor and all the other Spaniards that the Incas, their captains, and all the lords of vassals should accept the Christian religion and permit it to be preached throughout the empire. The second request was that as the Spaniards were strangers and had no villages or land on which to support themselves, they should be given food like the other inhabitants of the kingdom, and Indian men and women to serve them, not as slaves, but as servants.

The reply given them was that as regards the Christian religion, the Indians not only did not reject it, but begged them, as soon as they reached their general's camp, to send preachers and priests to teach them the Christian faith, which they desired to know: they would welcome the priests and serve them like gods, for they fully realized that Christianity was a better religion than their own. The Inca Huaina Cápac had told them so on his death bed, and they had no need of any other bidding than that of their Inca. He had also bidden them obey and serve the new-comers to the empire, who would excel them in everything. Because of their Inca's command the Indians were obliged to obey and serve the Spaniards even though it cost them their lives, as Atahuallpa had done. Therefore the Spaniards might ask whatever they wished, and the Indians would seek to satisfy them in everything. When all this had been recorded by the historians on their knots, they told the Spaniards that they were free to depart whenever they wished.

They thereupon took leave and went in search of their governor, laden with presents and accompanied by many Indians. On the way, Francisco de Chaves and his companions discussed together what had happened and being serious men they declared that the acts and words of the Indians were so reasonable and enlightened that they could not proceed from idolatrous barbarians, but must have been the result of miracles and inspirations by our Lord God who had disposed the minds of the heathen to receive His doctrine and holy Gospel with love and gentleness. They therefore went on, full of good intentions to persuade the governor and all the other Spaniards; many of these—of whom the governor was one—desired the same thing. But the Devil, the enemy of the human race, used all his strength and wiles to prevent this and impede the conversion of the Indians; and though he could not completely stop the conversion, at least he did so for many years with the loyal aid of his diligent ministers, the seven deadly sins, for in a time of such liberty and opportunity each of the vices had free rein. Thus there arose the wars that shortly after broke out between Indians and Spaniards as a result of the failure to fulfil these terms, for pride did not consent to the restoration of the kingdom to its owners; and this led to the general rising of the Indians. Then followed the wars between the two partners Pizarro and Almagro, caused by wrath and envy, for each wanted to govern and be superior to the other. These wars lasted till the death of both leaders, Almagro beheaded by one of Pizarro's brothers and Pizarro killed by a son of Almagro. This strife was followed by the wars of the good governor Vaca de Castro (whom I knew in Madrid in 1562) against Don Diego de Almagro the younger, for pride and discord prevented this young man from obeying his lord and king; and thus he died, for his warlike deeds could not save him from being betrayed to his executioner by a treacher-ous subordinate. Next came the wars of the Viceroy Blasco Núñez Vela and Gonzalo Pizarro, the fruit of avarice and rebellion. A few years after there followed in due order, the risings of Don Sebastián de Castilla and Francisco Hernández Girón, who were provoked by lust and gluttony. The Devil stirred up all these wars one after another, over a period of twenty-five years; and we shall, with divine aid, recount them all in their due order. These were the obstacles that prevented the Gospel from being preached as it otherwise would have been, for the faithful could not preach the faith owing to the daily disturbances that took place, nor could the infidels receive it because during the whole of that period there was nothing but war and murder with fire and the sword. The Indians were affected no less than the Spaniards, and indeed they had the worst of it, for both sides waged their wars at the expense of the natives, who were required to furnish supplies and ordered to carry the army's baggage on their backs, and perform all other tasks, great and small, some of which I myself witnessed.

CHAPTER VII

The Spaniards enter Cuzco and find great treasures.

As soon as Inca Titu Atauchi had sent Francisco de Chaves and his companions with these terms, he made his own half-brother Manco Inca his messenger, to convey the same conditions to the Spaniards and report to him what happened, so that he would be prepared for whatever negotiations might take place with the Spaniards. The commander Quízquiz sent to warn him not to disband his army, but rather to try to increase it until he had reached an agreement with the Spaniards as to how they were to live together; the commander also urged him to beware lest he should suffer the same fate as his brother Atahuallpa.

The Indians sent these and similar warnings to Manco Inca and with them their recognition of him as supreme lord of the whole empire, for though they had hitherto been his enemies and desired to kill him so that Atahuallpa should be unopposed, on the latter's death and the disappearance of his hopes and ambitions, they adopted as a good military policy the course of restoring the empire to its legitimate owner, so that all the Indians should be united in their resistance and in ejecting the Spaniards from their kingdom, or else in coming to a *modus vivendi* with them. In this way the Indians would be more respected and feared than if they were divided into rival parties.

Prince Manco Inca received warnings of his brother and the commander Quízquiz, and was glad to have them, since they showed that these personages, who had been so much opposed to him, were now on his side and wanted to restore the empire to him. He thought the Spaniards would wish to do the same, since they declared themselves so strictly attached to justice. In this hope he made ready to visit the Spaniards in order to ask them in the name of peace, friendship, and simple justice, to give him power and command in his kingdom, according to the terms put forward by his brother Titu Atauchi. We shall now leave him with his preparations until his due time, and return to the governor, Don Francisco Pizarro.

After having suffered the havoc we have seen at the hands of Titu Atauchi and Quízquiz, Pizarro collected his men together and set off with more circumspection than hitherto. He was involved in no more encounters of any moment, but merely a few trivial alarms. When he had nearly reached Cuzco, its inhabitants came out armed to bar his way, but they made little resistance before returning to their homes, collecting their wives and children and such wealth as they could and retiring to the hills, for they had heard what had happened at Cajamarca. The city resisted because it was controlled by Atahuallpa, who had seized power when he captured Huáscar; but its inhabitants desired to avenge the latter's death if they could. López de Gómara here writes as follows:

Next day the Spaniards entered Cuzco without any resistance, and at once some began to pull down the walls of the temple which were of gold and silver, others to dig up the jewels and jars of gold that had been buried with the dead, and still others to seize idols made of the same metal. They also sacked the houses and the fortress, which still contained much gold from the time of Huaina Cápac. Finally they obtained from Cuzco and its surroundings more gold than they had got by the capture of Atahuallpa in Cajamarca. However, as they were now much more numerous than formerly, the quantity each received was less. For this reason, and because it was the second occasion and there was no king to capture, it caused no such stir in Spain. One Spaniard walking through a dense thicket found a whole silver tomb worth 50,000 Castilians. Others found many less valuable tombs: for the rich in Peru used to be buried in the country near some idol. They also went in search of the treasure of Huaina Cápac and the ancient kings of Cuzco, which was so famous; but it was never found then or since. The Spaniards were not satisfied with what they had, but wearied the Indians by digging everything up and turning it inside out, and treated them very badly, committing many cruelties to get them to talk about the treasure and show them tombs.

Thus López de Gómara, and this is taken literally from his ch. cxxiv. Zárate, in his Book II, ch. viii, speaking of some Spaniards who were pursuing an Indian captain, speaks as follows: "And being unable to catch him, they returned to Cuzco, where they found as great a treasure as at Cajamarca, consisting of gold and silver, which the governor divided among his people." Thus Zárate. These authorities give ample proof of our statement that the Spaniards found as much wealth in Cuzco as in Cajamarca, and more. I am glad to be able to quote these passages with their authors' names, so as to show that I do not wish to adorn myself, like the crow, with others' plumes, and also to produce Spanish witnesses for what I am saying.

To return to López de Gómara's statement about the treasure the Spaniards found buried in Cuzco and its surroundings, the fact is that during the seven or eight years that followed these events, when the Spaniards were in peaceful possession of the empire, treasure was found both within the city and outside it. When the houses in the city were shared out among the Spaniards, it happened that in one of them, a royal palace called Amarucancha which fell to Antonio Altamirano, a horseman was galloping in the yard, when his horse sank its foot into a hole, which had not previously been there. When they went to look at the hole to see if it was the bed of some former stream passing under the house, they found that it was the mouth of a golden jar holding eight or nine arrobas. These jars are made in various sizes by the Indians to serve as vats for brewing their drink. It was accompanied by many silver and gold vessels to a value of over 80,000 ducats. And in the part of the house of the chosen women which fell to Pedro del Barco and was later owned by an apothecary, one Hernando de Segovia whom I knew, this Segovia happened to dig part of a foundation and found a treasure of 72,000 ducats. With this and more than 20,000 he had earned at his trade, he returned to Spain, and I saw him in Seville, where he died a few days after his arrival of sheer misery and grief at having left the city of Cuzco. Others who have returned, and who were known to me in both Peru and Spain, have died of the same form of misery. There were thus many treasures found in the city when it was first won and since. It is believed that there are many more, for the Indians hid the greater part of their treasures on the arrival of the Spaniards, as we have stated elsewhere.

CHAPTER VIII

The conversion of an Indian who asked for the true religion of mankind.

ON THIS day, the first on which the Spaniards set eyes on the imperial
city of Cuzco, there occurred a marvellous incident involving a Spaniard and an Indian. A gentleman from Trujillo called Antonio [? Alon-
so] Ruiz, while sacking the city with the others, happened to enter a
house, whose owner came to receive him with a peaceful expression on
his face and addressed him in his own language as follows: "Be very
welcome, for I have been expecting you for many days, since Pachacámac
has told me by means of signs and auguries that I shall not die until a new
people arrives, which will teach me the new religion we are to observe.
All my life I have lived with the desire of it in my heart, and I am sure
that it must be you who are to teach me it." The Spaniard, who could not
follow all the Indian had said, understood the first two words; for they
were then beginning to pick up the commoner Indian phrases, and the
Quechua tongue expresses the four Spanish words for welcome in two.
Understanding this and seeing how glad and delighted the Indian was to
see him at a time which seemed to call for mourning rather than pleasure,
he suspected that he wanted something, and in order to find out what it
was he decided to stay with the Indian, who tried to entertain him as best
he could.

After two or three days, when Christians and infidels alike had settled
down a little after the sack, Alonso Ruiz went to look for the dragoman
Felipe and brought him back to speak to his host. Having fully understood what he had said, he plied him with questions about his life and
customs. From the answers given Ruiz realized that the Indian was a man
of peace who had been content with his natural life and had done no harm
to anyone, and desired to know the true religion of mankind, since he said
that his own did not give the satisfaction his soul was seeking. Thereupon
the Spaniard sought as best he could to teach him the principles of our
holy Catholic faith so that he might believe in the true God, three in one.
And as the Indian language lacks all these words, as we have said above,
and even the verb "to believe," he told the Indian that he was to have in
his heart what the Christians teach, which was to hold what Mother

Church of Rome believes. Having repeated this often and heard the Indian always say yes, he called a priest, who was told the whole occurrence and informed that the Indian wanted to become a Christian, as he had repeatedly said. The Indian was then baptized, to the great satisfaction of all three, the minister, the convert, and Alonso Ruiz, his godfather. The Indian died a few days later, and was very content to die a Christian. Alonso Ruiz returned to Spain with more than 50,000 pesos he had gained from the spoils of Cajamarca and Cuzco and elsewhere; and like a good Christian, he always had scruples that his wealth was not honestly come by, and so went to the emperor and told him:

"Sacred Majesty, I am one of the conquerors of Peru, and I received more than 50,000 pesos in spoils, which I have brought to Spain. I am torn with anxiety that they are ill-gotten, and I do not know to whom to return them, unless to Your Majesty, who are lord of that empire. If Your Majesty wishes to grant me part of it, I shall receive it as from a lord who is entitled to give me it: but if you do not wish to grant me it, I shall understand that I do not deserve it."

The emperor accepted the restoration, and out of good will and Christian spirit awarded him an income of 400,000 maravedis a year, payable on a small town near Trujillo called Marta. This estate is now possessed as an inheritance by a grandson of Antonio [? Alonso] Ruiz. He was indeed well-advised to make restitution, for in addition to salving his conscience, he was given more in wealth and dignity than he could have bought with his money. The most remarkable fact is that the land was granted to him in perpetuity, and his descendants still own it, while the allocations in Peru are for two lives, and almost all of them have now expired. This estate will be enjoyed forever, while what is brought from the Indies—even though not in the form of allocations, but obtained in other ways—does not reach the third possessor in Spain or America. With this we must return to the theme of our history.

CHAPTER IX

Don Diego de Almagro goes to meet Don Pedro de Alvarado; and Belalcázar, to punish Rumiñaui.

PIZARRO and Almagro were busy collecting the many treasures which López de Gómara says they found in Cuzco and its district when news reached them that Alvarado had come to Peru with the intention of installing himself as governor of whatever lands he might conquer, and that he had with him five hundred men, most of them very noble gentlemen, the flower of Spanish arms, with a good supply of horses, weapons, and equipment. Those who were at Cuzco were greatly disturbed, fearing that he was going to deprive them of their possessions, for there is no human pleasure unmingled with sorrow. Thus alarmed, the governor sent his companion Almagro with a hundred Spaniards to prevent any harm from happening. He was to defend the coast and prevent Alvarado from landing, or if he could not resist the newcomers, he was to buy up his forces, using his best endeavors to this end. Almagro set off according to his instructions, and we shall say later what happened to him; for here we must treat of great events that occurred at the same time. Soon after the departure of Don Diego de Almagro, Francisco de Chaves and his companions reached Cuzco and informed the governor and the other Spaniards of the generous treatment they had received from Titu Atauchi and his captains, describing the care and attentions they had received, the gifts and escort they had been provided with, the agreement they had made with the Indians, and finally the execution of the scribe Cuéllar, carried out by the Indians with the aid of a crier and an executioner.

The governor and all the rest were delighted to see Francisco de Chaves and his comrades, whom they had mourned as dead, and they were astonished that the Indians should have treated them as they described. They also took note of the death of Cuéllar, on whom the Indians had taken their vengeance, instead of wreaking it on all their prisoners. They were more astonished at the conditions of peace than at anything else; and when they realized the desire of the Indians for peace and friendship with the Spaniards and for the preaching of the holy Gospel, they proposed that all the terms should be accepted. But the disturbance caused by the arrival of Alvarado prevented any talk of peace and religion for the moment, and their only concern was with war and cruelties, to the destruction of both Indians and Spaniards, as we shall see in the course of our history.

At almost the same time the governor received news of the rebellion and bloodshed caused by Rumiñaui at Quito, and of how he was raising men against the Spaniards. In order to punish this rebel and remedy the possible effects of his rising, the governor sent Sebastián de Belalcázar as captain of a well-furnished force of horse and foot to succor Almagro if necessary. They took their departure with every precaution so as to avoid the fate of Francisco de Chaves and his friends. On the road they found some of Atahuallpa's captains defending peaks and strongholds, though they had no forces to oppose them in the open field. These were minor leaders who on hearing of Atahuallpa's capture had raised men in their own districts without receiving instructions from the Inca. When they heard he had been killed, they did not dismiss their men but waited to see if some kinsman of his might call on them to avenge his death. These captains were thus scattered about the country, and were independent of one another, with no leader or governor, though if they had all been brought together, they could have done the Spaniards a great deal of harm, if only in the difficult passes and dangerous gorges there are on the roads. Sebastián de Belalcázar had a few clashes of little importance with these captains, but as they had too few men to make a serious resistance, they disengaged as best they could. Only one of them, called Súpay Yupanqui, or "Devil Yupanqui," lived up to his name and killed five Spaniards and wounded fourteen, and if he had had more men, would have butchered them all. Francisco López de Gómara, His Catholic Majesty's royal chaplain, writes of these encounters in his ch. cxxviii and says the captain was called Zopo Sopagui. The imperial treasurer Agustín de Zárate in his Book II, ch. x, calls him Sapa Sopagui, which is closer to his name. His real name was Súmac Yupanqui, "handsome Yupanqui," for as a young man this Indian had striking features and a well-formed body. His name was Yupanqui, and "handsome" was added as a nickname, from the participle *súmac*, which we have mentioned in dealing with the Indian poetry. He was a bastard son of a member of the royal family and his mother was from the kingdom of Quito. He had been brought up with Atahuallpa, and proved such a good soldier that he was made one of his captains. When Atahuallpa ordered all manner of cruel acts after defeating and capturing his brother Huáscar Inca, this captain noticed how the king delighted in these barbarities and sought to please him by exceeding all the other leaders whose mission it was to execute them, and invented other acts of sadism which neither his companions nor his king had even thought of. This often happens with servants of lords and princes, who seek to gain the good will of their masters without fear of God or shame before mankind. When Atahaullpa's captains and men saw him perform such devilish deeds they changed his nickname and substituted *súpay,* "devil," for *súmac.* After this Indian had resisted Sebastián de Belalcázar and done as much harm as he could, he withdrew and took refuge in a place where neither Spaniards nor Indians could reach him, for he feared the arms of the first, and the second hated him for his deeds. It was supposed that he despaired of living among his own people after his past devilries and dared not trust the Spaniards, and therefore buried himself among the wild forests of the Antis among tigers and serpents, as other captains who were his companions had done.

Sebastián de Belalcázar went onward and reached Quito intending to stop Rumiñaui's cruelties and punish him. The Indian leader came out to meet him, and as we have already said, they fought several engagements with little loss to the Spaniards but a great deal to the Indians, who were few and ill-prepared. As this commander had committed such barbarous acts against his own people, as putting his fellow captains to death, slaying the brother and sons of his own king, and burying the chosen virgins alive, without any cause or justice, he was so hated by the Indians, that although he summoned them to arms, saying that he intended to avenge Atahuallpa's death, no one obeyed the call. Thus being unable to resist Belalcázar, he despaired of his life and withdrew to the forests. Some Spaniards also took this course to escape from their enemies, as we shall see later.

CHAPTER X

*The fears and hopes of Almagro, the flight
of his interpreter, and the agreement
with Alvarado.*

T HE GOOD Don Diego de Almagro, on his way to intercept Don Pedro de Alvarado, also had brushes with Atahuallpa's captains whom he met on the road, but they were of so little importance that there is nothing to tell of them. Thus Almagro travelled slowly on, waiting till he should have definite news of Alvarado's whereabouts: he was anxious not to miss him, for he had heard that he had landed and was marching inland.

Belalcázar, who had instructions to come to Almagro's help, first put Rumiñaui and the other captains to flight from Quito, and then came hastily down to the coast in search of Almagro. Having joined forces, both leaders set about disbanding the groups of Indians who were scattered about those provinces. They did this because they dared not go in pursuit of Alvarado, knowing that he had a large number of excellent soldiers with him. They were even on the point of giving up their task, but shame prevented them from doing so. This continued until Alvarado came up with them and captured seven horsemen whom Don Diego had sent out to scour the countryside. He released these men as soon as they had told him the size of Almagro's forces and given him other information he needed; for indeed Alvarado never intended to prevent those engaged in the conquest of Peru from pressing it forward, but only to help them as far as he could. He therefore freed the prisoners, though he could easily have held them. The good Almagro was pleased by this display of generosity on Alvarado's part, and as he supposed it to be a sign of peace and concord which would tell in his favor, his preoccupations were somewhat allayed. But as Alvarado sent no message by the liberated scouts, he was not quite at ease, but wavered between hope and fear, awaiting the outcome.

At this time of trouble and perplexity for Almagro, an incident occurred which added greatly to his cares. The Indian Felipe, who had gone with him as his interpreter, on learning that Alvarado was at hand, took flight one night, taking with him a leading cacique, and warned Don Pedro of the smallness of Almagro's force, saying that all the Indian chiefs who were with him wanted to run away and serve Alvarado, and that all the others throughout Peru would do the same; and he offered to bring them to serve and obey Alvarado, and also to lead him to Almagro's camp so that he could take his rival unawares and easily capture him. But Don Pedro, though delighted to learn the news that was in his favor, refused to accept Felipe's suggestion, hoping to get better results by a different approach. The Indian committed this treacherous act because his own conscience accused him of his misdeeds, and he was afraid that he would be punished for giving false evidence to the effect that Atahuallpa intended to kill the Spaniards, which was the cause of the king's execution.

To shorten our account, we may say that Alvarado and Almagro met on the fields of Riuecpampa, which the Spaniards call Riobamba, where they faced one another under arms and ready to fight. But when they were on the point of attacking one another, as they were all Spaniards and most of them from Extremadura, they began to converse, and each party offered peace and friendship: the same thing happened near Lérida between the soldiers of the great Julius Caesar and Pompey's captains, Petreius and Afranius. Almagro was very glad of these negotiations, for his forces were less than a quarter of Alvarado's, though he and his followers were determined to die rather than give in to their rivals. Both parties tempered their excitement, and a truce for twenty-four hours was agreed by common consent, during which time the generals should meet and discuss the future. They had an interview, and by the mediation of Licentiate Caldera, a native of Seville, reached agreement that they should all share equally in what had been gained and what was still to be gained, and that Alvarado should proceed down the coast southward with his fleet to discover whatever provinces and kingdoms there might be there, while Pizarro and Almagro remained behind to pacify what they had discovered and nearly conquered. It was also settled that the soldiers of either group should go freely wherever they wished, either by sea on the new discovery or on the conquest by land. This was all that was made known of the agreement, so as not to annoy the followers of Alvarado; for, as Cieza de León and López de Gómara say, there were among them many very distinguished gentlemen who would have resented not being rewarded then and there.

The secret conditions, which they dared not reveal, were that Almagro promised to give Alvarado 100,000 pesos in good gold (meaning of 450 maravedis the peso) for his fleet and his horses and equipment, and that he should return to govern Guatemala, and should swear, as he did in fact swear, that he would never return to Peru during the lifetime of the two companions, Pizarro and Almagro. Both were very satisfied with this arrangement.

After reaching this agreement Almagro buried alive the *curaca* who had fled with Felipe the interpreter, because of his treachery in running away; and he would have done the same with the dragoman if Alvarado had not pleaded for him. With regard to this López de Gómara says the following in his ch. cxxix:

Almagro had no funds with which to pay the 100,000 gold pesos from what he had found on the present expedition, though he had taken a temple lined with silver at Caramba: or else he did not wish to fulfil the bargain with Pizarro, or wanted first to take Alvarado somewhere where he would not be able to get out of the bargain. They both therefore went to San Miguel de Tangarara, and took most of the best troops with them.

Thus far López de Gómara: this is what I would have written, but as he has done so, I have put it in his name. Almagro then reported all this to the governor, Don Francisco Pizarro.

CHAPTER XI

Almagro and Alvarado go to Cuzco; Prince Manco
Inca comes to speak to the governor,
who gives him a great reception.

WHEN THE Spaniards had celebrated this agreement to the general satisfaction of them all, the two governors, Almagro and Alvarado (who for the purposes of the treaty was given the same title of governor as Pizarro and Almagro) instructed Sebastián de Belalcázar to return to the kingdom of Quito and pacify it, for there was no lack of petty Indian leaders who were keeping the region in a ferment. The Spaniards thus tried to prevent the outbreak of any possible rising. This done, they took other necessary steps, including the establishment of a garrison town where Spanish troops coming from Panama or Nicaragua to take part in the conquest of Peru would find security—the fame of the great wealth of Peru was now drawing men together from all sides. This stronghold was supplied with arms and food, and sufficient men were left behind to guard it. Alvarado, who had undertaken by the terms of the agreement that had been made public to return to his ships and sail southward to the conquest of new provinces and kingdoms, announced that he intended to go overland to meet Pizarro so as to have the opportunity of seeing Peru and its wonders. He said this to conceal the effect of the secret capitulations. At this time it was agreed that Almagro should send a representative called Diego de Mora (whom I later knew) to see to the delivery of the fleet. Alvarado sent Garci Holguín to hand it over, and Mora received it on behalf of the joint expedition, for under the terms of the agreement the ships and all they contained were to be common property. Once these measures had been settled, the two governors took the road to Cuzco where Pizarro was. We shall leave them on the way,

and return to Pizarro and the events in Cuzco after Almagro's departure
on this expedition: we shall thus not have to return to tell this part of
our story, but keep everything that happened in its proper time and place.

After receiving the warnings of Titu Atauchi and the commander
Quízquiz, Manco Inca prepared to visit the governor and ask for the
restoration of his empire and the fulfilment of the other terms put forward by his brother and all the other leading captains in the kingdom.
He took council with his friends two or three or more times about the
manner of his going, whether he should be accompanied by warriors or
by civilians. His advisers were doubtful about this, inclining at first to one
side and then to the other, but they almost always tended to think that he
ought to go with a strong army, as Quízquiz recommended, so as not to
suffer the fate of his brother Atahuallpa. It should be assumed that the
strangers would be more moved by fear of war than by respect for
courtesies, for Atahuallpa's courtesies had done him more harm than
good. The Inca therefore addressed his counsellors when they were
assembled to decide this question, and spoke as follows:

"My sons and brothers! We are going to ask those whom we regard as
children of our god Viracocha for justice, for they entered our country
declaring that their main purpose was to do justice all over the world.
I do not think they will deny me it in so reasonable a matter as our
request; for according to the doctrine our ancestors have always handed
down to us, they should prove by their deeds what they have promised in
words, and so show that they are true children of the Sun. It will be of
little use for us to regard them as divine if they disprove their divinity by
acts of tyranny and wickedness. I prefer to trust in our rights and justice
rather than in our power and arms. Since they say that they are messengers
of the god Pachacámac, they will perhaps fear him, for as his messengers
they know that there is nothing he hates so much as the denial of justice
by those who are set over others to administer it and who take things for
themselves instead of awarding them to their rightful owners. We go
armed with the justice of our request: let us fix our hopes on the rectitude
of those we hold to be gods rather than on our own efforts, for if they are
true children of the Sun as we believe, they will behave like Incas. They
will give us our empire, for our fathers, the past kings, never deprived
those they conquered of their authority however rebellious their chiefs
had shown themselves. We have not been rebellious: on the contrary the
whole empire has yielded to them without resistance. Therefore let us go
to them in peace, for if we go armed it will appear that we are going to
make war on them and not to ask for justice, and we shall give them a

justification for refusing us; for any pretext is sufficient to cause the powerful and greedy to do what they want to do and refuse what is asked of them. Instead of arms let us take them what gifts we can, for these usually appease angry men or offended gods. Bring together all the gold and silver and precious stones you can; hunt whatever birds and animals you can find; gather the best and most delicate fruits we possess. Let us go as well supplied as we can, and even though we lack our ancient power as kings, our spirit as Incas shall not fail us. If all this is not enough to persuade them to restore our empire, we shall understand clearly that the prophecy of our father Huaina Cápac has been fulfilled, when he said that our monarchy is to be taken away, our state to perish, and our religion to be destroyed. We have seen part of this fulfilled. If Pachacámac has so ordained, what more can we do but obey him? Let us do what is right and just: let them do what they will."

The Inca said all this with great dignity: his captains and *curacas* were much affected by his concluding words and shed many tears, considering the line of their Inca kings to have ended.

After this mourning the *curacas* and officials prepared what the Inca asked them to produce, and everything else that was necessary in order for their ruler to travel with some royal dignity, even though he could not attain the majesty of past kings. He thus went to Cuzco accompanied by many lords of vassals and their kinsmen, though by very few of his own family, for they had all been consumed by Atahuallpa's cruelty. He was given a great reception. All the Spaniards, some mounted and some on foot, came out to welcome him a good distance from the city. The governor alighted close to the Inca, and he did likewise; for he was travelling in a litter, made not of gold like those of his ancestors, but of wood. Although his advisers had recommended him to travel in royal state, as he was entitled, with a golden litter and his crown on his head (which was the scarlet fringe), the Inca preferred to use neither, thinking it would be disrespectful toward the Spanish governor and his companions to assume the royal insignia when he was going to request the restitution of the empire: if he did, he would imply that he intended to be Inca whether they approved or not, since he had taken possession of the empire by assuming the scarlet fringe. He said that he would wear the yellow fringe so that the Viracochas—as the Indians called the Spaniards, and I may as well call them the same since I am an Indian—should realize that he was the legitimate heir.

The governor received the Inca with the usual Spanish courtesy, bidding him welcome. The Inca replied that he had come to serve and worship those whom he regarded as gods, sent by the almighty Pachacámac. Their speeches were short, for lack of good interpreters. As soon as the governor had spoken to the Inca, he moved off so as to give the other Spaniards the opportunity to speak. Then his two brothers Juan and Gonzalo Pizarro appeared.

On learning that they were the brothers of the *apu* or captain general, the Inca embraced them and received them with great courtesy. Before going to meet the Spaniards, he had arranged for one of the Indians who had been among them and was acquainted with their captains and other officials to be present when he spoke with them and tell him who they were. The Inca thus had an Indian who was in Spanish service to tell one of his lords of vassals standing by his side the rank of each Spaniard as he approached to address him, and the *curaca* passed the word on to the Inca. Thus warned, the Inca could address the captains and officers in the imperial service in different terms from the other soldiers who came forward in bands to speak to him. He treated them all very honorably, and displayed great affection toward them in his gestures and words. And at the end he made the same remarks as Atahuallpa had done after seeing Hernando Pizarro and Hernando de Soto: "These men are true sons of our god Viracocha, for they resemble his portrait in their faces, beards, and dress. They deserve that we should serve them, as our father Huaina Cápac bade us in his will."

CHAPTER XII

The Inca asks for the restoration of his empire; the answer he receives.

THERE the interview ended. The Spaniards mounted their horses, and the Inca returned to his litter. The governor placed himself on the Inca's left, and his brothers and the other captains went in front, each leading his own company. The governor ordered one to take the Inca's rear, and two dozen foot to be arranged round the royal litter. This greatly pleased the Indians, who thought that they were placed on a level with the Spaniards and raised to the height of those they regarded as divine by being bidden to proceed in the same company with them. They thus entered the city with great rejoicings; and its inhabitants came out with many songs and dances composed in praise of the Viracochas, for they were delighted to see their Inca, supposing that the legitimate heir was to rule and that Atahuallpa's cruelties were at an end. The street along which the Inca passed was strewn with reeds, and triumphal arches were raised at intervals and covered with flowers, as the Indians were in the habit of doing for their royal triumphs. The Spaniards took the Inca to one of the palaces called Cassana, which was in the main square, facing the place where the Jesuit College now is. They left him there full of satisfaction and hope, supposing that his reception would lead to the restoration of the empire. He said as much to his friends and they were all extremely satisfied, thinking that the peace and quiet they had grown accustomed to under the Incas would soon return.

When the king had reached his lodging, his officials at once produced the present they had brought for the governor and his Viracochas; the latter expressed their gratitude so graciously that the Indians could hardly contain themselves for pride. This was the happiest and most honorable day this poor Inca had in the whole of his life, for he had previously suffered great anguish and distress fleeing from the tyrannous persecution of his brother Atahuallpa, and the days that followed from now to the time of his death were no less wretched, as we shall see.

On finding himself settled in his house, the Inca sent to tell Francisco de Chaves and his companions that he wished to know them and to see them separately from the rest, owing to the report he had received about them from his friends. When they arrived, he embraced them with signs of great affection, and after drinking with them according to the Inca custom, he said, among other kindly remarks, that they had proved themselves true sons of the god Viracocha and brothers of the Incas by their action in trying to save Atahuallpa. He was grateful to them and hoped to reward them generously: let them regard him as a brother, for they were all of one lineage, children and descendants of the Sun. He bade them be presented with many jars of gold, silver, and precious stones which were set aside for this gentleman and his friends. Chaves replied that they were all His Highness' servants and would prove as much when opportunity offered. What they had done for his brother the king had been in fulfilment of their duties: let him bid them whatever he might wish in order to make proof of their good intentions, and he would find them very ready to serve him. The Inca again embraced them and dismissed them, full of satisfaction and enriched with gifts of gold, silver, emeralds, and turquoises.

Two days after his arrival, Prince Manco Inca proposed to the governor that the empire should be restored to him and the terms of the agreement between the Indians and Spaniards under which they might live in peace and brotherhood should be carried out. He asked for priests and ministers to preach the Gospel and teach the Christian religion to the Indians, as the Spaniards themselves had proposed when the agreement was reached; and he undertook to send them out with great reverence and every attention to the chief kingdoms and provinces in his empire to indoctrinate the Indians. The fact that his father Huaina Cápac had declared on his death bed that the Christian religion was superior to their own would be sufficient to guarantee that they would be very willingly received. He asked the Viracochas to say in what way they would like to be served and what part of the kingdom they wished to take for themselves: he would duly satisfy their desires and they would find themselves obeyed, for his father had also left instructions in his will that the Spaniards were to be obeyed and served with every mark of love and attention.

The governor replied that His Highness was very welcome in his imperial city, and he hoped he would rest at ease. He was very glad to know the Inca's desire so as to be able to comply with it, and the terms of the agreement were so just that it was only reasonable that they should all be adopted. After this, they spoke of other matters, but the conversation was short for want of interpreters.

The governor consulted his brothers and the other captains about the Inca's requests, about which there were various opposing opinions, but as it was known that the symbol of taking possession of the empire was the wearing of the scarlet fringe, he went next day to the Inca's house, accompanied by his friends, and without more ado, said that he begged Manco Cápac to take possession of his empire forthwith. If he had known before what was involved, he would not have permitted him to be an hour without the imperial crown on his brow. As regards the division of the kingdom, this would be dealt with later when both sides had come to an agreement and settled down, for at present both Indians and Spaniards were in a state of excitement. The services the Indians were to perform for the Spaniards and the conditions of peace between them should be settled by the Inca according to his will and pleasure, and the Spaniards would more willingly obey him. They could not for the moment supply ministers to teach the Indians the Christian religion, for there were so few priests that they had not even enough for themselves: when more came, and they were expected, they would be sent in ample numbers, for the Christians had come to Peru only to undeceive the natives about the errors and barbarities of their heathen faith. The Indians were very satisfied at this, and the Inca assumed his scarlet fringe with the greatest festivities and celebrations, though they could not compare with those of past times, since all the members of the royal blood— who contribute principally to the majesty of all the courts in the world— had disappeared. Moreover many of the lords of vassals who had been swept away by Atahuallpa's cruelties were missing. The older Indians who remembered the days of the great Huaina Cápac mourned the decline of the house and court of the Inca: the younger, who had never seen its ancient majesty, were full of rejoicing.

CHAPTER XIII

The two governors go in quest of the commander Quízquiz.

As we have said above, Alvarado and Almagro were travelling with their splendid company toward Cuzco, where they knew they would find the governor, Don Francisco Pizarro. On the road they heard that Quízquiz was in the direction of the province of the Cañaris, with many warriors and plenty of gold and silver, a great quantity of the precious royal textiles and innumerable flocks of sheep. Such was the report; and as is usual in such cases, all the details were greatly magnified by rumor. The governors marched in this direction to disband the army and kill the rebel leader, for they had heard from the Indians that this was the only remaining force under arms. Although Quízquiz had his army with him, he remained quietly where he was, with no intention of fighting the Spaniards, since after he and Inca Atauchi had sent the above-mentioned terms accepted by Francisco de Chaves and his friends to Pizarro, he had remained waiting for their ratification and for the establishment of universal peace between Indians and Spaniards, and was quite unaware that the Spaniards were coming to kill him. His lack of concern had been fortified by the policy Inca Titu Atauchi had enjoined on him on his death bed. The poor Inca died a few days after releasing Francisco de Chaves and his friends; and his death was caused by grief and pain at the death of his brother Atahuallpa and the knowledge of what the traitor Rumiñaui had done to his nephews and brothers and the captains and chosen virgins in Quito. He considered that such excesses and disorders on the part of a vassal against the Inca's own blood constituted a clear sign of the loss and destruction of the empire and of the majesty of his line. In these tribulations and finding himself near death, he called the commander Quízquiz and his captains and bade them seek peace with the Viracochas, offering to serve and respect them, and remembering that their Inca Huaina Cápac had bidden them do so in his will: his prophecy would certainly be fulfilled in its entirety, for they had already seen how most of it had come to pass. They should therefore try to please those whom they had accepted as descendants of their father the Sun and children of their god Viracocha, just as Huaina Cápac, himself a child of the Sun, had enjoined them.

Because of these arguments and of his hopes that the conditions of peace would be accepted, Quízquiz neglected to prepare for war, and though he knew that the governors were approaching, he did not stir or give the alarm. He simply sent a company of a hundred men—which was the smallest unit the Incas had in wartime—led by a centurion whom the historians López de Gómara and Zárate call Sotaurco, for Soctaorco, "six hills" (*socta,* "six," and *orco* "a hill"), so named because he was born among the great mountains of Peru where his father was fighting in the wars, accompanied by his mother: this must have been owing to some inescapable necessity. He was therefore given this name to preserve the memory of his strange birth in time of war, which was all the more unusual in that women never accompanied their husbands on campaign. At the place where he was born there were six high hills standing out above the rest; so that the name he was given summarized the whole story including the time and place of his birth.

The annals of the Indians consisted of similar traditions, which were reduced to a few words containing the gist of the matter so that it might more easily be remembered; or else they recorded it in succinct poems, which recalled some event or embassy, the reply of a king or official, a speech made in time of peace or war, the content of some law with the penalties for breaking it, and everything else that took place in their commonwealth. These matters were memorized by the historians and accountants, and were taught by tradition to their sons and successors. These figures and short verses and odd words, such as the name of this captain and others we have mentioned and shall mention if opportunity arises, were intended only to bring the subject to the mind of the historian or accountant, who would already know the tradition concerned.

By the use of his notes, which were the knots, marks, and cyphers, he could read off his history better and faster than a Spaniard with a book, as Padre Acosta says in his Book VI, ch. viii. This was because they knew the traditions by heart and studied nothing else by day or by night, so as to acquit themselves well in their duties. We have said all this before, but have felt impelled to repeat it here because the name of this captain Soctaorco offers such an excellent example.

Soctaorco was therefore sent forward by Quízquiz, when he learnt of the coming of the Spaniards, to find out their intentions and report what he could discover. The captain took fewer precautions than he might have done, for he was captured by the scouts and brought before Alvarado. When the latter had found out where Quízquiz was and what forces he had, he determined to travel rapidly and on finding him near to overtake him by means of a night march and catch him unawares. He took his departure accompanied by a large band of horsemen; but they found the roads so rough that when they came within a day's journey of Quízquiz almost all the horses had lost their shoes. They spent the night without sleeping and shod the horses by the aid of torches, as both our authors agree. The next day they went on at great speed "lest any of the numerous people they met on the way should turn back and let Quízquiz know of their arrival. They did not stop until the following day, when they came within sight of Quízquiz's camp toward evening. When he saw them, he withdrew to one side with all the women and servants," etc. Thus Zárate, extracted word for word; and López de Gómara says almost the same. This is sufficient proof that the commander Quízquiz had no idea of making war on the Spaniards or that they would make war on him: otherwise he would not have been surrounded by women and servants; and his soldiers were not so green that they would have failed to warn him if he had bidden them do so, for it would have been sufficient for them to have passed the word for the news to have reached him almost at once. But Quízquiz's negligence was an act of providence on behalf of the Spaniards, who were to preach the holy Gospel. Moreover the Spaniards were ignorant of Quízquiz's desire of peace and friendship and of the terms Francisco de Chaves had brought from the Indians, for when Chaves had reached Cuzco where Pizarro was, Almagro (who might otherwise have brought news of this) had left Cuzco in search of Alvarado. Thus the Spaniards were anxious to destroy Quízquiz, not knowing his peaceable intentions; if they had known of them, they would have accepted them most willingly, for they too desired peace, like the Indians. But the Devil went sowing discord with all his arts and wiles and frustrating the teaching of the Catholic faith so that those gentiles should not escape from between his claws and free themselves from his cruel oppression.

CHAPTER XIV

Three battles between Spaniards and Indians; the number of dead.

WHEN Quízquiz saw the Spaniards hastening toward him, he realized that they intended to fight, and repenting of his over-confidence and full of shame and anger at his own negligence and amateurishness, collected his followers as best he could and retired to a high range of mountains to protect them from the horses. He could not have done otherwise, for he had no warriors but only servants, and they are more apt to be in the way than to help in an emergency. He sent one of his captains to assemble the fighting men and hold off the Spaniards while he got his rabble to safety: this warrior is called by the Spaniards Guaipalcon and is said to have been a brother of Atahuallpa's, though he was relative on his mother's side and called Huaipallca: as this is from the language of Quito I cannot say what it means. Huaipallca assembled what soldiers he could, but did not attack Alvarado, who had plenty of horses and was on favorable ground. Instead he engaged Almagro who had hoped to catch Quízquiz between Alvarado and himself and had therefore taken a slope that was so rough that he was almost lost, as Zárate says in the following words:

Almagro came across Huaipallca and his warriors at the top of a slope when the horses were so tired that they could not get up even though led and the Indians threw down a great many rolling stones called *galgas*, in such a way that a single stone in falling five or six times the height of a man dislodges thirty more and so by the time it gets to the bottom is followed by an innumerable quantity of them,

etc. Thus Zárate; and López de Gómara says the same, as we shall see. Almagro was greatly troubled by the shower of stones which killed some of his men and horses, and he himself was in danger of perishing; he therefore decided to withdraw with all speed and take another less rugged road, so as to cut Huaipallca off. When the Indian found himself between the two governors he retired to some extremely steep rocks, where he defended himself valiantly till nightfall, for neither the Spanish cavalry nor the infantry could attack him, since in these inaccessible mountains the Indians are superior to the Viracochas in attack and withdrawal, not being burdened with clothes and weapons of defence. Under cover of night Huaipallca and his men withdrew to a place of safety. Next day the Spaniards sighted Quízquiz's rear guard. As the Indian leader did not intend to fight he was marching with his army divided into a vanguard and rear, with a wing on each side separated by a distance of fifteen leagues or more, as Zárate says in his Book II, ch. xii. A little later in the same chapter he adds:

Don Diego and Don Pedro collected all the Spaniards, and the Indians went off under cover of darkness in search of Quízquiz. It was later found that the three thousand Indians travelling on the left wing had butchered fourteen Spaniards whom they had cut off from the rest; and continuing their march, they came upon Quízquiz's rear. The Indians took up positions at a river crossing, and prevented the Spaniards from going over for the whole of that day: on the contrary, they themselves crossed upstream from where the Spaniards were and held a high mountain, inflicting heavy loss on the enemy when the latter offered battle. Although the Spaniards wished to withdraw, they were unable to do so owing to the difficulty of the land, and a great many were therefore wounded, especially Captain Alonso de Alvarado whose thigh was transfixed, and another commander of St. John. All that night the Indians remained on guard; but at daybreak, they had freed the river crossing and made themselves strong in the high mountains where they were left alone, for Almagro was unwilling to delay any longer there,

etc. Thus Zárate; López de Gómara speaks as follows in his ch. cxxx:

A few leagues from the road, while Quízquiz was fleeing the Spaniards came up with his rear, and when he saw them, he took steps to prevent them from crossing a river. The Indians were numerous, and some held this crossing while others passed it much higher up, fighting their way and hoping to cut off the Christians and kill them. They took possession of a very rough range of hills, where they were safe from the horses, and there fought with courage and success. They killed a few of the horses, which could not maneuver owing to the difficulty of the land, and wounded many Spaniards, including Alonso de Alvarado of Burgos by transfixing his thigh: they almost killed Don Diego de Almagro,

etc. Thus López de Gómara. The Spaniards who fell fighting, and those who later died of their wounds in these three encounters numbered fifty-

three, with the fourteen mentioned by Zárate. Eighteen more recovered
from their wounds. Thirty-four horses were killed: one was that of Don
Diego de Almagro, which had a hind leg broken by a rock which hit it
at an angle so that both horse and rider were brought down, and Don
Diego was badly shaken. It was fortunate that the rock did not hit them
full on, or they would both have perished. A little more than sixty Indians
were killed, for the inaccessibility of the place, which spelt death to the
Spaniards and their horse, was their protection.

For this reason Almagro did not wish to stay and fight the Indians
when they had made themselves strong on their hilltop, since the place
offered every advantage to the Indians and none to the Spaniards, who
could neither operate themselves nor use their horses. Almagro wished to
avoid any further losses among his companions, for they had suffered
heavily in the last two days: Padre López de Gómara suggests this briefly
in the title of the chapter in which he records these events: "Chapter
cxxx: On a Reverse We Suffered at the Hands of Quízquiz's Rear
Guard," etc. Padre Blas Valera, mentioning the memorable battles fought
by the Spaniards in Peru and their losses, names eight major and dangerous engagements, apart from others of less moment, and puts this first,
calling it "the battle of Quito," because it took place in the territory of
Quito. He says that the Spaniards would have lost if Divine Providence
had not fought on behalf of its Gospel. The Spaniards themselves who
were present used to say the same, and I heard many of them affirm that
they had often been so nearly lost in their battles with the Indians that
they saw no human means of escape, yet they suddenly found themselves
victorious after they had given up as defeated, and this could only have
been by the special favor of heaven. And when they spoke of their pressing danger in this fight, they would say that if Quízquiz had done so
much havoc and put them in such danger, when he had not intended to
fight and had his army divided into four contingents, what would he not
have done if he had all his troops together and ready, and under his
direct command—for he was regarded as a famous leader, as López de
Gómara says when describing his death at the hands of his own men?
Almagro collected the spoils, which were said by the historians to have
exceeded fifteen thousand head of sheep, and more than four thousand
Indian servants of both sexes, who were captives and when freed at once
went over to the Spaniards. None of the fine textiles was obtained, for the
Indians burnt them when they found they could not carry them. They did
the same with the gold and silver they had, hiding it where it was never
found. Almagro sent Indian messengers with letters about all this to

Pizarro, reporting the outcome of these battles, and Alvarado's decision to go to Cuzco to see Pizarro, so that the latter might be forewarned and take what steps he thought necessary.

CHAPTER XV

The governor leaves Cuzco, sees Alvarado, and pays him the sum agreed on.

PIZARRO was distressed by the loss of the Spaniards and their horses at the hands of Quízquiz's men, for it seemed as though the Spaniards were losing the reputation they had won in the eyes of the Indians. But as he could do nothing to remedy what was past, he himself resolved and he warned his men to be more careful in the future. On hearing that Alvarado was coming to Cuzco to see him, he wished to spare him part of the journey and to hasten the settlement that Almagro had agreed with him, so as to get Alvarado out of his jurisdiction and prevent any disturbance that might arise from the presence there of three leaders at once. Even the two remaining leaders, having enriched themselves, could not live in the same peace and brotherliness as when they were poor, for power brooks no equal, or even a rival; and this spirit of ambition was to lead to the total destruction of both men, as we shall see in due course. The governor thought he would speed the departure of Alvarado by going to the valley of Pachacámac, so as to prevent Don Pedro from leaving the coast and travelling the 240 leagues each way from Pachacámac to Cuzco and back, and from setting eyes on the imperial city and its glories, lest this should cause some alteration in the pact that had been made, which had from the first seemed advantageous and desirable to Pizarro. He consulted his brothers and the other leaders of his army before beginning his journey, and recommended them to take care of the Inca's person and take all other necessary steps to keep the peace with the Indians. He spoke to the Inca and told him that he had to go away for some days and visit the valley of Pachacámac so as to settle certain affairs with some Spaniards who had newly arrived in Peru, affairs of great importance to both Indians and Christians, especially with regard to the fulfilment of the conditions of peace, which would be applied as

soon as he returned. He begged the Inca to give him leave to undertake
this journey, for he would soon return, and in the meantime his two
brothers and the other Spaniards remaining with the Inca would serve
His Highness, and he might consider them as recommended to him since
he regarded them as his brothers and children of the Sun. The Inca
wished him godspeed and a speedy return, and hoped the journey would
be successful: let him have no fear about his brothers and the other
Viracochas who were to remain, for they would be well treated, as he
would see on his return. This said, he ordered the lords who owned
estates on the route the governor was to follow to send vassals to serve
him as if he were the Inca himself, and to prepare a guard of two hundred
men to accompany Pizarro, which was to be renewed every three days so
that it should be fresh and serve him better.

When the governor had understood the Inca's commands, he took
leave of him, and chose thirty horsemen to accompany him. On reaching
Jauja he heard that Almagro and Alvarado were to pass through Pachacámac to see the great temple there. He therefore hastened on so as to be
able to receive them in that beautiful valley, and entertain Alvarado and
show him the honors so brave a captain deserved. Pizarro was therefore
ready to welcome his guests, when they arrived at Pachacámac twenty days
after him. They were very well received, and suitably entertained. Pizarro
entrusted Alvarado with all his powers and gave strict orders to his men
to call him governor and to name himself and Almagro by their names,
with no other title. He refused to judge any case, great or small, during
the whole time Alvarado was at Pachacámac, ordering them all to be
referred to Alvarado, whose decisions were to be obeyed as the superior
of them all. He was greatly delighted to see such illustrious gentlemen
as Don Pedro had brought with him, and accorded them all possible
honors and courtesies.

This common rejoicing lasted several days. At the end of this time
Pizarro gave Alvarado the hundred thousand pesos that had been agreed
to, together with an allowance of twenty thousand and a great many
valuable emeralds and turquoises and much gold and silver plate. As a
man with long experience in warfare, he understood and duly appreciated
the benefit Alvarado had conferred on him by bringing such an excellent
and powerful force, so well supplied with arms and horses as he had
produced on this occasion: it was indeed enough to cause Atahuallpa's
commanders and the whole of the Inca empire to surrender formally to
him. And having truly estimated the value of these reinforcements, he
paid the price we have mentioned for the agreement; though many, as

López de Gómara and Zárate state, advised him not to pay it, but to arrest Alvarado and send him to Spain for having trespassed on his jurisdiction with armed forces. Almagro, they said, had only come to terms with Alvarado because of fear occasioned by the latter's greatly superior forces. If Pizarro wanted to pay him, let him give him no more than fifty thousand pesos, for the ships were worth no more, and two of them belonged to Pizarro: the men, arms, and horses should not come into the bargain, for Alvarado was selling things that were free and not his own property.

But Pizarro looked on the counsel offered him by his followers as a gentleman rather than as a cheat and a pettifogger, and paid Alvarado as generously as we have seen, for he recognized that gentlemen owe a duty to themselves in these and similar matters. He also considered the advice he was given from the point of view of a good soldier, so that he could not be accused of failing to take account of either of the two professions. He therefore thought it more important to keep the word given by Almagro in the name of both of them than to consider his interests under the agreement, however great these were. He refused to accept the points adduced by his counsellors on his behalf, to the effect that Almagro had given his word under compulsion and that the ships were not worth half the price that had been promised. To these arguments Pizarro replied that before a gentleman gave his word he should consider the circumstances; for once he had given his faith and made his promise, he was obliged by the rules of chivalry and military law to fulfil whatever he had undertaken to do, as Atilius Regulus had done to his own detriment. With regard to the allegations brought forward in his own favor, Pizarro considered that Alvarado might suggest that they should both return to the state of affairs before the agreement was made, so as to free himself from the contract. Such was military law which, however, he said was not satisfied by those who took such a course, for a man's plighted troth could only be redeemed by the fulfilment of his promise.

He replied to the suggestion about the excessive price of the ships by saying that anyone who considered how useful they had been in bringing arms, horses, and artillery for the arming and pacification of that great and wealthy empire would realize that they were worth the hundred thousand ducats freighted, let alone bought. For these reasons he held it to be a noble and generous deed to fulfil the promise, and add whatever they could to the bargain; for it would all be money well spent. Finally, when his advisers wanted to answer back, he told them not to give him advice to the advantage of the treasury at the expense of his honor, for he would not accept it. He thus dismissed the flatterers, and turned his thoughts toward serving and entertaining the good Don Pedro de Alvarado with every display of respect in word and deed that he could muster up.

CHAPTER XVI

Alvarado's unfortunate death.

THE *adelantado* Don Pedro de Alvarado was very grateful for the courtesies shown him by Pizarro, and when they took leave of one another, each offered the other any assistance he might need on the great conquests in which he was engaged. Alvarado then returned to govern Guatemala. He was not content to rest as he might have done on his wealth and success and on the trophies and feats he had personally performed since boyhood: it seems rather that the greater his deeds, the more his spirit to attempt new exploits, until at last he found his death in them, as we shall now see. For although it falls outside the scope of our history, we may properly include it, since it was so unfortunate and unexpected that it greatly distressed all those who had known so noble a gentleman, who had performed so many deeds in the exploration of numerous lands which he discovered with the famous Juan de Grijalba, and in the conquest of Mexico with the great Hernán Cortés, and in that of Guatemala or Huahuti-mallan, which he conquered himself, and many other provinces of New Spain, apart from the deeds we have described in support of the conquest of Peru, for to him is due the securing of that great empire. His death is told by López de Gómara in ch. ccx of his history of the Indies: as this chapter contains many notable matters I shall copy it literally, as follows:

While Pedro de Alvarado was peacefully and prosperously engaged in governing Guatemala and Chiapa, which he had exchanged with Francisco Montejo for Honduras, he obtained permission from the emperor to go and discover and settle Quito in Peru, which was said to be very wealthy and where there were no other Spaniards. He therefore fitted out five ships in 1535 and took two more in Nicaragua; in this fleet he transported five hundred men and many horses. He landed at Puerto Viejo, and went to Quito, suffering greatly on the way from cold, hunger and thirst. He caused a good deal of anxiety, and even alarm, to Pizarro and Almagro. He sold them his ships and artillery for 100,000 castilians, as we have mentioned in dealing with the affairs of Peru. He returned to Guatemala wealthy and proud. He later fitted out ten or twelve ships, a galley and several smaller vessels with oars with the money he had brought from Peru, intending to go to the Spice Islands or to discover the Point of Whales, which others call California. In 1538 Fray Marcos de Niza and other Franciscan friars entered the land of Culhuacán and travelled three hundred leagues westward, beyond the region explored by the Spaniards of Jalisco. They returned with great news from these parts, extolling the wealth and excellence of Cíbola and other cities. As a result of the reports of these friars, Don Antonio de Mendoza, viceroy of New Spain, and Don Fernando Cortés, marquis del Valle, captain general of New Spain and discoverer of the southern coast, wished either to go to these new parts or send a fleet and army there, but they failed to agree. In fact they quarrelled about the expedition, and Cortés came back to Spain while the viceroy sent for Alvarado, who had the above-mentioned ships, and negotiated with him. Alvarado and his fleet went to the port (I think the one called Navidad) and thence overland to Mexico. He agreed with the viceroy to go to Cíbola, heedless of the ingratitude and harm he was doing Cortés, to whom he owed all he had become. On his return from Mexico he went to Jalisco to settle and reduce certain peoples there who were in revolt and fighting the Spaniards, and came to Ezatlán where Diego López de Zúñiga was making war on the rebels. He went with him to a crag where many Indians had fortified themselves. Our Spaniards attacked the crag, but the Indians repulsed them in such a manner that they killed thirty and put the rest to flight, and as the slope was steep and rough, many horses fell as they came downhill. Alvarado dismounted to avoid a horse that was coming straight at his own, and thought he had placed himself in safety, but the horse had come rolling from a height and was hurtling down with great speed and fury. It struck a rock very hard and was deflected into Alvarado, who was dragged down the slope after it. This was on St. John's day, 1541. He died a few days later at Ezatlán, three hundred leagues from Guatemala, fully conscious and in a Christian spirit. When he was asked where he was hurt, he always replied "in his soul." He was a merry and easy-going man,

etc. Thus López de Gómara, who adds at the end of the same chapter: "He left behind no estate or memorial of himself but this, and a daughter he had by an Indian woman, who married Don Francisco de la Cueva." Here he ends his chapter.

We may add that the same account reached Peru with the same details as López de Gómara gives: the only difference is that the Peruvian version says that Alvarado was struck by a large rock dislodged by a horse and rolling down the slope. He may have been hit by both, for the horse was preceded and followed by many stones as it rolled. In addition to his daughter, I knew a son of his, a mestizo called Don Diego de Alvarado, a worthy son of such a father. He resembled him in all his virtues, and even in his unfortunate death, for he and many other noble Spaniards were slain by the roadside after escaping from the battle of Chelqui Inca, as we shall say in due course if we reach so far. Such was the end of the good Don Pedro de Alvarado. He had the habit of Santiago and was one of the best lances to cross to the New World. His unfortunate end was much regretted in Cuzco by all those who had accompanied him to Peru. They had many masses said for him at the time and for years after: I can bear witness to some of them, which were said in my own time. Whenever he was mentioned, these gentlemen spoke up in praise of his goodness and virtue, and many of them could recount particular instances of his generosity toward each of them.

Among proofs of his excellent character which I heard in my father's house—where, as I have said, this was the main theme of conversation during their leisure—it was said that when they were coming to Peru they suffered terribly from lack of water at sea, so much so that when they reached Túmbez many of them were so weakened by fevers brought on by sheer lack of water that they could not jump ashore. When Alvarado had landed and been brought water to drink, he refused to touch it, although he was as thirsty as any of them, but sent it to the sick on shipboard and did not drink until he knew they had all been supplied. All the anecdotes told of this gentleman's good qualities were of this kind, and contrast with the account given by López de Gómara in the same chapter of Alvarado's character. We can only suppose that he had his information from one of the many jealous rivals Alvarado had, who could not conceal his great deeds since the whole world knew of them, but sought to blacken him by describing his nature and character very differently from what they were. The same author excuses himself on this account, realizing that some of the information given him must have been false; and so in his ch. cxcii, speaking of the accounts he had received, he says: "Let anyone who did well and is not praised lay the blame on his companions," etc. He says this knowing that in all societies there are many envious and ill-speaking companions who are unworthy of the company of the good and prefer to tell lies rather than the truth. With this we had best return to Peru, and say what happened after Alvarado left it.

CHAPTER XVII

The foundation of Lima and Trujillo.

As SOON as the governor had dealt with Alvarado, he sent his companion Almagro to Cuzco with most of the gentlemen who had come with Alvarado, so as to confer with Prince Manco Inca and his two brothers Juan and Gonzalo Pizarro. He recommended them to serve the Inca and treat the Indians well, so that the natives should not be provoked or the Inca lose his affection for the Spaniards, to whom he had come of his own free will. The governor remained in the valley of Pachacámac, desiring to establish a city on the coast and take advantage of the traffic over the sea. Having consulted his friends, he sent people who were experienced in nautical affairs to explore the coast in both directions to find some good port, which was essential for what he had in mind. He learned from them that four leagues north of Pachacámac there was a good port at the bottom of the Rímac valley. He went there and inspected the advantages of the port and the valley; and decided to transfer thither the town he had begun to build at Jauja, thirty leagues inland from Rímac. The city was founded on the Day of the Kings, Epiphany 1534.

With regard to the years of these events there is some disparity between the various authors, some of whom place events earlier and others later, while others give the decades, such as 1530, but leave the last number blank, so as to avoid errors. We shall leave opinions aside, and count the years by the most notable occurrences. It is certain, and all authors agree on this, that Pizarro, Almagro, and the schoolmaster Hernando de Luque established their triumvirate in 1525. They spent three years on the discovery before reaching Túmbez for the first time, and took two years more to come to Spain and obtain the right to conquer Peru, and to return to Panama and prepare the expedition. They reached the island of Puna and Túmbez in 1531. The capture of Atahuallpa took place in December of the same year, and his death was in March 1532. In October of this year they entered Cuzco, where Pizarro remained until April of 1533, when he learned of the coming of Alvarado. In September 1533 he left Cuzco to pay Alvarado the sum agreed in their bargain, and he founded Lima on the Day of the Kings at the beginning of 1534. It was for this reason that Lima took as its arms and device the three crowns of the holy Kings and the shining star that appeared to them.

The city was beautifully laid out, with a very large square, unless it be a fault that it is too big. The streets are broad and so straight that the country can be seen in four directions from any of the crossroads. It has a river that runs to the north of the city, from which many irrigation channels are drawn. These water the fields and are brought to all the houses in the city. When seen from a distance, the city is ugly, for it has no tiled roofs. As there is no rain in that region or for many leagues around on the coast, the houses are covered with thatch of excellent local straw. This is covered with two or three fingers' thickness of mud mixed with the straw, which suffices for shade against the sun. The houses are well built inside and out, and are daily improved. It stands two short leagues from the sea, and I am told that the part that has been built in recent years is approaching the sea. Its climate is hot and damp, a little less than Andalusia in summer: if it is less so, it is because the days are not so long and the nights not so short as they are here in July and August. The degree of heat lost by the later rising and earlier setting of the sun and the greater freshness of the night, which begins earlier and lasts longer, explains its greater coolness as compared with Andalusia. But because in Lima the heat is constant throughout the year, the inhabitants grow accustomed to it and take the necessary measures against it. They have cool rooms, wear summer clothes, and use light bedcoverings; and take steps so that the flies and mosquitoes (which are numerous on the coast) shall not molest them by day or night. There are day and night mosquitoes in the hot valleys of Peru. The nocturnal ones are like those of Spain, with long legs and of the same color and shape, though they are much bigger. Spaniards emphasize how fiercely they sting by saying they can penetrate a leather boot. They say this because knitted stockings, even if of kersey or worsted, provide no defence, not even when linen is worn underneath. The mosquitoes are more savage in some regions than in others. The day mosquitoes are small and exactly resemble those found in wine cellars in Spain, except that they are as yellow as weld. They are so bloodthirsty that I have been assured that, not content with sating themselves, they have been seen to burst while sucking. In order to test this, I let some of them prick me and take their fill of blood: when sated, they were unable to rise and could only roll away. The sting of these smaller mosquitoes is somewhat poisonous, especially if the flesh is unhealthy, and produces small wounds, though they are not serious.

Owing to the hot damp climate of Lima, meat soon spoils. It has to be bought daily for consumption. This is very different from what we have said of Cuzco, for the two cities are quite opposite from one another, one being cold and the other hot. The other Spanish cities and towns on the Peruvian coast all resemble the city of Lima, for the region is the same. The inland cities from Quito to Chuquisaca, over a distance of seven hundred leagues from north to south, are of a very pleasant climate, neither as cold as Cuzco nor as hot as Lima, but sharing temperately in the conditions of both, except in the settlement of Potosí, where the silver mines are: this is a very cool region with extremely cold air. The Indians call the region *puna,* meaning that it is uninhabitable on account of the cold; but the love of silver has drawn so many Spaniards and Indians there that it is today one of the largest, best supplied, and most comfortable towns in Peru. Among its other glories, Padre Acosta says in his Book II, ch. vi, it is two leagues in circumference. And this shall suffice for the Spanish towns and cities in Peru: what we have said of them in general makes it unnecessary for us to repeat it of each one in particular.

To return to the city of Lima in particular, we should add that after Pizarro had founded it and divided the land in the city and the fields and estates and Indians among those who were to settle there, he marched up the coast to the valley of Chimu, eighty leagues north of Lima, where he founded the city now called Trujillo. He gave it the name of his native town, which he wished to commemorate in this way. He gave the first conquerors allocations of Indians, assigning by name the province or provinces that each was to receive in payment for the labors he had undergone in the winning of the empire. He did the same in Lima, to the great satisfaction and approbation of them all, for it seemed as though the country was now quiet and becoming settled, and the first comers were now being rewarded according to their various merits; and that all of them would be treated in the same way. In this task, as excellent as all those this famous gentleman performed in the course of his life, we shall leave him, to return to other matters which occurred among the Indians at this time.

CHAPTER XVIII

*The commander Quízquiz is killed
by his own men.*

WE MUST now say what happened to the commander Quízquiz, the captain Huaipallca and all their forces, lest any of the memorable events which then occurred in Peru should be omitted. After their victory in their three encounters with Alvarado and Almagro, they were filled with vainglory and thought they could easily expel the Spaniards from the whole empire. Huaipallca in particular, who had been the chief Indian commander in these conflicts in the absence of Quízquiz, was full of pride and self-conceit as a result of his success. The two leaders travelled toward Quito intending to raise new forces and collect supplies for the war they proposed to wage against the Spaniards. But after a few days' journey they became disillusioned of their vain hopes, for the *curacas* and the Indians in common had taken warning from the treachery of the commander Rumiñaui and feared a repetition of this experience: they therefore fled rather than follow these leaders, and they disobeyed the summons to produce supplies, for in the whole army they did not see a single Inca of the royal blood to obey, nor did they know who was to reign in the kingdom of Quito, whether some successor of Atahuallpa or Manco Inca, who was the legitimate heir to the whole empire.

Harassed by these difficulties and by lack of food, Quízquiz continued his march until his scouts fell into the hands of Belalcázar. Friendly Indians had warned the Spaniard of his approach, for they desired to enjoy their newly established peace with the Spaniards and detested those Indians who were still under arms; and as there was no other army left but this, they wanted to see it disposed of and so advised Belalcázar, who easily defeated Quízquiz's scouts and captured many of them. Those who escaped reported their defeat to Quízquiz and told him that the Viracochas were numerous. He was thus undeceived of the idea that all the Spaniards had gone with Alvarado and Almagro, as he had thought when he saw so many of them together on the previous campaign.

Quízquiz then summoned the captains to a council of war to decide what should be done. He proposed that they should retire to obtain supplies, of which they were in great want, and then return to attack the Viracochas and not cease until they were defeated. The captains, including

Huaipallca whose superior standing was acknowledged after his recent victory, said that it seemed more prudent to go to the Spaniards and surrender, asking them for peace and friendship, since it was folly to hope to defeat them by force of arms when past experience had shown them to be invincible. They should consider their plight as regards supplies; for the Indians avoided obeying them, and if they had no food they could hardly make war on and defeat their victors. It would be better to try to persuade the Spaniards than to oblige them by force, and to trust them rather than resist them, for as people sent from heaven they would make good friends. Let them no longer try the fortunes of war, since they hourly saw the prophecies of their Inca Huaina Cápac being fulfilled, to the effect that these strangers were to become masters of his empire.

Quízquiz, a warlike and brave man, was disinclined to give way, and grew angry at the cowardice of his captains, rebuking them for their pusillanimity and lack of spirit. He arrogantly told them that he had no need of their counsel, for he knew what needed to be done then and in any other contingency. As their commander he required them to obey and follow wherever he might lead, which was what was necessary to achieve victory. The captains had gradually lost their respect for Quízquiz since the battles with Alvarado and Almagro, thinking that it was due to his cowardice and unwillingness to fight the Spaniards at that time that they had not secured a complete victory. They were now inflamed by discord and sought to show how little respect they had for him. They therefore freely told him that since he was so opposed to peace and friendship with the Viracochas, and so desirous to continue the war, and so assured of victory, he had better not delay it, but go and offer battle to the Castilians straight away, since they were near at hand. Let there be no talk of withdrawing, for that would be real cowardice, and he was accusing them of cowardice when he was guilty of it himself: it would be more honorable to die like good soldiers in the fight than to perish of hunger looking for supplies in the deserts, like a defeated army. This was their last word on the matter.

Quízquiz was angered at hearing his captains speak so freely, and the suspicion he had felt for some days that a mutiny was brewing in his army was strengthened, for he had noticed that the captains had been daily withdrawing their respect from him and transferring it to Huaipallca. He intended to show them that he had perceived this so that they would abandon any treacherous thoughts they might have had and mend their ways before punishment fell on them. He therefore rebuked them for their freedom and boldness, and told them that it smelt of mutiny to show so little obedience to their captain and commander. He would hold an enquiry and severely punish the rebels and the instigator. Huaipallca took this as a reference to himself and was full of indignation. Being puffed up by his past victory and aware of the regard the other captains had for him, he made bold to do something which would never have occurred to any of the other captains, namely to tear away from him the commander's insignia he held in his hand. This was a dart, which corresponded to the baton captains have in Spain. They are called *chuquiapu,* or "captain's lance." He struck Quízquiz with it on the breast, and it pierced him from side to side. The other captains followed suit, each striking him with the weapon he had in his hand. Thus died Quízquiz, the last and most famous of Atahuallpa's captains and officials. He died at the hands of his own men, like all his comrades, for it is the judgment of heaven that tyrants shall never lack other tyrants. Huaipallca and the other captains dismissed the soldiers and disbanded the army, each of them repairing secretly and in disguise to wherever he fancied he would be best concealed, here to live in perpetual fear and suspicion of his nearest neighbors.

CHAPTER XIX

Almagro declares himself governor without royal authority; his agreement with the marquis.

DISCORD, having achieved a success among the Indians with the death of Quízquiz, now introduced itself among the Spaniards to see if it could do the same, as it well might, had not peace and friendship, its foes, stood in the way and prevented it. A few months after the foregoing events, news reached Peru of Hernando Pizarro's arrival in Spain, of the welcome given to him and his treasure, and of his successful negotiations at court, resulting in the award of the title of marquis to his brother, the governor. Zárate describes this as follows in his Book III, ch. v:

Among other requests the governor Don Francisco Pizarro made of His Majesty, as a reward for his services in the conquest of Peru, was one that he should receive 20,000 Indians for himself and his descendants in perpetuity, in a province called Los Atavillos, with their revenues, tribute, and jurisdiction, and the title of marquis. His Majesty was pleased to grant him the title of marquis of this province: as regards the Indians, information would be sought as to the value of the land and the advantages or disadvantages of awarding them to him, and he would receive such favor as might justifiably be shown him. In this letter he was addressed as marquis, and he gave instructions that he was so to be addressed in future, which was done. We shall call him by this title in future in our *History*.

Thus Zárate. Apart from the title, he was permitted to extend the limits of his jurisdiction a certain number of leagues. This is mentioned by Zárate, though he does not say how many. Hernando Pizarro also obtained for himself a habit of Santiago and other favors, which were said to have included the title of marshal of Peru and the award of a jurisdiction a hundred leagues long from north to south, beyond that of the marquis, for Almagro. This second administrative division was called New Toledo, as the first was New Castile. Almagro received all this news in Cuzco (where he was with Prince Manco Inca and the marquis' brothers Juan and Gonzalo) by means of letters from Spain. Without awaiting the arrival of the royal appointment or any other assurance but the first news, he could not help assuming the title of governor straight away; such is the desire of the ambitious for power and command. And as he thought the marquis' jurisdiction extended two hundred leagues from the equator southward, measurable along the coast, or inland, or as the crow flies, and as this did not reach Cuzco, he concluded that the city fell within his own administration, and began to award allocations of Indians, as though he had already had the royal letter of appointment. And in order to show that he gave these grants as absolute governor and not by anyone else's authority, he renounced the power he had received from the marquis to govern that city. In this he was advised and incited by many Spaniards, for there was no lack of ministers of discord. These (apart from their own ambition) told him that this was in his own interest and declared themselves his partisans. On the other hand Juan and Gonzalo Pizarro and many other gentlemen from Extremadura who had come with Alvarado objected. They included Gabriel de Rojas, Garcilaso de la Vega, Antonio and Alonso de Altamirano, and the greater part of the army. Passions rose between the two parties: and they often came to blows with dead and wounded on each side. When the marquis heard of this, he hastened alone from Trujillo, where the news reached him, and was carried the two hundred leagues to Cuzco on the shoulders of Indians. He dared to trust his person to the Indians and make this long journey alone because he had Prince Manco Inca (whom we call prince and not king, since he never came to reign) in his brother's hands. Out of love for Manco Inca, the Indians outdid one another in offering services and presents to the Spaniards, in the hope of obliging the marquis to restore the empire to them.

The marquis thus arrived in Cuzco, and his presence extinguished the flames lit by discord and ambition, for the long-standing and brotherly friendship that had long existed between these two distinguished men soon brought them together in any case of rivalry or unpleasantness, once evil counsellors were removed from the scene. Almagro was ashamed of what he had done without seeing the royal letter, though he said that once His Majesty had granted a favor, he had thought it unnecessary to receive papers. The marquis forgave him and restored him to favor, as if there had been no ill-feeling between them. Then they both again swore before the holy Sacrament that they would not break their alliance or oppose one another. And in order to strengthen this pact of peace and concord, they agreed with the common consent of their followers, that Almagro should go and conquer the kingdom of Chile, which was said by the Peruvian Indians to be very rich in gold and had belonged to the Inca empire. In this case they would ask His Majesty to make Almagro governor of it, and if it did not satisfy him, they would divide Peru between them.

They were all very satisfied by this arrangement, though there was no lack of malicious people who said that the Pizarros had forced Almagro out of Peru despite his having been so good a companion and played so great a part in its conquest. It was said they wished to enjoy Peru for themselves and whetted his appetite for a whole great kingdom instead of a hundred leagues of land, so as to get rid of him. This measure was taken also because as a result of the fame of its wealth, many Spaniards had come to Peru from all sides, and what had been conquered was insufficient for the first conquerors, according to what they quite justifiably thought their merits entitled them to expect. It was thus necessary to stimulate new conquests like that Almagro was to make to provide more land and more Indians to go round, and so that the Spaniards engaged in the conquest should not be idle and plot some rebellion, as a result of the envy that was kindled by the sight of the great allocations granted to the first conquerors. It was therefore agreed that Captain Alonso de Alvarado should go to the province of Chachapoyas, which, though a part of the Inca empire, had refused to acknowledge the Spaniards, confiding in the inaccessibility of the country, where horses would be of little use, and presuming on its strength and warlike spirit. Captain Garcilaso de la

Vega was given the conquest of the province the Spaniards ironically call Buenaventura. Captain Juan Porcel was sent to the province the Castilians call Bracamoros and the Indians Pacamuru. Help was also sent to Sebastián de Belalcázar who was engaged in conquering the kingdom of Quito.

After the agreement between Almagro and Pizarro and the announcement of the new conquests, each of the captains made preparations and raised men. Alonso de Alvarado raised 300 for his conquest, Garcilaso de la Vega 250 for his, and Porcel as many again. All three then left for their districts, where each underwent great privations owing to the thick forests and great rivers in those provinces, as we shall later say. Sebastián de Belalcázar was sent 150 men as reinforcements. Almagro raised over 550 men, including many of those who already had allocations of Indians, but were glad to leave them, thinking to do better in Chile, according to the fame of its wealth; for in those days any Spaniard, even a poor soldier, thought all Peru together too little for himself alone. Almagro lent his followers more than 30,000 pesos in gold and silver to buy horses and arms, and good equipment: he thus had a very fine expedition. He sent Juan de Saavedra, a native of Seville whom I knew, with 150 men to go ahead as scouts, though the whole country was at peace and quite safe to travel in, since Prince Manco Inca was with the Spaniards and all the Indians hoped for the restitution of the empire. Almagro left in Cuzco Captain Ruy Díaz and his bosom friend Juan de Herrada, who were to raise more men and bring them to his help: he thought this would be necessary owing to the great fame of the kingdom of Chile for difficulty and warlike spirit.

CHAPTER XX

Almagro enters Chile; his army is much weakened;
his welcome by the Inca's representatives.

AFTER taking these steps Don Diego de Almagro left Cuzco at the beginning of 1535. He took with him a brother of Manco Inca called Paullu, whom we have already mentioned, and the then high priest of the Indians named Uíllac Umu, and called by the Spaniards Villaoma. They were also accompanied by many Indian nobles and many others as servants bringing arms and supplies. Altogether there would be more than fifteen thousand Indians; for Prince Manco Inca did all he could to serve the Spaniards in the hope of regaining his empire, which he thought he could oblige the Spaniards to return to him. He therefore ordered his brother and the high priest to accompany the Viracochas so that the Indians should respect them and serve them the more readily, though the historians have confused the order of events and say that he planned with them to kill Almagro and his companions at Los Charcas, or wherever they might find the best opportunity. But these instructions were sent later by messengers when the prince found that the Spaniards would not restore the empire, as we shall say later. Juan de Saavedra, who was travelling ahead, reached Los Charcas, two hundred leagues from Cuzco, without meeting with any experience worthy of note: the country was peaceful and the Indians showed him every consideration. At Los Charcas he found Gabriel de Rojas who had been sent by the marquis a few days before, with sixty soldiers to represent him as captain in this province. Saavedra wished to arrest him without any just cause, for when discord could accomplish nothing among the Indians because of their soft and peaceful nature, she sought to stir up her fires among the Spaniards. Rojas was warned and left on some pretext, making his way to Lima by a different road from Almagro, so as to avoid meeting him. Most of his sixty men went to Chile.

Almagro reached Los Charcas without any noteworthy incident. He had the necessary preparations made for the journey, intending to go by the mountains and not by the coast, for he had heard that this was the shorter route. Although Paullu and Uíllac Umu told him that the mountain road was only possible at certain seasons when there was less snow in the gorges and passes of the great cordillera, he refused to believe them, saying that the discoverers and conquerors of Peru would be obeyed by the earth and the other elements and favored by heaven, as they had been hitherto. Nothing therefore was to be feared from the inclemencies of the weather. He then took the mountain road, which was discovered by the Incas after they had won the kingdom of Chile, since the coast road by which they had originally entered it involved a much longer march. But this mountain road can only be used during the summer, at about Christmas time (which is wintertime here) and then only with care, for the snow is to be feared the whole year round.

Almagro left the Charcas, and rejecting the advice of Paullu, whose good faith he doubted and whose advice he regarded as suspect, took the mountain road. But after they had marched for a few days through the mountains, they began to regret their choice, for the road proved extremely difficult. They could not advance because of the thickness of the snow, and they often had to push it aside with their hands in order to pass, so that they could only go a little way in a day. Supplies began to fail them, since they only carried enough for so many days, and they had taken three times as long. They experienced the most intense cold, for according to the cosmographers and astrologers the great chain of the snowcapped mountains reached up to the middle region of the air; and as the air is extremely cold there and the ground is covered with snow, and the days were the shortest and coldest in the year, about St. John's day, many Spaniards, Negroes, Indians, and horses were frozen. The Indians suffered the most, for they wear very light clothes. More than 10,000 of the 15,000 were frozen to death; and even of the Spaniards, though they had thicker clothes against the cold, more than 150 died, while many others had their fingers and toes numbed and frozen, and could feel nothing till they fell off. I knew one of them called Hierónimo Costilla, a native of Zamora and a member of one of the very noble families in that city.

They lost their baggage, not by having it taken by the enemy, for there was none in this spot, but because the Indians who were carrying it died. The Spaniards reached the other side of the mountains worn out and exhausted by the privations they had undergone. Here they found, instead of enemies, friendly Indians who welcomed them and served them and waited on them affectionately like their own sons, for they had belonged to the Inca empire and were of the Copayapú tribe. When they knew that Paullu, the brother of their Inca, and the high priest were travelling with the Spaniards, they came out to receive them and entertained them with every possible attention. If they had found enemies as hostile as these people were hospitable they would have been utterly ruined, so grievous was their state.

While the Viracochas were recovering from their recent ordeal, which surpassed description, Paullu Inca and his relative Uíllac Umu addressed the chiefs and captains of the Inca empire, telling them what had happened in Peru in the struggle between Huáscar Inca and Atahuallpa and how the Spaniards had killed the latter and avenged the death of their king and the whole of the royal line, and now had Prince Manco Inca, the legitimate heir to the empire, in their hands, and treated him with much respect and honor, making great promises to restore him to his power and majesty. All the Indians were therefore obliged to serve and succor the Viracochas so as to oblige them to fulfil their promise to restore the empire. Prince Manco Inca expected this with great confidence, for these men were the children and descendants of the Sun, the father of the Incas, and were therefore called Incas and recognized as their relatives. In particular they had been given the title of their god Viracocha, and the general who had come with them was a brother and companion of the one who had remained behind in Cuzco. Any services rendered to either of them were regarded as services to both, and the best offering that could be made to them was to give them plenty of gold, silver, and precious stones, for they were very fond of these things. And as there was only gold in this country, let them collect all they could and make a great present of it; and their prince Manco Inca would be greatly obliged. The Indians of Copayapú were overjoyed at the possibility of a restoration of the empire, and collected more than 200,000 ducats' worth of bricks of gold that very day. These were drawn from the presents they usually sent to the Incas, for as soon as news of the war between the two brothers Huáscar and Atahuallpa had reached Chile, the Inca captains who sustained and governed the kingdom ceased sending gifts to the Inca and waited to see which of the two would be master. They did not go to help their king for fear of leaving Chile unprotected and because of the length of the journey, and especially because they had no instructions from their Inca. Paullu brought the gold to Almagro, and offered him it in the name of his brother Manco Inca and the whole kingdom of Chile.

Almagro and his friends were delighted to find so great a quantity of gold in so short a time in a single place, and took it as evidence of the great wealth of the country. Almagro told Paullu that he was grateful, and would presently and in the future reward him with many privileges. On hearing Almagro's promises, Paullu tried to please him more and more with similar gifts, and therefore sent to the peoples in the other valleys to ask them to bring the gold they had stored to be offered to the Inca, for he needed it to give to the Viracochas, the Inca's brothers. On these instructions the Indians brought a further sum of 300,000 ducats' worth of gold in a few more days, and they were presented to Almagro. When he saw the wealth of the land that had fallen to his lot, and which he regarded as already won, he made a great display of liberality, as a sign of joy at his good fortune, and to win honor and fame, of which he was very desirous, and also to oblige his followers to be loyal companions. He produced in front of them the bonds and receipts he had for the money he had lent them for this expedition, which amounted to more than 100,000 ducats, and tore them up one by one, telling those concerned that he presented them with the sum they owed him, and regretted he could not give them much more. To the rest he gave subsidies and expense allowances, so that they were all content. López de Gómara mentions this act in his ch. cxlii, and adds: "It was a liberality more worthy of a prince than of a soldier, yet when he died he had no one to lay a cloth on the execution-block for him," etc.

CHAPTER XXI

New claims prevent the conquest of Chile; Almagro prepares to return to Peru, and the reason why.

WHEN ALMAGRO and his followers had rested and refreshed their horses from their past labors, he took up the question of reducing the remaining valleys and provinces of the kingdom of Chile, which had not been subjugated to the Inca empire; for all those that had been subjugated had accepted his authority on seeing that he was accompanied by Paullu, the brother of their king. He informed Paullu of his intention and asked his assistance in carrying out this conquest. Paullu saw that this was to the advantage of his brother's empire, and brought together all the men he could from the garrisons and strongholds in Chile. He sent out for large quantities of supplies, which were produced, and accompanied Almagro to the conquest of the provinces of Purumauca, Antalli, Pincu, Cauqui and others in that area, as far as that of Araucu. He had several serious clashes with the natives, who proved brave and very expert in the use of their weapons, especially bows and arrows, with which they shot wonderfully well. We shall not recount all this in detail, or speak of the battles that were fought, except to say that they were severely contested, for we must return to our Peru.

Despite the resistance of their enemies, the Spaniards were successfully advancing with the aid and support of Paullu and his Indians, so that it was expected that the whole of that kingdom would be won in less than two years. But discord cut short their progress and prosperity, for it even sought opportunities to kindle the fires of passion between these two famous brothers, and did not cease till it had consumed them both, as we shall see later.

While Almagro was gaining these victories, though at great cost in Spanish and Indian blood, rather more than five months after his arrival in Chile he was joined by Captain Ruy Díaz and Juan de Herrada with a hundred Spaniards; for, as we have said, these two had remained in Cuzco raising men to help Almagro. They came by the same route, and though it was November, which is summer there, and they found the passes much freer of snow, they still lost many Indians and some Spaniards from the great cold they experienced; those who escaped nearly perished of hunger from which they suffered most severely. They fed on the flesh of horses they found dead: they had been frozen when Almagro passed that way, and though five months had passed, their meat was as fresh as if they had been killed that day.

After suffering these hardships and more which we omit, they came up with their captain general. They were received with great rejoicing, the more so when they knew that Juan de Herrada had brought His Majesty's concession of a grant of a hundred leagues of land beyond the jurisdiction of the marquis. This document had been brought by Hernando Pizarro on his return from Spain to Peru, and had been sent post-haste from Lima to Herrada, since it was known that he was on the point of leaving for Chile. Of this López de Gómara writes literally as follows in his ch. cxxxv:

While Almagro was fighting in Chile, Juan de Herrada arrived with the documents of his jurisdiction which had been brought by Hernando Pizarro. He was more delighted with these—even though they cost him his life—than with all the gold and silver he had won, for he was ambitious for honor. He held a council of his captains to decide what should be done, and it was decided by a majority to return to Cuzco where, since it fell within the limits of his jurisdiction, he would assume his new authority. Many pleaded with him to establish a settlement there or in the rich territory of the Charcas before returning, sending in the meantime messengers to find out what was the attitude of Pizarro and the town council at Cuzco, for it would be wrong to precipitate a breach first. Those who most urged him to return were Gómez de Alvarado, Diego de Alvarado, and his particular friend Rodrigo Orgoños, Finally Almagro decided to return to Cuzco and govern by force, if the Pizarros were not willing to allow him to do so.

This is from López de Gómara. The passion of Almagro and his captains to return to Peru was not to enjoy the hundred leagues' jurisdiction to which he was entitled, for they had won much more in Chile, where the natives received them and served them as we have said, and they were gaining many more leagues, all land productive of gold, according to the evidence they had found. But none of this seduced them unless they possessed the imperial city of Cuzco; and this was the apple of discord that the Devil threw down between the governors, and the desire for it led to civil wars and delayed the preaching of the holy Gospel, so that many of the faithful died, as well as innumerable infidels, without the sacrament of baptism; for the enemy of mankind and his myrmidons prevented its administration and that of the other sacraments that are the medicine of our souls.

With this attachment to or passion for the imperial city of Cuzco, Almagro and his friends decided to leave Chile and return to Peru, not by the road by which they had come, for they had learned from experience not to try it again, but by another which proved equally difficult, for while the first had submerged them in snow and water, the second nearly finished them with lack of these things and excess of sand, as we shall see. The historians Zárate and López de Gómara are very confused about Almagro's expedition to Chile and say that he returned by the same road by which he went, and that he prepared wine skins to carry water, of which he suffered great lack. But as there is no lack of water wherever there is snow, it is clear that whoever gave them this information jumbled together what happened on the outward journey and what happened on the return, making one single journey out of two very different ones. These authors also say that the gold presented by Paullu and the people in Chile to Almagro was obtained by Juan de Saavedra from the Indians in the Charcas, who were taking it to offer to their king, though this road was closed as soon as the wars broke out between Huáscar and Atahuallpa. Because of this the old conqueror whom we have mentioned elsewhere as having made marginal notes in López de Gómara's *History,* seeing the confused account given to López de Gómara about these events, writes rather peevishly over ch. cxxxv as follows:

There is a great deal to add and to subtract in all this author writes about Cuzco and Chile; for according to what he says here he seems to be following the account of someone who did not know the facts any better than himself, as the passage shows. The truth of the matter is that Almagro did not return by the same road as he had come, for they went by the mountain road and suffered greatly from hunger and cold. And when they crossed the passes to enter Copayapú, the first valley in Chile on that road, there was such heavy snow and such great cold that many were frozen, Indians, Spaniards, and horses alike, and many escaped with their toes frozen off, Negroes, Indians and Spaniards. Five months later Ruy Díaz and Juan de Herrada reached the same place with the reinforcements they had stayed behind to raise in Peru, on

Almagro's orders. They too suffered greatly from cold, hunger, and fatigue. The pass cannot be crossed in less than four or five days whatever one's haste. They found themselves very short of food because the Indians had taken it. The passes had less snow on them, and they crossed them in better weather, though they suffered greatly from the cold and some died. They relieved their hunger, which was very great, on the horses which they found frozen, and as fresh as the history says.

Almagro, as I say, did not return by the mountain road, but by the coast road or the llanos, which is now generally used. There is a desert from Atacama, the last town in Peru, to Copayapú, the first in Chile, a distance of eighty leagues. On the road there are a few pools of standing water. As it is stagnant and rarely drawn on, it smells foul; the pools are at intervals of six or seven or more leagues. As the water was too little to supply the whole army, Almagro ordered the horsemen to cross the desert in bands of five or six; and as the first groups cleared the pools, more water appeared so that the number of horse and infantry that crossed increased, until the whole army had passed. After crossing the desert, Almagro embarked in a ship brought by Noguerol de Ulloa, one of his captains, who was the son of the governor of Simancas killed by the bishop of Zamora. Jerónimo de Alderete, who was governor of Chile many years after, was once in Copayapú, and on seeing that there was not much snow on the passes, thought he would go up with many of his companions to see if there were any traces of the memorable losses suffered when Almagro made his crossing. They found a Negro leaning against the rocks in a standing position and also a horse standing as if carved of wood with its reins, now rotten, in the Negro's hands. This was five or six years after Valdivia went out as governor: he was succeeded by Alderete.

This is the note the old *conquistador* wrote in López de Gómara's *History*. We shall explain it further in the following chapter.

CHAPTER XXII

*Almagro abandons Chile and returns to Cuzco; Prince
Manco Inca again asks for the return of his empire,
and the answer given him; Hernando Pizarro's
arrival in Peru; and the arrest
of the Inca.*

KNOWING Paullu Inca's faithfulness and attachment to him, Almagro
informed him of his decision to return to Peru (which was to be
the destruction of them all) and asked him his opinion about the route
they should follow; for he feared they might fall into another danger as
great as the last, when by scorning and ignoring the Inca's warning, he
would have come near to perishing with his whole army if God's mercy
had not saved him, as it saved them from many other dangers we have
seen and many more we shall mention: it protected them because they
were to be the preachers of His Gospel and His Catholic Faith, which
they were to teach to these gentiles. When Inca Paullu had consulted his
Indians about the roads, he informed Almagro of the coastal route, and
told him how it had been shut since the wars between Huáscar and
Atahuallpa and how the springs or wells used by travellers were choked
with wind-blown sand since they had not been used for a long time, and
they contained very little water, and that too foul to drink. He however
would send Indians ahead to clear the wells and remove the foul water,
and according to their reports of the quantity of water in the pools, the
army could be sent forward in bands and the size of the bands increased
in proportion to the amount of water available; the more water they took
from these wells, the more they produced, and the army could divide into
small bands since there were no enemies on the road. As the sources
were some six or seven leagues apart, skins would be made to carry water
between them so that the men might not suffer from thirst. This was the
method used by the Incas, his forefathers. Paullu Inca's plan seemed excellent to Almagro and his captains; and they relied on him, and told
him to arrange things as he thought fit for their common safety according
to the lore of the Incas in the past. Inca Paullu was very proud that the

governor and his Spaniards should trust their safety and lives to him, and at once sent Indians forward to clear the springs with orders to report their progress. He gave orders for the flaying of the number of sheep he thought would be needed for the waterbags and for their skins to be kept whole. He instructed that supplies be collected for the eighty leagues' march through the desert, and while all this was being done, the Indians who had gone ahead to clean the springs reported on the work and said that the Spaniards could begin to advance.

Almagro was reluctant to place entire confidence in the Indians in a matter of such moment as the safety of his whole army but preferred that some Spaniards should accompany them to confirm their reports on the road and the springs. He therefore sent four horsemen to report in writing and not verbally on what they saw on each day's journey. According to their reports, the other Spaniards went off in increasing numbers until none were left in Chile. They travelled thus to Atacama, where Almagro heard that Noguerol de Ulloa was not far away with a ship which the marquis had sent to discover what ports were on that coast and to visit Chile and find what had happened to Almagro, and return with a report on the advantages of that kingdom so that help could be sent to Almagro in case of need. Almagro wrote to Noguerol de Ulloa to come for an interview and report to him what had happened in his absence in Peru. When Noguerol replied the two of them met and discoursed at length; and, in order to have an opportunity to talk further of the events of the two kingdoms without delaying his army, and also to please Noguerol de Ulloa, who was a good friend of his, Almagro said he would go on toward the ship and be a seaman and soldier under Noguerol for a few days, while his army travelled overland: the ship would soon overtake them, however far ahead they were. Thus agreed, they went on by sea and land; and after sailing for a few days, Almagro returned to his army, where we shall leave him for the time being, to return to describe the general rising of the Indians which took place while Almagro was still in Chile.

As soon as Almagro had left Cuzco for Chile and the other captains had gone about their conquests, as we have said, Prince Manco Inca, finding the governor at ease after Almagro's departure, again proposed to him that the conditions agreed between Indians and Spaniards should be carried out. He said that Pizarro had promised to execute them and restore his empire, and begged and urged him to do so, so that the natives might live in peace and realize how they could best serve the Spaniards. The governor and his brothers were at a loss, for they found no sufficient reasons for putting off the Inca's request and expectations. But they told him as best they could, so as not to rouse his suspicions, that they intended to fulfil the conditions which were to the advantage of both sides, Indians and Spaniards alike; but that the past disturbances and present circumstances were inopportune, principally because they hourly expected the reply of their lord the emperor, to whom they had sent a long account of the conditions and the question of the restoration of the empire. They expected the answer would be brought by Hernando Pizarro and that it would satisfy His Highness, for it was not to be expected that so great, so just, and so religious a prince would do less than ratify the conditions; let the Indians await the arrival of Hernando Pizarro, who would remove all their anxieties with the emperor's instructions.

With these vain hopes they held the Inca off for some days. Then came the news of Hernando Pizarro's landing at Túmbez. The marquis saw that this was a good opportunity for him to leave Cuzco, as he desired to do, partly to avoid the Inca's demand and partly to return to the new settlement at Lima, which, as he had founded it, he desired to see completed. He therefore spoke to the Inca and told him that, in order to expedite His Majesty the emperor's commands with regard to His Highness the Inca's request, he must go and receive his brother Hernando Pizarro. He begged him to give him leave to undertake this journey: he would soon return and they would then reach the agreement that would be to their mutual advantage. In the meanwhile, it would be best if His Highness for his own tranquility and the comfort and security of the Spaniards, would kindly retire to his royal fortress and remain there until the marquis' return: during this time the marquis' brothers and his other companions would serve His Highness as they were bound.

Pizarro made this request of the Inca because it seemed necessary to him, to his brothers, and to all the rest. They perceived that Manco Inca had a proud and brave spirit, and knew how to dissimulate, as he had done hitherto. They were afraid lest he should begin some disturbance on finding that they delayed restoring the empire to him and fulfilling the conditions, and wanted to have him in a secure place and to be safe from him. The Inca saw that this was not a good augury for the result of his request and the restoration of his kingdom, discreetly disguised his true feelings so as not to alarm the marquis to greater wrongs, and consented to his request or order. He therefore went to the fortress with apparent willingness and climbed the steep slope on foot, refusing to be borne in his litter, so as to make less ceremony. As soon as he was inside, he was shackled, as López de Gómara says in his ch. cxxxiv:

"Manco, the son of Huaina Cápac, to whom Francisco Pizarro gave
the scarlet fringe at Villcas, was a man of spirit and proved troublesome,
for which reason he was put in the fortress of Cuzco in iron shackles."
These are López de Gómara's words. The Indians greatly resented the
imprisonment of their Inca, and the reversal of the promises and hopes
that had been held out to them. They wept and lamented bitterly. Prince
Manco Inca consoled them saying he wished to obey the Spaniards cheerfully in everything, and they should do the same, since their Inca Huaina
Cápac had bidden them so in his will; let them not give way till they saw
the final outcome of the affair, for he hoped that his arrest would lead to
his being treated more liberally and that his release and the restoration
of his empire would occur at once, so that the generosity of the Viracochas
might resound throughout the world. Let the Indians trust them, for
they were people from heaven.

The marquis took leave of the Inca, entrusting him to the care of his
brothers Juan and Gonzalo Pizarro, and went to Lima, where he received
his other brother Hernando, bringing the new grants awarded by His
Majesty with great rejoicings and festivities. López de Gómara describes
this in his ch. cxxxiii:

Soon after Almagro left for Chile, Hernando Pizarro reached Lima, bringing
the title of marquis of Los Atavillos for his brother and the governorship of
New Toledo, a hundred leagues of land south and east of the border of
Pizarro's jurisdiction of New Castile, for Almagro. He asked the conquerors
for a contribution for the emperor, who said that as monarch he was entitled to
the whole ransom since Atahuallpa was also a king. They answered that they
had already paid the royal fifth, which was the emperor's due; and there was
nearly a mutiny because people in the court and in Spain regarded them as
rogues who were undeserving of such wealth. I do not say that this occurred
then, but those who have not been to the Indies but have stayed in Spain have
said it before and since; they are perchance men who do not deserve what they
have and should not be heeded. Pizarro placated them saying that they had
deserved their rewards by their efforts and qualities, and indeed deserved all
the rights and privileges won by those who helped King Pelayo and the other
kings to wrest Spain from the Moors. He told his brother he must seek some
other way to meet his promise, for none of them wanted to give anything, and
he would not take back what he had given them. Hernando Pizarro then took a
percentage of what they smelted, an action that roused great resentment.
However he did not desist from his demand, but went off to Cuzco to seek as
much again, and tried to persuade Manco Inca so that he would produce a
great quantity of gold for the emperor, who was much reduced by the expenses
of his coronation, and the affairs of the Turk and Vienna and Tunis.

This is taken from López de Gómara, who finishes his chapter here. We should say that the marquis sent his brother to Cuzco with a commission and power to govern the city in his name and to look after the Inca, for he himself proposed to stay in Lima and settle and develop it.

CHAPTER XXIII

The measures taken by Prince Manco Inca to recover his empire.

PRINCE Manco Inca who was under arrest in the fortress—the fortress built with such splendor and majesty by his ancestors as their grandest trophy, never thinking that it would become the jail of their descendants —tried discreetly to ease his bonds by flattering and serving the Spaniards. He plied them, superiors and inferiors alike, with many presents of fruits, birds, meat, and other delicacies, and with gold, silver, emeralds, and turquoises. His friendly and brotherly intercourse with them, and his lack of resentment for his imprisonment, reassured them all, and they removed his bonds and let him walk freely about the fortress. Meanwhile the Inca had heard that Hernando Pizarro was coming to Cuzco to take charge in that city. He then did his best to obtain permission to go down to the city and live in one of his palaces. This was easily gained, for the Spaniards were so attached to him that they readily granted whatever he asked. His anxiety to get out of the fortress was in order that Pizarro should not find him shackled and suspect him, or withhold his confidence from him, or deny what he had asked and the Spaniards had promised. He was indeed fortunate in this, as López de Gómara and Zárate confirm, almost in the same words. Zárate (Book III, ch. iii) says:

When Hernando Pizarro reached Cuzco, he made friends with the Inca and treated him well, though he still had him carefully guarded. It was thought that this friendship was due to an intention to ask the Inca for some gold either for His Majesty or for himself. Two months after his arrival in Cuzco, the Inca asked his permission to go to the land of Incaya to celebrate a certain festival, promising to bring back a life-sized statue of his father Huaina Cápac made of solid gold. In his absence he completed the plan he had hatched as soon as Almagro had left for Chile,

etc. Thus Zárate.

The Inca asked permission to go to Y'úcay, which was, as we have said, the garden of the Inca kings, with their cemetery, called Tampu, a league lower down the river: here their intestines were buried after their removal for the embalming of their bodies, and it is probable that the golden statue was kept there as a monument to his father. On reaching this place, the Inca, under pretext of the festivities that were to be celebrated, summoned together some of his father's old captains and some of the chief lords; and addressed them on the disloyalty and obstinacy of the Spaniards in refusing to carry out the terms his brother Titu Atauchi had made with them, and on their arrest of the Inca and his confinement in irons without any justification, and on the fact that the captain general had twice disappeared so as to entertain him with false hopes and to avoid restoring the empire to him. He said that though he had been aware of this faithlessness from the first, he had dissimulated in order to strengthen his case in the sight of God and men: no one could accuse him of disturbing the peace agreed between himself and the Spaniards. But now that he had done all he had been obliged to do on his side, he wished to wait no longer for the fulfilment of vain promises, for it was well known that the Spaniards were dividing the land among themselves in Cuzco, Lima, and Túmbez, which was a clear sign that they did not mean to restore the empire. He had no desire to expose his person to the risk of being treated as on the previous occasion, when they had not hesitated to put him in handcuffs and chains, though he had done nothing to annoy them or offered any occasion for such treatment. He therefore enjoined them as loyal servants and faithful vassals to give their prince the benefit of their advice in this important matter, for he proposed to recover his empire by force of arms, being confident that neither Pachacámac nor his father the Sun would allow him so unjustly to be deprived of it. The captains and *curacas* chose one of the oldest of the captains to speak for them all: and he, after showing the deference due to kings, said:

"Sole Lord, it never seemed safe nor yet fitting to the members of your Council that Your Majesty should place his person in the power of these strangers, nor that you should trust them to restore the empire. But we have submitted to your will since we realized how devoted you were to the peace concluded with them by your brother, Titu Atauchi. We now know that there is nothing to be expected of this, since we have seen what they have done to your brother Atahuallpa, whom they killed after they had received the ransom he had promised them in return for his freedom. It has been a great mercy of Pachacámac that they have not done the same with your royal person, since they have had you in their power and under arrest. Nor is the restitution of your empire to be hoped for any longer, for people who have shown such covetousness for the fruit are not likely to think of returning the tree to its owner; it is more to be feared that they will seek his death and that of all his family so that there shall be none who can aspire to the empire. According to what they themselves have taught us, Your Majesty should therefore distrust their promises and give orders for as many warriors as possible to be summoned with all haste and for the necessary supplies to be brought together; let us not lose the opportunity they have offered us by dividing into so many groups, for it will be easier to put them to death than if they were all together. We must attack them all at once so that they cannot succor one another. The roads must be blocked so that they may not have news of one another; and they will thus all perish on the same day, for Your Majesty's men can fall upon them in such multitudes wherever they are that the mountains will be flung down on them if you so order. And if your vassals do not aid them, as they will not, they will undoubtedly die at our hands or from the hunger they will suffer in the siege. The suddenness of the attack is what is most important, for no one can doubt its success, since we have justice on our side."

Here the captain ended, and the rising was decided upon. They very secretly sent messengers the length and breadth of the kingdom to raise what warriors there were, and bid them murder all the newcomers from Castile on a certain day. All the supplies to be found in the royal or communal stores were to be brought forth, and if these had been lost or used in Atahuallpa's wars, more were to be collected from private houses, wherever they might be found; and as soon as their enemies had been killed, any damage or loss suffered by any of the Inca's vassals would be made good. Let them recall that on this deed depended the lives, security, and liberty of them all, great and small, and especially of their Inca. On these instructions from Manco Inca the warriors from Lima to the Chichas, a distance of three hundred leagues and more, rose up in arms. The rest of the kingdom from Lima to Quito could not raise warriors, for they had all been killed in those parts in Atahuallpa's wars and with the havoc wrought by the Spaniards when the king was captured and killed.

The Inca also sent disguised messengers to the kingdom of Chile who said in public that they were going to enquire after the health of the infante Paullu and the high priest Uíllac Umu, though they were secretly to warn them of the Inca's decision. They were to give assistance and to execute Almagro and all his companions, which would be necessary for the recovery of their empire, for there was no longer any hope that the Spaniards would return it peacefully. When the rising was launched, the Inca ordered the inland Indians from Antahuailla and the coastal ones from Nanasca in the region of Chinchasuyu to go to Lima and kill the governor and his companions, while those of Cuntisuyu, Collasuyu, and Antisuyu went to Cuzco to slay Hernando Pizarro and his brothers and the other Spaniards, who numbered two hundred in all. He appointed captains for both armies. In our next chapter we shall describe the events that took place in Cuzco, the greatest of which were the Lord's mercies which He performed for the Spaniards for the benefit of those heathen idolators.

CHAPTER XXIV

Prince Manco Inca's rising; two miracles on behalf of the Christians.

THE INCA ordered his warriors to make for Cuzco and Lima to fight and destroy the Spaniards. He also ordered all those Spaniards who were scattered about the kingdom obtaining gold from the mines to be killed: owing to the peace and the obedience of the Indians, they went about as unconcernedly as if they were in their own country. Many of them were killed in different places. The Indians thus reached Cuzco on the appointed day, having travelled with the greatest possible secrecy. On the following night they suddenly attacked the Spaniards with loud war cries and a great hubbub, for there were more than two thousand Indians in the attack. Most of them were armed with bows and arrows, and carried lighted tinder for firebolts. They shot these at all the houses in the city in general without respect for the royal palaces, but only sparing the house and temple of the Sun and all the apartments it contained, and the house of the chosen virgins, and the workshops in the four streets inside the house. They did not touch these two houses out of respect for their owners; they had already been stripped of their wealth and largely abandoned by their inhabitants but the Indians still revered them and avoided what they feared would be an act of sacrilege in their vain religion, one being the house of the Sun and the other that of his women. They also spared three great halls that had been used for their festivals on rainy days, wishing still to have places for celebrations when they had butchered the Spaniards. One of these halls was in the upper part of the city, among the houses that had belonged to the first Inca Manco Cápac, as we mentioned in our description of the city. The other hall was one of the houses of Pachacútec, called Cassana. The third was among the houses of Huaina Cápac, called Amarucancha, which now belongs to the holy Society of Jesus. They also spared a fine round tower standing in front of these. All the rest of the houses were fired, and none was left standing.

The bravest Indians, who had been picked to burn the house of Inca Viracocha where the Spaniards were lodged, attacked it vigorously and set fire to it from a distance with their incendiary arrows: it was burnt down and not a trace of it remains. The great hall inside it, where the cathedral now is, and where the Christians then had a chapel to hear mass, was saved by our Lord from the flames, and though innumerable arrows were shot at it and it began to burn in many places, the flames were put out again, as if there were as many men throwing water on them. This was one of the marvels performed by our Lord in that city to establish His holy Gospel there; and the city has proved this, for it is certainly one of the most religious and charitable in the New World today, among both Spaniards and Indians.

Hernando Pizarro and his two brothers and the two hundred others with them always lodged together because they were so few; and like good and experienced soldiers they did not sleep, but always had sentries carefully stationed round their dwelling and watchmen on the roof. As soon as they heard the noise of the Indians, they armed themselves and harnessed their horses, for they kept thirty of them ready saddled every night in case of any emergency; and thus went out to reconnoiter the enemy. They saw how numerous the Indians were, and as they could not tell what weapons they had against the horses (which were what the Indians most feared), it was agreed to withdraw into the main square, where, owing to its great size, they could more easily dominate the enemy than in the streets. This was done, and they drew up there in formation. The infantry, numbering 120, were in the middle, and the 80 horse stationed themselves in twenties on either side and in front of and behind the square, so that they would be able to resist the Indians from whichever direction they launched their attack. When these saw the Spaniards all gathered together, they fell on them with great ferocity, hoping to overrun them at the first onset. The cavalry attacked them and held them up valiantly, and both sides fought with great courage till daybreak when the Indians re-formed. Arrows and stones shot from slings rained on the Spaniards in a remarkable way; but the horses and lances were sufficient to cope with them, and they made no onset without leaving at least 150 or 200 Indians dead on the ground. This was because the Indians had no defensive arms and did not use pikes (though they had them) against the horses, since they had no experience in facing cavalry, but always fought their wars on foot and unprotected. But owing to their weight of numbers they withstood the advantages the Spaniards had in arms and horses, and despite their great losses, bore up in the hope of shortly butchering all the Spaniards.

The Spaniards were held by the Indians in the square of Cuzco for seventeen days without being able to leave it, such was the obstinacy of the attack. During all this time, night and day, the Spaniards remained in formation to resist their enemies, and even marched in formation to drink from the stream that runs through the square, or to search the burnt houses to see if there was any maize left to eat, for they felt their horses' need more than their own. They did find some supplies, and though they were much damaged by fire, hunger made them appetizing. Zárate writes of this as follows:

Thus the Inca came with all his forces against Cuzco and surrounded it for more than eight months, and each full moon there was fighting at many parts. Hernando Pizarro and his brothers defended it valiantly, with many other knights and captains who were within, especially Gabriel de Rojas, Hernán Ponce de León, Don Alonso Enríquez, the treasurer Riquelme, and many more. They did not put down their arms by night or day; for they felt certain the governor and all the other Spaniards had been killed by the Indians, having heard how the latter had rebelled throughout the country. They thus fought and defended themselves like men who had no hope of succor but from God and their own strength, though the Indians daily reduced their numbers, killing and wounding them.

Zárate thus briefly describes the dangerous plight of the Spaniards in the siege of Cuzco, where their strenuous efforts to find food would not have saved them from dying of hunger if their Indian servants had not succored them like true friends. These went over to the hostile Indians by day, giving out that they had forsaken their masters, and even pretending to fight against them, though at night they would return to them bringing all the food they could carry. This is also mentioned by López de Gómara and Zárate, though very briefly. Their account of all the Inca's rising is short, especially with regard to the miracles performed by our Lord Jesus Christ on behalf of the Spaniards in Cuzco, where the danger was greatest and the fury of the Indians most fierce. The danger became so acute that after eleven or twelve days the Spaniards and likewise their horses grew very weary from the continuous alarms and daily fighting, and the intolerable hunger they experienced. Thirty Christians were dead, and almost all were wounded, with no means of healing their wounds. They were afraid they would all die in a few days, for they could do nothing themselves and they could hope for no help from anywhere except heaven, whither they directed their groans and prayers, begging God's mercy and the Virgin Mary's intercession and protection.

The Indians had noticed that in the night when they had burnt the whole city they had been unable to set fire to the hall in which the Spaniards were living, and they now went to burn it down, for there was no one to prevent them. They repeatedly set fire to it over a period of many days and at all times of the day and night, but they never succeeded in carrying out their intention, and were astonished because they could not understand the reason. They said that fire had lost its virtue against the house because the Viracochas had lived in it.

Finding themselves in such a plight, the Spaniards decided to perish bravely together in the fray and not to wait until they died of hunger and their wounds, or let their enemies kill them when they could no longer take up their arms. They therefore prepared to sally forth when the Indians attacked, and do what they could until they died. Those who could confessed to the three priests they had, when and as the Indians allowed them; the rest confessed to one another; and they all called on God and the saints of their devotion in order to die like Christians. At dawn on the following day the Indians came forth with their usual ferocity, full of anger and shame that so small a band of Spaniards could ward off such a multitude of enemies for so many days; for there were a thousand Indians for every Spaniard, and they were determined not to give up the struggle until they had slain them all. But the Spaniards attacked the Indians with the same courage and ferocity, calling aloud on the name of the Virgin and on that of their defender the apostle St. James. Both sides fought obstinately with much slaughter among the Indians and many wounds among the Spaniards. After five hours of this the Christians felt weary, and their horses were exhausted from their labors on that and previous days. They expected death and felt it hovering near, while the Indians grew hourly fiercer as they sensed the flagging of the horses, and more determined to slay the Spaniards to avenge the losses they had suffered. Prince Manco Inca watched the battle from a hill and encouraged the Indians by calling on the various tribes and provinces, full of confidence in becoming lord of his empire that day.

In this hour of need our Lord was pleased to favor His faithful with the presence of the blessed apostle St. James, the patron of Spain, who appeared to the Spaniards. Both they and the Indians saw him mounted on a splendid white horse, bearing a shield showing the arms of his military order and carrying in his right hand a sword that seemed like a flash of lightning, so brightly did it shine. The Indians were terrified at the sight of this new knight and asked one another: "Who is the Viracocha with the *illapa* in his hand?" (meaning, lightning, thunder, and thunderbolt). Whenever the saint attacked, the Indians fled as if they were lost, madly trampling one another down as they fled from this wonder. As soon as the Indians attacked the Christians on the opposite side from the saint, they found him among them and fled madly before him. Thus the Spaniards took heart and fought on, killing innumerable Indians who could not defend themselves and lost courage so rapidly that they fled helter-skelter and abandoned the fight.

Thus the apostle succored the Christians that day, depriving the infidels of a victory that lay within their hands and granting it to his own people. He did the same the next and each subsequent day when the Indians tried to fight; as soon as they attacked the Christians, they lost their heads and did not know which direction to take, and returned to their posts, where they asked one another: "What is this? How have we become *útic, sampa, llaclla,* (fools, cowards, weaklings)?" Nevertheless they did not cease to persist in their quest, as we shall see, and kept up the siege for over eight months.

CHAPTER XXV

A miracle of Our Lady on behalf of the Christians;
and a duel between two Indians.

WHEN THE Indians had retired to their quarters, the Inca ordered his captains to be called together and publicly rebuked them for the cowardice and weakness they had shown that day, when so many Indians had fled from so few weary and hungry Viracochas. He told them to look to the future; for if they did not fight like men, he would send them to spin with the women and pick others to take their places who better deserved the responsibilities of captains. The Indians excused themselves on the ground that a new Viracocha with the *illapa* in his hands had so bewildered and alarmed them that they did not know if they were fleeing or fighting, and promising to act thenceforth like good soldiers and amend their past errors. The Inca told them to have their troops ready for the fight on the second night: he hoped that if they fought by night the darkness would keep them from seeing the warrior who frightened them. The Christians meanwhile knew of the mercy our Lord had shown them, and gave Him thanks and offered up many promises and vows. They were as full of courage and good spirits for the future as they had reason to be, and regarded themselves as masters of the kingdom since heaven showed them such favors. They prepared their arms and refreshed their horses against any contingency, assured now of victory and in a very different frame of mind from hitherto.

On the night chosen by the Inca for his attack, the Indians came out with their weapons ready, fiercely threatening to avenge their past reverses and butcher all the Spaniards. But these were warned by their servants, the friendly Indians who acted as spies, that the enemy was about to attack, and took up their arms and devoutly called on our Lord Christ and the Virgin Mary His mother, and the apostle St. James to succor them in that hour of need and danger. When the Indians were about to fall on the Christians our Lady appeared in the air with the child Jesus in Her arms in great splendor and beauty and stood before them all. When the infidels beheld this marvel they were astonished. They felt a dust fall into their eyes—sometimes like sand, sometimes like a dew— and it prevented them from seeing so that they did not know where they were. They thought it best to return to camp before the Spaniards should fall on them; and they were so alarmed that they dared not leave their quarters for many days. This was the seventeenth day since the Indians had surrounded the Spaniards, and during all this time the latter had not dared to leave the square, or to abandon their battle formation, either by day or by night. From this time onward the Indians were so alarmed by the appearance of our Lady that they gave them more room and were much afraid of them. But infidelity is so blind that after a few days they began to lose some of their fears and once more attacked the faithful. This was due to their great desire to restore the empire to their prince Manco Inca. But owing to the miracles they had seen, their desire exceeded their courage, and they were too cowed to do more than advance and utter their war cries and give the alarm by day and night, so as to upset the Spaniards, though without offering battle any longer. When the Spaniards saw that the Indians could not prevent them, they retired to their lodgings in the above-mentioned hall. They went in with great satisfaction, and gave thanks to God for having preserved that place where the wounded, who had suffered greatly till then, might be cured and those who were still sound might find shelter, of which they were sorely in need. They determined to dedicate the place as a temple and house of prayer to the Lord when He freed them from the siege.

The friendly Indians were of great help in curing their wounds and in ministering to all their other needs, bringing healing herbs and food to eat: as we have mentioned, some of them are great herbalists. On seeing this, many of the Spaniards themselves said that they were in such straits that they did not know what would have happened to them if it had not been for the help of those Indians who brought them maize, herbs, and everything they needed to eat and to cure their wounds, and went without food themselves so that their masters might eat, and served them as spies and watchmen, warning the Spaniards day and night of their enemies' intentions by secret signs. It was also regarded as a miracle of God that the Indians should do so much on behalf of the Spaniards in their own country and in opposition to their own people. In addition to divine providence, it is also a proof of the love and loyalty which, as we have already mentioned, these Indians show toward those who have conquered them in war. They had all been beaten in the various engagements and battles that occurred, and because of their military training and their natural loyalty, as well as through God's will, they were so faithful to their masters that they would have died a hundred deaths for them.

It was for this reason that after this revolt had been suppressed the natives of Cuzco and the other tribes who had been present at the siege, on seeing that the Virgin Mary had vanquished them with the beauty of Her appearance and the dew which She cast in their eyes, were so filled with love and affection for Her—apart from that which they have since learned from the Catholic Faith—that, not satisfied with learning from the priests the titles given to the Virgin in Latin and Spanish, they have tried to render them in the general language of Peru and add others so as to be able to address Her in their own tongue and not in a foreign language when they adore Her and seek favors and mercies of Her. We shall now give some of these names so as to show how the Indians translate and interpret them.

They say *Mamánchic*, "our Lady and mother"; *Coya*, "queen"; *Ñusta*, "princess of the royal blood"; *Sapay*, "unique"; *Yurac Amáncay*, "white lily"; *Chasca*, "morning star"; *Cítoc Coillor*, "shining star"; *Huarcarpaña*, "immaculate"; *Huo Hánac*, "without sin"; *Mana chancasca*, "untouched, inviolate"; *Tazque*, "pure virgin"; *Diospa Maman*, "mother of God." They also say *Pachacamacpa Maman*, "mother of the creator and sustainer of the universe"; and *Huacchacúyac*, "lover and benefactor of the poor," or "mother of pity," "our advocate"—having no words with these meanings in their own language, they use what is nearest. After their affection for the Virgin comes their devotion and love for Saint Ann, whom they call *Mamanchicpa Maman*, "mother of our mother"; *Coyanchicpa Maman*, "mother of our queen"; and the other names given above similarly adapted. They also say *Diospa Payan*, "grandmother of God." The word *paya* really means "old woman," and as grandmothers are necessarily old, especially in a country where marriages were as late as in Peru, the word was not regarded as an insult but as an honor, for it meant the same as grandmother.

To return to Prince Manco Inca and his captains and soldiers, they were so astonished and discouraged by the marvels they had seen that they dared not even speak about them, for the very memory of them filled them with fear. Nevertheless they persisted in the siege in case their fortune should change, though without daring to come to grips, since whenever they did they had the worst of it because of the assistance the divine St. James gave the Christians. When the Indians saw that he alone terrified them and repulsed them more than all the other Spaniards together, they would shout out: "Keep the Viracocha on the white horse from attacking us, and you shall see what befalls you all."

After five months of siege, it happened that an Indian captain who regarded himself as a brave leader thought he would encourage his men by trying his fortune in single combat in the hope that he would fare better than they had in the common fray. He therefore presumed to ask his superiors for leave to challenge a Viracocha to fight to the death, and as the Spaniards on horseback fought with lances he took his spear and a small axe, called a *champi,* but no other weapon. He thus departed, and standing opposite the guard the Spaniards kept in the square near their lodging, he shouted aloud that if any Viracocha dare face him in a single combat, let him leave the Spanish lines and he would receive him with the arms he was carrying. None of the Spaniards was willing to accept the challenge, thinking it below their dignity to do battle with a single Indian.

Then a Cañari Indian went to Pizarro's brothers, Hernando, Juan, and Gonzalo, and told them that this man had rashly come forward to defy the Viracochas on behalf of the Indians, and offered, as their servant, to take up the challenge. He was one of the nobility of his tribe and had as a boy been page to the great Huaina Cápac. He had been forced to surrender by Pizarro, and had taken his master's name, calling himself Don Francisco: I knew him and he was still alive in Cuzco when I left. He begged for permission, saying that he was confident that their good fortune would bring him victory. Hernando Pizarro and his brothers thanked him, praised his courage, and gave him leave to fight. The Cañari went out with the same weapons as the other and both fought for a long spell. They came to grips three or four times and even wrestled, but neither could throw the other, and they broke away, took up their weapons and resumed the fight. This continued until the Cañari slew the other, plunging his lance into his enemy's chest, cutting off his head and dragging it by the hair to the Spanish quarters where he was welcomed as his victory merited.

The Inca and his captains were greatly shocked by the Cañari's victory. It would not have impressed them so much if it had been won by a Spaniard; but as it had been gained by one of their Indian vassals they took it as a very bad omen, and as they are very superstitious they lost heart at this augury to such an extent that they performed no more deeds worthy of note during the siege, except perhaps the unfortunate killing of the good Juan Pizarro, which we shall shortly describe.

Whenever I recall these marvels and others that our Lord God wrought for the Spaniards in the siege of Cuzco and that of Lima, I am astonished that the historians do not mention them despite the fact that they were so important and so generally known that as a boy I heard them recounted by both Indians and Spaniards, who alike were filled with wonder. After the siege the hall in which the Spaniards lodged was dedicated to our

Lady, in memory of these events; and today it is the cathedral church and is dedicated to St. Mary of the Assumption. They dedicated the city to the Spanish St. James, and commemorated his protection with very great celebrations every year on his day, consisting of a procession, sermon, and solemn mass in the morning and a bull fight, a tourney with canes, and many rejoicings in the afternoon. On the façade of the cathedral that juts out into the square they painted Santiago on a white horse with his shield on his arm and his sword in one hand; the sword was serpentine, and he had many Indians dead and wounded at his feet. When the Indians saw this painting, they used to say: "It was a Viracocha like this that destroyed us in the square." The painting was still there in 1560 when I came to Spain. The Inca's rising was in 1535 and it ended in 1536; and I was born in 1539, so that I knew many Indians and Spaniards who had taken part in the war and seen the wonders I have mentioned, which I heard about from them: I myself have fought with canes on St. James' day. Because of this I am astonished that those who have sent back accounts of affairs in Peru should not have told the historians of such important matters, unless of course they wished to ascribe the victory to their own efforts.

Many days after writing this chapter, I was glancing through Padre Acosta's book and lit on his reference to the many miracles that our Lord Christ and His mother, the Virgin Mary, the queen of the angels, have performed in the New World on behalf of their holy religion. Among them he mentions those I have referred to as having happened in Cuzco, and I was indescribably glad to find this; for though it is true that I am proud to write of such things, which are the most important in history, I nevertheless shrink to do so when I find that the Spanish historians have not touched on these high matters as a whole or in part, lest it should be thought that I am inventing fables, which I should hate to do, or am flattering the reader. Padre Acosta therefore says in his Book VII. ch. xxvii:

In the city of Cuzco when the Spaniards were besieged and in such a plight that they could never have escaped without the aid of heaven, it is reported by trustworthy informants (and I myself have heard them say it) that when the Indians threw firebolts on the roof of the Spaniards' lodging, which was where the cathedral now is, although the roof was of straw called *chicho* (for *ichu*) and the torches were very large, the fire never caught, because a lady in the sky at once put the flames out. This the Indians saw with their own eyes, and they were filled with wonder. It is known for certain from various accounts and histories that in several battles fought by the Spaniards both in New Spain and

Peru the enemy Indians saw a knight in the air, sword in hand, mounted on a white horse and fighting for the Spaniards. Hence the great veneration throughout the Indies for the glorious apostle St. James. On other occasions the image of our Lady, from whom the Christians in those parts have received incomparable blessings, was seen in these conflicts. If these works of heaven were to be recounted at length as they have happened, it would make a very long story,

etc. Thus Padre Acosta, who, as he says, heard the story of these miracles though he visited Peru nearly forty years after they had occurred. With this we shall return to our Spaniards, and with such favors, it would hardly be surprising if they won a hundred new worlds!

CHAPTER XXVI

The Spaniards win the fortress, but the good Juan Pizarro is killed.

IN CH. V of Book Eight of our First Part, we promised to speak of the loyalty of the Cañaris to the Inca kings and of how they later repudiated them because of the friendship of one of the Cañaris with the Spaniards. We did in fact speak of their loyalty in Book Nine, ch. xxxix, and it remains to say why they went back on it. The Cañari in question received so many favors from the Spaniards at the time of their victory and later, that the whole tribe became attached to the newcomers, and not only withdrew the love and obedience they owed the Incas as their natural lords but became cruel enemies of them and went over to the Spaniards and served them thenceforward as spies, agitators, and executioners against the other Indians. Even in the civil wars between the Spaniards until the rising of Francisco Hernández Girón, the many Cañaris living in Cuzco under the command of this Don Francisco Cañari acted as scouts and double spies for the royalists and the rebels, astutely dividing into two parties, one on each side, so that when the war was over those who had taken the losing side might save themselves from death by pretending they had all been on the winning side. They were able to keep up the pretence since they did not deal directly with the Spaniards for the purpose of taking or giving messages except for a few of their leaders, so that the rest were unknown, and they could thus all pass for loyal though they had been double-dyed traitors and had exchanged information with their kith and kin about all that was happening between the two armies. I heard of this trickery from one of the Cañaris who was telling another Indian how those who had been with the rebels had escaped after the war against Francisco Hernández. Don Francisco Cañari was so full of pride and favor that years later he boldly poisoned Don Felipe Inca, the son of Huaina Cápac, whom we have already mentioned, or so public report has it; and this was confirmed by the fact that he soon after married Don Felipe's wife, who was very beautiful. He won her more by force than by persuasion, and less by request than by the threats uttered by his partisans, to the great scandal of the Incas, though they had to put up with the outrage because they were no longer in authority. We shall later give another instance of this Indian's boldness, which caused great scandal among those living in the city.

When the Spaniards saw that they were daily more favored by divine aid and that the Indians grew hourly more discouraged, and thought no longer of attacking them, but merely of besieging them, they sought to break through the surrounding forces and show that though they were so few and their foes so many, they were not afraid. They put this to the proof by attacking the Indians and pressing them back as far as they wished, without any defence being made. This happened often on many different days, and twenty-five or thirty Spaniards attacked any Indian company however large, and scattered them like children; for if God fought for His own, who could stand against them? They thus drove the enemy back clear of the whole city and its surrounding fields, and did not stop till they reached some cliffs and crags where the horses could not dominate the Indians. But even these did not avail the Indians much, for the horses climbed the rocks like goats. This comparison is my own, but I heard a better from one of the conquerors called Francisco Rodríguez de Villafuerte, one of the thirteen companions who stood by Pizarro when the rest abandoned him, as we have mentioned in describing the incident.

This gentleman was in a large company escorting some noblemen on their way to Spain by the road to Arequipa, and I was going with them as a boy: this was at the end of 1552. The whole way from Cuzco to Quespicancha, or three leagues, Francisco de Villafuerte was telling the story of the siege and pointing out the places where various deeds had been done, which he duly recounted, naming those who had performed them. He said: "Here such a one did this gallant deed, and here another did that, and over there a third did something else." All these were remarkable deeds, and among them he told one of Gonzalo Pizarro, which we shall mention later, for we have still not reached the time for it: this he told stopping at the very place where it had happened by the wayside. After telling a great many of these episodes, he said: "There is no cause to be astonished at these things, though they are indeed great, for God visibly and marvellously lent His aid. One of the miracles we saw was that our horses ran as nimbly and easily up the mountains as that flock of pigeons over there." The mountains he was referring to were those to the left of the road which are very rough.

I wish I had not forgotten what I heard that day, or I could have filled many sheets of paper with the prowess of the Spaniards in that siege. Suffice it to say that 170 men resisted 200,000, supporting hunger and sleep and weariness and wounds, with no surgeon or medicines, not to mention the other discomforts and hardships that occur in such rigorous sieges. All this must be left to the imagination of the reader of this history, for it is impossible to describe these great labors in detail as they took place. The Spaniards suffered these hardships and conquered by the strength of their spirits because God had chosen them and formed them to preach His Gospel in that empire.

Once they had forced the Indians aside, the Spaniards decided to attack the fortress, because the enemy was congregated thickest there, and they thought they had done nothing until they had conquered it. They therefore left a garrison in their quarters and climbed up to the fortress. The Indians fought hard and in six days could not be reduced. One night, after both sides had fought bravely all day, they retired to their posts, and Juan Pizarro, the marquis' brother, who had been wounded days before and could scarcely bear to wear his helmet, took it off too soon, and as soon as he did so a stone slung from a sling struck him hard on the head, and he died of this wound within three days. Zárate says of his death: "It was a great loss for the whole of Peru for Juan Pizarro was very brave and experienced in warfare with the Indians, and much loved by everyone." These are Zárate's words.

So died this good gentleman, and his death was then greatly mourned, and since that time fame too has mourned the passing of so generous, brave, kind, and much loved a man in such unfortunate circumstances. His virtues were indeed all that could be desired in a knight. When I left, his body was buried in the high chapel of the cathedral of Cuzco, with a great slab of blue stone over his grave, with no inscription, though it would have been proper to put one as he deserved. It must have been omitted for want of a sculptor, for in those days and for long after chisels were unknown in my country, and men used only spears, swords, and arquebusses. The Spaniards won the fortress of Cuzco and expelled the Indians from it, with the great losses we have mentioned above. The historians mention this incident at the outset of the siege, but the Indians tell the story in the order we have followed: they do not depart from the historical truth, but their version coincides with that of the Spaniards.

CHAPTER XXVII

The deeds of Indians and Spaniards during the siege of Cuzco.

WITH THE death of the good Juan Pizarro the Indians took courage again, since he was brother to the governor and a brave and famous leader such as the Indians set great store by. They again strove to offer battle, and though they were gradually losing all their forces, they did not lose their desire to kill the Spaniards and so restore the empire to their prince Manco Inca. They were now much wearied by their determination, though they did not give it up. As the Indians no longer pressed them, the Christians were able to move freely for a space of a league round the city, but they were still harassed and when their Indian servants brought up supplies they were molested. The Christians were therefore obliged to range the countryside in search of food. During the siege, they had been short of it and obtained it by force, for what their Indian servants stole for them was little and insufficient to maintain them. Zárate describes one of these raids as follows:

During this siege Gonzalo Pizarro went out with twenty horsemen to range the countryside as far as the lake of Chinchero, five leagues from Cuzco, where he was beset by so many Indians that though he fought hard he would have been defeated if Hernando Pizarro and Alonso de Toro had not come to his help with some more horsemen, for he had ventured too far into enemy country in proportion to his small force, and shown more courage than prudence.

Thus Agustín de Zárate. Lake Chinchiru, as the Indians call it, lies two leagues north of the city, and is a fine sheet of water drained by a stream from which the Incas built a splendid channel to irrigate the fields in the valley of Cuzco. This channel was destroyed in the wars and disturbances among the Spaniards; but was restored later in 1555 and 1556 by my lord Garcilaso de la Vega when he was corregidor. It was in existence when I left, and must be still, for it is most necessary. With regard to what Zárate says of the danger Gonzalo Pizarro was in when his brother came to his aid, we may mention (as we said in our history of Florida) that his lance was without contradiction the best in the New World. He and his men fought very bravely that day, but they would certainly have been lost had they not been rescued, for they were overwhelmed by the force of Indians that fell on them. It was regarded as a manifestation of providence and divine mercy that help was given them; for they did not ask for it and Hernando Pizarro did not know they needed it.

On another day there was a great battle in the field of Las Salinas, a short league to the south of the city where famous deeds were done on both sides. All fought bravely, and though the Indians were numerous and did their best, they were at last defeated and fled. A few of their captains carried on the fight, preferring to die in the sight of their Inca, who was watching them from a hill, rather than flee in his presence. A gentleman I knew who was mounted with a lance in his hand fought one of these Indians who was standing on the road to Collao. The Indian bravely waited for him with his bow and arrows ready, and as the Spaniard aimed his lance at him, he caught it in his bow, which he then dropped and seized the lance, dragging it away from the Spaniard. Another gentleman, whom I also knew, had been watching the single combat and had not attacked with his friend, since there was only one Indian; he charged when he saw that the Indian had seized the lance and bore down on him with his own lance. The Indian warded off the blow with the lance he had won, forced it out of his hands, dropped the first lance and seized the second, standing with it against the attack of the two Spaniards, whose names are not given out of respect for their descendants, one of whom was my fellow pupil in the grammar school.

Gonzalo Pizarro, who had been fighting elsewhere and had put his opponents to flight, happened to be close by, and on seeing what was happening rode up, shouting: "Off, off!" when he realized that the two Spaniards were about to attack the Indian. They stood aside when they recognized him, to see if he would have better or worse luck than they. When the Indian saw him approach, he stood on the first lance he had won, and with the second in his hands, received his third opponent, dealing the horse a blow in the face before its rider could strike at him and causing it to rear in such a fashion that it almost tipped him off backwards. When the Indian saw Gonzalo in these difficulties, he dropped the lance he was holding and seized the Spaniard's, as he had done with his two former adversaries. In order not to lose his lance, Gonzalo grasped it in his left hand and seized his sword in his right, so as to cut off the Indian's hands. Thus threatened, the Indian let go of the lance and stooped for one of the others. At this moment the two men who were watching, alarmed by the Indian's boldness, rushed forward to kill him. Then Gonzalo Pizarro shouted aloud: "He does not deserve to be harmed; he ought to be rewarded."

The two men stopped, and the Indian, realizing that Gonzalo's words had saved him, dropped the lance he had just picked up in token of surrender, and went to Gonzalo and kissed his right leg, saying: "You are my Inca, and I am your servant." Thereafter he served him most loyally, and Gonzalo loved him like a son, till at last the Indian died in the battle of Canela, as we shall say later. I heard this account from Francisco Rodríguez de Villafuerte, who was present at the battle, and from many others. Gonzalo Pizarro used to say he had never been in such a dangerous plight in any passage of arms as in his fight with this Indian.

A little later, toward mid-day, another strange event occurred, which Francisco Rodríguez de Villafuerte also used to tell. This was that a man was riding slowly along the road on his horse, when there were no longer any Indians to be seen to fight, and the horse suddenly fell with him. Although its owner hastily got clear, the horse had difficulty in rising and could stand on only three legs, for an arrow had pierced the lower part of one of its forelegs. The rider looked round to see who could have shot it, for there were no natives about, and beheld an Indian leaning against one of the long, deep ravines there are thereabouts, though it seemed impossible that he could have shot the horse from where he was. But judging from the wound the arrow seemed to have come from that direction, and in order to find out, they went over, and found a dead Indian standing propped up against the ravine with a bow in one hand and an arrow in the other. He had been wounded by a Spanish lance which had passed through his shoulder to his waistband and had thrown himself over the ravine to avoid the horse. Finding himself so sorely wounded, he had wanted to perform some noteworthy deed before he died, and had shot the arrow at the passing horseman. He had aimed well, but the distance and his own wound had prevented him from hitting the Spaniard in the head or body as he intended, and he had hit the horse's leg.

These were two of the famous deeds, among others, that the Indians performed that day, one of the last days of the siege. Here we shall leave the affairs of Cuzco and give an account of what happened at Lima, where the governor was at first unaware of the ordeal his brothers were undergoing, but as soon as he realized it, he did all he could to relieve them, like a good captain, as we shall see.

CHAPTER XXVIII

The number of Spaniards killed by the Indians on the roads, and the events of the siege of Lima.

AS SOON as his brothers ceased to write regularly to him as was their custom, Pizarro became uneasy, and was greatly distressed because he could not guess what had happened, so as to take the proper steps. Using the friendly Indians the Spaniards had, he ordered them to find out from their relatives what was happening in Cuzco and in the rest of Peru, for he feared, and not without cause, that the roads had been cut. The *yanacunas,* as the Indian servants are called, investigated, and learned that the Inca had rebelled and had many warriors in Cuzco, but they could not obtain details of what was happening there and could only give the marquis a confused account. He at once wrote to Panama, Nicaragua, Mexico, and Santo Domingo to ask for aid. Zárate gives the following account of this:

When the marquis saw such a host of Indians against Lima, he felt sure that Hernando and the rest of those at Cuzco were dead, and that the rising had been so general that those in Chile had worsted Almagro and his friends. He then sent the ships to Panama so that the Indians should not think that the Spaniards were holding them back through fear in order to escape in them and so that the Spaniards should not rely on getting away by sea. He also sent to the viceroy of New Spain and to all the governors in the Indies to ask for help, informing them of his great straits.

Thus Zárate. We may add that he also wrote by means of faithful *yanacunas* to Alonso de Alvarado who was engaged in the conquest of

Chachapoyas and Sebastián de Belalcázar at Quito, both of whom were prospering. He likewise wrote to Garcilaso de la Vega who on the contrary was meeting with great difficulty in the conquest of the province ironically called Buenaventura, where the five large and turbulent rivers called the Quiximíes flow down to the sea (his difficulties rose not from the resistance of the natives, for there are almost none, but from the inaccessibility of the land, which is rendered uninhabitable by wild mountains—we shall say something of the labors of this expedition later on). Pizarro also wrote to Juan Porcel who was engaged in conquering the Pacamurus. He bade them all come to Lima as soon as possible so that they could all resist the Indians together. Until these captains should arrive, the marquis tried to send urgent help to his brothers as best he could, though he did not fully appreciate their need or how many Indians were pressing against them. He prepared such men as he could and sent 70 horse, as Zárate says, and 30 foot under Captain Diego Pizarro, a kinsman of his.

The Indians who were coming from various directions to kill the marquis and his companions, on learning from their spies that he was sending help to his brothers, turned aside from Lima and began to occupy the roads so as to cut off the reinforcements and kill them in the difficult places, which are very numerous everywhere between Cuzco and Quito. They therefore cunningly permitted Diego Pizarro and his friends to travel for seventy leagues without molesting them. They were thus at a considerable distance from the governor, and, although they had already passed several difficult places, the Indians had not attacked, lest the governor should find out what had happened, for they wanted him to think the reinforcements had reached Cuzco in safety. When the Spaniards came to a steep slope called the hill of Parcos, the Indians threw down so many of the stones called *galgas* that they were all killed and none escaped, though not a blow was struck with sword or lance. The same was done to Captain Francisco Morgovejo de Quiñones, who had 60 horse and 70 foot. And behind him they killed Captain Gonzalo de Tapia who had 80 horse and 60 foot, and Captain Alonso de Gahete, with 40 horse and 60 foot. Thus 470 Spaniards, 250 horse (though Zárate says 300), and 220 foot perished in different places on the road. Cieza de León (ch. lxxxii) speaks as follows of the Spaniards killed by the Indians in the general rising:

They affirm that the Indians of the province of Cunchucu were warlike, and that the Incas had difficulty in subjugating them, though some of the Incas always tried to attract other peoples by good deeds and friendly words. These Indians have killed some Spaniards in various places, so that Pizarro sent Captain Francisco de Chaves with some Christians to make war on them with all severity; some Spaniards say that a great many Indians were burnt at the stake. And at that time or a little earlier there occurred the general rising of the other provinces and the Indians killed over 700 Christian Spaniards between Cuzco and Quito, and those who were taken alive and carried off were put to death with great cruelty. May God preserve us from the fury of the Indians, which is certainly greatly to be feared when they can carry out their intents. Although they said that they were fighting for their freedom and to put an end to the harsh treatment they had received, and that the Spaniards were fighting to remain masters of the country and of them,

etc. Thus Cieza de León.

Padre Blas Valera also says there were more than 700 Spaniards killed in the rising, about 300 butchered at the mines and on the estates where they were scattered about in search of gain, while 460 were the reinforcements collected by the marquis and sent off piecemeal, as they could be got together. He did not send them all together, hoping that the first to arrive would bring relief earlier, and not realizing that there was such danger on the road or that the Indians were strong enough to kill 10 on horseback, let alone 60 or 70 together, apart from infantry. Although he thus overrated his own men, he was extremely preoccupied at not hearing from them, for neither the first nor the last wrote to him. In order to settle his mind and get news of his brothers he sent yet another captain, Francisco de Godoy, a native of Cáceres, with 45 horse, to ride rapidly forward, not to reach Cuzco, but simply to find out what had happened on the road and return with some account of their predecessors. López de Gómara describes this in his ch. cxxxvi:

Pizarro was alarmed at not hearing from his brothers or from these captains, and fearing what had in fact happened, sent 40 horsemen under Francisco de Godoy to bring news. He returned with his tail between his legs, as they say, bringing two of Gahete's Spaniards who had escaped at the gallop; and the bad news was thus brought to Pizarro, who was greatly distressed. Then Diego de Agüero came fleeing to Lima with the news that all the Indians were up in arms and had tried to burn him in his villages, and that a large Indian army was not far away. This greatly alarmed the city, especially as there were few Spaniards there. Pizarro sent Pedro de Lerma of Burgos with 60 horse and many friendly Indians and Christians to prevent the Indians from reaching Lima, and he himself sallied forth with the rest of the Spanish forces. Lerma fought very well and drove the enemy back to a crag, where he would have completed his victory and dispersed them if Pizarro had not called the retreat.

One Spanish horseman died that day in battle: many others were wounded and Pedro de Lerma's teeth were broken. The Indians gave many thanks to the Sun for saving them from such dangers and offered up great sacrifices. They moved their headquarters to a range of mountains near Lima, and on the other side of the river, where they stayed ten days skirmishing with the Spaniards, but refusing to attack other Indians.

These words of López de Gómara are repeated almost exactly by Zárate; they suggest if read carefully that the Indians were more successful than the Spaniards. What really happened was that the infidels had killed so many Spaniards on the roads and felt so full of victory that they went to Lima perfectly confident of being able to kill the marquis and all his companions. So resolved, they met with Pedro de Lerma and his friends eight or ten leagues from the city, where both sides fought with great valor. As the battle began on a plain, the Spanish horsemen killed many Indians, using their advantage in weapons and mounts. The Indians therefore withdrew to the crag where they drummed and trumpeted and shouted till more than 40,000 Indians were gathered. The ground was difficult and the horses were tiring, so the Indians dared to emerge and fought bravely. Pedro de Lerma's teeth were broken by a stone from a sling, and he was in a bad way. Many other Spaniards were wounded, and 32 of them later died, to the great regret of all their companions; 8 wounded horses also died, though in the battle itself only one Spaniard and one horse were killed. The governor, who was following behind, saw that the Spaniards were hard pressed and sounded the retreat so that they should realize that he was supporting them and the Indians should take fright and cease fighting. Thus the battle, which had been very bloody, ended for that day. The Spaniards retired to the city, and the Indians retired also, and by calling their forces together collected more than 60,000 men under their general Titu Yupanqui (whom Zárate calls Tiso Yopanqui and López de Gómara Tizoyo). They put their army near the city, but across the river so as to be safe from the horses.

There they made sacrifices and offered thanks to the Sun, thinking that they had had the better of the Spaniards that day since they had forced them to retire to the city and give up the fight. The historians say they gave thanks for their escape from such danger, though they immediately add that the Indians fought continuously with the Spaniards and refused to do battle with the other Indians. This was because they disdained to fight those who had been their vassals after fighting the Spaniards. They thus continued the fight daily, though with little harm to the Spaniards, for here the ground is flat and the horses could drive them back. Nevertheless the Indians were so numerous that they kept the Spaniards hemmed in and sorely tried by repeated alarms and excursions by day and night, depriving them of sleep and supplies and exhausting them. The tame Indians who were the servants and friends of the Spaniards, used to go over to the enemy as they did in the siege of Cuzco and pretended to have forsaken their masters; but returned to them at night and brought food and news of the enemy's plans, which were of great use and helped them to take steps and be prepared against an enemy attack. Diego de Agüero and other soldiers, who, as Zárate says, came galloping back to Lima, did so because their Indian servants had warned them of the Inca's rising and the approach of armies coming to kill them. These Spaniards were enjoying the estates the marquis had awarded them, and only escaped death owing to the loyalty and help of their Indian servants.

Apart from such human succor there were also miracles of God in this siege, as at Cuzco, on behalf of the Christians. The river which the Indians regarded as the protection of their army turned against them and became their ruin and destruction, for whenever they crossed it to attack the Christians during the siege, or whenever they returned over it, it swelled into a great sea and they had no lack of misfortunes, many being drowned by the pressure of their enemies or even without this, despite the fact that the river is smaller than others on the coast, except when it is winter in the mountains and there are great spates. The Spaniards crossed it with spates or without, just as if it were level ground. The Indians noticed this, and being very superstitious, said that even the elements had turned against them and befriended the Viracochas, and that Pachacámac, the sustainer of the universe, had forsaken them and favored their enemies; for as soon as the Indians saw the Spaniards in the field, before they came to grips and without knowing why, they lost heart and stomach for battle. If so many thousand men could not vanquish or even resist so few Spaniards, it was clear that the Maker wished it to be so, and was defending the latter.

With these suppositions, or rather works of God, the Indians daily weakened and thenceforth achieved nothing of moment, continuing the siege out of a sense of duty toward their elders rather than in the hope of success. The domestic Indians informed their masters of all their enemies said and feared. The Spaniards noted the marvels our Lord God had accomplished on their behalf and, knowing that the Indians had seen them and spoken about them, rendered Him many thanks for everything, saying that the river had been to them and their Indian enemies what the Red Sea had been to the people of Israel and the Egyptians. And as their greatest battles and victories took place on both banks of that river, they became particularly devoted to the blessed St. Christopher, recalling the Lord's mercy and favor toward this saint in a river, which is commonly reported and is depicted in churches. They therefore called on this saint together with the apostle St. James in these battles. And after the siege, they called the hill where the Indians had most of their forces the hill of St. Christopher in memory of the saint. It stands near the city across the river, and it was here that they completed their victory and the destruction of the Indians.

CHAPTER XXIX

The flight of Uíllac Umu; the punishment of
the interpreter Felipe; Prince Manco Inca
abandons his empire.

WE HAVE said above that Prince Manco Inca sent messengers to Chile to warn his brother Paullu and the priest Uíllac Umu of his determination to kill all the Spaniards in Peru and recover his empire and urging the Chileans to do the same with Almagro and his companions. These messengers reached Chile before Almagro's departure and delivered the prince's warning; but Paullu and his friends, after consulting together, dared not make an attack on the Spaniards, thinking their forces too small for a direct onslaught, since more than ten thousand Indians had perished of suffocation and cold and snow in crossing the mountains. Neither dared they fall on the Spaniards secretly at night, for they saw that the latter were on the watch and vigilant, and there was no hope of a successful surprise attack. They therefore decided to conceal their intentions and serve the Spaniards faithfully until an opportunity should occur to carry out what they desired. When Paullu and Uíllac Umu found themselves in Atacama in Peru and out of the Chilean desert, as we have said in ch. xxi of this book, they agreed that the high priest should take flight and that Paullu should remain with the Spaniards in case of emergency, if only to be able to warn his brother the Inca of their hostile intention. And though López de Gómara says they both fled, Zárate mentions only the flight of the priest in his Book III, ch. i; and in ch. iv of the same book, he says the following of Paullu: "Don Diego de Almagro made Paullu Inca, and gave him the imperial fringe because his brother Manco Inca had fled after doing all this with many warriors to some very wild mountains called the Andes."

Such is Zárate's account, and we have already explained that when these authors differ, Zárate is to be followed for preference; for he was in Peru, and the other was not. The interpreter Felipe, who was with Almagro, also fled; for he had been frightened since the death of Atahuallpa and wanted to be away from the Spaniards. He now fled, not because he knew of the Incas' intention; for they would have concealed it from him and certainly not have revealed it to him, but in imitation of the other Indians who were escaping, and to get away from those whom he hated. But he was unlucky and, as he did not know the ground well, fell into Almagro's hands. The latter remembered how he had fled to Don Pedro de Alvarado, and suspected that he knew about the flight of the high priest but had failed to warn him; he therefore gave orders that Felipe was to be quartered. Of this López de Gómara says in his ch. cxxxv (though this is out of place): "The villain confessed at the time of his death that he had falsely accused the good king Atahuallpa in order to be able to lie safely with one of his wives. Felipillo de Pohechos was a bad man, fickle, inconstant, a liar, and fond of intrigues and bloodshed; a poor Christian, though baptized." So López de Gómara; and we must again ponder and deplore that the first interpreter Peru had for the preaching of the Catholic faith should have been such a one.

Almagro ignored Uíllac Umu's flight since Paullu had remained with him, and advanced toward Cuzco, having now been informed of the Inca's rebellion. Hitherto he had had his suspicions but they had not been confirmed, for Paullu and his followers had shown themselves friendly and served him diligently. He went by Collao and was not molested by the Indians; for as the ground is flat, there were no difficult places where they could attack him with advantage as there are between Cuzco and Lima. When he reached Cuzco Prince Manco Inca had already abandoned the siege, on learning of Almagro's approach to relieve the other Spaniards, though he did not know of Almagro's hostile intentions toward the Pizarros. Almagro tried to see the Inca and speak with him to win him over to his side, for they had known one another of old. The Inca agreed to the interview, hoping to capture Almagro and kill him, if he could; for he thought that if this were done, it might still be possible to kill the rest. They met and talked, but neither had his way, for Almagro, like a prudent soldier, was well escorted by Spaniards on horse and on foot, so that the

Inca did not dare to attack, and on the other hand the Inca did not wish to join Almagro's side. After the interview the Inca said that as his object was to recover his empire he did not wish to favor or help either side; and though his friends urged him to accept the suggestion and keep the war going until the Spaniards should have exhausted themselves and killed one another, when it would be much easier to fall on those who remained and finish them off, the prince replied that it was not for Inca kings to go back on their word once it had been given, or to harm those they had received under their favor and protection: he would rather lose his empire than do anything an Inca should not do.

While Almagro had gone to see the Inca, Hernando Pizarro had sent a message to try to persuade Juan de Saavedra, who had remained in charge of Almagro's troops, to hand them over to him, offering great honors and profit. But Juan de Saavedra, who was a gentleman of the very noble family of that name in Seville and himself a man of great goodness and virtue, disregarded the offer, refusing to do anything dishonorable. Thus the three parties remained facing one another without wishing to close in. When the Inca saw that Almagro had come back from Chile and had more than 450 Spaniards, despite the fact that nearly 200 had been lost crossing the mountains and in the conquest of Chile, he realized that as he had not been able to reduce 170 Spaniards in so many months, he had no chance at all of reducing 600. Although they were at the moment divided and at odds with one another, as soon as either party was attacked they would all join together against the Indians. It would therefore only bring death and destruction to continue the war, as experience had shown; for in a little less than a year since the rising had begun they had lost over 40,000 either at the hands of the enemy, or by hunger, or from other hardships that war involves. It was wrong to let them all perish in pursuit of an object that grew daily harder to achieve. He therefore discussed these matters with his few remaining relatives and decided to abandon the war. He then summoned the chief commanders and captains and told them in public:

"Brothers and sons! I have seen the love you have shown in my service since you have so bravely and readily offered your lives and possessions and wives and children to see my empire restored to me; it seems to me that Pachacámac is visibly opposed to this, that he does not wish me to be king, and that we should not go against his will. I believe you all know that if I wished and sought to recover my empire, it was not because of my desire to reign but so that my realms might enjoy the peace and ease they knew under the gentle sway of my fathers and ancestors; for a good king must study the welfare and prosperity of his vassals, as our Incas did. I fear that the rule of these men we call gods sent from heaven will be very different; but as I can do nothing to remedy this, it would be wrong for me to persist in my quest at so great an expense of life and effort, when what I desire is the opposite. I would rather be deprived and dispossessed of my empire than see my vassals slain, whom I love as my own children. So that I shall give the Viracochas no cause to misuse you by seeing that I am still in one or other of my kingdoms and fearing that you may desire to restore my empire to me, I shall go into exile. They will then lose their suspicions, and treat you better and hold you as friends.

"Now I see the prophecy of my father Huaina Cápac fully realized, to the effect that strangers should deprive us of our empire and destroy our commonwealth and our religion. If before we had begun our war against the Viracochas we had pondered on the words of the king my father's will, we should not have rebelled, since he bade us obey and serve these men, saying that their law is better than ours, and their arms more powerful than ours. Both these things have proved true, for as soon as they entered our empire our oracles fell silent, which is proof that they were conquered by theirs! Then their arms overcame our arms: though we at first slew some of them, only 170 of them were able to resist us, and we may even say they defeated us, for we could not execute our plan, but were forced to retire. We can in truth say that it was not they who defeated us; nor can they boast that they did so. It was rather the marvels we have all seen—fire lost its force, for it did not burn their houses but did burn ours; then when we had surrounded them there appeared the man with lightning, thunder, and thunderbolts in his hand and destroyed us all; then at night we saw that beautiful princess with the child in her arms, and with the softness of the dew she cast in our eyes, she blinded us and bewildered us so that we could not return to our lodgings, let alone fight against the Viracochas. Moreover we have seen how so few men have defended themselves against such a number of us without food or sleep or an hour's rest, showing themselves braver and stronger when we thought they were dead or exhausted.

"All this clearly shows that it is not the work of men but of Pachacámac, and as he favors them and forsakes us, I am going to betake myself to the Antis, so that their wilderness may defend me and protect me from these men, when all my might has failed to do so. There I shall live quietly, not molesting the strangers lest they should misuse you for my sake. In my solitude and my banishment I shall be relieved and comforted to know that you are prospering under the new rule of the Spaniards. Instead of a testament, I shall accept my father's will, and bid and charge you to obey and serve them as best you can, so that you may be well treated and not abused. Remain in peace, for I would willingly take you all with me so as not to leave you in the power of strangers."

Here the Inca ended his discourse. His friends wept many tears, and groaned and sobbed so that they choked. They did not answer, and did not dare to resist him, for they saw that this was his resolution and will. The warriors and their caciques were soon dismissed and sent to their provinces to obey and serve the Spaniards. The Inca brought together all those of the royal blood he could find, men and women alike, and retired to the wild forest of the Antis to a place called Villcapampa where he lived in exile and solitude as one can imagine a dispossessed and disinherited prince would live, until one day he was slain by a Spaniard whom he had sheltered and protected from enemies who had sought his death: this we shall see in due course.

CHAPTER XXX

An author on the Inca kings and their vassals.

PADRE BLAS Valera speaks at length of the ingenuity, skill, endurance, and courage of the Peruvian Indians; and as his words have much bearing on various parts of our history, I shall quote them here, in order to have his authority for a great deal of what I have said and shall say:

The keen ingenuity and wit of the Peruvians exceed those of many peoples of the Old World; for despite their ignorance of writing they achieved many things that the Egyptians, Greeks, and Chaldaeans failed to achieve, and it may be argued that if they had had letters as they had knots they would have surpassed the Romans, Gauls, and other peoples. Their present rudeness is not due to any want of ability or wit, but because they are unused to European customs and devices, and no one teaches them anything that requires wit, but only what is to their interest or profit. Those who do find a teacher and free time and permission to study, even though they are not taught, but merely copy what they see, turn out skilled craftsmen and excel many Spaniards. Similarly in reading and writing, in music, instruments, and other acquirements, and even in Latin, they would not be the worst pupils if the Spaniards would only teach them. We moreover are slower in understanding their books

than they in following ours; for we have been dealing with them for more than
seventy years without ever learning the theory and rules of their knots and
accounts, whereas they have very soon picked up not only our writing but also
our figures, which is a proof of their great skill. The tenacity of their memories is noticeably superior to that of Spaniards, even those of outstandingly
good memory. The Indians are ingenious in memorizing with the aid of knots,
the knuckles, and places; and they can moreover use the same knots for various
themes and subjects, and when a subject is mentioned they can read off the
account as fast as a good reader reads a book, and no Spaniard has yet contrived to do this or to find how it is done. All this springs from the Indians'
ingenuity and good memory.

As regards military science, the Peruvians excel Europeans under equal
conditions, and with the same arms. Give me the most famous captains of
France and Spain without their horses, harnesses, and arms—either lances or
swords—without bombards and firearms, but clad only in shirts and loincloths,
with slings about their waists and their heads covered with crowns of feathers
or flowers instead of helmets and vizors, and their feet bare among the thorns
and brambles, with herbs and roots for their food and pieces of matting in their
left hands as shields; set them thus on the battlefield to face bronze axes and
tridents, stones slung from slings, poisoned arrows, and archers firing at the
heart and eyes; and if they can conquer in these conditions, I would say they
deserved the reputation of valiant soldiers among the Indians. But as it would
not be possible for them to stand up to this sort of weapons and warfare, it
would, humanly speaking, be impossible for them to be victorious. But if on
the other hand the Indians had the powerful weapons used by the Europeans
and their military skill on land and sea, they would be harder to defeat than
the Grand Turk. Experience itself shows this to be so, for when Spaniards and
Indians fought with the same weapons, the Spaniards fell in droves, as at Puno
in Mexico. Yet when the weapons have been quite unequal, and Spaniards have
been laden with arms and the Indians naked, the former have often been
defeated in pitched battle, as in Quito, Chachapoyas, Chuquisaca, Tucumán,
Cunti, Jauja, Parcos, Chile, and elsewhere. Thus it is impossible to compare
the Spaniards with the Indians of Mexico and Peru in order to prove the
bravery of the former, since their weapons are unequal, and it is the invention
of firearms rather than human feats of courage that has made all the difference.
The victory that was won in the New World, and especially in Peru, was due
to God's providence and His struggle on behalf of the Gospel, and not to the
strength of the Spaniards. The comparison can only be made between Europeans and Asiatics, where the weapons are equal, and in this case Spain has the
advantage.

But setting this apart, and comparing Indians with Indians, with equality of
arms, there is no doubt but that the Peruvians and the Incas bear the palm;
for in a short space of time they conquered the land we now enjoy, and this
took place not yesterday, as some pretend, but more than five or six hundred

years from where we are. Among them many of their kings were of great valor, such as Manco Cápac, Inca Roca, Viracocha Inca, Pachacútec, and his descendants down to the great Huaina Cápac, who was their emperor, and many captains of the same blood, all of whom we shall speak of at length in their proper place.

These are the words of Padre Valera, with which we shall return to the Spaniards.

CHAPTER XXXI

*Differences between the Almagros and
the Pizarros; the arrest of
Hernando Pizarro.*

DON DIEGO de Almagro and Hernando Pizarro, on seeing that the Inca had disappeared and disbanded his army and left the empire to the Spaniards, now openly displayed their passions and turned their arms against one another, the first seeking to command and rule and the second to prevent him; for this is a calling that brooks no superior, or even an equal. Almagro bade Hernando Pizarro evacuate the city and leave it to him, since he knew that it fell within his administration and not Hernando's brother's. Almagro alleged that Cuzco fell within his domains, arguing that the 200 leagues belonging to the marquis should be measured from the equator southward along the seacoast, including the headlands and creeks the sea makes in the land, and if he wished to measure them in the interior, he should mark them off on the royal road from Quito to Cuzco. Almagro's friends put forward these measurements because the 200 leagues would not go further than Túmbez if taken along the coast, and although his majesty had granted Pizarro a further 100 leagues, this still fell short of Lima. The same effect would be produced by measuring inland, and even less; for it is commonly reckoned that it is 500 leagues from Quito to Cuzco. The marquis' jurisdiction thus fell short of Lima, and much more so of Cuzco, by either manner of reckoning; and this was Almagro's reason for saying that the government of the imperial city was his. He and his supporters had invented these measurements and irrelevant arguments so as to come hurrying back from Chile to Cuzco and Peru, where their return caused so many evils.

Hernando Pizarro, having sought the opinion of his companions, replied that he was not in Cuzco by Almagro's authority but by the governor's, who was his captain general and to whom he had taken an oath of loyalty not to deliver it to anyone else: he would not be fulfilling the laws of chivalry or his military obligations if he handed it over without his captain's orders and unless he were first freed from his oath. Let them write to the marquis; and if he countermanded his orders, he would at once hand the city over. But apart from this he said that the imperial city fell within his brother's jurisdiction, and put forward arguments against Almagro's and different calculations to disprove his. He pointed out that it was obviously unfair to measure the 200 leagues down the coast and to take in all capes, creeks, and bays, for an inlet of the sea in the land or a point of land projecting into the sea might take up half the distance allocated. This had been shown by experience on that very coast, taking into account the inlets and points between the Isle of Palms and Cape St. Francis. Neither was it fair to measure the leagues overland along the royal highway, since the road wound in and out owing to the rough nature of the country; and if a smoother route was sought to the east or west, without so many twists and turns, then the road would be broken by ravines with slopes 2, 3 or 4 leagues long up and down the mountainsides, when the distance as the crow flies was less than half a league from hill to hill. All this indicated that the reckoning should be made by degrees, as seamen measure distances at sea. The Pizarros insisted on this reckoning because it was only eleven degrees from the equator to Lima, and if each degree was reckoned as 17½ leagues, as seamen do, it would be 192½ leagues to Lima in a north and south direction, or 245 leagues to Cuzco, which is 14 degrees south. Hernando Pizarro thus claimed that both cities fell within the jurisdiction of the marquis, including the number of leagues added by His Majesty, though he did not say how many these were.

Almagro's companions argued that if the reckoning was to be as the crow flies, it should not be north and south, but east and west, where each degree is 80 leagues, and if this reckoning were not acceptable, then an average should be taken between the two kinds of sea leagues and each degree reckoned as 49 leagues, setting leagues of longitude off against leagues of latitude. In this way the marquis' jurisdiction would only stretch 6 degrees south of the equator, at 49 leagues to the degree. Whichever of the three ways of reckoning the Pizarros might choose, Cuzco and also Lima would remain outside their jurisdiction.

Each side kept up its demands and replies for many days, and they would often have come to blows but for Diego de Alvarado, who was a very noble and wise and prudent gentleman, an uncle of the *adelantado* Don Pedro de Alvarado and of Gómez de Alvarado, who had gone to Chile with Almagro. He desired to see peace and concord established between the governors, foreseeing the harm that could befall them all if they resorted to force, and he acted as mediator between them. After many attempts he at last persuaded Hernando Pizarro to write to his brother the marquis in the sense Almagro demanded, each side to remain peacefully in its quarters until a reply was received. A truce was made to this effect, and peace reigned for some days. But discord, which desired an end of the peace that had hitherto existed between them, now roused its myrmidons and inspired them to tell Almagro that he was wrong to accept terms and seek his rival's consent to what the emperor had granted him as his own. They told him that Hernando would not write to his brother as they had agreed, for fear of being dispossessed from his government of the city; and if he did, his brother would not reply, for fear of alienating so important a place as the imperial city. And having given their word and agreed that they would stay where they were until the marquis replied, he could keep them dangling all their lives. It was public knowledge that Cuzco was in his jurisdiction, so let him take possession of it and not await the consent of his rivals, for it would be wonderful indeed if they willingly gave up so great and rich a prize. He ought rather to think what was at stake and take such steps as were necessary forthwith. Almagro needed few sparks to kindle the powder that was laid up in his soul and readily accepted the urgings of his evil companions—for such counsels never proceed from good advisers—and hastened to put them into action without waiting to consult his true friends.

One dark night he went with an armed band to the lodging of Hernando and Gonzalo Pizarro, who were off their guard as a result of the truce, despite the fact that a little before one of Almagro's followers had come to them and said that he intended to arrest them. Hernando Pizarro had then answered that this was impossible, for Almagro was a gentleman and would not break the word he had given in his truce. At this the noise of people was heard, and the man who had come to warn the Pizarros said: "Well, since you don't believe, here they are."

The Pizarros and their guests and servants hastily picked up their arms and began to defend the gates of their lodging which had been repaired since the Inca's departure, like many of the other places where the Spaniards were dwelling in the city. Almagro's companions could not get in and therefore set fire to the house on all sides. Those within surrendered to save themselves from burning to death. Hernando and Gonzalo and many of their kinsmen and friends from Extremadura were captured. They were all put in a very small apartment in Cassana, and closely shackled so as to keep them quite safe. The ministers of discord persuaded Almagro to kill Hernando Pizarro, bidding him remember how Hernando had shown himself his enemy since he first arrived from Spain, and had never spoken well of him, and was a tough and vengeful man, of a very different character from his brothers, and would avenge himself when he could, and that such a man was better out of the way. Almagro was about to do this, but Diego and Gómez de Alvarado, Juan de Saavedra, Bartolomé de Terrazas, Vasco de Guevara, Hierónimo de Costilla, and others, who were of noble character and partisans of peace and friendship, dissuaded him, saying that it would be wrong to break altogether with the marquis, when they had been such good companions in the past. To return to uphold his reputation and take possession of his governorship was right enough, though he had put himself in the wrong in breaking the recent truce. But if he killed Hernando Pizarro, everyone would regard it as a detestable crime, and it would be accounted a very shameful act on his part. He should think what he was doing, and take counsel with reason and prudence and not with wrath and vengeance, which would lead him to a dangerous cliff. With such and similar arguments these gentlemen calmed Almagro. He made the city council take the oath to him as governor of the city and a territory of a hundred leagues, according to His Majesty's authorization. Here we shall leave him and turn to other events that occurred at the same time.

CHAPTER XXXII

Hardships undergone by Garcilaso de la Vega
and his companions in the discovery
of Buenaventura.

WE HAVE mentioned how Pizarro, on finding himself besieged and faced with the Indian rising, feared that his brothers in Cuzco and Almagro in Chile had all been butchered and sought help from Mexico, Nicaragua, Panama, Santo Domingo, and the other Windward Islands; and that he also instructed his captains Alonso de Alvarado, Sebastián de Belalcázar, Garcilaso de la Vega, and Juan Porcel to give up the conquests in which they were engaged and come to his help, for they must all rally together to resist the might of the Indians.

Alonso de Alvarado was the first of these to appear, since he was the nearest; but he could not arrive until after the Indians had relaxed the siege of Lima, and when he came they abandoned it altogether. Captain Sebastián de Belalcázar and Juan Porcel, the captain of the Bracamoros, did not come because the governor's orders did not reach them, the Indian messengers having been killed. Garcilaso de la Vega appeared soon after Alvarado, returning from the bay called Santa Marta [San Mateo?] and La Buenaventura, where, as we have said, he had had a difficult time since the land is uninhabitable. He and his men suffered great privations in the incredible forests there are in those parts, which are denser and harder to pierce than a wall, for the trees are so thick that eight or ten men cannot put their arms round one, and their wood is extremely difficult to cut. And between them there is such a quantity of bushes and smaller trees that the forest is rendered too dense for men or beasts to pass, nor is fire of any avail in these forests, since it is perpetually raining.

At first, at the beginning of this conquest, they thought they would find Indians in the interior, and they therefore advanced as best they could, forcing a way by the strength of their arms, and climbing and descending along the watercourses which served as a road for them, as indeed such streams still serve in the forests, for the force of the water prevents the trees from growing in them. Amidst these hardships they travelled for many days. The Indian servants they had brought from Peru often told them to turn back, for they were lost and there were no inhabitants for leagues in that region, which the Inca kings had never settled, regarding it as uninhabitable. But the Spaniards refused to believe them and thought they were decrying these regions so as to be able to return to their own. They persisted and travelled over a hundred leagues, suffering greatly from hunger and maintaining themselves on herbs and roots, toads, snakes, and any other creatures they could kill, which they said were as good as rabbits and hares in the straits they found themselves in. They found the big snakes less bad to eat than the small.

After this long and difficult journey, finding their hardships grow daily greater, intensified by the pangs of hunger, the officers of the army and the representatives of the royal treasury went to the captain and told him that it was clear from long experience that the trials of the discovery were unbearable, and that as they had been five months among those forests without seeing an Indian to conquer, or any land to till or settle, or anything at all but undergrowth and rivers, lakes, and streams, and constant rain, it would be well if he looked to his own safety and that of his followers, for he had persisted so long that it looked as if he deliberately meant to kill them and himself with starvation and misery. He should return, and persevere no longer in a journey of such manifest danger.

The captain replied that he had realized for many days what they had told him about the difficulties of the conquest, and he would have left the forests two months after they had entered them, except that his respect for his own honor and that of all the rest of them had led him to persist thus far; and it still urged him to press on with the quest, lest their rivals should say they wanted to return to the fat sheep and wealth of Peru. He begged and urged them not to turn their backs on their task, for the greater the difficulties they had undergone, the greater would be the honor and fame they would enjoy. This was the prize of victory: let them seek to gain it like good soldiers, striving until they were successful, or at least until they had deprived slanderers of any excuse to wrong them, for they would do so if they returned so soon. The sufferings of each of them pained him as much as they did the victim, and he did not flee; he begged them to follow him as their captain, which their military discipline and nobility as Spaniards obliged them to do.

With these words those good soldiers gave way, and went on with their quest. They continued the discovery almost three months more; but their hardships became so unbearable that their health gave way. Many Span-

iards and Indians fell sick, and many died, of hunger more than of anything else. Seeing that the number of sick and dead was daily increasing
and that they could get no further, they all agreed by common consent to
return, not by the road by which they had come, but by turning east and
then south, hoping that by taking this course they would come across some
Indians within the area and at least to have explored it all to their greater
satisfaction. They passed through some more forests, no better than the
last, but worse if that were possible. Their hunger increased, and with it
the number of deaths. They killed the poorer horses so as to relieve the
sick and hungry. What they regretted most was that most of those who
perished did so because they were too weak to walk, and they had to be
abandoned in the forests, since they could not help one another, all being
in the same plight. They left eleven dead one day, and thirteen another.
When hunger and weakness overcame them, they found their lower jaw
dropping so that they could not close their mouths, and so when they
abandoned a man they said, "Remain with God," and the unfortunate
man would reply, "Go with God," but could not pronounce the words,
and only moved his tongue. These details were told by common report
and also by a soldier called ———— de Torralva. I heard him more than
once and he wept as he spoke, and said he wept with grief to remember
how they had left their comrades alive, for if they had left them dead, he
would not have remembered them. In this way more than eighty Spaniards
died of hunger, without counting the Indians of whom many more
perished.

They had the greatest trouble in crossing the rivers called the Quiximíes, for the wood they cut for rafts was useless and sank in the water,
being heavy and green. The rivers had no fords, and were very full and
rough, with many of the lizards they call caimans, twenty-five or thirty
feet long and very dangerous in the water, for they are carnivorous. The
rafts were made of branches lashed together, and so they managed to
cross, though with the difficulty that can well be imagined. At one of
these rivers as they were looking for a place to cross they chanced to find
two large trees, one facing the other on opposite sides of the stream with
thick branches intertwined above it. They thought they would cut away
part of the foot of the tree on their side so that it would fall on the other
tree and they could thus make a bridge. It turned out as they hoped, and
all the Spaniards and Indians crossed in single column, in groups of three
or four, clutching the branches as best they could. In the last group there
were six men left, three Indians and three Spaniards, including the captain, who wanted to be the last to cross. The Indians were sent first,

carrying their arms and those of two of the Spaniards and two saddles, and thus they all crossed. But when they reached the top of the fallen tree and were near the standing one, it gave a great crack and the part they had left uncut came apart at the trunk. The two Spaniards and three Indians firmly gripped their branches; but the captain, who realized the danger quickest, leapt over his companions and managed to seize a branch of the standing tree, though he pulled it down with his weight and was submerged under the water. Those who were clinging to the other tree were also plunged into the river and reappeared no more. Two or three of the captain's group who were waiting on the other side held out their lances when they saw them in such danger. The captain was aware of this and clutched one of them. The man holding it called two more and the three of them pulled him ashore, giving thanks to God for saving him from death.

On this journey wherever they found any store of food, such as wild fruit or roots better than the usual, they stopped two or three days to collect them, and take them with them where there were none. At one of these halts, after they had been more than a year in these forests, the captain climbed one day up a high hill near his camp, full of distress at his and his companions' ordeal, and hoping to see some way out of their prison from the hilltop. And as the undergrowth was so dense and high that it was impossible to see the land even on top of the hill, he climbed one of the biggest trees, which are like high towers. From here he could see these forests stretching a great way on all sides, but there seemed to be no way out. While he was watching he saw a great band of parrots pass, chattering loudly. He noticed they were going straight ahead between east and south, or southeast, as sailors say. After a long flight they all suddenly came down to the ground. The captain calculated how far it would be from where he was to where they were, and guessed it would be six or seven leagues, and thought that as parrots are very fond of maize, there might be some where they had dropped. With these feeble hopes he took careful note of the place so as not to lose the direction, and returned to his men, telling them to make a great effort, for he saw signs that they might soon find cultivated land. They were all encouraged, and next day left that place, and cut their way most of the eight leagues between this and the other point. This took them thirty days, at the end of which they found a little Indian village of about a hundred houses, with plenty of corn and other vegetables, and good land capable of supporting many more people than there were. They gave thanks to God for getting them out of that desperate maze.

When the Indians saw men with beards, most of whom were naked, for their clothes had rotted away from being constantly wet and the best dressed of them had leaves or barks of trees instead of loincloths, they were astonished at the sight, and more so when they beheld the horses, a few of which had avoided being eaten. They began to call one another to take to the hills, but when the newcomers made signs to them not to be afraid they soon lost their fear, and called their cacique who was in the fields. He received them very kindly and with great regret at seeing them naked, full of burrs and twigs, and as weak and pale as dead men. He entertained them like brothers, and gave them clothes from among their own cotton blankets. He became so attached to them, and especially to their captain that he begged them not to leave his country, or if they did to take him with them to theirs.

They stopped thirty days there and would have stopped longer, such was their need, but in order not to waste all those poor Indians' food—which they gave with good will—they left that land as soon as they had refreshed themselves a little. They did not find out what it was called, for they were more concerned to escape than to ask names. The cacique left with them to escort and guide them and took thirty Indians laden with the food they could collect, which was very necessary for the wilderness they had to cross. The presence of the Indians was of great help in getting them over one of the great rivers they still had to cross for they made rafts and could sail them better than the Spaniards. So they came to the first valley in the district of Puerto Viejo. The cacique and his Indians then returned with many tears on taking leave of the Spaniards, and in particular of the captain, to whom he had become greatly attached on account of his kindness.

The Spaniards reached Puerto Viejo. There were little more than 160 of them, for 80 or more had died of hunger out of 250 who had left on that conquest. In Puerto Viejo they heard about the Inca's rising, but could not learn anything about the course of events. With this news they hastened to reach Lima. On the way they found the marquis' orders that they were to return and succor him, whereupon they doubled the length of their daily march and reached Lima some days after Captain Alonso de Alvarado. They were received with great relief by the marquis, on account of the pressing need in which he found himself.

CHAPTER XXXIII

Alonso de Alvarado goes to succor Cuzco;
the events of the journey.

As SOON as the marquis had received the succor of these two captains, Alonso de Alvarado and Garcilaso de la Vega, he gave orders for help to be sent to his brothers. He was still ignorant of all that had happened in Cuzco, both of the withdrawal of Prince Manco Inca and of the return of Almagro from Chile and the arrest of his brothers. He prepared 300 men from the best of those brought back by the captains and those he already had with him: 120 were horsemen and 180 foot. He appointed Alonso de Alvarado general in place of Pedro de Lerma of Burgos, who had held the office since the Inca's rising and had proved a good captain and a good soldier, fighting bravely whenever necessary, and losing his teeth by a blow with a stone in a battle between Spaniards and Indians, as we have said. Not content with removing Lerma from his office and giving it to another, Pizarro sent him with Alvarado, though naming him captain of the horse. The marquis was warned that this was careless or ill advised, and told that as he had deprived him of his office, it would be less insulting to keep him in Lima than to put him under his rival's orders: and Pedro de Lerma felt this more than the loss of his office, for both of them were from the same region and both were nobles. The natural arrogance and presumption of men more readily suffers a stranger as superior, even though he be of lower rank, than one from one's own country who is an equal. This jealousy later led to the ruin of the expedition, as we shall see. When the day of departure was at hand, Garcilaso de la Vega asked the marquis' permission to go with these captains and succor his brothers. The marquis bade him be patient; for he was thinking of sending more forces soon, and Garcilaso should go as their leader. Garcilaso replied saying that he would be glad if his lordship would let him go at once, for his spirit did not brook the idea of being among the second party when His Lordship's brothers were in peril, for they were all from the same region and all friends, and their friendship and common origin made it impossible'for him to delay: there would be no lack of officers for the next expedition. With this the marquis gave him leave to accompany Alvarado.

It was decided to take the coastal road as far as Nanasca so as to avoid the many difficult places on the mountain road. Four leagues from Lima, in the beautiful valley of Pachacámac, they had a very bloody battle with the Indians who were still in revolt, even though their prince had already retired into the forests. As the Indians had so far been successful against the bands that had gone to relieve Cuzco, they attacked Alonso de Alvarado with great spirit and fought fiercely for a long while. But many Indians were killed; for they always had the worst of it when there were no mountains or forests where they could defend themselves from the horses, and did better on rugged terrain. Nevertheless they killed eleven Spaniards and seven horses in this battle. Thence Alonso de Alvarado pressed on, and was in such a haste that he travelled all day, though his Indians tried to dissuade him, saying that it was impossible to cover those barren sands by day, but that they should be crossed by night, for the sands were wide and the sun strong, and travellers underwent the danger of thirst unless they carried supplies of water. The Spaniards refused to believe this, thinking that the Indians were hanging back because the expedition was against their Inca, and threatened them with death if they did not make haste. The Indians humbly obeyed, and at the end of that day's march, at about one in the afternoon, they and the Spaniards were sorely tried by the drought. The Indians, being burdened, felt it most, and more than five hundred of them collapsed, unable to stand anymore. The same would have happened to the Spanish foot, had not the horsemen, realizing that there was a river not far away, galloped to it and fetched a supply of water, as Zárate says in his Book III, ch. vi, in the following words: "And when Alonso de Alvarado continued his way toward Cuzco, he suffered greatly in crossing a desert, where more than five hundred of his Indian servants died of thirst; and if his horse had not run to fetch jars of water to succor the foot, it is thought that they would all have perished, such was their state of exhaustion," etc.

Thus Zárate. The lack of the Indians who perished caused them to stop until more were obtained to carry the burdens. And in order to avoid another such emergency, they left the desert road and made for the mountains, where they were joined by two hundred more men, seventy horse and the rest on foot, who had been sent by the marquis under Gómez de Tordoya de Vargas, a close relative of Garcilaso de la Vega. With these reinforcements Alvarado had five hundred men, with whom he continued to advance and fought with the enemy, who now dared to bar the way as the ground was rough. But the Spaniards, having learned from the experiences of the previous contingents which had been slaughtered by the Indians, proceeded carefully lest they should suffer any misfortune. They thus reached a bridge called Rumichaca, "stone bridge," where the Indians made a last attempt to try their strength, as the place was a difficult one. They held many points at which to resist the Spaniards, and the latter sent bands of forty or fifty arquebusiers to take them. These bands were accompanied by large parties of Indians who guided the Spaniards and took the enemy in the rear and diverted him while the Spaniards went by. Innumerable Indians invaded the bridge and fought with great valor. The Spaniards did likewise, and after the battle had lasted many hours they prevailed with great losses to the Indians, on account of the arquebuses, which numbered more than a hundred. These were aimed at the enemy in the narrow passes and gorges: and if it had not been for them, the Indians would have had the advantage at the place, since the Spaniards could not use their horses. But the arquebusiers opened fire and won the victory, though twenty-eight Spaniards and nine horses were lost, as well as many Indian servants, as López de Gómara says in his ch. cxxxviii:

Alvarado travelled without difficulty to Lumichaca, the bridge of stone, with five hundred Spaniards. There a multitude of Indians attacked, hoping to kill the Christians as they crossed, or at least worst them. But Alvarado and his friends, though surrounded on all sides by the enemy, fought so well that they won the victory and killed many Indians. These battles cost many Spanish lives and many of those of the friendly Indians who acted as servants and auxiliaries,

etc. These words are taken from the imperial chaplain.

From Rumichaca, Alonso de Alvarado advanced, still fighting the Indians, who though battered and losing refused to learn from experience and attacked the Spaniards wherever there was a difficult or dangerous point on the road, hoping at least to molest them, if they could not defeat them. The attacks no longer led to pitched battles as at first, but they did not fail to cause losses on both sides. They thus travelled twenty leagues to the bridge of Amáncay, where Alonso de Alvarado learnt from the Indians of the Inca's retreat, the arrival of Almagro, the arrest of Hernando Pizarro and the death of Juan Pizarro and the others who had fallen in the siege, together with other news, of all of which he had been in ignorance. He thought, with the opinion of his friends, that he had better not go on until he had fresh orders from the marquis, to whom he reported what had happened. And in case Almagro should attack him, he fortified himself and collected what supplies he could.

When Almagro heard that Alvarado was at the bridge of Amáncay with an army, he sent him a message by Diego de Alvarado and eight other gentlemen of the noblest who were with him proposing peace and friendship, and saying that as it was common knowledge that His Majesty had made him governor of Cuzco, Alonso de Alvarado should go away and leave him in peace: if not, the blame for the death and destruction that might follow would lie at his door. Alonso de Alvarado arrested the messengers as soon as he had heard them and then told them that this warning should have been conveyed to the marquis and not to him: he was not authorized to do what they asked without orders from the governor. Garcilaso de la Vega, Pero Alvarez Holguín, Gómez de Tordoya, and other prominent men in his army pressed him to release the messengers so that they could convey their request to the marquis, reminding him that messengers and ambassadors were regarded as privileged and exempt from harm by all nations of the world, even the most barbarous, and even in the midst of cruel wars and discords. They added that this was the surest way to increase and kindle the fires of passion that already existed between the two governors, rather than to quell them. They urged him to recall that they had all come to conquer the empire and that it was wrong for them to kill one another over the division of the spoils instead of enjoying the fruits of their labors in peace and quiet, and that the whole world would curse and abominate them for this deed and for the discord they themselves were fomenting among themselves. But Alonso de Alvarado refused to hear their arguments. On the contrary, he persevered in what he had begun with all his natural ruthlessness, to the great discontent of his men, who all desired to enjoy in peace and friendship those fruits of Peru that had already cost them so many labors and so much hardship.

CHAPTER XXXIV

The battle of the river Amáncay and capture of Alonso de Alvarado and his followers.

WHEN ALMAGRO, who had left Cuzco behind his messengers, saw that they did not return in due time, he suspected some untoward result and retired to the city, where he remained in some trepidation and perplexity about the outcome. His fears were due to the fact that Alonso de Alvarado had more men with better arms than his, and that he could not rely on many of his followers who had been on the side of Hernando Pizarro and would repudiate him when they saw others of their own party. It was therefore dangerous for him to risk an engagement. He also thought that the gate of peace had been shut with the arrest of his messengers.

While Almagro was harassed by these anxieties and fears and did not know what line to take, he received letters from Captain Pedro de Lerma, who felt aggrieved by the marquis for the reasons we have given and seeing an opportunity offer itself for vengeance, now wrote to Almagro revealing all that was in his breast and informing him of the resentment amongst Alvarado's men caused by his harsh nature and his arrest of the ambassadors, an action that all had condemned. Let Almagro not hesitate to stand up for his fame and honor; for he, Lerma, would help him to regain them with great ease. He could assure him that he had a hundred friends on his side who would go over to him as soon as they saw him at hand, and he hoped to bring the rest over to loyalty to him, for they were very dissatisfied with their captain. At this news Almagro took courage, and having laid in supplies, which took over a fortnight, he left Cuzco in search of Alvarado, capturing Pedro Alvarez Holguín, who had been sent to scout and find out Almagro's intentions, on the way. It was easy to take him, for most of those with him had given their pledge to Pedro de Lerma. Most of those left with Alonso de Alvarado had taken the same step; and when he knew of Holguín's capture, he tried to arrest Pedro de Lerma, because as López de Gómara says in his ch. cxxxviii: "he spoke too freely and came from Burgos, and knew Alvarado." These are López de Gómara's very words. Lerma had instant information of Alvarado's most secret counsels and now fled with some of his friends, almost without concealment, for he had established such an ascendancy over the men that if he had waited four days more he could have taken them all. He told Almagro to hasten and have no fear of victory; for he had made sure of it with the men who had remained. And he arranged what was to be done and how and where and when the attack was to be made, as he had planned. He said it must take place at night, for that was the sinners' cloak. He personally led them to the bridge where he knew many of the confederates would be, and he sent the cavalry across the ford, telling them that they would cross in safety.

They thus went forward with great expectations of victory; and though Alvarado and his officers gave the necessary orders to fight and defend themselves, they were not obeyed. As it was night and most of them were in the plot, the horsemen pretended their lances had been stolen and flung in the river and the foot soldiers that their arquebuses, crossbows, and pikes had been hidden; and though none of this was true, they failed to respond to their captains' orders, and fled in disorder wherever they wished. And those who came out to defend the bridge and the ford, instead of fighting, told Almagro's men to cross without fear; for they could be sure of the bridge and the ford and surer still of the men. And as Almagro's men dared not enter the river, since it was night and they did not know the ford, their opponents went in to show them the way. The same happened at the bridge, where they were invited and persuaded to pass without fear. In this way Almagro won the day, and captured Alonso de Alvarado, Garcilaso de la Vega, Gómez de Tordoya, and Captain Villalva, and the other captains and officials, as well as a hundred soldiers who had not joined the plot. This occurred without a casualty on either side, except that Rodrigo de Orgoños paid for them all when a stray stone flung by an unknown hand broke his teeth. Almagro and his friends returned full of pride and victory to Cuzco and spoke very freely against the Pizarros, saying they would not leave a *pizarra,* or slate, to trip over in all Peru, and if they wanted something to govern they could go and govern the mango swamps and forests on the seacoast under the equator. The suspects were imprisoned, and as they were numerous they were divided between two jails, some being taken to the fortress, while others were left in the house called Cassana in the city.

As to the marquis Don Francisco Pizarro, having sent Alvarado and soon after Gómez de Tordoya to succor his brothers, he stayed in Lima collecting the men who were coming in from all sides in response to his appeal, as López de Gómara says in his ch. cxxxvii:

Alonso de Fuenmayor, president and bishop of Santo Domingo, sent his brother Diego de Fuenmayor, a native of Yanguas, with many Spanish arquebusiers who had just arrived with Pedro de Vergara. Hernán Cortés sent Rodrigo de Grijalva from New Spain in one of his own ships with a quantity of arms, cannon, harnesses, gear, silk clothes, and a sable robe. Licentiate Gaspar de Espinosa sent a good company of Spaniards from Panama, Nombre de Dios, and Tierra Firme, and Diego de Ayala brought back a good number from Nicaragua and Guatemala. Others also came from elsewhere and in this way Pizarro had a fine army with more arquebusiers than ever before; and though they were not very necessary against the Indians, they proved of infinite value against Almagro, as we shall say,

etc. Thus López de Gómara.

When the marquis found himself at the head of such a large and excellent army, consisting, according to Zárate, of over seven hundred Spanish horse and foot, he decided to go personally to his brothers' help to relieve the anxiety that is usually caused by waiting for news from a distance.
He marched out with his people along the coastal road, and after a few
days received Alvarado's message about the retreat of the Inca, Almagro's
return, and the arrest of his brothers, and death of the third of them,
which greatly grieved the marquis. And to give him more to weep about,
he received two days later the second report of the loss of his army and
capture of Alvarado, which caused him indescribable sorrow. As the force
he had with him was better equipped for fighting against Indians than
against Spaniards, he decided to return to Lima, though he had already
gone twenty-five leagues, and to equip himself with arms and gear specially for his new undertaking. He also thought he would try the door
of peace and concord, for having received two adverse strokes of fortune, he feared a third. When he saw his rival surrounded by many men,
with plenty of arms and horses, he began to wish to put out the fire of
passion and restore their previous partnership and brotherly association,
which they had ratified by so many oaths. And as they had won that great
and rich empire as partners and friends, he began to hope that they might
enjoy it in the same way and not slay one another on the threshold of their
old age.

With this in mind he sent Licentiate Espinosa to Cuzco to see if he
could make some accommodation between him and Almagro. Among
other things the marquis told him to remind Almagro that if His Majesty
knew what had happened, and that the governors had failed to agree,
and were full of passion against one another, he would send another
governor in place of both of them, who would thus without stirring a
step enjoy what they had won with such hardship and at such cost in
blood and treasure. A good peace was better than a bad war, and though
the saying was usually the reverse, in their case it sounded better so.
Finally the marquis told Espinosa that if he could not obtain anything
else, he was to persuade Almagro to release his brothers and to remain
himself in Cuzco and not advance on Lima, governing that city for the
time being until His Majesty knew what had taken place and decided
what each of them was to have.

Espinosa went off with this mission and laid the proposals before
Almagro and his captains; but they were puffed up with pride and might
after their recent victories and would accept no terms. Although Diego de

Alvarado, with his usual discretion and good sense, reminded them that the terms offered were what they themselves had been asking for hitherto since they were allowed free enjoyment and possession of Cuzco, they turned down his advice, and replied that they would have no limits imposed on them and not be told they were not to advance on Lima. In their own jurisdiction and in their situation of strength and good fortune, they would not obey other people's laws or accept conditions, but make them. And although Diego de Alvarado replied that the conditions were so favorable that it seemed almost as if they had set them and not received them, they refused to heed him. It is noteworthy that until then each of the governors had asked the other to relinquish Cuzco and to accept the whole area outside the narrow valleys as his jurisdiction, the one to the north and the other to the south. And now that Almagro was offered it, he refused to accept it, thinking that as he already had the city in his possession, the fact that his rival was now willing to offer him it, though he had coveted it so much before, was proof that Pizarro was afraid of losing his whole jurisdiction. And as fortune favored him with flags unfurled, he preferred to follow it as far as it led and see if he might not enjoy the whole empire to himself. Stirred by these insatiable passions of ambition and covetousness, Almagro refused to accept the terms the governor offered him.

This attitude was contributed to by the sudden death of Espinosa, who died at the height of the negotiations before he could conclude them. His judgment, prudence, and good counsel gave promise of a satisfactory result, but death prevented him from seeing the fruit of his efforts and desires, and God too in his mysterious designs denied him it. Espinosa died prophesying the death and destruction of both governors, seeing their reluctance to recognize what was to their own advantage. Almagro left Cuzco at the head of his army, as a sign that he rejected the conditions the marquis had sent. He left Gabriel de Rojas as his deputy in the city with charge of all the prisoners, who numbered more than 150, including the first group taken with Hernando Pizarro and the second with Alonso de Alvarado, divided between two prisons, as we have said.

Almagro took Hernando Pizarro with him, not daring to leave him with the rest lest he should escape. He went by the coastal road, left the district of Cuzco and entered that of Lima reaching the valley of Chincha, a little over twenty leagues from Lima, where he founded a settlement as a sign of possession, indicating and even proving that he claimed both jurisdictions. He remained there with his army to see how the marquis would take this act of defiance, suggesting that if he did not like it, he should take up the challenge, and he, Almagro, would wait for him in the field like a good captain and accept the arbitrament of war.

CHAPTER XXXV

The marquis appoints captains for the war; Gonzalo Pizarro escapes from prison; the sentence of the judges on the question of the jurisdictions; the interview of the two governors and the release of Hernando Pizarro.

As soon as the marquis reached Lima, he prepared for the war he was expecting against Almagro. Drums were beaten and messages were sent along the coast with information about what had happened. New troops arrived daily, and as the army increased he appointed captains and officials. He made Pedro de Valdivia commander and Antonio de Villalva, the son of Colonel Villalva, sergeant major. Pero Ansúrez, Diego de Rojas, and Alonso de Mercadillo were appointed captains of horse, and Diego de Urbina, a native of Orduña and nephew to the commander Juan de Urbina, was made captain of the pikemen. Nuño de Castro and Pedro de Vergara (who had been a soldier in Flanders and brought a great band of arquebusses to the Indies with all the necessary ammunition) were made captains of the arquebusiers. These captains raised eight hundred picked men, six hundred on foot and two hundred horse, with which the marquis left Lima to meet Almagro, announcing that he was going to defend his rights as governor, which Almagro was trying to usurp.

While the affairs of the marquis and Almagro were proceeding in this way, the prisoners in Cuzco did not sleep, but sought the precious gift of liberty by all possible means. As everything can be bought in civil wars, especially the most important things, they found some who were ready to sell their loyalty to their captain Almagro and his deputy Gabriel de Rojas. They did not sell it for cash, but for credit, relying on the promises of Gonzalo Pizarro and Alonso de Alvarado, who were with fifty or sixty others in the prison of Cassana. The sellers were forty of the guards who left their own arms in the cells when they went to visit the prisoners, and removed the bolts from their shackles and chains. They also tried to find mounts for them, and as the other soldiers were their friends they were trusted with anything they asked for. When the prisoners and their allies were ready to slip away in the silence of the night, it happened that Gabriel de Rojas came to visit them very late, as he had on many previous nights. On opening the prison, he found that all the prisoners were loose, and he himself was the only captive; for they surrounded him and told him he must go with them or die on the spot. He had no other course but to agree to what they asked, or rather forced on him.

Thus about a hundred men went off to find the marquis. They could take the mountain road quite freely, for Almagro had gone by the coastal plains. There was no lack of malicious people who said that Gabriel de Rojas was in the plot with them; but they were deceived in their malice, for if he had been, he would not have left the others in the fortress in prison; they numbered nearly a hundred more, and included many of the first conquerors, such as Francisco de Villafuerte, Alonso de Mazuela, Mancio Serra de Leguíçamo, Diego de Maldonado, and Juan Julio de Hojeda, Tomás Vázquez, Diego de Trujillo, and Juan de Pancorvo, whom I knew and who had great allocations of Indians in Cuzco. In addition, Garcilaso de la Vega, Gómez de Tordoya, and Pero Alvarez Holguín remained in prison. It would have been a great victory if the plotters had carried them all off, but it turned out as I have said. The marquis was full of joy at the arrival of his brother and his friends, for he feared that his enemies might have been stirred by wrath and spite to slay them. He was also glad to see how his men took heart on receiving these excellent reinforcements. He made Gonzalo Pizarro general of the infantry and Alonso de Alvarado general of the cavalry. Many horsemen became foot soldiers, so as to call themselves Gonzalo de Pizarro's men, for he was much beloved, even by his opponents.

When Almagro knew the size and quality of the marquis' force, and heard of the freeing of his prisoners and the capture of his deputy, he found his anticipated victory snatched from his hands. Before he should lose it altogether, he asked for terms, regretting now that he had not accepted the conditions offered earlier. He therefore sent three gentlemen, Don Alonso Enríquez, the factor Diego Núñez de Mercado, and the treasurer Juan de Guzmán, who were officials of His Majesty's treasury, and who were to go with full powers. He chose them because, as servants of his royal master, they could decide dispassionately what befitted the interests of the crown. The marquis received them, and they all discussed many important conditions together, but they could not agree on some points. The marquis therefore suggested that they should refer to a person of legal training and good conscience, and that they should abide by his verdict. Almagro accepted this and they agreed to stand by the decision of Fray Francisco de Bobadilla, provincial of the Order of Mercy in those parts. Here our authors differ, for Zárate mentions only this religious, and López de Gómara names another, who he says was nominated by Almagro and called Fray Francisco Husando. Whether there were two judges or one, both historians agree on the decision, using the same words. Zárate says in his Book III, ch. viii:

Fray Francisco exercised his power of judgment and decided first that Hernando Pizarro should be released and Cuzco restored to the marquis' possession, as it had been at first. The armies should be disbanded and the companies sent out as then constituted to make new discoveries in various directions, while His Majesty was informed of all the circumstances so that he might take what steps he thought fit. And in order that the marquis and Almagro might meet and converse, he arranged that they should appear each attended by twelve horsemen at a village called Malla, which was between the two armies. They thus came to the interview, though Gonzalo Pizarro, not trusting the terms of the truce or Almagro's word, at once followed with the whole army and took up positions secretly near the village. He then ordered Captain Castro to make an ambush with forty arquebusiers in a canebrake on the road along which Almagro would pass, with orders that, if Almagro brought more men than had been agreed, they were to let off their arquebusses and he would come up at the signal.

This is Zárate's version, and he says nothing of Almagro, though López de Gómara gives the following account of him in his ch. cxl:

Almagro said that he would be glad to see Pizarro, though he thought the verdict a very harsh one. On leaving for the interview with twelve friends, he recommended his general Rodrigo Orgoños that the army should be prepared in case Pizarro did anything, and they should kill Hernando Pizarro, who was in their power, if any force were brought against him. Pizarro went to the agreed place with twelve others, and Gonzalo came up behind him with the whole army. I do not think anyone knew whether he did this with his brother's consent or without it. What is sure is that he stationed himself near Malla and bade Captain Núñez [Nuño?] de Castro make an ambush with his forty arquebusses in a canebrake near the road by which Almagro must pass. Pizarro reached Malla first, and when Almagro came up they embraced cheerfully and spoke of agreeable things. One of Pizarro's men went up to Almagro before the business began and whispered to him to go away, for his life depended on it. He then rode off and turned back without saying a word about this matter or the business in hand. He saw the ambush of arquebusiers and believed what he had been told. He railed bitterly against Pizarro and the friars, and all his followers said that no sentence so unjust had been given since Pilate's day. Pizarro, though advised to capture him, let him go; he had given Almagro his word; he protested greatly that he had not ordered his brother to come up and had not bribed the friars.

Here López de Gómara ends his chapter; and Zárate gives the same account of the interview.

In his next chapter López de Gómara says:

Although the interview was in vain and led only to greater hatred and indignation on both sides, there were those who tried sincerely and dispassionately to bring about an understanding between Pizarro and Almagro. Diego de Alvarado at last arranged that Almagro should release Hernando Pizarro and that the marquis should give Almagro a ship and a safe port, which he lacked, so as to be able to send his reports and messengers to Spain. Neither was to attack the other before new instructions had been received from the emperor. Almagro then released Hernando on his oath, which was guaranteed by Diego de Alvarado, though Orgoños was greatly opposed to this and suspected some harm would result from Hernando's harsh nature. Almagro himself soon repented of the idea and wished to arrest him again, but he made his mind up too late.

Everyone said that Hernando Pizarro would stir up everything again, and they were not mistaken, for when he was set free, there were great new disturbances. Pizarro himself was not very sincere in the negotiations; for he had received a royal order in which the emperor bade each of them remain where he was when he received the order, even though he might be in the territory and jurisdiction of the other. Once Pizarro had freed his brother and had the benefit of his advice, he summoned Almagro to leave the land he, Pizarro, had discovered and settled, since new instructions had been received from the emperor. Almagro, having read these instructions, replied that he had heard and obeyed by remaining quietly in Cuzco and the other towns he then possessed, which was what the emperor required in the royal order. And the order further said that he was to be left in peaceful possession where he was. Pizarro replied that he had pacified and settled Cuzco, and Almagro had taken it from him by force, saying that it fell within his jurisdiction of New Toledo. He must therefore leave it and take his departure: if not, he, Pizarro, would expel him without in any way infringing his oath, for the arrival of the king's new instructions put an end to the agreement they had made. Almagro replied firmly and flatly.

Pizarro then led all his army to Chincha, taking his original captains and Hernando Pizarro as his adviser, and giving out that he was going to expel his enemies from Chincha, which lay clearly within his jurisdiction. Almagro returned toward Cuzco so as not to fight. However, as he was being followed, he shortened his journey and withdrew to Güitara, a high and rough range of mountains. Pizarro pursued him with a bigger and better force, and one night Hernando took the arquebusiers up into the mountains and took the pass. Almagro, who was ill, hastily retired leaving Orgoños behind to withdraw in good ·order without fighting. Orgoños did this, though Cristóbal de Sotelo and others said he would have done better to have fought the Pizarrists, who were suffering from mountain-sickness, as Spaniards usually do when they first leave the hot plains and go up to the snowy mountains, owing to the changes caused by the difference in altitude.

Thus Almagro collected his men and returned to Cuzco, breaking the bridges and forging weapons of silver and copper, and arquebusses and other firearms, and gathering supplies of food in the city and defending it with ditches,

etc. This is López de Gómara's account and Zárate says the same, though more briefly. And as these writers are obscure about some of the events just described, which they told in this way to avoid prolixity, I should make some comments on their account, which I will do in the following chapter, lest this should grow too long.

CHAPTER XXXVI

Comments on the foregoing; Hernando Pizarro attacks Almagro.

As we have said, Don Diego de Alvarado was an accomplished gentleman in all respects. He was a model of good sense and discretion, and therefore realized what would happen if the governors were swept ahead by their passions. He tried to bridle these passions, as we have seen in the events of the past and shall see in the present and future. When he saw that the sentence of the friars had increased the fires rather than damped them down, he acted as mediator, and sincerely tried to establish peace and concord between the marquis and Almagro, going repeatedly from one to the other. He did not stop until he had persuaded Almagro with good arguments to release Hernando Pizarro, and obtained a ship and a port from the marquis for Almagro. In order to establish this agreement, he made all three of them swear an oath of homage to him, and he acted as guarantor to both parties, undertaking to oblige each of them to respect their undertaking and fulfil the oaths they had taken as Christians and their words to him as gentlemen. For this reason López de Gómara says the agreement was made at Diego de Alvarado's instance: he was in fact both negotiator and guarantor. Orgoños was opposed to the release of Hernando Pizarro, and on seeing Almagro's decision and realizing that his arguments had not been accepted, he foretold Almagro's destruction, saying: "Your lordship has let the bull loose: he will attack you and kill you without respect for the fulfilment of his word and oath."

When López de Gómara says the Pizarrists were suffering from sickness, we should explain that both newcomers from Spain (called *chapetones* in the language of the Windward Islands) and those who are accustomed to the country (the *baquianos*), if they have spent long in the plains or seacoast, fall sick if they go back to the mountains. The sickness is like that of those who have newly gone to sea, but much worse; for they may be a day or two, according to their different natures, without being able to eat or drink or stand, but suffer from continuous vomiting, if they have anything to cast up. The snow is also painful to the eyes, and many are blinded by it for two or three days, and then recover their sight. The cause of this is said to be the change from so hot a region as the coastal plains to a very cold one like the snowy mountain range that stands between the coast and the interior. The distance is quite small, for in less than six hours one passes from one region to the other; this does not happen to those who go down from the mountains to the plains.

Padre Acosta writes of the sickness that affects people who go up into the mountains, and he gives a very scholarly and copious account of the causes and effects of it in Book III of his *Natural History of the Indies* (ch. ix), to which I refer anyone who wishes to see it. In view of this, it was good counsel that Cristóbal de Sotelo and others gave to Orgoños, that he should turn back and give battle, for the enemy were in such a bad state that they would easily be defeated. Zárate says:

Rodrigo de Orgoños refused to do this because it was against the governor's instructions, though it is thought that he would have succeeded if he had made the attempt since the marquis' men were suffering from sickness and from the great quantity of snow on the mountains, and were much the worse for their journey. Because of this, the marquis returned with his army to the plains and Almagro went to Cuzco,

etc. Thus Zárate.

Almagro had left orders with his captain general not to fight; for the two governors always desired a compromise in their claims and hoped to avoid open war, as can be seen from the interview they had in Cuzco before Almagro went to Chile, when they readily reached agreement, and the fire that had been kindled between them was easily extinguished. The same thing happened in the interview at Malla, as both historians say, for when they were about to meet, they both embraced in a friendly and cheerful way and spoke of agreeable things, despite all that had happened. But neither ever lacked evil counsellors and these never left them free to do as they wished, but forced them to come to the state of affairs they eventually reached—to come to blows and kill one another. Nor did the counsellors gain anything, but all shared in the fruits of their ill counsel, as usually happens in such cases.

Continuing with his story, Zárate says in his Book III, ch. xi:

While the marquis was with all his army on the plains, on his return from the mountains, he found that his people differed about what should be done next, and at length it was decided that Hernando Pizarro should go with the army that had been prepared, as the marquis' deputy in the city of Cuzco, taking his brother Gonzalo as his captain general. Their expedition was under pretext of obtaining justice for many of the *vecinos* of Cuzco who accompanied him and who had complained that Almagro had entered and occupied their houses by force and seized their allocations of Indians and other properties in the city of Cuzco. Thus the army departed and the marquis returned to Lima. When Hernando Pizarro at length reached the city one evening, all his captains were in favor of going down to the plains to sleep that night, but he himself would only establish his camp in the mountains. So when the next day dawned, Rodrigo Orgoños was already in the field, waiting for the battle, with all Almagro's men, including Francisco de Chaves, Juan Tello, and Vicencio de Guevara (this should be Vasco de Guevara; Francisco de Chaves was cousin to another of the same name, an intimate friend of the marquis) as captains of his horse. He had many Indian auxiliaries, as well as a few Spaniards, in the mountains, and held all the friends and servants of the marquis and his brothers who were in the city prisoner in two towers of the fortress of Cuzco, and they were so numerous and the room so small, that some were suffocated.

Next morning, after hearing mass, Gonzalo Pizarro and his men came down to the plain, where they entered their lines and marched toward the city, intending to occupy a height above the fortress; for they thought that when Almagro saw their full might he would not dare to offer battle, which they themselves wished to avoid by all means, because of the loss they expected to suffer. But Rodrigo Orgoños was on the royal highway with all his men and cannon in readiness, with very different thoughts.

Thus Zárate, and López de Gómara says the same. To this we may add something of what these authors omit, so as to throw more light on the story, for the events are worthy of note. First, for those who have never seen the place where the battle was fought, we should explain that it was a gross error to say that Pizarro's men intended to occupy a hill so as to dominate the fortress, for the battle took place on a plain the Indians call Cachipampa, "field of salt," which is more than a league south of the fortress, near a fine saline spring where the inhabitants of the city and its surroundings make salt in some great pans which are built down the stream and lie between the city and the battlefield. Because the battle took place so near this it was called the battle of Las Salinas.

Orgoños ranged his men in formation, determined to die rather than show weakness, though he saw and realized the great force of men and arquebusses his opponents had. He had fought in Italy and had won a single combat on horseback there, for he was an excellent soldier. And as a good soldier, he had resented deeply a message Hernando Pizarro had sent him two days before as a challenge, saying that he, Hernando, and a companion would enter the battle on horseback, armed with coats of mail and cuirasses and would each wear slashed doublets of orange velvet over their mail. This message was sent as a warning in case he or anyone else wanted to seek out Hernando Pizarro, whom they would know by these signs. Hernando Pizarro sent this message because he was angry at some things that had happened while he was under arrest, which he regarded as insulting to his person. Orgoños took it as a challenge to a pitched battle, and called on Captain Pedro de Lerma, who, as we have said, had a grudge against the Pizarros and had offended them in the fight of Amáncay. Orgoños told Lerma:

"Our enemy is so full of himself that he is already singing victory over us, for this is what he means by sending us the description of himself. He has no doubts of his victory, and we cannot very well deprive him of it, for our strength is as small as our spirit is great. We can however make sure that he does not enjoy his victory, or live to see it. There are two of them with this description; let us see to it that both of them die at our hands; we shall thus avenge our own deaths and the insults offered us."

Thus agreed, they prepared for the day of the battle, which was bitter and bloody, as we shall see in the following chapters.

CHAPTER XXXVII

The bloody battle of Las Salinas.

RODRIGO Orgoños, like the brave soldier he was, prepared his men early in the morning and set his infantry in formation, with bands of arquebusiers on either flank, though his arquebusses were few and those of the enemy many: it was this that defeated and destroyed him. His infantry captains were Cristóbal de Sotelo, Hernando de Alvarado, Juan de Moscoso, and Don Diego de Salinas. The horse were divided into two detachments; Juan Tello and Vasco de Guevara were in one and Francisco de Chaves and Ruy Díaz in the other. Orgoños, as leader, wished to be unattached, with his friend Pedro de Lerma, so as to control the battle; but his real intention was only to be free to range the field in search of Hernando Pizarro and fight him. He placed his artillery by the side of his battleline, where it might do the enemy much harm. He left a stream that runs through the plain and a small marsh in front of his lines, supposing that they would be serious obstacles to his opponents.

Pedro de Valdivia, who was commander, and Antonio de Villalva, sergeant major, arranged their forces on similar lines. Their main formation was flanked by very fine bands of arquebusses, which were to gain the day. Two squadrons of a hundred horse each were ranged against those of Orgoños. Hernando Pizarro with his friend, who was called Francisco de Barahona, led one of these squadrons, and Alonso de Alvarado the other. Gonzalo Pizarro, as general of the infantry, chose to fight on foot. Thus they advanced against Almagro, crossing the stream and marsh without opposition; for before doing so they had fired a volley of shot that did much damage, and even disordered the enemy so that his lines were easily broken, both infantry and cavalry withdrawing from their stations to get away from the arquebus fire. When Orgoños saw this, he lost hope of victory, and ordered his artillery to shoot. One ball entered the opposing squadron and hit five soldiers in a row, which so alarmed them that if four or five more such shots had been fired the whole squadron would have been put to flight. But Gonzalo Pizarro and Valdivia went to the fore and encouraged their soldiers, bidding them shoot their wire shot at the enemy's pikes where they would do much execution. Almagro's forces, for want of arquebusses, had been armed with pikes, and the Pizarrists wished to deprive them of them so that the horses could break their formation more easily. Two volleys broke more than fifty pikes, as Zárate and López de Gómara say.

For those who have not seen it, wire shot is made in the same moulds as ordinary shot. A *cuarta* or a *tercia* of iron wire is taken, and the end of each wire is twisted into a loop, like a small fish hook. One end of each wire is put in one half-mould and the other in the other half-mould. The half-moulds are divided by placing a piece of copper or iron sheet as thick as a sheet of paper in the middle. The molten lead is then poured on, and it sets round the hooks of the iron wire, and the ball comes out in two halves both attached to the wire. They are put together to load the arquebus, as if they were a whole ball, but they separate as they are fired, and cut anything they hit by means of the wire between them. Because of this cutting power they were used against pikes! as the historians say; for ordinary balls will not break as many pikes as these. They did not fire at the pikemen, whom they would not have hurt so much: they wanted to show the enemy the superiority their arquebusses gave them. This invention was brought to Peru from Flanders by Pedro de Vergara with the arquebusses he introduced. I saw some of them in my country, and have seen them and made them in Spain. I also knew in Peru a gentleman called Alonso de Loaisa, a native of Trujillo, who was wounded in this battle by one of these shot which broke his lower jaw with all its teeth and some of the molars. He was the father of Francisco de Loaisa who lives in Cuzco today, and is one of the few sons of the conquerors who enjoy their father's allocations. The invention of this wire shot must have been derived from the use of pieces of chain to increase the effect of artillery against the enemy.

To return to our account of the battle, when Rodrigo Orgoños and his friend Pedro de Lerma saw the havoc the arquebusses were doing, they attacked the squadron of cavalry in which Hernando Pizarro was, to see if they could kill him, which was what they desired, for they already saw the victory in the battle dropping into the enemy's hands. They ranged themselves in front of him and his companion who were easily distinguished by the doublets of orange velvet. They charged, and the others came out boldly to meet them. Rodrigo Orgoños, who carried his lance on a rest, faced Francisco de Barahona and struck him in the jaw-piece: in Peru, for lack of Burgundian helmets, horsemen wear these jaw-pieces on infantry helmets so as to protect their faces. The lance broke the jaw-piece, which was of silver and copper, and split open his head. Orgoños felled him, and passing on, drove his lance through another man's breast. He then pulled out his sword and went on performing miracles of bravery. But this did not last long, for he was wounded with a pellet from an arquebus in the forehead, and so lost his sight and strength.

Pedro de Lerma and Hernando Pizarro met with lances. As they were using light lances which are not held on a rest, we must explain how they wielded them. In those days and since, in all the civil wars the Spaniards have waged, they have made leather bags which are fastened by strong belts hanging from the front saddlebow and the horse's neck; the head of the lance is fixed in the bag and it is tucked under the arm like a lance rest. This led to very fierce encounters between Spaniards in the battles in Peru, for the blow carried all the weight of the rider and the horse. This was not necessary in fighting the Indians, who could be wounded with a blow of the arm without using a rest at all. After the first encounter, if the lance remained whole, it was taken out of the bag and used like a light lance. We give this detailed account of the weapons of offence and defence used in my country so that the reader may understand better what we are saying. To return to the duel between Hernando Pizarro and Pedro de Lerma, the lances were long and quivered more than the combatants would have wished, so they each aimed low. Hernando Pizarro wounded his opponent severely in the thigh, breaking his cuirass and the coat of mail he was wearing. Pedro de Lerma hit Pizarro's horse in the top of the forelock so that the iron point of the lance cut off some of the skin and broke the head-piece before crashing into the top of the front saddle-bow, which, though armoured, was dislodged and shifted from its place. The lance then passed on and broke the cuirass and mail and wounded Hernando Pizarro in the belly. The wound was not a mortal one, for the horse was carrried over by the force of the thrust and fell to the ground, thus saving its rider from death. Otherwise the lance would certainly have pierced him through.

Here both historians use almost the same words in praise of Orgoños' prowess. Zárate concludes his praise with these words: "And when Rodrigo Orgoños charged, they wounded him with a charge of shot in the forehead which pierced his helmet. After being wounded, he killed two men with his lance and thrust his sword down the throat of a servant of Hernando Pizarro's, thinking he was his master, for he was very well arrayed." Thus Zárate: here it may be observed that whoever gave him the account of this battle in Spain must have been on the opposite side from Hernando Pizarro, for in this particular he twisted the facts, saying that Hernando had dressed a servant in the dress and tokens he had said he would wear in the battle, so that those who were seeking for him would see the servant so decked and ignore him. This stigmatizes him as a coward and caitiff; and this aspersion was spread through Spain and reached Peru, and the Council of the Indies, in order to find out the truth of the matter, called a famous soldier who was at the battle fighting for Almagro, Gonzalo Silvestre by name, and asked him, among other things, if Hernando Pizarro was regarded as a coward in Peru. Although this soldier was on the opposite side, his reply bore out all we have said of Hernando Pizarro and his challenge and Orgoños and their companions, for this was public knowledge at the time in Peru. This incident occurred in Madrid toward the end of Hernando Pizarro's captivity, which lasted twenty-three years. The soldier told me what had happened in the Royal Council of the Indies. Whoever spread this discreditable story sought to lend color to it by describing the companioh of Pizarro as his servant. He saw that he was well arrayed, and this was true, for he wore the same device as Hernando, which was a slashed doublet of orange velvet. He denied the truth and added a lie in saying that this was a servant when it was his companion.

When his friends saw Pizarro fall, they thought he was dead, and fell on Almagro's men, and both sides fought bravely with great loss of life; for their passions were kindled more than they thought, and they wounded and killed one another with great fury and desperation, as though they were not all of the same nation and one religion, and forgetful that they had been brothers and companions in arms in the great hardships they had suffered in gaining that empire. The fight lasted much longer than they had thought, without any decision. Though Almagro's men were much weaker in numbers, they were equal in valor and spirit to Pizarro's, and they resisted the might of their foes and the superiority of their arquebusses at the expense of their lives, which they sold dear until they found themselves worn out, or dead or wounded, when those who could turned their backs. Then the fury with which they had fought showed itself more pitiless than ever, for although they surrendered and were seen to be defeated, they were not spared. On the contrary the rage of the victors was even greater, as Zárate, Book III, ch. xi, and López de Gómara, ch. cxli, agree. López de Gómara's words are given in full in the following chapter.

CHAPTER XXXVIII

*The lamentable events that took place after
the battle of Las Salinas.*

WHEN THE followers of Almagro and Gonzalo Pizarro rushed forward and all fought like Spaniards with great bravery. But the Pizarros prevailed and made cruel use of their victory, though they laid the blame for this on those who had been defeated with Alvarado at the bridge of Amáncay, who were few in number and wished to avenge themselves. When Orgoños surrendered to two gentlemen, one came up and threw him down and slew him. While Captain Ruy Díaz was leading another who had surrendered at the rear of his horse, a soldier struck him with a lance and killed him. Many others were likewise killed after they had been disarmed: Samaniego stabbed Pedro de Lerma to death in bed at night. Captains Moscoso, Salinas, and Hernando de Alvarado died in the fight, and so many Spaniards perished that if the Indians had fallen on the few wounded survivors, as they used to do, they could easily have finished them off. But they were absorbed in robbing the fallen, leaving them naked, and in stealing from the camps which were left unguarded as the vanquished fled and the victors pursued them. Almagro did not fight because of his illness. He watched the battle from a mound and shut himself up in the fortress when he saw that his friends had lost. Gonzalo Pizarro and Alonso de Alvarado followed him and captured him and fastened him in the shackles they themselves had been kept in.

Thus López de Gómara, who here ends his chapter. We shall mention some of the notable events of that day, which our author failed to record. One was that while a gentleman was leading behind his horse Hernando de Sotelo, a relative of Cristóbal de Sotelo, who had surrendered, a soldier shot the captive with his arquebus and killed him, and also wounded his captor, though not fatally. This cruel deed was done in the supposition that Hernando de Sotelo was his kinsman Cristóbal, whom the Pizarrists had their eyes on because he had given Orgoños the advice we have mentioned above, to offer Hernando Pizarro and his men battle when they were sick, after leaving the plains. His death was caused by a soldier who shouted: "They're bringing Sotelo." The arquebusier did not know him, but shot him, thinking he was doing an agreeable service to his side because of their common hatred for Sotelo. The victors performed many other acts of cruelty unworthy of the Spanish nation: so much so that it was said that more were killed after they had surrendered than had died fighting in the battle.

The death of Pedro de Lerma was another act of most barbarous cruelty, so much so that we shall tell how it happened. As we have said, Lerma was seriously wounded in the fray both from the blow Hernando Pizarro dealt him and from other wounds. He went to the house of a gentleman who was a friend of his to be treated. This was Pedro de los Ríos, a member of one of the many noble families of this royal city of Córdova: I knew him when I was a child. A soldier called Juan de Samaniego bore a grudge against Lerma, and therefore sought him out after the battle in order to take vengeance on him. Two days later he heard that he was lying wounded in the house of Pedro de los Ríos. He went there, and finding no one in the house to say him nay, and since everything was just as things usually are in time of war, he walked boldly in and searched the whole house until he found Pedro de Lerma lying in a poor bed. He sat on the bed and said coolly:

"Master Pedro de Lerma, I have come to satisfy my honor by killing you, because you struck me on such and such an occasion."

"Sir," replied Lerma, "you know you were the aggressor, and I was forced to strike you because of your excesses, by which you had earned the blow. It will be little or no satisfaction to your honor to kill a wounded man who is lying in a bed. If God spares me, I swear I will give you the satisfaction you seek, and you shall have my word or I will set it in writing with all the formalities of strict military usage, so that you may be fully satisfied."

"No, by ———," said Samaniego, "I'll not wait so long, but kill you now as my honor requires!"

"You'll lose honor rather than gain it," said Lerma, "if you kill a man who's half dead. But if I live, I'll see you get full satisfaction."

These words were repeated three or four times, the one threatening death and the other offering satisfaction. After all this, when Pedro de Lerma thought that his enemy would be satisfied with the promise, and with having put him in this position—which in military usage was enough to satisfy him—Samaniego got up, drew his dagger and stabbed him many times till he saw that he was dead. He then went out into the street and boasted he had killed Captain Pedro de Lerma to satisfy his honor. And in order to magnify his feat, as he thought, he repeated word for word what he had said and the other had replied, which greatly angered all his hearers. And wherever he was he spoke of nothing else till his very boasting brought about his own death, so that his punishment came from his own hand, as the crime had done. And though we anticipate in time and place, we may as well include this here so that our hearers may lose the feeling of indignation that Samaniego's cruelty may have inspired in them, for his deed was certainly abominated throughout Peru.

About five years later, when the kingdom was at peace and the passions between Pizarros and Almagros had abated, Juan de Samaniego was living in Púerto Viejo where he did not forget his doughty deed, but often spoke boastingly of it, and in order to exaggerate it, would repeat that in satisfaction of his honor he had stabbed a captain who had been lieutenant general to the governor, Don Francisco Pizarro, and no one had gainsaid him. He added some other arrogant adornments. An *alcalde ordinario* of the town, who was weary of hearing these things, sent a message by a friend of Samaniego's that he had better stop talking in this vein, which sounded ill and did him little honor. Since he had avenged himself, let him be satisfied and say no more. Instead of being grateful for this good advice and following it, Samaniego became very angry and went out into the square, where he saw the alcalde engaged in friendly conversation with fifteen or twenty other Spaniards (which must have been nearly the whole Spanish population of the place). He went up to them, and joining the circle, remarked angrily: "Well, I hear that some are annoyed by my having satisfied my honor when I killed Pedro de Lerma. Whoever it is let him speak up clearly and in public, and not send whispering messages, for I swear I am man enough to answer back and stab him too, whoever he be."

The alcalde, seeing himself referred to thus, attacked Samaniego and grasped him by the collar and shouted: "In the king's name, stand by justice against a traitor and murderer!" The bystanders seized Samaniego and thrust him into a house, for everyone was angry at his excesses. The alcalde took evidence of four witnesses concerning all they had heard him say about how he had killed Lerma, one of His Majesty's captains who had served the crown well in the conquest, and had acted as lieutenant general to Pizarro. They recorded that Samaniego said he had killed him when he was wounded in bed, and not in battle. On this evidence he was condemned to death, and while the witnesses were reciting their evidence, the Indians were ordered to raise a gallows of three poles in the square. Samaniego was marched out, and the Indians were given the task of acting as crier (in their own language) and executioner, and he was hanged. The sentence pleased all who saw and heard it.

To return to the thread of our history, the Indians did not, as they had planned, kill all the Spaniards after the battle, for they realized what both would be reduced to. If they failed to do this, it was because God preserved the Christians for the teaching of His holy Gospel, and permitted discord to work among the Indians, for those who were the servants of the Spaniards refused to let them be killed out of natural loyalty to their masters. They said they would rather die defending them than attack them, and recalled that their kings Huaina Cápac and Manco Inca, his son, had bidden them serve and please the Spaniards. By their opposition they dissuaded the unfriendly Indians from their evil intentions. The Indians were also greatly influenced in the sense of not carrying out their wicked plan by their lack of a leader to govern them; for if they had had one, neither the winners nor the losers would have escaped, as the histories say.

This battle was fought on April 6, 1538, the Saturday after Lazarus Friday. As it was so near his day, the Spaniards dedicated a church to him. When I left, it still stood on the plain where the battle was fought, and all those who died on both sides were buried there. Some say it took place on the 26th, but I say this was an error of the printer or narrator who put 26 for 6. Padre Blas Valera mentions this battle in writing of the greatness of the city of Cuzco, and says:

There is on the battlefield a church dedicated to St. Lazarus, where the bodies of those who died there were for long buried. A noble and pious Spaniard, one of the conquerors, often went there to pray for the souls of the dead. It happened that after he had continued his devotion for many days, he heard groans and weeping in the church, and one of his friends who had died in the battle appeared to him, but he said nothing except that his friend was to visit him often at certain hours of the day and night. At first the Spaniard was much afraid; but habit and the words of his confessor, Padre Andrés López, of the Society of Jesus, overcame his fears, and he continued his devotions, praying no longer for his friend alone, but for all the dead, and asking others to help him with their prayers and alms. And at his suggestion, the *mestizos,* the sons of those Spaniards by Indian women, moved their fathers' bones to the city of Cuzco in 1581, where they were buried in a hospital. Many masses were said here; and much alms given, and other pious works performed. The whole city joined in with great charity, and the vision then ceased to appear.

These are the words of Padre Blas Valera.

It remains to describe the most cruel deed perpetrated after that lamentable battle, which was the killing of the good Don Diego de Al-

magro, which caused the total destruction of both governors and of most
of their supporters and Peru in general. It is described by the two historians in the same terms, by Zárate in his Book III, ch. xii, and by López
de Gómara in his ch. cxlii. Their words are reproduced in the following
chapter.

CHAPTER XXXIX

The lamentable death of Don Diego de Almagro.

THE VICTORY, with the capture of Almagro, enriched some and impoverished others, as is the custom of wars, and especially of what are
called civil wars between neighbors and relatives. Hernando Pizarro seized
Cuzco without opposition, though not without grumbling. He gave something
to many, for it would have been impossible to give to all. But as it was little in
comparison with what all those who had taken part in the battle claimed, he
sent most of them off to conquer new lands where they could enrich themselves; and so as not to stand in danger and to relieve himself of anxiety, he sent
Almagro's friends with his own. He also sent Don Diego de Almagro the
younger to Lima under arrest, lest his father's friends should start a rising with
him. He brought accusations against Almagro, announcing that they would be
sent with the prisoner to Lima and thence to Spain; but as he was told that
Mesa and many others would appear on the road and release him, or else
because this was his real will, and he wanted to avoid further trouble, he
sentenced him to death. The grounds were that he had entered Cuzco by force
and caused the death of many Spaniards, that he had plotted with Manco Inca
against the Spaniards, that he had given and taken allocations without powers
from the emperor, and that he had fought against the royal justice at Amáncay
and Las Salinas. Other accusations were also made, which I do not mention as
they were less criminal charges.

Almagro was greatly distressed by the verdict, and said such pitiful things
that hard hearts were softened. He appealed to the emperor. But Hernando,
though many begged him earnestly to do so, refused to allow the appeal.
Almagro begged Pizarro not to kill him for the love of God; he reminded him
how he, Almagro, had not killed Hernando when he could have done so, and
had not shed the blood of his kinsmen and friends when he had them in his
power. He recalled that he had done most to raise Hernando's beloved brother,
Francisco Pizarro, to the pinnacle of honor where he stood. He begged him to
consider how old, weak, and gouty he was, and revoke the sentence by appeal,
allowing him to spend the few sad days that remained to him in prison where

he could weep over his sins. Hernando Pizarro was very harsh against these words, which might have softened a heart of steel, and said that he was surprised that a man of such spirit should fear death so much. Almagro replied that as Christ had feared it, it was not surprising that he should too; but that he would compose himself, for at his age he could not live long. Almagro refused to confess, hoping to escape in this way, when he saw no other open. Yet he did confess, and made his will, and declared the king and his son, Don Diego, his heirs. He refused to accept the verdict for fear of execution; and Hernando Pizarro refused to grant leave to appeal lest the sentence should be revoked by the Council of the Indies: he had, moreover, authority from Francisco Pizarro. At last Almagro agreed to hear the sentence. At his earnest request he was strangled in prison and afterwards beheaded publicly in the square of Cuzco in 1538. Many regretted Almagro's death and missed him greatly. Who missed him most, apart from his son, was Don Diego de Alvarado, who had acted as guarantor to the dead man for his executioner, and had saved Hernando Pizarro from death and imprisonment, though he had never been given any credit for the deed, despite his pleas. He therefore came back to Spain to complain against the conduct of Francisco Pizarro and his brothers, and to summon Hernando Pizarro before the emperor to keep his oath. While engaged in this, Diego de Alvarado died at court in Valladolid; and as he died within the short space of three or four days, some said he had been poisoned.

Diego de Almagro was a native of Almagro. It was never known for certain who his father was, though enquiries were made: it was said he was a priest. He could not read. He was brave, persistent, fond of honor and fame, and liberal, but full of vainglory; for he always wanted everyone to know what he gave. His soldiers loved him for his gifts, though he often abused them and laid hands on them. He pardoned debts of over 100,000 ducats, tearing up the bonds of those who went with him to Chile. This liberality was worthy of a prince rather than of a soldier. But when he died he had no one to lay a cloth on the block for him. His death seemed worse as he was not cruel himself and would never kill anyone who was connected with Francisco Pizarro. He was never married, but had a son by an Indian woman in Panama who was called after him and well brought up and educated, though he came to a bad end, as we shall say.

This is López de Gómara's account, and Zárate says the same. We shall add something for the better understanding of this. After his victory Hernando Pizarro sought to send his enemies away from him so as to avoid the danger of being killed by them. Because of the acts of cruelty committed after the battle the two parties continued full of hatred and enmity, and though Hernando Pizarro did all he could to make friends of the leaders on the other side, he failed to do so: and they daily displayed their hatred and rancor more openly, speaking freely of taking revenge when they could. Moreover his friends also turned against him when they saw their hopes of reward undone, for each of them had promised himself a whole province. And though Hernando Pizarro gave something to many of them, as López de Gómara says, it was impossible to reward them all, and most of his friends were left as dissatisfied as his enemies. And in order to save himself the trouble of rewarding the former and to avoid his fears and suspicions of the latter, he began offering both new conquests, as we shall say in the next chapter.

Almagro was condemned to death and his property confiscated for the royal treasury. At first Hernando Pizarro had no intention of killing him, but only of sending him to Spain with the case against him. This was until he saw that Almagro bore his imprisonment badly and openly said that they would have to release him, declaring that Hernando Pizarro was more guilty than he of the charges brought against him, for he had been the chief cause of the discord between the two governors. If Hernando had not incited his brother, the marquis, against Almagro, their passions would never have reached such a pitch; and now he wanted to avenge his own disappointment by executing and robbing of his jurisdiction one who had done more and spent more in conquering Peru than all the Pizarros: all this was intolerable, and the very stones would rise up against them.

When Hernando Pizarro heard this, and knew in particular that one of his officers called Gonzalo de Mesa, who had been a captain of artillery, but had been unrewarded and bore a grudge, as we shall say, was proposing to go out with his friends and release Almagro on the road, he hastily decided to kill Don Diego. He thought by thus getting rid of him all the passions that had been aroused would die down and they would all remain in peace and quiet; but everything turned out very differently, as our history will show. When López de Gómara says that it was never known who Almagro's father was, though enquiries were made, this is true and Zárate confirms it, adding that he was left at the church door. This may well be so, for the church regards such as well-born and admits them to all its dignities and prelacies. But when López de Gómara adds that his father was a priest, this is not to be borne: this must be the tale of some envious slanderers and desperate characters who could not sully his great deeds and sought to condemn him for his birth with poisonous tongues, and without evidence or even the appearance of truth. The sons of unknown fathers should be judged by their deeds and virtues, and when their acts resemble those of the *adelantado* and governor Don Diego de Almagro, one can only say that they are well born, for they are the children of their own virtue and their own right arms. What is the benefit of nobility to the children of noble fathers, if they are unworthy of it and do not confirm it with their own virtues? For nobility was born of these virtues and is sustained by them. We can therefore truthfully say that Don Diego de Almagro was the son of very noble parents: these were his own works, which have magnified and enriched all the princes of the earth, as we have already said and proved at length.

This heroic man was thus garrotted in prison, and as if this were not enough, beheaded in the public square, to the great grief and distress of the onlookers, for he was more than seventy-five at the time, and his health was so broken that it was thought that his end was very near, even if it had not been hastened. Slanderers said that he had been killed twice, to show the better the great hatred in which he was held and to take revenge on him. The executioner exercised his rights and claimed his spoils, removing all Almagro's clothes down to his shirt; and he would have taken that if he had not been prevented. His body was left in the square for a great deal of the day, with no one friend or enemy willing to remove it; for his friends were dejected and humbled and could not, and his enemies, though many of them regretted his death, dared do nothing for him in public for fear of angering their friends. This shows how the world rewards those who do it the greatest services. And about nightfall there came a Negro who had been the dead man's slave, bringing a wretched sheet, which was all he had in his poverty or could get as alms, to bury his master in. He wrapped Don Diego in it with the aid of some Indians who had been his servants and carried him to the church of Our Lady of Mercies. The religious charitably and tearfully buried him in a chapel below the high altar. So ended the great Don Diego de Almagro, of whom no memory is left but that of his deeds and his pitiable death, which seems to have been a model and pattern of that suffered by the marquis Don Francisco Pizarro in revenge. For Pizarro's death was very similar, as we shall see; and these two conquerors and governors of the great and rich empire of Peru remained equal partners in everything.

CHAPTER XL

The captains who went out on new conquests;
the return to Spain of Hernando Pizarro
and his long imprisonment.

AFTER HERNANDO Pizarro had captured Almagro he sent out many captains on new conquests, partly to free himself from the importunity of his friends, and partly from fear and suspicion of his enemies. He sent the commander Pedro de Valdivia with many excellent men to undertake the conquest of the kingdom of Chile, which Almagro had abandoned. There Valdivia had both extremes of fortune, as we have said in telling the life of Inca Yupanqui, the tenth king of Peru. Francisco de Villagra, whom I later knew, and Alonso de Monroy went with him. Captain Francisco de Olmos was sent to the bay of San Mateo, where Garcilaso de la Vega had been. López de Gómara speaks of these conquests in his ch. cxliii:

> Gómez de Alvarado went to conquer the province of Guánucu, and Francisco de Chaves to make war on the Conchucos who had beset Trujillo and its inhabitants, and brought an idol with their army to which they offered the spoils of their enemies and even the blood of Christians. Pedro de Vergara went to Bracamoros, near Quito, in the north. Juan Pérez de Vergara went against the Chachapoyas, and Alonso de Mercadillo to Mullubamba, and Pedro de Candía beyond Collao. He however could not get where he intended, either because of the difficulty of the land, or that of his men, for many of them mutinied as they were friends of Almagro under Mesa, Pizarro's captain of artillery. Hernando Pizarro went there and beheaded Mesa as a mutineer, because he had spoken ill of the Pizarros and tried to go and free Almagro if he had been taken to Lima. He gave Candía's three hundred men to Pero Ansúrez, and sent him on the same conquest. In this way the Spaniards dispersed and conquered more than three hundred leagues of territory from east to west, with admirable rapidity, though with infinite loss. Hernando and Gonzalo Pizarro reduced Collao, a region rich in gold which they use for plating their oratories and chambers, and abounding in sheep, which are like camels in the forequarters, or perhaps rather deer.

Thus López de Gómara, who adds further on in the same chapter:

Hernando Pizarro returned to Cuzco where he saw Francisco Pizarro, whom he had not met since before the arrest of Almagro. They talked for many days of this event and of matters concerning the government of Peru. It was decided that Hernando should return to Spain to report to the emperor on behalf of both of them concerning the case of Almagro and the royal fifths and the number of expeditions they had made. Many of their friends, who knew the situation, advised Hernando not to go, as they did not know how the emperor would take Almagro's death, especially as Diego de Alvarado was at court and had made charges against them: it would be much better to negotiate from Peru than in Spain. Hernando said the emperor would show him great favor on account of his numerous services, and because he had pacified the country and punished those who had stirred up disorder. On leaving he urged Francisco not to trust any of the Almagrists, especially those who had gone with Almagro to Chile, for they had been very constant in their attachment to their dead leader. He recommended his brother not to let them gather together, or they would kill him; for he, Hernando, knew that they talked of this whenever five of them came together.

So he took leave, and returned to Spain and the court with a great show of wealth and splendor; but it was not long before he was taken from Valladolid to the castle of La Mota at Medina del Campo, whence he has not yet emerged.

Here López de Gómara ends his chapter: we may add in explanation that Gonzalo de Mesa, who had served Hernando Pizarro as captain of artillery, was, like many others, very bitter against him, partly because he had not been rewarded and partly because he had been sent on the conquest under the flag of Captain Pedro de Candía, though he had wanted to be honored by being made leader of them all. Finding himself without honor or profit, he made bold to speak ill of Hernando Pizarro, saying he would rescue Almagro when they took him to Lima. He called his friends together for this purpose quite openly, and without considering the danger to his life, and found many on Almagro's side who rallied to him. This obliged Hernando Pizarro to go to find Mesa with all speed. He was in the Collao, having returned from the expedition with Pedro de Candía to the Musus, to the east of Collao, a country of great forests and rushing rivers, as we have said at length in telling the life of king Inca Yupanqui. On account of these difficulties the Spaniards had not been able to complete the conquest and had returned to Collao, where Hernando Pizarro found them. He beheaded Mesa and took the army from Pedro de Candía and gave it to a gentleman called Pero Ansúrez of Campo Redondo, who went off on the expedition and achieved more than the others, though even his labors also proved vain and fruitless owing to the difficulty of the country.

Pedro de Candía was angry at being deprived of his men to form an expedition for another, and nursing this grudge in his bosom, went over later to the side of the Almagros, but came to a bad end, as we shall say. Although Candía concealed his grievance, Hernando Pizarro did not fail to notice it, for a man's face reveals his pleasure or pain, even when his tongue is still. Many others shared his feelings. When Hernando saw that the more he did to try to reduce his enemies, the more they multiplied, he decided to kill Almagro, which he did on his return to Cuzco from the expedition to Collao. He thought that if the cause of all these risings and disturbances were removed, they would die down and peace and quiet would be restored. But the opposite happened; for Hernando Pizarro incurred such hatred with the lamentable death of Almagro that he thought it safer to bring his suit to Spain, despite the fact that Diego de Alvarado was there with charges against him, than to stay in Peru, where the Almagrists would doubtless have killed him. And as Hernando Pizarro was shrewd, he chose his return to Spain as the lesser of two evils, against his friends' advice; for he thought that he would do better by negotiating on the strength of the great wealth belonging to His Majesty and to himself, even if he did so badly, than by waiting for his enemies to kill him. He thought too that he could justify himself by saying that he had pacified the empire and performed many services in its conquest and undergone great hardships in the siege of Cuzco. But when his enemies saw that he had left Peru and that they could not take vengeance on him, they turned their hatred against his brother, the marquis, and did not stop until they had killed him, as we shall say.

When Hernando Pizarro reached Spain, Diego de Alvarado brought very grave charges against him and asked that he should be tried in either the civil or military court, as His Majesty thought fit, saying that he defied him to single combat and would prove by trial of arms that he had broken his plighted word and was himself responsible for the deeds for which he had blamed Almagro. He also accused him of many other matters, which we omit to avoid prolixity. Because of this Hernando Pizarro was arrested and taken to the Mota at Medina del Campo. Continuing his charge, Diego de Alvarado accused him of having given certain very rich presents and gifts of gold, silver, and precious stones. Some of these cases he proved by showing the evidence, which led to the showing up of certain important people. We leave this in obscurity, as it is an odious subject. And as Diego de Alvarado died while pursuing his case with such justification and his death was very sudden, it was suspected, as López de Gómara says, that he was poisoned. However, he left his suit well launched, and there were serious sentences as a result of it.

But in time these were moderated, and Hernando Pizarro left prison in

1562 after 23 years. He showed the same courage as he had against all the adversities fortune brought him, with the death of his brothers and nephews, the loss of his Indians, and the incredible expense of his lawsuit and arrest. All this the world gave him in return for his great deeds and the innumerable hardships he suffered in helping his brother the marquis Don Francisco Pizarro, as captain general in the conquest of that great empire. With this we must close our second book, giving thanks to our Lord God for suffering us to reach this point.

End of the Second Book

BOOK
THREE *of the*
SECOND
PART

It contains the conquest of Los Charcas; the departure of Gonzalo Pizarro to conquer La Canela, the land of cinnamon, and the many great privations he underwent; the treachery of Francisco de Orellana; a conspiracy against the marquis Don Francisco de Pizarro and how he was killed; Don Diego de Almagro sworn as governor of Peru; opposition to his claims; the arrival of Licentiate Vaca de Castro in Peru; his choice of captains for the war; Gonzalo Pizarro's return to Quito; the cruel battle of Chupas; the death of Don Diego de Almagro; new laws and ordinances sent from the Spanish court for the empires of Mexico and Peru; the crisis successfully surmounted in Mexico owing to the prudence and good sense of the visitor.

It contains twenty-two chapters.

CHAPTER I

The conquest of Los Charcas, and some battles between Indians and Spaniards.

ITH THE death of Don Diego de Almagro and the departure of Hernando Pizarro the whole weight of the conquest and administration of Peru lay on the shoulders of the marquis. He grappled with the two tasks; for God had given him powers to handle both, but they were curtailed by the work of evil counsellors. He sought to bring peace to the country by sending the captains off on the conquests we have mentioned in the previous book. He sent his brother Gonzalo to conquer Collao and Los Charcas, 200 leagues south of Cuzco. He was accompanied by most of the gentlemen who had come with Don Pedro de Alvarado, so that these might have the opportunity to gain new lands; for those already won, consisting of what is now the jurisdiction of Cuzco and Lima and all the coastal valleys as far as Túmbez, had been divided between the first conquerors who were present at the capture of Atahuallpa, and it was necessary to win more land to distribute among the second conquerors who had come with Almagro and Alvarado.

Gonzalo took a large and splendid company with him to the Collao. At first the Indians made little resistance, but when the Spaniards reached the limits of Los Charcas some 150 leagues from Cuzco, they fell upon them and fought a number of battles in which many were slain on both sides and the Indians also killed many of the horses. Their main object, on which they staked all their hopes of victory, was indeed to destroy the horses, for they thought that if they did this they would have little trouble in killing their masters, over whom they had an advantage on foot. In one of these battles it happened that after both sides had fought very bravely and many Indians had been killed the Spaniards were finally victorious. Gonzalo de Pizarro followed the course of events over the whole battlefield and was accompanied by three companions. One of these was Garcilaso de la Vega, the second Juan de Figueroa, and the third Gaspar Jara, all three of whom had Indians in the city today called Silver City, which was known in the Indian tongue as Chuquisaca. They were later given better allocations in Cuzco, where I knew them.

As these four were riding across a plain some distance from the place of the battle in order to give their mounts a breathing space after their toils, they saw seven Indian nobles appear over the crest of a low hill. They came armed with bows and arrows for the battle and wearing their war plumes and finery. As soon as they saw the Spaniards, they deployed, each taking up a position ten or twelve paces from the next, so as to divide their enemies and force them to attack singly and not all together. They prepared their weapons for the fray, and although the Spaniards made signs to them not to be afraid, for they did not want to fight, but to be friends, the Indians did not seek terms, and so both parties attacked with great spirit and gallantry.

The Spaniards, as they themselves said, were annoyed and ashamed to attack seven Indians, on foot, naked and without defensive armor, when they were four knights, well armored on their horses, with their lances in their hands. But the Indians received them as bravely as if they wore strong breastplates and fought like men, all coming to one another's help, so that when one was free from the attack of a Spaniard, he helped another who was engaged with one, laying on now from the side, now from behind, with such skill and ferocity that the Christian had to beware of each equally as the Indians arranged their onslaughts, for there were two Indians against each Spaniard almost all the time. After a long struggle the Spaniards won, each of them killing an Indian. And as one of them was pursuing an Indian who was fleeing, the latter stooped to pick up a stone from in front of him and flung it at the Spaniard and hit him in the chin-piece with which his face was protected, half stunning him. If he had not been so protected, he would probably have been killed, such was the force with which the stone was cast. Though sorely hurt, the Spaniard finished by killing the Indian.

The three remaining Indians escaped by flight; and the Spaniards were glad to let them go, for they were so distressed after the two battles that they had no wish to follow them or to enjoy such a victory as they might have achieved by killing three Indians. This indeed seemed unworthy.

All four then gathered to assess the damage. Three were found to be wounded, each with two or three blows, though of no great importance, while the horse of the fourth had been struck severely by an arrow and took many days to recover. When telling the story of the event, the man with the wounded horse used to say:

"All four of us were wounded; and I the most grievously, for I would rather have suffered my horse's wound in my own body, so greatly did I miss him."

I heard the man himself say this when I was a child. It was a common phenomenon for the Spanish conquerors who won the New World to feel their horses' wounds more than their own; and thus this gentleman put it in this way. They then returned to the army, where they told their companions that the fight with the seven Indians had been tougher and more dangerous than the battle against six or seven thousand of them earlier the same day. There were many similar engagements in this campaign, and in one of them there occurred the incident mentioned at the end of the last chapter of Book One of this Second Part, where we spoke of the loyalty and affection of the Indians toward the Spaniards who had defeated them in battle.

They thus travelled on, with severe battles every two or three days, until they came to a place called Chuquisaca, whose population was very warlike. There many thousands of Indians attacked, and held the Spaniards sorely pressed with continuous fighting and hunger and many casualties, as the historians López de Gómara (ch. cxliii) and Zárate (Book III, ch. xii) say, though their account is brief. Gonzalo Pizarro succeeded in discovering the country as far as the province of Los Charcas, where he was surrounded by many Indian warriors who came against him, and reduced him to such straits that he had to beg for help, which the marquis sent him from Cuzco, with many horsemen. In order that this succor might arrive more promptly the marquis pretended that he himself was coming too, and marched two or three days along the route.

The siege described by these authors was very severe; so much so that the Spaniards reached the end of their resources, and were afraid they would all perish, so they sent messages to the marquis by the Indian servants they had, who always served as messengers in such perils, as we have seen. These Indians were sent by diverse routes, so that if the enemy killed some, others would escape.

When the marquis realized the plight of Gonzalo and all his companions, he sent a captain to go and aid them, and himself made the sortie mentioned by Zárate so that the help might arrive the sooner. But neither the efforts of the captain nor the marquis' pretence would have sufficed to save the besieged, if God had not fought for them. For while the messengers were seeking help and the relief was coming, they were so closely beset that they regarded themselves as lost, until the divine St. James, patron of Spain, fought visibly for them, as he did at Cuzco.

When the Christians saw his favor and protection, which succored them so patently in their trials, they strove to such effect that when help at last arrived they were already victorious. And because of the favor that our Lord performed for them there, they decided to found a Christian town on the spot. It now has a cathedral church and is the seat of a royal chancery, and is eighteen leagues from the mines of Potosí, which have enriched and ennobled it as is seen today. Padre Blas Valera, in his short account of the memorable battles fought between Indians and Spaniards in Peru, tells the story of the battle that occurred in this province and says that God fought there for His Gospel.

CHAPTER II

The marquis divides the kingdom and province of Los Charcas, and Gonzalo Pizarro goes to the conquest of the land of cinnamon.

AFTER the war was over and the Indians had been pacified, the marquis divided them among the principal Spaniards who had been present at the conquest. He gave a good allocation to his brother Hernando and another to Gonzalo, in whose district the silver mines of Potosí were discovered years later. Hernando Pizarro received a mine as a *vecino* of the city, though he was already in Spain, and it was placed in the hands of his officials so that they could send him the silver that was extracted; it proved so rich that for over eight months it produced fine, pure silver, with no other treatment but melting it. I mention this wealth at this point, because it slipped my memory when discussing the famous hill of Potosí in the first part of these *Commentaries*. The allocation called Tapac-Ri was awarded to my lord Garcilaso de la Vega, and Gabriel de Rojas was given another excellent one, as were many other gentlemen, over an area of more than a hundred leagues which then constituted the jurisdiction of the city: part of this area was later given to the city called La Paz.

The value of these allocations was small at the time when they were awarded, though they had many Indians and their soil was very fertile. It was only with the discovery of the mines of Potosí that their rents increased tenfold, and the allocations that had produced two, three, or four thousand pesos later produced twenty, thirty, and forty thousand.

The marquis ordered the foundation of the town called La Plata, now called the city of La Plata, and divided the Indians in its jurisdiction among the Spanish conquerors and settlers, all of which took place in 1538 and 1539. Then having rested less than two years from the past civil wars and conquests, he engaged in new and more arduous enterprises, as we shall say. With the death of Almagro he was left as sole governor of a country extending more than seven hundred leagues from north to south, from Los Charcas to Quito, where he had much to do in pacifying and arranging the new conquests his captains had made in various directions, and in administering justice and maintaining the peace among the towns and peoples that had already been subdued. But as the desire to command and rule is insatiable, not content with what he had, he sought new discoveries, for his warlike spirit wished to press on with the successes he had thus far had.

He had heard that beyond Quito, and beyond the limits of the land ruled by the Inca kings, there was a large and broad country where cinnamon was produced, and which was therefore called La Canela, the Land of Cinnamon. He thought he would send his brother Gonzalo to conquer it, so that the latter might have as much land to rule as he had himself. And having consulted with the members of his privy council, he surrendered the government of Quito to his brother, so that the inhabitants of this city would give him all necessary help, since it was to be the starting point of the expedition, as La Canela lies to the east of Quito. Having decided this, he sent for Gonzalo, who was in Los Charcas, attending to the settlement of the new city of La Plata and preparing to enjoy the allocation of Indians his brother had assigned to him. Gonzalo at once came to Cuzco, where his brother was, and after they had discussed the conquest of La Canela, he accepted the task with a good will in order to show his courage in such undertakings and began to make the necessary preparations.

He raised more than 200 soldiers in Cuzco, 100 horse and the rest on foot: he spent over 60,000 ducats on them. He marched the five hundred leagues to Quito, where Pedro de Puelles was governor. On the way he fought the Indians who were in revolt, and had several small battles with them, though those of Huánucu pressed him hard; so much so that the marquis sent him help by Francisco de Chaves, as Zárate says in his Book IV, ch. i.

When Gonzalo had escaped this and other lesser dangers, he came to Quito, and showed Pedro de Puelles his brother's instructions. He was obeyed; and installed as governor, began to make ready what was necessary for his expedition. He raised more than 100 more soldiers, making 340 in all, 140 horse and the rest on foot. He was accompanied by more than 4,000 friendly Indians carrying his arms and supplies, and such requisites as iron, axes, hatchets, hemp ropes and cables, and nails, against any emergencies. They also drove a herd of about 4,000 stock, consisting of pigs and Peruvian sheep, which also helped to carry part of the munitions and baggage.

He left Pedro de Puelles in Quito as his lieutenant, and having attended to certain matters in which reforms were necessary, left Quito at Christmas 1539. His journey was peaceful and he received every help from the Indians until his road went beyond the limit of the Inca empire. He then came to a province the historians call Quixos. And as López de Gómara and Zárate are in close agreement about the events of this expedition, telling them in almost the same words, and I myself heard the accounts of many of those who accompanied Gonzalo Pizarro on this occasion, I shall say what happened drawing on all these sources.

In this province of Quixos, which is to the north of Quito, many hostile Indians came out against Gonzalo, but as soon as they saw how many Spaniards and horses he had, they withdrew into the interior and did not appear again. A few days later there was a violent earthquake, in the course of which many houses fell down in the village where the Spaniards were. The earth opened in many places, and there was such thunder, lightning, and thunderbolts that the Spaniards were filled with amazement. It also rained so hard for many days that the rain seemed to be poured out of buckets. The nature of the country, so different from what they had seen in Peru, filled them with surprise. After this storm had gone on for forty or fifty days, they tried to pass over the snow-covered cordillera; and though they were well supplied the mountains are unpredictable, and they were met with such snow and cold that many of the Indians were frozen, for they wear few clothes and what they have gives little shelter. In order to avoid the snow and cold of this difficult region, the Spaniards abandoned the cattle and food they had brought, supposing that they would be able to replace it wherever there was an Indian village. But it turned out very differently, for after they had passed the mountains they were greatly in need of supplies, for the land they found was barren and uninhabited. They hastened to get away from it, and reached a province and town called Sumaco, on the side of a volcano, where they obtained food; but at such a price—though they were there two months it never stopped raining for a single day, which caused them much harm and rotted much of the clothing they had brought.

In this province called Sumaco, which is on the equator or near it, the trees called cinnamon, of which they were in search, grow. They are very tall and have big leaves like laurels; the fruit consists of bunches of small fruits growing in husks like acorns. And though the tree and its leaves, roots, and bark all smell and taste of cinnamon, these husks are the most perfect spice. A great many such trees grow wild and produce fruit, but it is not so good as that obtained from trees planted and tended by the Indians, who trade in it with their neighbors, though not with those of Peru. These latter have never wanted any other spices but their *uchu*, which the Spaniards in Peru call *"aji"* and in Spain *"pimiento."*

CHAPTER III

The hardships of Gonzalo Pizarro and his
followers; how they made a wooden bridge
and a brigantine to cross
a large river.

IN SUMACO and the surrounding district the Spaniards found the Indians going naked, with no clothes at all; the women wore a little cloth in front of them for decency's sake. They go naked because it is a very hot district, and as it rains so much that their clothes rot, as we have said. The Spaniards said that the Indians were wise in not troubling about clothes, for they had no use for them and they were not necessary to them.

Gonzalo left most of his people in Sumaco, and took the most athletic with him to go ahead and see if there was any road to advance by; for the whole distance they had come, which was nearly a hundred leagues, was through dense forests through which they often had to open a way by main force with hatchets. The Indians they took as guides lied to them, and often set them on the wrong direction, and led them away from their own lands and those of their friends and allies toward inhospitable deserts where they suffered greatly from hunger and had to sustain themselves on herbs, roots, and wild fruit: and they counted themselves fortunate when they could find this.

After these ordeals and others that can be better imagined than described, they reached a province called Cuca, rather more populated than the rest, where they found supplies. Its lord greeted them peacefully and entertained them as best he could, offering them food, which was what they most needed. A very large river passes this place and it is thought to be the chief of the rivers that join to make the great river called the Orellana, or by others the Marañón.

There he stopped nearly two months waiting for the arrival of the Spaniards he had left at Sumaco, whom he had given orders to follow him by his trails if they could not find guides. When they appeared and had rested from the trials of the journey, they all travelled together down the banks of that great river, and for fifty leagues found no ford or bridge to cross over, for the river is too wide for either.

At the end of this long journey, they found that the river went over a fall more than two hundred fathoms high, making such a noise that it could be heard more than six leagues before they reached it. They were astonished at this great and wonderful sight, and even more so forty or fifty leagues further down when they found that that immensity of waters narrowed down and streamed through a gorge in another enormous rock. This channel is so narrow that it is not more than twenty feet from bank to bank, and so high that the brink (along which the Spaniards passed) is two hundred fathoms above the water, or as far as the waterfall they had seen. It is indeed wonderful that there are things in those parts that far exceed all that can be said of them, such as these two places and a great many others that may be noted in the course of this history.

Gonzalo and his captains, seeing that there was no easier route than this to cross the river and find out what lay on the other side, since their whole way so far had lain through a wretched, poor, and barren country, decided to build a bridge over the channel. The Indians on the other side, though they were few, defended it bravely, and the Spaniards were therefore forced to fight them, though they had not hitherto had hostilities with any of the Indians of those parts. They fired their arquebusses, and when a few natives had been killed, the rest fled in astonishment at so strange a thing as seeing their companions slain at a distance of a hundred or two hundred paces. They went off spreading reports of the wildness and ferocity of the newcomers, saying they wielded thunderbolts and lightning to kill any who disobeyed them. When the Spaniards found the way open, they built a wooden bridge. It may well be considered how difficult it was to lay the first beam across; for the height above the water was so great that it was rash even to look down, and one Spaniard who dared to look from the brink of the precipice down into the rushing stream in the gorge grew giddy and fell into the torrent below. When the others saw their comrade's misfortune they went more carefully, and with great toil and trouble laid down the first beam, and with its aid the others that were necessary. They made a bridge over which men and horses were able to pass in safety, and left it as it was in case they should need to cross it on the way back. They then travelled downstream through some forests which were so dense and wild that they often had to make a way with axes.

With such toils they reached a land called Guema, as poor and starving as the rest. They found few Indians; and such as there were, on seeing the Spaniards, took to the wilderness and did not reappear. The Spaniards and their Indian servants maintained themselves on herbs, roots, and tender shoots of trees which could be eaten as vine shoots are here. Many Indians and Spaniards fell sick and died from the hunger and labors of the road, and from the great quantities of rain that fell, for their clothes were always wet. In spite of all these difficulties, they travelled many leagues until they came to another country where they found Indians rather more civilized than the others they had met: they ate maize bread and wore cotton clothes. But the country was as rainy as ever. Messengers were sent out in all directions to see if they could find any open road but they all soon returned with the same tale: the whole country consisted of wild forests, full of marshes, lakes, and pools that led nowhere and could not be forded. They therefore decided to build a brigantine and use it for crossing the river from one side to the other; for it was now so wide that it stretched about two leagues across. They set up a forge to do the riveting; and made charcoal with considerable difficulty, for the rain was so frequent that it prevented them from burning their fuel. They made shelters to cover it, and also huts to shelter from the rain, for though the country is under the equator and extremely hot, they had no way of protecting themselves from the downpour. Part of the riveting was made with the shoes of the horses which they had killed to give the sick food, and also to nourish those who were well when they had no other resources. Another part of the riveting was made of their own armor, which they valued more than gold.

Gonzalo Pizarro, like the great soldier he was, was the first to cut wood, forge iron, make charcoal, or undertake any other duty, however menial, so as to set an example to the rest and prevent anyone from avoiding similar duties. They made pitch for their brigantine from the resin of trees, which they found in abundance. Tow came from cloaks and old shirts, or to be exact rotten shirts; each of them vying with his neighbor to supply one, even though he remained shirtless, for they all thought that their common salvation lay in the brigantine. So they finished it, with such efforts as we have said, and launched it with the greatest rejoicing, thinking that that day was the end of their labors: but within a few days they were wishing they had never made it, as we shall soon see.

CHAPTER IV

Francisco de Orellana rebels, seizes the
brigantine, and sails to Spain to claim
this conquest; his death.

T HEY LOADED the brigantine with all the gold they had, which amounted to more than 100,000 pesos, and many rich emeralds, and the iron and shoes and everything else they had of any value. They also shipped the weakest of the sick, who could not travel overland. In this way they escaped from this place after travelling nearly two hundred leagues, and made their way downstream, some by land and some by water in the boat, but not getting far apart from one another and gathering at night so as to sleep together. They all travelled with great difficulty, for the land party often had to open a road with hatchets and billhooks in order to advance, and those on the brigantine had to resist the current for fear of being separated from their companions. When the forest was too thick to permit them to advance down the bank, they had to cross to the opposite shore in the boat and four canoes they also had; this was their most difficult task, for it took two or three days to cross in this way and they were sorely troubled by hunger.

After continuing for over two months amidst these tribulations, they came across some Indians who told them by signs and by certain words which the Indian servants could understand that they would find an inhabited country ten days' journey away, with plenty of food and rich in gold and everything else they sought. They indicated by signs that this country was on the banks of another great river that joined the one where they were. This news encouraged the Spaniards. Gonzalo Pizarro appointed a captain called Francisco de Orellana to take charge of the brigantine and fifty men to go with him where the Indians had told them, which would be a distance of about eighty leagues from where they were.

On arrival at the meeting place of the two rivers, they were to leave all their cargo, load the brigantine with supplies and return upstream to help their companions, who were so tormented by hunger that men were dying every day, both Spaniards and Indians; though the latter had the worst of it, for of 4,000 who began the expedition, more than 2,000 had already perished. Francisco de Orellana went his ways, and sailed the eighty leagues, and as he thought, more than a hundred, in three days without the use of sail or oars. They did not find the promised supplies; and as he thought that if he tried to return with the news to Gonzalo Pizarro, it would not be possible to sail in a year the distance he had come in three days, so strong was the current, and realizing that if he waited there it would help neither himself nor the rest, for he had no idea of how long it would take Gonzalo to arrive, he changed his plan and without consulting anyone, set sail and went on downstream with the intention of forsaking Gonzalo and returning to Spain to claim the conquest and government of the area for himself. Many of his companions opposed this, suspecting his ill faith; they told him that it was not necessary for him to go beyond the captain general's orders, or abandon him in such a time of need, for it was obvious how necessary the brigantine was. In particular a religious called Fray Gaspar de Carvajal told him of this, together with a young gentleman from Badajoz called Hernán Sánchez de Vargas whom the opposition adopted as their leader. They would have come to blows had not Orellana pacified them for the moment with fair words, though after, when he had suborned his rivals with great promises, he abused the poor priest with words and blows, and would have marooned him there if he had not been a priest. He did maroon Hernán Sánchez de Vargas, who, so as to assure him a more cruel and lingering death, he did not kill, but left abandoned in that desert, surrounded on one side by the wild forest and on the other by this vast river, so that he could not escape by land or water, but must perish of hunger.

Orellana continued his journey; and on the following day, in order to make public his purpose, he repudiated the powers he had been given by Gonzalo Pizarro, so as not to do anything as his subordinate, and had himself elected as His Majesty's captain, independent of anyone else. This feat, which better deserves the name of treason, has been performed by other leaders in the conquests in the New World, some of which cases are recounted by Captain Gonzalo Hernández de Oviedo y Valdés, His Catholic Majesty's chronicler, in Book XVII, ch. xx, of his *General His-*

tory of the Indies. He adds that those who did so were paid in the same coin by those who succeeded them in their offices, in confirmation of which he quotes the proverb that says: "Kill, and you shall be killed; and so shall whoever kills you." If we may go on with this author's observations on this matter, we could tell of deeds of great cunning and treachery that took place after the chronicler's time, but in circumstances such as those he describes. However, we shall leave them, for they are offensive and involve the thunder, the lightning, and the thunderbolt itself, for all sorts have been involved, and we had better not mention them.

Orellana had some brushes with the Indians dwelling on the banks of the river further down. They showed great ferocity, and in some places the women came down and fought beside the men. For this reason Orellana thought he would blow up his achievements by describing the country as a land of Amazons; and he thus asked His Majesty for the right of conquest. Beyond these provinces, further down the river, he found other tamer Indians, who received him peacefully and were astonished to see the brigantine and such strange men as it contained. The Spaniards made friends, and were brought all the food they needed. They stayed there some days and built another brigantine, for they were very crowded in the first. They thus came down to the sea, which they reached two hundred leagues from the island of Trinidad according to the mariners' chart, after experiencing the trials we have mentioned and great dangers on the river, where they often gave themselves up as lost and thought they were on the point of drowning.

At Trinidad Orellana bought a ship with which he returned to Spain and asked His Majesty for the conquest of the land, exaggerating his undertaking by saying that the country was full of gold, silver, and precious stones and offering as proof such supplies of those things as he had. His Majesty granted him the conquest and government of whatever he might win. Orellana then raised over five hundred excellent soldiers, including some distinguished gentlemen, with whom he embarked at Sanlúcar for his expedition; he died at sea, and his followers were dispersed in various directions. Such was the end of this journey, an appropriate end to its ill-starred beginnings. We shall now return to Gonzalo Pizarro, whom we left in great straits.

After he had sent off Orellana with the brigantine, he built ten or a dozen canoes and as many rafts so as to be able to cross the river from one bank to the other whenever the forest became too dense to pass, as had occurred on previous occasions. They travelled in the hope that the brigantine would soon relieve them with supplies to abate the hunger that tormented them, for they met with no other enemy on this journey. After two months they reached the junction of the two great rivers, where they thought they would find their brigantine laden with provisions, supposing that it had not been able to return for them owing to the strength of the current. They were disillusioned, and lost hope of emerging from that hell, a name that can well be applied to a place where they had suffered such trials and miseries with no remedy or hope of escape. At the meeting of the rivers they found the good Hernán Sánchez de Vargas, who, with the spirit and constancy of a noble knight, had remained in his place suffering from hunger and the other trials that beset him, in order to give Gonzalo Pizarro a full report of what Orellana had done against his captain general and against Hernán Sánchez himself, for trying to oppose his wicked plan. At this Gonzalo was full of wonder that there could be men in the world who turned out so differently from what might be expected of them. The captains and soldiers were so downcast and grieved at finding their hopes shattered and themselves deprived of any relief that they were on the brink of despair.

Their general, though he felt the same grief as all the rest, consoled and encouraged them, bidding them be of good cheer and support these and greater misfortunes, if there could be such, like Spaniards; the greater their misfortunes, the more honor and fame they would leave to posterity. Since it had befallen them to be the conquerors of that empire, let them behave like men chosen by divine providence for such a great enterprise. At this they all took heart on seeing the captain general do so; for their common belief was that his disappointment must be greater than that of all the rest. They still continued their journey down the banks of that great river, first on one side and then the other, crossing over whenever they were obliged to do so. The labor of getting the horses over on the rafts was incredible, for they still had more than 80 out of the 150 they had left Quito with. They also had nearly 2,000 of the 4,000 Indians who left Peru. These served their masters like children in all their toils and needs, searching for herbs, roots, wild fruit, toads, snakes, and other vermin, if any could be found in the forests, for all tasted good to the Spaniards, who would have fared much worse if they had been without these vile things.

CHAPTER V

Gonzalo Pizarro seeks to return to Cuzco; the
Chilean party plans to kill the marquis.

AMIDST these miseries they journeyed another hundred leagues downstream without finding any improvement in the country or any
ground for hope of such, since it grew daily worse and offered no promise
to them. When the general and his captains had seen and discussed this,
they decided to return to Quito, if this were possible: they were more than
four hundred leagues from it. And as it was impossible to sail upstream
the way they had come, they resolved to try a different route and go to the
north of the river, since they had noticed that there were fewer lakes and
marshes there than on the other side. They penetrated the forests, cutting
a way with axes and billhooks, to which work they were now so accustomed that it would have been the least of their hardships if they had had
food. Here we shall leave them in order to say what happened to the
marquis while his brother Gonzalo was engaged in these labors. For it
seems that these gentlemen, just as they had been chosen for such famous deeds, were likewise destined to undergo all manner of toils and misfortunes, of which they had no lack till their lives ended in deaths that
gave great grief and pain to those who knew them.

When the marquis had divided the provinces of the Charcas among the
conquerors of the kingdom and repaired some damage caused by the late
passions between his own followers and those of Almagro in Cuzco, he
left all in peace and quiet and went to Lima so as personally to assist in
its settlement. In Lima was Don Diego de Almagro the younger, who had
been sent there, as we have said, by Hernando Pizarro immediately after
the execution of his father. The marquis found that some of the most
prominent of the Almagrists now surrounded Almagro's son, who fed
them at his table from the proceeds of a good allocation of Indians his
father had given him: this he did because all his followers had been deprived of their Indians as traitors for being on his father's side. As the
marquis was a man of noble and generous character he tried to satisfy
these gentlemen by offering them large subsidies and appointing them to
positions in the administration of justice and the royal treasury. But they
hoped to see the Pizarros punished for the undeserved death of Almagro

and for the cruelties they had committed in the battle of Las Salinas and afterward, and refused any sort of reward, so as to have nothing to thank the marquis for, and no cause to lay down their rancor against the marquis and his friends, for they wished to give no opportunity to anyone to say that they had taken gifts from him and still remained his enemies. They thus went on supporting one another and refusing to receive anything from the Pizarrists, however great their need. When some of the marquis' familiars and advisers saw this and pondered over it, they advised him, like evil counsellors, that as the Almagrists would not become his friends by fair means, he should force them to do so, or at least reduce them by hunger and want. The marquis reluctantly complied with his advisers' opinions—though they were not his own, for he never deliberately harmed anyone, however hostile to him—and took away the younger Almagro's Indians. It was in Almagro's house that the others used to meet for their meals; and it was thought that if they had no food they would go and seek it elsewhere and so leave the city. But this action, instead of reducing the Almagrists to obedience, simply roused them to greater indignation and wrath, which is the usual result of tyrannical rigor, especially if it is undeserved.

So when Almagro's followers saw how harshly they were misused, they wrote letters to many places where they knew there were Spaniards who were well disposed toward them, summoning their friends to Lima to help them press their claims. Among those who came out on their side there were many who had not been with them in the late wars, but who had recently come to Peru: some of these joined one side or the other without any special cause, as always happens when there are divisions. Thus more than two hundred soldiers gathered in Lima, having come three or four hundred leagues. When they found themselves so numerous, they took courage from one another, and began freely to acquire arms; hitherto they had not even dared to mention them, for they were as if under arrest. But because of the mildness which the marquis had assumed toward them, they acted with complete freedom and began to plan to avenge the death of Almagro on the marquis, now that Hernando Pizarro, who was the cause of all their past, present, and future evils, had gone to Spain. Their negotiations were not so secret that they did not come to the ears of the marquis' advisers, and these last importuned him earnestly to punish the rebels by killing the leaders and banishing the rest before they began a rising against him and his followers. The marquis, as Zárate says in his Book IV, ch. vi:

was so confident and in such good heart that he said it would be best to leave the poor wretches, who had enough trouble with their poverty and humiliation and defeat. Thus Don Diego and his friends relied on the marquis' patience and equanimity, and gradually treated him with less and less regard, so much so that the leaders on several occasions passed him without removing their caps or showing any sign of respect.

Thus Zárate.

The fact is that their poverty was such that there were groups of seven soldiers with only a single cloak among them, and that not new, but worn out; and each would take his turn to go out and about his business in it, each waiting for the one who was abroad wearing it to come back before he ventured forth. Likewise with their food; they all gave what money they had to Juan de Rada, and also anything they won by gambling, and he acted as treasurer and housekeeper for them all. Their liberty and shamelessness in the face of the marquis' forbearance were in proportion to their poverty. Their most brazen action was to tie three ropes from the gallows in the city square one night; the first was fastened to the house of Antonio Picado, the marquis' secretary, the second to that of Dr. Juan Velázquez, the mayor, and the third to the marquis' own house, a piece of shameless impudence that would have sufficed to hang them all with the same ropes. But the marquis' character was so noble that he not only did not punish or investigate the affair, but even excused its perpetrators in the face of their accusers, saying that they were defeated and broken and did that because they could do no more: leave them alone, for their misfortune was enough. When the Chileans knew this, instead of being appeased they grew more and more shameless and embittered, until they finally killed the marquis, as we shall see.

CHAPTER VI

*A provocation drives the Chileans to kill the marquis;
how they perpetrate the deed.*

FOR ALL their impudence and defiance, the supporters of Almagro were still vacillating, not knowing what course to take, for though they had agreed to kill the marquis, they wished to wait for His Imperial

Majesty's commands with regard to the punishment of the murder of Don Diego de Almagro, since they knew that Diego de Alvarado, who, as we have said, came to Spain to accuse the Pizarros, had succeeded in getting a judge appointed to try the case, though they had also heard that the judge's jurisdiction was very limited. He was not to punish anyone or to remove the marquis from his post, but merely to obtain information about what had happened and take it to Spain, where His Majesty would decide on the punishment that was to be applied to the guilty. This greatly annoyed the followers of Almagro who wanted a judge with full powers to investigate and cut off as many heads right and left as they thought fit to name, and to confiscate property, and award it to themselves. In this state of doubt they decided to wait until the judge's arrival so as to see how he executed his commission and find how he would proceed and whether his powers would be as limited as they had been told, or wider, as they hoped. Privately they plotted together like conspirators saying that if the judge did not arrest the marquis as soon as he arrived and apply other severe penalties, they would kill them both and raise the standard of revolt, avenging themselves for the wrong the marquis had done them and also for the emperor's omission in not punishing a crime so atrocious as they thought the death of Almagro to be. The plan to raise the standard of revolt throughout Peru they later executed, as we shall see.

It was public knowledge in Lima that the Chilean party was discussing the killing of the marquis, and many of his friends who heard about it duly warned him. He replied, as Zárate says in his Book IV, ch. vii,

saying that their heads would protect his, and behaved so carelessly that he would often walk outside the city to some mills he was building accompanied by only a single page. And when he was asked why he did not take a bodyguard he would say that he did not want to have it said or thought that he was protecting himself from Licentiate Vaca de Castro, who was coming as judge over him. Therefore the Chilean party tried to put the marquis off his guard by spreading the report that Vaca de Castro was dead. One day Juan de Rada and some of his friends went to see the marquis and found him in a garden, and asked him why his excellency wanted to kill him and his companions. The marquis swore that he had never had any such intention; on the contrary, he had been told that they wanted to kill him and had bought arms for the purpose. Juan de Rada replied that it was not surprising that if his excellency bought lances, they bought breastplates to defend themselves with. He made bold to say this because he had left a body of more than forty well-armed men quite close behind him. He also said it to lull his excellency's suspicions so that

he would give Don Diego and his friends permission to leave Peru. The
marquis suspected nothing from the words, but was on the contrary sorry for
his enemies, and reassured them with kind words, saying that he had not
bought the lances against them. Then he picked some oranges and gave them
to Juan de Rada, for as these were the first fruit of the kind grown in Peru
they were then highly prized; and he whispered to him to let him know what
they needed, and he would see to it. Juan de Rada kissed the marquis' hand,
and leaving him reassured, said farewell and returned to his lodging where he
agreed with the chief of his supporters that they would kill the marquis the
following Sunday, since they had failed to do so on St. John's day, as they
had agreed.

This is Zárate's version, and López de Gómara says the same. Thus the
good marquis was as heedless of being killed by the Chilean party as
they were impatient to kill him. But, as we have said, they awaited the
arrival of the judge so as to see how he would handle the case. Their hesitation, however, was turned to rabid indignation and rage by an action of
the marquis' secretary, Antonio Picado, at this time.

As the Chileans had fastened ropes from the gibbet and one of them
had been directed at him, and as they were full of such brazen impudence
toward the marquis—though they seemed only to threaten to take up arms
without actually daring to do so—Picado mocked them for their cowardice by putting in his cap a rich gold medal with a picture of a fig on it and
a scroll reading: "For the Chileans." The brave soldiers were so insulted
and furious at this that they decided to carry out the murder of the marquis without waiting for the judge to arrive. They thus discussed the matter more openly than hitherto, and the marquis heard about it through a
priest who had learned in secret how and when they meant to do the deed.

The marquis took counsel with the mayor, Dr. Velázquez, and his
secretary, Antonio Picado. They calmed his fears, saying that there was
no need to set any store by such wretched people who only said such
things to calm their hunger and forget their misery. But the marquis
had now changed his first idea and was afraid. He did not go to mass
in the cathedral on St. John's day, 1541, which was the day they had
fixed for his death, and he did not go the Sunday following, June 26,
excusing himself on the ground of ill health, though his real desire was
to stay in the house for a few days and decide with his friends and advisers how best to put an end to the impudent boldness of his enemies,
which now passed all bounds. The *vecinos* and chief gentlemen of the
city called on the marquis after mass that Sunday, having noted his ab-

sence, and after seeing him, retired to their houses, leaving with him only Dr. Velázquez and Francisco de Chaves, who was his intimate friend.

The Chileans, aware that the marquis was now more suspicious than hitherto and that his supporters had visited him in such numbers, suspected that a plan was being arranged to kill them. Thus they grew alarmed, and like desperadoes that very Sunday, at the hour when all were at dinner and the marquis himself had just dined, they all came out into the corner of the square to the left side of the cathedral church, where Don Diego de Almagro the younger and his chief followers lodged, and they crossed obliquely over the square, which is very long, to the marquis' house in the opposite corner. There were thirteen of them. Twelve are named by López de Gómara, though he does not say where they came from. They are Juan de Rada, who was leader of the rest; Martín de Bilbao; Diego Méndez; Cristóbal de Sosa; Martín Carrillo; Arbolancha; Hinojeros; Narváez; San Millán; Porras; Velázquez; Francisco Núñez; and Gómez Pérez, who was the one not mentioned by López de Gómara.

They crossed the whole square with their swords bared shouting: "Down with the traitor and tyrant who has killed the judge the emperor sent to punish him!" The reason why they came out so openly and made so much noise was to cause the people of the city to think that they must be very numerous, since they dared to do such a deed so publicly, and thus prevent them from coming out of their houses to help the marquis. The manner in which they did it was astonishingly bold and rash, but it was the marquis' misfortune that the partisans of Don Diego de Almagro should succeed in their aim under pretence of avenging their leader's death, as we shall see.

CHAPTER VII

The death of the marquis and his poor funeral.

HEARING the noise made by the Chileans, some Indians in the marquis' service entered his room and warned him of their approach and their threatening appearance. The marquis was talking to the mayor, Dr. Velázquez, Captain Francisco Chaves, who acted as his deputy, and Francisco Martín de Alcántara, his half-brother, as well as twelve or thirteen of his servants, and he suspected what was afoot when the Indians brought the warning. He bade Francisco de Chaves shut the door of the room and the hall where they were, while he and his friends got their arms and prepared to defend themselves from the attackers.

Francisco de Chaves thought that the affair was a private quarrel by some soldiers and that his authority would be sufficient to stop it; and instead of shutting the door as he had been ordered, he went out to meet them and found them already climbing the stairs. Much disturbed at finding what he had not expected, he asked them: "What do you want?" One of them thrust at him with a sword for answer. Finding himself wounded, he laid his hand on his own sword, but they all attacked him and one struck him so hard in the neck that, as López de Gómara says in his ch. cxlv: "his head was smitten off and his body went rolling down the stairs." The marquis' servants who were in the room came out at the noise, but on seeing Francisco Chaves lying dead, they turned back and fled like mercenaries, flinging themselves down from windows that gave on to a garden of the house. These included Dr. Juan Velázquez, who had his wand of office in his mouth so as to free his hands, and hoping apparently that the attackers would respect it. These last forced their way into the room, and finding no one there, went on into the hall.

When the marquis realized they were so close, he went out half armed without having had time to tie the laces of a breastplate he had put on. He had a shield on his arm and carried a sword in his hand. He was accompanied by his brother Francisco Martín de Alcántara and two pages, fully grown men, one called Juan de Vargas, the son of Gómez de Tordoya, and the other Alonso Escandón. They wore no armor, for they had no opportunity to get any. The marquis and his brother stood at the door and defended it bravely for a long time without letting the attackers pass. The marquis, full of spirit, told his brother: "Kill them, they are traitors!" Both sides fought hard, until the marquis' brother was killed, for he had no armor. One of the pages took his place, and he and his master defended the door so manfully that the enemy began to doubt whether they could force a way through. So, fearing lest help would come for the marquis and they would all be killed if the struggle went on long, Juan de Rada and one of his companions seized Narváez and threw him through the door, so as to keep the marquis busy while the rest of them got past. So it fell out; for while the marquis received Narváez at the point of his sword and dealt him several wounds of which he soon died, the rest came in, and some attacked the marquis and others his pages, who fell fighting like men, having severely wounded four of their opponents. When they found the marquis alone, they all fell on him and surrounded him on all sides. He defended himself like the great man he was for a long while, leaping from side to side and wielding his sword with such force and skill that three of his assailants were severely wounded. But as there were so many of them, and he was more than seventy-five years old, he soon wearied, and one of them approached and struck him in the throat with his sword, whereupon he fell to the ground, shouting for confession. So lying, he made a cross with his right hand, put his lips to it, and died kissing it.

This was the end of Don Francisco Pizarro, famous above all famous men, who so enriched and extended, and still does extend, the crown of Spain and the whole world with the riches of the empire he gained, as can be seen and as we have often repeated. With all his greatness and wealth, he was so wretched and poor when he died that there was no one to bury him. In less than an hour fortune matched the favor and prosperity she had shown him throughout his life with no less disfavor and misery. In confirmation of which Zárate says in his Book IV, ch. viii:

Thus he gave his soul to God, and his two pages died at the same time. Of the Chileans, four were killed and others were wounded. When the news was known in the city, more than two hundred men rallied to Don Diego, who, though they were prepared, had not dared to show themselves till after the deed. They now ran about the city, arresting and disarming all those who came out in support of the marquis. And as the murderers came out with blood on their swords, Juan de Rada made Don Diego mount a horse and ride about the city saying that there was no other governor or king in Peru but he. And after sacking the houses of the marquis and his stepbrother and Antonio Picado, he made the city council receive Don Diego as governor, under pretext of the agreement made with His Majesty at the time of the discovery by which Almagro was to be governor of New Toledo and his son or nominee after him. Certain vassals who were servants and retainers of the marquis were killed, and the weeping and wailing of the wives of those who had been killed and plundered was pitiable to hear.

The marquis was almost dragged to the church by some Negroes, and no one dared bury him until Juan de Barbarán, a native of Trujillo, who had been a servant of the marquis, and his wife buried him and his brother as best they could, after receiving Don Diego's permission to do so. They were in such haste that they hardly had time to dress him in the habit of the Order of Santiago and put on his spurs after the fashion of members of the order, for they were warned that the Chileans were coming in a hurry to cut off the marquis' head and expose it on the gibbet. So Juan de Barbarán buried him, and then performed the honors and exequies, finding the wax and other expenses himself. Having buried him, he went to rescue his children, who were scattered and in hiding, while the Chileans remained in possession of the city.

This shows how the things of this world are and how great is the mutability of fortune; for in so brief a time a gentleman who had discovered and conquered as great realms and lands, and possessed as much wealth, and given out as many grants of land and income as the most powerful prince in the world of that time died, without confession and without opportunity to order the affairs of his soul or of his descendants, at the hands of a dozen men in broad daylight in a city where all the chief residents were his servants or kinsmen or soldiers, all of whom he had amply fed and provided for. Yet now no one came to his aid, but even his household servants fled and abandoned him. And he was buried as ignominiously as we have said, and from all the wealth and prosperity he had possessed he descended in a moment to the stage where he had nothing left even to buy candles for his funeral. And all this happened to him despite the fact that he had been forewarned by the means we have mentioned above, and by many others, of the plots against him.

These are the words of Agustín de Zárate, and they might be a repetition of those describing the death and burial of Almagro, so similar were the two; and in this and all the other events of their lives and deaths the two seem to have been equals, as they swore to be when they formed their association for the conquest of the empire of Peru. The similarity of their experiences applied to everything, as Zárate himself says and as we shall see in the following chapter. Many years later, after the wars that disturbed the empire had been ended, the bones of this valiant gentleman were removed from their grave; and in order to honor him as he merited they were put in a coffin in a space dug in the front of the cathedral church of Lima, a little to the right of the high altar, where they still lay when I left for Spain in 1560. The marquis' death occurred on June 26, 1541.

Zárate, like an excellent historian, imitating the great Plutarch, draws the parallel between these two famous and unfortunate Spaniards, never adequately praised yet ill rewarded by the world. And comparing the two of them and their customs, life, and death, he makes a separate chapter, which is the ninth in his Book IV, and shall be the eighth in Book Three of the second part of our *Commentaries*, though it is by another hand. It runs, as follows, copied with its title word for word.

CHAPTER VIII

"On the customs and qualities of the marquis Don Francisco Pizarro and the adelantado Don Diego de Almagro."

As the whole of this history and the discovery of the province of Peru with which it deals have their origin in the two captains of whom we have been speaking, the marquis Don Francisco Pizarro and the *adelantado* Don Diego de Almagro, it is fitting that we should write of their customs and qualities and compare them together, as Plutarch does when he writes of the deeds of two captains who have anything in common. And as we have said all that can be discovered of their lineages, we may add that in other respects both were full of courage and resolution, very patient of hardships and most virtuous men, both of them inclined to please everyone even though at their own expense. They bore a close resemblance to one another in their inclinations, especially in regard to their state of life, for neither of them married, though neither was under sixty-five when he died.

"Both were inclined to warfare, though the *adelantado* was fond of husbandry when there was no occasion for fighting.

"Both set out on the conquest of Peru at an advanced age, and both labored on it as we have said above, though the marquis suffered great dangers and many more than the *adelantado*; for while the former was engaged on the greater part of the discovery, the latter remained in Panama, providing whatever was necessary, in the manner we have described.

"Both were men of great spirit who always conceived high thoughts and strove to put them into execution, despite the great hardships they involved and notwithstanding their humanity and friendliness toward their followers. They were also liberal in giving, though in appearances the *adelantado* was the more so, for he very much liked his generosity to be published abroad and talked about. The marquis was rather the reverse, and was inclined to be annoyed if his liberality became public, and sought to hide it, being more concerned to meet the needs of those on whom he bestowed his gifts than to gain honor by them.

"Thus it happened that he heard that a soldier's horse had died and went down to the court for playing at ball in his house hoping to find the man, and carrying in his bosom a gold brick weighing ten pounds, which he meant to give him with his own hand. He did not find the man; meanwhile a game of ball was arranged and the marquis played without undressing so as not to show the brick, which he did not dare to remove from his bosom for above three hours, when the soldier who was to receive it arrived. Pizarro then secretly called him to a private room and gave it him saying that he would rather have presented him with three such bricks than have suffered the discomfort the man's delay had given him. Many other examples could be adduced of this quality. And it was extraordinarily rare for the marquis to give anything except by his own hand, and he always sought not to have it known.

"For this reason, the *adelantado* was always regarded as the more openhanded, for though he gave much he did it in such a way as to make it seem more. Yet with regard to the quality of magnificence, they may justly be matched with one another; for, as the marquis himself used to say, because of the conditions of their association with regard to all their property neither gave anything without the other contributing half.

"In this way the one who knowingly permitted the gift gave as much as the giver. This point of the comparison may be sufficiently illustrated by the fact that though the two of them were very wealthy men both in money and revenues in their lifetime, and either of them could give or hold more than many uncrowned princes in the past, yet both died so poor that not only is there no record of their having left any estates or wealth, but there was not even enough money found in their possession for their burial; the same is written of Cato, Sulla, and many other Roman captains who received public funerals.

"Both were very devoted to the interests of their friends and followers, whom they enriched, promoted, and saved from danger. The marquis had this quality to excess, so much so that once in crossing a river called the Barranca, it happened that the great stream carried off a Yanacona Indian in his service, and the marquis threw himself in after him and drew him forth by the hair, exposing himself to great danger owing to the furious force of the stream, which none of his whole army, however young and bold, dared face. And when some of the captains rebuked him for his excessive boldness, he replied that they did not know what it was to be fond of a servant.

"Although the marquis governed longer and more peacefully, Don Diego was much the more ambitious and desirous of command and government. Both preserved old-fashioned ways, and were so attached to them that they almost never changed the dress they wore in their youth. This was especially the case with the marquis who usually never dressed otherwise than in a black cassock with skirts down to the ankle and the waist halfway up his chest, and white deerskin shoes and a white hat, with his sword and dagger worn in the old-fashioned way.

"On some feast days, at the behest of his servants, he would put on a sable cloak the marquis del Valle had sent him from New Spain, but as soon as he came out of Mass he would cast it aside and remain in his house clothes. He usually had some napkins round his neck, for he spent most of the day in time of peace playing at bowls or at ball, and they served to wipe the sweat off his face.

"Both captains were very long suffering against toil and hunger, and the marquis was particularly so in the games we have mentioned, for there were few youths who could outlast him. He was much more inclined to all kinds of sport than the *adelantado,* so much so that sometimes he spent the whole day bowling, without caring who he played with, if it were a seaman or a miller, or without allowing others to hand him the ball or perform other courtesies due to his rank.

"There were few affairs for which he would break off his game, especially when he was losing, unless it were the news of some Indian disturbance. In this case he would at once don his armor and rush through the city with lance and shield to the place where the tumult was, without waiting for his followers, who afterwards caught up with him, running at all speed.

"These two captains were both so courageous and skilled in warfare with the Indians that either of them would have taken on a hundred Indian braves single-handed without the slightest hesitation. They had excellent judgment and were full of experience in all questions of warfare and government, particularly so as neither of them was well read: indeed they could not read or write or even sign their names, which was a great defect in persons of standing, apart from their need of it in business of such great consequence. Yet in all their qualities and pursuits they never appeared to be anything but noble, except in this matter alone which the learned men of old esteemed a mark of base birth.

"The marquis had such confidence in all his servants and friends that he delivered all his documents referring to questions of administration and the allocation of Indians by making two marks between which his secretary, Antonio Picado, signed the name of Francisco Pizarro.

"This may be excused as Ovid excused Romulus for being a bad astrologer, saying that he knew more of arms than of letters and was more con-

cerned with conquering his neighbors. Both were simple and unpreten-
tious among their followers and fellow citizens, and went unescorted from
house to house, visiting the *vecinos* and dining with whoever invited
them. They were similarly abstinent and temperate, both in feeding and
eating and in curbing their sensuality, especially as regards Castilian
women; for they considered that they could not indulge themselves except to the detriment of the *vecinos* and their daughters and wives. Even
as regards the Indian women of Peru, the *adelantado* was much the more
temperate, for he was never known to have children by them or intercourse
with them, though the marquis had a liaison with an Indian lady, a sister
of Atahuallpa's by whom he left a son called Don Gonzalo, who died at
fourteen, and a daughter called Doña Francisca. And he had a son called
Don Francisco by another Indian of Cuzco. The *adelantado* had the son
who killed the marquis by an Indian woman of Panama.

"Both received favors from His Majesty, for Don Francisco Pizarro was
given the title of marquis and governor of New Castile and awarded the
habit of Santiago. And Don Diego de Almagro was given the governorship of New Toledo and made *adelantado*.

"The marquis in particular was much attached to His Majesty and
fearful of his name, so much so that he abstained from doing many things
which he had power to do, saying that he did not wish His Majesty to
say that he was exceeding himself. Often when he was in the smelting
house he would rise from his chair to pick up grains of gold and silver that
fell from the chisel as the royal fifth was being cut, saying that the royal
treasury must be gathered up with the mouth, if there was no other way.
They resembled one another even in the manner of their death, for the
marquis' brother killed the *adelantado* and the *adelantado's* son killed the
marquis.

"The marquis was also very devoted to the development of Peru by
improving its agriculture and buildings. He made some fine houses in
Lima and left two sluices for mills in the river there, to the building of
which he devoted all his idle moments, spurring on the workmen.

"He was very solicitous for the building of the cathedral of Lima and
the monasteries of St. Dominic and the Mercedarians, and gave them allocations of Indians for their support and the repair of the buildings."

Thus Zárate: in the following chapter we shall comment on this author's words and add other excellencies of this never sufficiently praised
gentleman.

CHAPTER IX

The affability of the marquis; his inventions
for succoring those he felt to be in need.

T HE MARQUIS had only one son and one daughter, and Gonzalo Pizarro
one son, as we said in Book IX, ch. xxxviii, though Zárate makes them
all children of the marquis. The mother of the marquis' son was a daughter
and not a sister of Atahuallpa. His daughter was by a daughter of Huaina
Cápac called Doña Beatriz Huaillas Ñusta, as we have explained at length
in the above chapter.

It is quite true as this author says that though the two governors had
been very rich they died so poor that there was scarcely enough in their
possession to bury them. They had no property at all, but were buried by
charity. Almagro was buried by a man who had been his slave, and the
marquis by one who was his servant, as the same author says. Those who
carried both to their burial were Negroes and Indians, as both authors
say. Let this suffice to show how the world treats and repays those who
serve it best when their need is greatest.

The marquis was so kindly and gentle by nature that he never said a
hard word to anyone. When playing bowls he would not let anyone get
up to give him his ball: and if anyone did so, he would take it and throw
it to a distance, and then go after it himself. Once when he picked the
ball up he dirtied his hand on a piece of mud sticking to it: he lifted his
foot and cleaned his hand on the sandal he was wearing, for in those days
and much later, even in my own time, it was regarded as a piece of gallantry and ostentation to wear sandals and not shoes in warfare. One of
the marquis' favorite servants, on seeing him clean his hand thus, came
up to him and said: "Your Lordship could have cleaned your hand on the
handkerchief you have in your belt and not on your sandal."

The marquis smiled and replied: "Bless my soul, it looks so white I
wouldn't dare touch it."

One day when the marquis was playing bowls with a good soldier
called Alonso Palomares (a cheerful and conversable man whom I
knew), he happened to be losing and was excessively annoyed and
grumbled about Palomares at every ball, so that everyone noticed that his

vexation was greater than usual, either because of some hidden annoyance or because of the loss of his stake, which was more than eight or nine thousand pesos. Many days passed, and though the winner often claimed his money, the marquis did not pay. One day the marquis grew angry at being asked for the money so often and said: "Don't ask me any more because I'm not going to pay you."

Palomares replied: "Well, if Your Lordship wasn't going to pay me, why did you grumble so much at losing?" This answer amused the marquis very much, and he ordered the money to be paid at once. He played with many people at all sorts of games, and the marquis himself used to invite many to play with him when he knew they were in need, so as to help them by losing at play: in this way the recipient was not humiliated as he would be by being given alms as a pauper, but rather seemed to have gained honor by showing himself a better player than the marquis; and the money seemed to have been won and taken by force and not given freely. When he played ninepins in these circumstances he aimed short or wide and did not knock over the pins he could have done, so as to let the other win. And when he played cards, which was usually at *primera*, he used to stake his main on the worst cards he could, and if by any chance he had a flush he would shuffle his cards without looking at them and pretend to be angry at having lost. In these and similar ways he made himself as much beloved as by his deeds and generosity.

López de Gómara, speaking of the death of this prince—and more than prince, for there is no title on earth that fully expresses his greatness and merits—speaks as follows in his ch. cxlv:

He was a bastard son of Gonzalo Pizarro, a captain in Navarre. He was born at Trujillo and left at the church door: he was suckled by a sow for various days, being unable to find anyone to give him milk. His father later recognized him, and brought him to look after his pigs. In this way he never learned to read. One day he annoyed the pigs and lost them. He did not dare to return home out of fear, and went to Seville with some travellers, and thence to the Indies. He was in Santo Domingo, passed to Urabá with Alonso de Hojeda, and went with Vasco Núñez de Balboa to discover the Southern Sea, and with Pedrarias to Panama. He discovered and conquered what is called Peru,

etc.

Such are the words of this author, and there is much in them that calls for reproach, if such may be permitted, both in the case of the writer and in that of his informant, for it was not right to say such low things of a gentleman of whom he himself had written such great deeds of arms;

even if they had been true, they should have been suppressed, the more so as they have no verisimilitude whatever. I should like to ask the informant where he heard such details about the birth of so poor a child, for he himself says Pizarro was left at the church door and sucked the milk of a beast because there was no one to give him milk. If such things happen to the sons of great kings and princes, it is unusual for them to be recorded, much more so in the case of an abandoned child left at the church door. To say that his father after recognizing him as his son sent him to keep his pigs clearly shows the envy and malice of the informant, for it does not make sense that a noble gentleman like Gonzalo Pizarro, the marquis' father, a captain of men-at-arms in Navarre, should set his son to keep swine once he had recognized him.

To say that he annoyed the pigs and that they got lost, so that he did not dare return home from fear, also argues great malice on the part of the narrator, for I have taken special care on this point, and have consulted many famous pig breeders, to find out if it is true that they can be so annoyed and they all in general have told me that there is no such thing.

Envy in countries where there are rivalries usually produces similar calumnies against the most valiant men there are in these rival parties; for when it is impossible to tarnish and belittle their great deeds, especially if they are as great and famous as those of the marquis Don Francisco Pizarro, their enemies seek to invent similar fables about their birth and upbringing, which were less famous than their deeds and liberality.

The truth is that the marquis Don Francisco Pizarro, the conqueror and governor of the great empire called Peru, was the natural son of his father and mother, and recognized as such even before he was born. His father, Captain Gonzalo Pizarro, married the marquis' mother, who was an old Christian, to an honest farmer called ——— de Alcántara, whose son was Francisco Martín de Alcántara, whom López de Gómara himself describes as Pizarro's half-brother. He died at the marquis' side, as we have said. Thus such things cannot be permitted to be said of such a prince, who may be equalled with all those recorded by fame, and should not be said, even if they were true. With this, since I cannot praise this great gentleman as he deserves, I will let his superhuman deeds and conquests praise him, the last of which was the conquest of Peru, and pass on with my history.

CHAPTER X

Almagro the younger has himself sworn in as
governor of Peru; he sends instructions
to various parts of the kingdom;
they are defied.

T HE MARQUIS died, as we have seen, through the overconfidence of
Francisco de Chaves, who failed to shut the gates as he was bidden.
If he had done so, those who were with the marquis would have had time
to arm themselves while the attackers were breaking in, and would possibly have overcome the Almagrists. Since only four of them, the marquis,
his brother and his two pages, all ill armed, killed four of their assailants
as the historians say, it may well be believed that if they had been better
prepared these four and those who got away through the windows would
have been sufficient to ward off their enemies and even to defeat them,
for even though they themselves did not win the fray, help might have
come in due course. But when misfortune occurs, it is hard to remedy it
through human counsel.

The Negro López de Gómara mentions as being killed by the Chileans
had heard the hubbub caused by the fight with the marquis and gone up-
stairs to help his master or die with him, but on reaching the door found
him already dead. He tried to bolt it from the outside so as to shut the
murderers in and call the justice, but as he was pulling the doors together,
one of those within happened to come out, and realizing the slave's intention, attacked him and killed him with his sword. Seven of the marquis'
followers died, including a servant of Francisco de Chaves. Then the
Almagrists came out into the square with bloody swords, singing victory.
Such was the end of the good marquis, due to the neglect and overconfidence of his friends rather than to the power of his enemies.

With the news of his death a great to-do was raised throughout the
city. Some shouted: "Help in the king's name, they're killing the marquis!" others cried: "The tyrant is dead and Don Diego de Almagro is
avenged!" Amidst this shouting and confusion many came out to support
either side, and there were many quarrels and frays in the square, resulting in dead and wounded on both sides. But when it became known for

certain that the marquis was dead, his followers at once gave up. The Chileans now brought out Don Diego de Almagro the younger into the square, saying that there was no other king in Peru but he. Once the disturbances had settled down, he had himself sworn in by the city council as governor of Peru and nobody dared gainsay him, though all the members of the council were on the opposite side. Yet no one dared speak up or oppose the demands of the victors. The ministers of justice were removed and others of the winning side put in their stead. The richest and most powerful men in Lima were arrested because they were on the other side; and in short Almagro took possession of the whole city. He seized the royal fifths, for which a very large sum was in store. The same was done with the property of the dead and absent. All this was needed to help the Almagrists, who were as poor as we have said.

He named Juan de Rada as his captain general, and appointed as captains Juan Tello de Guzmán, a native of Seville, and Francisco de Chaves, a close kinsman of the other Francisco de Chaves who was killed with the marquis; such is the effect of civil wars in which brothers are against brothers. He also made Cristóbal Sotelo a captain and appointed other officers. The report of these events brought all the Spaniards who were wandering idly and ruinously round Peru flocking to Lima, and in this way Almagro raised more than eight hundred soldiers. He sent messengers to Cuzco, Arequipa, the Charcas, and down the coast as far as Trujillo and inland to Chachapoyas to require and demand absolutely that he should be acknowledged as governor of the whole empire. In one or two cities he was obeyed, though from fear rather than from affection, for they had no forces with which to resist the fifty men Don Diego sent against them; the other cities resisted, as we shall say.

In Peru it is usual to say up-coast and down-coast, not because there are ups and downs on the coast, for generally speaking there are none, but down-coast is applied to the new sailing route followed by those travelling before the south wind from Peru to Panama. This is down-coast, as that wind always blows. And they use the word up-coast for the journey from Panama to Peru referring to the opposition of the same wind, which forces them to struggle as if they were going up hill.

Juan de Rada took all the steps we have mentioned in Don Diego's name with absolute powers, and without informing the other captains and companions who had been present at the marquis' death. This led to envy and ill feeling among the leaders, and they considered killing Juan de Rada. When this plot was known, they garrotted Francisco de Chaves, who was the ringleader, and killed many others, including Antonio de

Orihuela, a native of Salamanca, though he had but recently arrived from Spain, for they had heard that on the way he had said they were rebels; and he had so little regard to his own interests that after saying this he appeared among them.

One of the officials sent by Don Diego to go along the coast and take possession of the towns, raise recruits, and seize horses and arms from the *vecinos* who were on the other side (for most of them were his enemies) was a gentleman called García de Alvarado, who went to Trujillo, and removed Diego de Mora from the office of judge there, although he was a lieutenant of Almagro's. This was because it was known that he gave information about all that was going on to Alonso de Alvarado, who was on the opposite side. In the city of San Miguel he beheaded Francisco de Vozmediano and Hernando de Villegas, and committed other excesses; and in Huánucu he killed Alonso de Cabrera, who had been steward to the marquis Don Francisco Pizarro, because he had collected some companions together to flee with them to the royalist side.

Another of Don Diego's ministers called Diego Méndez went to Los Charcas, to the town of La Plata, which he found abandoned, for the *vecinos* had gone off in various directions to join those of the city of Cuzco and take the king's side with them, as we shall see. Diego Méndez took a great deal of gold which the settlers had hidden in the hands of their Indians, who are usually so feeble that they will tell all they know on the slightest threat.

He also took more than sixty thousand pesos of pure silver from the mines called Porco, for those of Potosí had not then been discovered. He confiscated the Indians and the very valuable estates that had belonged to the marquis and placed them under the control of Don Diego de Almagro; and he did the same with the Indians belonging to Captain Diego de Rojas, Pero Ansúrez, Gabriel de Rojas, Garcilaso de la Vega, and all the other *vecinos* of the place, who were all friends of the Pizarros.

Another messenger was sent to the province of Chachapoyas, which was being pacified by Alonso de Alvarado. The latter, on seeing Don Diego's letters and instructions, though these offered great rewards if he obeyed and made great threats in case he refused, replied by arresting the messenger and persuading a hundred Spaniards who came with him to take His Majesty's side. With their agreement he raised the royal flag. And though Don Diego sent him other messengers, he refused to obey him, and replied that he would not acknowledge him as governor until he had seen an express order from His Majesty to that effect. This he knew His Majesty would not send, and he hoped with the aid of God and his own friends to avenge the marquis' death and punish the disrespect that had been shown His Majesty. In making this reply Alonso de Alvarado was relying on the inaccessibility of that province, the difficulty of which we have often referred to. Although Alvarado had few men, he hoped to hold out until other Pizarrists gathered to serve the emperor, for he well knew that many would rally to him. Thus he waited to see what would happen, summoning to him those who were on the coast; and we shall leave him there and turn to others who did likewise.

The messengers who took Almagro's powers and instructions to Cuzco did not dare to commit any of the outrages that had taken place elsewhere; for though they had many partisans in the city, there were many more royalists, and these included the richest and most powerful inhabitants who had allocations of Indians, while Don Diego's party consisted of poor soldiers newly arrived in Peru who desired such disorders in order that they too might prosper. The alcaldes of the city were then Diego de Silva, whom I have mentioned before, the son of Feliciano de Silva and a native of Ciudad Rodrigo, and Francisco de Carvajal, who was later commander under Gonzalo Pizarro. When these had seen the letters, they wished to avoid irritating the Almagrists and they and the whole council made reply neither obeying nor opposing, but saying that in a matter of such gravity it was necessary for Don Diego to send fuller powers than he had done; and when he did this, he would be accepted as governor. They said this not meaning to accept him but only to keep him waiting so that there should be time and opportunity for those who were on the Pizarrist side and were then absent to come to Cuzco: most of them were out of the cities on their allocations or at their gold mines, which most of the allocations of Cuzco have.

CHAPTER XI

Steps taken by the vecinos of Cuzco in the king's
service, and those adopted by Don Diego; the
appointment in Spain of Vaca de Castro
to be judge of the events of Peru.

GÓMEZ DE TORDOYA, who was one of the chief members of the city
council of Cuzco, was not in the city when Don Diego de Almagro's
instructions and powers arrived. He had gone hunting seven or eight
days before, and his retainers sent a messenger to warn him of what had
happened. As soon as he read the letter he was so stricken with grief at the
death of the marquis, of whom he was a close friend and servant, that he
wrung the neck of his falcon, saying: "This is a time for fire and the
sword rather than for hunting and pastimes." For, like an intelligent man,
he realized that these events would lead to great disorders and cruel
deaths. He then went to the city, which he entered by night, so as not to
alarm his opponents, and spoke to the leading members of the council,
telling them that they ought to summon people from Arequipa and Los
Charcas and the whole region to the south of Cuzco and bring in the Spaniards who were dispersed. Messengers should be sent to convey the news,
and he offered himself as one of them. This done, he left the city the
same night and went in search of Captain Nuño de Castro, who was fifteen or twenty leagues from the city, among his Indians. Both sent messengers to Pedro Ansúrez and Garcilaso de la Vega with orders to collect
all His Majesty's servants and bid them rally to his service like loyal
subjects.

After sending this message, Gómez de Tordoya went off in all haste in
pursuit of Captain Pedro Alvarez Holguín, who had taken over a hundred Spaniards on an expedition to the east of the Collao to conquer some
Indians in those parts who have still not been reduced even today. By
making all haste he overtook him, and informed him of the marquis'
death and of how Almagro the younger was claiming to be governor of
the empire. He urged Holguín to shoulder the task and undertake so
just a quest in the service of his God and king, begging him to act as
leader of the forces that were being collected, and telling him, as a further inducement, that he offered himself as the first and least of his sol-

diers. Holguín, seeing the honor that was done him and the justice of the cause, accepted the task and at once raised His Majesty's flag and sent messengers to Los Charcas and Arequipa, to report his intentions and to say how he was going to march slowly with the forces he had toward Cuzco so that those who came behind would catch up with him before he reached the city. The messengers found many coming from Arequipa and Los Charcas, for the whole country was already in an uproar at the confused news that rumor had spread about the marquis' death. The men from Arequipa and Los Charcas joined Holguín and marched to Cuzco as a group of about two hundred men.

When the supporters of Don Diego who were in the city heard about this, they were afraid that they would be subjected to some rigorous punishment, and one night more than fifty of them fled in a band, meaning to join Almagro: there was no one of any prominence among them. Captain Nuño de Castro and Hernando Bachicao went out after them with twenty arquebusiers, and after a rapid night march captured them and brought them back to Cuzco unharmed. Meanwhile Pedro Alvarez Holguín reached the city with his good company, which included many leading gentlemen. The council of Cuzco received them with great content, and those in the city and the newcomers at once set about choosing a captain general, for Holguín resigned the post of captain on reaching the city. There was some delay and difference of opinion in making the choice, not because of passion but out of courtesy toward one another, for there were many gentlemen in the city who were equal in rank and merits and who deserved this office and other higher honors. But by the common consent of those who had newly come and those who were already in the city, Holguín was chosen and sworn as captain general and chief justice of Peru until His Majesty should decide otherwise. The citizens were within their rights in doing this; for in default of a governor appointed by His Majesty, the council of Cuzco, as the capital city of the empire, was authorized to nominate officials for war and the administration of justice until His Majesty should make appointments. They elected Gómez de Tordoya as commander; Garcilaso de la Vega and Pedro Ansúrez as captains of cavalry; Nuño de Castro and Hernando Bachicao as captains of infantry; and Martín de Robles as bearer of the royal standard.

They publicly declared war on Don Diego de Almagro, and the *vecinos* of Cuzco bound themselves to repay His Majesty all that Holguín might spend on the war from the royal treasury, if His Majesty did not approve the expense. In addition to guaranteeing the royal treasury in this way, the people of Cuzco also offered their persons and property for the campaign, and those of Arequipa and Los Charcas did likewise. And everyone displayed such promptitude and willingness to serve His Majesty that in a short time more than 350 men were recruited, captains and picked soldiers. Of these 150 were horse, 100 arquebusiers, and the remaining 100 pikemen. Holguín had heard that Alonso de Alvarado had raised his flag for the emperor in Chachapoyas, and he and all his men rejoiced at it, for they had feared that the whole area from Lima to Quito was for Don Diego de Almagro. They also knew that Almagro was coming to Cuzco to make war on them, bringing more than 800 men. When the captains had discussed this together, they considered that it would not be safe to wait for the enemy in Cuzco, but that it would be best to join Alonso de Alvarado, taking the mountain road so as to avoid meeting Almagro and to collect the friends and servants of the marquis who had fled from Almagro to the mountains and fastnesses along the road. With this determination they left Cuzco, leaving the old and sick behind so as to suggest that the city was still on their side. They also appointed a justice to govern it. They set out well equipped, with their scouts in front to explore the land and determined to fight Don Diego, if they could not capture him.

While these preparations were being made in Cuzco, Don Diego de Almagro and his captains had not been idle in Lima. They had heard by secret letters from their friends what Holguín had done, and how he had decided to go across the mountains to join Alonso de Alvarado since he had too few men to resist the Almagrists. Then Don Diego decided, with the approval of his captains, to go forward and meet them. To this end he sent to summon his captain García de Alvarado to come back with all haste: he had gone down the coast below Trujillo and was gathering men, arms, and horses. When he received Don Diego's orders he obeyed, though he had previously resolved to go to the Chachapoyas against Alonso de Alvarado, thinking he was the stronger. When García de Alvarado arrived, Don Diego left Lima to go to Cuzco against Holguín. He had 300 horses, all excellently equipped, 120 arquebusiers and more than 160 pikemen, making nearly 600 in all, all picked men. Many noble and rich gentlemen went with them, having been taken by Don Diego when he killed the marquis.

On departing Almagro expelled the children of the marquis and of Gonzalo Pizarro so that none of his enemies should remain behind and the supporters of the marquis could not raise up one of his sons as their leader, as Almagro's men had raised him up. In order to find out if the marquis had left some secret treasure he had his secretary Antonio Picado severely tortured, and having got nothing out of him, hanged him, in payment of the medallion he had worn in his hat to mock the Chileans. This done, he marched on Cuzco, taking all military precautions on the way.

We shall leave him on his journey, and Holguín on his, to return to say what His Imperial Majesty decided in Spain when news of the troubles in Peru up to the time of the death of Almagro the elder came to his ears. His Majesty chose Licentiate Vaca de Castro, a member of his royal council, to go and obtain information about Almagro's death, but without making any alteration in the marquis' powers. However Vaca de Castro held a commission to become governor of Peru if the marquis should die in the meanwhile. This illustrious gentleman, as his works will prove him to be, was a native of the city of León, a member of the family of Vaca de Castro of Quiñones, very noble names among the many there are in that royal city.

He embarked in Seville for Peru, and after difficulties in the Northern Sea, reached Nombre de Dios later than he had intended. He crossed thence to Panama, where he embarked for Peru in a ship that was but poorly equipped to speed the journey of one entrusted with so important and grave a mission. After sailing a few leagues, it pulled inshore because the wind was contrary. And it was so contrary that they lost an anchor, for lack of which the currents bore the ship away and carried it to the place called the Seno de la Gorgona, after the island of that name, a very difficult place for any ship that enters to leave, especially if it is sailing toward Peru. Therefore Vaca de Castro, after waiting to see if the mariners' efforts to get away would be successful and finding that they were all in vain, decided to go overland, as he could not progress by sea.

It was a long and very laborious journey, and took him longer than he would have wished because of the difficulty of the forests, the great rivers, and the rough mountains, which he crossed with some sickness and lack of supplies. His delay also gave Almagro the opportunity to hasten the vengeance of his murdered father, since the king's punishment was postponed. With these difficulties, Vaca de Castro reached the confines of Quito where Pedro de Puelles was acting as deputy for Gonzalo Pizarro. As soon as he found himself in the territory over which he had jurisdiction and heard what had happened in Peru and the divisions that had appeared, he wrote to all concerned announcing his arrival and the powers he held from the emperor, so that they should all accept him as their governor. He sent commissions to all the cities of Peru, naming as judges those whom he was told were independent of the passions of the two parties.

CHAPTER XII

The people of Lima and other places accept Vaca
de Castro as their governor; Holguín and his
men deceive Don Diego de Almagro and
join Don Alonso de Alvarado.

AMONG the instructions Licentiate Vaca de Castro sent out, that to Lima
was addressed to Fray Tomás de San Martín, who was then provincial of the Order of St. Dominic, and to Francisco de Barrionuevo
and Jerónimo de Aliaga, who were to undertake the government of the
city and those beyond it, until he himself should arrive. These despatches
were received in the convent of St. Dominic a few days after Don Diego
had left the city. The provincial was away, for Don Diego had taken him
with him in order to give his expedition the prestige that might be
derived from his presence, but the council met by night and agreed
unanimously to obey the instructions and receive the Licentiate Vaca de
Castro as governor of the empire, and Jerónimo de Aliaga as his lieutenant, since the instructions were also addressed to him. This done, the
vecinos at once fled to Trujillo, for Don Diego was near and they were
afraid. He, on hearing of this change in the city, was on the point of
returning to sack it, burn it, and level it to the ground for so soon turning
against him. But he did not dare to do this, lest Holguín should pass him
in the meantime; for this was the prey he most desired to capture and
the one of greatest importance to him. Because of this fear he went on in
search of Holguín, but not without misgivings, for when it became
known in his army that the emperor's governor had arrived in Peru,
many of the leading men fled, including the provincial, Juan de Saavedra,
the factor Illén Suárez de Carvajal, Diego de Agüero, and Gómez de
Alvarado. Despite these reverses Almagro went on, and to his greater
distress and undoing, his lieutenant general Juan de Rada fell sick,
which troubled him greatly, for he did not dare leave him behind lest
the enemy kill him, and could not travel with him, for the illness was too
serious. However, he continued his search for Holguín, which was his
main objective, as best he could.

When Pedro Alvarez knew that the enemy was near and had a much
larger force than he, he decided not to risk an encounter, since his small

army was of great importance for His Majesty's service, but agreed, with the approval of his captains, to avoid an open conflict with Don Diego and to get past him by tricking him with a stratagem. He sent twenty chosen horsemen, and bade them go ahead as scouts and do all they could to capture one of Don Diego's soldiers. This they executed so well that they arrested three of the enemy spies. Pedro Alvarez hanged two of them, and made great promises for the future to the third, and said he would give him 3,000 gold pesos to return to Don Diego's camp and tell some of his friends to come over to his side and stand by him in the battle, for Holguín had decided to attack Almagro's army the following night or early in the morning. He would strike from the east, crossing the skirt of the snowy mountains, which would be the road the enemy would least expect him to take. The man was to make similar offers of rewards and grants to his friends, and was told that all such promises would be amply redeemed, as the service they would do their lord the emperor merited. They made him swear an oath of fealty that he would not tell anyone and told him they had trusted their greatest secrets to him as to a good friend. The soldier returned to Don Diego's camp, and as Don Diego knew that the other two had been hanged and this one set free for no legitimate reason, he became suspicious and arrested the man and had him tortured. The soldier confessed the secret he had been entrusted with, and told how Holguín was thinking of attacking him across a skirt of the snowy mountains, because he thought his enemy would think the crossing impossible and be taken unawares. When Don Diego saw that the soldier was acting as a double spy, he gave orders that he was to be hanged, but gave credit to his words (which was what Holguín wanted) and set off with his men to cross the snowy mountains, which took him three days amid much suffering from the cold. Meanwhile Holguín gave him the slip. Almagro followed him for a few leagues, but seeing that he could not catch him, turned back to the road to Cuzco. Holguín continued his march and joined Alonso de Alvarado. Both parties met with great content and rejoicing, for most of them or almost all had entered Peru with Don Pedro de Alvarado and the bonds of this first brotherhood still subsisted among them. They then agreed to write to Licentiate Vaca de Castro reporting what had happened and bidding him come with all haste, for his presence was necessary.

When Vaca de Castro had sent out the messages we have mentioned, he went to the city of Quito in order to collect the men who were there. Lorenzo de Aldana, who was the marquis' deputy governor in Quito, came in to receive him, and so did Pedro de Puelles who was deputy for

Gonzalo Pizarro. Captain Pedro de Vergara, who was engaged in the conquest of the province called Pacamuru, which the Spaniards call Bracamoros, also came out to meet Licentiate Vaca de Castro, abandoning a village he had fortified to defend himself in in case Almagro came or sent men against him. Before Vaca de Castro left Quito, he sent Pedro de Puelles on ahead to Trujillo so as to make the necessary preparations for war there. He also sent Gómez de Rojas, a native of the town of Cuéllar, with powers to repair posthaste to Cuzco and try to get Vaca de Castro accepted as governor. He made such speed that he reached Cuzco before Almagro, who had been held up at Jauja by the illness and death of Juan de Rada, which occurred there. Gómez de Rojas was well received in Cuzco, and the governor's instructions were accepted and he was obeyed, for the people of the city had remained obedient to His Majesty, as Holguín had left them. Licentiate Vaca de Castro left Quito and went to Trujillo. On the way many noble gentlemen who had been scattered about Peru came out to greet him, as did many soldiers who desired to serve His Majesty. Holguín and his followers, who were now at Trujillo, decided to send two persons to offer, on behalf of all the rest, their obedience to His Majesty's governor, as we shall call him henceforward. Gómez de Tordoya and Garcilaso de la Vega were appointed to undertake this mission. The governor was delighted to see them and to find his party growing from day to day, for with those he had collected when he reached Trujillo, he had more than two hundred soldiers, including those who had fled from Don Diego de Almagro, who were the provincial, Illén Suárez de Carvajal, Gómez de Alvarado, Juan de Saavedra, and Diego de Agüero, who were all leading men in the country, as well as many others who went with them. At Trujillo the governor was received with the military solemnity customary in wartime, with music and the sound of trumpets, fifes, and drums, and many salvos of arquebus fire, and not with the solemnities of peace, for it was not a time for laws, but for arms.

CHAPTER XIII

*The governor chooses captains; he sends his army
forward, and takes other necessary steps in His
Majesty's interest; the death of Cristóbal de
Sotelo at the hands of García de Alvarado,
and that of García de Alvarado by
Don Diego de Almagro.*

HOLGUÍN and his captains and soldiers, in addition to offering their
duty to the governor by proxy, repeated their obedience in a solemn
public announcement in writing and delivered the army up to him, each
of the captains placing his commission and banner in the governor's
hands. The *regidores* and justice of the city of Trujillo did likewise. The
governor received them properly, and again confirmed them in His
Majesty's name in all the offices of peace and war they formerly held.
He appointed six cavalry captains, Pedro Alvarez Holguín, Alonso de
Alvarado, Pero Ansúrez, Gómez de Alvarado, Garcilaso de la Vega, and
Pedro de Puelles. He also appointed Pedro de Vergara, Nuño de Castro,
and Juan Vélez de Guevara captains of arquebusiers; for

though he [Vélez de Guevara] was himself a lawyer, he was a good soldier
and a man of such skill that he personally saw to the making of the arquebusses
with which the men of his company were equipped. But he never failed to
attend to legal matters, for both at this time and during the disturbances of
Gonzalo Pizarro (which will be described later) he was appointed alcalde, and
until mid-day he used to be dressed neatly as a lawyer and held audience and
settled suits, while from mid-day onwards he wore soldier's dress, with hose
and a gallant colored doublet with gold embroidery and a plume and a leather
jerkin and carried his arquebus on his shoulder, as he and his men practised
shooting.

Thus Zárate (Book IV, ch. xv), who thus amply shows that both
offices can be wielded at once by anyone who is capable of performing
them. The governor appointed Hernando Bachicao captain of the pikemen and Francisco de Carvajal sergeant major (he was later Gonzalo

Pizarro's commander). Gómez de Tordoya he made commander; and he kept the royal standard for himself and acted as general. With these captains and ministers in their various offices, the governor sent his army forward. It consisted of 700 men: 370 arquebusiers, 160 pikemen, and the rest horse. He ordered Captain Pedro de Puelles to go in front with 30 horsemen to spy out the land; he was to take the mountain road and not go beyond Jauja, but wait there for the governor who intended to go by the coast to Lima. He also ordered Diego de Mora to remain as deputy governor and captain.

Having done this, Vaca de Castro went to Lima, where he received the men and arms that were coming in from all sides. He left Francisco de Barrionuevo as his lieutenant there and made Juan Pérez [Vélez?] de Guevara captain by sea; and then followed his army to Jauja. He left instructions that if Almagro came down to Lima, Pérez [Vélez?] de Guevara, and Barrionuevo were to put the wives and children of the *vecinos* of the city and the aged and infirm aboard the ships that were in the port, so that the enemy could not harm them; he would then pursue Don Diego.

We shall leave him on his way, and return to say what happened among the Almagros in Cuzco. Discord was not content with kindling the fire of passion between the two sides, but, aided by envy, now stirred up enmities and caused bloodshed among the members of one of the parties, and among its chiefs and leaders, for these beasts are not content with underlings. As Don Diego was travelling toward Cuzco, as we have said earlier, he chose, on the death of Juan de Rada, Cristóbal de Sotelo and García de Alvarado to be the counsellors and ministers closest to his person and of greatest authority in his army. He sent the first of these ahead with a band of chosen men to reach Cuzco and take possession of the city and reduce it to loyalty and obedience to him, so that he would be welcomed when he arrived. Sotelo did as he was required, and entered Cuzco, where he found no defence capable of resisting him. He removed the officials Holguín had left, and replaced them with others of his own faction. He collected what supplies he could, for the Indians gave their own food to both parties, and themselves remained starving. When Almagro reached Cuzco he made a great deal of excellent gunpowder, for there is a fine saltpeter there, which is superior to that of the rest of Peru. He founded cannon, with the skill and industry of certain Levanters, which is the name given in the Indies to the Greeks. These rallied to him very willingly out of their regard for Pedro de Candía, who had gone over to the Almagros' side as a result of the wrongs he had suffered at the hands of Hernando Pizarro, as we have said. A great deal of excellent artillery was forged, for there is plenty of metal in Peru for the purpose; and Pedro de Candía was made captain of artillery. The Levanters, with the help of the Indian silversmiths, also made many helmets and corselets of copper and silver, which turned out excellently. Prince Manco Inca, who was in voluntary exile in the forests, recalled his past friendship with Don Diego de Almagro the elder, and wished to favor his son by offering the objects he had in his possession: coats of mail, cuirasses, helmets, lances, swords, and saddles, the plunder taken by the Indians from the Spaniards they had killed on the roads.

The Inca sent a great quantity of this to Don Diego; there were two hundred coats of mail and breastplates alone. But in the midst of his good fortune when Almagro was feeling that everything was turning out for him better than he could have asked, one of those incidents that discord seeks to sow everywhere occurred. Cristóbal de Sotelo and García de Alvarado were the heads and leaders of the army, but instead of joining together and agreeing on what was necessary for the conquest of the empire to which they aspired, they disagreed about everything, however trivial. The result was that they were almost declared enemies, as they were in their hearts; so much so that one day they quarrelled in the public square. Their quarrel reached such a pitch that quite unexpectedly García de Alvarado slew Cristóbal de Sotelo. And as they were both such prominent men, they had many friends, who flocked to the scene and caused a great disturbance, in which many would have been killed had not Don Diego appeared. He pacified the parties with soft and discreet words, but greatly regretted the death of Cristóbal de Sotelo, who had rallied to him promptly and with good will on all occasions. However, he dissimulated for the moment and reserved the punishment for the right opportunity. García de Alvarado did not fail to suspect this, for Almagro, however much he tried to hide his anger, could not prevent Alvarado from being aware of it. The result was that Alvarado, fearing his own downfall and seeing no way to placate Don Diego, behaved with great circumspection. But realizing that in the long run this would not save him, he decided to kill Almagro, hoping thus to obtain the governor's pardon for himself and his friends. He consulted with some of the boldest of them and they agreed that Alvarado should hold a solemn banquet and invite Don Diego, who could be easily killed in Alvarado's own house and among his friends. They invited Don Diego for a certain day and he accepted, so as not to disclose his feelings about Alvarado. But he was wise enough to realize what lay behind the invitation, and on the day he pretended to be ill, so as to avoid attending. Of this Zárate writes as follows:

And when García de Alvarado saw this, after having made all the necessary arrangements, he determined to go, with a good escort of his friends, and beseech Don Diego to attend. On the way it happened that he told a certain Martín Carrillo where he was going, who replied that he should not go, for he thought they would kill him. Another soldier told him almost the same thing, but this was not enough to dissuade him. Don Diego was lying on his bed, and had a number of gentlemen secretly carrying arms in his room. As García de Alvarado entered the antechamber with his companions, he called out: "Get up, Your Lordship. Your indisposition can't be anything serious; come and relax a little; for even if you don't eat much, you'll be the guest of honor for us."

Don Diego said he would, and called for his cloak, for he was lying down dressed in his coat of mail and with his sword and dagger. And as everyone began to leave the room, when García de Alvarado, who was in front of Don Diego, reached the door, Juan de Rada, who was holding the door, shut it with a slam and grappled with Alvarado saying: "You are under arrest!"

And Don Diego pulled out his sword and struck him, saying: "Not under arrest, but dead!" Then there appeared Juan Balsa, Alonso de Saavedra, Diego Méndez, the brother of Rodrigo Orgóñez, and others who were on guard; and they dealt Alvarado so many blows that they finished him off. When this was known throughout the city, a disturbance began. But Don Diego went out into the public square, and calmed the people, though some of García de Alvarado's friends took flight,

etc.

This is from Zárate's Book IV, ch. xiv, and López de Gómara says the same almost in the same words in his ch. cxlix. The soldier who Zárate says warned García de Alvarado not to go, but whom he does not name, was called Agustín Salado. When he says that Juan de Rada shut the door, he is making a slip of the pen, for he has already told how Rada died at Jauja. The man who shut the door was called Pedro de Oñate, and for performing this service in such good season Don Diego created him his commander.

CHAPTER XIV

*Almagro goes out in search of the governor; and
Gonzalo Pizarro leaves La Canela after having
undergone incredible hardships.*

S OME DAYS after settling the disturbance caused by the death of García
de Alvarado, Don Diego determined to go out and face Governor
Vaca de Castro, who he knew had left Lima and come in search of him.
He wished to suggest that he was not afraid of the governor, but that the
latter had more reason to be afraid of him owing to the large and
impressive force he had, consisting of 700 Spaniards, 200 of them
arquebusiers and 250 pikemen, many of whom had halberds. He had
250 horse, with mail and breastplates, and many wearing the harnesses
they had manufactured. As López de Gómara says in his ch. cxlix:
"Neither his father nor Pizarro had such well-armed people. He had also
much good artillery in which he had great confidence, and a large force
of Indians," etc.

These are López de Gómara's words; he adds a little further on: "He
took Juan Balsa as his general and Pedro de Oñate as commander," etc.
With this army and equipment Almagro set off in search of Governor
Vaca de Castro in order to offer him battle. He travelled fifty leagues
until he came to the province of Villca, where he heard that the royal
army was less than thirty leagues away.

We shall now leave both parties and return to Gonzalo Pizarro, whom
we left with his companions in the midst of the greatest difficulties and
hardships, for they were struggling against torrential rivers, marshes,
and bogs that could not be crossed, incredibly wild and thick forests,
with trees as large as López de Gómara says at the end of his ch. lxxxv
in describing the discovery of that region by Vicente Yáñez Pinzón. After
describing what happened to the discoverer he mentions the following as
the last of the monstrous things he saw there: "The discoverers brought
back the bark of certain trees which resembled cinnamon and the skin of
the animal that hides its young in its bosom, and they told as a great
marvel that they had seen a tree too big to be embraced by sixteen men,"
etc.

In addition to these difficulties, Gonzalo Pizarro's expedition fought against hunger, the cruel enemy of men and animals that has consumed so many in that uninhabitable land. Gonzalo, as we have said, decided to return to Peru, striking away from the river to the north; and they travelled through forests and other country no better than what they had visited before. They had to cut their way by main force, eating herbs, roots, and wild fruit, of which they found very little, and when they found any at all they counted themselves fortunate. The sick and feeble had to be carried over the lakes, marshes, and bogs; and Gonzalo and his captains toiled more than all the rest at this task, so as to encourage their followers to imitate them. In this way they travelled more than three hundred leagues without getting past the obstacles we have mentioned and with no diminution of their labors; the reader can well imagine how many and how great these would be in the course of the four hundred leagues they covered on the outward journey and three hundred on the return. Their hunger was such that they gradually killed the horses, driven by necessity, until all had been eaten. Before that the greyhounds and mastiffs had been consumed, which, as we mentioned in our *Florida*, have been of great benefit in the conquest of the Indies: all these were eaten. And as López de Gómara says in his ch. cxliv, "they were on the point of eating the Spaniards who died, after the evil custom of the barbarians of those forests," etc.

Many Indians and Spaniards perished of starvation, for though the horsemeat was shared among them all it was insufficient. It helped to keep them going with the grasses they ate, but when it gave out, they died the sooner. Indians and Spaniards remained by the wayside in threes and fours, left alive in the forests, for they could not walk, as we said in describing Garcilaso de la Vega's expedition, and there was nothing for it but to forsake them.

One of their greatest wants was the lack of salt, of which they found no trace for more than four hundred leagues, as Zárate says in Book IV, ch. v. As they were travelling through uninhabitable country they neither found it nor met anyone who could tell them how to remedy the lack of it, because of which they weakened and sagged so that they could not strive or work or move. They were thus alive, but rotting and stinking, as we have said in our history of Florida, in describing the lack of salt there. Because of the incessant rain and the water on the ground they were always drenched, and their clothes rotted on their backs. They were reduced to going naked, leader and men alike, and had nothing with which to cover themselves. They covered their private parts with the leaves of trees with which they made belts round their bodies which covered them in front and behind. The fact that the region was very hot helped them to stand their nakedness, but they were sorely tried by thorns, spines, and rough undergrowth in the virgin forest which tore at them as if it were going to flay them as they cut it down with their axes.

Their labors and their lack of food caused Gonzalo Pizarro and his men such cruel suffering that the 4,000 Indians who took part in the discovery all died of starvation (which was the plague that consumed them), including Gonzalo Pizarro's favorite Indian, who had deprived two mounted men of their lances, as we have told. Gonzalo regretted and wept his death as if it had been that of one of his brothers, and he often said as much. Likewise 210 Spaniards died out of 340 who set out, apart from the 50 who were taken off by Francisco de Orellana. The 80 survivors, having penetrated three hundred leagues of forest, reached an opener country with scrub and less water, where some game was found, both birds and animals, including deer, of which they killed as many as they could with crossbows and arquebusses, using such powder as they had saved. With their skins they made short pantaloons, which were enough to cover their private parts but no more. They wore their swords without scabbards and covered with rust, and they were on foot and unshod, and so black and withered and weak that they did not recognize one another. Thus they reached the borders of Quito. They kissed the earth and thanked God they had escaped from so many great labors and perils. They began to eat with such a desire to stuff themselves that they had to use restraint so as not to burst of a surfeit. Others were made of a different nature and could not eat what they wanted, for their stomachs were so used to fasting and abstinence that they would not receive what they were given.

The city of Quito was warned of their approach; and it was half empty because its leading citizens had gone off to the wars with Don Diego de Almagro. Those who were left strove to find clothes for Gonzalo and his followers, of which they were in the greatest need: but as those in the city were few and there was a lack of merchants owing to the wars, they could not find all the clothes they wanted. Six suits were obtained, when each of the inhabitants had brought what he had, a cloak or smock, hose or trousers, a cap or hat, and shirts: this was enough for Gonzalo and five of the leading men to clothe themselves; the rest could not be accommodated.

They were brought a dozen horses; more could not be found, for they had all been taken away for His Majesty's service in the war against Almagro. Much food was sent with the horses; the residents would have liked to send them all the fine things in the world, for Gonzalo Pizarro was one of the best beloved men there ever were or will be in Peru: his nature was so noble that he endeared himself to strangers, and much more so to his own friends and followers.

A dozen of the chief people in the city were chosen to take these offerings to him. They went and found Gonzalo more than thirty leagues from the city, where they all welcomed one another with much rejoicing and many tears: it was impossible to say then which of the two was the more abundant. Gonzalo Pizarro and his friends greeted the men from Quito with very great rejoicing and delight, for they had never imagined they would reach such a place after all their toils and troubles. The men from the city wept with pity and grief to see the state they were in, and on learning that those who were lost had perished of hunger, and that most of them had been forsaken still alive in the forests. They each comforted one another, seeing that there was no remedy for what was past and that their tears did them little good.

CHAPTER XV

Gonzalo Pizarro enters Quito; he writes to the governor offering his person and his men; the answer; the terms offered by the governor to Don Diego de Almagro.

GONZALO Pizarro and his captains and men received the presents and entertainment with due gratitude, but seeing that there were only enough clothes and horses for the leaders, they refused, as Zárate says (Book IV, ch. v), "to change their clothes or ride the mounts, wishing, like true soldiers, to preserve equality in everything, and they entered the city of Quito one morning in the state we have mentioned, going straight to the cathedral to hear mass and give thanks to God for bringing them safely through so many dangers."

This account of Zárate's lacks the following details which I heard from eyewitnesses. The twelve persons who took the gifts to Gonzalo Pizarro, seeing that neither he nor his captains wished to put on the clothes or mount the horses, decided to appear as he and his men were, shoeless and naked, in order to share in the honor, fame, and glory those who had suffered so many great hardships deserved. They thus entered as equals, and the city was very grateful to its ambassadors for this. After hearing mass, they received Gonzalo Pizarro with the celebrations they could provide, mingling joy and content at seeing him and his men alive with sorrow and pity at the state they were in. This return took place in early June 1542, after the expedition had been away two and a half years, though one writer by a slip says they came back after a year and a half. They stopped in the city where each repaired his wants as best he could. When Gonzalo Pizarro heard of the death of his brother the marquis and of the rising of Don Diego de Almagro, and his disobedience to His Majesty, and of the arrival of Vaca de Castro as governor of the empire and his expedition against Don Diego accompanied by all the friends and supporters of his brother the marquis, it seemed to him wrong that he should not serve His Majesty in the company of those gentlemen, most of whom had been his companions and comrades; he therefore wrote to the governor and reported on his journey and offered his person and his men to serve the governor as soldiers.

The governor replied acknowledging his goodwill and desire to serve the crown and thanked him in His Majesty's name, expressing his own great gratitude for the offer of his person and of men so experienced in military affairs. He begged him, however, and bade him in His Majesty's name to remain in Quito and rest from his past labors; and in due course he would advise him how he should serve His Majesty.

The governor did not want Gonzalo Pizarro to join his army since he was not without hope of coming to some agreement with Almagro and wished to avoid open conflict, fearing that, as the two parties were so impassioned, the struggle would lead to the destruction of both sides, and like a prudent man he wished to avoid so much bloodshed. He thought that if Gonzalo Pizarro were in his army, Almagro would not accept or even heed any offer of terms, or dare to place himself in his hands, fearing that Gonzalo Pizarro should wreak some cruel vengeance on him. He knew how popular Gonzalo was with everyone, and must necessarily be so with the whole army.

Such was the governor's intention. Some malicious persons thought it insufficient, and said that he was afraid that if Gonzalo came to the royal camp, he would be acclaimed general by common consent because of the universal affection for him and of his valor and authority and military experience.

Gonzalo obeyed the governor's orders and stayed in Quito till the end of the war. The governor also sent to instruct those who were in charge of the children of the marquis and of Gonzalo to keep them where they were in San Miguel and Trujillo and not bring them to Lima until they received new instructions. He said they would be safer at that distance than nearer at hand: his critics said he wanted to keep them away from him although they were only children.

When the governor had given these instructions, he travelled toward Huamanga, for he was told that Don Diego was already near that city and intending to enter it, as it was considered a stronghold, being surrounded on all sides by deep ravines and gorges and difficult of access. He sent Captain Castro ahead with his arquebusiers to hold a very steep hillside on the road, known to the Indians as Farcu and to the Spaniards as Parcos. On the way the governor heard that Almagro had already entered the city. This he greatly regretted, for the site was very favorable, and his own people had still not come up but were strung out along the road.

Alonso de Alvarado went back to collect them, and made such haste that they all reached the place where the governor was. Many of them had covered four leagues and some five or six in the course of that day, in order to arrive as soon as possible, and were very weary owing to the difficulty of the road. They spent the night drawn up in formation, for they had news that the enemy was two leagues away. But next day they heard from scouts that the news was wrong and that Don Diego was at a distance from the city. This calmed them and they went on to Huamanga. The governor did not stay there long, for he feared that if a battle was to be fought, as seemed likely, it would be disadvantageous to fight it there, since little use could be made of his horses in which he was superior to his enemy and which ought to tell very much in his favor. He therefore left the city and marched to some fields called Chupas, whence he sent two messengers to Don Diego, one called Francisco de Idiáquez and the other Diego Mercado, who told him that the governor offered him in His Majesty's name pardon for all that had happened if he would place himself under the royal standard and disband his army; he also offered rewards. Don Diego replied that he would accept the terms provided a general pardon was extended to all his followers and he were made governor of the new kingdom of Toledo and the gold mines and allocations of Indians his father had had.

Don Diego was inspired to make these excessive demands by a priest who had newly come from Panama and who had told him a few days be-

fore the terms were offered that he had heard in Panama that it was publicly said that His Majesty had pardoned him and awarded him the governorship of New Toledo, which included Cuzco. The priest had asked for
a reward for bringing the good news. He had also told Almagro that
Vaca de Castro had few men, that they were ill armed and dissatisfied.
Though this information was hard to believe Don Diego accepted it
because it was favorable, and took such courage that he replied making
these demands, supposing that the governor, being as weak as the report
said, would grant any concession he asked for.

After Vaca de Castro had sent the above-mentioned messengers he also
sent a soldier called Alonso García with official letters to many captains
and leading gentlemen, promising them pardon for what had happened
and great allocations of Indians. The messenger went disguised as an
Indian and kept away from the road so as not to be stopped. He was unfortunate, for as it had recently snowed, Don Diego's scouts, who were
very alert, found Alonso García's track in the snow, and followed it till
they found him and brought him to Don Diego with all his despatches.
Almagro was furious at this double dealing as López de Gómara says in
ch. cl and Zárate in Book IV, ch. xvi, and declared that it was not for
gentlemen and imperial officials to make offers of peace on the one hand
and attempts to bribe and spread mutiny among captains and soldiers on
the other. Thus enraged, he ordered the messenger to be hanged, both
for bringing the message and for appearing in disguise; and he then prepared his men for the coming battle in the presence of the governor's
other messenger. He promised to give anyone who killed the owner of
an allocation his Indians, his wife, and his property; and he told the
governor that he had no intention of obeying him so long as he was accompanied by his enemies, Pedro Alvarez Holguín, Alonso de Alvarado,
Gómez de Tordoya, Juan de Saavedra, Garcilaso de la Vega, Illén Súarez
de Carvajal, and Gómez de Alvarado, and all the other gentlemen who
had been on the Pizarros' side. He gave this reply to break the governor's
confidence in arriving at an agreement; for if he separated from those
who had been on Pizarro's side, as Almagro asked, he would have been
left alone. Almagro also sent to tell the governor that he need not count
on anyone deserting; he had better set aside any hopes he might have
entertained of this, for all his followers would do battle with great spirit
and would hold their ground against the whole world, as he would prove
by experience if he would but wait: he was setting off at once to meet him.

And Almagro did so, making his men ready and marching toward
the governor's camp. Not only he but all his followers were anxious to

offer battle, for they were all indignant at the attempt at double dealing. His followers were rather strengthened than shaken in their friendship and devotion to Almagro, saying that the governor would deal as falsely with them as he had with their leader and would not keep his promises. They therefore proposed to die fighting and hear no more terms. It was thought that but for this, and if there had been a pardon with His Majesty's signature, Almagro would have accepted any reasonable terms.

CHAPTER XVI

The manner in which Vaca de Castro and Almagro order their forces; the beginning of the battle; the death of Captain Pedro de Candia.

THE GOVERNOR realized on receiving Almagro's reply that many of his own followers were hesitant about giving battle, for they said they were alarmed and perturbed that His Majesty should not have accepted the battle of Las Salinas, for he had thrown Hernando Pizarro into a dungeon for fighting it, and they were afraid of committing a similar misdeed. In order to remove this difficulty and to settle his followers' fears, the governor ordered a list of the crimes of Don Diego de Almagro to be drawn up, how he had killed the marquis and many other persons, had confiscated the property of others and assumed control of them, had allocated Indians without having a commission from His Majesty, and was at present leading an armed force against the royal standard, and had challenged the governor to a pitched battle. In order to justify his action the governor signed this in the presence of them all, and pronounced sentence against Don Diego de Almagro, declaring him a traitor and rebel, and condemning him and all his followers to death and the confiscation of all their property. Having delivered sentence, he summoned all the captains and the whole army to aid and assist him to execute it as minister of His Majesty and governor of the empire.

Having issued this sentence, Vaca de Castro considered that there was no purpose in discussing terms any longer, in view of Almagro's desperate reply and pertinacity in his rebellion; he therefore prepared his forces for battle, knowing that Don Diego was now at hand.

He led his troops forth and delivered a harangue, bidding them remember who they were, whence they came, and why they fought. The possession of the empire depended on their strength and efforts: if they were defeated, neither they nor he could avoid death, and if they won, in addition to having fulfilled the obligations they owed their king as his loyal vassals, they would remain lords of their allocations and properties and enjoy them in peace and quiet. And to those who had no Indians he would give some in His Majesty's name, for it was precisely in order to reward those who had served him loyally that His Majesty wanted the land of Peru. He said that he realized that there was no need for him to exhort and encourage such noble gentlemen and brave soldiers: he indeed would rather take courage from them, which he did and would go ahead and break his lance before the rest. They all replied that they too would be cut to pieces and die rather than be defeated, and each of them regarded the quarrel as his own. The captains earnestly begged the governor not to take the van where there was such great danger, for the safety of the whole army depended on that of its general. Let him go to the rear with thirty horsemen, and wait there so as to lend help where it was most needed. On the earnest request of his captains the governor agreed to stay with the last, though he wished to be among the first. In this agreement they waited for Don Diego, who was two leagues away. On the following day two scouts arrived with news that Don Diego was less than half a league away and resolved to give battle.

The governor set out his men in formation. On the right of the infantry he set the royal standard which was entrusted to Alonso de Alvarado and borne by Cristóbal de Barrientos, a native of Ciudad Rodrigo and *vecino* of Trujillo, where he had an allocation of Indians. Pedro Alvarez Holguín and Gómez de Alvarado, Garcilaso de la Vega and Pero Ansúrez, the captains of the cavalry, were to the left of the infantry, and each, as Zárate says in his Book IV, ch. xviii, had his standard and company in good order and was himself stationed in the front line. Between the two squadrons of cavalry were Captains Pedro de Vergara and Juan Vélez de Guevara with the infantry. Nuño de Castro and his arquebusiers went ahead as an advance party to open the skirmishing and retire in due course upon the main formation. Vaca de Castro remained in the rear with his thirty horsemen, a little apart from the army, so that he could see where he was most needed in the battle and lend help, as he did.

These are Zárate's words. Holguín wore over his armor a doublet of slashed white damask, saying: "They usually aim at the mark, and few or none hit the white." In the above order the governor waited for Don Diego de Almagro, who reached the plain and occupied a mound at a distance from the royal formation and even beyond the range of artillery fire. His sergeant major, called Pedro Suárez, who had been a seasoned soldier in Italy and knew all about warfare, saw that the position was better than the enemy's and soon drew up the army on the same lines as theirs. He placed the cavalry on either side of the infantry, with the captain general Juan Balsa and his commander Pedro de Oñate, and Captains Juan Tello de Guzmán, Diego Méndez, Juan de Oña, Martín de Bilbao, Diego de Hojeda, and Malavez. They all had excellent companies and their men were keen to fight to win the empire and become lords of vassals. The sergeant major placed his artillery, with Pedro de Candía as its captain, in front of the squadrons, pointing toward the direction from which the enemy could attack. Having arranged the army in this fashion, he went to Don Diego, who was between the cavalry and infantry with a guard of eight or ten men, and said:

"Your Lordship has his army drawn up in order with so many advantages of position and artillery that the enemy can be defeated without running a lance or striking a blow with a sword, but merely by staying quietly here without budging. Wherever the enemy may attack, you can defeat him and cut him to pieces with the artillery before he comes within arquebuss range."

By the time Don Diego had drawn up his battle array, it was already late, and less than two hours of daylight remained. Vaca de Castro's advisers disagreed whether they should fight that day or not. Francisco de Carvajal, his sergeant major, being a man of experience in such matters, said that they should by no means fail to give battle that day, even though it were necessary to fight in the dark, for otherwise they would encourage the enemy and discourage their own men, many of whom would go over to Don Diego on seeing a sign of weakness. The governor therefore determined to offer battle forthwith, and said he would be glad to have the power of Joshua to bid the sun stand still.

They marched toward Don Diego's position, and he ordered his artillery to fire in order to frighten them. Francisco de Carvajal perceived that if they advanced straight at the enemy they would suffer heavy losses from the artillery which was numerous and extremely good, and took another direction, where he was sheltered by the slope of a hill. Passing round this they came out into the open, where they stood in obvious danger from the artillery; but Pedro de Candía, who was captain

The battle of Chupas continues

of it, fired high and did no damage. When Don Diego saw this, he fell upon him and slew him with his lance over the cannon. He then sprang down from his horse, and was so furious at his captain's treachery that he leapt up on to one of the pieces, and standing near the mouth of the cannon, lowered it a point by the weight of his body and ordered it to be fired, as he stood on it. The ball was aimed at Vaca de Castro's formation and cut a lane in it from van to rear, as Zárate says in Book IV, ch. xix, and López de Gómara (ch. cl), though they do not mention the death of Candía or how many died from that cannon ball: it struck down seventeen men. Four more such balls would have won the day and made it unnecessary for Don Diego to fight, as his sergeant major Pedro Suárez had assured him; but owing to the treachery of his captain, he lost it.

Realizing that Hernando Pizarro, who had offended him and caused him to go over to the Chileans as we said in the appropriate place, was under arrest in Spain, and the marquis, under whose authority Hernando had committed the offence, was dead, Pedro de Candía considered that he was sufficiently avenged on both of them, and that as there was now a new governor in Peru, he had better not lose the merit he had acquired by his efforts in helping to conquer the empire, but ought to return to His Majesty's service. He therefore sent a secret message to the governor telling him not to fear the artillery; for he was in charge of it and would see that it did no harm, as he did. This was the main reason why the governor decided to offer battle when he did. But Pedro de Candía did not live to enjoy his reward.

CHAPTER XVII

The cruel battle of Chupas continues; a
miscalculation by Don Diego's followers;
the victory of the governor and flight
of Don Diego.

WHEN HIS Majesty's captains and his sergeant major Francisco de Carvajal saw their battle array cut open and their infantry in confusion, they filled the front of the lane cut by the cannon ball and closed ranks, encouraging their men and ordering them to attack with all possible ferocity, so as not to give the enemy the opportunity of firing any more cannon balls by further delay. In order to advance more rapidly, they forsook the artillery so as not to be held back by it.

Almagro's captains were ill advised about their own interests and not very experienced in such cases. When they saw the enemy advancing on them at all speed, they began to shout: "They are winning honor from us: they see us standing here quietly and think we are afraid of them, so they attack us as though we were cowards! Up and at them, for we can't stand such an insult!" They thus forced Don Diego to advance with his whole army, which they did with such little thought that they got in front of their own artillery.

When the sergeant major Pedro Suárez saw this, he went to Don Diego and shouted to him: "Sir, if Your Lordship had kept my order and followed my advice, we should have won the victory today. But you have taken other counsel, and we shall lose. I will not be defeated, and as Your Lordship won't let me win on your side, I'll do so on the other." So saying, he spurred his horse and rode over to Vaca de Castro, bidding him hasten to close with his enemies and telling him about the disorder they had produced among themselves.

Vaca de Castro took Pedro Suárez's good counsel and ordered his formation to march rapidly forward. Francisco de Carvajal considered himself victorious on hearing Pedro Suárez's account, and as if in triumph at the enemy's ignorance, he took off his coat of mail and a vizor he was wearing, and threw it on the ground, telling his men not to be afraid of the artillery, for it would not hit him though he was as big as any two of them.

At this time a gentleman of very high descent who was in the cavalry squadron, seeing both sides were now within arquebus shot and that he would have to fight, left Vaca de Castro's squadron, saying: "Gentlemen, I am one of the Chileans: you all know I went with old Don Diego de Almagro on his expedition there; and if I am no longer with them, that is no reason why I should be against them." Thus saying, he went some distance aside from the battle array, where there was a priest called Hernando de Luque, a kinsman of the schoolmaster of Panama of the same name who had been a partner with the two governors, Almagro and Pizarro. The priest was accompanied by a sick gentleman, who being unable to fight was watching the battle. The cowardice of the first gentleman, who wanted to secure his life by not being on either side, was condemned by everyone in the squadron, and served to add to his infamous reputation, for he was already noted as a coward. Vaca de Castro's arquebusiers wanted to shoot him, but did not do so, because he left in such haste that when they had found out what he had done he was already between the two others, and they did not fire at him for fear of hitting them. I knew him and he was still alive in a city in Peru when I left. I remember his name, but it would be wrong for me to set it down here: I have said enough of his cowardice for all noble gentlemen and good soldiers to abominate it.

Vaca de Castro's men hastened to the top of the hill and found that Don Diego's army had almost lost its original formation. His arquebusiers received them with a shower of bullets and did much execution against the infantry. Gómez de Tordoya, the commander of the army, was hit by three balls and died within two days. Captain Nuño de Castro was badly wounded, and many others killed. When Francisco de Carvajal saw this, he ordered the cavalry to attack, in which he had great confidence because they were much more numerous than Don Diego's. On receiving the command they fell on Don Diego's and fought a very fierce engagement which lasted a long while without advantage to either side. Captain Pedro Alvarez Holguín was killed by a shot from an arquebus, for as he was so clearly marked out by his white dress, and they knew who he was, all the most notable shotsmen wanted to try for him. On the other side, Vaca de Castro's infantry attacked and fought bravely till they captured the artillery which was idle because Don Diego's own men had shown so little military skill, or rather none at all, and placed themselves in front of it. Both sides fought so obstinately that though the sun had set and the night fallen, they still went on, only able to distinguish one another by their war cries, some shouting "Chile!" and others "Pachacámac!" instead of Almagros and Pizarros, for these names were also given to the two parties. The mortality of the cavalry was very great, for in addition to encounters with lances much damage was done among them with swords, clubs, and axes.

Their stake in the victory sharpened their cruelty toward one another, for they knew that the winners would enjoy the empire and its great riches and the losers would forfeit them, and their lives too. It was now more than two hours after dark and four since the battle began. The governor with his thirty horse attacked Don Diego's formation from the left, where the men were still fresh, and the battle seemed to begin all over again. But at last the governor won the victory though ten or twelve of his men were killed, including Captain Jiménez, Mercado de Medina, and Nuño de Montalvo. Both sides sang victory, and the battle still went on, though Don Diego's were weakening. As he became aware of this, he attacked the enemy with the few men he had left, and made an inroad into them, performing marvels himself in the hope that he would be killed; but he was neither killed nor wounded, for he was well armed and not recognized. He fought, as López de Gómara says in his ch. cl, with courage.

It was now acknowledged that the governor had won the day; and some of Don Diego's leading supporters, on seeing this, shouted their names: "I am so-and-so, and I am so-and-so who killed the marquis." Thus they died fighting desperately and were cut to pieces. Many of Don Diego's men saved themselves by removing the white armlets they wore under cover of darkness, and putting on red ones taken from the dead on Vaca de Castro's side. Don Diego, on seeing that victory had slipped between his fingers and that death too avoided him, left the battle with six friends, who were Diego Méndez, Juan Rodríguez Barragán, and Juan de Guzmán, and three others whose names have been forgotten. He went to Cuzco where he met with the death his enemies had not been able to give him at the hands of those he himself had made men of by granting them the administration of justice and military posts. As soon as they saw him coming back defeated, Rodrigo de Salazar, a native of Toledo, whom he had left as his deputy, and Antón Ruiz de Guevara whom he had made *alcalde ordinario* of the city, arrested him. They also arrested those who came with him so as to add to their cruelty. Of this Zárate says in his Book IV, ch. xix: "Thus ended the command and government of Don Diego, who in a day saw himself lord of Peru, and in the next was arrested by his own alcalde whom he himself had given authority. And this battle was fought on September 16, 1542."

Thus Zárate, who here finishes the chapter in question. The victory was obtained by Vaca de Castro at about nine at night, though in such confusion that it was not regarded as sure, for some were still heard fighting on the field. And for fear lest Don Diego should return—for they did not know if he had gone or not—the governor ordered through the sergeant major that all the infantry and cavalry should remain in formation until it was known for certain if they had won or if they had to win it again. So they resumed their positions, and remained awaiting whatever might happen till the following day.

CHAPTER XVIII

*The names of the leading gentlemen who were
in the battle; the number of the dead; the
punishment of the guilty and the death
of Don Diego de Almagro.*

THE GOVERNOR spent much of the night praising the bravery and
spirit of his captains and the other gentlemen and soldiers, the
ferocity and determination with which they had fought, the valor they
had shown in the royal service and the noteworthy deeds some had performed in particular, and these he mentioned by name. They had proved
their loyalty, love, and attachment toward the marquis, for they had not
shirked facing any danger to avenge his death. He also spoke of the determination shown by Don Diego, who had shown courage and fought
bravely to avenge his father's death: he said he had done more than was to
be expected of his youth, for he was little more than twenty years of age.
He also praised some of Don Diego's captains who had behaved bravely.
In particular he praised the military skill of Francisco de Carvajal, who
had shown no fear of the artillery and arquebusses, but had always been at
the head of his men and had brought his experience and judgment to bear
on each need as it arose. Since the governor had watched the battle, he had
been able to see and take note of the deeds of courage that had occurred,
and he recounted them one by one. The chief participants on His Majesty's
side who distinguished themselves were the commander Gómez de Tordoya and the factor Illén Suárez de Carvajal and his brother Benito de
Carvajal; Juan Julio de Hojeda; Tomás Vázquez; Lorenzo de Aldana; Juan
de Saavedra; Francisco de Godoy; Diego Maldonado, who afterwards acquired the nickname of "the Rich"; Juan de Salas, brother of the archbishop of Seville, the inquisitor-general Valdés de Salas; Alonso Loaisa,
brother of the archbishop of Lima, Jerónimo de Loaisa; Juan de Pancorvo;
Alonso Mazuela; Martín de Meneses; Juan de Figueroa; Pedro Alonso
Carrasco; Diego de Trujillo; Alonso de Soto; Antonio de Quiñones and
his brother Suero de Quiñones and his cousin Pedro de Quiñones, an old
soldier of the Italian wars (all three close kinsmen of the governor);
Gaspar Jara; Diego Ortiz de Guzmán; García de Melo, who lost his right

hand in the battle; Pedro de los Ríos and his brother Diego de los Ríos, natives of Córdova; Francisco de Ampuero; Don Pedro Puertocarrero; Pedro de Hinojosa; Diego Centeno; Alonso de Hinojosa; Juan Alonso Palomino; Don Gómez de Luna, first cousin of Garcilaso de la Vega; Gómez de Alvarado; Gaspar de Rojas; Melchor Verdugo; Lope de Mendoza; Juan de Barbarán; Miguel de la Serna; Jerónimo de Aliaga; Nicolás de Ribera and Jerónimo de Ribera who were distinguished, as we have said elsewhere, as Ribera the younger and Ribera the elder.

All these and many others whose names have been forgotten distinguished themselves by their valor in this battle, going in the front ranks of their companies, and almost all of them were wounded. In short, there was not a man of note in the whole of Peru, as López de Gómara says, who was not present in the battle on His Majesty's side. The dead were three hundred Spaniards on the king's side, and many, though less, of the other party. Thus the battle was very bloody and few captains escaped alive, so hard did they fight. More than four hundred were wounded, and many of these were frozen to death that night, for it was extremely cold. All these are López de Gómara's words, with which he ends ch. cl of his history. On Don Diego's side two hundred died; so that López de Gómara is right in describing the battle as bloody, since of fifteen hundred men who were present in it five hundred died and another five hundred were wounded; of these one hundred were on Don Diego's side and four hundred on that of the king.

One of the royalist soldiers behaved so cruelly that even after the victory was won he went on killing Almagrists and accounted for eleven of them. He himself boasted of his misdeed after the battle, saying that he had been robbed of eleven thousand pesos somewhere or other, and he considered himself avenged by having killed eleven men.

Many other similar events occurred that night. So many of the wounded were frozen because the Indians robbed them, taking their arms and clothes and stripping them naked, respecting neither side, since as it was nighttime, they could not tell them apart, nor would it have made any difference if they had, for to the Indians all was grist to their mill. Nor could the victors bring in their wounded because they were all in such a state that they could not even take care of themselves, and in any case the tents had not arrived and they all passed the night in the open air. Only two tents were erected, for Gómez de Tordoya and Pedro Ansúrez, Gómez de Alvarado and Garcilaso de la Vega, and other severely wounded captains who were dying. Those less grievously wounded remained in the open air, and it was a lamentable thing to hear their cries from the pain of their wounds and the lack of treatment for them.

Nor did the Indians spare those who fled from the battlefield, pursuing them too; for there are none who dare not attack the vanquished. They killed Juan de Balsa and ten or twelve others, who were with him by the wayside; his title of captain general did not secure him any respect. They did the same elsewhere, killing many Spaniards who fled in vain from the battlefield.

At daybreak the governor ordered the wounded to be brought in to be treated, and the dead to be buried in four or five great pits that were dug, in which they were all flung except Pedro Alvarez Holguín, Gómez de Tordoya de Vargas, and other leading gentlemen, who were borne to Huamanga, where they were buried as well as possible. More than a hundred horse and fifty or sixty foot fled from the battlefield and reached the city of Huamanga. The few who were there came out like victors to meet them, discomfited them and took away their arms and horses, which they surrendered very willingly in order that their lives might be spared.

The charitable work of burying the dead on the battlefield was accompanied also by the punishment of the guilty that day, for among the dead the bodies of Martín de Bilbao, Arbolancha, Hinojosa, and Martín Carrillo were found. They were those who had shouted during the battle that they had killed the marquis, in the hope of being killed. Although they were cut to pieces in the fray, a new sentence was executed on them, for they were drawn and quartered and their crime cried by a crier. The same was done with others who had been defiant and insulting toward the royalists.

On the next day the governor went to Huamanga, where he found that Captain Diego de Rojas had beheaded Captain Juan Tello de Guzmán and Pedro de Oñate, Don Diego's commander. The governor entrusted the punishment of the rest to Licentiate de la Gama, and he beheaded the chief followers of Don Diego who were under arrest in Huamanga. They were Diego de Hoces and Antonio de Cárdenas; and he hanged Juan Pérez, Francisco Peces, Juan Diente, and Martín Cota, and thirty others of the guiltiest. The rest were pardoned and exiled to various places outside Peru.

While justice was being done in Huamanga, the governor learnt of the arrest of Don Diego in Cuzco. He at once went there and on his arrival ordered the sentence he had pronounced on Don Diego to be executed, for as he had been tried before the battle, he did not want to waste time on a new trial (though Zárate says he did). He was beheaded in the same square as his father and by the same executioner, who stripped him of his clothes, as he had his father, though not of all of them, for someone paid him to leave him his doublet, hose, and shirt. He lay there almost the whole day so that his punishment should be manifest to everyone. Afterwards his body was taken to the convent of the Mercedarians, and a grave was made for him by the side of his father's, or the same one was used. He was thrown in with no shroud apart from the dress he wore, and a few masses were said for his soul from charity.

This was the end of Don Diego de Almagro the younger: it was so similar to his father's that it would seem that fortune wished to make them equal in all things. Apart from being father and son, both had the same name and equal courage and determination in war and equal prudence and judgment in time of peace. Though young, Don Diego's judgment was very great, for he had been well taught from childhood and had much ability and natural intelligence. He and his father suffered the same death in the same place, where both were beheaded; their burial was the same. They died in such poverty after having been wealthy and powerful that they were buried by charity. And to make them father and son in everything, they were both destroyed on the same day, for each of the two battles was fought on a Saturday.

So ended poor Don Diego de Almagro the younger, the best mestizo ever born in the New World, had he only obeyed the king's minister. He was a fine horseman in both styles of riding. He died like a good Christian, full of repentance for his sins. After his execution they hanged Juan Rodríguez Barragán and the ensign Enrique and eight others who had succeeded in following Don Diego to Cuzco. Gómez Pérez, Diego Méndez, and another companion of theirs fled from prison, and finding no place of safety to seek refuge in all Peru, they went off to the forests to which Prince Manco Inca had withdrawn. Five others did the same and sought shelter there. The Inca received them very affably and entertained them as best he could. Later we shall tell how ill they repaid him, for one of them killed him.

CHAPTER XIX

*The good government of Licentiate Vaca de Castro;
peace and quiet in Peru; the cause of the
disturbances there.*

WITH THE death of Don Diego de Almagro the younger and of the
most prominent and guiltiest of his followers and the exile of the
less guilty, peace and quiet settled on the empire of Peru, for the name
and party of the Almagros was brought to an end. Licentiate Vaca de
Castro, like a prudent man, governed with great rectitude and justice, to
the general applause and satisfaction of Spaniards and Indians alike, for
he made laws of great advantage to both. The Indians in particular received great pleasure and favor from his laws, and said they were very
like those of their own Inca kings. The governor divided the Indians who
had no masters among the most deserving Spaniards who had served His
Majesty in the wars. He also improved the fortune of many who already
had Indians, giving them better allocations and changing them from one
city to another as they wished. Many *vecinos* then moved from Los Charcas
to Cuzco, one of whom was my lord Garcilaso de la Vega, who left the
province of Tapac-Ri, as we have already said, for that of Quechua and
the people of Cotanera and Huamanpallpa.

Although the governor carried out this allocation as justly as everyone said, there was no lack of discontent among those who had received
no Indians, for they very often thought they deserved the best allocations
in Peru. One of the malcontents was a gentleman called Hernando Mogollón, a native of the city of Badajoz, whom we have referred to in our history of Florida (Book I, ch. iii). His deserts were great on account of the
many services he had rendered in the conquest of new lands; and it was
public knowledge that he had fought like a good soldier in the battle of
Chupas and Vaca de Castro himself had seen it. As he received no Indians
at all in the allocation, he went to the governor and told him:

"Sir, in this country as Your Lordship well knows, everyone eats
à la mogollón (sponges), for they take it from its owner, and only
Mogollón is left starving, though he was present at the discovery of
Florida and other conquests of import to the crown of Spain, and lastly
at the battle of Chupas under Your Lordship's standard. It is fitting that

you should bear me in mind, for I have never forgotten to serve His Majesty."

When the governor saw that Hernando Mogollón was only asking for justice, he rewarded him with an allocation of Indians, albeit a small one. And to help the remaining malcontents and the poor soldiers, who were numerous, and prevent them from starting a mutiny, he sent them in companies to conquer and settle various parts of Peru, following the policy of the marquis. He hoped that in this way there would be estates and Indians to share among them. He sent Captain Pedro de Vergara back to the province of Pacamuru on the conquest of which he had been engaged when he was called to serve·His Majesty in the war: he had a large and excellent force.

He sent Diego de Rojas, Nicolás de Heredia, and Felipe Gutiérrez, a native of Madrid, to the province called Musu, and known to the Spaniards as Moxos. They had an excellent company of men, and underwent great hardships in reaching the river Plate: we may later refer to their expedition. He sent Gonzalo de Monroy to the kingdom of Chile to help the captain and governor Pedro de Valdivia, who was engaged in the conquest of the provinces and tribes of that kingdom. Captain Juan Vélez de Guzmán was sent to conquer another province called Muyupampa [Moyobamba]; he himself had recently discovered it, and had heard news of other extensive lands and provinces stretching eastward between the rivers called Orellana, Marañón, and the Plate; but it is a land of such great forests, lakes, and marshes that it is almost uninhabitable, and the few Indians who live there are so brutish and beastly that they have no religion or civilization, but eat one another, and the region is so hot that they cannot wear clothes and so go naked.

Having cleared of soldiers the whole length and breadth of Peru, which measures seven hundred leagues from Quito to Los Charcas, Vaca de Castro was left free of the importunities and troubles they caused him and governed in peace and quiet to the satisfaction of everyone. He made such laws as we have said, obtaining information from the old *curacas* and captains about the administration of the Inca kings, and choosing from these reports whatever seemed to him best adapted to the interests of the Spaniards and the improvement of the Indians' lot. He summoned Gonzalo Pizarro, who was still in Quito, and having thanked him on his own behalf for his past conquests and undertakings and rewarded him on His Majesty's behalf according to his merits, he sent him to his home and his Indians in Los Charcas bidding him go and rest and look to his health and his fortune. The Indians set to cultivating the land

and producing a great abundance of food, now that they were free of the vexations and persecutions they had suffered during the recent wars; for both sides had waged the struggle at the expense of the lives and property of the Indians, and a million and a half of them had perished, as López de Gómara says at the end of his ch. cli. By the industry of the Spaniards who also enjoyed the peace and sought their own prosperity, very rich gold mines were found in many parts of Peru, but the richest were to the east of Cuzco in the province called Callahuaya, or by the Spaniards Caravaya, where much very fine gold of 24 carats was extracted, and still is today, though not in such abundance. To the west of Cuzco in the province called Quechua, which contains many tribes of the same name, in the region called Huallaripa, they found other mines of gold, less fine than those of Callahuaya, though they still reached 20 carats, more or less; but in such quantity that I remember seeing, nine or ten years after the discovery, one of the *vecinos* who had a share in them receive two thousand pesos in gold dust every Saturday from his Indians.

We call gold dust the gold that is brought out in its natural state; it resembles the filings of blacksmiths, and there is another kind rather coarser like the bran from flour. In this they also find the grains called *pepitas* which are like the pips of melons or gourds and are worth three, four, six, or eight ducats, more or less, as they chance to be discovered. Of all this gold a very large quantity was retained at the melting works for His Majesty's fifth, which was an incalculable treasure, for he received one mark out of five, one peso out of five, and so on down to the last ha'penny. The volume of trade with Spain was in proportion to the amount of treasure found and extracted. With all this prosperity and the administration of a governor so Christian, so noble, so wise, so zealous in the service of our Lord God and his king, the empire flourished and improved from day to day. And what is most important, the teaching of our holy Catholic Faith was spread throughout the whole land with great care by the Spaniards, and the Indians accepted it with no less gladness and satisfaction, for they saw that much of what they were taught was what their Inca kings had taught them and bidden them observe under their natural law.

In the majesty of the preaching of the holy Gospel and the prosperity of peace, quiet, and the enjoyment of spiritual and temporal goods that Indians and Spaniards alike then possessed, the Devil, that enemy of the human race, ordained that all these good things should be spoiled and reversed. He therefore roused his ministers—who are ambition, envy, covetousness, avarice, wrath, pride, discord, and tyranny—and bade each perform his functions and stop the preaching of the holy Gospel and the conversion of the gentiles to the Catholic Faith, which was what most distressed him, for he was losing the ascendancy he had established over those heathens. And our Lord God permitted him so to do, in His secret wisdom and for the chastisement of many, as we shall see.

Certain persons, showing themselves very zealous for the well being of the Indians without considering the difficulties and the harm that would result to the very persons they wished to assist from their ill advice and folly, proposed in the Royal Council of the Indies that new laws and ordinances ought to be adopted for the good government of the empires of Mexico and Peru. The one who most insisted in this was a friar called Fray Bartolomé de las Casas, who years before, as a secular priest, had travelled through the Windward Islands and Mexico, and after becoming a regular, put forward many proposals which he said were for the good of the Indians and their conversion to the Catholic Faith and to the advantage of the royal treasury.

On this matter we shall quote López de Gómara, His Imperial Majesty's chaplain (ch. clii and following), and Zárate, accountant general of the royal treasury in Peru (Book V, ch. i, and following). And we shall add what a modern historian of the affairs of the Indies, called Diego Fernández, a citizen of the city of Palencia, says of the disturbances caused in Mexico and Peru by the new laws and ordinances: this historian begins his story with them, and follows the other two in the substance of the facts, without departing from the truth. I shall say what all three have written, quoting passages from each; for as I am opposed to appearing as the author of odious things (as many of those that have to be said in truth in the course of the history perforce are), and as these matters were the real cause of the misfortunes suffered by the inhabitants of Peru on each of the two sides, I shall set them down quoting literally what these authors say; and though it would be sufficient to mention the authors in the margin, mentioning the book and chapters referred to, as I have done previously, it seemed best to quote them word for word lest any slanderer should say I had suppressed anything from or added to what they say. This shall only be with regard to the odious part: for the rest I shall serve as commentator, explaining what is confused and adding what they omitted to say when there are things that actually happened which I heard from many of the participants in these disturbances. For when Viceroy Blasco Núñez Vela went to Peru, I was already four, and thereafter in the course of my life I knew many of those who are named in the history.

We shall first speak of the troubles caused by the ordinances in Mexico, and how these were brought to a fortunate conclusion by the prudence and good sense of the judge appointed to apply them. We shall then return to Peru and speak of the misfortunes, deaths, havoc, and ruin caused by the imprudence, inflexibility, and harshness of the viceroy sent to apply them and govern that empire. And though the Mexican side of the matter is not necessary to our history, I thought I should include it so as to show the events that occurred in each of the two kingdoms, which were so different although the cause was the same. Princes, kings, and monarchs may then note—since histories serve as examples of how they are to govern—and may beware of allowing such rigorous laws to be made, and of electing judges so severe that they oblige and force their vassals and subjects to lose respect and withhold the obedience they owe, and enable other princes to seek to command and govern them. For from divine and human history, ancient and modern, we see from long experience that no kingdom ever rebelled against its king because he gave it good treatment, but only on account of his harshness, cruelty, and tyranny and the excessive taxes and tributes he imposed. And Peru was on the verge of being lost and alienated from the Spanish crown on account of the rigorous laws applied to it, had not the mildness and gentleness of the emperor restored it, as we shall see in our history.

CHAPTER XX

New laws and ordinances made in the court of Spain for the two empires of Mexico and Peru.

IN 1539 Fray Bartolomé de las Casas came from New Spain and arrived in Madrid, where the court then was, and in his sermons and private discourse he showed himself extremely zealous for the welfare of the Indians and spoke very warmly in their defence. He proposed reforms which, although they seemed good and holy, nevertheless proved very harsh and difficult to put to effect. He put them forward in the Supreme Council of the Indies where they were not well received, for the good cardinal of Seville Don García de Loaisa prudently rejected them. He was a member of the council and had been a governor in the Indies for many years, and knew more about them and what was necessary for their good than many of those who had conquered them and settled there; and with his discretion and good counsel he was never of opinion that what Fray Bartolomé asked should be granted. The latter therefore suspended his claims until 1542, when the emperor Charles V returned to Spain after a long journey through France, Flanders, and Germany. His Majesty, being a very religious man, was easily persuaded to do as the friar wanted, for fear of the burden on his conscience if he failed to execute the new laws and ordinances that were necessary for the well being of the Indians. His Imperial Majesty, having listened attentively to the friar, summoned his councils and various other grave lawyers, prelates, and religious. The case was put before them and discussed, and finally Fray Bartolomé's claims were approved, though against the opinion of the cardinal and president above-mentioned and of the bishop of Lugo, Don Juan Suárez de Carvajal (whom I knew); the *comendador mayor* Francisco de los Cobos, His Majesty's secretary; Don Sebastián Ramírez, bishop of Cuenca and president of Valladolid, who had been president at Santo Domingo and Mexico; and Don García Manrique, count of Osorno and president of the Orders, who, as López de Gómara says, had dealt with affairs of the Indies for a long time in the absence of the cardinal Don García de Loaisa. All these, being men of experience in Indian affairs and having dealt with them for a long time, were opposed to the ordinances, which were forty in number.

The emperor signed them in Barcelona on November 20, 1542, as López de Gómara says in his ch. clii. The battle of Chupas between the licentiate Governor Vaca de Castro and Don Diego de Almagro the younger occurred on September 15 of the same year, two months and five days before the ordinances were signed. This clearly shows the diligence and solicitude of the Devil in preventing the preaching of the holy Gospel in Peru, for scarcely had so great a fire as that been extinguished than he endeavored to kindle another and greater one, as we shall see from the results produced by the ordinances. We shall only mention four of these ordinances, though our authors say more of them, for these are germane to our history: they are as follows.

The first ordinance was that on the death of the conquerors and settlers who were *vecinos* in the Indies with allocations of Indians entrusted to them and placed under their control by His Majesty, their sons and wives should not succeed to them but they should come under the royal control and the children should be granted a sum drawn from their revenues, on which to maintain themselves.

No Indian was to be forced to labor except in places where no other solution was possible, but their work was to be remunerated. No Indians were to be forced to work in the mines or pearl fisheries, and the tribute they were to pay their master should be established and the personal service abolished.

The *encomiendas* and *repartimientos* of Indians held by bishops, monasteries, and hospitals should be suppressed; those who were or had been governors, presidents, judges, magistrates, or their deputies, or officers of His Majesty's treasury should likewise be deprived of their Indians and be prohibited from having Indians even if they offered to resign their offices.

All the *encomenderos* of Peru, or those who had Indians, and had taken part in the disturbances and struggles between Don Francisco Pizarro and Don Diego de Almagro, should lose their Indians, on whichever side they had been.

This ordinance meant, as Diego Fernández says, that practically nobody in Peru could have Indians or estates, and none of the people of standing in New Spain or Peru could have them, under the third law; for all or nearly all of them had been corregidors, alcaldes, or justices or deputies or officials of the royal treasury. So that these two laws alone were like a sort of net that enclosed the whole of the Indies and excluded their owners.

For the better understanding of these ordinances we must say something of the motives of those who discussed and approved them. As to the first ordinance, we must explain that the conquerors of the Indies were awarded the allocations of Indians in return for their services, and were to enjoy them for two lives: their own and that of their eldest son, or daughter if they had no son. Later, when they were bidden to marry because it was thought that if they were married they would settle down and cultivate the land and live quietly on it instead of seeking changes, the award of the Indians was extended to the wives of the conquerors, who would inherit them in default of children. The second ordinance which prevented them from forcing the Indians to work was adopted because of reports that the Indians were made to work without being paid. This was true of some conscienceless Spaniards, but not of all of them in general, for there were many who paid their Indians and treated them like their own children; and the Indians were and are prepared to work without pay, for they are like day laborers in Spain who hire themselves out to dig or reap and work for their food. To forbid Indians to work in this way was to do them much harm, for it deprived them of their right to earn. What should have been done was to order those who did not pay them to be very severely punished.

With regard to the law against putting Indians to work in the mines, I have no comment to offer, except to refer to the Indians who still today in 1611 work by order of the governors in the silver mines of the hill of Potosí and in the quicksilver mines in the province of Huanca: if they ceased to do so, neither the silver nor the gold of the empire would be brought every year to Spain.

And with regard to the regularization of the tributes to be paid to the *encomenderos,* this was a good law; and it was received with general approval when President Pedro de la Gasca established the norms in Peru, as I myself saw. As to the removal of personal service, I can only say that they must have been misinformed about this. Each *vecino* was given a number of Indians for service in his house as part of the tribute; for this purpose, in addition to the main allocation, they were allowed some villages of forty or fifty houses, or sixty at most, with obligation to provide what is called personal service, which entailed supplying the owner's house with fuel and water and fodder for his horses (for there was no hay in those days), and they paid no other tribute. In this fashion my father had three little villages in the valley of Cuzco, one of which was called Caira, and many other *vecinos* of Cuzco had them in the district round the city. And when there were no small villages to be awarded for personal service, the main allocation was required as part of its tribute to supply Indians for this service, which they did willingly and performed the tasks with ease and content. Thus as President La Gasca found this custom well established and accepted by both parties, he made no attempt to alter it, but left it as it was.

The third law, by which allocations of Indians were to be removed from bishops, monasteries, and hospitals wherever governors had awarded them to these, was acceptable to everyone. It was thought that no wrong was done in removing these Indians, for the intention of the governors in awarding them had not been to go beyond the powers conferred on them by His Majesty to allocate Indians for two lives and no more. As monasteries, prelacies, and hospitals are permanent, they were done no wrong by being made equal to the conquerors of the empire. The last and fourth ordinance which remains to be commented on will be discussed later in our discourse on the objections raised by those who were deprived as a result of it.

CHAPTER XXI

The ministers who went to Mexico and Peru to put the ordinances into execution: and the description of the imperial city of Mexico.

TOGETHER with these ordinances instructions were given that the *audiencia* of Panama should be abolished and another erected in the regions of Guatemala and Nicaragua, and that the province of Tierra Firme should be subject to this *audiencia*. It was also established that there should be another chancellery in Peru, consisting of four judges and a president, with the title of viceroy and captain general, and that a suitable person should go to New Spain as visitor to the viceroy, the *audiencia* of Mexico, and all the bishops, and inspect the accounts and actions of the officers of the royal treasury and all the magistrates of the kingdom.

These measures were set out together with the ordinances, which, as we have said, numbered more than forty. And as there were always Spaniards from all parts of America at court, these latter at once sent to Mexico and Peru many transcripts of the ordinances and the other laws, to the great scandal, discontent, and anger of the *vecinos* and settlers in the two empires, who at once began to seek a remedy, as the three historians say.

Within a few days of the publication of the ordinances, His Imperial Majesty appointed Don Francisco Tello de Sandoval, a native of Seville, to be visitor. He had been inquisitor in Toledo, and was then a member of the Royal Council of the Indies, and was a person of great rectitude and prudence; and it was his duty to take the new laws and ordinances to New Spain, and apply them in that empire and make the tour of inspection of the above-mentioned officials.

In the same way Blasco Núñez Vela, a native of the city of Avila, who was then inspector general of the guards of Castile, was appointed president and viceroy of the kingdoms and provinces of Peru. Zárate adds in his Book V, ch. ii, the following: "As His Majesty had experience of what he had already accomplished both in this office and in that of corregidor which he had formerly held in the cities of Málaga and Cuenca, and he was an honest gentleman who gave justice without fear or favor, and applied the royal commands absolutely without any compromise." Thus Zárate.

His Majesty further appointed as judges of the *audiencia* of Peru, Licentiate Diego de Cepeda, a native of Tordesillas, who had been judge in the Canaries; Licentiate Lisón de Tejada of Logroño, who was alcalde of the nobility in the royal *audiencia* of Valladolid; Licentiate Alvarez, an advocate in the same *audiencia*; and Licentiate Pedro Ortiz de Zárate, a native of the city of Orduña, who was *alcalde mayor* in Segovia. These four lawyers were the judges appointed to Peru. His Majesty also appointed Agustín de Zárate, then secretary of the royal council, to go as accountant to the kingdoms, provinces, and Tierra Firme. And the ordinances were delivered to him, and when the *audiencia* had been established in Lima, which was where His Majesty had decided that it should be set up, they were to be applied strictly and literally as inviolable laws.

Thus Diego Fernández in his ch. ii, and Zárate says almost the same. These instructions were sent off in the month of April 1543.

We shall now speak briefly of the fortunate outcome of the ordinances in Mexico, and then turn to the events of Peru, where they caused great distress to all the inhabitants of the empire, both Spaniards and Indians. In the month of November of the same year of 1543 the viceroy, judges, and officials, and the visitor Don Francisco Tello de Sandoval embarked at Sanlúcar de Barrameda. Their fleet was a fine one of fifty-two ships and with a favorable wind they reached the Canary Islands in twelve days. After taking on supplies they continued their journey, and part of them turned to the right toward New Spain, while the rest went to the left toward Peru, where we shall leave the viceroy so as to say what happened to the visitor in the kingdom of Mexico. Omitting a full description of the voyage which is given by Diego Fernández of Palencia, we may say that he safely reached the port of San Juan de Ulúa in February 1544, and went thence to Veracruz and continued his journey to Mexico. He was received with humility and veneration in the villages and towns he passed through, which celebrated his arrival as best they could.

The people of the city of Mexico, having had news of the ordinances he was bringing and of his approach, decided, as Diego Fernández says, to go out and receive the visitor in mourning, to show the sorrow and regret caused by his arrival. When the viceroy Don Antonio de Mendoza knew this, he rebuked them and prevented it, bidding them on the contrary to receive the visitor with every display of pleasure and rejoicing. Thus the viceroy himself went out with the royal *audiencia*, and its officials and the city council and cathedral chapter, and more than six hundred other very rich gentlemen with fine mounts and trappings. They received the visitor half a league from the city, and the viceroy and he greeted one another with great respect and ceremony, as did all the rest. They then repaired to the monastery of St. Dominic, and Don Fray Juan Zumárraga, of the Order of St. Francis, the first bishop of Mexico, appeared at the gate to receive the visitor. When the viceroy and all the rest had taken leave, the visitor remained as a guest in the monastery.

Having recounted these events, Diego Fernández continues with a description of the city of Mexico. I may be permitted to reproduce his account, for I am, as an Indian, much attached to the former greatness of that other Rome. He says:

This great city of Mexico is founded in a plain on water, like Venice; for the whole body of the city stands on the water and has a very great number of bridges. The lake on which it stands appears to be one, but is in fact two very different bodies of water, one of bitter salt water and the other sweet and fresh. The salt water ebbs and flows, but the fresh water is the higher and thus the good water falls into the bad, and not the reverse.

The salt water is five leagues broad and may be eight long: the fresh is almost the same.

There are 200,000 small boats on these lakes. The natives call these *acales* and the Spaniards canoes: they are made in a single piece like troughs, and are large and small, according to the size of the tree trunk from which each is made.

At that time there were 700 very large, well-built houses there, excellently built of stonemasonry. None of these houses has a tiled roof, but they have splendid terraces so that one can walk on the roofs.

The streets are well designed and level and straight, and so broad that seven can ride abreast along any of them, with lances and shields and without crowding one another.

The house where the royal *audiencia* is contains nine courts and a very fine garden and square which could well have been used for running bulls. The viceroy, Don Antonio de Mendoza and the visitor Don Francisco Tello de Sandoval were very comfortably lodged in this house, with three judges and the royal accountant. It also held the royal prison, the smeltery where bells and artillery were founded, and the mint.

On one side of this house runs the street called Tacuba and on the other that of St. Francis. Behind it is the street of La Carrera, all of which are main streets, and in front of it lies the square where they fight bulls. The house is so large that it faces eighty doors of houses of the leading citizens in these streets and the square.

The Indian population of the city is in two large quarters called Santiago and Mexico, where there would be 200,000 Indians in those days. Four roads leave the city, one of them two leagues long, and it was by this road, leading south, that Hernán Cortés entered Mexico. Another road is a league long, and the others less.

Thus Diego Fernández, and when he says that Mexico had seven hundred very large houses in those days, he might have said seven hundred great suburbs, as can be seen clearly from his own description of the house where the viceroy and visitor lodged, since in addition to them the judges and other royal officials lived there, and it had the royal prison, the mint, and the foundry for bells and artillery, each of which things would need quite a large suburb. Our author proves this when he describes the periphery of the house and says: it "is so large that it faces eighty doors of houses of the leading citizens in these streets and the square." This clearly shows the size of a single house of those days, which might, as we have said, be more properly described as a suburb than a house; and the rest were similar. In particular it might be said of the imperial city of Mexico that it is one of the greatest in the universe, if not the very first, as a Flemish gentleman told me, who out of curiosity and for his own pleasure had seen all the famous cities of the Old World and had gone to the New solely to see Mexico. In addition to seeing it he won 20,000 ducats in his own country in bets staked on whether he would be man enough to go there.

In order not to make this digression too long, I shall not say all the details he told me about this and the long journeys he made and the many years he spent in seeing everything. Suffice it to say that he spent more than fourteen years there. And when Diego Fernández says that the viceroy came out to receive the visitor with the royal *audiencia* and its officials, and the city council, and cathedral chapter and more than six hundred other gentlemen with very rich mounts and splendid trappings, this was no exaggeration, but perfect truth; for among its other excellences Mexico had this, that in those days on Sundays and feasts five or six hundred gentlemen used to walk abroad in the streets, without the attraction of a tourney or any other diversion, but as an ordinary practice on days of rest: this is a very royal thing for a city without a king in residence.

CHAPTER XXII

*They elect persons to appeal against the
ordinances, which are proclaimed publicly;
the disapproval and disturbances resulting
from them, and how they are put down,
and the successful issue brought
about by the prudence and wisdom
of the visitor in the whole
empire of Mexico.*

TO RETURN to our history, on the day following the visitor's entry into the city of Mexico there was a general discontent and disturbances everywhere. It was said that he had come to apply the new laws, and each discoursed as he thought fit on the subject of his arrival. A meeting was publicly called to discuss what action should be taken, for it was said that he was doing them a grievous injustice. Everyone agreed that an appeal should be drawn up against the ordinances and lodged forthwith with the visitor. And that night and the following day, Sunday, the chapter and officials of His Majesty's treasury and the *vecinos* discussed nothing else. On Monday at daybreak they summoned one another to a meeting and all the *regidors* and the clerk of the town council with a great throng of people went to the monastery of St. Dominic bearing their appeal duly drawn up. The throng was so great that though the monastery is a very spacious building there was not room for them all inside. And though the visitor hesitated and was somewhat alarmed at their boldness, he went out to meet them with a cheerful countenance and explained the cause of his arrival to them. He gently admonished the city council, telling them that as he had not presented his powers nor stated the purpose of his coming, they could not appeal, as they did not know what they had to complain of. He begged them to disperse at once and to choose two or three *regidors* as representatives of the city, who could come in the evening to discuss the matter with him, when he would hear them and give his reply. At this they all took their leave, and among themselves they chose the chief procurator and two *regidors* and the clerk to the municipality and council, Miguel López de Legaspi, who went back to the monastery at two in the afternoon.

The visitor received them with apparent pleasure, and took them to his lodging, where he reproved them for the great disturbance that had taken place in the morning. He exaggerated their fault and described to them all the possible consequences to the disservice of God and His Majesty. He also told them that he had not come to ruin Mexico, but to favor them in every way he could. He promised to act as a good mediator and intercessor between them and His Majesty, to whom he said he would write on their behalf in favor of the suspension of the ordinances, the most rigorous of which he had no intention whatever of applying.

In short he spoke to them so persuasively that they went back very satisfied and took no steps about the petition they had been entrusted with. They themselves quieted the people, who had been so disturbed and scandalized. In this way three days passed until Monday, March 24, when the new laws were publicly proclaimed in the presence of the viceroy, the visitor, and the whole *audiencia*. As soon as the proclamation was finished, the chief procurator of the city broke through the throng making some stir, so as to get to where the visitor was, and laid before him the petition which was already drawn up, while many of those present gave clear proof that they were outraged and ready to go even further with the liberty they had taken. The visitor therefore, fearing some overt act of disobedience, began there and then in the presence of all of them to excuse himself with signs of great regret for having had the ordinances proclaimed, which he had done rather by force than willingly. He gave earnest assurances that nothing that ran counter to the interests of the conquerors and *vecinos* should be executed, and that he would not fail in any of the matters he had discussed with the deputies of the city council or in the promises he had made them. He displayed great regret, and even complained that he had not been fully trusted. He protested and solemnly swore that he desired the well being of all the inhabitants of New Spain more than they did themselves.

He promised under oath to write to His Majesty and report to him favorably on behalf of the conquerors and settlers, saying that he would not only assist them in the sense of seeing that His Majesty did not reduce the revenues and estates they already had or remove their rights and privileges, but that he would support them in obtaining confirmation of these and the award of new grants, and the allocation of everything in the country that was at present unoccupied. The bishop of Mexico, who was present, seeing the city so sad and discontented, strove all he could to support the visitor's intentions, and invited all the people to meet on the following day, March 25, the festivity of Our Lady, in the cathedral, where he would preach and the visitor would say mass.

With this the people dispersed, still very sad and confused, but consoling their anxieties and fears a little with the doubtful hopes they had been offered. All that night was passed restlessly, for they were full of care. Next day, the viceroy, judges, and council, and all the other *vecinos* gathered in the cathedral, where the visitor said mass and the bishop of Mexico preached, quoting many scriptural texts with reference to the present plight of them all, and discoursing so well and with such understanding that he gave them all much consolation. They then began to show more content and to deal more reasonably with the matter. Thereafter the chief procurator and the *regidors* visited Don Francisco Tello, and discussed with him the procedure they would follow with His Majesty to obtain redress. With his advice they appointed two leading religious and two *regidors* as deputies for the city council and the whole kingdom, and these at once departed for Germany where they knew the emperor then was, engaged on his wars against the Lutherans. The visitor offered to write a letter for them to take to His Majesty to explain how greatly it would benefit his service and God's and the peace, quiet, and preservation of Mexico that the ordinances should be suspended, and adding that he would refer to the harm and difficulties that would ensue from their application.

He fulfilled his promise like a gentleman; he wrote a report on his journey and on the events following his arrival in New Spain and sent it to His Majesty, pointing out a great many issues regarding the promulgation and execution of the new laws, and in particular what should be modified or extended in the case of each law. His letter included a long and notable chapter in favor of the conquerors and settlers of the country, urging that they should be granted Indians and rewarded for their services and labors, and laying much blame on the governors who had distributed the allocations unfairly in the past. The letter contained twenty-five chapters, including the conditions under which Indians should be allocated for the preservation of the country and betterment of its inhabitants. Almost all the chapters were in favor of the *vecinos* entrusted with Indians.

The procurators embarked for Castile with this letter, and a great many others also set sail to flee from the new laws. Some days after the publication of the ordinances the visitor tried with great care and tact gradually to fulfil and execute some of them as best he could. Thus the third of the rigorous laws touching the then holders of royal offices was put into execution, for it seemed reasonable and just that it should be applied to them though not to those who had held office in the past or those who were deputies. The Indians were removed from the convents, prelates, and hospitals, and a long account of this was sent to His Majesty. The procurators, deputies, religious, and *regidors* who left New Spain arrived safely in Castile after a prosperous voyage, and departed thence for Germany to negotiate with the Catholic emperor; the religious assumed the dress of soldiers, for at that time the heretics in those parts were persecuting the monasteries and religious. Having carried out their negotiations successfully and obtained royal decrees to that effect, they wrote by the first fleet sailing to New Spain of the success of their dealings with His Majesty and of the great attention he had shown them on account of the visitor's report.

When their despatches reached Mexico and were seen by the council, they all at once went out, as they were, with the scribe of the municipality and repaired to the visitor's house, with very different expressions from those they had had when they went to appeal against the ordinances. They thanked him greatly for the letters he had written on behalf of them all, and showed him His Majesty's decree, by which the visitor was expressly bidden to suspend the new laws, and not to proceed with their application until further advice. It was also said that His Majesty would give instructions for the allocation of the country among the conquerors and settlers. After this, His Majesty sent powers to Don Antonio de Mendoza by the first fleet to allocate whatever was unassigned in Mexico. The city and council then gave orders for celebrations to be held for joy at the good news, and they jousted and ran bulls more joyously and solemnly than had ever been done before.

Thereafter they were so full of pleasure and content that they thought of nothing else but festivities. And to confirm their good hopes that the royal decree about the suspension of the new laws would in fact be applied, it happened at this time that a married conqueror who had Indians, but no children, died, and the viceroy and visitor entrusted his Indians to his widow. All the owners of Indians were overjoyed at this, for they were still full of fears and suspicions whether the new laws would be executed or not.

When Don Francisco Tello de Sandoval had done all we have said in New Spain and carried out the other instructions he had received from His Majesty, he returned to Castile, and was later appointed by His Majesty to be president of the *audiencias* of Granada and Valladolid and president of the Royal Council of the Indies; and in December 1566 His Majesty gave him the bishopric of Osma.

This ends our account of the ordinances in Mexico. We shall now describe the misfortunes that arose from their application in Peru, where, as will be seen from our history, the result was quite different from the fortunate issue they had in Mexico. These misfortunes were caused by the unhappy destiny of that empire and its great wealth, and by the harshness and severity with which they were applied there, which produced so many deaths and disasters, robbery, tyranny, and cruelty. Not a tenth of what the Indians and Spaniards suffered can be written down, for the calamities caused by the war to both sexes and all ages, throughout seven hundred leagues of territory, are impossible fully to describe.

End of the Third Book

BOOK
FOUR *of the*
SECOND
PART

*It contains the going of Blasco Núñez Vela to Peru;
his journey thither; what he did before and after his
arrival in Peru; what was said against the ordinances;
the viceroy's reception; the arrest of Vaca de Castro;
discord between the viceroy and his judges; the death
of Prince Manco Inca; the election of Gonzalo Pizarro
as procurator general; how the viceroy raises men,
appoints captains, and again arrests Vaca de Castro;
the rebellion of Pedro de Puelles and of many more with
him; the death of the factor Illén Suárez de Carbajal;
the arrest of the viceroy and his release; how Pizarro is
named governor of Peru; the war between the two;
Pizarro's attacks on the viceroy, and Francisco de Carvajal's on Diego de Centeno, who is defeated; the battle
of Quito; the death of the Viceroy Blasco
Núñez Vela and his burial.*

It contains forty-two chapters.

CHAPTER I

The doings of Viceroy Blasco Núñez Vela on his arrival in Tierra Firme and on the confines of Peru.

AVING in the last book told of the prosperous outcome in the kingdom of Mexico, brought about by the good sense and discretion of the visitor Don Francisco Tello de Sandoval, we must now attempt to give an account of the misfortunes, bloodshed, and calamities in the empire of Peru, which arose from the severe, harsh, and uncompromising character of the viceroy Blasco Núñez Vela, who so resolutely persisted in putting these rigorous ordinances into force, against the opinion of the judges of his own *audiencia* and without in the least considering what was in the best interests of his king. We should recall that the two fleets for Peru and Mexico separated in the Gulf of Las Damas. The viceroy sailed on and had fair weather till his arrival at Nombre de Dios on January 10, 1544, whence he went to Panama and at once released many of the Indians the Spaniards had brought there from Peru and ordered them to be sent back to their various provinces. Many were angered by the removal of these Indians from their masters, both because they had been trained for work and because they were now Christians; the release was also against the wishes of many of the Indians themselves. The viceroy was repeatedly addressed on this matter, and efforts were made to dissuade him on the ground that the step was contrary to the service of His Majesty and of God, since it was notorious that the chief object of the Spaniards was to make the Indians Christians and this could not be put into effect if they were under the control of the caciques. In particular it was obvious that if an Indian had become a Christian and then returned to his cacique's authority, he would be sacrified to the Devil. Moreover, His Majesty's express command was that the Indians were to be set at liberty, and those who were in that province wanted to remain there, and it was against their own will that they were being sent to Peru, with moreover so little provisions that it was certain that many of them would die. The viceroy's reply to all this was that His Majesty had expressly ordered them to be sent, and he could and would do nothing else. He therefore bade the Spaniards who had Indians to send them off at their own expense.

About three hundred Indians were removed from private persons, and these were forthwith embarked and sent to Peru; most of them died for want of food or because they were abandoned on the coast. When the people who had advised the viceroy realized the great dangers which it was feared would follow the execution of the ordinances, they sought to prevent him from proceeding with it, adducing many arguments to bring these dangers home to him, and reminding him of the great wars that had taken place in Peru and of the dissatisfaction and unrest existing among the settlers. The viceroy listened to all this reluctantly, and replied sharply that as they were not within his jurisdiction he could not hang them all. In this way he raised a complete barrier against any persuasion as to what required to be done. He stayed twenty days in Panama, during which time the judges obtained information about many aspects of Peruvian affairs. In particular they realized two things: first, how deeply outraged the conquerors were by the ordinances, and second, the great danger of trying to put them into force so soon after Licentiate Vaca de Castro had fought Don Diego de Almagro the younger, and defeated and executed him with a loss of 350 men in the battle: as a result of which the survivors were all expecting to receive great favors for the real services they had done His Majesty. When the judges understood this, and considered the nature of the task and the character of the viceroy, they ceased to urge him, but thought that once they arrived in Peru, and he saw what the country and people were like, he would be more disposed to take their advice.

The viceroy, annoyed for little or no reason at what the judges had told him, resolved to leave before them and said that he had sworn to show them what sort of man he was by having the ordinances obeyed and executed by the time they arrived. As Licentiate Zárate was at the time ill and confined to bed, the viceroy paid him a visit before his departure. The licentiate said to him that, as he was determined to leave without them, he begged and prayed him to enter Peru gently and not try to execute any of the ordinances until the *audiencia* had been set up in Lima and he was in full control of the whole country. When this was so, he could put into execution whatever laws were necessary, both for His Majesty's conscience and the good government and well being of the natives. With regard to the laws that were too harsh and any others that seemed inappropriate, it would be best to send His Majesty a report on them:

then, if His Majesty again instructed him to carry them out, in spite of the information he was given, he would be in a better position to execute them, since he would have established himself more firmly in Peru and justices of his own choosing would have been appointed to all the towns and villages.

Licentiate Zárate said all this and more; but it was not to the viceroy's taste. On the contrary he was greatly annoyed by it, and replied with some asperity, swearing to carry out the ordinances according to the stipulations contained in them and to brook no delay or postponement: when the judges got to Peru, he would have done their work for them. With this he embarked alone, refusing to wait for all or any of the judges, though they begged him to do so. On March 4, he reached the port of Túmbez, where he landed, and continued his journey by land, executing the ordinances in each of the settlements he came to, assessing the Indians some of them had and depriving others of their Indians and placing them under the crown. In this way he passed through Piura and Trujillo, promulgating the new laws and refusing to accept any petitions, though the *vecinos* alleged that all this could not be done without a formal sentence, if the ordinances were to be applied, or until the *audiencia* had been set up, since these were His Majesty's express commands in one of the laws which stated that a viceroy and four judges were being sent to execute them. However, the viceroy intimidated and threatened those who persisted, spreading great distress and confusion in the hearts and minds of all of them when they considered how harsh the laws were, embracing them all at large and sparing none. Even before this, as soon as the viceroy reached the coast of Peru, he had sent forward his credentials and instructions to Lima and Cuzco with orders that he was to be acknowledged and obeyed and that Licentiate Vaca de Castro should lay down his authority, as he himself was now in the country as viceroy.

Some days before these messages were received in Lima, it had become known that His Majesty had appointed Blasco Núñez Vela, and a copy of all the ordinances had also been received. At this the city council had sent Don Antonio de Ribera and Juan Alonso Palomino to inform Licentiate Vaca de Castro, who was in Cuzco. He too had had letters from Spain announcing the appointment of Blasco Núñez Vela and the despatch of the ordinances. These letters were brought him by his servant Diego de Aller, who had gone to Spain and came hastening back with the news.

All this is from Diego Fernández of Palencia; and the other historians say the same.

CHAPTER II

*Licentiate Vaca de Castro goes to Lima and takes
leave of his companions on the way; the
disturbance caused by the news of the
execution of the ordinances and the
insubordinate talk that ensues.*

GOVERNOR Vaca de Castro, on hearing the news of the coming of
Viceroy Blasco Núñez Vela and of the ordinances he was bringing,
and how he was executing them without listening to anyone or admitting
any appeal, thought that he had better cover himself by going to Lima
and receiving the viceroy. He therefore refused to receive the embassy of
Don Antonio Ribera and Juan Alonso Palomino from the council of Lima
or to listen to the representatives of the municipality of Cuzco and the
vecinos who had come from other places. These all urged him not to receive the viceroy but to appeal against the severity of the ordinances in the
name of all of them and against the viceroy's instructions on the ground
of his harshness and incapacity for the office. They further suggested that
they should not accept the viceroy as governor, since he had proved himself unworthy of the office by refusing a fair hearing to His Majesty's
vassals and showing such obduracy in even the most trivial business. They
told Vaca de Castro that if he did not undertake the task, there would be
others in Peru who would.

All Peru was full of the viceroy's harshness and the severity with which
he was executing the ordinances. The disturbance was fomented by the
very messages the viceroy had sent out in all directions to bid the inhabitants receive him as governor, for they had spread news of the ordinances far and wide, and rumor had added its part, as usually happens in
such cases, to further incense those who heard the news. Licentiate Vaca
de Castro brushed them all aside and prepared to go to Lima. He was
honorably escorted by gentlemen who were *vecinos* and by soldiers from
Cuzco, for he was so beloved that if he had permitted them, not a man
would have failed to accompany him and remained in the city. On the
way he was notified of the viceroy's instructions that he was to abandon
the governorship of Peru and acknowledge him as governor. Vaca de
Castro duly obeyed and laid down his office, though before committing

this to writing he awarded a large number of allocations of Indians to persons who had deserved them by serving His Majesty: he had either witnessed their deeds with his own eyes or been informed of the services they had rendered before his arrival in Peru.

Those who brought the viceroy's instructions told how he had set about executing the ordinances; how he had deprived the Spaniards in Panama of their Indians and shipped the latter back to Peru against their own wishes; how he had assessed certain allocations and confiscated others, placing them under the control of the crown, according to the ordinances; and how he had refused to hear any petitions or respect any rights, saying that such was His Majesty's bidding. Licentiate Vaca de Castro's companions were outraged at this, and most of them returned to Cuzco without taking leave of the governor, saying that they would not dare to appear before such a harsh man who would have them all hanged for no reason at all. When the judges arrived and the *audiencia* had been established, they would come back and put forward the justice of their case. But all their excuses showed clearly that they were scandalized and disaffected; and they themselves openly proved it, for when they reached Huamanga they took the artillery that had been left there after the defeat of the younger Almagro and carried it off to Cuzco. The perpetrator of this was a *vecino* called Gaspar Rodríguez, who collected a large number of Indians to transport the artillery, to the great scandal of all who saw and heard it.

Vaca de Castro was ignorant of this misdeed and continued his journey. On the way he met a cleric called Baltasar de Loaisa who was greatly attached to him and had come to warn him that he was being much criticized in Lima for coming down with such a large company and with too many arms. The licentiate, on hearing this, asked those who were still with him to return home, and many did so. Those who did not wish to return he asked at least to leave behind the lances and arquebusses they had brought with them: in those days and for many years after it was customary to travel with these arms.

The arms were left there, and within a few days they arrived at Lima. Vaca de Castro was accompanied by Lorenzo de Aldana, Pedro de los Ríos, Licentiate Benito de Carvajal, Don Alonso de Montemayor, and Hernando Bachicao. They were received with great rejoicing in Lima, though this was tempered by sadness at the news of the ordinances and the severity of his successor, who was so different from him. Vaca de Castro at once sent his steward, Jerónimo de la Serena [Serna], and his secretary, Pedro López de Cazalla, with letters to the viceroy, welcoming

him and offering his person for his lordship's service and that of His
Majesty.

While these things had been happening on the road from Cuzco to
Lima, other more serious events had occurred on the viceroy's journey
from Túmbez to Rímac. Wherever he found any of the ordinances applicable, he executed it rigorously, admitting no argument in favor of the
conquerors of the empire, saying merely that these were his king's orders
and they must be obeyed. At this the *vecinos* and other inhabitants were
completely outraged; for, as Diego Fernández says, they were all participants in the damage without a single exception. They spoke shamelessly
against the ordinances, saying that they had been recommended to His
Majesty by prejudiced persons who were envious of what the conquerors
of Peru had won and now possessed because they were not capable of
doing as much themselves. They added that others had hypocritically
tried to promote their own interests by forcing him to sign the ordinances
and sending them out with a judge who was so rigorous and contuma-
cious that he refused to hear anyone, as López de Gómara says in his ch.
clv, in these words. The title of the chapter is:

> What passed between Blasco Núñez and the people of Trujillo and the
> complaints and arguments they all put forward against the ordinances

Blasco Núñez entered Trujillo, to the great sorrow of the Spaniards. He
had the ordinances publicly promulgated, assessed the Indians for tribute and
freed them; and forbade anyone to oblige them to work without payment.
He removed all the vassals he could under the ordinances and placed them
under the crown. The council and inhabitants petitioned against the ordinances,
with the exception of those which required the assessment for tribute and tax-
ations to be carried out, and ended forced labor among the Indians, which they
accepted. He turned down their appeal; and applied very severe penalties to
magistrates who flouted his orders, saying that he had the emperor's express
command to execute the laws without hearing or heeding any appeals. He told
them however that they were justified in complaining of the ordinances and
should take the matter up with the emperor—to whom he himself would write
saying that he had been misled in decreeing these laws. When the *vecinos* saw
how inflexible he was despite these fair words, they began to curse. Some said
they would forsake their wives, and some indeed did so, for many had married
their concubines and kept women since they had been instructed that they
would lose their estates unless they did so. Others said it would be much better
not to have a wife or children to support if they were to be deprived of the
slaves who kept them with their work in the mines and on the farms, and in
other ways. Others asked to be paid for the slaves who were taken from them,
since they had bought them from the royal fifth and they were marked with the

king's brand. Others thought their toils and services had all been wasted if they had no one to serve them in their old age. Some showed teeth missing from eating the toasted maize of Peru; others displayed many wounds and bruises or great alligator bites. The conquerors complained that after they had spent their wealth and shed their blood in winning Peru, the emperor had taken away the few serfs he had rewarded them with. The soldiers said that they would not go and conquer any more lands, since any hope of getting serfs had been removed, but that they would rob right and left as best they could.

The royal officials and placeholders were extremely offended at being deprived of their allocations, though they had not mistreated the Indians; for they had not been given Indians with their offices, but in return for their labors and services. The clergy and friars also said that they could not sustain themselves or the churches if their villages were taken away from them. The most outrageous critic of the viceroy and even of the emperor was the Mercedarian Fray Pedro Muñoz, who enlarged on how ill His Majesty repaid those who had served him, saying that the laws had more of the odor of duplicity than of sanctity, since they took back the slaves he had sold, but did not restore the purchase price, and took the Indian villages for the crown from the monasteries, churches, hospitals, and conquerors who had won them. Worse still, the Indians thus recovered in the king's name were burdened with double taxes and tribute, and they themselves wept because of this.

Thus López de Gómara.

CHAPTER III

What was said in Peru about the formulators of the ordinances, and especially about Licentiate Bartolomé de las Casas.

THEIR shameless disrespect increased, and they did not spare the advisers and formulators who had been responsible for the ordinances. They said a thousand hard things about these advisers, especially as they knew that Fray Bartolomé de las Casas (who Diego Fernández describes as a former conqueror and settler) had petitioned for them and devised them. The Spaniards in Peru told a thousand fantasies about what he had done before he took orders. They repeated his particular misdeeds, how he had tried to make himself conqueror and colonizer of the island of

Cumaná, and had caused the death and ruin of many Spaniards with the false reports and great promises he had made to the emperor and his foreign servants about increasing the royal revenues and sending great quantities of gold and pearls to Spain and to the Flemings and Burgundians who dwelt at court. They said that many Spaniards who had been conquerors in the Windward Islands and had known Las Casas before he took orders had later come to Peru and they knew what had happened when he had promised to convert the natives of Cumaná. This is given by López de Gómara in ch. lxxvii of his *History*, and I suspect he had his version from one of these conquerors, for what he says in this chapter is in agreement with what the people in Peru used to say: in order to quote an author who has dealt with this matter I shall give his chapter with its title:

Chapter lxxvii. The death of many Spanish crusaders taken by the priest
Bartolomé de las Casas

Licentiate Bartolomé de las Casas, priest, was in Santo Domingo when the monasteries of Cumaná and Chirivichi were flourishing, and heard this country praised for the fertility of its soil, the gentleness of its inhabitants, and its abundance of pearls. He came to Spain and asked the emperor to make him governor of Cumaná, telling him how he was deceived by those who were governing the Indies and promising to increase the royal revenues. Juan Rodríguez de Fonseca, Licentiate Luis Zapata, and the secretary Lope de Conchillos, who understood Indian affairs, opposed him, bringing forward information about the matter and regarding him as incapable of exercising the position because he was a cleric, with insufficient experience of the country and the matters he had taken up. He then had recourse to Monsieur de la Chaux, the emperor's chamberlain, and other Flemings and Burgundians, and attained his object because he seemed to be a good Christian in saying that he would convert more Indians than anyone else by adopting certain measures and would enrich the king by sending him a great quantity of pearls. Many pearls were then arriving in Spain, and Chièvres' wife had 170 marks of them out of the royal fifth, and every Fleming was begging and seeking them.

Las Casas asked for farmers to take out saying that they would do less harm than swashbuckling, greedy, and insubordinate soldiers. He asked that they should be armed knights with golden spurs and a red cross, different from that of Calatrava, so that they should be ennobled and freed of taxation. He was given what ships and sailors he wanted in Seville at the royal expense, and went to Cumaná in 1520 with some three hundred farmers with crosses. He arrived as Gonzalo de Ocampo was building Toledo. He was dismayed to discover so many Spaniards there with this gentleman, sent by the admiral and the *audiencia*, and to find the land quite different from what he had thought and declared it to be at court. He presented his credentials and demanded that they should abandon the land to him and clear it for him to settle and rule. Gonzalo de Ocampo said that he would obey the instructions, but that it was not proper to put them into effect and he could not do so without orders from the governor and judges of Santo Domingo. He made a good deal of fun of the priest, whom de la Vega had known from some of his past actions: he also made fun of the new knights and their crosses like *sanbenitos*. Las Casas was very annoyed at this and distressed by the home truths Ocampo told.

He could not enter Toledo, and so built a house of mud and wattle near the former Franciscan monastery, where he established his farmers and the weapons, articles for barter and supplies he had brought. He then went off to bring his suit in Santo Domingo. Gonzalo de Ocampo went off too: I do not know whether because of this or because of troubles with some of his companions, all of whom went after him. Thus Toledo was abandoned and the farmers were left by themselves. The Indians were delighted by the Spaniards' disagreements and attacked the house, killing almost all the golden knights. Those who could escape took refuge in a caravel, and there was not a Spaniard left alive in the whole of the pearl coast.

When Bartolomé de las Casas heard of the death of his friends and the loss of the royal investment, he became a Dominican friar in Santo Domingo. So he neither increased the royal revenues, nor ennobled the farmers, nor sent pearls to the Flemings.

Thus López de Gómara.

All the above and much more was told to the discredit of Las Casas by those who were hit by the ordinances: even López de Gómara does not give the full gist of it in what he says, but abridges it. The people in Peru went far beyond this, saying that Las Casas had become a priest so as to avoid being punished by His Majesty for the inauspicious account he had given him without having seen or known anything about the country of Cumaná. They also said that in order to make restitution to His Majesty for the loss he had caused the royal treasury, he had recommended the ordinances and insisted so much on them, pretending to be zealous for the welfare of the Indians: the effects of his zeal would speak for themselves and show how good he was. They spoke a great deal on these lines, and we cannot set it all down. The emperor appointed Las Casas to be bishop of Chiapa in the kingdom of Mexico, as Diego Fernández says, but he did not dare to go there because of what he had done in the Indies. I met him in Madrid in 1562, and when he knew I came from the Indies he gave me his hand to kiss, but on learning that I was from Peru and not Mexico he had little to say to me.

CHAPTER IV

*The reasons for their complaints adduced by the
victims of the ordinances; how they prepare
to receive the viceroy.*

MANY OTHER things were said about the ordinances, not only in
Lima, but also throughout Peru. In order to explain these complaints and lamentations, we should mention that it was then the custom
in both Mexico and Peru, and still was in 1560 when I left, that as offices
were not held for life, four gentlemen of the greatest credit and trust
should be elected in each Spanish settlement to act as officers of the royal
treasury and keep the fifth of the gold and silver mined throughout the
country: this was the first tribute the Catholic monarchs laid on the
whole of the New World. The officials of the royal treasury were the
treasurer, accountant, factor, and inspector whose duty it also was to collect tribute from the Indians when a *vecino* died and they were placed
under the control of the crown. In addition to these offices each Spanish
settlement elected annually two ordinary alcaldes, a corregidor and his
deputy, and six, eight, or ten *regidors*, in proportion to the size of the
place; elections were also made to the other offices that were necessary for
the good government of the republic.

Under the third ordinance, these officials were treated in the same way
as governors, presidents, judges, and magistrates and their deputies. All
who had held such offices or were now holding them were to lose their
Indians under the new law. For this reason the victims said:

"We won this empire at our own cost and risk, and have augmented
the crown of Castile with all the great kingdoms and dominions it now
possesses. In payment for these services we were given the Indians we
have, and we were given them for two lives, though they should have
been perpetual as seigniories in Spain are. The reason why our Indians are
now being taken away is that we have been elected officials of the royal
treasury, or magistrates, or *regidors*. If we perform these duties well and
do no one any harm, why should we be deprived of our Indians because
we have been elected as men of standing? Yet, they order us to keep our
offices, which may be an excuse to deprive us of anything we may gain in
the future on some other occasion. If this is what we have come to, we

should have done better to be thieves, bandits, adulterers, and murderers, for the ordinances do not mention these, but only those of us who have been respectable citizens."

Those condemned under the fourth law spoke as freely, or more so. This laid down that all those who had taken part in the rivalries between Pizarros and Almagros should be deprived of their Indians: this law, as Diego Fernández says, meant that no one in all Peru could have Indians or estates.

To this they asked what blame attached to those who had obeyed His Majesty's governors, for both were legitimate governors and had ordered the settlers to do what they had done. Neither of them was against the royal crown, but had been drawn into rivalries and discord by the Devil over the question of the division of the two jurisdictions. If one party had done such wrong as to have their property confiscated, it was obvious that the others should remain free for their services to their king. But to condemn the two sides equally was more like the tyranny of Nero and other such oppressors than a desire to favor the vassals of the crown.

They also uttered iniquities and blasphemies against the authors of the ordinances who had persuaded and forced His Majesty to sign them and order them to be put rigorously into force by telling him that this was in his interest.

They said that if these people had been in the conquest of Peru and undergone the toils the conquerors had experienced they would certainly not have made such laws but would have opposed them. They bolstered up these statements and blasphemies with examples from ancient and modern history like the wars and hatred between Almagros and Pizarros. They said that if when there had been wars in Spain between the two kings Peter the Cruel and Henry, his brother, to whom the lords and landowners rallied, serving them until one died, if any succeeding king had ordered all the estates and properties to be taken away from both sides after the wars were over, what would the leading men in Spain have said or done? Similarly with the wars between Castile and Portugal over the inheritance of the so-called Beltraneja, who was twice sworn princess of Castile and was supported by many of the lords of Castile: when Queen Isabella spoke of these and called them traitors, the duke of Alba heard her and said: "Let Your Highness pray to God that we may win, for if they win we shall be the traitors."

They argued from this that if the successor to the throne had taken away the estates of all the lords who had taken part in the war, what would they have done? They said a great many more shameful things, which we shall not write down lest we give offence to our readers: these roused their indignation till they came to the pass they later reached.

To return to the viceroy, who was on the road to Lima, he received gratefully and in good heart the messages and messengers sent by Vaca de Castro, and answered them and sent them back to Lima. But when they reached the city, they brought a long account of the severity with which the new laws had been applied and of the harshness and inflexibility of the viceroy and his determination to put them into execution throughout Peru without admitting any appeal or postponement. This kindled new fires in Lima, Cuzco, and throughout the kingdom.

It was generally mooted whether they should refuse to receive the viceroy and obey the ordinances, for they said that the day he entered Lima and proclaimed the new laws, they would have no Indians and no estates. Apart from the intention of depriving them of their Indians, they said, there was such a jumble of various orders in the new laws that it was inevitable that all their property would be confiscated, and their lives too were in danger; for on the same grounds as they were to lose their Indians, for taking part in the wars between Pizarros and Almagros, they might also lose their heads, which was not to be tolerated even if they were slaves.

With these follies the people of Lima almost convinced themselves not to receive the viceroy, but the factor Illén Suárez de Carvajal and Diego de Agüero, who were the leading figures in the council and much beloved on account of their virtues and characters, soothed them with good arguments. It was therefore generally decided that the viceroy should be received with all possible pomp and solemnity to see if they could prevail upon him to hear their case by receiving him and showing their humility and vassalage. They hoped he then might apply the laws the Catholic monarchs and the emperor himself had made in favor of the conquerors of the New World, and especially in favor of those of Peru, for they had been the most favored and best rewarded under these laws, like the dearest children of the rulers of Spain, in recognition of their conquest of that wealthy empire.

Having so decided, everyone prepared his finest dress and harness against the day of the viceroy's entry. The factor Illén Suárez de Carvajal and Captain Diego de Agüero did not escape the criticisms that were current about all this. It was said that they had proposed that the viceroy should be received and persuaded the rest out of regard for their own interests; for both had lost their Indians, the first as royal factor, and the second as a participant in the late wars, and both together as *regidors*, so that their object was to secure their own advantage rather than to serve the emperor.

During all this time the viceroy was travelling on, and wherever he passed he put any part of the ordinances that was applicable into execution; and though he was aware of the disturbances and complaints this was producing, he did not cease to do so, but daily displayed greater rigor so as to prove that he was not afraid of the settlers and was determined to be a good servant of the crown and do the king's bidding: he kept saying that he would respect the king and no one else.

In this way he reached the valley called Huaura where he slept at the inn and found no Indian serfs and no supplies. This neglect was due chiefly to the council at Lima, whose duty it was to provide for the viceroy on his journey. But he laid the blame on Antonio Solar, a native of Medina del Campo and *vecino* of Lima, who had been awarded this valley. The viceroy therefore conceived a great hatred for him, which was increased by his finding a squib written on a blank wall of the inn, which is the writing paper of the bold, as the saying is: "Who seeks to throw me out of my house and land I'll seek to throw out of the world." He suspected that Solar, whose house it was, had written this piece of impertinence, or bidden someone else do so, and so conceived a monstrous hatred for him, though he dissimulated for the time being, to show it later, as we shall say.

CHAPTER V

The viceroy's reception; the arrest of Vaca de Castro; the public scandal and the passions aroused in the viceroy and the rest.

AMIDST these conflicts and troubles (though he tried to conceal them), the viceroy came within three leagues of the city of Lima where a great many of the leading gentlemen came out to escort him. They included Vaca de Castro and Don Jerónimo de Loaisa, bishop of Lima, who was later archbishop. The viceroy received them all with great pleasure, especially the bishop and Licentiate Vaca de Castro; and so they travelled on, the viceroy discoursing on the excellence of the valley, and its fertility and beauty. On reaching the river crossing they found awaiting them Garci Díaz de Arias, bishop-elect of Quito, together with the chapter of his holy church and the rest of the clergy. The meeting was attended by great festivities and rejoicings.

A little further on, at the entry to the city, they found the city council and all the *vecinos* and principal gentlemen, including (as all three authors say) the factor Illén Suárez de Carvajal as the principal personage of the council. In the name of the whole city he took the oath from the viceroy to the effect that he would respect the privileges, rights, and favors granted by His Majesty to the conquerors and settlers of Peru, and also give a legal hearing to their petition against the ordinances. The viceroy swore that he would do whatever was for His Majesty's service and the well being of Peru. Many said and put it about that he had taken the oath falsely and with reservations.

Thus Diego Fernández. All, ecclesiastics and laymen alike, regretted that the viceroy should have sworn thus, without making himself clear or showing any sign of meeting their requests. They then lost their rejoicing, which turned to tears and suppressed grief. They said that no good could be expected to come of this oath; but they feared a great deal of harm, and that next day they would find themselves dispossessed of their Indians and estates and unable to earn anything else to keep themselves with, for they were old and wasted by their past toils. Though the viceroy was received under a brocade canopy and the *regidors* carrying it wore trailing robes of crimson velvet lined with white damask, and though the bells of the cathedral church and the convents were rung, and music was played in the streets, which were strewn with rushes and covered with many triumphal arches made, as we have said, of a great variety of beautiful flowers by the Indians; yet all this seemed more like a sad and sorrowful funeral than the reception of a viceroy, so great was the silence and their inward grief. Thus they went to the cathedral; and after he had adored the Blessed Sacrament, they escorted him to the house of the marquis Don Francisco Pizarro, where the viceroy and all his retinue were lodged.

On the next day, when the viceroy had heard about the disturbed state of mind in which those who had come down with Vaca de Castro had returned to Cuzco, he suspected, as Zárate says in Book V, ch. iii, as well as the other authors, that Vaca de Castro had known about their rebelliousness and had been the origin of it. He thereupon had him arrested and flung in the public prison, and his goods confiscated.

The people of the city, though not in agreement with Vaca de Castro, went to beg the viceroy not to permit a person of his standing, a member of His Majesty's council who had been governor, to be cast in the public jail, for even if he was to be beheaded next day he could be put in a safe and decent place of custody. The viceroy therefore had him put in the royal house, on a surety of 100,000 Castilians, in which the *vecinos* of Lima bound themselves. Having seen these proofs of his severity, the people were angry and gathered in little groups; they gradually left the city for Cuzco, where the viceroy had not been received.

Thus Zárate, and Diego Fernández says the same almost in these very words, adding that Vaca de Castro was in the public prison, as follows:

Those who were in the city held a thousand meetings and conclaves to discuss the harm that would befall Peru and the settlers. They said that the cutting off of the wealth, liberty, and authority of the conquerors and lords of Indians would lead to the depopulation and impoverishment of the country. It was impossible to acquiesce in His Majesty's commands, and it would be impossible to make new discoveries and even more so to preserve the population and trade of Peru: they all thought of a thousand other objections.

In the midst of the general confusion and fears some of them went to the viceroy under pretext of a social visit, in the belief that they might find some solution or some mitigation of his severe intentions after he had seen what the country was like and how disturbed it was. Some who made bold to address him about this depicted some of these disadvantages as moderately as they could —for they knew he at once grew angry when these things were mentioned— but this did little good, for he soon put down his rod of office and interrupted the discussion on the ground that he was obeying his prince's will. Thus he would not allow anyone to conclude his discourse, and refused to answer or satisfy anyone who said anything to him about this matter, but at once cut them short, interposing the royal will. This caused even greater scandal in the hearts of many of them, and added to their enmity and rancor toward the viceroy.

Within a few days of his reception three of the judges who had remained behind arrived, though Licentiate Zárate was still ill at Trujillo.

He then began to set up the *audiencia* and the royal courts in the house where he was lodged, as being the most suitable place on account of its position and size. He ordered a sumptuous reception for the royal seal, as befitted the case of an *audiencia* newly established in the country. It was received carried in a box on a well-harnessed horse covered with a cloth of gold, under a brocade canopy borne by the *regidors* of the city, clad in their trailing cloaks of crimson velvet, one of the *regidors* leading the horse by the bridle. This is the way in which the royal person is received in Castile.

The *audiencia* was then established and business was begun. Matters of administration and of justice were dealt with, since this seemed to enhance the authority of Peru. The lesser sort and the poor were very glad of this, for these are usually more glad than the rich to see plenty of justices. And as the Devil had already set about plotting the fall of the unfortunate viceroy, stirring up the land when it had only so recently been pacified, he ordained that this disturbance should multiply and spread. He made those first ill humors burgeon and sowed discord and dissension between the viceroy, the judges, and the whole kingdom, on the question of whether the execution of the ordinances should be carried through, and the viceroy's refusal to receive the petitions of the city council of Lima and other places further south which had sent representatives.

Thus Diego Fernández of Palencia (ch. x). As this author says, the Devil sought to bring the viceroy down by stirring up the land; but the Devil and discord, his chief minister in the destruction of kingdoms and empires, were not satisfied by kindling fires between the viceroy and the conquerors of Peru, but also tried to start them between the viceroy and his four judges, who should rightly or wrongly have been all of one mind. And the Devil succeeded, for the judges tried to temper the viceroy's wrath in the matter of executing the ordinances, since they were dispassionate, prudent, and far-sighted men who realized that as the mere news of the ordinances had caused such a disturbance, their execution would lead to much greater disorders, and a kingdom that had only just laid down its arms after the recent wars could not stomach such severity, which might well bring about the perdition of them all and of the empire itself.

With these fears they tried to soften the viceroy, if this were possible. But he took umbrage and suspected that they had been bribed, and grew angry, declaring that he would regard as his enemy anyone who thought he could prevent the execution of His Majesty's orders. And he showed his wrath by bidding them each find houses to live in by themselves, and not to reside in the houses of *vecinos* or live at their expense.

There were sometimes high words about this and about the obstacles the judges placed in the way of the execution of the ordinances; but as they were forced to be in permanent contact to deal with public affairs, they had to restrain themselves from exhibiting their passions in public. But as the intention of executing the ordinances grew daily plainer, so did the confusion and anger of their victims increase. As Diego Fernández says in his ch. x:

on the one hand they contemplated the determined will of the viceroy to put the ordinances into effect, on the other they realized that His Majesty the emperor was too far away for them to seek a solution to their ills from him. They furthermore feared that if they were once deprived of their authority over the Indians they had, they would find it very difficult to get them back. These were like three ulcers in their bowels, which worked them into a frenzy, and they were all in a state of confusion, madness, and folly. It seemed that this disease had not only come over the people, but over the viceroy himself, for on seeing the people in a state of exaltation and rebellion and finding that many of them had run away from him, he also became exalted and disquieted, and uttered a thousand insults in consequence. This increased the obstinate spirit of those concerned, who decided to fling their lives and honor after their estates, as they later did.

Thus Fernández, copied word for word.

CHAPTER VI

The secret discord between the viceroy and the judges becomes public; Prince Manco Inca and the Spaniards with him write to the viceroy.

DISCORD was not satisfied with entering the inner hearts of the viceroy and the judges, but had to appear openly, for its pleasure is to walk in the squares and run through the public streets. It therefore reminded the viceroy of the lampoon he had read in the inn at Huaura belonging to Antonio Solar; suspecting that he had written it or had it written, the viceroy summoned him and discussed the lampoon with him in private, saying also that he had uttered some very disrespectful words: Zárate and Fernández say this in the same terms. The viceroy then ordered the palace gates to be shut, called one of his chaplains to shrive Solar and wanted to hang him from a beam under a balcony overlooking the square. Antonio Solar refused to confess and the tussle lasted so long that the news of it spread through the city and the archbishop and other persons of quality with him came and begged the viceroy to suspend his sentence for the time being, which they could not persuade him to do. Finally he agreed to postpone it for that day, and had Antonio Solar cast in jail and laden with shackles. Once his rage had subsided, he thought it would be unwise to hang Solar, and so kept him in prison for two months, without bringing any charge against him in writing or opening a case against him. At length the judges went to visit the prison one Saturday, and being informed of the facts and petitioned on behalf of Antonio Solar, they saw him and asked him the cause of his arrest. He said that he did not know, and no case against him was found in the hands of the scribes, nor could the governor of the prison say more than that the viceroy had sent him to the prison, thus loaded with irons.

On the Monday following the judges told the viceroy at their joint session that they had found Solar under arrest and that no charge seemed to have been made against him, but it was said that he was there on the viceroy's orders; if there was no information with which to justify his arrest, they could do no less than release him in conformity with justice.

The viceroy answered that he had had Solar arrested and had wanted to hang him too, both because of the lampoon in his *tambo* and because of certain disrespectful remarks made about his person, of which there were no witnesses. By virtue of his powers of government as viceroy he could have Solar arrested and even killed without being obliged to give them an account of his reasons. The judges replied that there was no government but that which conformed to justice and the laws of the kingdom. They thus remained in dispute, and on their visit to the prison on the following Saturday, the judges ordered Solar to be released and placed under house arrest. On their next visit they discharged him. This annoyed the viceroy extraordinarily, and he found an opportunity for getting his own back on the judges in the fact that all three of them were residing in the houses of the richest *vecinos* in the city who fed them and supplied them with all they and their servants needed. Though this had at first been done with the viceroy's consent, it was only a temporary arrangement until they found houses and had them made ready to receive them. But seeing they continued there, the viceroy sent to tell them to find houses for themselves and not eat at the *vecinos'* expense, for it would not look well in His Majesty's eyes, and was moreover not permitted. Nor should they consort with the *vecinos* and merchants.

The judges answered this by saying that they could not find houses until the tenancies expired, but that they would eat at their own expense in future. As to the company they kept, this was not forbidden, but was very proper, and it was the custom in Castile in all His Majesty's councils, for the merchants attended to the judges' business as they came and went and brought them information. The judges and viceroy were thus still at odds, and this emerged whenever they met together. So much so that one day Licentiate Alvarez took evidence from a procurator on a report that he had given the viceroy's brother-in-law Diego Alvarez de Cueto a sum in gold pesos in order to have himself appointed to the office. The viceroy deeply resented this.

So Zárate, and Fernández, having said as much, adds the following:

So that the viceroy and judges appeared to be two opposing factions. Solar too, on being freed and discharged, secretly inflamed the *vecinos* and others against the viceroy, and they added fuel to the flames by saying publicly that the viceroy had said and done things that had never entered his head. All this was fully believed, for Blasco Núñez was already so generally detested by everyone that on his account the very name of viceroy was then as odious in Lima as that of king had been among the Romans after Tarquin the Superb was driven from Rome, notwithstanding that Blasco Núñez Vela was the first viceroy Peru had had.

This is Fernández' addition.

Dr. Gonzalo de Illescas, dealing with the affairs of Peru in his *Pontifical History*, speaks as follows of Blasco Núñez Vela's terrible temper: "After this Vaca de Castro continued to govern Peru peaceably for the space of a year and a half until Blasco Núñez Vela went there as viceroy. The latter was a leading gentleman of Avila, and took some extremely rigorous ordinances, though they were not so rigorous as their bearer," etc. The doctor says in a few words all that our historians could not or dare not say in all they wrote on the subject.

While this was happening in Lima, other and greater events were occurring elsewhere, where the ambitions, envies, rebelliousness, and passion for power that held sway in Lima were unknown. But discord overran all Peru, and found a means of troubling and slaying poor Prince Manco Inca, who was happy and peaceful in his voluntary exile, though deprived of an empire for the mastery of which there had been such bloodshed and such cruel wars as in the past, the like of which, and worse if possible, were feared for the present.

It should be recalled that Diego Méndez and Gómez Pérez and six other Spaniards fled from prison in Cuzco, as we have mentioned, and escaped the persecutions of the Pizarros, their enemies, and the justice of Governor Vaca de Castro when he had recently punished those most guilty of the death of the marquis. They now learnt through the Inca of the coming of the new governor and of the discord prevailing throughout Peru, for it was said that he had come to inflict more punishments and make alterations in the Spaniards' possessions in Peru. The Inca's subjects indeed did not fail to send daily reports to him about what was happening in the outside world, so that he should not be in ignorance in his isolation in those wild forests.

Diego Méndez and his companions were delighted at the news, and persuaded the Inca to write to the viceroy begging his permission to leave his prison and go and serve His Majesty by the governor's side on whatever occasions might offer. The Inca did this on their advice, since they told him that it would be a step toward the restoration of his empire, or a good part of it. The Spaniards also wrote on their own behalf, begging forgiveness for the past and safe conducts to go and serve His Majesty as he might command.

They chose Gómez Pérez as their ambassador to the viceroy, and he appeared before the viceroy, accompanied by ten or twelve Indians the Inca had sent to serve him. He presented his letters and his message, making a long report on the Inca's situation and his intention of serving the crown. The viceroy was much gladdened by the news, and readily granted the Spaniards their pardon, answering the Inca in terms of great friendship, courtesy, and affection, for he thought that the Inca's company would be of great assistance to him in any emergency, whether of peace or war. Gómez Pérez returned to his friends with this answer, and they and the Inca were overjoyed at it, and made ready to depart as soon as possible to place themselves at the viceroy's orders. But the adverse fortune of Blasco Núñez Vela did not consent to this, and everything turned out quite differently, as we shall see in the following chapter.

CHAPTER VII

The unfortunate death of Prince Manco Inca;
the disturbances among the Spaniards
about the ordinances.

THE INCA was playing ninepins one day with Gómez Pérez, for such was his custom with him and the other Spaniards; they had had a set of ninepins made for their and his amusement: the Indians had not previously known the game. Gómez Pérez was a man of little discretion and no refinement, and whenever he played with the Inca, he would dispute excessively about the placing of the ninepins or any little incident the game offered. The Inca was now very annoyed by him, but did not wish to show his contempt, and played with him as he did with the rest who were more civil and courteous. So one day when Gómez Pérez was playing he disputed much more than usual—now that the viceroy had shown him such favor and he had hopes of soon leaving his present abode, he thought that he could treat the Inca like one of the Indian servants the Inca himself had given him. Gómez Pérez was so discourteous at one stage in the game and behaved so freely and contemptuously toward the Inca that the poor prince could stand no more and gave him a punch or butt in the chest, saying: "Get away, and remember who you're talking to!" Gómez Pérez was as choleric as he was melancholy, and without a thought for the harm he was doing himself and his friends, raised his hand with the ball in it and struck the Inca so rudely on the head that he felled him and killed him.

The Indians who were present fell on Gómez Pérez, and he and his companions fled to their quarters where they defended the door with their swords so that the Indians could not get in. The Indians then set fire to the house; and the Spaniards, in order to avoid being burnt alive, came out into the open, where the Indians fired arrows at them as if they were wild beasts, filled with the greatest fury in the world at seeing their Inca dead. After killing them, they were on the verge of eating them raw to express their consuming anger. Though already dead, the Indians intended to burn them and cast their ashes into a river so that no trace should be left of them. But they finally decided to throw them on the ground where the birds and beasts would eat them, for they could think of no greater punishment for the corpses.

So ended poor Prince Manco Inca at the hands of those he had sheltered from death and regaled with all he had as long as he lived. His voluntary exile in these wild forests where he had sought refuge and protection availed him naught, for the hands of a senseless lunatic fool sought him out there. López de Gómara touches on his death in ch. clvi of his book, though he differs about the manner of the Inca's death. I heard it however from the Incas who were present at that unheard of act of folly. It was tearfully and tenderly described to my mother by her kinsmen who came down with Inca Sairi Túpac, the son of this unfortunate prince, when he left the wild forests on the orders of Viceroy Andrés

Hurtado de Mendoza, marquis of Cañete, as we shall tell, if it pleases God that we should get so far.

The Devil, our deadly enemy, found great opportunities and an excellent concatenation of events for his main aim, which was to put an end to, or at least defer for many years, the preaching of the holy Gospel in the great and rich empire of Peru; and he determined not to let his chance go by. So he sent his ministers to set fire to all parts of the kingdom, however remote, using arguments false or not false and twisting them to their purpose. He hoped that this would bring to an end the good teaching of the Catholic Faith and the peace, concord, and friendship that had obtained while Peru was governed by Vaca de Castro. And it seemed to him that there were the most victims of the ordinances in Cuzco, for there were eighty *vecinos* with allocations of Indians there, so he directed against it all his wickedness and the efforts of his ministers in order that they might achieve what they did. As we said at first, copies of the ordinances had circulated throughout Peru and caused the greatest scandal, for all the conquerors saw themselves dispossessed of their Indians and estates overnight, without a single exception.

The scandal and alarm was increased by the rigid character of the viceroy, his refusal to hear the petitions of any of the cities and his determination to apply the ordinances in their full rigor. The settlers in the four cities, Huamanga, Arequipa, Chuquisaca, and Cuzco, where the viceroy had not yet been acknowledged, decided that they would elect a procurator to represent them all and the whole kingdom: his election by Cuzco, the head of the empire, was regarded as his election by the whole country, and it was hoped that this would remedy the calamity they all feared. The matter was discussed and letters were sent to and fro in an effort to select a person with the necessary qualifications for the undertaking.

With this intent they fixed their eyes on Gonzalo Pizarro, for there was no one else in the whole country who might more reasonably accept the office, principally because he was brother to the marquis Don Francisco Pizarro and had helped to win Peru and suffered all the toils and labors we have mentioned, though our account has fallen short of the truth. By nature he was full of nobility and virtue, and because of his character he was beloved and respected by everyone. For all these reasons, even if he had not been appointed by the kingdom at large, he was bound to be the protector and defender of the Indians and Spaniards of the empire.

The councils of these four cities therefore wrote to Gonzalo Pizarro, who was at Los Charcas where his allocation was, begging him to come to

Cuzco to discuss a matter of general concern to all of them, and of no less interest to himself, for he was the principal loser, since apart from the loss of his Indians the viceroy had often said that he had His Majesty's orders to cut off Gonzalo's head. When Gonzalo had read the letters, he collected what money he could from his own estate and that of his brother Hernando, and left for Cuzco with ten or twelve friends, where, as Zárate says in Book V, ch. iv,

everyone came out to receive him and show their joy at his coming, and every day people fleeing from Lima reached Cuzco, and told what the viceroy was doing, each adding something so as to rouse the *vecinos* more. Many meetings were held of the city council of Cuzco, both sessions of the *regidors* and meetings of all the *vecinos*, and they discussed what steps they should take as a result of the viceroy's arrival. Some said he should be received, and that procurators should be sent to His Majesty to get redress against the ordinances. Others said that if he were once received and the ordinances were applied, as he was in fact applying them, they would lose their Indians, and once dispossessed, they would have great difficulty in recovering them. It was finally decided that Gonzalo Pizarro should be elected by the city of Cuzco and that Diego Centeno, who had come with powers from the town of La Plata, should be his deputy. He would thus go to Lima with the title of procurator general and petition against the ordinances in the royal *audiencia*.

At first there were differing opinions about whether he should take armed men with him, and it was finally decided that he should, though on various pretexts. The first was that the viceroy had beaten his drums in Lima with a view to punishing the removal of the artillery. It was also said that he was a harsh and stern man who had executed the ordinances without accepting the petitions that had been laid before him or waiting for the royal *audiencia* which was also entrusted with the execution, and that he had repeatedly said that he had orders from His Majesty to behead Gonzalo Pizarro for his part in the late disturbances and the death of Don Diego. Others, who took a more respectful view of the matter, gave as an excuse for calling up armed men the fact that in order for Gonzalo to get to Lima he would have to pass through places where the Inca was up in arms and he would thus need to have soldiers for defence. Others were franker about the whole affair, and said that the men were being raised for defence against the viceroy, for he was a tough character with no respect for the forms of the law, and it would not be safe to raise legal questions with him. They had the evidence of so many witnesses about this that there was no lack of lawyers who gave it as their considered opinion that there was no question of disrespect in this and they could do it legally, since force can and should be met by force, and a judge who proceeds *de facto* can be resisted *de facto*. It was thus decided that Gonzalo should raise his standard and enlist men, and many of the *vecinos* of Cuzco offered him their persons and property, and there were even some who said they were prepared to see themselves damned in their quest for justice.

Thus Zárate in the fifth book of his *History of Peru* (ch. iv). What follows is from López de Gómara (ch. clvii).

⚬

CHAPTER VIII

The disturbances continue; four cities write to
Gonzalo Pizarro; he is elected procurator
general of Peru and raises men
to take to Lima.

M ANY OF the conquerors of Peru wrote to Gonzalo with such arguments that they raised him up in Charcas, where he was, and brought him to Cuzco after Vaca de Castro had gone down to Lima. When he arrived, many of those who were afraid of being deprived of their vassals and slaves rallied to him, together with others who hoped to enrich themselves if there were changes. They all begged him to oppose the ordinances Blasco Núñez had brought and was applying without respect for anyone, either by appeal or even by force, if necessary. They had taken him as their leader and would stand by him and follow him. Either to test them or to make his own position safe, he told them not to send him, for opposition to the ordinances, if only by petition, was opposition to the emperor who was so determined to have them executed. He urged them to consider how lightly they began wars, when the next stage would be difficult and the end uncertain. He did not wish to accede to their request if it were not in the royal interest, or to accept the office of procurator or captain. They brought forward many justifications of their procedure in order to persuade him. Some said that as the conquest of the Indies was lawful, they could lawfully have Indians taken in war as slaves: others that once he had granted them the emperor could not justly take away villages and vassals during the period of the grant, and this was especially true of dowries granted on condition they married. Still others said they could defend their vassals and privileges by force of arms, as the nobles of Castile had defended the liberties they had been granted for having aided the kings to win their realms from the power of the Moors, just as they had won Peru from the hands of idolators. Finally, they all said that they were doing no wrong in appealing against the ordinances, and some said that there was no wrong in opposing them, since there was no previous engagement on their part to agree to them and accept them as laws.

There was no lack of those who said that it was a headstrong and foolish policy to make war against their king under pretext of defending their properties. It was not within their competence and would be disloyal to do so. But it was of little use to speak to those who did not wish to listen. For they not only said all this because it was in their favor, but passed the bounds of military discipline by speaking ill of their king and emperor, supposing that they could twist his tail and frighten him by their swaggering. It was said too that Blasco Núñez was tough, headstrong, opposed to the wealthy, and an Almagrist, and that he had hanged a priest in Túmbez and quartered a servant of Gonzalo's who was against Don Diego de Almagro. Moreover, he had express orders to kill Pizarro and punish those who had been with him in the battle of Las Salinas. And to prove his ill disposition, they alleged that he had forbidden the drinking of wine and eating of spices and sugar, and wearing of silk and travelling in litters.

Some of these reasons were feigned and some true, but Pizarro was glad to become captain general and procurator, thinking and hoping he could go in by the sleeve and come out by the collar. So he was elected procurator general by the council at Cuzco, capital of Peru, and those of Huamanga and La Plata and other places, while the soldiers made him their captain with full powers over them. He took the proper oath for the purpose.

He raised his standard, ruffled his drums, and took the gold that was in the royal chest; and, as many arms that had been used in the battle of Chupas were at hand, he instantly armed four hundred men, horse, and foot. This caused a good deal of scandal among the authorities, who repented of what they had done on seeing that Gonzalo had taken the hand when he was only offered the finger. But they did not revoke his powers, though many secretly protested against the authority he had been given. These included Altamirano, Maldonado, and Garcilaso de la Vega.

Thus López de Gómara, copied word for word. To explain these authors, who are a little contradictory on this point and suggest that the rebellion that broke out later was anticipated in the thoughts of the citizens, we should say that in fact when Pizarro was elected procurator general there was no idea of his going armed, but that he should appear plainly and simply as the representative of loyal vassals who had gained that empire and extended the realms of the Spanish crown. They were confident that if their appeal were fairly heard, their case could not be denied, even by a court of savages. Such was the true intention of the four cities at first, and they sent their procurators with sufficient powers, and by common consent elected Gonzalo Pizarro. But the terrible inflexibility of the viceroy's character and the news of his deeds that came every day to Cuzco caused Gonzalo not to trust his person any more to papers and written laws, even if they were in his favor, but to prepare arms to ensure his safety, as we shall say.

On his election as procurator general of Peru, Pizarro decided to form a company of two hundred soldiers both to deal with a viceroy who had shown himself so uncompromising about the ordinances and to make himself safe from having his head cut off, as it was publicly reported the viceroy had repeatedly threatened to do. He did not raise his standard or appoint captains, for he did not wish his actions to smell of rebellion or resistance to the royal authority; he only wished to have a bodyguard. The *regidors* and the whole city addressed him on this point saying that it was not their intention or that of the empire to resist His Majesty's commands in his ordinances by force of arms, but to petition submissively since they felt their case was so strong that their prince and king would not deny them justice. He ought therefore to dismiss the men and go as procurator and not as captain, since their intention was to be obedient subjects, as they protested they were. He replied that they knew of the viceroy's character and how he had said he had special orders to cut off Gonzalo's head; how then could they send him to the slaughterhouse with his hands in his pockets, for he might be beheaded with no gain to them and without even being heard? If they wanted him to go to certain death, he would give up the office of procurator and return home, where he would wait and see what the viceroy tried to do with him: this would be better than irritating him into hastening his death and destruction. The councillors and the representatives of the other cities saw that Gonzalo was right, in view of the viceroy's character, conduct, and policy and allowed him to raise men for a bodyguard. They then produced the pretexts mentioned by our two authors for appointing him captain, the chief of which was that he would have to pass through the forests in which Manco Inca had shut himself up. Having obtained permission to raise men, he increased their numbers till they reached the four hundred horse and foot mentioned by López de Gómara, and there were even many more. When the citizens saw this, they regretted having elected him, for it seemed more like a rebellion than a request for justice, and so the three López de Gómara mentions protested, and so did many others, as we shall see.

Pizarro took great care in preparing himself for his claim, urgently writing to all parts where he knew there were Spaniards, not only to the three cities, but also to the Indian villages and allocations, appealing to them with the best arguments he could think of and offering them his person and wealth for any contingency, either present or future. This aroused suspicions, and even the certainty, that he wanted to resume his claim to govern Peru; for, as all three historians say, he had powers from his brother the marquis, Don Francisco Pizarro, to govern after the marquis' death, under a document of the emperor's when he was awarded the governorship for two lives, his own and a nominee's, just as the allocations of Indians had been for two lives.

CHAPTER IX

Gonzalo Pizarro appoints captains and leaves Cuzco with his army; the viceroy summons men, chooses captains, and arrests Licentiate Vaca de Castro and other leading men.

WITH THIS object in view Pizarro was moved to make such a display with his soldiers that it looked more like war than a representation. To reveal his intentions more clearly he sent Francisco de Almendras (my godfather) down the road to Lima with twenty soldiers and the Indians, and gave him orders to take great care not to let anyone pass him going down from Cuzco or coming up from Lima. He took the silver and gold that was in the royal chest and that of the deceased and the other common funds, under pretext of borrowing it to pay his men. This clearly revealed his purpose. He prepared the large quantity of excellent artillery that Gaspar Rodríguez and his friends had brought from Huamanga to Cuzco, and had a great deal of good powder made, for round the city the best and largest quantities of saltpeter in Peru are found. He appointed officers to his army, Captain Alonso de Toro to be commander, Don Pedro Puertocarrero as captain of cavalry, Pedro Cermeño captain of arquebusses, and Juan Vélez de Guevara and Diego Gumiel as captains of the pikemen. Hernando Bachicao was made captain of the artillery, with twenty excellent fieldpieces. As Zárate says in his Book V, ch. viii:

he prepared the powder, shot, and other necessary munitions, and having collected his men in Cuzco, he delivered a general and particular justification for his illegal undertaking, or rather tried to explain away the causes of it. He declared that he and his brothers had discovered the country and placed it under His Majesty's rule at their own risk and expense, and had sent him much gold and silver, as was well known. After the death of the marquis the emperor not only failed to award the governorship to his son or his brother, as he had undertaken, but had now ordered them to be deprived of all their estates, for there was no one who was not included under one head or another of the ordinances. He had moreover sent out Blasco Núñez Vela to enforce them, and he had applied them rigorously, denied the settlers' right to appeal and uttered most harsh and offensive words to them, to all of which and much else they were witnesses. And above all it was public knowledge that the emperor had bidden the viceroy behead him, though he had never done anything to His Majesty's disservice, but had served him as well as everyone knew. For these reasons he had resolved, with the approval of Cuzco, to go to Lima and petition against the ordinances in the royal *audiencia*, sending procurators in the name of the whole kingdom to His Majesty to tell him the truth about what had happened and what should be done, and hoping that he would supply some remedy. If he did not after they had made their approach to him, they would dutifully obey whatever commands His Majesty issued. As Gonzalo was not sure of the viceroy on account of the threats he had made and the men he had called up against them, it had been decided that he too should go with an army, solely for his own safety and with no intention of doing any harm with it unless he were attacked. He therefore requested them to go with him and keep good order and military discipline: he and the other gentlemen would reward them for their work, for they were going in just defence of their estates.

With these words he persuaded the people to believe in his justification for calling up men, and they offered to go with him and defend him to the death; he thus left the city of Cuzco, accompanied by all the *vecinos*.

Thus Zárate. Gonzalo Pizarro left for Lima in his declared role of procurator with all this display and more than five hundred soldiers and over twenty thousand Indians, since twelve thousand were needed to carry the artillery alone. He reached Sacsahuana four leagues away, and there we shall leave him to say what happened in Lima between the viceroy and his followers, and in other places.

Viceroy Blasco Núñez Vela, though set up on his throne and acknowledged as governor of the empire, neither sat quietly in his place nor enjoyed his monarchy, feeling that everyone was upset and indignant at the ordinances. In order to secure himself against any act of defiance and increase the authority of his office, he bade Captain Diego de Urbina raise fifty arquebusiers, as López de Gómara says (ch. clviii), to escort him. No one dared speak to him about the suspension of the ordinances, for although the city council, as Zárate says (Book V, ch. v):

had put forward their petition with many arguments for their suspension, he refused to do so. He did however promise that after executing them, he would write to His Majesty and say how necessary it was for the royal service and the protection of the natives that the ordinances should be revoked, for he frankly admitted that they were prejudicial to His Majesty and to Peru: if those who had drawn them up had had the present situation in mind, they would not have advised His Majesty to pass them. They should therefore send their procurators to Spain, at the same time writing to His Majesty about what required to be done. The viceroy was confident that the crown would take remedial measures, but he himself could not discuss the suspension of execution which he had begun and which constituted his only instructions.

So Zárate, and further on he and the other authors say:

During all this time the road to Cuzco was closed, and there was no news of what was happening there either from Indians or Spaniards, except that it was known that Gonzalo Pizarro had come to Cuzco and that all those who had fled from Lima and other places had repaired there on rumors that there would be war. The viceroy and the *audiencia* sent off instructions that all the *vecinos* of Cuzco and elsewhere should receive Blasco Núñez as viceroy, and come down to serve him in Lima with their arms and horses. Although all these instructions were lost on the way, some of them did reach the hands of certain individual *vecinos* of Cuzco, as a result of which some of them came down to serve the viceroy, as we shall say.

At this stage reliable news reached the viceroy about what had happened in Cuzco. This caused him energetically to increase his army, drawing on the good supply of money that was available, since Vaca de Castro had shipped up to 100,000 castilians brought from Cuzco for His Majesty and these were now landed again and were soon spent in soldier's pay.

He appointed Don Alonso de Montemayor captain of cavalry, and also his brother-in-law Diego Alvarez de Cueto; Martín de Robles and Pablo de Meneses captains of infantry; Gonzalo Díaz de Piñera captain of the arquebusiers, and his brother Vela Núñez captain general. Diego de Urbina was commander and Juan de Aguirre sergeant major. There were six hundred soldiers in all, without counting the *vecinos*; one hundred were horse, two hundred arquebusses, and the rest pikes.

He collected a great many arquebusses, both iron ones and others founded from certain bells he removed for the purpose from the cathedral. And suspecting that Licentiate Vaca de Castro, whom he had already confined to the city limits, was negotiating with some of his servants and friends, he had a false alarm sounded one day at dinner time, giving out that Gonzalo Pizarro was at hand. The men were drawn up in the square, and he sent his brother-in-law Alvarez de Cueto to arrest Vaca de Castro. Other officials arrested in various places Don Pedro de Cabrera; Hernán Mejía de Guzmán, his son-in-law;

Captain Lorenzo de Aldana; Melchor Ramírez; and Baltasar Ramírez, his brother. They were all taken out to sea and placed on a ship of the fleet, commanded by Jerónimo de Zurbano, a native of Bilbao. Aldana was released after a few days; Don Pedro and Hernando Mejía were banished to Panama, and Melchor and Baltasar Ramírez to Nicaragua. Vaca de Castro was left under arrest on the same ship. None of them were ever given charges or accused of anything so that proceedings might be taken, nor was any information received for the purpose.

Thus far Zárate (ch. vi).

CHAPTER X

Two vecinos of Arequipa take two of Gonzalo Pizarro's ships to the viceroy; the vecinos of Cuzco flee from Pizarro's army.

WHILE Viceroy Blasco Núñez Vela was in the midst of these cares and troubles, an event happened which gave him much satisfaction. Two *vecinos* of Arequipa, one called Jerónimo de la Serna and the other Alonso de Cáceres, being desirous of serving the king, entered two ships that Gonzalo Pizarro had in this port, which he had bought to carry his artillery and make him master of the sea, this being of great importance to him. The two men bribed the seamen, seized the ships, and sailed to Lima, where the viceroy received them with great joy, thinking that his opponents' forces were coming over to his side and growing therefore more hopeful of success.

Meanwhile, in Gonzalo Pizarro's army, which we left at Sacsahuana, the *vecinos* who had come with him found that his intentions were the opposite of theirs, for it had never occurred to them to ask for justice with their arms in their hands, but only with due submission and homage. The leaders therefore decided to flee from Gonzalo and not go with him as they had secretly planned and discussed.

The chief of these were Gabriel de Rojas, Garcilaso de la Vega, Juan de Saavedra, Gómez de Rojas, Hierónimo Costilla, Pedro del Barco, Martín de Florencia, Jerónimo de Soria, Gómez de León, Pedro Manjarrés, Luis de León, Licentiate Carvajal, Alonso Pérez de Esquivel, Pedro Pizarro, Juan Ramírez.

These are named by Zárate and Fernández. Those not named by them were Juan Julio de Hojeda, Diego de Silva, Tomás Vázquez, Pedro Alonso Carrasco, Juan de Pancorvo, Alonso de Hinojosa, Antonio de Quiñones, Alonso de Loaisa, Martín de Meneses, Mancio Serra de Leguíçamo, Francisco de Villafuerte, Juan de Figueroa, Pedro de los Ríos and his brother Diego, Alonso de Soto, Diego de Trujillo, Gaspar Jara, and others whose names have slipped my memory. They were forty in all, and I knew many of those named.

All these fled from Gonzalo Pizarro and returned toward Cuzco. On reaching their homes, they took what they needed for the road and hastened down to Arequipa, for they knew that Gonzalo had the two ships there and thought they would go in one or both of them to Lima to serve His Majesty and the viceroy in his name. But everything turned out against them, for when they got to Arequipa they found that Cáceres and Serna had carried off the ships to Lima, with the same object of serving His Majesty.

Disappointed in their hopes, they could think of no other safe course but to begin building a large ship in which to sail to Lima, for they feared Gonzalo would have seized the coastal road as he had the mountain road. It took them forty days to build the ship, but as the shipwrights were not skilled and the wood was not seasoned, it sank with all its cargo.

So seeing they had no other remedy, they decided to risk falling into enemy hands and follow the coast to Lima. This decision turned out well, for the road was clear. But when they got to Lima they found that the viceroy had already been put under arrest and shipped off to Spain, as we shall see.

Their ill-luck caused the viceroy's downfall and that of the *vecinos* who had gone to serve him, for because they had lingered forty days in making the ship, the viceroy's arrest took place. If these gentlemen had reached Lima in time things would have turned out very differently: on seeing such leading gentlemen, the flower of Cuzco, in Lima, the people would have overcome their fear of Gonzalo and not have arrested the viceroy. But, as our authors say, they arrested him and shipped him off out of pure fear before Gonzalo should reach Lima, lest he should kill the viceroy if he found him there. But as the *vecinos* found him already arrested and despatched, they separated and each betook himself where he thought his life was safest. Some stayed in the city, and of them we shall speak later.

Gonzalo Pizarro, on finding himself repudiated by those in whom he had most confidence and who constituted the command and authority of his army, thought he was lost and, as the historians say, decided to return to Los Charcas or go to Chile with fifty friends who would not fail him, but would die with him. This decision would have been carried through if he had not then received news that Pedro de Puelles was coming to help and serve him. This news encouraged Gonzalo, and so as not to show weakness, he returned to Cuzco and deprived the *vecinos* who had fled of their Indians, assuming control of them himself. Later, when Pedro de Puelles arrived, he awarded him those belonging to Garcilaso de la Vega, whose house was sacked by the soldiers: one of them wanted to set fire to it, and even had the torch in his hand. Another, less vindictive, said to him: "What harm has the house done you? If we could catch the owner, we'd take it out of him; but what do the walls owe us?" So they did not burn the house, though they left nothing worth a penny in it, nor any Indian servants, for they were all threatened with death if they entered the house. Eight persons remained abandoned within: my mother was one, and a sister of mine and a serving woman who preferred the risk of being killed to denying us, myself, and Juan de Alcobaça, my tutor, and his son Diego de Alcobaça and a brother of his, and an Indian serving woman who also refused to deny her master.

Juan de Alcobaça was saved from death by his good and exemplary life, for he was regarded as a man above all passions and worldly interests. My mother and the rest of us, whom they also wished to kill, were protected by the friendship of some of the intruders, who, though on Gonzalo's side, were also friends of my father. They turned to us and said: "How are the children to blame for the deeds of their elders?" We should have died of starvation if the Incas and Pallas, our kinsfolk, had not succored us, by secretly sending us food at all hours of the day. But it was so little, because of their fear of the rebels, that it did not suffice to sustain us.

One of my father's caciques called Don García Pauqui, the lord of two villages on the banks of the Apurímac, seven leagues from the city, one of which was called Huaillati, was braver and more loyal than the rest, and risked the death they had been threatened with. He came to the house one night, and arranged for us to be on the watch the following night when he would send twenty-eight *fanegas* of maize. Seven or eight nights later he sent twenty-five more, which sustained us, though our hunger lasted eight months, until Diego de Centeno entered Cuzco, as we shall see. I have mentioned these details, though they are of no significance, to show the loyalty of the good *curaca,* so that his children and descendants may take pride in it.

In addition to the aid of the good Don García Pauqui, I had other relief in particular from a nobleman called Juan de Escobar, who was then without Indians, but was awarded some many years after by Licentiate Castro. He married a daughter of Vasco de Guevara and Doña María Enríquez, two very noble and eminent people. This good gentleman Juan de Escobar, who then owned the houses of Alonso de Mesa over the street from my father's, seeing our hunger and taking pity on it, asked my tutor Juan de Alcobaça to send me every day to dine and sup with him. The dinner was accepted, but the supper refused, so as not to open the door of the house at that hour, for we feared every moment to be butchered and were continually threatened. And Hernando Bachicao, the captain of the artillery, which had not yet left the city, cannonaded our house from his, which, as we mentioned in our description of Cuzco, faced us across the two squares. He did a good deal of damage, and would have levelled the house to the ground, but we had protectors who stood by us. The same happened in the houses of the other *vecinos* who had fled, though they were not treated so harshly. They wanted to show their anger against my father because he had been one of the two originators of the escape. The other was Gabriel de Rojas, but they had nothing to avenge themselves on in his case, for his houses were in Chuquisaca, the city of La Plata.

Having done this damage to the houses of the *vecinos* who had fled from him in Cuzco, Gonzalo once more took the road to Lima to receive Pedro de Puelles and his companions. He travelled slowly as far as Huamanga because he was hindered by the artillery. Jerónimo de la Serna and Alonso de Cáceres, who brought the two ships to Lima, informed the viceroy, among other things, of how Gonzalo had been elected procurator general of the empire, and had raised arms, munitions, and artillery to come against Lima.

When the viceroy and the judges learned this—as the roads were closed all they had known hitherto about Gonzalo was that he had come from Los Charcas to Cuzco—they sent instructions to the four cities, requiring and commanding them to acknowledge Blasco Núñez Vela as His Majesty's viceroy and to come to Lima or send their procurators to ask for such justice as they thought fit. And as López de Gómara says in his ch. clviii, "the viceroy sent Fray Tomás de San Martín to assure Gonzalo that he had no instructions whatever to do him any harm; on the contrary the emperor wished to reward his services and hardships very richly; and he begged him to drop his present course, and come and see him simply and sincerely so that they could discuss the affair." This López de Gómara; we now turn to the rebellion of Pedro de Puelles.

CHAPTER XI

How Pedro de Puelles rebels against Blasco Núñez Vela and goes over to Gonzalo Pizarro, and others whom the viceroy sends after him do the same.

A PART FROM the instructions he sent to the four cities and this message to Gonzalo, the viceroy also sent to bid Pedro de Puelles to come and serve His Majesty. Of him Diego Fernández says in his ch. xvi and Zárate in his Book V, ch. x, the following, both in the same words:

When the viceroy was received in Lima, Pedro de Puelles, a native of Seville, who was then the governor's deputy in the town of Huánuco, came to kiss his hand. He had been appointed to this post by Vaca de Castro, and had been so long in the Indies that he was highly respected. So the viceroy gave him new powers to return and be deputy in Huánuco: he bade him have the people there in readiness, so that he could call him if the crisis grew more acute, and all the *vecinos* with their arms and horses would come down to Lima.

Pedro de Puelles did as the viceroy bade, and not only had all the people in the city prepare themselves, but also arrested certain soldiers who had come from the province of Chachapoyas in company with Gómez de Solís and Bonifaz. He then awaited the viceroy's orders. The latter in due course sent Jerónimo de Villegas, a native of Burgos, with a letter to Pedro de Puelles, to come to him with all his men. On reaching Huánuco, they all discussed the situation and thought that if they joined the viceroy, it would be a step toward bringing his affairs to a successful head. Having overcome Gonzalo Pizarro he would execute the ordinances that were so much to their detriment, for the removal of the Indians from those who had them would not only harm the *vecinos* their owners, but also the soldiers, since they would cease to receive their keep from the owners of the Indians. So they all agreed to go over and serve Gonzalo Pizarro and set off to find him wherever he might be.

The viceroy was warned of this expedition through an Indian captain called Illatopa who was on the war path. When he knew, he was much upset by the reverse, and thinking he might waylay them in the valley of Jauja through which they would have to pass, he hastily sent off his brother, Vela Núñez, who took forty people speeding off to catch Pedro de Puelles and his friends. He sent Gonzalo Díaz, the captain of arquebusiers, with Vela Núñez, taking thirty men with him. In order to hasten their progress, the viceroy instructed that thirty-five mules be bought for them from the royal chest: they cost over 12,000 ducats. The other ten soldiers who made up the forty were raised from among Vela Núñez's relatives and friends. They were well equipped and left Lima, continuing their way till news was brought to them from Guadachile, twenty leagues from the city, that the men had planned to kill Vela Núñez and go over to Gonzalo Pizarro. Certain runners were sent on ahead and four leagues from Guadachile, in the province of Pariacaca, they came up with Fray Tomás de San Martín, the provincial of Santo Domingo, whom the viceroy had sent to Cuzco to negotiate with Gonzalo. Then a certain soldier from Avila took him aside and told him what was being planned so that he could warn Vela Núñez and his friends, and put them on their guard; otherwise they would be killed that very night.

The provincial pressed forward and took the scouts back with him, for they told him that Pedro de Puelles and his friends had passed through Jauja two days before and it would be impossible to catch up with them. On reaching Guadachile, he told the rest this news and said that it was a waste of effort to go on with the journey. He secretly warned Vela Núñez of the danger in which he stood so that he could take precautions. He told four or five of his kinsmen what was happening; and at nightfall they took their horses as if they were going to water them, and guided by the provincial, escaped under cover of darkness. On finding them gone a certain Juan de la Torre and Piedrahita and Jorge Griego, and other soldiers who were in the plot, attacked the night watch and accosted each of the men in turn and placed an arquebuss at his chest if he did not decide to go with them.

Almost all accepted, especially Captain Gonzalo Díaz, who, though he appeared to be afraid and they tied his hands and made other pretences of intimidating him, was believed to be in the plot and even to be its originator. It was certainly supposed by all those in the city that he must have been, for he was Pedro de Puelles' son-in-law, and had been sent after him; and it was scarcely to be imagined that he would arrest his father-in-law, with whom he was on good terms. So they all rebelled and mounted their mules which had cost so dear, and went to Gonzalo Pizarro whom they found near Huamanga. Pedro de Puelles and his friends had arrived two days before and found the camp so discouraged by the lukewarmness evinced by Gaspar Rodríguez and his allies that if they had arrived three days later the whole army would have dispersed. But Pedro de Puelles infused such courage into them with his support and his words that they decided to go on; considering that if Gonzalo and his followers refused to go, Puelles and his friends would be enough to arrest the viceroy and expel him from Peru, so cordially was he hated.

Pedro de Puelles had just under forty horsemen and twenty arquebusiers, and all were confirmed in their purpose by the arrival of Gonzalo Díaz and his company. Vela Núñez reached Lima and told the viceroy what was happening. He was naturally distressed, for his fortune seemed to go daily from bad to worse. Next day there arrived in Lima Rodrigo Niño, the son of Hernando Niño, *regidor* of Toledo, and three or four more who had refused to go with Gonzalo Díaz. Because of this they had been insulted in every possible way and deprived of their arms, horses, and clothes, and Rodrigo Niño appeared in a doublet and some old cuishes with no half-hose, and only his sandals and a reed spear in his hand, having walked the whole way. The viceroy received him with great affection, praising him for his faithfulness and constancy, and saying that he looked better in that guise than if he had come dressed in brocade, considering the reason for his coming.

Thus these two authors, who agree about all the foregoing. Fernández adds:

When the viceroy knew what had happened, he was exceedingly distressed, for he saw clearly how ill things were turning out for him and what a sorry pass he was in. He wanted to do justice and avenge himself somehow for the great treason committed by Gonzalo Díaz, a person in whom he had had such trust, but who had broken his plighted word: and as he could not do justice on him in person, he had his flag brought and dragged all round the square in front of all the captains and soldiers and in view of the whole city. He then bade all the sergeants and ensigns, both those of Gonzalo Díaz's company and the rest, to tear it to shreds with the points of their lances to the greater shame of the absent captain.

Gómez Estacio, the ensign of the company, was not a little angry and affronted by this, like some of his companions under his captain's flag, particularly as the viceroy had made Estacio himself trail the flag. From this time he was opposed to the viceroy and a great friend and servant of Gonzalo Pizarro's. And though some thought Gonzalo Díaz had done wrong and that it was only proper that he should be dishonored by having his flag trailed in the dust, yet others rejoiced, for they saw the viceroy's power waning and Gonzalo Pizarro's waxing, and desired his fall and ruin and expulsion from Peru. So he could do nothing, however good, that was thought well of. This distressed him greatly, though he disguised his feelings.

Thus Fernández. The malicious spoke against the viceroy's advisers, because they had recommended him to send Captain Gonzalo Díaz against his father-in-law, despite their being on good terms, as our authors say. The viceroy was also condemned for taking their advice without considering its disadvantages.

They also stood up for the honor of Gómez Estacio, Gonzalo Díaz's ensign. They said he had been insulted needlessly by being forced to trail his own flag in the dust though he had had no share in his captain's treason. In this way they spoke ill of the viceroy out of hatred for him because he had tried to execute the ordinances so literally.

CHAPTER XII

*Pardon and safe conduct for Gaspar Rodríguez
and his friends; his death and
that of some others.*

To CLARIFY what these authors say of Gaspar Rodríguez, whom Zárate sometimes calls Gaspar de Rojas, it should be explained that he was a brother of that good captain Pero Ansúrez of Campo Redondo, who died in the battle of Chupas, and had inherited his Indians on his death, by grant of Licentiate Vaca de Castro. It was this gentleman who had very irresponsibly carried off the artillery from Huamanga to Cuzco, and had committed himself to Gonzalo Pizarro. But on finding that the *vecinos* most friendly toward Gonzalo had repudiated him and fled from him and that his affairs were going awry, he decided to forsake him too. Yet since he had been concerned in such a grave affair as that of the removal of the artillery, which had so incensed the viceroy, he was afraid to put himself directly in Blasco Núñez's power without any security for his life. Indeed he said that as the viceroy was so harsh by nature, he would have him killed even though he went back to offer his services. He tried to induce some of his friends to accompany him so that it should seem that he had done a great service in having deprived Gonzalo Pizarro of part of the noblemen on his side.

He and his friends then decided to beg the viceroy's pardon for what had gone before and ask for a safe conduct to go and serve him. Pedro de Puelles found them in the midst of these dealings, as our authors say, and if he had delayed three days more in arriving, all Gonzalo Pizarro's followers would have disbanded. Though they saw these reinforcements come to Gonzalo Pizarro, Gaspar Rodríguez and his friends still sought to realize their desires. They revealed them to a priest, a native of Madrid called Baltasar de Loaisa, whom I knew in Madrid in 1563; I never knew him in my own country because of my extreme youth, though he knew me very well, as a mutual friend of my father and all the noble people in the empire. Gaspar Rodríguez of Campo Redondo and his friends approached this priest (who was more cut out to be a commander) with a view to his going to Lima to beg the viceroy's pardon and secure a safe conduct for them. He was to tell the viceroy how many and who would serve him, and say that with their departure and that of those who had already fled, Gonzalo Pizarro's party would be completely undone.

Baltasar de Loaisa secretly left Pizarro's camp, and when Gonzalo knew of it he sent men after him, but they could not catch him, for he had left the royal highway. He reached Lima, where he was well received by the viceroy on account of the good news he brought, for intimations of Gaspar Rodríguez and his friends' intention had already reached Lima through Jerónimo de la Serna, and the viceroy had made the news public so as to encourage his supporters. But the affair turned out to his disadvantage, for Gonzalo Pizarro was at once warned of what was afoot and it contributed greatly to the death of Gaspar Rodríguez and those who were executed with him when their secret was revealed. Baltasar de Loaisa was given his pardon and safe conduct, and this was at once made known in the city, as Zárate says, whose account we follow in all these affairs rather than those of other writers, since he was present at the time. Many of the *vecinos* and others who were secretly attached to Gonzalo Pizarro and his aims, which coincided with their own interests, were disappointed at this. They thought that the arrival of these gentlemen would be followed by the collapse of his army, and there would be no one left to oppose the viceroy in executing the ordinances. Baltasar de Loaisa left Lima with his favorable despatches, and as soon as it was known that he had left with such a successful outcome to his negotiations, it was generally feared that his message would result in the collapse of Gonzalo Pizarro and that they would then be exposed to the loss of their Indians and estates. Certain *vecinos* and soldiers decided to go off in haste after Loaisa and catch him and take away his despatches. Loaisa had gone with only one companion, called Hernando de Zavallos, in September 1545.

Next day, under cover of darkness, about twenty-five horsemen set off after him in great haste. The chief of them were Don Baltasar de Castilla, son of the count of La Gomera; Lorenzo Mejía, Rodrigo de Salazar, the hunchback, who had arrested Don Diego de Almagro the younger in Cuzco; Diego de Carvajal called "the gallant"; Francisco de Escobedo; Jerónimo de Carvajal; Pedro Martín de Cicilia otherwise called Pedro Martín de Don Benito; and others up to the number we have said. They travelled on with such haste that they overtook Loaisa less than forty leagues from Lima and seized his despatches and instructions, which they sent off at once to Gonzalo Pizarro with a soldier who travelled by by-roads. When Gonzalo received them, he told Francisco de Carvajal about them in confidence. He had made Carvajal his commander a few days before owing to the illness of Alonso de Toro, who had left Cuzco as the holder of the office.

Gonzalo also told the other captains and leading personages in his army who had not been concerned in sending to ask for the safe conduct. Some of them had private enmities, others were jealous, and still more hoped to be given Indians, so they advised him to apply an exemplary punishment which would serve as a warning tp the rest not to think of such acts of mutiny and treachery. It was therefore decided to kill Captain Gaspar de Rojas [Rodríguez?]; Felipe Gutiérrez, son of Alonso Gutiérrez, His Majesty's treasurer and a citizen of Madrid; and a Galician gentleman called Arias Maldonado who had stayed behind in the town of Huamanga with Felipe Gutiérrez two or three days earlier, under pretext of making arrangements for the road. Gonzalo Pizarro sent Captain Pedro de Puelles with some horsemen back to Huamanga to arrest them and cut their heads off. Gaspar Rodríguez was with the army as captain of nearly 200 pikemen, and as he was such a wealthy, prominent, and highly esteemed person they did not dare openly to carry out their designs against his person. They therefore used the following procedure: Gonzalo Pizarro forewarned 150 arquebusiers from Cermeño's company and issued secret orders to them to fall in and parade. He also had the artillery made ready, and summoned all the salaried captains together, saying that he intended to show them certain despatches he had received from Lima. When they were all assembled, with Gaspar Rodríguez among them, the tent was surrounded and all the artillery trained on it. Then Gonzalo left it, pretending he had other business. All the captains were left together, and Francisco de Carvajal went up to Rodríguez, placed his hand on the hilt of the other's sword and drew it from its scabbard, and then told him to confess to a priest who was called, for he was to die on the spot. And though Rodríguez refused as long as he could and offered to make full explanations of any charge that was brought against him, it was of no avail and he was duly beheaded.

These executions greatly alarmed the whole camp and more especially those who had a share in the matter which caused them. They were the first executions carried out by Gonzalo Pizarro since he began his rebellion. A few days later Don Baltasar and his friends reached the camp, bringing Baltasar de Loaisa and Hernando Zavallos prisoner, as we have said. And the day Pizarro learnt that they would arrive at his head-quarters, he sent his commander Carvajal down the road by which they were expected to come with orders to strangle Loaisa and Zavallos on meeting them. Such was public report; but as fortune had it they left the highway by a by-road and the commander missed them. When they reached Gonzalo's presence there were so many who interceded for them that he spared their lives, sending Loaisa off on foot and without supplies, and taking Zavallos with his army.

So Zárate (Book V, ch. xi). Gaspar Rodríguez and those killed with him were incriminated and their death was hastened by the safe conduct they had sought in order to save their lives; for as López de Gómara says in his ch. clxiv, "the viceroy gave them all a safe conduct except Pizarro, Francisco de Carvajal, and Licentiate Benito de Carvajal, and some others like them. This greatly angered Pizarro and his commander, who strangled Gaspar Rodríguez, Felipe Gutiérrez, and the rest." These are all López de Gómara's words. So this poor gentleman Gaspar Rodríguez of Campo Redondo hastened his own death, and because of his wavering he was not accepted by those called rebels or by those who regarded themselves as loyal.

CHAPTER XIII

The death of the factor Illén Suárez de Carvajal
and the scandal and unrest it causes
throughout Peru.

WHILE THESE executions were taking place at Pizarro's headquarters, a regrettable event occurred in Lima, which López de Gómara describes in his ch. clix, in these words:

Luis García San Mamés, who was corregidor at Jauja, brought letters in cypher from Licentiate Benito de Carvajal to his brother the factor Illén Suárez. The viceroy was suspicious of the cypher, for he was on bad terms with the factor, and showed the letters to the judges, asking if he could kill him. They said he should not until he knew the contents of the letters; so the factor was summoned. He appeared, and was not put out of countenance by what they said, though they used hard words. He read the letters, and notes were taken by Licentiate Juan Alvarez. The purport of the cypher was the number of men and the aims of Pizarro and the names of those who were at odds with him, and the writer said that he would at once come and serve the viceroy when he could slip away, as the factor had told him to do. The code book was then sent for and it agreed with what he had read: in fact Licentiate Carvajal reached Lima two or three days after Blasco Núñez's arrest and still ignorant of the factor's death.

Thus López de Gómara. The suspicions roused against the factor were like a diabolical disease that continually itched and inflamed the viceroy, and it led to a terrible deed no one had anticipated which took place in the viceroy's own apartments. This was the death of the factor, which caused a deeper and more alarming impression than the executions in Pizarro's camp. There was thus mourning on both sides. This event took place on the very night when Don Baltasar de Castilla and the rest fled. The three authors give almost the same account. We shall give the treasurer Zárate's version, and append the points the others give but he omits. His words (Book V, ch. x) are:

To return to the course of our history, a few hours after Don Baltasar and his friends had left Lima in pursuit of Loaisa, the news, which could not be concealed, came to the ears of Captain Diego de Urbina, the viceroy's commander. He was going the rounds of the city, and calling at the lodgings of some of those who had fled, discovered that they and their arms and horses were missing, and likewise their Indian *yanaconas*. He therefore suspected what had happened, repaired to the viceroy's house, found him already in bed and assured him that most of the people in the city had fled, as he himself believed.

The viceroy was naturally much disturbed, and got up, ordered the alarm to be given and summoned his captains. He at once sent them scurrying from house to house throughout the whole city until he knew who was missing. In addition to the rest they found that the factor's nephews Diego and Jerónimo de Carvajal and Francisco de Escobedo were absent. The viceroy already suspected that the factor favored Gonzalo Pizarro, and felt certain that the departure of the nephews had taken place by his orders or at least that it could not have occurred without his knowledge, since they lodged in his house, though they used a side door and not the main gate. The viceroy therefore sent his brother Vela Núñez to investigate his suspicions, and aided by a group of arquebusiers, to bring back the factor under arrest. The factor was found in bed, made to dress and taken to the viceroy's lodging. The latter had hardly slept all night and was lying dressed and armed on his bed. The factor came in by the door leading into the hall. Some of those present say that the viceroy rose and said to him: "So traitor, you have sent your nephews to serve Gonzalo Pizarro!"

The factor replied: "Let not Your Lordship call me traitor, for I am not."

The viceroy is said to have answered: "I swear to God you are a traitor to the king!"

And the factor rejoined: "I swear to God I am as good a servant of the king as Your Lordship."

At this the viceroy was so enraged that he attacked the factor, dagger in hand. Some say he wounded him in the breast, though he himself said he did not strike him, but that his servants and halberdiers, on hearing how disrespectfully the factor had spoken, seized some partisans and halberds lying near and dealt him so many wounds that he died before he could confess or even utter a word. The viceroy ordered him to be buried at once. He was afraid that as the factor was very popular, there would be a disturbance if the body were taken down in front of the soldiers (for every night a guard of a hundred men was mounted in the courtyard of the house). He therefore had the body lowered from a balcony into the square, where certain Indians and Negroes took it and buried it in the church nearby, without a shroud, but wrapped in the long scarlet robe he had been wearing.

Three days later when the judges arrested the viceroy, as we shall see, one of the first things they did was to take cognisance of Illén Suárez's death, beginning the proceedings from the fact that the factor had been taken to the viceroy's house at midnight and had not reappeared, and having his body exhumed and his wounds verified.

When the people knew of his death, there was a great scandal, since everyone thought the factor had helped the viceroy's affairs, especially in his efforts to have him received in Lima, against the judgment of most of the *regidors*. These events took place on Sunday night, September 13, 1544.

Thus Zárate; Fernández, having said the same, adds (ch. xvii):

They lowered him from a balcony and buried him in a corner of the cathedral nearby. Within a few hours the viceroy's fit of impassioned anger passed and his reason returned. He then regretted what he had done, and it was regarded as certain that he wept. But the death of the factor became known throughout the city, and the viceroy called some of the chief *vecinos* and justified himself by saying that there was ample cause for killing the factor and ascribing his death to his own disrespectful words. He said that no one was to make a disturbance, for whether he had done right or wrong he would respond to God and his king. But everyone was outraged and indignant against him. In this way the flight of the citizens caused this bloody occurrence, which in turn gave an opportunity and excuse for arresting the viceroy. This was certainly an unjustifiable act of rebellion. The truth is that the viceroy much regretted the deed afterwards, and often repeated that at the death of Illén Suárez he had been confused and beside himself with rage, and blamed his brother Vela Núñez for bringing the factor before him, calling him a fool and a beast, since his brother knew his character and realized that he was in a temper; yet he had still brought the factor, though if he had had any sense he would have only feigned obedience and have said that he could not find the factor until the viceroy's fit of rage had passed.

So Fernández; López de Gómara adds that when the factor replied and rebutted the accusations levelled against him, "the viceroy struck him two blows with a dagger, shouting: 'Kill him, kill him!' His servants came up and finished him off, though some threw some clothes over him to save him from being killed." These are López de Gómara's words (ch. clix). He ends by saying: "The factor's death caused an uproar, for he was a very important personage in Lima. People were so afraid that many *vecinos* of Lima left their own houses at night, and Blasco Núñez himself told the judges and many others that the death of the factor would be his undoing, for he realized what a mistake he had made," etc.

The death of this gentleman led to the complete downfall of the viceroy, for his own followers became so alarmed at his temper after he had committed this unexpected murder that they all avoided him and hid, so as not to appear in his presence, at which his opponents were encouraged and emboldened by finding their opinions about him thus justified.

CHAPTER XIV

The various decisions of the viceroy in the face of Gonzalo Pizarro's advance on Lima; the open opposition of the judges.

REINFORCED BY Pedro Puelles and those who had come over to him from the viceroy, Gonzalo Pizarro travelled forward with greater courage and confidence than hitherto. His progress was slow owing to the weight and cumbersomeness of the artillery which greatly reduced the length of the day's march, as it had to be carried on the backs of Indians over a very rough road with many hills to go up and down. The viceroy knew that the enemy was daily drawing closer, and that many of those about him openly showed their dissatisfaction at the execution of the ordinances, while those who concealed this feeling were very lukewarm in his service and were perceptibly discontented. As he pondered on this and saw the spirit of his men grow hourly more adverse, he decided to change his policy, though it was now late, and suspend the ordinances, supposing that by publishing this he could extinguish the fires that were raging, and that Gonzalo Pizarro would no longer have any excuse for acting as procurator general and would disband his army, after which the disorders would die down and the country would be pacified. So he announced the suspension of the ordinances, as Fernández says, until such time as His Majesty had been informed and had issued new instructions.

López de Gómara says (ch. clviii):

Blasco Núñez was worried because Pizarro had so many arms and artillery, and the people were so well disposed toward him. He suspended the ordinances for two years until the emperor should dispose otherwise, though it was at once said that he had done so under protest and had recorded in the minute book that the suspension had been forced on him, and it was believed that he would execute the ordinances as soon as the land had been pacified, which they all found odious. He made an order and had it cried abroad that anyone could kill Pizarro and others with him, and promised to reward whoever killed him with Pizarro's allocation of Indians and estates, which greatly angered the inhabitants of Cuzco and did not please those in Lima. He even distributed some of the allocations of those who had gone over to Pizarro.

So López de Gómara. Though the suspension came very late, it would still have done much to settle things if it had contained any provision for negotiations and an avoidance of the open breach that followed. But as the news of the suspension was accompanied at once by that of the viceroy's protest and the report that he had acted under constraint and meant to apply the ordinances as soon as the country was at peace, the result was to anger everyone rather than to appease them. The incident clearly revealed the obstinacy of the viceroy in pursuing their common disadvantage. They were therefore more rebellious and more obstinate even than before, and they went on resolved to die in their quest. The viceroy was scandalized when he learnt this and found that a measure designed to appease them had only inflamed them. His own followers were dejected, and many of them inclined to Pizarro who had risked his neck for the sake of them all. The viceroy decided to shut himself up in the city, and not wait for the enemy in the open.

He therefore fortified the city, cleared the streets, made embrasures, and brought in supplies in case the siege should last. But as fresh news came in daily of the strength of Pizarro, he thought he had better not wait in Lima but withdraw to Trujillo, eighty leagues away. He planned to take the wives of the *vecinos* in ships while the army marched down the coast.

He thought of depopulating and destroying the city, breaking up the mills and taking away everything that could be of use to the enemy, and collecting all those coastal Indians and taking them inland, so that Gonzalo Pizarro would find no supplies or Indian serfs and have to disband his army and abandon his plans. He put these ideas before the judges, who when they saw his purpose opposed it openly. They said that the royal *audiencia* could not leave the city since His Majesty had ordered it to sit there: they could not accompany His Lordship or permit anyone to abandon his home. So the judges and the viceroy appeared in open conflict and the *vecinos* were more inclined to take the part of the judges than that of the viceroy, for the judges had spoken in favor of them and tried to prevent their wives and supporters from being taken away by soldiers and sailors. When the viceroy left his meeting with the judges, at which nothing was decided, he thought he would put into effect his plan of escape by sea, sending his brother by land with the soldiers. He therefore ordered Diego Alvarez Cueto, as Zárate says in his Book V, ch. xi:

to go with a detachment of cavalry and take the sons of the marquis Don Francisco Pizarro to the coast and put them on a ship, where he was to remain on guard over them and over Vaca de Castro, acting as admiral of the fleet. This was because he feared that Don Antonio de Ribera and his wife, who were in charge of Don Gonzalo and his brother and sister, might hide them.

This caused a very great commotion, and the judges were very much displeased, especially Licentiate Zárate who insistently begged the viceroy to bring Doña Francisca back from the sea, since she was now a grown-up young lady, and rich and beautiful, and it was improper that she should be in the company of soldiers and sailors. But he had no satisfaction from the viceroy, who made it obvious that he was determined to withdraw and found them of a very different opinion.

So Zárate, and to abridge what our authors have to say on the subject, we may add that the judges ordered Martín de Robles, though he was the viceroy's captain, to arrest him. When he tried to excuse himself from doing so on the grounds of the danger to himself, they assured him that it was in His Majesty's interest and it would pacify the whole empire if a stop were put to the troubles the viceroy was causing. Nevertheless

Martín de Robles asked for written orders, signed by all the judges, in order to cover himself, which they gave him, admonishing him to keep them secret till the proper moment. They also took a measure binding the *vecinos* and inhabitants of the city to cease to obey the viceroy's instructions about delivering up their wives for embarkation and abandoning their houses. They were all to assist Martín de Robles to arrest the viceroy, which would be a service to the emperor and in the best interests of Peru. This decision was also kept secret until it seemed to be time to announce it.

While these measures were being taken on both sides, the people were confused and at sixes and sevens, not knowing which side to join. Respect for the king inclined them toward the viceroy, but self-interest and the vision of the loss of their Indians if he prevailed forced them to take sides with the judges, since their opinion about the ordinances was the opposite of Blasco Núñez's.

They spent the whole day in this confusion, though the viceroy sought to assure himself against any steps the judges might take against him by calling up his captains and men. They guarded him till midnight. The judges, for their part, seeing that the viceroy had sounded the alarm and had over four hundred men with him, were afraid he would have them arrested. They called on some of their particular friends, but so few responded that they were afraid they would not be able to do anything against the viceroy. So they remained shut in the lodgings of Licentiate Cepeda, and fortified themselves there in case any attempt were made to arrest them.

During the confusion a leading colonist, whom López de Gómara calls Francisco de Escobar, a native of Sahagún, spoke up and said: "Good God, gentlemen, let's go out into the street and die fighting like men and not cooped up like chickens," etc.

So the judges came out to the square in desperation, rather inclined to surrender to any demands than harboring hopes of having their way. But it turned out well for them, for the viceroy had been out in the square until late at night and his captains had now persuaded him to retire to his house and enter his lodgings. The soldiers and captains then found themselves released from the respect they had had to show in his presence, and two of the captains, Martín de Robles and Pedro de Vergara, went over to the judges with their companies. More and more followed them until there was no one left at the viceroy's door to defend the house, with the exception of the hundred soldiers chosen as his bodyguard, who were inside the courtyard.

CHAPTER XV

The arrest of the viceroy and its results on land and at sea.

THE JUDGES, though supported by the men who had gone over to them and those who hourly rallied round them, were still afraid to carry out the arrest of the viceroy, since they had been told that he was in the square with a large force and determined to come and arrest them. To allay their fears they went to the square, where they sought to justify their actions and summon more men to their side by having the crier read the dispositions they had drawn up, though there was such a hubbub that few could hear them. When the judges reached the square, as Zárate, who was present at the viceroy's arrest, writes in Book V, ch. xi, it was already daybreak, and some shots were fired at them from the viceroy's balcony.

This so angered the soldiers accompanying the judges that they determined to force their way into the house and kill all who resisted them. The judges pacified them with soothing words and sent Fray Gaspar de Carvajal, the superior of St. Dominic, and Antonio de Robles, brother to Martín de Robles, to tell the viceroy that all they sought of him was that they should not be put on shipboard against their will and against His Majesty's commands, and that he should not offer to oppose them but repair to the cathedral and they would await him inside. Otherwise he would imperil himself and his companions.

When these messengers went to the viceroy, the hundred soldiers at his door waited no longer, but passed over to the judges. The rest of the soldiers, finding the way clear, all entered the viceroy's house, and began to loot his servants' quarters, which gave on to the courtyard. Licentiate Zárate now came out of his lodgings to join the viceroy, but falling in with the judges on the way and finding himself unable to pass, he entered the church with them. When the viceroy heard their message and saw his house full of armed men, and found that his own soldiers, in whom he had placed his trust, had forsaken him, he went to the church where the judges were and placed himself in their hands. They brought him to the house of Licentiate Cepeda, armed as he was in a coat of mail and a breastplate. When he saw Zárate with the other judges, he said: "You too, Licentiate Zárate! Have you come to arrest me, when I placed all my confidence in you?" And Zárate answered that whoever had said such a thing had lied, for it was public knowledge who had arrested him and whether he, Zárate, had been present or not. It was then arranged that the viceroy should take ship for Spain, since if Gonzalo Pizarro found him under arrest he would kill him. They also feared that some kinsmen of the factor might kill him in revenge: in either case the blame would be laid at their door. It occurred to them that if they sent him off alone, he would land again and come back against them. They were so confused that they could not come to any agreement, and showed signs of regretting what they had done. They made Cepeda captain general and they all escorted the viceroy to the sea, determined to put him on shipboard. But this was almost impossible since Diego Alvarez Cueto, who was admiral of the fleet, on seeing the crowd bringing the viceroy under arrest, sent Jerónimo Zurbano, his naval captain, in a boat with some arquebusiers and cannon to collect all the ship's boats on board his flagship, while he went to demand that the judges release the viceroy. No notice was taken of this, for they refused to hear him, but some of the arquebusiers shot at him from the land and he replied from the sea, and retired. The judges then sent out rafts to bid Cueto hand over the fleet and the marquis' children, saying that they would deliver the viceroy to him in a ship. Otherwise his life would be in jeopardy.

With the viceroy's consent this embassy was accompanied by Fray Gaspar de Carvajal who went out on a raft and on reaching the flagship gave the reason for his appearance. Diego Alvarez Cueto, in the presence of Vaca de Castro, who, as we have said, was under arrest in the ship, now saw that the viceroy was in danger and therefore sent ashore by the same rafts the children of the marquis and Don Antonio and his wife, despite the fact that the judges had not yet fulfilled their part of the bargain but were threatening to cut off the viceroy's head unless the fleet were handed over. And though the viceroy's brother, Captain Vela Núñez, went to and fro several times, the sea captains refused to give way. The judges then returned with the viceroy to the city, well guarded.

Two days later those in the fleet heard that the judges and the captains on their side were planning to bring out rafts with crowds of arquebusiers and seize the ships. This was because they could not prevail on Jerónimo Zurbano to hand them over, though they had made him generous offers if he did so: they realized that he had more importance than Cueto since he influenced all the soldiers and sailors, who were Biscayans. The captains of the ships answered the threat by deciding to sail out of the port of Lima and stand off the coast until despatches or instructions came from His Majesty about what should be done. They considered that there were servants and friends of the viceroy in Lima and throughout Peru, as well as others who had not taken part in his arrest, and many supporters of the crown who came down daily to the ships. The ships themselves were mediocrely armed and stored, having ten or twelve light iron pieces and four bronze cannon, with more than forty cwt. of powder. They also had above four hundred cwt. of biscuit, five hundred *fanegas* of maize, and plenty of salt meat. These supplies would be enough to gain time, especially as they could not be prevented from watering, as they could put in at any point on the coast. They had only twenty-five soldiers; and since there were not enough sailors to man the ten ships in their power, and it was unsafe to leave any of them behind lest they should be followed, they burnt the four smallest ships the day after the viceroy's arrest: these they could not sail out. They also burnt two fishing boats which had been beached. They then set sail with the six remaining ships. The four ships were all gutted, for there was no going aboard to save them; the two fishing boats were saved and the fire extinguished, though they were somewhat damaged. The ships put in at the port of Huaura, eighteen leagues below that of Lima, to take on fuel and water which they needed. They had brought Licentiate Vaca de Castro with them, and they decided to stay in Huaura and await the result of the viceroy's arrest. When the judges heard this, and realized that the vessels would not go far away since the viceroy was still under arrest and in great danger of his life, they resolved to send men by land and sea to seize them by hook or by crook. So Diego García de Alfaro, a *vecino* of Lima, was charged with the repair of the two ships that had been beached, for he was very skilled in nautical matters. When they had been repaired and floated, he went aboard with some thirty arquebusiers and sailed down the coast. By land they sent Don Juan de Mendoza and Ventura Beltrán with certain others. Having ascertained that the ships were at anchor in Huaura, Diego García sailed his boats under cover of darkness behind a rock in the harbor quite close to where the ships were, though out of sight from them. The land party began to fire; and those on the ships thought it must be some supporters of the viceroy or people who wanted to embark, so they sent Vela Núñez ashore in a boat to find what was happening. As he came in, but before he could jump ashore, Diego García attacked from one side and began firing, reducing him to such straits that he had to surrender with the boat. They thereupon told Cueto what had happened, and said that if he did not surrender his fleet they would kill the viceroy and Vela Núñez. Cueto feared that this would be done, and delivered up the fleet, against Zurbano's advice. He took the ship of which he was captain, and sailed off to Tierra Firme; for two days before Diego García's arrival Cueto had told him to sail down the coast and bring in all the ships he could find lest they should fall into the judges' hands.

The judges, as soon as the fleet had left Lima, feared that the factor's kinsmen would kill the viceroy, as they had already tried to do, and decided to take him to an island two leagues from the port, and put him on it with twenty persons to guard him, sailing thither on some rafts of dried reeds, which the Indians call *enea*. Once the fleet had surrendered, they resolved to send the viceroy to His Majesty together with the information that they had collected against him. Licentiate Alvarez, one of the judges, would go with him and take him under arrest: he was given 8,000 castilians for his expenses and the necessary documents were drawn up, but Licentiate Zárate refused to sign them. Alvarez went overland, and the viceroy was taken by sea in one of Diego García's boats. At Huaura he was handed over to Alvarez with three ships. These set sail without waiting for the *audiencia's* despatches, which had still not come. And Licentiate Vaca de Castro was brought back in one of the captured ships, as before, to the port of Lima.

Thus Zárate (Book V, ch. xi): as he was present at these events, we have followed his version alone. The other writers do not depart from the truth, but we shall not quote them in particular unless they have anything to add that Zárate omits.

CHAPTER XVI

Lamentable occurrences with the viceroy; a plot
in Lima against the judges, and its results;
the viceroy's release.

LÓPEZ DE GÓMARA gives all the foregoing, though rather confusedly and adds the following: as it is so pathetic about the poor viceroy in his tribulations, I have included it in the author's words (ch. clxi):

Seeing that the captains would not take him in exchange for the ships, the people abused his guard saying: "A man who brought such laws deserves such a reward. If he had come without them, he'd have been worshipped. Now the country is liberated, since the tyrant is under arrest." With these carolings they returned him to Cepeda, keeping him under guard and disarmed in charge of Licentiate Niño, though he ate with Cepeda and slept in his bed.

Blasco Núñez was afraid he would be poisoned, and said to Cepeda the first time they ate together in the presence of Cristóbal de Barrientos, Martín de Robles, Licentiate Niño, and other leading men: "Can I eat safely, Master Cepeda? Remember you are a gentleman."

To which he answered: "What, sir, am I such a villain that if I wanted to kill you I wouldn't do it openly? Your Lordship is as if with my lady Doña Brianda de Acuña (his wife). And in order that you may believe it, I will taste everything." And he did so during the whole time the viceroy was in his house.

One day Fray Gaspar de Carvajal went in to Blasco Núñez and told him to confess, for such was the judges' order. The viceroy asked him if Cepeda was there when the order was given, and he said no, but the other three were. He called Cepeda and protested. Cepeda comforted him and reassured him by saying that no one but he had power to do such a thing, referring to the division of duties between the judges. Blasco Núñez then embraced him and kissed him on the cheek, before the friar.

Thus López de Gómara, word for word: it is certainly a pathetic thing that a prince chosen as governor of an empire such as Peru should be placed amidst such tribulations and torments by his closest collaborators. Fray Gaspar de Carvajal, who was mentioned in the above chapter, was the priest who opposed Francisco de Orellana when he rebelled against Gonzalo Pizarro on the expedition to the land of Cinnamon. He had remained in the island of Trinidad and thence returned to Peru, where he spoke at length of the hardships he had seen and suffered on the expedition.

We have also mentioned Don Juan de Mendoza, a gentleman I knew as a *vecino* of Cuzco. A strange thing occurred to him in Mexico, which was so extraordinary that it had better be recorded, for I doubt if anything like it has occurred anywhere in the world. He was playing canes in a solemn celebration in the square of the royal city of Mexico, before he came to Peru (he was one of those who came with the famous Don Pedro de Alvarado); and it happened that after the joust, when the gentlemen were scattered about the square throwing lances and canes, as they often do at important festivities, this gentleman threw a cane to show his dexterity and knightliness. As he was gathering himself for the throw, his horse, which was galloping, suddenly stopped. He was very tall, longlegged and spindly and not such a good rider as he fancied, and fell forward over his horse's head with his feet still in the stirrups and his hands sticking down to the ground so as to save his head: he was thus left draped round the horse like a breast leather. His life would have been in danger if he had not been succored forthwith; he thus escaped owing to the attentions of the bystanders from many of whom I heard this story, and one of them was my lord Garcilaso de la Vega, who was present at this festivity. I may be pardoned for this digression since the story is so strange; with this let us return to our history.

While the viceroy was under arrest on the island two leagues from the port, Don Alonso de Montemayor and the rest of those who had accompanied him in pursuit of the other party that had gone to arrest Fray Loaisa returned to Lima. They were arrested by the judges and some were disarmed; they were then placed under house arrest in the homes of Captain Martín de Robles and other *vecinos* together with some of the viceroy's captains and those who had come down from Cuzco. Because they were misused in this way, they determined to kill the judges, release the viceroy, and restore him to his office and liberties, which they set about in the following manner: certain arquebusiers were to fire at night in Martín de Robles' house, whereupon Francisco de Aguirre, the sergeant who with others formed Licentiate Cepeda's guard, would kill him and arquebusiers would take up stations at the corners of the street leading into the square by which Dr. Tejada and Licentiate Alvarez must perforce pass on their way to Cepeda's house on hearing the alarm. They would then be killed and the city would declare for the king. All this would have been easily accomplished, if a *vecino* from Madrid who had been informed of the affair had not revealed it to Licentiate Cepeda that night, an hour before it was to be carried out. Cepeda at once ordered the arrest of the ringleaders: Don Alonso de Montemayor; Pablo de Meneses, a *vecino* of Talavera; Captain Cáceres; Alonso de Barrionuevo; and certain other servants of the viceroy. After investigating the affair, they condemned Alonso de Barrionuevo to death, though on reconsideration they cut off his right hand: he was found to be the originator of the conspiracy which was thus stifled. Thus Zárate.

We may add that the judges found many others who were guilty of a share in the mutiny and might well have been punished with death, but in order to avoid bloodshed and new disturbances, and in view of the supplications of many leading personages in Lima, they condemned Alonso de Barrionuevo as we have said and banished Don Alonso de Montemayor and the other participants from the city to various places to the north. They later joined the viceroy and shared his hardships, a worse fate for many of them. Continuing with his history, Zárate says:

After this Gonzalo Pizarro was daily informed of what had happened, for it was thought that it would cause him to disband his army. But his idea was very different, for he thought that all the affair of the viceroy's arrest was a deliberately invented rumor intended to make him break up his camp, after which he would be arrested and punished as soon as he was alone. He therefore continued to advance in battle order, though more cautiously than hitherto.

When Licentiate Alvarez sailed with the viceroy and his brothers, he went up to the viceroy's cabin that very day and sought to make peace with him over what had gone before: for he had been the chief promoter of all this and the most diligent in bringing about the viceroy's arrest and in punishing those who had wanted to restore him to liberty and authority. Alvarez said that his object in accepting that mission had been to serve the viceroy and get him out of Licentiate Cepeda's power and save him from Gonzalo Pizarro, who was expected so soon. To prove this he would deliver the ship to him forthwith, and place him at liberty and put himself under his command. He begged to be forgiven for his past errors, for taking part in the viceroy's arrest and the subsequent events, for which he now made amends by saving his life and liberty. He then ordered ten men whom he had brought to guard the viceroy to do whatever the latter ordered them. The viceroy thanked him for this, accepted it and took over the ship and arms, though he soon after began to abuse him, calling him a rogue, a troublemaker, and other insulting words, and swearing to hang him: if he did not do so then, it was because he needed him. This abuse lasted almost all the time they were together. So they went down the coast to Trujillo where the events we shall next tell occurred.

Thus Zárate, word for word; the same author then goes on as follows in ch. xiii.

CHAPTER XVII

The judges send a summons to Gonzalo Pizarro;
the unfortunate fate of the vecinos
who had fled from him.

WHEN ALVAREZ had sailed, it was realized in Lima that he had made terms with the viceroy, for he had shown some signs of this before embarking and had gone off without awaiting the despatches the judges were to give him: as Zárate had not signed they had been held up and were to be sent on next day. The judges were very annoyed at this, since Alvarez had been the originator of the viceroy's arrest and had negotiated it and given the order for it to take place. And while they waited to know the truth of the matter, they decided to send to Gonzalo Pizarro, telling him what had happened and summoning him to obey the royal commands. They were there in His Majesty's name to take the necessary steps for the administration of justice and the government of Peru, and had suspended the ordinances, granted the appeal against them, and sent the viceroy to Spain, which was far more than they had said they would do to pacify the country. They therefore bade him break up his camp and disband his men, and if he wanted to come to Lima, come in peace without an army: should he wish to bring some men to guard his person, he could come attended by fifteen or twenty horsemen, for which permission was now given.

After this the judges sent some *vecinos* to notify Gonzalo Pizarro, wherever they might find him on the road. No one wished to accept this mission, both because of the danger attending it and because they said that Gonzalo and his captains would blame them, saying that although he had come to defend their property, they had opposed him. The judges thereupon formally despatched Agustín de Zárate, the royal accountant for Peru, to go with Don Antonio de Ribera, a *vecino* of the city, and carry the notification to Gonzalo Pizarro, giving them a letter of credence with which they left for Jauja, where Gonzalo's camp then was. He had already been forewarned of the summons that was being sent him, and feared that if the notification arrived, his people would mutiny, on account of their great desire to reach Lima as a duly constituted army and even to sack it, if they could find any opportunity. Wishing to take suitable steps, he sent his captain Jerónimo de Villegas with some thirty mounted arquebusiers down the road by which the messengers would arrive. He found them, and let Don Antonio de Ribera pass to the camp and arrested Agustín de Zárate and took the instructions he was carrying from him, sending him back by the road he had come as far as Pariacaca, where he was held for ten days. The men did all they could to intimidate him and make him abandon his embassy, and he stayed there until Gonzalo arrived with his army.

So Agustín de Zárate. The council of the city of Lima had elected Don Antonio de Ribera and Agustín de Zárate because they were two of the least suspect in the eyes of Gonzalo who could be found. Don Antonio was as it were his brother-in-law, having married the wife of Francisco Martín de Alcántara, the marquis' brother, and Agustín de Zárate was a newcomer to the country and had not become involved on either side. Thus Jerónimo de Villegas let Don Antonio pass because of his relationship, and kept the treasurer Zárate under arrest. Diego Fernández says the same, but adds in ch. xxiv that at the meeting of his captains Gonzalo called to decide on their reply to the judges' message, nothing was said except a single speech made by the commander, that great soldier Francisco de Carvajal. When the judges said that Gonzalo should go down with a squadron of fifteen or twenty, the captains retorted that it was to the common interest that Gonzalo should be made a governor. If this were done, they would do as the judges asked: if not, they would attack the city with fire and the sword, and then sack it, etc. So Diego Fernández.

As we have already noted, Gabriel de Rojas, Garcilaso de la Vega, and the other *vecinos* and gentlemen from Cuzco who had fled from Gonzalo had gone to Arequipa; as they could not go by sea, they came down the coast. When they reached Lima, they were lost, for the viceroy whom they had set out to serve was under arrest and had been shipped to Spain. Since the judges had carried out the arrest, these gentlemen preferred not to approach them, thinking that having arrested the viceroy, they must be more inclined to Gonzalo Pizarro than to Blasco Núñez.

In fact the judges' intention was not what malicious tongues suggested.

They wanted to avoid greater scandals such as the killing of the viceroy, who was so deeply hated by all those who would be affected by the ordinances he had wished to execute. When the band of gentlemen considered this, they did not declare for the judges, which seemed to them to be no better than returning to Gonzalo's party. As there was no one who took up His Majesty's interest, they remained isolated in the midst of their enemies, unable to flee from them by sea or land; for after the arrest of the viceroy the whole country joined Gonzalo. Most of these gentlemen remained in Lima as there was nowhere else they could go. They stayed secretly in the houses of friends and companions, for as they had all shared in the conquest of Peru, they helped one another as far as they could. Others did not wish to stay in the city. They went as far as they could from it and hid among the Indians. These fared best, for they escaped the risk of being killed that all the rest ran; and some were indeed killed.

The same happened to Luis de Ribera, Antonio Alvarez, and twenty-four or twenty-five gentlemen and *vecinos* of La Plata, who had come from that town, three hundred leagues from Lima, to serve the viceroy. Having undergone many hardships on the way, trying to avoid meeting Gonzalo or his supporters, they were already quite near Lima when they heard that the viceroy had been arrested and put on a ship. At this news they were all lost and ruined. They dared not enter the city, thinking the whole country had come out for Gonzalo, and that it would be dangerous deliberately to place themselves in their enemies' hands. Each of them went off to hide where best he might. Many other gentlemen scattered about the country did the same. They had come to serve His Majesty in the person of the viceroy, and on his arrest they scattered and hid in various places. Some of them did not think themselves safe in Peru and went off to the wild forests of the Antis where they perished of hunger and were eaten by tigers. Others, who went to the provinces of unconquered Indians, were killed and sacrificed to the idols. Such is the power of the fear of death at the hands of one's enemies; it seems a lesser evil to venture where a lesser cruelty may be expected from savages and wild beasts than from rebels, for these are more cruel than either of the others. All these misfortunes sprang from the passionate temper of the viceroy. If he had proceeded more moderately, he would not have been arrested, for this succor would have reached him, consisting of many rich, noble, and powerful people, the flower of Cuzco and Los Charcas. But now they and he were lost and delivered over to the cruelties of war and their enemies, who executed many of them.

CHAPTER XVIII

Gonzalo Pizarro approaches Lima; the death of some
of the leading citizens because the judges
delayed appointing him governor.

G ONZALO Pizarro travelled with his army to Lima by easy stages, hampered by his artillery which was heavy and hard to carry. So he
reached the province called Pariacaca, where Agustín de Zárate was held
under arrest. He had him brought to ask him why he had come. Zárate
himself describes this in his Book V, ch. xiii:

And as Zárate had been warned of the danger to his life if he tried to announce
the judges' order, he spoke to Gonzalo Pizarro apart and told him what he had
been instructed to do, whereupon Gonzalo took him into a tent where all the
captains were assembled and told him to tell them all he had just said. Zárate
perceived his intention and conveyed to him on behalf of the judges various
matters touching His Majesty's service and the good of Peru, using the letter
of credence which had been given. In particular, he said that as the viceroy
had been deported and the petition about the ordinances had been accepted, it
was necessary to repay His Majesty what Blasco Núñez had spent as they
offered in their letters to do. They should pardon the *vecinos* of Cuzco who
had left their camp to serve the viceroy, for they had had good reason for
doing so. They should also send messengers to His Majesty and clear themselves with regard to what had happened. Zárate said other similar things, but
they gave him no reply save that he should tell the judges that it was in the
interest of Peru that Gonzalo Pizarro should be made governor. If this were
done, all the measures they had spoken about would be seen to: if it were not
done, the city would be sacked.

Zárate returned with this reply to the judges, though he several times refused
to take it. The judges much regretted hearing Pizarro's frank intention, for
hitherto he had not claimed anything but the viceroy's departure for Spain and
the suspension of the ordinances. They now sent to tell the captains that they
had heard their demand, but could not grant it or even discuss it in those
circumstances, unless the claimant appeared and put his claim in writing in the
usual form of such requests. When this was known, the procurators of the
cities who were in the camp went forward, and meeting those of the other cities
who were in Lima, they put a petition before the *audiencia,* formally requesting
what they had asked for verbally. The judges thought the matter a dangerous
one; and having no commission or liberty to refuse, since Gonzalo was then
close to the city and had occupied all the roads and byways so that no one could

leave, they therefore resolved to put the case before all the most authoritative people in the city and get their opinion. They made a minute of this, and ordered the following to be summoned: Don Fray Jerónimo de Loaisa, archbishop of Lima: Don Fray Juan Solano, archbishop of Cuzco; Don García Díaz, bishop of Quito; Fray Tomás de San Martín, provincial of the Dominicans; and Agustín de Zárate, His Majesty's treasurer, accountant, and inspector. They were to take cognisance of what the procurators asked and give their opinion, explaining their reasons in full. This was done not to follow or reject their opinion, for it was clearly understood that no one was free to do anything except what Pizarro and his captains demanded, but merely to get witnesses to the oppression they were all under.

While this business was being discussed, Gonzalo Pizarro reached a point a quarter of a league from the city and established his camp and parked his artillery. Seeing that the despatch of the document in his favor was delayed, the following night he sent his commander with thirty arquebusiers who arrested some twenty-eight persons who had come from Cuzco and others with whom he had a quarrel because they had favored the viceroy. These included: Gabriel de Rojas, Garcilaso de la Vega, Melchor Verdugo, Licentiate Carvajal, Pedro del Barco, Martín de Florencia, Alonso de Cáceres, Pedro de Manjarres, Luis de León, Antón Ruiz de Guevara, and others who were among the foremost people in Peru. Francisco de Carvajal flung them in the public prison, which he seized, deposing its governor and taking the keys, without the judges being able to stop or contradict him, though they saw what was happening: there were no more than fifty armed men in the city, all the soldiers of the viceroy and the judges having gone over to Gonzalo Pizarro. With these and those he had before, he now had twelve hundred well-armed men. Next morning some of his captains came into the city and told the judges to make out the order at once; otherwise the city would be exposed to fire and bloodshed and they would be the first victims.

The judges evaded them as best they could, saying they had no powers to issue the order; so Carvajal in their presence brought four of the men he had arrested out of prison and hanged three of them, Pedro del Barco, Martín de Florencia, and Juan de Saavedra, and he mocked them and made jokes about them as they died. Moreover he did not allow them half an hour to confess and compose their spirits. To Pedro del Barco in particular, who was the last of the three to be hanged, he said that he wanted to give his death a noteworthy preeminence because he had been a captain and conqueror and was such a leading figure, being almost the richest man in Peru; he might choose which branch of the tree he would like to hang from. Luis de León's life was saved by one of his brothers, a soldier in Gonzalo's army, who begged for it as a special favor.

When the judges saw this, and the commander threatened that if they did not issue the document on the spot he would hang the rest of the prisoners and let his soldiers sack the town, they ordered the persons who had been informed about the affair to bring their opinions. They all without exception said that the powers of government should be conferred on Pizarro. The judges then passed an order that he should be governor until His Majesty ordered otherwise, respecting the superiority of the *audiencia* and swearing to obey it and surrender his office whenever His Majesty or the judges should bid him, and also to guarantee he would do justice to all those who had cases against him.

Thus Zárate, and here we cut the thread of his story lest this chapter grow too long and wearisome.

CHAPTER XIX

Pizarro is named governor of Peru; his entry into Lima; the death of Captain Gumiel; the release of the vecinos of Cuzco.

THE DEATH of Pedro del Barco, Martín de Florencia, and Juan de Saavedra caused a great stir in the city and in Pizarro's camp, for, as Diego Fernández says in his ch. xxv, it was thought and feared that Francisco de Carvajal would kill all those he had arrested and many others it was suspected he would arrest. With these fears many went to Gonzalo Pizarro, both *vecinos* of Lima and captains and soldiers in his army, to beg him not to allow so many noble people who had all helped him to conquer the empire to die; however justifiable his case in killing them, their deaths would be odious to the whole world. Gonzalo was by nature compassionate, and gave them a rich medal he was wearing and a well-known ring so that Francisco de Carvajal should kill no one else.

What occurred at the time of these executions I heard from many of those who were present: Gonzalo had no intention that Francisco de Carvajal should kill any of these *vecinos*. He had sent him to pacify the city and told him: "Calm these people down—meaning the *vecinos* who had fled from him—so that they are glad we've come."

Carvajal knew quite well who he was referring to, and replied: "I promise Your Lordship I'll quieten them so that they come out to receive you." In fulfilment of this promise (for he used to settle such matters with military rigor), he hanged those rich and influential men by the side of the road by which Gonzalo would make his entry, as though he had put them there to receive him. He also intended to terrify the judges and the whole city, so that they should delay no longer in issuing the appointment of governor which all the procurators had demanded. Gonzalo much regretted the death of these three gentlemen when he knew of it, and ordered them to be taken down from the tree before he should see them, for he had no desire to see them hanging: he had not ordered it or wished it. His appointment as governor caused the city and army much pleasure, as Fernández says in his ch. xxv:

for they all thought that it was necessary for the pacification of the empire. They said that His Majesty would confirm it, both on account of the services of his brother the marquis and of the reasons advanced in praise of Gonzalo Pizarro. His fortune now raised him on a pinnacle in the opinion of the people in his guise of liberator, so that he seemed to be universally beloved. What most favored this was the fact that they had so cordially hated the viceroy, a sentiment prompted by their own interests.

Thus Fernández. On receiving the document, as Zárate says in his ch. xiii:

Gonzalo Pizarro entered the city, ranging his troops in battle order, as follows. The vanguard was held by Captain Bachicao with 22 pieces of field artillery and more than 6,000 Indians carrying the cannon and munitions on their backs. They were fired in the streets. There were 30 arquebusiers as a guard over the artillery, and 50 artillerymen. Then came Captain Diego de Gumiel's company with 200 pikemen, and behind it Captain Guevara's with 150 arquebusiers, and behind that Captain Pedro Cermeño's with 200 arquebusiers. Then followed Gonzalo Pizarro, preceded by these three companies of infantry like lackeys. He was on a fine horse and wore no armor but a coat of mail with a brocade tunic over it. Behind him came three captains of horse. In the middle was Don Pedro Puertocarrero with his company's standard in his hand: on the right Antonio Altamirano with the standard of Cuzco, and on the left Pedro de Puelles with Gonzalo's own standard. They were followed by all the cavalry, armed for battle. In this order he went to the house of Licentiate Zárate, the judge, where the other judges were gathered; for he had feigned illness so as not to go to the *audiencia* to receive Gonzalo. Having drawn up his army in the square, Gonzalo went up to where the judges were, and they received him and took his oath and pledges. He then went to the council chamber where all the *regidors* were gathered, and they received him with the customary solemnities. Then he went to his lodging and his commander billeted the horse and foot, using the houses of the *vecinos* as barracks and bidding them feed the soldiers.

This entry and reception occurred at the end of October, 1544, forty days after the viceroy's arrest. Thenceforward Gonzalo Pizarro exercised his office in regard to military and similar matters, but did not interfere with the administration of justice, which was done by the judges, who held their *audiencia* in the house of the treasurer Alonso Riquelme. Then Gonzalo sent Alonso de Toro to Cuzco as his deputy, and Pedro de Fuentes to Arequipa, and Francisco de Almendras to La Plata, and others to other cities.

So Zárate. Fernández (ch. xvi) adds that when Diego Centeno reached Lima with Gonzalo as procurator for La Plata and saw that Almendras, whom he considered a close friend, had been appointed captain and justice in La Plata, he begged him to persuade Gonzalo to send him too to the same place, as he had his Indians and house there. Almendras obtained this request and took him to Los Charcas, where Centeno later killed him when he went over to His Majesty's side. This was an ungrateful act, though it was in the king's service; for throughout the conquest, which Diego Centeno entered as a very young man, Almendras, who was a wealthy and eminent personage, had always helped him in his need and his illnesses, some of which were very serious, treating him as his own son, and that Centeno recognized these benefits privately and in public by calling him father, and Almendras called him son. It was therefore regarded as most ungrateful of Centeno to kill him: but the force of obedience to the prince and the commonwealth is great and cancels private obligations.

When Gonzalo Pizarro found himself governor of the empire, in virtue of the rights held by his brother the marquis and on the nomination of the judges, he appointed the captains and corregidors we have mentioned, and began to deal with business in the *audiencia* with great authority and good report. He did justice and gave all the satisfaction he could to the merchants, so that the whole city was content. But in the midst of this good fortune there was no lack of rifts. Captain Diego Gumiel, who had hitherto been a passionate supporter of Gonzalo's, now turned against him and spoke very ill of him because he had not granted an allocation of Indians that Gumiel had sought for a friend of his. He spoke ill of the judges too, saying that they had deprived the marquis' son of the right to govern, though it was his by law as the heir to his father and by virtue of His Majesty's grant. They had given the governorship to one to whom it did not belong, and he would see that it was restored to the marquis' son. Diego Gumiel said all this and much more so lightly that he did not take care when he said them or to whom. Thus they came to the ears of Gonzalo Pizarro, who ordered his commander to investigate and silence the captain and bring him to his senses, for he was out of his mind. He said this, not meaning that Carvajal should kill him, which was certainly not his intention. But Carvajal never needed spurring in these matters, and after an enquiry which proved Gumiel's excessive boldness and contumacy, he went to the captain's lodging and strangled him in his room. He dragged the body forth to exhibit it in the square and said: "Stand aside! Make way, gentlemen, for Captain Diego Gumiel, who has sworn never to do it again!" Thus ended poor Gumiel, for talking too much, which is usually harmful.

CHAPTER XX

The festivities and rejoicings of the Pizarrists;
a general pardon granted to those who had fled;
the place where Garcilaso de la Vega had
withdrawn and how he obtained pardon
from Gonzalo Pizarro.

G ONZALO Pizarro and his captains displayed their rejoicing and satisfaction at becoming lords of Peru. They organized many solemn festivities with bullfights and games of canes and the ring. Some wrote very good poems on these, and others maliciously satirized them. They were so satirical that though I remember some of them, I thought it better not to include them here.

In the midst of the general rejoicings he had ordered the release of the gentlemen *vecinos* from Cuzco who had fled from him when he left that city: all of them had been arrested by Carvajal as we have said. He declared a general pardon for all those who had not rallied to him, except Licentiate Carvajal, who had fled though Gonzalo had been such a friend of his, and Garcilaso de la Vega. Fernández mentions this in his Book I, ch. xxvii. We shall soon say how it happened, for these authors did not obtain a full account of this episode, and though he and Zárate touch on it they do not say how it came to pass. Gonzalo also forbade anyone to leave the city without his permission; and when Rodrigo Núñez and Pedro de Prado asked for it, it caused their death, for they raised suspicions about themselves and it was thought that they meant to escape. There were thus no rejoicings without executions and no executions without rejoicings on one side and mourning on the other, for all things are possible in civil wars.

In explanation of what was happening in Lima, we may mention that Francisco de Carvajal had arrested most of the *vecinos* who had fled from Gonzalo, but not Garcilaso de la Vega (in spite of what the historians affirm); for the night that Carvajal knocked at his door to arrest him, it was opened by a soldier called Hernando Pérez Tablero, a native of Almendral in the duchy of Feria, and a foster brother of my uncle Don Alonso de Vargas, my father's brother. This Hernán Pérez accompanied and served my lord Garcilaso de la Vega because they were from the same place, both Extremadurans, and because he and his parents and grandparents had been servants of my own. Recognizing Carvajal by his speech, he ran to my father without answering and said: "Sir, Carvajal's knocking at the door." My father got away through the yard as best he could and went to the convent of St. Dominic where the religious received him and hid him in the hollow vault of a grave: he remained hidden in that house with great secrecy for over four months. Next day, when Carvajal knew that he had hidden in a monastery, as St. Dominic was the nearest to his lodging, he suspected that that was where he was, and went there with a great force and searched it high and low, even the garrets and lofts. He left no stone unturned short of pulling down the house, such was his desire to find and kill my father. This was because Gonzalo Pizarro was particularly angry with him, saying that they had been companions and comrades in the conquest of Collao and Los Charcas and had eaten at the same table and slept in the same room, and my father should not therefore have turned against him for anything in the world, let alone become the instigator and leader of the fugitives.

Apart from this, Carvajal came to look for him four times more and once he lifted the altar cloth on one side of the high altar, which was hollow, where the Blessed Sacrament was, supposing that he was hiding there: he found a good soldier who had also run away and was hiding, but it was not he Carvajal wanted, and he pretended not to see him and dropped the altar cloth, saying aloud: "Our quarry isn't here."

Behind him came one of his officials ———— de Porras, who wanted to show his dutifulness and lifted the altar cloth and saw the wretch Carvajal had spared, seeking to stop anyone else from looking there by saying: "Our quarry isn't here." Porras saw him without recognizing him and shouted: "Here's the traitor! Here's the traitor!"

Carvajal regretted that the man had been seen and said: "Yes, I'd noticed him." But as the man was one of the guiltiest, he could not fail to hang him, and had him shriven and taken away. But Porras did not go unpunished by heaven, as we shall tell.

On another occasion it happened that Carvajal came into the convent unexpectedly, and Garcilaso de la Vega was unprepared for the visit. He could find no other refuge but to enter a cell, which was absolutely empty, with no bed or anything else to conceal himself behind except a bookshelf opposite the door, standing a little away from the wall. It was draped with a cloth about a vara long, and my father got in it between the wall and the books. Two or three of the searchers came into the cell, but finding it quite bare and supposing that the bookshelf was against the wall, and that there could be nothing behind it, they came away saying: "He's not here."

My father suffered many of these alarms during the whole time Gonzalo was in Lima. His many friends pleaded for him, and though Gonzalo was obdurate about pardoning him, he spared his life on condition that he did not appear before him, for he did not wish to set eyes on one who had repudiated him despite their common origin and friendly companionship. Thus pardoned, my father left the convent, and passed many more days withdrawn in his lodgings, and not going out. Finally the importuning of his friends resulted in Gonzalo's pardoning him completely, seeing him and taking him with him as a nominal prisoner. Gonzalo Pizarro never again let him leave his house or eat anywhere but at his table; and in the camp he slept in his tent. This continued until the day of the battle of Sacsahuana. As he went with Pizarro as a prisoner, none of the three historians of these events mentions him. I can affirm what happened because I was closely affected by my father's tribulations and necessity: for he was without his Indians for three years, having been dispossessed of them. During this time he and his family, who, as I said, numbered eight, lived on charity. The reason why Gonzalo kept my father by his side and would not let him leave his tent was to make sure that he did not escape. He fed him at his own table because my father had none; and as he had to eat with someone, it would have looked bad if Gonzalo had not helped him. My father's needs were such at this time that he had to buy a horse in the city of Quito, after the viceroy's death, from a soldier called Salinas, so the horse was called Salinillas. This was one of the famous horses of Peru; it cost him 800 pesos or 960 ducats, but he had no money at all, but confided in his friends giving it him or lending it until he could get some. One friend lent him 300 pesos and had no more. But when Gonzalo knew of the purchase of the horse, he had it paid for from his own funds, knowing that my lord Garcilaso had no means.

CHAPTER XXI

The punishment of a profanation of the Blessed
Sacrament, and of some blasphemies; Pizarro
and his friends appoint procurators
to come to Spain.

IT REMAINS to speak of Porras' punishment. Three months after his
profanation of Our Lord, he was sent by Carvajal on certain business
to Huamanga. He happened to pass a stream with less than an arm's depth
of water. The horse was heated, tired and thirsty, and began to drink from
a little pool to which Porras himself took him to drink. Having watered,
he fell in the pool with one of his master's legs under him. Porras happened to fall in the upper part from which the water flowed, and could
not get out from under his horse, which must have hurt his leg as it fell
on him. He could find no means of making the horse rise, and they remained there until Porras was drowned in the pool formed by the horse
blocking the stream. He was drowned in so little water that the horse
only had to raise its head to survive until other travellers came up and got
it on its feet. Porras was buried beside the stream, and everyone felt sure
that this had been a punishment from heaven for his profanation and this
became known throughout Peru.

We could tell of other cases in which God had manifestly chastened
men, especially blasphemers who commonly abused his name in their
oaths. These were not content with such common oaths as: "I swear to
goodness!" or "By Jove!" in their conversation, but said "I don't believe
in ———", "By ———'s life" and "By ———!" They were well-
known blasphemers, some of whom I knew and they all died of wounds
in the mouth either in private quarrels when they fell out with one another, or in the battles, being found dead with shot wounds or sword or
lance thrusts in the mouth. This was constantly observed in Peru as long as
I was there. In particular, a year before I left Cuzco, a certain Aguirre, a
rough sort of soldier, joined in someone else's quarrel with Juan de Lira,
who was on the contrary a pleasant and agreeable person. He put on a
sleeved coat of mail for the dispute, with knickerbockers of the same and
an iron helmet, and thus lay in wait for Lira in the square before St.
Dominic's monastery one Friday in Lent as he was going home after hear-

ing a sermon in the cathedral. They fought for nearly an hour by the clock, for there was no one to come between them. At the end of this time, Lira closed with Aguirre and dealt him a sword thrust in the mouth that came out more than half its blade's length through his nape. Aguirre dealt Lira a downward slash through the cloak he had in his left arm and cut through eleven folds in it and shore off the finger the Latins call the index. Aguirre died of the wound that night in jail, for he was taken there by ill luck, while Lira took refuge in the divine St. Dominic's, where I visited him and saw his hand with a finger missing and the eleven folds in the tattered cloak.

Other notorious blasphemers have died in the same way. Two or three fell in the battle of the Salinas and as many in that of Chupas. Four died at Huarina, one of whom was called ―――― Mezquita. All, as we have said, died of mouth wounds. This was noted by the Spaniards, and led not only to the end of these blasphemies but also to an improvement in common swearing. Thus all the Spaniards in Peru have received a special boon from the Lord, in that they are all careful about swearing, and regard it as a blemish and defect in those who do so. The good custom of Peru has spread beyond its borders, and on the voyage to the Indies, whether to Mexico or Peru, it is held disgraceful to swear, especially among soldiers. Anyone who utters an oath is severely punished by being made to swallow it, so that he takes care not to swear again. The captains and officers who have introduced this good custom and enforce it in their armies deserve much praise.

I will not say the same of my kinsmen, the mestizos, lest it be said that I speak in their favor as one of them. Speaking without passion, they should be esteemed in this particular, for as in the heathen times of our maternal ancestors swearing was nonexistent and no one knew what an oath was, they follow their mother's milk, for which many thanks should be given to God.

Although Gonzalo was much taken up with festivities and rejoicings in celebration of the title of governor he had gained, he did not forget what needed to be done, and therefore discoursed privately with his captains and particular friends and later in public with the *vecinos* of Lima and the procurators of the other cities he had with him, to the effect that it would be as well to send ambassadors to His Majesty to report on what had happened and beg him in the name of the whole empire to confirm Pizarro's governorship, for this was necessary for His Majesty's service and the common peace and welfare of Spaniards and Indians alike. The procurators should make this request on their own behalf and Gonzalo should send another ambassador to represent him with the same request, bringing forward his services and labors in extending Spanish rule. This proposal was accepted by common consent, and it was thought that His Majesty would accede to it, for it was to his service and to the common advantage of all, both that of the royal treasury and the vassals. Only Francisco de Carvajal was in opposition, saying, as Fernández writes in his ch. xxviii:

that the true procurators were many arquebusiers and soldiers, and arms and horses. He said that vassals should never take arms against their lords and kings, but if once they did, they should never put them down. What ought to have been done at the very outset was to arrest the judges and send them to His Majesty so that they would have to account for the viceroy's arrest, for which they were responsible.

This opinion was approved by Hernando Bachicao, but in spite of these two it was decided to send Dr. Tejada to Spain in the name of the *audiencia,* as a member of it, and that he should be accompanied by Francisco Maldonado, Gonzalo's steward, in the name of the whole kingdom. The two of them were given powers as procurators, and the *audiencia* gave them instructions for all contingencies. It was decided to send them on a ship that was in the port of Lima, for there were no others. This was the one on which Licentiate Vaca de Castro was held prisoner. He waited to see what they would do with him, not wishing to go to Spain without orders from his superiors, since the viceroy had ordered his arrest.

It was agreed that Hernando Bachicao should take the necessary artillery and men and escort the procurators to Panama. Vaca de Castro was told of this by a friend and kinsman, called García de Montalvo. The licentiate feared that if he were taken off the ship, incidents unbecoming to his rank and authority would take place, and he decided with the favor and help of his kinsman Montalvo, and the servants he had with him, to seize the ship and sail to Panama. He succeeded in doing this; for there was no one of Gonzalo's faction on board to prevent him, and the seamen were glad to satisfy Vaca de Castro, who had been extraordinarily popular and beloved in Peru. Gonzalo Pizarro was extremely annoyed that the journey of his ambassadors should be thus blocked, for he thought it would turn out greatly to his advantage.

CHAPTER XXII

Gonzalo Pizarro's anger at the escape of Vaca de Castro; Bachicao goes to Panama; and the viceroy issues orders calling up soldiers.

PIZARRO'S suspicions were further inflamed by the idea that others had helped Licentiate Vaca de Castro to do this. All the authors say as much. An alarm was given and all suspect gentlemen in the town were put under arrest, whether they had been among those of Cuzco who had fled or had come from other parts to join the viceroy. They were all cast in the public prison, and among them was Licentiate Carvajal, whom the commander Francisco de Carvajal made confess and draw up his will, as he was determined to kill him. The factor's brother began to do as he was bidden; and though he was told to make haste, he lingered over his confession. The executioner was there with a halter and garrotte in his hand, ready to put him to death. Doubtless they decided to kill him because many declared that in view of his rank, which was above such treatment, it was a mistake to have used him so if they were going to let him live. It was also feared that when he had been killed there would be a massacre of the other prisoners, which would have been a great disaster, since they were the leading inhabitants of Peru, who had rallied to His Majesty's service. While Licentiate Carvajal was in this plight, some people went to see Gonzalo Pizarro and tell him to remember Licentiate Carvajal's standing in Peru; for after the death of his brother, the factor, who had been so completely blameless, since the chief ground for killing him was said to have been the fact that the licentiate was with Gonzalo, it would be an injustice to put him to death. He might be expected to serve and follow Gonzalo rather than oppose him, if only to avenge his brother's death: let him reflect, and not decide so hastily on the death of a man who could be so useful to him. As to the flight of Vaca de Castro, they said they were all satisfied that neither the licentiate nor the others had been a party to it, but that they had been maliciously arrested and troubled, and no attention had been paid to any circumstances but the suspicion that had been put about with regard to the present business.

Gonzalo Pizarro became so angry that he refused to hear anyone, and it was impossible to get him to say any more than that no one was to mention the affair to him. So Licentiate Carvajal and his friends decided to go another way about the business. They gave the commander a block of gold of 2,000 pesos, and secretly offered him much more. He accepted it, and soon relaxed his persecution, going off to see Gonzalo. Finally Licentiate Carvajal and the rest were set free.

Preparations were then made for the departure of Hernando Bachicao, a brigantine having newly arrived in port from Arequipa; other ships were prepared too, and some of the cannon Gonzalo had brought down from Cuzco was put aboard. Bachicao then left, with Dr. Tejada and Francisco Maldonado, and sixty arquebusiers who were raised and wanted to go with him. So he went down the coast, having had news that the viceroy was at the port of Túmbez. One morning he reached this place; he was at once seen by the viceroy's men and the alarm was given. The viceroy thought that Gonzalo Pizarro was arriving by sea with a large force and he therefore hastily fled toward Quito with 150 men. Some of them stayed behind and Bachicao received them. He took two ships that were in the port, and sailed to Puerto Viejo and other places, collecting 150 men in his ships. The viceroy repaired to Quito without stopping.

So Zárate: we have clarified a few points he left in doubt. With regard to the block of gold Francisco de Carvajal received, he used to take whatever those accused of any crime would offer when the charge against them was false; and so as not to kill the accused in their innocence, he would stay the execution of the penalty while intercessors went to Gonzalo and obtained a pardon. On these occasions Carvajal was thus bribed to give an opportunity for intercession to be made. When the crime was proved, however, neither gifts nor prayers availed, and the death sentence was at once carried out, for he genuinely performed whatever was to the interest of his party, both in punishing its enemies and in succoring and entertaining its friends and supporters. Historians exaggerate his covetousness and cruelty: he did indeed show these qualities, but not so much as they say. All the misdoings and cruelties he committed were on behalf of his party, as we have said, for he prided himself on being a true soldier, captain, and commander. In due course we shall say remarkable things about his character. I knew him, and all Gonzalo Pizarro's other captains; and I heard many private things about them from those who were intimate with them.

We have said how Licentiate Alvarez freed Viceroy Blasco Núñez Vela, and another ship at once joined him, carrying his brother Vela

Núñez. They thus sailed to Túmbez, where they landed and set up an *audiencia*; for, as the historians say, he had special powers from His Majesty to establish an *audiencia* with only a single judge. Many instructions were sent off to different places with reports of his arrest and release and of the arrival of Gonzalo in Lima and all the rest. All Spaniards were ordered to rally to His Majesty's service. He sent captains to raise men in Puerto Viejo, San Miguel, and Trujillo; he bade Captain Jerónimo de Pereira go to the province of Pacamuru, which the Spaniards call Bracamoros. He ordered supplies to be sent to him from all directions and also His Majesty's gold and silver in the royal chests. All this would be needed to resist so many foes as he had. There were also divisions and rivalries in the cities to which he sent his orders, and many went off to join Gonzalo and take him the news. Others fled to the hills to avoid falling into his hands. Despite these difficulties 150 Spaniards joined the viceroy, all armed and with such horses and supplies as they could raise. The viceroy was very satisfied that they should come to help his schemes when his future was so adverse. These rejoicings did not last long, for his ill luck soon put an end to them for him, using Bachicao as its instrument; and he had to withdraw inland, where he underwent many great privations until his death.

Pizarro, learning that the viceroy was in Túmbez raising men against him, thought he had best not neglect so important a matter. He sent captains to harass and resist the viceroy as far as possible. And the viceroy's own despatches warned him what to do for the best, since they almost all fell into his hands, brought by the messengers themselves. So he sent Captains Jerónimo de Villegas, Gonzalo Díaz, and Hernando de Alvarado down the coast toward the north. They were to collect what men they could find, so as to keep them out of the viceroy's hands, and harass him as much as possible without giving battle even though they had enough men to do so.

CHAPTER XXIII

Bachicao's doings in Panama; Licentiate Vaca de
Castro comes to Spain; the end of his affairs;
the viceroy retires to Quito.

AFTER HERNANDO Bachicao had taken the viceroy's ships and freed
him to retreat inland, he continued his voyage to the port of Panama.
He fell in with two or three ships on the way. To avoid prolixity we shall
not say whose they were or what passed: Fernández gives a full account in
his ch. xxix. He took them with him and as he had no fear that any enemies would molest him, he sailed from port to port. These are numerous
on that coast, and he took on supplies at each one. When he got to the
islands called the Pearls, twenty leagues from Panama, as Zárate says in
ch. xvi, the people in the city were warned of his coming and sent two
vecinos to find out his intentions and summon him not to enter the jurisdiction of Panama with armed men. Bachicao answered that if he had
soldiers, he had brought them for defence against the viceroy; he had no
intention of harming anyone in that country, but came only to escort Dr.
Tejada, His Majesty's judge, who brought a commission from the royal
audiencia to report on events in Peru, and he would do no more than set
this gentleman on shore, obtain the necessary supplies and return.

In this way he reassured them and they made no opposition to his entry.
On his reaching the port, two ships there unfurled their sails to depart. He
stopped one with a brigantine and made it return to port, with the master
and boatswain hanging from the lateen yard. This caused a great scandal
in the city, for it was realized that his intention was quite different from
what he had stated. But as it seemed too late for defence, no attempt was
made to resist; they remained fearing for their lives and properties, submitting to the will of Bachicao, whose conduct was very extravagant. As
he entered the city, Captain Juan de Guzmán, who was raising men for
the viceroy, did not dare wait for him, and his soldiers all went over to
Bachicao, who also seized the artillery Vaca de Castro had brought in the
ship he had fled in. Bachicao tyrannized over the place, doing whatever
he wanted with the property of the inhabitants and oppressing the magistrates so that they dared do nothing but what he bade them. He arrested
and publicly beheaded two of his captains who had plotted to hang him,
and carried out other sentences with public proclamations saying: "Cap-

tain Hernando Bachicao has ordered thus and thus," exercising full jurisdiction there.

Licentiate Vaca de Castro, who was then in Panama, fled to Nombre de
Dios on knowing of his coming and took ship in the Caribbean. Diego
Alvarez Cueto and Jerónimo Zurbano, who were the viceroy's ambassadors, did the same. Dr. Tejada and Francisco Maldonado also went
with them to Nombre de Dios, and they all travelled to Spain like good
companions though they were of three different parties. Dr. Tejada died
on the way in the strait of Bahama. Maldonado and Cueto reached Spain
and posted to Germany, each to convey his embassy to His Majesty.

Licentiate Vaca de Castro stayed at Terceira in the Azores, and travelled
thence to Lisbon and after to court, saying that he had not dared to come
by Seville for fear of placing himself in a region where the brothers and
kinsmen of Captain Juan Tello de Guzmán, whom he had had executed
at the time of the defeat on Don Diego de Almagro the younger, held
sway. On arriving at court, he was placed under house arrest on the orders
of the Council of the Indies and a certain charge was made against him.
He was after imprisoned in the fortress of Arévalo while the case was in
progress: it lasted more than five years. Later he was sent to a house in
Simancas, and when the court moved he was ordered to remain in the
town of Pinto or its jurisdiction until a verdict was given. This is from the
royal treasurer Agustín de Zárate, who however does not say what the
verdict was, for he finished writing his history before Vaca de Castro's
affair was settled.

As the licentiate had many rivals who uttered great calumnies out of
envy rather than with any truth, the case dragged on and on. He was glad
of this, for he knew that he would be completely cleared—as he was, being described as a good official and governor of Peru and restored to his
place in the Royal Council of Castile. As the affair dragged on so long,
when he went to take his place he was the oldest judge in the whole royal
council: I found him in Madrid at the end of 1561 when I went to Madrid. After being freed and restored to the dignity of his office, he was
rewarded for his services to the Imperial Majesty in Peru: his son Don
Antonio Vaca de Castro was given a habit of Santiago, as was his father,
with an income of 20,000 pesos in Peru chargeable against whatever allocations he might choose. I met this gentleman in Nombre de Dios when
he was accompanying the count of Nieva who was going as viceroy to
Peru in 1560. He thus went to enjoy the reward granted to his father,
who without flattery and without offence to anyone else was acknowledged throughout the whole of Peru to have been the best governor ever

to have gone there. This can be seen from all three historians who speak of him, none of whom say that anything he did was ill done. So we may return to Peru, and say what Viceroy Blasco Núñez Vela did.

After the viceroy's withdrawal (Zárate, ch. xvi) with some 150 men following Bachicao's seizure of his fleet at Túmbez, he marched to the city of Quito, where he was readily received. There he mobilized up to 200 men with whom he stayed in that fertile and well-supplied region, having resolved to await His Majesty's further commands, once he had heard the news of what was happening from Cueto. He had good guards and spies on the roads to find out what Gonzalo Pizarro was doing, though it is more than three hundred leagues from Quito to Lima, as we have said. Meanwhile four of Gonzalo's soldiers who had had some trouble with him stole a ship and fled with it along the coast from Lima, rowing until they came to a good point from which to begin the land journey to Quito. On their arrival they told the viceroy how dissatisfied the *vecinos* of Lima and other places were with Gonzalo Pizarro on account of his oppression: he had deprived some of their homes and property and billetted guests on others, or imposed other intolerable vexations. They were now so weary of these that as soon as anyone came in His Majesty's name, they would be glad to join him so as to end Pizarro's tyranny and oppression. This news, and many other things the soldiers told him, stirred him to leave Quito with the men he had, and march toward San Miguel, taking as his general a *vecino* of Quito called Diego de Ocampo, who had rallied to him as soon as he reached Túmbez. Ocampo had given him every assistance personally and in money, spending more than 40,000 pesos of his own fortune. Licentiate Alvarez followed the viceroy on his journeyings in virtue of a decree of His Majesty in the viceroy's possession which enabled him on his arrival in Lima to set up an *audiencia* with one or two judges who arrived first, without awaiting the rest. The same applied in case two or three of them died. The viceroy therefore struck a new seal, which he delivered to Juan de León, *regidor* of Lima, who had been appointed by the marquis of Camarasa, *adelantado* of Cazorla and grand chancellor of the Indies, to be chancellor of the *audiencia:* he had fled from Gonzalo Pizarro. The viceroy thus took whatever measures were necessary in the name of King Charles, and his orders were sealed with the royal seal and signed by himself and Licentiate Alvarez. So that there were now two *audiencias* in Peru, one in Lima and the other with the viceroy. It often happened that two decisions were taken on the same matter, one the opposite of the other.

Thus Zárate.

CHAPTER XXIV

*Two captains of Pizarro's behead three of the
viceroy's; he avenges them by force of arms;
Gonzalo embarks for the city of Trujillo.*

Z ÁRATE continues his history, the same chapter:
When the viceroy decided to leave Quito, he sent Diego Alvarez de Cueto, his brother-in-law, to Spain, to tell His Majesty all that had happened and ask for help in returning to Peru and making war on Gonzalo Pizarro with great power. Cueto passed to Spain in the same fleet as Vaca de Castro and Dr. Tejada, as we have said above. So the viceroy reached the city of San Miguel, 150 leagues from Quito, determined to reside there until His Majesty's commands arrived. He still proclaimed His Majesty's royal name, and thought that this would be a good place to gather all the men who came from Spain and from other parts of the Indies to Peru. As we have said, it is a compulsory stop and cannot be avoided by those who come by land and bring horses or other beasts. In this way he hoped his army would daily grow in size and strength. Most of the *vecinos* there received the viceroy willingly and entertained him, providing him within their powers with all he needed. Each day men, horses, and arms arrived until he had 500 men, poorly prepared, for some lacked defensive armor and made corselets of iron and dried cowhides.

When Gonzalo Pizarro sent Captain Bachicao in the brigantines to capture the viceroy's fleet, he also sent two of his captains called Gonzalo Díaz de Piñera and Jerónimo de Villegas to go overland and collect men in the cities of Trujillo and San Miguel, and hold the frontier against the viceroy. They managed to bring together 80 men and stayed in San Miguel until they knew of the viceroy's coming. They did not dare confront him and marched overland toward Trujillo, lodging in a province called Collique, 40 leagues from San Miguel. They warned Gonzalo of the viceroy's movement and that his army was daily increasing, pointing out the great danger that would follow unless steps were taken in time. These captains then learned that the viceroy had sent one of his captains, Juan de Pereira, to the province of Chachapoyas to convoke everyone he might find there, though few Spaniards reside in those parts. These captains thought Pereira and his companions would be unprepared, and decided to go down the road by which he would come, and one night they overpowered his guards and fell on his party. Taking them sleeping and unsuspecting, they cut off the heads of Pereira and two leading men who were with him.

All the other men, some 60 horsemen, were brought over to the service of Gonzalo Pizarro under fear of death. They then returned to their quarters.

The viceroy was much saddened by the news and decided to seek an opportunity for revenge. He therefore left San Miguel secretly with some 150 horsemen, and reached the place where Captain Gonzalo Díaz and Villegas were. They were less careful and well guarded than they should have been, like persons who had carried out such a successful attack on their enemies a few days before. Thus the viceroy reached Collique one night almost unperceived. The captains were so surprised that they had no time to order themselves or make a fight of it, but all escaped as best they could, so dispersed that Gonzalo Díaz went off all alone to a province of warlike Indians who attacked him and killed him. Hernando de Alvarado did the same. Jerónimo de Villegas afterwards collected some men and marched overland toward Trujillo, while the viceroy repaired to San Miguel.

When Pizarro had heard how his captains were worsted and how the viceroy was daily gathering strength, arms, and equipment, he decided to go with all possible haste and undo the viceroy and his army. He felt sure that more men from Spain and other parts of the Indies would arrive from day to day, and they must necessarily land at or near the port of Túmbez, where the viceroy was. He was also afraid that some despatch might come from His Majesty in the viceroy's favor, which would have broken the spirits of his followers.

With this thought he determined to take his army before things got worse and seek out his enemies, and bring matters to the test of arms, if the viceroy waited for him. He therefore instructed his captains, paid the men, and sent the horses and equipment on to Trujillo, while he and the chief men in his army remained alone, to follow on behind.

A brigantine from Arequipa then arrived in Lima with a sum of over 100,000 castilians for Gonzalo Pizarro, and another came from Tierra Firme belonging to Gonzalo Martel de la Puente who was sending his wife and children to Cuzco, where his house was. Gonzalo Pizarro and his friends were puffed up with pride at their good fortune with the ships, which they very much needed. Indeed they were so cock-a-hoop that they feared no one in all the world.

So Zárate; and Fernández adds that they made bold to utter:

follies and nonsense, and even blasphemies, for some said Gonzalo should crown himself and call himself king. Cepeda argued that all kings descended from tyranny in their origins, and nobility sprang from Cain and common people from the just Abel. So much was clear from the devices and insignia nobles carried and depicted on their arms. Francisco de Carvajal very much liked this, and talked loud about producing the will of Adam to see if the emperor King Charles or the kings of Castile commanded in Peru. Gonzalo Pizarro heard all this very readily, though he dissimulated with words of moderation,

etc. Thus Diego Fernández, taken literally from his Book I, ch. xxxiv.

The Pizarrists put a great many arquebusses, pikes, and other equipment and armor on the ships. They embarked more than 150 leading men, and took Licentiate Cepeda, the judge, and Juan de Cáceres, His Majesty's accountant, in order to give the expedition greater authority. Cepeda's departure dispersed the *audiencia,* for no judge was left in Lima but Licentiate Zárate. And to protect himself further from royal commands, Gonzalo carried the royal seal with him. Having to depart from Lima, a place so important to his plans, he thought that he should leave the city under the control of a man who would hold it for him come what might. For this purpose he chose Lorenzo de Aldana, a most prudent, discreet gentleman, well beloved by everyone and rich, for he had a great allocation in the city of Arequipa. Pizarro left him eighty men as a guard, which was sufficient for the security of the city, for all the *vecinos* who had Indians were going with him. He embarked in March 1545, going by sea to the port called Santa, fifteen leagues from Trujillo. Here he landed and spent Easter at Trujillo where he waited some days until the men he had sent to various places rejoined him. As there was some delay, he thought he had best take his army out of the Spanish town so as not to give too much annoyance with billetting, and went to the province called Collique, where he spent some days until the men he was expecting appeared. He held a review and found he had more than six hundred foot and horse. Though the number was not greatly in excess of the viceroy's, he was better armed and equipped; his soldiers were veterans and skilled in warfare, and had been in other battles and knew the country and its difficulties, being inured to military hardships in their previous battles from the time they had arrived to conquer the empire. The viceroy's men, on the contrary, had mostly come recently from Spain and were raw recruits unaccustomed to fighting, ill armed, and with poor powder and lacking many other things necessary for warfare.

CHAPTER XXV

Gonzalo Pizarro's great precautions crossing a
desert; he comes within sight of the viceroy,
who retreats to Quito; Lorenzo de Aldana's
prudence and good government.

G ONZALO made great efforts in Collique and thereabouts to collect
supplies and all that was necessary for his army, especially as he had
to pass through a desert more than twenty leagues wide with no water or
refreshment, and nothing but sand and great heat. He tried to forestall
this obvious danger by seeing to it that there was plenty of water for the
road. He ordered all the neighboring Indians to bring great quantities
of jars and pitchers; and depositing all the baggage that was not essential,
such as clothes, coverings, and beds, he made the Indians who had been
transporting these things carry water for the crossing of the desert to supply the horses and other beasts as well as the human beings. The Indians
were loaded; and everyone marched fast, carrying no baggage lest they
should run out of water. Thus prepared, they sent forward twenty-five
horse along the usual road through the desert with orders to show themselves to the viceroy's men so that his scouts would report Gonzalo's coming. The rest of the army took another road, also through the desert. Thus
they travelled, carrying their food on their horses.

But the viceroy had spies on both roads, and knew of the enemy's approach shortly before they arrived. He had the alarm sounded, saying
that he intended to go out and do battle. But as soon as the men were
drawn up and out of the city, he marched them off in the opposite direction to the hill of Cassa, moving at great speed. Four hours later, Gonzalo learned of his escape. He did not enter the city of San Miguel or
wait for more supplies, but ordered the army to take the road by which
the viceroy had gone, and marched after him for more than eight leagues
that night, capturing some of his men. In this way he continued to harass
the viceroy, capturing many men and seizing everything he had with him
in his camp. They hanged some, as seemed necessary, and travelled on
over rough roads without stopping to eat, though every day they made
more arrests among those of the viceroy's men who could not keep up
with him and fell behind.

They sent off letters at a venture, despatching them by Indians to the chief persons in the viceroy's camp and offering great promises of pardon and rewards to anyone who killed him. This caused great scandal and sowed suspicion, so that later there were some very regrettable killings without any justification. As these were civil wars, those who had private passions and enmities sent letters to one another under false signatures. Gonzalo Pizarro never wrote letters to try to have the viceroy killed, nor did the viceroy's followers write to Pizarro, as these authors say: hidden treachery caused many evils in this war, as it does in all human passions. After Gonzalo had followed the viceroy for many leagues, undergoing many difficulties from the roughness of the road and suffering much from hunger for want of supplies as the viceroy seized them wherever he went, he reached a province called Ayahuaca. Here he stopped to rest his men, who were in a bad way as a result of their many recent hardships. He gave up the pursuit of the viceroy because of the distress of his men, having learnt that the enemy was too far ahead to be overtaken. In Ayahuaca he got what supplies he could, and left it in good order, and, making great speed, followed the viceroy's tracks. On the way he found many of the viceroy's men who had fallen out from tiredness or dissatisfaction. The viceroy went on to the city of Quito, as that region was rich in food and other supplies and he needed to relieve his men's needs.

Gonzalo Pizarro, though following at a distance, refused to take with him any of the viceroy's stragglers who fell into his hands, as Zárate says (Book V, ch. xx):

partly because he did not trust them and partly because he thought he had more men than were necessary to cope with the enemy's small numbers, especially in a pursuit with a shortage of food.

Pizarro therefore sent all these stragglers overland to Trujillo, Lima, and other places, wherever each one wished, though he hanged some of the leaders against whom he was especially incensed. But wherever they went they began to spread reports favorable to the viceroy and against Pizarro's rebellion. These reports were welcomed by many people, some because they thought the cause a just one, others because the people who reside in that province are fonder of upsets than those of the rest of Peru, particularly the soldiers and idle people. The *vecinos* and leading men always seek peace, which is so much to their advantage, for in time of war they are oppressed and harassed and made to pay contributions of various kinds; and if they do not put a good face on it, they stand in more danger than the rest, for any excuse is enough to cause the governor to kill them so as to reward his followers with their estates.

This talk could not be so secret but that it came to the ears of Gonzalo's deputies, who each in his own jurisdiction punished it as he thought most fitting. In Lima in particular, where most of these people repaired, many were hanged by an *alcalde ordinario* called Pedro Martín de Cicilia, a great partisan of Gonzalo and his cause; for Lorenzo de Aldana, who was deputy governor there, was always careful not to become involved in anything which might lead to accusations against himself later. Indeed he did his best to prevent killings and confiscations; and such was his conduct that during the whole time he exercised justice on behalf of Gonzalo he did so little in his favor that the Pizarrists thought he was suborned, since he readily received all who were inclined toward the viceroy. Thus all those who held these opinions in other provinces repaired to Lima, which they found the safest place; and the extremists of Pizarro's part were greatly incensed, especially a *regidor* of the city called Cristóbal de Burgos. Lorenzo de Aldana had to rebuke him publicly; he reprimanded him and even laid hands on him, putting him under arrest for a time. There were those who wrote to Gonzalo about their suspicions, and although he regarded them as confirmed, he never ceased to place his trust in Aldana. Being at such a distance he thought it would be unwise to depose him, since Aldana had many soldiers with him and had gained the esteem of the leading men in the city.

Thus Zárate.

CHAPTER XXVI

Gonzalo and his captains pursue the viceroy; the
hunger and hardship experienced by both sides;
the violent deaths of the viceroy's
commander and captains.

GONZALO thought he would persist in his pursuit of the viceroy and press him harder and harder until he could finish him off. So as not to be hampered by the presence of the whole army, he sent Francisco de Carvajal after him with 50 chosen horse and this party duly followed his rear. He also wrote to Hernando Bachicao, who was on the coast, to leave the ships at Túmbez under guard, and make for Quito to meet him. After this, he marched furiously after the viceroy to stimulate and encourage Carvajal. The viceroy progressed with difficulty; he encouraged his men as best he could and having covered eight leagues in the day, rested for the night, thinking he had escaped from his enemies. But Carvajal did not sleep and came up with him at four in the morning, sounding the alarm with a trumpet.

The viceroy got up and collected his men as best he could. They fell in and continued their march. Carvajal, coming up, caught some of those who were left behind for lack of horses. At daybreak the two parties were within sight of one another, and the viceroy, seeing how few the enemy were, stopped and prepared to fight. He formed his men, some 150, into two squadrons. Carvajal did not wish to risk his hand, but sounded the trumpet and withdrew a little. The viceroy took the opportunity to resume the journey, though his men were too hungry and weak to go on, and they and their horses were in a sorry state. He therefore gave permission for any who wished to fall out, but none of them accepted, all preferring to die with him. So they struggled on, hungry, tired, and sleepless, for they were given no chance to rest. Gonzalo heard that Carvajal had given the viceroy the alarm, and his rivals were so jealous of him that they asserted that he could have taken the enemy unprepared and killed them if he had not sounded his trumpet. The historians indeed blame him for this. But I knew him, and I heard many who knew about warfare say that there had been no such soldier as Carvajal since Julius Caesar. Carvajal refused to fight so as not to endanger his enterprise, since he had only 50 men against the viceroy's 150, as historians themselves state. Because of this Carvajal said: "For a fleeing enemy make a bridge of silver."

It was also said that he had instructions not to fight for fear of being defeated. It is necessary to be aware of all the causes before condemning captains in deeds of war; and it is usually difficult to find the facts owing to the secrecy with which plans are, or should be, kept. Gonzalo sent reinforcements of 200 men under Licentiate Carvajal. These pursued the viceroy to the province and village called Ayahuaca and kept gaining part of his men, horses, and baggage; and when he reached the place, he had barely 80 men left. He then pressed on, hoping to reach Quito and relieve his men with the food they would find there, of which they were greatly in need. They were forced by hunger to eat the horses as they tired. Gonzalo Pizarro's force did the same, and they suffered as much or even more from hunger, for the viceroy was careful to leave nothing anywhere that could be of use to the enemy. Carvajal killed some of the leaders taken in the chase, Montoya, a *vecino* of Piura, Briceño of Puerto Viejo, Rafael Vela, and another ——— Balcázar. Pizarro sent up more reinforcements under Captain Juan de Acosta, who took 60 men with the best horses in the army, and as these were fresh, they pressed the viceroy hard. Fernández says (ch. xli) that the viceroy:

travelled day and night with the few he had left after the recent pursuit, and they often had only wild herbs to eat. He was so desperate that he cursed Peru and the day he had reached it, and the Spaniards for going there and the ships he had come in: they were all traitors. Juan de Acosta followed hot on his heels till he came to the village of Callua. It was late when he arrived, and he rested a little that night, thinking that after so long a chase there would be time to sleep. But Juan de Acosta arrived at daybreak and suddenly attacked. The first royalists they met held them off, and the viceroy succeeded in getting away with some 60 men with the best horses, including all the captains. Acosta took the others and the baggage, and then pulled up to rest, thinking that he could do no more damage. This gave the sad and weary viceroy a respite and relieved him of immediate danger. But on reaching the province and village of Callua, Captains Jerónimo de la Serna and Gaspar Gil rode on ahead of the company and its banners, and he suspected that they were going to cut the road in front of him. When he had come to Piura, he had built a wooden bridge from a rock overhanging a wide river, just short of Tambo Blanco in the province called Amboca: it had been difficult to build and if destroyed would have taken a long time to mend. He had other suspicions and even warnings about these captains, and thought they wished for a reconciliation with Gonzalo Pizarro and had written to him. So he decided to kill them, and did so, having them strangled and beheaded in the brief resting space his enemies allowed him. He now journeyed with less fear and difficulties, and reached the town of Tomebamba, where he also had his commander, Rodrigo de Ocampo, killed. This man he had considered to be a great and intimate friend, for he had passed on his suspicions about the two captains he had executed after they had served him and followed him in all his trials.

There were many conflicting judgments and opinions about these deaths in Peru, some critical, some palliatory. From the town of Tomebamba, Blasco Núñez marched on to Quito without any further reverses and no longer suffering from hunger and need. A little before reaching Quito he had news that Francisco de Olmos and those who had accompanied him from Puerto Viejo had uttered ill-intentioned words against the royal service, so as soon as he reached the city he made enquiries about how they had left Puerto Viejo and what they had done since. As a result, after consulting Licentiate Alvarez, he executed many of them, hanging some and beheading others and branding them as traitors. Those killed were Alvaro de Carvajal, Captain Hojeda, and Gómez Estacio, but Olmos was spared, as he was deemed not to have been guilty.

So Fernández. López de Gómara describes the death of these captains differently, in his ch. clxviii, which runs:

Pizarro sent Juan de Acosta with 60 companions on horseback posting after the viceroy, so as to provoke him. The viceroy made all speed to Tomebamba, suffering equally from hunger, hardship, and fear. He had his captains Jerónimo de la Serna and Gaspar Gil speared, suspecting that they had corresponded with Gonzalo, though it is said that they did not: at least, Pizarro never received their letters. He also had Rodrigo de Ocampo, his commander, put to the sword for the same reason. All agreed that he was blameless and undeserving of such a fate after supporting and following the viceroy. In Quito he bade Licentiate Alvarez hang Gómez Estacio and Alvaro de Carvajal, *vecinos* of Guayaquil, on suspicion of plotting to kill him,

etc. Thus López de Gómara.

The executions caused great scandal throughout Peru, and slanderers said whatever occurred to them on the subject. They did a great deal of harm to the viceroy's cause, for as the guilt of the victims was not manifest, and there was no proof, but only suspicion, many who had wished to go and serve the viceroy did not do so for fear of suffering the same fate.

We shall leave the viceroy in Quito and Gonzalo on the road, coming up behind him, in order to tell what had happened in the meanwhile in the province of Los Charcas, seven hundred leagues away at the opposite end of Peru. It is remarkable that the same conflict should have gone on over seven hundred leagues of land.

CHAPTER XXVII

The death of Francisco de Almendras; the rising
of Diego Centeno; Alonso de Toro resists him,
and the long chase after him.

WE HAVE said above that many *vecinos* of La Plata came to serve the viceroy in answer to his summons, though on learning of his arrest on the way they returned home. Gonzalo Pizarro, as we have also said, sent Francisco de Almendras, a genuine partisan of his, as his deputy there. One day Almendras heard that a leading gentleman of the town, Don Gómez de Luna, had stated in his house that it was impossible but that the emperor should rule again some day. He arrested him and flung him in the public prison under guard. The members of the town council begged that he should be freed, or at least put in a place appropriate to his rank, and when Almendras replied unfavorably, some retorted that if he would not set the prisoner free they would. The deputy took offence at this, though he disguised his annoyance. At midnight he went to the jail, and strangled Don Gómez and had the body beheaded in the public square. This, as Zárate says (Book V, ch. xxi):

was much resented by the *vecinos*, who thought they were all involved in this affront. One *vecino* called Diego Centeno, a native of Ciudad Rodrigo, who had been a great friend of Don Gómez, particularly resented it. And although Centeno had followed Pizarro in his first rising and accompanied him down to Lima as one of the most influential men in his army, representing the province of Los Charcas, later, on finding that Pizarro's designs went far beyond what he had at first declared, he obtained permission to return to his home and his Indians, and was living there when Don Gómez's death occurred, which he resolved to avenge as best he could,

saving from Almendras' tyranny all those who lived under his rule.

He informed the leading *vecinos* of the province, especially Lope de Mendoza, Alonso Pérez de Esquivel, Alonso de Camargo, Hernán Núñez de Segura, Lope de Mendieta, Juan Ortiz de Zárate, his brother, and others in whose intentions he could confide. They all decided to kill Almendras, and did so one Sunday, meeting at his house to accompany him to mass. They stabbed him, and as he did not die at once, they took him into the square and beheaded him as a traitor, raising standards in His Majesty's name. They had no difficulty in calming the town, for Almendras was unpopular. They placed themselves on a war footing, appointing Centeno captain general and he named captains of horse and foot and began to call up men and diligently to provide arms and supplies. He posted guards on the roads, so that it should not be known what he had done. He sent Lope de Mendoza to Arequipa to try to capture Pedro de Fuentes, Pizarro's governor there. But when Fuentes heard from the Indians what was happening in Charcas, he forsook the city, and Lope de Mendoza entered it. He, with the men, horses, and treasure he could collect, rejoined Centeno in La Plata. They now found themselves with 250 well-equipped men. Centeno assembled them and delivered a long harangue about what Pizarro had done with regard to the ordinances. He condemned Pizarro's intentions, reminding them of the men he had killed under pretext of serving the crown and how he had used threats and force to get himself appointed governor of Peru, and had taken property from

His Majesty and many private persons, whom he had deprived of their Indians, taking them for himself; he had also allowed his people to speak openly against the crown. He added a great deal more against Gonzalo, and finished by reminding them of their obligations toward the king as good vassals and of the ill fame that would attach to them if they did not serve him. So Centeno persuaded them to offer to obey him and follow wherever he might lead.

He then sent a captain to guard the road to Cuzco and tried to prevent the news of what he had done from reaching that city until he should have collected more men and prepared arms, horses, powder, and supplies. But all his precautions to keep secrecy were insufficient, for the news reached Cuzco through the Indians and was conveyed a hundred leagues north of it on the road to Lima, where Alonso de Toro was deputy for Gonzalo. Toro was guarding the road, for Gonzalo feared that the viceroy might make through the mountains to Cuzco, and had sent him with a hundred men to hold the passage. Here Toro had news, not only of Centeno's rising and Almendras' death, but of how many men and the number of horses and arquebusses there were and everything else that had been done, which the Indians told him at length. Toro then hastened to Cuzco, raised men, notified the *vecinos* and *regidors* of the city, and persuaded them to defend Gonzalo against Centeno. He said that he proposed to go against Centeno, as there were enough armed men and horses to resist and overcome him. In order to justify his case, he said that Centeno had no title or authority to start his rising, but that he had been moved by his private interests and was using His Majesty's name: Gonzalo Pizarro was the legitimate and accepted governor of Peru which was peaceful and undisturbed awaiting news of His Majesty's commands, which would be obeyed. Centeno had thus unjustly and causelessly begun this revolt, and it was necessary to oppose and punish it as such a scandalous deed deserved.

He also tried to justify Pizarro's party, reminding them of what he had done for all the *vecinos* and soldiers of the empire by standing up for the revocation of the ordinances in defence of all of them. In this he had staked his life and property for the common good, for it was notorious that if the ordinances were executed, not a single *vecino* would be left with his property, nor could a single soldier stay in Peru, since the *vecinos* fed and kept them. Because of the good he had done they were all bound to take his side. Gonzalo had not opposed His Majesty's orders or done anything in his disservice; for when he went to petition against the ordinances he found that the *audiencia* had arrested the viceroy and expelled him. Gonzalo, as governor, ruled Peru and was responsible for it, and if he had gone against the viceroy, this was because of the formal summons and sentence issued by the royal *audiencia*. To show how just was his cause, he told them to remember that Licentiate Cepeda, His Majesty's judge and the senior member of the *audiencia*, had gone with Gonzalo Pizarro. He said that it was wrong for them to discuss whether the judges were or were not entitled to make Pizarro governor: this was a case for His Majesty to decide. So far nothing had been said against it, and no one had more merits or was better qualified to govern the empire to the general satisfaction, for he had conquered it with his brothers at their own expense and risk, and he knew all the other conquerors and was acquainted with their deeds and merits, and could reward them better than governors newly arrived from Spain.

All this and much more like it he said, and he was so harsh and rude that he had himself obeyed and no one dare contradict him. So they prepared to follow him against Diego Centeno. Toro raised men, entitled himself captain general, appointed captains, took all the horses in the city from those who were sick or infirm and unable to fight, and made the *vecinos* accompany him in person. By this means he raised nearly three hundred men, all fairly well equipped. He marched six leagues to the south of Cuzco, where he waited twenty days without news of his opponents. At the end of this period he went off to look for Centeno, thinking he was wasting time in waiting for information.

He came to within twelve leagues of Centeno, who withdrew as his men were divided into two parties. However, messengers and hostages were exchanged in order to open negotiations in an attempt to avoid open conflict; but it was soon found that there was no room for compromise. Toro prepared to give battle. Centeno and his friends decided not to risk so important an affair, for if they lost, their enemies would be greatly strengthened, and His Majesty's party would be ruined. They therefore withdrew, driving off many sheep laden with food and taking the principal chiefs of the provinces. They entered a desert more than 40 leagues across. Toro pursued them to La Plata, 120 leagues from Cuzco: he found it nearly abandoned, and ill equipped for a sojourn, for there was no food and the Indians had taken to the mountains in the absence of their chiefs. He decided to follow no further, but return to Cuzco. He went ahead with fifty horse and left Captain Alonso de Mendoza with thirty men on picked mounts to hold the rear and defend the main body from Centeno in case he attacked. They would also return to Cuzco, where they would rejoin him.

CHAPTER XXVIII

Centeno sends men after Alonso de Toro; suspicions of disorders in Lima; Lorenzo de Aldana pacifies them; Pizarro sends his commander Francisco de Carvajal to Los Charcas; his deeds on the way.

CENTENO learned from the Indians of Toro's withdrawal to Cuzco, and was astonished that he should have retired so needlessly after bringing such a large force. He supposed that this hasty retreat with the men divided into three groups could only mean that Toro had found his followers untrustworthy and reluctant. He therefore decided to seize his opportunity. He sent Captain Lope de Mendoza with fifty men on good horses with light saddles in pursuit of the enemy to bring back any deserters. Lope de Mendoza overtook some fifty men in the second party, for Alonso de Mendoza had still not left La Plata; he took their horses and arms, though he soon returned them and gave them some money, as they promised to serve him in the campaign. He hanged some who were suspect or too close to Toro, though the historians do not say how many. Lope de Mendoza then turned against Alonso de Mendoza, who duly avoided him, and they did not meet. Centeno then reached La Plata. It was decided to establish headquarters there, and collect the men who would come to them, and fit themselves out with arms and other necessaries. Toro arrived at Cuzco, with no explanation of his sudden and disorderly retreat, which had given the enemy an opportunity to make a sudden attack and obtain an advantage that would have been even greater if he had had the courage to follow it up. All this became known in Lima, where there were people of both parties. The viceroy's followers took courage and spoke almost openly of joining Centeno. Aldana's remissness in punishing them spread the suspicion among the Pizarrists that he had given his consent and wanted to become their leader.

With these fears they went to him and reported the outrageous remarks of those who spoke freely. At that time the news reached Lima of the viceroy's execution of his own followers and his discomfiture at the hands of his pursuers. The news of the viceroy's reverse and misfortunes and of his treatment of his adherents discouraged those who had spoken up for him, and animated the Pizarrists, whose leaders decided to speak frankly to Aldana, telling him that there were suspicious persons in the city who were harming their party with scandalous utterances. They ought to be punished with executions and exile; and information would be provided of who and how many they were. Aldana replied that he had known nothing about this, but would investigate and punish them severely.

The informers then arrested fifteen persons. Alcalde Pedro Martín de Cicilia, or de Benito as he was also known, wanted to torture them. They would have been in great danger if this had been done; for however little they confessed, Pedro Martín, who was completely devoted to Pizarro's party, would have put them to death. Aldana deplored this and took them from him, removing them to his own lodging on the pretext that they would be safer and less able to flee. He gave them all they needed, and under pretence of punishing them, exiled them from the city in a ship he gave them. He spoke to some of them privately, revealing his intentions so that they would know for the future. The Pizarrists were very dissatisfied at Aldana's failure to punish these men; and their suspicion that he was on the other side was strengthened. They warned Gonzalo, but he did nothing against Aldana, whom he regarded as a friend. In any case he was far away in Quito, and Aldana was so popular it was doubtful if he could be successfully removed.

Now Gonzalo learned of Centeno's revolt and he wanted to restore the situation in Los Charcas, which seemed more important than that of Lima. Having consulted with his captains, he gave powers to his commander Francisco de Carvajal to carry this through. The captains urged Gonzalo to do this with great insistence, some because they wanted to take command and others because they were afraid of Francisco de Carvajal's brutality. Everyone agreed that an expedition such as this required a man of his experience and ability. He left the confines of Quito with only twenty reliable companions, and reached the city of San Miguel, where he was received with signs of satisfaction. He arrested six of the leading *regidors*, and told them of Gonzalo's complaints against them, for having opposed him and having favored the viceroy's side so strenuously. He had been determined to sack and burn the city and not leave a man alive in it; but considering that the plebeians had done no harm, but only the leaders, he had resolved to punish only those he had chosen and so limit the destruction. He ordered them to confess, and had one whom he regarded as most guilty strangled: this man had shown how to make the royal seal which the viceroy was using, being skilled in this craft. The others escaped on the pleadings of their wives and friends, while a cluster of priests and friars went to beg him to spare them. He granted this, and sentenced them to exile from the province and to be deprived of their Indians, each paying 4,000 pesos. He then moved on to Trujillo, gathering what men and money he could. He levied loans, which he speedily collected, and went to Lima, where he assembled two hundred well-equipped men (including those he already had), and so left for Cuzco by the mountain road. He reached the town of Huamanga and, as our authors say, laid a tribute on it which he collected.

Meanwhile a new plot to kill Aldana was hatched in Lima, where the people were always ready for mutinies without any regard to where they would lead: most of their originators perished. This, which was the third rising planned in Lima, was put down with the death of three or four ringleaders, and led to the execution of five or six more killed by Francisco de Carvajal in Huamanga, on being denounced by those in Lima. In Huamanga Carvajal learned of Centeno's retreat and of Toro's pursuit and his victorious return to Cuzco. Thinking he had nothing to fear from Centeno, he decided not to go on and returned to Lima. He did this also to avoid meeting Alonso de Toro, who was his rival, since Gonzalo had removed Toro from the post of commander owing to an illness and had replaced him by Carvajal: for this reason they were on bad terms.

Carvajal returned to Lima, but had hardly reached the city when news reached him that Centeno had left the forests and followed Toro, capturing and winning over more than fifty of his men; and also that Alonso de Mendoza had retired in a different direction. He thought he had better go out against Centeno, and so he did. To avoid meeting Toro he did not go by Cuzco but by Arequipa, and so reached that city down the coast. When Alonso de Toro and the *regidors* of Cuzco learned this, they wrote to him not to attack Centeno from Arequipa but from Cuzco, or he would give offence to that city, the capital of the empire. Carvajal did as he was asked, not so much because he was moved by these pleas as because it was to his interest to raise more men in Cuzco. He hastened to the city where he and Toro received one another with fear and suspicion, though there was no trouble in public. Next day Carvajal arrested four *vecinos* of Cuzco who were not on his side, and hanged them without informing Toro, which annoyed his rival even more. Carvajal took three hundred well-equipped men, a hundred horse and the rest foot, with whom he marched to Collao where Centeno was, and came to within ten leagues of him. Centeno thought, as everyone told him, that Carvajal's men were very discontented and would come over to him, so he made a surprise attack one night with eighty men, and got so near that the two sides spoke to one another. But he was disappointed in his fond hopes, for Carvajal had his force so well drawn up that no one dared leave the ranks. In any case they were not so dissatisfied as rumor said: if they had been, it would not have been possible for a single man to stop the three hundred of them from filtering away.

The authors say that Carvajal was unpopular because he treated his men badly and only paid them with ill use and coarse words. But the great deeds they themselves ascribe to him and the ease with which he performed them show how he treated his men, for they helped him to do these things. He was cruel, that cannot be denied. But not toward his own party, only toward the enemy, and then not toward all, but only those he called shuttlers, who came and went from one side to the other like the shuttle of a loom: hence his name for them. Later on we shall take the opportunity to say more about Carvajal, who was certainly a good soldier and showed he had fought under the Grand Captain, Gonzalo Fernández de Córdoba, duke of Sessa, and other leaders of his day.

When Centeno found that no one came over as he had expected, he retired in good order: he always kept good order during all these brushes with the enemy, till he was finally destroyed.

CHAPTER XXIX

Carvajal pursues Centeno; he commits a strange
act of cruelty against a soldier; a trick
another played on him.

AT DAYBREAK Francisco de Carvajal followed his enemy with his infantry drawn up in companies and the horse ranging ahead to harass Centeno's rear. The latter withdrew, attacking Carvajal that night and for three or four more. He still hoped that some would desert to him, but finding himself deceived, he began to withdraw his own force lest the enemy should worst him. He travelled furiously twelve, thirteen, or fifteen leagues a day, as our authors say. He sent the baggage on ahead, and he himself and the fastest and best armed stayed behind. Carvajal pursued him so constantly that however fast he went, he was hardly ever out of sight of the army in formation. Carvajal had two dozen pikes and said that they were always raised and would destroy the enemy, as indeed they did. Centeno took his chosen men and faced Carvajal, holding the narrow places on the road. He was able to hold him up for two or three days, but not to stop his advance. Meanwhile he ordered all the heavily armed soldiers and the baggage to travel at full speed. When he thought they would have gone twenty leagues or more, he left Carvajal and hastened to rejoin his men, who all said: "Thank God, the rebel will have to give us two days' rest while he catches up." But I heard many of those who were with Centeno tell how they had hardly rested five or six hours when they saw the raised pikes above the horizon: it seemed as if they were carried by devils, not by men. So they resumed their retreat in all haste, and Centeno again took the rear to defend his column.

One day in a narrow defile through a gorge between cliffs Centeno held off the enemy for more than half a day; but at nightfall they withdrew. One of them, whose name I forget, an arquebusier riding a mare, wanted to fire a good shot without considering the danger to himself. He dismounted and hid behind a rock, so as to fire from a sheltered position and not waste his ball. Nor did he, for he killed a good horse in front of Carvajal; but when the poor arquebusier went to get his mount, having lingered behind all the rest of his party, trusting in his speed, the mare ran away, scared by the sound of the arquebus and attracted by the other horses which had already gone. He was thus forsaken. Carvajal's men captured him and took him before their leader. He was furious at the brave and prolonged resistance of the enemy and angry at the temerity of this soldier; so in order to torment him more than if he were killed on the spot, he had him left as naked as when he was born, tied hand and foot in a swamp. It is so cold there that the Indians take care to put their jars, pitchers and other earthenware vessels under cover, for if they heedlessly leave them out overnight they are cracked by the intense cold in the morning. The wretched soldier passed the whole night in that cruel plight, shouting and screaming for mercy. "Christians, won't any of you take pity on me and kill me, and release me from my torment? It'll be the greatest charity in the world, and God will repay you." With these repeated lamentations, the poor fellow passed the night, and at daybreak, when it was thought that Carvajal would regard his punishment as completed, he had him strangled. I for my part regard this as the greatest of his cruelties.

He then set off after the enemy, harassing him as hard as before. Centeno's men could not stand the daily and nightly ordeal and many weakened, as did their horses. Carvajal captured all he could, and killed his most notorious enemies without sparing any. Others, less implicated, were pardoned at the request of his followers. We should not forget to mention a trick a soldier played on Carvajal during these attacks: it was one of many that took place during the campaign. Many poor soldiers came to Carvajal during the whole time he was commander, and offered themselves to him saying: "Sir, I've come so many leagues walking and barefoot, just to serve my lord the governor. I beg Your Worship to fit me out so that I can do so."

Carvajal would thank them for their intention and repay them for the trouble of the journey by giving them arms, horses, clothes, and money, as best he could. Many of the soldiers remained in his service and served him well till the end of the war. Many others only went to get arms and horses, and then ran away, when they could, to the king's side. One of these soldiers was given a mare, for Carvajal had nothing else to offer. The soldier intended to flee and was very slow in the attack, always being amongst the last to come up. But he bragged greatly, saying that if he had a good mount, he would be first after the enemy. Carvajal was angry at hearing this repeated so often, and exchanged the mare for a very good mule, saying: "Soldier, here's the best mount in the company. Take it, and don't complain about me. And by the life of my lord the governor, if you don't get twelve leagues ahead of us by morning, you'll pay very dear for it."

The soldier mounted and heard the threat; to prevent it from being carried out, he fled that night, taking the opposite road from the one followed by Carvajal and hoping that no one would be sent after him. And he rode so hard that by daybreak he was eleven leagues away. At that moment he met another soldier, an acquaintance of his, who was going after Carvajal: he told him: "Be so good, sir, as to tell the commander I beg his pardon. I haven't been able to do what he bade me, for I've only come eleven leagues, but by mid-day I'll do the twelve, and four more into the bargain."

The second soldier did not realize that the first had fled, and told Carvajal, thinking it was an urgent message. Carvajal was more annoyed by this piece of impertinence than by the soldier's misdeed, and said: "These shuttlers—his word for those who joined him and deserted to the king's side—had better go shriven; for all those I find will have to pardon me for hanging every man of them. I won't have them come and take my arms and horses, and then when they get them run away from me. And I'll do the same to the priests and friars who act as spies. Let the religious and clergy stay in their churches and convents and ask God for peace among Christians, but let them not trust in their habits and orders and stoop to spying. If they themselves scorn what they should prize, it won't be surprising if I hang them, as I've often seen done in the wars I've been in."

Carvajal said this very angrily, and he carried it out, as the historians say. He vented his anger and cruelty on the shuttlers who deceived him, but honored straightforward soldiers who served the king and did not pass from side to side; and when he arrested them, he treated them well to see if they would join his party. Let us leave Carvajal in his rage, chasing Diego Centeno, and return to Gonzalo's pursuit of the viceroy: both took place at the same time, and almost on the same days.

CHAPTER XXX

Gonzalo pursues the viceroy and expels him from Peru; Pedro de Hinojosa goes to Panama with Pizarro's fleet.

WE HAVE told how the viceroy entered Quito with Gonzalo at his heels, and how the Pizarrists were as weary and ill-supplied, and even worse off than their enemies, since the viceroy took care to leave behind no supplies that could be of use to them. Yet the Pizarrists' anxiety to finish off the viceroy was so great that they did not cease to pursue him by day or night, as Zárate says (Book V, ch. xxix):

Gonzalo Pizarro followed the viceroy from San Miguel, whither he had retired, to Quito, 150 leagues, persisting so hard with the chase that hardly a day passed without the scouts meeting and speaking. Neither side unsaddled its horses the whole way, though the viceroy's party was the more watchful; for if they rested at night, they remained dressed and held their horses by the halter, without waiting to erect tents or take other usual precautions for horses at night. This was especially the case in the sandy wastes where there are no trees. Here necessity has shown a remedy: they take bags or small sacks, which they fill with sand on reaching the place where they intend to spend the night. They then dig a deep hole, put the sacks in, tie the horses to them, and fill in the hole again, treading down the sand round it. Both armies suffered from hunger, but Gonzalo's the more since the viceroy diligently took away the Indians and their caciques to prevent him getting supplies on the way. The viceroy was in such a haste that he took eight or ten horses for himself, the best that could be found. They were led by Indians, and when an animal grew tired it was hamstrung so that the enemy could not use it.

On the way Gonzalo was joined by Captain Bachicao, who came from his expedition to Tierra Firme, bringing 350 men, 20 ships, and plenty of artillery. He had landed as near Quito as he could and came up to meet Gonzalo. In Quito, Gonzalo had more than 800 men altogether in his camp: they included the principal people of Peru, both *vecinos* and soldiers, and were as peaceful and prosperous as ever the followers of a rebel governor have been, since the province has plentiful supplies of food, and only a little before very rich gold mines had been found there. There was a great store of gold from the allocations of *vecinos* who had repudiated him, and the royal fifths, and the chests of the deceased. Here Gonzalo heard that the viceroy was forty leagues away in the town of Pasto, which is in the governorship of Benalcázar. He determined to go in search of him (though the whole chase was almost continuous and with hardly a pause, since Gonzalo was only in Quito a very short time). On his leaving Quito there were skirmishes between the two sides at a place called Río Caliente. When the viceroy heard Gonzalo was coming, he left the city and marched overland to Popayán. Gonzalo followed twenty leagues beyond Pasto and then decided to return to Quito, since the land beyond was desert and lacking in food. The chase had gone on so long when he turned back to Quito that it can be said that he followed the viceroy from La Plata, where he first went out against him, to Pasto, a distance of seven hundred leagues, but long leagues which would amount to more than one thousand ordinary Castilian leagues,

etc. Thus Zárate.

In addition to what the historians say of this expedition, we should add that when the viceroy had crossed the Río Caliente, he thought that his opponents would be satisfied by expelling him from the limits of Peru, beyond his jurisdiction; and that they would not follow any longer, but leave him in peace to decide what to do for the best. But a few hours after he had talked with his captains in this sense, they saw Gonzalo's army appearing, descending a long slope down to the river in their usual furious haste. Then he raised his hands to heaven, and exclaimed aloud: "Is it possible that anyone would believe it if they were told there were Spaniards who would pursue their king's royal standard four hundred leagues from Lima here, as these have done?" So saying, he hastily called his men together and went on, as the enemy had not tired of the chase. Pizarro returned to Quito where, as Zárate has said, he was so puffed up with pride after his victories and successes that he began to make very disrespectful remarks about His Majesty, saying that he would have to give him the governorship of Peru willy-nilly. He said why the king must do so, and added that he intended to resist if he did anything different. Though Gonzalo sometimes dissimulated, his captains publicly persuaded him of it and had him openly announce his disobedient pretension.

He resided for a while in the city of Quito, with daily feasts, rejoicings, and banquets. He had no news of the viceroy or his plans: some said he meant to go to Spain by Cartagena, others that he would go to Tierra Firme so as to hold the isthmus and collect men and arms to carry out what His Majesty had bidden him. Still others said he would await the royal commands where he was at Popayán, for no one thought he would be able to re-form his army there, or take any new step in the affair. In any case Gonzalo and his captains thought they had better seize Tierra Firme so as to cut the viceroy off in case of emergency. For this reason, and to prevent the viceroy from getting there, he sent back the fleet Hernando Bachicao had brought and made his chamberlain, Pedro de Hinojosa, admiral of it. He took 250 men, and left forthwith, sending Captain Rodrigo de Carvajal by ship from Puerto Viejo to take Gonzalo's letters to Panama. These asked the *vecinos* there to stand by him, and assured them that he was sending the fleet to give satisfaction for the lootings and other misdeeds perpetrated by Bachicao, which had been done quite against his will: he had not ordered them or even thought of any such thing. Rodrigo de Carvajal came within three leagues of Panama, and learnt from a landowner there that two of the viceroy's captains, Juan de Guzmán and Juan de Illanes, were in the city. They were raising men to help him in the province of Benalcázar, where he was waiting, and they had more than a hundred soldiers, a good quantity of arms and five or six pieces of field artillery. Although they had had everything ready for some days, they had not gone to the viceroy, but were lying low there to defend the city against the Pizarrists, being assured that he would send to occupy it. Rodrigo de Carvajal sent a soldier secretly with letters to certain *vecinos,* who informed the authorities. The man was arrested, and when the authorities learned of Hinojosa's coming and of his intentions, the alarm was given in the city and two brigantines were sent to seize Carvajal's ship. But he guessed what had happened when the soldier delayed, and set sail: the two brigantines failed to find him and returned.

CHAPTER XXXI

Pedro de Hinojosa arrests Vela Núñez on the way;
the preparations made to resist him in Panama,
and how the fire was quelled.

T HE GOVERNOR of Panama, Pedro de Casaos, a native of Seville,
hastened to Nombre de Dios, prepared the forces that were there,
and collected armor and weapons which he brought to Panama, and made
ready to resist Pedro de Hinojosa. The viceroy's two captains did the
same; and though there had previously been some rivalry between them
and Casaos about seniority, Casaos was elected general. After sending off
Rodrigo de Carvajal, Hinojosa continued his journey to Panama, seeking
information about the viceroy along the coast. In the port and river of
San Juan he landed men to find out what was happening and they brought
in ten Spaniards under arrest. From one he discovered that the viceroy,
because of the delay of his captains, Guzmán and Illanes, had sent his
brother Vela Núñez to Panama to fetch the men who were there. In order
to increase this force he had given him a great deal of money from the
royal chest and delivered to him a natural son of Gonzalo Pizarro's.
Vela Núñez had sent the arrested man forward to find out what was
happening on the coast, and he himself was a day's journey away. On
learning this, Hinojosa sent two captains and some men who divided and
took two different roads, following the information given by the spy.
They were fortunate, for one party captured Vela Núñez and the other
Rodrigo Mejía, a native of Villacastín, who was in charge of Gonzalo's
son. In each case much valuable booty was seized. They were taken to
Hinojosa, who was overjoyed, for Vela Núñez might have impeded him
in Panama, while the restoration of Gonzalo's son would delight his
father. They were all full of rejoicing at such a rapid and notable success.

In these good spirits, Hinojosa was sailing to Panama when Rodrigo de
Carvajal met him and told him what had occurred, explaining that the
city was armed and ready to resist. He was glad at the news, and put his
force on a war footing, sailing on till one day in October 1545, he sighted
Panama with his fleet of 11 ships and 250 men. The city was in a great
uproar: everyone rallied to the colors, and Pedro de Casaos acted as

general. He had over 500 men, though most were merchants and artisans with so little experience of war that they could not shoot or handle the arquebusses; worst of all, they had little desire to fight, since they had always held the opinion that the function of the people in Peru was to bring them profit rather than loss in their bargainings and dealings, while many of the merchants, including the wealthiest, had their property in the hands of partners or factors in Peru. These were afraid that Gonzalo would seize their possessions if he found they had resisted him. However they prepared to defend themselves and drew up in form of battle. Their leaders were the general, Pedro de Casaos, and Arias de Acevedo, who later came to Spain and settled in Córdova, where his grandsons still live. The other captains were Juan Fernández de Rebolledo and Andrés de Araiza, and the viceroy's captains Juan de Guzmán and Juan de Illanes, with many other noblemen, who all desired to defend the city, both because it was in the king's service and because they had been warned by the excesses of Bachicao and feared Hinojosa would do the same.

On finding himself resisted Hinojosa landed with 200 well-armed veterans, leaving the other 50 on guard over the ships. He marched along the coast, bringing in the ship's boats plenty of artillery which would suffice to destroy the enemy if they were attacked. He had left orders on board the ships that if the enemy offered battle Vela Núñez and other prisoners were to be hanged. Governor Pedro de Casaos realized that Hinojosa was determined to fight, and came out to meet him, resolved to conquer or die. When they were about an arquebus shot apart, all the priests and friars came out of the city with many crucifixes and other holy insignia covered in mourning in token of sadness and grief. They loudly appealed to heaven and men for peace and concord, saying that they were all Christians who had gone to those parts to preach the Gospel to the heathen and not to turn their arms against one another to their common discredit and destruction. With these words they restrained the two armies from coming into open conflict, and going to and fro between them, negotiated a truce and succeeded in arranging an exchange of hostages. Hinojosa sent Don Baltasar de Castilla, son of the count of La Gomera, and the Panamanians sent Don Pedro de Cabrera, both natives of Seville. Hinojosa's party argued that they could see no reason why their entry should be resisted, since they had not come to harm anyone, but only to repair the wrongs done by Bachicao in the city and to buy with their own money the clothing and supplies they needed for their journey. They had express orders from Gonzalo not to hurt anyone or to fight unless they were forced to do so. Once they had taken supplies and refitted their ships, they would go away. Their purpose in coming had been to find the viceroy and oblige him to go to Spain, as the royal judges had bidden him, for he was disturbing the peace ot Peru; but as he was not in Panama, they had no reason to stay, and they begged the Panamanians not to force an issue since they intended to observe as rigorously as possible the orders given them by Gonzalo Pizarro. But if they were obliged to fight, they would do all they could not to be the losers.

On Governor Pedro de Casaos' behalf different arguments were advanced to show how wrong it was thàt the Pizarrists should trespass on another's jurisdiction with their men drawn up for battle. Even if Pizarro governed legally, as his men maintained, there was no excuse for interfering in another region; and Bachicao had made promises similar to theirs, but after establishing himself there he had caused the destruction and havoc they said they had come to repair. Commissioners were appointed to settle the difference, and they ruled that Hinojosa might land and stay thirty days in the city, with fifty soldiers for the security of his person: the fleet and the other men should withdraw to the Pearl Islands and there seek the shipwrights and equipment they needed. At the end of the thirty days they would return to Peru. Both sides took an oath to observe these conditions, and hostages were exchanged.

Hinojosa went to the city with his fifty soldiers and took a house where he gave dinner every day to anyone who appeared, and permitted his companions to gamble and converse openly with the citizens. As a result, as Zárate says in Book V, ch. xxxii—for all we have said is his—within three days almost all the viceregal soldiers raised by Captains Guzmán and Illanes went over to him. All the other idle folk in the city did the same, except the *vecinos* and merchants, and they were all very enthusiastic for Hinojosa and wanted to go with him to Peru. The viceroy's captains, finding themselves abandoned, secretly took a ship and went off with the fourteen or fifteen persons who were left. Hinojosa remained at peace: he set about strengthening his army, and did not interfere with the government or administration of justice in Panama, or let his followers do any harm. He sent Don Pedro de Cabrera and Hernando Mejía de Guzmán, his son-in-law, with men to Nombre de Dios, to guard the port and try to get the information he needed for his security from Spain and elsewhere.

CHAPTER XXXII

What Melchor Verdugo did at Trujillo, Nicaragua, and Nombre de Dios; how he was expelled from the last-named city.

AT THIS time there occurred in the city of Trujillo an event that caused much scandal, and led to great hatred against its perpetrator, a *vecino* of the city called Melchor Verdugo, who had been allocated the province of Cajamarca, famous as the scene of the arrest of King Atahuallpa and the great doings we have described.

This man came from the viceroy's native city of Avila, and therefore wanted to perform some notable feat to distinguish himself in his service. As the viceroy knew of this before his arrest, he had given him a commission to do what he could in the question of evacuating Lima. For this reason Verdugo was very much in the bad books of the Pizarrists; and he therefore tried to leave Peru before they could lay hands on him. Before doing so he wanted to perform some doughty deed against the enemy, and therefore collected some soldiers, bought arms in secret, and made some arquebusses and fetters in his own house; for his purpose was to achieve his ambition even by molesting his fellow *vecinos,* if need be. His plan was assisted by the fortunate arrival of a ship coming from Lima at that moment. He sent for the master and pilot, saying he wanted them to see some cloth and maize he wished to load for Panama. When he had them in his house, he put them in a dungeon he had made. Then pretending to be suffering from a disease of the legs he had, he went to the window of the house, and seeing the alcaldes and a notary with them, called on them to come up to where he was to execute some documents, for he was too ill to go down. When they came in, he found a pretext for taking them to the place where the master and pilot were, and then deprived them of their rods of office and put them in chains with six arquebusiers standing guard over them. He then returned to his window and called any *vecino* who appeared in the square, pretending he had some business with him, and duly clapped him in his prison, without anyone outside suspecting anything. He soon had more than twenty of the leading citizens who had been left, the rest having gone with Gonzalo Pizarro. Then he went out into the square with some twenty soldiers whom he regarded as friends, and shouted out in the king's name. He arrested any who did not rally to him forthwith, and told all his prisoners that he was going after the viceroy and needed men and arms; they could all ransom themselves for whatever they could pay, and pay on the spot, or he would take them with him as prisoners. His prisoners paid what they had promised in cash, and he also took what was in the royal chest. All this with his own possessions (for he was a rich man) amounted to a great sum in gold and silver; and he embarked with it, bringing his prisoners down to the beach with him so that they could do no harm: there he left them in their fetters. At sea he met a ship laden with a great deal of merchandise which was being taken to Bachicao as part of his plunder from the city. Verdugo seized all this and divided it among his followers and himself. He did not dare to put into Panama, fearing that Pizarro's fleet would be there, and went to Nicaragua.

Hinojosa found out about this and sent after him Captain Juan Alonso Palomino with 120 arquebusiers in two ships. He caught Verdugo ashore and seized his ship, but dare not land himself since the *vecinos* of Granada and Léon were ready to resist him. Palomino then returned to Panama with such ships as he found on the Nicaraguan coast: he carried off those that were of use and burnt the rest. On arriving at Panama he reported to Hinojosa. Verdugo was now unable to do any of the things he had planned in the Pacific, having lost his ship and being unable to buy another, as Bachicao and his friends had taken them all. He thought that if he went by the Caribbean to Nombre de Dios he might achieve some great feat there, supposing that Hinojosa had few men and that they would not be on their guard; so that he would meet with no resistance. With this idea he prepared four frigates and launched them in the lagoon of Nicaragua with a hundred well-armed men, and passing down the channel between it and the sea, he entered the Caribbean and sailed along the coast to Nombre de Dios. At the river called Chagre he took a boat with some domesticated blacks, from whom he learnt what was going on in Nombre de Dios and what captains and men there were there. Guided by these blacks he reached the city at midnight. He landed and surrounded the house where Captains Don Pedro de Cabrera and Hernán Mejía were with some men; these awoke at the noise and began to defend the house. Verdugo's party set fire to it and those within were in great danger and obliged to force a way out through the assailants, who however were more intent on loot and their own profit than on killing people, and did little to stop them. The refugees escaped under cover of night and hid in the great forests there are there, which almost touch the houses. They repaired to Panama as best they could and reported to Hinojosa what had happened. He was very vexed, and wanted to avenge himself with legal justification. So he brought the matter up before Dr. Ribera, the governor of Nombre de Dios, who was in Panama; and complained to him of Verdugo's conduct, emphasizing that he had improperly entered Ribera's jurisdiction without orders or authority, and had arrested the alcaldes, released the prisoners, and made a disturbance on both seas and in the city, all on his own responsibility. They asked the doctor to order him to be punished, and Hinojosa offered to accompany him and help him with his own men. Dr. Ribera accepted the accusation and Hinojosa's offer, and as a precaution took an oath of him and his captains that they would obey him as captain general and not exceed his orders. Thus they left Panama for Nombre de Dios. Melchor Verdugo, on receiving the news, put his men in order and placed the *vecinos* among them. Hinojosa attacked, and several died on both sides in the first exchange of shots. When the *vecinos* found that their governor was leading the opposition, they withdrew to a hill nearby. Verdugo's men dispersed to arrest the fugitives, and being unable to resist, went back to their frigates. They took the best ship in the port, equipped it with the cannon they found in the other ships and raked the town, though they did little damage as it lies in a hollow. Verdugo realized that he could not carry out his plans, and that many of his men had remained on shore; so he went to Cartagena with the ship and the frigates to await an opportunity to strike against the enemy if he could. Dr. Ribera and Hinojosa pacified the city as far as possible, and leaving the same captains in it with rather more men than before, returned to Panama.

CHAPTER XXXIII

Blasco Núñez Vela reforms his army at Popayán;
Gonzalo Pizarro pretends to go to Quito
[Los Charcas] to drive him out; the
viceroy pursues Pedro de Puelles.

MEANWHILE the viceroy was at Popayán, as we have said. To avoid
being idle he collected all the iron to be found in the province, sent
for craftsmen, built forges and soon had two hundred arquebusses made
and finished, together with the necessary equipment; he also fitted his
men out with armor. He wrote to Governor Sebastián de Belalcázar and
to one of his captains, Juan Cabrera, who was busy with a new conquest
among the Indians on the governor's orders. He reported on what had
happened since his arrival in Peru, on Gonzalo's risings, his own expulsion, and his determination to face him as soon as he had an adequate
army. He asked them to come and join him, thus rendering His Majesty
a notable service. Once the rebel had been killed, he would make new
allocations in Peru and they should have the largest and best of them. In
addition to these promises he tried to encourage them by saying that
Centeno was standing out at the other end of Peru in His Majesty's name,
and was daily receiving more men: if the rebel were attacked from both
sides, he could not fail to succumb. He sent them powers to take thirty
thousand pesos to pay their men from the royal chests in the cities and
towns round about. The captains at once obeyed on seeing these instructions, and came to Popayán with a hundred well-equipped soldiers. They
kissed the viceroy's hand; and he duly sent despatches to their kingdom
of New Granada, Cartagena, and other places, in the same sense as the
last. Every day more men came in, so that shortly he had 400 fairly armed
men. He now learned of the arrest of his brother and the loss of Captains
Illanes and Guzmán: this he regretted for he had hoped for much help
from Panama. However Gonzalo Pizarro thought and planned of nothing
but how to lay hands on the viceroy, feeling that he himself would never
have an hour of security while Núñez Vela was alive and had an army.
As he could not enter the province where the viceroy was for lack of

supplies, he thought of a stratagem: he put it about that he was going off to Los Charcas to put down Centeno's rising, and was going to leave Captain Puelles in Quito with 300 men facing the viceroy in case he tried to escape. He soon arranged for his plans to be bruited abroad, and decided which captains and soldiers were to accompany him and which were to stay. He paid both, and left Quito after reviewing both forces. In getting this brought to the viceroy's notice, he availed himself of a villain whom the viceroy had sent to spy on him. This man revealed himself to Pizarro out of self-interest, and showed him the cypher he was to use in writing to the viceroy. Gonzalo told him to write all that had happened and sent an Indian who knew nothing of the deceit to carry the letter. He also told Puelles to write to some friends of his in Popayán and say he was remaining with 300 men, and if they wanted to visit him they could do so; for they were his friends and the country was quiet now that Gonzalo had gone. The Indians who took the letters were present at Gonzalo's departure, so that they could describe it. They were told to travel openly so that the viceroy's guards would seize the letters given them. Having made these arrangements, Gonzalo left Quito, as we have said. After travelling three or four days, he pretended to be ill and halted.

The viceroy meanwhile received the letters from his spy and the false ones from Puelles; and believing them both, thought that he would be stronger than Puelles with his 400 men and would easily defeat him and then follow Gonzalo and destroy him. He had no news of Gonzalo's whereabouts as the roads were closed, but he decided to go to Quito, confident that he would be welcomed. But Gonzalo knew hourly from the Cañari Indians what the viceroy was doing and where he was going. On learning that he was twelve leagues from Quito, he hastily marched back and joined Puelles, and both groups went out joyfully to meet the viceroy, although they had heard he had 800 men. But Gonzalo relied on the fact that his men were seasoned and the viceroy's raw. He held a review and found he had 200 arquebusiers, 350 pikemen, and 150 horse, all well equipped and with plenty of good powder and resin. His captains of arquebusiers were Juan de Acosta and Juan Vélez de Guevara, of pikes Hernando de Bachicao, and of cavalry Puelles and Gómez de Alvarado: his standard was borne by Francisco de Ampuero with 60 horse, Licentiate Benito Suárez de Carvajal, brother to the factor Illén Suárez, went with Gonzalo: he had 30 men, his relatives and friends, as a separate company of which he was captain. Knowing that the enemy was two leagues away, Gonzalo advanced to hold a river crossing which the viceroy would use, intending to discomfit him there. The place was strongly fortified; and this was Saturday, January 15, 1546, as Zárate says.

Viceroy Blasco Núñez Vela came, full of courage, against Captain Pedro de Puelles, hoping to defeat him first and then go against Gonzalo and do the same. He always thought that the rebel's companions would desert him and come over to serve His Majesty. Thus confident, he approached so near Puelles, without realizing Pizarro was there, that the scouts spoke to one another, calling one another traitors, and each side insisting that it was serving the king. Although the spies were within sight, the viceroy never knew Gonzalo was there, but thought that he was going to fight Puelles. Early next night, as Zárate says (Book V, ch. xxxv): "he consulted with his captains, and they decided that it would be less risky to go to the city than to give battle, so before midnight he bade his own men take up their arms as silently as possible. Leaving his camp with his tents and Indians, he marched out toward the left." He crossed many mountains, where, as Fernández adds (ch. lii): "it rained all night, and he crossed many large rivers and ravines, and often the horses went sliding down on their buttocks into the rivers. They travelled thus all night, leaving some horses dead and losing some soldiers who failed to come up in time for the battle. At daylight they were a league from Quito."

Thus Fernández; the viceroy's motive in undertaking this difficult march was to take the enemy from behind and fall on him at daybreak. But he had not expected the road to be so rough or so long; for, as Zárate says, he was less than three leagues from Quito, but it took him eight to get there by his circuitous route. This is attributed to a serious error by his advisers, who having decided to give battle next day, nevertheless wearied their men and horses by their eight-league night march over rough, mountainous roads. But when misfortune threatens, especially in war, advice thought to be good turns out amiss.

CHAPTER XXXIV

The beginning of the battle of Quito, in which the viceroy is defeated and killed.

THE VICEROY entered the city of Quito. He found no resistance, but a woman told him that Pizarro was coming against him, at which he was astonished and perceived the deception that had been practiced on him. But Pizarro did not know the viceroy had reached Quito, imagining he was still in his camp until next morning when the scouts came near the tents and saw how little stir there was. They went into the camp and learnt from the Indians what was afoot and told Gonzalo. He hastily sent out scouts in all directions, and thus learnt that the viceroy was in Quito. So he struck camp with all speed, and marched in good order to give battle wherever he found the viceroy. The latter knew what was happening and that the enemy had the advantage over him, yet he had no remedy but to risk a decision, hoping that all His Majesty's servants would desert to him. He came out of the city to receive the enemy and encouraged his men with great vigor; and they all marched along as if victory was already assured; for despite Pizarro's advantage in numbers, the viceroy had very valiant captains and other noteworthy men. His captains of infantry were Sancho Sánchez de Avila and his cousin Juan Cabrera and Francisco Sánchez; of cavalry Adelantado Sebastián de Belalcázar, Cepeda, and Pedro de Bazán.

The armies came within sight of one another and advance parties of arquebusiers came out on both sides and skirmished. Pizarro's were much stronger than the viceroy's, because they were skilled from long practice and had plenty of good powder; the viceroy's were the opposite. The armies were so close that it was necessary to recall the skirmishers to the banners. On Gonzalo's side Captain Juan de Acosta went out to bring them in, accompanied by another good soldier called Páez de Sotomayor. Then Gonzalo ordered Licentiate Carvajal to attack the enemy's right with his company. He placed himself in front of the cavalry, but the captains would not consent to his exposing himself and put him with seven or eight companions on one side of the infantry so that he could direct the battle. The viceroy's cavalry, some 140 men, seeing that Carvajal's were attacking, went out to meet them, and all rushed forward without any sense of order or timing, so that, as Zárate says, when they reached the enemy they were already half discomfited. A picket of arquebusiers awaiting them on one side did much execution among them, and Licentiate Carvajal and his men handled them severely. Although Carvajal's were few, they had the advantage over the viceroy, for they and their horses were fresh and strong, and his were weak and weary. Many were unseated by lances in the charge, and all of them came to close quarters and fought with swords, axes, and clubs. The battle grew very hot. Gonzalo's standard now moved forward with a hundred horsemen, and finding the enemy already worsted, easily completed their confusion. On the other hand the infantry fought hard, and there was such shouting and noise that the forces engaged seemed much larger than they were. At the first shots Captain Juan Cabrera was killed, and soon after Captain Sancho Sánchez, who had fought valiantly with a broadsword and cut his way through several of the enemy's ranks.

But Pizarro's army was so much more numerous and better armed that they overwhelmed their opponents, surrounding them on all sides and killed their captains and most of the men. The viceroy fought along with his cavalry and performed many brave feats. In the first encounter he felled Alonso de Montalvo, and engaged others with courage and vigor. He was disguised, wearing an Indian shirt over his arms, and this was the cause of his death. Seeing that his men were lost, he tried to retire, but could not, for a *vecino* of Arequipa called Hernando de Torres engaged him without recognizing him, dealt him a two-handed blow on the head with a battle axe, which felled and stunned him. Here Zárate (Book V, ch. xxxv) says as follows: "The viceroy and his horse were so tired from their labors the night before, when they had not stopped or rested or eaten, that he was easily brought down. Although the battle was still raging between the infantry, at the sight of the viceroy's fall, his followers, who recognized him, weakened and were defeated, and many of them were killed."

So Zárate. If Hernando de Torres had recognized the viceroy by the habit of Santiago worn openly on his breast, he would certainly not have struck to kill, but have tried to capture him with the help of his comrades. But because of the Indian dress he took the viceroy for a private person, and even a poor soldier, and so did as he did and caused his death. The viceroy was blamed for going in disguise, but his purpose was to avoid being taken prisoner if he were worsted. He wished to be unrecognized so that he should not be accorded the honors of a viceroy, but treated like a private soldier: and this was the cause of his misfortune.

Licentiate Carvajal saw that the enemy was beaten and scoured the field in search of the viceroy, wishing to satisfy his anger at the death of his brother. He found Pedro de Puelles about to kill him, though he was nearly dead from his fall and an arquebus shot he had received. One of the viceroy's soldiers revealed his identity to Puelles, who otherwise would never have recognized him in his disguise. Licentiate Carvajal was about to dismount and finish him off, but Puelles stopped him, saying that it was an unworthy act to lay hands on a man who was nearly dead. Then the Licentiate ordered a Negro to cut his head off. This was done and it was taken to Quito and placed on the gibbet, where it was exposed for a short time, until Gonzalo Pizarro found out about it. He was very angry, and had it removed and put with the body for burial. One author says of this: "Having taken the viceroy's head to Quito, they set it up on the column of the square where it hung for some time. But some thought this disgraceful, and took it down and placed it with the body which was shrouded and buried," etc.

This author does not say that Gonzalo had the head removed from the gibbet, but only that some thought it disgraceful and took it down, which suggests that Gonzalo was to blame for having it put there, or at least gave his consent. But this was not so: Gonzalo deplored the affair, and as López de Gómara says, ordered it to be taken down as soon as he knew it was on the gibbet. But flattery greatly influences those who wish to please and not to do justice and they add to or suppress material facts. López de Gómara himself, speaking of the viceroy's death and having mentioned all the foregoing, says:

Hernando de Torres, a *vecino* of Arequipa, found and laid low Blasco Núñez, though, as some say, without recognizing him, since he wore an Indian shirt over his armor. Herrera, Pizarro's confessor, had time to shrive him: seeing him lying on the ground, he asked who he was, for he too failed to recognize him. Blasco Núñez said: "That has nothing to do with you: get on with your job." The viceroy feared some deed of cruelty,

etc. So López de Gómara.

Then there arrived some who cut off his head and took it to the gibbet. Some of the soldiers were very unrestrained, and pulled off part of his beard, saying: "You've been brought to this pass by your choler and severity." A captain I myself knew wore part of the beard as a plume for some days until he was told to take it off.

Such was the end of this good gentleman, who had persisted so in the application of laws that were not in the king's interest, nor in that of Peru, causing the death and destruction of Spaniards and Indians we have described and shall describe in our history. But he was not so much to blame as has been said, for he had explicit orders to do what he did, as we shall see from the historians and as he himself often said.

CHAPTER XXXV

The viceroy's burial; Gonzalo Pizarro's actions
after the burial; he spares Vela Núñez; the
good laws he makes for the
administration of the empire.

WHEN PIZARRO saw that he was victorious, he had the trumpets sound the retreat, since his men were scattered in the pursuit and doing great execution on the defeated enemy. In the battle and the subsequent pursuit two hundred of the viceroy's men were killed, but no more than seven of Gonzalo's, as Zárate testifies. The viceroy's men were so tired from their long march and sleepless night that they were not fit to fight, but only to let themselves be killed, and this they did, showing their attachment to the royal service. All were buried in the field, and six or seven bodies were thrown into each grave. The viceroy, Sancho Sánchez de Avila, Juan Cabrera, Licentiate Gallego, Captain Cepeda of Plasencia, and other leaders were taken to the city and buried with great solemnity in the cathedral. Gonzalo put on a mourning robe, and his chief followers did the same. Don Alonso de Montemayor, Governor Sebastián de Belalcázar, Francisco Hernández Girón (whom López de Gómara calls Francisco Hernández de Cáceres and Zárate does not mention) were wounded. Fernández says of the last:

Pizarro wanted to kill Captain Francisco Hernández Girón and had even given orders to do so, which would have been no loss, considering the trouble he later caused in Peru. But he was begged to spare him because the captain was popular and had fought well, and was respected as a relative of Lorenzo de Aldana; so Gonzalo pardoned him,

etc. Thus Fernández.

Licentiate Alvarez, the judge the viceroy always kept with him, was badly wounded in the fray and died some days later of his wounds, though certain slanderers say that he was killed by the surgeons by agreement with Gonzalo Pizarro. All three historians mention this, but it is false testimony against Gonzalo and the surgeons; then as always whenever there is civil strife, people try to say all the ill they can, especially of the fallen. Gonzalo pardoned Belalcázar, and sent him back to his own jurisdiction with part of his force in return for an oath that he would favor and serve him forever. He exiled Don Alonso de Montemayor, Rodrigo Núñez de Bonilla, treasurer of Quito, and other leading men to Chile, though on the voyage they seized the ship and went to Mexico. Gonzalo caught all the vanquished he could lay hands on, and had Pedro Bello and Pedro Antón hanged for having fled from Lima in a boat. The rest he told of his reasons for condemning them, saying that they had opposed him and themselves when he stood up for the common good of *vecinos* and soldiers; but that he would pardon them as some had been deceived and others compelled. He promised them that if they did their duty by him, he would show them as much consideration as his own followers and reward them as well. So he ordered them to remain in his camp and supplied them with everything they needed. He instructed his followers that no one was to misuse or abuse them, but they were to treat them like brothers. He sent messengers to all parts of Peru with news of his victory, so as to encourage his supporters and depress his enemies. He sent Captain Alarcón by sea to Panama to take the news to Hinojosa and bring back Vela Núñez and the other prisoners.

He next received the opinions of those who were attentively considering the next steps in his campaign, and they recommended him to send his fleet along the coast of Nicaragua and Mexico to collect and burn any ships it could find, thus forestalling any attempt at a counterattack by sea. After this he should bring his fleet back to Lima, in case His Majesty sent despatches to Tierra Firme, which there would then be no means of sending on to Peru. This would give him a lever to negotiate on his own terms, and was very important for the ultimate success of his undertaking, as we shall see. But Pizarro confided in Hinojosa and his friends, most of whom he had saved from poverty and want and had enriched with rank and Indians: he expected them to be as grateful as noblemen should be, and repudiated his friends' advice, thinking that it would be regarded as cowardice and weakness. His own boldness, which often deceives those who pride themselves on it, led him to suppose that he could openly resist and defeat any opposition.

Captain Alarcón completed his journey and brought back Pizarro's son and Vela Núñez and three other prisoners: he hanged two of them for uttering scandalous statements and would have hanged the third, but Gonzalo's son won a pardon for him by saying that he had always treated him with respect and courtesy. He took Vela Núñez to Quito, and Gonzalo pardoned him for all that was past, warning him not to place himself under suspicion in future or he would stand in great danger. He took him to Lima, and treated him more freely than seemed proper in the case of one who had been so opposed to him. But Gonzalo trusted in others as they might trust him, for he was a straightforward and guileless man. Licentiate Cepeda, the judge we have most neglected, accompanied Gonzalo during the whole campaign, and was present at the battle, in which he fought like a soldier and not like a judge.

After all this Gonzalo lingered in Quito. It seemed to him that as governor he should now undertake the administration of the whole empire, since he was now alone and the *audiencia* had been scattered by his actions. Cepeda was with him; Licentiate Alvarez was dead; Dr. Tejada had been sent as ambassador to Spain; and Licentiate Zárate was in Lima alone and ill, and could settle none of the *audiencia's* business. So Gonzalo, like a man who wishes to give a good account of himself, tried to make laws and ordinances for the good government of Peru, and the peace and prosperity of Indians and Spaniards, and the expansion of Christianity, as López de Gómara says in ch. clxxiii of his *History,* which, with its title, runs as follows:

How Well Gonzalo Pizarro Governed in the Absence of Francisco de Carvajal, and How Finally He Wanted To Declare Himself King, Urged on by Many of His Followers

While his commander Francisco de Carvajal was away, Gonzalo would never consent to kill a Spaniard except with the approval of all or a majority of his council: and then only according to legal process and after confession. He passed laws that the Indians were not to be forced to pay taxes (this was one of the ordinances) or "ranched," which means seizing Indians' property and money by force, under pain of death. He also ordered all owners of Indians to have priests in their villages to teach the Indians Christian doctrine, under pain of being deprived of their allocation. He did much to swell the royal fifth and add to the crown properties, saying that his brother Francisco had done the same. He bade them pay only one in ten, and as it was no longer time of war, since the viceroy was dead, told them all to serve the king, in order that he might revoke the ordinances, confirm the existing allocations and pardon them for what they had done. Everyone praised his administration; and even La

Gasca said on seeing his laws that he had governed well for a rebel. His good government continued, as I said at first, until Hinojosa delivered the fleet to La Gasca.

So López de Gómara; the rest of this chapter we shall leave till later, for many famous deeds were done in the meantime, and in order to narrate them it is necessary to leave Gonzalo in Quito, and make a jump of seven hundred leagues, to where we left Carvajal and Centeno in great strife, pursuing one another and doing what damage they could, as we shall see in the next chapter.

CHAPTER XXXVI

A brave stratagem employed by Centeno against Francisco de Carvajal; other occurrences until the end of this campaign.

As WE SAID earlier, Francisco de Carvajal went in search of Diego Centeno without losing a moment in coming to grips with the enemy. He marched with his company of infantry in formation, and daily seized part of Centeno's baggage and men. One day, as he was still driving them before him, within sight, they had to pass through a deep ravine, with a drop of more than a league down to a small stream and a climb as long on the other side: we have mentioned many such ravines in Peru. The two sides of the ravine were less than an arquebus shot apart; and Carvajal, who knew the road ahead very well, was delighted at the thought that he was chasing his rival to the slaughter. He imagined that while Centeno was descending the slope to the stream, he would reach the top of it so that his arquebusiers could catch Centeno climbing the other side, and kill him and his followers by aiming carefully and coolly from protected positions. So Carvajal was very cock-a-hoop, and his followers as well, for they felt sure they would settle their business that day. Centeno however was on his guard and saw the danger he was running. He therefore took precautions, and a league before reaching the ravine, he called his leaders together.

"Gentlemen," he said, "You can see the danger we are in, for while we are climbing the slope facing up on the other side of the stream, the enemy will be at our backs, and shoot us down from cover without being able to miss. Six of you, with the best horses, must get behind this hill to the right of the road, and lie there quietly unseen. When Carvajal and his vanguard have passed the hill, you must attack his rear and lance all the Negroes or Indians or Spaniards you can, and the horses and beasts of burden. Spare nothing and make all the noise you can, so that the alarm reaches Carvajal's ears and he goes back to the rescue, leaving us to pass freely. Otherwise we shall all perish." He named the six who were to stay in order to avoid discussion; for all wanted to stay, and there were fifteen or sixteen in the council.

With this precaution taken Centeno went on his way, pressing his party forward as fast as he could. The six horsemen rode round the hill, and when Carvajal and his vanguard—which contained all the able fighting men, since he suspected no attack from the rear—had passed, they fell on the rearguard and furiously lanced Indians, Negroes, and Spaniards who were with the train. They killed the horses and beasts they found, and so obliged the enemy to sound the alarm for help. Carvajal, hearing this quite unexpected sound, halted, but hesitated to turn back suspecting that it was a false alarm. He realized that if it were and he turned back, he would lose the opportunity that lay within his grasp.

But the six horsemen did their duty so well that Carvajal's men no longer sounded the alarm, but begged and cried for help. They brought down and killed a mule carrying two hundredweight barrels of gunpowder, and set fire to it, so that it gave a roar like thunder which reverberated through the hills and valleys. This assured Carvajal that the alarm was not a false one, but real and dangerous. He sent his men back to help their companions who were in such dire need. The six horsemen, seeing the soldiers approach, turned tail and went back the way they had come, and by byways and cuts shown them by the Indians, they finally rejoined Centeno six or seven days later. Carvajal spent the rest of the day and the following night on the spot after helping his followers —he could not pursue the enemy because the damage done by the six horsemen was so great. They had lanced everything before them, as they had time and were unopposed; and in this way they allowed Centeno to escape from the trap unharmed. Carvajal was furiously chagrined and affronted that a captain he regarded as a raw recruit should have practiced such a skilful stratagem on him, so successfully that he had escaped from obvious danger and caused great loss to his enemy. Carvajal was in such dudgeon that he did not speak a word all day except to take what steps were necessary, and refused to eat in the evening, saying that he was fed up for that day and plenty more by the trick he had had played on him. Late at night, when his anger and discomfiture had somewhat passed, he told his followers: "Gentlemen, in the course of my soldiering in Italy, for more than forty years, I have seen retreats by the king of France, the Grand Captain, Antonio de Leiva, Count Pedro Navarro, Marcantonio Colonna, and Fabrizio Colonna and other famous captains of my day, Spanish and Italian alike, and I've never seen any of them retreat so gallantly as this boy today." These were Carvajal's very words unaltered, and I had them from one who heard him utter them.

Early next morning, he pursued the enemy with more haste and heat than hitherto, daily gaining men, horses, and baggage that could not go on. After a chase of more than two hundred leagues along royal highways and throughout hills and valleys, Centeno was left with only eighty men. These were so weary and reduced that he decided to go down to the coast at Arequipa and escape by sea, as he could not by land. He sent one of his captains called Ribadeneyra with instructions that if he could find a ship on the coast he was to buy it or seize it and bring it in to Arequipa where they would embark and escape. Ribadeneyra duly found a ship bound for Chile: he and his companions attacked it silently on a raft and easily won it, finding it well manned with sailors. They then sailed toward Arequipa to find Centeno. But Centeno was so harried by Carvajal that he reached the port before the ship; and realizing that the enemy was close behind and that they had nowhere to go, he decided to tell his men to disperse, saying that as Ribadeneyra had not appeared, and there were no ships in which to flee, they had better divide into bands of five or six or go singly in various directions, so that the enemy might follow some but not all; he would hide as best he could. So he bade his men farewell, and entered a ravine between crags and mountains with a companion called Luis de Ribera and a servant. They found a cave and spent nearly eight months hidden in it, until President La Gasca entered Peru. All this time they were fed by the *curaca* of an allocation of Miguel Cornejo's, on whose land they chanced to be. We shall leave them there till their due time.

During all the foregoing episodes from the time when he raised His Majesty's standard, Diego Centeno was accompanied by Gonzalo Silvestre, a native of Herrera de Alcántara, of whom we have spoken at length in our history of Florida. Carvajal reached Arequipa in pursuit of Centeno, and there lost track of him, though hé knew that he and his companions had scattered in various directions. He went to the port of Arequipa, and next day at daybreak Ribadeneyra appeared in his ship.

Carvajal knew who he was from one of those he had arrested, and knowing his purpose and his password, tried to seize the ship. But Ribadeneyra was very cautious, and on asking to speak with one or other of his friends and finding that no one came out to speak to him, he raised his sails and left the port. Carvajal heard that Lope de Mendoza was fleeing inland with seven or eight comrades, and sent one of his captains with twenty arquebusiers who followed them for nearly a hundred leagues, until he drove them into the jurisdiction of Captain Diego de Rojas, whence he returned to tell Carvajal what had happened. Seeing that Centeno was lost and none of his men appeared, Carvajal went to La Plata to collect money from Gonzalo Pizarro's estate and from those who had opposed him.

To return to Lope de Mendoza, he entered the jurisdiction of Diego de Rojas, who was one of the captains on whom Governor Vaca de Castro had bestowed new conquests, after putting down the disturbances that followed the punishment and death of Don Diego de Almagro the younger. We shall say what befell them in the next chapter.

CHAPTER XXXVII

The affairs of Lope de Mendoza; the kinds of
poison used by the Indians for their arrows;
how Lope de Mendoza
returned to Peru.

LOPE DE MENDOZA's purpose was to see if he and his companions could hide in the wild forests of the Antis that cover all the east of Peru until the king were proclaimed again. With this intention, and little expecting to find Spaniards in those parts, he came upon Gabriel Bermúdez, one of those who had accompanied Diego de Rojas there. He and his companions had performed great deeds against the Indians on this conquest, and suffered incredible privations and hunger; but when they reached the River Plate and came to the fort built there by Sebastian Cabot, they fell into discord among one another, on the death of their captain general Diego de Rojas, about who was to command their brave little army. Those who wanted to rule were so full of ambition that many were killed and the rest divided into various groups. As if they had no enemies to use their weapons on, they turned them against one another.

Diego de Rojas' death was produced by an arrow wound treated by the Indians with an extremely poisonous herb which takes effect after three days and finishes off the victim in another week: he dies raging, biting his hands, and beating his head against the wall, and thus hastening his own end. The Spaniards wanted to find the antidote, which the Indians would not reveal under threats or for promises; so they wounded an Indian prisoner in the thigh and let him go. He sought two kinds of wild herbs, crushed them separately, and drank the sap of one and rubbed the other on his wounds, which he first opened with a knife to remove the barbs of the arrow. These are so skilfully made and arranged that when the arrow is withdrawn the barbs remain behind, and they have to be removed for the antidote to work. The Indian did all this and recovered. With this remedy many Spaniards were saved from poisoned arrows, though some died because they could not extract the barbs. In the Windward Islands and all the country called Brazil, and Santa Marta and New Granada and other places where there are savage Indians, a different kind of poison was used (it is not known what the one mentioned above was). These peoples would take the leg of an Indian they had killed, hang it in the air and sun and stick all the barbs they could into the limb: after so many days they were taken out and dried in the air away from the sun without being wiped, and later fastened to the arrows. The poison was most cruel, very difficult to cure, and worse to heal; in due course I shall tell an incident I myself witnessed in proof of this. With the arrival of the Spaniards and their wars with the Indians, the latter changed the type of poison, and instead of using Indian flesh as hitherto they used that of such Spaniards as they could catch or kill. If they caught a ruddy Spaniard with what is called saffron hair, they used him for poison rather than any other, thinking that such a strange fiery color would be more deadly than the rest. It is said that they had heard the saying current among Spaniards to the effect that redheaded men were good for making red arsenic.

To return to this expedition, when the Spaniards saw that their disputes had gone so far that there was no possibility of peace or friendship, part of them decided to leave that country and return to Peru, since they were so divided that they could do nothing against the Indians, who were warlike and brave. The reference to the poison, as well as all the events of the expedition and the despatches of the Spaniards, is given fully in Fernández's history, which has some strange episodes: to shorten my account, I refer to his. The Spaniards were moved to return to Peru (as well as by their own discord) by the news of the disturbances there brought them by an Indian, though they did not know any details beyond the fact that there was war between the Spaniards. So they sent Gabriel Bermúdez toward the Peruvian border to find out what was happening, so that they could join whichever side they preferred. While on this mission he fell in with Lope de Mendoza, who told him all that had occurred in Peru since Diego de Rojas had left. Gabriel Bermúdez's companions collected and by common consent sent messengers to Nicolás Heredia, the leader of the opposite faction, who came in with his companions. Mendoza reconciled them and both parties agreed to make him their captain general and swore to obey and follow him. They were 150 men in all, almost all mounted, and soldiers of courage who were capable of standing up to any privation, want, or hunger, as could be expected of explorers who had been away three years on end and had discovered nearly six hundred leagues of land, without a day's rest, and nothing but incredible ordeals, worse than any writer can describe.

When Mendoza found he had such stalwarts with him, he left the forests to try if he could resist Carvajal and see if anyone else had proclaimed the king, so that he could join with him. He reached the village and province called Pucuna, where he rested some days to refresh his men and horses, who were fatigued by their hunger and trials. Francisco de Carvajal, who never neglected any of the duties devolving on a good commander, heard of Mendoza's coming and that the expeditionaries (such was the name given to these soldiers) were with him and that they had been at odds with one another. He decided to seek them out before they reached agreement, supposing he would defeat them more easily while they were still disunited. Mendoza knew of his coming and fortified himself in the village with trenches and loopholes for defence. But when Carvajal came near he changed his plan; he was afraid Carvajal would surround him and reduce him by hunger, as he had no supplies. He also realized that as his men were nearly all cavalry they were superior to the rest and would fight better in the open field than behind defences. He also thought Carvajal's men would more easily desert to him in the open and he could round them up better than if there were a wall between them: the idea that Carvajal's men were dissatisfied and would flee if they could had often deluded Diego Centeno, and it now did the same with Lope de Mendoza. He came out to receive Carvajal, who had his men drawn up to fight him in the village. On seeing his enemy leave the fort, he made a great show of attacking and giving battle; but his aim was only to trick him into leaving the fort, and he made great fun of them when he saw them come outside. It was indeed a very amateurish manoeuver, and to prove it on them Carvajal marched straight upon them, and Mendoza followed suit. But when they were within arquebus shot Carvajal veered to one side and marched into the village in good order without resistance. Since none of his men went over to Mendoza, as the latter had hoped, there was no opposing him, for he had double the number of men and plenty of experienced shots. They had thus changed places, and Carvajal was in the fort and Mendoza in the open. Carvajal's men sacked the village, in which his rivals had left all their property, and won their clothing and 50,000 pesos in silver bars which Lope de Mendoza had had brought out on leaving the forests: he and Centeno had hidden them during their flight from Carvajal, and he intended to use them to pay the expeditionaries, but they were so generous that few, or rather practically none of them would take anything, thinking that later they would lay claim to great rewards for serving the king at their own expense and risk without pay or subsidy—and they did subsequently allege this in their petitions. It was in fact a common custom, not only among the expeditionaries but among all the noble soldiers of Peru, not to receive pay or assistance, and to spurn what they were offered; for it was a point of honor with them not to serve for present interest, but for future reward. If anyone received money because he was in great need, it was not regarded as payment, but as a loan, with the obligation to return it to His Majesty's treasury when he had anything of his own. This was done with great regularity, for they staked their honor on keeping their words as soldiers.

CHAPTER XXXVIII

The stratagems of Carvajal, whereby he defeats and kills Lope de Mendoza, and goes to Los Charcas.

WHILE Carvajal's men were sacking the village, Lope Mendoza seems to have lost an opportunity by not attacking, for sacking has often led to the defeat of the victors and victory of the vanquished. But they feared Carvajal would not be so careless that they could prevail; and in fact he realized that his men were scattering and called them back and spent the night drawn up in formation. In order to trick the enemy so that he should not slip away by night, he wrote a false letter in the name of one of his followers and gave it to a Spanish-speaking Indian telling him what to say and do in order to be believed. The letter urged them to attack Carvajal that night from two sides, for there were a great many malcontents who would desert and had not done so the day before so as not to be killed by the arquebusses while crossing over.

Carvajal used this device so as to turn to account his opponents' general belief that his people were always misused and dissatisfied, and would run away if they could. When Lope de Mendoza saw the letter, although he did not know whom it was from, as it was unsigned, he believed it, since it fitted in with his preconceived idea. He prepared his men, and at midnight they attacked on two sides as they had been recommended, though without any effect; for there was strong opposition and no one deserted. This discouraged him, on seeing himself deceived; and he retired with the loss of seven or eight men killed and others wounded by the arquebus fire. He learnt from the Indians that Carvajal had left all the property and baggage six or seven leagues away, and thought he would avenge himself and pay Carvajal back in his own coin, by stripping him as he himself had been stripped. He went straight away to the spot and won all Carvajal's baggage, to the great joy of all of them, since they found much gold, arms, and powder, as well as clothing.

All three historians say that Carvajal was seriously wounded in the fray that night by an arquebus shot that passed through his thigh, and that he was attended in secret so that no one should know he was hit, and went about all night giving orders. They say that he was wounded by one of his own men. But on their own showing the wound could not have been of any significance, since he kept going all that night and pursued the enemy next day, to find them asleep and unheeding the following night, and defeat and disband them, and capture many of them; those he could not catch scattered in many directions under cover of night, Lope de Mendoza among them. When day dawned and Carvajal saw that Mendoza had gone, he trailed him, discovering on the way that his opponents had sacked his companions' and his possessions.

Then he turned to his followers and said: "Master Lope de Mendoza has misjudged by taking the dagger of his own death with him." He implied that he and his men must do their utmost and either recover their baggage or die in the attempt. So he hastened after Lope de Mendoza, who, having gone eight or nine leagues, and thinking that Carvajal would be too busy to follow that day or the next, crossed a river and stopped on the further bank, where they slept, being overcome with sleep after their night marches. Some were sleeping and others eating at leisure when Carvajal appeared over a hill leading down to the river. Mendoza's men lost their heads at this sudden onset, supposing Carvajal's whole force was upon them, and fled in all directions, without waiting for their enemy, who numbered only sixty, for Carvajal had picked those with the best horses, thinking that this would be enough to pursue the fugitives. Many of Mendoza's men were captured, and Carvajal lingered there collecting the loot that had been taken from him. He found part of the stolen gold in the hands of two or three groups of soldiers who were gambling; and this brought forth some characteristic utterances which Fernández gives in full. He spent the whole day there; and Lope de Mendoza meanwhile had time to escape with five or six followers. The rest scattered without knowing where they were going, as long as they got away from the enemy.

When Carvajal had recovered his possessions, though not all that had been lost, he pursued the fugitives, and happened to follow the trail of Lope de Mendoza, not because he knew whose it was, but because his was the largest group. He made great speed, and although they had five or six hours' start, he overtook Mendoza in a small Indian village before dawn on the second night. Within the space of thirty hours since Carvajal's last attack, he had come twenty-two leagues; and thinking that Carvajal had too many men to move so fast, he had stopped there. He was also compelled to do so by the weariness and want of sleep from which he and his friends were suffering after travelling so long by day and night without eating or resting or feeding the horses. So they were all cut to pieces and put to sleep as corpses.

Carvajal reached the village with eight men, having distanced the rest so as to catch Mendoza that night wherever he was and give him no chance to rest or stop, but slay him as he fled. The Indians told him which house Mendoza and his friends were in and how many there were of them. This gave him greater confidence, and holding the two doors of the house, which was a large hall belonging to the chief, he shouted the names of his various captains, not because they were with him, but to frighten the enemy and deceive them into thinking he had more men than he actually had, so that they would not resist. He said: "Captain so-and-so, you and you guard this door; and you, so-and-so; and you the other. And you, Master ———, bring fire and burn this hut down."

With this shouting he terrified the occupants and went into the house with three men, and disarmed them and bound them all, except Lope de Mendoza, whose office of captain general he respected. They were then brought out and saw how few men he had. Such was the capture of Lope de Mendoza, though the historians give it only in brief and do not speak in detail of Carvajal's stratagems. He had Mendoza strangled and beheaded, and also Heredia and three others; the rest he pardoned. He also spared the other expeditionaries he found, restoring their arms and horses, and giving a subsidy in money to them, and mounts to those who had none, trying to make friends of them and induce them to take his side. He similarly pardoned Luis Pardomo and Alonso Camargo, who fled with Lope de Mendoza when they left Centeno, and told him where Centeno had buried more than 50,000 silver pesos.

After this victory, Carvajal found there was no more opposition in the land, and went to Charcas to spend a few days at La Plata and collect what he could from the mines of Potosí, which were discovered that year, and from the Indians belonging to the dead *vecinos* and those who had fled. He took their allocations in the name of Gonzalo Pizarro for the expenses of the war. The day he entered La Plata those in the town came out to receive him and pacify him. One was a certain Alonso Ramírez whom Centeno had made ordinary alcalde. He had his rod in his hand. Carvajal said: "Master Ramírez, take the cross off your rod and make a dart of it and throw it at a dog; and if you don't hit it in the arse, I swear I'll hang you." This was to show the man what a clumsy fool he had been to come out to receive him holding a rod neither Carvajal nor any other Pizarrist had given him, but which he had received from an enemy. Ramírez set it down, realizing too late what should have occurred to him before.

CHAPTER XXXIX

*Carvajal sends Lope de Mendoza's head to Arequipa;
a woman's saying; a revolt against Carvajal
and his punishment of it.*

T HE DAY after Carvajal entered the city of La Plata, he sent Mendoza's
head to Arequipa by a certain Dionisio de Bobadilla, later Gonzalo
Pizarro's sergeant major, whom I knew. It was to be placed on the gibbet
in the town as a reminder and punishment of its having been the scene of
Mendoza's and Centeno's rising. Bobadilla took it; and we may as well
tell what happened between him and an honest woman, for it is too noteworthy to be overlooked. A very virtuous and charitable woman called
Juana de Leitão lived in Arequipa; she had been servant to Doña Catarina
Leitão, a noblewoman of the Portuguese family of that name, who had
married Francisco de Carvajal, though some maliciously say she was his
mistress. In fact she was his wife and much esteemed by him and all the
gentlemen of Peru, as she deserved to be for her qualities and noble birth.
This lady reared Juana de Leitão, who therefore took her name; and she
married her to an honest man called Francisco Vosso. She was such an
excellent woman that Carvajal respected her like a daughter.

During Gonzalo's rebellion she always favored the royalists, pleading
with her master Carvajal for some, helping others from her purse, and
even hiding them in her own house, so that when Pizarro first entered
Lima and there were all the arrests and executions we have mentioned,
Juana de Leitão had three *vecinos* hidden in her house. Francisco de
Carvajal, from whom nothing was hidden, went to her and said privately:
"What about the three men you are hiding?"

She denied it, but Carvajal retorted that she had and named one of
them, either on suspicion or because he knew. This confounded her, and
seeing that she could not deny it, she manfully said: "They're inside, in
such and such a room: I'll bring them down to you with a knife to cut
their throats with and drink their blood and eat their flesh, if that will
sate you. Gorge yourself, gorge yourself on human blood, for which
you're so thirsty!" So she began to go to fetch the fugitives.

But Carvajal, seeing this, said: "Leave them alone, and leave me too, and to the devil with you!" And he went, leaving Juana victorious. I heard this from one of Carvajal's greatest enemies, a very truthful man called Gonzalo Silvestre, whom I have already mentioned.

Soon after Juana de Leitão went, as we have said, to live at Arequipa, where Dionisio de Bobadilla brought the heads of Mendoza, Heredia, and three or four more. But before visiting Pedro de Fuentes, Pizarro's deputy in the city, he called on Juana, because he knew it would please his master Carvajal if he did so. She received him very politely, and after asking about his health and Carvajal's, and knowing that he had brought the heads to exhibit on the gallows, she said: "Master Dionisio de Bobadilla, I beg you to give me Mendoza's head and I'll bury it as best I can, though it won't be as well as he deserves; for he was a great gentleman and a true servant of the king." Bobadilla excused himself, saying that he could not, for he well knew his master's character; and if he did so, he would be quartered for it. She replied: "Give me it, for God's sake, and I'll give you two hundred pesos for you to pay one of your men. The head is no good to you on the gibbet. It's quite enough to have cut it off, without dragging it round on the ground." Bobadilla again excused himself three or four times with the same words, as she insistently repeated her request. At length seeing that neither prayers nor promises availed, she was almost in a temper and cried: "All right, set it up then, and much good may it do you. The two hundred pesos I offered you for his head I'll spend in masses for his soul; and as to you, I tell you it won't be long before the head's taken down and properly buried and yours is hanging in its place."

And her saying came true to the letter, as our history will show. Bobadilla came out bursting with laughter, but struck by the conversation. He took the heads to Pedro de Fuentes, and as the Indians could not unwrap them from the blankets they were in, he went and uncovered them more skilfully. Some Spaniards who were present said the heads stank, and Bobadilla said: "No, gentlemen, no, when we cut off the heads of our enemies they smell, not stink." This he said since he prided himself on being an apt pupil of Carvajal, who said such things.

When Commander Carvajal had defeated Centeno and killed Mendoza, Heredia, and others, and collected and presented the soldiers of the River Plate expedition with arms, horses, and money, he established his quarters at La Plata, to collect all the silver he could to send to Gonzalo. The expeditionaries were now ashamed and annoyed on realizing how easily Carvajal had defeated and dispersed them and killed their chief captain, Heredia, and his companions. So they planned to kill Carvajal, out of revenge rather than greed, as some maintain, though they were so lacking in greed that shortly before they had refused payment from Lope de Mendoza, when he offered it them, and generously. The leading conspirators were Luis Pardomo, Alonso Camargo, and others who had earlier been pardoned by Carvajal, as we have said. There were thirty others, less well known. The plot was to kill him on a certain day, and they swore on a crucifix that they would all carefully keep the secret. But Carvajal always watched his own safety with great care, and had also intimate friends who knew about the plot. He arrested some of the conspirators, and had them quartered in a great rage, uttering the words that Fernández here sets down: "Master Balmaceda and many other expeditionaries from La Plata wanted to kill me after I had treated them well, and honored them more than those who serve the governor Gonzalo Pizarro," etc.

After executing six or seven of the leaders, he pardoned the rest, so as not to kill so many. To secure himself from them, for he thought they were very embittered, he sent them off by various routes as a sort of banishment to Gonzalo Pizarro, whom he had just informed of all the above events in a long written report, showing that all their enemies were defeated and dispersed. In return Carvajal received from Pizarro news of the battle of Quito, the death of the viceroy and his subsequent measures. Pizarro announced his intention of going to Lima and Carvajal was instructed to do the same, so that they might meet and take whatever steps seemed necessary for the future.

CHAPTER XL

What Carvajal wrote and said to Gonzalo on the question of his becoming king of Peru; the persuasions of others on this matter.

A T THIS news Carvajal gave much thought to Pizarro's affairs, considering how he might perpetuate his rule over the empire, not only as governor in the emperor's name, but as its absolute master, since he and his brothers had won it. He wrote him a long letter urging him to take the title of king, which Fernández mentions (ch. xil). But when he met Gonzalo in Lima, he said (though this is out of its proper place):

"Sir, when a viceroy is killed in a pitched battle and his head is cut off and placed on a gibbet, and the battle was against the royal standard, and there were as many deaths and as much looting as there have been since, there's no pardon to be hoped for and no compromise to be made, even though Your Lordship makes ample excuses and proves himself more innocent than a suckling or babe. Nor can you trust their words or promises, whatever assurances they give, unless you declare yourself king; and take the government yourself without waiting for another to give it you, and put a crown on your head; and allocate whatever land is unoccupied among your friends and supporters; and as what the king gives is temporary for two lives, you give it as a perpetual title and make dukes and marquises and counts, such as there are in all the countries of the world, so that they will defend Your Lordship in order to defend their own estates.

"Set up military orders with the same names and titles as those in Spain and other saints as patrons and such insignia as you think fit. Give the knights of the orders revenues and pensions to keep themselves and live at ease, as military knights do everywhere. With all this I have said in brief Your Lordship will attract to your service all the Spanish chivalry and nobility in this empire, fully rewarding all those who conquered it and who have served Your Lordship, which is not now the case. And to attract the Indians and make them so devoted that they will die for Your Lordship as they would for their Inca kings, take one of their princesses, whichever is closest to the royal line, to wife, and send ambassadors to the forests where the heir to the Incas is and bid him to come forth and recover his lost majesty and state, asking him to offer you as your wife any daughter or sister he may have. You know how much this prince will esteem kinship and friendship with you, and you will gain the universal love of all the Indians by restoring their Inca and at the same time make them genuinely willing to do whatever their king orders them on your behalf, such as bringing supplies, abandoning the villages, holding the roads against your enemies—in short all the Indians will be on your side, and if they do not help your enemies with supplies and porters, no one can prevail against you in Peru. Their prince will be satisfied with the title of king and the fact that his vassals obey him as they used to do; and he will govern his Indians in peace as they did in the past, while Your Lordship and your officials and captains govern the Spaniards and have charge of military affairs, requiring the Inca to tell the Indians to do whatever you command. Thus you will be sure that the Indians do not deceive you or act as double spies, as they now do, serving first one side and then the other.

"In addition, Your Lordship will receive from the Inca not only all the gold and silver the Indians produce in this empire, for they do not regard it as treasure or wealth, but also all the treasure of the kings their ancestors which they have hidden, as is well known. All this will be given and delivered to Your Lordship both on account of your relationship with the Inca and because of his restoration to his former majesty. With all the gold and silver they were reputed to have Your Lordship can buy the whole world, if you want to be master of it. And pay no attention if they say you are a traitor to the king of Spain: you are not, for as the saying goes, no king is a traitor. This land belonged to the Incas, its natural lords, and if it is not restored to them, you have more right to it than the king of Castile, for you won it at your expense and risk, together with your brothers. Now, by restoring it to the Inca, you are simply doing what you should by natural law; and in seeking to govern it yourself as its conqueror and not as the vassal and subject of another, you are doing what you owe to your reputation, for anyone who can become king by the strength of his arm should not remain a serf for lack of spirit. It all depends on the first step and the first declaration. I beg Your Lordship carefully to consider the import of what I have said about ruling this empire in perpetuity, so that all those who live and shall live here may follow you. Finally I urge you whatever may happen to crown yourself and call yourself king, for no other name befits one who has won an empire by his strength and courage. Die a king. I repeat many times, die a king and not a vassal, for whoever lets a wrong be put on him deserves worse."

I have omitted some even more improper remarks in Carvajal's discourse so as not to offend the ears of faithful and loyal subjects, or please the malicious. Gonzalo Pizarro willingly heard what his commander had to say, and seeing that he had considered what should be done in the circumstances to such good effect and how well he had understood the situation, he thenceforward called him father, and regarded him as such for having sought his well being and the continuance of his authority. Pedro de Puelles, Licentiate Cepeda, Hernando Bachicao, and his most intimate friends, who were numerous, all said the same, as López de Gómara says (ch. clxxiii):

Francisco de Carvajal and Pedro de Puelles wrote to Pizarro urging him to call himself king, which he was, and not to consider sending procurators to the emperor, but to collect plenty of horses, breastplates, cannon, and arquebusses: these were the real procurators. And let him apply the royal fifth and the royal towns and revenues to himself, and the dues that Cobos unworthily levied. Some said they would not let the king have the land unless he gave them permanent allocations; others that they would make whoever they wanted king, and that was how Pelayo and Garci Jiménez had been made kings in Spain; others that they would call upon the Turks if Pizarro were not given the governorship of Peru and his brother Hernando released. All in fine said that the land was theirs and they could share it up, since they had won it at their own expense and spilt their own blood in the conquest.

So López de Gómara, who ends his chapter here. Diego Fernández (Book II, ch. xiii) says of all this:

This done he continued his journey to Lima, and his followers continually discussed the future, some saying that His Majesty would forget the past and would not fail to confirm Pizarro as governor. Others spoke more openly and shamelessly, saying that even if His Majesty wanted to do otherwise, it should not be allowed. Cepeda (who applauded and flattered Pizarro in everything) went even further, and Hernando Bachicao and others agreed with him, saying that he had a just and legal title to the kingdom of Peru, and quoting examples of kingdoms and provinces which had rebelled after their original foundation, and in course of time the title had become good and the rebels had remained lords and kings. They discussed the dispute about the kingdom of Navarre, and the manner in which kings were anointed, and similar matters, always seeking to incline Gonzalo Pizarro to go beyond the governorship, and affirming that never had a man who had sought to become king done so with such rights over the land governed as Pizarro had over Peru. Gonzalo heard all this willingly, for all men in general desire to rule and have power, and are driven by ambition. This was especially so as Gonzalo Pizarro was rather dull of understanding, could not even read, and was a man who rarely considered obstacles. And as Licentiate Cepeda was regarded as a man of learning and an expert of excellent judgment, everyone approved what he said and no one contradicted him. Whenever there was leisure and conversation, this was the only topic discussed.

So Fernández. We should explain López de Gómara's allusion to the tribute Cobos unworthily levied: His Imperial Majesty had granted his secretary Francisco de los Cobos 1½ per cent of all the gold and silver taken to be assayed at the royal smeltery and treasure house, but this was on condition he supplied at his own expense smelters and coal to melt the ore, and assayers to assay the silver and gold. When the secretary had met these obligations, he was the loser rather than the gainer; but as each of those who went to pay the fifth wanted to know how much he had and how much he had to pay for the fifth in taxes and how much he would be left with, they used to produce the gold and silver already smelted and purified at their own expense, so that Secretary Cobos did not carry out any of his obligations. For this reason López de Gómara says he unworthily collected his levy, meaning that he did not fulfil his part of the bargain.

CHAPTER XLI

The respect of Gonzalo Pizarro for the royal service; he leaves Quito and goes to Trujillo and Lima; the celebrations on his arrival.

G ONZALO wished to avoid a decision about assuming the title of king, for his natural respect for his prince was stronger than the pleas of his friends, and he never lost hope that His Imperial Majesty would grant him the confirmation of his governorship of Peru, on the grounds that he and his brothers had won it, and in return for his personal services, realizing that he knew all those who had served His Majesty in Peru and was in the best position to reward them. All these things were arguments in favor of the award of the governorship, in addition to the fact that the emperor had issued a grant to the marquis his brother by which he could appoint his successor as governor and he had in fact appointed Gonzalo. In the late conflict with the viceroy it was thought that he had sufficient justification because of the viceroy's severity in applying the ordinances without heeding the kingdom or its procurators, wherefore the whole of Peru had elected Pizarro its procurator general. In any case the judges, not Pizarro, had arrested the viceroy and sent him to Spain. In the light of all this, Pizarro thought that he not only deserved a pardon for the past, but the award of the governorship anew; for it is a natural habit among men of war to esteem their own deeds, even if they are guilty ones. As Pizarro had not dared to venture on an undertaking so much to his advantage, as his friends maintained, the common people attributed it to lack of sense, and not to excess of respect toward the king. They regarded him as mean spirited and mocked his lack of judgment. The historians have respected this, because they were given a distorted version, and do not say what really happened. For it was the common opinion of those nearest to Gonzalo Pizarro who knew him best that he was a man of good judgment, who never cavilled or deceived or made false promises or spoke evasively. He was simple, sincere, noble, and good, and trusted in his friends, who destroyed him, as the historians themselves say. How should we blame those who have written thus, for those who gave them their information tried to press their own interests by flattery. Fernández was even ordered to write, as he says in his dedication in these words:

But when I wished to proceed, my pen shrank back, and I refused the task on ground of certain difficulties that arose. Thus in doubt, I then came to His Majesty's court, where I displayed the first history I had written (which is now the second in order) to your Royal Council of the Indies. They thought the discourse truthful and considered that it would be useful and even necessary for me to finish the history I had begun, and gave orders to that effect, holding out the hope of recompense and reward, which gave me new courage to carry out the instructions of this high court, casting aside the fears and doubts I had had about finishing the undertaking I had begun,

etc. This being so, is it surprising that they should speak of their enemies, and especially the leaders, according to the reports given them by interested parties? On the contrary, they behaved soberly by modern standards.

Gonzalo Pizarro resolved to leave Quito for Lima and reside there, as it was in the middle of the empire and he could move north or south as the affairs of peace or war required. He left Pedro de Puelles as his lieutenant and captain general in Quito, with 300 soldiers. He had great confidence in Puelles who had served him so loyally and rallied to him when he would otherwise have been lost. On reaching San Miguel, he heard that there were many Indians in the district on a war footing, and sent Captain Mercadillo with 130 men to conquer them. He founded the city now called Loja. He sent Captain Porcel with 60 men to his former conquest of Pacamuru, and ordered Licentiate Carvajal to go by sea with the party of soldiers Palomino had brought from Nicaragua, executing his instructions in each of the ports up the coast. Carvajal carried this out fully and went as far as Trujillo, while Gonzalo reached the same place by land; on joining forces they made arrangements for the journey to Lima. Gonzalo left Trujillo with 200 picked soldiers, including Licentiate

Carvajal, Juan de Acosta, Juan de la Torre, Licentiate Cepeda, Hernando Bachicao, Diego Guillén, and other noble people. He advanced on Lima.

On his arrival his friends differed about the manner of his entry. Some said it should be under a canopy as a king, for such he was and would soon be crowned: those who said this were of course those who had urged him to call himself king. Others spoke more moderately, and said that he ought to make a new gate and street in one of the quarters of the city in memory of his entry, as they did in Rome when the emperors entered in triumph after their great victories. Both parties were obstinate in their views and tried to get their own way, but Gonzalo refused to accept either of them but agreed to what Licentiate Carvajal might decide. He then arranged for Gonzalo to enter on horseback with his captains walking in front of him and their horses led before them, the infantry following behind drawn up in ranks. The cavalry was also to enter on foot, along with the infantry, since it seemed that if the captains went on foot the men should not ride. Pizarro rode after his comrades on a splendid horse. He was flanked by four bishops: on his right the archbishop of Lima with the bishop of Quito by his side, on his left the bishop of Cuzco and the bishop of Bogotá, who had come to Peru to be consecrated by the other three prelates. After them came another band of soldiers on foot, forming as it were a rearguard for Pizarro, though none of them carried arms such as pikes or arquebusses or wore armor, so as to avoid appearing as if they were going to war. They had only swords and daggers, as in time of peace. Behind these came Lorenzo de Aldana, as Pizarro's deputy, with the city council, the *vecinos,* and the other citizens, who had come out to receive the governor and congratulated him with great acclamations and thanksgivings by each and all, in return for what he had done in saving their property and for having undergone such privations and risking his life for them all. So Gonzalo made his entry, and went to the cathedral to worship the Blessed Sacrament. There was much music in the streets, with singing, trumpets, and excellent minstrels he had: the bells of the cathedral and the convents rang out joyfully through the city. After adoring the host Gonzalo went to his house, which had belonged to the marquis, his brother. The historians say that he now lived with much greater pomp and pride than before. One says he had a guard of eighty halberdiers and that no one now sat in his presence; another says he gave his hand to be kissed by everyone. This is said partly as a form of flattery by slandering an enemy, and partly to shock the reader. Most of what they say about this gentleman and his officials is in the same slanderous strain; but I can swear as a Christian that I am telling the truth when I say that I never saw a halberdier in his guard or heard tell that he had one. I have already mentioned that when the marquis entered Peru he had an edict from His Majesty permitting him to raise twenty-four halberdiers as his bodyguard, but that this impossible as no one, except two men I knew, wanted to be a halberdier, which was regarded as a low sort of employment. I do not know how it was possible to find eighty of them later when people were prouder and more presumptuous. Our historians themselves have said that the Spaniards in Peru pride themselves on their free-handedness and will not even take pay from the king in time of war. Possibly this was a printing error and the author put halberdiers instead of arquebusiers (as another writer has it), being unaware of the pride of the Peruvian Spaniards and not realizing that a bodyguard could be of arquebusiers and not halberdiers. They also say that he used poison to kill whoever he wished. This is certainly false witness, for no such thought ever entered his head. If anything of the sort had happened, I would have heard about it then or later, as they did; such wickedness would have caused him to be hated by everyone, yet the historians often said he was greatly loved. I hope I may be permitted to say truly without offending anyone what I saw, for my only purpose is always to tell plainly what happened without hatred or flattery, since I have no motive for either.

CHAPTER XLII

*The author says how Gonzalo Pizarro treated his
friends; he tells of the death of Vela Núñez
and the arrival of Francisco de Carvajal in
Lima, and his reception.*

I KNEW Gonzalo Pizarro by sight in Cuzco, where he went after the battle of Huarina and stayed till that of Sacsahuana, almost six months; most of those days I was in his house and saw how he behaved both at home and outside. Everyone honored him as their superior and accompanied him wherever he went on foot or on horseback, and he treated them all, both *vecinos* and soldiers, so kindly and so like a brother that no one complained of him. I never saw anyone kiss his hand, or him give it, even if anyone asked out of courtesy. He took his cap off civilly to ev-

eryone, and never failed to call anyone who merited it "your honor."
As we have said, he called Carvajal "father": I once heard him do so, for
when I was with the governor, who took me about with him as a small
boy, Francisco de Carvajal came to speak to him, and though there was
no one in the room to hear but myself, my presence made him cautious
and he spoke into Gonzalo's ear so that I could not even hear his voice.
Gonzalo Pizarro replied briefly, and said: "Look, father."

I sometimes saw him dine. He always ate in public: a long table was
laid with places for at least a hundred men. He sat at its head and no one
sat for two spaces on either side. Below this all the soldiers who wished
sat down to dine: the captains and *vecinos* never ate with him, but in their
homes. I twice ate at his table because he bade me. Once was the day of
the feast of the Purification of Our Lady: his son Don Fernando, and his
nephew, the marquis' son, Don Francisco, and I ate standing, all three at
the space where there were no seats and he fed us from his own plate. I
saw all this when I was about nine years old, celebrating my birthday on
April 12 following, and can vouch for all this as an eyewitness. The historians must have had informants who were moved by hatred or rancor to
have told them what they wrote. They also say that though he collected all
the royal fifths and revenues, and the tributes of the undistributed Indians and those belonging to men who had opposed him, all of which
came to more than two-thirds of the revenues of Peru, yet he did not pay
his soldiers, and they grew very discontented. But when he was killed,
they do not say that any hidden treasure was found, which clearly reveals
the slanderous intention of the informants. He is also accused of adultery,
and they greatly stress this fault; as indeed it is proper that such wrongs
should be criticized, especially in those who govern and rule.

To return to our history, we should say that while Gonzalo was in
Lima on this occasion, the unfortunate death occurred of the viceroy's
brother, which was caused by Captain Juan de la Torre, who had years
before married an Indian, the daughter of a chief in the province of
Puerto Viejo. The Indians were pleased by their kinship with him, which
they valued more than their treasures, and showed him the tomb of their
ancestors and lords, where there were more than 150,000 ducats in gold
and fine emeralds. When Juan de la Torre found himself so rich, he desired to escape from Gonzalo and come to Spain to enjoy his wealth; but
he thought that he would not be safe because of the crimes he had committed against His Majesty, having been one of those who cut off the
viceroy's beard and wore it as a medal. He therefore tempted Vela Núñez
to flee with him in one of the ships in the port, so that in Spain he and his

relatives would take him under their wing in return for helping Vela Núñez to escape from the rebel leader. But after getting Vela Núñez' agreement, he changed his mind, having heard certain tittle-tattle that was concocted to the effect that His Majesty would confirm Gonzalo as governor: he did not want to lose Gonzalo's favor and friendship if this were so, for he hoped for great rewards. And lest Vela Núñez or anyone else should tell Pizarro about their negotiations, which would have cost him his life, he decided to forestall his possible delator, and therefore told Gonzalo Pizarro, who promptly had Vela Núñez beheaded and another man quartered. It was rumored, however, that he did this at the behest of Licentiate Carvajal rather than from any desire of his own to kill him, for Pizarro always suspected from Vela Núñez' conciliatory nature that he was more likely to be incited than to incite anyone else. Thus this good gentleman perished, through one who was a traitor on all counts.

Francisco de Carvajal, having received some days before news of Gonzalo's journey to Lima and his summons, came from Los Charcas to meet him there. Gonzalo Pizarro came a good way out of the city to greet him, and made him a solemn and triumphal reception as a captain who had won so many victories and dispersed so many enemies. Carvajal left Alonso de Mendoza as captain and deputy for Gonzalo Pizarro in La Plata, and brought with him nearly a million pesos of silver, which he had obtained from the mines of Potosí and the undistributed Indians: Pizarro thus had plenty to spend. Carvajal repeated what he had written in his letter about Pizarro becoming king. We shall leave them and their ministers and friends, particularly the *vecinos* of the cities of the empire, who occupied themselves in pacifying the Indians and Spaniards and spreading the Catholic faith, indoctrinating the natives and increasing their own wealth and that of the merchants and traders, for no one had dared to trade during the late wars and disturbances. Everything then might be taken from its owners, either robbed by pretended rebels or removed allegedly in the king's service, for troubled waters make good fishing, as the saying is. We shall now return to Spain and speak of His Imperial Majesty's steps on hearing of the rebellion in Peru and the arrest of the viceroy.

End of Book Four

BOOK
FIVE *of the*
SECOND
PART

It contains the appointment of Licentiate Pedro de la
Gasca to restore order in Peru; his powers; his arrival in
Tierra Firme; how Gonzalo's fleet is handed over to the
president by his own friends and captains; Licentiate La
Gasca's voyage to Peru; the death of Alonso de Toro;
Diego Centeno's emergence from his cave and how he
took the city of Cuzco; how the president sends Lorenzo
de Aldana with four ships to Lima; how Gonzalo Pizarro is repudiated by his supporters and they go over
to La Gasca; how Gonzalo retires to Arequipa; how
Diego Centeno goes out to meet him; the cruel battle
of Huarina; Pizarro's victory; his going to Cuzco; President La Gasca's doings, and his administration of the
army; the battle of Sacsahuana; the president's victory;
the death of Gonzalo Pizarro and that of his captains.

It contains forty-three chapters.

CHAPTER I

*The selection of Licentiate Pedro de la Gasca
by the emperor Charles V to restore
order in Peru.*

HILE these events were taking place in Peru, Diego Alvarez Cueto and Francisco Maldonado reached Spain, the first representing the viceroy and the second Gonzalo Pizarro. They went to Valladolid where the court was residing and Prince Philip was governing in the absence in Germany of his father the emperor, who was then personally conducting the war he was waging as a Catholic prince to reduce the Lutherans to the service of the Holy Mother Church of Rome. Each of the ambassadors informed His Highness and the Royal Council of the Indies as best he could of events in Peru up to the time of their departure, when the death of the viceroy had still not taken place. The news of the disturbances caused great regret, and the prince ordered the wisest and most experienced advisers in his court to discuss the situation and recommend a solution. These were Cardinal Don Juan Tavera, archbishop of Toledo; Cardinal Don Fray García de Loaisa, archbishop of Seville; Don Fernando de Valdés, president of the royal council and bishop of Sigüenza; the duke of Alva; the count of Osorno; the *comendador mayor* of León, Francisco de los Cobos; and the same of Castile, Don Juan de Zúñiga; Licentiate Ramírez, bishop of Cuenca and president of the royal *audiencia* of Valladolid; the judges of the Royal Council of the Indies, and other persons of authority.

All these and the court in general were astonished that the laws and ordinances framed for the universal welfare of Spaniards and Indians in Peru should have gone so awry as to cause the destruction of both and bring the kingdom to such a pass that the emperor was in danger of losing it. In this mood they held many meetings to decide how to remedy the evident danger of losing the empire, of which they were so conscious. There were divergent opinions. Some proposed that it should be reconquered by force of arms with the despatch of an army led by experienced captains. But the difficulty of raising so many men, arms, horses, munitions, and supplies, and sailing them so far over two seas forced them to drop the idea. Other opinions held by less warlike people and cooler heads were that as the trouble had sprung from the severity of the laws and the harsh character of the viceroy, it would be best to remedy it with antidotes: annulling the former laws, and making new and contrary ones, and sending out a gentle, kindly, prudent, experienced, astute, and resourceful person who would be able to conduct peaceful affairs, or warlike ones if necessary. They selected Licentiate Pedro de la Gasca, a priest of the Council of the Inquisition, who they were satisfied possessed all the qualities they required; and so they wrote to His Majesty asking him to approve their choice. On receiving their report, he ordered what López de Gómara mentions at this point, and as his account is briefer and more compendious than that of the other writers, who run to length without saying more than he does, I shall transcribe exactly with this historian says in his ch. clxxv:

When the emperor heard of the rebellion in Peru over the new ordinances and of the arrest of the viceroy, he disapproved of the boldness and disrespect of the judges who had arrested him and regarded Gonzalo's undertaking as a disservice. But he tempered his wrath in view of the appeal against the ordinances and on hearing from the letters and from Francisco Maldonado (for Tejada had died at sea) that the viceroy was to blame for applying the new laws so rigorously without allowing any appeal. The emperor also regretted that he had given instructions for the execution of the ordinances without leave of appeal, having been informed, or rather misinformed, that he was acting in God's service, for the welfare and security of the Indians, and for the discharge of the royal conscience and the increase of his revenues. He also regretted these new difficulties when he was immersed in the German war against the Lutherans, which filled him with anxiety. But realizing the importance of relieving his vassals and realms in Peru, which were so rich and profitable, he decided to send a calm and discreet negotiator to repair the harm done by Blasco Núñez, who was hot-headed, indiscreet, and disinclined to reason. As a lion had done no good, he resolved to send a lamb; and so he appointed Licentiate Pedro de la Gasca, a cleric on the Council of the Inquisition, a man of much better understanding than his appearance suggested, who had shown his wisdom in the'troubles with the moriscos of Valencia. He gave him the powers he asked, and such letters and blank signatures as he needed. He revoked the ordinances and wrote to Gonzalo Pizarro from Venlo in Germany in February 1546.

So La Gasca left with few people and little display, though with the title of president and with great hopes and a high reputation. He spent little on freight and shipping so as to spare the emperor expense and prove his simplicity to the Peruvians. As royal judges he took with him Licentiates Andrés de Cianca and Rentería, men in whom he had full confidence. He reached Nombre de Dios, but did not reveal his business, answering anyone who asked about his mission according to his opinion of the questioner. He thus shrewdly misled them, and said that if Pizarro would not receive him, he would return to the emperor; for he had not come to make war, which would not be fitting in one of his cloth, but to bring peace by revoking the ordinances and presiding over the *audiencia*. He sent to tell Melchor Verdugo who was bringing men to serve him not to come, but to remain on the watch. He took several other steps and went on to Panama, leaving García de Paredes as captain, with the men Hernando Mejía and Don Pedro de Cabrera, Pizarro's captains, gave him; for it was rumored that the French were plundering the coast and meant to attack the town, but they did not arrive since the governor of Santa Marta slew them at a banquet.

Thus López de Gómara.

CHAPTER II

The powers taken by Licentiate La Gasca; his
arrival at Santa Marta and Nombre de
Dios; his reception and the events
and negotiations that occurred there.

ADDING what this author omits about the powers taken by Licentiate La Gasca—for although he says the emperor gave him what he asked for, he does not say what it was—we should explain that he asked for absolute power in all matters, to the full extent of His Majesty's authority in the Indies, so that he could raise men, arms, horses, money, ships, and supplies anywhere he needed them. He asked for the revocation of the ordinances the viceroy had taken with him, and a pardon for all past criminal offences with a bar against the starting of proceedings either by the crown or by private parties; a guarantee of unmolested possession of property; power to send the viceroy back to Spain if this seemed necessary for the peace of Peru; the right to draw on the royal treasury for any expense needed for reducing Peru, and for its government and the administration of justice; and liberty to award all the vacant allocations of Indians and any that might fall vacant, and to appoint the officials of the whole empire, governors to the parts that had been discovered, and conquerors to what remained to be discovered. For himself he asked to have no salary, but only a royal treasurer to spend whatever he required and give account to the officials of the exchequer afterwards.

Licentiate La Gasca asked for all this, wisely looking to the past and to the future, so that it should not be said that he had been induced to face the enormous difficulties and dangers that lay ahead in the hope of reward, but that he was moved by zeal for the king's service for which he sacrificed rest, peace of mind, and life itself, etc.

And in explanation of López de Gómara's remark that his abilities greatly surpassed his appearance, the fact is that he was very small and oddly built, being as large as a tall man from the waist down and barely a third of a yard from the waist to the shoulder. On horseback he looked even smaller than he was, for he was all legs. His face was very ugly. But what nature had denied him in physical gifts, she had doubled in his mind and spirit, since he had all the qualities this author says and more, and reduced an empire so lost as Peru was to the king's service. I knew him, and in particular watched him all one afternoon when he was on the balcony of my father's house overlooking the square, where many solemn festivities were being held in his honor. The president watched the bull running and jousting from this balcony, and was lodged in the house that belonged to Tomás Vázquez and now belongs to his son Pedro Vázquez, where Gonzalo Pizarro also lodged. This house is to the west, opposite the convent of Our Lady of the Mercies, and although it has a corner in the square with a large window from which Licentiate La Gasca could have watched the festivities, he preferred to see them from my father's balcony which gives onto the middle of the square.

Now we must proceed to tell of his deeds, which, though they were not affairs of the sword and lance, were yet so full of wisdom and prudence that he took all the measures necessary to end the war and secure his object, after which he left the country free and unoppressed. It required great patience and restraint to suffer the labors that presented themselves and put up with the shameless disrespect of the military people. It needed much astuteness, discretion, and skill to penetrate and foil the stratagems of his enemy, who showed great ingenuity. The proof is that he succeeded in a way that would seem incredible to anyone who considers what a state the empire was in when he accepted the task. We shall omit the voyage of the president (as we shall call him from now on) to Nombre de Dios, which Fernández describes, and say only what happened after.

At Santa Marta the president learned of the death of the viceroy from Licentiate Almendárez, then governor of that province and of New Granada. Licentiate La Gasca and all his friends were deeply distressed, thinking that it would be impossible to reduce people who had committed so great a villainy against their king as to kill a viceroy in pitched battle. But the president disguised his emotions so as not to cause greater alarm, and in order to seek a solution spoke very openly to the effect that his powers enabled him to pardon as much and even more, if there could be more to pardon. His powers had been signed after the deed had been committed, so there was no doubt that it was covered by the general pardon. He also realized that the disappearance of the viceroy would contribute greatly toward reducing the empire to His Majesty's service, by removing the general hatred he had inspired by his harshness. In addition it avoided the obstacle that would have been created if it had become necessary to expel the viceroy from Peru in order to pacify it, for he might have resisted, saying that it was an outrage after he had served his king so zealously against rebels who had defied his commands.

These thoughts consoled President La Gasca, and he sailed on toward Nombre de Dios, where he was received with plenty of arms and arquebusses by Hernán Mejía and his soldiers and those of the city who accompanied him with their governor. They all showed La Gasca little respect and no affection. The soldiers in particular uttered many shameless and disagreeable remarks about his stunted physique and ugly features. But the president politically turned a deaf ear to it all, and beamed on them all, as Fernández says. The clergy of the city behaved like ministers of God, coming out in a procession with their crucifix, receiving the president, and escorting him to church singing *Te Deum laudamus*. It gave him great pleasure to see that there were well-conducted people in the country, as well as the others.

Next night, his joy was increased when Hernán Mejía, who was a captain of Gonzalo's and much indebted to him, came to talk in private and offered to bring Gonzalo's other captains and soldiers over to the king's service. He gave a full report on the state of the country and the fleet at Panama and its officers and men, of whom Pedro de Hinojosa was general. The president thanked him and promised to reward him in His Majesty's name, bidding him keep secrecy. So peace and friendship were established between them, and they had nightly discussions in which

Mejía passed on all the news he received from Panama. The president daily won over both soldiers and civilians, some of whom came to live and talk with him. He showed himself unassuming and kindly, and gained the love of all of them, and in his conversation he discussed nothing but how to reduce them to His Majesty's service by peace and love and the offer of grants and benefits at the king's hands with a general pardon for all that had gone before. If they refused to give in peaceably, he would return to Spain and leave them alone: he wanted no quarrels with anyone, and his cloth and profession as a priest would permit him to have none. He often repeated all this in public, hoping that report would spread it all over the empire.

A few days after his entry into Nombre de Dios Melchor Verdugo, whom we have already mentioned, appeared with two ships, proposing to enter the port. Those in the city were greatly troubled, for they hated him and even suspected he was under the president's orders. When the latter realized this, he wrote a letter by a priest who was a close friend of Verdugo, saying that he was not to come to Nombre de Dios under any circumstances, but to go wherever he thought fit and restore the ships to their owners, and also all the loot he had taken.

This was the contents of the letter in brief, but by word of mouth he ordered him to return to Nicaragua and wait there until he was told what had happened, and in what way he could serve His Majesty. But Verdugo came to Spain, thinking he was not safe in America, since he had made himself hated everywhere. His Imperial Majesty awarded him a habit of Santiago. I saw him in the antechamber of Philip II in 1563, when he was vexed and distressed by the charges his rivals and enemies had made against his misdeeds in Peru, Nicaragua, and Nombre de Dios. He feared that these accusations would lose him his habit, and he took this so to heart that his face was pitiful to see. But the king gave him a pardon, and he returned peacefully to Peru.

CHAPTER III

The president sends Hernán Mejía to Panama to pacify Hinojosa, and despatches an ambassador to Gonzalo Pizarro, who, on learning of the president's arrival, sends ambassadors to the emperor.

T HE PRESIDENT hastily prepared to go to Panama, where he hoped by dint of skill and persistence to reduce Pedro de Hinojosa and the other captains to His Majesty's service. He had heard from Mejía about their state of mind, which was like his own, and hoped therefore to succeed. So he went as rapidly as possible to Panama, taking Marshal Alonso de Alvarado with him, whom, as Palencia says (ch. xxxviii), "he had had released from the arrest under which the Council of the Indies had placed him, obtaining permission for him to return to Peru as his companion and helper," etc.

This gentleman had been in the battle of Chupas against Don Diego de Almagro the younger, and came to Spain, where the Council of the Indies arrested him for his part in the quarrels between Pizarros and Almagros. We shall leave him and the president on the road, and tell what Hinojosa did meanwhile in Panama. He was very distressed to know that Mejía had received the president with every appearance of friendship and obedience, and no sign of opposition. He resented this because he did not realize what powers the president had, and because he had not been consulted. He wrote sharply about it; and some friends of Mejía warned him not to come to Panama because Hinojosa was angry with him. Nevertheless, as Zárate says:

having informed the president, it was decided that Mejía should depart at once for Panama to negotiate with Hinojosa, allaying his fears and relying on his close friendship with him and knowledge of his character. So Mejía discussed the case of La Gasca's reception with Hinojosa, explaining that whatever happened little would be lost by it. He satisfied Hinojosa and returned to Nombre de Dios. The president then went to Panama, and discussed his affairs with Hinojosa and all his captains so shrewdly and quietly that he won them all over unbeknown to one another. He then dared to speak to them openly and convinced them of his views and objects. He supplied many soldiers with what they required, regarding the courtesy and consideration with which he treated them as the best way to success; for the soldiers in those parts were most susceptible to good treatment,

etc. Thus Zárate (ch. vii).

When Hinojosa had learnt of the arrival of the president at Nombre de Dios, he had written to Gonzalo Pizarro, and his captains did the same, boastfully asserting that he must be stopped from reaching Peru. But after dealing with the president in Panama, they changed their opinions, and wrote the opposite; for the president had frequently visited them and won their confidence. They therefore permitted him to send one of his companions who had come from Castile with letters for Gonzalo Pizarro, announcing his coming and his intentions and authority. So the president decided to send a gentleman called Pero Hernández Paniagua, a *vecino* and *regidor* of the city of Plasencia, and a very suitable person for the task, for apart from being a noble knight, he had a wife and children and a fine estate in Spain, and Gonzalo would respect him, as he came from his own region and was an ally of his own kinspeople. He departed for Peru in a frigate with a letter from His Majesty to Gonzalo and another from the president, as well as other secret missives for some leading personages, one of which was from the bishop of Lugo to Licentiate Benito de Carvajal, a relative of his, whom he told what he should do to serve the king. We shall leave Paniagua on his voyage and say what Gonzalo did in the meantime.

When Gonzalo's hopes of becoming permanent governor of Peru were at their highest pitch, he received letters from his general Pedro de Hinojosa with news of the president's arrival. This set off a great dispute among his followers, and at a council attended by the captains and *vecinos* they all aired many conflicting opinions. Finally, they reduced them to two—some said that he should publicly or privately have the president killed; others that he should be brought to Peru, for when he came and they had seen his powers it would be easy to get him to concede all they wanted. If this did not succeed they could delay him for a long time by saying that they had to collect all the cities of Peru at Lima, so that their procurators could decide whether to receive him or not: as the places were so far apart, the meeting could be delayed more than two years, and meanwhile they could keep the president waiting on the island of Puna under a reliable guard so that he could not write to His Majesty and accuse them of disobedience. Others said that the best and quickest thing would be to send him back to Spain with a good supply of money and comforts for the journey, to show that he had been treated as a minister of the crown.

They spent many days in this confusion of ideas; and at last by common consent they decided that procurators should be sent to His Majesty to take whatever steps were necessary for the empire, and giving an account of the latest events, especially justifying the battle of Quito and the killing of the viceroy, laying the blame on him as the aggressor, and saying that he had forced them to kill him by attacking them and that they had done so in battle in self defence. At the same time they begged His Majesty to appoint Gonzalo governor of the empire because he had conquered it and deserved the office for many reasons, and had His Majesty's engagement to the marquis that the latter should appoint the next governor to succeed him. The procurators were to ask the president in Panama not to come to Peru until His Majesty was informed and sent new instructions about what should be done.

This done, they began to select the ambassadors to go to Spain, and in order to give the mission greater authority, they begged Don Fray Jerónimo de Loaisa, archbishop of Lima, to accept the leadership, for as prelate, father, and pastor of the city he would command more attention in Spain. They also asked the bishop of Santa Marta and Fray Tomás de San Martín, provincial of the Order of St. Dominic, and sent Lorenzo de Aldana and Gómez de Solís to accompany these three. They were given money for the journey so that they could spend what was necessary; and Gómez de Solís, who was Pizarro's chamberlain, was also given thirty thousand pesos for Hinojosa's expenses in Panama. Lorenzo de Aldana was earnestly requested, as a friend and fellow countryman, to send rapid and reliable news of the outcome of the journey and whatever he could find out in Panama about the president's powers. So they sailed in October 1546, with the title of ambassadors of the empire of Peru to His Majesty. Nothing of moment worth recording occurred on the voyage.

CHAPTER IV

*The ambassadors reach Panama; they and those
already there repudiate Gonzalo and deliver
their fleet to the president;
Paniagua reaches Lima.*

A S SOON as the ambassadors reached Panama, Lorenzo de Aldana went
to lodge with Pedro de Hinojosa, and having burned the instructions he had brought from Gonzalo about what he was to do in Panama
and Spain, he went to kiss the president's hand. They soon came to an
understanding, and continuing their familiarity and conversation, Aldana,
Mejía, and Hinojosa decided to go over to the president's service, though
for the first three days they made difficulties, till at length they all spoke
their minds openly. On finding themselves unanimous, they and all the
other captains revealed their intentions, and on the fourth day they went
to the president and all offered their obedience and turned over to him
Gonzalo's fleet with its supply of arms and munitions and swore to serve
him faithfully and obey all his commands. They agreed to keep the matter
secret among themselves until they knew how Gonzalo took the message
delivered by Paniagua. They were moved by their zeal for the royal service
to repudiate Gonzalo and go over to the king's side—let us put it like this,
so as not to be accused of slander. But they kept their agreement secret,
since each of them thought of the rewards that would be offered when
Peru was pacified: and in this way they were not disappointed, for they received more than they asked, as we shall say in due course. The most important influence in all this was the revocation of the ordinances and the
pardon and absolution for what had gone before. Once they saw themselves secure in the possession of their Indians and freed from the threat
of death as a result of the killings and damage that had been done, they
did not wish to lose this opportunity, but promptly grasped it despite the
fact that it meant the ruin and destruction of the man who had lifted
them up and made them captains and ambassadors with hopes of further
advancement, for though they were men of rank, they were not conquerors, excepting only Palomino. The secret was kept only a few days,

for the president did not wish to waste time after winning so auspicious a success so soon. A general review was called; they gave their standards to the president and the captains publicly offered him their allegiance. He accepted it in the king's name and returned them their flags, appointing them captains in the imperial forces, as López de Gómara says in his ch. clxxix:

> Hinojosa then surrendered the ships willingly, for no one could have forced him to do so. He received promises from La Gasca, who made a highly successful bargain. This began the downfall of Gonzalo Pizarro. La Gasca took the fleet and made Hinojosa general of it, returning the ships and standards to the captains whom Pizarro had appointed, and so making honest men of traitors. He was beside himself with joy at seeing the fleet, and thought he had negotiated very well, for without it he could scarcely have succeeded and he could not have gone by sea to Peru, and the land journey, which he at first contemplated, would have been beset with hardships and hunger and cold and other dangers.

Thus López de Gómara, speaking of the measures the president took and the promises made by both parties. Having established friendship and agreed on the price of it, La Gasca openly appointed Pedro Hinojosa to be captain general of the land and sea forces. He had four ships made ready, with Aldana, Mejía, Illanes, and Palomino as captains, and Aldana in charge of all four. They took three hundred of the best soldiers, well armed and fully equipped, and carried many copies of the order revoking the ordinances and of the general amnesty which they sent and scattered throughout the country. So the four captains continued their journey, carrying out the duties assigned to them. The president wrote to Don Antonio de Mendoza, then viceroy of Mexico, with a report on what had happened so far, and asking for reinforcements of men and arms for the expedition. He sent Don Baltasar de Castilla to Guatemala and Nicaragua, and others went to Santo Domingo, Popayán, and other places for the same purpose; for all this was thought to be necessary. But it was the revocation and the general pardon that fought the war with Gonzalo Pizarro and gave the empire to La Gasca.

To return to Paniagua, whom we left at sea on the way to Lima and omitting the story of his voyage, which the historians narrate, we shall give the gist of his story. He arrived in Lima and gave Gonzalo the emperor's and the president's letters, and his letter of credence for the whole kingdom to the effect that he had been sent by the president, so that credit should be given to what he said as well as what the letters contained.

Gonzalo received him favorably and after hearing his message sent him away, bidding him discuss the president's business with no one, or it would go ill with him. He summoned Licentiate Cepeda and Francisco de Carvajal and the three alone heard the contents of the letters. His Majesty's letter is given by Zárate:

Contents of His Majesty's Letter.

The King.

Gonzalo Pizarro: By your letters and from other reports I have received news of the disturbances and events that have occurred in the provinces of Peru since the arrival of Blasco Núñez Vela, our viceroy, and the judges of the royal *audiencia* who accompanied him, as a result of their having attempted to execute the new laws and ordinances made by us for the good government of those kingdoms and the good treatment of the natives. We are assured that neither you nor those who have followed you had any intention to be of disservice to us, but only to avoid the harshness and rigor with which the said viceroy acted in refusing to accept any petition. Wherefore, having been informed of all this and having heard Francisco Maldonado's statements on behalf of yourself and the *vecinos* of those provinces, we have resolved to send to them as our president Licentiate de la Gasca, of our Council of the Holy and General Inquisition, to whom we have given commission and powers to pacify the country and take whatever steps he may see fit in the service of Our Lord God and to the ennoblement of the provinces and benefit of their inhabitants, our vassals, who have gone to settle there, and of the natives. Wherefore I charge and command you to do and perform whatever the said licentiate bids you on our behalf, as though we ourselves had bidden it, and to lend him all the aid and favor he may ask and need to perform and fulfil what we have committed to him, according as he may command you on our behalf and as we confide in you, for we do and shall recall the services you and the marquis Don Francisco Pizarro, your brother, have rendered us so that his sons and brothers may be rewarded.

At Venlo, the 16th of the month of February, 1546.
I, the King,
by His Majesty's command,
Francisco de Eraso.

The president's letter to Gonzalo Pizarro ran as follows:

Illustrious Sir:
Expecting to have left sooner for Peru, I have not sent your honor the letter of our lord the emperor which accompanies this, nor have I written to you to announce my arrival, since it seemed disrespectful to His Majesty not to hand

you the letter in person and improper that mine should precede his. In view of the delay in my departure, however, and as I am told your honor has gathered the representatives of the towns in Lima to discuss past events I decided to send it to you by a special messenger: I have therefore sent His Majesty's letter and this by Pedro Hernández Paniagua, a person of the necessary rank to carry a letter from His Majesty and of standing in your country, and a great friend and servant of it. I may say that the news of the disturbances in Peru since the arrival of Viceroy Blasco Núñez (whom God pardon) caused much concern in Spain; and after His Majesty had heard and considered the various opinions, he decided that there was no reason to think that any of the late disorders had been caused in disobedience to him and in his disservice, but only because those of this province had defended themselves from the unrightful rigor and harshness with which their appeal to His Majesty had been received and to gain time for the king to hear this appeal before the execution of the laws. His Majesty was persuaded of this by the letter you addressed him, reporting that you had accepted the office of governor as the *audiencia* had entrusted it to you in His Majesty's name and under his seal, and begging his approval, saying that any other course would have been to his disservice, and that you had therefore accepted it until His Majesty should command differently, whereupon you would obey as a good and loyal subject.

When His Majesty knew this, he bade me come and pacify this country by revoking the ordinances, as he had been petitioned, and gave me powers to grant a pardon for what had occurred and to summon and consult the inhabitants as to what should be done in God's service, and for the good of Peru and benefit of the settlers and *vecinos*. I am further to assist and give employment to the Spaniards whom it has been impossible to reward with allocations, despatching them on new conquests; since the proper solution for those who cannot find a living in the existing conquests is that they should find one in future discoveries and there gain wealth and honor, as the conquerors of the existing possessions did. I beg your honor to consider this as befits a noble Christian gentleman and with prudence and the love and desire you have always shown for the good of the country and its inhabitants; and to thank God and Our Lady to whom you are devoted, as a good Christian, that in an affair of such moment as that in which you are involved and have hitherto undertaken, His Majesty and the rest of us in Spain have never regarded what you have done as rebellious or disloyal to the king, but simply as a defence of your just rights which you had claimed by appeal to your prince. And as your king is so just and so Catholic as to have given you and the other inhabitants of Peru what was yours and what you begged for in your appeal, undoing the wrong said to have been done in the ordinances, your honor should return to the king what is his, in other words obedience. You should therefore fulfil all His Majesty's commands, for in so doing you will not only fulfil the natural obligation of fidelity you owe the king, but also your duty toward God, who ordained in the law of nature and scripture and grace, that each should be given his own, and kings especially should be given obedience, and that those who did not obey this commandment should not be saved.

Consider this too as a noble gentleman, an illustrious title your ancestors have won and bequeathed you by their loyalty to the crown, since they came forward and served it better than those who have not deserved the title. It would be a serious fault if your honor lost it by not being as they were, and stained the honor of your line by showing yourself unworthy of it. And as after the soul, nothing is more precious to men, especially to good men, than honor, its loss is to be accounted greater than that of anything else except that of the soul; and a person like yourself is obliged to look to it, recalling that your ancestors left it to you, and their honor, no less than yours, will be smirched if you do not do your duty toward the king; for he who does not give God what is due to religion and the king what is due to fidelity, not only loses his reputation, but also besmirches and destroys that of his lineage and relatives.

Consider the matter too as a man of prudence, recognizing the greatness of your king and your own small ability to stand up against his will. As you have not been in his court or his armies you have not seen the power and persistence he displays against those who have displeased him, yet ponder on what you have heard about him and think who the Grand Turk is, and how he came in person with 300,000 and more warriors, and another great horde of pioneers, to wage war, but when he was near His Majesty, not far from Vienna, he thought he was not strong enough and would be discomfited if he fought; and was in such a plight that he forgot his authority and was forced to retire, and in order to do so lost so many thousand horsemen whom he had sent forward so as to engage His Majesty and conceal his retreat with the rest of the army,

etc. The president's letter is given in a much longer form by the historians; but I preferred to cut it short here, as the rest is the catalogue of the emperor's victories over his foes, on the same lines as that over the Grand Turk, so as to persuade Gonzalo Pizarro to surrender and submit to his prince, against whom his forces were not sufficient to prevail. In the following chapter we shall speak of the meetings held about these letters and the opinions expressed.

CHAPTER V

*Consultations about the revocation of the ordinances
and the pardon for past offences; the secret
messages given to Paniagua, and Gonzalo
Pizarro's reply.*

WHEN THE three members of the first council, Gonzalo, Licentiate
Cepeda, and Francisco Carvajal, had read the letters twice and more,
Gonzalo asked the others their opinion. Cepeda asked Carvajal, as the
oldest, to speak first, and though each courteously tried to give way, Carvajal finally spoke first, saying: "Sir, these are very good bulls. I think
you should take them and we'll all do the same, for they bring very great
indulgences."

Licentiate Cepeda said: "What is there good about them?"

Carvajal replied: "Sir, they're very good and very cheap, since they
offer the revocation of the ordinances and a free pardon for the past, and
for the future the opinions of the *regidors* of the cities are to be sought, so
as to order what seems serviceable to God and good for the country and
its *vecinos* and settlers. This is all we've desired and can desire; for the
revocation of the ordinances secures us our Indians, which was our reason
for taking up arms and risking our lives, and the arrangements for the
future, whereby Peru is to be governed according to the opinions of the
regidors, make us lords of the whole country, for we shall govern it. For
this reason I say we should take the bulls and pick new ambassadors to go
to the president with our reply, and have him carried aloft into the city
and pave the streets with bricks of silver and gold, and show him all the
attentions we can, to show how thankful we are for his good news and
oblige him to treat us as friends, and tell us if he has sufficient powers to
make Your Lordship governor of the empire, which I don't doubt he has.
The proof of this is the stake he has placed on the first trick, which
shows he has more to overbid it with. Bring him here as I say, and if it
doesn't turn out well, we can do as we like with him."

Cepeda said that all Francisco de Carvajal had said was wrong, for the
promises were verbal ones, and were quite unsure: the mighty never ful-

filled their promises if the fancy so took them, and once the president had landed, he would attract to himself all the inhabitants and do what he liked. He had not been sent as a simple and forthright man, but on account of his cunning, astuteness, duplicity, and falseness. In his opinion the president should certainly not be received, for this would lead to their total destruction.

Such in brief was what the two advisers said, though they both advanced many more arguments. Gonzalo did not declare for either view, but was more inclined to agree with Cepeda than with Carvajal, thinking that he was already being deprived of the governorship and control of Peru. Licentiate Cepeda's opinion was colored by ambition and interest, for he thought that as soon as the president came he would lose his authority, and possibly lose his seat as judge and even his life; for though he had been one of His Majesty's ministers, he had stopped the ordinances and opposed the viceroy until he was killed in pitched battle.

Gonzalo Pizarro left the council still undecided, and ordered a great meeting of all the *vecinos* who had Indians, and the captains and other nobles and lawyers of the city so that they could all decide what was to be done and answer His Majesty's and the president's letters with the opinion and authority of the whole country. More than eighty persons gathered in this meeting, where many strange and conflicting opinions were voiced. Some were serious and sensible, and favored both Spaniards and Indians and God's service; others were not so, for each spoke according to his whim. Some were frankly ridiculous, for it is inevitable that there should be a little of everything among such a number of different people. The best opinions coincided with Carvajal's, but they were not accepted since ambition and the desire to rule ran counter to them. Carvajal repeated in public that the bulls were good and they had better take them.

Cepeda said: "The commander's afraid!"

Some of the other hot-heads said the same, and Carvajal resented it and shouted: "I'm a loyal servant of my lord the governor, gentlemen, and I want to see him prosperous, strong, and peaceful, and I give the advice I think most likely to bring about what I desire for him because of my love toward him. If I ever do otherwise—well, I have lived many years and have as long a neck for the rope as any of you."

Fernández gives part of Carvajal's advice but inserts it at a later stage in his *History*. He must have received the news late, and got it from someone who cut it short: it was at this meeting Carvajal gave his opinion, and at much greater length than we have said. López de Gómara and

Zárate do not mention it; I do not know why, for when the war was over, everyone publicly praised Carvajal's wisdom and good advice, which would have been very sound if Gonzalo's judgment had been sound enough to accept it.

The discussions we have mentioned took place in public. There were other secret meetings against Gonzalo in the lodgings of Paniagua, to which many repaired unsummoned by him that first night and during the rest of his stay in Lima. They thought to gain his favor by saying that they were servants of His Majesty and were dominated by Pizarro against their wills: as soon as the president entered Peru they would all go over to him and forsake Pizarro. They begged him for the love of God to remember carefully their names and tell the president who they were, for they offered themselves thenceforward for the president's service. All this was privately communicated to Paniagua by the leading *vecinos* who had pledged themselves most firmly to Gonzalo and spoke hardest against the president in the recent meetings, where they had suggested he should be stabbed or poisoned or drowned by sinking his ship on his way to Peru, as our historians say.

The secret messages brought to Paniagua by night prevented him from speaking frankly to Gonzalo Pizarro. He had instructions from the president, who had spoken to him in private on his departure, saying: "Take very great care and pains to find out the intentions of Gonzalo's companions. If you see that they are all unanimous, tell him from me that he can be tranquil and not worry, for I have orders from His Majesty to confirm his governorship of Peru. In fact, when I left Spain, the members of His Majesty's council told me that if the whole of Peru was behind Pizarro, I was to leave him as governor, and the last words they said were these: 'So long as Peru remains under our lord the emperor, the Devil can govern it.' This secret I now tell you," said the president to Paniagua, "as they told it me. Now remember in all you do your obligation as a gentleman to serve your king."

Paniagua himself used to tell all this after the land had been pacified and the president had gone back to Spain, for he remained in Peru with a good allocation of Indians. He used to say that on hearing such divergent opinions he was often on the point of revealing his secret to Gonzalo Pizarro and had often since regretted not having done so. Paniagua sought an answer to his message and obtained one through the good offices of Licentiate Carvajal. He was glad of this, for he was afraid Gonzalo would learn of his conversations with the Pizarrists by night and have him killed, as he had at first threatened. He left Lima in January 1547. Gonzalo gave him money for his journey and a letter to the president, which Fernández gives but Zárate suppresses. It runs:

Most Magnificent and Reverend Sir:

I have received yours written in the city of Panama on September 26 of last year, and kiss your hand many times for the warnings you send me, for I realize that they come from a mind as sincere as one of your standing, conscience, and letters must be. With regard to myself, pray believe that my desire has always been, and is, to serve His Majesty. My desire may speak for itself without my saying anything, since my actions and those of my brothers give clear proof of it, for to my mind he who serves his prince with words alone does not serve him at all. And though those who achieve things at His Majesty's expense also serve him, they have less reason to boast of it than I, who have served him for sixteen years since I came to Peru, not with words, but with deeds and with my person and those of my brothers and kinsmen, who have added to the royal crown of Spain more and greater lands and greater store of gold and silver than anyone ever born in Spain, and all this I have done at my own expense without His Majesty's spending a peso. Yet all my brothers and I have left is the mere fame of having served His Majesty, for all we have won here we have spent in the royal service; and when Blasco Núñez came, the sons of the marquis and Hernando Pizarro and I had no gold or silver (though we had sent so much to His Majesty) and owned not an inch of the land we had added to his royal crown. Nevertheless we were as stalwart in his service as on the first day we came. There is therefore no need to suppose that one who has served His Majesty in this way needs to be informed of his prince's power, unless it be to praise the Lord for His mercy in giving us such a lord and for making him so powerful that victories fall naturally to him and all princes, Christian and infidel alike, fear him. And though I have spent less time at His Majesty's court than in wars in his service, pray believe that I am so anxious to know about His Majesty's doings, and especially his achievements in time of war, that there can be few at court who know better than I the true course of all the wars he has waged; for everyone knows my interest in the matter and those who come from Spain always write and tell me the news and I always seek to remember it, since it is a thing that pleases and satisfies me so: it is a curious fact and may be attributed to my love of truth in general,

etc. The rest of the letter may be omitted as irrelevant, it merely blames Viceroy Blasco Núñez Vela for everything that had happened and excuses himself on the ground that all the cities of Peru had elected him procurator general, and that the royal judges, by order issued under the royal seal, had bidden him expel Blasco Núñez from the kingdom. He had done nothing on his own account, but merely followed instructions.

Paniagua sailed away with this letter, and we shall leave him to bide his time. When the letter says "without an inch of the land we had added to his royal crown," he means as a grant in perpetuity, such as is held by lords in Spain from past kings whom they aided in the conquest and in expelling the Moors. For though Gonzalo and Hernando Pizarro had allocations of Indians, they were not in perpetuity but only for life, and though the marquis had them too, his had lapsed with his death and his children did not inherit them.

CHAPTER VI

The death of Alonso de Toro; Diego Centeno comes forth from his cave, and other captains rally to serve His Majesty; Gonzalo burns his ships; Carvajal's remarks on the subject.

AFTER dismissing Pedro Fernández Paniagua [*sic*], and finding that Aldana had sent him no account of his mission or of the fleet in Panama or any news about La Gasca, though there had been plenty of time for him to have done so, Gonzalo Pizarro's suspicions were aroused and he wrote to his deputy and captain in Quito, Pedro de Puelles, and to Captain Mercadillo in San Miguel, Captain Porcel in the Pacamurus, and Captain Diego de Mora at Trujillo, warning them to be ready when he sent for them, which would be soon. But when the messengers arrived, all three captains had already heard of the revocation of the ordinances and the general pardon from the letters and copies of his powers the president had sent out (for, as we have said, he secretly and skilfully circulated them throughout the whole kingdom). They were therefore resolved to repudiate Gonzalo, which they did soon after. Gonzalo also sent Antonio de Robles as his captain to the city of Cuzco, to collect such men as were there and in the district and hold them in readiness.

He sent this captain to Cuzco because he knew that Diego González de Vargas (whom I knew) had killed his deputy Captain Alonso de Toro, who held authority from him in that city. The death was not planned by the murderer and not expected by his victim, for Alonso de

Toro was Diego González's son-in-law. González had entered Toro's quarters, for they all lived close together, and found him quarrelling and shouting with his wife, a most virtuous woman, though Toro was arrogant, choleric, and quarrelsome. As the old man entered a room that led to his daughter's apartment, Toro happened to come forth, and finding him there and supposing he had come to take his daughter away, attacked the old man, who was over seventy-five, and shouted rude insults at him. Diego González, intending to hold him off rather than to harm him, laid hands on an old two-eared dagger he had hanging from his waist (which I also saw in his possession), and held it before him in an attitude of defence. Alonso de Toro, seeing this, attacked the old man with greater fury and wounded himself on the dagger. Diego González, seeing that there was no way out of the affair, gave him three or four more wounds in the belly, and turned his back, fleeing lest Toro should seize the dagger and kill him. The wounded Toro pursued him for more than fifty paces, to the staircase of his house, where he fell and died. So ended poor Alonso de Toro, killed by his own savagery and vile temper, which was so curst that he forced his father-in-law to slay him in pure fright.

Diego González was absolved, and I knew him years later. A son of his born in Peru, Diego de Vargas, was my fellow pupil at the primary school and after at our classes of Latin. The incident happened in a house opposite my father's where I was when it took place. On the death of Alonso de Toro the people of the city chose Alonso de Hinojosa as captain and alcalde in Gonzalo's name. Soon after, Antonio de Robles entered with his commission and was received as captain, at which Hinojosa took offence, as he later showed, though at the time he dissimulated.

The letters announcing the president's arrival also reached the city of Arequipa and town of La Plata and were carried throughout Collao where there were many people scattered about and in hiding after Carvajal had put Centeno to flight and broken up his force. They all rose up at the news, and a *vecino* of Arequipa called Diego Alvarez, who was then on the coast with nine or ten companions, raised a linen napkin as a standard and made himself captain. He went in search of Centeno, who then left his cave, and soon nearly fifty men had gathered. They unanimously set up Centeno as captain general of the new undertaking, and discussed where they should go, whether to Arequipa or Cuzco, where they knew Antonio de Robles had three hundred well-armed men. They hesitated to decide, for it seemed risky to attack a captain like Robles, who had such an advantage in numbers. But they were confident in the king's name, and determined to go thither. We shall leave them on the way and relate other deeds and events that occurred simultaneously in various places. They are so many that I fear I shall not find my way out of this maze, but we shall endeavor to report them as best we can; if our account is not so complete as it should be, I must be pardoned and my good intention accepted.

Aldana, Mejía de Guzmán, Palomino, and Illanes, whom we left sailing toward Peru on the president's orders, arrived at Túmbez, where there was a captain called Bartolomé de Villalobos as Gonzalo's deputy. When he saw that the four ships had been four days outside the port without coming in, he suspected that they were not on his side, and on this suspicion, with no other assurance, he wrote to Gonzalo Pizarro about what he had seen at sea and what he suspected. He directed the messenger to Diego de Mora at Trujillo, more than a hundred leagues from Túmbez, to inform him and ask him to tell Pizarro at once. Mora sent the messenger on to Lima, and was in doubt what to do himself, whether to stand by Gonzalo or forsake him. While he was hesitating, he had news of the revocation of the ordinances and His Majesty's pardon for what had passed. Then collecting all the gold and silver he could raise from his estate, he put it on a ship in the port and went off to Panama, taking his wife with him and forty more soldiers, including some *vecinos* of Trujillo.

The news of the four ships reached Lima, and though it was not known who was in them, Gonzalo and his friends were greatly perturbed, and without further news began to prepare for the war which they feared was imminent. They appointed captains of horse and infantry. After this, the news came of what Diego de Mora had done, and it was decided to sent a certain Licentiate León to Trujillo to take over Mora's duties. But he also repudiated Gonzalo, for after sailing for a few days he fell in with Aldana and his friends and joined up with them. Mora also met Aldana, and returned with him to Peru. They all put in at Trujillo, where Mora landed with forty men who were sick and needed to be attended to ashore. He marched inland to Cajamarca with news of the revocation of the ordinances and the general pardon so as to muster together all the people of those provinces. The news brought many men to serve His Majesty, including Juan de Saavedra, a native of Seville, Gómez de Alvarado, and Juan Porcel, whom Gonzalo had asked to be in readiness for when he should summon him. In short, in all those regions more than three hundred men joined Diego de Mora to serve the emperor.

When Bartolomé de Villalobos, who was at Túmbez, knew this, he collected what men he could to march across the mountains to join Gonzalo. But on the way he was arrested by his own men and persuaded to change sides and heart, and return to Piura and hold it for His Majesty, as he had formerly done for Gonzalo. He saw that this was not a bad solution and accepted it, though against his will, if one may put it so.

The same happened at Puerto Viejo, where Francisco de Olmos was deputy for Gonzalo. When he heard that many had submitted to serve His Majesty, he went to Huayallqui with some trustworthy companions, and dissimulating his intentions, surprised Manuel Estacio, who was Gonzalo's deputy there, and stabbed him before he could strike, raising his standard in the king's name. In this way all these people, Gonzalo's deputies and captains, gave in on the mere news of the revocation of the ordinances and the general pardon: no other persuasion was necessary.

Gonzalo and his friends heard all this; on hearing daily and hourly news of misfortunes and untoward events, they were as shocked as they might well be, for they saw the whole country denying them and suspected that those who were with them would soon do the same. They had councils, but there was such confusion and alarm that the decisions were of little avail. One of the things they did was to burn five good ships in the port and the smaller vessels. Gonzalo had this done on the advice of Licentiate Cepeda and Benito de Carvajal, who had most influence over him; and being more skilled in laws than warfare, they persuaded him to burn them, saying that it would be best to remove opportunities from any who might desert, for if there were ships in the port many would flee; but if not, they would follow him willy-nilly.

The burning of the ships took place during [Francisco de] Carvajal's absence; he was away for seven or eight days attending to affairs of importance twenty leagues from Lima. When he was told about the ships on his return, he wept the loss tenderly, and told Gonzalo: "Your Lordship has burnt five angels you had in port to guard and defend the coast of Peru and attack and destroy your enemies. You might at least have kept one for me, for with it I'd have made bold to serve you to your satisfaction: and everyone would have envied me when I went out in it with a good company of arquebusiers and faced the enemy, who is sure to arrive tired and sick. Experience has shown that the coast between Panama and here is unhealthy, and their arquebusiers will be out of training and have their powder damp and useless, so that a ship of yours will be worth more than four of the enemy's." Carvajal's rivals, the two licentiates, secretly told Pizarro that it was to be suspected that Carvajal spoke thus of the burning of the ships because they had destroyed his means of escape. Later we shall see how much better was Carvajal's advice than that of the lawyers, and how Gonzalo proved this by experience of events.

CHAPTER VII

The president leaves Panama and reaches Túmbez;
Aldana reaches the valley of Santa; he sends
spies out against Gonzalo, who appoints
captains and pays them; a suit
against the president.

LICENTIATE Pedro de la Gasca, His Majesty's president, had sent Aldana and his companions in four ships to Peru, and then collected all the men, arms, horses, and supplies he could find in the whole region so as to follow them. Among those who rallied to him was a famous soldier, Pedro Bernardo de Quirós, a native of Andújar, who had gone to the Indies years before and served His Majesty in the Windward Islands, Cartagena, and Tierra Firme, and had been standard bearer. He was now given the same position, as there was no captaincy available. He played a distinguished part in the wars against Gonzalo Pizarro and after served as captain against Don Sebastián de Castilla and Francisco Hernández Girón, which earned him an allocation of Indians called Cacha in Cuzco with a pension for the lances raised at that time for the defence of the kingdom. Many other gentlemen and soldiers, including the noblest in those coastal provinces, came with him to serve His Majesty, and there were soon more than five hundred. When the president saw this, he thought he would not need the help he had asked for from Mexico and elsewhere, and so again wrote to the viceroy Don Antonio de Mendoza and the other governors, reporting on what had happened so far and telling him not to send the men he had asked for, as they no longer seemed necessary. After writing this and giving instructions for the administration of Panama and Nombre de Dios, and writing to the king a long report on what he had done so far, he left with the whole fleet for Peru; and though they met with some storms in the early part of the ocean voyage, their journey was not impeded. Continuing their way, they met Paniagua bringing Gonzalo's reply. The president was glad to see him and even gladder to find the readiness of Gonzalo's companions to serve the crown and come over to him in due course. He was so overjoyed that he refused to read Gonzalo's letter, so as not to hear any impertinence it might contain, and had it burnt, and continued his voyage successfully as far as Túmbez, where we shall leave him to speak of Lorenzo de Aldana, who was sailing with his four ships to Lima, and Gonzalo's distress on learning that he was being abandoned.

Aldana thus continued up the coast from Trujillo. Some of his men were ill, and on reaching a river called the Santa, he stopped for refreshment. From here he sent on by land a Mercedarian friar called Pedro de Ulloa to give Gonzalo news of his arrival, and under this pretext to speak to such persons as he knew to be friendly and warn them to leave Lima as best they could. He would send boats ashore as he went down the coast to pick up the fugitives. Gonzalo found out about this and had the religious put in a place apart so that he could not speak to anyone in public or in private. He complained bitterly of Aldana and of his treachery to their common origin and the friendship Gonzalo had always shown him; and said that if he had followed the advice of his chief followers, he could have put him to death long ago. His followers all blamed him publicly for this, saying that it was his fault for not believing them.

It was now public knowledge that Aldana was coming to Lima and that Gonzalo's fleet had gone over to La Gasca; so Gonzalo declared war, ruffled his drums, enlisted men, and appointed captains, and offered them all pay and presents. In particular he favored many noble and famous soldiers with a thousand or two thousand pesos, as befitted their individual merits. He held a general review, and himself went out on foot as general of infantry. Zárate (Book VI, ch. xi) says he had a thousand men, all as well armed and equipped as any seen in the most prosperous days in Italy, for none was without silk doublet and hose, and many had cloth of gold and brocade, and others embroidery in gold and silver, and gold ornaments on their hats and on their powder flasks and gun boxes. The cavalry captains Pizarro appointed were Licentiates Cepeda and Carvajal, whom he regarded as most attached to his cause. Those of arquebusiers were Juan de Acosta, Juan Vélez de Guevara, and Juan de la Torre. Captains of pikes were Hernando de Bachicao, Martín de Almendras, and Martín de Robles. The commander of all of them was Francisco de Carvajal, as in the past, and he had a company of arquebusiers who had always followed him. The standard was borne by Antonio Altamirano with a guard of eighty cavalry. Some captains had devices on their banners with Gonzalo Pizarro's name surmounted by a royal crown. One of the devices was a *G* and a *P* intertwined, and another captain had a heart with the name of Pizarro. The banners were all newly made and of various colors.

By order of Francisco de Carvajal a practice was introduced—which I have not seen in Spain in time of war—whereby each soldier in every company wore among the plumes in his hat a badge consisting of a little flag the same color as the company's flag to show which company he belonged to: and if he had no plume, he wore the little flag instead. Only Carvajal refused to have a new flag: he raised his old one, under which he had won so many victories so that his men should see it and strive to win greater ones. He handed out forty, fifty, or sixty thousand pesos for each company of infantry or cavalry. He bought all the horses, mares, and mules there were to mount his followers and paid for them. If there were other mounts he did not pay for, as one of the authors says, this was because many merchants of Lima enlisted as soldiers so as not to show cowardice; some days later they bought themselves out at the cost of their arms and horses, or if they had none, by giving their value in money. Gonzalo and his ministers approved this, since they did not want to take anyone against his will: for a forced soldier never fights a good war.

With these preparations for battle Licentiate Cepeda produced a fabrication of laws to flatter Gonzalo and collected all the lawyers present and proposed that a criminal process should be drawn up against Licentiate La Gasca and Pedro de Hinojosa and his other captains, the latter for having delivered up Gonzalo's fleet and the former for receiving it. Witness was called to show that it was treason and robbery on the part of the captains to have given away a fleet that had cost Gonzalo more than a hundred thousand pesos and on the president's to have received another's property. The process was heard, and sentence of death, drawing, and quartering pronounced on all the guilty parties. Cepeda signed the sentence; and Gonzalo was asked to sign it as governor of the empire, and also all his advisers.

When it was Carvajal's turn to sign, Cepeda told him that it was very necessary that he should do so, at which he smiled as if in mockery of Cepeda's insistence, and said: "Undoubtedly it must be a matter of great importance, though we don't understand why we should sign the sentence." And turning to him he said: "Sir, if these lawyers and I all sign this sentence, is it going to be carried out and are these traitors going to die?"

Cepeda replied: "No, sir, but it is as well that the sentence should be signed and pronounced, so that we can carry it out when we catch them."

Carvajal burst into roars of laughter, and said: "God bless my soul, I thought from all your insistence that when I signed the sentence a thunderbolt would strike them all dead where they stood. If I had them under arrest, I wouldn't give a pin for the sentence. I'd put them all where you want without any signatures." He followed this with a great many characteristic jokes.

Licentiate Polo, whom we have already mentioned, was at this meeting, and said apart to Gonzalo that it would be a mistake to sign and publish such a sentence, first because La Gasca was a priest, and all who signed would be excommunicated, and second because it was hoped that many captains who had gone over to him would come back to Pizarro, because they had been coerced by Hinojosa: but when they heard they had been sentenced to death and the sentence had been made public, they would finally turn their backs on him and become mortal enemies. At this the session closed, and only Cepeda signed the sentence.

CHAPTER VIII

Gonzalo sends Juan de Acosta against Aldana;
they lie in wait for one another; the
death of Pedro de Puelles.

IN THE midst of these furious councils, processes, and ridiculous and irrelevant sentences which the lawyers tried to fulminate against the enemy, Gonzalo had news of the four ships bringing Aldana and the other captains toward Lima. They had gone up the coast and had now left Trujillo. He ordered Captain Juan de Acosta to take fifty picked mounted arquebusiers and ride down the coast to prevent Aldana's fleet from taking on water or fuel or landing at any of the ports. Acosta reached Trujillo, but dared not stay more than a single day, fearing the arrival of Diego de Mora, who was in Cajamarca and might oppose him. He marched back up the coast, trying to capture someone who had landed from the fleet, but Aldana had heard from his spies of Acosta's approach and arranged an ambush of more than a hundred arquebusiers whom he hid in a canebrake through which Acosta must pass, with orders to catch him or kill him or do what harm they could. Acosta meanwhile waylaid a watering party from the fleet and killed three or more and took as many more prisoner, while fourteen or fifteen came over willingly and went with him. From these he found out about Aldana's ambush and avoided it, and Aldana's men did not dare to come out and relieve him of his prey, though they were superior in numbers, for they had not enough powder for their arquebusses and their men were on foot and the enemy mounted, and the country was all bare sand.

Acosta sent the deserters to Gonzalo Pizarro, who received them kindly and gave them arms, horses, and money. He learnt from them that the four ships were very short of supplies and that there were few men left on board, for all the rest had gone ashore sick and many had died and been thrown overboard, while the survivors were ailing and ill equipped with arms and ammunition and had no news of the president, nor knew when he would arrive, but thought he would not appear that year. Gonzalo and his friends were delighted at this certain news; but considering the want of the people in the four ships, Gonzalo clearly perceived how ill advised he had been to burn the five ships he had had, and how right Carvajal had been to reproach him, saying that a single one of those ships would be worth more than all four of Aldana's. Acosta reached the port of Huaura, where Fernández says that there was such a remarkable quantity of excellent salt that all Italy, France, and Spain could have been supplied from it.

When Gonzalo knew Acosta was returning to Lima and had heard of Mora's doings in Trujillo, he decided to send Licentiate Carvajal with three hundred men to prevent Aldana from landing or taking water or supplies, and also to punish Diego de Mora and take other steps. When they had prepared for the journey and the licentiate was ready to start, Francisco de Carvajal raised objections, saying that the plan was a bad one, since his namesake would flee and take all those men with him. If he had stayed with Pizarro so far, it was merely to avenge the death of his brother, the factor; but now that he had a pardon for all he had done and the ordinances had been revoked, and as all his relatives held prominent offices of profit under the crown, there could be no doubt but that he would flee, especially when he recalled how they had had him with the rope round his neck ready to strangle him for no fault at all. These arguments of Francisco de Carvajal were supported strongly by Juan de Acosta, for as soon as he knew of what was proposed he came out strongly against it and criticized it as a slight on himself.

So Gonzalo changed his mind, and sent Acosta to do what it had been proposed that Licentiate Carvajal should do. Juan de Acosta went on his way with three hundred men. He felt that many were faint-hearted and prepared to flee, and the disappearance of twelve of his best-known men confirmed this. His friends, falsely or truly, assured him that others wished to do likewise, and that their ringleader was Lorenzo Mejía de Figueroa, the son-in-law of the count of La Gomera, whom he beheaded merely on this suspicion. This gentleman had married Doña Leonor de Bobadilla, formerly wife of Nuño Tovar, deputy general of Governor Hernando de Soto on the expedition to conquer Florida, which we have fully described in our history of Florida. He had a son and a daughter, Doña María Sarmiento, who married Alonso de Loaisa, a *vecino*, in Cuzco: it was on their wedding night that Francisco Hernández Girón began his revolt, as we shall say, with God's help. The son was called Gonzalo Mejía de Figueroa, a gentleman who though young was most accomplished. He was at the grammar school with me, and died very young, to the regret of all who knew him and hoped great things of him. We shall leave Acosta on his way and the rest on the coast, to say what happened to Pedro de Puelles in Quito.

On hearing of the revocation of the ordinances and the pardon for all past crimes, however grave, he thought he would take advantage of the royal bulls and return to the royal service, repudiating Gonzalo Pizarro, for whom he had done so much in the past. He decided to send a formal summons to all his captains and men and point out to them the necessity of returning to the royal service, since they were pardoned and freed from the ordinances. Rodrigo de Salazar, the hunchback, heard this from a famous soldier called Diego de Urbina, in whom Puelles had confided secretly, as his friend. Salazar, seeing the deed was inevitable, wanted to have the honor for himself, and to prevent Puelles from getting the credit from the president or from His Majesty, for so notable a service as the winning over of three hundred picked men. He therefore decided to forestall him, and have the honor and glory for himself. He told four special friends, whose surnames were Bastida, Tirado, Hermosilla, and Morillo, and were so known. He told them what Puelles was thinking of doing, and that they ought to enjoy the reward for winning the men over, and that they should therefore kill Puelles, which they agreed to do. Next day, a Sunday, all five went to his house early in the morning, and said that Captain Salazar had come to visit him and accompany him to church to hear mass. Puelles was grateful and invited them into his room, as he was still not up. The four of them went in, and Rodrigo de Salazar stayed at the door, unwilling to go in until he saw the result. Some say he did go in: but I often heard the tale from those who spoke about him, and they told it as we have said. Puelles was killed by the four of them with swords and daggers, whereupon Captain Salazar came out into the square and declared for the king, and everyone in the city supported him with great good will.

CHAPTER IX

*A single combat over the death of Puelles;
Centeno's entry into Cuzco and his fight
with Pedro Maldonado.*

SALAZAR and his friends at once prepared to go in search of President La Gasca, and they came up with him in the valley of Jauja, where they were received with great applause and praise and many thanks for their service to the crown and the promise of rewards in the future— though in this we anticipate. Diego de Urbina, a friend of Puelles, realized that Salazar had won these favors, which properly belonged to the dead man, as a result of his having revealed the secret, and was conscience stricken and full of grief at his friend's death. He openly displayed his anger against Salazar and publicly revealed Puelles' intention of serving His Majesty, saying that he himself had told Salazar, and that the latter was a cunning double-dealer who had repudiated the viceroy and gone over to Gonzalo and followed him hitherto until he had seen that if Puelles took the force over to the king he would get no credit and not even be thought of, so he had decided to steal the other's glory, as he had when he had arrested Don Diego de Almagro the younger, though he was an officer under him, on seeing he was lost. He had always been an astute and treacherous fellow who had followed the principle of "Long live the winner!" So Urbina said he defied him to single combat in which he would make him confess the truth of the charges.

Salazar had no such confidence in his skill and arms as to dare to face a man of Urbina's rank and courage, and as it was true that Urbina had revealed Puelles' secret and so caused his death, he relied more on his astuteness and ingenuity than on his sword and lance, and replied that all Urbina said about Puelles was true, but that he had killed Puelles on suspicion that he was putting off the decision and might repent of it when the appointed day arrived. Because of this and of the president's approval, Urbina and other leading soldiers on his side were satisfied, and admitted that the cause was sufficient for killing Puelles. Others said they had accepted very weak excuses for getting out of the single combat: the dead and the absent have few friends.

We left Captain Diego Centeno on the road intending to attack Captain Antonio de Robles, who held Cuzco for Pizarro with a large force. Although it seemed an act of temerity rather than of courage to lead forty-eight ill-armed foot, who had recently emerged from the caves into which they had fled from Carvajal, against a man with three hundred well-equipped soldiers, nevertheless he boldly went on. Alonso de Hinojosa, who had taken offence at the appointment of Antonio de Robles in his stead, solicited the leading men in Cuzco, and they all wrote to Centeno promising to be on his side and help him if he would come against Robles. This greatly encouraged Centeno and he hastened on. Robles knew of the enemy's approach and prepared to resist. He consulted his captains about the best means, and sent out a scout in whom he had great trust, a certain Francisco de Aguirre, who rode out till he came to Centeno six leagues from the city and warned him of Robles' decision and how he proposed to draw up his army and oppose Centeno's entry. Captain Centeno and his colleagues, of whom the chief were Pedro Ortiz de Zárate, Francisco Negral, Luis de Ribera, Diego Alvarez, and Alonso Pérez de Esquivel, agreed that the attack and entry should be under cover of night, so as to surprise their enemies and so that their friends, who included almost all Robles' army, should be able to avoid fighting and come over to them.

They used a very ingenious stratagem, removing their horses' reins and hanging lighted fuses from their harnesses and saddles. The Indians were then made to drive the horses before them, and on reaching a certain place spur them hard so that they would enter the city at a gallop. The street by which they were to enter was that we have called the Street of the Sun in our description of the city: it debouches into the middle of the great square. While the Indians were doing this, Centeno and his men went in by another street to the west of the first, leading to a corner of the square. When Robles knew of the night attack, he drew up his three hundred men in the middle of the square, facing the Street of the Sun, for there was no other approach for the enemy unless he took a circuitous route. Centeno's Indian servants brought the horses in with a great hubbub, so that they seemed far more numerous than they were. They entered the square, and broke Robles' formation without his seeing who they were, for when he came forward to face them he found the horses riderless, and was perplexed. Now Diego Centeno came out of the other street, shouting loudly and firing off his few arquebusses.

In those days the house that had belonged to Hernando Pizarro, and now belongs to the Society of Jesus, was occupied by a quiet and peaceable man called Pedro de Maldonado, who was no soldier, and did not pretend to be. He was saying Our Lady's hours, being devoted to her. On hearing the alarm, he put the hours in his breast, took up his sword and a pike that was lying nearby, and went out into the square, where the first person he met was Centeno. Without knowing who he was, he dealt him a blow with the pike, which pierced his left hand, and a second blow in the left thigh, which was not pierced because the point of the pike was an old iron one of the type known as "eared," having a couple of fleur-de-lis–shaped protuberances on either side of the spike, so that the iron could not go right through the thigh. But when Maldonado was pulling the pike out to deal another blow, these ears caught in the slashings of his velvet breeches, and he knocked Centeno over. Meanwhile a page of Centeno's, a grown man, whose name has escaped my memory, seeing his master brought down, shot at Maldonado with an arquebus, and laid him low, though he soon got up again to fight Centeno. Now others came up to help Centeno, and attacked Maldonado and disarmed him. Centeno's men now completed their victory, for some of Robles' squadron had run away and most had come over to the king. No other event worthy of note occurred in the attack, but only the fray between Pedro de Maldonado and Captain Diego Centeno, both of whom I knew; and no blood but that of this famous leader was shed that night.

CHAPTER X

*A remarkable result of Pedro Maldonado's fight;
the death of Antonio de Robles; the election
of Diego Centeno as captain general; the
reduction of Lucas Martín to the
royal service; the agreement
between Alonso de Mendoza
and Centeno.*

MALDONADO was the tallest and biggest man I have ever seen in Peru or in Spain. He did not die of the arquebus shot, nor was he even wounded, though he fell to the ground, for it seems that the Virgin Mary, Our Lady, to whom he was so devoted, wished to save him from death. The shot hit the book of hours from which he had been praying and which he had put in his bosom, and the force of the blow was so great that it knocked him over like a child. I saw the hours years later, for I was near Maldonado at a mass to the Mother of God which was sung every Saturday in the Mercedarians, and asked him for the book, desiring to see the miraculous hours, as they were generally considered to be. He gave me it and I opened it: the shot had entered the cover and pierced and cut up the first thirty or forty pages, and had torn through as many more, while the next twelve or fifteen were bored in the shape of the ball. The last page to be torn was the one before the mass of Our Lady, for in those days they used to print in books of hours not only the office and mass of the Virgin, but many other devotions as well, as the printers thought fit, for books were not controlled as they have been since the Holy Council of Trent. The book was as large as a modern prayer book.

Our authors say that there was fighting and casualties that night, but in fact there was only the fray between Maldonado and Centeno: the historians were misled by their informants. I was almost an eye witness of the affair, for six days later I reached Cuzco with my uncle Juan de Vargas, Captain Rodrigo de Pantoja, and nine other Spaniards, who had been at an allocation of Indians thirty leagues from Cuzco, where all my father's family, or the few of us there were, had taken refuge from the Pizarrists, not daring to remain in the city. My uncle and the other Spaniards then went to Cuzco to serve His Majesty. My mother and I and the rest went after them, and on the day following our arrival I went to kiss the hands of Diego de Centeno on my mother's behalf. I remember seeing his left hand swathed in a black taffeta band over the white bandage. I found him up, for the wound in the thigh was also not dangerous. He was lodging in the house of Hernando Bachicao, which now belongs to Don Luis Palomino. This occurred shortly after the feast of Corpus Christi in 1547, and I wrote it down originally at about the same season in 1605, so that I can say I was almost an eye witness.

The whole struggle was as if among friends; for if they had fought as the historians say, 48 ill-armed men could scarcely have resisted the 300 well-equipped men of Antonio de Robles, especially as many of them had daggers fastened to poles instead of pikes or lances, as the historians themselves state.

When Captain Robles found himself forsaken and lost, he fled into the convent of the divine St. Francis, not the present one, to the west of the city, but its predecessor to the east. Centeno had him brought forth next day, with no intention of killing him, for he was kindly and in no wise cruel, but hoping to bring him over to serve the king. But Robles, who, as Zárate says, was quite a youth, and not very intelligent, on finding that they were not going to hang him, at once concluded he could still become leader and head of the city, and said many brave things on behalf of Pizarro and some shameful ones against His Majesty. Centeno grew angry and ordered him to be beheaded, which was an honor many deplored, for they thought he should have been hanged although he was a nobleman.

Some who were very devoted to Gonzalo fled that night from Cuzco and came post-haste to Lima to tell him of the loss of his captain and men, which deeply grieved Gonzalo, though he disguised his sorrow at the time and took steps which we shall mention. On hearing of Centeno's victory, all those who had been in hiding for more than forty-five leagues round the city rallied to him. There were many leading *vecinos* and noble and famous soldiers, so that with those already in Cuzco they numbered over 500 men. These by common consent elected Centeno captain general of all of them. He appointed captains of infantry and cavalry, whom we shall mention in speaking of the battle of Huarina.

When Centeno had reformed his force, he returned to Collao, determined to attack Alonso de Mendoza who was holding La Plata in

Gonzalo Pizarro's name, so as to reduce it to His Majesty's service peaceably if he could, or otherwise by force.

Centeno's victory quickly became known in the city of Arequipa, where there was a captain called Lucas Martín Vegasso, a *vecino* of the place whom Gonzalo had sent there as his deputy after the battle of Quito. This captain did not know what had happened in Cuzco, but had decided to take 130 men he had with him to help Gonzalo. A few leagues out of the city he was arrested by his own men, who wanted to go over to the king, and had no love for him. They put him in irons lest he should escape.

When they got back to Arequipa, they heard of Centeno's success, and as they were all friends, they went to Lucas Martín and persuaded him to change his mind and do willingly what he would have to do by force, going over to the royal service. They would then restore him to his command, and go with him as captain to tell Centeno they wanted to serve the king. Lucas Martín agreed, though under compulsion, as he himself used to declare afterwards.

In Arequipa they found thirty or forty thousand pesos which Lucas Martín had sent for Gonzalo Pizarro; they took them and shared them out and went to Centeno, who received them with much gratitude for their service to His Majesty, and all went together to Los Charcas in search of Alonso de Mendoza, who had come forth from that province with 300 men to join Gonzalo.

When they were close to one another, Centeno tried to avoid a battle and wrote a letter asking the others to forget their hostility and strife, dating from the time of Alonso de Toro's and Francisco de Carvajal's attacks, and to come over to His Majesty, and forsake Pizarro, who had declared against the king, if they themselves did not want to be called traitors to their natural lord. A dignitary of the cathedral of Cuzco, the schoolmaster Pedro González de Zárate, was given this letter and embassy. He had been brought out of his church to act as mediator, for he was a person of authority, prudence, and good sense.

While the schoolmaster was negotiating with Alonso de Mendoza for his return to the royal service, and the latter had still not decided, since he did not like the idea of repudiating Gonzalo, Centeno received despatches the president had sent him, containing the president's powers to govern the empire, the revocation of the ordinances, and the general pardon. All this Centeno at once communicated to the schoolmaster, his ambassador, for him to show Alonso de Mendoza, thinking that this would certainly succeed in convincing him, however deeply involved he was. He was not deceived, for as soon as Mendoza saw the despatches, he changed his mind and resolved to come over to the king. He agreed with the schoolmaster that he would join Centeno, but only on condition that he remained captain general of his own men and commanded and governed them as he had done hitherto: his men were 300 picked soldiers, very well armed and mounted. Centeno accepted the condition, ignoring the difficulty of having two captain generals in the same army; and so both parties came together and celebrated and rejoiced. Finding themselves so strong, as Zárate says—for they had more than 1,000 men—they decided to go in search of Gonzalo and hold a certain place so that he could not pass, intending to wait for him there and go no further as they were short of food. We shall leave them here, near Huarina, where that bloody battle later took place, and return to speak of President La Gasca whom we left sailing the Southern Sea.

CHAPTER XI

The president reaches Túmbez; the measures he
takes there; Gonzalo sends Juan de Acosta
against Centeno; Aldana approaches
Lima, and Gonzalo takes an oath
of loyalty from his followers.

WITH SOME difficulties on the way the president safely reached the port of Túmbez with his whole fleet, for only one ship fell behind because it was poor at sailing on a bowline: its captain was Don Pedro Cabrera, who, finding that he could get no further in his ship, put in at Buenaventura and travelled overland with his small party, reaching the president at Túmbez, where he was provisioning his army of some five hundred men. Here he received letters from important persons, both *vecinos* and captains and soldiers, to whom he replied with expressions of gratitude and promises of rewards on His Majesty's behalf. He decided that Hinojosa, as captain general, should go ahead with the soldiers as far as Cajamarca and join the captains and men already there; Pablo de Meneses was to sail up the coast with the fleet, while he himself, with such men as seemed necessary for his safety travelled across the coastal plains to Trujillo. He had news of the captains and others who had rallied to serve the king and who were waiting for him in the villages and farms. He sent messengers out in all directions to bid these volunteers collect and march over the mountains to the valley of Cajamarca, there to await his orders. After taking these steps, he travelled across the plains, sending his scouts in front to get news and make the way safe.

While all this was happening to the president and his army, Gonzalo had heard the news of the victory of Centeno at Cuzco and of the death of Robles and capture of Lucas Martín Vegasso, which distressed him exceedingly, for he saw the fabric he thought he had built to become governor of the empire falling about his ears. He speedily summoned Captain Juan de Acosta, whose journey to Trujillo to remedy the danger threatening there we have already mentioned. Francisco de Carvajal now beheaded Antonio Altamirano, Gonzalo's ensign general, because he had become very lukewarm in serving Gonzalo since hearing of Centeno's success, and this was a good enough excuse for executing him. When Acosta arrived, Gonzalo ordered three hundred men to accompany the captain against Centeno. He made Martín de Olmos captain of cavalry, and Diego Gumiel captain of arquebusiers (both of whom I knew); Martín de Almendras was captain of pikemen; and he gave the standard to Martín de Alarcón. Páez de Sotomayor was commander, and Juan de Acosta, whom I also knew, was general of the whole army.

Gonzalo sent them to Cuzco by the mountain road, proposing to sally forth himself by the plains a few days later, so that they would attack Centeno on all sides. He was most angry with Centeno, because he said he had been one of the first and most vocal to beg him to accept the office of procurator general of Peru; yet now, on the simple receipt of news, false or true, that they had been pardoned and the ordinances revoked, Centeno had repudiated him as rapidly and whole-heartedly as he had voted for him and followed him until Gonzalo became procurator and governor of Peru; all the others who had raised him up had done the same, but Gonzalo trusted that God would punish them and avenge him.

Gonzalo made these and similar complaints in talking to his intimate friends, but in public he was full of courage, as he always was in his greatest undertakings: the historians say this in his favor at this point.

Fortune swelled these complaints and reverses with others even worse, for when she begins to show disfavor, she never shows it sparingly. She ordained that at that juncture Aldana should arrive with his four ships at a point only fifteen leagues from Lima, where he was quite safe, though he was so short of men and supplies, for he had heard how Gonzalo had burnt the ships in the port. He remained perfectly quiet and undisturbed and took courage to reach the port of Lima, for his intention was not to fight but simply to bring in in his boats those who ran away from Gonzalo. The news of his arrival in Huaura was known in Lima, and caused a great scandal in the whole city. Aware of how many had already repudiated him and fearing that those still with him would do the same, Gonzalo sought to bind them to him by the force of religion. By the orders of Licentiate Cepeda, the originator of the idea, he summoned all the *vecinos* who had Indians, and there were a great many of these, men of eminence from all the cities of Peru who were still with him. He also called the captains, knights, and chief soldiers, and delivered a harangue, explaining the duty and obligation they and all the rest of the empire had incurred toward him by virtue of his having undergone such dangers and strife and hunger and privations in defence of their cities and the Indians they possessed through the grace and favor of his brother the marquis. Let them recall that he had justified his case by sending messengers to report all that had happened in Peru to His Majesty, and the president had detained them, and had deceived his captains and plotted with them and taken his fleet, which had cost him a mint of money; finally, they had entered his jurisdiction and distributed letters which were very detrimental to everyone in the empire, showing the intention of making war, for which reason he intended to resist the president's entry. This resistance was in the best interest of them all; for if the president entered Peru and took possession of it, he would do the same as the viceroy had done. He would execute the ordinances and punish those involved in all that had gone before. He, Pizarro, therefore wished to know the intentions of each and all of them, for he would not force anyone who did not wish to follow him. He begged and prayed them each to say openly if they wished to follow or not; for if they did not, he would at once give them leave to go to their Indians, or to the president, if they wanted. Those who wished to remain by him and pursue so just a cause, must give him their plighted troth as noblemen and their oath as Christians to keep and fulfil the promise they had made. They all said they would die a hundred deaths for him, and swore it and signed a long screed in which Cepeda wrote all this down: he was the first to sign.

Francisco Carvajal, a man so shrewd and experienced in these matters, laughed and mocked at these proceedings among his close friends, saying: "You'll see how they fulfil their promises and how they respect the solemnity of their oath!" He said a great deal else, and if we had collected it all, we could make a fine speech—as fine as his speeches were on all subjects, for he was certainly one of the most extraordinary men in the world.

CHAPTER XII

*Hostages are exchanged, with trickery on both
sides; many leading men desert Gonzalo.*

TWO DAYS after this session Aldana's four ships reached the port of Lima, causing a great disturbance in the city. Gonzalo had the alarm sounded and formed the soldiers in the square: they numbered more than six hundred. It seemed safest to go out of the town, for those who were disaffected would not dare to flee in the open in sight of everyone. He established his camp one league from the city and one from port, and placed watchers on horseback to prevent them from escaping. In order to settle his dilemma and find what Aldana intended, he sent a *vecino* of Lima, Juan Fernández, with instructions to stay with Aldana as hostage for another gentleman whom Aldana would send to him to state the reason for his coming and make known his intentions. Captain Peña was sent from the fleet, and he gave Gonzalo the president's powers, together with the general pardon for all culprits and the revocation of the ordinances; verbally he urged on him how important it was to obey His Majesty and submit to his will, as it was not his pleasure that Gonzalo should be governor. In this place Fernández inserts what we have said about the bulls; but he was misled, for by now the time for discussing powers and bulls, as they called them, had passed; and there was nothing but confusion, scandal, and a general desire to flee, as we shall see in the course of our history. Gonzalo replied angrily to Captain Peña's message. He said that Aldana, Hinojosa, and all the rest who had pretended to be good friends had betrayed him and put him in the position of being called a traitor, when he had justified his case by sending ambassadors to His Majesty and had never intended to offend the king, but only to pacify Peru and remove obstacles to peace in the king's service. He added a great deal more; for he was deeply offended and complained bitterly that those whom he had most befriended and made men of by granting them positions of responsibility should have sold him so unjustly. He ordered Captain Peña to speak with no one, and to remain in the tent of Don Antonio de Ribera, so that he could not tell anyone about the despatches he had brought, which Gonzalo wished not to be made public. The historians say that that night Gonzalo sounded him about the possibility of seizing Aldana's ship; for if it were gained, all the rest would be his, and he promised Peña a hundred thousand pesos for the deed. But Captain Peña replied that he was not the man to commit such treason for any interest, nor should it have been suggested to him.

Next day Gonzalo sent him safe and sound back to the ships, where his own people discussed stratagems with Juan Fernández more successfully than Pizarro had with him. When Aldana heard from Peña that Pizarro had not wished the news of the despatches to be made known, he thought that the whole success of the affair lay in publishing the royal pardon and the revocation among the *vecinos* and soldiers in the form of an official notarial document, for hitherto the news was only known in Lima from the letter the president had sent to Gonzalo. So he had two copies of the pardon and revocation made with all haste, with many other letters to private persons, and he delivered the whole to Juan Fernández with instructions about what he was to say to Gonzalo and what he was to do with the papers. On reaching Gonzalo, Fernández took him aside and told him that Aldana had made him many promises if he would bring the pardon and revocation and secretly make them known to the *vecinos,* so as to make them forsake Pizarro and go over to the president.

"And I," said Fernández, "I lulled Aldana with vain hopes, and promised I would do so, and received from him these papers which I now deliver to Your Lordship, for I wouldn't betray you when you trusted your personal well-being to me, as you did when you sent me among your enemies as a hostage—indeed I value your trust so much that I shall hand it down as an honor to my heirs."

All this and other flattering phrases he uttered to remove any suspicion or uneasiness Gonzalo might have felt about him. Gonzalo, like a noble character, with no suspicion of malice or deceit, for such things never entered his breast, believed all he was told and placed all his confidence in Fernández, thanking him for having handed over the papers and promising him much consideration for the future. After this Juan Fernández made the papers known among such persons as he thought fit and gave the letters to those who were his friends or left them lying about or thrust them through doors and windows in the case of persons he could not be sure of. So that soon everyone was in the conspiracy against Gonzalo. None of the letters was wasted, and all had their effect, as we shall see.

The publication of the letters and the great promises they contained, together with a hint from Aldana that anyone who fled to him at sea would find boats on the beach ready to receive them, produced such confusion among Gonzalo's followers that all were suspect, for there was scarcely a man among them to be trusted. The first to flee were those most engaged to him. As he had pitched his camp in the open and announced that he would advance across the plains, many of the leading men, who were not prepared for a journey, took the opportunity to ask him for leave to go back to the city to obtain what they would need for the road. The chief of these were Vasco de Guevara, Martín de Meneses, Nicolás de Ribera, Hernán Bravo de Laguna, Diego Tinoco, Francisco de Ampuero, Alonso de Barrionuevo, Diego de Escobar, Francisco de Barrionuevo, and Alonso Ramírez de Sosa, all of whom had Indians in Lima or Cuzco, as well as many other soldiers of note. Gonzalo gave them permission and they went to their houses; but having collected what they needed, instead of returning to Gonzalo as they had promised, they repudiated him and went toward Trujillo.

When Pizarro was warned of this by his guards, he sent Captain Juan de la Torre with twenty reliable arquebusiers to pursue them and bring them back, or kill them if they refused. He followed them for more than eight leagues, but being unable to overtake them, returned, and on the way fell in with Hernán Bravo de Laguna, who had lingered behind with the idea of hiding in the city in a relative's house, though when he and his relative realized the risk they and everyone in the house would run if he were found, they decided that he should go after his friends. This was why he was late in leaving and met Juan de la Torre on the road. The latter brought him before Gonzalo Pizarro, who turned him over to Francisco de Carvajal to be hanged. A prominent lady, the wife of Nicolás de Ribera, one of the fugitives, called Doña Inés Bravo, a woman of great courage and goodness, on learning that Hernán Bravo, who was her cousin, had been taken and would doubtless be killed, went straight to Gonzalo's camp, accompanied by her father; and though she was involved in the guilt of her husband and cousin who had denied Gonzalo, she did not hesitate to lay herself at his feet, trusting in this gentleman's compassionate nature toward those who asked for mercy. So, kneeling and shedding many tears, she begged him to have pity. He hastily raised her from the ground; and though he at first refused to grant the pardon, at last he did so on the prayers of many bystanders, and handed her the token he usually gave in such cases, which was his cap with the medallion he wore on it. It was carried with all speed to Francisco de Carvajal; and they arrived in the nick of time, for he had already put Hernán Bravo under a tree with a rope round his neck. Carvajal accepted Gonzalo's pardon, at the instance of many who were with him, for they were all obliged to take the lady's part; and so Hernán Bravo de Laguna escaped. I knew him well, and he was still living in Cuzco with an allocation of Indians, though not a very large one, when I left. Here Zárate (Book VI, ch. xvi) says the same and adds:

And another point worthy of mention with reference to this pardon was that one of Gonzalo's captains called Alonso de Cáceres, who was with him when he spared the life of Hernán Bravo, kissed him on the cheek, crying aloud: "Oh, prince of the world, cursed be whoever denies you, unto death!" But within three hours he and Hernán Bravo himself and others had fled, which was regarded as a marvellous thing, for he had scarcely had time to breathe after the plight he had been in with the rope round his neck,

etc.

CHAPTER XIII

Martín de Robles uses a trick and flees.

THE FLIGHT of so many noble and eminent people, the first who had forced Gonzalo to take up the defence of their lives and properties, caused a great disturbance in the camp, for as Zárate himself says, some had followed Pizarro from the first and were deeply implicated with him, so that it could never have been suspected that they would fail him. Gonzalo was so furious that no one dared appear before him. He ordered the guards to lance those who were outside the camp. They hanged a poor soldier who was found to be wearing two shirts, which was thought to be sign of flight; and though he was poor, he still did not lack someone to denounce him.

To add to Gonzalo's and his adherents' troubles, it happened on the following night that Captain Martín de Robles, in order to have a good pretext to go into the city, astutely sent a secret warning to Diego Maldonado the Rich, a *vecino* and *regidor* of Cuzco, that Gonzalo wanted to kill him and had discussed it with his captains, so he should go into hiding; for Robles could render no greater service to the friendship between them. Maldonado believed this, as he had been one of the *vecinos* of Cuzco who had fled from Gonzalo to come and serve the viceroy, as we have already said. After this he had been severely tortured, because of certain anonymous letters that had been found in Gonzalo's tent when he was going to fight the battle of Quito; but he was not to blame, for the culprit was afterwards found. Moreover, Gonzalo had recently had his intimate friend, Antonio Altamirano, killed on suspicion.

For these reasons and the fear of cruel death that stalked among them, Diego Maldonado believed Robles' warning, and slipped out of his tent and out of the camp without waiting for a horse to be saddled, though he had excellent mounts, or telling any of his servants. All he had was his sword and cloak, and though he was a man of more than sixty-eight, he walked all night long until he reached some canebrakes three leagues from the sea, where the ships were; and there he hid. But fearing that search would be made for him next day and that he would be killed if they found him, and even if not, he might perish of hunger and thirst, he left his cover and happened to find a passing Indian, whom he called and told of his need. The Indian took pity on him, with that natural compassion they all have, and led him to the sea. On the beach he made a raft of reeds, such as the Indians use to cross rivers and sail on the sea (on the few occasions when they do so). They both straddled the raft like a horse, and the Indian rowed them to the ships. They were in great danger of being drowned, at least Maldonado was, for when they reached the ships the raft had nearly disintegrated for lack of cords to tie the rushes.

So the good Diego Maldonado made his escape. He was one of the first conquerors, and was still living in Cuzco when I left. Next day, early in the morning, Martín de Robles went to Maldonado's tent to see how he had taken the false alarm; and finding that he had fled by night, he went to Gonzalo, pretending to be very loyal to him and strongly on his side, and said: "Sir, Diego Maldonado has fled. It seems to me that as Your Lordship sees the army shrinking hourly and people fleeing at every step, you should move your camp and march to the place you had determined, Arequipa. Don't give anyone leave to go to the city to make preparations, or they'll all make it an excuse to run away, and that must be avoided. In order that my own company shan't ask leave, but will set an example to the rest, I would like Your Lordship's permission to go to the city with a few reliable friends, so that they can get what is needed, without my letting them out of my sight. On the way I propose to visit the convent of St. Dominic, where I'm told Maldonado is, and I'll get him out and bring him to Your Lordship, so that you can punish him publicly and then no one else will dare to flee from now on."

Gonzalo liked these words, which were favorable to his cause, and trusting in Martín de Robles' implication in the affair—for he had arrested the viceroy and pursued him till he was killed—he told him to go to the city and do all he proposed. Robles first of all took Maldonado's horses, as though he had confiscated them from a traitor, and then his own. He next called on his most intimate friends in the company, numbering more than thirty, and went to Lima; and without stopping there, they all rode on toward Trujillo saying publicly that they were going to the president and that Gonzalo was a rebel.

This news reached Gonzalo's camp and caused such astonishment that many refused to believe it. It seemed impossible that Robles should deny Gonzalo after he had shown himself so much in favor of his party on every previous occasion. But the fact was corroborated, and it was feared that everyone else would flee that day, or that someone would kill Gonzalo and finish the whole business, for there was nothing else to be done. But no one thought of killing Gonzalo, for he was too good to inspire such a thought; they were content to repudiate him and flee, and no one sought to do more. Gonzalo put down the stir as best he could, and declaring that if only ten good friends stayed with him he would hold out and reconquer the whole of Peru. These words are from Fernández (ch. lxiv).

CHAPTER XIV

The flight of Licentiate Carvajal and that of
Gabriel de Rojas, and many other vecinos
and famous soldiers.

T HE FLIGHT of Pizarro's supporters did not end with that of Martín de Robles: this rather hastened the departure of others who wanted to escape. On the following night Lope Martim Pereira, a Portuguese whom I knew, fled; he was one of the first conquerors. When Pizarro heard this, he wanted to secure his camp, at least from the direction of the city; and ordered Licentiate Carvajal, in whom he should rightly have been able to confide because he was so deeply involved, to take his company of horse and guard that quarter so that no one could pass. But this step turned out very differently from what he intended, for instead of avoiding the losses he feared, it gave an opportunity to open the gates of his camp and let everyone get away. For though Carvajal pretended as hitherto to be an enthusiastic supporter of Pizarro, now that he saw the people so cool, he changed sides, and left the camp for Trujillo with his whole company and Pedro Suárez de Escobedo and Francisco and Jerónimo de Escobedo, his nephews, who had caused the death of their uncle, the factor Illén Suárez de Carvajal, by their flight, as we have already said. Licentiate Polo, Marcos de Retamoso (a famous ensign), Francisco Miranda, Hernando de Vargas, and many other renowned soldiers went with him.

The flight of all these could not be a secret. It was noised abroad by those nearest that quarter; and Gabriel de Rojas, whom Gonzalo had recently made standard bearer instead of Don Antonio Ribera, followed their example. Gonzalo had left Ribera as his deputy in Lima, for he had great trust in him on account of their relationship and his pledges in their chimerical cause. Many others fled with Gabriel de Rojas, including his nephews Gabriel Bermúdez and Gómez de Rojas, who were persons of rank. They got away unperceived, leaving by the quarter that had been guarded by Licentiate Carvajal, which Pizarro and his friends thought was securely held.

But in the morning when Licentiate Carvajal's flight and that of Gabriel de Rojas and the rest became known, Pizarro was naturally very angry, especially because of the defection of the first named. He was much perplexed about the cause of Carvajal's dissatisfaction and pique, and regretted not having married him to his niece Doña Francisca Pizarro, as he had once intended, for this would have bound him to him forever by bonds of kinship. He also wondered if the licentiate had taken offence at being replaced by Captain Juan de Acosta after he had been appointed for the expedition. In this connection Gonzalo complained to Francisco de Carvajal, blaming him for his bad advice which had led to the change.

Carvajal replied that: "As the licentiate had made bold to run away in his presence, when if perceived, his life would have been in danger, it was much better that he should be at a distance; and the damage would have been much worse if he had taken with him the three hundred men under his command. They came to Your Lordship when they needed you to stand up for their estates and lives and honor; but just as they then forsook the emperor and pursued the viceroy until they killed him, so the very same people now deny and sell Your Lordship and flee from you because they no longer need you. You've guaranteed them their possession of what they'd lost, and they worship no other idol and have no other king but their own interest. They've repaid Your Lordship like the people they are, and their own deeds will reward them as they deserve."

Such were the commander's words, and I saw his prophecy duly fulfilled in the case of most, or almost all of them; for few of the leading ones died a natural death, and most came to a violent end in the risings that followed. The departure of Licentiate Carvajal finally discouraged Gonzalo's followers. They thought that if this gentleman, who was so deeply involved in the affair and had even beheaded the viceroy, turned against Gonzalo their whole party must be bankrupt. So, many resolved to quit and did so. Next day, while the army was on the march, all those who could fled secretly, and they began to defect so openly and boldly that two famous soldiers, Pedro Villadán and Juan López, rode off in full view of the whole camp and of Gonzalo himself. They went off shouting for His Majesty, and crying death to the traitor Gonzalo. Soon after two others did the same, one called Francisco Guillada and the other Juan Páez de Soria. Gonzalo refused to pursue them, fearing that the pursuers would not bring them back even if they overtook them, but would go with them. With these fears Gonzalo hastened to cross the plains to Arequipa. Many arquebusiers fled on the way, leaving their guns behind so that Pizarro should be satisfied to have the weapons and not try to follow them. So many fled that, as Zárate says (Book VI, ch. xvii), he had no more than two hundred men when he reached the province of Nanasca [Nasca], sixty leagues from Lima. Francisco de Carvajal, like an experienced captain, collected the arquebusses and any other weapons left behind by the fugitives, so as to arm new soldiers if any appeared.

CHAPTER XV

Lima declares for His Majesty; Aldana lands;
a great disturbance in the city.

ILL FORTUNE was not content to dog Gonzalo with all these defections
from his army, reducing it from the thousand soldiers with whom he
had left Lima a few days earlier to no more than two hundred. It also
ordained that those he had left in Lima as his most trustworthy friends,
both because of pledges they had given him and their ties of kinship,
should now turn against him and go over to the king's side. Two days
after Gonzalo's departure for Arequipa, Don Antonio de Ribera, who
had remained as his deputy in Lima, and the alcaldes Martín Pizarro and
Antonio León, and other *vecinos* who, on grounds of old age or illness,
more feigned than real, had obtained permission to stay behind on condition they exchanged their arms and horses for their persons—these old
and sick men, finding the enemy twelve or fifteen leagues away, took the
city flag out into the public square, called together the people, and raised
it in His Majesty's name, announcing the president's bidding and the
general pardon.

Fernández says that this was done by order of Gonzalo, who had left
instructions to this effect so that those who had forsaken him should get
no credit for going over to the king. However, Fernández himself con-
tradicts this, saying that it must be a malicious invention. But it was in
fact the case; for Gonzalo did give such instructions: and it was for this
reason that he left as his deputy Don Antonio de Ribera, to whom he was
so attached both on account of their kinship and of Ribera's service to the
marquis, his brother, and himself. He realized that by getting the city to
declare for His Majesty (after his own departure) Ribera would gain
credit and honor in the eyes of President La Gasca; for Gonzalo was well
aware that as soon as he was out of sight, the people in the city would turn
against him as the other captains and deputies had done in various parts
of Peru, and he thought that it was better that this should be done by his
orders, even if they had to be kept secret. This would assist Don Antonio
de Ribera; moreover his niece, the marquis' daughter, Doña Francisca
Pizarro, remained in Ribera's hands.

When the city had risen against Pizarro, Aldana was informed of the fact. He celebrated the event with incredible delight, for he had not expected those within to come over so easily, and was some distance out at sea, where he was cautiously collecting all those who came over to him. Captain Juan Alonso Palomino was on the shore for this purpose and had fifty men with him. Boats were kept ready so that they could retire if necessary, for it was feared that Gonzalo would return to the city when he knew what had taken place there. In order to learn immediately of Pizarro's approach, if he did return, twelve horsemen were stationed on the road: these were men who had fled to Aldana, and were therefore regarded as more loyal than those who had simply declared for him, since they had turned their backs on Gonzalo. Captain Illanes was sent in a frigate to sail southwards and where possible to land a religious and a soldier who were to convey the president's despatches to Centeno and others to well-known men who were with Acosta; the Indians would spread them throughout the country and so they would reach their destinations. The letters did Acosta a great deal of harm, as we shall see.

Captain Aldana, whom I knew and of whom I shall later make special mention, took the above measures on shipboard, still not daring to land; for as both elements were disturbed, he feared that some might try to kill him and then desert to Gonzalo Pizarro. In addition to the many who went over to the king, there were some who left the king and came over to Gonzalo; and the historians give their names. Aldana was afraid that one of these might attempt to perform some striking act such as killing him. Because of these fears he stayed quietly out at sea until he knew that Gonzalo was 80 leagues from Lima; and by the time the news arrived he was 110 leagues away. Then Aldana and all his followers landed. Everyone in the city, captains, soldiers—though there were few of these—even children, came out solemnly to receive him. He left the fleet in charge of the *alcalde ordinario* Juan Fernández after the necessary ceremonies of handing it over. He then entered the city and sought out such arms and munitions as there were.

Meanwhile it was reported that Gonzalo was returning to the city, and though this was so impossible that the news should have been disregarded, fear made them insecure and they believed it and even supposed that the enemy was four leagues away. They thought that they were not strong enough to resist him, and those who had no horses to escape by land went out to sea to seek refuge in the ships, while those who had mounts rode to Trujillo by the royal highway. Others who were unable to take such precautions scattered and hid in secret places, such as canebrakes and farmsteads or wherever they could. They thought they were lost for a day and a night, until they received assurances that the news was false. Those who had not gone far away retired into the city. Zárate says that Aldana landed on September 9, 1547. Here we shall leave him, to return to Acosta, who was marching on Cuzco by the mountain road, accompanied by three hundred men, with a commander, ensign general, and captains of arquebusiers and pikemen, as though it were an army of thirty thousand.

CHAPTER XVI

Acosta's captains and soldiers flee; Gonzalo Pizarro reaches Huarina, and sends a message to Centeno; the reply.

WHILE Acosta and his men were near Cuzco, they received news of the reverses of Gonzalo and the numerous desertions that had taken place; and though Acosta tried to suppress the news, he could not do so, for some of his soldiers had received the letters that had been scattered abroad and knew what was happening, though they did not dare to talk about it for fear of arousing suspicions. But when the bad news became public property, the commander, Páez de Sotomayor and Captain Martín de Olmos, whom I knew, each decided to kill Acosta. They did not at first dare to reveal themselves to one another, but at length each guessed the other's intention and they discussed the matter and informed some reliable soldiers. However it came to the ears of Acosta, who took precautions and doubled his bodyguard.

The two captains now became suspicious, and hearing one day that Acosta was closeted in his tent with Captain Martín de Almendras and another close friend called Diego Gumiel, they were afraid that he was planning to kill them, so they decided to escape, as they could not kill him. So they passed the word on, and soon thirty men were ready with horses and arms, and left the camp in full view of the rest and went to Lima.

The leaders of these were Páez de Sotomayor, Martín de Olmos, and the ensign general Martín de Alarcón, Garci Gutiérrez de Escobar, Alonso Rengel, Hernando de Alvarado, Martín Monge, Antonio de Avila, and Gaspar de Toledo. Acosta followed, and overtook three or four of them and killed them; but seeing that it was a waste of time to pursue them any further, he retraced his steps to Cuzco, where he deposed the alcaldes Centeno had left and appointed others.

Here he received a message that he was to join Gonzalo Pizarro in Arequipa as best he could. Juan de Acosta left Cuzco, and after he had gone twelve leagues his captain Martín de Almendras, in whom he had great confidence, fled one night with thirty of the best men. Almendras returned to Cuzco and deposed Acosta's alcaldes, as though this would bring victory in the whole campaign. After this Almendras marched toward Lima, leaving Acosta astonished that a man in his position could turn his back on Gonzalo, who had treated him like a son out of regard for his uncle Francisco de Almendras, who was killed by Centeno. Acosta did not dare to follow Almendras lest all his men should desert; so he continued his journey, increasing his daily march. Many still fled in twos and threes, so that by the time he joined Gonzalo in Arequipa he had no more than a hundred men, as Fernández says (Book II, ch. lxviii), and Zárate (Book VI, ch. xviii). There they discussed what they should do to defend their lives, for there was now nothing left to lose: their honor they regarded as already lost since they were called traitors to their king, and their estates were in the hands of their enemies.

Pizarro and his captains decided to travel on by the way Centeno had taken, for there was no other means of reaching their destination, which was one of the many trails in eastern Peru leading into the wild forests the Indians call Anti. They thought they would try to win some province where they might end their days, if they were allowed to do so. If this could not be done, they would cross into Chile and help in the conquest of the warlike tribes there, supposing that they might get a pardon for their past crimes in return for these services, once they had left Peru. If Centeno would not let them pass, they meant to stake all and win or die in battle with him, though it was realized that he was superior in the number of his men. So Pizarro left Arequipa, and by daily stages came nearly to Huarina through which the road toward the forests passed.

Captain Diego Centeno heard of Pizarro's approach, left his fortified position, and burnt the bridge over the river that drains Lake Titicaca so that the enemy could not cross. In order to prevent Pizarro's escape, he went out determined to give battle, for he was confident of an easy victory in view of the large number of good men he had.

Pizarro was afraid to come to grips for the same reason, and sent him a messenger with a letter reminding him of their former friendship in the conquest of the Collao and Los Charcas, and of the great benefits he had conferred on Centeno then and since, especially in sparing his life after he had killed Gaspar Rodríguez and Felipe Gutiérrez: Gonzalo had then pardoned Centeno, against the advice of all his friends, though it was clear from the list of plotters that he was one of the ringleaders. Let Centeno remember that he had been one of the first and leading procurators of Peru, who had made Pizarro procurator general when they needed him, and later governor; that Centeno had followed him to Lima and had not left him till he was made governor. Let him forget the past, and they would meet and discuss calmly what should be done for the benefit of all of them and of the land of Peru: he, Pizarro, would do all he could for Centeno, treating him as his own brother. They sent this letter by a soldier called Francisco Vosso, the husband of Juana Leitão, whom we have already mentioned; he was very closely attached to Francisco de Carvajal and therefore selected as the most trustworthy.

Zárate (Book VII, ch. ii) tells how Vosso gave the letter to Centeno and offered to serve him, warning him that Diego Alvarez, his ensign, was in correspondence with Gonzalo. Centeno did not punish him, however, for Alvarez had already revealed the correspondence to him, saying that he had begun it in their own interest. Centeno replied to Gonzalo's letters very courteously, thanking him for his offer and acknowledging the benefits he had received from him; he hoped to repay him for them by advising him and begging him to consider the circumstances and His Majesty's generosity to him and all the rest in offering a pardon for all that had gone before. If Gonzalo would join him and submit to the king, he, Centeno, would plead with the president on his behalf to make the best and most honorable terms possible, without jeopardizing Gonzalo's life or property, and assuring him that if the affair had been against any other than His Majesty, Gonzalo would have found no better friend or collaborator than himself. He made other observations of the same kind in the letter.

Thus Agustín de Zárate.

CHAPTER XVII

*Centeno writes to the president by Gonzalo's own
messenger; Gonzalo's despair; the president
reaches Jauja where he
finds Francisco Vosso.*

CENTENO saw that Vosso was anxious to serve His Majesty, as he had
offered his services unsolicited and had revealed so great a secret as
that of his ensign, and therefore decided to entrust him with a message
for the president, consisting of a long letter reporting what had happened and how he had trapped Pizarro so that he had no way of escape.
He said how many cavalry and infantry he had himself, and how few
Gonzalo had, and said that he hoped he would not get away. He also
passed on the message Francisco Vosso had brought and enclosed Gonzalo's own letter in full testimony of what he said. Centeno told Vosso of
his reply to Gonzalo, and explained that he was trusting him with his
message to the president. He gave him a thousand pesos of gold for the
journey, and told him that on reaching Gonzalo's camp, he was to deliver the reply and answer any questions Gonzalo might put, then secretly to buy the best mule he could find in the camp and hasten off to find
the president, wherever he might be, and give him the despatch and all
the news he had about the affairs of both armies. In order that his information should be exact, Centeno gave him an account of all the men
and arms he had. And so that he should not lack a reward for his deeds as
a double spy, he gave him a signed document granting him in the king's
name a small allocation of Indians that was vacant in the district of Arequipa. He also wrote to the president begging him to confirm this reward, which Vosso deserved for his good intentions and services.

Vosso returned to Gonzalo Pizarro, who, on learning of his approach,
sent Francisco de Carvajal to examine him and get to the bottom of all
that had passed between Centeno and Vosso: he was confident that Vosso
would conceal nothing from his patron Carvajal. The latter interrogated
him thoroughly and Vosso gave complete answers, reporting in detail on
the captains of infantry and cavalry and the number of soldiers. He said

that Centeno had told him all this, and added what he had written in his reply to Gonzalo to the effect that he would intercede with the president to spare his life and property, and make it worth his while to submit to the king.

Carvajal, having heard all this, took Vosso to Gonzalo Pizarro and repeated all he had said. When Gonzalo heard that Centeno was offering him patronage and rewards, he said that he would receive none from one who had himself received them from his brothers and himself. He refused to read the letter, not wishing to set eyes on such arguments; and like a man despairing of any compromise, had it burnt in public so that there should be no talk of an agreement. He ordered Vosso to say that Centeno had no more than seven hundred men, lest they should be discouraged if they knew he had twelve hundred.

Having carried out his duty as messenger, Vosso on the same day bought a mule for eight hundred pesos through a friend, without telling him why he wanted it. That night he rode off on it and at daybreak was twelve leagues away from the camp. He went straight to the president without visiting Arequipa, where his wife and children were. Gonzalo was astonished to hear of his flight, and told Carvajal privately that he could not understand why it was that those in whom he most confided because they were most pledged to their undertaking were the first to deny him. Even Francisco Vosso, a servant of Carvajal's, had repudiated him. Carvajal told him not to be surprised, for it was typical of mean-spirited people anxiously to desire pardon when they found they were blamed. Thus the deepest involved had turned their backs on him, while those least pledged to him were still with him. That was the way of this wretched world. No one honored another for the other's deserts, but only for his own needs; and when these were past, he denied all the benefits he had received.

Gonzalo Pizarro realized that he had been tricked by Centeno when Vosso fled, and was filled with disdain, complaining of his ill fortune that those who had received most benefits of him were most ungrateful to him. So he prepared to go on and fight to win or die, for there was no longer anything to be gained from negotiations.

The president, whom we left on the road from Trujillo to Lima, had hourly news of what Gonzalo was doing and of the desertion of so many of his followers. As they reached the president they gave him full reports of everything. Thus he knew that Gonzalo had gone down the coast toward Arequipa, and he sent orders to the captains who were in Cajamarca to travel in good order with the men they had to the valley of Jauja, which he had been told was a good place to collect supplies and to bring together the men in the region and the deserters coming over from Gonzalo Pizarro. After this, he pressed on, and soon heard how completely lost Pizarro was; he had now only two hundred men, who were those who had not been able to flee; and Juan de Acosta was also broken and beaten, for of three hundred men he had brought from Lima, two hundred had fled with their captains. The president learnt that Lima had declared for the king and that Aldana had good control over it from his ships. This greatly encouraged him and he sent new messengers to his captain general Pedro de Hinojosa, with a full report and orders to hasten to Jauja; he himself decided not to enter Lima, so as not to waste time.

The president took the mountain road and went to Jauja, where he found his captains, who received him with great celebrations and rejoicings at seeing him in their midst. He spent many days there, bringing in arms and supplies of all kinds, and set up forges and sent for craftsmen. In short he took all the steps a good leader should to ensure that the enemy should be completely destroyed and that those who had abandoned him should not fall again in his power.

Francisco Vosso added to their encouragement and good fortune by the good news of Centeno's army he brought and the bad news of Gonzalo's, which he reported to the president as an eye witness of both. This crowned the content of them all. He gave the president Centeno's letters and the document granting him his allocation of Indians, which the president confirmed. Vosso was unlucky that it was not the best in Peru, which he might have been given just as readily as a reward for his good news. The captains and officers of the army decided that no more men should be raised and that the army should be disbanded, as Centeno's force would be sufficient to finish off Gonzalo Pizarro. We shall leave them in their councils and rejoicings, and tell the story of the cruel battle of Huarina, which occurred during these very days.

CHAPTER XVIII

*Pizarro decides to give battle; he sends
Acosta to make a night attack; Centeno
draws up his men and Pizarro
does likewise.*

GONZALO and his captains were much incensed with anger and humiliation at finding that when peace negotiations were opened their own messenger should have been deceived into becoming a double spy against his master. Blinded by their wrath, they decided to march on in search of a means of escape, and if Centeno barred their way, to fight him till they won or died.

This decision was the result of Pizarro's council meeting with his commander and captains to discuss the flight of Francisco Vosso. They prepared their arms (though they had never neglected them), and so marched toward Huarina, first spreading the rumor that they were going by a different road, so as to throw Centeno off the scent: in order to convince him, Francisco de Espinosa was sent to collect Indians and supplies along the road they were not going to take. But Centeno soon heard from the Indians of Espinosa's journey and of the route taken by Gonzalo, for the Indians diligently brought him information of all Pizarro did. This was by order of Don Cristóbal Paullu Inca, of whom we have already spoken at length.

When Centeno knew of the direction Gonzalo had taken he went out to bar his way, and they came so near that their scouts talked together and returned with news of their opponents. Centeno had his men made ready and made them keep watch that night drawn up in formation, for he feared that Carvajal might try some night attack, like those he had often practiced in the past. He did not however avoid a midnight attack by Acosta with 20 arquebusiers which caused such a stir in his camp that Zárate says (Book VII, ch. ii), "that many in his lines fled to their tents, and others, from Valdivia's company, dropped their pikes and ran away, while Acosta returned to his camp without losing a man." Thus Zárate.

With regard to Valdivia's company, Captain Pedro de Valdivia heard in Chile of the struggles in Peru, and came by sea to observe them with some of his companions. On reaching the Peruvian coast he heard of Gonzalo's downfall, and that President La Gasca was at Jauja preparing to attack him. He decided to go there and serve His Majesty, and so as to get there more quickly, landed his men and ordered them to join Centeno: these are the men Zárate refers to.

Next day Centeno's and Pizarro's armies marched almost within sight of each other, and drew their men up in formation. Centeno had 1,212 men, according to López de Gómara (ch. clxxxii), though Zárate says a little under 1,000, and Fernández over 900. I always heard that there were 1,200: 260 horse, 150 arquebusiers, and nearly 800 pikes. All the pikemen and arquebusiers formed an infantry squadron with picquets of arquebusiers on either side, though as these were few the picquets were weak.

The captains of infantry were Juan de Vargas, brother to my lord Garcilaso de la Vega, Francisco de Retamoso, Captain Negral, Captain Pantoja, and Diego López de Zúñiga. These five with their ensigns on their left hand formed the first rank some twenty paces in front of the main body. There followed eleven ranks of the best soldiers forming the vanguard. Behind came the standard bearers with their banners, and after that the rest in order, arquebusiers mingled with pikemen.

To the right of the infantry squadron Centeno stationed three companies of horse, under Captains Pedro de los Ríos, a native of Córdova of the noble family of that name, and Antonio de Ulloa, a native of Cáceres, a very noble gentleman. With them was Diego Alvarez, a native of Almendral, as ensign general with the royal standard. Diego Centeno was sick and did not enter the formation or take part in the battle, which he watched from a litter. The formation included 160 horse, who were to attack Gonzalo's infantry from the left. To the left of his own infantry Centeno drew up another squadron of 97 horse, consisting of men from Arequipa and La Plata, led by Alonso de Mendoza and Jerónimo de Villegas. They were accompanied by the commander, Luis de Ribera; a gentleman called Luis García de San Mamés was sergeant major.

The opposing army was drawn up by the commander Francisco de Carvajal, who would have been the flower of the armies of Peru, if he had served the king; for this alone sullied his honor and caused the historians to write so ill of him. He was a man so experienced in warfare and so skilled in it that he knew in how many moves he could mate his opponent, as an expert chess player playing against a beginner. With his experience he drew up his men on a very level plain. He had 400 men, rather less

than more, though the historians say nearly 500, having said just before
that when Gonzalo reached Arequipa he had only 200, and that Acosta
had only 100 when he joined him. The truth is that he put about 400 men
into this battle: 85 horse, 60 pikes, and 250 arquebusiers. The authors
exaggerate Pizarro's force and diminish the others, so as not to give so
much glory to Carvajal for defeating so many with so few, and to spare
Centeno from ignominy at being beaten by so few. But they do not perceive the secret of the one's victory and the other's defeat, which we shall
soon mention.

He formed a small squadron with his limited number of infantry on a
flat plain where there was nothing to hinder the shooting of the arquebusiers. He had a very fine company of these under Captain Diego
Guillén, Juan de la Torre, and himself. Juan de Acosta, though a captain
of cavalry, exchanged his men for those of Captain Master Guevara, who
was lame and could only fight on horseback. These four were the captains
of the arquebusiers, and Hernando Bachicao of the 60 pikemen. Picquets
of arquebusiers were placed on either side of the squadron.

The captains of cavalry included Gonzalo Pizarro himself, armed in a
fine coat of mail with a green velvet breast guard over it, which I have
seen him wear. This was covered by a tunic of slashed crimson velvet. At
his sides were Licentiate Cepeda, as captain of cavalry, and Master Guevara.

Carvajal placed this squadron of cavalry to the right of the infantry,
not level with it, but fifty paces back, for he wished to have the front and
sides of the infantry clear so as to give free play to the arquebusiers on
whom he relied for his victory.

Carvajal was armed like a horseman with a coat of mail, a breastplate,
and a helmet of the type called Burgundian with a flat visor, varnished
with the black varnish they used for sword hilts. Over his armor he wore
a tunic of soiled green cloth. He rode a common nag, and looked like a
very poor soldier who had been rejected from the cavalry: he wished to
pass unrecognized. Thus he continued to arrange his forces, often going
to the front and flanks to set them in order and give what commands were
necessary.

So both armies were drawn up, with the main formations more than
six hundred paces apart. Centeno's imagined the victory was already
theirs; and many of them, on leaving the camp to join the lines, told their
Indian servants to prepare double their usual amount of food, for they
would invite their friends, the vanquished, to dine with them.

The Indians contradicted these vain expectations, saying to their mas-

ters: "Sir, you'd better tell us where you want us to put this baggage before the enemy takes it. There aren't many of them, but they'll beat you."
They said this with such warmth and conviction that some Spaniards
were angry and wanted to lay hands on them; but they went off cursing
them to join the lines. One of these was Martín de Arbieto, who was
talking to a friend about this ill omen, when Gonzalo Silvestre came up
and confirmed that his own Indians had said the same. They had hardly
gone a few steps before Juan Julio de Hojeda, a *vecino* of Cuzco, and one
of the first conquerors of Peru, came up shouting: "By ————! I've been
on the point of killing my Indians, for they've told me we're going to be
beaten! I don't know how these dogs get their information unless they
talk to the Devil by witchcraft." At this point another *vecino* of Cuzco,
called ———— Carrera, joined them and said the same. And another leading soldier approached from another direction with the same tale; so that
six or seven of them brought this ill omen from the Indians, and still
cursing them, they took their places in the cavalry squadron to the left of
the infantry.

CHAPTER XIX

The battle of Huarina; Carvajal's stratagem,
and the personal deeds of Gonzalo Pizarro
and other famous knights.

THE TWO armies were some time observing one another without making a move. Then Gonzalo Pizarro sent a chaplain called Fray Herrera
to ask Centeno to let him pass, for there was no need to fight a battle: if
not, the responsibility for all the casualties and havoc would be with him.
The chaplain carried a crucifix in his hand, but they did not let him approach, suspecting that he had come to reconnoiter the disposition of Centeno's army. The bishop of Cuzco and Centeno, who were together, summoned him, and after hearing him, had him arrested and taken to the
bishop's tent. Centeno's men thought their victory was certain when they
heard of the priest's message; and wished to gain the honor of being the
first to attack; so they left their station and advanced toward the enemy.
After they had gone a hundred paces they drew up. Carvajal's interest was

to stay quietly where he was and wait for the enemy to arrive, and in order to incite them to attack he sent Acosta with 30 arquebusiers to begin a skirmish, pretending later to retreat so as to draw the enemy after him. A similar number of arquebusiers came out from the other side and they skirmished, though little harm was done as they were too far apart for the shots to reach home.

Carvajal, as the historians say, and especially Zárate (Book VII, ch. iii),

seeing that Centeno's army had stopped, tried to make him move again and ordered his men to advance ten paces, very slowly. Centeno's men saw this and some began to say that the enemy was winning honor at their expense. Then they all began to march, and Pizarro's army stopped. As they came on, Carvajal ordered a few arquebusses to be fired to provoke the enemy into letting off a round, which they did. Centeno's infantry quickened its step and raised its pikes, and the arquebusiers fired another round, but still did no harm, for they were three hundred paces away. Carvajal refused to let any of his own arquebusses fire until his enemy was a little over a hundred paces away, when he ordered a round. The arquebusiers were numerous and highly skilled, and the first volley killed more than 150 men, including two captains, so that Centeno's squadron began to break: a second volley shattered it and the men began to flee in disorder.

So Zárate; and this brief account is the beginning, middle, and nearly the end of the battle. López de Gómara and Fernández say the same with no discrepancies. I shall pass over what they say, and give some details about the battle which I heard from those who fought on one side or the other. Carvajal's insistence on provoking the enemy to attack while he remained still was because his arquebusiers, though they were no more than 250 in number, had over six and nearly seven hundred arquebusses. Carvajal was so experienced that he shrewdly took precautions against emergencies before they occurred, and as we have said, he assiduously collected the arms of those who fled, especially the arquebusses, and seven or eight days before the battle he had them carefully made ready and distributed among his men, almost all of whom had three arquebusses and some four. And as they could not march carrying three or four arquebusses, or use them if they were on their backs, he used these devices to get the enemy to come to him and not to have to go to the enemy. To show his skill, and the wit and humor of all he said and did, we shall mention in particular two of his sayings at that time.

The first was when, two days before the battle, a famous soldier came up to him and said: "Have them give me a little lead to make balls, for I have none for the day of the battle."

"I can't believe," said Carvajal, "that a soldier of your eminence is without shot when the enemy is so near."

The soldier replied: "No, sir, I haven't any."

Carvajal said: "You must excuse me if I don't believe you. I find it impossible that you shouldn't have any."

The soldier, being so pressed, said: "On my oath, sir, I've only three."

Carvajal said: "I was sure that a person like yourself wouldn't be without shot. Of those three I beg you to lend me the one you have over, and I'll give it to one who has none; and with one of the ones you keep kill a bird today and with the other kill a man tomorrow, and don't fire another shot."

Carvajal implied that if each of his arquebusiers killed a man his victory would be assured. Nevertheless he did not neglect to supply this soldier and all the rest with all the powder and shot and other arms they needed. Such was his humor toward his intimates: he had another and more telling style for his enemies.

His second speech was a short harangue to his arquebusiers. When he saw the enemy approaching, he urged them to shoot at the lower half of the body, not at the head or chest. He said: "Remember, gentlemen, that the shot that goes high, even if it's only two inches over the enemy's head, is a wasted shot. The one that goes low, even if it hits the ground ten paces before him, does damage, not only the shot itself but anything it throws up. Moreover, it's an advantage to hit the enemy in the thigh and legs, for it's a miracle if a man with an arquebus wound there stands on his feet. They usually fall at once, and that's what we want. If you hit their arms or body, and it's not a mortal wound, they still stay on their feet."

With these instructions he had the arquebusiers fire when he saw the enemy a hundred paces away, as Zárate says, and the volley of shot poured into them was so cruel and devastating that not ten were left standing of the first rank of captains and ensigns or the eleven ranks of picked men marching in front of the banners. They all fell, dead or wounded, and it was a grievous sight. Damage was also done to the squadron of cavalry led by Alonso de Mendoza and Jerónimo de Villegas, in which ten or twelve men were brought down, one of whom was the Carrera we have mentioned. The commander, Luis de Ribera, seeing that if the horse advanced slowly they would all be killed before they reached the enemy, ordered them to attack Gonzalo's horse.

Gonzalo, though he saw the enemy approach, stayed where he was without attacking, for the commander had bidden him do so, in order to give the arquebusses a chance to punish the enemy before they came to grips. But when Centeno's horse had passed to the right of his infantry, he advanced some thirty paces to receive them. Centeno's men, coming on with the impetus of a long charge, drove Gonzalo's back and overran them like sheep. Horses and men fell, and the historians say (and I with them) that not ten men were left on their horses. One was Gonzalo, who, finding himself alone, took shelter with the infantry. Three famous gentlemen who knew him went after him to kill him or force him to surrender. They were Francisco de Ulloa, Miguel de Vergara, and Gonzalo Silvestre. The latter took Pizarro's right and the other two his left. The two who were nearest Gonzalo lunged at his back; but as he was well armed they did not hurt him. Miguel de Vergara shouted: "The traitor Pizarro's mine! The traitor Pizarro's mine!" So all four went galloping toward the infantry. Silvestre's horse pressed Gonzalo hardest, for its rider spurred it so hard that its chin rested on the rump of Pizarro's horse and hindered it from running. Pizarro perceived this and turned round with a short-handled battle-axe which was hanging from his right wrist. With this he dealt three blows at the horse: two were on the muzzle which he cut to the teeth on either side of the nostrils and the other was above the right eye-socket. It broke the horse's headpiece, though without injuring the eye. Gonzalo did all this as coolly and smoothly as if he were tilting in the yard. I heard Gonzalo Silvestre himself say this. He often told this episode in the battle, as well as many others that took place that day. So all four reached the infantry squadron.

CHAPTER XX

The cruel battle of Huarina continues;
individual feats of arms; Gonzalo
Pizarro's victory.

PIZARRO's men recognized him and raised their pikes to receive him. Gonzalo Silvestre saw that the blows he had aimed at his back had done no harm, and therefore dropped his hand and struck out at the horse's right haunch, but the wound was a very slight one; and later, when peace was restored and the blow was mentioned, Silvestre never dared say that he had struck it, lest anyone should say that his arm was as feeble as the wound. Pizarro's men, after receiving their leader, went out to kill his pursuers. Silvestre's horse was struck in the face with two blows with the pike, which made it rear; and another pike pierced both its fore-legs. The horse tried to turn round to escape its enemies, and broke the pike transfixing its legs, so that it and its rider escaped with no more harm than we have said.

Miguel de Vergara fared worse, for he was so carried away by the thought that the traitor Pizarro was his, as he said, that he penetrated three or four ranks deep into the enemy's lines and was cut to pieces with his horse. Francisco de Ulloa did no better, for as he turned his horse to retire, an arquebusier ran forward, placed the muzzle of his gun against Ulloa's left kidney, fired it and blew a hole through his body. Another soldier at once knifed Ulloa's horse and hamstrung it in both legs above the hocks. But the horse, a grey (I heard all these details down to the color of the horses), was so good that, wounded as it was, it bore its master more than fifty paces from the place where it was struck, until both of them fell dead. Such was the encounter of the cavalry of Centeno and Pizarro, which was so cruel that next day 107 dead horses were counted at the place of the combat. Of 182 horses on both sides these 107 were all slain within two *fanegas* of land, without counting those that fell further away. My father told me this; and the clash was so cruel that when it was first spoken of the listeners refused to believe it until the narrator said that it was Garcilaso de la Vega who had counted the dead horses. Then they believed it and were astonished at so remarkable an occurrence.

When Centeno's cavalry found that Pizarro had retreated into his infantry lines, they turned on the few horses left in their hands and killed almost all of them, shouting victory. One of those killed was Captain Pedro de Fuentes, Pizarro's deputy at Arequipa. Another gentleman struck him a two-handed blow with an Indian club on the helmet. He hit so hard that poor Pedro de Fuentes leapt more than half a yard in his saddle and fell to the ground dead with his head crushed in his helmet, for the blow had smashed it in. Captain Licentiate Cepeda was also taken and badly wounded in the face, with a slash right across it through the middle of the nose: I saw him later in Cuzco when the wound had healed, and he still wore a finger's breadth of black taffeta plaster across his face.

Hernando Bachicao, the captain of Gonzalo's pikes, hearing Centeno's men cry victory, now secretly went over to them in the heat of the fray and obtained witnesses to his coming to serve the king. Centeno's other squadron of horse, which was to the right of the infantry and led by

Pedro de los Ríos and Antonio de Ulloa, attacked Pizarro's infantry from the left, as had been arranged at the beginning of the battle. But they received such a volley of shot that Pedro de los Ríos and many more were killed before they could come to blows, and those who were left turned aside and tried to avoid closing with the squadron which was well defended with pikes and arquebusses and still unbroken, since the enemy had not yet done it any damage. They passed the whole left flank and rearguard of Pizarro's squadron and suffered great damage, for the little band was well equipped on all sides with *illapas,* which, as we have said, means thunder, lightning, and thunderbolts in the Indian language. And such were the arquebusses to Centeno's noble and splendid army, which certainly contained most of the best riders and horses of the time in Peru, almost all of whom perished in this bloody and disastrous battle. Gonzalo Pizarro wanted to leave his ranks and fight with the cavalry as best he could till he died. But Carvajal heard him and said: "Let Your Lordship stay still, for that won't help. Leave it all to me, and I'll give you your enemy beaten, dead, and fleeing; and I won't be long about it."

Centeno's horse re-formed, some having passed Gonzalo's lines on the right and some on the left. But they were still not safe, for Carvajal ordered the rearguard to fire with all speed, which they did, doing great execution and forcing them to abandon their station and flee across country. The whole conflict was so brief that Centeno's men had hardly stopped singing victory when Pizarro's began. When Bachicao saw this, he returned to his squadron, very exultant because of the victory. One of the horsemen, a native of Herrera de Alcántara whose name has escaped my memory, passed in front of Gonzalo's lines, where Carvajal happened to be on his nag. Without recognizing him, but simply to do something worthy of note, he slashed at him as he ran and struck him in the visor. The sword was a good one and so was the arm behind it, and Carvajal's visor was broken, but he was not wounded. The blow and its result were so remarkable that all who beheld it were astonished. After the battle, when quiet was restored, Carvajal showed Pizarro the helmet and said: "How do you think that gentleman would have left me if I hadn't had this defence?" A third of Centeno's infantry died, as we have said. Another third broke ranks when they heard their own men shouting victory and tried to sack Pizarro's camp; and they did sack a great part of it. This was one of the reasons why the battle was so quickly lost, for the soldiers forgot to fight, and were fully engaged in stealing what they could find. A few more foot remained, not above 60, and they crossed pikes with Gonzalo's.

Then Juan de Acosta came out to fight them. One of Diego Centeno's soldiers, a certain Guadramiros, whom I knew, a tall, well-built man, though very peaceable, and with less pretentions to soldierliness than to civility, struck him in the gullet with his pike, which sank into his back, and Juan de Acosta fell to the ground, raising both legs in the air. Then a Negro came up, a certain Guadalupe, whom I also knew, and he slashed him in both calves. The Negro was a little runt of a man and the sword no better than its owner, so he did not cut them both off, but only slightly wounded him. Pizarro's men attacked Centeno's few survivors and killed almost all of them. Guadramiros and Guadalupe were saved from death by Juan de Acosta, who got in front of them and shouted to his followers that they deserved honor and reward. As I have said, I knew them both: I later saw Guadalupe in Cuzco as an arquebusier in Gonzalo's companies, full of plumes and decorations and prouder than a peacock, for everyone honored him for his spirit. I may be pardoned for including these details which may seem trifling: they happened, and as I was an eye witness of them, I have set them down.

CHAPTER XXI

The dead and wounded on both sides, and other
occurrences; what Carvajal did
after the battle.

GUADRAMIROS' feat was the last in the battle; and Gonzalo's victory was now fully established. Less than a hundred of his men died; more than 70 were cavalry, for not 15 of the infantry were killed. The wounded included, as we have said, Captain Cepeda, Juan de Acosta, and Captain Diego Guillén. On Centeno's side more than 350 were killed, including the commander and all the infantry captains, ensigns, and leading foot soldiers, as well as Pedro de los Ríos, a captain of horse, and the ensign general Diego Alvarez: all these lay dead on the field. Of the 350 more who were wounded, over 150 died owing to the lack of surgeons, medicines, and comforts, and because the air is always so cold up there, despite its being the torrid zone. Gonzalo came out in pursuit with 7 or 8 more on wounded or lame horses. They went to Centeno's tents, rather to prove their victory than to follow it up or harm the fugitives; for, as López de Gómara says (ch. clxxxii), the victors were too badly damaged to pursue the vanquished.

At one side of the battlefield, on the wide plain, there was a long narrow bog or fen, thirty or forty feet wide, and so shallow that only the horses' hooves sank in. Before reaching this bog one of Pizarro's men said to one of Centeno's, who was riding among them with his horse and himself covered in blood: "Sir, that horse will soon fall." This much distressed the royalist, who wanted to get away from the enemy and relied on the horse, which was an excellent one. He was Gonzalo Silvestre, whom we have so often mentioned. He told me this episode, and many others that took place in the battle. He said that at that moment he turned his head to the left and saw Gonzalo and his followers moving across the flank toward Centeno's tents. Gonzalo was crossing himself and saying aloud: "Jesus, what a victory! Jesus, what a victory!" And he repeated this many times.

Soon, before they reached the bog, Silvestre was approached by one of Pizarro's soldiers called Gonzalo de Nidos, whom Silvestre had defeated in the battle. As he had begged for mercy, Silvestre had done him no harm, but let him go. Recognizing Silvestre as an enemy, the man now began to shout: "Kill that traitor! Kill that traitor! He's one of the traitors!"

Silvestre turned to him and said: "Sir, let me be, for God's sake; for my horse and I are in such a state that we shall soon die without your killing us."

"No, by ———," cried the other, "you shall die at my hands!"

Silvestre looked at him and recognized him as the man he had spared, and said: "Show a little courtesy, sir, as I did to you not long ago."

Then Nidos shouted even louder: "So you're the rogue. I swear by ——— that I'll kill you for it, and draw your heart out and throw it to the dogs."

Silvestre told me that if the soldier who addressed him so rudely had spoken otherwise to him, he would have given in; for, as the other had said, he was almost falling off his horse. But as his opponent was so rude and ungrateful, he was angered into not surrendering if his horse could help him escape. These words took place while they were crossing the bog, during which the floundering of the horses prevented them from coming to blows. When they got to the other side Silvestre tried spurring his horse to see how it went. It leapt forward as if there were nothing wrong with it, but at the same time snorted and tossed its head, scattering much blood over its master from its head wounds. Silvestre then galloped off, to draw his assailant away from his companions. Nidos followed him, shouting: "Death to the traitor who's fleeing!"

When they were a good distance from Gonzalo Pizarro, Silvestre turned on Nidos, and gave him a blow with the flat of an old rapier he had taken from a Negro in the battle, after breaking his own two swords in it, one of which he carried girt to his waist and the other in his saddle-bow—for this was how good soldiers fought in their battles in those days, with double arms. Silvestre did not wound Nidos, but greatly surprised him and sent him running back to his own companions, crying out for help and saying: "They're killing me! They're killing me!" for cowards never have hands, but only tongues.

When Pizarro saw this brave deed, and sent one of his companions called Alonso de Herrera very courteously to ask Silvestre to come to him, for he wished to honor him for his courage, Herrera went to him; but however he spurred his horse, he could not get it to go any faster than a trot, for it was so badly wounded it soon after fell dead. He shouted: "Sir, come back, come back, for I swear by ———— the governor will honor you more in one day than the king in all his lifetime!"

Silvestre spurred his horse without troubling to reply. I heard this both from those who were with Gonzalo and from Silvestre, and I write it here from the accounts of all of them.

After the victory, Gonzalo did not wish to enter Centeno's camp, realizing that his soldiers were furiously sacking it. He returned to his own, which had also been sacked by Centeno's men when they thought the victory was theirs; and they had taken many horses and mules on which they ran away. Carvajal followed up the victory in another direction, though not so as to kill the beaten Spaniards with clubs carried by two of his Negroes, as Fernández says (ch. lxxx), who asserts that he slew more than a hundred. It is a strange thing that anyone should seek to flatter and adulate by saying such evil of one who did no such thing: surely it is enough for a flatterer to say good about the object of his flattery, even though it did not exist. Carvajal killed no one after the battle: he was content with the victory alone, which he had won by his good skill and strategy, as everyone knew. This satisfied him and he was so proud of his achievement that he boasted of having killed more than a hundred men in the battle by himself—he might have said he accounted for them all, for he killed them by his military skill. López de Gómara (ch. clxxxiii) comments on this saying of the commander's: "Francisco de Carvajal boasted of having killed a hundred men, including a priest, for his own satisfaction. A typical piece of cruelty, unless he meant it glorying in his victory and meaning that he attributed it to his own doing." Thus López de Gómara.

Francisco de Carvajal had won all this honor, fame, and glory, and thought more of succoring and relieving his enemies than of persecuting them. For the day after the battle, learning that some of Centeno's leading adherents, sworn supporters of His Majesty, were wounded, and that his own men had hidden them in their tents out of friendship and were tending them, he went and diligently sought them out. Everyone thought that he was going to kill them. He found eight of them. One was Martín de Arbieto, a native of Biscay, a brave and noble man whom we have already mentioned, and shall have cause to do so again; another was a native of Salamanca called Juan de San Miguel; another from Zafra, Francisco Maraver. I knew all three: I do not remember the names of the other five. He found them all sorely wounded and spoke to each of them in person, saying among other kindly things that he much regretted seeing them in such a plight. He begged them to take care of themselves and ask for anything they needed, which he promised to supply as if they were his own brothers. When they had recovered, if they wanted to go, he gave his word of honor that he would give them leave without making the slightest difficulty. If they wanted to stay with him, he would take care to serve them all his life.

Apart from this particular instance, he also had a proclamation made to his whole army that all Centeno's soldiers who were wounded were to ask for what medicines and money they needed, and he would see that they were attended to just like his lord the governor's own men. Francisco de Carvajal did this to attract soldiers to him and inspire devotion: he was well aware that benefits were more effective than the cruel punishments he applied to declared enemies and those he called shuttlers.

The flight of Centeno

CHAPTER XXII

*Pizarro has the dead buried, and sends
officials in various directions; the
flight of Centeno, and incidents
among the vanquished.*

As soon as Gonzalo reached his camp, he found my father there and asked him for his horse Salinillas, while his own, which he greatly valued, was being cured of the small wound it had been dealt by Gonzalo Silvestre. He rode round the camp on my father's horse, and ordered the dead and wounded to be brought in. Most of them had already been stripped of the clothes they wore, for the Indians had looted them all, without respecting friend and foe. He gave instructions for the dead to be buried in ten or twelve pits which were dug on the battlefield. The captains and noblemen killed on both sides were buried in the village called Huarina, not far away, after which the battle was given its name. They were buried in a church the Indians had built, and where they were taught Christian doctrine when there was an opportunity to hear it. Four years later, when the empire was at peace and the Spanish settlement of La Paz had been founded, the bodies were taken there and buried in the cathedral with solemn masses and sacrifices, which lasted many days. All the gentlemen of Peru contributed toward the cost, for all were connected with the dead by bonds of kinship or friendship. Having seen to the dead and wounded, Gonzalo next day appointed officials to go in all directions and carry out missions on behalf of their enterprise. He sent Dionisio de Bobadilla to La Plata to collect what silver he could find and bring it to pay the men. Diego de Carvajal, called "the gallant," went to Arequipa for the same purpose, and Juan de la Torre to Cuzco. All three took thirty arquebusiers each and commissions to enrol what men they found and bring them back to Gonzalo.

Centeno, whom it is long since we mentioned, was not fit to fight because of his illness: the historians say that he was bled six times for a pain in his side. Finding his men defeated, he got down from his litter and mounted a horse he had nearby, and with that fear of death and love of life that is natural to all of us, took to flight without waiting for the bishop. And to avoid Carvajal and his wiles and tricks, of which he had long experience, he did not go by the royal highway, or by Cuzco or Arequipa, but through uninhabited places, accompanied only by a priest called Fray Vizcaíno. He reached Lima without Carvajal or any of his men knowing which way he went; he seemed to have disappeared by magic. And although he heard on the way that the president was in the valley of Jauja, he did not go there, but contented himself with sending a letter by Fray Vizcaíno, for he had to go to Lima to dress himself as befitted his rank and the office he had held.

So we leave him in Lima, and return to Carvajal, who was continuing the pursuit, as the historians say, in the hope of coming up with Don Fray Juan Solano, bishop of Cuzco, with whom he was very incensed, because, as he put it, instead of staying in his church praying for peace among Christians, he had set up as commander in Centeno's army. As he could not catch him (and it is not known what he would have done with him if he had), he hanged the bishop's brother, a certain Jiménez, and a friar who was a companion of his. He then went down the road to Arequipa, where we leave him to say something of what happened to the fugitives. The little we shall say will indicate what hardships and misfortunes the maimed and wounded had to suffer, with no doctor or medicines and not even a hut in which to shelter at night from the great cold that reigns perpetually in those deserts, the very thought of which is horrible.

Having escaped from Pizarro's soldiers, Silvestre went to his tent, and the first thing he asked his Indians for was his horse's tool box, for in those days and for long after the Spaniards always used to travel with apparatus for shoeing their horses in case they cast a shoe on the road: they had a leather bag with a couple of hundred nails and four shoes ready to fit, and a hammer and tongs and hoofparer, for as the Spanish settlements are so far apart, the nearest being sixty leagues from one another, and the roads are so rough, it was necessary to be prepared for this contingency: I am told that nowadays each inn is equipped in the same way as inns in Spain. The old custom still sticks with me, for I knew how to shoe and bleed the horses in my father's stables when it was necessary to travel.

Silvestre asked for this equipment because it was most necessary for the road. Then he asked for a scarlet cloak: in those days noble people often wore scarlet. So he departed, leaving his Indian servants very tearful because he had not believed them when they said he would be defeated and ought to hide the baggage. He left them without heeding them, and as he travelled he saw numberless people, both Spaniards and Indians, fleeing without knowing where to escape but wandering where chance took them. Among them, just over a quarter of a league from the camp, he overtook a wounded Spaniard on a worthless nag; he had several wounds, including one above the right kidney and was leaning over the animal's neck since he could not ride erect. An Indian serving woman was walking with him, and she had her left hand on her master's wound and a little stick to beat the horse in her right, and was saying: "Try and flee from these traitors, sir, for I won't leave you till you're safe and sound, never fear." Silvestre went on and came up with many more who were sorely wounded, the most remarkable of which encounters we shall describe.

After he had gone little more than three leagues night fell, and he left the road or track and went into a deep dell where there were bushes and green grass for the horse to eat. He had brought no food either for himself or for the horse, and when he dismounted and removed the horse's bit it was so famished that it ate every blade of grass and every leaf. Its master was glad of this, and consoled himself for his own fast by watching his horse sup.

Within two hours more than twenty Spaniards had arrived, some wounded and some whole. More than a score of Indians came with them, and this proved a great blessing, for they soon made a fire and shared a little maize they had with the Spaniards. The wounded did not know what to do to be cured, but groaned with pain, for one of them had twenty-three wounds between himself and his horse, some large and some small. God provided for them in this hour of need, for among other Indians who came there was one who carried one of the boxes they make of straw, which might be called a hamper or trunk. They thought he might be bringing some delicacy to eat or other comfort, but when they opened the box they found that it was full of tallow candles. The Indian must have picked up the box in the camp thinking it contained some treasure; for the Spaniards used these cases to carry all they possessed when on the road or in time of war, as they hold just as much as an Indian can carry. The Indian servants with the Spaniards told their masters that they could cure their wounds with the tallow, and they melted it in two iron helmets the Spaniards happened to have, and brought some llama's dung which was scattered about the fields, and pounding it with the tallow, put it on the wounds as hot as the patients could bear it. They filled the wounds with this, however deep, and cured the horses in the same way. They all consoled themselves for God's mercy in providing them with this remedy when they had no other treatment; for the whole party was cured, and they all told it afterwards as a miracle of our Lord of Mercies. After midnight, they resumed their journey, separating into groups so that the enemy should not follow them, as he might if he knew that they were in a party.

Fifteen days later Silvestre met the wounded Spaniard attended by the Indian woman. He was safe and well in an Indian village of fifteen or twenty houses, where she had taken him to her relatives, and they all cured him and entertained him. I had particular reports about these events that took place in the desert; many others, as anyone can imagine, occurred in other places, but as I had no accounts of them I do not write of them. Here I must return to the scene of the battle, and quote what the three authors say of what my lord Garcilaso de la Vega did in the fray.

CHAPTER XXIII

The author quotes authorities for what he has said; and in case he is not believed, takes pride in what the historians say about his father.

LÓPEZ DE GÓMARA (ch. clxxxii), in telling of the battle of Huarina, says who was killed and wounded, and adds: "Pizarro would have been in danger if Garcilaso had not given him a horse," etc.

Zárate (Book VII, ch. iii), describing the same battle, says: "When the cavalry saw the discomfiture of the infantry, they attacked their opponents, and did much execution on them, killing Gonzalo's horse and bringing him to the ground, though he suffered no hurt," etc.

Fernández (Book II, ch. lxxix), speaks of the battle in these words:

Pedro de los Ríos and Antonio de Ulloa attacked the cavalry from the other side, but not the infantry, as they had been instructed. The attack was such that almost all Pizarro's men were brought down and not ten remained on their horses. Like men who regarded victory as assured, they began to disarm their opponents and plunder them. Gonzalo was brought down in this encounter, and Garcilaso, who had remained in his saddle, alighted and gave him his horse and helped him to mount. Licentiate Cepeda had surrendered. Hernando Bachicao, thinking Centeno had won, fled and joined the royalists,

etc.

This is what these authors say of my father. I have written what actually happened in the battle, for Gonzalo Pizarro's taking of my father's horse did not occur during it but afterwards. I am not alarmed that the historians should say otherwise, for I remember that some mestizos who were my fellow pupils at school told me that they had heard what Fernández says about my father—that he dismounted, gave Pizarro the horse and helped him to mount. In order to disabuse popular opinion, my father gave formal evidence before magistrates after the battle of Sacsahuana and produced twenty-two witnesses, all supporters of Centeno and none of Pizarro, who said that when Gonzalo Pizarro asked my father for the horse, none of Centeno's men were left to fight within a distance of half a league, and that the wound suffered by Pizarro's horse was so small that it could have gone on fighting all day if necessary. I also heard it said that what we have told of Francisco de Ulloa's horse, that it was hamstrung above the hocks, happened to Gonzalo Pizarro's. This is a fiction, for Pizarro's horse died twenty-two leagues from the scene of the battle. Its wound was healed, but it was debilitated by the rigorous diet it was subjected to; for though the horse doctor warned Pizarro's stableman, a certain Mescua, a native of Guadalajara, whom I knew, not to fill the animal with plain water, but to give it him with a brew of maize flour, the stableman forgot to tell the Indian who led the horse (which was muffled up against the intense and perpetual cold of that region). The Indian, not knowing the horse doctor's orders, let the horse drink its fill as they crossed a stream, and a quarter of a league further on it fell dead and lay stiff. All this was revealed at the enquiry.

The historians therefore did not write as they did without cause; and I write what passed, not to justify my father, or in the hope of reward or with any idea of claiming one, but merely to tell the truth about what happened. For this crime has been imputed to my lord Garcilaso, and I have done penance for it without any guilt or blame. I asked His Majesty to reward my father's services and restore my mother's property—for as my father's other widow died so soon after him, we brothers and sisters were all impoverished. But when the Royal Council of the Indies studied the evidence I presented about all this, and they were convinced of the solidity of my case, a member of the court, Licentiate Lope García de Castro, who was after president of Peru, said to me: "What reward do you expect His Majesty to grant you when your father did as he did at the battle of Huarina and gave Gonzalo Pizarro that great victory?" And although I replied that this was false witness that had been brought against me, he said: "The historians have written it: are you going to deny it?"

With this they dismissed my claims and closed the door against others I might have made since for my own services. For by God's mercy and through the favor of the lords I have had and gentlemen I have served under, especially that of Don Alonso Fernández de Córdoba y Figueroa, marquis of Priego, and lord of the house of Aguilar, and of Don Francisco de Córdoba, second son of the great Don Martín de Córdoba, count of Alcaudete, lord of Montemayor, and captain general of Oran, I have served His Royal Majesty with four commissions as captain, two from King Philip II of glorious memory, and two from Don John of Austria, his brother, who is in glory. Each of these honored me and bettered the other's reward as though competing with one another. This was not for any deeds I performed in their service, but because the prince recognized my anxiety to satisfy him with my services, and he informed his brother of it. Yet the reverses I had suffered were so great that I did not dare to revive my former or present claims and hopes. Moreover I emerged from the war so impoverished and burdened with debts that it was impossible for me to return to court, but I took refuge in these nooks of poverty and solitude, where, as I said in the foreword to my *History of Florida,* I spend a quiet and peaceful life, like a man disillusioned who has taken leave of this world and its changes, and asks nothing of it, for there is no longer any cause, and most of life is gone by; and for what remains the Lord of the Universe will provide, as He has done hitherto. I hope I may be pardoned for this tiresome outburst, which I have included in dudgeon against my ill fortune in this matter: one who has written the lives of so many others can hardly be criticized for saying something of his own.

To return then to what these authors say about my father, I should repeat that I have no reason to contradict three such grave witnesses, nor should I be believed, nor is it right that anyone should believe me in view of my interest in the matter. I am satisfied to have said the truth, and the reader may choose; for if I am not believed, I shall do without, accepting the truth of what they have said of my father, and taking pride in being able to call myself the son of a man of great courage, heart, and spirit, who in so cruel and fiercely fought a battle had the courage and valor to dismount from his horse and give it to a friend and help him to mount, thus giving him the victory in so important a battle. There can have been few deeds in the world like this.

This I shall take as my device and trophy, since honor and fame are so coveted by mankind, which often prides itself on what others regard as infamy. There will be no lack of someone to say that what he did was against the royal interest: to which I shall reply that such a deed, wherever it is done, deserves honor and fame, for itself alone, without anyone else's favor.

With this we return to the fugitives, one of whom was the bishop of Cuzco. He and Centeno separated without waiting for one another, and the bishop came to his cathedral, though he was in too much haste to look at it. In his company came Alonso de Hinojosa, Juan Julio de Hojeda, and forty other prominent citizens, *vecinos,* and soldiers: though I saw them in the city I do not remember their names. I knew the three I have mentioned. The bishop, as I have already said, lodged in my father's house with fourteen or fifteen others, and early next morning they all gathered in the smaller square of the city nearer the convent of the Mercedarians, and went off post-haste toward Lima, for Captain Juan de la Torre was coming after them. We shall speak of him in the next chapter.

CHAPTER XXIV

What Juan de la Torre did in Cuzco, and what other bad officials did in various places.

CAPTAIN Juan de la Torre reached the city of Cuzco in his pursuit of the fugitives from the battle. There he executed Juan Vázquez de Tapia, who had been *alcalde ordinario* for the king in the city. He also hanged one of his assistants called Licentiate Martel. They died through their own indiscretion, for believing Centeno to be victorious because of his superiority over Gonzalo, they had made great demonstrations for the king and against the rebels. They were then so ill advised as to stay in the town and await Juan de la Torre, although the bishop himself had fled. Juan de la Torre punished them for their ignorance. However, he proclaimed a pardon for all Centeno's soldiers who enlisted in his company. He collected all the arms he could, and prepared a great many triumphal arches and other magnificent decorations for Gonzalo's reception in the city, whither he expected to repair to enjoy his victory. Juan de la Torre sought all the supplies that were available for the use of the army, and sent out officials in various directions to this end. They included Pedro de Bustincia, a nobleman who was married to Doña Beatriz Coya, the legitimate daughter of Huaina Cápac; and he went to the province of Antahuailla, because it and its neighbors have abundant supplies of food. This gentleman was chosen for the mission, since it was thought that the caciques and their subjects would serve him more readily and show greater willingness to bring him supplies out of respect and affection for his wife, the princess. But he was unfortunate and imprudent with regard to his own life, for he brought his own death upon himself when he could have avoided it, as we shall see.

Dionisio de Bobadilla, who had gone to La Plata on behalf of Gonzalo Pizarro, collected what silver he could find from the estates of Gonzalo and his brother Hernando and from the tribute of the allocations of Indians that had been confiscated because their owners were serving with the royalists. This was a great sum in gold and silver, and with it he returned in all haste, finding Gonzalo Pizarro in Cuzco, where he was well received on account of the funds he had brought for the soldiers.

Diego de Carvajal, called "the gallant," who went to Arequipa on the same errand as Bobadilla, misused many women there, as Fernández says (ch. lxxxi), because their husbands had made themselves prominent on His Majesty's side or as friends of Centeno. Fernández says he sacked them and even took their clothes, and that he and one of his companions, Antonio de Biedma, raped two of them who took poison in revenge for the affront to their honor, thus imitating the good Lucretia who killed herself for the same reason.

All this is not gallantry, but downright wickedness and tyranny so abominable that no adequate name can be found for it. For he who is reputed gallant must be so in everything, not only in his array, but in his words and deeds, so forcing everyone to love him. But these soon paid for their villainy as they deserved. Francisco de Espinosa, who went on the same mission to Los Charcas, did no better, but even worse. He robbed all he found on the way, which Fernández says amounted to more than sixty thousand ducats; and in Arequipa he killed two Spaniards, one of whom had Indians. In La Plata he hanged a *regidor* and an alguacil, all four on charges of serving the king. On his way back to Cuzco, he burned alive seven Indians on the pretext that they had warned certain Spaniards of his coming, who duly fled.

He did all this without any commission from Gonzalo Pizarro, or from his commander or any other officer, but simply to be rewarded and make a show of loyalty and service to a master who did not thank him for it, but rather abominated it. For Gonzalo did not like such cruelties, and disapproved of many of those of Carvajal. But Espinosa also paid for his crimes, as did the other two, and as we shall see in due course.

And to take away the indignation and distaste these wicked deeds will have inspired in our readers, we shall mention a generous deed (for completeness' sake) that a man of ill repute performed at this time, so that it may be seen that he was not as black as the historians paint him.

CHAPTER XXV

*What Carvajal did in Arequipa in gratitude
for the benefits he had received from
Miguel Cornejo years before.*

AMIDST the many bad deeds others have ascribed to him Francisco de Carvajal gives us something good to say. We left him on the road to Arequipa pursuing the vanquished. Those in the city, both those who had escaped from the battle of Huarina and the few who still lived there, some forty in all, fled from the city when they knew Carvajal was coming and took the coast road to Lima. He learnt of their flight as soon as he entered the city and without resting an hour sent a famous soldier after them with twenty-five arquebusiers who regarded themselves as pupils of the old master, and whom he distinguished by calling them his sons. They made such haste that they caught up with the fugitives in two days, and brought them all back to Arequipa, without letting one escape. Among them was a nobleman, one of the first conquerors and a *vecino* of the city, called Miguel Cornejo, who had done a service to Carvajal and helped him years before when he first arrived and had no Indians or fame in Peru. Carvajal had been travelling to Los Charcas with his wife Doña Catarina Leitão, a serving woman, and two men servants, and reached Arequipa. In those days and for many years after, there were no inns or lodging houses in Peru: and even in 1560 when I left there were none. Travellers therefore used to lodge in the houses of natives of their own region or province, for in those days the *vecinos* or lords of vassals were so generous that this was enough for them to receive a traveller into their house and give him good entertainment, not only for days and weeks, but for months and years, giving him food and clothes until he was capable of earning his own by the dealings they all engaged in.

As Francisco de Carvajal had no relative or friend in the city, he stopped for a time, which lasted more than three hours, with all his family on their horses in a corner of the square. Miguel Cornejo saw them as he passed on his way to church and again as he came back, and went up to him and said: "What are you doing here? For I saw you here more than three hours ago."

Carvajal said: "Sir, as there are no inns in this country, and I've no relatives or friends in this town, I don't know where to go, and that's why I'm here."

Cornejo replied: "While I've a house, you have no need to go to an inn. My lodging shall be your house, and we shall serve you with all our hearts, as you shall see."

So saying, he took them to his house and entertained them well, keeping them there until the marquis Don Francisco Pizarro gave Carvajal an allocation of Indians in the city, for Carvajal was one of the distinguished soldiers sent by Don Antonio de Mendoza, viceroy of Mexico, to help the marquis, when he was in trouble with the rising of Prince Manco Inca, which we have duly described.

When Carvajal knew that Cornejo was among the prisoners, he ordered them all to be brought before him; and having recognized them, he took Cornejo aside into a private room and gently reproved him, saying: "Master Miguel Cornejo, do you think I'm so ungrateful as to forget all the kindness you showed me years ago in this very city? Don't you expect me to show my gratitude and serve you whenever you need me? Do you think I forget how you saw me waiting in the square with my wife and family without knowing where to go, and how in my moment of need you took me into your house and entertained me for days and months until the marquis Don Francisco Pizarro of glorious memory gave me one of my own? Were the kindnesses you did me in your house of so little moment that I should ever forget them? Well, so that you shall realize how well I've remembered them, I'll tell you that I was given full information of how and where Diego Centeno hid on your allocation, and which was the ravine and cave where he was concealed, and how your Indians were feeding him. I pretended not to know all this, feigning ignorance so as not to involve you in trouble and set the governor, my master, against you. I could easily have sent a couple of dozen soldiers in three or four directions to bring back Diego Centeno to me. And I did this for you, though you were my enemy, and never gave the matter a thought at the time, for one doesn't give much thought to a man who has chosen a cave as a hiding place. But when he came out, as he did, and presumed to oppose my lord the governor, then I presumed to put him in another cave, and even smaller, as I've recently done in the battle of Huarina, with the aid of God and my lords and friends. Now, having respected so great an enemy as Centeno out of regard for you, wouldn't I respect your person and those of your friends and acquaintances very much more, and the whole of this city, because you live here? I shan't forget my quarrel with you as long as I live, but so that you may prove what I've just said, I give you leave to go to your home and have yourself cared for in peace and quiet, and assure the safety of the city and all your companions, for your sake. I free and exempt them from any punishment or harm I might have done them."

With these words Carvajal dismissed Miguel Cornejo and pacified the city, which was very much afraid of being severely punished, as its inhabitants had very often shown their allegiance to the king and their support for Centeno. I heard this anecdote of Carvajal and Miguel Cornejo privately from Gonzalo Silvestre who was Carvajal's greatest enemy and a very close friend of Centeno's, being his companion in all his reverses and misfortunes until Centeno died, as we shall say later. I mention this very trustworthy witness, for I have no wish to flatter anyone in good fortune or ill by adding to or taking away from what actually happened.

When Carvajal had collected whatever arms, horses, and men he could raise in Arequipa, he returned to Gonzalo Pizarro, who was now marching toward Cuzco; for he had not been able to leave Huarina before, owing to the many sick and wounded he had with him after the battle. And as the thing is worth recording, I should explain that the richest and most prominent of Gonzalo's supporters, on seeing how many wounded men of Centeno's were left with them, divided the worst cases among themselves and took them to their tents to be cured and brought them with them. My father took charge of twelve of them: six died on the way and the others were saved. I knew two of them, one of whom was Diego de Tapia, a very honorable and virtuous gentleman, who proved most grateful for what my father did for him. When I came to Spain, he was in the house of Diego de Silva, my godfather at my confirmation. The other was called Francisco de la Peña, whose constitution was shown by the name *Peña* ["rock"], which was not his surname but was given him because he was like a rock. Among other wounds he had three cuts in the head, all close together. From the first to the third there were three fingers' breadth of skull which was smashed and had to be removed. The man who performed the operation, though not a surgeon, had nothing better to remove the bone with than a horse doctor's tweezers, and so he cured him. And though the treatment was so rude, he showed himself much ruder and tougher, for he recovered from all these wounds without a fever or anything else that prevented him from eating all he could lay hands on. The tale was afterwards told as a monstrous occurrence, perhaps never seen or heard before, and he was called Francisco *Peña,* and not *de la Peña.* Here we must return to the president.

CHAPTER XXVI

The president's distress and that of his army at Gonzalo Pizarro's victory; the new measures he takes.

HOW BRIEF and frail are the prosperities and expectations of this life was amply seen in the valley of Jauja, where we left the president and all his army celebrating and rejoicing with great content and pleasure because of the good news Francisco Vosso had brought them of the might of Centeno's army and its superiority over Pizarro's in men, arms, and horses. As a result of this news the president and his council had decided not only not to raise more men, but to disband the army and dismiss the soldiers who had joined him from such distant lands and provinces, since the cost of maintaining them seemed superfluous and excessive now that the enemy seemed to be defeated, killed and dispersed.

The decisions of the council went so far along these lines that it was decided that the army should be dissolved, as Zárate says (Book VII, ch. iv):

And at this stage the president received news of Centeno's defeat, which distressed him greatly, though he pretended it was of no importance and displayed great good spirits in public. His whole army expected the opposite of what happened, so much so that it had often been considered that the president should not raise an army, since Centeno's alone would suffice to defeat Gonzalo Pizarro, etc. So Zárate. It was the president's luck and his adversary's misfortune that the decision had not been made known and no orders had been issued; for if it had been carried out, it would have been a most difficult and laborious process to reconstitute so great a force of men and supplies.

At this juncture the bishop of Cuzco reached Jauja with the sad news of the defeat and loss of Diego Centeno, of which, as an eyewitness, he was able to give a full account. The president and all the *vecinos* who had Indians lamented this bitterly, for the war they thought was finished had flared up again, and the enemy seemed so strong and brave and famous that they thought he was invincible, and they in turn began to think they were vanquished.

The captains and soldiers were not sorry at this bad news, but on the contrary were glad, for the wealth of all soldiers is in war, and the longer it lasts, the more the honor and the greater the reward they hope to get out of it, especially in the empire of Peru, where captains and soldiers seek no other boon than to be given allocations of Indians and become lords of vassals. The president did not wish to discourage his friends any more, and concealed his misgivings as best he could, making a brief harangue in which he said that they must not be surprised at such reverses of fortune, which were usual in time of war, but they should praise God, for he himself thought that the Divine Majesty had permitted Gonzalo to win this victory so that theirs would be the greater when they defeated him. In order to obtain this honor they must all carry out their duties and functions, carefully taking all the necessary steps to counter such a foe. He said that there was no need for him to exhort gentlemen so valiant and experienced in warfare. He would follow their example and take their advice in so grave a matter; for he was fully satisfied that everything would turn out to His Majesty's service, and he would reward them according to their deserts and make them lords of the whole empire.

After this discourse, he sent Marshal Alonso de Alvarado to Lima to collect the men who had remained there and bring the artillery from the ships, and Spanish clothes, arms, and horses, and everything else needed for the war. He also gave orders that the craftsmen (though they had not hitherto been neglectful) should press on with their tasks of making arquebusses and powder, and collecting lead, and making pikes, helmets, chin guards, and copper corselets, which the Indian silversmiths made with much skill. The craftsmen hastened to carry out their duties, for they were picked for their skill in these tasks.

The president also sent Captain Alonso Mercadillo and after him Lope Martim Lusitano, with fifty men to go to Huamanga and thence in the direction of Cuzco, and advance as far as they could to collect the fugitives from Centeno's army. We shall leave the president making these arrangements to speak of Gonzalo Pizarro, whom we left on the field of Huarina, where he won that famous victory.

CHAPTER XXVII

Licentiate Cepeda and others persuade Gonzalo Pizarro to ask for peace and make terms with the president; his reply; the death of Hernando Bachicao; Gonzalo's entry into Cuzco.

HAVING DONE his duty toward the dead, Gonzalo Pizarro intended to go to Cuzco, but he could not do this for many days, as he was greatly impeded by the many wounded he had with him. He and his officers were much troubled by them, for they could travel only in short stages. On the way Licentiate Cepeda reminded Gonzalo Pizarro of a promise he had made him earlier, that he would discuss terms of peace with President La Gasca when a favorable opportunity presented itself. Cepeda said that now was the most suitable moment to get good conditions. Many others agreed with Vepeda, for the affair was discussed at a meeting of the leaders, and most of them desired peace and quiet. They were so insistent that Gonzalo grew angry, as López de Gómara says in his ch. clxxxiii:

At Pucarán Pizarro and Cepeda disputed over the question of coming to terms with La Gasca, Cepeda saying that that was the best opportunity and reminding him that he had promised to take it at Arequipa. Pizarro, following the views of others and influenced by his good fortune, said that it was a bad policy, for if he began negotiations it would be regarded as weakness and all his followers would desert, and many of his friends who were with La Gasca would fail him. Garcilaso de la Vega and some others were of Cepeda's opinion.

So López de Gómara.

Gonzalo turned down Cepeda's advice, which would have been advan-

tageous, and took that which was later given him by Captains Juan de
Acosta, Diego Guillén, Hernando Bachicao, and Juan de la Torre, who
were young and bold, and thought themselves invincible after the great
victory of Huarina, and had no wish to negotiate, for they would not be
satisfied with less than the whole empire of Peru. Two days after this meeting the commander, Francisco de Carvajal, returned from his journey to
Arequipa, and two days later he had Captain Hernando Bachicao strangled
for having gone over to Centeno at Huarina. Carvajal had known about
this on the day of the battle, but he postponed the punishment, not wishing to spoil so great a victory as he had won by killing a captain who had
been so long in his service and was so committed to his party as Bachicao.
After this, Gonzalo and his army reached Cuzco, still harassed by the number of wounded.

Captain Juan de la Torre had arranged a solemn reception with many
triumphal arches in the streets down which Pizarro would pass. They
were made of many different flowers of various pretty colors, as the Indians used to make them in the time of the Inca kings. The infantry came
first, each company separately with its banners raised, the men marching
in order, three in each rank, preceded by their captains. Next came the
cavalry in the same order. Long after the army had been billetted, Gonzalo Pizarro entered, attended only by his servants and the *vecinos* who
were with him. He had not wished to enter with the soldiers, lest it should
be said that he was exulting over his enemies. On his entry the bells of
the cathedral and convents were rung, though there were few of them at
that time. The Indians in the city appeared in the square from their various
quarters and in their tribal groups, and acclaimed him with loud shouts,
calling him Inca and giving him other royal titles which they used in the
triumphs of their own kings. They had been ordered by Captain Juan de
la Torre to celebrate as they did in Inca times. There was music of trumpets and minstrels, for Gonzalo had excellent musicians. He entered the
church of the Mercedarians to worship the Blessed Sacrament and the
image of his mother, our Lady the Virgin. Then he walked to his lodgings
in the house belonging to his deputy and commander Alonso de Toro, opposite the Mercedarian convent.

I entered the city with them, for the day before I had gone out as far as
Quespicancha, three leagues from Cuzco, to receive my father. I walked
part of the way, and was borne part of it on the backs of Indians who took
turns to carry me. For the return I was given a horse and a man to lead
it, and I saw all I have described, and could still say in which house each
captain was lodged, for I knew them all and remember the houses, though

it is nearly sixty years since all this happened. Memory retains what is seen in childhood better than what happens in later years.

As soon as Gonzalo and his army had entered Cuzco, Francisco de Carvajal began to take the necessary steps for the continuance of the war. He sought to make up the number of weapons lost in the battle of Huarina, and made much gunpowder and collected plenty of lead. The spare arquebusses, which were numerous, for he had collected all that Centeno's men had left on the battlefield when they were killed or fled, were put in order. This was done with great care and attention, for he esteemed arquebusses above all other weapons of offence and said that it was not in vain that the pagans had armed their god Jupiter with this weapon which wounds and kills from a distance as it does near at hand. He had pikes made, though not of ash, which is not found in Peru, but of other woods, equally good and stronger. He collected plenty of cotton or wicks, and left no detail, however small, unprepared for its proper time and season. He saw to everything himself, and never trusted to his subordinates to see to it, for he was afraid of negligence on their part. He was so solicitous and painstaking in all these tasks that he was never idle, and it seemed as if he never ate or slept.

He always rode a big mule of a color between dun and red: I never saw him on any other mount during the whole time he was in Cuzco before the battle of Sacsahuana. He was so single minded in seeing to all his army's needs that his soldiers came across him at all hours of the day and night doing his own duty and other people's. Carvajal thought they would criticize his earnestness, and as he passed by with his hat in his hand, instead of saying: "I kiss your hands," he would say: "What you can do today, don't put off till tomorrow." This phrase he had constantly in his mouth. When they asked him when he ate and when he slept, he would say: "Those who have work to do find time for everything." In the midst of all this activity Francisco de Carvajal did not forget to keep his followers up to the mark, and committed a characteristic act in having a noble woman of Arequipa strangled, because after the battle she had railed womanishly against Gonzalo Pizarro, saying that his tyranny would be put down like that of others more powerful than he, who had won greater victories than Huarina, but had still lost in the end. She quoted instances from the ancient Greeks and Romans, and said it all in public so often and so fearlessly that Carvajal hanged her from a window in her dwelling after she had been strangled.

CHAPTER XXVIII

The capture and death of Pedro de Bustincia;
the captains selected by the president;
how he leaves Jauja and comes
to Antahuailla.

T O PUNISH and avenge this execution it appears that God permitted a similar deed to take place in the royal army, lest Francisco de Carvajal should boast of so discreditable a deed as the killing of a woman, which greatly distressed Gonzalo Pizarro, as he said in secret to his friends, though he did not mention it to the commander. In order that Gonzalo should not prevent the deed, if it had reached his ears, and rescue the victim from his hands, as he had done before, Carvajal had her strangled in her own dwelling with no stir at all, and later had her hanged from the window. The other death was that of Pedro de Bustincia. While he was collecting supplies in Antahuailla and its district, as we have said, Captains Alonso Mercadillo and Lope Martim, who were on the same errand, heard that Bustincia was there, and agreed that Lope Martim should ride forward and make a night attack and capture Bustincia if possible, for his capture would be very useful to them in ascertaining the strength and intentions of the enemy. Lope Martim contrived this so well that, although he had fewer men than Bustincia, he surprised him with a night march and caught him. In doing so he was greatly assisted by the fact that twelve of his, Bustincia's, party were from Centeno's army, who, having been defeated by Gonzalo Pizarro, were only too glad to see him suffer any reverse, and so did not fight or make any resistance. Lope Martim captured them all and killed three of them: one of these, a Pizarrist, who was bolder than the rest, died in the fight though it was brief enough. The other two were Levanters who wanted to be thought brave soldiers and, without regard for their own safety, boasted of having killed ten men at Huarina. This caused their death. Lope Martim released the twelve soldiers of Centeno's, and carried off the Pizarrists as his prisoners, with Bustincia among them: he was very proud of such a good prize.

The president greatly esteemed his coup, and learnt from Centeno's men about Pizarro's doings and many details of his army he desired to know. Pedro de Bustincia was not satisfied with being under arrest in the president's power, but took it upon himself in prison in the midst of his enemies to talk boldly in praise of Pizarro's undertaking. These words brought about his death, which was the same as that of Doña María Calderón at the hands of Carvajal. He was strangled: so the two deaths resembled one another in both manner and cause.

Licentiate Pedro de la Gasca, his Imperial Majesty's president, had called up all the captains and soldiers in Quito, Cajamarca, Lima, and other places; and having received them had sent Alonso de Alvarado to Lima to collect men, arms, horses, money, and Spanish clothes for his army and also to bring the ship's cannon; finally, having obtained all the supplies he could, he left Jauja in search of Gonzalo Pizarro. To perfect the organization of his army, he appointed captains and officers, as all three historians say. In particular, Zárate (Book VII, ch. iv) says:

The army was organized in the following manner: Pedro Alonso de Hinojosa was captain general, as he had been when he handed over the fleet at Panama. Marshal Alonso de Alvarado was commander, and Licentiate Benito de Carvajal ensign general, and Pedro de Villavicencio sergeant major. The captains of cavalry were Don Pedro Cabrera, Gómez de Alvarado, Juan de Saavedra, Diego de Mora, Francisco Hernández, Rodrigo de Salazar, and Alonso de Mendoza. Captains of infantry were Don Baltasar de Castilla, Pablo de Meneses, Hernando Mejía de Guzmán, Juan Alonso Palomino, Gómez de Solís, Francisco Mosquera, Don Hernando de Cárdenas, Adelantado Andagoya, Francisco de Olmos, Gómez Darias, and Captains Porcel, Pardavel, and Serna. Gabriel de Rojas was captain of artillery. He had with him the archbishop of Lima and bishops of Cuzco and Quito, and the provincials of St. Dominic, Fray Tomás de San Martín, and of the Mercedarians, as well as many other religious, friars, and priests. At the final review he found he had seven hundred arquebusiers, five hundred pikemen, and four hundred horse, though by the time he reached Sacsahuana the total reached nineteen hundred men. He left his camp at Jauja on December 29, 1547, and marched in good order up the road to Cuzco, to find the best place to cross the river Abáncay.

Thus Zárate. So that without the four principal officers, that is the general, commander, ensign general, and sergeant major, there were seven captains of cavalry and thirteen of infantry, as well as the captain of artillery. All were very noble and eminent men, most of whom I knew. With them the president left Jauja and continued his quest for the enemy. He reached the city of Huamanga, which he found empty of supplies, and he therefore had to hasten on to the province of Antahuailla where he intended to go into winter quarters, for as we have said, this province had abundant supplies of food. Here the president and the whole army stopped, awaiting the arrival of Marshal Alonso de Alvarado who was bringing reinforcements, and that of other captains and men who he knew were flocking to the royal colors. These numbered three hundred, as Zárate says, and we shall speak of them in the next chapter.

CHAPTER XXIX

The leading men, captains, and soldiers, who repair to Antahuailla to serve His Majesty; the rejoicings that take place there.

THE PRESIDENT remained for more than three months in quarters at Antahuailla. During this time many men rallied to him from all sides, including a certain Alonso de Mendoza who had escaped after the battle of Huarina. He had reached the army at Jauja, though we forgot to mention this at the time, and was therefore one of those appointed captains of cavalry. A month and a half after the president's arrival at Antahuailla, Marshal Alvarado appeared with 100 soldiers, the ships' cannon, and part of the money, arms, and clothing. The rest of this was brought by the accountant Juan de Cáceres, and it was used to supply the need of the soldiers, which was very great. There also arrived Licentiate Pedro Ramírez, judge of the *audiencia* of Nicaragua, with twelve horsemen in his company and 120 infantry following behind: they arrived eight days after the judge. Adelantado Belalcázar also arrived with 20 more horse, after travelling more than four hundred leagues. Captain Diego Centeno appeared with 30 horse who had escaped from the battle of Huarina and rejoined him. One of these was Gonzalo Silvestre, his great friend and companion in his toils. Apart from these there were many more of less note, reaching 300 in all. The president was delighted to see them, and to find his army so enlarged and prosperous, and he was glad that they had come such a great distance to serve the king. He was particularly pleased to see Captain Diego Centeno on account of the latter's great loyalty and qualities of mind and body: he was a fine and handsome man.

Among the last to arrive was Pedro de Valdivia, governor of Chile, with 8 more horsemen: Fernández and Zárate praise him in the same words, and Zárate (Book VII, ch. v) says:

When the president had left Jauja, Captain Pedro de Valdivia reached his camp. He, as we have said above, was governor of the province of Chile and had come from there by sea and landed at Lima, in quest of men, munitions, and clothes in order to complete the conquest of Chile. But on landing and learning of the state of affairs, he equipped himself and his friends, for they had a great deal of money with them, and went off to join the president. This was regarded as a stroke of great good fortune, for though there were eminent and rich captains with the president, there was none so skilled or experienced in military matters as Valdivia—though even he could not equal the wiles and stratagems of Captain Francisco de Carvajal, which had won so many fights for Gonzalo Pizarro, and especially that of Huarina against Centeno, a victory that everyone attributed to Carvajal's knowledge of the art of war. This victory had frightened the president's whole camp, and they were therefore much encouraged by Valdivia's appearance.

Thus Zárate, who, in praising Valdivia, praises Carvajal much more, and rightly so, for in the art of war he stood head and shoulders above all those who have gone to the New World. The historian Fernández of Palencia, having said the foregoing about Pedro de Valdivia, adds (Book II, ch. lxxxv):

And as any curious reader will desire to know the reason for the coming of Pedro de Valdivia, and it is necessary for a better understanding of the narrative, I shall give it here. It was as follows:

While Valdivia was in the province of Chile, he received news that Gonzalo Pizarro had rebelled against His Majesty, and it is even said (and is true) that he had received letters from Pizarro, but Valdivia dissimulated, and pretended he knew nothing. He asked for loans of gold from those he thought would have any, saying that he needed the money to send Francisco de Villagra to Peru to raise men to complete the conquest of Chile; but though he tried hard, no one would lend him anything. So Valdivia quietly summoned them all together and said that if they would not give him gold willingly, all those who wished should go to Peru, and he would give them leave. By taking gold with them they would prove the value of Chile and draw people to it. So many of them prepared to go to Peru and took ship in the port of Valparaíso, ten leagues from Santiago. They included Villagra, who was the person chosen to bring back the people from Peru.

Valdivia remained in the city of Santiago; but when all the rest had gone and he thought they would be ready to sail, he went out secretly by night and reached the port just as they had all embarked. They had built a hut of branches on the foreshore, where Valdivia had an excellent dinner cooked to which he invited them all, a party of about twenty persons. After the meal, he earnestly recommended to them Francisco de Villagra, whom he regarded as a son, saying that as he was going to collect settlers for Chile, they should lend him any gold he might need. They all promised very willingly to do so. Then Valdivia secretly left the hut and went down to the sea where a boat was waiting in which he rowed out to the ship. There he seized all the gold they had put on board, which amounted to over eighty thousand castilians, and noted down what he had taken from each of them. Then he brought on board Jerónimo de Alderete, Gaspar de Villarroel, Juan de Cepeda, Captain Jofré, Luis de Toledo, Don Antonio Beltrán, Diego García de Cáceres, Vicencio de Monte, Diego Oro, and his secretary, before whom he declared that he was going to Peru to serve His Majesty against Gonzalo Pizarro. So leaving those from whom he had taken the gold ashore, he set sail with these friends, leaving Francisco de Villagra as his deputy. On reaching Peru, they heard that the president was going against Cuzco and went straight to Lima, where they bought what they needed and made for Andahuaillas, knowing that the whole army would wait there until the rains abated and summer came, when they would begin to advance and finish off the war.

Thus Fernández; this particular deed is like many others now practiced in the world, which the ministers of the Devil countenance with the new doctrine they have invented called reason of state.

On the occasion of the arrival of Pedro de Valdivia and so many noble captains and soldiers, and especially to encourage Captain Diego de Centeno and his followers who were very depressed by the memory of their late defeat, many rejoicings and solemn festivities were held. They jousted and tilted at the ring, though they had no lance rests. These celebrations had the same effect as music is said to have, cheering the cheerful and saddening the sorrowful. The president wintered in Antahuailla with all his army. It was a very hard winter with a great deal of continual rain which rotted the tents, which are there called *toldos* and here *tiendas*. As the accommodation for the common troops was little and bad, and many of them were raw and new to Peru, many fell ill. But by the aid of a hospital which the president had thoughtfully provided under the charge of a Trinitarian religious called Fray Francisco de la Rocha, a native of Badajoz, few died.

CHAPTER XXX

The army leaves Antahuailla; it crosses the river Abáncay;
the difficulty of crossing the river Apurímac; a
project to make four bridges; a plan
of Carvajal's rejected
by Gonzalo Pizarro.

AFTER THE fury of the winter had passed, the president decided to leave
Antahuailla and go in search of Gonzalo Pizarro, who was at Cuzco.
He travelled with his army as far as the river Amáncay, which the Spaniards call Abáncay, and which is twenty leagues from the city. They found
the bridge badly burnt, for then, as we have said, all the bridges in the
empire were made of osier cables. They began to repair it, which was not
difficult, as the river is particularly narrow at the point where the bridge
is attached. After crossing it, they held a council about where they should
cross the Apurímac, which was more difficult. They were doubtful about
crossing it by the royal highway, for the river is very broad there, and
though the bridge is made across the narrowest point, it is still two
hundred paces across. There was also another obstacle, namely that there
are few Indian villages on the road and these poor, so that they would
find no food. It was therefore decided that the army should cross by one
of three bridges, which would be built up river where it passes through
wild mountains and has a narrow channel over which the bridges could
more easily be built. One of the three places chosen was Cotapampa; the
second, higher up, Huacachaca; and the third Accha. The road to all three
places was very difficult, and almost impassable for an army in formation
owing to the steepness of the mountains, which would be incredible to
anyone who had not seen them. Nevertheless they decided to pass through
them, as there was no other road.

In order to divert the enemy they pretended to build bridges in four
places so that Gonzalo should not know for certain by which of them the
army would pass. The Indians were therefore ordered to convey materials to these four points, as though fifteen or twenty loads of osier were
sufficient for each bridge, when any one of them requires three or four

thousand loads of osier, and branches, and many ropes and cables: all this equipment for every bridge, and much more, is provided at the expense of the poor Indians. The site of each bridge was entrusted to a special officer, who was to collect the material there. Fernández says in his ch. lxxxvi that Pedro Alonso Carrasco went with some men to the bridge on the royal highway; Lope Martim to Cotapampa, Don Pedro Puertocarrero and Tomás Vázquez to Accha, and Antonio de Quiñones and Juan Julio de Hojeda to Huacachaca. I knew all these gentlemen, who were *vecinos* of Cuzco, and four of them were among the first conquerors.

Although these steps were taken it was decided to cross at Cotapampa, for the difficulties were less there than elsewhere: the decision was kept very secret, lest the enemy should discover it. The persons mentioned went to their stations and executed what was required of them. The president and his army travelled with enormous difficulties through the rough mountains covered with so much snow that, as our authors say, many of the Spaniards were blinded. We have explained elsewhere that they do not lose their sight permanently, but that it is a sickness like the evil eye which lasts three or four days. We shall leave them in the midst of these labors on their road, and say something of the plans Francisco de Carvajal was devising at the very same time, for the preservation of Gonzalo Pizarro's authority.

As soon as the president had left Antahuailla with his army on the way to Cuzco, Pizarro knew about it, for he was informed hourly where the enemy was and what he was doing. In time of war the common Indians cannot be relied on to keep any secret, for they act as double spies, and not knowing which side will win, try to please both of them, warning each of what the other is doing so that the victors will not afterwards harm them for not having done so. I believe we have mentioned this before, but we repeat it here, because one of the historians greatly emphasizes the secrecy that the president enjoined on Indians and Spaniards. Though Gonzalo knew that the president was approaching, he made no attempt to cut the roads or bar the difficult places which were so numerous. He simply remained still, quite unperturbedly waiting to give battle, and confident in the result after the many victories he and his army had won in that war.

His commander Francisco de Carvajal did not rest by day or night studying means to make Gonzalo Pizarro master of the whole empire after the great things they had already done to that end. But seeing that Pizarro now thought of nothing at all but the coming battle, he went to him and begged him to consider carefully what he was about to propose, saying: "Sir, considering what has passed and our present situation, and remembering that in every battle there is a risk of losing or winning, it seems to me that Your Lordship should avoid an issue but try to delay and draw out the fighting until your success is assured. Now I'll make a speech that might be made before either army, so that Your Lordship won't deny that what I have to say is for your good, and is necessary to achieve your aims and what we all desire.

"In order to obtain victory over your enemies, Your Lordship must go out of this city and leave it without a single inhabitant, breaking the mills, taking away all the food, banishing the inhabitants, removing their merchandise, and burning everything you can't take with you, so that the enemy find nothing of the slightest use to them. Your Lordship has two thousand men coming against you: one thousand are seamen and ship's boys and such people and they'll all arrive naked, shoeless, and starving. All their hopes are set on getting to this city to repair their hunger and nakedness. If they find it as I've described, they'll be utterly discouraged. The president won't be able to maintain them, and he'll be forced to dismiss them as useless people.

"Your Lordship shall also dismiss Centeno's men: for they've been defeated and will never make good friends. You can take more than five hundred men with you, for many soldiers have joined our army since the battle of Huarina to enjoy your success. They'll be picked men, and not one of them will fail you or deny you in any emergency. You'll set two picquets of fifty arquebusiers apiece on either side of the road, and they'll be twenty or thirty leagues from your army, bringing in sheep and any supplies they find. What they can't carry they'll burn or destroy so that it won't be of any use to the enemy. Your Lordship's men will be eating kids and calves and Peruvian lambs and all the best there is in the provinces in front of us. Your enemies can't follow you with their present army of two thousand, because it's too cumbersome and half the men are useless. The thousand who could follow you will be starving because they'll find no food on the road. Any they do get will come from a hundred leagues and more away, for they too will have used up all the supplies in the provinces they've come through, and every day they'll be further away from them.

"They won't be able to follow you with a thousand men. If they do try to follow, they'll have to divide in two. Your Lordship can fight either half with advantage, and if you don't want to fight, you can travel at leisure from province to province, spinning out the war and taking it easy, until you tire out the enemy and force him to surrender or offer very advantageous terms."

Gonzalo rejected this very profitable advice, saying that it would be cowardice to retreat from the enemy when he did not appear to have any marked advantage, and that they would besmirch and disgrace their past victories and surrender and destroy the fame and honor they had won.

Carvajal answered: "You'll not lose honor, you'll add to it; for great captains who are skilled in warfare should know how to spin it out with true military ingenuity until they weaken and break their enemy without risking a battle in which there is no certainty whatever of victory, as you can see from the many battles that have been fought all over the world. The battle of Huarina is good proof of this, for Your Lordship won it quite against the expectations of the enemy, since they'd ordered their servants to prepare double rations for the prisoners they thought they'd take from us. Remember that that victory was won more by the special grace of God than by any human force or skill, and it's wrong to tempt God to perform miracles like that at every touch and turn."

Pizarro still said that he thought it looked ill to turn their backs on the enemy. He wanted to wait and try his fortune: it had given him many victories and never allowed him to be defeated and it wouldn't deny him this final victory. So their conversation ended, to the great regret of Carvajal that Pizarro would not accept his good advice. Fernández (ch. lxxxviii), telling part of this conversation, attributes the following among other things to Carvajal: "Let Your Worship do as I say, and we'll give a lance apiece of Centeno's to Centeno's men and let them go. They'll never make good friends and we'll withdraw better without them."

All these words are from Diego Fernández, and they are clearly Carvajal's, for that remarkable man, never sufficiently praised by his own followers or others, had some such saying for every occasion. The reason why Gonzalo Pizarro did not take Carvajal's excellent advice, or other similar suggestions we shall mention later, was that the commander had lost credit in the general's eyes since the day in Lima when Gonzalo and his captains held the council about whether to receive President La Gasca or not. Carvajal then said the letters were good bulls, and he thought they should take them and enjoy them until they saw exactly what powers the president had. These words sowed the suspicion in Gonzalo's mind that Carvajal was playing a double game, for the advice was not to his liking and ran counter to his ambitions: Gonzalo did not want anyone to advise him that there should be any other governor, since he regarded himself alone as entitled to the office. As it is natural for those in command not to brook rivals or equals, this quite unfounded suspicion was sufficient to undermine Carvajal's credit and to cause Gonzalo to believe a thing so contrary to Carvajal's character and record. Neither the miracles Carvajal performed in his service, nor the victory at Huarina were sufficient to restore him to his former position. And this suspicion did cruel harm to Pizarro himself, who was ruined the sooner for his refusal to believe Carvajal or take his advice: if he had done so, he might have proved more fortunate, as those who knew these secrets affirmed.

CHAPTER XXXI

Lope Martim throws three cables of the bridge
across the stream; Gonzalo's scouts cut two
of them; the disturbance in the royal army;
Carvajal recommends Juan de Acosta
to defend the river crossing.

T HE GENTLEMEN appointed to build the bridges went to their stations and collected the necessary materials. Lope Martim Lusitano, who was assigned to Cotapampa, having prepared the necessary cables, laid the three that form the floor of the bridge across the river on learning that the army was only a day's march away, despite the fact that he had instructions not to lay any till the president arrived. However, he wanted to show his diligence and therefore anticipated the orders by a day, though his action seriously embarrassed the whole army, and especially the president and his officers; for Gonzalo's scouts, who were patrolling the river and watching what was being done, seeing that the cables had been laid and were very carelessly guarded, boldly came out and cut them the following night. There were three Spaniards and eight of the domestic Indians called *yanacunas,* and they did this work with hatchets they had brought with them in case of need, using fire to help them attain their end. Two of the cables were cut before their opponents received succor. The scouts thereupon returned to Cuzco to report what they had done and seen to Gonzalo: the deed was much more than was expected of them. Here Fernández speaks as follows (ch. lxxxvii) :

As the president was travelling, Fray Martín, of the order of St. Dominic, arrived and told him that Lope Martim had laid three of the cables the day before, and that during the night three of Pizarro's soldiers had come down with some Indians, and burnt two of them, and then fled. The president was much annoyed by this news, partly because he had lost authority through the imprudent and stupid laying down of the cables before the proper time, and partly because so little care had been taken to guard them. What distressed him most was the thought that his enemy would already have been informed, and while his force was going down to the bridge and preparing to cross, they could come out and stop him either from completing the bridge or from crossing it. In this way they would either pass at great peril to themselves, or would be forced to go and cross at Accha, which would be difficult and troublesome and would involve a loss of credit and reputation on their part and a corresponding gain by the enemy. It might also occur that the enemy would learn what route they would take and block their road to Accha. After pondering all these considerations, it seemed that the solution lay in speed. It was therefore decided that the general should join Valdivia and Captain Palomino with the arquebus companies of Pablo de Meneses and Hernán Mejía. They were to try to reach the bridge that night if possible, and cross the river on rafts so as to defend the remaining cable from being burnt and help the others to lay it and build the bridge. Gabriel de Rojas and the artillery also went up so that the Indians could help with the same work. Other companies were sent after the general; and the president, pretending to be in conversation with him, also went on. The bishops and many others missed him and left to follow him, and the marshal remained with the army,

etc. So Fernández.

We shall leave the president and his captains on the road and toiling to repair the bridge, and say what Gonzalo Pizarro and his friends were doing and what Francisco de Carvajal was planning and plotting to forestall such military contingencies as he thought might arise. As soon as Gonzalo's scouts reported what was happening on the river Apurímac, he called his commander and captains to a council and laid the scouts' report before them, asking them to give their advice about what to do against the enemy at the crossing and who to send to defend the river and take such other steps as the chances and changes of war might require.

Francisco de Carvajal spoke before any other, and said: "Sir, this expedition's mine; there's no call to discuss who's to go, for it's mine by right."

Gonzalo said: "Look, father, I need you near me for future contingencies. We have young and bold captains, and any of them can undertake this task."

Carvajal replied: "Sire, the task is mine. I beg Your Lordship not to take it from me; for good fortune has offered me the opportunity to obtain honor in the last days of my life and to achieve our object of defeating and destroying our enemies. I promise Your Lordship, on my word as a good soldier, that if you grant my request, I'll bring you the crown of the empire within four days and put it on your head. Your Lordship has long experience of my great desire and enthusiasm to see you elevated to this position of majesty, of which my small services have given ample proof. I beg you many and many times not to refuse me this favor, for I only beg you it for Your Lordship's greatness and my glory and that of all your men."

Gonzalo Pizarro repeated what he had said before, and said that he was well aware of his enthusiasm and did not forget his deeds, through which he had reached his present position. But he did not want to let Carvajal go away, but keep him by him like a good father. He then ordered a vote to be taken as to who should go on the expedition. By common consent Captain Juan de Acosta was elected, for they realized Gonzalo wanted it: on previous occasions, as we have said, he had sent Acosta on such errands, and had picked him for the greatest and most important missions, believing him to be very brave, as indeed he was. But in addition to bravery, a captain needs skill, prudence, and experience in war, and all these things were as lacking in Acosta as they were present in Carvajal. The advisers of the powerful are usually flatterers who express opinions according to the taste and will of the prince, and not according to his need.

When the commander Francisco de Carvajal saw that Acosta had been selected, he turned to him and said: "Captain, you're as fortunate as I am unfortunate; for all the glory, honor, and fame I'd have won on this expedition has been taken from me and bestowed on you. But as my fortune will have it so, I'll tell you what I'd have done so that you can come back victorious and bring the crown of the empire I promised my lord the governor. You'll leave this city at nine in the morning. The bridge is nine leagues away. Cover seven leagues at a moderate pace, neither fast nor slow. Get to such and such a place, four leagues from here, by two in the afternoon and stop there an hour to eat and to feed the horses. Leave at three and ride slowly so as to arrive late, and you'll come to the top of the hill on this bank of the river at nine in the evening. A little below the crest, a league and a half from the river, there's a fine spring of excellent water near the roadside. When you get there stop and sup and get yourself a bed set down with four mattresses and fine

Holland sheets, and sleep in it. You can post half a dozen arquebusses charged but without balls round you: you won't need them. The president and his army, however fast they march, can't reach the bridge until such and such an hour the next day; and though all the devils in hell come and help them build the bridge they can't lay the first cable till such and such an hour of the afternoon, and it'll be night before they lay the second.

"They'll begin to cross at nine at night, and they'll come up the hill on this side without any order or preparation, for they won't expect there to be any enemies near. They certainly won't expect us to have thought of this plan.

"Their vanguard will reach your bed at twelve at night: they'll be dying of thirst and anxious to drink water from the spring. Then you order all the arquebusses round your bed to fire. You do that, and nothing else, and don't even see the enemy. Then come back to the city, and we'll crown my lord the governor." This was the plan that skilled and experienced commander gave to Captain Acosta, who did something so different that he lost the crown and all their lives, as we shall see.

He was to take two hundred of the best soldiers in the army, and they were to ride, accompanied by thirty lances, with no baggage but the food they would need for themselves and their horses. When Carvajal told him to take a bed with four mattresses and Holland sheets and post his arquebusses without shot, he meant that the task would be easy, implying that without any special effort and without killing the enemy, they could discomfit and defeat them by means of a single real alarm. And when he said "even if all the devils in hell come out and help them," he was emphasizing the exertions of his rivals in building the bridge; for that brave soldier and great captain had such turns of phrase for all occasions.

CHAPTER XXXII

The president reaches the river Apurímac; the
difficulties and dangers with which they cross
it; Juan de Acosta comes out to defend the
crossing; his carelessness and
negligence with regard to
the whole expedition.

HOWEVER fast the president and his captains moved, they could not
reach the bridge that day, but pulled up two leagues from it, where
night fell. But as soon as the moon came out, they continued their journey,
and for a great part of it they went on foot, because the ground was so
rough. They reached the bridge at eight in the morning, and for all their
exertions could not lay the first cable till twelve, and the second till seven
in the evening. Then they began to lay the floor of the bridge with many
branches covered with small pieces of wood intertwined like a cane
hurdle. At ten at night the first men began to cross, and a few soldiers
also ferried themselves over on a raft made of the plant called *maguey,*
which is very light, like the common fennel that grows over here, though
the *maguey* that is chosen for rafts is thicker than a man's leg. They ferried the raft across on long ropes attached to it and pulled from the two
banks. The horses were swum across with great difficulty and ran much
danger of drowning, for in that place the river has no flat bank for beasts
to go in by, and they had to be spurred and forced to jump headlong into
the stream. The force of the current swept them away and dashed them
against some rocks in a bend or elbow in the river. Zárate (Book VII, ch.
v) says that more than sixty horses were drowned in these turbulent
waters, and many others injured. Despite the fact that the place is too
difficult for fighting on horseback, they made this cruel haste in getting
the animals across, fearing that the enemy would descend on them before
they had got over.

These fears were certainly well founded, for the place is a very dangerous one in wartime with the enemy at hand. Anyone who seeks to defend

it and gain honor in the defence, as Francisco de Carvajal confidently intended, will find the place of great advantage to himself and correspondingly disadvantageous to an enemy trying to pass, both because of the difficulty of the river crossing and the immediate surroundings and because of the long rough slopes on either side, which are nearly two leagues up and down and almost perpendicular, as I myself have seen. And Carvajal had good grounds for complaining when he asked to be entrusted with this expedition and it was refused him. He had remarked that his good fortune had offered him this opportunity to win honor in the last days of his life and to accomplish their object in destroying and annihilating the enemy. Carvajal was thoroughly experienced in warfare, and having inspected all the passes by which the enemy could get at them, he felt certain that he could win a victory at any of these places, especially at Cotapampa, which was rougher and more difficult than the rest.

With all the difficulties we have described, half the army had crossed by midnight. The first to reach the other side resumed their order of march as best they could and climbed up the opposite bank, intending to reach the top of it before the enemy took it, which was what they most feared. Having occupied this point, they would assist and secure the ascent of the whole army. When the leaders were half way up, a false alarm was sounded. It was never known who sounded it, but it caused such a fear, bewilderment, and chaos that even many of those who had not yet crossed the river fled on horse or foot without seeing whom they were fleeing from, as though they were being charged. There was such disorder that Captains Porcel and Pardavel and the captain of artillery, Gabriel de Rojas, and many other prominent soldiers who were in the rear and formed the guard on the other side of the river all remarked when they saw this senseless flight: "If this is a real alarm, we're all lost this very night." But as, fortunately, it was false, calm was soon restored; the fugitives returned to their places, and everyone hurried on. The vanguard who were climbing the slope also fell into disorder and fled at the alarm; but they soon recovered their confidence when they found it was false and made such haste that before daybreak they reached the spring where Acosta should have been lying in wait for them if he had followed the instructions of Carvajal, who considered that victory could be gained at that spot. The advance party drank thirstily at the spring, and on reaching the top of the hill, drew themselves up in formation. But there were few of them and they were uncaptained, so that fifty opponents could have defeated them in an attack. Shortly more and more soldiers arrived; for the general, Pedro de Hinojosa and Governor Valdivia, who had crossed the bridge and were at the bottom of the slope, urged them on and pressed them to reach the top. The other half of the army, which was still on the other side of the river, could not cross as a result of the alarm until nine in the morning, when the artillery was brought over with great difficulty. They then hastened after the rest, where we shall leave them to speak of Acosta, who had left Cuzco to defend the river crossing.

This captain had been sped on his way by the commander, and left the city with two hundred mounted arquebusiers and thirty lances, all picked men. He covered the first four leagues, and then stopped without trying to go any further, ignoring the instructions he had received. He spent the night there, and was so careless as to let two soldiers escape, and they gave news of his approach. Next day, after seven in the morning, he resumed his march, though not at all according to the plan Carvajal had given him when he was appointed to lead the expedition. That day another soldier, Juan Núñez de Prado, a native of Badajoz, also fled, and he reported how near the enemy were and the scheme Carvajal had drawn up with its carefully calculated times and distances. The president's advisers were much perturbed, and even more so when they heard that the alarm should have been given at a certain hour during the night; it seemed to them that everything would have turned out exactly as Carvajal planned. They said, if they had been so disordered by a false alarm, what would have happened if there had been a real one? On account of Acosta's negligence Gonzalo Pizarro was blamed for not having defended the crossings, as Zárate says in his Book VII, ch. iv, when, having referred to the company of Indians and Negroes in the president's army, he goes on:

And when Acosta had reconnoitered, he thought that his numbers were too unequal to attack, and returned for more men. Meanwhile the president got his whole army across the bridge, which had now been finished. It was regarded as very negligent of Gonzalo not to have come near enough to prevent the crossing, for a hundred men would have sufficed to defend that particular place.

So Zárate, who here ends his chapter. He is quite right about this, for it is true that the crossing is extremely difficult and no description would be adequate to depict it as it is. When Acosta was not far from the hill which dropped down to the river, as his scouts told him, he went out with six companions to inspect the land and locate the enemy. He found them already lodged on the hilltop, but they were so scared that, as the historians say, the Negroes and Indians were mounted on the horses and given lances and partisans and drawn up in formation, so as to make the enemy think they were more numerous than they were. In order that this rabble should not be recognized by the enemy, three or four ranks of well-armed Spaniards were placed in front to cover the Negroes and Indians, and the infantry made another squadron nearby. Acosta was deceived by appearances and refused to fight. Although the writers say that he sent to Gonzalo for a reinforcement of three hundred arquebusiers, this was only to make the governor think that he was able to score a victory. But he did none of the things Carvajal said he would have done if he had been entrusted with an expedition so much after his own heart. And although the reinforcements were sent, when Acosta received them, he saw that he could not discomfit the president's army and retired without doing anything at all, or even firing an arquebus; he hastened to Cuzco, where he reported all that had happened and told Gonzalo that the president was at hand.

CHAPTER XXXIII

Gonzalo announces his departure from Cuzco;
Carvajal tries to prevent this, recalling
a prophecy about his life; the
president marches toward Cuzco,
and the opposing army comes
out to meet him.

WHEN PIZARRO saw that Acosta's expedition had borne little or no fruit, he decided to go out and receive the president and do battle with him, for he staked all his hopes on this, on account of the victories he had invariably won over both Indians and Spaniards. He had it announced that everyone was to be ready on the fourth day to go to Sacsahuana, four leagues from the city, which was done without consulting Carvajal.

When the latter knew of it, he was very angry, and went to Gonzalo and said: "It's quite the wrong plan to go out and receive the enemy, for if Your Lordship does you'll merely lighten his task and simplify things for him, and at the same time complicate them for yourself instead of adding to his difficulties. I beg Your Lordship to believe this and have a little confidence in me."

Pizarro replied that he had chosen a certain position at Sacsahuana as the place of battle, where the enemy could only attack from in front, and he hoped to defeat them with the artillery, without coming to grips.

Carvajal replied: "Sir, there are plenty of such strong places in this country, and if Your Lordship bids me, I'll find one that'll assure us of victory. What I suggest is that instead of going out four leagues to meet the enemy, you withdraw the same distance and wait for him at Orcos five leagues away. Give the enemy this distance to march and you'll see what confusion and straits he'll get into, and how difficult it will be for him to follow you. When you've seen this, you can choose whichever seems the best policy, either give battle as you wish or continue to withdraw, as I beg you. And I beg you again to retire instead of waiting to receive them. Do this, if it is only to avoid spurning the advantages and countenancing the disadvantages of a horoscope the astrologers have cast for Your Lordship.

"It is well known that they've said you run great danger of losing your life in such and such a year, but that if you survive it, you'll live long and very happily. The year in which Your Lordship's life is in danger is this present year, and the crucial point is not many months, maybe weeks, ahead. Now, as the horoscope is just as unfavorable as it is favorable, you should take the course that is most likely to save your life, and avoid and abominate anything that may threaten it, at least until the year's out. Otherwise you may have cause to blame yourself and your present and future adherents will weep for pity that you didn't set such store by these things as you should have done; for although there's not enough certainty in horoscopes for us to believe them, it seems to me that we should always wait for the period they mention to expire, in order to see if they're true or false. There's nothing to force Your Lordship to give battle, and plenty of reasons for obliging you to put it off and get more advantages than you now have. Who obliges us to risk what we can make quite sure of by marching quietly from place to place at our own ease and comfort and with a great deal of trouble to our enemy, at least until this astrological year, at once so promising and so threatening, is out?"

Pizarro's reply was brief. He said that no one was to advise him to retreat near or far, much or little, for the only thing that befitted his fame and honor was to follow his fortune and finish his resolve, which was to await the enemy at Sacsahuana and give battle without looking at the moon or the stars. So their conversation ended, and Carvajal came away very distressed, telling his friends that their lord the governor had made a fatal decision at the end of his days. Everyone else thought so too, when they realized how precipitately he was delivering himself into his enemy's hands without regard for his safety and authority. They said that it was not for lack of understanding, for he had no lack of that; but it must be the excessive influence of signs and planets that had blinded him and obliged him to place his throat under the knife, since he refused to accept such wholesome advice as his commander had offered.

Returning to the president, for we must frequently move from one side to the other like a weaver, since both sides make the cloth, we should say that on the withdrawal of Acosta, the way lay open for the royal army to advance without fear of its adversaries. But it was so encumbered by artillery, munitions, and supplies that it could not leave that place until the fourth day; for it took three to bring the whole of the baggage train up the hill from the river to the place where the army was. The president then ordered the army to advance in good order; but despite the efforts of the officers the impedimenta were so great that they could not move as fast as they wished. The longest day they were capable of was of two leagues, and most were only one; and after each day they had to stop a day or two for the rearguard to catch up.

Meanwhile Gonzalo was hastening to get his followers from Cuzco to Sacsahuana where he was to await the enemy and offer battle. His captains were all young and bold, and thought of nothing but their own bravery, in which they were full of confidence. They therefore hastened to march forward and conclude the campaign imagining themselves already as masters of Peru. Carvajal and those who sided with him and shared his views—and these were the most esteemed and practiced members of the army—were very critical of the policy of going out to meet the enemy, especially as they had many men to whom they could not trust their lives and fortunes as Gonzalo trusted his own followers; for they had more than three hundred followers of Diego Centeno, people who had surrendered to them so recently that many of them still had plasters on their wounds. These men were enemies and therefore more likely to seek their destruction than to desire their success; and on the day of the battle they were to flee instead of fighting, thus dispiriting and discouraging those who were Gonzalo's faithful friends.

They were therefore very discontented, and Carvajal continued whenever opportunity offered to try to dissuade Gonzalo and see if he could not make him reverse his decision and so avoid the evident destruction of his life and honor and everything else that was his. But God had ordained, as his rivals used to say, that Gonzalo's crimes should lead him to the punishment he deserved, and he refused to follow any advice but his own. This so angered his adherents that they prepared in their hearts to repudiate him when they could. On this point I can affirm that after the battle of Sacsahuana when peace had been restored, I heard some of Gonzalo's leading supporters, who were talking of these events, state that if he had retired as his commander had advised him, they would have died rather than deny him; for they regarded Carvajal as an oracle, and on account of his wisdom and long experience expected his military recommendations to bring them success and prosperity.

Gonzalo Pizarro, obdurate in his own destruction, left the city of Cuzco at the end of March 1548 and reached Sacsahuana, less than four leagues away, in two days. He took so long because he too was encumbered with artillery, supplies, and baggage, wishing to have everything necessary to avoid hunger and meet all kinds of needs in case the enemy were delayed. And although he undertook this journey against the advice of most of his friends, as we have said, they did not dare to oppose him, for they saw that he was quite determined on it. So almost all of them were confirmed in their resolve to look to their own particular interests, in other words to repudiate Gonzalo Pizarro, who was clearly surrendering himself to death, which now called him at the best and most successful moment of his life. He was forty-two years of age, and had won every battle he had fought against Indians and Spaniards, and less than six months before had obtained the victory of Huarina, which raised him above all the famous captains of the New World. All this prosperity and his hopes of the future, and his life to boot, were buried in the valley of Sacsahuana.

CHAPTER XXXIV

*The two armies reach Sacsahuana; Gonzalo's
distrust of Centeno's men incorporated in
his army, and the president's confidence
that many will desert to him; Pizarro's
request and protestations and La Gasca's
reply; they decide to give battle;
the array of the royal army.*

G ONZALO stationed his army in a corner of the valley between a small
river that flows through it and a steep mountain. These two natural
features are close together, and the place is so strong that it cannot be attacked from the sides or from the rear. The river has very deep ravines
toward the side of the mountains, and Gonzalo had the tents pitched between these and the river, leaving the level space between the ravine and
the mountain free so that he could draw up his army on it. As we have
said, the president was travelling slowly, and he reached the spot three
days after Gonzalo. Three days more were spent in skirmishes between
isolated groups, but nothing worthy of note took place. Meanwhile all the
imperial army came up: it had not been able to arrive earlier because of
the difficulty of the road and the great quantity of impedimenta it had.
For two more days the armies observed one another without coming to
grips. Gonzalo and his captains took care that none of his men should flee
and desert to the president, though it would have been better to have had
more confidence in his men, having come out with the intention of offering battle. Gonzalo's mistrust was aroused, though late, by the presence of
more than 300 of Centeno's men in his army. Carvajal had suggested
giving them one of Centeno's lances each and letting them go, for a surrendered enemy can never be regarded as good enough friend to trust with
life, honor, and property all at once. López de Gómara also refers to Gonzalo Pizarro's mistrust in his ch. clxxxvi: "Pizarro therefore marched
forth with 1,000 or more Spaniards of whom 200 had horses and 550

arquebusses. But he did not trust all of them, for 400 were Centeno's men. He therefore took great precautions lest they should escape, and lanced any who did," etc. Thus López de Gómara.

The president on the other hand was full of confidence that some of the enemy would come over to him, especially Licentiate Cepeda, who, as our author says in the same chapter (a very long one), had sent him a promise that if Gonzalo did not come to terms, he would go over to the royalists in time to undo Pizarro. This promise was conveyed by Fray Antonio de Castro, a predicant who was then prior in Arequipa.

In this confident mood the president held a council with his captains to decide whether to give battle or avoid it in order to prevent the casualties that might be caused on both sides. They would all have liked to avoid a battle, but they thought it best not to put it off because of their lack of supplies, fuel, and even water, which they had to bring from a great distance. Their enemy had plenty of all these things, and the president and his captains feared that their men might be driven by hunger to desert. They therefore decided to give battle next day. On the same day Gonzalo sent a request and a protestation to the president, as our author says in the same chapter:

Pizarro sent two priests separately with letters requesting La Gasca to say if he had any instructions from the emperor that he, Gonzalo, was to give up the governorship. If such an original document were produced, he was ready to obey, and abandon his office and even Peru. But if no such document were produced, he declared that he would fight, and the blame would be the president's and not his. La Gasca was warned that the priests would suborn Hinojosa and others, and had them arrested. His reply was that Gonzalo should surrender, whereupon he and all his followers would be pardoned. The president reminded Gonzalo of the honor he would have gained in getting the emperor to revoke the ordinances, if he remained in His Majesty's good graces, and pointed out how deeply obliged they would all be if he gave way without fighting, some because they would be pardoned, some because they would be enriched, and all because they would be alive, and not dead in the fight. But this was the voice of one preaching in the wilderness: Gonzalo and his advisers were quite obdurate, either through despair or because they regarded themselves as invincible. And in truth, their position was a strong one and they had plenty of Indian servants and food.

Thus López de Gómara, who thus says briefly what we have said at length. It is true that Gonzalo had plenty of Indian servants, for all the Indians in general served him with very great affection, regarding the first Spaniards to reach them as children of the Sun and brothers of their own Inca kings. They therefore used to call them Incas; and as Gonzalo was one of them and brother to the marquis Don Francisco Pizarro, they never lost the love and respect they felt toward him as an Inca; and they wept his death tenderly.

The night before the battle, Acosta decided to take 400 arquebusiers and attack the royal army, to see if he could do something to repair his negligence and the failure of his recent expedition. The soldiers who had gone with him grumbled loud and long at his carelessness and lack of military skill. And when Carvajal knew how things stood, he wept his ill fortune that had deprived him in his old age of the greatest deed that would have crowned his whole career. When Acosta was ready for the attack, it was found that one of Centeno's soldiers had escaped; and suspecting that he would have given warning of Acosta's attack, they abandoned it. Gonzalo Pizarro was not sorry, for he thought that the safest way to obtain a victory was to fight a pitched battle, and not to try alarms and night attacks. López de Gómara here says that he told Acosta: "Juan, as we've as good as won, don't let us risk it," which "was fatal arrogance and blindness."

So López de Gómara. The arrogance and blindness of Pizarro and his captains lay in supposing that the whole army would fight as well as themselves, in which case they could not have failed to win. But this was not so: neither those who thought themselves valiant, nor those reputed cowards fought.

The soldier who deserted warned the royal army that Juan de Acosta and his men were ready to make a surprise attack by night and offer battle. This obliged the president and his army to pass the whole night drawn up in formation; they were so cold that, as López de Gómara and Zárate say, their lances fell from their hands, which were too numb to hold them. At daybreak, April 9, 1548, the royal army resumed its formation after recovering a little from the previous night. The infantry was placed together, under the captains we have already named, with picquets of arquebusiers on either side. To the left of the infantry they stationed 200 horses, under Diego de Mora, Juan de Saavedra, Rodrigo de Salazar, and Francisco Hernández Girón (whom Zárate calls Aldana). To the right were Captains Gómez de Alvarado, Don Pedro Cabrera, and Alonso Mercadillo, with 200 more horse forming a guard for the royal standard carried by Licentiate Carvajal, the ensign general, who accompanied these captains. To their right, at a good distance, was Captain Alonso de Mendoza. He was accompanied by Diego Centeno, and they had a company of 60 horse, most or almost all of whom had escaped from the battle of

Huarina. As companions in their past reverses and hardships they wanted no other captain but Mendoza. These were stationed near the river to help those who might flee to the royal army on that side: they were well aware that there were men everywhere who would desert to the royalists, and such fugitives would run the greatest danger at that point. Captain Gabriel de Rojas strove to bring the artillery down to the plain, which was done with great difficulty owing to the steepness of the mountainside. General Pedro de Hinojosa, Commander Alonso de Alvarado, Sergeant Major Pedro de Villavicencio, and Governor Pedro de Valdivia disposed the squadrons. Behind them all was the president with the three bishops of Lima, Cuzco, and Quito, and the provincials of the order of Preachers and the Mercedarians, as well as a great many other priests and friars who had come with the army. In their rear there were 50 horsemen to protect them in case some impudent wretch attacked them.

CHAPTER XXXV

The events of the battle of Sacsahuana up to the defeat of Gonzalo Pizarro.

O N THE other side, Gonzalo Pizarro sounded the call to arms as soon as it grew light and ordered his men up to the plain between the ravine and the mountain where they were to draw up. The artillery was brought up and placed on an eminence. Licentiate Cepeda, as López de Gómara says, was instructed to arrange the troops, for Francisco de Carvajal refused to perform his usual duty as commander that day out of pique that Gonzalo Pizarro should have refused to follow his advice. He thought the day was already lost, and placed himself as an infantry captain at the head of his company. Thus the historians make no mention of him in describing the disposition of the troops.

While they were all busily taking up their stations, my lord Garcilaso left them, and on the pretence that the Indian who should have brought him his lance had not done so, he went down to the river shouting for the man. As soon as he was covered by the ravine, he went toward the royal standard, and having crossed a small bog between the two armies, he went down to the river, climbed up the side of the ravine and presented himself to the president in full view of both armies. The latter welcomed him and embraced him with great satisfaction, saying: "My lord Garcilaso, I always expected your honor would render His Majesty such a service."

My lord Garcilaso then replied: "Sir, as a prisoner deprived of his liberty, I have not been able to serve His Majesty or Your Lordship hitherto, though I have never lacked the desire to do so."

When Gonzalo Pizarro knew that Garcilaso had gone, he was much distressed, though he did not show it for fear of discouraging his men. He came upon a cousin of my father called Gómez Suárez de Figueroa, and said to him: "Garcilaso has left us; do you think he'll fare well if we win?" He spoke thus because he was deceived by his false hope of victory; but it was not long before he was disillusioned.

My father's departure took place as I have described it, though two of the historians mention Licentiate Cepeda first, and then my father and others, as if they left together. But they did not hear his account of how the incident occurred. The other historian tells it as we have said, and mentions first my lord Garcilaso, and a cousin of his and some others, saying that it was a great calamity for Gonzalo. Then continuing, he says: "And soon after these, Licentiate Cepeda came away and fled as well." My lord Garcilaso de la Vega left alone, without any companion at all, and had arranged beforehand to escape in this way. As soon as Gonzalo Pizarro pitched his camp in that place, three days before the president arrived, my father went out to reconnoiter and see how he could get away most safely, for he knew that Gonzalo and his captains were very much on the watch for fugitives. In order to have an excuse for going away from them, my father told the Indian who should have brought him his lance not to do so, but to leave it in his tent so that he would have to go and look for it, as he did. My father was covered by the ravine, so that the men above did not see him. I heard him tell all this himself later when peace was restored and the doings and events of those times were being discussed.

I also heard my lord Garcilaso say that after Gonzalo Pizarro took his horse Salinillas in the battle of Huarina, as we have said, he purposely did not buy himself another good horse, expecting that when Gonzalo saw him on foot, he would either return Salinillas or give him another, for he had others like it. And this was in fact the case, for four days before Gonzalo left Cuzco for the battle of Sacsahuana, he sent him the horse Salinillas, and when my father saw it back in his house he thought it had been brought by an angel from heaven. I have mentioned these details not to justify my father; for all that is now past history, as I have said elsewhere, but simply in order to set down the truth about every event and give its day, hour, and moment. I do not wish to offend anyone by depriving him of his place and putting another in it, for there is no reason for me to do so: it is the duty of historians to tell the simple truth. With which let us return to the course of the battle.

Gonzalo's army was drawn up as seemed best to Licentiate Cepeda. On the side toward the mountain there came forth a picquet of arquebusiers to skirmish with the royalists. Captains Hernán Mejía de Guzmán and Juan Alonso Palomino came out against them with their companies of arquebusiers and drove them back without loss to either side. Meanwhile, the artillery of both armies was fired. Gonzalo's did no damage because the president's army was stationed in a hollow like a cup, and the balls passed over their heads. The president's artillery was very well placed, for it dominated the opposing camp, in which it landed many balls, according to the historians, killing two men. This is the truth; and one of them was a page to Gonzalo Pizarro.

Licentiate Cepeda, who was arranging the troops in order of battle and desired to go over to the royalists, pretended to go and look for a better position than that which the army was occupying, and as soon as he was at a little distance, spurred his horse. This was a very handsome animal, a dark chestnut with its neck, breast, and rump covered in handsomely decorated black cowhide, an original and singular trapping which was unique in those days and which I have never seen since I left Peru. Nevertheless the splendid covering harmed both horse and rider, for while they were still running and had already gone some distance from Pizarro's lines, Pedro Martín de Don Benito came out in pursuit on a big, long horse as thin as a rake, which I also knew: it was a chestnut and covered more ground in a single stride than others in three or four. He overtook Cepeda as he was entering the small bog near the royalist camp; and lanced the horse in the rump (bringing it down in the mire) and its rider in the thigh. He would have killed him if four of Mendoza's company had not come to the rescue: as we have mentioned, they were stationed there for this purpose. The covering impeded Cepeda's horse, for without it it would have run more freely and avoided Pedro Martín de Don Benito, who was a big old man, hard and tanned. After performing this feat, he hastened back to his own lines, and Cepeda as a result of the timely aid he had received, was able to get out of the bog and go and kiss the president's hand. He received him with great joy, as López de Gómara says (ch. clxxxvi): "La Gasca embraced Cepeda and kissed him on the cheek, though he was all muddy. He regarded Pizarro as beaten without him." So López de Gómara.

Meanwhile many other soldiers came over at various points, both horse and foot. One of them happened to be Martín de Arbieto, whom we mentioned in the battle of Huarina, and promised to say something of his doings. Here we shall insert one of them. He was riding a good horse with a long-stirruped harness and a lance on a rest, such as were and are rarely seen in Peru. With him was a soldier called Pedro de Arenas, a native of Colmenar de Arenas, a small, neat man, very honest and a good soldier: I knew him later. He had a fine sorrel and white pied mare, small in size like its master, and more suitable for riding through city streets than for the battlefield. Martín de Arbieto reined in his horse so as not to forsake one who had placed himself under his protection. Pedro Martín de Don Benito had lanced four or five foot, and seeing these two riding away, set off after them to lance them too. Martín de Arbieto, who was riding in front of his companion, easily cleared the bog, but Pedro de Arenas' mare became stuck and in floundering threw its rider into the mud, for his saddle was a long-stirruped one and the girths were loose. Arbieto, on seeing this, went back through the marsh and rode straight at Pedro Martín de Don Benito to prevent him from killing his friend. When Pedro Martín saw that Arbieto meant to fight him, he pulled up and stood waiting. Arbieto called to him: "Come on, you rogue; we'll see who sucked the better milk!" But his opponent refused the challenge and returned to his own ranks without saying a word.

On one of these excursions Pedro Martín was hit by a stray shot which pierced his right hand and made him drop his lance. Having lost it, he went to Gonzalo Pizarro and said, "I'm of no use to Your Lordship now," and so saying joined the rear rank of the horse. While this was going on both horse and foot continued to desert to the royalists. Francisco de Carvajal, seeing that they were losing because Gonzalo had not paid any attention to him, began to sing aloud:

> "Mother, my little hairs are gone away
> Gone two by two with the wind away."[1]

And he went on singing this song in mockery of those who had rejected his counsel, until there was not a soldier left on his side. Thirty-two arquebusiers left the picquet to the right of Gonzalo's formation, pretending to be going to skirmish with the enemy, as though they were still quite loyal. But when they were some distance away, they ran helter-

---

[1] *Cabellicos*: "little hairs," a pun on *caballicos*, "little horses."

skelter for the royal lines. They and those who had already fled advised the royalist general and his officers not to come forward to fight, but to stay where they were, for very soon all Pizarro's men would abandon him and leave him alone. And so it turned out, for Gonzalo sent thirty horse to follow the arquebusiers and stop them, which they did so dutifully that they too delivered themselves up to the president. Another forty of the arquebusiers who were on Pizarro's left deserted, and no one dared pursue them as they withdrew in good order, facing their former companions and showing signs of firing on anyone who tried to resist them. They also ceased the pursuit because Mendoza and Centeno with their sixty horse had crossed the bog and come nearer to help the deserters. When the pikemen saw that the arquebusiers on both wings had fled and that they themselves could not pretend that they were going to skirmish with the enemy, they dropped their pikes as one man, and began to flee in all directions, thus completing the dispersal of Gonzalo Pizarro's army.

Such was the battle of Sacsahuana, if it can be called a battle, for there was no more fighting than we have said, not a sword thrust, nor a clash with lances, nor an arquebus shot between the two sides. Gonzalo's defeat was so rapid that it will have taken longer to read this chapter than he took to suffer the reverses we have described. On his side ten or twelve were killed, as López de Gómara says. They died at the hands of Pedro Martín de Don Benito and others who were trying to stop the deserters: the president's men did not kill one of their enemies. Although the historians say that the two armies were within arquebus shot, it was a very long shot, for there were more than five hundred paces between them. On the royalist side only one was killed, shot by the carelessness of one of his companions.

CHAPTER XXXVI

Gonzalo Pizarro surrenders, as this seems less
shameful than flight; his conversation with
the president; the capture of
Francisco de Carvajal.

T HE LAST straw in Gonzalo's destruction was the action of the pikemen in dropping their pikes and taking to their heels. This left him
and his officers aghast, for they had not imagined such a thing to be possible. Gonzalo turned to Acosta, who was near by, and said: "What shall
we do, brother Juan?"

Acosta, showing more valor than discretion, replied: "Sir, let's attack
and die like the ancient Romans!"

Pizarro said: "It's better to die like Christians."

Here López de Gómara comments (ch. clxxxvi) : "It was the word of
a Christian and of a brave man: he preferred to surrender rather than
flee, for no enemy ever saw his back," etc. A little further on he adds:
"He was very gallant on his powerful chestnut horse, and wore a coat of
mail and a rich breast guard with a surtunic of crushed velvet and a golden
casque on his head with a gold chin guard," etc. Thus López de Gómara.
Zárate adds that the tunic he wore over his arms was of yellow velvet
covered almost all over with gold plates, and that he said to Acosta:
"Well, as they've all gone to the king, I'll do the same," etc.

So he rode toward the royal army with such captains as wished to follow him: Juan de Acosta, Maldonado, and Juan Vélez de Guevara. Diego
Guillén had already gone over to the president. On the way Gonzalo
came upon Pedro de Villavicencio and seeing that he was well attended,
asked him who he was. On learning that he was the sergeant major, he
said: "I am Gonzalo Pizarro, and I surrender to the emperor." So saying
he handed him a sword he was carrying in his hand; for he had broken
his lance on his own men as they fled, as Zárate mentions. Villavicencio
was delighted at his good fortune; and he therefore courteously thanked
Pizarro for the honor he did him by surrendering to him. In recognition

of this he refused to accept his sword and dagger, which were of great value, for the hilt and guard were of gold.

A little later they met Diego Centeno who went up to Gonzalo Pizarro and said: "I am very sorry to see Your Lordship in this case."

Gonzalo smiled somewhat, and said: "There's no use in talking of that, Captain Centeno. I have finished today: tomorrow you'll weep for me." And without saying any more they went to the president. He received Pizarro, as all three authors say, and we shall quote the words of each of them literally. Zárate (Book VII, ch.vii) says:

And thus he was taken to the president, and exchanged certain remarks with him. The president thought they were disrespectful and handed him to Diego Centeno to guard,

etc. López de Gómara (ch. clxxxvi) says:

Villavicencio was delighted at having taken such a prisoner, and took him off to La Gasca just as he was. The latter said, among other things, did he think it right to have rebelled against the emperor. Pizarro replied: "Sir, I and my brothers gained Peru at our own expense, and I did not think that I was doing amiss in seeking to govern it as His Majesty had commanded." La Gasca then twice said angrily that he was to be taken away. He entrusted him to the care of Diego Centeno, who begged for the privilege,

etc. Fernández (ch. xc) says as follows:

Gonzalo Pizarro was taken before the president, to whom, having alighted, he made obeisance. The president tried to comfort him, at the same time rebuking him for the error of his ways, but Pizarro remained obstinate and unrepentant. He replied that he had won Peru, and began to add explanations somewhat in justification of what he had done. He spoke in such a manner that the president was forced to reply sharply, for it seemed necessary to do this to satisfy those who were listening. He said that Pizarro had not been content to depart from the loyalty he owed his prince, but still appeared obdurate and ungrateful. Although His Majesty had granted his brother the marquis all he had given him, which was enough to raise him and his brothers from poverty to great wealth, and to lift them out of the dust, they had shown no gratitude, especially as he himself had done nothing toward discovering Peru, and his brother, who had done everything, had always shown that he realized His Majesty's generosity and had displayed loyalty and also respect. The president did not wait for any further reply, but told the marshal to take him away and deliver him to Centeno.

Thus Fernández: and as each of the three authors are somewhat brief on this point, and do not attempt to describe what happened in full, we shall give the historical truth of what occurred.

When Gonzalo Pizarro reached the president, he found him alone with the marshal, the magnates having withdrawn to a distance, so as to avoid seeing the leader they had abandoned and sold. Pizarro greeted the president on horseback without alighting, for they were all mounted. The president did the same and asked him if he thought it right to have stirred up Peru against the emperor and to have made himself governor of it against His Majesty's will, and to have killed his viceroy in pitched battle. He replied that he had not made himself governor, but that the judges, at the behest of all the cities of Peru, had bidden him become it and had authorized it in the light of the power vested by His Majesty in his brother the marquis to appoint his successor as governor. His brother had appointed him, as everyone knew, and there was nothing surprising in the conqueror of Peru becoming its governor. As to the viceroy, the judges had also ordered him to be expelled from Peru, saying that it behove His Majesty's service and the peace and quiet of the empire. He had not killed the viceroy: what had happened was that the viceroy had caused so many wrongs and deaths by his precipitate and unjustifiable actions that the relatives of the dead had been forced to seek revenge. If the messengers he had sent to report to His Majesty (who were those who had sold him and caused him to be called a traitor) had been allowed to pass, His Majesty would have regarded himself as well served and have acted in quite a different manner; for everything Pizarro had done then and since had been at the instance of the *vecinos* and procurators of the cities of the whole of Peru, and had been approved by all the lawyers in the country.

The president then said that he had shown himself very ungrateful for the grants His Majesty had made to his brother. This had enriched them all, though they had been so poor before, and had raised them from the dust; and in any case Gonzalo Pizarro had played no part in the discovery of Peru. Gonzalo answered: "My brother alone was enough to discover the country; but all four brothers were necessary, and the rest of our relatives and friends, to conquer it, as we did at our own risk and expense. The only honor His Majesty did my brother was to confer on him the title of marquis: if he did more, tell me what it was. He did not lift us up from the dust, for we have been noblemen and gentlemen with our own estates since the Goths came to Spain. Those who are not may very well be raised from the dust by His Majesty's offices and commissions. If we were poor, that was why we ventured out into the world, and won this empire, and gave it to His Majesty, though we might have kept it ourselves, as many others who have won new lands have done."

This angered the president, and he twice shouted: "Take him away; take him away. He's as much of a rebel today as he was yesterday." Then Centeno led him away, having requested the president for the privilege. The other captains were sent to various places where they could be safely guarded.

Francisco de Carvajal, though eighty-four years old, was prompted by a natural hatred for dying to take flight and see if he could not lengthen the days of his life a little. He was on a small, old chestnut horse, which I knew: it was called Boscanillo and had been a fine work horse. On crossing one of the many little streams there are in the countryside there, with a slope of seven or eight paces down and a rather steep climb of the same height on the other side, the horse went down rather fast—which indeed was necessary for their escape—and having crossed the stream, rushed at the opposite bank. Carvajal was old and bulky (for he had run to fat), and could not assist the horse, though it would have sufficed to have grasped its mane. On the contrary he slipped sideways and pulled the horse with him. Both fell in the stream and the horse caught his leg under its body so that he could not rise. His own men, who were running away, found him in this state, and were glad to have caught him, for they decided to take him under arrest to the president, so that he would pardon them their own misdeeds in return for such a prisoner.

CHAPTER XXXVII

What happens between Francisco de Carvajal
and Diego Centeno and the president;
the capture of the other captains.

WHEN THE cry went up that Carvajal was taken, many others of the president's followers came up to see so famous a man. But instead of comforting him in his troubles, they held lighted torches against his neck and tried to thrust them between his body and his shirt. While this was being done, Carvajal saw Captain Centeno who had returned to the army after having placed Gonzalo Pizarro in his tent in the care of half a dozen of his friends, all distinguished soldiers. When Carvajal saw that he was passing by without noticing him, he shouted to him: "Captain Diego Centeno, I hope you won't regard it as a small service if I present myself to you!" He meant that in good military usage captains and soldiers should think it a very notable thing that a commander who had so often been victorious, even until the recent battle of Huarina, should now present himself as a prisoner so that Centeno might satisfy himself for his past losses and triumph over his enemy. Centeno turned toward him, and said that he was sorry to see him in that plight. Carvajal replied: "I believe your honor; and I think that as a Christian and a gentleman, you'll do as you should. Let's talk no more of it, but tell these gentlefolk to stop what they're doing"—that is tormenting him with torches. They had not stopped doing this despite Centeno's presence, for they thought that he was such an enemy of Carvajal's he would rejoice at any harm they might do him. But Centeno fell on them and beat them with the flat of his sword, for they were all low fellows: sailors and ships' boys accompanying the army, who were capable of playing such vile pranks on one who deserved very different treatment.

When Centeno had got Carvajal away from these rogues, he ordered two of the soldiers who were with him to escort the captive and see that no harm was done to him. As they were going on their way, they came across Governor Pedro de Valdivia, who, on learning that they had got Francisco de Carvajal, wanted to have him taken before the president, wishing to appear in his presence with such a prisoner. He therefore asked Centeno to give him up, which he did, saying that after Carvajal had been presented, he should be brought back to Centeno's tent, for he wished to be in charge of Carvajal. Centeno said this because he thought that if Carvajal were anywhere else he would be mishandled by impudent and lawless soldiers who wanted revenge for injuries they themselves had suffered. Pedro de Valdivia took him before the president, who reprimanded him for his cruelty and rebelliousness, saying that they were contrary to the king's service. Carvajal did not say a word in reply, or humble himself, or show any sign of listening to what was being said. He looked around him with such a grave and lordly air that he might have been master of all those present. When the president saw this, he ordered him to be taken away; and he was led to Diego Centeno's camp and put in a separate tent by himself, so that he and Gonzalo Pizarro should see one another no more.

All the other captains and officers were captured, some that day and others later: none escaped. Only Captain Juan de la Torre hid in Cuzco

for four months in the straw hut of an Indian servant, so that no one
knew what had become of him during all this while. It was as though the
earth had swallowed him up, until a Spaniard unfortunately discovered
him without knowing who he was; and he was hanged like the rest,
though belatedly.

CHAPTER XXXVIII

Francisco de Carvajal's visitors while he is
under arrest; his conversations with
those who come to triumph
over him.

ALL WE HAVE told of the events of the battle of Sacsahuana occurred
before ten in the morning of April 9, 1548, for as the affair began
so early, all was quiet by that hour. The president then sent two captains
to Cuzco, to catch fugitives from the battle and to prevent any bold spirits
from trying to sack the city. The same afternoon many of the leading men
in the army, captains and soldiers, went to visit the prisoners, some because of former friendships with them, some as relatives, and some as
their fellow countrymen. Some went to comfort them; and others were
moved by interest, to see if they had left any hidden property they might
inherit. Only Francisco de Carvajal's visitors lacked these motives, for he
had no friend, relative, or countryman: even his most intimate friends
avoided him. Nevertheless many leading gentlemen went to see him,
especially some of the younger and naughtier ones, who went to mock
him and triumph over him rather than to console him. But as Francisco
de Carvajal was wise and wily enough to realize their intention, he triumphed over them, and made fun of them, as we shall say. I shall tell
some stories that I remember occurred on that day. Some of these are
mentioned by the historians, though not as they happened, but very differently: I shall add others that they do not mention.

While Carvajal was under arrest, a merchant came up and pretending
to be very distressed, said: "Your honor's soldiers robbed me of so many
thousand ducats of merchandise at such and such a place. You, as their

captain, are obliged to make restitution. I leave it to your conscience to discharge this debt, as you have to die soon."

Carvajal looked round and found in his sword belt the scabbard that had been left when they took away his sword. Taking it from its place, he gave it to the merchant and said: "Take this, brother, as the first instalment, for they haven't left me anything else." He meant to emphasize the man's stupidity in wishing for thousands of ducats from one who had nothing but a scabbard.

A little after this man had gone, another came with a similar request. Carvajal had nothing with which to pay, and replied that he couldn't remember owing anyone anything except half a real to a woman with a tavern in the Puerta del Arenal in Seville. This piece of nonsense was intended to match the folly of one who asked restitution from a man who had not even been left a cloak or a hat on his head; for the conquerors had sacked everything. In fact, the richest spoil taken that day was what Carvajal lost, for he always carried his property with him, in gold, not silver, because it was less bulky.

From the above-mentioned requests and replies it can be guessed what others were made; but these we shall pass over, and turn to the remarks of more important people. Carvajal's visitors included a very notable gentleman, one of His Majesty's captains. He was a very gay and cheerful man, a great courtier and was fond of joking about everyone, for he had a jest for each. Among his other achievements, he was much devoted to Venus and Ceres, and showed it openly. After talking with Carvajal for a while, he concluded the conversation by saying: "Your honor has some heavy burdens on your conscience. Remember that you won't be allowed to live much longer. You had better examine your conscience and repent of your sins, and confess and beg God to pardon you, so as to die like a Christian and obtain God's forgiveness."

Carvajal replied: "You've spoken like a gentleman and like the good Christian you are. I beg you to take the same advice to yourself, for you need it as much as I do; and be so good as to bring me a bowl of that stuff those Indians are drinking."

On hearing this reply, the gentleman got up, and not wishing to hear any more, went to where the Indians were, got a bowl of the brew and took it to Carvajal. He received it, and in order not to seem ungrateful, took a swig and threw the rest behind him. With this the gentleman went off, so well rewarded for his good counsel and so chastened that afterwards whenever he made fun of one of his friends and would not leave him alone, the victim would say: "Peace, peace! Let's go to Carvajal: he'll restore peace!" This remark so abashed him that he found no reply.

Another gentleman of standing, younger than the last and less restrained in his youthful pranks and follies, and very fond of broadcasting them, made almost the same observation to Carvajal, pretending to be very solicitous for the welfare of his soul, as he was about to die. Carvajal replied: "Your honor speaks like the saint you are; that's why people often say that when boys are great scallywags they'll grow up into honest men." This silenced him, and he dared say no more, for they were talking in public.

Another gentleman fared worse. He had come to get his own back for an old grudge rather than to console Carvajal, and the latter realized this from the terms in which he spoke, saying: "I kiss your honor's hands, master commander. Though your honor wanted to have me hanged at such and such a place, I haven't taken it to heart, but have come to ask what I can do to serve you. Anything I can I'll very gladly do without any thought for my own injury."

Carvajal answered: "What *can* your honor do for me, which you offer with such enormous generosity? Can you save my life or do anything else to help me? When I wanted to hang you, I could have done so, but I didn't because I never killed such a villainous fellow as you. Do you think I don't know what you can do? Why do you want to sell me what you haven't got? Now, be off with you, before I say any more."

In this way he scored off and triumphed over those who thought they would triumph over him. Never, even at the height of his power, did he show such authority and serenity as that day when he was under arrest. The incidents I have mentioned happened in the case of these gentlemen, all three of whom were known to me, and whose names I remember; but it is not proper to mention them in this connection, but only when they performed great deeds. They were later *vecinos* of Cuzco and lords of the best allocations of vassals in the city.

CHAPTER XXXIX

*The captains who were executed, and how their
heads were taken to various parts of Peru.*

AFTER THESE conversations there followed a very different one with
a soldier called Diego de Tapia, whom I knew and of whom I spoke
at length in the *History of Florida* (Book VI, ch. xviii). He had been a
soldier under Carvajal, a member of his own company and a favorite
with him, for Tapia was a good soldier and very able in any sort of task.
He was a small and neat man, and had fled from Carvajal before the
battle of Huarina. He now appeared before him and wept bitterly with
great passion and tenderness, and amidst many other pathetic things, he
said: "Oh, sir, my father, I'm very grieved to see your honor in this plight.
Would to God they'd be satisfied to kill me and let you go, for I'd willingly give my life for yours. Oh, sir, how sad I am to see you in this
state! If you had run away when I did, you wouldn't be here like this!"
Carvajal said that he understood his grief and sorrow and much appreciated his readiness to give his life for another's, which amply showed
what great friends they had been. And as to the question of running away,
he said: "Brother Diego de Tapia, as we were such great friends, why
didn't you tell me you were going to run away and we'd have run away
together?"
This reply greatly amused all who knew him, and they were astonished
at the self possession with which he answered anything that was said to
him. All this and much more happened to Francisco de Carvajal on the
day of the battle. Gonzalo Pizarro was alone and no one saw him, except
Diego Centeno and six or seven other prominent soldiers who were
guarding him, for such were his own wishes.
The following day Gonzalo Pizarro and his commander and captains
who had been captured on the day of the battle were executed. As López
de Gómara says (ch. clxxxvii), they were Juan de Acosta, Francisco Maldonado, Juan Vélez de Guevara, Dionisio de Bobadilla, and Gonzalo de
los Nidos. He mentions that in the case of the last of these they pulled his
tongue out through the back of his neck, though he does not say why: it

was because he uttered great blasphemies against the Imperial Majesty. All these and many others were hanged, and though they were gentlemen their privileges were not respected since they were traitors to the king. After being hanged, their heads were cut off and sent to various cities in Peru. Juan de Acosta's and Francisco Maldonado's were placed on the gibbet in the main square of Cuzco, each in an iron cage: I saw them there, though one of the historians, Fernández (ch. xci), says that Acosta's was taken to Lima. Dionisio de Bobadilla's and that of one other were taken to Arequipa, thus fulfilling the prophecy the good Juana de Leitão made to Bobadilla himself when he brought Lope de Mendoza's head to the city: her words were that it would soon be taken down and his own set up in the same place. This thus came about, exactly as she said. Gonzalo Pizarro and his officers were executed in haste, for, as the authors say, it was feared that the country would not be safe while he was alive. They sentenced Pizarro to be beheaded as a traitor; his houses in Cuzco were pulled down and the site sown with salt, and a stone pillar was erected with an inscription reading: "This is the house of the traitor Gonzalo Pizarro," etc.

I saw all this carried out. The houses were those granted to him in the allocations of Cuzco, when he and his brothers conquered the city. The place is called Coracora, or "meadow," in the Indian tongue. Pizarro spent the day of his arrest in the tent of Captain Centeno, where he was treated with the same respect as during his greatest prosperity and power. He refused to eat that day though he was invited to do so. He spent almost the whole time walking up and down alone, brooding. Late at night he called to Centeno: "Sir, are we safe tonight?" He meant would they kill him that night or wait till next day, for he well knew that each hour was a year for his rivals until they had killed him.

When Centeno understood him, he said: "Your Lordship can sleep safely; there's no need to brood over that." And after midnight he lay down a little on the bed, and slept about an hour. Then he resumed his pacing up and down till daylight. At dawn he asked for a confessor, and lingered with him till mid-day, where we shall leave him to return to Francisco de Carvajal, and say how he spent the day.

Carvajal did not behave so extravagantly as one of the authors says, but very differently. I shall recount this, not because I have any obligation for having received anything from him: on the contrary, he wanted to kill my father after the battle of Huarina, and tried to find reasons for this drawn from his own suspicions and imaginations. For this reason I might be expected to speak ill of him rather than seek to defend his honor.

But the obligation of one who writes the history of those times for the information of the whole world binds me, and even forces me, if I may put it so, to tell the truth about what happened without passion for or against. And I swear as a Christian that I have clipped and cut short many passages so as not to seem to speak with passion against the versions of the historians, especially Fernández, who must have gone to Peru very late and have heard many fables invented according to the party passions of their authors. What I have said above, and other details I shall give of these days, I heard as a child from people who were talking of those things: at that time and for many years after there was no theme of conversation among noble people which did not touch to some extent on these matters. Later, when I was older, I heard them from a person or persons who were on guard over Francisco de Carvajal and Gonzalo Pizarro, for the tents they were in were very close together and the soldiers on guard, all eminent men, went between them relieving one another; so they saw everything and described all the details as eye witnesses.

And to show the difference between what this author says and what I have said of the incidents that happened to Carvajal and Gonzalo Pizarro after their capture, I shall quote some of the remarks he sets down, which are obviously the sayings of the dregs of the common people and not the words or deeds of such eminent and educated persons as were involved. The following is from his ch. xc:

Then Francisco de Carvajal, who had been taken after falling under his horse in a bog, was brought before the president by Pedro de Valdivia. He was surrounded by people he had aggrieved who wanted to kill him, so that the president could scarcely protect him. Carvajal himself declared that he wanted them to kill him on the spot, and cordially besought them not to prevent his being put to death. Then the bishop of Cuzco came up and said to him: "Carvajal, why did you kill my brother?"—referring to his brother Jiménez, who was hanged after Huarina.

Carvajal replied: "I didn't kill him."

The bishop again asked: "Then who did?"

And Carvajal said: "His bad luck."

This angered the bishop, who, with a vision of his brother's death before him, attacked Carvajal and dealt him three or four cuts in the face. Many others then came up, and uttered abuse and insults, reminding him of many things he had done. At all this Carvajal was silent, and Centeno strongly rebuked those who were maltreating him. Carvajal then looked at him and said: "Sir, who are you to show me such favor?"

At this Centeno replied: "Doesn't your honor recognize Diego Centeno?" And Carvajal exclaimed: "Good heavens, as I always saw your back, now I see your face I didn't recognize it"—implying that Centeno had always run away from him.

Then Carvajal was led away under arrest, and Centeno continued to offer to help, despite what Carvajal had said to him: he declared that if there was anything he could do for him, he was not to hesitate to say so, for he, Centeno, would do it willingly, even though Carvajal would not if he were in his place. To this Carvajal, accompanying him to the tent where he was to be kept, stopped a little and said: "Diego Centeno, sir, I'm not a child or a boy, and fear of death won't make me commit such a feeble and cowardly act as to ask you to do anything for me. I don't remember having heard anything to make me laugh so much for days as your offer." And at this they put him in the tent.

In the whole royal army not a single man died in the battle, and on Gonzalo's side fifteen, for just as God supplied the means—in His almighty power and in recompense for His Majesty's merits and holy zeal in dealing mildly with Gonzalo and his men—so by His blessed and mighty hand, He ended the war with such little bloodshed, despite the fact that there were 1,400 arquebusiers, 17 field pieces and more than 600 horse, and a large number of pikes on both sides. For when the royalists saw that their opponents were dispersed and lost and made no resistance at all, they did nothing but arrest them,

etc.

In his following chapter (xci), after stating the sentence passed on Gonzalo Pizarro, he speaks as follows:

And though some recommended and urged that he should be quartered, and the quarters placed on the four roads into Cuzco, the president would not consent out of respect due to the marquis, his brother. He died well, showing proof of repentance for the wrongs he had committed against God, his king and his fellow men.

On the same day Francisco de Carvajal was executed. He was drawn and quartered, and the quarters placed round Cuzco. His head was sent to Lima with that of Gonzalo; and his house in Lima was pulled down, and the site sown with salt, and an inscription erected. Francisco de Carvajal, from the time of his arrest till his execution, was as unperturbed as in the days of his greatest prosperity. When informed of the sentence and all of its contents, he said without any emotion: "Death's enough." Carvajal asked that morning how many had been executed, and on being told none, calmly replied: "The president's very compassionate, for if we'd had his good fortune, I'd have scattered the quarters of 900 men around here." He was persuaded to confess only with great difficulty, and when they tried to induce him he said he knew his own business and had confessed not long since. When they spoke of restitution, he laughed heartily and said: "I've nothing to confess about that: I swear by ———— that I've no other debts but half a real I owe in Seville to a woman who keeps a tavern in the Puerta del Arenal, from the time when I came to the Indies." When they put him in a native chest instead of a hamper, he said coolly: "I began in a cradle and ended in a cradle." On being brought to the place of execution so many people had come to see him that they hindered the executioner; and he said: "Gentlemen, don't stand in the way of justice." In all he died more like a gallant than a Christian.

Thus Fernández: he must have heard this from people who had some grudge against Carvajal, and being unable to avenge themselves on his person, sought to do so on his reputation.

CHAPTER XL

What Francisco de Carvajal said and did on
the day of his death; what the authors
say of his character and
military skill.

To RETURN to our author's words, it is scarcely to be credited that a bishop so religious as that of Cuzco should have stabbed an old man of eighty-four publicly or in secret, or that a man of such discretion and good sense as Centeno should have so persistently offered his help to a man who he knew would be executed within a few hours. Nor would Francisco de Carvajal, to whom all three historians ascribe such brave deeds and such witty sayings as he uttered on all sorts of occasions, have expressed himself in these stupid terms at a time when he most desired to exhibit his courage and character. The author must certainly have picked these words up from some of those who invent what in Cuzco are called *trónicas,* which are lies invented to be credited as true, such being the meaning of the word *trónica,* which I have never heard used any-where else.

Carvajal did not pretend not to recognize Centeno, but spoke as I have said, and I heard the words from those who were in the company of both of them, and not from the *hoi polloi.* And though López de Gómara (ch. clxxxvii) says almost the same in different words, and Palencia may have followed him, the fact is that one of the first and foremost soldiers of Peru, who came to Spain soon after López de Gómara's history appeared, happened to meet him in Valladolid, and in the midst of a conversation about these events, asked him why he had written such a great lie and allowed it to be printed, when it had never happened. López de Gómara replied that he was not to blame, but those who gave him biassed accounts. The soldier said that a historian's judgment was intended precisely for such cases, and he should either not get his reports from such people, or not write at length without considering at length, so as not to defame those who deserve all honor and praise in his writings. At this López de Gómara took his leave, full of confusion and regret at having brought false witness against Carvajal by saying that he did not recognize Centeno. Nor did Carvajal utter the piece of braggadocio about scattering around the quarters of 900 men: he was neither so mad nor so vain as that. I shall say what I heard from those who were in his company that day, among whom I was reared from the age of nine—my ninth birthday was the day following these events—till I was twenty, when I left Peru.

To return to our history, the fact is that as soon as it was day Francisco de Carvajal sent for Pedro López de Cazalla, La Gasca's secretary, and spoke with him alone for a long time. At the end of the conversation he produced three very fine emeralds which were pierced like beads: the two largest were egg-shaped and the third round, and he had them fastened round his left arm. With these in his hand, he separated the largest of them and said: "Master secretary, this comes from the heirs of Antonio Altamirano; it's valued at five thousand pesos, or six thousand ducats. I beg your honor will have it returned to its owner. This other is from ———— (the name has slipped my memory); it is valued at four thousand pesos; you will please have it returned too. The third and smallest is mine, and cost me two thousand pesos before the war. I beg your honor to have it sold and give what it brings as alms for masses to be said so that the Lord may take pity on my soul and pardon me."

The secretary was sorry for him and said: "Master Francisco de Carvajal, if your honor wishes to make further restitution, I can offer you ten thousand pesos of my own, and will give them to anyone you desire."

Carvajal answered: "Sir, I didn't begin this war, or even cause it. On the contrary, because of it I came many leagues out of my way, for I was on my way back to Spain. I couldn't avoid it. I followed the party I happened to be with, as any other good soldier might have done, and as I did in the emperor's service when I was sergeant major to Licentiate Vaca de Castro, who was His Majesty's governor in Peru. If there have been robberies on either side, that's because there must be in wartime. I never robbed anyone: I took what they gave me of their own free will, and at the end of the day they took this and the rest from me; I mean what I was given and what I had before. All of which I refer to the infinite pity of our Lord God, whom I beg to forgive my sins and to keep and prosper your honor, and reward you for your charity toward me, for I esteem your intention as highly as such a deed should be esteemed."

At this the conversation ended and the secretary left. After mid-day the secretary sent him a confessor, for which Carvajal had asked and he spent the afternoon confessing to him; and although the officers came two or three times to try to hasten the execution, Carvajal lingered over his confession as long as he could so as not to go out by day, but by night. But he failed to achieve this object, because the royal judge Cianca, and the commander, Alonso de Alvarado, who were the judges, felt every moment to be a day or a week. At last he emerged, and at the tent door he was put in a native chest (we have described elsewhere what these are like) instead of a hamper, and sewn up, so that only his head stuck out. The hamper was then attached to two beasts of burden to be dragged along the ground. After the beasts had gone two or three steps, Carvajal's face struck the ground, and raising his head as best he could, he cried to those who were nearest: "Gentlemen, let your honors remember I'm a Christian."

The words were not out of his mouth before some thirty prominent soldiers of Centeno's had lifted him off the ground in their arms. I heard one of them in particular say that when he rushed forth to take the hamper, he thought that he was one of the first, and when he managed to get his arm under it, the whole space was taken and he seized the arm of a man who had got there before him. He was thus carried as a dead weight to the foot of the gallows that had been made. On the way he was praying in Latin, but as this soldier did not understand Latin, he did not know what the prayer was. Two seculars who were with him said from time to time: "Recommend your soul to God."

Carvajal replied: "I'm doing so, sir," and said not another word. In this way he reached the place where they hanged him, and he accepted his death with humility, not uttering a word or making a gesture. Such was the end of the brave Francisco de Carvajal, of whose death López de Gómara (ch. clxxxvii) says: "He was eighty-four, was ensign in the battle of Ravenna, and a soldier under the Grand Captain; and he was the most famous warrior of all the Spaniards who crossed to the Indies, though not particularly valiant or skilful in the use of weapons." So

López de Gómara: I do not know what greater valor or skill a commander can have than to win battles and gain victories over his enemies.

The historians say that he was a native of a village near Arévalo called Rágama: it is not known of what family he was. He was a soldier all his life, and an ensign at Ravenna as has been said. He was present at the capture of the king of France at Pavia and at the sack of Rome, where because he fought like a good soldier, he obtained nothing in the sack. It happens commonly enough that while the good soldiers are fighting the rest are sacking and winning the prizes of war: such was the case with Carvajal. Finding that he had gained nothing, three or four days after the sack he happened to enter the house of a prominent notary and found a great quantity of law suits; he thought the papers might possibly be of some value and loaded five or six beasts with them and carried them off to his lodging. After the fury of the sack had abated, the notary returned to his house and found that what he thought nobody would touch had been sacked. He caused a search to be made for the papers and having traced them, paid Carvajal more than a thousand ducats for them. With this money Carvajal went to Mexico, taking his wife Doña Catarina Leitão, as we have said before. Some say she was his mistress, but she was his wife and was respected as such by everyone in Peru: she was an honorable and noble woman, for this name Leitão is of great nobility in the kingdom of Portugal.

From Mexico Carvajal passed to Peru, as we have already said. Throughout his life military service was his idol, which he worshipped, prizing himself more on being a soldier than on being a Christian. All three historians condemn him; but he was not as bad as they say, for like a good soldier he was proud of being a man of his word, and was very grateful for any service or present he was offered, however trivial. Zárate says the following of Carvajal (Book V, ch. xiv):

He was a man of average height, very stout and ruddy, and extremely skilled in warfare owing to his long experience. He was better able to support hardships than might have been suspected from his age, for the way in which he never took his arms off day or night was marvellous, and if necessary he did not lie down or sleep, except that the hand on which he supported his head as he lay back in his chair would tire from time to time. He was very fond of wine; so much so that when he could not get Castilian wine, he would drink the brew the Indians make in much greater quantities than any other Spaniard. His character was very cruel: he killed many people on the slightest pretext, and some for nothing they had done at all, but merely because he thought that it was politic for the preservation of military discipline. He killed men pitilessly and with jests and humorous sallies, though he was always courteous. He was a very bad Christian, and proved it by word and deed.

Thus Zárate.

CHAPTER XLI

Francisco de Carvajal's dress; some of his stories and jests.

COMMANDER Francisco de Carvajal prided himself on his soldierliness, and almost always wore instead of a cloak a purple Moorish burnoose with a hood and fringe and I often saw him dressed so. On his head he wore a lined hat of black taffeta with a plain silk braid. He had a lot of black and white plumes in it from the wings and tail of ordinary chickens, and crossed like X's all round the hat. This ornament he wore to set an example to his soldiers, for one of the things he most exhorted them to do was to wear plumes of any kind at all, for he said that that was a proper ornament and the true mark of a soldier and distinguished him from a citizen, on whom it was a proof of frivolity, though on soldiers it showed gallantry. He promised that any soldier who wore them would be so full of valor and spirit that he would kill one, lie in wait for two, and not run away from three. This was not his own phrase, but a very old soldier's saying about plumes.

Francisco de Carvajal had some very amusing tales and witty sayings which he had for all occasions and contexts. I should like to be able to remember them so as to write them down here, for they would provide good entertainment. We shall set down the ones that occur to us; and also the more decent ones, so that his indecent ribaldry, which was very great, may not give offence.

When Carvajal came across a new and very small soldier of poor build and worse expression, he said: "What's your honor's name?" The soldier replied Stealing [Hurtado], and Carvajal remarked: "Not worth finding, let alone stealing."

When Carvajal was on one of his campaigns, he came across a lay brother, and as there were no lay brothers in Peru in those days (I do not know if there are any now), he suspected that he was a spy and was about to hang him, and in order to be surer he invited him to dine. To test whether the man was a friar or not, he had him served with wine in a bigger bowl than the usual ones, to see if he would take it with two hands or one: when he saw him drink with both hands, he was sure the man was a friar, and said: "Drink father, drink, for it's your salvation. Drink, for it's your salvation." Carvajal said this because if he had not drunk in that way, his suspicions would have been confirmed and he would have hanged him forthwith.

When Carvajal captured one of his greatest enemies and was going to hang him, the man, as if to threaten him as being the cause of his death, said: "Tell me openly why you're killing me."

Carvajal guessed his intention and replied: "I perceive you want to have a pedigree for your death so that you can point to it and pass it on as an heirloom. Well, I'm hanging you because you're a loyal servant of His Majesty. Now, good-bye; for he'll regard it as a great service and will reward you very well." Saying this, he had him hanged at once.

Whilst Carvajal was travelling through Collao, he fell in with a merchant who had fourteen or fifteen thousand pesos worth of Spanish wares purchased in Panama. Carvajal said to him: "Brother, in good military usage all that property is mine."

The merchant was astute and prepared for any sort of peril that might occur, and said: "Sir, in war and in peace this is your property, for I bought it in Panama in both our names so that we could share the profits. And in proof of this I've brought from Panama two pitchers of red wine and two dozen shoes for your beasts with nails"—in those days, as we have already said, each horseshoe was worth a silver mark. So saying, he sent for the wine and the shoes, and showed Carvajal a document naming the two as partners. Carvajal took the wine and the shoes, for which he was very grateful, and he wished to show this by honoring his partner. He gave him a captain's commission and an order for the Indians along the road to serve him and supply him with anything he needed. He also ordered that no merchant in Potosí should open his stall or sell anything until his partner had got rid of all his goods.

The merchant was full of pride at these favors, and sold everything at his own price, making a great profit of more than thirty thousand pesos. In order to make sure of Carvajal's collaboration he returned in search of him, and having found him, told him briefly: "Sir, we made eight thousand pesos under our partnership, here's four thousand for your honor."

Carvajal put on a very businesslike air, and in order to make his soldiers laugh, said: "I can't pass this account until I've seen the stockbook."

The merchant drew it out and read the entries, including pieces of brocade and velvet, satin and damask, fine Segovia cloth, Holland, Rouen, and everything else that was imported from Spain, with their prices. The last entries read: "Three dozen combs, so much."

Carvajal, who had listened so far in silence, said: "Stop, stop, read that again." Having heard it, he turned to his soldiers and said: "Don't you think my partner's charging me a great deal for these combs?"

The soldiers laughed heartily, on seeing that he had raised no objection to the other prices, which were very high, but boggled at the combs, and realized he only meant to make them laugh. This brought the partnership to a close, and Carvajal took his share of the profits and sent his partner off very well entertained and satisfied. Carvajal would always do this if he were given something. One of the authors tells this story or one like it in a very different manner.

While Carvajal was pursuing Diego Centeno so hotly, he captured three enemy soldiers one day; and having hanged the two most important of them, came to the third, a foreigner from Greece called Master Francis who acted as a surgeon, though he was not one, and said: "This one's a poor specimen: hang him from the highest pole."

Master Francis said: "Sir, I haven't done your honor any harm, or anything to make you want to kill a poor specimen like me, especially as I can serve you by tending your wounds, for I'm a famous surgeon."

Seeing him so distressed, Carvajal replied: "All right, be off with you: I'll forgive you now and for always. Now go and tend my mules, that's the trade you know."

In this way Master Francis escaped, and a few months later he fled, and went off to serve Centeno. After the battle of Huarina Carvajal captured him again and ordered him to be hanged at once. Master Francis said: "Your honor mustn't kill me, for last time you forgave me then and for always, and being such a great soldier and so proud of it, you'll keep your word to me."

Carvajal said: "Devil take you, do you remember that still? I'll keep my word. Be off and tend my mules; and run away as often as you please, for if all the enemies of my lord the governor were like you, we shouldn't regard them as such." One author applies this tale of Master Francis to a friar, and the characters must have been changed in the report he was given.

While pursuing Centeno, he took three of the soldiers he called shuttlers, who went over from one side to the other to supply their own wants. He never spared these if he caught them, and at once ordered them to be hanged. After two had been strung up, the third tried to find some pretext for getting a pardon and pretended to have been one of his servants, saying: "Pardon me, your honor, if only because I've eaten your bread." And as Carvajal's soldier he had often eaten at his table.

Carvajal exclaimed: "A curse on such a waste of bread!" and turning to the executioner said: "Hang this gentleman from the highest branch for eating my bread."

And lest this chapter grow too long, we shall divide it into two parts.

CHAPTER XLII

*Other similar anecdotes; the last of which
tells of what happened to a boy with
one of Carvajal's quarters.*

O N ANOTHER occasion, as he was leaving Cuzco and marching toward Collao, he took three hundred soldiers in formation, for he often led his men drawn up in order of battle partly to amuse himself and partly to train the men in the art of war. Just over a league from the city, a soldier left the ranks and went behind some rocks by the roadside to perform a natural necessity. Carvajal, who was going at the back of the formation to see how they marched, went after the soldier and reprimanded him for breaking ranks. The soldier pleaded the call of nature. Carvajal replied saying: "Good ———, a good soldier in Peru, because he's in Peru, has to be better than all the others in the world, and eat a loaf in Cuzco and pass it out in Chuquisaca." This was to stimulate martial spirit, for the two places are at least two hundred leagues apart.

On another occasion, when Carvajal and six or seven companions were travelling, they were brought one morning a roast leg of a Peruvian sheep, which has more meat on one quarter than there is on half a Spanish sheep. One of his comrades, a certain Hernán Pérez Tablero, a great friend of Carvajal's, began to carve, but being very inexpert, cut some very thick slices. Carvajal saw this and said: "What are you cutting, Hernán Pérez?"

He replied: "One slice for each of you."

Carvajal said: "You're right, anyone who came back for more would be a villain."

On returning victorious from his pursuit of Captain Centeno, he held a banquet in Cuzco for his leading soldiers in celebration of his success. As wine was then worth more than three hundred pesos the arroba, the guests let themselves go, and like people unaccustomed to drinking it, they suffered certain of its effects and some of them fell asleep in their seats, others wherever they happened to drop, and still others anywhere where they could find a place. Doña Catarina Leitão came out of her room, and seeing them in this state, railed at them, saying: "Alack for Peru, look at the state of those who're governing it."

Carvajal heard her and said: "Quiet, you old besom; let them sleep a couple of hours and any of them'll be fit to govern half the world."

On another occasion he had arrested a rich man for having said certain things about him, but not finding enough proof (not that he needed any to despatch his enemies), he kept him in prison. When the prisoner found that his execution was delayed, he thought he might save his life by giving money; for it was notorious that on such occasions Carvajal would take money and make friends. With this idea the man sent for one of his friends and requested him to bring two blocks of gold he had in a certain place. When they had been brought, he sent his friend to beg Carvajal to come and listen to his explanations of the charges that had been brought against him. Carvajal went to see him, for the prison was inside his own house. The prisoner said: "Sir, I'm not guilty of what I'm charged with. I beg you to use this trifle, and pardon me for the love of God: I promise that from today on I'll be your most loyal servant, as your honor shall see."

Carvajal took the blocks, and said aloud so that the soldiers in the courtyard could hear: "Oh, sir, when you've so authentic and authoritative a letter of credential, why didn't you show it me before? Go in peace and live in safety, for even though we're against the king, there's no reason why we should be against God's church."

We have already said how Carvajal strangled Doña María Calderón and had her hung from the window of her house. We did not quote the words that passed on this occasion, so as not to interrupt the current of our history and because it was no place for jesting. We shall now set down the missing words. Doña María Calderón, although she was in her enemy's power, spoke quite openly against Gonzalo Pizarro and his tyrannies; and her ordinary conversation was nothing but criticisms of him. Carvajal knew this and sent to warn her once or twice or more times to desist from these jests which were indiscreet and not likely to be good for her health. She was given the same advice by other persons who feared for her safety. But instead of restraining herself and mending her ways, Doña María Calderón spoke thereafter even more freely and disrespectfully, so that Carvajal was obliged to go to her lodging to arrest her, and said: "Do you know, madam gossip, I've come to strangle you?"

She thought Carvajal was joking, and replied lightly: "Go with the Devil, you drunken lunatic, I don't want to hear it even in jest."

Carvajal said: "I'm not jesting. I've come to squeeze your throat so that you don't speak so much and so ill; and in order to convince you, I now bid these Ethiopian soldiers to strangle you."

There were three or four Negroes he always had with him for such deeds. They at once suffocated her and hung her from a window over the street. Carvajal, passing below, raised his eyes and said: "By ———'s life, madam gossip, if that doesn't chasten you, I don't know what to do with you."

Carvajal spent some time in a city in Peru, and had his soldiers billetted on the inhabitants. He had to leave the place with his men to go on a certain expedition, and at the end of two months returned to the city. A jealous artisan who had had a soldier as his guest during their last sojourn came up to Carvajal and said: "Sir, I beg your honor won't billet so and so on me."

Carvajal understood and nodded his head in reply. When he got to the square, he billetted the soldiers, saying to each of them: "You can go to so-and-so's house, and you to so-and-so's." He used to lodge his men anywhere he went as easily as this, just as if he had a written list of the inhabitants. When he came to the soldier in question, he said: "You go to so-and-so's house," a long way from that of his former host.

The soldier said: "I know a house where I can go, sir."

Carvajal replied: "You go where I say and nowhere else."

The soldier returned to the charge: "I don't need to go to a new house; I'll go where I'm known."

Carvajal nodded his head very gravely and said: "You go where I send you, for you'll be very well attended to there. If you want anything else, here's Doña Catarina Leitão."

The soldier, seeing that Carvajal had read his thoughts and ministered to his desires, went where he was sent without another word.

They cut off Francisco de Carvajal's head to take it to Lima and place it on the gibbet there beside Gonzalo Pizarro's. His body was quartered, and the quarters were placed, with those of other captains who suffered the same fate, at the four royal highways leading out of the city. And as in Book IV, ch. xxxvii, I promised a story in proof of the poison the Indians of the Windward Islands made for their arrows by sticking the latter into the quarters of dead men, I shall say what I saw in the case of one of the quarters of Carvajal which was placed on the road to Collasuyu, to the south of Cuzco.

On Sunday, ten or twelve of us schoolboys, all mestizos, children of Spanish fathers and Indian mothers, and all of us under twelve, went out, and hearing that Carvajal's quarter was lying on the ground said in unison: "Let's go and see Carvajal!" We found the quarter, which was one of his thighs: a good piece of ground was covered with grease from it, and the flesh was already greenish and rotten. As we were all standing round looking at it, one of the boys said: "Don't any of you dare touch it?"

Another said: "But I do."

"But you don't."

And this went on for some time till the boys were divided into two groups, the do's and the don'ts. Then a boy called Bartolomé Monedero, bolder and naughtier than the rest, came forward and said: "I dare to touch it," and poked it with his right thumb so that it sank right into the quarter.

The others of us ran away from him, crying: "You dirty beast. Carvajal'll kill you, he'll kill you for that."

The boy went to a ditch nearby and carefully washed his thumb and hand, rubbing it with mud, and then went home. The next day, Monday, in school he showed his thumb swollen where it had entered Carvajal's quarter, as though it had the finger of a glove fitted over it. That afternoon the whole hand was swollen as far as the wrist and looked very ugly. By Tuesday morning the swelling had gone up to the arm to the elbow, and he had to tell his father what had happened with Carvajal's quarter. The doctors were then summoned and they tied up his arm above the swelling with a tourniquet, swathed the hand and arm, and gave him other drastic treatment against poison: nevertheless he nearly died. All this was caused by Carvajal after he was dead, and it resembles what he did while he was alive. It proves what I wrote about the poison the Indians use for their arrows.

CHAPTER XLIII

How Gonzalo Pizarro was beheaded; the charity
he asked for at the hour of his death;
his character and good qualities.

IT REMAINS to speak of the pitiful death of Gonzalo Pizarro. He spent the whole day confessing as we have already noted, and we left him confessing until mid-day. He continued after the priests had dined, though he himself refused to eat and remained alone until the confessor returned: he stayed with him until very late. The ministers of justice came and went and tried to speed the execution. One of the gravest of them, annoyed at the delay, called out: "Come, haven't you finished with the man yet?" All the soldiers who heard this were offended at this disrespect, and uttered a thousand insults: although I remember many of them and knew the man, it would not be proper for me to set them down here or to mention his name. He went off without saying a word before anyone laid hands on him, as it was feared they would, on account of the indignation and wrath the soldiers displayed at his uncalled-for remark.

Soon after Gonzalo Pizarro appeared, and mounted a mule which was ready saddled. He was covered with a cloak, and though one author says his hands were bound, this was not so. A rope's end was hung over the mule's neck in compliance with the law. He carried in his hands an image of Our Lady, to whom he was most devoted. He begged her to intercede for his soul. After going half way he asked for a crucifix. One of the ten or twelve priests who accompanied him happened to have one and gave it to him. Gonzalo took it, and gave the priest the image of Our Lady, kissing the hem of the image's robe with great devotion. With his gaze fixed on the crucifix in his hands, he went to the platform that had been prepared for his execution, and mounted it, standing on one corner of it, and talked with the spectators, who included all the soldiers and *vecinos* of Peru: only the magnates who had denied him were missing, and even some of them were there in disguise or muffled in their cloaks. He said aloud: "Gentlemen, you know that my brothers and I won this empire. Many of you have allocations of Indians the marquis my brother gave you. Others have allocations I gave you. Moreover many of you owe me money I lent you. Others have received money not as a loan but as gifts. I die so poor that even the garment I wear belongs to the executioner who is to cut off my head. I have nothing with which to seek the good of my soul. I therefore beg those of you who owe me money to give this money, and those of you who do not owe me any to give your own money as charity for as many masses as possible to be said for my soul, for I trust to God that, through the blood and passion of our Lord Jesus Christ His Son and through the charity you will give, he will have compassion on me and forgive my sins. God be with you all."

He had not finished this speech when a general wail went up, with groans and sobs and the shedding of many tears, when such pathetic words were heard. Gonzalo Pizarro knelt before the crucifix he had brought, which was placed on a table on the platform. The executioner, called Juan Enríquez, placed a bandage over his eyes. Gonzalo said: "It's not necessary. Leave it." When he saw the man draw his scimitar to cut off his head, he said: "Do your task well, Brother Juan." He meant that he was to do it generously and not torture him, as often happens.

The executioner replied: "I promise Your Lordship." So saying, with his left hand he lifted his beard, a long one about a palm long and round, for in those days they were worn full and untrimmed. Then with a single stroke he cut off the head as easily as if it were a leaf of lettuce, and remained with it in his hand; the body took some time to fall to the ground.

Such was the end of this good gentleman. The executioner wished to exercise his rights and denude him, so as to enjoy the spoils. But Diego Centeno, who had come to recover Gonzalo's body, ordered him not to touch it and promised him a good sum of money in exchange for the clothes. So they carried him to Cuzco and buried him in his clothes, for no one offered to give him a shroud. He was buried in the convent of the Mercedarians, in the same chapel in which the two Almagros, father and son, lay, so that they were equals and companions in everything—in their conquest of Peru and in all being beheaded and buried by charity all three in a single grave, as though there was not even enough earth to cover them. They were made equal in everything by fortune, lest any should presume over the others or over the marquis Don Francisco Pizarro, the brother of one and companion of the other, who was killed as we have said and also buried by charity: thus all four were·as brothers and companions in everything and for everything. It is the usual reward of the world to those who serve it best, as those who saw these things dispassionately observed: for those who finished thus had conquered the empire called Peru.

None of the three authors speak of Gonzalo Pizarro's appeal for charity at the hour of his death, despite the fact that he spoke as publicly as we have said. This must have been so as not to distress their hearers. I set out to tell simply what happened, and this is what I have done.

Once the storm of war was passed, all the *vecinos* of the empire, each in the city where he lived, had many masses said for Gonzalo's soul, both because he himself had asked for them as charity, and because of their general and common obligation toward him, since he had died for them. His head and that of Carvajal were taken to Lima, which his brother the marquis Don Francisco Pizarro had founded and settled. They were placed on the pillar in the square there, each in an iron cage.

Gonzalo Pizarro and his four brothers, of whom history speaks at such length, were natives of the city of Trujillo in the province of Extremadura, the great mother that has borne and bred such heroic sons who won the two empires of the New World, Mexico and Peru; for Don Hernando Cortés, marquis del Valle, who conquered Mexico, was also from Extremadura, a native of Medellín. And Vasco Núñez de Balboa, the first Spaniard who saw the Pacific, was from Jerez near Badajoz; and Don Pedro de Alvarado, who after the conquest of Mexico went to Peru with eight hundred men, and Garcilaso de la Vega, who came as their captain, and Gómez de Tordoya were natives of Badajoz. And Pedro Alvarez Holguín and Hernando de Soto and Pedro del Barco, his companion, and many other gentlemen of the Alvarado and Chaves families, together with many other noble people who helped to conquer these realms, were mostly from Extremadura and took most of the inhabitants with them. And to praise the greatness of such a motherland it is enough to point to its famous sons, and their heroic deeds will praise and glorify the mother that brought such sons into the world. Gonzalo Pizarro was of the name and genealogy of the Pizarros whose blood is noble and illustrious throughout Spain. The marquis del Valle, Hernando Cortés, was of the same blood and kinship, for his mother was called Doña Catalina Pizarro, so that this lineage should receive the honor and glory of having won both those empires.

Gonzalo Pizarro and his brothers, in addition to being men of such a noble line, were the sons of Gonzalo Pizarro, captain of men-at-arms in the kingdom of Navarre, a position of such eminence that all the soldiers in the company must be nóbles by common repute or by letters-patent. In witness whereof I may say that I knew a gentleman, a grandee of Spain, Don Alonso Fernández de Córdoba y Figueroa, marquis of Priego, lord of the house of Aguilar, who held the same office of captain of cavalry of the kingdom of Navarre, which he held until his death and regarded himself as greatly honored by his association with such a place.

Gonzalo Pizarro was a knightly man, with handsome features, good health, and great endurance under hardships, as our history has shown. He was a fine rider with both saddles and a skilful shot with arquebus or crossbow: he could make any design he liked by firing clay pellets at a wall. He was also the best lance who crossed to the New World. Such was the conclusion of all who spoke of the famous men who have gone there.

He prided himself on his horses, and had some excellent ones. At the beginning of the conquest of Peru he had two chestnuts, one called Villein, because it was not of good build, and the other Zainillo, Little Chestnut. One day when the gentlemen of those days were talking of this horse in conversation, I heard one of them, who had been a companion of Gonzalo's, say: "When Gonzalo Pizarro, may he be in glory, came out on Zainillo, he took no more notice of armies of Indians than if they were flies."

He was of a noble, clear, and guileless mind, without malice, deceit, or cunning. He was a true man who confided utterly in his friends and in those he thought were his friends, and this was his undoing. Because he was so lacking in wiles and deceptions and wickedness the authors have called him foolish: on the contrary, he was of good understanding and strongly inclined toward virtue and honor. By character kindly, universally loved by friends and foe alike, he had all the good qualities a nobleman should have. As to the riches he personally won, we may say that he was lord of all Peru, for he possessed and governed it for a length of time with such justice and rectitude that the president himself praised him, as we have said above. He distributed many allocations of Indians, worth ten, twenty, or thirty thousand pesos a year, though he himself died as poor as we have said. He was a good Christian, and was very devoted to Our Lady the Virgin Mary, the mother of God, and the president set this down in the letter he wrote. He was never asked for anything for the love of Our Lady that he refused, however great it was. Having experience of this, Francisco de Carvajal and his other ministers, when they were going to kill any of their adversaries who deserved to die, always took care that no one should contrive to ask Gonzalo to spare his life, for they knew that if the request were made in Our Lady's name it would never be refused, whoever the petitioner. He was loved by everyone for his military deeds and moral qualities, and though it was necessary to put him to death, leaving aside the question of the royal service, everyone in general regretted it on account of his many good qualities. Thus I never afterwards heard anyone speak ill of him; they all spoke well and respectfully, as of a superior. And when Fernández says that there were some who thought and urged that he should be quartered and the quarters placed on the roads out of Cuzco and that the president refused to allow it, this was a very false account he was given, for no such thing was thought of: if it had been, it would have been spoken of later when peace was restored, as many other things even more secret were spoken of, and I should have heard it. But the thing was never thought of, for all the members of the council (except the president) were deeply indebted to Gonzalo Pizarro, having received great benefits and honors at his hands, and they would not have expressed an opinion so much to his shame. It was enough to have consented to his death in His Majesty's service and for the quiet of the empire.

End of the Fifth Book

BOOK
SIX *of the*
SECOND
PART

It contains the punishment of Gonzalo Pizarro's party; President La Gasca's allocation of the Indians; the great rewards which fell to some and the complaints of others; the unlucky death of Diego Centeno; the patience of President La Gasca toward the insolent soldiery; the galley slaves sent to Spain; the second distribution made by President La Gasca; the death of Licentiate Cepeda; the entry of the president into Panama; the theft of His Majesty's gold and silver by the Contreras; the good fortune of the president in restoring all that was lost; his arrival in Spain, and his honorable end and good death; a revolt by the soldiers of Francisco Hernández Girón in Cuzco; the departure of the viceroy Don Antonio de Mendoza for Peru; his short life; the rebellion of Don Sebastián de Castilla; the death of General Pedro de Hinojosa and that of Don Sebastián; the punishment of his followers.

It contains twenty-nine chapters.

CHAPTER I

New measures by the president for the punishment
of the rebels; the scandal caused among
the Indians by the sight of Spaniards
being whipped; the harassing of the
president by the claimants, and
his departure from the city
to carry out the
allocation.

ITH the death and destruction of Gonzalo Pizarro and his captains and commander, the empire called Peru still did not remain safe from risings and revolts. On the contrary, there were even greater scandals, as our history will say. It must be mentioned that after his victory in the battle of Sacsahuana, the president sent two captains, Hernando Mejía de Guzmán and Martín de Robles, the same day to Cuzco with reliable soldiers to arrest those of Gonzalo Pizarro's men who had taken flight and also to prevent the large number of royal troops that had advanced on the city from sacking it or killing people to avenge their private wrongs and enmities, for in the heat of victory there were those who said that they were free to do whatever they liked to their enemies. The day after the punishment and execution of Gonzalo Pizarro and his friends, the president left the place, which has become famous on account of the battle that was fought there, and though it is no more than four leagues from the city, it took him two days to make the journey.

On his arrival he sent Captain Alonso de Mendoza with a good force of trustworthy men to arrest the captains sent by Gonzalo Pizarro to Charcas and Potosí. These men were Francisco de Espinosa and Diego de Carvajal, "the gallant," whom we have already mentioned. He also sent Licentiate Polo Ondegardo as governor and captain general in these provinces with orders to punish all those who had favored Gonzalo de Pizarro and those who had not come forward to serve His Majesty. These were the people known as "the onlookers" because during the course of the wars they had simply looked on, without being either loyal or traitors: they were therefore punished with heavy fines for their cowardice. He sent Captain Gabriel de Rojas with Licentiate Polo to act as His Majesty's treasurer in those provinces and collect the royal fifths, the revenue of the royal estates and the fines levied on the traitors and onlookers. In a short time, as Agustín de Zárate says (Book VII, ch. viii), Polo sent more than 1,200,000 pesos, having taken over the office of treasurer, since Gabriel de Rojas departed this life almost as soon as he arrived in Charcas.

While all this was happening in the great province of Charcas, the president was in Cuzco, where he was received with regal and very costly bull fights and tilting, the performers all wearing velvet of various colors. He watched the celebrations from the balcony of my father's house, where I saw him, as I have mentioned. The judge Andrés de Cianca and the commander Alonso de Alvarado were entrusted with the task of punishing the rebels. Many famous soldiers of Pizarro's army were hanged; others quartered; and more than a hundred Spanish soldiers were flogged in groups of four and six. I saw all this, for the boys of my own age went out to see the flogging. It caused a great scandal among the Indians when they saw with what contumely and infamy Spaniards treated fellow Spaniards. Until then, though many had been hanged, they had never seen any Spaniard flogged. As a greater disgrace, horsemen led them on llamas taken from among the Indians' pack animals, and although there were mules and nags that could have been used to carry those who were to be flogged, the administrators of justice insisted on their being driven on llamas, to their greater shame and punishment. They were all condemned to the galleys.

The president at the same time announced a general pardon from blame and sentence for all those who had followed the royal standard in the battle of Sacsahuana. This was to apply to any crimes committed during Gonzalo Pizarro's rebellion, even though they had taken part in the death of the Viceroy Blasco Núñez Vela and others of His Majesty's officials. The pardon covered only crimes: civil suits and the disposal of property were referred to legal process, according to the president's commission, as Agustín de Zárate says (Book VII, ch. viii), it being considered that Gonzalo de Pizarro had cancelled criminal charges against his followers by his death.

Even though he had attained victory and had executed his enemies, the president, in this period of peace and calm, was more downcast, troubled, and distressed than he had been during the war, for then he had found many to assist him in bearing the burden of his military responsibilities, but now that peace was restored he was called upon to suffer the importunities, demands, and woes of 2,500 men who claimed pay and reward for their services. Not a single one of them, however little he had done, failed to think himself worthy of the best allocation of Indians in all Peru. And the persons who had been of most assistance to the president in time of war, were precisely those who molested him most with their petitions and demands now that peace was declared. They were so tenacious and troublesome that in order to avoid their importunities to some extent, he decided to go to the valley called Apurímac, twelve leagues from the city, to attend to the allocating of the Indians more calmly. He took with him the archbishop of Lima, Don Jerónimo de Loaisa, and his secretary, Pedro López de Cazalla, and left instructions that no *vecino* or soldier, or any other person, was to follow him or disturb him in his task. He also ordered that no *vecino* in all Peru should go home until the distribution of the Indians had been completed, for he imagined that by keeping them together he could ensure against any attempt at revolt on the part of the common people. His wish and concern was to spread the soldiers over various parts of the kingdom, or to send them to make new conquests and win new lands, as those who had won the empire had done. But he dispersed very few of them, for he was in a great hurry to get away from the country before there should be some rising among the many people who were dissatisfied, as he imagined, some having reason for their complaints and others none.

CHAPTER II

After making the allocation, the president
goes secretly to Lima; he writes a letter
to the unlucky claimants, which drives
them to desperate deeds.

T HE PRESIDENT spent more than three months in the valley of the Apurímac, engaged in the allocation of the land. Many petitions and statements were sent him by claimants who alleged and described their services, but he paid little or no heed to them, for he had already made his mind up and decided and appointed which were to enjoy the great rewards. They were all the leaders who were with General Pedro de Hinojosa in Panama and Nombre de Dios when they delivered Gonzalo Pizarro's fleet to the president. On that occasion the allocations each was to receive were already agreed, and they were now duly awarded them, as the historians of the time aver. Having divided the land without consulting anyone but himself and the archbishop Don Jerónimo de Loaisa— both of whom knew very little of the deeds and deserts of the claimants, as the latter were quick to point out when they found they had been passed over—the president went to Lima, leaving orders for the archbishop and the secretary Pero López to return to Cuzco twelve or fifteen days after his own departure, and inform those who had been favored of the result of the distribution.

To the unfortunates who received nothing he addressed a very solemn letter, assuring them of his good will and his intention to gratify them out of such estates as might be disposable in the future. The letter is the following, taken literally from Book II of the first part of Fernández's *History* (ch. xcii), and is addressed thus:

To the most magnificent and noble lords, the knights and noblemen who serve His Majesty in Cuzco.

Most magnificent and noble lords: Since it often transpires that the attachment men feel to their own interests renders them incapable of a fitting and free use of their reason to give thanks where they are due and display love and gratitude, I have decided to write this letter to beg you to continue to show your love and gratitude toward me, not only because of the credit I am entitled to expect from each of you, but also because of all I have done, am doing, and shall do to your advantage, as long as I live, in Peru and out of it. And setting aside the consideration and memory of special services I have rendered some of you, you should bear in mind that more generally I have never failed to do anything that lay within my power in your interests. I think that, as you know, as regards the cost of the recent war, never before in Peru (or outside it) has so much been spent on so few in so short a time. And everything that was disposable in Peru I have distributed among you with all the equality and justice I could, toiling all day and into the small hours to consider the merits of each one of you so that in the light of them I might reward each of you according to what he had deserved, considering only his merits without favor: nor have I given so much to those with the greatest claims as to disappoint those with less merit of their deserts. I shall pursue the same policy, with regard to everything I have to dispose of while I am in Peru: it will be awarded only to you, according to your deserts as gentlemen and loyal subjects in the royal service. And so that you alone may enjoy this enormously rich land, I shall not only seek to expel from it those who have shown themselves wicked, and even those who have stood aside and failed to do what you have done, but also to procure that none shall enter it from Spain or Tierra Firme, Nicaragua, Guatemala, or New Spain whose presence might reduce your enjoyment of the wealth of Peru. Since all this is no less than the truth, and it is all I have been and am able to do on your behalf, I beg you to be satisfied and content as God Himself is satisfied when men do what they can in His service. With this in mind, be satisfied with your fortune, even though it may not be as great as you hoped, remembering that more could not have been done for you, and that he who gave you this earnestly wished there were enough to give you much more, and this he will do as soon as the opportunity arises. Anyone who has not been favored should remember that this was because there was less material than I could have wished to dispose of, and rest assured that whenever anything of value shall fall disposable so long as I am in Peru, it shall only be bestowed on you, so that those not now rewarded shall be rewarded in the future, if almighty God wills. And as I neither seek nor claim any reward for my own labors by land and sea after embarking on this expedition, the last third of my mortal span, except the knowledge that I have used my small talents according to the duty of a Christian toward his God, of a subject toward his king, and of a neighbor and faithful servant toward you all, I should be deeply wounded if you failed to understand this, and were ungrateful for the love and good will I feel for the betterment of each one of you, and for what I have done and shall do on your behalf. For, as I have said, you will not find me to fail in anything that I have been or shall be able to do. And as I must depart for Lima to establish the *audiencia* and deal with other matters relating to the city, and as His Reverend Lordship the archbishop can express better all that remains to be said here, I have besought his lordship to do me the favor of going to Cuzco to deliver to each of you his lot and offer in my name what I have promised for the future. Wherefore I have nothing more to add but to beg Our Lord to grant that I may see you enjoy all the prosperity and preferment in His holy service that you and I desire, for you may be assured your desires are mine. Given at Guainarima, on August 18, 1548. Your Graces' servant.

In addition to this letter, Licentiate La Gasca instructed the provincial, Fray Tomás de San Martín, to deliver a sermon on the day the distribution was made known, and to speak to the claimants and try to persuade them to accept it as it was drawn up. All this is described at length by Diego Fernández of Palencia, and I have abbreviated it to avoid prolixity.

When they learnt in Cuzco that the president had gone off alone and turned a deaf ear to them all, Captain Pardavel exclaimed to a group of other captains who were engaged in conversation: "I'll swear that since Madalena de la Cruz has gone off in secret, she's foisted some *harana* on us!" *Harana* was a word used in Peru for any trickery or deceit used to avoid paying gambling debts; and the president was known as Madalena de la Cruz (among other nicknames), meaning that he was a trickster and witch, like that good woman who was punished by the Holy Office here in Córdova.

To avoid hearing this and similar pieces of effrontery that were uttered in Cuzco, the president had left the city to draw up the allocation and went even further off at the time of its publication, as Fernández says in ch. i of Part II of his *History,* in these words:

It was realized that he had left Cuzco so as not to be present when the distribution was published. He was shrewd and cautious, and had enough experience of the inhabitants of Peru to fear the effrontery of the soldiers and avoid hearing their complaints and curses and blasphemies. He was not mistaken about this, for when the archbishop of Cuzco had reached the square where nearly all the citizens and soldiers were assembled, and began to publish the distribution, on August 24, St. Bartholomew's day, many of the citizens and soldiers at once began to blaspheme and insult the president, and shamelessly and openly uttered words of treason inciting one another to rise in a new rebellion.

They plotted together and attempted to kill the judge Andrés de Cianca and also the archbishop, whom they regarded as the real author of the allocation. The cause of this scandal and of their anger was the belief that the chief *repartimientos* and *encomiendas* of Indians had been given to the chief followers and adherents of Gonzalo Pizarro and others who had done the king disservice. Francisco López de Gómara says as much and more strongly in ch. clxxxviii:

He therefore went to Apurima, twelve leagues from Cuzco, and discussed the distribution there with the archbishop of Lima, Loaisa, and the secretary, Pero López, and gave 1,500,000 in income and more to various persons, and 150,000 Castilians in gold which he took from the *encomenderos.* He married many rich widows to men who had served the king, and enriched many who already had allocations: there were those who had 100,000 ducats a year, an income fit for a prince except that it terminated on their death, for the emperor did not make such grants hereditary. Hinojosa was the one who received most. La Gasca went off to Lima to avoid hearing the complaints, denunciations, and curses of the soldiers, and perhaps out of fear, sending the archbishop to Cuzco to announce the awards and make promises to those who received neither money nor vassals, promising them great honors later. For all his eloquence the archbishop could not appease the wrath of the soldiers who had received no part in the share-out, nor that of many who had received little. Some complained that La Gasca had given them nothing, and others little;

others because he had rewarded those who had been disloyal to the king and turncoats, swearing they would bring charges against him in the Council of the Indies. There were thus some, such as the commander Alonso de Alvarado and Melchor Verdugo, who later wrote accusingly about him to the fiscal. Finally, they discussed rebellion, planning to arrest the archbishop, the judge Cianca, Hinojosa, Centeno, and Alvarado, and to ask President La Gasca to revise the allocations, by dividing the very large ones or providing pensions chargeable on them: otherwise they would seize them themselves. This plot was soon discovered, and Cianca arrested and punished the ringleaders, whereupon peace was restored.

This is quoted from López de Gómara.

CHAPTER III

Marriages of claimants with widows; the allocations given to Pedro de Hinojosa and his companions; the surprise of the recipients.

I N EXPLANATION of this author's reference to widows, it requires to be mentioned that many of the colonists who had Indians had been killed in the later wars, and their widows had duly inherited the Indians. In order that they should not make second marriages among those who had not served His Majesty, the governors arranged marriages for them. This occurred throughout Peru, and many widows were so treated. Moreover many were the losers, since they found themselves wedded to husbands much older than the ones they had lost. The former wife of Alonso de Toro, Gonzalo Pizarro's commander, who had a great allocation of Indians, was married to Pedro López Cazalla, President La Gasca's secretary.

Martín de Bustincia's wife, who was a daughter of Huaina Cápac and herself (not her husband) the owner of the Indians, was married to a very good soldier called Diego Hernández, a very worthy man, who was said in his youth to have been a tailor—though it is more likely that this was false than true. The princess learned this and refused the match, saying that it was unjust to wed the daughter of Huaina Cápac with a *ciraca-*

mayo, meaning tailor. Although the bishop of Cuzco and Captain Diego Centeno, as well as other personages who went to attend the ceremony of betrothal, begged and pleaded with her, it was all to no purpose. They then sent to fetch her brother Don Cristóbal Paullu, whom we have already mentioned. When he came, he took his sister into a corner of the room and told her privately that it was impolitic for her to refuse the match, for by so doing she would render the whole of the royal line odious in the eyes of the Spaniards, who would consider them mortal enemies and never accept their friendship again. She agreed, though reluctantly, to her brother's demands, and so appeared before the bishop, who wished to honor the betrothed by officiating at the ceremony.

When the bride was asked through an Indian interpreter if she consented to become the bride and spouse of the aforesaid, the interpreter said "did she want to be that man's wife?" for the Indian language had no verb for consent or for spouse, and he could therefore not have asked anything else.

The bride replied in her own tongue: *"Ichach munani, ichach mana-munani,"* meaning: "Maybe I will, maybe I won't." Whereupon the ceremony continued. It was held in the house of Diego de los Ríos, a *vecino* of Cuzco. They were still alive and living as man and wife when I left Cuzco.

Other marriages of this kind took place throughout the empire, and were arranged so as to give allocations of Indians to claimants and reward them with other people's properties. Many, however, were dissatisfied, some because their income was small and others because their wives were ugly: there is no perfect satisfaction in this world.

As our authors say, the allocation of the land caused these disturbances because General Pedro de Hinojosa was given the Indians Gonzalo Pizarro had in Charcas, who produced an annual revenue of 100,000 pesos. With them he received a very rich silver mine so that within a few months this gentleman's income exceeded 200,000 pesos: the amount of silver extracted from these mines at Potosí was incredible, and, as we have already mentioned, iron came to be worth more than silver. Gómez de Solís was granted the *repartimiento* called Tapac-Ri, worth more than 40,000 pesos a year. Martín de Robles was given another as valuable, but Diego Centeno, despite his labors and services which we have mentioned, received nothing but the allocation he already had called Pucuna, and others who served with him got nothing. These *repartimientos*, not to mention others of less value, were in the province and kingdom of Charcas. Lorenzo de Aldana received an allocation in addition to the one he had, in the city of Arequipa, the two together being worth 50,000 pesos. In the city of Cuzco Don Pedro de Cabrera was awarded one called Cotapampa, worth more than 50,000 pesos a year. His son-in-law, Hernán Mejía de Guzmán, received another in Cuntisuyu worth more than 30,-000 a year. Don Baltasar de Castilla had one in Parihuana Cocha that brought him 40,000 pesos a year all in gold, which is produced in great quantity in those parts. On Juan Alonso Palomino was bestowed a second allocation in addition to the one he already had: the two together were worth 40,000 pesos. Licentiate Carvajal was given another as valuable, but he did not live long to enjoy it. While corregidor in Cuzco, he had the misfortune to fall from a window while courting a lady and was killed. I saw his funeral and recall that it was the feast of St. John the Baptist. Hernán Bravo de Laguna had another allocation of less value, not above 8,000 pesos, for he was not one of those who had handed the fleet over.

These and similar prizes were awarded to those who had delivered the fleet to the president in Panama. And he did well to repay so handsomely the service rendered to him and the king by those gentlemen, for it had enabled him to win the whole empire of Peru, despite the fact that it seemed to be utterly lost when the president arrived, as will not have escaped the notice of the attentive reader of this history. The rest who received Indians in all the other towns of Peru were much less amply repaid: it was merely a case of adding richer allocations to poor ones and finding others for those who had had none. But however poor the allocations, they were worth 8,000, 9,000, or 10,000 pesos a year. The ten allocations we have mentioned, in Charcas, Arequipa, and Cuzco, were worth nearly 540,000 pesos of assay, or nearly 650,000 ducats in Castile.

As soon as they reached Cuzco, Archbishop Loaisa and the secretary Pero López de Cazalla published the division and read the president's letter to the unfortunates who were given nothing. And the provincial preached his sermon urging them to be patient. But the only signs of patience they evinced were curses and blasphemies, as our authors agree, especially on hearing the president's letter. They were moreover angered and astonished at the abundance and prodigality of the distribution and the overpayment of some who expected nothing, for the truth is that among those appointed to receive 40,000 or 50,000 pesos a year there were many who not only had no hope of reward, but rather feared the death penalty or at least banishment from the empire, and counted themselves lucky not to have been expelled from the country when they recalled what they had done in support of Gonzalo Pizarro, in defiance of the Viceroy Blasco Núñez Vela whom they arrested, persecuted, and finally slew, cutting off his head and impaling it on the gibbet. Although a general pardon from all blame and punishment had been declared, they suspected it was merely to lull them into a sense of security with the purpose of punishing them when the land should have been pacified. So one of them, Martín de Robles, on hearing what had been awarded him together with the other awards, remarked ironically to the bystanders: "Well, well, well! So much good bodes ill," implying that it was wrong to confer such great honors on those who not only did not deserve them or expect them, but rather deserved great punishment. A few months later, when he was informed of a sentence of the royal *audiencia* fining him 1,000 pesos, or 1,200 ducats, for having been present at the arrest of Viceroy Blasco Núñez Vela and having favored Gonzalo Pizarro, the fine being awarded to the viceroy's son-in-law Diego Alvarez Cueto who brought a suit accusing some of the followers of Gonzalo Pizarro, he exclaimed: "Is that all they make me pay because I arrested the viceroy?" The notary replied that this was the sum of the penalty, and he replied, "Well, at that price, I'll take ten more."

Those who had done such deeds were so puffed up with presumption that they boasted of them and not only dared to say such things, but said them to the president's very face. We shall repeat some of them, but not all, for they are not fit to be committed to paper.

CHAPTER IV

Francisco Hernández Girón unreasonably takes great offence at the distribution, and is granted a commission to explore and make new conquests; the punishment of Francisco de Espinosa and Diego de Carvajal.

THE DISTRIBUTION was so rich and abounding in gold and silver that it amounted to more than 2,500,000 pesos, though one author says only 1,000,000, and another 1,400,000 odd. Yet the claimants were disgruntled and offended, either because they themselves had received nothing, or because such excessive rewards were bestowed on those who had neither conquered the country, nor performed any service there for His Majesty, but who had supported the rebel and followed him until he slew the viceroy, and had later sold themselves to the president.

The man who displayed the greatest dissatisfaction the most publicly, and with the least reason, was Captain Francisco Hernández Girón. He had not served in Peru at all, but at Pasto, where (as Fernández says in the last chapter of Part I of his *History*) he had less than 600 pesos a year: he was given an allocation called Sacsahuana in Cuzco, formerly the property of Gonzalo Pizarro and worth above 10,000, but he openly complained of not having been given more than all the rest, because he thought he deserved more. He worked himself into a passion and complained so openly and in such scandalous terms that everyone thought them treasonable, for they reeked of rebellion. He spoke to the archbishop to beg permission to go to the president to complain of the slight done him in offering him the worst allocation though he had deserved the best because of his outstanding services. The archbishop rebuked him for these scandalous words, and refused his permission. Then Francisco Hernández took the liberty of boldly setting out, announcing that he was going to Lima, whether the authorities liked it or not.

When Licentiate Cianca, who was governor and chief justice in Cuzco jointly with the archbishop, learnt this, he wrote a letter advising him to return and not add to the great scandal and uproar that existed throughout the kingdom, provoked by complainants who had as much or more right than he: let him remember that he would forfeit the claims of his past services and make himself odious to all royal officials in future. The messenger carrying the letter came upon him at Sacsahuana, four leagues from the city; and when Francisco Hernández had read it, he sent a reply saying that he was leaving the city so as not to be involved in some revolt which he feared would break out, lest the soldiers should make him their leader and chief. He was going to warn the president of certain matters of importance touching His Majesty's service. He added other liberties that incensed the judge Cianca, who at once instructed Captain Lope Martim—though Fernández says Captain Alonso de Mendoza, who was then at Charcas, where, as we have said, he had gone to punish the rebels and "onlookers"—to take half a dozen reliable soldiers and pursue Francisco Hernández, and arrest him and bring him back to Cuzco wherever they found him. Next day Lope Martim went off with six companions, and covering the usual distances on the road, four to five leagues a day, came up with Francisco Hernández at Curampa, twenty leagues from the city. The latter cunningly tried to run with the hare and hunt with the hounds, assuring His Majesty's ministers that he was serving the king, and pretending that the soldiers who were aggrieved by the recent distribution thought he was aggrieved too and that he would do what they wished, as he had said in his answer to Cianca when he had seen the latter and excused his action by saying he had left the city so that the soldiers who were on the point of rebellion should not make him their general.

The judge ordered him to be detained in the house of Juan de Saavedra, one of the leading citizens of Cuzco, but having drawn up the case against him and despatched it to the president, he released him on parole, after extracting an oath that he would place himself at the disposal of his superiors. Francisco Hernández then went to Lima, but spent more than three months on the way, for the president did not grant him permission to enter the city. Only at the end of this long period did he obtain permission to kiss the president's hand.

The president received him affably, and after a few days, in order to satisfy the stirrings of his restless spirit and rid the kingdom of one band of the many idle soldiers, granted him the honor of conquering the region known as Chunchu, with the title of governor and captain general of whatever he won and conquered at his own expense and risk, on condition that he observed the boundaries of the cities bordering on his conquest: Cuzco, the city of La Paz, and Silver City. Francisco Hernández received this dispensation with great satisfaction since it afforded him the opportunity to exercise his intention, which had always been to rebel against the king, as we shall see. He remained at Lima until the president took ship to return to Spain, as we shall tell in due course.

While the president was making the *repartimiento* of the Indians in the Apurímac valley, Cianca received news that Licentiate Polo, who had gone as judge to Charcas, was sending back under arrest Francisco de Espinosa and Diego de Carvajal (the gallant), the two persons sent by Gonzalo Pizarro on his service to the city of Arequipa and Charcas after the battle of Huarina. Their insolent actions we have already described. Before their arrival at Cuzco, they now wrote to Diego Centeno, begging him to intercede for them and obtain forgiveness for their misdeeds, so that they might merely be expelled instead of being executed. Diego Centeno answered that he would have been very glad to do as they wished if their offences had been such as to permit him to lay their petition before the judges of the case; but as they were so heinous, especially the burning alive of the seven Indians without any cause or blame on their part, the gate of mercy was shut and no one had the temerity or inclination to intercede for such violent deeds. A few days after this reply, the accused were brought into Cuzco and hanged and quartered, the quarters being exhibited by the roadside, to the satisfaction of Indians and Spaniards, for such cruelty rightly deserves and requires a like retribution.

CHAPTER V

Pedro de Valdivia is given the governorship of Chile; the conditions imposed on him by his followers, and the president's ingenuity in releasing him.

AMONG THE great honors and notable awards made by President La Gasca in the Apurímac valley was that of the government of the kingdom of Chile, granted to Pedro de Valdivia with the title of governor and captain general of all that great kingdom, which extends more than five hundred leagues. Pedro de Valdivia was given powers to grant the land to those who conquered it and showed themselves deserving, and he used these powers largely and prosperously. However, this very prosperity and the abundance of riches in Chile caused his death and that of 150 other Spanish gentlemen who died with him, as we told in our First Part in narrating the life of the great Inca Yupanqui, where we anticipated the death of Pedro de Valdivia as being a matter worthy of note though excluded from our history since we do not deal with events in Chile. The present incidents are included because they occurred in Peru, as described by Diego Fernández of Palencia whom we follow literally, reproducing the title of his chapter. It will be seen how the same human law can lead to the condemnation and death of some and the salvation and preservation of others, as a result of the same crime. The title of the chapter and its contents are as follows:

Chapter xciv. How the president sent to have Pedro de Valdivia arrested, and the conditions imposed by the conquerors of Chile, and the way in which the President saved him.

The history has already told how Pedro de Valdivia came to leave Chile and how the president later granted him powers to conquer that kingdom. In order to prepare for the expedition, Valdivia went from Cuzco to Lima where he provided himself with all that was needed and gathered as many men as he could to complete the conquest. Among his followers were some who had been exiled from Peru and others condemned to the galleys for participation in the rebellion. As soon as he had made ready the necessary men and supplies, he embarked everything on ships which sailed from the port of Callao, and Pedro de Valdivia went to Arequipa by land. In the meantime the president was notified that he had enlisted rebels and committed various misdeeds on the way in defiance of instructions given by himself. The president therefore sent Pedro de Hinojosa to employ some device to bring him back under arrest, suggesting a way to do this. Hinojosa overtook Valdivia on the road and asked him to return to satisfy the president, but as he refused Hinojosa rode with him for a day in amiable converse. Having disarmed the suspicions of Valdivia, who was as confident in the loyalty of his companions as in Hinojosa's friendship, the latter found a way to arrest him with the aid of only six arquebusiers and brought him to the president.

At the same time some of those whose gold Valdivia had taken on his departure (as we have said) arrived from Chile. They set down in writing various charges and allegations against Pedro de Valdivia as soon as he appeared with Hinojosa, accusing him of taking the gold, of killing various people, of living with a certain woman, and even of abetting Gonzalo Pizarro, saying that he had left Chile to help him in the rebellion; and they had a great many more grievances. Finally they asked to be repaid the gold that had been taken from them.

All this put the president in a quandary: if he condemned Valdivia, it would mean putting off the expedition, which seemed highly impolitic in the state of Peruvian affairs because of the number of idle people who were going on it. Yet it seemed an injustice and indeed an infraction of the law not to make him disgorge and restore the gold he had been shown to have taken. Any failure on the president's part would certainly be much criticized. Assailed by these doubts, the president hit on a device to spare Valdivia from having to make this restitution. Before serving notice of the accusations levelled against Valdivia or formally acknowledging them, he collected statements about how many people and who had formulated and lodged the accusations, without anyone noticing or perceiving why he did so. To this end he took depositions from all those who had been interested in the Chilean affair, which proved that all of them had been concerned in framing them and drawing them up, so that no one could legally bear witness in his own suit. Having collected this evidence, the president ordered a copy of the accusations to be served on Valdivia, and he replied by presenting a long document denying all the allegations. And as the affair could not go to court for lack of legal witnesses—for there were none— the president himself took cognisance of the case and declared none of the accusations proven or supported by evidence to the extent of warranting his preventing Valdivia from going on the expedition, though there were some suggestions of guilt in his relations with Gonzalo Pizarro and other matters. The president therefore ordered Valdivia to proceed with his journey and continue the conquest, provided he undertook not to take those guilty of rebellion. He stipulated that a judge should be sent to satisfy those who complained about the gold that had been seized, and urged Valdivia to return it on his arrival. Valdivia promised to do so and at once left for Chile.

This is from Fernández, who finishes the chapter here.

CHAPTER VI

The unfortunate death of Diego Centeno in Charcas, and of Licentiate Carvajal in Cuzco; the foundation of the city of La Paz; the establishment of the audiencia at Lima.

AFTER President La Gasca had made his distribution of the Indians in the Apurímac valley and gone to the city of Lima, all the *vecinos*, who are the owners of vassals in Peru, took leave to return to their homes and the towns where they resided, some to take possession of the new allocations they had been given, others to see to their houses and estates which had all been ruined in the late wars. Although the president had not given leave, because of his haste in leaving the Apurímac valley, they all took it. Diego Centeno, like the other citizens, went to his house in the town of La Plata, now called Silver City, on account of the great quantity of silver extracted then and now from the nearby hill called Potosí.

His intention was to gather all the silver and gold he could from his estate and make ready to return to Spain to represent his numerous services to His Imperial Majesty, in the hope of being rewarded for them, for he was annoyed and offended that the president should not have borne him in mind when there was such good reason for doing so. He revealed this determination to some friends of his and consulted with them about his journey, and very soon his intention was public knowledge throughout the kingdom, through the exchange of letters. Some of the principal people were scandalized that Diego Centeno should carry his complaints to Spain. Some of them became his rivals and sought to put obstacles in his way under the guise of friendship; but seeing they could find no way of dissuading him, they resolved to cut short his journey by a surer means. Certain citizens met together, some with malice and others in ignorance, and wrote to Diego Centeno to come to Silver City where they would hold general consultations about his journey to Spain and entrust him with business that he should take up personally with His Imperial Majesty on their behalf.

Diego Centeno prepared to go to the city, although his Indians whose villages he was visiting earnestly begged and prayed him not to go, or he would be killed. But he only speeded the preparations for his journey, and disregarded the superstitions and witchcraft of the Indians. In the city he was received with great pleasure and joy by those who had invited him, though some of his companions in arms who had been prominent in his campaign against Francisco de Carvajal and in the battles of Huarina and Sacsahuana called on him privately to express their regret and grief at his coming, since their Indian servants on learning that he was on his way had apprised them of the same forebodings Diego Centeno had heard from his own Indians, that he was coming to his death. His friends could see no cause or reason why anyone should want to kill him, but discussed this evil omen with Centeno. He brushed it aside, saying that it was wrong to heed or even talk about the prophecies of the Indians, since they were the result of communications with demons or lies. But events soon showed whether this was so or not. Four days after his arrival in the city, he was invited to a formal banquet in the house of one of the leading citizens whose name need not be mentioned in the course of our history, to avoid calumny; for all those concerned have gone to the place where each must render his own account. At this banquet Centeno was served a dose of poison which was so well concealed that it despatched him in three days without any sign of the cruel torments and vomitings that usually accompany poisoning.

His passing was regretted and wept throughout the kingdom on account of his goodness and kindness. He was one of the best-liked gentlemen in the country and a good companion to everyone, having been one of those who came to Peru with Don Pedro de Alvarado at the time of the conquest of the empire. When the news of his death reached Spain, a brother of his went to inform His Majesty the emperor Charles V of the manner of it, pointing out that he had left two natural children, a boy and a girl, by Indian women, and that they were left poor and unprovided for, since his grant of Indians expired on his death. His Majesty ordered the daughter to be given a capital of twelve thousand Castilian ducats for her dowry, and the son, Gaspar Centeno, who was a schoolfellow of mine, to have four thousand pesos a year drawn against His Majesty's treasury in Silver City. I heard it said that this income was in perpetuity, though I cannot affirm as much, for grants in my country were never in perpetuity, but always for a single lifetime, or two at most.

The death of Captain Diego Centeno was followed a few months after by that of Licentiate Carvajal who, as we have already noted, died of a fall from a high window when they cut the cords of a rope ladder he was either scaling or descending, without respect for the office of corregidor he then held in the city.

The deaths of other citizens of less note occurred in other cities of Peru, and their Indians became disposable so that the president was able in this way to reward some of those who were offended by the first distribution, but they nevertheless were just as dissatisfied for, as we shall see, every man of them imagined he deserved the whole of Peru.

While the deaths and misfortunes we have mentioned occurred in Silver City, Cuzco, and other places, President La Gasca was in Lima attending to the restoration and reform of the royal chancery that is now established there. He also ordered the settlement of La Paz. Both of these achievements are described by Diego Fernández of Palencia in Book II of Part One of his *History* (ch. xciii), as follows:

Don Jerónimo de Loaisa left with this letter—the letter the president wrote to the claimants who had been passed over in the distribution of the Indians—and went to the city of Cuzco. From this arose the events already recounted in the history of Francisco Hernández's revolt, a shameless rebellion said to have originated from the distribution.

President La Gasca left Guainarima for Lima and on the way sent Alonso de Mendoza with powers as corregidor of the new town, which he had ordered to be founded in Chuquiabo in the general distribution and to be named the City of Our Lady of Peace [La Paz]. The place was so nàmed because it was founded in time of peace after so many wars, and at that place because it is half way along the road from Arequipa to Charcas, a distance of 170 leagues. It is also half way from Cuzco to Charcas, a distance of 160 leagues. Because the distance between these places was so great and there was no Christian settlement between them, and the trade was so considerable and of such value, it had become necessary to found a town there to put an end to the robberies and other disorders that occurred in the region.

Having made this decision, the president continued on his way, and on

September 17 entered Lima, where he was received with great celebrations and dances and tourneys after the following fashion. The president and his seal rode under a rich canopy: the seal was on his right hand in a handsomely made and well-decorated coffer mounted on a white horse covered with a brocade cloth hanging to the ground, and the horse's reins were held by Lorenzo de Aldana, the corregidor of the city. The president's mule was led by Jerónimo de Silva, an *alcalde ordinario*. Lorenzo de Aldana, the alcaldes, and others who held the rods supporting the canopy wore trailing robes of crimson velvet, with their heads bare. The guard raised by the city to escort the seal and the president was given liveries, and the participants in the dances and tourneys colored silks.

A brave dance was performed by dancers each representing one of the chief towns of Peru, and each recited a verse in the name of his town in praise of its demonstration of loyalty. The verses were:

Lima
The city of Lima am I,
that always had most law.
Thus I set the crown
on things of renown,
and I still stand by the king.

Trujillo
Trujillo is my name,
a city of great fame.
I came out loyally
to greet His Majesty
and welcome his entry.

Piura
Piura am I, I desire
to stand firm and serve.
Like a lion in rage
I showed much courage
to put down the tyrant.

Quito
I'm Quito on the loyal side;
although I was sorely tried.
I followed with fidelity
the banner of His Majesty
as soon as I was set free.

Guánuco and the Chachapoyas
Guánuco and Chachapoy
kiss your feet and hands with joy.
In order to help the king to win

men poured forth from our Troy
and brought their fellow townsmen in.

Guamanga

I'm Guamanga and I made
a change
unknown before on land or sea.
I changed the P for G.
God it was who wished it so.

Arequipa

I'm glorious Arequipa's town
whose beauty is of much renown.
My one regret is this alone,
that on Huarina's bloody field,
my people perished one and all.

Cuzco

Illustrious sir and noble lord,
I'm Cuzco the famous.
I was your loyal servant too,
although the rebel traitor's force
held me in thrall.

Charcas

O eminent and noble sir,
light of our obscurity,
Parnassus of perfection
in this Christian region
by divine clemency.
Centeno very prudently
in the Charcas flourished he,
and if he did not prevail
it was God's will to reserve
to the president the victory.

These are the verses which Diego Fernández of Palencia records as
being spoken by the dancers in the name of the chief towns of the empire. They are so crude, clumsy, and lifeless that one would think they
were written by Indians from the various cities, and not by Spaniards.

To return to our author's reference to the foundation of La Paz and
the choice of site being governed by the distance between the Spanish
settlements and the need to prevent the robberies and outrages that occurred thereabouts, it was in our opinion perfectly right to establish the
city at that place to increase the number of Spanish towns, but not to prevent robberies and outrages. The generous spirit of the whole of the

empire called Peru is such that its equal cannot be found anywhere in the world, and since it was conquered in 1531 until the time of writing this, in 1610, it has never been asserted in public or in private that people were robbed, or that traders or merchants were attacked, despite the great number of them and the value of the quantities of gold and silver that daily come and go on the highways that stretch three or four hundred leagues. Travellers go their ways with no other protection than that afforded by the general honesty and excellence of the whole empire, sleeping in the field where they happen to find themselves at nightfall with no greater security or defence than the sheets they carry to cover their merchandise. This is something which has been quoted in the Indies and in Spain to the credit and honor of the empire.

The foregoing, of course, applied, and still applies, to times of peace: in wartime anything could happen, for such is the effect of rebellion, as has been seen in the past and will be seen again in the future.

CHAPTER VII

The preoccupations and labors of President
La Gasca; the suppression of a rising; his
patience in the face of insulting words
applied to him; his skill and
ingenuity in holding off
the claimants.

HAVING set up the *audiencia* in the city of Lima, the president applied himself to the pacification of the empire and the indoctrination and instruction of the natives. He ordered a general visitation to be made, and an assessment to be made of the tribute the Indians were to pay their masters, the result being set down in writing for each allocation, so that the Indians should not be required to pay more than was just. To this end Licentiate Cianca, as His Majesty's judge, went to the city of Lima, after having lightly punished a certain rising that took place in Cuzco as a result of the past distribution.

He hanged one soldier and banished three others, but avoided pressing the punishment or investigating further for fear of causing a scandal and disturbances. For the same reason the president raised the sentence of banishment before any of those who had been sentenced craved pardon, for he saw that it was better to appease people who were full of grievances —and many with justification—with softness and suavity rather than provoke them with stern and harsh treatment. Licentiate Cianca, obeying President La Gasca's instructions, left as corregidor in Cuzco one Juan de Saavedra, a very noble knight from Seville, who had Indians in the city.

The president sent the commander Alonso de Alvarado to the "New Town" with a commission as corregidor, enjoining him to pay particular attention to the settlement of the city of La Paz: the city had both names at first. He had an allocation of Indians near the city.

Meanwhile citizens came from all parts of the empire to the city of Lima to kiss the president's hand and thank him for the many great allocations he had bestowed on them. A great many of the leading soldiers who had served the king also appeared to ask for rewards for their services and satisfaction for their grievances, since the pay that was due to them had been given to others who deserved rather to be punished and executed for having betrayed His Imperial Majesty. News arrived of the deaths of Diego Centeno, Gabriel de Rojas, Licentiate Carvajal, and other citizens, and although the president was aware of the news, it was duly communicated to him with urgent and passionate demands that he should revise the past allocations, and rearrange them in such a way that all might have the wherewithal to eat, instead of their starving while those who had done most for the rebel leader died of apoplexy and surfeit. This is confirmed by López de Gómara, in ch. clxxxiv, which I have already cited, in these words: "Lastly they discussed a request to President La Gasca that he should revise the allocations, so that all should have a share, and either divide the greater ones or award them pensions payable from them. Otherwise they would seize them themselves, etc." These are López de Gómara's words.

The president was very distressed and exhausted because of his inability to satisfy so many claimants with so little to award and divide among them, they being so presumptuous about their merits and services that if the whole of Peru had suddenly become disposable, it would have seemed little in relation to the overweening arrogance with which they put forward their deserts. But the president, discreet, prudent, astute, and ingenious, held them off for the year and a half he was in the city. During this time several shameless and disgraceful incidents occurred, as the historians mention, but the good president suffered them with prudence and discretion. He did more than conquer and win all the empire: he conquered himself, as will be seen from some incidents I heard at the time and later since I came to Spain. I mention the more decent: there were others more impudent still.

In the midst of the trouble put upon him by the importunate claimants, the president wished to have the services of one of the captains, a man I knew, and said: "Captain so-and-so, do me the kindness to disabuse these people and tell them to go away, for His Majesty has nothing to grant them, or I to bestow."

The captain replied unabashedly: "You deceived them: you disabuse them. I have no reason to disabuse them." The president was silent as if he had not heard. A similar thing happened with a soldier of less account who insistently begged for a reward for his services. The president told him he had nothing to give, since everything had been distributed. The soldier retorted like a desperate man: "Let Your Lordship give me that cap with which you have deceived so many, and I'll consider myself satisfied." The president looked at him and bade him go with God's blessing.

Another person I knew who assumed the title and rank of captain, though he never was one and had an ordinary allocation of Indians worth not more than 7,000 or 8,000 pesos a year, said to the president: "Your Lordship must order my Indians to be increased, as you have done in the case of many who have done nothing to deserve it like I. I was one of the first conquerors and one of the discoverers of Chile. Nothing of any magnitude or importance has happened in the whole of this empire without my being on the spot to serve His Majesty, so I deserve very great rewards."

This and similar bragging impertinences were uttered with great arrogance and presumption; and the president, considerably annoyed by the man's vanity, replied: "Come, sir, you have quite enough for what you are. They tell me you are the son of a so-and-so in your home country," mentioning his father's trade.

The self-appointed captain said: "Anyone who told Your Lordship that is a liar, and so is anyone who believes it," with which he hurriedly left the chamber, fearing someone might lay hands on him because of his boldness and impudence. The president put up with it well, and used to say he would suffer very much more to please and serve the king his master. In addition to his patience he used to talk to the soldiers, holding out hopes and even promises of what was in store for them, as Diego Fernández of Palencia says in Book I of the Second Part of his *History* (ch. iii), in these words:

During the whole time the president was in Lima, some seventeen months, he was continually approached by people wanting him to remedy their needs and reward their services, for as we have seen many of those who had served the king were disgruntled at the first distribution. And by now many great allocations had fallen vacant by the deaths of Diego Centeno, Gabriel de Rojas, Licentiate Carvajal, and other citizens now deceased. Consequently new dispositions had to be taken, and the president was much harassed and importuned by everyone, but held them off with great dexterity, pleasing each of them by his replies. As he was travelling, he asked them privately to pray God to grant him a safe journey, for he had put their affairs into good shape.

The claimants buttered up his servants in the hope of hearing from them what they were going to be given. Some of the servants gave the captains and soldiers they were friendly with or had accepted gifts from to understand that they had seen the book of the allocations and that the president was going to grant a certain *encomienda* to one of them and something else to another. Today some believe they did this for their own profit and invented what they said: others hold that the president shrewdly wrote such things down and left his papers about with feigned carelessness so that some servant might see them and believe them, and then reveal the contents in confidence, so making his followers happy. What is true is that even today there are men who believe they have been deprived of what the president intended to give them and it can truly be said that some went out of their wits because of this idea. President La Gasca was very intelligent and took care to take the emperor a great sum in silver and gold and collected 1,500,000 castilians, which is more than 2,500,000 Spanish crowns of 350 maravedis cash. This was after he had paid out a great sum expended on the war.

When the time came for him to depart, which he was very anxious to do, he therefore made great haste lest some despatch should arrive bidding him delay his departure and hoping that if such should happen, he would already have left. Having completed his distribution, he had it covered and sealed and gave instructions that it was not to be opened or its contents to be made known until a week after he had set sail. He gave the archbishop a document authorizing him to hand over the allocations he had awarded to the recipients. He left Lima for the port of Callao, which is two leagues from the city, on January 25, but on the following Sunday, before setting sail, he received a message from His Majesty, which had just arrived from Spain, and it contained a document in which the king ordered him to put an end to the personal serfdom of the Indians.

Feeling that the peace of the country was very brittle, since the people were dissatisfied and full of ill intentions after the redistribution of Guainarima because many good servants of the king were left unprovided for and many who had at first been on Gonzalo Pizarro's side were richly rewarded, the president, who was quite determined to depart, decided for these and other reasons to suspend the execution of the royal decree, and issued an edict to the effect that as he was on his way to report the state of the country to His Majesty and to make recommendations, the decree should be suspended and personal serfdom should not be abolished until His Majesty should have been informed about it by word of mouth and had given new instructions. Thereupon, on the following Monday, he put to sea, carrying off with him all the gold and silver he had collected.

This is from Fernández, whose chapter ends here.

CHAPTER VIII

The cause of the risings in Peru; the delivery
of the galley slaves to Rodrigo Niño to bring
to Spain; his great ingenuity and cunning
in escaping from a pirate.

FROM WHAT our author says of the president's decision about His Majesty's edict on the serfdom of the Indians, it is quite obvious that the previous regulations and the harsh and obdurate character of Viceroy Blasco Núñez Vela were the cause of the rising of the whole empire and of the death of the viceroy himself and of innumerable Spaniards and Indians, as we have seen in our history. And since the president had brought about the revocation of the regulations, by means of which and because of his skill and patience he won over the empire and restored it to the emperor, it was not just or decent to His Imperial Majesty or to the honor of the president to make any innovation about the regulations, especially in the question of the serfdom of the Indians, which was one of the most scandalous and hateful matters. He himself said as much to some of his friends, declaring that he would not promulgate the order, nor did he wish it to be promulgated until His Majesty should have heard him personally. He had seen by experience how scandalous this regulation was and what trouble was stirred up whenever it was mentioned. But the Devil, as we have had occasion to observe before, sought by all the means within his power to destroy the peace of a country where the spread of Christianity and the preaching of the Holy Gospel had advanced so far; and in order that it should not settle down he impeded and cast a cloud over the prudence and discretion of the royal councillors, so that the advice they gave their prince was not that most fitting for the security of the empire, but rather the contrary. This is seen from the wars of Don Sebastián de Castilla and Francisco Hernández Girón which followed the earlier rebellions, and rose from no other source but that of the past regulations and others similar to them, as is stated by Diego Fernández, whom we shall quote.

To interrupt the thread of a tale so melancholy as that of the aforementioned chapters, it will be well that we should say something of a more stimulating nature so that we may continue with less melancholy. In the midst of these events Hernando Niño, *regidor* of the city of Toledo, sent a letter to his son Rodrigo Niño whom we have mentioned in Book IV of the Second Part of these *Commentaries* (ch. xi), in speaking of the misfortunes of the Viceroy Blasco Núñez Vela. In it the father bade the son to go straight to Spain, as he was unoccupied after the wars of Gonzalo Pizarro, and take possession of and enjoy an estate bequeathed to him by a relative. The president and his ministers thought that this gentleman, who had shown himself so loyal to His Majesty in the late war with the rebels, could perform a useful service in conveying to Spain eighty-six galley slaves, former soldiers of Gonzalo Pizarro condemned to the galleys. He was therefore asked to do this, being informed that it would be a great service to His Majesty and that he would be rewarded in Spain for it as well as for his other services in Peru. Rodrigo Niño accepted, though reluctantly, for he did not wish to be troubled with galley slaves. Yet as the hope of reward overweighs all obstacles, he made ready his arms to go as captain of these people, and thus left the city of Lima with the eighty-six condemned Spaniards, who included six of Gonzalo Pizarro's musicians whom I knew, one I remember was called Agustín Rodríguez, a half-breed from the imperial city of Mexico. All six were excellent performers, and on instructions took their instruments with them to play wherever they stayed, and profited by gifts from several prominent and wealthy gentlemen, who had enjoyed their excellent music.

With good weather and a prosperous voyage Rodrigo Niño reached Panama. All along the way while he was in the district of Peru, the justices of the towns helped him to guard and watch over the galley slaves, who behaved peaceably and with humility since they had offended His Majesty in that region. But on passing to Panama and Nombre de Dios, some of them tried to avoid the fate of rowing in the galleys by taking flight. The reason was that they were almost unguarded; no guards had been provided because the ministers thought Rodrigo Niño's authority would be sufficient or because it was hard to find anyone who wanted to leave Peru to go and guard galley slaves.

Beset by these problems, Rodrigo Niño reached a place off the islands of Santo Domingo and Cuba, where a French corsair came up with him— in those days there were no corsairs of other nations, as there now are. The Spanish captain, seeing he had neither weapons nor men for his defence since the people on board were hostile rather than friendly, employed an amusing military ruse. Armed head to foot with corselet and visor and many plumes, and with a partisan in his hand, he climbed the mainmast and ordered the seamen and the rest of the company to lie low and not appear, only the musicians were to sit on the poop and play their instruments when they saw that the enemy was near at hand. Everything was done as Rodrigo Niño ordered; the ship's course was not changed and no notice was taken of the enemy, who was full of confidence in an easy victory. But when they heard the royal music from a ship that appeared empty they were highly perplexed. One of the ideas that crossed their minds was that the ship belonged to some great lord exiled on account of some grave crime against his king or dispossessed of his estates by some suit or trickery such as there are in the world, wherefore he had turned corsair and appeared in full dress. With this in mind they halted, not daring to attack Rodrigo Niño, but sailing off and letting him continue on his way. This was known later, when the president passed these islands on the way to Spain, for the corsair himself had said as much at the ports he put in at peaceably to buy supplies for money. The president was very glad to have selected such a person to escort the galley slaves to Spain.

CHAPTER IX

All Rodrigo Niño's galley slaves take flight,
and he drives off one who remains behind
with his dagger; the penalty for this,
and the favor shown by
Prince Maximilian.

HAVING escaped from the corsair with his musical stratagem, Rodrigo Niño sailed on and reached Havana, where a good number of the galley slaves fled because of the insufficiency of the guards given him when they were handed over to him to guard. A few others had fled at Cartagena; others did the same at the Azores, and so many had fled by the time they crossed the bar at Sanlúcar that only eighteen were left, and seventeen of them fled between there and the Arenal at Seville. With the single one that was left of the eighty-six that had been entrusted to him, Rodrigo Niño landed, and took him to the Casa de la Contratación, where he was supposed to deliver them all, according to the instructions given by the president in the city of Lima. Rodrigo Niño entered Seville with his galley slave by the Póstigo del Carbón, a gate that is very little frequented.

Seeing no one about, Rodrigo Niño laid hands on his galley slave, seizing him by the hair in the middle of the street and exclaiming, dagger in hand, "By the emperor's life, I could stab you twenty times, and if I don't do so, it's because I don't want to soil my hands by killing a man as base and vile as you, a fellow who has been a soldier in Peru, but doesn't disdain to row a galley. Couldn't you have run away like the other eighty-five who came with you, you dog? Go to the Devil, and never let me set eyes on you again, for I'd rather be alone than in such bad company."

With which he gave him two or three blows with the dagger and turned him loose, and went off to the Contratación to report that he had guarded his galley slaves as best he could but explaining that they had taken to their heels because he had been given no men. He alone had been unable to guard them or hold them: on the contrary they had done him a kindness in not killing him, which they might well have done, the better to secure their escape. The justices of the Contratación were puzzled until they discovered the truth of the matter. The last galley slave unburdened himself in the first tavern he entered and told others as vile as himself what Rodrigo Niño had said and done to him. They told others, and the story circulated until it came to the ears of the justices, who were very angry and arrested Rodrigo Niño. His Majesty's fiscal accused him formally of having set at liberty eighty-six of His Majesty's slaves and demanded that he pay so much a head for the loss of them. The case dragged on for a long time. Rodrigo Niño's explanations were not accepted, and he was sentenced to serve six years in the cavalry in Oran with two others at his expense and was prohibited from returning to the Indies.

He appealed from this sentence to Prince Maximilian of Austria, who was then occupying his uncle's place in the government of Spain while His Imperial Majesty was absent. His Highness listened to Rodrigo Niño's sponsors at length while they told him of what had happened in Peru to the rebels who took sides with Gonzalo Pizarro when the Viceroy Blasco Núñez Vela had sent them to arrest others, and how they had mistreated Rodrigo Niño for being unwilling to go with them, as the historians narrate at length and we have repeated in ch. xi of Book IV of this Second Part. They also related the stratagem he adopted with the corsair, and the whole story of the galley slaves down to the last he drove away and his words to him. The prince heard this kindly and said that he thought the blame lay rather with those who did not provide the necessary guards and that the galley slaves had shown some restraint in not killing Rodrigo Niño to cover their flight.

Rodrigo Niño's sponsors, finding the prince well disposed, begged him to do the delinquent the favor of granting him an audience. His Highness consented, and when Rodrigo Niño appeared questioned him like a lawyer, and said: "Are you the man who was entrusted to bring eighty-six galley slaves, and let them all flee but one, whom you drove off with blows from a dagger?"

Rodrigo Niño replied: "Most Serene Highness, I could not do more because they gave me no guards to help in keeping the galley slaves. My will to serve His Majesty is known to all the world. If I let the last galley slave go, it was from pity; for it seemed to me that he alone was to slave and toil for all those who had fled. I did not wish to earn his curses for having brought him to the galleys, or to repay him so ill for having been more loyal than all his fellows. I beg Your Highness to order me to be punished for these crimes, if crimes they be."

The prince replied: "I shall punish them as they deserve. You behaved like a gentleman. I absolve you of the sentence and set you free. You may return to Peru when you wish."

Rodrigo Niño kissed his hands, and years later returned to Peru, where he told at length what we have briefly narrated. He used to say: "In all Spain, I never found a man to say a good word to me, or show me favor but the good Prince Maximilian of Austria, God save him and increase his kingdoms and dominions, amen, for he behaved like a prince to me."

CHAPTER X

The second distribution is published; the president leaves for Spain; the death of Licentiate Cepeda; the arrival of the president in Panama.

PRESIDENT La Gasca was so desirous of leaving the empire of Peru that the hours seemed years to him, and he did everything he could to expedite matters. In order to avoid further delay, he left orders, as Fernández has said, for the archbishop of Lima to deliver the deeds drawn up and signed with his name bestowing the second distribution of *repartimientos*. He thought this would suffice and at once embarked with all haste, sailing from the port called Callao and bequeathing his blessing to Peru, which had kept him in such a state of turmoil and fear. The eight days he had appointed to elapse before the publication of the distribution expired, and it was published, as Fernández says in these words, from ch. iv of Book I of his Second Part:

The term appointed by President La Gasca for publishing the allocations passed, and the day so greatly desired by the claimants dawned. They regarded it as the time and season for the fulfilment of their ambitions and all repaired to the chamber of the *audiencia*. The judges being seated on their daises, the distribution, which the president had left covered and sealed, was opened and read in public. Many of those who had been most confident proved unlucky, and others who had had no such hopes, obtained good allocations. It was extraordinary to hear what some of them said, and to see the ill will displayed by others, and even the despair shown by some: they cursed the president, because they no longer had hopes of anything,

etc. Thus far from Fernández.

The president had fled the country not to hear the curses and blasphemies. He made all haste to reach Panama by sea, so abhorring the people he left behind that he would not put into any port even to take on fresh supplies. With him he brought under arrest Licentiate Cepeda, formerly one of His Majesty's judges in those provinces. He refused to take cognisance of the case himself, though he might have done so, since he did not wish to judge cases he had previously amnestied, but referred the matter to the Supreme Royal Council of the Indies.

When they reached Spain, the case was dealt with at Valladolid where the court then was: the royal fiscal brought serious charges, although Cepeda defended himself by maintaining that what he and the other judges had done had been with the intention of serving His Majesty so that those who deemed themselves wronged by the regulations might not commit any act of open defiance, like those caused by the obstinate character and harsh treatment exhibited by Viceroy Blasco Núñez Vela as past events had shown. He brought up many of the actions of the viceroy described in our history, hoping they would appear favorable to his case, but they contributed little to abate his fear, and even certainty, that he would be condemned to a traitor's death. His friends and relatives, realizing that they could not save his life, tried to free him from the imputation of treachery and arranged for him to be given a potion that sped him on his way from prison to the other life. The sentence was thus not carried out in public, and in fact was never published though it had been pronounced. All this was recounted quite freely in Peru, where I heard it; and I also heard it later in Spain from some people from America who were discussing the death of Licentiate Cepeda.

After Gonzalo Pizarro's death, Cepeda himself, speaking on more than one occasion of past events and Pizarro's sentence and execution, and the way in which they had condemned him as a traitor, pulled his house down, strewn the gate with salt, and exhibited his head in an iron cage hanging from the gibbet, used to say that he would defend Gonzalo Pizarro who had never been a traitor to His Majesty but had served him loyally and desired nothing but the preservation of the empire. If he, Cepeda, were condemned in this defence, he had nothing to lose but his life, and was ready to offer his head on the block provided the case were tried and settled in the Parliament of Paris or the University of Bologna or any

other court not subject to the imperial jurisdiction. It was supposed that
he offered this defence as a pretext for defending his own part.

Dr. Gonzalo de Illescas in his *Pontifical History* says almost what we
have said in speaking of Cepeda. His words are:

One of the notable and outstanding figures who had a hand and even played
a prominent part in the Peruvian disturbances was one Licentiate Cepeda, a
native of Tordesillas, one of the judges who went out with Viceroy Blasco
Núñez Vela. There is no reason to conceal his name for he was very prominent
in His Majesty's service while he was a free agent, and in Pizarro's party after
the latter rebelliously won him over together with the rest of Peru. Cepeda
went over to the imperial camp at the last moment when the armies were
ranged for the final battle, and risked his life in so doing, for Pizarro had him
pursued and he was left for dead in a marsh. La Gasca received him with great
affection, though he afterwards flung him in prison here in Spain and his case
was taken to the criminal court. Cepeda brought forward many telling arguments in his defence. According to himself, he had a good case and it was
thought he might be honorably discharged from prison. But as he died of illness in prison in Valladolid, the case was never settled. I have had in my hands
a very skilful statement he drew up in his defence, and indeed anyone who
read it could hardly fail to acquit him and regard him as a loyal servant of the
crown. His legal ability was greater than his fortune in this matter, for after
having enjoyed incalculable wealth and the greatest of honor, I saw him in
prison in great need and distress.

This is taken from Dr. Illescas, who, in speaking of the death of Count
Pedro Navarro, a very famous soldier of the day, gives the story we have
told of the death of Licentiate Cepeda, that the governor had him arrested, and being a close friend of his, strangled him in prison to avoid
his being beheaded as a traitor, after he had won the whole kingdom of
Naples, etc. Fortune allows similar events to take place in various parts of
the world, so that there shall be no lack of those who help the unfortunate
to weep.

President La Gasca safely reached Panama City with more than 1,500,-
000 in gold and silver which he was bringing to Spain for His Majesty,
apart from as much, or rather much more, in the private possession of
those who accompanied him. The historians record a curious incident
about this. As Agustín de Zárate puts it most clearly and gives the causes
of the misdeed—which was one of the ordinances our history has mentioned: they caused risings, disturbances, and scandals everywhere—we
shall follow his account of the origins of this rebellion, and then extract
from all three authors the substance and truth of the deed and the extent

of the robbery of gold and silver and other objects which the Contreras carried out in Panama. If they had been satisfied with their plunder and being able to salt it away to enjoy it later, they could have avenged their wrongs with a handsome profit. But their youth and lack of skill in military affairs caused them to lose it all, and their lives into the bargain, as our history will tell. Agustín de Zárate gives the following account, which comes word for word from Book VII of his *History of Peru* (ch. xii): it and its title are as follows, being the eleventh chapter in our *Commentaries*.

CHAPTER XI

"What happened to Hernando and Pedro de Contreras, who were in Nicaragua and went in pursuit of the president"

WHEN Pedro Arias de Ávila discovered and governed the province of Nicaragua, he married one of his daughters called Doña María de Peñalosa to Rodrigo de Contreras, a native of the city of Segovia, where he was a leading citizen of some substance. On the death of Pedro Arias, the government of the province passed to Rodrigo de Contreras, on whom His Majesty conferred it at Pedro Arias' nomination, out of regard for his merits and services. He governed for several years until a new *audiencia* was set up with its seat in the city of Gracias a Dios, named after the territory of Guatemala. The judges not only relieved Rodrigo de Contreras of his post, but applied one of the ordinances we have mentioned above and deprived him and his wife of their Indians because he had been governor. They also removed all those he had granted to his sons and daughters during his term of office. He therefore came to Spain to seek redress for the wrong he claimed he had been done, alleging the services he himself and his father-in-law had rendered. His Majesty and the members of the Council of the Indies decided that the regulation must be enforced and confirmed the ruling of the judges.

When Hernando de Contreras and Pedro de Contreras, Rodrigo's sons, learned this, they were much incensed by the result of the business their father had gone to negotiate, and decided like foolhardy youths to start a rebellion, relying on the support of one Juan Bermejo and other soldiers who had come in his company from Peru, some out of dissatisfaction because the president had not given them a living as a reward for their service in the war against Gonzalo Pizarro, and others because they had been banished by the president from Peru after serving Pizarro. These men encouraged the two brothers to undertake the deed, assuring them that if they landed in Peru with the two or three hundred soldiers they could gather, and using the shipping and navigating equipment they had, most of the people in Peru, who were disgruntled because Licentiate La Gasca had not remunerated their services, would come over to them.

Thus resolved, they started secretly to gather men and weapons, and as soon as they felt strong enough to resist the authorities, began to put their purpose into action. They considered that the bishop of the province had been opposed to their father in all the matters that arose between them, and began by taking vengeance on his person. One day some men from their company forced their way in on the bishop while he was playing chess and slew him. They then raised their flag, calling themselves the Army of Liberty, and, taking the ships they needed, sailed into the Pacific with the idea of lurking in wait for the president and seizing and robbing him on the way, for they had heard that he was preparing to come to Tierra Firma with all His Majesty's bullion. They decided they ought first to put in at Panama, which was as well or better placed than Nicaragua for them to sail the return route from Peru: they also hoped to get information, so they took on about three hundred men and put in at the port of Panama. But before they did so they ascertained the state of affairs there from some settlers they arrested, learning that the president had already arrived with all the royal treasure. From this and other information they gathered, they concluded that good luck had brought their prey into their very hands. They waited till nightfall, and secretly descended on the port with great stealth, in the belief that the president was already in the city and that they could carry out their purpose without any precautions or danger,

etc. This is from Agustín de Zárate.

López de Gómara's account is almost the same. He adds in his ch. cxciii:

(the Contreras) collected together the Pizarrists who were fleeing from La Gasca and other outlaws, and decided to make the attack to enrich themselves, declaring that the treasure and all the riches of Peru belonged to them as grandsons of Pedro Arias de Ávila who had been associated with Pizarro, Almagro, and Luque, and had sent them on their discovery, but they rebelled. The tale was an unlikely one, but good enough to attract rogues for their purpose. Finally they made the attack and achieved a notable haul, if they had only been satisfied with it,

etc. This is from López de Gómara.

The Contreras entered Panama by night, and in the city, in the house of Dr. Robles, and in four ships that were in the harbor, they seized 800,000 castilians, some belonging to the king and some to private persons, as Fernández says in ch. viii. In the house of the treasurer they found 600,000 pesos more, which, as López de Gómara says, were to be taken to Nombre de Dios (ch. cxciii). In addition to these sums of gold and silver, they robbed many shops belonging to rich merchants in Panama, finding Spanish goods in great abundance, in fact in surfeit, since they could not take them all. They sent one of their henchmen, called Salguero, with a band of arquebusiers down the road of Las Cruces to the Chagre River, hearing that a great deal of gold and silver had been taken to Nombre de Dios along that road. Salguero found seventy loads of silver awaiting shipment, and sent it all to Panama. It was worth more than 560,000 ducats, so that without the merchandise, pearls, and golden jewels, and other ornaments they seized in the city, there were nearly 2,000,000 pesos of gold and silver taken from the president and other passengers. The latter had no suspicion of pirates or robbers and took part of their gold and silver with them, leaving the bulk of it in Panama to be transported gradually across to Nombre de Dios: they could not have transferred it in a single journey, or in four or even eight, for as López de Gómara says in the chapter we have quoted, the sum carried by the president and his fellow travellers exceeded 3,000,000 pesos in gold and silver.

All this excess of wealth and prosperity that fortune poured upon them so suddenly and with such abundance was lost because the youthful bandits gave themselves up to the follies and stupidities into which the young often fall. Their misadventures after seizing this prize were increased by the futile desire of Juan Bermejo and his companions, the Pizarrists, to lay hands on President La Gasca and avenge themselves on his person for the wrongs he had done them, as they believed, whether by underpaying them or over-punishing them. They boasted that they would make gunpowder of him: a thing they needed and said he would do very well for, judging by his sharpness and subtlety. But they were wrong in these vain imaginings, because it would have been a greater torment and pain to the president, and so a greater vengeance for them, to have him return to Spain alive but without the store of gold and silver, which was the greatest of his achievements in Peru.

CHAPTER XII

The amateurishness and folly of the Contreras
which lost them their treasure and their lives;
the pains and ingenuity of their enemies
in seeking their punishment
and death.

WITH LICENTIATE La Gasca in the plight we have described, it seemed as if the good fortune that had favored him in winning and recovering so great an empire as Peru took exception to the rashness of a group of unpracticed youths and abandoned and desperate rebels who had brought him to such a state of impoverishment, and wished to restore him to his honors and continue the favor and protection it had hitherto shown him, and it therefore availed itself of the arrogance and ignorance they displayed in their moment of success. Such was their blindness and stupidity that although many of the soldiers had known Francisco de Carvajal and followed his party in Peru, they nevertheless brought about their destruction and death by their inexperience and folly.

The first piece of folly they committed was in arresting many of the chief citizens after they had won Panama and sacked it. Among those arrested were the bishop, the royal treasurer, and Martín Ruiz de Marchena, and other *regidores*, who were carried off to the gibbet to be hanged. Their colonel Juan de Bermejo would have done this with pleasure if Hernando de Contreras had not stopped him, as a result of which Juan Bermejo was greatly annoyed, and declared that if he wanted to favor his enemies and displease his friends by not letting them kill their enemies, he had better not be surprised if one fine day they hanged him and all his followers.

This foreboding was soon fulfilled. Hernando de Contreras was content with extracting an oath from the prisoners that they would not oppose him in what he had done, but that they were in favor of it, as if it had been in His Majesty's and God's service and in the interest of the citizens themselves, which was another misjudgment.

Moreover the soldiers were divided into four companies, though they were so few, barely exceeding 250. One company of 40 men remained with Pedro de Contreras to guard the four ships they had brought and four more they had seized in the harbor. Hernando de Contreras sent Salguero with 30 more, as we have said, to capture the silver at Río de Chagre. He himself took 40 men and went off down the Capira road to seize the president and sack Nombre de Dios, expecting to achieve both objects easily by surprise. Juan Bermejo remained on guard at Panama with 150 more, and one of the steps he took, as impotent and foolish as those already mentioned, was, as Fernández says, to return all the spoils they had seized from the merchants and other persons of substance under arrest in return for a written pledge that they would be delivered to him or to Hernando de Contreras on his return from Nombre de Dios. This display of folly was due to their belief that they were already masters of all the New World without any opposition. He ordered all the horses in the city to be handed over to him so that he could go off with all his men to help Hernando de Contreras if necessary. And so, he suddenly departed from the city, leaving it quite exposed. He thought that it was as safe as if it had been his own house, though he would have done better to have had the loot of gold, silver, jewels, and merchandise loaded on the ship and to have gone off wherever they wished, leaving the president and his friends completely destroyed and undone. But they did not deserve to enjoy their ill-gotten gains any more than the president deserved the harm they had done him. Thus his good fortune returned, as we shall soon see.

At daybreak, Arias de Acevedo, who was one of those who escaped arrest in the attack of the previous evening and who has already been mentioned, sent one of his servants at all speed to Nombre de Dios to warn President La Gasca what the rebels had done at Panama. Although the account was not a complete one, which would have been impossible, at least it was sufficient for the president and all his men to be forewarned and on their guard.

Meanwhile in the city both those who had at first fled and those who had shown themselves friendly to Juan Bermejo to the extent of becoming repositories of what had been stolen, recovered courage on finding that the rebels were divided and that he had gone off with all his men. They rang the bells and collected together, hastily fortifying the city, both in the direction of the sea, so that Pedro de Contreras could not attack them, and on the side of the Capira road, so that if their enemies returned they could not easily enter. The sound of the bells attracted many Spaniards from the estates, which are called *estancias,* with such arms as they had and many Negroes who came to help their masters. Very soon above 500 soldiers were assembled, both white and black, determined to die in defence of the city.

Two soldiers left behind by Juan Bermejo for lack of mounts fled when they saw the stirring of the people and went to warn their captain that the city had risen and resumed its allegiance to His Majesty. Juan Bermejo passed the news to Hernando de Contreras saying that he proposed to return to Panama to draw and quarter the traitors who had broken their oath to him. He supposed that it would be as easy to win the city a second time as it had been the first. But things turned out very differently, because the citizens, to avoid having their city (which is mainly of wood) burnt, came out to meet him on the way and finding him encamped on a steep hill, attacked it with great vigor and spirit, annoyed and outraged by the insult he had put upon them when he caught them unawares. Desiring vengeance, they fought like men, and although at the first onslaught neither side had any perceptible advantage, at the second clash the people from the city attacked desperately like injured people determined to avenge their wrongs. Although their opponents fought courageously, they were at length defeated and most of them were killed, being outnumbered by the crowd of whites and blacks who flung themselves upon them. Juan Bermejo, Salguero, and above 80 others perished. As many more were captured and taken to the city, where they were herded in a courtyard. The alguacil mayor, whose name had best remain unrecorded, brought two Negroes and stabbed them all to death, ignoring their cries and screams and pleas for confession. One author, Fernández (ch. x), says that having died without confession they were buried beside the sea.

The news of the reverse travelled far and wide, and soon reached Hernando de Contreras, who had heeded Juan de Bermejo's warning and was returning to Panama. Finding himself now ruined and utterly abandoned, he desperately dispersed his men, giving them orders to get through to the sea coast, each as best he might, where his brother Pedro would take them on board. He proposed to do the same and thus they separated. A few days later, while the king's men were scouring the mountains, marshes, and bogs in search of them, they came across the body of Hernando de Contreras, drowned in a bog. They cut his head off and took it to Panama. His followers recognized it, though it was much disfigured, because a peculiar hat he wore was found with it, together with a gold *agnus dei* he wore round his neck.

His brother Pedro heard of the misfortunes of Juan Bermejo and the death of his followers, and not knowing what to do tried to escape by sea. But neither wind, nor water, nor land favored him: on the contrary all three elements showed themselves hostile. Abandoning the ships, he tried to escape in boats, but made off without knowing where to go, for every man's hand was against him. The inhabitants of the city prepared boats themselves and recovered their own ships and the others, thereupon setting off after Pedro de Contreras, though they had to proceed by guesswork, for they had no idea where he was going. The pursuers found some of the fugitives in the wilds. They had separated and scattered in various directions, like Hernando de Contreras' men. It was not known what happened to Pedro de Contreras, but it was suspected that hostile Indians or tigers or other savage beasts (and there are very fierce animals in those parts) killed and ate him. Nothing more was heard of him.

Such was the hopeless and fatal end of this incident: no other result could have been expected since it began with so dire and abominable a deed as the murder of a bishop. Although some people later tried to excuse the murderers on the ground that the bishop was a bad and foul-mouthed man and that they were obliged to do away with him, no excuse can possibly justify so wicked an act. Their retribution we have already seen.

CHAPTER XIII

The president recovers his lost treasure, punishes the guilty, and reaches Spain, where he finishes his life happily.

LICENTIATE La Gasca was greatly perturbed by the news of the descent of the Contreras and the sack of Panama, which reached him in the city of Nombre de Dios—the more so as fate seemed to have reserved to the end of his journey this astonishing event and (as one author puts it) unlooked-for peril that no amount of forethought could possibly have provided against. He sought as best he could to secure the treasure he had with him, and prepared the men escorting him and those who were in Nombre de Dios to return to Panama, recover what had been lost, and punish the bandits, though his experience and good sense suggested to him that they would have already gone off and salted away their loot. Nevertheless, in order not to fail in his duty—which in the past he had never missed any opportunity of fulfilling—he hurriedly left Nombre de Dios with such arms and men as he could scrape together, and at the end of the first day's march received news of the fortunate outcome of events in Panama and the death of Juan Bermejo and Salguero and the flight of Hernando de Contreras into the forests and that of his brother by sea. This consoled the good president and he pursued his journey much encouraged and pleased, thanking Our Lord, as López de Gómara says, for "events as remarkable as they were fortunate for his honor and memory," etc.

The president reached Panama more triumphantly than all the victors in the world, since he had overthrown, slain, and destroyed enemies who would have displayed every cruelty if they had not been so mad and foolish. His victory was achieved without arms or any force or stratagem but the favor of good fortune. He recovered the lost treasure and asked those with whom it had been deposited to take care of it. He even gained a great deal of gold and silver, for as the bandits had collected everything whether belonging to the king or to travellers or citizens, the president ordered it all to be sequestrated for His Majesty and demanded that private persons who claimed to have lost their property should provide proof by declaring the marks on their silver bars or gold ingots. It was a very ancient custom among those travelling to and from Peru to cut figures or other distinguishing marks with a chisel on the gold and silver they were carrying: thus if a ship goes aground on those shores, they can each distinguish their own. I did the same with the few poor things I brought back, so I can warrant that the practice existed. Those who could give the marks, proving by them that the precious metal was theirs, were allowed to take it, but those who could not produce signs lost it, and the unclaimed part went to the king, so that the president rather won than lost by the incident, a thing that often happens to fortune's favorites.

Having recovered his treasure, the president punished those guilty of making bold to take the bars collected by Salguero: although they had not been members of Contreras' band, they had dared to take advantage of the disturbance in the city to steal whatever they could from the loot. Some were whipped, and others pilloried, so that in addition to the rebels some were punished who were not rebels, for fishing in troubled waters.

The president had Hernando de Contreras' head exhibited on the gibbet in an iron cage with his name written on it. He himself punished none of his enemies: they were all dead when he returned to Panama. This done, he embarked with all speed to continue his journey to Spain, as Fernández says in the following words in ch. x of his Second Part:

Thus President La Gasca crowned the good fortune that had been his in Spain and Peru with this other fortunate incident, in which he recovered the results of the notable robbery practiced upon him, as well as a vast sum belonging to private persons. He embarked for Spain with all his treasure, and on his safe arrival went to inform His Majesty, who was in Germany. He had already been granted the bishopric of Palencia, which had become vacant on the death of Don Luis Cabeza de Vaca of good memory, and held it until 1561, when His Catholic Majesty King Philip gave him the bishopric of Sigüenza. This he held till November 1567, when God was pleased to call him from this life: he died in Sigüenza.

This is from Fernández. Francisco López de Gómara adds the following, from his ch. cxciii:

La Gasca embarked therefore in Nombre de Dios, and reached Spain in July 1550, having won great riches for others and a great reputation for himself. The emperor made him bishop of Palencia and summoned him to Augusta in Germany, so as to have a full and direct account of the people and affairs of Peru from his own mouth.

This is from López de Gómara, who ends his chapter here. Although he says President La Gasca fought the rebels and defeated them, he means the president's good fortune defeated them and brought him the victory he had won and recovered for him the treasure he had lost. The president never set eyes on them alive or dead. The worthy man ended his days as we have said, deserving of eternal memory, for by his good fortune, skill, prudence, sagacity, and other good qualities he conquered and recovered an empire thirteen hundred leagues broad, and restored it to the emperor Charles V, with all the treasure he brought back from it.

CHAPTER XIV

*Francisco Hernández Girón announces his
expedition; many soldiers hasten to join
it; they cause a great disturbance and
rising in Cuzco which is pacified
by the prudence and good 'sense
of some of the citizens.*

LEAVING the good President La Gasca, bishop of Sigüenza, surrounded
with honors and good works, we must make a rapid leap from Sigüenza back to Cuzco, where events worthy of record now occurred. On the
president's departure for Spain, the citizens went back to their towns and
homes to see to their estates, General Pedro de Hinojosa among them.
Captain Francisco Hernández Girón went to Cuzco with the authorization
he had received to undertake the expedition: he gave it out on the way and
sent captains nominated by himself to raise men in Huamanga, Arequipa,
and Pueblo Nuevo. In Cuzco he had the expedition solemnly proclaimed
with trumpets and drums, and the noise and fame of it attracted more
than two hundred men from all sides, for he was highly esteemed. When
this number was gathered together, they began to give unbridled expression to their feelings about past events, cursing the president and the
other governors he had left throughout the empire.

This wild talk led the citizens, who heard a great deal of it, to address
Juan de Saavedra, then corregidor of the city, with a view to his urging
Francisco Hernández to hasten his departure and rid the place of the
soldiers. All but a few of these men, who were in the captain's house,
were billeted on the other citizens and residents. Fernández, in mentioning this in ch. iv, says: "The citizens were distressed both in their own interests and because they thought that if the soldiers left and any untoward
event occurred they would not be able to supply soldiers for His Majesty's service as they had on past occasions and were left defenceless without them," etc., but I do not know who could have told Fernández this or
who could have imagined such a thing, for the citizens stood to gain far

more from ejecting all the soldiers from the place on such missions than from keeping them at home, where they had to support and feed them at their own expense. Many citizens had four, five, six, or seven soldiers in their houses, supplying them two solid meals a day at their tables and finding them clothes, lodging, and all necessities. Other citizens did not have a single soldier: I could name some who did not as well as those who did, but it would not be proper to speak against them. But when our author says the citizens regretted being rid of the soldiers, I cannot imagine how this can be credited, since the fact that they were spending their own money on those men, as I have said, was public knowledge.

Fernández could not have witnessed personally many of the things he describes, but must have based his accounts on the records of others, for on some points his statements are wrong and contradictory. He talks so much of risings at every touch and turn that there are more risings than columns in his history, and the result is to turn all the inhabitants of Peru, whether citizens or soldiers, into traitors. We shall omit all this, as not necessary to history, and give the substance of all that happened, for I was in Cuzco when Francisco Hernández and his men created the first disturbance, which I shall describe. I was also there at the time of the second, three years later: I was so near to those concerned that I saw everything, without attracting any attention because I was so young—at that time I had not left boyhood behind, or even reached the end of it. So I shall tell plainly all I saw and heard from my father and many others who discussed these and succeeding events of the empire in our house.

The soldiers proved, as we were saying, so arrogant and rude that orders were publicly given for some remedy to be found. They resented this and had recourse to their captains. They agreed together not to let themselves be downtrodden, since the authority granted them by President La Gasca for this campaign freed and exempted them from any other jurisdiction, and the corregidor had no power over them: he could not give them orders and they had no obligation to obey him. The disturbance went to such lengths that all the soldiers assembled armed in Francisco Hernández's house. The city and the corregidor sounded the alarm, and the citizens, and many of their kinsmen, and other soldiers who were not enrolled for the expedition, and many rich and worthy merchants gathered in the main square with their arms and formed a company. Their opponents formed another in the street outside the captain's house, near the square, and the two parties remained so for two days and nights, in great risk of open conflict. This would undoubtedly have occurred, but that men of experience and discretion who deplored the late unfortunate happenings tried to reconcile them. Some approached the corregidor and others Francisco Hernández Girón, and urged them to meet and discuss the situation.

The chief intermediaries were Diego de Silva, Diego Maldonado (the Rich), Garcilaso de la Vega, Vasco de Guevara, Antonio de Quiñones, Juan de Berrio, Jerónimo de Loaisa, Martín de Meneses, and Francisco Rodríguez de Villafuerte, the first of the thirteen who overstepped the line Francisco Pizarro drew with his sword. Many other citizens accompanied them, and persuaded the corregidor not to let the disturbance go any further lest it should end in the destruction of the whole city and even of the whole kingdom. They told Francisco Hernández the same, reminding him that he would lose the credit for all his past services and not be allowed to proceed with his conquest, which was the thing that most closely touched his honor and estate. Finally they arranged a meeting between him and the corregidor in the cathedral. But his soldiers refused to let him go without receiving hostages for his safe release. Four of the citizens went as hostages, my lord Garcilaso, Diego Maldonado, Antonio de Quiñones, and Diego de Silva.

The two leaders met in the church, and Francisco Hernández behaved in so free and insolent a manner that the corregidor was on the point of arresting him, if he had not feared that the soldiers would kill the hostages. He therefore restrained his indignation so as not to rouse Francisco Hernández, and let him go back to his house. They met again the same afternoon, the above-mentioned citizens again acting as hostages. Having pondered on the misfortunes that the disturbance might lead to and consulted privately with some of his friends, Francisco Hernández showed himself more amenable and ready to listen to reason, and they agreed on a longer interview on the following day to decide what should be done. They thus met once more, and after many accusations, defences, and other judicial forms and ceremonies, it was agreed that Francisco Hernández should dismiss his men in the interests of peace and hand over to the corregidor eight of them who had been the most insolent and shameless and had fired the arquebuses on the king's company, though without doing any harm. Francisco Hernández himself was to go to the royal *audiencia* and give an account of the rising and the scandal his people had caused.

This was agreed and sealed with a solemn oath on both sides, and it was set down in writing that the corregidor should let him go free on parole and under oath of loyalty. Francisco Hernández thereupon returned home, and informed his soldiers of the agreement. They were so angry that he had to allay them with words and promises, or they would have closed with His Majesty's squadron and wrought great havoc on the royal party, for the soldiers numbered two hundred and had nothing to lose, while the rest included nearly eighty lords of serfs and the rest were merchants, property owners, and men of substance. God was pleased to prevent a clash by the prayers, intercessions, and promises of the priests, secular and regular, and women and devout persons, though the tension on both sides was even greater, and all spent the night under arms with sentries posted. But early next day when the corregidor saw that Francisco Hernández had not dismissed his men, he sent a protest and a summons for him to appear in person.

Francisco Hernández realized that if his soldiers knew that he was going to the corregidor, they would not allow him to leave the house, and would get completely out of hand, and so he slipped out stealthily in his house-clothes so as to suggest he was going to talk to a neighbor. He thus reached the corregidor's house, who promptly arrested him and flung him into prison. On hearing this, his men scattered and fled in various directions. The guiltiest, eight in number, withdrew to the convent of St. Dominic and made themselves strong in the bell tower. Although surrounded and attacked for many days, they refused to surrender, for they had suffered no harm in the fighting and the tower was narrow and strong, dating from Inca times. Because of these desperadoes, the tower was pulled down and levelled, so that others might not dare to follow their example and use it as a fort—though it deserved a better fate. The eight men gave in and were punished, but not as rigorously as their misdeeds deserved.

CHAPTER XV

Juan Alonso Palomino and Jerónimo Costilla flee from Cuzco; Francisco Hernández Girón appears before the royal audiencia, and returns to Cuzco a free man and married; the story of another rising in Cuzco.

WHEN THE soldiers had taken flight and Francisco Hernández Girón had been arrested, the disturbance was at an end. On the second night after the settlement, Juan Alonso Palomino and Jerónimo Costilla, brothers-in-law and lords of serfs in the city, fled, prompted by unknown motives. I can speak of their flight as an eye witness for I was in Cuzco when it happened, though Fernández, following someone who must have been dreaming, sets it two years later and connects it with other disturbances he tells of as occurring in the city, which everyone then regarded as trifling. These gentlemen went off at midnight, for no perceptible reason, as we have said. Had they gone two or three nights earlier, they would have had reason enough, for the whole city stood in imminent danger of destruction. As it was everyone made fun of their purposeless departure and criticized them severely when it was heard that they had burnt the Apurímac and Amáncay bridges which were built by the labor of the poor Indians and at their expense. The two brothers-in-law spread unrest near and far by announcing that Francisco Hernández Girón had started a great rebellion and was holding Cuzco. Juan Alonso Palomino was amply repaid for this in the second rising of Francisco Hernández, who slew him at a dinner, as we shall tell: Jerónimo Costilla escaped because he was not at the feast.

To return to the affairs of Francisco Hernández, once his men had been disbanded and the worst culprits punished, the agreement that had been made with him was ratified, and it was confirmed that he should betake himself under solemn oath to the city of Lima and present himself before the *audiencia* with an explanation of what had happened. Out of friendship and because they were neighbors living in opposite houses in the same street, Diego Maldonado (the Rich), accompanied him as far as Antahuailla, which is forty leagues from Cuzco; the place was in Diego Maldonado's allocation and the Indians were his, so that he also made the journey because it was useful for him to visit his vassals, and so kill two birds with one stone.

About this Fernández says that Francisco Hernández was handed over to the alcalde Diego Maldonado and Captain Juan Alonso Palomino, who were to accompany him to Lima at his expense with twenty arquebusiers and that the corregidor extracted an oath of loyalty from him for greater security. I do not know who could have given him an account so different from the truth, unless it were someone who wanted to set up as a writer for the stage. Francisco Hernández reached the city of Lima and appeared before the royal *audiencia*. The judges ordered his arrest, but after a few days they gave him the whole city as his cell, and a little later, attaching small importance to his misdeeds, they accepted all the explanations he produced and set him free on assurances; they were quite satisfied to let him marry a young, beautiful, virtuous, and noble woman who was certainly undeserving of all the hardships her husband thrust upon her at the time of his second revolt, as we shall tell. He returned with her to Cuzco, and remained quiet for some days and months, though not years. His conversation was always with soldiers and he avoided intercourse with the citizens.

He even lodged a suit against a leading person in the city about a valuable horse that he said was his, though it was not, and maintained that he had lost it in the later wars at Quito. It was true that the citizen had bought it at that time for a great sum of money from a very good soldier who had won it fairly on the field. All this was known to another good soldier who knew both parties, but who was in hiding for having sided with Gonzalo Pizarro. No one knew his whereabouts but the owner of the horse, who however preferred to lose his prize rather than betray the fugitive who would have been killed or sent to the galleys. Francisco Hernández sold the horse at far less than its value and the case did no good except to reveal his friendly feelings toward his fellow citizens and equals who were lords of vassals—so much so that I never knew him having anything to do with them in general or in particular. He only mixed with soldiers who were his friends and boon companions, as he was later to demonstrate.

On seeing the small importance and even less punishment assigned by the judges to the insolence and misbehavior of Francisco Hernández Girón and his men, others were emboldened to follow his example; they did not want to be thought less brave or daring than he and his men. But these were few and leaderless, and did not include a single *vecino* (or lord of vassals). They sought however to pursue their aim by hook or by crook, and so openly that it became known in the city of Lima. And although the corregidor in Cuzco was warned of what was afoot and asked to make an investigation and punish the ringleaders in the interests of the peace of the city, he replied that he did not want to make any more enemies than already existed, in other words Francisco Hernández and his men. He said that as the *audiencia* had paid little attention to the defiance of these, they would pay even less in the present case: if his superiors would not punish such deeds, he was absolved from intervening. All this became generally known, whereupon there arrived a citizen of Cuzco called Don Juan de Mendoza, a troublemaker who mixed a great deal with soldiers, though he was the sort of person who incites and provokes others, rather than does anything himself, whether to good or to harm. As soon as he reached the city, he had talks with chiefs of the malcontents, called Francisco de Miranda, Alonso de Barrionuevo, who was then alguacil mayor of the city, and Alonso Hernández Melgarejo. Miranda told him that all the soldiers wanted to elect him general and Barrionuevo his lieutenant. Mendoza repeated this to some of the *vecinos* who were friends of his, and advised them to flee the city since their persons were in great peril from the soldiers. When he saw that they ignored his advice, he fled to Lima, declaring on his way that Cuzco was in revolt, though the city had taken no notice either of his coming or of his going. Fernández sets the flight of Juan Alonso Palomino and Jerónimo Costilla on this occasion, but it took place two years earlier, where we have included it.

CHAPTER XVI

The judges of the audiencia send a new
corregidor to Cuzco, who executes
justice on the rebels; the causes of
these risings set forth.

AFTER the disturbance caused by Don Juan de Mendoza in Lima, the judges appointed Marshal Alonso de Alvarado as corregidor of Cuzco with instructions to punish the rebels severely, so as to put an end to the licence and impudence of the soldiers. As soon as he reached Cuzco, he arrested some of the soldiers, together with a *vecino* called Don Pedro Puertocarrero on whom the soldiers had laid blame in their statements to the judge, the better to excuse themselves. After thorough investigations, he hanged the ringleaders, Francisco de Miranda and Alonso Hernández Melgarejo, without regard for their rank, for they were both sons of noblemen. When Alonso de Barrionuevo, who was one of those arrested, knew this, he sent a request to the corregidor that he should not be hanged, but beheaded like a gentleman, which he was: if he were hanged, he would despair of salvation and be condemned to hell. The intermediaries begged the corregidor to grant this request and not to allow the man to be so condemned. He did so, though reluctantly, and ordered him to be beheaded. I saw all three after their execution, for I always wanted to see such things close at hand, as boys do. He banished six or seven others from the country. Others fled and could not be caught. Don Pedro Puertocarrero was handed over to the judges, who soon set him free.

Fernández refers to Francisco de Miranda as a *vecino* of Cuzco. He must have used the word in the Castilian sense, where any dweller in a town is called citizen [*vecino*], while we, in accordance with the usage of Peru and Mexico, say *vecino* for a man who has an allocation of Indians and is a lord of vassals. Such a person was, as we have said elsewhere, in the Foreword to the First Part of these *Commentaries,* obliged to reside in the town where he had his Indians; but Francisco de Miranda never had any. I knew him well, because a niece of his, a *mestiza,* and a very respectable woman, was brought up in my father's house.

A few months after these punishments for the last rising there was an investigation of another which Fernández describes at great length, but in fact this was merely a pretext to take vengeance on and execute a poor gentleman who had spoken of and reported certain cases of bastardy in the families of some dignified and established people, both on the male side and on the female. He spoke without malice, and it would be wrong and unpermissible for us to say who they were. The affair was mixed up with certain expressions of dissatisfaction that occurred at that time and blown up into a rebellion, but the punishment was visited on only one person, Don Diego Enríquez, a youth from Seville barely twenty-four years old. His death was greatly regretted by the whole city, especially as a poor gentleman quite without blame in the riot was made to pay for a disturbance in which more than two hundred people were involved, as Fernández says in a chapter eight columns long. Rough justice of this sort was visited also on leading Indians, the vassals and servants of some citizens, among them the noblest and richest in the city. This was done more out of vengeance against their owners than as punishment for any crimes of their own.

The many and lengthy disturbances Fernández mentions are always ascribed to the decrees and regulations issued by the judges of the *audiencia,* depriving the citizens of the personal service of the Indians and refusing to allow those whose interests were impaired to appeal through a common advocate, but insisting that each should present his own case separately and appear in person before the *audiencia.* As we have said on previous occasions, all this was an invention of the Devil designed to foster discord among the Spaniards and so impede the teaching and conversion of the Indians to the Catholic Faith. President La Gasca, who was a very prudent man, perceiving that the decrees that Viceroy Blasco Núñez Vela took to Peru and put in force there caused the rising of the whole empire and would have led to its utter loss if they had not been revoked by himself, realized that they would cause the same disturbances again and refused to put into effect His Majesty's instructions about the abolition of the personal service of the Indians. The judges of the *audiencia* thought differently, and sent the royal instructions out to all parts of the kingdom, thus giving the soldiers the opportunity to talk of risings and rebellions, this time without displeasing the citizens, as Fernández describes at length in his Second Part, Book II, ch. i, ii, and following.

CHAPTER XVII

*The arrival of Viceroy Don Antonio de Mendoza in
Peru; he sends his son Don Francisco to visit
the country as far as Charcas, and sends
him to Spain with a report on it;
a severe sentence by a judge.*

AT THIS time there arrived in Peru as viceroy, governor, and captain
general of the empire Don Antonio de Mendoza, second son of the
house of the marquis of Mondéjar and count of Tendilla, who, as we
said in the *Florida del Inca,* was viceroy in the empire of Mexico, a saintly
and religious man with all the good qualities of a Christian and a gentleman. The city of Lima received him with due solemnity and festivities. A
canopy was brought out for him to make his entry, but though he was entreated by the archbishop and all the city, he would not be persuaded to
enter under it. He refused it as though it would have been treason to accept, a thing very different from what we see today, when men think more
of such an honor, even though they are only acting a part, than of all their
natural life. He brought with him his son, Don Francisco de Mendoza,
who was later generalissimo of the galleys in Spain, and I saw him both
in Peru and here. He was a worthy son, who throughout the whole of his
life, in youth and in age, always imitated his father's virtue and goodness.

The viceroy reached Peru in very poor health, owing it was said, to his
many penitences and the abstinence he practiced. Because of this he lost
his natural warmth, and although the region is so hot, he tried to recover
it by means of violent exercise: for this purpose, as well as for recreation
and to raise his spirits, he would ride out after mid-day into the fields to
hunt such owls or other birds as the little falcons of Peru could kill on the
sandy stretches. This was how the good viceroy busied himself on days
when he was spared the usual tasks of government and the affairs of the
empire. Because of his own lack of health he sent his son Don Francisco
to visit the cities between Lima and Charcas and Potosí, and bring back
a full report about them for presentation to His Majesty.

Don Francisco went on this visitation and I saw him in Cuzco, where he was given a solemn reception with many triumphal arches and dances and a great display of horsemen who rode before him in squadrons through the streets as far as the cathedral and thence to his lodging. After a week they arranged a bull fight and a joust, the finest celebrated in the city before or since, for the liveries worn were of velvet of various colors and many of them embroidered. I remember my father's and those of his companions, which were of black velvet with the tunic and cape embroidered at intervals with two pillars about a span apart and a scroll joining them, with the words *Plus ultra*; above the pillars was an imperial crown, also in yellow velvet, and through both ran a cord of thread of gold and blue silk, all of which looked very well. There were other very rich and costly liveries which I do not remember well enough to describe, though I remember my father's because it was made at home. The squadron of Juan Julio de Hojeda, Tomás Vásquez, Juan de Pancorvo, and Francisco Rodríguez de Villafuerte—all four among the first conquerors—had a livery of black velvet embroidered with various kinds of foliage in scarlet and white velvet. In their turbans they wore so many emeralds and other precious stones that they were valued at more than 300,000 pesos, or above 360,000 Castilian ducats. All the other liveries were similar to the ones described. Don Francisco watched from the balcony of my father's house, where I saw him in person.

He then went to the city of La Paz, La Plata, and Potosí, where he gathered a great deal of information about the silver mines and everything else he needed to know to pass on to His Majesty. He returned by Arequipa and the sea coast to the city of Lima, travelling a total of over 650 leagues. He brought back a written description and illustrations of the hill of Potosí, the silver mines, and hills, volcanoes, valleys, and plains there are in those parts, all of strange forms and shapes.

On his return to Lima, his father the viceroy sent him to Spain with his reports and illustrations. According to Fernández, he left Lima in May 1552, and we shall leave him at this point to recount an incident that occurred at this time in Cuzco, where Alonso de Alvarado was corregidor: the matter was regarded as the more serious and ominous because he was considered to be a very vigilant and strict judge.

About four years earlier a large party of over two hundred soldiers had left Potosí for the kingdom of Tucma, which the Spaniards call Tucumán: most of them set out with Indian porters, though the regulations laid down by the *audiencia* prohibited this. An *alcalde mayor,* whom I knew, went out to inspect the companies of soldiers, and having permitted them all to pass with their Indian porters, laid hands on the last of them and arrested him, called so-and-so Aguirre, on the grounds that he had two Indians carrying his property. A few days later he sentenced the man to two hundred strokes of the lash, since he had no gold or silver with which to pay the fine established for those guilty of using Indians as porters. Aguirre, on being informed of the sentence, tried to find patrons to intercede and prevent it from being carried out, but they had no effect on the alcalde. When Aguirre saw this, he sent to beseech the alcalde to hang him instead of whipping him, for although he was a gentleman, he preferred not to avail himself of his privilege so as not to reveal in public that he was the brother of a man who was a lord of vassals in his own part of the country.

All this had no effect on the licentiate, who was a gentle, peaceable, and conversable person in private life; but it often happens that honor and responsibility change the natural character of people, and so this man of law, instead of being appeased, sent the hangman with a mule and attendants to carry out the sentence forthwith. They went to the prison and mounted Aguirre on the beast. The leading and most respected citizens of the town, on being made aware of the injustice, sought out the magistrate and begged him not to carry out the sentence because it was excessive. The alcalde, not so much willingly as under compulsion, granted a week's suspension. When they got to the prison with these new orders, they found Aguirre already naked and mounted on the ass.[1] When he heard that the only mercy shown him was a week's stay of execution, he said: "I hoped not to have to get on this beast or go naked like this, but since things have come to this pass, let the sentence be carried out, and I accept it, and so we shall save the trouble and pains there would have been for these eight days in searching for intermediaries and advocates who would probably have gained as little as the present ones." So saying, he pressed the ass forward and ran his course, to the great regret of Indians and Spaniards alike, who grieved to see such a cruel wrong so causelessly executed on a gentleman. But he had his own back, according to the way of the world.

---

[1] The penalty of the *azotes* was carried out by mounting the victim naked on an ass which was driven round a set course, the *calles acostumbradas*, while men posted at intervals lashed him as he passed.

CHAPTER XVIII

*The vengeance Aguirre obtains for the wrong
done him, and the pains the corregidor
takes to lay hands on him;
how Aguirre escapes.*

AFTER this Aguirre did not proceed on the expedition though the inhabitants of Potosí were ready to help him with anything he needed; but he refused it saying that the only thing he needed for his comfort was to find death and to hasten its coming as much as possible. He remained in Peru, and when Licentiate Esquivel finished his term of office as corregidor, Aguirre began to pursue him like a desperate man with the intention of killing him by hook or by crook, in order to avenge his wrongs. Esquivel, informed by his friends of this intent, decided to go away and put a distance between himself and the aggrieved Aguirre—not merely a short way but a good 300 or 400 leagues—hoping that the latter would forget him if he were so far away.

The more Esquivel fled, the bolder Aguirre grew, following his tracks wherever he went. At first Esquivel journeyed to Lima, 320 leagues away, but within a fortnight Aguirre arrived. On hearing he was in the city, Esquivel returned and hurried off to Cuzco, a distance of 500 leagues; but a few days later Aguirre appeared, travelling on his bare feet and declaring that one who had suffered a public whipping should not ride a horse or show himself where people might see him.

In this way Aguirre pursued Esquivel for three years and four months, at the end of which time the latter, wearying of these long and useless journeys, decided to settle in Cuzco, thinking that, as the judge in that city was so strict and stern, Aguirre would not dare to make any attempt against him. So he took a dwelling house opposite the cathedral, and lived there very quietly. He always wore a mail shirt under his doublet and carried dagger and sword, though this was against his profession.

At that time a nephew of my father's, the son of Gómez de Tordoya, who was known by the same name, spoke to Esquivel, both being from

Extremadura and friends, saying: "Everyone in Peru knows that Aguirre means to kill you and how doggedly and persistently he goes about it. Let me come to your house and sleep, for if Aguirre knows that I am with you, he won't dare to enter the house."

Esquivel thanked him, and said that he was on his guard and was safe because he never took off the mail shirt or laid down his weapons, which should be enough, for any further precautions would scandalize the city and suggest that he was afraid of a little fellow like Aguirre. He said this because Aguirre was a small and ill built. But his thirst for vengeance gave him such courage and strength that he might be compared with Diego García de Paredes and Juan de Urbina, the champions of the day.

One Monday at mid-day he made bold to enter the licentiate's house, and having made his way the length of it by a low balcony high above the street, and passed through a high hall and a stable, a chamber and study where Esquivel kept his library, he found him sleeping over a book, and stabbed him through the right temple. The blow was a fatal one. He stabbed him again several times in the body, but without wounding him because of the coat of mail, though the blows could be seen by the rents in his doublet. Aguirre then retraced his steps, but on reaching the street door, discovered he had dropped his hat. He had the courage to go and get it, and so went out into the street. But having gone so far, he lost his head and continued without any plan. Instead of taking refuge in the cathedral which was just opposite, he went toward St. Francis, the convent then being to the east of the church, but after walking down most of the street, he avoided going into the monastery either. Turning left he followed a street to a place which led to the place where the convent of St. Clara was founded.

In the little square there he found two young gentlemen, the brothers-in-law of Rodrigo de Pineda, and went up to them saying: "Hide me, hide me!" He was so wild and stupefied that he could not utter any other word.

They knew his purpose and asked him: "Have you killed Esquivel?"

"Yes, sir," he replied, "hide me, hide me!"

They then put him in their brother-in-law's house, at the back of which were three large yards, and in one of them a sty where they shut up pigs for fattening.

They put him in this place and told him not to come out or show his face under any circumstances, in case some Indian chancing to enter the yard might see him, though as there were no cattle in the yard, there was no reason why anyone should go in. They promised to bring him food without anyone knowing, and did so. They ate at their brother-in-law's table, and each secretly transferred to his pocket all the meat, bread, and other food he could, and after eating, pretended he was going to obey the call of nature and went out to the gate of the sty and supplied the wretched Aguirre. They kept him in this way for forty days and nights.

As soon as the death of Licentiate Esquivel was brought to the corregidor's notice, he ordered the bells to be rung and Cañari Indians to stand guard at the gates of the monasteries and sentinels to be posted round the whole city, while the crier announced that no one was to leave the city without his permission. He entered the convents, combing them all and doing everything short of pulling them down. The city remained thus on the alert for over thirty days without any news of Aguirre, who seemed to have been swallowed up by the earth. At the end of this period, these measures were relaxed, and the sentries were dismissed, but not the guards on the royal highways, which were still closely watched.

Forty days after the deed, the gentlemen who were hiding Aguirre— one of whom was called something Santillán and the other something Cataño, both noblemen whom I knew well (I met one of them in Seville when I came to Spain)—thought it time to get Aguirre to a safer place and also avert the peril to which they exposed themselves by keeping him in their power, for the judge was strict and they feared some mishap would befall them. They therefore decided to get him out of the city publicly and not by stealth, dressing him in a black coat, shaving his hair and beard, and dyeing his head, face, neck, hands, and arms up to the elbows in water prepared with a wild fruit the Indians call *uitoc,* which is inedible and of no other use at all. It is the shape, color, and size of a large aubergine, and when broken in pieces and steeped in water for three or four days, can be used to wash the face and hands, which after being washed three or four times and dried in the air become as black as those of an Ethiopian, and even though they are afterwards washed with clean water, the dark color stays fixed for ten days, and then can be removed with peel of the same color, leaving the face as it was before.

So they dressed Aguirre as a Negro laborer in poor and tattered garments, and took him out one day at mid-day through the streets and the main square as far as the hill called Carmenca which is on the road to Lima. It is a tidy step through the streets of the town from the house of Rodrigo de Pineda to the hill of Carmenca, and the Negro Aguirre went on foot in front of his masters, carrying an arquebus on his shoulder, while one of them carried another on his saddlebow, and the other had a small Peruvian falcon on his wrist. With this pretence that they were going hunting, they reached the end of the town where the guards were. These asked them if they had a permit from the corregidor to leave the town.

The one with the falcon exclaimed to his brother, as though annoyed at his own forgetfulness: "Wait for me here or go on slowly, and I'll go back and get the licence, and I'll soon catch you up."

With these words, he returned to the town, and of course did nothing about the licence. His brother hastened on with the Negro until they were out of the jurisdiction of Cuzco, a matter of forty leagues in that direction. Having bought Aguirre a horse and given him a little money, he said: "Brother, now you are in a free country and can go where you like, and I can do no more for you." He returned to Cuzco and Aguirre got to Huamanga where he had a close relative, a rich and noble citizen who was one of the chief people there. This man received him like his own son and lavished a thousand embraces and attentions on him, sending him on his way many days later with everything he needed. We do not mention his name here because he had harbored a criminal in his house and succored him in defiance of the royal justice.

Thus Aguirre escaped. It was one of the most remarkable occurrences of the time in Peru, both because of the severity of the judge and the extraordinary pains he took and because of Aguirre's folly on the day of his deed which helped rather than hindered him. If he had entered some convent, he could not possibly have escaped, so closely were they all searched, though there were then only three: Our Lady of Mercies, the seraphic St. Francis and the divine St. Dominic. The corregidor was furiously angry that all the numerous steps he had taken to punish Aguirre as he intended were in vain. The unruly and swaggering soldiers used to say that if there were more Aguirres in the world and they went to such pains to avenge their wrongs, the investigators would mind their own business better and not be so high handed.

CHAPTER XIX

Many citizens go to kiss the viceroy's hand;
an incident with a gossip; a revolt in Lima
and its punishment; the death of the
viceroy and the scandals
that follow.

WE HAVE mentioned the arrival of the good viceroy Don Antonio de Mendoza at the city of Lima. He lived there a very short time, and in such sickness and pain that he seemed more dead than alive. There is therefore little to say of his viceroyalty. As soon as he reached the city, many citizens from all parts of the empire from Quito to Los Charcas gathered to kiss his hand and congratulate him on his arrival. One of them kissed his hand with great affection and many compliments, and ended: "I pray, Your Excellency, that God may take many days from your life and add them to mine."

The viceroy replied: "I am afraid they will be few and unprofitable."

The citizen, realizing that he had put his foot in it, said: "I beg pardon, sir, I did not mean what I said, but the opposite. May God take many days from my life and add them to yours."

The viceroy answered: "That was what I understood you to mean, and there is nothing to beg pardon for in that." He then dismissed the visitor to the amusement of those who remained.

A few days later a captain, well known in our history, came in for the purpose of tendering to the viceroy advice which he thought essential to the security and good government of the empire. Among other points, the most important he made was this: "Sir, Your Excellency really must take action in the case of two soldiers who live in such-and-such an allocation. They live among the natives. They have guns and live off what they kill. All this shooting ruins the country. What is more, they make their own powder and shot, which is a very serious matter in this country. The whole of Peru is scandalized! There have been serious disturbances here, and it's high time they were punished. The least they deserve is to be dismissed from Peru."

The viceroy asked if they ill-treated the Indians, or sold powder and shot, or committed other serious wrongs, and when the captain replied that all they had done was what he had said, the viceroy gave his reply: "The crimes you mention are things to be grateful for, not things to punish. If two Spaniards live among the Indians, and eat what they shoot themselves, and make their own powder and don't sell it, I don't see what harm they are doing. On the contrary, it sounds a very good example for others to follow. Now good-bye, but don't let you or anyone else come back with this sort of tittle-tattle, for I don't like to hear it. The men you mention must be saints, if their life is what you describe as criminal." The captain went off, well rewarded for his charitable intentions.

The viceroy governed the empire gently and well in the little time he lived. Perhaps my country did not deserve such goodness: he was soon taken off to heaven. While he was sick, the judges ordered the serfdom of the Indians to be abolished, and it was published in the city of Lima, Cuzco, and other places with such rigorous conditions that another disturbance was caused. A gentleman called Luis de Vargas was beheaded as ringleader, but the punishment of the affair was not pressed forward for fear of inciting and scandalizing many others, since the investigation cast suspicion of responsibility on General Pedro de Hinojosa, three witnesses having accused him in their statements, though not directly. The judges elected him corregidor and chief justice in Los Charcas, to make an honest man of him, as Fernández says in Book II, ch. iii, for they had news that many soldiers were out of hand. Although the general at first refused the office, the senior of the judges, Dr. Saravia, spoke to him and persuaded him to accept, which in effect he did. The blame attributed to him was a question of suspicion rather than of fact. The soldiers themselves said that he held out hopes, some said certain hopes, others vague ones, that on getting to Charcas he would do what they wanted: let them go there and he would provide for them as best he could. Although the words were vague, the soldiers, who were in favor of any rebellion, took them and explained them according to their own taste and wishes. Whether the general intended to rebel or not was not then made clear, though signs were not lacking that he was ill rather than well disposed. All the soldiers in Lima who could went off to Charcas and wrote to their friends in various parts of the kingdom to follow them.

On this news, many soldiers reached Charcas. Among them was a gentleman called Don Sebastián de Castilla, a son of the count of La Gomera and brother to Don Baltasar de Castilla, who is often mentioned in our history. This gentleman left Cuzco with six other noble and famous soldiers, because Vasco Godínez, the chief promoter of the desired rebellion, had written to him in cypher, briefly announcing what they were proposing to do and saying that Pedro de Hinojosa had promised to be their general. Don Sebastián and his friends left Cuzco by night without saying where they were going, lest the corregidor should send people in pursuit of them. They threw the spies off the scent and travelled by devious paths and by-ways through villages, heaths, and deserts till they reached Potosí, where they were warmly received. Although the corregidor of Cuzco, on learning of their departure, sent men after them and warned the Spanish settlers to arrest them wherever they might be found, he had no success, for Don Sebastián's companions were experienced in the arts of peace and war. Don Sebastián himself was rather cut out for a court gallant than for the general of a rebellion such as was planned. Thus the poor gentleman soon perished, more owing to the treachery of those who had set him up as leader and because he would not execute the cruelties and murders they wanted than because of his own wicked acts, of which indeed he was innocent, as our history will say.

During these disturbances occurred the death of the good viceroy Don Antonio de Mendoza, an irreparable loss to the whole empire. His obsequies were attended with great mourning and all possible solemnity, and he was buried in the cathedral of Lima in a niche in the wall to the right of the high altar. The body of the marquis Francisco Pizarro lay on the viceroy's right, and some cavillers complained that as the marquis had been the conqueror of the empire and founder of the city his body should properly have been nearer the high altar than the viceroy's.

The *audiencia* appointed a gentleman called Gil Ramírez de Avalos, a servant of the viceroy, to be corregidor of Cuzco, and the marshal went to the city of La Paz, otherwise known as Pueblo Nuevo, where he had his allocation of Indians.

CHAPTER XX

Disturbances in the province of Charcas, and
many private quarrels, one of which is
recounted in particular.

AT THAT time the soldiers were so unruly in Peru, especially in Charcas and Potosí and their districts, that there were daily quarrels and duels, not only between the leading soldiers of renown, but also between merchants and traders, even including the people called *pulperos,* a name applied to the poorest dealers, because on one occasion an octopus [*pulpo*] was found for sale in one of their shops. These quarrels were so numerous and so continuous that it was impossible for the authorities to deal with them all. They hit upon the remedy of announcing publicly that no one was to make bold to reconcile those involved in duels, under pain of incurring the same penalties as for the crime itself. But this measure had no effect; nor did those of the ecclesiastical authorities, or the warnings included by preachers in their sermons. It seemed indeed that discord and all its ministers were scheming, plotting, and striving toward the revolution and open war that was to break out in that province a few months later.

Among the duels that occurred, some we might mention were worthy of record, for the participants agreed to fight in their shirts and breeches, or naked from the waist up, or in scarlet taffeta shirts and hose so as not to faint at the sight of the blood from their wounds. Some of the conditions were quite ridiculous; in short anyone who was challenged imposed any weapons and conditions he thought fit. They fought with seconds, each choosing his own, and usually went out into the fields in case anyone should try to stop them in the towns.

Fernández tells of one of the most famous combats of the time in his Book II, ch. iv. His version is short and confused, and we shall therefore tell it at length as it happened, for I knew one of those involved, whom I met in Madrid in 1563, when he still had the marks he had won in the encounter, which were the loss of the use of both arms, so that he could barely feed himself. The combat was between two famous soldiers, one called Pero Núñez, the one I knew (though Fernández calls him Diego Núñez), and the other Baltasar Pérez, both gentlemen who had a notable conceit of themselves.

Their quarrel arose from the satisfaction or nonsatisfaction of a point of honor in a combat between two others a few days before, when they had been the seconds. Baltasar Pérez now chose as his second a gentleman from Seville called Egas de Guzmán, one of the most famous knights in Peru among the many doughty swordsmen of the day. Another gentleman, Hernán Mejía, also from Seville, whom Egas de Guzmán used to speak ill of, out of the great conceit he had of his own valor, heard of the affair and on learning that Egas de Guzmán was to be the second of Baltasar Pérez pestered Pero Núñez until he agreed to take him as his second, his object being to pick a quarrel with Egas de Guzmán, a thing he greatly desired. When Egas de Guzmán heard this, he sent to Pero Núñez to say that as the two contestants and himself were noble gentlemen, they could not admit as second a man of base origin, the son of a mulatto woman who sold fried sardines in the square of San Salvador in Seville: let him pick someone else as second, even if he were not a nobleman, provided it were not anyone as base as Mejía. Pero Núñez, seeing that Egas was right, tried to persuade Mejía to release him from his promise to take him as second, but failed to move Mejía, who declared, among other things, that Egas was trying to prevent him from being present because he knew that he, Mejía, was greatly superior to him in the exercise of arms. When Egas heard that Mejía had refused to release his principal from his promise, he sent a message to him to say that he had better present himself well armed and warning him that he himself would appear in coat of mail and helmet, though their principals were to be naked from the belt up.

Consequently the two duellists went out naked and the seconds fully armed. The combat took place in the fields at a distance from Potosí. In the first encounter Pero Núñez, who was the strongest man then known, struck his opponent's sword from his hand, closed with him and knocked him down, and sitting athwart him threw handfuls of earth in his eyes and pummelled his face and chest, to avoid killing him with his dagger. In another part of the field, at a distance, the seconds were fighting, but Hernán Mejía feared to close with Egas de Guzmán because the latter was the sturdier and stronger of the two. Mejía held him off with his skill with the sword and quickness, in which he had the advantage, leaping from side to side, but without wounding or being wounded.

Seeing his principal in such a sorry plight, and himself unable to lay hands on his opponent, because he held him off, Egas de Guzmán took his sword by the guard and flung it at Mejía's face. To avoid the sword, Mejía looked away and thus permitted Egas de Guzmán to follow up and close with him, dagger in hand. He dealt Mejía a blow on the face, and the dagger entered a couple of fingers deep, where it broke off. Distracted with pain, Mejía fled across the field; and as he passed the place where the principals were situated as we have said, without looking who he was aiming at, he dealt a blow at his own principal and went on running, regardless of where he was going.

Egas de Guzmán hastened to help his principal and heard Pero Núñez saying to him: "It wasn't you who gave me this wound. It was my own second." With which words he pummelled him and threw earth in his eyes.

Egas de Guzmán came up, and exclaiming: "Damn it all, Master Pero Núñez, didn't I ask you not to bring such a vile second?" dealt him a blow with his knife. Pero Núñez defended himself with one arm and received a bad wound in it, then with the other, while Egas de Guzmán dealt him blows over his whole body until he was like a bundle of rags on the field.

Egas de Guzmán picked up his principal and collected all four swords, Mejía having dropped his in his distraction, and stuck them under his left arm. Taking his principal, who was unable to walk, on his back, he carried him to the nearest house, which was a hostel for sick Indians. There he left him, and told them that there was a dead man on the field, whom they had better go and bury. He took refuge in a church. Pero Núñez was taken to hospital and treated; he recovered from his wounds, but his arms remained useless, as we have said. Mejía died of the wound in his head, it being impossible to extract the point of the dagger.

There were a great many more duels in those days, not only between residents in the towns, but between travellers on the roads, some of whom I knew and whose quarrels I could relate. But let the one incident I have mentioned stand for all.

CHAPTER XXI

*A single combat between Martín de Robles and
Pablo de Meneses; the satisfaction given in
it; Pedro de Hinojosa's departure for
Charcas; the great number of soldiers
he found ready for a rising; the
warning given the corregidor;
the vain hopes with which
he entertained the soldiers.*

FERNÁNDEZ mentions other duels and private quarrels such as that between Martín de Robles and Pablo de Meneses and other persons of consequence. I could repeat a great deal of what I heard at the time in conversation about these affairs, but most of what was said was making fun of those involved and not of any moment. In order to inflame passions and stir up public scandals with a view to serving their own purposes, the soldiers used to circulate falsehoods and bear witness to the detriment and dishonor of the wealthy citizens, inventing calumnies touching their honor, so as to give greater offence and provoke them to seek vengeance more furiously. They thus put it about that Pablo de Meneses, then corregidor of Charcas, had committed adultery with Martín de Robles' wife. Fernández has long chapters on this, but we shall only give the substance of the matter, to avoid prolixity.

The fact is that when the supposed wrong had been much noised abroad by soldiers who supported one side or the other and it was expected that an armed conflict would break out, the parties agreed that Pablo de Meneses should prove that what was said was false and a clear and manifest lie by announcing his betrothal to a daughter of Martín de Robles, who was then a child barely seven years old, while he was more than seventy. Both sides agreed to this, and the soldiers of both parties regarded themselves as defrauded and insulted, the more so when they knew that Martín de Robles, who prided himself on his witticisms, was going about ridiculing his own supporters as well as those of the other side. One of his jokes was to say: "What do you think of my friends and enemies? Don't you think they look a pretty parcel of fools?"

Fernández, mentioning the betrothal in his Second Part, Book II, says:

So that after many discussions and toings and froings it was concluded that Pablo de Meneses should marry Doña María, Martín de Robles' daughter, who would then have been about seven. Her father offered a dowry of 34,000 castilians, which he undertook to pay when his daughter was twelve. Thus ended the differences between Pablo de Meneses and Martín de Robles, to the consequent sorrow and despair of a great number of soldiers who had hastened to enlist with both sides on the supposition that somehow or other the whole country would fall into civil strife and they would all repair their own fortunes by calmly robbing other people, each already imagining himself as the master of a great allocation.

With this our author terminates the five long chapters he writes on these quarrels to which evil speakers used to apply one of the great oaths. The marriage did not last long owing to the disproportion between the ages of the parties. Pablo de Meneses died within a few years of its consummation. His spouse, though still not twelve years of age, inherited her husband's Indians, and exchanging the old pot for a new one (as Pedro de Alvarado's ladies used to say), she married a youth of twenty, a relative of Pablo de Meneses: it seemed a sort of recompense. We have somewhat anticipated events here, but the anecdote is relevant at this point.

Shortly before the pact just mentioned, General Pedro de Hinojosa reached Charcas to take up his duties as corregidor and chief magistrate of the Silver City and its provinces. He found far more soldiers than he had expected, for they had been drawn there by the hopes he had given them, or they thought he had given them from his vague speeches, some calling others. The general was sorely perplexed to know how to find them lodging or supplies, and had an angry altercation about this with Martín de Robles and Pablo de Meneses, who objected to putting his guests up. The general said that as they had summoned the soldiers to make use of them in their notorious quarrels, it was up to them to supply them with the necessities of life and see that they did not starve. Martín de Robles replied that they alone were not to be blamed for calling in the soldiers, since many others were involved. He spoke in broad terms implying that the general had called them in, for Martín de Robles was proud of speaking deviously on all occasions, as we shall see later in reporting his sayings.

These people and others like them thus cast the blame for their actions on the shoulders of others, and the Silver City and its neighborhood reached such a pitch of disturbance that some of the citizens went away, some repairing to other towns and others to their Indians, thus avoiding the unruly licence of the soldiers. These were now so open in their preparations for rebellion that on many occasions they addressed the general with requests that he should fulfil the promise he had more than once made them, to become their chief and leader when he arrived in Charcas. The time had fallen due, so let the rebellion begin: they could wait no longer. The general held them off with new hopes, telling them that he was expecting the authorization of the royal *audiencia* to act as general in any new war that might break out, and that this would be a better pretext and enable him to do what they wanted with more authority.

He held off the soldiers with this and similar devices, but was in reality far from falling in with their expectations. Although it is true that he had made promises in confused and equivocal terms in the city of Lima, as has been said, now that he saw himself the possessor of an income of 200,000 pesos a year, he wanted to enjoy it in peace, and not to lose in a second rebellion what he had won so easily at the expense of others in the first. Seeing his lukewarmness, the soldiers tried to divert their rebellious designs in another direction. They arranged to kill the general and make Don Sebastián de Castilla their leader. He was their great favorite.

This was talked of so openly that everyone knew about it, and many citizens and others who only desired the peace of the land warned the corregidor to take care of his own safety and to rid the land of the soldiers before they killed him and ruined it. In particular Licentiate Polo Ondegardo spoke to him, and among other things, said: "Corregidor, make me your deputy for a month, no longer, and I will guarantee your life, which is in great danger, and free the city of the fear of revolt, which these military gentlemen are so set on."

But the corregidor was so confident in his great wealth and the influence of his office, and his valiant deeds (as though he had ever performed any) that he took no notice of what he was told, or of what he saw with his own eyes.

CHAPTER XXII

*Many other warnings conveyed to the general
in various ways; his bold words and
lukewarmness; the soldiers
plot to kill him.*

THE SOLDIERS went a good deal further than we have said, dropping strong letters addressed to Don Sebastián de Castilla or to famous leaders, warning them to beware of the corregidor because he wanted to kill them. They also sent letters to the corregidor threatening to murder him. These letters were then made known and circulated to kindle indignation, as Diego Fernández de Palencia writes at length with much repetition. In order to conclude what we have to say of these stratagems and wiles, we shall quote part of his ch. xi of his Second Book, as follows:

At the same time Licentiate Polo had often warned Pedro de Hinojosa about all this, and urged him to order an investigation and apply the appropriate penalties; but as his pleas were in vain, he addressed himself to the superior of St. Francis after mass on Saturday, March 4, begging him to speak to Hinojosa, and persuade him to take steps to mend matters, telling him that he had been asked to do so under the seal of confession. This was done, but it met with a poor response from Hinojosa.

The same day after dinner, Martín de Robles said as much to him in the presence of some of the citizens, telling him roundly that the soldiers meant to kill him. But as Hinojosa was still on bad terms with Robles and the quarrel about billeting men on him was recent, Hinojosa told him he only said this to get witnesses. Licentiate Polo, who was present, told him with some heat to look to his own safety: if Martín Robles gave him the sort of information he had given, he had better accept it and act on it, for should it turn out to be false, he would have good reason to punish Robles. Nevertheless, he, Polo, was sure that everyone, down to the very stones in the streets, would say the same. He should therefore institute an investigation at once, since the case was a thorny and difficult one, and if things did not turn out to be as he had been told, he could take him, Polo, and cut his head off. But Pedro de Hinojosa refused steadfastly to temporize, haughtily and boastfully asserting that all the soldiers together would not dare to lift a finger if he set about them. Then he changed the subject, forbidding anyone to say any more about the business.

The next day, Sunday afternoon, Hinojosa was talking amicably with Martín de Robles, Pedro Hernández Paniagua, and others and that evening Juan de Huarte and some other soldiers went to visit him to see what sort of attitude he would adopt toward them, so as to judge from his appearance, like good astrologers, the inclination of his heart. They certainly regarded him as a straightforward man with little power of dissimulation. After talking with him, they concluded that he had received them with pleasure and was glad to converse with them. As far as the presence of the soldiers was concerned, he said that he was delighted to see so many brave men as he had in his jurisdiction and swore that all the flower of Peru was in the town. They were not a little pleased with this and took leave of Pedro de Hinojosa, reporting their impressions to Don Sebastián and the other conspirators. They then decided to force an issue in the game, and all swore to gather that night and go forth in the morning to begin the revolt, their long and laborious pregnancy thus ending in an abortion.

Thus Fernández ends the chapter under question. The soldiers were unable to abide further delay in a culmination they so greatly desired and agreed by common consent to slay the general and rise up in revolt. The ringleaders in this were Don Sebastián de Castilla, Egas de Guzmán, Vasco Godínez, Baltasar Velázquez, Licentiate Gómez Hernández, and other prominent soldiers. The most part and the best of them were then in the Silver City, and as has been said they had summoned one another for the purpose. Egas de Guzmán had come to this consultation with the intention of asking the general to obtain him a royal pardon for the death of Hernán Mejía. The good general was so careless of his own interests and the peril he was in that he agreed and gave Guzmán letters of recommendation addressed to the secular and ecclesiastical authorities in Potosí, because it was there that Guzmán said he had to clear himself.

The soldiers, now resolved on rebellion, sent a message to the garrison of Potosí by Egas de Guzmán that as soon as they heard of the death of the general they were to rise with all their friends in Potosí. They made the plans that seemed good to them, and foregathered in the house of one of their number, Hernando Guillada, where they planned to execute the deed the following morning at daybreak. So Don Sebastián de Castilla chose seven companions to go with him to kill the general. They all agreed not to go about in a large group, lest they should arouse suspicions and cause the general's doors to be shut, or the alarm to be given, and so miscarry. Garci Tello de Guzmán stayed in the house with fourteen or fifteen companions. They were to go separately by different streets to the general's house and help Don Sebastián if he needed them. Nine or ten more soldiers shut themselves up in Hernando Pizarro's house, which was now ownerless and abandoned: these were led by one Gómez Mogollón and had the same scheme as the others. Thus the night passed. At dawn, they sent spies out to the crossroads, to see if there was any stir in the city or in the general's house, with instructions to give the word at once if they found it open, so that the attack could take place and the general be slain in bed before he could get up.

CHAPTER XXIII

*Don Sebastián de Castilla and his companions kill
the corregidor Pedro de Hinojosa and his deputy
Alonso de Castro; some of the citizens flee and
others are arrested; the officers
appointed by the rebels.*

WARNED by his spies that the general's house was open, Don Sebastián left his lair with his seven companions. Although they were all picked men, they were so frightened that some were on the point of swooning and others as overwrought as Fernández says, just as if they had to attack a whole company in battle formation, whereas they were going to kill a gentleman who, as they knew, had taken no precautions for his safety. At last, they entered the house, coming first on the corregidor's deputy, Alonso de Castro. Seeing that they were in revolt, he tried to override them with the authority of his office, crying: "What disturbance is this, gentlemen? Long live the king!"

Don Sebastián laid his hand on his sword and said: "It's too late to go into that."

The deputy, seeing the naked sword, turned on his heel and fled, and one of the soldiers, Anselmo de Ervias, ran after him and catching him up, ran him through with so strong a blow that it pinned him to the wall and the point of the sword was bent back a little, and when he tried to strike him two or three times more, the sword would not enter, and Ervias exclaimed: "Oh, you treacherous dog, what a tough hide you've got!"

Some others then helped to finish him off. They then went to General Pedro de Hinojosa's apartment, but not finding him there or elsewhere in the house, they began to be badly scared, supposing or suspecting that he had fled.

Two of them leaned out of the windows giving on to the street, shouting: "The tyrant's dead! The tyrant's dead!" but without having found him; the only motive of their cries was to call their friends to help them before the townspeople should come to save the general. Those who had stayed in the courtyard then went in and searched the whole house, as far as the outhouses, and it was in one of these where he had gone to relieve himself that he was found by a soldier, who said: "Come out, for Don Sebastián de Castilla and some other gentlemen have come to kiss your hand and have speech with you." This he said jestingly, making fun of the general.

The general came out in his dressing gown, and at the courtyard gate a soldier called Gonzalo de Mata blocked his way, saying, as Fernández records in his ch. xii: "Sir, these gentlemen want you to be their general and father."

The general raised his voice and said with a smile: "They want me? Well, here I am, gentlemen; tell me what you wish."

To which Garci Tello de Guzmán replied: "It's too late, damn you. Don Sebastián's a good enough general for us."

So saying, he ran him through with his sword which sank in almost to the hilt, and he fell to the ground at once. He struggled to rise, but Antonio de Sepúlveda and Anselmo de Ervias ran up and struck him down again with two more blows. He began to shout "Confession, gentlemen!" And so they left him for dead.

At this moment Don Garci Tello came down, and when they told him the general was dead, he ordered them to go back and make quite sure, so that there could be no possibility of mistake, for so much depended on it. Anselmo de Ervias then returned to where the general was lying on the ground, and struck him a great blow in the head with his dagger; which finished him off at once. They then ran out into the square crying: "Long live the king! The tyrant is dead!"—the word is commonly applied to traitors in Peru. They at once robbed and sacked the whole house, and nothing at all was left in it, etc.

This is from Fernández. The great blow in the head which he says Ervias dealt the general was not with his sword, but with a bar of silver he took from one of the rooms, where he found a pile of them like bricks in a kiln. As he struck the blow, he said: "Take your wealth, since you had so much of it that you wouldn't keep your promise to us to be our leader."

When the general was dead, they went about shouting: "Long live the king, long live the king. The skin-flint traitor who broke his word is dead!"

At this point Garci Tello de Guzmán appeared with his fifteen companions, and they divided into two groups, one to go and kill Pablo de Meneses and the other Martín de Robles: all the soldiers were greatly opposed to both of them because of the way in which they had brought the soldiers together to make use of them in their past quarrels and then deceived and taunted them, as our history has told.

Martín de Robles was warned by an Indian servant what was afoot, and had no other recourse but to leap into the yard of the house in his shirt, and so avoid being murdered. Pablo de Meneses had left the city during the night, out of fear and anger at the mounting lawlessness of the soldiers. He repaired to a property he had near the city, where he was warned by his followers and fled in haste to avoid capture.

Finding they had left their houses, the soldiers stole everything they found in them and went out to the square to join Don Sebastián. They attacked the homes of other citizens, all of whom they hated and envied. They arrested Pedro Hernández Paniagua, the gentleman who had acted as President La Gasca's messenger and borne his letters to Gonzalo Pizarro. The reward of this journey had been a good allocation of Indians in the Silver City. They also arrested Juan Ortiz de Zárate, Antonio Alvarez, and such other citizens as they could lay hands on. Although these people knew that the soldiers were out of hand, they took no precautions and were therefore captured. Licentiate Polo escaped on a good horse, after being forewarned by an Indian house servant, or *yanacuna*.

The other soldiers, who had scattered throughout the city, soon collected in the square. One of them, Tello de Vega, nicknamed "Fool," got an Indian flag and hoisted it in the square, as Fernández says in his ch. xiv:

Drummers and criers announced that all residents and visitors in the town must appear in the square, and form companies under arms, on pain of death. There appeared one Rodrigo de Orellana, who was an *alcalde ordinario*, though he left his wand of office at home. Juan Ramón and Licentiate Gómez Hernández also presented themselves. A roll of those present was made, as they went into the church by one door and came out by another, and 150 men were counted. Don Sebastián was named captain general and chief justice, and two days later he freed the arrested citizens who elected him at a town meeting, nominating Licentiate Gómez Hernández as his deputy. He appointed Hernando Guillada and Garci Tello de Vega captains, Pedro del Castillo captain of artillery, Alvar Pérez Payán treasurer and quartermaster general, and Diego Pérez de la Entrada senior alguacil and Bartolomé de Santa Ana junior.

This is quoted word for word from Fernández. Rodrigo de Orellana was a citizen of Silver City; he joined the rebels out of fear rather than conviction. The same was true of other citizens and many well-known soldiers, who were good servants of His Majesty, but now joined the rebels because they were the more numerous and were equipped with all manner of weapons to kill any who opposed them: there was therefore no alternative.

CHAPTER XXIV

Precautions and measures taken by Don Sebastián;
his instructions to Egas de Guzmán to rebel
in Potosí and the strange events
that took place there.

DON SEBASTIÁN also appointed one of the soldiers who was his most intimate friend, called Diego Méndez, to be captain of his guard. Thirteen others chosen from among the bravest and most friendly toward Don Sebastián were appointed to form the guard, so that the leader's person might be as well protected as possible. But when the poor gentleman needed them, he found none of them.

He then sent another soldier called García de Bazán with a troop of men to Pedro de Hinojosa's allocation to seize the slaves, horses, and other property of the dead general, and also to bring in all the soldiers who dwelt in that district, many of whom lived among the Indians because they had no money to buy clothes: what was imported from Spain was very dear, and among the Indians they managed as best they could. Don Sebastián instructed them to arrest Diego de Almendras, who was on Hinojosa's allocation. He despatched the soldiers in pursuit of Licentiate Polo, but neither of these troops did what it was ordered, for Polo reached the place where Diego de Almendras was and warned him of Hinojosa's death. Almendras collected what slaves he could of the many Hinojosa possessed, together with seven horses belonging to the general, and made off with Polo, putting a good distance between themselves and the rebels so as not to fall into their hands. Don Sebastián likewise sent two soldiers to Potosí, to advise Egas de Guzmán of what had happened and instruct him to rebel in that town.

All these steps, like those mentioned in the last chapter, were taken on the day of Hinojosa's murder, and simply served to hasten Don Sebastián's own death. The messengers who went to Potosí made such good speed that they arrived the next morning at daybreak, despite the fact that they had eighteen leagues of rough road to cover and a sizable river to cross. When Egas de Guzmán heard the news, he called together the soldiers he had ready for the deed, and they, together with the messengers who brought the news, armed only with swords and daggers and wrapped in their cloaks, went to the houses of Gómez de Solis and Martín de Almendras, the brother of Diego de Almendras, and arrested them with the greatest of ease, conveying them to the town hall, where they were manacled and chained and put in a room with guards to watch them. The news of this great feat brought in more soldiers who joined Egas de Guzmán and went to the royal mint. They seized the treasurer, Francisco de Isásiga, and the accountant, Hernando de Alvarado, broke open the royal treasure chests, and stole all they found—a quantity of silver worth more than 1,500,000.

They then announced that everyone was to assemble in the square and form companies, under pain of death if they disobeyed. Egas de Guzmán appointed a soldier called Antonio de Luján as senior alcalde. He celebrated his assumption of office by killing the accountant Hernando de Alvarado, whom he accused of plotting a rebellion with Pedro de Hinojosa, and whom he had executed on this charge. Egas de Guzmán hurriedly detached six or seven soldiers to go to the place called Porcu, and collect all the men, weapons, and horses he could find there and in the district. At the time a certain knight of the order of St. John was there among his Indians, of whom he had a considerable allocation. When he heard of the death of Hinojosa, he wrote a letter to Don Sebastián congratulating him on this feat, and suggested that he should send twenty arquebusiers to arrest him and he would then go with them to arrest Goméz de Alvarado and Lorenzo de Aldana, who were nearby. He warned Don Sebastián not to send the men by the main road, but by paths and by-ways, to avoid being noticed and raising suspicions of the purpose of their journey. The good knight later paid for this, as we shall tell.

The day after the death of General Hinojosa, Baltasar Velázquez and Vasco Godínez reached the city: the latter was the heart and soul of the rebellion, and did more than anyone to bring it about, as we shall see. The two of them came for the same purpose as Don Sebastián, and Fernández describes how they reached Silver City on the morrow of Hinojosa's death in his ch. xv:

When Don Sebastián was preparing to go out and receive them they appeared in the town square. Don Sebastián went cheerfully toward them, and Godínez advanced to meet him. Both dismounted and greeted one another warmly, embracing with every sign of mutual trust. Vasco Godínez said to Don Sebastián: "Sir, this glorious deed that I so much desired came to my ears five leagues away."

Don Sebastián, standing bareheaded, replied: "These gentlemen have chosen me as their general and entrusted me with this responsibility. I accepted it until such time as you should arrive: now that you are here, I renounce it and confer it on you."

Vasco Godínez answered: "No, indeed: the responsibility is in good hands, and I have labored for no other purpose than to see you exercise it."

After this exchange of compliments, the two of them retired and conversed together for a while in secret. After this Don Sebastián ordered an announcement to be made that everyone should obey Vasco Godínez as commander under pain of death, and that Baltasar Velázquez was appointed captain of cavalry. This done, Don Sebastián told Vasco Godínez: "Sir, it was not possible to await your arrival for time was pressing, but so far all has gone well. From now on command as you think fit."

Godínez replied saying that they could not go wrong then or in the future by following this plan and that he trusted in God that the labors the present affair involved him in would bring them all ease. He then said publicly that it had been a good thing that the affair began in his absence, since they had not killed Alonso de Alvarado. If the news had caught him not so far away, he and his companions would have returned to see to this. Don Sebastián then ordered a council of war to discuss this. Those who took part were Vasco Godínez, Baltasar Velázquez, Juan Ramón, Licentiate Gómez Hernández, Hernando Guillada, Diego de Avalos, Pedro del Castillo, and Don Garci Tello, with a few others. Vasco Godínez offered to lead the expedition, but Don Sebastián said he had already promised Juan Ramón the duty, and therefore a band of twenty-five soldiers was prepared to go under the command of Juan Ramón and Don García and take the city of La Paz. Vasco Godínez said that if they wrote letters to Juan de Vargas and Martín de Olmos, this could be achieved without difficulty: he offered to write the letters and did so.

Thus far Fernández.

CHAPTER XXV

*Don Sebastián and his officers send captains and
soldiers to kill the marshal; Juan Ramón, their
leader, disarms Don García and his supporters; at
this news, Don Sebastián is killed by those
who made him their leader.*

CONTINUING his story, the same writer says in his ch.xv:
Then they drew up the roll of those who were to go and made them ready
to leave the next day, giving them arms and horses for the journey. Thus on
Wednesday morning, the party left: it consisted of Juan Ramón, Don Garci
Tello, Gómez Mogollón, Gonzalo de Mata, Francisco de Añasco, Almansa
(Hernando de Soria), Pedro de Castro, Mateo de Castañeda, Campofrío de
Carvajal, Juan Nieto, Pedro Franco de Solís, Baltasar de Escobedo, Diego
Maldonado, Pedro de Murguía, Rodrigo de Arévalo, Antonio Altamirano,
Lucena, and Hermosilla. As they left the town, Vasco Godínez sent a message
to Egas de Guzmán to send what men he could to help Juan Ramón and
Don García. The letter he wrote is as follows:

"My beloved brother: The general has sent our brother Don García and
Juan Ramón to Pueblo Nuevo to arrest our friend the marshal. Once he is
taken and killed, nothing will stand between us and victory. Twenty-five
mounted men are going on this mission and they are such that I would make
bold to confront the whole human race with them, so I am sure that there is
no possible risk of failure. I therefore urge you to prepare and take up arms,
brother, for the general says, and I fully agree, that you should send well-
equipped men to help our friends. As seen from here, we all think you have
shown great mercy in sparing the life of Gómez de Solis; mercy is all very well,
but not too much of it."

When Egas de Guzmán received this letter, he at once ordered fifty-five men
to prepare to go to Juan Ramón's help, sending Gabriel de Pernia as captain
and Alonso de Arriaza as ensign, with orders to follow Juan Ramón as far as
Pueblo Nuevo. They duly made ready and set off with their flag flying. Among
them were Ordoño de Valencia, one-eyed Diego de Tapia, Francisco de Chaves
(a mulatto), Juan de Cepeda, Francisco Pacheco, Pero Hernández de la En-

trada, Alonso Marquina, Pedro de Benavides, Juan Márquez, Luis de Estrada, Melchor Pacho, Antonio de Avila, and others, fifty-five in all.

Thus far Fernández. Once Don Sebastián de Castilla's rebellion was achieved, the soldiers who planned and executed it set about unseating and killing the leader they themselves had set up, for in the empire of Peru from the wars of Gonzalo Pizarro onwards, whenever a rebel leader set up, his followers at once turned their backs on him and killed him, and then represented it as great service entitling them to be rewarded with allocations. Juan Ramón, who was picked as leader with Don García to go to the city of La Paz and kill Marshal Alonso de Alvarado, before leaving Silver City, discussed with some of his friends the advisability of repudiating Don García and Don Sebastián and going over to His Majesty's service. As they all harbored the designs we have said, they readily assented to Juan Ramón's plan, and set off with this excellent intention. On the way Don García heard what Juan Ramón proposed to do, for the plotters betrayed one another, but he did not act on the information, and being an inexperienced youth with little practice of warfare, he cherished illusions that were to do him more harm than good, and went on his way without even advising his friends to be on their guard.

On the second day out Juan Ramón discovered that Don García had heard about his amiable intentions, for all the men doublecrossed both parties repeating what was said by each to the other. Juan Ramón therefore decided to anticipate events, and giving the word to his friends, disarmed and dismounted five of Don García's closest adherents who had remained behind, Don García himself having gone on ahead. They then caught up with Don García and four others who were with him, and removed their lances, arquebusses, and horses, but left them their swords, so as not to offend them too much. Don García now regretted he had not done to Juan Ramón what Juan Ramón had done to him, and offered to go in his company to serve His Majesty, but his opponent refused so as not to share the merits of this service.

Seeing how they were left, Don García and his friends decided to return to Don Sebastián de Castilla, sending a soldier called Rodrigo de Arévalo to warn him what had happened. He reached the city, as Fernández tells, at nine at night on March 11. The people in the city were still camped in the square in battle formation, and when they saw Arévalo coming on foot and with a downcast and forlorn expression on his face, such as can be readily imagined, all those who saw him were dismayed, and so was Don Sebastián when he was told. He called a council of those he regarded as his best friends, Vasco Godínez, Baltasar Velázquez, and Tello de Vega, and asked them their opinion. They disagreed, and could not decide on any course of action.

Then Vasco Godínez, who had been the most active in stirring up this treacherous rising, as he himself had said, took Don Sebastián aside and said to him in private: "Sir, in order to assure yourself of success, you must give orders to kill eighteen or twenty well-known soldiers from the company in the square, who are notoriously supporters of the king. If we get rid of them, all the rest are our friends, and we can rely on them and carry on with our scheme with every prospect of success."

Don Sebastián who, as we have said, was a high-minded youth, of very different character from Vasco Godínez, replied: "What have those gentlemen done to me that I should kill them and commit so great and surprising a piece of cruelty? If it is necessary for me to kill them, I would rather they killed me."

Hardly had Vasco Godínez heard him than he changed his mind, and determined to kill Don Sebastián, as the latter would not kill those he regarded as enemies. Godínez said: "Wait for me here. I shall come straight back."

He then went out into the square where the company was and sought out one by one the men he had suggested should be killed. Finding them dispersed and being unable to speak to them because of the number of people who were present, he took each of them by the hand and pressed it hard two or three times. This was a pre-arranged signal to warn them to stand by him in the act of treachery he was contemplating. This done he returned home, and finding Licentiate Gómez Hernández, outlined to him what he had in mind, saying that it was to the advantage of them all, for His Majesty would naturally reward such an outstanding service: let him call his known friends, so that they might help to execute the deed. Gómez Hernández went out into the square and called some of them by name, but none dare reply to his call, for they all feared some disaster.

Gómez Hernández went in again, and accompanied Vasco Godínez to where Don Sebastián was. Both came to grips with him and stabbed him many times, and though he was wearing a coat of mail, they wounded him badly. Baltasar Velázquez, who was near Don Sebastián at the opening of this inspiring scene, when he saw they were attacking him, shouted and ran away, but finding that they were killing him, went to help them, so as to have a share in the victory. He stabbed Don Sebastián, while another came up with a partisan and dealt many blows, not sparing the friends who were busy stabbing, and who received their share, as Fernández says, in ch. xvi.

Don Sebastián got away from them, sorely wounded, and retired to a dark closet: if, having got so far, he had managed to get out by the street door into the square where the armed company were waiting, there would have been further bloodshed and butchery. Baltasar Velázquez and four or five others entered the room where Don Sebastián was, but as it was dark, they dared not hit out with their weapons for fear of wounding one another. However, Baltasar Velázquez bade them go out into the square and announce that Don Sebastián was dead, so as to prevent his friends coming in to help him, saying that he would stay and finish him off. So he and they went about their tasks: Baltasar Velázquez found Don Sebastián and stabbed him repeatedly in the head and neck. The poor gentleman pleaded for confession, shouting and screaming until he could no longer speak. Then Velázquez left him to go and look for someone to help to drag the body out to show to the company. He called for Diego de Avalos and Licentiate Hernández, and when they reached the place where he had left Don Sebastián, they found that he had crawled to the door of the room

where he lay panting, and there they dealt him many more blows until they were sure he was dead. It was about ten o'clock at night. Vasco Godínez was wounded in the right hand in the struggle. They then dragged Don Sebastián's body outside to the company, shouting: "Long live the king, the tyrant is dead!"

And Vasco Godínez came out crying: "Long live the king. The tyrant is dead, and I killed him!" Though to my mind, anyone who thought that the murderers were just as much tyrants as the dead man, or more so, would certainly not be far wrong. They were as great rebels as he or greater, and their offence was the greater in that they were officers of justice.

Thus far Fernández, in the aforementioned chapter.

CHAPTER XXVI

The election of civil and military officers;
Vasco Godínez's election as general;
the death of Don García and many
others without confession.

As has been said, Don Sebastián was slain by the very men who persuaded and forced him to kill the corregidor, General Pedro de
Hinojosa. And now the corregidor's murderers set themselves up as
judges to gain credit and merits in His Majesty's service, having betrayed
their king and their own friends once, twice, and three times, as the
sentence passed on Vasco Godínez a few months later ran. He indeed
was the architect of the whole villainous episode. Only five days passed
from the death of General Pedro de Hinojosa to that of General Don
Sebastián de Castilla: the former is said to have taken place on March 6
and the latter on March 11, 1553. Having killed Don Sebastián, Vasco
Godínez and his companions released Juan Ortiz de Zárate and Pedro
Hernández Paniagua from prison and chains and set them free, impress-
ing on them that they had done everything in order to free them and the
whole city from inevitable death and destruction at the hands of the
rebels, and therefore in His Majesty's service. In particular, Vasco Godínez made the following remarks, recorded by Fernández in his ch. xvii:
"Gentlemen, I beg you for the love of God that, since I am deprived of
the use of my hand, you will go to this company and encourage the men,
and exhort them to serve His Majesty." But as Juan Ortiz de Zárate saw
that all the delinquents and murderers of Hinojosa were in the company
and its captain was one of the chief aggressors, Hernando Guillada, partly
because he was afraid of being killed and partly because he thought it
politic, he shouted to everyone to accept Guillada as captain.

Thus far Fernández. Juan Ortiz de Zárate's suggestion was accepted,
since it seemed to offer protection against his enemies. Vasco Godínez
went in to treat the wound in his hand, making more of it than of the
death of Don Sebastián. The same night he sent six arquebusiers to stand
guard on the road to Potosí, so that the news of what had happened
should not reach Egas de Guzmán. He arrested three of the soldiers who

had been his most intimate friends and had them garrotted before day-break, because they knew all about his intrigues, trickeries, and betrayals.

As soon as day came, he called Juan Ortiz de Zárate, Pedro Hernández Paniagua, Antonio Alvarez, and Martín Monge who were citizens of the place (there were no others at the time), and explained to them with great exaggeration all the dangers he had incurred in killing the rebel and the great service he had rendered His Majesty, the city in general, and themselves in particular. In gratitude for his services, he begged them to elect him chief justice of the city and its district and appoint him captain general in the war, since Egas de Guzmán was still in power with a great force at Potosí; he also asked that Hinojosa's Indians who had been left ownerless, should be entrusted to him. The citizens replied that they had no power to make such elections and were afraid of being punished if they did. But Juan Ortiz, seeing that they would be in trouble if they resisted, said, more out of fear than any sense of gratitude, that if Licentiate Gómez Hernández, who was a man of law, would give his opinion that they were qualified to elect, they would willingly do so. The man of law said they were, especially as Vasco Godínez had requested it, for his services certainly deserved such recompense. They then called a scribe, and in his presence appointed Vasco Godínez chief justice and captain general, depositing General Pedro de Hinojosa's Indians in his hands: together with the mines they were worth, as we have said, 200,-000 silver pesos. A worthy reward for two such notable betrayals as this man conceived, elaborated, and carried through: his intention was always to possess himself of that allocation by hook or by crook. The worthy man of law also arranged for another large allocation called Puna to be entrusted to himself. Of this Fernández says: "It certainly seems that they wanted to feather their own nests, and to make a good bargain and return for the esteem the soldiers had held them in, the terror the citizens had of them, and the fear that they would turn out to be harsher than Don Sebastián had been." Thus far Fernández.

They then appointed Licentiate Gómez Hernández deputy general of the army, and Juan Ortiz de Zárate and Pedro del Castillo captains of infantry. This choice was intended to show that they did not want to monopolize the military offices, but share them with the *vecinos*: the latter accepted them out of fear, rather than as honors. It was proclaimed that everyone was to obey Vasco Godínez as general and Baltasar Velázquez as commander. Six soldiers were sent to arrest Don García and the soldiers accompanying him on their return from the glorious expedition to murder Alonso de Alvarado.

On taking over his duties as commander, Baltasar Velázquez had two famous soldiers who came from Potosí with despatches from Egas de Guzmán to Don Sebastián de Castilla drawn and quartered. He also had another soldier called Francisco de Villalobos garrotted, and gave orders for two soldiers who were among his closest supporters to have their hands cut off. The other soldiers interceded for them, and he granted that each should lose only one hand. The good commander achieved all this within four hours of his appointment.

The next day Martín de Robles, Pablo de Meneses, Diego de Almendras, and Diego Velázquez, who were fleeing from the soldiers so as not to fall into their hands, entered the city. Others of less account came with them. When Vasco de Godínez, who was in bed pretending to be severely wounded, heard this, he sent for Ortiz de Zárate and asked him to persuade Pablo de Meneses and Martín de Robles and the other newcomers to hold a town meeting and approve and confirm his election as chief justice and captain general and the bestowal on him of Pedro de Hinojosa's Indians. They gave answer that they had no authority to approve anything of the sort, but advised him as friends to drop his claims so that it should not appear that he had killed Don Sebastián de Castilla to feather his own nest and not to serve His Majesty. This reply greatly angered Vasco Godínez who shouted that he would be damned if he didn't make short work of anyone who tried to cast aspersions on his honor. He ordered them all to attend a town meeting and put seventy or eighty soldiers at the door of the council chamber with orders to kill anyone who opposed anything he wanted. When Pablo de Meneses and his friends saw this they gave their consent to the appointments and a great deal more than they were asked, though very much against their real feelings. This was because Licentiate Gómez Hernández persuaded and assured them that otherwise they would all be killed. Vasco Godínez was delighted to have been approved by two town meetings, though the fact was to contribute to his undoing.

Riba Martín, who had gone as the leader of five arquebusiers told off to take Don García Tello de Guzmán, arrested him five leagues from the city. Don García was full of confidence in the favor and protection he expected to receive from Don Sebastián and his friends, and when he heard that Vasco Godínez, Baltasar Velázquez, and Gómez Hernández, who were Don Sebastián's closest friends and those who had been most prominent in the rebellion and in killing Pedro de Hinojosa, had turned on Don Sebastián and killed him, he was astonished and bewildered, for it seemed impossible that those who had so urged Don Sebastián to kill

Hinojosa, should have killed him, especially as each of them was incomparably more guilty and more deeply implicated in the revolt than the latter. As one well versed in their intrigues and trickery, he told Riba Martín that he had no doubt that they would murder him in the heat of the moment, so as to prevent his having time or opportunity to say what he knew of their misdeeds. So it turned out. As soon as he entered the city, Vasco Godínez, as Fernández tells in his ch. xix, "ordered Baltasar de Velázquez to despatch him at once so that he should not reveal their intrigues." These are our author's own words, and he adds a little later:

He warned him that he was soon to die and that he had better ask for confession. Juan Ortiz de Zárate had come in, and Don García begged him to try to arrange for him to be given time that day to meditate over his sins and beg God's forgiveness for them, for he was young and had been a great sinner. Then Baltasar Velázquez came in, but took no notice of Juan Ortiz's pleading, turning him out and telling Don García that he was to die in less than an hour, and therefore had better quickly compose his spirit. When he had confessed, Velázquez was in a great hurry to make an end of him, and the confession was hardly over when they took him to the garrotte. The cord broke, and while a new one was being put round his neck, it seemed to Baltasar Velázquez that the delay was excessive, and he pulled his sword out of his belt and cut off Don García's head with it. Juan Ortiz de Zárate had the body covered and buried. Some others were then executed, and no confession or trial was permitted in the case of those who might reveal that they were the authors and instigators of the rebellion.

Thus far Fernández (ch. xix). A little before he says the following on the same subject:

The core of his policy was to kill a great many people without letting them confess, for fear they should reveal his schemes and intrigues. As to those who were not guilty in the recent plot, if he felt absolutely confident that they would keep secret his part in bringing it about, he let them off with light punishments, shook hands with them, and gave them help on their way. In all this he twisted justice according to the dictates of his own interests.

This is from Fernández and is the end of his ch. xviii. He is quite right. Thus, and even more, should we abominate the cruelty and wickedness these men committed against their own friends, having themselves devised and executed the murder of Pedro de Hinojosa, a deed they had planned more than three years before, if he should refuse to become their leader. It cannot be overemphasized that to cover up their own villainy and to silence those who knew about it, they had themselves elected to important civil and military offices so as to be able to punish and kill those they had made guilty by their own treachery and wickedness. But heaven did not fail to punish them, as we shall see.

CHAPTER XXVII

The events of Potosí; Egas de Guzmán drawn and quartered, and other excesses committed by the soldiers; the death of many famous men; preparations in Cuzco against the rebels.

ALL WE have told and a great deal more—for matters so unnatural and abominable cannot be told in full—took place in the Silver City. We shall now narrate what happened at Potosí, where His Majesty's treasury was sacked, and a sum so vast as to be worth more than 1,500,000 silver pesos vanished into thin air, for not a penny of it was found, and His Majesty's treasurer, Hernando de Alvarado, was done to death. This last deed was committed by Antonio de Luján, who made himself chief justice of the town and its surrounding district and had the crier proclaim that his victim had planned to rebel with General Pedro de Hinojosa and seize power. A certain Juan González, a friend of Antonio de Luján, wrote him a letter giving news of the death of Don Sebastián and the arrest of Don García, and the departure of Juan Ramón and others to meet the marshal Alonso de Alvarado. This letter was sent by an Indian house servant or *yanacuna*, who are the best spies in that region. The Indian took the letter in the sole of his shoe so as to be able to pass the guards on the road. The message in it was that Luján should at once stab Egas de Guzmán, since their object had been thwarted by the death of Don Sebastián.

In his capacity as self-created chief justice in Potosí, Antonio de Luján ordered the alarm to be sounded and a company to be formed in the square, whereupon Egas de Guzmán appeared and demanded to know what was happening. Luján, to find if the letter was true or false, and also to make Egas de Guzmán trust him as a friend, showed him the letter in the presence of the rest. It was doubted whether the signature was that of Juan González or a forgery, but they finally decided that it probably was genuine. This bewildered Egas de Guzmán, and he revealed in his face the turmoil in his heart. All those who claimed to serve His Majesty now wavered and turned against him, which was what Antonio de Luján had intended in exhibiting the letter, so that everyone should know of Don Sebastián's death and they should then change their colors and do as the letter suggested, and kill Egas de Guzmán. They therefore came to an understanding at this meeting, by merely looking at one another, and without exchanging a word. Although there were some who still adhered to Egas de Guzmán, most were against him, and Antonio de Luján and others made bold to lay hands on him and arrest him and release Gómez de Solis and Martín de Almendras. The manacles and chains used on them were transferred to him, and a coat of mail he had was taken and put on by Gómez de Solis. Six hours later they drew and quartered Egas de Guzmán, whose boldness availed him nothing, and one Diego de Vergara with him.

Such was the result in Potosí of Juan González's letter. The people at Silver City, led by Vasco Godínez, Baltasar Velázquez, and Licentiate Gómez Hernández, consulted the other citizens and soldiers in the place and all agreed to go together to make war on Egas de Guzmán at Potosí, unaware of what had happened to the poor gentleman. Vasco Godínez went as general chief justice of the army, for such they called it, though it consisted of less than a hundred soldiers, and looked more like a boy's game. It included two infantry captains and one of cavalry, with a deputy commander.

When they had gone two leagues they had news that Egas de Guzmán was dead and the town restored to His Majesty's service. It was then agreed that Vasco Godínez should return to Silver City and Baltasar Velázquez and Licentiate Gómez Hernández with fifty picked men should continue to Potosí and press on in search of Gabriel de Pernia, who, as we have said, had been sent by Egas de Guzmán to the city of La Paz to kill Marshal Alonso de Alvarado. Gabriel de Pernia, having journeyed a long way with his men, heard how Juan Ramón had disarmed Don García, so he raised the banner he was carrying against the marshal for him, and sent to tell Ordoño de Valencia that he was coming to serve him. A few leagues further on Gabriel de Pernia was arrested by his own men, who raised Don Sebastián's flag, and went back with it, leaving Pernia and three others to go where they wished: they went to join the marshal and succeeded in reaching him. Pernia's soldiers, journeying without a leader and with no plan at all, heard that Don Sebastián was dead, whereupon, as Fernández writes in ch. xxi,

they returned to say that they had raised their flag in His Majesty's name. So the flag was like a weathervane which always points in the direction from which the wind blows freshest. Or we might say it went as disloyal people do, always with the stream.

These men therefore joined Baltasar Velázquez. Alonso de Arriaza, who carried the flag, with Pedro Juárez and two other soldiers, marched ahead and advanced to within thirty paces of Baltasar Velázquez's flag, dipped their own three times and handed it over. Baltasar Velázquez then sent Riba Martín and Martín Monge to the city of La Paz to inform the marshal that the garrison and town of Silver City were pacified and restored to His Majesty's service. He then returned to the fort, with the following prisoners: Alonso de Arriaza, Francisco Arnao, Pero Juárez, Alonso de Marquina, Francisco Chaves the mulatto, and Juan Pérez. A league and a half from the fort, he ordered Francisco de Arnao to be quartered, and on entering it, he had Alonso de Marquina drawn and quartered. The same night he entered the monastery of the Mercedarians and seized Pedro del Corro, who had gone as a friar (because he had been present at the murder of the general), and hanged him.

Thus far Fernández. To be brief, for our narrative is growing long, we must add that Baltasar Velázquez handed over his other captives to Vasco Godínez (who had set himself up as chief justice) to do what he liked with them—which was to kill all those who knew about his intrigues. He banished many of them to various places, four, five, or seven hundred leagues from Silver City. He quartered Garci Tello de Vega— whom Vasco Godínez himself had chosen to be Don Sebastián's captain. Another soldier, Diego Pérez, had both his feet cut off and was condemned to the galleys. A fine galley slave he would have made without feet! One would say such decisions were intentional follies. He sent Baltasar Velázquez and another famous soldier called Pedro del Castillo to "go to Lima to enlarge upon and exaggerate the services Vasco Godínez and they had performed." These are Fernández's words, and end the chapter we have mentioned.

By his absence from Charcas, Baltasar Velázquez saved himself from the death he would have suffered at the hands of Alonso de Alvarado. But it did not save him from an even worse fate that heaven had in store for him. The news of the rebellion of Don Sebastián de Castilla soon spread throughout the empire to the great scandal of the *vecinos,* for they were the ones who footed the bill in all the wars that occurred in Peru. On the one hand as lords of vassals their substance was wasted, and on the other their lives hung by a thread, for their enemies did all they could to kill them so as to inherit their Indians. As soon as the news reached Cuzco, preparations were made to resist the enemy. A town meeting was called and they elected Diego Maldonado, called "the rich," as general, since he was the senior *regidor,* and Garcilaso de la Vega and Juan de Saavedra as captains of cavalry; the infantry captains were Juan Julio de Hojeda, Tomás Vázquez, Antonio de Quiñones, and another citizen whose name has escaped my memory. These people raised an army with all haste, and Juan Julio de Hojeda was so active that within five days he camped in the square with three hundred well-armed and equipped soldiers. The speed astonished everyone. Three days later, making eight in all, news arrived of the death of Don Sebastián, which ended the war for the moment.

The same happened at the city of Lima, as Fernández says in his ch. xxii:

The *audiencia* received reports of these disturbances and the storm that had burst, for news of the death of the general and the rebellion of Don Sebastián de Castilla arrived at the end of March: six days later they heard about Egas de Guzmán's rising in the fort at Potosí: four days after came news of the death of the rebels, which caused great rejoicings and festivities in Lima.

Thus Fernández. In the following chapter we shall say what steps were taken to punish these misdeeds.

CHAPTER XXVIII

*The royal audiencia appoints Marshal Alonso de
Alvarado as judge to punish the rebels; the
judge's measures and those taken by the
soldiers; the arrest of Vasco Godínez
and other soldiers and citizens.*

AFTER the rejoicings and festivities that took place in the city of Lima on the news of the death of Don Sebastián de Castilla and the downfall of the rebels, Ordoño de Valencia, whose good fortune permitted him to bring the news of Don Sebastián's death, was rewarded by the royal judges with a grant of Indians in the city of Cuzco worth five or six thousand pesos a year. I left him in enjoyment of it when I came back to Spain. He was undoubtedly the one who throve most by the rising, for he had been on both sides, as Fernández often mentions in his history. Others improperly seized or acquired property. In order to punish and execute them the judges of the royal chancery issued a decree giving Marshal Alonso de Alvarado a commission to punish the whole rebellion. He was known to be a strict and rigorous judge, qualities that were obviously necessary to punish all the great offences that had been committed against God Almighty and the emperor Charles the Fifth, king of Spain. The royal judges also ordered Licentiate Juan Fernández, the fiscal of the *audiencia,* to go to Charcas and perform his duties in the case of the criminals. They also made a secret order appointing Alonso de Alvarado chief justice in all the provinces concerned and captain general with powers to raise men and pay all necessary expenses from the royal treasury, in case the rebellion was not yet extinguished.

Alonso de Alvarado received these instructions in the city of La Paz, where he at once set about punishing the rebels. He sent trustworthy persons to various places to arrest the criminals who had fled and sought refuge in the Indian villages. One of these commissioners, called Juan de Henao, pursued them to the extent of entering the great lake of Titicaca with rafts and searching the islets and the reeds, rushes, and osiers with which the lake abounds. He took more than twenty of them there, including some of the guiltiest, and handed them over to Pedro Enciso who was corregidor in Chucuitu. The latter took confessions from them and sent them on to the marshal, well secured and guarded.

When it was known in Charcas and Potosí that the marshal was commissioned to deal with the past disturbances in those parts, many soldiers who were implicated advised Vasco Godínez, whose crimes seemed to be beyond pardon, to have regard to his safety and form an army with which to resist the marshal. Fernández mentions this in his ch. xxii, in the following words:

it would be possible to do this successfully, and they even persuaded him to announce that the marshal, Lorenzo de Aldana, and Gómez de Alvarado meant to rebel and set up their own government, and use this as a pretext to kill the marshal, in which they would give him all possible assistance, for once it was done there could be no other obstacle in their way. But Vasco Godínez was full of confidence in his great services to the crown, and Juan Ramón, when he heard of the scheme, rebuked its authors and Vasco Godínez, so no attempt was made to carry it out. The marshal had some information about all this and decided to try a ruse. In publishing the news of the commission he had been entrusted with, he also announced that he had been given authority to reward those who had brought about the death of Don Sebastián and ended the rebellion, and that he was empowered to deliver Alonso de Mendoza's *encomienda* of Indians to Vasco Godínez and Juan Ramón. When this news was known, he sent Alonso Velázquez with some troops to Potosí where he was to arrest Vasco Godínez; at the same time the marshal put it about that Alonso Velázquez was taking the authorization for Vasco Godínez to take over the Indians.

Thus Fernández, whose ch. xxii we follow literally. Vasco Godínez was then at Silver City where he heard in a letter from a relative that Alonso Velázquez was bringing him the decree of the royal judges granting him Alonso de Mendoza's Indians. Vasco Godínez was very angry and even insulted that he was not being awarded Pedro de Hinojosa's Indians of whom he had rebelliously and wrongfully taken possession. When he was given the letter, he complained in this sense to those who were present, and though they consoled him with the thought that what he was offered was a good start and he would do better later, he cursed like a heretic, and so did some of the soldiers with him, who also claimed to be rewarded with some of the best allocations in Peru, each assuming his merits to be what he himself imagined.

Soon after Vasco Godínez received the letter with the news of his Indians (which there was no question of his being given), Alonso Velázquez reached Silver City and went to Godínez's lodging, accompanied by some friends. They exchanged polite greetings and other remarks, and Godínez was on the one hand in fine feather, but rather melancholy and chagrined because he had not been awarded the whole of Peru. Alonso Velázquez put an end to these festivities by bringing out a letter from the marshal and others even blacker, for they were forged in order to allay his suspicions.

As he was reading them, Alonso Velázquez approached, and laying his hand on his arm, said: "You are under arrest, Sr. Godínez."

The latter, much bewildered, asked him to show him where it said this in the letters. Alonso Velázquez replied in the words recorded by Fernández in ch. xxii:

that he was to go with him and he would show him later by what authority. Godínez asked him to call a meeting with those who were present so as to show his despatches and let them decide what was to be done. Alonso Velázquez grew angry at this, and said he did not want any discussion, but that Godínez was to go with him, and began to lead him off in the direction of the prison by force. Thus treated, Godínez gave way to despair, seizing his beard in his right hand and turning his eyes to heaven. Some of those present tried to comfort him by saying he should be patient and put up with the arrest, for the result would be to bring into the open the great services he had done His Majesty, and justice would prevail. Vasco Godínez replied with curses, saying let the Devil take him, since he had brought him to such a pass. Finally Alonso Velázquez flung him into jail with chains and fetters, and set a strong guard over him. He then wrote to inform the marshal what had happened.

The latter duly came to Potosí and set about punishing the culprits, arresting a large number of soldiers and *vecinos,* and bringing charges against Martín de Robles, Gómez de Solis, Martín de Almendras, and others. He proceeded according to law in those cases and took cognisance of their explanations and the evidence they advanced in their own favor, especially the *vecinos.* They and many others saved their lives by long justifications of their conduct and drawing out their defence. This indeed was more effective than the defence and explanations they offered, as we shall see.

Thus far Fernández word for word, and this ends his ch. xxii. His last remarks suggest he had an account from someone who was embittered against the *vecinos* who were lords of vassals in Peru, or that he was embittered against them, for he mentions no crime committed by those now arrested by the marshal, having stated on the contrary that the rebels arrested Gómez de Solis and Martín de Almendras, and that Martín de Robles only escaped from them by fleeing in his shirt; yet now he asserts that they only saved their lives by prolonging their cases and not by the defence and explanations they offered. This seems obviously a question of prejudice, which he also shows in other places we shall mention.

CHAPTER XXIX

The judge punishes many rebels in the city of La
Paz and in the fort at Potosí, condemning them
to death, the lash, and the galleys; he does
the same in Silver City; the sentence and
death of Vasco Godínez.

THE MARSHAL began to punish those responsible for the rebellion in the city of La Paz, which was his headquarters. He sentenced all the prisoners that Pedro de Enciso sent after their capture in the great lake, and others arrested in various places. Many were hanged, others beheaded, or sentenced to the lash or the galleys, so that all were duly rewarded.

From the city of La Paz the marshal went on to Potosí, where he found many prisoners, including the famous stalwarts of Egas de Guzmán and Don Sebastián de Castilla, among whom he likewise apportioned heavy penalties, condemning some to be beheaded, a great number to be hanged, and a few to be whipped or sent to the galleys. He arrested Hernán Pérez de Párraga, a knight of the order of St. John; and because of the already mentioned letter he wrote to Don Sebastián asking him to send twenty arquebusiers to arrest him so that it should not appear that he went over to him of his own free will, he was deprived of Indians he had in Silver City and delivered over to the grand master at Malta with a strong guard and in shackles.

Having completed his duties in Potosí, the marshal went to Silver City, where Vasco Godínez was under arrest, together with many of the most famous and unruly soldiers in those parts. They were punished in the same way as the culprits at Potosí and the city of La Paz, by hanging, beheading, whipping, and the galleys. Few were sentenced to the galleys, because it was a laborious business to send them to Spain and deliver them over to the commanders of the galleys. Hitherto this penalty was rarely fully applied, and most of those condemned fled in the course of the long journey, as did those entrusted to Rodrigo Niño, when only one out of eighty-six reached Seville.

The number of persons punished, either killed or flogged, is not recorded, for they were too many to count, or at least to describe. From the last day of June 1553 till the end of November, when the news of Francisco Hernández Girón's rebellion was received four, five, or six soldiers were sentenced every working day, and executed on the morrow. This was necessary to clear the prisons and put the country in a state of security. The recent rebellion with its attendant strife and destruction had given rise to much disquiet, and no one regarded himself as safe. Yet scandalmongers accused the judge of cruelty and called him Nero, seeing so many leading soldiers and others executed so ruthlessly, despite the fact that many of them had been beguiled or forced to rebel. They said that the judge, after condemning five or six soldiers to death every day went from the jail to his house laughing and joking with his deputy and fiscal as if the condemned men were so many capons and turkeys for a banquet. A great many other unbridled criticisms were made against the justice, which might have been acceptable in the case of any other crime but rebellion. In the month of October, as Fernández says in his ch. xxiii:

he had Vasco Godínez drawn and quartered, accusing him and finding him guilty of a great many heinous offences, which are enumerated in the sentence. There is no doubt that the marshal much regretted not having caught Baltasar Velázquez (who had gone to Lima), for if he had been there, he would certainly have treated him the same as Vasco Godínez,

etc. Vasco Godínez's treason and other crimes were briefly set out in the proclamation made when he was drawn, which said: "This man is to be drawn and quartered for betraying God, the king, and his friends." It was the best sentence ever delivered in the empire, for those three words contained the essence of what cannot be expressed in many chapters.

Justice was then done with the other culprits, and many were put to death, until in the middle of November news arrived of the rising of Francisco Hernández Girón, which put an end to the butchery and scourging of these soldiers. Only when a new revolt broke out in a different place did the fear it inspired temper the penalties applied to the first.

The Indians of Cuzco foretold the new uprising, as I myself beheld. It was the eve of the feast of the blessed Sacrament, and I as a boy went out to see the decorations in the two chief squares of the city, for in those days the procession did not go round the other streets, as I am told it now does, making the route twice as long as before. I was near the corner of the great chapel of the church of Our Lady of the Mercies at one or two in the afternoon, when a comet fell to the east of the city near the highway to the Antis. It was so large and bright that it filled the whole town with a greater glow than the full moon at midnight. It fell straight down, and was as round as a ball and as big as a large tower. When it was about twice the height of a tower above the ground, it broke up into fiery sparks and particles, but did no damage to the houses of the Indians on whose property it fell. At the same time a dull and deep sound of thunder was heard reverberating across the sky from east to west. Hearing and seeing this, the Indians in the two squares all together shouted: "Auca! Auca!" repeating the word a great many times. It means "rebel, traitor, caitiff, perfidious, cruel," and all the epithets that can be applied to a traitor, as we have said. This happened on June 19, 1553, on the feast of Corpus Christi. The prophecy of the Indians was fulfilled on November 13, the same year, when Francisco Hernández Girón rebelled, as we shall see in the following book.

End of Book Six

BOOK
SEVEN *of the*
SECOND
PART

It deals with the rebellion of Francisco Hernández Girón; the steps he took to accomplish his rising; his search for the royal judges; their choice of captains to go against the rebel; misfortunes on both sides; the clash at Villacori and Francisco Hernández Girón's victory; Alonso de Alvarado's arrival with his army in search of the enemy; the events of the expedition to the battle of Chuquinca, which the marshal lost; how Francisco Hernández sends officers to various parts of the kingdom; their robberies; how the judges pursue the rebel; the conduct of both sides on this expedition until the battle of Pucara; the flight of Francisco Hernández and his friends, the battle having gone against them; the capture of his men, who are sentenced to death; the arrest and execution of all of them.

It contains thirty chapters.

CHAPTER I

On hearing of the severe punishments administered in Charcas, Francisco Hernández Girón conspires to rebel.

AME SOON spread throughout the empire the report of the severe and rigorous punishment applied in Charcas to the rebellion of Vasco Godínez, Don Sebastián de Castilla, and their companions. Rightly or wrongly—for my lady Fame can carry truth or lies alike—it was rumored that the marshal was collecting charges against other delinquents who lived outside his jurisdiction. As Fernández says (ch. xxiv), it was said:

that the branches had been cut in Potosí, but the roots remained to be pulled up in Cuzco, and a letter said to have been written without any malicious intent by Juan de Arreinaga bore this out. On this news, Francisco Hernández Girón became very cautious and watchful, posting spies on the road to Potosí so as to have news of anyone who was coming, for he was afraid the marshal would send men to arrest him. He likewise forewarned his friends so that they would find out if Gil Ramírez, who was then corregidor, received any despatches from the marshal.

This is taken literally from Fernández, who says a little further on that all the citizens of Cuzco were disaffected by a proclamation made there about ending the personal service of the Indians, and that the corregidor tore up a petition signed by all of them on this subject, etc.

I am surprised that anyone could have given him information so remote from verisimilitude, for the only citizen in Cuzco who was scandalized by the punishments was Francisco Hernández Girón, who had already shown signs of disaffection and rebellion, as our history has said. Nor would the corregidor, a very distinguished gentleman brought up in the household of a good and saintly prince like the viceroy Don Antonio de Mendoza, have done so hateful and detestable a deed as to tear up a petition from a city which then had eighty lords of vassals and was capital of the empire. If he had, he might well have been stabbed fifty times (with all respect for His Majesty), as our author declares, in a later column of the same chapter, Francisco Hernández Girón and his friends planned to do, either in the town council or in the office of a scribe in which the corregidor used to give audience. Thus Fernández. I must not of course flatly contradict what he says: in many instances he must have drawn on popular report and not on authentic sources. I shall, however, leave his account at this point and tell what belongs to history and what happened in Cuzco: this I saw with my own eyes.

The only *vecino* of Cuzco who was scandalized by the punishment of the rebels of Charcas was Francisco Hernández Girón, for the reasons we have given. He was an intimate friend of many soldiers, but not of the *vecinos,* which in itself is enough to arouse suspicion of his intentions and disposition. He was therefore put on his guard when he heard that the marshal was starting an investigation about him; and seeing himself accused by his very deeds, he tried to carry out his rebellion as soon as possible. Accordingly he spoke with a few friends among the soldiers, not above twelve or thirteen in number, and including Juan Cobo, Antonio Carrillo (whom we have mentioned in our *Florida*), Diego Gavilán and his brother Juan, Nuño Mendiola, and Licentiate Diego de Alvarado, who set up to be a braggart soldier rather than a jurist, and with reason, for his learning amounted to nothing and he never exhibited it in either peace or war. They were soldiers and poor, though noble and men of rank.

Francisco Hernández also spoke to Tomás Vázquez, who was a rich citizen and one of the leading figures in Cuzco, being one of the first conquerors who had been present at the arrest of Atahuallpa. The opportunity to approach him about the conspiracy was provided by a quarrel he had had with Gil Ramírez de Avalos, the corregidor, a few months earlier. On this occasion the corregidor had acted in a fit of anger and arrested Tomás Vázquez with little or no reason, clapping him in the public jail and proceeding more like an enemy than a judge. Tomás Vázquez took great offence at this, for citizens of his standing and seniority were held in much honor and esteem. Consequently, Francisco Hernández approached him from this side, urging him to seek vengeance for his wrongs, and Vázquez, blinded by rancor, agreed to join the rebels. Francisco Hernández further approached another citizen called Juan de Piedrahita, who was a person of little consequence in the city and of small income, and who spent most of the year away from Cuzco among his Indians. He was easily led, and behaved more like a quarrelsome soldier than a peaceful citizen. He joined Francisco Hernández with great readiness. For his restless spirit desired nothing better.

These two *vecinos* and a third called Alonso Díaz joined Francisco Hernández in his revolt, though Fernández mentions also a fourth called Rodrigo de Pineda. But he and others who went with him to the city of Lima were not companions of Francisco Hernández in his conspiracy and revolt; but followed him afterwards, as our history will say, more out of fear than for any other consideration or interest. They thus all repudiated him as soon as they could, and went over to His Majesty's side, and were in effect the cause of Francisco Hernández Girón's downfall.

Fernández, having mentioned all these we have named in the plot, but without distinguishing between *vecinos* and soldiers, says that other citizens and soldiers were involved in the conspiracy to kill the corregidor and spread rebellion in the city and throughout the kingdom, but this must have been based on the information of some malicious person or someone who had a grudge against some *vecino* or *vecinos* of Peru, for whenever he speaks of them he tries to represent them as traitors or at least to throw out suspicions that they were.

I am a son of Cuzco, as I am of the empire of Peru, and I deeply regret that he should condemn as traitors or at least put under suspicion men who won a great and wealthy empire that has enriched the whole world, as has already been amply proved, and who were guiltless of any offence against His Royal Majesty. I claim as a Christian to tell the truth without any prejudice or passion, and where Diego Fernández was in the right I shall say so, and where he was wrong, or confused and in the dark, I shall also say so; and I shall be briefer than he, and try to avoid unnecessary complications.

Francisco Hernández Girón plotted then with those we have named and another soldier named Bernardino de Robles and one called Alonso González, a low and mean man, both by rank and in character, face, and figure. As the revolt went on, he turned out to be the greatest butcher in the world, who slew with his sword men Francisco Hernández had pardoned, and beheaded them before the news of their pardon was brought to him so that he could say they were already dead when the orders reached him. Before the revolt he lived by raising pigs in the valley of Sacsahuana, which was Francisco Hernández Girón's own allocation of Indians: it was there that they met and became such fast friends.

Having elaborated the plot, they waited before carrying it out till the day of a solemn wedding that was celebrated on November 13, 1553. The bridegroom was Alonso de Loaisa, a nephew of the archbishop of

Lima, and one of the most prominent and richest citizens there; the bride
was Doña María [Sarmiento] de Castilla, a niece of Don Baltasar de
Castilla, the daughter of his sister, Doña Leonor de Bobadilla, and Nuño
Tovar, a gentleman from Badajoz. We have spoken about them at large
in the history of Florida. In our next chapter we shall say something of
the beginnings of this rebellion which was so costly and onerous to the
whole empire.

CHAPTER II

*Francisco Hernández rebels in Cuzco; the events
of the night of the rebellion; the flight
of many citizens from the city.*

O N THE DAY of the wedding, all the citizens and their wives came
out to escort the bride and bridegroom, dressed in the finest clothes
they had, for on every possible occasion whether of gladness and joy or
of grief and sorrow, the citizens of Cuzco used to foregather to do honor
to one another like members of one family, and there were no divisions
or rivalries or enmities among them, whether in public or in secret. Many
of the *vecinos* and their wives dined and supped at the wedding, which
was followed by a solemn banquet. After dinner there was a tourney in
the street, though as it was narrow the number of riders was limited. I
watched the celebrations from the top of a stone wall opposite the house
of Alonso de Loaisa. I saw Francisco Hernández in a room giving onto
the street, sitting on a chair with his hands crossed on his breast, and his
head bowed, more pensive and brooding than Melancholy itself. He must
have been brooding on the deed he was to do that night, though our author
says he spent the day rejoicing at the wedding, etc. He may have said
this because Francisco Hernández was at the wedding, but he did not
display any joy.

After the tourney, it was time for supper and more than sixty sat down
to table in a downstairs room which was very broad and long. The ladies
dined within in another large room, and both tables were supplied with
viands from a courtyard between the two rooms. Don Baltasar de Castilla, who was the bride's uncle, and himself a very gallant man, presided.

I went to the celebrations almost at the end of the supper to return home with my father and stepmother, who were guests. On entering I went as far as the head of the table, where the corregidor was sitting, and though he was a very distinguished and courtly gentleman and I but a boy of fourteen he noticed me and called me to him, saying: "There's no chair left for you, so come and stand by me, and try these cakes and mulled wine. That's the stuff for boys."

At this moment there was a knock at the door of the room and Francisco Hernández Girón was announced. Don Baltasar de Castilla, who was near the door, said: "You've left it very late to give us the honor of your company," and ordered the door to be opened. Then Francisco Hernández came in with a naked sword in one hand and a small shield in the other, flanked by two of his companions, each carrying a partisan.

Those who were eating were taken aback by such an unexpected scene, and all got up from their chairs. Francisco Hernández bade them: "Keep still. That goes for all of you."

The corregidor waited to hear no more, but slipped out by a door on his left and went to the room where the women were. In another corner of the hall there was a door leading into the kitchen and the inner rooms of the house, and those who were sitting on that side all went out by it and the other door. Those on the other side, nearest the street door, were in great danger because they had no way of escape. Juan Alonso Palomino was sitting in front of the street door, but with his back to it, and as Licentiate Diego de Alvarado and his companions recognized him, they dealt him five blows, for they had all agreed to kill him and his brother-in-law Jerónimo Costilla for the part they played in upsetting Francisco Hernández's first revolt, as we have mentioned. Juan Alonso Palomino died of these wounds next day in the house of Loaisa, for he was unable to get home to be treated.

They also slew a rich merchant called Juan de Morales, an excellent man, who was present at the wedding feast. He was noted for his good qualities among all the citizens. Without realizing what was going forward, he tried to put out the candles on the table thinking to escape the more easily in the dark. He pulled the tablecloth and ten of the eleven candles toppled over and went out. Only one remained alight. One of Francisco Hernández's men carrying a partisan struck him on the mouth, saying: "You traitor! Do you want us to kill the lot of you?" and cleft his mouth open from ear to ear. Another rebel soldier drove a sword through his left nipple, and he fell to the ground dead. The unfortunate man had not even time to tie a golden jar to his belt, as his detractors told the historian who mentions it. I saw his body next day with the wounds I have mentioned. Those who had done these deeds talked of them at great length afterwards, as though they took pride in having committed them.

My father—with Diego de los Ríos; Vasco de Guevara; two brothers, the Escalantes, who were his brothers-in-law; Rodrigo de León, a brother of Pero López de Cazalla; and other *vecinos* and soldiers, numbering thirty-six altogether—went out by the same door as the corregidor, and I with them. They did not go to the room where the women were, but turned to the right so as to find their way out through the yard. They found a ladder and got up onto the roof. They realized that the house next door was that of Juan de Figueroa, a leading citizen, whose front door was in another street, not that in which Alonso de Loaisa's house was. My father, seeing that this was a good means of escape, said to the rest of them: "Wait here for me. I'm going to fetch the corregidor, and get him to deal with this misdeed."

Thus saying, he went to where the corregidor was, and told him that there was a way of escape, and a number of men ready to stand by him and help: if he would go to the square and ring the bells and call the people to arms, the disturbance would be settled, for the rebels would at once take flight. The corregidor refused to adopt this advice, and gave no reply but to ask to be left where he was. My father returned to his companions, and found them all on the roof at the place where the house touched that of Juan de Figueroa. He begged them to wait while he returned and pressed the corregidor. So he went in again, but with no better result, however much he urged and importuned, showing the corregidor ample reason why he should stir from where he was. But the latter shut his ears, fearing that they were all in the plot and wanted to kill him, as Francisco Hernández had declared at the door of the chamber.

My lord Garcilaso then went out, despairing of persuading him, and took his slippers off at the foot of the ladder, remaining in the socks of his buskins which he had worn for the tourney. He climbed up to the roof and I followed him. They then pulled up the ladder and carried it across the roof so as to cross to Juan de Figueroa's house, and all of them climbed down it, I among them. There they opened the street door and sent me out ahead as a scout, since no one would take any notice of a boy, and I was to whistle at each crossing for them to follow me. We went in this way from street to street until we reached the house of Antonio de Quiñones, who was my lord Garcilaso's brother-in-law, the two of them having married sisters. We found him at home, to my father's great joy, for he was very worried at not knowing what had become of him. One of the conspirators, Juan Gavilán, had come to Quiñones' assistance in return for some friendly services rendered by the latter in the past. Finding him near the main door of the chamber, Gavilán had pushed him and Juan de Saavedra, who was with him, out into the street, telling him: "Go home now, and take Master Juan de Saavedra with you; and don't leave it till I call for you tomorrow."

Thus my father found them in the house, and they were all very glad to see one another. They had scarcely met in the house of Antonio de Quiñones than they agreed to leave the same night for the city of Lima. They invited Juan de Saavedra to join them on the journey, offering to supply him with everything, such as a mount, a hat, a scarlet cloak, and riding boots; for at first he excused himself saying that he could not travel for lack of all these things. But when they were brought to him, he again excused himself on grounds of poor health which he said made it impossible for him to travel. They, therefore, ceased to insist and he stayed in the city. Further on we shall mention the chief cause of his reluctance, by reason of which he was to lose his possessions and his life.

The remaining citizens and soldiers who were with my father all went home to make ready for the journey to the city of Lima. My lord Garcilaso sent me home, only a short distance away, to bring a horse, the best he had, which was still saddled for the journey. On going to fetch the horse I passed the gate of Tomás Vázquez's house, and saw two horses saddled in the street and three or four Negroes with them, talking together. When I came back I found them still there, and told my father and his friends about it. They were all alarmed, wondering if the horses and slaves belonged to the conspirators. At this moment Rodrigo de León, the brother of Pero López de Cazalla, called me and bade me go to his brother's house in the same street, though some distance away from where we were. I was to tell the Indian porter to hide the coat of mail and helmet in his closet, for he feared the rebels would sack the city during the night. I went off on this errand in a hurry and when I returned found that my father and his two kinsmen, Diego de los Ríos and Antonio Quiñones, had already gone, following a circuitous and difficult route so as not to pass by Tomás Vázquez's gate. I then returned to my father's house facing the two squares—in those days the houses that now stand further down the street in each of these two squares had not yet been built. I stayed there watching and waiting for the outcome of that unfortunate and fearful night.

CHAPTER III

Francisco Hernández arrests the corregidor, goes
out into the square, releases the prisoners
from jail, and has Don Baltasar de Castilla
and the treasurer Juan de Cáceres killed.

FRANCISCO Hernández Girón and his companions, who had remained
in Alonso de Loaisa's house desiring to seize the corregidor, since they
thought that if they caught him they would have the whole city at their
mercy, made every effort to find him. Being informed that he was in the
room where the women were, they broke down the outer door with a
bench, and when they reached the inner door those inside asked them to
give their word not to kill the corregidor or do any other harm. Francisco
Hernández gave his word, whereupon the door was opened and he arrested the corregidor and carried him off to his own house, where he left
him well guarded and shackled and went out to the square with his band
of companions, who numbered no more than twelve or thirteen.

The seizure of the corregidor, his transfer to Francisco Hernández's
house, the posting of the guard, and their departure for the square was
not done very rapidly, taking at least three hours, so that it is obvious that
if the corregidor had come out when my father and his friends asked him
to and had taken his stand in the square and sounded the alarm, the rebels
would have fled and hidden themselves wherever they could. Everyone
who knew the facts later agreed about this. At this time I went out to the
square to see what was happening, and found this small group of men,
who would have been quite at the mercy of anyone who had been there
to resist them. But because of the darkness of the night and the boldness
of the rebels in entering a house full of people, as Alonso de Loaisa's had
been, the corregidor was terrified, and the citizens and soldiers who might
have rallied in His Majesty's service and helped the corregidor took
flight.

After I had been in the square for more than half an hour, Tomás
Vázquez appeared on horseback, together with another man. They had

lances in their hands and Vázquez said to Francisco Hernández: "Tell us what we are to do."

Francisco Hernández answered: "Do the round of these squares, and tell anyone who comes out not to be afraid; let them come to the main square, and they will find me there, at the service of all my good friends."

Soon afterwards there appeared Alonso Díaz, another *vecino*, also on horseback and lance in hand; and Francisco Hernández told him the same as he had told Vázquez. Only these three *vecinos*, Tomás Vázquez, Juan de Piedrahita, and Alonso Díaz, joined Francisco Hernández that night. The other who had come with Vázquez was not a *vecino*, but a guest of his: this shows clearly that there were no more conspirators with him. And although some other *vecinos* followed him later, it was, as we have said, more out of fear than friendship, and they repudiated him as soon as they could.

The wretched rebels, finding themselves so few and ill-supported, went to the jail and released all the prisoners and brought them with them to the square, so as to make a larger and more impressive number. There they stayed till daybreak, still less than forty in number. Although Fernández (ch. xxiv) says they went out into the square shouting for liberty, that they carried a number of pikes and arquebusses and hoisted a flag, that Francisco Hernández made a proclamation ordering everyone to go to the square under pain of death, that some people joined them that night, and that they posted watchmen and guards throughout the city, to see that no one escaped; I can affirm that nothing more happened that night than what I have said. I, an unnoticed boy, spent the night among them, and they had not enough men to guard themselves, let alone post guards or watchmen throughout the city, which was then more than a league round.

Next day they went to the corregidor's lodging and seized his papers, where they are said to have found seventeen despatches from the judges of the *audiencia* containing various orders to the detriment of *vecinos* and soldiers about the personal service, and not sending Indians to the mines, and not having soldiers as lodgers or maintaining them either publicly or secretly. All this was put up by the rebels to inflame the soldiers and bring them over to their way of thinking.

On the third day of the rising Francisco Hernández began to visit the chief citizens in their own houses. He went to my father's house among others, and spoke to my stepmother in my presence. Among other things he told her he said that he had taken that action on behalf of all the soldiers and *vecinos* of the empire; but he proposed to give the chief

authority to the person who had the best right to it and deserved it more
than he himself did. He asked her to beg my father to come out into the
square and not skulk in his house at a time when he was so much needed.

He held the same language in other houses he visited, supposing that
those who had fled to the city of Lima were in hiding, for he refused to
believe they had left. Thus, when my stepmother assured him that she
had not seen my father since the night of the wedding and that he had
not returned home, Francisco Hernández was astonished. My stepmother
repeated it four times, the last time with a solemn oath in order to persuade him to believe it, and she asked him to have the house searched,
and anywhere else he thought my father might be. Then he believed what
she said and appeared very upset. He then cut the conversation short, and
went off to visit the other houses, with the same result. The truth was
that not all of those who were missing had gone off that night; some
went three or four or five nights later, for as there was no one to guard
the city there was nothing to stop them from going as they liked.

Eight days after Francisco Hernández Girón began his rebellion one of
his followers, called Bernardino de Robles, a seditious troublemaker,
assured him that Don Baltasar de Castilla and the treasurer Juan de
Cáceres were trying to escape and take some of the men with them; and
that they had got a force together, and had put their coined silver and
other moveable property in a monastery. Hearing this, Francisco Hernández sent for his man of laws, Licentiate Diego de Alvarado, and after
consulting him, turned the case over to him for the punishment of the
culprits. The lawyer had no need to collect much evidence, for two
months earlier he had quarrelled with Don Baltasar de Castilla in the
main square of the city, and both were wounded in the dispute. Although
no offence was given by either side, the man of law was angry at not
having killed his adversary, for, as has been said, he prided himself more
on his arms than his letters. Using his commission, he vented his spite on
his victim, though neither he nor the other was to blame, and it was
generally known that this was a fact. The licentiate himself went for them
that night and brought them to his house, where he gave them a few
minutes to confess. Before they had had all the time they needed for the
purpose, he had them strangled, the executioner being Juan Enríquez,
the town crier, who had beheaded Gonzalo Pizarro and hanged and
quartered his captains and commander. On the morrow of Francisco
Hernández's rebellion, this man had come out, prepared for his noble
duty, laden with cords and garrottes to throttle and torture anyone the
rebels wanted to have killed or tormented. He also brought a scimitar to

do any beheading that was required. But he paid for all this later, as we shall see. He quickly throttled the two poor gentlemen and stripped them to despoil them of their possessions. Don Baltasar was left as he was born, and Juan de Cáceres only with his shirt because it was not so fine as his companion's. They were taken out to the square in this state and placed at the foot of the pillar, where I saw them: it would be about nine at night.

The next day it was said that Francisco Hernández rebuked his man of law for killing the two gentlemen without informing him. But this was more to win favor with the people than because he regretted their deaths: in secret he gloated in the fear and astonishment caused by this great deed, for one of the victims was His Majesty's treasurer and the other had been his captain in the late wars and had an allocation of Indians yielding fifty thousand ducats a year. Because of this cruel deed all the citizens surrendered, thinking that those who had fled had chosen the better part, since the two victims had been killed quite without guilt and the murderers were full of vainglory and even more arrogant than before.

CHAPTER IV

Francisco Hernández appoints a commander and
captains of his army; two cities send envoys
to him; the number of citizens
who fled to Lima.

F RANCISCO HERNÁNDEZ, having collected a number of soldiers from the district round the city, now found himself in a powerful position; he had now more than 150 followers, and therefore decided to appoint a commander and captains and officers for his army. As commander he chose Licentiate Diego de Alvarado, and as captains of horse Tomás Vázquez, Francisco Núñez, and Rodrigo de Pineda. He had to flatter the last two after making his rebellion, for they were *vecinos,* and he offered them the rank of captain in order to make sure of them: they accepted, but more out of fear than on account of the honor or profit of the rank. As infantry captains he appointed Juan de Piedrahita, Nuño Mendiola, and Diego Gavilán, and Alberto de Orduña as ensign, and Antonio Carrillo as sergeant major. They all hastened to assume their responsibilities and coax men to enlist in their companies. They made themselves very showy flags with devices and mottoes referring to liberty; so the army was called "The Army of Liberty."

During this time the news that Cuzco had rebelled reached the neighboring towns, but as it was not known in what circumstances or under whose leadership it was assumed that the movement represented the whole city, and Huamanga and Arequipa sent envoys to request that Cuzco should admit them into a league of defence, since it was the mother city and capital of the whole empire: they wished to join Cuzco in submitting petitions to His Majesty against the harmful measures that the judges of the *audiencia* were notifying them of from day to day. The envoy of Arequipa was a certain Valdecabras whom I knew, though Fernández says he was a priest called Fray Andrés de Talavera: there may have been two envoys. The spokesman from Huamanga was called Hernando del Tiemblo. These ambassadors were well and warmly received by Francisco Hernández Girón, who boasted arrogantly of having done a deed of such importance that the whole kingdom was rushing with all haste to support it. And to add stature to his achievement, he put it about that Marshal Alonso de Alvarado had been killed in Charcas and that the murderers had been prompted by it.

When the inhabitants of Huamanga and Arequipa discovered that what had happened in Cuzco was not a general rising of the whole city, but a personal movement begun by a man who was afraid he would be punished for his past misdeeds, and when they learnt that most of the *vecinos* had fled from the city, and how many and who these were, they changed their minds and by common consent all those of both cities who were able went off to serve His Majesty, as those of Cuzco itself had done. These latter included my lord Garcilaso de la Vega, Antonio de Quiñones, Diego de los Ríos, Jerónimo Costilla, and Garci Sánchez de Figueroa, my father's first cousin, who was not a *vecino,* but a senior and honored soldier. These five gentlemen left the city of Cuzco for Lima on the same night as Francisco Hernández Girón began his revolt. The others we shall mention left two, three, four, or five nights after, as they were able to prepare for the journey. Vasco de Guevara, a *vecino,* and the two Escalantes, his brothers-in-law, who were not *vecinos,* left two nights later. Alonso de Hinojosa and Juan de Pancorvo, both *vecinos,* left on the fourth night, and Alonso de Mesa, also a *vecino,* on the fifth, for he lingered to put a small quantity of silver in a safe place, which his enemies later seized as we shall tell.

My lord Garcilaso and his companions continued their journey and nine leagues from the city came upon Pero López de Cazalla on a property he had there, which we had cause to mention in Book IX of the First Part of our history (ch. xxvi). His brother Sebastián de Cazalla was with him, and both were *vecinos*. On learning what was going on in Cuzco, they resolved to accompany the party and offer their services to His Majesty. Pero López's wife, a very noble and beautiful woman called Doña Francisca de Zúñiga, a person of perfect goodness and discretion, wanted to undertake the journey too, to serve not His Majesty, but her husband, and though she was a delicate woman in poor health, she bravely travelled those rough roads and precipitous places riding on a mule with a chair saddle, and made the journey as easily and successfully as any of the rest of the company. At the halting places she succored them all by providing for their supper and breakfast, soliciting supplies from the Indians and showing the Indian women how to prepare the food.

I heard all this and much more about this excellent lady from the lips of her companions. They continued their journey and at Curampa, twenty leagues from Cuzco, they found Hernán Bravo de Laguna and Gaspar de Sotelo, *vecinos* who had Indians at that place, and took them with them. They were similarly joined by the other *vecinos* and soldiers they met on the road to Huamanga. At this place the inhabitants were much encouraged by the arrival of men of such eminence, and were strengthened in their earlier decision to serve His Majesty in such good company. So all who could went with them and those who could not go then followed later, as soon as they could prepare for the journey. To return for a moment to when my lord Garcilaso and his friends passed the bridge over the Apurímac River, they realized that people would come from the city of Cuzco and elsewhere to place themselves at His Majesty's service, and decided that it would not be right to cut them off by burning the bridge and so leaving them isolated at the mercy of the rebels, and agreed that two of them should remain on guard to receive those who might come during the next five or six days and then burn it, so as to protect the road and prevent the rebels from giving pursuit. This plan was duly carried out, so that those who were late in leaving Cuzco were able to cross the bridge, though they arrived at it in fear of finding it already burnt. Some other leading citizens of Cuzco went to Lima by other routes, because the rebellion caught them with their Indians on their allocations to the west of the city. These were Juan Julio de Hojeda, Pedro de Orué, Martín de Arbieto, and Rodrigo de Esquivel; they passed through the allocation of Don Pedro Cabrera, who joined them, and they all advanced together.

CHAPTER V

Letters written to the rebel leader;
he banishes the corregidor
from Cuzco.

AT THIS point Fernández, in his ch. xxv, says:
Miguel de Villafuerte now arrived at Cuzco with a letter in cypher for
Francisco Hernández from Don Pedro Luis de Cabrera, who was at Cotapampa
at the time of the revolt with some soldiers who were friends of his, including
Hernando Guillada, Diego Méndez, and others previously implicated in Don
Sebastián de Castilla's rebellion. The message was to the effect that since Don
Pedro had not been the first to rebel, and Francisco Hernández had beaten him
to it by four days, the latter should go on and carry the movement throughout
the country at large. He, Don Pedro, had raised a standard in his name, and was
marching on the city of Lima to obtain nomination as captain general from the
royal *audiencia*. As soon as he was invested with this office, he would arrest the
royal judges and ship them back to Spain.

After Francisco Hernández had received this letter, Don Pedro sent him
another, also in cypher, by a son of Gómez de Tordoya. This was to tell Francisco Hernández that he could take it for granted that if Garcilaso de la Vega,
Antonio Quiñones, and others had gone to Lima, it was not to favor the above
plan, but because they and Don Pedro could not carry out what had been proposed, because Francisco Hernández had anticipated it. He also said that on
leaving his Indian villages he had had mass said and then taken communion at
a consecrated altar, telling his companions not to worry about him since his only
purpose in going to Lima was to arrest the royal judges and send them to Spain.

But Francisco Hernández regarded Don Pedro as a shrewd and sly fellow
and concluded that these assurances were intended to permit him to slip away
safely and without impediment, together with the soldiers he had with him.
He therefore sent Juan de Piedrahita and some arquebusiers to take Gil Ramírez, remove his wand of office, and expel him from the city, escorting him
under guard more than twenty leagues from Cuzco and then setting him free
to find his way to Lima, without Francisco Hernández having taken anything
from him. He also told Piedrahita to try to find Don Pedro, and tell him not to
think of going to Lima, but to do him the favor of returning to Cuzco, and if

he refused, to arrest him and bring him back under guard. But Don Pedro had already gone, and it would have been extremely difficult to have caught up with him, so Piedrahita returned with his men to Cuzco,

etc. Thus far our author in his own words. As he tells them some of these events are set forward and others put back, and we shall therefore describe them as they occurred, and how Piedrahita arrested the corregidor.

The truth is that Don Pedro de Cabrera had no need to send assurances to Francisco Hernández that he would join him, for no such thing ever entered his head. In person, behavior, conversation, and way of life he was quite the reverse of a martial figure, being the fattest man I have ever seen, either in America or Europe, especially about the belly. In proof of this I may mention that some two years after the battle of Sacsahuana a Negro slave of my father's, who was an excellent tailor, made a leather waistcoat for Don Pedro de Cabrera decked with many gold fringes. When he had made it and was ready to decorate it, four mischievous boys all about ten or eleven years old, of whom I was one, went into the tailor's workshop and found the waistcoat on a table laced up in front with a silk cord. Seeing how big it was, we all four got into it, each in one corner, and there was enough room left in the middle for a fifth boy as big as ourselves. Moreover his belly was so big that he could not ride a horse with an Andalusian saddle, for the fore-peak prevented it; and he always rode with long stirrups, or on a mule. He never tilted or raced on horseback, however the animal was saddled, and although he had been a captain of cavalry in Gonzalo Pizarro's war, this was merely because he was present when Gonzalo Pizarro's fleet was handed over to the president and he was rewarded with a company of cavalry, receiving after the war was over the excellent allocation of Indians we have already mentioned.

As to his love of good things, his way of life, behavior, and conversation—he was a tremendous trencherman and a great joker and entertainer full of most amusing anecdotes and dialogues, which he made up himself; and he used to joke with his pages, lackeys, and slaves. We could recount some very witty and laughable incidents that come to mind, but it would not be proper to repeat such childish things, and the episode of the waistcoat must suffice. His house was near my father's, and they were kinsmen, for my lady Doña Elena de Figueroa, his mother, was a member of the house of Feria, and there was therefore a good deal of intercourse between them, and he never called me by any other name but nephew. We shall repeat some of what we have said about him later, when we refer to his death, which took place in Madrid in 1562.

Because of all this, I can affirm that he was very far from following Francisco Hernández Girón or becoming a rebel. He had indeed no reason to do so, for he lived at ease and in all the peace and content anyone could desire; and he had nothing to do with Francisco Hernández because he spent most of the year with his Indians in the company of half a dozen friends. The messages he sent were to ascertain exactly how Francisco Hernández's revolt had taken place and what had happened after it, and what citizens had fled, and who were with the rebels; for as he and his friends planned to go to Lima they wanted to know just what had happened at Cuzco so as not to be in the dark and to be able to tell the news on the road. And he sent the letters in cypher so that Francisco Hernández should not suspect the messengers and so that he could send them back with the answer. Don Pedro could get to Lima in perfect safety, for his allocation, where he then was, is more than fifteen leagues from Cuzco on the road to Lima, and the Apurímac River crosses the road, so that once he had burnt the bridges over it, he could be quite sure his enemies could not follow. Thus Don Pedro and his friends, on receiving the information they wanted, made for Lima without caring a fig for the rebels.

Francisco Hernández ordered Juan de Piedrahita to take a dozen arquebusiers and accompany the corregidor Gil Ramírez de Avalos, not northwards in the direction of Lima but southwards by the Arequipa road, and having taken him a distance of forty leagues from the city, to set him free to go wherever he wanted. Piedrahita's journey was not at the outset of the rising when Don Pedro de Cabrera's messengers came (which was within eight or ten days of the outbreak), but more than forty days later. The object in sending the corregidor by Arequipa and not by the direct road was to delay his arrival at Lima and deprive him of the pleasure of travelling with the citizens going thither. This clearly shows that Fernández's version was that commonly repeated by the populace, most of whom speak according to their fancy and repeat what they hear at second hand and not what really happens.

CHAPTER VI

Francisco Hernández has himself elected procurator and captain general of the empire; the royal judges appoint officers for the war; and the marshal does the same.

A FORTNIGHT after his rising, Francisco Hernández Girón found himself at the head of a considerable force and generally feared because of the cruelty with which he had treated Don Baltasar de Castilla. He therefore thought it was time to give his rebellion greater authority by assuming, as he thought in his folly, a better title, so as to induce those who saw him elected and supported by the capital city of the empire to embrace his policy, which he himself did not clearly understand. He therefore ordered a town meeting to be called. Those present were 25 *vecinos,* lords of Indians. Fernández mentions their names, and I knew them all. They included only an *alcalde ordinario* and 2 *regidors,* none of the rest being officials of the city council. He asked them to free themselves of the tribulations the royal judges daily put upon them with their edicts by electing him procurator general of the whole empire, so that he could make whatever requests they wished to His Majesty. He also asked them to name him captain general and chief justice of the city and of the whole kingdom so that he could rule them and keep the peace and administer justice. The citizens behaved very nicely, as children say, and agreed more out of fear than respect, for he had a squadron of over 150 arquebusiers with 2 captains, Diego Gavilán and Nuño Mendiola, stationed before the gate of the city hall. After the assembly was over, a proclamation of the powers granted to Francisco Hernández Girón was made in the square. His object in seeking nomination by the meeting was not only to strengthen his authority, but especially to get the citizens and other residents to pledge their support for, and confidence in, his great work, as if they had invited him to do of their own free will what he had asked and forced them to do.

While this was happening in Cuzco, the news reached the city of Lima. At first, the royal judges thought it was false, and suspected some trickery, for the bearer of it was a great friend, and, it was said, a foster brother of Francisco Hernández Girón. They thought that he had come to try out the inhabitants of Lima and find out which were for the rebel and which against him. With this suspicion they arrested Hernando Chacón, the bringer of the tidings, but they soon released him, because his news was duly confirmed from many other sources. The royal judges then nominated captains and other officials for the threatened war. We shall not mention those nominated, for some of them did not accept the posts they were offered, thinking they deserved to be generals, and even more. We shall leave them at this point, and say later who were elected and served in the war; the selection gave rise to many jealousies, rivalries, and troubles, as usually happens when there is no leader and many try to command.

News of Francisco Hernández's rising also reached Potosí, where Marshal Alonso de Alvarado was still punishing the murderers of General Pedro de Hinojosa and the followers of Don Sebastián de Castilla. These punishments were at once halted, though there were many culprits who deserved the death sentence as much as those who had already been punished. But on the outbreak of the new revolt it was politic to pardon the guilty and placate the faithful, both of whom were scandalized by the severity of the sentences and the large number of executions. Those condemned to death were reprieved on condition they served His Majesty at their own expense. They included a soldier called ———— de Bilbao, and when one of his friends visited him to congratulate him on gaining his life and liberty and bid him give thanks to God for such an abounding mercy, the soldier answered: "I thank his Divine Majesty and St. Peter and St. Paul and St. Francisco Hernández Girón, through whose merits grace was given me." He then prepared to go off and serve his benefactor wherever he might find him, which in fact he did, as we shall see.

In addition to this soldier, forty odd more were freed from prison: most of them had been in imminent fear of death, and the luckiest expected to row in the galleys. The citizens and many soldiers who deserved smaller penalties would have been freed by the marshal without any sentence, but they themselves refused this, as Fernández tells in the following words in ch. xl:

When they heard this, some of those who were under arrest suspected that he wanted to release them without sentence in order to be able to arrest them again and punish them at some future time. Thus some of the leading prisoners objected to being released without first having had their cases disposed of. In view of this, the marshal began to deal with them, condemning Gómez de Solís to pay five hundred pesos as the cost of his guards. Martín de Almendras and Martín de Robles received the same penalty, and others were fined two hundred, one hundred, fifty, or twenty, according to the resources of each of them and without reference to the penalty they deserved.

Thus Fernández. In addition, the marshal prepared weapons for the campaign. He ordered pikes to be cut in the neighboring districts where there was wood, and powder to be made in readiness for events. A few days later two orders from the royal judges arrived, the first suspending the legislation about the personal service of the Indians for two years, together with all other measures adopted to the detriment of the citizens and soldiers of the empire, for the governors already perceived that it was this legislation that was causing unrest through the land, and not the temper of the inhabitants. The other order named the marshal as captain general in the war against Francisco Hernández, with general powers of administration to charge the necessary expenses of the campaign against His Majesty's revenues and to borrow if these were insufficient. The marshal appointed captains of infantry and cavalry, and the other officers we shall mention. He offered the post of commander to Gómez de Alvarado, but he did not accept it, because it was much sought by a brother-in-law of the marshal himself, his wife's brother called Don Martín de Avendaño, on whose behalf his wife pleaded so insistently that he at length gave way, reluctantly, for the candidate was very young and had little or no experience of military affairs. The marshal did however appoint him to prevent the outbreak of war in his own house.

He also ordered the Indian chiefs to produce a great quantity of supplies, and provide eight or nine thousand Indian carriers to accompany the army. He sent officials out in various directions to collect men, arms, horses, and slaves, and we shall now leave him in the midst of his preparations to return to Francisco Hernández Girón, for we must go backwards and forwards to preserve the continuity of our story.

While all this was happening in the cities of Lima and Potosí, Francisco Hernández Girón did not neglect the pursuit of his undertaking. He sent Tomás Vázquez with fifty well-armed men to the city of Arequipa, to take possession of it in his name and negotiate with the citizens for his election as captain general and chief justice of the kingdom, as Cuzco had done. He also sent Francisco Núñez, a citizen of Cuzco, whom he had brought over to his side with flattery and fair words and the offer of a company of cavalry. Still, fear was of more avail than profit in making these friendships. He sent Juan Gavilán and forty other soldiers to the city of Huamanga with the same objectives as Tomás Vázquez, and orders to tell the inhabitants that as it and Arequipa had agreed with his aims and had sent ambassadors to him, they should comply with his request to have him appointed by the city council, so as to give fuller authority to his position. Francisco Hernández sent the captains on these missions in order to spread it abroad throughout the empire that these cities were for him, rather than in any hopes that they would grant what he asked, since he knew perfectly well that they had renounced and revoked all their envoys had offered at the outset of his revolt.

In addition to this commission, each of the captains was entrusted with many letters to private persons who were citizens in these places, and Francisco Hernández also wrote privately and separately to the councils, and ordered the city of Cuzco to write to them to support him on the ground that it was to their advantage and that of the whole empire. He also got it to write to Silver City; and he, in particular, wrote to many citizens of Charcas and to Marshal Alonso de Alvarado and his wife Doña Ana de Velasco, but the tenor of the letters was too ridiculous to be taken seriously, and no one replied. Anyone who wishes to see them will find them in Fernández (ch. xxvii).

CHAPTER VII

The captains and officials nominated by the royal
judges for the war; candidates for the position
of captain general; Francisco Hernández leaves
Cuzco to oppose the judges.

THE ROYAL judges decided to select captains and other officers for the army since they knew that Francisco Hernández was daily increasing in strength, reputation, and authority. They named Pablo de Meneses as commander and Don Antonio de Ribera, Diego de Mora, Melchor Verdugo (a knight of the order of Santiago), and Don Pedro Luis de Cabrera as captains of horse. The last two refused the commissions, thinking they were entitled to be generals in a larger army. As captains of infantry they chose Rodrigo Niño (of the episode of the galley slaves), Luis de Avalos, Diego López de Zúñiga, Lope Martim Lusitano, Antonio de Luján, and Baltasar Velázquez who escaped punishment at the hands of Marshal Alonso de Alvarado for his part in Don Sebastián de Castilla's recent rebellion, as we have already mentioned. Lope de Zuazo was ensign general. Melchor Verdugo refused the commission, but contrived to get it bestowed on Pedro Zárate. A citizen of Arequipa called Alonso de Zárate was also appointed captain of horse. Francisco de Pina was elected sergeant major, and Nicolás de Ribera the younger, captain of the judges' guard, though in order that their presumption might not appear so openly Fernández says that he assumed the title of captain of the guard of the royal seal. These are Fernández's words (ch. xxviii).

There was a great deal of disturbance and confusion in the election of the captain general, for there were three serious claimants, each of whom made a fuss on his own behalf. One was Licentiate Santillán, one of His Majesty's judges, and he was the favorite of the other judges and connected with many of the noble gentlemen who won the empire, and who wished to see him appointed. The second claimant was the archbishop of Lima, Don Jerónimo de Loaisa. No one quite knew what cause prompted a religious of the Predicant Order and an archbishop of God's church to want to be captain general of an army of Christians engaged in making war on other Christians. The boldest of the soldiers—and most people agreed with them—said that the only cause was ambition and vanity, adding that it would look better if an archbishop and a regular stayed in his church praying for peace among Christians, the conversion of the natives, and the dissemination of the Gospel throughout the empire, now so sorely divided by the Devil with civil strife. The third claimant was Dr. Saravia, one of the judges of His Majesty's *audiencia*. Although disabused of the belief that he would be elected, he pressed his candidature with great energy, partly for the purpose of bringing his party to the support of Archbishop Loaisa, and partly to increase the number of opponents of Licentiate Santillán and to prevent his election. There was,'in fact, secret hatred and rivalry between these two members of the court, and Saravia desired that, since he himself would not be chosen, the archbishop would win and not Santillán. The confusion continued for some days with no decision in favor of any of the parties. But when the electors, who were two of the royal judges and some responsible citizens of Lima, saw that time was being wasted and the authority of the army impaired, they agreed to pick two generals, for the sake of peace and to placate the claimants and their supporters. One was Licentiate Santillán and the other the archbishop of Lima: by choosing the latter they thought they would satisfy Dr. Saravia, who supported him.

At this point the royal judges had news of the citizens of Cuzco and also letters from them giving details of who and how many were coming to serve His Majesty. But the judges were so nervous and suspicious since the outbreak of the rebellion that they did not even trust one another, much less those from outside and from the rebel zone of Cuzco. They therefore sent instructions that they were to stop and not continue their journey until further orders. Hardly had the messenger left with these instructions when they realized that it was a mistake to reject and dismiss from His Majesty's service men of such standing as those, who were on the way and who had left their homes and wives and children undefended to avoid the rebel leader. The judges now feared that by treating them with disregard and contempt they might drive them to return to the rebel zone to look after their houses and estates and wives and families whom they had left unprotected in enemy lands in defiance of their natural responsibilities. A messenger was therefore at once sent with a conciliatory letter warmly thanking them for coming and couched in the most expressive language. The second messenger was bidden to make all haste to overtake the first and recover the first order and destroy it before anyone should see it. All this was done, and the citizens of Cuzco reached Lima, where they were well received and given all the attentions they deserved.

After electing the captains and generals, the royal judges sent orders to all the other cities of the empire, informing them of Francisco Hernández Girón's revolt, and warning them to make ready to serve His Majesty. They nominated captains of horse and foot for each town, and ordered a general pardon to be proclaimed for all those who were guilty in the late wars of Gonzalo Pizarro and Don Sebastián de Castilla provided that they rallied to His Majesty's service—it was known that many concerned in both wars were in hiding in the Indian villages and dared not return to the Spanish settlements. Among the precautions taken the first was to defend and control the sea: for this purpose they instructed Lope Martim to take forty men and embark in a good galleon that was in the port and inspect the other ships there. He did so, but he held the position for only a few days, less than a week, for his temper tended to choler rather than to phlegm. His successor was Jerónimo de Silva, who performed his duties in a sailorly, soldierly, and gentlemanly manner. Lope Martim returned to his infantry command, where we shall leave him to return to Francisco Hernández Girón.

The rebel leader, now well supported since more than four hundred men had rallied to him from various quarters, apart from those he had sent off to Huamanga and Arequipa, decided to march on the city of Lima to meet the army of the judges—he never called it by any other name than the "army of the judges," implying that if it had been His Majesty's army he would not have gone out to fight it. He was accompanied then by more than four hundred well-armed and well-mounted men with plenty of munitions and supplies and a full range of weapons, though on the other hand he was much downcast and depressed by the fact that the cities, towns, and villages of the empire in whose service and honor he pretended to be acting, had not rallied to him.

Before deciding to go to Lima, he had hesitated whether or not to attack the marshal first. This would have been more profitable to his cause, for all the marshal's people were dissatisfied, both those who were loyal servants of His Majesty and those who were disloyal, on account of the rigor of the recent punishments: many of those executed were relatives, friends, or fellow townsmen of the loyalists, who deeply deplored the loss of most of them and said they had died of a surfeit of punishment rather than of a sufficiency of crimes. All those most experienced in warfare said that it would have been better if Francisco Hernández had first attacked the marshal, for no captain can succeed with a discontented army. On this point Fernández has the following in his ch. lx:

Francisco Hernández was ill-advised and hapless in not choosing to march on Potosí rather than Lima, for it would undoubtedly have been better to have seized the former province. If he had attacked the marshal, who was very unpopular at the time, none of his men would have deserted as they did on the way to Lima, and the marshal's men would not, and indeed could not, have resisted because of the delay there had been in preparing for the campaign and the numerous enemies the marshal had around him,

etc. Thus far Fernández.

God did not permit Francisco Hernández to judge aright at this point, or this havoc and harm wrought would have been irreparable. He pressed on against Lima, as our history will say. Licentiate Alvarado, his commander, stayed in the city to prepare the remaining men, as they could not all march together.

Before leaving Cuzco, Francisco Hernández displayed his generosity by offering permission to all *vecinos* who preferred to remain at home and not go with him, to do so freely. This he did, because he thought they disapproved of the venture; for they had not been very friendly toward him, and he did not want to have doubtful elements in his army, especially if they were *vecinos*, who were powerful people and would have to be accompanied by a large number of soldiers in the event of an emergency. Only Diego de Silva he begged and pleaded to accompany the army to increase its authority and standing by his presence. Diego de Silva obeyed, though more out of fear than regard for Francisco Hernández, and returned to his own people as soon as he could, as we shall see. There were thus six *vecinos* who accompanied Francisco Hernández on his departure from Cuzco: the three who were with him the night of the rebellion, who were Tomás Vázquez, Juan de Piedrahita, and Alonso Díaz; and three more won over later by flattery and the offer of captaincies, Francisco Núñez (who was given a company of horse), Rodrigo de Pineda (one of infantry), and Diego de Silva (who, as we have said, was gained by words of friendship concealing threats).

A week after Francisco Hernández had left, the commander followed with more than two hundred men. They included Francisco de Hinojosa, who had arrived a few days before from Cuntisuyu with more than twenty soldiers—everyone who used the description of "soldier" wanted to follow and support Francisco Hernández Girón, and a great many rallied to him because he offered to stand up for them against the many orders made by the royal judges to the detriment of soldiers and *vecinos*. Apart from Hinojosa there came another soldier from the direction of Arequipa. He was called Juan de Vera de Mendoza and had been on the king's side, but being very young and a good horseman, he was passionately anxious to be a captain, even though he had no standing as a soldier; as the royal officials did not appoint him captain, he came with a friend called Mateo Sánchez to Cuzco, where Francisco Hernández was, a few days before he set out, in order to obtain the rank of captain and that of ensign for his friend. They brought a hand towel fastened to a stick as their banner, and hoped and expected that Francisco Hernández as captain general would confirm both of them in these titles. We shall tell the outcome of the expedition in the following chapter.

CHAPTER VIII

*Juan de Vera de Mendoza flees from Francisco
Hernández; the people of Cuzco go off to join
the marshal; Sancho Duarte recruits men and
makes himself their general; the marshal
puts him down; Francisco Hernández
reaches Huamanga; the scouts of
the two sides meet.*

T HE COMMANDER Alvarado came up with his general, who had waited
for him to arrive, eight leagues from Cuzco. They continued the
journey together, crossing the river Apurímac and bivouacking for the
night two leagues beyond it. It took four days to get the whole company
of men, horses, munitions, and supplies over the river. Juan de Vera de
Mendoza, who had been more than a fortnight in Francisco Hernández's
army without being promoted or confirmed in the rank of captain he had
awarded himself, took it into his head to leave the rebel army and rejoin
the king's. The affair sounds more like play acting than warfare, and we
repeat it as such. Juan de Vera agreed with four other soldiers no older
than himself and his companion (making six in all) to take flight that
night. They did so, and, returning to the bridge in all haste, crossed it and
burnt it to protect themselves from being followed. They reached Cuzco
the next night and rode in, sounding the alarm, so that the whole city
was in a commotion fearing that the rebels had returned to do some harm.
So no one dared go out into the square. At daybreak, finding it was only
Captain Juan de Vera de Mendoza, still flying his flag, the citizens came
out and together resolved to go to the marshal, knowing that he had
formed a good army. They elected Juan de Saavedra, a citizen, as their
captain. Juan de Vera de Mendoza decided to go on ahead with his own
group so as not to march under any flag but his own, but although he
reached the marshal, he failed to get a better flag or the title of captain;
all his industry only sufficed to make his puerile pretensions public
property.

The people from Cuzco gathered, but amounted in all to fewer than forty men. Fifteen were *vecinos* with their own Indians and the rest tradesmen and artisans who had been left behind as useless by the rebels. They all made for Collao, where Marshal Alvarado was, but when he heard of their approach, he sent to tell them not to leave the city limits but to wait for his arrival in Cuzco.

Sancho Duarte, who was then corregidor in the city of La Paz, gathered a force to serve His Majesty, raising his banner and marching toward Cuzco with more than two hundred men in two companies: one of infantry captained by Martín de Olmos, and one of horse, of which he appointed himself captain with the title of general. He reached the bridge over the Desaguadero, where he lingered several days, and learning that Francisco Hernández had left Cuzco for Lima, pressed on his way with the idea of reaching Cuzco and then pursuing Francisco Hernández. Everyone wanted to give orders and not receive them, and his purpose was to avoid the marshal so as not to be under his orders. When the latter knew about this, he sent him a double message: the first was a letter asking him to return to his own jurisdiction and wait there, since it was not in His Majesty's best interests that there should be so many little armies. Together with this letter he gave the messenger a strict injunction in his capacity as captain general, telling the bearer that if Sancho Duarte did not do as he was asked, the injunction was to be presented to him. This was done, and Sancho Duarte meekly returned to his jurisdiction, though before seeing the injunction he had tried to avoid complying with the letter so as to pursue his design.

We shall leave him here to return to Francisco Hernández, whom we left at Apurímac. He went on with his march and learned at Antahuailla that all the *vecinos* and soldiers of Huamanga had gone off to serve the king, and that Juan Alonso de Badajoz, who had been made commander of them, was with Captain Francisco Núñez and the few soldiers this captain was able to bring from Cuzco to Huamanga. Francisco Hernández took this news badly, complaining to his followers that the cities that had at first approved his movement now as readily repudiated it without any reason. He marched on to the river Villca, where his scouts sighted those of His Majesty's army, for when the judges heard that Francisco Hernández was advancing toward them they sent Captain Lope Martim with a band of thirty soldiers to get news of the enemy and find out where he was and report without delay. Lope Martim did this; as soon as he sighted the enemy, he retired and reported their position.

Francisco Hernández still continued toward Huamanga, where he

awaited Tomás Vázquez, having told the latter when he sent him to
Arequipa that he, Hernández, would not go beyond Huamanga until he
returned. Tomás Vázquez had done little or nothing at Arequipa and
returned by the coast road to meet Francisco Hernández. Although the
people of Arequipa, thinking that all the citizens of Cuzco were unanimous in electing a procurator general to speak on their behalf and ask
His Majesty and the royal *audiencia* for what they wanted, had at the
outset sent an envoy to Cuzco, as we have said, when they later discovered
that this was a private rebellion, they repented and all the *vecinos* went
off to offer their services to His Majesty. Thus Tomás Vázquez, finding
no one to treat with, returned from his idle quest; and so that the quest
might not be absolutely idle he killed Martín de Lezcano, a great companion of his, on the way because he suspected him of wanting to kill him
and declare for His Majesty. He hanged another leading soldier called
Alonso de Mur because he fancied he wanted to desert after being given
a horse and supplies by Francisco Hernández.

On learning of Tomás Vázquez's approach, Francisco Hernández went
out to meet him with a crowd of people in no sort of order or array, and
they all entered thus together. Francisco Hernández did this so that it
should not be seen how few people Tomás Vázquez had brought with
him. Captain Francisco Núñez, who left Cuzco with forty soldiers to
seize Huamanga and carry out the other duties assigned to him, found
there what Vázquez found in Arequipa—that all the *vecinos,* repenting
of their original decision, had fled to Lima to serve His Majesty. He was
left with only Juan Alonso de Badajoz and Sancho de Tudela, an old
man of eighty-six who followed Francisco Hernández till the end of the
revolt and was after put to death by him.

With these two and his small number of soldiers, Francisco Núñez
went out to receive his general, and found him very sad that those who
had at first welcomed his undertaking should now have repudiated it. To
relieve his distress, two famous soldiers went over to him from Lope
Martim, one of whom was later ensign to the commander Licentiate
Alvarado, and told him all he wanted to know about His Majesty's forces.
With this information he left Huamanga with more than seven hundred
men. On reaching the Jauja valley, he sent two captains with bands to
range in various directions. One was Juan de Piedrahita with sixty
soldiers, and the other Salvador de Lozana with forty.

From the royal camp Jerónimo Costilla, a *vecino* of Cuzco, was sent
out with twenty-five soldiers to explore and find out the whereabouts of
the enemy. His path happened to be that taken by Juan de Piedrahita,

and on learning that they were four leagues away and sixty in number, he retired, as he could not have offered resistance. On the other hand Juan de Piedrahita learnt from the Indians (who, as we have mentioned, are on both sides) that Jerónimo Costilla was so close and with very few men, and marched through the night so as to come up with them by daybreak. Finding them unprepared, he worsted them and captured three, with whom he returned to his army.

CHAPTER IX

Three of the king's captains capture a rebel
captain and forty men, and hand them over to
one of the royal judges; Francisco Hernández
decides to attack the royal army;
many of his followers desert.

As THE events of war are various and changeable, it happened that as Jerónimo Costilla retired, he chanced to meet Jerónimo de Silva, whom the judges had sent after him. Both fell back, fearing that Francisco Hernández with the main body of his army was pursuing them, but they succeeded in capturing an Indian who was in the service of Captain Salvador de Lozana, and by pressing him to answer their questions, they learnt where Lozana was and how many men were with them. They duly informed the royal judges and asked for men to go out and meet him and capture him. The judges instructed Lope Martim to take 60 men to their help, and these, joining Jerónimo Costilla and Jerónimo de Silva, managed the affair so well that although their opponents were noted soldiers, all armed with arquebusses and in a fort, they forced them to surrender and promised them that their crimes would be pardoned if they came over to the king's side. The rebels were demoralized and came out of the fort, and were all taken but one man who carried the news to Francisco Hernández Girón. The latter was very distressed by the news of this loss, because he had great confidence in Lozana and the soldiers were picked men. They were taken as prisoners to the royal army, and the judges ordered them all to be hanged, but when the royal soldiers heard this, they complained of the verdict, saying that they would refuse to go out scouting or do anything else against the enemy, since the latter would copy the judges and order any they arrested to be hanged, even if they had done nothing to justify the penalty. The complaints of the soldiers were supported by some of the captains who wanted to please their men, and the *audiencia* was begged to modify its decision. In order to get Lozana and his men away from the army the judges referred the case to Licentiate Altamirano, one of His Majesty's judges, who was at sea, with authorization for him to do as he thought fit with them. He ordered Lozana to be hanged, together with two others of the guiltiest, and the rest were exiled from Peru.

Though disheartened by the loss of Captain Lozana and his soldiers, Francisco Hernández Girón marched on with his army, confiding in the ruses and stratagems of war he had planned. On reaching the valley of Pachacámac, four leagues from the city of Lima, he called a council of war to decide what to do. Among other things, he and his advisers decided to attack the royal army, which was camped outside the city, during the course of the next few nights: they were to drive some of the numerous cattle to be found in that valley with lighted fuses fastened to their horns and a great number of Indians and Negroes and a few arquebusiers among them to goad them on and divert the royal forces so that the rebel army could fall on them in a favorable place. It was decided to execute this plan in four nights' time. Diego de Silva, a *vecino* of Cuzco whom Francisco Hernández had asked to accompany them to lend his authority to the campaign and whom he invited to all their councils to involve him more deeply, was present at this meeting.

The scouts of both armies meanwhile sighted one another and reported what they saw. The judges and their two generals prepared for any eventuality, and the captains likewise. Their soldiers were well drilled; for they had spent many days in skirmishing and shooting at the mark, the best marksmen being rewarded with prizes and trophies. There were more than 1,300 men in the camp, 300 mounted, about 600 arquebusiers, and 450 pikemen.

On hearing that Francisco Hernández Girón had passed Huamanga and was advancing to attack them, the royal judges thought fit to satisfy their men and placate the whole community of citizens and soldiers by suspending the orders they had had announced about the personal service of the Indians and against the use of Indians as bearers on the roads, or travelling with Indian men or women even when the latter were servants, and other regulations which annoyed and discontented all the inhabitants of the empire. The judges therefore decided to suspend all the orders, and in consultation with the *vecinos* who were present agreed that for their greater satisfaction they should elect two procurators to go to Spain in the name of the whole empire and petition His Majesty to grant their requests. They chose Don Pedro Luis de Cabrera, a *vecino* of Cuzco, whose enormous belly prevented him, as we have said, from taking part in the war, and Don Antonio de Ribera, a *vecino* of Lima. The two procurators duly made ready to go to Spain: Don Antonio de Ribera got there, but Don Pedro Cabrera stopped on the way and did not complete the journey.

Two days after Francisco Hernández reached Pachacámac, part of his force went out to skirmish with the royal army. The engagement began slowly and gradually increased, for each side was very anxious to test the strength of its opponents. Diego de Silva went out making much of his adhesion to Francisco Hernández, but as soon as an opportunity presented itself he went over to His Majesty's side and brought with him four famous soldiers, one called ———— Gamboa who was ensign to Captain Mendiola. The ensign's flight did the captain great harm, as we shall say. In addition to Diego de Silva and his friends, many other soldiers deserted the rebels that day and went over to the king, with which the fray ended.

The same thing happened next day, and each day following as long as Francisco Hernández was at Pachacámac. Men came over to the king in twenties and thirties, and the enemy could do nothing to stop it. This decided Francisco Hernández Girón to withdraw and fall back on Cuzco before all his followers abandoned him. The device of attacking by driving cattle in front now seemed useless, since Diego de Silva would already have warned their opponents about it, and the judges would be on their guard to resist and take the offensive.

In this frame of mind, the rebel leader made a magnanimous gesture, intended rather to test and reveal the spirit of his men than as evidence of his generosity. He announced that anyone who did not want to follow him could go over to the judges' camp at once, and he would give them free licence. A few took advantage of the offer, but they were the least useful, and the commander Licentiate Alvarado did not hesitate to deprive them of their horses and arms and their very clothes, if they were of any use to his own men.

So Francisco Hernández left the valley of Pachacámac in as good order as possible, prompted more by alarm lest his own men should all slip away than by fear that his enemies would follow him; for it was notorious that there were so many giving orders in the judges' camp that nothing was decided in its due time and season as circumstances required.

CHAPTER X

Francisco Hernández withdraws with his army;
much confusion of purpose in His Majesty's
camp; a revolt in the city of Piura
and how it ended.

FRANCISCO HERNÁNDEZ left Pachacámac determined to withdraw, as indeed he did. His men left everything unnecessary that they could not carry in their quarters, which were at once sacked by the king's men, who broke ranks in disorderly fashion. The judges summoned a meeting of the council of war, attended by the captains and in addition by many of the *vecinos*, whose judgment was the better because of their greater experience. But in the midst of a multitude of opinions, everyone claimed and demanded that his own plan should be followed. After a great many views had been expressed it was resolved that Pablo de Meneses should follow Francisco Hernández with all speed, accompanied by six hundred men, the best in the camp.

These men were ready to leave next day, when the two generals insisted that not more than a hundred men should go, on the ground that it was wrong to leave the camp so denuded of good and gallant men. The judges and their advisers, overruling this objection, again ordered the six hundred picked men to depart, and the same scene was re-enacted, the generals countermanding their orders and permitting only a hundred men to go to raid the enemy and bring in those who wanted to desert him. Thus Pablo de Meneses went off very dissatisfied and angry at so many changes of orders and at the severity of the generals, who now refused to sanction the departure of some private persons who were his special friends and wished to accompany him. We shall leave them here, to tell what happened at the same time in the city of San Miguel de Piura.

In this city there dwelt a man of good character and reputation called Francisco de Silva. The royal judges, as we have said, sent instructions to all the corregidors in the kingdom advising them of the rebellion and ordering them to prepare and recruit men to resist and punish the rebel leader. The corregidor of Piura, called Juan Delgadillo, commissioned

Francisco de Silva to go to Túmbez and collect all the soldiers he could find on the coast and bring them back. He went as instructed, and returned to Piura with a company of twenty-six or twenty-seven men. These, after being twelve or thirteen days in the city and finding that they were given neither food nor quarters and being poor and without means of support, went to the corregidor with Francisco de Silva as their leader, and begged his permission to go to the city of Lima to serve His Majesty there. The corregidor gave permission, though only as a result of requests and pleadings by the whole city. When the soldiers were ready to leave next day, he revoked his permit without any reason, and ordered them to go back to their lodgings and not to leave them or the city without his express authority.

Seeing that their prayers and protests went unheeded, Francisco de Silva and his companions all agreed to kill the corregidor and sack the city, and then go off to join Francisco Hernández Girón, since they were not allowed to serve His Majesty. Thus agreed and well supplied with arms, twelve or thirteen of them went to the corregidor's house and arrested him, killing an *alcalde ordinario*. They robbed the corregidor's house, where they found arquebusses, broadswords, swords, shields, lances, and partisans, and plenty of powder. They took the royal standard and announced that everyone was to come out and join the flag under pain of death. They unlocked the royal treasure chest, and stole what was in it, even the sums belonging to the estates of deceased persons, and then did the same in all the houses in the city, sacking them without leaving anything of value behind.

When a soldier chanced to arrive at Piura after being exiled from Lima and taking flight on the way, they put it about and proclaimed (by arrangement with the soldier) that he should say that Francisco Hernández Girón was descending in great force on the city of Lima and that the whole country was for him, even Judge Santillán, and that many of his friends and relatives had gone over to the rebel leader. He told other lies as well, as big, or bigger, if such were possible, and the petty rebels puffed themselves up as if it were all true and they were lords of Peru. And as the soldier said he wanted to go and find Francisco Hernández and enlist with him, they all wanted the same and set out in search of him.

They had the corregidor under arrest, secured by a stout iron chain and eight or nine other *vecinos* and leading residents with him, all in iron collars and chains like galley slaves. They travelled more than fifty leagues this way, as bold as brass, till they arrived at Cajamarca, where they found two Spaniards living by their own labors as farmers, from whom they heard the state Francisco Hernández was reduced to, and how he was in flight with the judges after him, and might at that very moment be dead and done with. They wept for their ill-considered folly, and agreed to return to the coast and try and escape on some ship, if they could find one. They freed the corregidor and their other prisoners, leaving them unprovided for lest they should do them any harm. The rebels, to the number of over fifty, then divided into little bands each consisting of three or four companions, so as not to be noticed as they passed by.

The corregidor, on being set free, summoned people to his side in the king's name, and arrested a few of the rebels, and had them quartered. The royal judges heard of the outrageous and disorderly conduct of these men and sent a judge called Bernardino Romaní to pursue them: he arrested and hanged almost all of them; some were sent to the galleys. Francisco de Silva and some of his companions went to Trujillo and entered the monastery of St. Francis the divine and took his habit; thus dressed, they left the city and went to sea, embarking in a ship that took them away from Peru and so saved their lives.

At the same time a native of Santiago, called Gaspar Orense, came from the kingdom of Chile with the sad and lamentable news of the rising of the Araucanian Indians there and the death of the governor Pedro de Valdivia and his companions, which we have related at length in Book Seven of the First Part of these *Commentaries*. The news was much deplored in Peru, because of the rising of the Indians, which began in the last days of 1553; still today, almost at the end of 1611, as we write these lines, the war is not finished—on the contrary, these Indians are even more arrogant and obdurate than at first because of the many victories they have won and cities they have destroyed. May the Lord God repair this harm as behooves His service. Perhaps in our next book we shall say something of the deeds of the Araucanians.

CHAPTER XI

Misfortunes of both armies; the death of Nuño
Mendiola, a captain on Francisco Hernández's
side, and of Lope Martim, a captain on
His Majesty's side.

To RETURN to events in Peru, when Francisco Hernández Girón left
Pachacámac, he moved very cautiously in marching order and with
his baggage and camp followers well covered, as though he were afraid
that his opponents would follow and pursue him to the end. But finding
after the first three or four days that they were not on his heels, and discovering through his spies that his opponents were deeply divided in all
their council meetings, that whatever the judges decided the generals reversed, and that all was confusion, rivalries, and opposition, he took
courage and marched on more freely and with greater confidence. Nevertheless, he still had difficulties and differences with his closest friends, and
when he reached the valley called Huarcu, he hanged two of his leading
soldiers merely because he suspected that they intended to desert: already
they were in such a state that mere suspicion was a strong enough prosecutor to condemn his most trusted followers to death.

Continuing his march, he reached the valley called Chincha, which
abounds in food and commodities. Captain Nuño Mendiola advised him
that it would be as well to stay there for three or four days in order that
the men might rest and stores be assembled for the road. Francisco Hernández rejected this advice; and on contemplating its author, it seemed to
him that Mendiola had taken its rejection with a bad grace, which encouraged certain friendly parties to insinuate that Mendiola intended to
go over to the king. The rebel leader had little difficulty in believing this
when he recalled how Mendiola's ensign Gamboa had fled with Diego de
Silva a few days before, supposing that the ensign must have taken messages to the judges to ensure the captain's safety when he should take
flight too. The suspicion sufficed to cause Francisco Hernández to send his
commander to deprive Mendiola of his arms and horse and dismiss him.
But the commander fulfilled his instructions to the point of depriving him

also of his life: such was the end of poor Captain Mendiola and the reward he received for being one of the earliest supporters of the rebel. Moreover, a number of soldiers left Francisco Hernández, and went over to Pablo de Meneses and informed him that the rebels were in a bad way, many of their people having fled and hardly three hundred of the original five hundred being left.

This news stimulated Pablo de Meneses to discuss with his friends the possibility of a night march to overtake the enemy and discomfit him. Only when they had resolved on this plan and already begun their march did they notice what they would have done well to consider earlier, that they had no maize for their mounts and nowhere to get it. One of the soldiers who had come over from Francisco Hernández, Francisco de Cuevas by name, then came forward saying that he knew where there was plenty and would bring all that was necessary. Pablo de Meneses sent him off with a dozen Indians who were to return laden with maize. The soldier went with them and sent them back with the maize, telling them that he himself would follow as soon as he had fed his horse; but as soon as he was alone, he returned not to Pablo de Meneses but to Francisco Hernández, whom he informed of the strength of the enemy and of their plan to fall on him the next night. He begged forgiveness for having fled, and said that he thought it was God's will in order that he should hear of the enemy's proposed attack and prevent Francisco Hernández from being taken by surprise. The reason the soldier returned to the rebels was that he had heard one of Pablo de Meneses' men say, speaking of the rebels in general, that the luckiest of them would be flogged and sent to the galleys when the war was over, even if they had gone over to the king. On hearing this, the soldier decided to return to the rebel leader and win his pardon by telling everything he knew.

Francisco Hernández at once made ready and spent the whole afternoon and the following night in battle order, awaiting the enemy. But Pablo de Meneses, Lope Martim, and their friends suspected what was afoot when Francisco de Cuevas did not return, and guessed that he had gone back to the rebels and told them of the plan, and that the enemy would come out to attack them when he knew how few they were. They decided therefore to withdraw, and ordered their people to march at once to a place called Villacori, five leagues from the place where they were on the Ica River, leaving thirty men mounted on the best horses as a rear guard to warn them in case of emergency.

Captain Lope Martim offered to stay with three others to watch out for the enemy and act as sentinels and scouts for the purpose of giving warning of danger. Pablo de Meneses and all his men then went off to Villacori, while Lope Martim and his companions climbed a high hill overlooking the Ica River so as to have a better view of the enemy. But their design miscarried, for the whole valley is full of trees and it is impossible to see through them. As they stood watching, a Cañari Indian belonging to Francisco Hernández happened to spot them and warned the rebels. The latter climbed the hill Lope Martim and his three friends were on from both sides, so as to take him from the rear. In this they succeeded, and Lope Martim and his friends, with their eyes fixed on the distance, failed to notice that the enemy was close at hand. This was possible because the river passes under the hill on which Lope Martim was and runs so near to its foot that those on the summit cannot see people climbing up the sides until they are near the top.

I and some companions of mine, when travelling on that road, climbed the hill to see how it was possible for Lope Martim and his friends to suffer the misfortune we are about to relate, and we discovered that it was because they had placed themselves in such a position that they could not see their opponents climbing up until they were just behind. On finding themselves cut off, Lope Martim and his companions began to flee in both directions, but though they strove hard, three of them could not escape and were caught, among them Lope Martim. The enemy did not recognize him until a Barbary Moor who had belonged to Alonso de Toro, Tomás Vázquez's brother-in-law (for they had married sisters) came up and told Alonso González that it was Lope Martim who had been captured. This news overjoyed them and they reported it to Francisco Hernández. He refused to see the prisoner, and remembering the death of his captain Lozana, whom Judge Altamirano had had hanged, said that he was to be killed at once, together with another soldier taken with him, who had deserted from the rebels. This was done. They cut off Lope Martim's head, put it on the point of a lance, and carried it as a trophy and standard on the journey to Villacori we shall now describe. Such was the end of good Lope Martim, one of the first conquerors of the empire, who was present at the capture of Atahuallpa and was a *vecino* of Cuzco.

CHAPTER XII

The royal judges send men to help Pablo de Meneses;
Francisco Hernández turns on him and delivers a
fierce attack; the unlucky death of
Miguel Cornejo; the loyalty of a
horse to its owner.

WHILE IN pursuit of Francisco Hernández Girón, Pablo de Meneses wrote to the generals of the army, Judge Santillán and Don Jerónimo de Loaisa, archbishop of Lima, saying that as the enemy had a large force and he only a small one, he needed them to send him help with all speed, since he hoped to destroy the rebel army then and there. The generals at once complied with his request, sending him more than a hundred men, including many *vecinos* of Lima, Cuzco, Huamanga, and Arequipa, all well armed and equipped. By making great haste on the road they reached Villacori just before Pablo de Meneses entered it. Both forces were much encouraged at finding one another. They learned that the enemy was five leagues off, and that Lope Martim had remained with three companions as watchmen and scouts in order to give warning of any emergency. This fact reassured them and made them think that they were quite safe. But in time of war captains, if they do their duty properly, should never rest assured even when the enemy is far away, let alone when he is near at hand, or they risk the fate that now befell the royal forces.

On learning from Lope Martim and his companions where Pablo de Meneses lay and in what circumstances, Francisco Hernández made ready his forces to give pursuit with all speed. Good fortune helped him to gain the victory, for the soldier of Lope Martim's who had escaped capture by the rebels was so frightened that he hid in a grove of locust trees to avoid being killed, and failed to execute the important task of warning Pablo de Meneses. The latter had no idea of the approach of the enemy, thinking that Lope Martim and his companions, who were considered honest and reliable fellows, were on the watch. They therefore slept without sentries or other precautions and without fear.

At daybreak a soldier who had left the royal camp to look for a little maize in the cultivated patches heard the noise of men, and looking out, saw a band of thirty horse, which Francisco Hernández had sent forward to raid Pablo de Meneses and hold him in skirmish until the main body of the rebels came up. The soldier gave the alarm and reported the approach of the enemy. Pablo de Meneses, thinking that he was faced with no more men than the soldier had reported, was reluctant to retire, and ordered his men to stand their ground and fight the pursuers, not heeding the advice of those who insisted that this was very dangerous and would allow the enemy to come up in force. At this point they saw more and more of the enemy appear among the sand hills. Then Pablo de Meneses ordered his men to retire at all speed, he himself remaining in the rear to hold the enemy back. A skirmish took place, and men were wounded and killed on both sides. The fighting went on during most of the day, for the royal force was unable to march away.

Then Francisco Hernández Girón came up with his whole force, and a scene of great confusion occurred. Neither those in pursuit nor those pursued could tell their own men from the enemy for dust and hubbub. The engagement covered a distance of more than three leagues. In it Captain Luis de Avalos was wounded and five or six more beside. Fourteen or fifteen lay dead, among them brave Miguel Cornejo, a *vecino* of Arequipa, one of the first conquerors, for whom Francisco de Carvajal, Gonzalo Pizarro's commander, did the friendly act we have mentioned in return for what he owed him. He was wearing a Burgundian helmet with the visor down; and being out of breath because of the great dust raised by those fleeing and giving pursuit and the intense heat that is always found in those valleys and thereabouts, he was unable to raise the visor in the sudden onrush and fear inspired by the enemy, and was suffocated. His loss was much mourned by all who knew him, for he was a man of great goodness and held in high esteem: proof of his goodness is his conduct toward Francisco de Carvajal and his wife and family when he found them abandoned and homeless in the square at Arequipa, and with no one to look to for protection.

The rebels called for the retreat, for although they were victorious, they felt they were losing men, since many of those who went in pursuit of the enemy were going over to the king. The engagement was therefore broken off, and they hastily withdrew lest a mutiny should break out. Among those who fled from Francisco Hernández that day was a citizen of Cuzco called Juan Rodríguez de Villalobos whom the rebel leader had sought to attach to his party after the rising, marrying him to his wife's sister. But the bond of relationship availed the rebel nothing, for he went over to the king's side in the fray. On learning this, Francisco Hernández pretended to be glad to be rid of him, and declared disdainfully that he was damned if he didn't care more about a sword the fellow had gone off with than about his absence. Becoming even more presumptuous, he declared that anyone who did not want to serve him could go freely over to the judges, and he gave them full liberty, for he did not want the company of pressed men, but of friends and volunteers.

Pablo de Meneses, thus pressed by the enemy, left his own men with three others and went on to Chincha, as Fernández relates, in his ch. xxxviii, in the following words: "When Pablo de Meneses saw that his men were beaten and that they were fleeing pell-mell, he cut away from the road and crossed the sandy flats to the river Pisco with three followers, and thence went to Chincha," etc. Thus Fernández.

The rebels, on re-forming after the attack, collected everything they could find by the roadside; for the royal force had thrown down everything they had to lighten their horses and mules, even cloaks, capes, and weapons, as sailors do when they are afraid of drowning in a storm. The royal captains and soldiers had so managed things that they found themselves in flight from the rebels and in a position to destroy them and wipe them out all in the same moment.

I may as well tell one incident that occurred in this engagement. As such things rarely happen in the world, the reader will give me leave to recount it: it concerns the faithfulness of a horse, which I myself saw. In this encounter there was a gentleman on the royal side called Juan Julio de Hojeda, a *vecino* of Cuzco, who had been one of the first conquerors of the empire. Among other horses he possessed a bay with a black tail and mane, which he was riding on the day of the battle of Villacori. Riding off pell-mell, as Fernández says, Juan Julio de Hojeda fell from his horse. Seeing him fall, the animal stopped, though it was galloping off in the midst of more than three hundred others, and did not stir until his owner picked himself up and remounted. The loyalty of the horse saved his life, and the incident was much remarked on as something extraordinary.

I myself witnessed a similar incident involving the same horse in the city of Cuzco. After the war was over, the gentlemen of the city were taking their exercise—for at least every Sunday there were public races—and a mestizo fellow pupil of mine called Pedro de Altamirano, the son of Antonio Altamirano, one of the first conquerors, who was taking part in the race, happened to see a pretty girl at a window in one of the houses belonging to Alonso de Mesa where she lived. The sight of her caused him to forget the race he was going to begin, and though he had passed the window he turned his head two or three times to look at her. The third time, the horse had already reached the starting point and feeling the rider turn back, sharply called his attention back to the race by furiously swerving into the course. The rider, more intent on looking at the girl than in racing the horse, slipped over its right shoulder and fell to the ground. But when the horse saw he had fallen, it pulled up sharp and did not stir, although it had started off so furiously and was wearing a breast plate with bells. The youth picked himself up, got on the horse and finished the course, to the amusement of the bystanders. All this I saw from the little balcony of my lord Garcilaso de la Vega, and the second feat of the horse confirmed the first, and satisfied those who had not seen it of its truth.

Here we shall return to the judge's army, in which there was great conflict and ill feeling and many changes of command and office, as we shall soon see.

CHAPTER XIII

The judges dismiss the two generals; Francisco
Hernández reaches Nanasca; a double spy brings
him much information; the rebel leader
raises a force of Negroes.

IN HIS Majesty's camp, there was a great deal of contradiction and division between the two generals, so much so that the captains and soldiers grumbled and swore in public because the two leaders avoided one another on every occasion and opposed one another's orders. This dissatisfaction was brought to the generals' ears, and on the intercession of a large number of leading citizens who brought Licentiate Judge Santillán from a place two leagues distant whither he had retired, the two dined together. Of their dining together and reconciliation Fernández says in his ch. xxxix that "the camp was very glad of it," etc.

Late on the same evening the news of the engagement at Villacori and the royalist defeat reached the camp. It caused great astonishment, for everyone thought from the news that had been received hourly that Pablo de Meneses was winning. The judges, captains, and other councillors were greatly incensed by the defeat of Pablo Meneses, and they saw by experience that the division and opposition of the two generals was responsible for this loss of prestige of the imperial army. They accordingly gathered together and decided to dismiss both generals by royal decree and appoint Pablo de Meneses as captain general, with Don Pedro Puertocarrero as his commander. This was also the cause of much grumbling and cursing in the camp, where it was thought that an officer who had lost an engagement like that at Villacori should have been reduced to the rank of the meanest private instead of being pushed up from commander to general, and punished and disgraced instead of being rewarded and honored. The decisions of the *audiencia* were conveyed to the generals, who were not a little put out; but they were at length mollified and accepted the decree.

Orders were given for the rebel to be hotly pursued by 800 men. But this gave rise to differences of opinion, just as in the past, so that three days went by before this force could leave. And as Licentiate Santillán returned to Lima, his numerous relatives and friends went with him, in all about 150 persons. At this point one of his friends advised him not to let them return with him in order to prevent talk, for his rivals and enemies would say that he was travelling with such a large escort because he was afraid of them or intended to rebel. Licentiate Santillán therefore dismissed his friends and kinsmen, and asked them to rejoin the army and serve His Majesty as circumstances required; he then went to the city with no other company but that of his servants.

Francisco Hernández was now at Nanasca, sixty leagues from Lima, which he reached without any untoward incident, being enabled to advance in peace and without opposition because of the confusion in the royal camp. To crown his satisfaction, the enemy sent one of the royal sergeants, a man who had taken part in Diego de Rojas' expedition, to go disguised as an Indian to the rebel camp and report what was going on there. The man was a volunteer, and the judges trusted him and gave permission for him to go. But he proved to be a double spy, and went to Francisco Hernández and told him how he had double-crossed the royal leaders to join him because there was a great deal of discord among the leaders and discontent among the soldiers in the royal camp, and no one wanted to fight. It therefore seemed certain that they would lose, and he preferred to save himself, and had come over to the rebels.

He added that the judges were dispirited and perplexed because they had received news that the city of San Miguel de Piura had risen against

His Majesty and in favor of Francisco Hernández, that another captain called Pedro de Orsúa was coming from New Granada with a large force for the same purpose, and that the kingdom of Quito had also declared for Francisco Hernández. All this filled the rebel leader and his followers with joy and they had it proclaimed as if it were perfectly true. The spy also reported that the judges had had news of the departure of the marshal from Charcas with a large and splendid army of more than 1,200 men, but this was suppressed and the man was ordered to say that the marshal had no more than 600, for fear of discouraging and spreading fear among the rebel army.

At the same time it was discovered that an Indian from the judges' camp was bringing letters and messages to one of the rebel soldiers. The Indian and the soldier were arrested and both were hanged. Though subjected to two tortures, the soldier did not confess, but after his death they found hanging from his neck a scroll containing a pardon from the judges for Tomás Vázquez. Francisco Hernández at once made this pardon public, adding that great rewards and allocations of Indians had been promised in the judges' name to anyone who killed him and other rebel leaders.

During this campaign and before the clash at Villacori, Francisco Hernández had formed a company of Negroes comprising more than 150 of the slaves taken in the towns, estates, and farms they had sacked. Later, as the rebellion proceeded, Francisco Hernández had more than 300 Ethiopian soldiers, and in order to do them honor and raise their courage and ardor, he gave them an independent command. Their captain general was a man I myself knew, called Massa John, a very skilful carpenter by trade. He had been a slave of Antonio Altamirano, already mentioned several times. The commander was Massa Antonio, who had received the surrender of one of the leading soldiers of the royalist forces at the affair at Villacori. I myself knew his prisoner, but I had better not mention his name, though the fame of the Negro commander who disarmed him reached Spain, and caused a certain gentleman who had known the soldier in the Indies and had been his friend to send him a brightly gilded sword and dagger, not so much as a token of their past friendship, but rather to underline his cowardice. All this was much spoken of in Peru after Francisco Hernández's war was over. Apart from the Negro commanders, the rebel leader appointed Negro captains, who picked their ensigns, sergeants, and corporals, and fifers and drummers, and raised their own flags, all of which they did very well. Many Negroes in the royal camp went over to the rebel side when they knew that Francisco Hernández had treated their relatives so honorably and they fought against their masters for the duration of the war. The rebel leader made full use of these soldiers, sending them out with Spanish corporals to collect supplies; and the Indians, to save themselves from the cruelties that were inflicted on them, gave what they had, depriving themselves and their wives and children. This later caused much dearth and starvation among the Indians.

CHAPTER XIV

The marshal picks captains for his army; he
reaches Cuzco and gives pursuit to
Francisco Hernández; the unfortunate death
of Captain Diego de Almendras.

WHILE THE events we have narrated were taking place in Cuzco, Lima, and Villacori, Marshal Alonso de Alvarado, who was in the kingdom and provinces of Charcas, was not idle. As we have said, he summoned people to His Majesty's service and collected pikes, arquebusses, and other arms, and gunpowder, supplies, and mounts for the men. He appointed captains and officers to help him in all this, and made a gentleman called Don Martín de Avendaño, who was his brother-in-law, commander, and a brave soldier called Diego de Porras ensign of the forces. Diego de Villavicencio was made sergeant major, a post he had occupied under President La Gasca against Gonzalo Pizarro. Two citizens of Charcas were made cavalry captains, Pero Hernández Paniagua and Juan Ortiz de Zárate, together with another gentleman of very noble family and character called Don Gabriel de Guzmán. These three were captains of horse. Licentiate Gómez Hernández was made judge advocate, and Juan de Riba Martín alguacil mayor. He chose six captains of infantry: three were *vecinos*, Licentiate Polo, Diego de Almendras, and Martín de Alarcón, and three were not, Hernando Alvarez de Toledo, Juan Ramón, and Juan de Arreinaga.

They all set about their duties in good earnest, and in a very few days the marshal had nearly 800 men, of whom Fernández writes as follows (ch. xli): "They were 775 of the finest and staunchest men ever seen in Peru, by reason of their soldierly qualities, their arms, their rich clothes, and their length of service. They demonstrated amply that they had come from that famous hill, than which none richer is known in all the world," etc. Thus Fernández, and his words are true, for I saw them a few days later in Cuzco, and they were just as gallant and fine as our author says.

The marshal, thus strongly provided with men, arms, and supplies, set forth for Cuzco, and on the way he was joined by groups of soldiers in 10's or 20's as they happened to come together to serve His Majesty. Nearly 40 men came from Arequipa, in spite of what that city had undergone. Sancho Duarte and Captain Martín de Olmos, who were at La Paz, came out to join the marshal with above 200 good men they had collected, and the meeting was attended with many salvoes of shot from both sides, and manifestations of great pleasure and rejoicing at this display of gallantry and strength. The army then advanced until it reached the limits of the jurisdiction of the great city of Cuzco, where Captain Juan de Saavedra was waiting for them with a band of men, which, though small in number, not exceeding 85, was notable for its valor and influence, since it included 13 or 14 *vecinos* of Cuzco, all participants in the first or second conquest of the empire. Of these, 60 were mounted and the rest on foot. The marshal was very pleased with them, especially on learning which and how many of the citizens of Cuzco had fled from the rebel, and gone to Lima to serve His Majesty. He was greatly encouraged by the thought that Francisco Hernández Girón must be very much weakened, since those he had thought were his supporters had abandoned him. So the marshal advanced in very good spirit and entered Cuzco with more than 1,200 men: 300 on horseback, 350 arquebusiers, and 550 with pikes and halberds. Each company marched in columns of five, and the whole army drew up in the main square, where there were infantry and cavalry skirmishes and all sorts of celebrations and rejoicings. They were billetted in the city.

The bishop of Cuzco, Don Fray Juan Solano, went out with the whole chapter to welcome the marshal and his army and gave them his benediction; but having learnt by experience from his campaign with Diego Centeno, he preferred not to go to war, but stayed in his church and prayed to God for all those concerned.

From Cuzco the marshal sent orders for the bridges over the Apurímac and Amáncay to be rebuilt, so that he could go out in pursuit of Francisco Hernández, whose whereabouts and doings were unknown. At this point news came from the *audiencia* of Pablo de Meneses' reverse at Villacori and of the fact that the rebel was in the valley of Nanasca. This caused the marshal to change his plans, and he decided to march back and cut off Francisco Hernández so as to prevent him from proceeding down the coast to Arequipa and so to Charcas, which would have wrought undue havoc throughout the country and have prolonged the war very greatly. He therefore left Cuzco, having ordered the newly made bridges to be burnt so that the enemy could not use them if he were to return to Cuzco. Moving toward Collao, he followed the royal highway for fourteen or fifteen leagues and then turned to the right in order to reveal himself to Francisco Hernández and find out by what route the latter would leave Nanasca to meet him.

Having no news of the rebels, he went on to Parihuana Cocha, though he had to pass a very rough waste more than thirty leagues across in order to get there. On the way four soldiers deserted and went over to Francisco Hernández. They stole two good mules, one belonging to Gabriel de Pernia and the other to Pedro Franco, both famous soldiers. When the marshal learnt who were the owners of the mules, he gave orders for them to be strangled, on suspicion that they had given the beasts to the deserters. This angered the army, who cursed the marshal for the cruelty of the sentence, as Fernández says in his ch. xli.

The four soldiers who fled came across Francisco Hernández's scouts and accompanied them to Nanasca. In private they revealed the great force with which the marshal was pursuing the rebels, and said that he was marching in the direction of Parihuana Cocha. But publicly, so as not to spread despondency, they announced that his army was very small. Nevertheless, Francisco Hernández undeceived his followers, as Fernández recounts in these words:

"Gentlemen, make no mistake, for I warn you that we have to grit our teeth. You have a thousand men before you down there, and twelve hundred up here, yet with God's aid, their numbers will be of no avail, and I trust to Him to defeat them all, if a hundred loyal friends will stand by me." Then he ordered his men to prepare to break camp, and on May 8 they left Nanasca for Lucanes by the mountain road, hoping to get to Parinacocha before the marshal,

etc. Thus Fernández (ch. xli).

Marshal Alonso de Alvarado pursued his way and crossed the Parihuana Cocha desert, where, owing to the rough ground and bad weather, he lost sixty of his best and strongest horses, which dropped dead on the way while being led, though well covered with blankets. The horse doctors were unable to determine the cause of this, saying that they lacked breath. This puzzled everyone, and the Indians took it as an ill omen. Fernández says the following of all this in his ch. xlii:

When the marshal reached Chumbibilcas and had supplied the army's needs, he entered the Parinacocha desert, which consists of thirty-two leagues of mountains, moors, and snowfields, with such rough and bad roads and so many steep cuts that many horses died of cold, it then being the very kidney of the winter in those parts; and there was great lack of food,

etc. Thus says our author, quoted word for word, as are all our extracts from the Spanish historians.

The marshal left Captain Sancho Duarte sick with diarrhea in Parihuana Cocha, where he died a few days later. As the army proceeded, its scouts captured one of the enemy's. He was taken to the marshal, and in order to avoid his being killed they told the marshal that he had come over to serve His Majesty. From him the marshal learned that Francisco Hernández was less than twenty leagues away. He therefore ordered his men to advance with caution lest the enemy should make bold to steal up to them by means of a night march.

Two days from Parihuana Cocha, a great alarm was given in the royal army. The cause was that Captain Diego de Almendras was in the habit of going off while the army was on the march and shooting such wild animals as are found in the desert. Among some rocks he came across a Negro belonging to the sergeant major Villavicencio, who had run away. He tried to tie the Negro's hands in order to bring him back to his master, and the man at first kept still to put Diego de Almendras off his guard, but when the latter approached, cord in hand, the Negro dropped to the ground, seized him by both legs, knocked him over with a butt of the head so that he fell on his back, and dealt him many blows with his own dagger and sword. At last the Negro left him almost dead, and fled to his fellows who were with Francisco Hernández, where he related his feat, and they all boasted about it as if they had each done it themselves. A mestizo lad who was with Diego de Almendras saw his master fall to the ground, beset by the Negro, and tried to free him by clinging to the Negro's back. But Almendras, finding himself fatally wounded, told the boy to run away before the Negro killed him, which he did, raising the alarm we have mentioned with his screams. Captain Diego de Almendras was carried to Parihuana Cocha, but the journey only expedited his end: the poor gentleman died as soon as he arrived. His misfortune, brought about by his attempt to recapture someone else's Negro slave, was regarded by both Indians and Spaniards as an ill omen for the expedition.

CHAPTER XV

*The marshal is warned of the enemies' approach and
sends men out to oppose them; a skirmish
between the two forces takes place,
and all those on the king's side
decide against giving battle.*

T HE DAY after Captain Diego de Almendras' misfortune, Marshal
Alonso de Alvarado, knowing that the enemy was near, marched with
his army eight leagues in search of them, travelling very light, for he had
given instructions at the outset that no one was to take more than his arms
and food for three days. They travelled, as Fernández puts it:

through a very cruel waste with a hundred marshes and snowfields. They slept
the night without the protection of any tents or shelters, and on the next day
marched eight leagues more. With great difficulty the army reached Guallaripa,
where they had news that Francisco Hernández had passed three days earlier
and that he was at Chuquinga, four leagues away, re-forming his forces, for
they too had arrived very fatigued from the roughness of the road and the hardships of the desert. Here the marshal was joined by Comendador Romero and
García de Melo with 1,000 fighting Indians, laden with food and some pikes,
from the province of Andaguailas. A full report about Francisco Hernández
was received, and it was learned how he had had Diego de Orihuela, a native
of Salamanca, strangled because he was going to the marshal's camp to serve
His Majesty.

Thus Fernández. Knowing that the enemy were so close and wishing to
have at them, the marshal decided to send two captains with 150 picked
arquebusiers to make a raid the following morning and bring in those
who were willing to come over to the king's side. The captains and citizens who took part in a council of war, realizing how strong Francisco
Hernández's position was, opposed him and brought forward solid reasons for not attacking the enemy in his stronghold. They were quite sure
that any attacker would be exposed to complete defeat and that it was
wrong to risk the 150 best arquebusiers in the army, for their loss would

mean the loss of the whole force. The marshal replied that he and the whole army would march behind them to give support and prevent the enemy from harming them. He then resolutely demanded that each captain should supply the roll of his company so that the 150 arquebusiers might be chosen, and ordered the commander and Captain Juan Ramón to go with them and get as near the enemy as possible. The captains and the 150 arquebusiers went out at midnight and the marshal left with the main force three hours later: they all marched in search of Francisco Hernández. The latter, knowing he had so stern a foe so near, took care not to be caught unawares, keeping his men in battle formation and guarding the only two passes by which he could be reached: the other sides were quite secure, and the position was a strong one.

Before daybreak the king's forces came up with the enemy and tried to get as close as possible without being seen, being separated from him by the river Amáncay. As they stealthily approached, an Indian from Francisco Hernández's forces discovered them and warned his master that they were at hand. He ordered the alarm to be given at once, and deployed men as necessary in case of attack. The two sides greeted one another with fusillades from the arquebusiers, but no damage was done for they were too distant.

At nine in the morning the marshal and his force came within sight of Francisco Hernández, whose men, on seeing them, began to skirmish with greater audacity and presumption than military science. Both forces were in places where there was no flat ground at all, but only the cliffs and woods and high rocks and ravines through which the Amáncay flows. Francisco Hernández's men scattered and hid among the trees. The marshal's descended boldly down a slope to skirmish, and on coming within gunshot shouted their identity so as to distinguish themselves better.

Juan Ramón's ensign, called Gonzalo Mata, got very near the enemy and cried very loud: "I'm Mata, I'm Mata!"

One of them who was well hidden, seeing him within range, cried: "And I'll mat you, I'll mat you!" shooting him in the breast and knocking him dead.

Others were killed and wounded in the same way without seeing who hit them, and although the marshal sent captains and men to intensify the skirmish and it lasted until three in the afternoon, his men gained no advantage in the fight, for more than forty of the leading men chosen for this excursion were killed or wounded. They included a youth of eighteen called Don Felipe Enríquez, whose loss was much regretted by both sides. Captain Arreinaga was wounded. The royal party received such havoc in the fray that they lost a great deal of the swagger with which they had begun it. During the fight two soldiers abandoned the rebels, one called Sancho de Bayona, and went over to the marshal. From the marshal's side the man we have mentioned called ———— de Bilbao went over to the rebels, as he had said he would whenever he found Francisco Hernández.

As the forces withdrew from the skirmish, the following events took place, which are described in Fernández's ch. xliv in the following words:

The marshal had a long discussion with Lorenzo de Aldana, Gómez de Alvarado, Diego Maldonado, Gómez de Solís, and other leading figures in his army. In debating what was to be done, he displayed the greatest desire to attack the rebels, since Bayona, the soldier who had come over, had told him that Francisco Hernández would undoubtedly take flight. When the marshal had said this, Lorenzo de Aldana and Diego de Maldonado took him aside and persuaded him not to give battle, begging him to be patient, since he had such obvious advantages over the rebels, both in men and morale, and in the strength of his position. Moreover, all the Indians and everyone else would be at his service, while the enemy could only rely on good fortune. By continuously harassing them with Indians, who could give them a sprinkling from all sides, he would reduce them to such a state of hunger and want that they would be forced to adopt one of two courses—to flee from the fort, in which case they could easily be defeated as they came out, or to come over to the royalist side as a whole or in great numbers, so that not a single man on the loyal side need be risked. All this could be done by sitting tight and at ease: it would only be necessary to keep a careful guard and constant watch on the rebels, especially from the top of the cliff or point that projected toward the river overlooking both camps. If this were carefully guarded, the marshal would be much stronger than the enemy. This advice recommended itself to many of the leaders, though Martín de Robles (to whom the marshal had given Diego de Almendras' company) and some others insisted on giving battle. But Lorenzo de Aldana was so insistent on the contrary course that the marshal promised and pledged his word not to give battle. On this assumption he at once sent to the camp established by the judges for some small pieces of artillery and arquebusiers so as to watch the enemy from the point of the cliff and force them to leave their fort and harass them so that they would either surrender or fight.

Thus Fernández, who shows clearly how much the marshal desired to give battle and the equally strong desire of his followers to avoid it and the good reasons they brought forward in support of their ideas. But their policy was not adhered to, and all was thus lost, as we shall see.

CHAPTER XVI

Juan de Piedrahita raids the marshal's camp;
Rodrigo de Pineda goes over to the king's
side and persuades the marshal to give
battle; the clash of opinions
about this; the marshal's
determination to fight.

AT NIGHTFALL Juan de Piedrahita went out with three dozen arquebusiers to raid the marshal's army. As they were in groups he attacked at three or four points but made no impression worth speaking of:
the marshal's men replied with their arquebusses to show that they were
not asleep, but paid little attention, and at dawn Piedrahita retired without having done anything useful. He had however made it possible for
Rodrigo de Pineda, a *vecino* of Cuzco who was a captain of horse with the
rebels, to go over to the marshal under pretence of going out to reinforce
Piedrahita in his scattered attacks.

Rodrigo de Pineda spoke as follows, according to Fernández in the
same chapter:

On his arrival he told the marshal for certain that many, indeed most, of
Francisco Hernández's men would come over but for the strong guard kept
over them. He could indeed be put to flight that self-same night, and the river
could easily be forded. The marshal then called the *vecinos* and captains to a
council of war, and when they were assembled, gave them the gist of Rodrigo
de Pineda's news. He said that this had determined him to attack the enemy
and he advanced some of his reasons. Many members of the council refuted
them, giving good cause for not attacking the fort in any circumstances.
Finding the leading men opposed, the marshal told Rodrigo Pineda to ex-
pound the views he had already mentioned to him before to the whole company, saying what he thought of Francisco Hernández and his army and what
he thought Francisco Hernández meant to do and how many people he had.
Rodrigo Pineda said that Francisco Hernández must have about 380 men, of
whom 220 were arquebusiers, though they were ill supplied and some were
serving against their will: he had more than a thousand mounts. What Fran-

cisco Hernández intended to do was to take flight that night unless battle were given, for he had no food and his men were afraid. If he fled and they tried to follow him, he might inflict great losses on his pursuers, because of the difficulty of the country and badness of the roads, and this would be to the detriment of the whole empire. But it would be easy to ford the river and give battle on the other side.

The marshal then said that he wanted to attack the same day so as to be sure the rebel leader should not give him the slip as he had the judges, and so as to avoid his doing more damage than he had already done: for he would not be able to follow him without great loss.

The others retorted that in their view it seemed that since Francisco Hernández was in the fort, it would be much better to let him take flight, for in that case he could be defeated with little danger and without risking a single man. But this did not satisfy the marshal, who said they were wrong, and that this plan did not fit in with his obligations, and it was discreditable to the honor of all the gentlemen and soldiers present that Francisco Hernández should be allowed to get away with his army and disturb and ravage the kingdom. Despite any objections, he was determined to give battle.

Many of the leading captains then left the marshal's tent, where the council was held, in great dissatisfaction. As they came out Gómez de Alvarado remarked bitterly: "Come on then; I can see that I've got to die."

Thus far Fernández, word for word. After leaving the council, the *vecinos* of Cuzco and Charcas returned to the marshal. They numbered more than 30 including Lorenzo de Aldana, Juan de Saavedra, Diego Maldonado, Gómez Alvarado, Pero Hernández Paniagua, Licentiate Polo, Juan Ortiz de Zárate, Alonso de Loaisa, the factor Juan de Salas, Martín de Meneses, García de Melo, Juan de Berrio, Antón Ruiz de Guevara, Gonzalo de Soto, and Diego de Trujillo, all of whom were among the conquerors of Peru. They spoke to Marshal Alonso de Alvarado apart and begged him to reconsider his decision about giving battle; remembering that the enemy's position was extremely strong, and that his own was no less so as a defence from the enemy. Even Rodrigo de Pineda had admitted that Francisco Hernández lacked supplies, and hunger would drive him to leave the fort within the next three days: let them wait just so long, and they could then plan better according to circumstances. The enemy was under their noses and when he did try to escape, he could not fly through the air, but would have to keep his feet on the ground, and they could follow him and get the Indians to block his path, and since the roads were so difficult, hold them so that he could not get away. To attack the enemy in such a strong place would risk the whole stakes at a throw, for there was nothing certain about battles, and it meant sending captains and men to the slaughter, for the enemy could shoot them all down with arquebusses. He should consider the advantages he had over the enemy. He had plenty of supplies, which they had not, and Indian helpers and everything else necessary for holding firm. Victory could be gained without any loss at all, particularly since the enemy was pinned down and exhausted. There was no sense in risking the loss of these advantages. But the marshal, forgetting that he had lost another battle like this on that very river, as we have described, replied angrily that he had considered the whole affair and that his duty obliged him to give battle. It was improper and offensive to his reputation and to theirs that a band of little rebels should go on raiding them quite impudently night after night. He was very annoyed by this and had determined to offer battle that very day. It might cost him 300 killed, but he wanted to have the lot of them drawn and quartered before sundown. There was to be no more talk of avoiding the battle or getting out of it; they were to go and get ready for it: those were his orders as captain general, and if they disobeyed he would hold them as traitors.

This determination ended the council, and the *vecinos* came away very much incensed. Some said that as the soldiers were not his sons or relatives or friends and cost him nothing, the marshal wanted to set them up as targets for the enemy to pick off; it was their misfortune and evil destiny that they had a captain general so black humored and full of bile that when he had victory in his hands he insisted on making a present of it to the enemy at their expense and with no purpose and nothing to oblige him at all. They said a great deal more, and their words foreboded their destruction and ruin, which was to occur six hours later.

In this desperate mood the wisest *vecinos*, captains, and soldiers prepared for the battle. Others thought simply that they would make hay of the enemy, since he had fewer than 400 men, fewer even than 350, while they had more than 1,200. But these had not considered the enemy's position or the difficulty of crossing the river to get at him and beat him, for it was a deep river and the enemy had many narrow and steep places and rough slopes in front of him as defences.

Because of these difficulties the marshal's cavalry was quite useless, for they could find nowhere to attack the enemy. The arquebusses were the weapons of the day, and the enemy had plenty of these and good ones, and excellent marksmen who could shoot down a bird with a ball. They included a number of mestizos, especially ——— Granado, from Mexico, who was an expert and had trained them all to shoot from cover or standing or in any position. It was moreover suspected, and almost certain, that

Francisco Hernández put some poison in the powder he had, for the surgeons used to say that arquebus wounds, provided they were not fatal, healed more easily and quicker than those inflicted by other weapons such as lances, swords, pikes, or partisans; yet those caused by arquebusses on the present occasion were incurable, however slight, and this was due to the effect of the powder and poison. With all these difficulties they set forth to engage in a battle that was to cost many of them their lives.

CHAPTER XVII

The marshal disposes his men for battle; Francisco Hernández disposes his defences; incidents in the struggle; the deaths of many prominent men.

IT WAS a little before mid-day when the marshal ordered the alarm to be sounded. When all the men were assembled in their respective companies, he ordered Captain Martín de Robles to cross the river with his arquebusiers and place himself on the enemy's left, so as to attack from that side. Similarly Captains Martín de Olmos and Juan Ramón were to take the enemy's right after crossing, and to attack with Martín de Robles. Both groups were ordered not to attack separately but at the same moment, the signal for starting the attack being a trumpet blast. The purpose of this was that the enemy, finding himself attacked on both flanks, should be fully occupied on both sides and have less resources to take the offensive. He also ordered the rest of the infantry and all the cavalry to descend by a very narrow path to the river; there was in fact no other way down. Having crossed, they were to form on a small piece of level ground near the enemy and attack with all fury. With these instructions they all went out to do battle.

Francisco Hernández Girón, who was watching their dispositions from his headquarters, guessed that they would attack on three sides and told his friends: "Well, gentlemen, today we must either win or die, for the enemy is going to fall on us with great fury!"

A professional soldier of long experience whom Francisco Hernández and his men called Colonel Villalva, finding the general and his companions rather half-hearted, as he thought, encouraged them by telling them (in Fernández's words) :

not to be in the least afraid, for the marshal could not possibly form his men, who would certainly be worsted while crossing the river. Because of this and of the roughness of the ground they could not maintain any sort of order, especially as they were coming in groups from various directions; and the fort was so strong that they could wait for the attack and defend it even if the enemy had 10,000 men. All who attacked would be lost. Villalva's words greatly rejoiced Francisco Hernández and all his men,

etc. It turned out exactly as Colonel Villalva had said. Francisco Hernández placed part of his arquebusiers and all his pikemen on a level space drawn up in battle order under the captaincy of Juan de Piedrahita and Sotelo. Their orders were to rally to the defence as a body or in two groups, as might seem necessary. Another large group of over 100 arquebusiers were scattered in 4's and 6's among the terraces, cliffs, and ravines, and clumps of trees on the river bank. There was no space down there for a force to form and the enemy would have to come one by one in loose order, so that they could be fired on from chosen positions without being able to reply, as indeed happened.

Martín de Robles duly crossed the river with his company of arquebusiers, and thinking himself already victorious—so low was his opinion of the enemy—he hoped to avoid sharing the honors of the day with anyone else and attacked hastily without even waiting for all his men to cross the river. Those who had crossed went straight into action. The water came up to their waists and even up to their chests, and many of them carelessly allowed it to wet the powder in their caskets; the more careful carried the caskets in their hands and lifted them above their heads together with their arquebusses. Captain Piedrahita and his friends, seeing Martín de Robles advance in such haste and disorder, went out to meet him with great spirit and gave him a good peppering from the arquebusses. Many men were killed, and captain and soldiers fled; they all returned across the river, while Piedrahita retired to his positions.

At this point captains Martín de Olmos and Juan Ramón approached the fort, and seeing that Martín de Robles' attack had led to nothing, they thought they would regain what he had lost and therefore attacked the enemy with all fury. The latter, after their success in the first brush, received them with another great volley, and though the struggle continued for a while, it ended with a victory for Piedrahita who drove the royalists back to the river bank with many wounded and dead; some recrossed the river, seeing how roughly the enemy was handling them. Captain Juan de Piedrahita, very proud of his two successful actions, returned to his position so as to sally forth as required.

While the marshal suffered these two reverses, which were due to Martín de Robles' refusal to wait for the trumpet call and obey the orders he had been given, the other captains and soldiers from the royal army went down to the river and tried to cross, though with great difficulty, for the water there was deeper than elsewhere and wetted the arquebusses and powder of the infantry, while the pikemen lost their pikes. Francisco Hernández's arquebusiers were, as we have said, scattered among the terraces, ravines, and cliffs of the river bank, and seeing the enemy getting into difficulties in crossing, they came out to meet them and received them with arquebuss fire. Many were killed in the river and never completed the crossing, for the rebels were able to fire from positions and pick them off as they liked.

A great many were killed and wounded during the crossing and on the level space, where they tried to form ranks but were prevented from doing so. Among those killed the chief men were Juan de Saavedra, Sergeant Major Villavicencio, Gómez de Alvarado, Captain Hernando Alvarez de Toledo, Don Gabriel de Guzmán, Diego de Ulloa, Francisco de Barrientos (a *vecino* of Cuzco), and Simón Pinto, ensign. These were killed. Those wounded included Captain Martín de Robles, Captain Martín de Alarcón, and Gonzalo Silvestre, of whom we have already spoken at length. He lost a horse killed in this engagement for which two days before he had been offered twelve thousand ducats by Martín de Robles (to whom the president awarded forty thousand pesos a year, as we have said), but he had not accepted because he wanted to have a good horse under him in the battle. This incident we have mentioned in Book Nine, ch. xvi, of the First Part of these *Commentaries,* but without naming those concerned, which we now have occasion to do. Gonzalo Silvestre had a leg broken by the horse as it fell to the ground, and escaped from the fight because an Indian servant brought up another but less valuable horse and helped him to mount. The Indian accompanied him as far as Huamanga, serving him to the very end of the war like his own son. Besides these prominent men who were killed or wounded and are mentioned by name, more than sixty other famous soldiers were killed before they could deal a blow with sword or pike.

These incidents were the most notable in the engagement, for what followed was merely disorder and confusion, and many of the marshal's men refused to cross the river to meet the enemy for fear of the arquebusses. The truth is that from the opening skirmish that took place the first day the two armies sighted one another, the marshal's men were frightened of the enemy's arquebusses, and their fear lasted until they were defeated.

A soldier called ———— Perales went over to the marshal's side and asked for a loaded arquebuss to shoot Francisco Hernández, saying that he knew him well and knew what color he was dressed in. When he was given it, he shot and killed Juan Alonso de Badajoz, thinking he was Francisco Hernández because he was dressed in the same color and was of similar build. He boasted publicly of having killed the rebel leader, but afterwards when it was realized that Francisco Hernández was winning, he again changed sides, saying that he had been captured. It was not long, however, before he paid for his treachery, for a few days later when Perales was in Cuzco with his commander Licentiate Diego de Alvarado, Francisco Hernández learnt that the man had boasted of having killed him and wrote to Alvarado to have him hanged. This was done and I saw him hanging on the city gibbet.

To return to the battle, when Juan de Piedrahita saw the confusion, disorder, and fear reigning in the marshal's army, he ordered his men to follow quickly and advanced running out of the fort with the arquebusiers who could accompany him—fewer than fifty in all—shouting victory and firing wherever they saw a group of twenty or thirty men, more or less. All surrendered and handed over their arms and powder, which was what the rebels most needed. In this way over three hundred men gave in, and he took them back with him. They dared not try to escape for fear that other rebels would attack them.

CHAPTER XVIII

*Francisco Hernández is victorious; the marshal
and his men take flight from the scene of
the battle; many of them are killed by
Indians on the way.*

WHEN Marshal Don Alonso de Alvarado saw that many of his men
refrained from giving battle and refused to cross the river, he himself crossed back to the other side to get them together and make them
fight. But the more he cried and shouted at them to this end, the less they
obeyed him and the more they ran away from the enemy who, led by Captain Juan de Piedrahita, was pressing on their heels. Some of the marshal's
friends told him not to fatigue himself by trying to bring them back, for
people who began to run away from the enemy would never turn round
and fight unless events took an unexpected turn or reinforcements appeared.

Upon this the marshal went off. Those who could followed him. The
rest fled in various directions, wherever they thought they would be safest.
Some went to Arequipa, others to Charcas, others to Pueblo Nuevo, others
to Huamanga, and others went by the coast route to join His Majesty's
army where the royal judges were. The smallest group went to Cuzco;
they were only seven soldiers and we shall relate their experiences further
on.

The Indians killed many Spaniards as they fled down the long, open
roads. They died without being able to defend themselves since they had
dropped their weapons. One who was killed was a son of Don Pedro de
Alvarado, the great gentleman who went to Peru with 800 fighting men,
as we have said at length in the proper place. The young man, whom I
knew, was called Don Diego de Alvarado, a son worthy of such a father,
and his unfortunate death caused great regret among all those who had
known the father. The Indians made bold to commit this outrage because the marshal's officers (and we shall not mention any special name),
thinking themselves certain of victory and desiring to prevent any of the
enemy from escaping, had ordered the Indians to kill all those they found

fleeing down the roads. This they did, and more than 80 perished in this way.

Those who died in the battle and skirmish on the first day numbered more than 120, and more than 40 others of the wounded (whom Fernández puts at 280) died of inadequate treatment and lack of surgeons, medicines, and comforts: in all of which there was great disorganization. So that those who died on the marshal's side numbered nearly 250 men, while the rebels lost no more than 17. As Fernández says, they looted the richest camp that ever was in Peru, because the marshal put into battle 100 of the richest and more prominent *vecinos* from the interior, and many of the soldiers had spent six or seven thousand pesos and others two, three, or four thousand on their equipment.

At the beginning of the engagement Francisco Hernández had bidden his sergeant major Antonio Carrillo to take 8 or 9 horsemen and guard an opening through which he feared some of his men might take flight because it was rather remote from the fighting. In the heat of the struggle Alberto de Orduña, Francisco Hernández's ensign general, appeared at this spot with his standard down and telling them to flee because the general was dead and his camp overrun. They all duly fled and travelled eight or nine leagues during the night. The next day they learned from the Indians that it was the marshal who was defeated and Francisco Hernández the conqueror. With this news they returned to their army much ashamed at their own weakness, though they said that they had been in pursuit of the marshal's men who were fleeing in the mountains. However, it was realized that they were the fugitives, and Francisco Hernández covered them by saying that he himself had ordered them to go out and round up the fleeing enemy.

After the victory, the rebel commander Alvarado, though he had shown himself unworthy of his duties, and indeed unworthy of being even a private soldier during the engagement, wanted to prove his valor and derring-do. Hearing that his people had captured a gentleman from Zamora called Comendador Romero, who, as we have said, joined the marshal's army four days before the battle with 1,000 Indians laden with supplies, the commander ordered his assistant Alonso de González (an assistant fit for such duties) to have Romero killed before he was brought into camp, as he knew that Francisco Hernández would pardon him if anyone interceded on his behalf. The merciless executioner did as he was bidden.

Then another prisoner, called Pero Hernández the Loyal, who well deserved the epithet for his faithfulness in His Majesty's service, was brought before Francisco Hernández. This man had served staunchly throughout Gonzalo Pizarro's war and was one of those who went with Captain Juan Vázquez Coronado, of Mexico, to discover the Seven Cities, an expedition we have described in our history of Florida. Later he served, as I have said, in the war against Gonzalo Pizarro and now in the marshal's army against Francisco Hernández Girón. He was named "the loyal" to distinguish him from others called Pero Hernández, such as Pero Hernández de la Entrada, whom we have recently mentioned, and who was so called because he had taken part in the Musu expedition or *entrada* under Diego de Rojas, which we have also described at some length.

Now Fernández says that Pero Hernández was a tailor, and that Francisco Hernández, after pardoning him at the request of Cristóbal de Funes, a *vecino* of Huamanga, rebuked him severely, calling him a blackguardly, mean villain of a tailor who had set up his flag like an inn sign in Cuzco in His Majesty's name. All this information given to our author is wrong; for I knew Pero Hernández the Loyal, who was a guest of my father's the whole time he was in Peru, sleeping in our house, and dining and supping at our board, for before coming to the Indies he was a trusted servant of the excellent and illustrious house of Feria, from which my father, by God's mercy, was descended from a cadet branch. And because Pero Hernández, a native of Oliva in Valencia, had been a servant of that house and a vassal of the duke of Feria, my father accorded him such treatment and honors as if he had been his own brother. And Pero Hernández was always treated as a very noble and honorable man: when I knew him, he always had one or two horses, and I remember that one of them was called Little Bird because it was so fast. A peculiar incident happened to me with this horse after Francisco Hernández's war was over, when Our Lord, in his great mercy, saved me from death. This man Fernández says was a tailor. I can only think that whoever gave him the information knew another of the same name who was a tailor, and added that he raised a banner in Cuzco against Francisco Hernández. It was not so, for during the whole time of the war I did not stir from that city, and Pero Hernández lodged in our house as I have said, so that if he had raised a flag or done anything else, I and everyone else would have known, and known better than Fernández. But nothing of the sort took place. The boy I have mentioned in Book Two, ch. xxv, of the First Part of these *Commentaries*, whom I cured by putting a medicinal herb on his eye when he was likely to lose it, was a son of this good soldier and was born in my father's house. Today in 1611, he lives in Oliva de Valencia, his father's native place, and is called Martín Leal. The most excellent duke of Feria and most illustrious marquis of Villanueva de Barca Rota employ him in their service and when they wish to buy horses or break them in, he is the man they send for, for he turned out to be an expert rider with the Andalusian saddle, which is the seat with which Peru was won, etc.

When Pedro Hernández the Loyal heard of Francisco Hernández Girón's rising, he was in the Antis, where he bought and sold the herb called coca and administered a large estate belonging to His Majesty called Tunu where the herb is produced. He at once repaired to the marshal's camp and faithfully served the king until he was captured at Chuquinca and presented to Francisco Hernández Girón as a person of quality because of his many loyal services rendered on behalf of His Imperial Majesty. Francisco Hernández, who had no use for loyalists, ordered him to be killed forthwith, and he was taken out to be executed. The executioner told him to kneel and put a halter round his neck to strangle him. At that point a soldier came up and asked the executioner something, and the latter turned his back on Pero Hernández the Loyal to answer. The victim, seeing the man busy with the soldier and himself unnoticed, boldly got up and, though a man in middle life, began to run so fast that even a horse could not have caught him, for his life was at stake. He reached Francisco Hernández, threw himself at his feet, flung his arms round the general's legs and begged him to spare him. All those present added their pleas, including Cristóbal de Funes, a citizen of Huamanga. Among other things they said that the poor fellow had already tasted death since he had had the rope round his neck; and Francisco Hernández, though himself reluctant, spared him to please all his friends. All this happened as I have told, and it was recounted many times in my father's house when peace was happily restored, sometimes when Pero Hernández the Loyal was there and others in his absence; later we shall tell how he escaped from the rebels and rejoined the king.

CHAPTER XIX

The scandal caused in His Majesty's camp by the marshal's defeat; the steps taken by the royal judges to repair the damage; their disagreements about whether to accompany the royal army or not; the flight of a rebel captain to the king's side.

JUST AS it happened in the battle of Chuquinca that the rebel sergeant major Antonio Carrillo and the ensign general Alberto de Orduña took flight because they heard someone shout that Francisco Hernández had been killed and it soon turned out that, on the contrary, he was victorious, in exactly the same way news of the result of the battle reached the royal headquarters. At first some Spaniards who were in the neighborhood heard from the Indians that Francisco Hernández was defeated and killed and wrote to the royal judges in great haste, asking to be rewarded for conveying the good news. But to prevent these rewards being paid for nothing, there arrived almost at once the true news of the defeat of the marshal and his companions. It caused the greatest scandal and disorder in His Majesty's army; so much so that Fernández writes (without citing causes or reasons) in his ch. xlvi, that the three other royal judges consulted whether to have their fellow-judge Licentiate Santillán killed or to arrest him and send him to Spain, as though he had caused the battle to be lost; but this was not done because Dr. Saravia was opposed to it.

We need not be shocked at this, for Francisco Hernández Girón's victory was so completely in defiance of the reckoning and expectation of all the most experienced men in Peru that everyone suspected and even believed that the marshal had been betrayed by his men and tried to think who could have done it, and they were as sure and convinced of this as if it had been revealed to them by an angel, until they saw many of their suspects come fleeing from the battle to His Majesty's headquarters, mostly wounded and in very bad shape. This testified to their loyalty and proved to the suspicious that there had been no treachery, but that the whole army had suffered a common misfortune.

After the disturbance had been settled, the royal judges ordered Antonio de Quiñones, a *vecino* of Cuzco, to go with sixty arquebusiers to the city of Huamanga to succor and protect all those who came fleeing from the defeat from that direction, and also to defend the city in case Francisco Hernández should send a force to it, which he was sure to do in order to get some of the many things he needed to supply his people. And indeed soon after the battle Francisco Hernández sent his captain Juan Cobo to the city to get a supply of medicine for those who were wounded or ill. But on learning that Antonio de Quiñones was approaching, Juan Cobo retired from Huamanga without doing anything.

In the meantime two letters from different quarters reached the royal judges almost simultaneously. One was from Marshal Don Alonso de Alvarado complaining of his ill fortune and of his followers who had disobeyed him and failed to observe the battle orders he had given, which was indeed true. The other was from Lorenzo de Aldana, who told the whole course of the battle in a few lines, saying that it had been fought against the advice of all the leading men in the camp. According to Fernández (ch. xlvii), whom we follow word for word, the letter ran as follows:

"Last Monday I wrote to Your Lordship and said what I suspected and feared. As soon as I had sent it, the Devil entered the marshal and he determined at once to give battle to Francisco Hernández in the fort where he was, against everyone's judgment and advice, quite apart from mine. Notwithstanding all this, he attacked in such a way that Francisco Hernández worsted us from his fort and killed a great many people, including some of the leaders. How many I cannot say, for as the engagement took place at the fort itself and the marshal withdrew, there was no opportunity to see. He was wounded: but not in the fighting, or in encouraging his men,"

etc. Thus far Fernández.

On receiving confirmation of the marshal's defeat, the royal judges ordered the camp to march and follow Francisco Hernández Girón, and the *audiencia* to accompany the army, as Fernández says:

both to give greater authority to it and to prevent people from complaining that they remained idle. In discussing this in their meeting, Licentiate Altamirano objected, saying that the *audiencia* could not accompany the army since His Majesty's command was that they should sit in Lima, and they could not leave it without express instructions; moreover, any orders the *audiencia* gave outside the city would be invalid. Dr. Saravia insisted that the *audiencia* must leave, and Licentiate Altamirano declared that he would not leave in any circumstances, for the king had not sent them to Peru to fight battles, but to sit in court and settle such cases and disputes as might arise. Dr. Saravia said that if he did not go he would suspend him from his duties and order the royal officials not to pay him his salary. This in effect was done, though there later arrived a despatch from His Majesty ordering that the salary be paid.

Thus Fernández. In view of these difficulties it was decided that the three royal judges, Dr. Saravia, Licentiate Santillán, and Licentiate Mercado should accompany the army and that Licentiate Altamirano, who refused to touch military matters and was only interested in civil strife, should stay in the city of Lima as chief justice. Diego de Mora, a citizen of Trujillo, who came with a good company of arquebusiers, as we have said, was left as corregidor of the city, and another captain, Pedro de Zárate, was put over his men.

When all this was done and precautions had been taken to guard the sea, the royal army marched to Huamanga. On the way a famous soldier called Juan Chacón, who had been captured by the rebels at Villacori, joined them. Because he was such a good soldier, Francisco Hernández tried to make friends with him and gave him a company of arquebusiers. But Juan Chacón, being a loyal servant of His Majesty, secretly negotiated with other friends of his to kill the rebel leader. And as in those times the only sort of loyalty consisted in selling each side to the other, someone told Francisco Hernández, and someone told Juan Chacón that he had been told. So before he could be arrested Chacón fled from Francisco Hernández and all his men. On the way he had been in great danger of losing his life, because the Indians applied the order they had received to kill all those who fled without any distinction between loyalists and traitors, and pursued Chacón very closely. They would have killed him if he had not had a gun which he aimed at them from a distance. In spite of all he arrived wounded at His Majesty's camp, where he reported all that Francisco Hernández intended to do. The royal judges and the whole army were overjoyed at this information, and marched into Huamanga, where we shall leave them to tell of Francisco Hernández and his doings at this time.

CHAPTER XX

What Francisco Hernández does after the battle;
he sends officers to various parts of the
kingdom to sack the cities; the silver
stolen from the citizens of Cuzco.

FRANCISCO Hernández Girón spent more than forty days at the place
where he won this battle. This was partly to bask in the glory he had
gained there and partly to attend to the needs of the many wounded royalists he had on his hands. These he comforted and flattered as much as
he could in the hope of gaining their friendship: many of them were won
over and followed him to the very end. At the same time he sent his commander Alvarado to Cuzco in pursuit of those who had fled thither. In
order that the sergeant major Antonio Carrillo should be shaken out of the
profound melancholy he had been plunged in since he ran away at Chuquinca, he was sent to the city of La Paz, Chucuitu, Potosí, and Silver City
to collect all the men, arms, and horses he could find up and down those
provinces. In particular he was ordered to seize the silver, gold, and
hidden supplies of wine that one of the marshal's soldiers called Francisco
Boloña said he knew of and could trace. So Antonio Carrillo went off with
twenty soldiers, taking Francisco Boloña with him. But of the twenty men
only two were attached to Francisco Hernández, all the rest being the
marshal's men. As a result it was publicly suspected and secretly whispered that Francisco Hernández was sending his sergeant major so that
they could beat him up, and not to his own benefit. Thus it turned out, as
we shall see. Francisco Hernández also bade his captain Juan de Piedrahita to go to Arequipa and collect what men, arms, and horses he could
find. For this expedition he gave him the rank and title of commander of
the Army of Liberty, which was what Francisco Hernández called his
force. The commander Alvarado was given the title of lieutenant general.
He thus promoted these two officers of his, adding to their presumption
and vainglory and prompting them to do the deeds they later committed.

Lieutenant General Licentiate Alvarado went his way to Cuzco in pursuit of those who had fled from the battle of Chuquinca. But one day be-

fore he got to the city, seven of the marshal's soldiers reached it with a certain Juan de Cardona as their leader. This little band brought news of the marshal's defeat, and the city was greatly afflicted, for it was never imagined that such a victory could be won by a man as near defeat and destruction as Francisco Hernández. They all agreed to flee before the rebels should come and kill them, and Francisco Rodríguez de Villafuerte, who was then *alcalde ordinario*, collected the men who were in the city, making barely forty with the seven soldiers who had just arrived, and they all marched to Collao. Some stopped for the night a league and a half from the city, the alcalde among them. Others went ahead three or four leagues. The latter were the luckiest, for when the excellent Juan de Cardona saw that the alcalde had stopped so near the city, he took the opportunity to give him the slip and run away to Cuzco, which he reached at midnight and where he told Licentiate Alvarado that Villafuerte and twenty others with him were a league and a half away. The licentiate instantly sent out the executioner Alonso González as leader of twenty others to catch Villafuerte. And Alonso González carried out his orders so well that next day by eight he had them all back at Cuzco, safely delivered to the lieutenant general. The latter made as if to kill Villafuerte and some of the others, but finding no particular crime, he pardoned them at the intercession of Francisco Hernández Girón's father-in-law and friends.

Among other rogueries committed by Licentiate Alvarado in the city of Cuzco on the instructions of the rebel leader was the theft of the bells of the cathedral and monasteries in the city. Of the two bells in the Mercedarian convent he took one, the larger of the two, and the same in the Dominican monastery. From the Franciscans he took none: they had only one and he would have taken it but for the pleadings of the religious. He took two of the five bells in the cathedral, and would have had all five if the bishop and clergy had not rallied round to defend them with maledictions and excommunications. The cathedral bells had been blessed by the bishop's own hands with oil and chrism, and were very large. He used the four bells to make six pieces of artillery, one of which burst when it was being tested. In founding the biggest piece he had it marked with the word *Libertas*, which was the name given to the rebellion. This artillery, being made of metal dedicated and consecrated to divine service, never harmed anyone, as we shall see.

In addition to this impious deed the lieutenant general also sacked and robbed the property of citizens who had fled and others who had died in the battle of Chuquinca, who were supposed to be rich because they were not so extravagant as others in the city and were known to have many bars of silver in store. Licentiate Alvarado, by means of questionings and threats, discovered from the Indians two pits that Alonso de Mesa had in a kitchen garden at his house and extracted from each sixty bars of silver, each so large that it exceeded 300 ducats in value. I saw them got out, for as Alonso de Mesa's house was opposite my father's, I went in when I heard them shout that they had found the silver bars. A few days later they got from Captain Juan de Saavedra's Indians 150 Peruvian sheep laden with three hundred bars of silver, all as big and as valuable as those just mentioned. It was then suspected that Juan de Saavedra had been unwilling to leave the city of Cuzco as my father and his friends had entreated him on the night of Francisco Hernández's rising, because he wanted to stow away and secure this large quantity of silver. His security assured him of nothing. He lost the silver, and his life into the bargain. These two hauls, according to the standard price of a bar of silver at the time, amounted to 126,000 Castilian ducats of 375 maravedis. Although Fernández says that part of the treasure belonged to Diego Ortiz de Guzmán, a *vecino* of Cuzco, I never heard of any but the two victims I have mentioned.

CHAPTER XXI

The theft committed by Antonio Carrillo and his death; the deeds of Piedrahita at Arequipa; his victory, owing to the divisions of the people there.

SERGEANT Major Antonio Carrillo went off to sack Pueblo Nuevo and the other cities of the district of Collasuyu, where he would have acted no less barbarously, if his life had lasted. In a few days in the city of La Paz he extracted from the local caciques an incredible sum out of the tribute they owed their masters and other things. Fernández in his ch. xlix says:

Antonio Carrillo arrested the stewards of all the *vecinos* and all the caciques, and while they were under arrest he terrified them until they delivered up all their masters' property and tribute. With this and many pitfulls of silver bars he got from the monastery of St. Francis and other sources, both inside the city and out, he collected and stole within the space of five days he spent there more than 500,000 Castilians in gold, silver, wine and other goods,

etc. Thus far our author.

All this was done on the information given by Francisco Boloña, who knew all these secrets, and the robbery and looting would have continued but that the informer's own conscience began to prick him and he was induced by Juan Vázquez, the corregidor of Chucuitu, to restore it all to its owners, whereupon he and some friends of his slew the wretched Antonio Carrillo with sword thrusts and knife blows in his own chamber, and reduced the city to His Majesty's service as before. Such was the end of the miserable Carrillo.

Francisco Hernández Girón's commander, now Juan de Piedrahita, was more fortunate in the city of Arequipa, because of the conflict that existed there between the corregidor and Captain Gómez de Solís, whom the royal judges had despatched there to carry on the war against Francisco Hernández. This angered the corregidor a great deal, because the other had been set over him, and he thought himself a much more experienced soldier than Gómez de Solís, as Fernández says in his ch. li:

When Gómez de Solís left His Majesty's camp, accompanied by Vicencio de Monte as ensign and bearing his instructions, news of his coming was received at Arequipa before he arrived and a great many made ready to come out and welcome him. But the corregidor Gonzalo de Torres stopped them, showing resentment at the appointment and declaring that the royal judges never decided anything properly. He also put it about that Gómez de Solís was not fit for the post he had been given, and that while he was corregidor in that city, no one else in all Peru ought to be appointed. So, exhibiting his prejudices in public, he would not let them go out to welcome Gómez de Solís,

etc. Thus Fernández.

While the people of Arequipa were taken up with these jealousies and divisions, news came of the approach of Juan de Piedrahita, who had more than 150 men, including more than 100 arquebusiers, Francisco Hernández's crack men. Everyone therefore retired to the cathedral, taking their wives, children, and moveable goods, and surrounding it outside with a high wall to stop the enemy from entering. The few arquebusiers they had were placed at the end of two streets down which the enemy might enter; they were to shoot from doors and windows without being seen.

But as nothing is secure in a place divided by jealousy and rivalry,

Piedrahita was warned about the ambush that had been prepared for him, and diverted his route so as to enter by a different street, from which he reached the bishop's palace, next to the cathedral, where there was some fighting, though it did not amount to much. Then Piedrahita sent them a Dominican religious with a message to say that he did not want any quarrel with them, but simply peace and friendship and the right for soldiers on both sides to be free to go and serve the king or Francisco Hernández, and also that they should give him their spare arms. Gómez de Solís was opposed to their accepting this offer, since it seemed disgraceful to deliver weapons to the enemy, even if they were to spare. But next day he accepted, and even begged to be allowed to do so, for during the night they burned some houses he had there (though he was a *vecino* of Charcas) and others belonging to the leading citizens. Although a truce was agreed for three days, it was broken by the rebels because they heard that some of Gómez de Solís' followers had fled, and that those who were left did not want to fight. At this the rebels brazenly came out to attack the fort; Gómez de Solís and the *vecinos* with him, seeing there was no one left to fight, fled as best they could, abandoning to Piedrahita all the property they had collected for safety.

The rebels thus returned rich and prosperous to join their captain general, Francisco Hernández. Although Piedrahita was deserted on the way by more than 120 soldiers of those who had been in the marshal's army, he did not care about that. His haul of gold, silver, jewels, and gems, arms, and horse remained with him and were ample compensation for the deserters, who had after all only been prisoners.

Francisco Hernández Girón, whom we left on the battlefield at Chuquinca, stayed there a month and a half, delayed by the large number of wounded men he had taken from the marshal. At the end of this long period he travelled with them as best he could to the valley of Antahuailla. He had been very angry with the Indians of the Chancas, who had harassed him in the battle of Chuquinca by boldly fighting his army and discharging showers of stones from their slings, which sufficed to crack the skulls of some of his men. As soon as he got to these parts he therefore ordered his soldiers, black and white alike, to sack and burn the Indian villages and lay waste the fields and do all the harm they could. From Antahuailla he sent for his wife Doña Mencía and for Tomás Vázquez's wife, both of whom were solemnly welcomed by the soldiers. They shamelessly called Francisco Hernández's wife "Queen of Peru," as Fernández says.

Only a few days were spent in the province of Antahuailla: they were content with having satisfied their rancor against the Indians. They marched toward Cuzco, knowing that the royal army had come out in search of them, and crossed the two rivers Abáncay and Apurímac. When Francisco Hernández saw how difficult the ground was on that road and how many places could be fortified and held against any attack, he repeated many times that if he had not sent Juan de Piedrahita on his mission with the picked men, he would have waited there and even have given battle to the royal judges at some natural stronghold there.

As Francisco Hernández was marching one day, six soldiers who had come from the marshal's army made bold to escape in full view of all the rebel army, taking selected mounts, arquebusses, and plenty of supplies. They succeeded in getting away because the rebel leader refused to have them pursued for fear all would take to their heels. He was satisfied only to lose six, for at the beginning of the trouble he feared many more would go off when these departed so openly and as bold as brass. The six men reached His Majesty's camp, and gave warning of Francisco Hernández's advance on Cuzco and his intention of pressing on to Collao. At this the royal judges ordered the army to march with haste and circumspection. This they did, though because of the quarrels and rancor that divided the leaders and chief officials, everything pertaining to His Majesty's service was done late and done ill.

CHAPTER XXII

Francisco Hernández avoids entering Cuzco; he takes his wife with him.

A CCOMPANIED by his whole army Francisco Hernández crossed the Apurímac River and left a soldier called ——— de Valderrábano with a company of twenty to guard it. Two days later, not trusting Valderrábano, he sent Juan Gavilán to take over with orders for Valderrábano to rejoin him. Gavilán remained on guard at the bridge, and after two days caught sight of scouts from the royal army; without waiting to find who they were, and why and in what numbers they came, he burnt the bridge and retired with all speed to the captain general's camp. The latter, according to Fernández, "much regretted its burning and unduly rebuked Juan Gavilán," etc. I do not understand the reason for this, for as he did not have to return across the bridge (since he was moving away from it) Juan Gavilán had done no harm in burning it, but had on the contrary served his master well by giving his enemies the labor of restoring it before they could pass.

Francisco Hernández went on to the Y'úcay valley to regale himself, albeit only for a few days, with the delights and joys of that pleasant vale. His army marched to within a league of Cuzco, and then turned to the left so as to avoid entering the city, since Francisco Hernández had been persuaded by his soothsayers, wizards, astrologers, and fortune tellers (with whom he consorted a great deal) that he ought not to enter because they had discovered by their witchcraft that the last to come out of it to do battle would be defeated. They proved this by instancing cases of leaders—both Indians before the conquest and Spaniards since—who had been defeated, but they omitted to refer to those who had been victorious, whom we could easily mention if it mattered at all. Fernández confirms all this in his chs. xxxii and xlv, and mentions four Spaniards and a Moorish woman who were regarded as wizards and necromancers and who gave out that they had a familiar who revealed to them what went on in His Majesty's camp and everything that was discussed in Francisco Hernández's. Our author adds that the rebels did not dare to try to run away or do anything else to their leader's disadvantage lest the Devil should tell him. I saw a letter Hernández had written to Juan de Piedrahita when the latter was ordered to Arequipa, as we have said; it was sent to Cuzco, and said: "You are not to leave the city on such-and-such a day of the week, but on such-and-such, because Juan is not written with *u* but *o*." There were other things of the same style in the letter, which I cannot remember well enough to repeat: I can only say that he was publicly known for a charlatan and liar. As we shall see, this only speeded his ruin, which is the sure reward of such men.

Francisco Hernández Girón's own men who knew of the traffic and dealings he had with wizards used to ask one another why he did not use the magic and prophecies of the Indians of Peru, as they were reputed to be great masters in these diabolical arts. The answer given was that the general did not heed Indian magic because most of it was childish nonsense and not real traffic with the Evil One. This was in part true, as we said in speaking of some Indian practices in the First Part of these *Commentaries*. In Book Four, ch. xvi, we referred to the good or ill omens drawn from the blinking of the eyes and alluded likewise to their interpretation of buzzing in the ears, which we will now explain, our authority for it being the confessional of the Catholic faith prepared on the instructions of a synod held in Peru. Among other precepts for confessors, it states that the Indians have superstitions connected with the sight and hearing. The superstition about the hearing is the following, which I have seen practiced: if the right ear buzzes, they said that some relative or friend was speaking well of the person concerned, and to identify the friend they thought of someone they knew and breathed on to the right hand and then transferred it from the mouth to the ear; if the buzzing continued, they thought of another friend and repeated the process, and so on until the buzzing stopped. The last friend when the buzzing stopped they were quite sure was the one who spoke well of them. The same theory was applied to the left ear, which they said buzzed when some enemy spoke ill of them, and to find out who it was they went through the same childish gestures as above, believing the last person they thought of when the buzzing stopped to be their enemy; if they had any grudge against him, their ill feeling was thereby reinforced.

As this witchcraft and other spells practiced by the Indians were so ridiculous, Francisco Hernández's friends used to say that he did not take any notice of them but merely used the wizards for his own ends.

Continuing its march the rebel army reached a level space behind the fortress of Cuzco, where Fernández says their leader was visited by Francisco Rodríguez de Villafuerte, an *alcalde ordinario* in the city. Francisco Hernández said a great many hard things to him about the *vecinos* of Cuzco and boasted a great deal that he would slay them and ruin them because they had not joined him in his rebellion. His remarks were all lies intended to blacken those who had refused to follow him. He then continued with his army along the road above the city and to the east of it, as his wizards advised. He took his wife with him, and when her parents objected, he told them he could not leave her in his enemies' hands so that they could take revenge on her for the harm he had done them. He then went on to the valley of Orcos, five leagues from the city, where we shall leave him to mention my experience with a son of this gentleman Francisco Rodríguez de Villafuerte here in Spain: we have never met, but only corresponded.

The man in question is his second son who came to Spain to study and has lived in Salamanca for some years, where he flourishes in all branches of knowledge. His name is Don Feliciano Rodríguez de Villafuerte, a good name for such a fine intellect. At the beginning of the present year of 1611 he presented me with a small retable, as broad and long as a half sheet of paper, full of holy relics, all labelled, and among them a piece of the *lignum crucis* covered with glass and protected on all four sides with wood, of very fine workmanship and marvellously gilded, so that it is a joy to look at.

With the reliquary he sent me two time pieces made by his own hand. One was a sundial of the usual kind with its style pointing north and its shadow-plate on which to see the hours of the day. The other is a handsomely made moon dial, astronomically perfect, with a circular movement divided into twenty-nine parts, corresponding to the days of the moon. It has a figure of the moon which waxes, wanes, grows to the full, and eclipses, all the phases being clearly observed as it goes round. It has also a gnomon to show the hours of the night, which can be adjusted according to the phase of the moon. It has also other features, which I shall not attempt to describe as I cannot explain them. He made the whole with his own hands and with no assistance from anyone, in either the scientific or material devising of the instruments, both of which have surprised learned men who have seen them and have filled me with great pride that a man born in my native country and indeed my native city should make such splendid and ingenious devices, to the astonishment of people in Europe. This proves the fine understanding and natural ability of the natives of Peru, both mestizos and creoles, in all the arts and sciences, a point we made earlier in citing the ease of our own preceptor and tutor, Licentiate Juan de Cuéllar, who was a canon of the cathedral of Cuzco and taught grammar in that city, though not for long. May our Lord God be praised for all, amen. With which we shall return to Peru to recount the events of the march of the royal army, which we left in the city of Huamanga.

CHAPTER XXIII

The royal army crosses the Abáncay River and the Apurímac with unexpected ease; its scouts reach the city of Cuzco.

HIS MAJESTY'S army left Huamanga in pursuit of Francisco Hernández Girón, knowing that he was moving toward Cuzco. It marched very cautiously, preceded by its scouts. It passed the Abáncay

River by the ford and restored the bridge for the infantry and artillery, no difficult feat, for the river is narrow there. A misfortune that was much regretted by everyone occurred here. This was that Captain Antonio Luján, after passing across, crouched down on the bank to drink from his hands, and as he got up his feet slipped on the stone he had been standing on and he fell on his back, striking the back of his head on the stone and so fell in the river. Two years later when my father was corregidor in Cuzco, the Indians brought a coat of mail he was wearing at the time of the accident to the city. Captain Luján's company of arquebusiers was given to Juan Ramón, as he had lost his own at Chuquinca.

With this misfortune the army reached the river Apurímac, where it was learnt that one of the scouts called Francisco Menacho, a bold and intrepid soldier who had gone ahead with forty companions, had rushed into the river at the place now called the Ford and crossed it without any danger, though no one previously had dared to do so. He had repeated the feat three or four times more before the royal army arrived, and the news, though alarming, encouraged the whole army to cross rather than wait in such a difficult place until the bridge was rebuilt, which would have wasted precious time. To protect the porters and baggage Indians and those who were carrying the artillery on their backs, they took all the horses into the river and stood them just upstream to break the force of the current; and behind the horses the infantry, the laden Indians and the artillery, borne on men's backs, all crossed over as safely as Fernández says (ch. i). And our Lord God showed them a very notable favor that day in making it possible for them to cross at such a dangerous place, where, though a whole army then went over, no one has since dared to pass. Then with great labor and difficulty owing to the roughness of the road, they climbed up the steep bank, and reached Rimactampu, seven leagues from the city, on the second day.

They went on the very night of their arrival, to the great annoyance of the officials of the army, for in almost everything respecting the conduct of the war those in command exhibited their rivalries and differences and what one ordered another countermanded. The present disagreement was caused by the fact that the scouts of the two armies were continuously in sight of one another as they advanced, and Francisco Hernández had taken care to change his men frequently so that it should seem not as if they were in flight, but as if they travelled very much at their ease. So the army reached Sacsahuana, four leagues from the city. At this point the citizens of Cuzco went out ahead to act as scouts so as to have the opportunity of visiting their homes and wives and children. They arrived at mid-day, and Lieutenant General Licentiate Alvarado had left the same morning. The citizens did not wish to sleep the following night in their own houses for fear the enemy should turn back and catch them separated from one another. They all collected, with the small number of soldiers they had, in the house of Juan de Pancorvo, a strong building with no entry but the main gate into the street. Around this gate they made a redoubt of adobe which projected seven or eight steps beyond the gate with embrasures so that they could cover with their arquebusses the three streets from which it was possible to deliver an attack, one straight in front and the others on either side. There they were safe all night with sentries placed along the streets that gave access to the house. I was with them, and made three or four visits to various houses on behalf of their owners, spending the night on these errands.

Next day, at about three in the afternoon, when I was on a balcony in my father's house, I saw Pero Hernández the Loyal come in by the gate from the street on his horse Little Bird, and without stopping to greet him I rushed in to tell my lord Garcilaso the good news. He rushed out and embraced Pero Hernández, and both of them were overcome with joy. My father's friend told how, on the previous day, as the rebel army was marching just over a league from the city, he left them, pretending urgency, and went among some rocks to the left of the road; concealing himself among them, he climbed up into the mountains a good distance from the army and so escaped from the rebels. He later joined my father in His Majesty's army, and served till the end of the war, when he returned with my lord Garcilaso to Cuzco. I can vouch for all this as an eye witness.

CHAPTER XXIV

His Majesty's army enters Cuzco and continues
beyond the city; how the Indians carried the
artillery on their backs; part of the
munitions reaches the royal army.

O N THE third day after the arrival of the citizens in Cuzco His Majesty's army entered, marching in by companies. The infantry formed up in the main square, and the cavalry skirmished with the foot soldiers in good military order with plenty of salvoes from the arquebusiers, which showed that the soldiers were skilled in all branches of military exercise. Fernández, in his ch. i, says that Don Felipe de Mendoza, who was captain of artillery, fired off all his pieces as he passed through the square, and that the men lined up round the square while the arquebusiers gallantly fired their salvoes. But his informants misled him, as in other matters we have already mentioned and some we shall refer to, for the artillery could not be fired off at every touch and turn since it was not dragged on its train, but both pieces and train were carried on the backs of Indians, of whom ten thousand were appointed, all of whom were necessary to carry eleven pieces of heavy artillery. And in order to record how the artillery was carried, I will describe the process, for I was in the main square of Cuzco the day they entered, and saw everything from first to last.

Each piece of artillery was lashed to a thick beam more than forty feet long. A series of poles ran under this beam each about two feet apart and sticking out about a yard on either side of the beam. Each of these poles was carried by a pair of Indians, one at each end in the style of palanquins in Spain. They bore the weight on their necks, where they wore pads so that the heavily laden poles should not hurt them too much, and the Indians were changed every two hundred paces, since they could not carry such a weight any greater distance. It may be imagined with what toil and pains the poor Indians bore these large and heavy burdens along the rough and stony roads of my country, where there are slopes of two or three leagues up or down. I have seen many Spaniards dismount on these slopes so as not to strain their steeds too much, especially on descending the slopes, many of which are so steep that travellers have to do this, or the saddles slip down the necks of the horses, since the cruppers are rarely strong enough to hold them and most of them break on such roads. I am speaking of the part from Quito to Cuzco, which is five hundred leagues by road. From Cuzco to Charcas the ground is level, and travelling is not so difficult. So that when Fernández says that Don Felipe de Mendoza fired all his artillery on crossing the square, it is clear that he says so to deck and embellish his story, and not because it really happened.

His Majesty's army passed within a league of the city where it stopped for five days, preparing what was necessary to press on, especially provisions which were supplied by the neighboring Indians, and the shoeing of the beasts which was very necessary. Both operations took about this length of time, and the delay was not, as our author states, due to other reasons: "The army was at the Salinas five or six days waiting for Indian carriers; but it finally departed without them, and indeed some of those who had accompanied it so far and came from allocations belonging to citizens of Cuzco ran away, and it was suspected and even regarded as certain that the *vecinos,* their masters, encouraged them to escape," etc.

I much regret to find such statements in Fernández's history, for they suggest that either the writer or those who gave him information was prejudiced, and particularly prejudiced against the *vecinos* of Cuzco, whom he continually blames for things that never entered their heads, as in this and similar passages. It was much more in the interest of the citizens that the army should march on promptly than that it should be held up by their getting the Indians to run away. The citizens indeed suffered a good deal from the presence of the army so near the city, which caused losses and damage to their houses and property. The same author indeed seems to contradict himself, for having stated that the army was awaiting Indian carriers and that some of those who had come with it fled, he adds: "Finally the army left without them." They could not thus have been essential, since it went on without their having appeared. What happened was what we have described: when our author says that the Indians were encouraged to flee by their masters, the *vecinos,* he means that the latter dismissed them, because from that point onwards the road was level, without slopes or ravines, and as it was possible to move more easily it was not necessary to have so many Indians as hitherto.

After the five days' halt, the army left the place, travelling in good order and in a state of preparedness in case it were necessary to fight. They suspected and feared that the rebels would wait to give battle until they came to the narrow passes on the way to Quequesana. But the enemy had no such idea, and they marched on without opposition, until they reached the town called Pucara, which is forty leagues beyond Cuzco. The rebels used their Negro soldiers to scour the countryside on both sides of the road and bring in what cattle and supplies were needed, while the royal army marched with great difficulty since the villages it came to had already been sacked and it had to draw supplies from a distance. On the way the scouts of both armies frequently met, but did not come to blows. The royal army learnt, however, that Francisco Hernández was awaiting them at Pucara to give battle. There was indeed no lack of traitors on either side: some soldiers fled from the royal army to the rebels and some from the rebels to the royalists.

The judges had to send a man back for the gunpowder, fuses, and lead which had remained behind at Antahuailla, where those who were supposed to be bringing them were negligently dallying; but the envoy, Pedro de Cianca, harried and pressed them, and part of the munitions reached the royal camp the day before the battle, a matter of great importance which caused much satisfaction, for the munitions were sorely needed.

CHAPTER XXV

His Majesty's army reaches the enemy's stronghold;
it camps on a flat piece of ground and fortifies
its positions; skirmishes occur and the
royalists suffer reverses.

O N THE march the judges heard of the defeat of Gómez de Solís at Arequipa, which greatly distressed them. They could, however, do nothing to remedy matters and disguised their disappointment as best they could, continuing the journey toward Pucara, where the enemy had camped in an advantageous position. It was indeed so strong that it could not be attacked from any side, being surrounded by rough and inaccessible mountains like a strong wall that twisted and turned, and the stronghold itself was very spacious. It could hold all the men and mounts the rebels had, and had even more room for their munitions, supplies, and baggage, of which they had a great deal, as was natural after they won the battle of Chuquinca, one of the greatest victories known in Peru. And the Negro soldiers went out every day and brought in whatever was needed from the surrounding countryside.

The royal camp, on the contrary, was on level ground open on all sides, with no fortifications to protect it, and few supplies and munitions, as we have said. Nevertheless, they fortified it as best they could so as not to be so exposed to attack. A mud wall was built breast high round the whole camp. As so many Indians had been brought to carry the baggage and artillery, they could be used as sappers when necessary, and it was not long before the wall embraced the entire camp, though this was very large. Francisco Hernández, on finding that His Majesty's army had made its camp, disposed his artillery on the top of the hill in front of his own camp, and harassed the judges and their followers by firing night and day and dropping as many balls as he wanted into the camp. Often he shot off whole salvoes for show and the balls soared through the air above and beyond the enemy, doing no harm either to the men or the horses, but bouncing across the ground like puff-balls. It was regarded as a divine mystery that what had been dedicated to God's service, as the bells now used for firing these cannon balls were, should not have been permitted to harm men who had not harmed them. This was observed by thinking men in both camps.

Once the two armies were settled within sight of one another, the captains and famous soldiers of both sides all sought to prove their valor. In the first skirmishes two leading soldiers on the royalist side met their deaths, and five or six of no account went over to the rebels and told them about everything in the royal camp. They said that a few days before reaching Pucara, General Pablo de Meneses had wanted to resign because the rivalries and differences between his officers had gone so far that they did not obey his orders, but countermanded them. He had said that he did not want a post, however honorable, with such a burden attached, but Dr. Saravia had persuaded him not to offer his resignation on the ground that his reputation would lose rather than gain by it. This greatly rejoiced Francisco Hernández and his friends, who hoped that their enemies' disagreements would tell in their favor, and even assure them of victory.

In the skirmishes the soldiers of both sides exchanged a number of witty repartees which Fernández mentions; as they are specimens of military speech, I shall include a few of them, taken from Fernández's ch. li, and explain the points he leaves obscure, for the better understanding of them.

And as in these skirmishes some who took part on one side had friends on the other, they always chatted together and assured one another that they would not do any harm. Scipio Ferrara, on the king's side, spoke to Pavía, who had been his companion in the service of the good viceroy Don Antonio de Mendoza and tried to bring him over with persuasive speeches, whereupon Pavía replied that the rebels had won him in fair fight and the royalists would have to get him back in fair fight,

etc. Pavía alluded to the battle of Chuquinca, where the rebels had forced him to surrender; he was satisfied to be with them and not to repudiate them, so he said he had been won in fair fight and therefore he would have to be won back in fair fight.

Fernández says:

Captain Rodrigo Niño spoke to Juan de Piedrahita, and in order to persuade him to come over to the king's side offered him a great reward from the *audiencia*. Piedrahita replied that he was well aware of the sort of favors the judges granted, and that if he ever took up arms again, he had his pieces well set out,

etc. Piedrahita said this because he and other followers of Francisco Hernández were bewitched by the lies his soothsayers had told him about their defeating the royalists. A few days later, he changed his mind, as we shall see.

Further on, our author says:

Similarly Diego Méndez and Hernando Guillada talked together, and so did Captain Ruibarba and his son-in-law Bernardino de Robles. But when the judges saw that these conversations had no result, they made an order prohibiting anyone, under pain of death, from conversing with the enemy. Captain Ruibarba and Bernardino de Robles had made an appointment to meet again another day, and arranged to recognize one another by both wearing scarlet cloaks. They each went out so dressed, but Bernardino had arranged with ten or twelve captains and soldiers to take his father-in-law prisoner by means of a trap, and then had him brought before Francisco Hernández and declared that he had come over of his own free will. When Ruibarba heard this, he said that anyone who said he had come over freely was a liar, and he would prove it on him on horse or foot with Francisco Hernández's permission, if his son-in-law had not taken him by means of a trick. Francisco Hernández was delighted by his arrival and took him to Doña Mencía, saying: "See what a fine prisoner I've brought you, madam. Take good care of him, for I am entrusting him to you." Doña Mencía said she was very happy to do so.

Thereafter Raudona went out and spoke to Juan de Illanes, who was Francisco Hernández's sergeant major, and attacked him, thinking to catch him by means of his horse's turn of speed. But Raudona's horse was badly harnessed, and he was taken prisoner. As he went off with his captors he said that he had promised the judges not to come back without capturing one of the leading rebels and that was why he had attacked the sergeant major. Some of the deepest-dyed rebels were very angry at this, saying that they would refuse to fight if he were not put to death, for it was a great mistake to spare presumptuous and brazen fellows like Raudona. He was then put in Licentiate Alvarado's tent and told to confess, and Alonso González was set on guard over the tent and told that if the rebel leader came, he was to put the prisoner to death before he approached. Licentiate Toledo, Francisco Hernández's *alcalde mayor,* and Captain Ruibarba begged the leader to spare Raudona's life, and he gave his gloves as a token to do so.

As Alonso González saw the messenger coming, he went into the tent and told the priest: "Get on, father, and absolve him. If you don't, he'll have to go as he is."

So the priest hastened to absolve him, and Alonso González at once cut his head off with a great knife he carried. He then went out of the tent saying: "Well, I've helped our little marquis to keep his word. He promised to take a head back with him or leave his own behind, and so he has." Thus saying, he had the body removed from the tent: the deed was much regretted by many who were present, and much more so in the royal camp when his death became known,

etc.

Raudona was a soldier who preferred to be thought brave than prudent. He had a good horse, if he had treated it properly; but in order to show off his skill he abused it by never giving it an hour's rest all day long from racing and curvetting. So when he really needed it, it let him down because it was exhausted, as Fernández says. His prudence can be judged from his telling the enemy that he had promised the judges not to return without a prize, a saying that caused his death at the cruel hands of Alonso González, the executioner.

Our author continues:

At this stage the royal judges issued certain pardons to individuals. They were sent by Negroes and *yanacunas* who were continually going from one camp to the other. The pardons all came into Francisco Hernández's hands, and he at once had them publicly proclaimed, saying :"So much for pardons." Not content with this, he had the hands and noses cut off the bearers and had them tied round their necks, and sent them back in this state to the king's camp.

Thus Fernández, who ends his chapter here.

CHAPTER XXVI

*Tricks of disloyal soldiers; Piedrahita raids
the royal army; Francisco Hernández decides
to do battle with the royal judges;
their precautions.*

THESE AFFRONTS and insults to His Royal Majesty occurred during
the whole of Francisco Hernández's stay at Pucara. In the skirmishes
that took place daily and even hourly he continued to gain men and horses,
for there were a great many unruly and turbulent soldiers who played
with both sides and got themselves posted missing by giving out that they
were going to skirmish with the enemy and as soon as they were surrounded by skirmishers cried out: "I surrender: I want to join you." They
then yielded up their arms and let themselves be led off, astutely pretending to be prisoners, so that if the royalists won they could say that they
had been captured by the rebels, and if the rebels won they could allege
that they had gone over to them and helped them to victory and to complete the conquest of the land. The royal judges became aware of this,
and prohibited skirmishing just as they had put an end to intercourse
between soldiers of both sides even though they might be relatives or
close friends, on the ground that no good came of such contacts.

On finding that the skirmishes and conversations between the two
forces had stopped, Francisco Hernández decided to annoy the enemy by
sending his commander Captain Juan de Piedrahita to make a raid on His
Majesty's camp with a party of 80 arquebusiers. He was to observe and
report whether the royalists were on the watch or neglectful and to go on
raiding by night and deprive them of rest until they were worn out and
could be destroyed.

Piedrahita went off with his men and performed the best raid he
could, but it was an affair of little moment and the royalists did not even
react, seeing that it was a mere puff of wind and not a real engagement.
Piedrahita returned and told Francisco Hernández and his friends of
great deeds of derring-do he had done, how he had found the royal camp

unguarded and without sentries, and the army carelessly sleeping, so that if he had had 150 arquebusiers he could have defeated them and captured the royal judges and their captains. He added a good deal more in the same strain, according to the custom of boastful soldiers who make better charlatans than leaders. And although Piedrahita was a captain of the rebels and fought several successful actions, he achieved no more than we have said on that particular night and boasted enormously about it.

Francisco Hernández Girón credited the exaggerated report his commander Piedrahita brought him, especially as some of the royalist soldiers who came over to him reported that His Majesty's camp was in great straits, with no fuses or powder. He therefore determined to offer battle to the royal army one night, and was encouraged to do so because they had not attacked him in his fort, a fact he attributed to lack of spirit or lack of strength, and concluded that because of their cowardly and pusillanimous conduct he had already got the better of them. He called his captains to a council and put his scheme forward, urging them most vehemently to adopt it because it offered every prospect of success; he added that this was confirmed by omens and prophecies, by which he meant his magicians.

His captains were opposed to the plan. They said there was no need to give battle, but only to keep still, since they were in a strong place well supplied with everything that was necessary, while their enemies lacked munitions and supplies. If he wanted to bring the enemy even lower, he could continue along the road he had followed hitherto so successfully as far as Charcas, where he could collect all the silver there was to be found there to pay his men, and return by the coast so as to enter the city of Lima, which he would find open and undefended by trained soldiers. His enemy would not have enough horses or enough shoes for those they had, and would not be able to give pursuit, unless by composing a very small force out of those who had the means to go on. If this were done, he would be able to defeat such a force whenever he liked to turn back on it. In any case, as things had gone well so far, it would be a mistake to change policy, for it was only too easy to lose battles: let him remember Chuquinca, where the enemy attacked so confidently and were so quickly and easily disposed of.

Francisco Hernández replied that he was determined to mount a night attack with the whole army. He had no desire to go on retreating before the judges, and the good old wise women said that that was the place to fight. He begged and prayed they would not try to thwart him, but prepare for the following night: he was determined to see his plan through.

So the council ended, with the captains highly disgruntled, since it was their common view that they were being asked to undertake a dangerous and doubtful task: they foresaw that they were being led to their ruin and were therefore very downcast. Although the general saw how strongly opposed they were to his policy and plan, he did not give way; on the contrary he persisted in following the advice and prophecies of his witches and magicians in the face of all of them.

It was arranged that all the army was to sally forth soon after midnight when the moon had set, wearing white shirts so as to be able to recognize one another. At sunset a roll was called; and it was found that two men from the marshal's army were missing, and it was suspected that they had gone over to the royalists. But those who wanted to please Francisco Hernández brought false news to the effect that one of these two, the one with the best credit and reputation, had been found by Indians on the road to Charcas, while the other, being a person of little account, would not be taken any notice of by the royal judges; indeed they would ignore his reports since he was a man of little skill. Francisco Hernández was content with these taradiddles and ordered everyone to be ready by the appointed hour.

The two soldiers who had fled at this late hour found their way to His Majesty's camp and gave warning of the rebels' plans: *i.e.*, that they would attack that night divided into two forces, boldly attacking the royalists in their stronghold since the latter had not dared to attack them, or even to come and look at them. The royal judges and their officers and advisers (who were the senior citizens of the whole empire, men who had become great soldiers and experts in military science by reason of the experience they had gained in the many wars they had had a hand in) agreed that it would be best to march the men out of the fort and draw them up by companies of cavalry and infantry on the plain, since the area they had fortified and where they were encamped was crowded with tents and shelters and crammed with beasts and Indians who would be more hindrance than help in the battle. This was done, though there were disagreements among members of the council who thought that the faint-hearted would fight better from behind a wall than in the open plain. Other arguments were advanced as well, but at last the men were marched out, and it was indeed by God's mercy and blessing that it was so, as we shall see. A fine body of infantry was drawn up, well stiffened with pikes and halberds and with the arquebusses very well disposed, and eleven pieces of heavy artillery.

CHAPTER XXVII

Francisco Hernández goes out to do battle; he retreats
as the attack miscarries; Tomás Vázquez
goes over to the royal forces; a prophecy
made by the rebel leader.

T HE REBEL leader left the fort at the hour appointed by his prophets
and soothsayers with 800 foot, according to Fernández, 600 being
arquebusiers and the rest pikemen: there were very few cavalry—less
than 30. In another direction he sent his company of Negroes, numbering over 250. They were accompanied by 70 Spanish arquebusiers to
guide them and instruct them what to do, but their only mission was to
cause a diversion so that the royalists should not know which party was
Francisco Hernández's. The Negroes were ordered to attack the fort of
the royal judges from in front, since Francisco Hernández intended to
attack it in the rear. They therefore advanced toward His Majesty's camp
as silently as possible, with their fuses covered so that they should not be
seen. The royalists were drawn up in companies, equally silent and on
the alert, with their fuses hidden so as not to reveal their whereabouts.
The Negroes reached the fort before Francisco Hernández did, as the
distance was shorter, and finding no resistance they went in and killed
Indians, horses, and mules, and whatever they came across; among the
Indians, they slew 5 or 6 cowardly Spaniards who had gone into hiding.

Soon after, Francisco Hernández reached the fort and trained all his
arquebusses on it; but the royalists made no reply at all until the rebels
had fired off all their shot. Then His Majesty's men let fly with arquebusses and artillery from their positions, which were quite unexpected by
the enemy, who thought they were in the fort. However, neither side did
much harm in this battle, because the night was very dark and they were
shooting at random and could not see one another. Considering the number of arquebusses engaged—more than 1,300 on the two sides—and
how near they were to one another, it would hardly have been surprising
to find them all lying stiff and cold on the ground, had they been able to
see one another.

When the rebel saw that the attack had misfired, he gave it up as lost, and his only aim was to withdraw into the fort in the best order he and his officials could procure. But all his efforts could not prevent his leaving behind more than 200 of the soldiers he had taken from the marshal, who dropped their pikes and halberds. His Majesty's men tried to attack and completely crush those who were fleeing, but the leaders of the force, who, except for the general and commander, were, as we have said, mostly *vecinos* of Peru, refused to let them break away and kept them still. This was sound tactics, for a group of cavalry that advanced, thinking the enemy had no intention of fighting or resisting, lost an ensign killed and three *vecinos* of Cuzco wounded: these were Diego de Silva, Antón Ruiz de Guevara, and Diego Maldonado the Rich. Diego Maldonado's wound was such a large one that it soon went beyond cure: he kept it open until he died eleven or twelve days after the battle, on the advice of doctors and surgeons who said that he would die if it were closed. By inflicting these losses the rebels assured their line of retreat, and it was very fortunate that the royalists were forbidden to go out and fight them, for if they had done so there would have been great mortality on both sides.

Francisco Hernández returned to his fort much downcast and with his former pride and arrogance greatly diminished, especially as he now realized that he had been deceived by the magic he had had such faith in, and which had made him believe he would vanquish all his enemies. Not to discourage his followers he put a cheerful face on things, but he could not disguise his feelings sufficiently to prevent the anguish in his heart from revealing itself.

In this engagement there was no more fighting than that we have mentioned: if what Fernández describes in his ch. liv had really happened, not a man would have remained alive. Proof of our version is given by his own words, for he mentions that the royal judges lost 5 or 6 killed and 30 wounded, and the rebels 10 killed and many wounded and taken prisoner, etc. The prisoners were those of the marshal's men who stayed behind, to the number of more than 200, as we have said: not more than 15 of Francisco Hernández's own men were captured. The killed and wounded in the royal army were killed and wounded by their own men, for as the night was so dark the rear guard could not tell where the enemy was and shot off at random to alarm them, thus killing and wounding some members of Juan Ramón's company which was stationed on one wing of the royal force. This was ascertained because all the wounds were inflicted from the rear. One of the dead was a gentleman called Suero de Quiñones, a brother of Antonio de Quiñones, a *vecino* of Cuzco, while a cousin of his called Pedro de Quiñones was among the wounded.

The day after the battle nothing happened on either side. At nightfall the royalists drew up in formation as they had the night before, having news that the enemy intended to try another night attack in the hope of covering the miscarriage of the previous night and having better luck. But this was an idle tale invented by someone or other, for the unfortunate Francisco Hernández was more concerned with taking flight and saving his skin than in giving battle, such was the extent of his disillusionment with the war and his superstitions.

On the third day after the battle, so as not to reveal this weakness and to prevent the royalists from thinking he was finished, he sent his captains and men out to provoke the enemy and skirmish with them. The resulting affray was on a small scale, but of great consequence; for Captain Tomás Vázquez and 10 or 12 of his friends who were acting in concert went over to the royalists, and moreover brought a token from Juan de Piedrahita in the shape of a silver helmet as proof that he would do the same, though not immediately, for later on he would bring over more men. Tomás Vázquez told the royal judges all this, and the news delighted them and all the royal army. The rebel seemed to be lost and his impudence at an end, for Tomás Vázquez was his main pillar of support, and once it was removed the rest would repudiate him.

The skirmishers retired to their positions, and Francisco Hernández encouraged his men so that they should not feel the loss of Tomás Vázquez too much by making a brief and pithy harangue, which Fernández reproduces in his ch. lv in these words:

"Knights and gentlemen. As you all know, I have before now explained the causes and motives that led me to begin this undertaking, and I have mentioned the events that have taken place in this kingdom to the detriment and undoing of the inhabitants, and the harm and trouble caused to *vecinos* and soldiers alike, the former being deprived of their property and the latter of their earnings and the rewards of their services. You know that my companions, the *vecinos*, who wanted this undertaking, left me in the thick of it, as Tomás Vázquez has now done. Do not regret his absence: he was one man, and no more.

"Do not trust those who say you will be pardoned: the day after you get it they'll hang you with your pardon round your neck. Remember that if you act like men, our chances are better than ever. I warn you that as soon as I am gone they will execute Tomás Vázquez and all the other deserters. I have no regrets for my own sake: I am just one man, and if my death would free all of you, I would willingly go to the sacrifice. But I can see very clearly that in that casé those who escape the gibbet will go to the galleys. So reflect carefully; pull yourselves together and encourage one another to see the affair through. We are 500, and 2,000 cannot harm us without coming off the worse. Our affairs are prospering, and our interests are clear; let us remember what is at stake and what will be the fate of one and all if I am not here."

He made these and similar remarks on the subject. Yet the flight of Tomás Vázquez produced great sorrow among his followers,

etc. Thus Fernández.

Francisco Hernández's remarks about their being hanged with their pardons round their necks was much nearer coming true than the prophecies he got from his soothsayers; for though Tomás Vázquez and Piedrahita were not hanged, they were strangled in prison with the royal pardons granted to them by the chancery in their hands. These pardons were sealed with the imperial seal and stated that crimes that had been pardoned could not be punished unless offences had been committed after the pardon. But all this did them no good, and Francisco Hernández's words came true to the letter. This is mentioned here out of its context, so that we shall not have to repeat it later.

CHAPTER XXVIII

Francisco Hernández flees alone; his commander with more than a hundred men takes another route; General Pablo de Meneses pursues them, captures them, and executes justice on them.

FRANCISCO HERNÁNDEZ was so bewildered and forlorn because of the flight of Tomás Vázquez that he resolved to abandon his followers that same night. The suspicion entered his breast that his own men wanted to kill him to save themselves by his death from the punishments they all deserved for having followed him against the Royal Majesty. So powerfully did this suspicion dominate him that it produced the effects described by the divine Ariosto in the second of his five additional cantos.

He had indeed grounds for suspecting and believing that they wanted to kill him, as Fernández says in his ch. lv: "Finally Francisco Hernández decided to flee that night because it was revealed to him in the greatest secrecy that his captains were contemplating killing him," etc. But they did not contemplate anything but following him and dying with him, as they later proved, if he had only trusted them at this point. However his suspicions were so great that he did not even trust his own wife, noble and virtuous woman that she was, nor any of his followers, however intimate and true.

So when night came, he told his wife and companions that he was going to see to some matters concerning the army and went off, calling for a horse named Almaraz, because it belonged to his brother-in-law, ————— de Almaraz. It was one of the best horses there were, and he mounted it, saying that he would soon be back, but not telling anyone where he was going. Such was his state of panic from the belief that they wanted to kill him that he could wait no longer to give his friends and supporters the slip, finding no security except in solitude, as Fernández says in the same chapter.

So poor Francisco Hernández made off, alone and unaccompanied. Two or three of his supporters followed his tracks, but when he realized that they were coming, he plunged into a deep ravine and continued along it so blindly that at daybreak he found himself still near the fort, and recognizing it, he fled among some snowy crests that were above it, without any idea of where he would emerge. Finally, owing to the excellence of his horse, he got out after having run great danger of suffocating in the snow. He departed from his army with no more ado than we have said, and when Fernández says that he had a long interview with his wife and that they both wept copiously, he is repeating the account of someone who did not know what happened; for his suspicion and fear of death prevented him from telling anyone that he was going away. His lieutenant general, who had remained in the camp, tried to assemble the men and follow him, and set out with 100 men. Some of these were the most deeply implicated, but others who were as deeply in it as they, and even more so—such as Piedrahita, Alonso Díaz, and Captain Diego de Gavilán and his brother Juan Gavilán, Captain Diego Méndez, Ensign Mateo del Sauz, and many others of the same type and quality—went over to the royal army on learning that Francisco Hernández had fled, and said that they wanted to abandon the rebels to serve His Majesty. They were well received, and in due course presented with a document sealed with the royal seal awarding them a royal pardon for their part in what had gone

before. The royal judges and the whole army spent that night in formation, awaiting events.

Next day, when the royal judges were assured of the flight of Francisco Hernández Girón and all his followers, they sent General Pablo de
Meneses with 150 men to catch the rebels, and arrest and punish them.
Leaving in haste, the general could only raise 130 soldiers. With them
he followed the track of the fugitives, and happened to trail Diego de
Alvarado, the lieutenant general, whose route was known, as he was
accompanied by 100 Spaniards and more than 20 Negroes. He caught up
with them after eight or nine days' pursuit, and though his band was
smaller than the enemy, since he had left behind many soldiers whose
horses could not stand the long marches, they surrendered to him without
making the slightest resistance. The general arrested them and executed
the leaders, who were Diego de Alvarado, Juan Cobo, Diego de Villalva,
———— de Lugones, Alberto de Orduña, Bernardino de Robles, Pedro de
Sotelo, Francisco Rodríguez, and Juan Enríquez de Orellana, who, despite his good name, boasted of being an executioner, though he was a
town crier by trade. He acted as executioner for Francisco de Carvajal and
Licentiate Alvarado.

General Pablo de Meneses said to him: "Juan Enríquez, since you are
accustomed to the job, you shall strangle these gentlemen who are friends
of yours, and their honors the royal judges will reward you for it."

The executioner went up to a soldier he knew and whispered to him:
"I expect the reward will be to have me hanged as soon as I've killed my
friends."

It turned out just as he said, for as soon as he had strangled the men
we have named and cut their heads off, two Negroes were ordered to
perform the same service for the executioner as he had performed for
the rest, who included eleven or twelve soldiers besides those mentioned.
Pablo de Meneses sent many of those he had captured under arrest and
with a strong escort to Cuzco, together with nine heads of the executed
ringleaders. I saw them exhibited at the house that belonged to Alonso
de Hinojosa, which was where Diego de Alvarado lived while he was
commander and lieutenant general. He always rode a mule, on which he
rushed about in the course of his duties: in this he copied Francisco de
Carvajal, whom I never saw on horseback.

One incident occurs to me which illustrates the impudence of some of
the rebel soldiers. The day after Francisco Hernández's flight, when my
lord Garcilaso was sitting at the table dining with eighteen or twenty
other soldiers who always ate with him (all the *vecinos* of the empire did

the same in time of war, according to their resources), he saw one of Francisco Hernández's men sitting among the soldiers. This was a fellow who had been with him since the beginning of the revolt and had acted with all the insolence and indiscipline one can imagine, yet he sat himself down to eat with these gentlemen. He was a blacksmith, but during the war he was clad more sumptuously than his companions.

When my father saw him sitting there, he said: "Diego de Madrid (such was his name), since you're sitting down, eat with these gentlemen and welcome. But don't come back another day, for it doesn't seem right to me that one who, if he could have cut my head off yesterday, would have gone running with it to his general to ask for a reward, should come here today to dine with these gentlemen who only wish me long life and health, and desire to serve His Majesty!"

Madrid answered: "Sir, I'll get up and go now, if you tell me to."

My father replied: "I won't tell you to get up; but if you feel like it, do as you wish."

The blacksmith got up and went out in peace, leaving everyone laughing at his impudence. Such was the hatred against Francisco Hernández's followers, for his rebellion was very outrageous toward His Majesty and toward the *vecinos*. It aimed at depriving the former of the empire of Peru and at killing the latter so that the rebels could seize their estates and Indians.

Francisco Hernández's wife remained in the hands of Captain Ruibarba, and the royal judges ordered Juan Rodríguez de Villalobos to take his sister-in-law as far as Cuzco and hand her over to her parents, which he did.

CHAPTER XXIX

*The commander Don Pedro Puertocarrero goes in
search of Francisco Hernández; two other
captains set out with the same purpose
by another road; they capture the
rebel and take him to Lima,
which they enter as if
in triumph.*

HAVING sent to Cuzco the prisoners and the heads of those he had
executed, General Pablo de Meneses could find no trace of Francisco
Hernández himself, and therefore decided to go back and report the
result of his expedition to the royal judges. As soon as the rebellion had
been scattered, the latter went to the imperial city, where they learnt that
Francisco Hernández was making for Lima. They therefore sent the commander Don Pedro de Puertocarrero with 80 men to pursue the rebel
leader across the plains; and two captains who had come to serve His
Majesty with companies they had raised at Huánucu were ordered to
return home by the mountain road in pursuit of the fugitive, so as to be
sure that he could not escape by either route. Both parties were authorized
to execute any prisoners they took.

The two captains, Juan Tello and Miguel de la Serna, did as they were
bidden and took 80 men with them. In the city of Huamanga they learnt
that Francisco Hernández was crossing the plains toward Lima. They
went in search of him, and after a few days heard that he was fifteen
leagues ahead and accompanied by 300 soldiers, including 150 arquebusiers. The next day the Indians said that there were no more than 200,
and the number daily diminished until it was said there were only 100.
The very contradictory reports the Indians made of the number of men
Francisco Hernández had were not entirely without foundation. As soon
as his men knew that he had fled, they scattered in various directions for
lack of a leader, usually in groups of 20 or 30. Many of these fleeing

parties came upon him, so that he soon had more than 200 soldiers, many those of the marshal's men who had grown devoted to him. But as they fled, the fear of attack and their lack of supplies, accentuated in defeat, forced them to straggle along the roads and go into hiding or seek their safety as best they could. Thus as the royalists approached, there were no more than 100 left. The first report the Indians gave showed a larger number, and the second those left a few days later, while the last report gave the final number. If therefore Francisco Hernández had not run away from his own men, but had gone out openly, a great many would have followed him, and it would have been much more difficult to capture them or wear them down.

When the captains were three leagues off, they checked how many rebels there were by sending a reliable Spaniard who was to travel light with an Indian guide and make a reconnaissance. The scout performed his task and wrote a note to say that there were up to 80 men, and no more. The captains then pressed on until the two groups sighted one another. The royalists advanced with flags flying and accompanied by 80 Indian warriors raised by the chiefs to serve the Spaniards. The rebels, seeing that they would have to fight and fearing the captains' horses which numbered about 40, climbed a hill in order to fortify themselves behind some walls there were at the top. Although the position was a favorable one, the captains followed, determined to fight and encouraged by the fact that they now had 200 armed Indian warriors, who had collected of their own accord to help put down the *aucas,* as they called the rebels.

When the captains were an arquebuss shot away from the rebels, 4 or 5 of the latter came forward, including one of Francisco Hernández's ensigns, who earnestly begged them to proceed no further, for all the rebels would come over, and there was no need to risk any of their own men being killed, as the enemy was ready to surrender. At this point 10 or 12 more soldiers came over, though the Indian warriors used their slings against them until the captains ordered them to stop. As soon as Francisco Hernández's followers saw this, they all came over, and only 2 men were left with him: one, his brother-in-law ———— de Almaraz, and the other, a knight from Extremadura called Gómez Suárez de Figueroa.

Finding himself thus abandoned by all his followers, Francisco Hernández left the fort for the royalists to kill him or do as they pleased with him. The two captains thereupon rushed forward with all their men to enter the fort and take Francisco Hernández. Those who reached him first were three noblemen called Esteban Silvestre, Gómez Arias de Avila, and Hernando Pantoja. The last of these seized the rebel leader by the helmet, and when he tried to defend himself with his sword, Gómez Arias caught hold of it by the guard and ordered him to drop it. He did not do so, and Esteban Silvestre then put his lance against the rebel's breast, and said he would kill him unless he obeyed.

Francisco Hernández then surrendered his sword to Gómez Arias, and climbed up onto the back of the victor's horse, and was led away a prisoner. When they stopped for the night Gómez Arias asked to be made guard over the prisoner, and promised to take the responsibility for him. The captains agreed, and had Francisco Hernández chained. Various soldiers were appointed to guard him. In this way they travelled on until they came to the mountain road to the city of Lima.

Captains Miguel de la Serna and Juan Tello had intended to carry out their commission by executing many of Francisco Hernández's followers whom they had arrested. But finding them honest, docile, and poor folk, they took pity on them and sent them into exile in various directions. But in order to make a show of rigorous justice as well as mercy, they had one of them called ———— Guadramiros killed: he had been with Don Sebastián and was the most shameless of Francisco Hernández's companions. Thus he paid for all his friends.

Rumor soon spread the news of Francisco Hernández's arrest: and the commander Don Pedro Puertocarrero and Captain Baltasar Velázquez, whom the royal judges had sent out from Cuzco a few days earlier with 30 men and two flags to find the rebel leader, hastened forward on learning the news, to enjoy their rivals' success and escort the prisoner to the city of Lima, as though they had caught him by their own labors and efforts. Thus, making all possible speed, they caught up with the captains and their prisoner a few leagues short of the city. They made their entry as if in triumph, displaying all four flags. Those of the two captains who had captured Francisco Hernández were carried between those of the commander and Captain Baltasar Velázquez, and the prisoner went between the four flags, with the three soldiers who actually took him in front and on either side. The infantry followed up, marching in order, as did the cavalry. Behind them all came the commander and the three captains. The arquebusiers fired salvoes as they marched, amidst great rejoicing and celebrations at the end of a rebellion that had wrought such havoc throughout the empire, to Indians and Spaniards alike: when one considers the whole episode and all its details, one realizes that what has been recorded is not a tenth part of the damage that was done.

CHAPTER XXX

The royal judges appoint corregidors; they have
difficult interviews with importunate soldiers;
they execute Francisco Hernández Girón; his head
is placed on the municipal pillar; a gentleman
steals it, with those of Gonzalo Pizarro and
Francisco de Carvajal; the strange death
of Baltasar Velázquez.

T HE JUDGES, on their return from Pucara, where Francisco Hernández
Girón was finally defeated, stopped in the city of Cuzco some days to
take important measures relating to the government of Peru, which indeed had been virtually without government for more than a year, and
had lain prostrate under rebels whose tyranny beggars description. Juan
Ramón was made corregidor in the city of La Paz, where he had his allocation of Indians; Don Juan de Sandoval, in Silver City and its provinces;
and Garcilaso de la Vega, corregidor and governor of the city of Cuzco.
As lieutenant he was given a lawyer called Licentiate Monjaraz, whom the
royal judges appointed lieutenant until such time as they should see fit.
On seeing this, the corregidor said that the lieutenant's appointment
should be terminable when he wished and not by anyone else, since if he
did not do his duty, the corregidor should be free to dismiss him and
appoint someone else in his place. The royal judges accepted this and had
the clause altered, but Licentiate Monjaraz governed so well under the
courteous and fair-minded corregidor that when his term of three years
had expired he was given another post as corregidor of no less honor; his
successor had a very different fate, as we shall see.

During the few days the royal judges spent in Cuzco, captains and
soldiers who claimed allocations of Indians for themselves importuned
them constantly for rewards in return for services rendered His Majesty
in the recent war and its predecessors. The judges made excuses, saying
that at the moment the war was not over, since the tyrant was still not

captured and many of his followers were still ranging the length and breadth of the kingdom. When peace was completely restored they would go into the distribution of favors in His Majesty's name; meanwhile the claimants would do well not to form associations as they were doing, for this or any other purpose, for such conduct was suspicious and gave rise to malicious gossip. The judges thus avoided being pestered.

Meanwhile they had news of the arrest of Francisco Hernández Girón, and therefore made all haste to complete their business in order to return to the city of Lima and busy themselves with the punishment of the rebel leader. Thus Dr. Saravia left six or seven days before his colleagues Licentiate Santillán or Licentiate Mercado.

Captains Juan Tello and Miguel de la Serna brought their prisoner to the *audiencia's* jail and delivered him to the governor, demanding a receipt for him, which was duly given. Two or three days later Dr. Saravia arrived, having made all haste so as to be present at the sentencing and execution of the prisoner. This was done within a week of the doctor's arrival, as Fernández says in his ch. lviii:

He made a confession and at the end of it declared that his opinions were generally shared by everyone in Peru, men and women, old men and children, friars, priests, and lawyers. He was taken out to execution at mid-day, dragged in a hamper fastened to a nag's tail, while a crier proclaimed: "Behold the justice ordained by His Majesty and the magnificent knight Don Pedro Puertocarrero, his commander, to be done upon this man as a traitor to the royal crown and a causer of rebellion in this kingdom, that he shall be beheaded and his head be affixed to the municipal pillar in this city, that his houses shall be razed and their sites strewn with salt, and a stone erected in their place with a notice declaring his crime." He died like a Christian, showing great repentance for the great harm and suffering he had caused.

Thus our author ends the chapter mentioned above. Francisco Hernández's end was as he says. His head was placed on the column in an iron cage to the right of those of Gonzalo Pizarro and Francisco de Carvajal. His houses in Cuzco, where the rebellion began, were never demolished, and nothing occurred beyond what we have said. His rebellion lasted from beginning to end thirteen months and a few days more.

It was said that the rebel leader was the son of a knight of the order of St. John. His wife became a nun in a convent in the city of Lima where she led a very religious life. More than ten years later, a gentleman called Gómez de Chaves, a native of Ciudad Rodrigo, who was impressed by the goodness, honesty and nobility of Doña Mencía de Almaraz, imagined that it would please her if her husband's head were removed from the pillar, and not knowing which of the three it was, he and a friend brought a ladder one night and removed one which he thought was that of Francisco Hernández Girón, but it turned out to be that of Francisco de Carvajal. Then they took another, which was Gonzalo Pizarro's. Finally the knight said to his friend: "Let's take the other, so as to be sure, and since God has permitted us to do this, none of them shall be returned." So they took all three, and buried them secretly in a convent there. And although the magistrates tried hard to find out who had removed the heads, they failed to do so, because the deed was generally approved of by all the people, especially because of the removal of the head of Gonzalo Pizarro, the sight of which in that place caused much grief. This account I received from a gentleman who spent some years of his life in the empires of Mexico and Peru with a post in His Majesty's service: he is called Don Luis de Cañaveral, and lives in this city of Córdova.

But at the beginning of 1612, a religious of the order of the seraphic St. Francis, a great theologian born in Peru, called Fray Luis Jerónimo de Oré, came here and told me, in speaking of these heads, that there were five of them in the convent of St. Francis in the city of Lima—those of Gonzalo Pizarro, Francisco de Carvajal, Francisco Hernández Girón, and two others he could not identify. The holy convent had them stored there —they were not buried, but merely deposited—and he had wished to know which was the head of Francisco de Carvajal, who had left such a reputation in the whole of the empire. I told him that he could tell which it was by the notice affixed to the iron cage, but he explained that the heads were not accompanied by the cages, but loose and without any distinguishing mark. The difference between the two versions must be that the religious would not wish to bury the heads that were brought to them, nor to be guilty of not having buried them, and they therefore kept them in that holy house, neither buried nor unburied, while the gentlemen who removed them from the pillar told their friends that they had them buried: this would explain the two versions.

The religious I have mentioned, Fray Luis Jerónimo de Oré, was travelling from Madrid to Cádiz on the instructions of his superiors and of the Royal Council of the Indies to send or to accompany two dozen religious on their way to Florida, where they were to preach the gospel to the heathen. He was not sure if he was to go with them or to return when he had seen them off. He asked me to give him part of my history of Florida to take to these religious so as to inform them about those provinces and the customs of the natives. I let him have seven books, three of the *Florida* and four of the *Commentaries,* for which his Paternity was very grateful. May God's Majesty aid them in their task so that the idolaters may be drawn up out of the abyss of their darkness.

I should describe here how Captain Baltasar Velázquez met his end, for it was a strange one; and so Francisco Hernández Girón may not go to his alone and unaccompanied. Some months after the events we have described, while Baltasar Velázquez was dwelling in the city of Lima and leading the life of a gallant young captain, two lumps appeared in his hair. He tried to show more courage than was wise by not having them attended to, to make them develop and burst, which is the safest way. He asked to have them squashed. The result was that he had an internal cancer on the fifth day, so virulent that he seemed to be burning alive. The doctors did not know what to do and applied vinegar to refresh him, but the fire grew and spread so that no one could bear to hold a hand a yard above his body which burned like a natural fire. Thus the poor captain died, leaving his friends who knew his past and present deeds much to talk of, even though he came to such a hard end.

The captains and soldiers who remained to claim rewards in Cuzco went off after the judges as soon as they heard of the arrest and execution of Francisco Hernández Girón, intending to insist on being given honors in return for their services. As soon as the judges were established in Lima, these men insistently repeated their demands. Many of them declared that they had spent all their wealth in the course of the war and were reduced to such poverty that they had nothing left for their ordinary expenses, and that therefore it was only right and just to fulfil the promises they had been given of some rewards when the revolt was over. The rebel was dead, and all that remained was the question of payment, but there seemed to be no intention of attending to it, as far as they could see.

The judges answered that loyal servants of His Majesty ought not to try to obtain the rewards that were owing to them by force and violence. They themselves and everyone else were aware that news was hourly, nay momentarily, expected that His Majesty had appointed a viceroy. No less was to be expected, for the service of the empire required that they should go no longer without one. If a viceroy arrived, and found that all the vacant allocations had been awarded, he would be angry with the judges for not having awaited his arrival, and with the claimants for having insisted on their rewards: thus everyone would start off on the wrong foot with him. Let them bide their time for three or four months, for it was impossible but that they should have news of the viceroy by then. If however no news came, they would then divide the land up and keep their word, for they were well aware that the claimants needed property and they regretted very much that they could not succor them in their need. But the time was a very short one, and so as not to displease the viceroy, it would be best to put up with necessity and hope for abundance. Any other course and any attempt to force payment would do them more harm than good. With these and similar arguments the judges placated the fury of the claimants, and God permitted that a few months after—less than six—news came of the departure of the viceroy, whereon all were appeased and awaited the reception of his excellency: he was the first to come to Peru with this title.

End of Book Seven

BOOK
EIGHT *of the*
SECOND
PART

It tells how Indians and Spaniards celebrated the feast of
the Holy Sacrament in the city of Cuzco; a remarkable
event that occurred there; the election of the marquis of
Cañete as viceroy of Peru; the appointment of new officials; the precautions taken against revolts; the death of
the citizens who followed Francisco Hernández Girón,
and that of Martín de Robles; the banishment of the
claimants to Spain; the heir to the empire comes out of
the forests in peace and dies soon after; the exiles reach
Spain; His Majesty rewards them with many favors; the
heirs of those killed by the rebels recover their Indians;
the departure of Pedro de Orsúa to the Amazon; the
election of the count of Nieva as viceroy of Peru; the
death of his predecessor and that of the count himself;
the election of Licentiate Castro as governor of Peru and
of Don Francisco de Toledo as viceroy; the arrest of
Prince Túpac Amaru, heir to the empire, and his execution; the return of the viceroy to Spain;
his end and death.

It contains twenty-one chapters.

CHAPTER I

*How the Indians and Spaniards celebrated the
feast of the Holy Sacrament in Cuzco;
a private quarrel among the Indians
at one of these feasts.*

S HISTORY requires that every event shall be told in its due
time and place, we shall place the two following incidents
at the beginning of this Eighth Book because they occurred
in Cuzco after the end of Francisco Hernández's war and
before the arrival of the viceroy, so anxiously awaited in
Peru. Following this precept, we must mention that the feast Catholics
call Corpus Christi was celebrated with great solemnity in the city of
Cuzco once these wars sown by the Devil to impede the preaching of the
holy Gospel in that empire had been brought to an end: the last of these
wars was that of Francisco Hernández Girón, and please God it may
remain so. The same solemnity will be observed now, and even greater,
for since that war, which ended at the end of 1554, there have followed
fifty-seven years of peace, up to the time of writing this chapter, in 1611.

My own intention is only to deal with the events of those days, and to
leave those of today to whoever is willing to take the trouble to write
about them. In the times I refer to there were nearly eighty *vecinos* in
that city, all noble knights and gentlemen; for as we have said before,
vecinos means lords of vassals with allocations of Indians. Each of these
took pains with the decoration of the floats his Indians were to carry in
the Corpus Christi procession. They adorned them with silks, gold, and
many rich jewels, such as emeralds and other precious stones. On the
floats they placed the image of Our Lord or Our Lady or some other saint
of the devotion of the Spanish lord or his Indian vassals. The floats were
like those carried by Spanish brotherhoods in such processions.

The chiefs from the whole district came into the great city to celebrate
the festivity, accompanied by their kinsmen and all the nobility of their
provinces. They used to bring all the decorations, ornaments, and devices

that they used in the time of the Inca kings for their great festivals, which we have described in the First Part of these *Commentaries*. Each tribe brought the coat of arms of the family from which it vaunted descent.

Some came dressed in lionskins, as Hercules is depicted, with their heads in the lion's head, since they claim descent from this animal. Others had the wings of a very large bird called *cuntur* fixed on their shoulders, as angel's wings are in pictures, for it was from this bird that they boasted of descending. Similarly others came with painted devices, such as springs, rivers, lakes, mountains, heaths, and caves, from which they believed that their earliest forefathers had emerged. Others had strange devices and dresses of gold and silver foil, or carried wreaths of gold or silver, or appeared as monsters with horrifying masks, bearing in their hands the pelts of various animals they pretended to have caught, and striking exaggerated attitudes and pretending to be mad or fools. They thus pleased their kings in many different ways, some with a show of pomp and wealth, and others with folly and poor trifles. Each province produced what it thought best devised either for solemnity, splendor, taste, or folly, or madness, realizing that variety gives delight to the eye and adds pleasure and contentment to the soul. With these things and much more that must be imagined, for I cannot describe them, the Indians used to celebrate their royal festivities; and in the same way in my time, with such additions as they were capable of, they used to mark the feast of the Blessed Sacrament, the true God, our Lord and Redeemer. This they did with great joy, like people now truly disillusioned about their former heathendom.

The chapter of the cathedral and the city council added each its contribution to the solemnity of the festivities. A platform was built against the wall of the cathedral which projects into the square, and the Blessed Sacrament was placed on it in a handsome monstrance of gold and silver. The chapter was ranged on one side of it and the city council on the other; and they were accompanied by the remaining Incas of the royal blood, thereby recalling that the empire had once belonged to them and doing them honor.

The Indians from each allocation marched past with their floats and accompanied by their kinsmen and friends, all singing in the special language of their province, not in the general language of the capital: thus each tribe could be told apart. They bore drums, flutes, horns, and other rustic instruments. In many cases the women of the province accompanied the men and joined in the singing and playing.

The songs they sang were in praise of Our Lord God, thanking Him for the great grace He had granted to them of permitting them a true knowledge of Himself. They also gave thanks to the Spanish clergy, both regular and secular, for having taught them Christian doctrine. From some provinces no women came, but only men; in a word everything was done according to the custom in the days of the Incas. On reaching the cemetery which stands seven or eight steps higher than the square, they mounted the steps to adore the Blessed Sacrament, in their tribal groups, each ten or twelve steps in front of the next so that they should not get mixed. They came down into the square again by the other steps to the right of the platform. Each tribe mounted according to its seniority, the date of its conquest by the Incas, the most recent first, then the second and third most recent until finally there came the Incas themselves. These went in front of the priests, a smaller and poorer band, since they had lost their whole empire and their private houses and estates.

As the bands were passing by in this way in the procession, that of the Cañaris arrived: although their province is outside the jurisdiction of the city, they have their own float, for a great many Indians of the tribe live in the city. Their chief then was Don Francisco Chillchi Cañari, whom we have mentioned in the episode of the close siege of Hernando Pizarro and his men by Prince Manco Inca, when this Cañari killed the Inca's captain in the city square as he challenged the Spaniards to single combat. This Don Francisco went up the churchyard steps with his cloak round him and his hands hidden in its folds: his float was not decorated with silk or gold, but painted in various colors, with four battle scenes of Indians and Spaniards depicted on the four panels of the canopy.

As he mounted the steps leading to the graveyard on the right of the city councillors where my lord Garcilaso de la Vega, then corregidor, was with his deputy Monjaraz, a lawyer of great wisdom and skill, the Cañari dropped the blanket he was wearing as a cloak and revealed his body with another blanket girt round it as they do when they intend to fight or engage in any other important affair. In his right hand he carried a model of an Indian head which he held by the hair. As soon as the Incas saw it, four or five of them attacked the Cañari, and lifted him up in the air so as to dash his head on the ground. The rest of the Indians on both sides of the platform with the Blessed Sacrament were now in a turmoil, and Licentiate Monjaraz had to go among them and pacify them. He asked the Incas what had upset them, and the oldest of them replied: "This dog of an *auca* instead of celebrating the festival comes with this head to stir up memories of the past that are best left forgotten."

The deputy then asked the Cañari what he meant, and he answered:

"Sir, I cut that head off an Indian who challenged the Spaniards when they were surrounded in this square with Hernando Pizarro, Gonzalo Pizarro, and Juan Pizarro, my lords and masters, and two hundred other Spaniards. None of them would go out and accept the Indian's challenge, thinking it was a disgrace and not an honor to engage a single fight with an Indian. So I asked their permission to go out and fight, and the Christians said yes, and I went out and fought the challenger, and beat him and cut his head off in this square." As he spoke, he pointed to the place of the battle, and then resumed his story: "The four pictures on my float are pitched battles between Indians and Spaniards, in which I saved the latter. Is it strange that on such an occasion as today I should take pride in the deed I did in the service of the Christians?"

The Inca answered: "Treacherous dog, did you do such a deed with your own strength, or by the virtue of the Lord Pachacámac, who is here before us, and the good fortune of the Spaniards? Do you forget that you and all your people were our slaves, and that you won no such victory by your own strength and valor, but only for the reasons I have mentioned? If you wish to try your fortune now that we are all Christians, go out into the square with your weapons and we will send out a servant, the meanest of us all, who will make mincemeat of you and all your people. Do you forget how at that very time and in this very square we cut off the heads of thirty Spaniards, and a single Inca won two lances from two mounted men and got them from their very hands, and would have taken Gonzalo Pizarro's, if he had not saved himself by his skill and strength? Do your forget how we gave up fighting the Spaniards and abandoned the siege, and our prince went into exile of his own will and left the empire to the Spaniards when he saw what great miracles Pachacámac wrought in their favor? Do your forget how on the road from Lima to Cuzco we killed nearly eight hundred Spaniards during the siege? What would you say if we produced all their heads including that of Juan Pizarro, whom we killed up there in the fort, on this occasion to do ourselves honor? Had you not better remember all this and a good deal else I could remind you of before you embark on a scandalous and foolish act such as you have just done?" With these words he turned to the deputy corregidor and said: "Sire, execute justice duly so that we are not disgraced by those who were once our slaves."

Licentiate Monjaraz, having heard the speeches of both Indians, took charge of the head the Cañari was carrying and ordered him to ungird the blanket he had on and not talk of those things again in public or in private, under pain of severe punishment. This satisfied the Incas and all the

Indians at the festival, who had been scandalized by the outspokenness and insolence of the Cañari, and they all cried out together, men and women alike: *"Auca, auca!"* and the word ran round the whole square. The procession then went on and ended with the usual solemnity. I am told that nowadays the route is three times as long as it used to be, for they go as far as St. Francis and return to the cathedral by a very circuitous way: in those times they merely went round the two squares, Cussipata and Haucaipata, which we have so often mentioned. May God's Majesty be praised for deigning to go with them and so illumine the gentiles and draw them up out of the darkness in which they lived.

CHAPTER II

A remarkable event that occurred in Cuzco.

T HE SECOND incident is the following: a strange occurrence that came to pass in Cuzco in the years after the war with Francisco Hernández Girón. As some grave and religious persons who heard me tell it told me that it would be a service to our Holy Mother Church to include it in the course of my history, I considered that I, as a son, however unworthy, of such a mother, was obliged to obey them, and repeat the story, which is as follows.

Eight or nine years before the events just recounted, the festival of St. Mark the Divine used to be celebrated annually in Cuzco, according to the abilities of the inhabitants. The procession used to come out of the convent of the blessed St. Dominic, which, as we have said, was founded in the house and temple that used to belong to the Sun in heathen times before the Gospel reached that city. From the convent the procession went to a chapel near the houses that belonged to Don Cristóbal Paullu Inca. A priest called Fray Porras, who had been many years in Peru and was devoted to the blessed Evangelist, used to solemnize the feast, leading a tame bull in the procession wreathed with garlands of many kinds of flowers. In 1556 the procession took place with the cathedral chapter, the city council, and the rest of the inhabitants, and the bull walked in their midst as gently as a lamb. When they reached the convent on their way back, the Indians and other common people stood in lines in the square before the temple, for there was not room for everyone inside. The Spaniards went in and lined the aisle from the door to the high altar. The bull, walking a little in front of the priests, had gone three or four steps beyond the threshold of the church, just as tame and gentle as we have said, when it lowered its head and caught a Spaniard called —— de Salazar between the legs with one of its horns, lifted him and tossed him over its back against one of the church doors, from which he fell into the street, unhurt. This action on the part of the bull spread panic among the people, who fled in all directions, but the bull remained as calm as during the whole procession and so advanced to the high altar.

The city was astonished at the occurrence, and thinking there must be some mystery about it, tried hard to arrive at the cause. It was discovered that six or seven months before, Salazar had had a dispute with an ecclesiastic and had been excommunicated. He had never troubled to get the excommunication absolved as he had not thought it necessary. He then did so, and learnt by experience not to fall into a similar error again. I was in the city at the time, and present when the incident occurred; I saw the procession and later heard the story from those who told it better and at greater length than I have done.

CHAPTER III

The election of the marquis of Cañete as viceroy
of Peru; his arrival at Tierra Firme; the fugitive
Negroes are recaptured; the burning of a
galleon with eight hundred
people aboard.

HIS IMPERIAL Majesty, on learning in Germany of the death of the viceroy Don Antonio de Mendoza, appointed the count of Palma viceroy of Peru, but he begged to refuse the post with good reasons. So also did the count of Olivares, who was also named viceroy of that great kingdom. The Peruvians supposed that they were unwilling to accept because of the length of the journey and the great distance from Spain, though one of the later viceroys used to say that the finest office His Majesty had in his gift would be the viceroyalty of Peru, if it weren't so near the capital in Madrid. He said this because he thought that when he gave offence to anyone news reached the capital in a very short time. Finally His Majesty appointed Don Andrés Hurtado de Mendoza, marquis of Cañete, lord warden of Cuenca, who accepted the post and left for Peru with the necessary royal decrees, and reached Nombre de Dios, where he made the usual investigation of the justices and officers of the royal treasury. He rewarded some of the early conquerors of the Windward Islands and Tierra Firme, as Fernández says (ch. ii), for he found them in great poverty. These were not, however, rewards of allocations of Indians, for the natives of those parts had already been exterminated: they were subsidies and offices of profit.

One so assisted was Pedro de Orsúa, a noble gentleman, a fine soldier, and a captain who had made great conquests in New Spain and settled a city called Pamplona. In order to get away from the persecution of a judge who wanted to reap the harvest Orsúa had sown, as the Reverend Juan de Castellanos writes, he went to live at Nombre de Dios, where Don Andrés Hurtado de Mendoza found him and commissioned him to find and apply a solution for the havoc wrought by the fugitive Negroes called *cimarrones*, who live in the mountains and come down to the roads to attack merchants and travellers, stealing their goods and killing many of them. This had become so intolerable that it was impossible to travel unless in parties of twenty or more. And the number of Negroes was increasing daily, for having such an asylum it was easy for them to run away without the slightest danger from their owners.

In order to clarify what Castellanos says (he mentions nothing of this), we must explain that Pedro de Orsúa raised a force to conquer the *cimarrones*—a word from the language of the natives of the Windward Islands —enlisting many of Francisco Hernández Girón's men who had either fled or been exiled to those parts, and the viceroy pardoned all who took part in the expedition. When the Negroes found themselves in a corner, they asked for terms. To restore peace, which was very necessary, all those who had hitherto fled from their masters were given their freedom, since their masters had lost them in any case. In return the *cimarrones* were obliged to hand over any who fled in the future or to pay what their owners asked for them; any Negro who was maltreated by his or her master could be freed by paying his master what he had cost him, and the Negroes were to establish themselves in places where they could live as settlers and residents, and not remain scattered in the wilderness. They could trade with the Spaniards as they wished. All this was agreed by both sides, so that they could live in peace. The Negroes gave sufficient hostages and thus guaranteed the treaty. Their king, called Ballano, came in person to deliver the hostages, but he himself remained as a permanent hostage, for they refused to release him. The poor Negro was taken to Spain, where he died.

Although it is not part of our history, I may include a strange incident that occurred at sea a little before the viceroy's voyage. Jerónimo de Alderete, who had come from Chile to Spain on the affairs of Governor Pedro de Valdivia, heard of the governor's death and claimed the succession, which His Majesty was pleased to confer on him. The latter had with him his sister-in-law, a very respectable and devout woman—what is called a *beata*. He sailed in a galleon with eight hundred on board and it was flagship of a fleet of six more vessels. They sailed from Spain two months before the viceroy. The good lady, to prove her piety, asked the master's permission to have a light in her cabin at nights to see to pray by. The master consented because she was the governor's sister-in-law. The weather was calm, and it happened that a doctor on one of the other ships wanted to come over to the galleon to visit a friend; the two were overjoyed to meet, though they were sailing in the same fleet. When it became late and the doctor spoke of returning to his own ship, his friend said: "Don't go, my dear fellow, spend the night here, and cross to your own ship in the morning, for the weather's perfectly calm."

The doctor remained and tied his jolly boat to the galleon so as to use it next day. But it happened that that night the pious lady, after saying her prayers or in the middle of them, fell asleep with the candle still lit, quite neglectful of the possible consequences. What follows shows how unwise it is to break any regulations that military or naval authorities have established for the preservation of order. One of these regulations is that there shall never be any other light on a ship at night except the ship's lamp, and it is a capital offence for a master to allow one. Misfortune had it that the pious lady's light was close to the timber of the galleon, which took fire and began to blaze.

When the master saw that there was no chance of extinguishing the flames, he ordered a seaman to bring up the jolly boat tied behind, in which the doctor had come over on the previous day. He then went to Governor Alderete, and silently roused him and told him what had happened. Accompanied by the governor and a boy, one of two sons he had with him, the master went to the boat, and the four men got in and rowed away from the ship without giving the alarm or making any sound at all for fear of waking the rest of the company and starting off a tumult in which everyone would have been drowned. In this way he hoped to escape death, leaving one of his sons behind as the penalty for having broken a rule that should inviolably be observed.

The fire, fed with the fuel of pitch and tar that ships can always supply, blazed away and woke the sleeping company. When great flames were seen spouting from the flagship, the other vessels closed in to pick up the company as they leapt into the sea, but the flames reached the artillery and set it off, and the other ships hastily withdrew for fear of the balls, the flagship being well armed and prepared against any possible attack. Thus the whole company of eight hundred souls perished either in the flames or by drowning, and the news of the disaster caused great dismay throughout Peru.

As soon as dawn came, Jerónimo de Alderete entered one of his ships and ordered his standard to be hoisted so that the rest should see that he had escaped fire and water. He then ordered the remaining ships to proceed to Nombre de Dios, himself returning to Spain to get new letters of authority and fresh supplies of everything he needed, for all his property was lost in the fire. He thus began the journey again in company with the fleet that took the marquis of Cañete to be viceroy of Peru, as Fernández tells, though he does not mention the disaster to the galleon.

CHAPTER IV

The viceroy reaches Peru; his appointment of new officials; he writes letters to the corregidors.

THE VICEROY Don Andrés Hurtado de Mendoza left Panama and reached Paita, where Peru begins, with fair weather. From here he sent letters to the kingdom of Quito and other places in the vicinity, and wrote to the corregidors of all the cities of the empire. He sent one young gentleman, a kinsman of his, on a special mission to the royal *audiencia* at Lima, and this person stopped in the city of San Miguel where he fell in with other gentlemen of his own age with whom he passed the time in a discreditable manner. The viceroy heard about this, and forbade him to go on. When he himself reached the city, he had the youth arrested and taken to Spain under guard to show that he would not allow his envoys and attendants to exceed the orders he gave them. He also sent back to Spain Don Pedro Luis de Cabrera and other married men whose wives had remained behind. The truth is that here the fault lay rather with the wives than with the husbands, for some of the latter had sent for their wives to come, with plenty of money for the journey, but they had not wished to leave Seville (which enchants all women who go there) and not only disobeyed their husbands but intervened with the justices to get them sent back. Three of these ladies, whose husbands I knew, lost allocations through not going to Peru: they would have inherited the property on the death of their husbands, and it was worth above 100,000 ducats a year. I could give their names, but it is only proper to respect their reputation and honor.

The viceroy continued his journey, displaying great courtesy and kindness and bestowing honors and generous speeches on all those who spoke to him and begged to be rewarded for their services. He did this with care and diplomacy so that the news should go ahead and serve to calm down those spirits that were still excited by the late disorders and misdeeds. Among other things, it was rumored that he proposed to form a private council of four of the leading and longest-established persons in the country. They were to be free of prejudices and attachments, but acquainted with everyone in the empire and familiar with their merits, so that they could advise the viceroy on how to treat the claimants and see that he was not taken in by cock-and-bull stories. Rumor had it that the Council was to consist of Francisco de Garay, a *vecino* of Huánucu, Lorenzo de Aldana, a *vecino* of Arequipa, and Garcilaso de la Vega and Antonio de Quiñones, both *vecinos* of Cuzco. Any of these four, as was well known, was capable of governing all Peru and more besides. The report stirred and delighted all the inhabitants of the empire, both Indians and Spaniards, ecclesiastics and laymen; and they all shouted that the viceroy had come from heaven since he proposed to govern the kingdom with such advisers.

He continued on his way to the city of Lima, still announcing that he was going to confer various rewards, as Fernández says (ch. ii) in the following words:

What most contributed to his reputation was the bestowal of great honors by him and the fact that he refrained from going into the past. For this reason a great many people rallied to Trujillo, many of whom had not been very steady in the royal service. The viceroy smiled upon them, and hinted in conversation that those of Francisco Hernández's men who had gone over to the king were responsible for the recovery of the whole country. He allayed their fears to such an extent that in Cuzco and in other districts many *vecinos* who had been living quietly among their Indians since the late disturbance and only came into the city well accompanied and with suitable precautions now began to relax,

etc. Thus far our author.

On this point we must explain that all the *vecinos* of Cuzco were calm and quiet and very glad of the arrival of the viceroy and the good reports rumor brought about his desires and intentions. The only ones who were dwelling among the Indians and not in the city were Tomás Vázquez and Juan de Piedrahita, more through a sense of shame at having followed the rebel from the beginning of his rising than from any fear of justice, for they had received pardons in the name of His Majesty from the *audiencia* in return for having turned against the rebel at the moment when they did, a very great service since it brought about his total ruin and downfall. They did not come into the city in company or with the precautions our author says, but stayed in voluntary exile on their allocations of Indians. In the period of over three years while my lord Garcilaso de la Vega was corregidor of the city, I never saw either of them in it but once, when Juan de Piedrahita came in by night on an urgent errand; he visited my father by night and described his solitary life, but he never went out into the street in the daytime. It surprises me therefore to find in writing an account so different from the truth. Alonso Díaz, another *vecino* who had accompanied Francisco Hernández, did not even leave the city, but lived in it as usual. This was the situation in the town, which was far from being as disturbed as our author's words would suggest to a listener.

The viceroy reached the city of Lima in July 1557, and was given a reception in accordance with the dignity of his royal office and his own rank and position, which was that of a lord of vassals with the title of marquis. The preceding viceroys had had the same rank, but not the title of lord of vassals. A week after he had settled he took possession of the empire in the name of King Philip II, since the emperor Charles V had abdicated from all his kingdoms and possessions because his failing health prevented him from governing such vast empires and kingdoms and dealing with such important and difficult business as they give rise to. The assumption of authority was celebrated with all the necessary solemnity, ceremonial, and accompaniment in the presence of the viceroy, the royal *audiencia,* the city council, the chapter of the cathedral, with the archbishop of Lima, Don Jerónimo de Loaisa, and the four convents of religious that then existed in the city—those of the Mercedarians, Franciscans, Dominicans, and Augustinians. After the ceremony in the square and the streets, they went into the cathedral where the archbishop celebrated a very solemn pontifical high mass. The same happened in all the other cities of the empire, everyone displaying according to his means his satisfaction and joy at the event. There were many splendid bull fights and jousts, with very costly liveries, as was, and is, usual in Peru.

Once he had taken possession of his office the viceroy Don Andrés Hurtado de Mendoza appointed corregidors and magistrates in all the towns in Peru. Among them a lawyer from Cuenca called Bautista Muñoz, who had come in the viceroy's train, was appointed to Cuzco. Licentiate Altamirano, one of the judges, who had refused to accompany the royal standard and army in the late war, was made corregidor in Silver City, and others were sent to Huamanga, Arequipa, and La Paz, where notable things occurred. Some of them we shall mention in the next chapter: it would be difficult to describe them all.

CHAPTER V

The precautions taken by the viceroy to prevent
risings and revolts; the execution of Tomás
Vázquez, Piedrahita, and Alonso Díaz
for having followed Francisco
Hernández Girón.

As Fernández says in ch. ii of his Third Part, as soon as the viceroy entered the city of Lima, he ordered all the roads from it to the cities of the empire to be guarded. For this purpose he appointed persons in whom he had full confidence, and instructed them carefully and vigilantly to watch if any Spaniards or Indians took letters from one place to another, "this he ordered so as to be aware if any trouble was brewing among them." These are Fernández's words, and what follows is his too: and I saw a great deal of it. The viceroy also ordered that no Spaniard should make a journey without a special permit from the magistrate of the town where he was, in order to obtain which he would have to show good reasons for the journey. He particularly forbade any Spaniards to come to the city of Lima to see the festivities and rejoicings there. This had little effect, since even before he arrived the city was already full of claimants and others who had business to transact and were waiting for him: as soon as he was known to be on the way everyone rushed to attend his reception and give him a welcome. He had the heavy artillery that was in the city brought into his own house, and also the arquebusses and other weapons. This was all done for fear of a new rising, for past experience suggested that rebellions were greatly to be feared in Peru. But the inhabitants were now so weary of warfare and so chastened that there was nothing to fear from them. So we shall leave the viceroy and turn to the corregidors he sent to Cuzco and Charcas.

Licentiate Muñoz reached Cuzco with his letter of appointment as corregidor and the city turned out to welcome him. On his entry my lord Garcilaso handed his rod of office over to him, and still holding it, the new corregidor at once asked him how much he charged for his signature. The answer was that he did not know, for he had never made any such charge. The licentiate replied that it was a mistake for judges not to insist on their rights, of whatever nature. Those present were astonished at the conversation, but were told that there was nothing strange in wanting to know what the office brought in apart from the established salary, since people only went from Spain to the Indies to make as much as they could.

As soon as the corregidor had taken his wand and appointed his alguacils, he sent two of them off, one to arrest Tomás Vázquez and the other Juan de Piedrahita, and within five or six days they were brought back under arrest and flung in the public prison. The relatives of both men tried to find sureties who would give pledges that they would stay in the city and not leave it, thinking that the motive of the arrest was to oblige them to reside in the city and not in Indian villages. My father was one of those asked to become a surety. He replied that the corregidor's purpose must be very different from what they thought, since if it were merely a question of their residing in the city, it would be quite sufficient to order them to do so, with some penalty, which might be quite light, if they did not comply. The fact that they had been sent for with every ostentation and brought in under arrest made him suspect that they were to be beheaded. It turned out as Francisco Hernández Girón had prophesied, for by daybreak next day they were dead. The pardons granted in His Majesty's name by the royal *audiencia* did nothing to prevent their being strangled. Their Indians were confiscated, and the viceroy gave Tomás Vázquez's allocation, which was one of the best in the city, to another citizen called Rodrigo de Esquivel, a native of Seville; this was a great boon to him, for although he already had an allocation, his Indians were poor and valueless. The same was done with the Indians belonging to Piedrahita and Alonso Díaz, who also was killed and despoiled of his property. No other steps were taken in Cuzco against the rebels in the late war.

Licentiate Muñoz made the usual examination of his predecessors and brought four accusations against his immediate predecessor. One was that he had jousted while a magistrate of the city; the second was that he sometimes left his house to visit some neighbors without carrying his rod, which might occasion a lack of the respect due to a corregidor; the third was that at Christmas he had let the *vecinos* and other leading inhabitants play in his house, and he had played with them while he was corregidor. The last charge was that he had allowed a man to become a notary of the city without complying with certain formalities prescribed by law. The answers given were that he jousted because he had done so all his life and would not cease to do so even though he held a higher and nobler office; that if he sometimes went out of his house without his rod it was to pay a visit so close to his own house that no one would notice it, and in any case he received the respect due to him with his rod or without it, since he was well-known throughout the empire and even beyond, and no offence was given to the rod by not carrying it. As to playing in his house at Christmas, he admitted it was true and he played with those who came in, because the fact that the gaming took place in his house prevented squabbling and quarrels such as might break out if he were not present, and indeed as occurred repeatedly in gambling, even among highly placed dignitaries. As to the notary, he himself was not a lawyer and did not know what the law prescribed, but he did know that the city needed someone to execute that office, and what he had looked for was a faithful and law-abiding man suitable for the job, such as the man had indeed proved and the whole city would vouch for it. Licentiate Monjaraz, who had been deputy corregidor, was confronted with similar and even more trivial charges. The examination was more for the purpose of allowing the new magistrate to say that he had conducted it than because there were any real charges to punish or faults to amend, so he absolved them completely.

CHAPTER VI

The arrest and death of Martín de Robles and the reason why he is killed.

LICENTIATE Altamirano, one of the judges of the *audiencia* of Lima, was sent, as we have said, to be corregidor in Silver City, and as soon as he took over his office he arrested Martín de Robles, a citizen of the place, and hanged him publicly in the square without bringing any charge against him. This distressed everyone in that district, as he was one of the leading citizens in the empire and so stricken in years and aged that he could no longer carry his sword in his belt but had an Indian boy to carry it behind him. The distress was the greater when the cause of his death was known, which Fernández describes in ch. ii of his Third Part, as follows:

The viceroy wrote a letter to Licentiate Altamirano with instructions to execute Martín de Robles, and it was reported that the reason for this was that the viceroy had been told and assured that Martín de Robles had said in the course of conversation: "Let's go to Lima and put the viceroy to school; he certainly has no manners in his letter."

The words were Martín de Robles', though he had no cause or pretext for saying them; and many, even most, affirmed that Martín de Robles had said no such thing. Some affirmed that what had upset the viceroy was not this trivial matter, but the fact that Martín de Robles had been very guilty on the occasion of the arrest and execution of Blasco Núñez Vela, the former viceroy of Peru,

etc. Thus Fernández.

In order to explain this passage, which is obscure and confused, we must mention that Martín de Robles used these words in another context. He was referring to the letters which, as we have mentioned, the viceroy wrote from Paita to all the corregidors in the empire to announce his arrival. The covers of these letters all ran *To the noble gentleman, the corregidor of so-and-so,* and in the letter they were all addressed as *"vos."* This style of address caused astonishment in Peru, for in those days, and much later, until the appearance of the decree about forms of address, the rich and noble men of Peru used to address their servants with the title "noble," writing on the cover: *To the very noble gentleman, so-and-so.*

Inside the letter they used the third person or *"vos,"* according to the office held by the person they were addressing. As all the viceroy's letters departed so far from the usual custom, slanderers and troublemakers who desired to stir up revolts and disorders seized the occasion to mock and complain and said whatever they thought fit, for the previous viceroys and governors had always written with respect and consideration for the qualities and merits of the individual they were addressing. There was therefore no lack of people who asked my father, who was then corregidor of the imperial city of Cuzco, how he could put up with such an improper style of address. My father replied that he could put up with it very well, for the viceroy was not writing to Garcilaso de la Vega, but to the corregidor, his subordinate: the next day or later the viceroy would write to himself, and his letter would obviously then be quite different from the present. And indeed within eight days of the viceroy's arrival at Rímac he wrote to my father under a cover addressed *To the very magnificent gentleman, Garcilaso de la Vega,* etc. And within he spoke as if to a younger brother, to the surprise of all who saw it: I had both letters in my hands, for I then served my father as secretary for all the correspondence he had with various parts of the empire, and I wrote the replies to these two letters in my own hand.

To return to the case of Martín de Robles, one of the first of the viceroy's letters was to the corregidor of Charcas, and it gave the troublemakers plenty to talk about. One of the things they said was that the viceroy was lacking in manners if he wrote in that strain to all the corregidors, many of whom were of as good stuff as himself. Thereupon Martín de Robles retorted: "Wait till he gets here, then we'll teach him manners." He said it as a witticism, for, as Fernández mentions, he was the sort of man who took the greatest liberties on the least occasion and never spared his own friends, however close, or even his wife, and we could tell a good many stories and sayings of his in proof of this, if they were not indecent and unworthy to appear in writing. Suffice it to say that when his friends upbraided him on account of the liberty of his quips, most of which were depreciatory and offensive and made him unpopular, he retorted that he would rather lose a friend than a good joke or a clever saying if it was to the point. So the poor fellow lost his life on this account. His part in the arrest of Viceroy Blasco Núñez Vela which Fernández gives as the cause was already forgotten, since thirteen years had passed since then, during which Martín de Robles had rendered His Majesty many services: he fled from Gonzalo Pizarro and went over to President La Gasca at a critical moment and with great danger to himself and served against Gonzalo Pizarro till the end of the war, being well rewarded by President La Gasca, as we have said. He also served in the wars against Don Sebastián and Francisco Hernández Girón, in which he spent a great sum of gold and silver from his own estate; and all his previous misdeeds were already pardoned in His Majesty's name both by President La Gasca and by the judges of the royal *audiencia*.

CHAPTER VII

How the viceroy deals with the claimants of rewards for their services; how he sends thirty-seven of them in exile to Spain as envious and disloyal schemers.

IN ANOTHER part of his ch. ii, speaking of the viceroy, Don Andrés Hurtado de Mendoza, Fernández says:

Using the festivities and rejoicings as a pretext, he collected in his own house all the artillery, arquebusses, and other weapons there were, and as soon as this had been done, he annulled the pardons and other letters issued by the royal judges, and tried out a great many people, both captains and soldiers, by offering them some small gratification in return for their services. And when he heard that they were greatly annoyed, and was told that they had even uttered some ugly words, he had a great many of them arrested at once in his own house (which he contrived by a piece of ingenuity) and had them taken thence under a strong guard to the port at Callao for shipment to Spain. He gave out that some were being sent for His Majesty to reward them for their services, which could not be done in Peru, and that others were being sent into exile as punishment. When some people tried to advise him and persuade him to despatch at the same time an indictment of the crimes they had committed either in word or deed (if any of them were guilty), he refused to do so and said that he did not mean to act as prosecutor but as mediator to see that His Majesty received them well, and honored and favored them,

etc. Thus our author.

Now these are episodes in the story which require some explanation so that the reader may understand how they came to pass, and as he has left them obscure, we shall give a historical account of each point. As regards the gathering of arquebusses and other weapons which our author says the viceroy collected in his house, it was the royal judges who had ordered all the corregidors in the empire to have this done, before even the viceroy appeared. My father, as one of the corregidors, had the order announced throughout his jurisdiction, and a great many leading gentlemen and soldiers who were loyal servants of His Majesty handed in their arquebusses and other arms, but none of the common people presented themselves, or if they did, it was to hand in some piece of worthless scrap. My lord Garcilaso therefore wrote to the royal *audiencia* saying what had happened and pointing out that the measure was doing more harm than good, for loyal servants of the crown were disarmed while those who were not remained armed. The royal judges then ordered that the weapons should be secretly returned to their owners, and this was done. And the question of collecting arms which Fernández mentions was simply this.

As regards the cancellation of the pardons and other letters issued by the judges to the followers of Francisco Hernández, this was done so that they could be sentenced, as we have related. And the truth about the test the viceroy made of many soldiers and captains, offering them some gratification in return for their services, is that many of the claimants we have mentioned were offered a gratification of some kind, but on a very niggardly scale in comparison with their services, and it was on condition that they married forthwith, since there were plenty of Spanish women in Peru. His Majesty gave these orders so as to restore peace throughout the kingdom and oblige the inhabitants to live in peace and quiet. In many cases the claimants were told which woman they were to marry. As the viceroy did not know them, he thought they were all honest and virtuous ladies, which many of them were not, and those who were supposed to marry them were scandalized and refused to have anything to do with them, since they knew all about them. This was sufficient to cause the rivals and enemies of the claimants, who were jealous of their merits and services, to go rushing to the viceroy with a great deal of gossip and tittle-tattle to the discredit of the claimants. This is why our author says the viceroy

heard that they were greatly annoyed and was told that they had even uttered some ugly words, [and] he had a great many of them arrested and taken under strong guard to the port of Callao for shipment to Spain, giving out that some were being sent for His Majesty to reward them for their services, which could not be done in Peru, and that others were being sent into exile as a punishment,

etc.

Those arrested and shipped to Spain were thirty-seven in number and included the staunchest and best-known servants of the crown. In proof of this we may say that one of them was Gonzalo Silvestre, whose labors and services are described at length in our history of Florida and in the present work. In the battle of Chuquinca, as we have mentioned, a horse of his was killed for which Martín de Robles had offered twelve thousand ducats a few days before. Many of them were of equal quality and length of service in Peru, which would have been glad to see their like again. And though Fernández says that some were exiled as a punishment, none in fact was exiled for any crime, for all of them were men of great deserts. He also says that

when some people tried to advise him and persuade him to despatch at the same time an indictment of the crimes they had committed either in word or deed (if any of them were guilty), he refused to do so and said that he did not mean to act as prosecutor, but as mediator to see that His Majesty received them well, and honored and favored them,

etc.

The truth is that there was no lack of people who went to the viceroy and spoke thus, and even added much more, about the disturbances and rebellions the soldiers would stir up because of the niggardly rewards offered them for their long and numerous services. But there were others who begged him not to permit such an injustice, instead of a proper recompense, for banishment from Peru to Spain was a punishment worse than death if they deserved it, since they were sent off as poor men after having done so much for the crown and wasted their substance on its behalf. The viceroy was also told that he would not help himself or his office by sending them off to Spain in that way since His Majesty would hear them and believe what they said, as there was nothing the viceroy could accuse them of having done against the service of His Majesty, to which they had indeed devoted their lives and fortunes. Many of them bore wounds they had received in battle, fighting for their king, and they could show them in proof of their loyalty and their labors.

But the viceroy, incensed and scandalized by the rumors of risings and disorders, replied angrily that he did not care a fig about how they went: it behoved the king's service and the peace of the empire that they should go, and it did not worry him what they said or did against him when they got back from Spain. Slanderers add that he finished up by saying: "It will take them a year to get to Spain, a year to do their business, and a year to get back. And even if they bring back letters in their favor, I can settle them by kissing the letters and placing them on my head, and saying that I obey the instructions but that they cannot be executed. And by the time they have gone back for letters of confirmation and reached here with them, three more years will have gone by: that makes six in all, and heaven knows where we shall be by then!"

So he dismissed his faithful advisers and packed the claimants off to Spain, so poor and ragged that the richest of them had not a thousand ducats to spend, even after selling his horse and clothes and the little movable property he had. Some had land and Peruvian sheep from which they drew revenues, but these were a long way off and they had to leave them unattended and lose everything. Even if they were able to give a friend charge of them, the distance between Spain and Peru usually led to their eventually losing their possessions: of this I can speak from personal knowledge, for I left a property behind in Peru in the charge of a friend, only for someone to take it away from him and get the benefit of it. Such was the fate of these poor gentlemen who left their estates. When I came to Spain, some of them asked me about the people in whose charge they had left them, wishing to know if they were still alive and what they could have done with their property. I could give them very little information, for I was too young to take much interest in other people's property.

The claimants of royal rewards for their services thus left Peru, and we leave them on their journey for the moment, to recount other events that occurred in Peru with its new viceroy at that time.

CHAPTER VIII

The viceroy tries to bring the Inca prince, the heir to the empire, out from the forests, and reduce him to His Majesty's service; the negotiations for this purpose.

THE VICEROY despatched these gentlemen to Spain as we have said, following the advice of envious and malicious advisers who urged him and intimidated him into doing it on the grounds that the claimants were responsible for the unrest in Peru, and that the remaining soldiers of less account followed their lead: once they were out of the country, the tumults and risings of the past would cease. The viceroy permitted them to go because he feared the outbreak of further unrest following the pattern of the many bloody rebellions of the past and wished to guard against this.

He took moreover other measures designed likewise to pacify the empire. He wrote to the corregidor of Cuzco, Licentiate Muñoz, and to Doña Beatriz Coya asking them to consider how to induce Prince Sairi Túpac, who was living in the wilds, to come to terms and live in peace and friendship among the Spaniards. If he came, he would receive a generous grant of land for the sustenance of his family and household. Negotiations were conducted through the *coya*.

The prince, the legitimate heir to the empire, was the son of Manco Inca, whom the Spaniards had killed after he had saved them from the hands of the enemies, as we have told in ch. iv of Book Four of this Second Part; and the *coya* was his father's sister. She was very anxious to see her nephew return to his city, even though he did not recover his empire, and received the viceroy's instructions with great good-will and compliance. She sent a messenger accompanied by Indian servants to the fastnesses of Villcapampa, where the Inca was, and so that the embassy might have greater authority and be assured of a good reception the envoy chosen was related to the royal blood.

The journey was a difficult one, for the roads and bridges were broken, but at last the party reached the first guards and informed them of the message they had brought for the Inca. Then there was a meeting of the captains and governors, who acted as tutors and regents for the prince, since he was not yet of an age to assume the scarlet fringe, the sign of royalty. When the captains had heard the messenger, they were afraid that he might be false, although he was a kinsman, and picked another envoy to represent the Inca and his regents in Cuzco, where he was to seek confirmation of the message. Remembering the death of Atahuallpa and other deeds of the past, they were afraid of some trickery on the part of the Spaniards. They therefore ordered Doña Beatriz's messenger and his companions to remain with them as hostages until their envoy returned.

He was charged first to verify from Doña Beatriz that there was no treachery in the offer, then to speak to the corregidor of Cuzco and anyone else in case of need, to make quite sure that the embassy was not false. He was next to ask the corregidor and Doña Beatriz to send Juan Serra de Leguíçamo, her son by Mancio Serra de Leguíçamo, one of the first conquerors, to allay the fears and suspicions they entertained. Unless the envoy returned with him, they would regard the whole business as a sham and a trick. The corregidor and the princess were delighted to receive the Inca's messenger, and sent Juan Serra back with him to give his assurance, as one of the Inca's closest relatives, that there was no deceit in what was proposed and that all his people would be delighted to see him come down from the mountains.

While all this was going on in Cuzco, the viceroy, who wanted to see the business completed and had grown impatient of negotiating through the good offices of third parties, sent a friar of the order of St. Dominic, whom Fernández calls Fray Melchior de los Reyes, together with a citizen of Cuzco named Juan de Betanzos, the husband of Doña Angelina, the daughter of the Inca Atahuallpa, whom we have already mentioned. Juan de Betanzos was supposed to be a great linguist in the general tongue of Peru; and because of this and of the relationship of his wife with Prince Sairi Túpac, the viceroy ordered him to go with the friar and act as interpreter and translator of the letters and other documents they would have to take. In obedience to the viceroy's instructions, the two ambassadors hastened on their way and tried to reach the Inca's fastness from the city of Huamanga, since the way into the mountains is shorter on that side than on any other: for this reason the Spaniards called that city San Juan de la Frontera, it being the frontier with the Inca's country and the first Spaniards having entered it at the conquest on St. John's day. But their efforts to gain an entry were all in vain, for the Inca's captains and governors, fearing that the Spaniards might try a surprise attack to seize their prince, had cut the roads in such a way that it was quite impossible to reach them. Discovering this, the friar and Juan de Betanzos went another twenty leagues down the royal road to see if they could get through at Antahuailla, but they found no way there either. The corregidor of Cuzco learnt all this from the Indians, and wrote to the ambassadors to stop wasting their labors, but come to Cuzco, where it would be decided what was to be done. In our next chapter, we shall copy Fernández's account of this, word for word, so as to show the mistrust of the Indians and their caution and cunning in making sure that there was no deceit or double-dealing in the embassy, as well as other things that are worthy of note among the Indians.

CHAPTER IX

*The suspicion and fears of the prince's governors
about the Christian embassy; their cunning and
devices to assure themselves.*

OUR AUTHOR says in his Book III, ch. iv, as follows:
On their arriving at Cuzco, Licentiate Muñoz and Doña Beatriz tried to
arrange that their mission should go on ahead with her son Juan Sierra Inca
while the friar and Juan de Betanzos remained safely behind. This was agreed,
and the friar and Betanzos left Cuzco three days before the others, but promised
to wait for them on the road. However, they wished to have the honor of being
the first ambassadors and hastened on to the bridge called Chuquichaca, where
the Inca's jurisdiction begins. They passed this bridge with a good deal of
labor, only to be arrested by the Indian warriors who were on guard there. No
harm was done them, but they were not allowed to proceed or to go back.
They were kept there till next day, when Juan Sierra was to be admitted in
safety, but no one else. Betanzos and the friar were therefore stopped, and
Juan Sierra and the ambassadors went on. But they had not gone far before
they were stopped until the Inca gave orders for them to pass. As soon as the
Inca knew that Juan Sierra was on the way and that the friar and Juan de
Betanzos had come as ambassadors from the viceroy, he sent a captain with
two hundred Indian warriors, Caribs—who are Indians who eat one another
in time of war—with instructions to find out the object of the embassy. The
Indian leader duly greeted them, but refused to hear their message till the next
day. When Juan Sierra came, the Indian captain rebuked him for bringing the
Christians with him, and Juan Sierra apologised, saying that it was on the
advice and instructions of the corregidor of Cuzco and the Inca's aunt Doña
Beatriz. He then described his mission to the Inca and read and explained the
letters from his mother and the corregidor and the letter from the viceroy to
Doña Beatriz.
Once Juan Sierra had described his mission, they called Betanzos and the
friar, and asked them for the same account as Juan Sierra had given, to see if
the two stories differed at all. They displayed the letter of pardon, and explained their mission, showing the present the viceroy had sent to the Inca,
consisting of pieces of velvet and damask and two cups of silver gilt and other
objects. This done, the leaders ordered two Indians who had been present

throughout to go and report to the Inca. The latter entered and sent back the reply that they were to go away at once, letters, documents, present, and all, and they would be done no harm, for he wanted nothing but that the viceroy should do as he saw fit, while he, the Inca, did as he saw fit, as he had hitherto. When Juan Sierra and the rest were about to leave, two more Indians arrived with instructions for them all to come forward and give the Inca and his captains their messages. They advanced to within four leagues of the Inca, when an order came for Juan Sierra to go on alone with the messages while the rest got everything ready to depart.

Next day Juan Sierra left for the Inca's headquarters, and when he had gone two leagues, he was ordered to stop and wait two days. Messengers were also sent for Betanzos and the friar to come back. After the two days had passed, the Inca sent for Juan Sierra, and when he appeared, received him with great affection like a close relative. Juan Sierra explained as best he could the purpose of his embassy and the purport of his messages. The Inca displayed great pleasure, but said that he alone could not decide, since he had not been sworn as lord of his people and had not received the fringe (which is like the king's crown), as he was not of age. It would be necessary to explain the messages to his captains, after which Fray Melchor de los Reyes would be ordered to come and explain the viceroy's embassy. This was courteously heard, and the present accepted. The captains answered that the friar and Juan Sierra must wait for a reply until they had held their council. After this had been held, they answered that the business had to be carefully studied and they would have to consult their huacas before deciding. Meanwhile, Juan Sierra and the friar should go to Lima with two Indian captains and kiss the viceroy's hand on behalf of the Inca. There they could discuss the question of the Inca's property, since the whole country naturally belonged to him by right of inheritance.

They duly left, and passed through Andaguilas on their way to the city of Lima, entering the capital in June on St. Peter's day. The Indian captains gave their embassy to the viceroy and were well received and entertained. The two captains spent eight days in Lima, during which time they frequently saw the viceroy to decide the grants of land and other concessions the Inca was to be given in return for coming down in peace and obeying the king. The viceroy took council with the archbishop and the royal judges, and it was agreed to offer him for his expenses and maintenance as a lord an income of seventeen thousand castilians for himself and his children, with the grant of the Indians of Francisco Hernández's allocation and the valley of the Y'úcay (the Indians that had belonged to Don Francisco de Pizarro, the marquis' son), and some lands above the fort of Cuzco where he and his Indians could dwell. The agreement, once decided on, was formally drawn up and entrusted to Juan Sierra, who was to go off alone with the two captains and present it to the Inca. In the agreement it was stated that the Inca should receive what was offered provided he came down from his dwelling place within six months, counting from the day the agreement was drawn up, July 5. When Juan Sierra returned, the Inca had already received the fringe, and showed great satisfaction with the viceroy's letters,

etc. Thus Fernández. I am very glad to have quoted this in his own words, for if I had said it myself, it might have appeared that I was exaggerating and overpraising Indian caution and shrewdness. I must now clarify some points in our author's account. The first is the reference to Caribs, who he says ate one another in time of war. This occurred in heathen times in Mexico, but never in Peru, for as I stated in the First Part, the Incas severely forbade the eating of human flesh. What our author says therefore refers to the usage of Mexico, but not of Peru.

The income awarded to the Inca fell short of seventeen thousand pesos, for Francisco Hernández's allocation, as we have seen, brought in ten thousand. When he refers to another allocation in the Y'úcay valley, formerly the property of Don Francisco Pizarro, the son of the marquis, this was almost nothing because, as the valley was a very pleasant one, it was all divided among the Spanish citizens of Cuzco for vineyards and farms, as it is today. So the Inca was given only the title of Lord of Y'úcay, and this because the valley was the most esteemed garden in the whole empire of the Incas, as we have said. The prince took the title as a great courtesy, but what Fernández writes is taken out of its proper time and place, for the grant of the Indians to the Inca was presented to him in person when he went to the city of Lima to visit the viceroy and promise obedience, as was demanded of him. The document that Juan Serra took to him was not a deed of grant, but a letter of pardon offered to him (without specifying for what crimes) and great promises of what was to be given him for his expenses and the maintenance of his house and family, but without defining which allocation or saying how much income he was to have. In the next chapter, we shall say how all this came about: what we have rather anticipated was merely to show another authority for the caution, cunning, suspicion, and mistrust exhibited by the captains in receiving the embassy and handing their prince over into Spanish hands.

CHAPTER X

*The prince's governors consult their omens and
prophecies about his departure; opinions
differ; the Inca decides to go; he arrives
at Lima and is received by the
viceroy; the Inca's reply to the
grant for his sustenance.*

T HE CAPTAINS and tutors of the Inca discussed among themselves the
departure of the Inca and his delivery to the Spaniards. They consulted their omens by sacrificing animals, by watching the birds of the air
by day and night, and by contemplating the sky. They looked to see if the
sun was serene and bright or sad and darkened with cloud and mist,
which gave them a good or evil omen. They did not consult the Devil, for,
as we have seen, he lost the power of speech in all the empire as soon as
the sacraments of our Holy Mother Church of Rome entered in. Although
the men were favorable, the captains had opposing views. Some said that
it was right that the prince should come out and see the empire and enjoy
it, and that all his subjects should see him in person, which they greatly
desired to do so. Others said that it was no use expecting any change: the
Inca had already been deprived of his empire, and the Spaniards had divided its peoples and provinces among themselves; it would not be returned to him, and his vassals would weep to see him disinherited and
poor. And though the viceroy had promised to give him the wherewithal
to sustain his house and family, they should remember that these were
mere words, for he had not said which provinces or which part of the empire he would give. If the gift was not in accordance with the Inca's rank,
it would be better for him to die in exile in the mountains than to go down
and face humiliation. What was most to be feared was that the Spaniards
should treat their prince as they had his father, who had freed them from
their enemies and saved them from the threat of death, only to be himself
killed by them without any cause or purpose, while he was playing ball
with them to relieve them of the perpetual melancholy and gloom those

Spaniards always carried with them. Let them also remember what had happened to Atahuallpa, who was lashed to a pole and strangled; it was to be feared and always would be, that such people would do the same to their prince.

These and similar deeds perpetrated by the Spaniards against Indian caciques and leaders were well known to them (and we ourselves have ceased to describe them since we cannot include them all). Having recalled them, the Inca's captains went to report to him the two opinions that existed about his departure. The prince listened and, recalling the death of his father and of his uncle Atahuallpa, he adopted the second view: that he should not leave his fastnesses or deliver himself to the Spaniards. It was then that the prince said what Fernández has put earlier; after listening carefully "he sent back the reply that they were to go away at once, letters, documents, present, and all, and they would be done no harm, for he wanted nothing but that the viceroy should do as he saw fit, while he, the Inca, did as he saw fit, as he had hitherto," etc.

But as our Lord God in His infinite mercy had determined that the prince and his wife, children, and family, should enter the bosom of his Roman Catholic Church, Our Mother and Lady, his negative attitude, deriving from ill will based on fear of death and perdition, soon changed completely and he took the opposite view. His anger and ill feeling were appeased; his fear turned to hope and confidence in the Spaniards, and he went out and gave himself up to them, as Fernández himself says continuing the narrative which we have interrupted: "as Juan Sierra and the rest were about to depart, two other Indians arrived with orders that they were all to go on and give the Inca and his captains the messages they had brought," etc.

Thus everything our author mentions occurred, though he puts some incidents too soon and others later. I have set it down as it was often told my mother by her Indian relatives who came down with the Inca and often visited her. So as not to prolong the tale unduly, we shall explain that when the prince's anger had abated, he said: "I wish to go and visit the viceroy to see if I can assist and protect those of my royal blood."

But the captains still pleaded with him and begged him to consider his life and safety, and not expose himself to such a risk. The Inca repeated that he was determined to do as he had said, for Pachacámac and his father the Sun bade him do so. The captains then referred to their omens, as we have said, and not finding them contrary, though they themselves might have wished it, they obeyed their prince and went out with him to the city of Lima.

On the way the caciques and Indians of the provinces through which they passed came out to receive him and celebrate as best they could, but their celebrations were fitter for weeping than for joy, so great was the misery of their present compared with the greatness of their past. The prince travelled in a litter, but not a golden one as his ancestors had. He was borne by his Indians, and three hundred went with him to serve him. The captains were unwilling that Indians who were already assigned to Spanish masters should carry the litter, for they were no longer his. And on the advice of the captains, the prince removed his scarlet fringe, which served as a royal crown, as soon as he left his own territory: they said that as he was dispossessed of his empire, the Spaniards would be offended if he still wore the insignia of possession. Thus the prince travelled till he came to the city of Lima.

He then went to visit the viceroy who, as Fernández says,

was waiting for him in his residence. The viceroy received him affectionately, rising to meet him and making him sit on a level with him. From the words of welcome they exchanged and their conversation until they took leave, the viceroy and the judges thought the Inca a wise and discreet young man, a worthy descendant of the prudent and valorous Incas of the past,

etc. Thus Fernández, word for word.

Two days later the archbishop of the city invited the Inca to dine at his house, and it was arranged by the authorities that the archbishop, Don Jerónimo de Loaisa, would hand him with his own hand at table the documents granting him the estate he was to have, which was thus more fittingly and worthily bestowed. Malicious tongues said that the presentation was merely a device to get the Inca to reward the good news of the allocation of Indians he was receiving with a payment of gold and silver and emeralds. The Inca however rewarded it with a mathematical proof which he made in the presence of the archbishop and the other guests at table. After the tablecloths had been removed, the butler brought in a great silver-gilt bowl containing the viceroy's document presenting him with the properties he was to have for the maintenance of himself and his family. Having heard the contents of the document and understood them, he took the table mat of velvet decorated with silver trimmings which was in front of him, and pulling out a thread of silver, raised it and said to the archbishop: "This cloth and the whole service was mine; now you give me this little thread to sustain myself and my whole house." So the banquet ended, and the archbishop and those with him were astonished at the aptness of the simile.

CHAPTER XI

Prince Sairi Túpac returns to Cuzco where his
people receive him with rejoicing; he and the
princess are baptized; the name he takes
and the visits he pays in the city.

Aᶠᵗᵉʳ the prince had spent a few days in the city of Lima, he asked the
viceroy's permission to go to Cuzco. This was granted with many
offers for the future. The Inca withdrew, and on his way the Indians
greeted him with many celebrations, as they had done before. As he entered the city of Huamanga, the citizens came out to receive him, celebrated his arrival, congratulated him on having left his mountain fastnesses, and accompanied him to the quarters where he was to lodge.

The next day he was visited by a citizen of the place called Miguel Astete, who brought him the scarlet fringe the Inca kings wore instead of a
crown, and presented it to him, saying that it had been taken from Atahuallpa at Cajamarca when the Spaniards arrested him, and was now restored to him as the heir to the empire. The prince received it with
feigned signs of joy and gratitude, and it was reported that he had rewarded the donor with gold and silver jewels. But this is hardly to be
credited, for the fringe was odious rather than acceptable to him, and he
and his followers later abominated it, as having belonged to Atahuallpa.
The prince was told by his kinsmen how Atahuallpa had betrayed and
fought the true king Huáscar Inca, and his rebellion had brought about
the loss of the empire. He must have burnt the fringe because that traitor-
ous *auca* had worn it, who did so much harm to all his line. This and
much more our relatives told my mother when they visited her at Cuzco.

The prince left Huamanga, travelled by stages to his imperial city, and
lodged in the house of his aunt, Princess Beatriz, which was behind that
of my father. All the members of the royal family, men and women alike,
came to kiss his hands and welcome him to his capital city. I went in my
mother's name, and asked his permission for her to go and kiss his hand.
I found him with his kinsmen playing one of the games the Indians

played which I have described in the First Part of these *Commentaries*. I kissed his hands and gave him my message. He bade me sit down, and two cups of silver gilt were brought, full of their maize drink. They were so small that there would be barely four ounces of liquid in each. He took them both, and handed one to me. He drank the other, and I drank mine, for as I have said, it is a usual custom among them and is a great honor.

After this ceremony, he asked me: "Why didn't you come to Villcapampa to fetch me?"

I answered: "Inca, as I'm only a boy, the governors didn't take any notice of me."

He said: "Well, I would have been better pleased if you had come and not the fathers (meaning the friars, whom the Indians usually call fathers because they hear them addressed as Father so-and-so). Tell my aunt I kiss her hand, and she is not to come here, but I will go to her house and kiss her hand there and felicitate her on our meeting."

He kept me awhile asking about my life and occupation, and then gave me leave to go, telling me to come back often. On saying farewell, I made my gesture of adoration in the Indian fashion, which pleased him a great deal, and he embraced me with every sign of joy on his face.

In Cuzco all the caciques from there to Charcas were gathered together—an area 200 leagues long and more than 120 broad. They made celebrations in the city with much more solemnity and grandeur than on the road, and some were filled with joy and happiness at seeing their prince in the city, while others were full of sadness and mourning when they saw his poverty and need: there were all emotions in that theater.

During the celebrations, the prince asked to receive the sacrament of baptism. My lord Garcilaso was to be his godfather, and this had been agreed long before; but owing to illness, he had to renounce the duty, and it passed to one of the leading gentlemen and oldest *vecinos* of the city called Alonso de Hinojosa, a native of Trujillo.

The Inca's wife called Cusi Huárcay was baptized at the same time as her husband. Fernández describes her as a daughter of Huáscar Inca, instead of granddaughter. To be a daughter she would have had to be at least thirty-two since Atahuallpa captured Huáscar in 1528, and the Spaniards entered the empire in 1530 or as some say 1531, and the baptism of this princess and her husband the Inca was in 1558, almost at the end of the year. She would thus have had to be more than thirty, but when she was baptized she was only seventeen. It is therefore a mistake to say that she was a daughter instead of a granddaughter of the unhappy

Huáscar Inca.[1] She was a beautiful girl, and would have seemed more so if her swarthy complexion had not detracted from it: this is frequently found in Peruvian women, though they usually have very good features.

The Inca took the name of Don Diego Sairi Túpac. He chose the name Diego because he had heard from his father and his captains of the marvels that the glorious apostle St. James had wrought in that city on behalf of the Spaniards when his father the Inca surrounded them. He learnt from the Christians that the saint was called Diego, and wished to assume his name because of his great deeds. The citizens of Cuzco celebrated the day of his baptism with great rejoicings and festivities including bull fights and jousting with very costly liveries. I can bear witness to all this, because I was one of those who took part.

After the celebrations of both Indians and Spaniards and the visit of the caciques, the Inca remained a few days relaxing and resting with his friends. He visited the famous fort his ancestors had built, and was surprised that it should have been demolished by those who might have maintained it in repair to their own honor and glory, having won it from so vast an enemy force, as our history has told. He also visited the cathedral and the convents of Our Lady of Mercies, St. Francis, and St. Dominic, where he devoutly worshipped the Blessed Sacrament, calling it "Pachacámac! Pachacámac!" and the image of Our Lady, whom he called Mother of God. However there was no lack of malicious tongues that said that when he knelt before the Blessed Sacrament in the church of St. Dominic, he was really worshipping his father the Sun and his ancestors, whose bodies had been in that place. He also visited the houses of the chosen virgins dedicated to the Sun, and passed the place where the palaces of the kings, his ancestors, had stood. These had all been pulled down and replaced by other buildings erected by the Spaniards. He did not visit all these places in one day nor yet in a week, but spent many weeks in this way, as an exercise and entertainment to occupy his leisure. He passed several months thus, and then went to the valley of Y'úcay to enjoy the sight of the beautiful garden that his forefathers had owned, rather than because of the little piece of ground he had been given there. He remained there the short time that remained until he died, which would be less than three years. He left one daughter, who later married a Spaniard called Martín García de Loyola: we shall say what he did and how he died in due course.

[1] Earlier Garcilaso has quoted Fernández as stating that this princess, "Cusi Huarque," is a daughter of Huáscar. See Part One, Book Nine, ch. xxxvii.

CHAPTER XII

*The viceroy raises a permanent force of infantry
and cavalry for the security of the empire;
the natural deaths of four
of the conquerors.*

WHEN THE viceroy had ejected the claimants for allocations of Indians from Peru, executed the followers of Francisco Hernández
Girón, and reduced the heir to the empire to serve His Catholic Majesty,
all of which were remarkable achievements, he raised a garrison of men-
at-arms and infantry to promote the security of the empire and act as a
guard for the royal *audiencia* and his own person. The cavalrymen were
called lances and the infantry arquebusses. To each lance he gave a thousand pesos a year in pay, with which they were to keep their own horse
and equipment: sixty lances were chosen. There were two hundred arquebusiers with five hundred pesos in pay, in return for which they were
obliged to keep an arquebus and other infantry weapons. Both bodies
were picked by trustworthy men who could be relied on in all circumstances to do their duty by His Majesty, though there were malicious
tongues that denied this, and held that the viceroy might in honest justice
have sent many of them to the galleys for their part in the rebellions of
Francisco Hernández Girón and Don Sebastián de Castilla, and for the
murders they had committed in private quarrels among themselves. But
this was hushed up, and the viceroy's commands were duly carried out.

The viceroy himself breathed a good deal more easily now that the
kingdom was at peace and those who had been reported to him as troublemakers had left it. His fears of new disturbances and rebellions were
allayed, and he devoted himself to administration and public works. His
spare time he gave to honest pleasures and entertainments, with no little
assistance from an Indian lad of fourteen or fifteen who became his jester
and used to say the most amusing things: he was in fact presented to the
viceroy, who was very pleased to have him and delighted in listening to
the nonsense he uttered at all hours, partly in his Indian language and
partly in Spanish. One of his jokes that amused the viceroy very much was

that he used to say "Your Pestilency" instead of "Your Excellency," at which the viceroy laughed heartily, though slanderers who laughed with him used to add in private that the name suited him better than the other, recalling his pestilential cruelty in killing some and disinheriting their children and confiscating their Indians, and the plague he laid upon those he sent in exile to Spain, so poor and ragged that he would have done better to have had them killed: these deeds they said were unworthy of the name of "Excellency." Peruvians who wanted to see the country governed less strictly made these and other malicious comments on the actions of the viceroy.

Among other incidents, some grave, some gay, that occurred in Peru, Marshal Alonso de Alvarado died of a long illness he had after the war with Francisco Hernández. His defeat in the battle of Chuquinca plunged him in deep melancholy and he never after enjoyed a day of pleasure or contentment, but gradually dwindled away until he died; and his end was so strange that I had better describe it. When he seemed to be dying, he was moved from his bed to a bier on the ground, with a cross of ashes, as the military rule of the knights of Santiago prescribes. When he had been a little while on the bier, he seemed to revive and recover consciousness, so they moved him back to his bed. But after a little while, he lost consciousness again and seemed to be dying, so he was once more placed on the bier, where he again recovered and breathed again. They again put him in bed, and he grew worse, and was returned to the bier. This continued for nearly forty days, during which the sick man suffered and his attendants toiled without cease, until at length he died. Soon after his eldest son died, and the allocation of Indians he had received as a grant from the emperor lapsed. His Majesty granted it to his second son, out of regard for the many services his father had performed, a favor conceded very rarely in Peru.

On the death of Marshal Don Alonso de Alvarado he was succeeded by Juan Julio de Hojeda, a man of noble family, one of the first conquerors and a leading citizen of Cuzco. He married Doña Leonor de Tordoya, a niece of Garcilaso de la Vega, being the daughter of one of his cousins. Their son, Don Gómez de Tordoya, inherited his Indians.

Some months later my lord Garcilaso de la Vega died, after a long illness lasting two and a half years. During this time he suffered various recoveries and relapses, and seemed at one point to be completely recovered: indeed he mounted his horse and rode about the city like a man in perfect health. But after three or four months, when he was full of equanimity his illness returned, and prostrated him. He was as long again shut up in the house without stirring abroad; and his illness lasted this long time until he died. He was buried in the convent of St. Francis.

In those days funerals were very solemn affairs in Cuzco. Three stations were made in the street, and a high catafalque was erected at each of them, on which to rest the corpse while the responsory was sung. A higher catafalque was erected in the church, on which the corpse lay during the funeral mass. But my father thought this over-pretentious, and left instructions that nothing of the kind was to be done at his funeral, but that a bier was to be brought and rested on the ground with a black cloth over it; and he was to be laid thereon. The same was to be done in the church; and his wishes were fulfilled. This innovation recommended itself to the people of Cuzco, and thenceforward they gave up the laborious erection of catafalques.

When I returned to Spain, I obtained a bull from his Holiness to have his bones brought to Europe; and they were duly removed from the convent and delivered to me; I placed them in the church of San Isidro, one of the parishes of Seville, where they are buried to the glory and honor of Our Lord God; may He have pity on us all, amen.

A year later Lorenzo de Aldana passed away at Arequipa. He also died after a long and serious illness. He was unmarried, and had no natural children. In his testament he left his allocation of Indians to his heir to be used in the payment of future taxation. He was a noble gentleman, one of the second conquerors, who came to Peru with Don Pedro de Alvarado. Shortly after the war with Gonzalo Pizarro two young gentlemen who were related to him, though not closely, came to Peru, and he received them in his home and treated them like sons. After he had had them with him for more than three years, he thought it was time they set about amassing some wealth of their own, and sent his steward to tell them that in Peru it was the custom for men to work, however noble they were, provided there was no war or new discovery afoot; if they liked, he would offer them 10,000 pesos (which are 12,000 ducats) with which to set themselves up and busy themselves in some occupation, abandoning their idle life and accumulating some wealth for the future.

In sending them this message, he intended to do them a favor by offering them the sum of money. But they took both the errand and the sum of money amiss, saying that they were gentlemen and had no intention of becoming merchants, or buying or selling things, which they regarded as an infamy. And although the steward assured them that it was quite usual for Spaniards to engage in business, however noble they were, and that it was not a question of measuring cloth or silk by the yard in a shop, but of

Indian textiles or the coca herb, or supplies of maize and wheat for the silver mines in Potosí, which was extremely profitable, and they would not have to do any of this personally, but could leave it to their servants, the *yanacuna* Indians, who were absolutely trustworthy and reliable; they replied that they would not do it at any price because they were gentlemen, and that meant more to them than all the gold and silver in Peru. Moreover all other gentlemen ought to think the same, and anything else was undignified and opprobrious.

The steward returned to his master with this answer, saying that his relatives thought so highly of themselves that they had listened to his mission with a very bad grace. Whereupon Lorenzo de Aldana gravely remarked: "If they think so much of themselves, why are they so poor? And if they are so poor, why do they think so much of themselves?" So Lorenzo de Aldana ceased to try to do anything for them, and they were in very reduced circumstances, as I myself saw them, though they did not actually lack food and clothes, for if they came from Arequipa to Cuzco, they put up with my lord Garcilaso, who gave them whatever they needed, and if they visited other cities, they stayed in the houses of gentlemen from Extremadura—in those days it was enough to be a native of that province to be received anywhere and treated like a son of the house.

The four gentlemen we have mentioned were among those who conquered and won the land of Peru. All four died a natural death. I do not know if any other four conquerors can be found in the course of history to have died as they did, for most of their companions came to violent ends, as will have been noticed in the course of our story. The decease of these worthies caused general grief and regret throughout the empire, for they had helped to gain it and settle it, and each and all of them were men of great quality and virtue and goodness.

Even though there were no commandments of God that sons should honor their fathers, natural law teaches this lesson to all of us, even the most barbarous peoples on earth, and disposes us not to let slip an opportunity to augment their honor. I find myself for this reason compelled by divine, human, and natural law to serve my father's memory by saying something of his many virtues, honoring him after his death, since I did not do so as I should while he was still alive. And that the praise may be the greater and the more disinterested, I shall include here a funeral oration in the form of an eulogy of his life made by a worthy religious who knew him well, for the comfort of his sons, relatives, and friends, and as an example to true gentlemen. I do not mention his name, since he asked me not to publish it when he sent me the oration; and although I would have preferred to name him, for his name would have added to my father's honor, I promised not to do so. I shall not include the exordium or the oratorical digressions with which it was embellished, but cut them all out, so as not to lose the thread of my historical narrative, and to be brief in this pious digression.

Funeral Oration of a Religious on the Death of My Lord, Garcilaso

In Badajoz, a city well known in Spain for its antiquity and nobility, founded by the Romans in the time of Julius Caesar, on the Portuguese frontier, in the region of Extremadura, there was born, among other gentlemen who helped to win this New World, Garcilaso de la Vega, a son of most noble parents. These were descended in the direct male line from that gallant knight Garci Pérez de Vargas, of whose glorious deeds and legitimate successors, and of those of the valiant knight Gómez Suárez de Figueroa, first count of Feria, his great-grandfather, and of Iñigo López de Mendoza, from whom the dukes of the Infantado descend, the brother of his maternal great-grandmother, and of Alonso de Vargas, lord of Sierra Brava, his grandfather, and of Alonso de Hinestrosa de Vargas, lord of Valdesevilla, his father, and their ancestors, he might well boast did he but lack virtues and deeds of his own with which to exalt himself and his lineage, or had he been one of those noblemen who rely on the fame and honor that their ancestors won by their strength, valor, industry, virtue, and superhuman deeds, and themselves live a life that, in comparison with his, is bereft of all but the boast of nobility and knows only the shame of degeneration from forebears who, had they been like these, would have deserved to be buried in oblivion.

But let us leave the illustrious deeds of his progenitors that only served him as a burning stimulus and incited him not to degenerate from what he was. Let us speak of his own deeds, in which his children should take such pride and honor; for they are such that if nobility had been lacking in his forebears, he could have supplied it plentifully to ennoble his house, however obscure. It is not my intention to rehearse in detail all those natural gifts with which God endowed him from childhood: the charm of his manner, his handsome countenance, his brave and graceful figure, the quickness of his understanding, the ease with which he learnt from his tutors and masters. Nor the beautiful flowers that sprouted on the tender branch of so generous a tree: his valor, prudence, equity, and moderation, with the true odor of which qualities he refreshed, sustained, and charmed his fellows and astonished his elders, as they can testify in this New World who knew him as youths in the Old, when, though his face was barely covered with down, his mind was covered already with the white hairs of mature judgment. I shall only say briefly something of what he revealed after his arrival in Peru with the *adelantado* Don Pedro de Alvarado and many other gentlemen from his mother country in 1531, until 1559, when he died.

Garcilaso de la Vega was a youth of twenty-five, a fine horseman in both styles of riding, skilled in the exercise of arms, and dextrous in their manipulation, for he had inured himself in time of peace, before he ever saw an enemy, to those things he would have to perform in time of war. He voluntarily offered himself to take part in the new conquests in Peru, and was appointed a captain of infantry while still in Spain, being the first with this title to come to these parts and justifying the choice by the excellent parts he himself displayed in such responsibilities. He displayed them so well that, unless I am blinded by passion or dazzled by the splendor of his deeds, it would be difficult to tell who was honored by whom, he by his ancestors or his ancestors by him. For all the illustrious qualities that gave each of them undying fame were found united in perfect proportion in the person of Garcilaso de la Vega. For what can be said in their praise that I cannot more justly say in praise of this invincible knight? In Garci Pérez de la Vega [Vargas] Spain praised his fortitude in suffering incomparable labors for his land and his king, his greatness of soul in the face of perilous passes, his skill in meeting them, and ability in overcoming them, his knowledge and application of military science, whereby he earned from the royal St. Ferdinand the honor of impaling and ornamenting his arms with those of Castile, an honor conferred on him at the capture of Seville, which noble city placed the famous eulogy over one of its gates, carved in solid marble, neither worn by time nor dismissed by envy: "Hercules built me, Julius Caesar walled and girded me about, and the Royal Saint won me with Garci Pérez de Vargas." Such an honor is assuredly due to the valor of his person.

But the honor that Peru renders Garcilaso de la Vega is much greater, for what tongue can recite the labors he underwent, the perils he faced, the hunger, thirst, fatigue, cold, and nakedness he suffered, the lands not seen before he visited them, and the immense difficulties he overcame? Witness his navigation from Nicaragua to Puerto Viejo under the torrid zone, burning with heat and tormented with thirst after having crossed the vast ocean sea from Seville. Witness the uncertain plains and crested peaks of Quito. Travelling through uninhabitable deserts, he and his companions would have perished for lack of water if He who makes it spring bubbling from the living rock had not reserved it for him in the *ipas* or canebrakes, to refresh him and his band. And when their supplies were exhausted, they lived on the herbs of the field, after eating their horses, which were then worth 4,000 or 5,000 ducats apiece. They climbed the snowy heights, where sixty of their companions were frozen to death. They clove their way through woods and forests so dense that they had to open a way for the foot to tread. They journeyed in sight of horrible volcanoes that covered them with ash, deafened them with their thunder, stopped their passage with fire and scorching stones, and blinded them with smoke. But nothing prevented him from forging ahead with his gallant band, aided by God who stirred and assisted him to greater things.

Witness his valor and fortitude in the conquest of the land that its inhabitants called Good Fortune, as well they might when Garcilaso de la Vega went to discover it as captain of 250 Spanish soldiers, the first in Peru, for when they knew that he had been appointed captain of that discovery all wished to accompany him, preferring toil to rest, war to peace, the doubtful future to the certain present, the untamed tribes of the hills to the docile tax-paying Indians they knew, and unknown lands to their own familiar country-side—such was the high opinion and good esteem they had of this gallant captain. But who shall say what he suffered in this expedition to increase the faith of Jesus Christ, to extend the royal patrimony and the confines of Spain, and to add glory to his person and his descendants? They might convey some idea of it if they spoke of dizzy peaks and marshy plains which swelled with pride under his foot, the ferocious beasts that found no safety anywhere from his gleaming arms, the dense woods, harder to penetrate than thick walls, cast down by the force of his strong arm, the raging torrents that murmured at the boldness of the strangers who waded through them and perhaps carried away the weakest or least fortunate with the furious rush of their waters, the man-eating alligators twenty-five or thirty feet long that hid in terror under the water and concealed their bodies from men who feared to lose their souls. But since they themselves cannot tell what I can feel only too well, I shall mention briefly what befell the captain and his noble company, for if it were to be told in full, it would fill a great book, and this I must leave to those who write his history.

This uninhabitable land is full of incredibly impenetrable mountains, for-ested with wild trees as big as great towers, for many have trunks five yards in diameter and sixteen in circumference, so that eight men cannot stretch their arms round him, interspersed with thickets so dense that men and beasts can-not set foot to earth, nor advance a single step without great difficulty, since they are hard enough to resist the stoutest steel, and in their cold damp recesses lurk fearful serpents, monstrous toads, fierce lizards, poisonous mosquitoes, and other repulsive creatures. The full rivers innundate the land with spates and floods caused by the incessant rainstorms and reduce the whole land to stinking and fuming marshes that even birds cannot cross in flight. Through such obstacles Garcilaso and his men journeyed for upwards of a year covering more than a hundred leagues, at first with a lively hope of the Good Fortune they sought, then with various effects from the ill fortune they encountered, and at last in dire necessity to return, for within a few days of their undertak-ing the expedition they lacked the supplies the Indian porters carried and were obliged to eat grass and roots, toads and snakes which the captain came to relish more than conies. In a few months they were stripped naked, for as they stretched themselves on the wet earth in their sodden clothes, drenched by the rains of heaven or rivers of earth, these rotted on their bodies, or fell apart from the continuous pulling of thorns, branches, rocks, brambles, spines, and trees; and they often laboriously scrambled to the top of a tree to see if they could sight a human habitation only to find a great serpent coiled at the top in the sun, wherefore they speedily descended, leaving in their haste not only part of their clothes, but their flesh too. As time went by their labors grew, their strength dwindled, the health of the strongest failed; but the good captain did not waver an inch or falter in his duties. Greater than the rest, but their equal in their labors, a brother in love, and a father in solicitude, he caressed some, assisted others, praised these, cheered those, and set an example of valor, patience, and charity to all, being the first in labor and the last in repose, and the solace of all in everything. His heart burst because he could not succor many of his men as they perished of hunger. He saw them emaciated, pale, fleshless, bloodless, their temples sunken, their eyes haggard, their cheeks sagging, their stomachs empty, their bones covered only with skin, like skeletons, incapable of moving a step or uttering a word. What would the good captain do on seeing such a sorry sight? What would he feel, what would he say? Death itself would have seemed a lesser thing to him than the sight of his companions suffering such agonies? He raised his heart to God (his hands he could scarcely lift from utter exhaustion); he begged God's mercy on himself and his men, and at once ordered all the horses he had to be killed, sparing only one or two of the best. With this meat he revived them, and they pressed on, for he was less afraid of death than of returning without having accomplished any deed of note.

He no longer had any soldiers, but only the image or shadow of dead men, men as we have seen frozen with cold, covered with sores, their feet full of blisters, without strength or clothes or weapons; they seemed the scum of the earth, yet with them and his undaunted courage it seemed to him a simple matter to conquer new provinces. But when he saw how they were dying, Indians and Spaniards alike, and that his soldiers were reduced to a few dozen feeble and emaciated creatures who looked like living pictures of death, he resolved to return at the request of the king's officers. In order to find his way, he scaled one of the largest and most prominent trees, as was his custom at daybreak, when he went up to spy out the land while his men still lay resting on the ground. But as he scanned the horizon he beheld nought but range upon range of mountains like those he had come through and was at present among. He thereupon lifted his eyes to heaven, whence alone succor could come, and prayed to the Father of Mercies through Jesus Christ, his Son and Our Comforter. Neither was his prayer in vain, for he soon heard the loud squawking of parrots, and on looking beheld a great band of them, which after flying for a long time settled suddenly on the ground. The prudent captain thought that there must be a settlement there, or at least some maize, a plant greatly esteemed by these birds.

They therefore marched in that direction, and after covering eight leagues in thirty days, forcing a way with their bare hands through the tangled thickets of the dense forest, they finally came out into a clearing, and found there human beings. They were greatly impressed by the captain, who, though naked, thin and emaciated, and scratched and bruised, yet seemed a man of distinction by his form, appearance, authority, and noble mien. The chief asked him to stay there or to take him away with them. He gave the captain all he had, served him, and regaled him. And in the thirty days he spent there he so won the favor of all those savages that they succored him and his men, obeyed them as their masters and provided them as brothers with the best of everything they had. When the time for departure came, the chief and many other Indians went with the captain, to show him the way and to bear him company as far as the first valleys of Puerto Viejo, where they took leave of him with many tears. He duly reached the port with just over 160 men, having lost through starvation and suffering more than 80 Spaniards, not to mention the Indians, all of which his companions in toil did not fail to recount for many years, as a witness of his fortitude and an advertisment of his virtues.

I have related this in few words, and in even less will I tell what remains, though all that I say is nothing in comparison with his sufferings, accomplishments, and merits. When he knew that the Indians had surrounded the marquis Don Francisco Pizarro in Lima, his valor, daring, and magnanimity were such that he forgot himself, his own comfort, sustenance, and life, and left like a thunderbolt to succor the marquis. From Lima he went to Cuzco with Alonso de Alvarado, to pacify that region, to calm the rebellious Indians and succor the marquis' brothers. He fought several battles on the way with the Indians at Pachacámac, at the bridge of Rumichaca, and wherever there was a rough or steep place, for on the plains the enemy feared his horses and feared him even more, since he was easily known as he always marched with the foremost and attacked with them. Yet the reward that awaited him in Cuzco after so many battles and the wounds he received was a long spell in prison, into which he was thrown by Diego de Almagro for following in the steps of justice and reason with the marquis. Suffering in his dungeon, he displayed no less fortitude than in fighting in the field.

Once released from these trials, he exposed himself to new labors even greater than those on the expedition to Good Fortune, for he accompanied Gonzalo Pizarro in the discovery and conquest of Collao and Charcas, which are two hundred leagues to the south of Cuzco. The natives were warlike and so bold that seven naked Indians, each armed only with his bow and quiver, attacked Gonzalo Pizarro, Garcilaso, and two companions who were mounted and well armed, and fought with great fury and courage and gave such a good account of themselves that, although four of the Indians were killed, three of ours were sorely wounded and the horse of the fourth was slain. Such were the inhabitants of this province, and such the battles they fought with the Spaniards. At length our men were reduced to such straits, without hope of succor from the marquis, that they would all have died at the hands of the barbarians if they had not felt the favor of heaven and seen the glorious Santiago fighting for them armed and mounted and leading the little band of Christians, whereupon they took heart, and Garcilaso especially, inflicting great carnage on the enemy. For this reason he was granted the allocation of Indians he had first at Chuquisaca, called Tapac-Ri, which came to be worth more than 40,000 pesos of assay a year, or more than 48,000 ducats.

With this he left the arms he had wielded for seven years to the glory of God and increase of our Holy Faith, and from a valiant Pompey, became a Cato in the republic. He thought himself now free of war's alarms, secure from his enemies, far from the front of battle, distant from danger, and ready to pluck the fruits of his labors. Oh, deceptive hopes! Oh, unstable wheel of fickle Fortune! He had rested barely two years when by the unlucky and violent death of the marquis Don Francisco Pizarro and the rising of Don Diego de Almagro the Younger, he was forced to take up the arms he had scarcely dropped and re-open his newly healed wounds. Fife and drum sound; a head of war gathers in Cuzco; the faithful vassals of His Majesty assemble from all sides; generals, commanders, captains, and officers are appointed. Garcilaso is captain of cavalry and he enlists a gallant band, with his cousin Gómez de Tordoya, a knight of the habit of Santiago and commander of the imperial army. In Cuzco's name they do obeisance to the governor, Licentiate Vaca de Castro, for they are the two leading and wisest gentlemen of the city. They are confirmed in their offices, their deeds are approved, and they are sent in pursuit of Don Diego de Almagro. In this undertaking the captain showed himself a faithful servant of His Majesty and inclined the hearts of all to his side.

A great gentleman, he freely spent his own estate to maintain, furnish, and equip many noble men. A great soldier, he fought valiantly in the battle of Chupas, in which he was sorely wounded. But the governor awarded him a good allocation of Indians in His Majesty's name, and our Lord God vouchsafed him good health, the better to show how devoted a vassal of the emperor he was; for when Viceroy Blasco Núñez Vela arrived soon after and Gonzalo Pizarro took the field against him (with justice on his side, it appears), Garcilaso urged many citizens of Cuzco to go and serve the viceroy, and so they did, undergoing great labors and peril of their lives, and leaving their wives, children, houses, and estates unprotected. And when they reached Lima, they found the viceroy already under arrest and the royal *audiencia* gone over to Pizarro.

Great heavens, what a blow of fate for Garcilaso! His houses were sacked, and not a stick left standing. They made plans to burn them, they cannonaded them with battering pieces, they turned out the Indian servants, and bade them never cross the threshold again under pain of death. His wife and children stood in great peril of being slaughtered, and would have perished of hunger if the Incas and Pallas had not come secretly to their aid, and a chief, one of his vassals called Don García Pauqui, had not brought them fifty measures of maize, on which they sustained themselves during the eight months their persecution lasted.

Garcilaso's friends blamed him, and laid on him the responsibility for their utter ruin and perdition: they were in disgrace with Pizarro, absent from their homes, despoiled of their property, their Indians, their persons, their lives, their honor were in jeopardy; yet he was happy to have done his duty. For true fortitude is characterized by largeness of soul in attempting great deeds, full of such perils, and in glorying in them even though they result in the utter loss of material goods—though he did not cease to grieve and lament when he saw all his companions under arrest and some of them hanged.

Thus despoiled of his Indians, and hunted and sought by Carvajal who would fain have executed him, he was obliged to spend more than four months hidden in the hollow of a tomb in the convent of St. Dominic, until Gonzalo Pizarro pardoned him, though he deprived him of all his possessions and kept him by his side as a prominent prisoner for three years, never letting him out of his sight, at table, in his house, in the tent, or anywhere else, fearing to lose so great a soldier and so skilled a counsellor. These precautions were multiplied when Garcilaso advised him to surrender to President La Gasca, as he had promised him and Licentiate Cepeda to do on several occasions. But as Pizarro would not keep his word, Garcilaso sought an opportunity to escape, though none offered until the battle of Sacsahuana, when he was the first to go over to the imperial army, and he led the way and stimulated the rest to do likewise, abandoning Gonzalo Pizarro and forcing him to follow his example and surrender, thereby restoring all Peru to the king of Spain, who would undoubtedly have lost it had Gonzalo Pizarro won the victory. For this reason President La Gasca rewarded him with a good allocation of Indians, which he kept for his lifetime and which brought him an income of 30,000 ducats.

I omit many other occasions on which he displayed his fortitude. I say nothing of what he did in the revolt of Don Sebastián de Castilla; nor do I tell what happened in the rising of Francisco Hernández Girón, though on both occasions he served His Majesty as a captain of cavalry and did not lay down his arms until all the land was quiet and the traitors reduced and executed, for in all his brave deeds he was always true to himself and a worthy descendant and imitator of Garci Pérez de Vargas. For if that noble knight served his king in the conquest of a single province, this illustrious captain served his in the conquest of a whole world. If the former risked his life in his own country to drive the Moors out of Andalusia, the latter left the land of his birth, crossed the seas, burst through thickets, discovered new lands, tamed nations of barbarous savages and innumerable hosts, and reduced them to the service of God and his king, banishing demons and their worship from all these provinces. If the former embellished his arms with those of Castile, the latter painted his with his own blood and ennobled them with those of the Incas. If the former was related by marriage to the royal house of Spain, the latter did not deign to join in marriage with the imperial house of Cuzco. Finally if the former was aided by God to emerge victorious from the war with the Moors, the latter was aided by the same God and by his apostle St. James to win so many victories over the Indians, to implant the Gospel, to reduce the barbarians, and pacify the Spaniards, showing proofs at all times of strength, magnanimity, and diligence, never swerving to the right hand of temerity, stubbornness, cruelty, arrogance, wrath, and ambition, or to the left of timidity, compliance, weakness, or pusillanimity. Avarice never induced him to despoil the conquered or plunder the rebellious. Sensuality never led him by the forelock to her vicious and slothful delights. Ease and comfort never shortened the steps of his labors and undertakings, nor could toil force him to take rest unless it was shared by his companions.

For these reasons and because of the many services he had performed for the king, the judges made him corregidor of Cuzco after the revolt of Francisco Hernández Girón had been put down, for it seemed that no one could perform those duties better than Garcilaso in such troublous and calamitous times. The inhabitants had destroyed themselves in the war. Youth was maimed, the harvests destroyed, the cattle lost, cottages burnt, farmsteads laid waste, houses and temples sacked, the old deprived of their children, children of their parents, matrons were widowed, maidens distressed, the laws subverted, religion forgotten, all reduced to confusion, weeping and wailing and desolation: that single measure seemed to the royal judges to put an end to all these evils. They were not mistaken, for when Garcilaso took up the rod of office, it became a magic wand of virtue, justice, and religion. The new judge prayed God to give him light to see aright, and his Divine Majesty enlightened his natural and acquired prudence with supernatural and instinctive powers so that he became an exemplar of Christian governors. He was armed with the holy fear of God to whose searching scrutiny he must submit his actions. He read the laws of the empire, those of Peru, and the municipal by-laws. He chose as his deputy a learned, wise, experienced, and God-fearing man, and always consulted him and other great lawyers. He went into the government of his commonwealth as a learned doctor enters a general hospital where there are patients sick with all manner of diseases, and he applied to each the medicine that was necessary to clear his infected palate, his wounds, and his chronic pains. He bled some with light penalties, and proffered others the emulsion of his timely advice. He purged some by rounding on them and anointed others with peaceful words and kind treatment, visiting them in their houses and showing himself more like a father than a judge.

In this way he treated citizens and soldiers alike, and in order not to grieve him they suppressed many of their grievances. On one occasion a certain leading soldier avoided a duel to the death with a rival who had given him grounds and laid hands on him, and the reason he gave for not fighting was that he did not wish to grieve or offend so good a corregidor, who disliked having to punish such disorders and preferred to prevent misdeeds rather than punish them when they had been committed.

He would rather be loved than feared. He was slow to anger, and not hasty in affairs, considering anger the enemy of good counsel and haste the mother of error. In speech he was soft and reasonable; in his reproaches restrained and self-controlled, for he was never heard to use an ill-bred or insulting word. He removed the pitfalls of his subjects, their stumbling blocks, the occasions when they might offend against the laws, annoy their neighbors, or set a bad example to the city: to this end he sought like a good father gentle and convenient methods. One such was the establishment in Cuzco of the sacred order of St. Francis, whose holy sons he and the other citizens sheltered and assisted with their alms, so that in two days and two nights they were given more than 22,000 ducats with which they bought the site of their convent and the buildings on it. The corregidor gave them possession, and they, in return for his money, gave him the high altar for his burial, where his arms were placed in memory of this benefaction.

What he did for the Indians was no less. He built them the hospital they have today in the imperial city, and went out to beg alms for the purpose, and on the first evening he and Fray Antonio de San Miguel, the guardian of St. Francis, collected from his close friends alone (those who had Indians) 34,200 ducats, a thing which caused great astonishment and proved how beloved he was among his fellow citizens. Yet it is surprising, since he never failed in his duty, either for fear of the powerful, which he never experienced, or from coveting bribes, which he never touched, or from special preferences, for he loved all alike; or out of hatred, which he never felt. He was the same to all, but all things to all men, according to their needs; and thus won over high and low, rich and poor, wise and ignorant, and indeed good and evil; he would do what he wished with them and what he wished was the good of all.

Who pacified the city and established laws and just ordinances in it? Garcilaso. Who broke up the factions and parties of restless men who often tried to disturb the peace? Garcilaso. Who repressed the insolent mutinies of rash soldiers? Garcilaso. Who stilled the raging waves and sudden spates of unexpected enemies? Garcilaso. I could quote many instances, but one shall stand for all.

There was in Cuzco a young and leading soldier, one of those who unreasonably complained of President La Gasca, named Francisco de Añasco, a brave, spirited, bold, cunning, and astute fellow, always agog for adventure and ready to risk his life and those of his numerous friends in defence of his interests or to establish himself as lord of Peru, as Francisco Hernández Girón had sought to do. He had prepared arms, raised men, named captains, and promised them masses of gold, for silver secured little. The rumble of rebellion was already heard when the corregidor had news of it, and he secretly investigated the matter, but without intimating that he knew what was afoot, the better to catch the culprit. He summoned the latter, invited him into his house, took him in, offered him a room, set him at his table, and conversed with him. At the same time he ordered eight gentlemen who were his friends and kinsfolk and honored his dwelling as his constant guests never to let the suspect out of the sight of two among them, whenever he himself could not be with him. In this way the ingenious governor compelled the other leaders of the conspiracy to reveal themselves, while keeping himself constantly informed of the state of their affairs and missing not a whit of their innermost thoughts, no less than their deeds, by means of the secret information he received.

Those who did not know the prudent sagacity and sagacious prudence of our corregidor and feared some disturbance from the reports they heard complained of his inactivity, for they seemed to see the rebels rush forth, weapons in hand and full of fury, sacking houses, slaughtering their owners, dishonoring their wives and daughters, burning the city. They rushed to the corregidor and pleaded with him not to let them be slain before his eyes for lack of action on his part after they had survived the fury of so many civil wars, begging him to save the lives of the citizens, to look to the honors of their wives and consider God's service, to defend the royal estates and public and private property and defend the city that had been entrusted to his care.

He thanked them for their warnings with moderate words, and begged them to be calm, for soon they would see the hopes of the malcontents brought to naught, and quiet restored, as indeed they did; for within a few days he had brought honest soldiers to their senses and dispersed the most unruly throughout the kingdom. And as to the gentleman who was responsible for the unrest, he upbraided him for his ill-intentions after he had been maintained in the corregidor's house for forty days and treated like a son; and threatening him with exemplary punishment if he did not mend his ways, he presented him with a horse from his own stable and 300 pesos of his own money and sent him in exile to Quito, five hundred leagues from here, for which Añasco was truly grateful, since instead of being executed, his life was spared and he was honorably provided for.

As soon as the president and the judges heard this, they praised the deed and the great prudence of the corregidor, whose experience had forestalled the havoc that might have ensued had he publicly arrested the ringleader, investigated the guilty, and arraigned them, fulminating rigorous sentences and executing exemplary punishments that could only have served to stir up others and induce them to continue the evil work. But the evils that threatened to arise from these disorders were averted by his blandishments and secrecy. Thus he put an end to the fears of the inhabitants and established the peace that continued in the city during the whole time of his government. The city indeed respected its corregidor as a man sent from heaven, and rightly for he was a man of deep religious feeling and of notorious piety. His desire for the common good was extraordinary, his good intentions toward all were known to all, his acuteness in interpreting the laws was just, his solicitude in despatching the cases brought before him incredible, and his affability and attentiveness in satisfying litigants those of a father and friend. And if we were to speak of his liberality, mercifulness, rectitude, and compassion, we should never end. When was he asked for anything in reason and did not grant it? When did he see an honest man in distress but that he offered him his house and supplied his every need? What beggar asked him for alms and went away empty handed?

What widow or orphan, what oppressed person sought justice from him and did not obtain it? Who wished to avail himself of his favor and was not favored by him? All this is well known to, and publicly attested by, the gentlemen who dined and supped in his house, which was usually full of such guests, whom he had not only sustained, but also dressed and supplied with horses from his stables when they wished to ride abroad. The religious widow and the modest beggar will mourn him, for he succored them secretly with copious alms, in addition to what was distributed in quantity at his door. Orphans and minors regret his passing, for he readily became their guardian to shelter them and see that their property was not squandered or consumed in law suits or by fraud. Once it happened that after he had fed for five years the orphan children of Pedro del Barco, a *vecino* of Cuzco, who was hanged by Carvajal for having taken flight with Garcilaso, the court awarded him 5,500 ducats for the food he had supplied them, but he refused to receive it, but paid it himself, saying that they were the children of his friend and that he would never charge anything for the food that was eaten in his house.

The prisoners and plaintiffs at law will miss him, for he dealt with them with all possible mildness and leniency, and never charged a fee for his signature. In civil cases he settled and composed as judge, arbiter, and friend; if pecuniary fines were applied, he forwent his part. In criminal cases he mitigated sentences and restrained his deputy from applying the full rigor of justice, lest the people should become exasperated, for many discontented soldiers were restless and sought to create disturbances and pick quarrels on the least occasion. But mild as he was in civil and criminal cases, he displayed every rigor in punishing any disrespect for God or profanation of his holy temple. Let the following stand as an example: when a certain citizen of Cuzco, more noble than patient, had words with an attorney, and the citizen used strong language against the attorney and the attorney replied with interest, the former laid his hand on his sword, and the latter, having no sword, fled into the church and only stopped at the high altar, where the citizen followed to slay him. And he would at least have wounded him, if passers-by, attracted by the hubbub, had not restrained him within the very choir. One of these was an *alcalde ordinario,* who took cognisance of the case and sentenced the citizen for disrespect for the Blessed Sacrament to a fine of four arrobas of olive oil, then worth more than 100 ducats, and four arrobas of wax, and 200 escudos for the service of the high altar.

The citizen appealed from the sentence to the corregidor, who greatly regretted that the case had not been brought before him and that the alcalde had dealt with it so leniently, and he said: "If I had sentenced him, the fine would not have been less than 12,000 ducats. For how can we permit ourselves to preach to these heathen Indians that the Lord that is in the church is the true God, the maker and creator of the Universe and our Redeemer, if we show Him such disrespect as to enter His house with naked sword and enter His very dwelling place, the high altar, to kill a man? How will the Indians believe what we preach, when they see our deeds belie our words, for these barbarians had so much respect for the house of the Sun, whom they worshipped as God, that they took off their shoes two hundred steps from the door when they were about to enter it?" So he doubled the fine applied by the alcalde, and the citizen readily paid it, seeing that it was decided not by passion but by reason.

That is why we all weep for him and mourn his loss. But especially do his Indian vassals prove it with the copious tears and heartfelt groans that make manifest how much they miss their lord, who was their father, defender, and sustainer. For if any of the Indians of Cuzco assigned to personal service fell ill, he tended them in his own house like sons. In one of his provinces he was satisfied with a fifth part of the tribute, for although he should have been paid so many Peruvian sheep and pigs which sold in the marketplace for 15 pesos, he was satisfied with no more than 3 pesos a head. The Huamanpallpas, who are forty leagues from Cuzco, were obliged to deliver a great quantity of wheat to his house every year, which they carried on their backs, but to favor them, he arranged for them to bring the wheat to a farm he had sixteen leagues from the city, situated on the road leading to the Indians' own land, and for the cost of transporting it he absolved the Indians from paying half what they were obliged to give him. These same Indians and the Cotaneras were supposed to give him so much Indian cloth a year from the wool they provided, but he supplied them with the wool in such quantity that there was some left over for themselves. Every four months they were supposed to bring him a certain number of baskets full of the coca herb, and he lightened their labors and spared them the expense of carrying it and saved them their keep (without any obligation to do so) by giving each one of them half a measure of maize, and lending them beasts of burden to carry their food and fetch the coca, things which I have never heard of any other lord doing for his Indian vassals. Wherefore this gentleman's Indians strove to serve him with extraordinary love, and the cloth they made and the coca they grew was the best in the kingdom.

I have heard and read much of the love of lords for their subjects, but nothing comparable with this. I have learned much of their gratitude for services rendered to them, but nothing greater than what I am about to relate. Garcilaso esteemed so highly the services of his vassal Don García Pauqui, who gave his family fifty measures of maize when they were in the straits I have described, that he made this cacique and the places he ruled free of all tribute they should have paid him and was content that they should give him some fruit such as *guayavas*, limes, and green peppers for his table as a token of vassalage. Could they but love such a lord? Could they but serve him? Could they fail to miss him and mourn him after his death?

Let them mourn him, for they have good reason to do so, for strong men too weep for him, seeing a firm column of fortitude shaken by his death. Let wise statesmen mourn him, for in him they have lost a rich store of civil prudence; let governors and judges mourn him, for in him they have lost a living portrait of justice. Lastly let all honest men mourn him, for in him they have lost a rare example of temperance in food and drink, in sleeping and manners, being liberal to his friends and dutiful to strangers; a pattern of clemency with which he soothed the vengeful spirit and filled it with good will toward all; of modesty, with which he won love and esteem, rendering everyone honor in excess of their deserts; of urbanity and restraint in speaking ill of no one, for he would not even allow anyone else to do so in his presence, but at once cut short the conversation, for he was always ready to gloss over the bad if the good were duly praised; of moderation, which he displayed even in death, disposing in his will that when he was buried, his body should be placed on a cloth on the ground while the responsory was being said, though it was the custom in Cuzco when a leading inhabitant was buried to erect great catafalques at three points in the streets through which the funeral procession passed and to raise the coffin on them, while everyone stopped for the responsory. And Garcilaso's excellent example was thereafter followed and is still imitated today.

What shall I say of his truly Christian virtues? We have already seen how he exposed himself to many perils and risks for the faith of Jesus Christ and its propagation. That faith he sustained throughout his life, not only by appointing virtuous, learned, and zealous priests to teach and indoctrinate his Indians and doing all within his power to see that our Holy Faith extended to the very corners of the land, but also by his example, performing all the duties our Faith requires of us, firmly believing what it teaches us, and adding to it the holy works of religion and piety. He heard mass regularly, and had many masses said for the souls in Purgatory: on a single festival he celebrated every year he spent 600 ducats. Who can explain the greatness of his firm hope and the warm glow of his charity? The Lord who gave him them alone knows the full extent of them, though he gave great proofs of them throughout his life and especially for two and a half years before his death, during which time God shaped him for heaven by means of a long illness that lasted all this time, confined to his bed for the most part, though not all of it, so that he might better dispose and prepare himself at leisure, as indeed he did, often confessing to the superior of St. Francis, Fray Antonio de San Miguel, who received the confession of no one else in Cuzco and who used to say that he wished he were like the man lying stretched on that bed. Now that he could no longer lay hand to sword, or lift his lance, or do heroic deeds in time of war, he put his hand in his purse and benefited all, clutching the cross of Christ crucified and begging His pity and forgiveness. He performed heroic deeds of charity, patience, and Christian humility, in the midst of a great peace of soul produced by a good conscience and especially by the confidence he had in the merits of Christ Our Lord. So there was a notable increase in alms-giving, prayers, masses and devotions, suffering and patience in time of grief; in hope of forgiveness and of attaining glory; in warm and living desires that God's will should be fulfilled in him, and that he might give his life for God's love, as indeed he did after receiving all the sacraments, at the age of fifty-nine, to the universal grief of Cuzco and all Peru, a grief fully justified, for with the death of Garcilaso there fell a strong bulwark of the Christian faith.

There died the exemplar of military valor; the ornament of peace; the honor of the nobility; the model of judges, of the good; the terror of the wicked; and lastly the defender of the natives. But while all are rightly mourning his death, he is enjoying eternal life; while his friends cry in dismay: "Can it be that the hero and champion of Spain is defeated? that the light and splendor of the house of Vargas is dimmed? that the civility and courtliness of Peru is ended? and the firm column of this empire has fallen?" he, making light of all earthly things, counting his strength as weakness, his light and splendor as darkness, his wisdom and prudence as ignorance, his fortitude as fickleness, triumphs in glory in Heaven wearing that inestimable crown of glory that he now enjoys and shall enjoy for ever and ever. Amen.

CHAPTER XIII

*Concerns the claimants who came in exile to Spain
and the great rewards conferred on them by His
Majesty; Don García de Mendoza goes as
governor to Chile, and his adventure
with the Indians.*

T O RETURN to the claimants of allocations of Indians whom we left embarking for exile in Spain, we must state that they reached that country exhausted with poverty and hunger. They appeared at court in the presence of His Majesty King Philip II, and he was much affected by their appearance and by the tale they told him of the reason for their arrival, impoverished and in exile. His Majesty comforted them by granting them honors in the Indies, if they wished to return, awarding them pensions from his treasury and the royal exchequer so that they should not be dependent on the viceroy of Peru. Those who wished to stay in Spain he rewarded according to their merits and rank, giving some more and others less, as I discovered when I arrived in Spain a little after these events. These rewards were payable from the Casa de la Contratación, in Seville: the lowest were of 480 ducats a year, and they went up to 600 or

800, and 1,000 or 1,200 for the most deserving, the same to continue to be paid all the days of their lives.

A little later, when His Majesty heard of the gossip there had been in Lima about the exiles, he desired to avoid provoking a revolt through the excessive rigor of the governor, and appointed as viceroy of Peru a very distinguished gentleman, endowed with every virtue and goodness: Don Diego de Acevedo, from whom the counts of Fuentes are descended. But he died of an illness while preparing for the voyage, to the great regret of everyone in Peru, when the news reached that empire. I heard grave and worthy men long established in Peru saying: "God took him straight to Heaven because we did not deserve such a viceroy." As this gentleman never reached Peru, his name is not included in the list of viceroys who have gone thither.

While all this was happening in the capital of Spain, the viceroy of Peru had appointed his son Don García de Mendoza to be governor and captain of the kingdom of Chile, which had remained without a governor since the death of Jerónimo de Alderete. The latter had expired on the journey just as he was approaching Chile, from distress and grief at the loss of eight hundred persons who had died on his galleon through the fault of his sister-in-law and himself. His mind dwelt on the fact that if she had not been his sister-in-law the master would not have given her permission to have a light in her cabin, which was the origin of the disaster.

The appointment of Don García was highly acceptable in Peru. Many citizens and leading soldiers offered to accompany him thither, thinking to acquire merit in the eyes of His Majesty and of the viceroy by escorting the latter's son. The viceroy appointed Licentiate Santillán, a judge of the royal *audiencia*, to act as lieutenant and governor for his son, begging him to do him the favor of accepting the appointment. Great preparations were made for the expedition in all parts of the kingdom, including arms, horses, dress, and other ornaments, which cost a great deal of money owing to the high price of goods brought in from Spain. The viceroy also made provision for three other expeditions; and three leading gentlemen were made captains of them: Gómez Arias, Juan de Salinas, and Antón de Aznayo. Each of these made every effort to fulfil the task assigned to him.

Don García de Mendoza departed to take up his post and took with him many eminent people. When he had assumed his duties, he made preparations for an expedition to reduce the Araucanian Indians, who were very arrogant and intractable since the victories they had won against the Spaniards, first against Pedro de Valdivia and later against others, as the poets of the day have written in verse—though they might better have written in prose, since more credit would have been given to them if they had composed history instead of poetry.

The governor entered the rebellious provinces with many gallant followers and a great display of everything needed for war, especially of weapons, munitions, and all kinds of supplies, rendered necessary because the enemy had put all their men on a war footing. Within a few days of their entry into enemy country, the Indians boldly ambushed them. The Spaniards were faced by a force of five thousand Indian warriors with orders to delay fighting and not to come to grips, but to retreat day and night in perfect order and with every possible precaution so that the Spaniards should not catch up with them and force an action upon them.

On learning from their scouts that the Indian horde was moving in front of them and not tarrying to meet them, the Spaniards prepared cautiously to follow. They did not disperse since the governor had been informed by Spanish residents as soon as he arrived in Chile how the Indians practiced all sorts of tricks and stratagems against them, and attacked or retreated as they found expedient. But the warning was of no avail, for the governor insisted on pursuing the enemy in the hope of executing a great slaughter of them so that the survivors would realize how warlike he was, lose their arrogance, and give in. With this intention he followed the Indian force for a day and a night. The enemy saw from their ambush that the governor was some distance from his camp, where he had left all his possessions, so they sallied forth and sacked everything they could find without any opposition. They made off with their loot unimpeded and left nothing behind. The news of this reverse was brought to the governor, who was obliged to abandon his pursuit and return to attack those who had sacked his camp. But his efforts were in vain, for the enemy had gone into hiding so as to run no risk of losing the loot.

The news of this misfortune reached Peru almost simultaneously with the news of the arrival of the governor in Chile, and the whole country was astonished that the Indians should have scored so striking a success and the Spaniards have been so discomfited and left with nothing but the arms and clothes they stood up in, in so short a time. The viceroy ordered help to be got together urgently so that it might arrive without delay. A great deal of gold and silver from the royal treasury was spent, which caused some grumbling, as Fernández writes in his Book III, ch. ii, though he ascribes it to the cost of the original expedition when the governor went to Chile and does not mention this second expense, or the fact that it was occasioned by the Indians, a fact that also gave rise to complaints, since it was said that the excessive payments made by the royal treasury were repeated twice or more times for the viceroy to help his son.

The events of Chile fall outside the scope of our history and we shall not say more except about the death of Loyola: the preceding remarks were inserted because the governor left Peru on the orders of his father, the viceroy. Those who may undertake the history of Chile will find much to write of, for the wars between Indians and Spaniards there have lasted fifty-eight years since the first rebellion of the Araucanians in 1553 to the latter part of 1611, the date of writing these lines. They will have to tell of the unfortunate death of Governor Francisco de Villagra and two hundred Spaniards who were with him, which took place on a hill called Villagra after him. They will also have to tell of the death of the commander Don Juan Rodulfo and two hundred more who were with him: they were slain in the marsh of Purín. I would indeed like to have a full account of all these deeds and others as great or greater that have occurred in that warlike realm, so as to include them in my history, but where the clash of arms has been so constant there will be no lack of skilled and elegant pens among the sons of Chile themselves, so that literature may flourish throughout that famous kingdom in the future, as I hope and trust in the Divine Majesty.

CHAPTER XIV

The heirs of those slain for their share in
Francisco Hernández Girón's revolt receive
their Indians; the departure of Pedro de
Orsúa for the conquest of the
Amazon; his end and death and that
of many of his companions.

THE VICEROY Don Andrés Hurtado de Mendoza, on finding that the claimants he had exiled from Peru were returning with great rewards conferred on them by His Majesty and payable from the treasure under triple lock in the royal chest—far from their not being allowed to return to Peru, as he had imagined—was greatly surprised, the more so when he

heard that His Majesty had appointed a new viceroy in his room. He regretted what he had done, and replaced the rigor he had so far exhibited
with every sign of meekness and mildness that can be imagined. This continued until his death, and those who observed it used to say publicly that
if he had begun as he finished, there would not have been a better governor in the world.

This display of mildness, together with the pacification of the country
and the mutation of the fury and rigor of the justices into gentleness and
mercy, emboldened those who had lately suffered from the application of
penalties to seek satisfaction for the wrongs and injuries they had received.
Thus the children and heirs of the citizens who had been executed for taking part in Francisco Hernández Girón's rebellion put their cases before
the royal judges, showing the letters of pardon that had been granted to
their fathers and pressing their claims until after sundry reviews they obtain a favorable sentence, and the allocations of Indians and any other
properties that had been confiscated from them were ordered to be restored. In this way they recovered their Indians, despite the fact that the
viceroy had redivided them and awarded them to others, so that some received better allocations than the ones they had lost and others new ones
they had never had. This caused the viceroy a great deal of embarrassment,
for the decision of the judges rescinded everything he had done in this
matter, depriving some and enriching others, and he had the perplexing
and troublesome task of satisfying with new rewards those who were now
dispossessed of what he had previously awarded them. All this I myself
witnessed in Cuzco, and the same happened in other cities where rigorous
sentences had been applied in the past, such as Huamanga, Arequipa,
Charcas, and Pueblo Nuevo.

In view of the sentence of restitution in favor of the heirs of those executed and the rescision of all the measures taken on the instructions of the
viceroy, Spaniards took the opportunity to say that the severity of the
former penalties had not been due to the orders of His Majesty or the
Royal Council of the Indies, but had been applied by the viceroy on his
own responsibility, for the purpose of causing himself to be feared and
securing his person against any such revolt as had occurred in the past.

In this mood of mildness and leniency, the viceroy disposed of the
right to explore and conquer the Amazons of the River Marañón. As we
have said, when Francisco de Orellana forsook Gonzalo Pizarro, he made
his way to Spain and obtained this right from His Majesty, though he died
on his journey and never reached the place he intended to conquer. The
viceroy now granted the right to a gentleman called Pedro de Orsúa, whom

I knew in Peru, a man of great goodness and virtue, who was one of his personal adherents and a very popular figure everywhere. He went from Cuzco to Quito gathering all the soldiers who wanted to go in search of new conquests, for in Peru there were no longer opportunities now that the whole country was divided among the oldest and most deserving settlers in that empire. Pedro de Orsúa also collected all the arms and supplies he could for his conquest, and the citizens and inhabitants of the Spanish settlements rallied to him willingly and generously, for he deserved all support on account of his excellent character.

Many soldiers left Cuzco with him, among them one Don Fernando de Guzmán whom I knew, a fresh arrival from Spain, and another of greater seniority named Lope de Aguirre, a very little man, very ill-favored, and of no good repute, whose misdeeds are mentioned in the *Elegies of Illustrious Men of the Indies* of Licentiate Juan de Castellanos, a beneficed priest of the city of Tunja in the kingdom of New Granada. It is an authentic and elegant history, though written in verse, and six cantos of it are devoted to this subject. They tell of Pedro de Orsúa's expedition—which consisted of five hundred well-armed and fully equipped men with plenty of good horses—and describe the leader's death at the hands of his own most trusted followers, who coveted a beautiful girl Orsúa had taken with him. This sort of passion has been the ruin of many great leaders in the history of the world, such as the brave Hannibal and others. Those chiefly responsible for Orsúa's death were Don Fernando de Guzmán, Lope de Aguirre, and Salduendo, who passionately desired the girl, as well as many others named by the author. The latter tells how the traitors made Don Fernando their king, and he was so remarkably discreet as to permit this and delighted in being called king, though instead of a kingdom all he had was constant misfortune, which ended in his being killed too by the very ones who had given him the title. Aguirre then became their leader and slew at one time and another more than two hundred men. He sacked the isle of Margarita, was beaten by its inhabitants, and killed a daughter of his who accompanied him before he himself died, simply so that no one should call her the daughter of a traitor after his death. Such was the tale of his cruelties, which were indeed diabolical, and such the end of that expedition, which began with such a brave array, as I myself saw in part.

CHAPTER XV

The count of Nieva elected viceroy of Peru; a
message sent by him to his predecessor; the
death of the marquis of Cañete and of the
count of Nieva; the arrival of Don
García de Mendoza in Spain; the
election of Licentiate Castro
as governor of Peru.

WHILE these events occurred in Peru, and Orsúa and his men were suffering such loss of life on the great river of the Amazons, His Majesty King Philip II had not forgotten the need to despatch a new governor to the empire. As soon as the good Don Diego de Acevedo died, he appointed Don Diego de Zúñiga y Velasco, count of Nieva. The latter prepared for the journey with all despatch and left Spain in January 1560, arriving in Peru in April of the same year. From Paita, which was the limit of his jurisdiction, he sent a servant of his with a short and succinct letter to the viceroy Don Andrés Hurtado de Mendoza to warn him of his arrival and instruct him to give up the government of Peru and cease all activities connected with it.

The viceroy heard of the approach of the messenger and ordered everything necessary to be made ready on the roads in abundance. In the city of Lima a very worthy lodging was prepared together with a handsome present of gold and silver jewelry and other gifts to the value of six or seven thousand pesos or more. But the messenger lost the whole of this because he had instructions to address the viceroy as "lordship" instead of "excellency," and the same form of address was used in the letter.

The viceroy Don Andrés Hurtado de Mendoza took this very ill, supposing that his successor meant to vaunt his superiority in public and without reason or justice. This so filled him with melancholy that his health gave way, and he declined day by day; being well stricken in years, he could not resist the malady and died before the new viceroy reached the city of Lima. The latter had no better fortune, for a few months after he had assumed his seat, with the solemnities that we have described in dealing with his predecessors, he too died. The cause of his death was a strange one, that he himself brought about, and he acted in such a way as to speed his own end. The matter is however too distasteful to be repeated; and we shall therefore continue, leaving this mystery unelucidated.

Don García de Mendoza, who was governor of Chile, hastened to leave that kingdom and return to Peru on learning of his father's death, arranging to leave in due course for Spain. This he did in such a hurry that malicious tongues said that he had got out of Chile in this haste in order to get away from the Araucanians, who had reduced him to a state of terror, and not to settle his father's affairs on his death. They also said that he left Peru in a hurry so as not to linger under someone else's jurisdiction. He came to Spain, and remained here until he returned to Chile as governor, when he imposed the tribute of *alcabalas* which the Spaniards today pay on their trade and contracts and the Indians on their harvests.

This particular point has been anticipated in time and place: it is not my intention to go beyond the death of the heir to the empire of Peru, the younger brother of Don Diego Sairi Túpac, whose descent from his mountain fastnesses and baptism and death we have already described. To this end we shall cut our story short, for the end is now in sight.

His Majesty King Philip II, on learning of the unfortunate death of the viceroy Don Diego de Zúñiga, count of Nieva, appointed Licentiate Lope García de Castro, a member of the Royal and Supreme Council of the Indies, whom we have already had cause to mention in speaking of my claims for the services of my father and his opposition to me on that occasion. He was appointed president and governor general of the empire, with the task of repairing the harm and allaying the disquiet caused by the sudden death of the two viceroys. Licentiate Lope García de Castro was a man of great prudence, experience, and good council for the governing of so vast an empire. He therefore departed at once and governed those dominions with mildness and benevolence, and returned to Spain, leaving them in peace and quiet. He returned to occupy his post, in which he lived with great honor and increasing esteem, and died as a good Christian.

My friends, on seeing this great figure return to his bench in the Supreme Council of the Indies, recommended me to resume my claims with reference to my father's service and the restoration of my mother's inheritance. They said that since Licentiate Castro had seen Peru and knew what my father had helped to win and my mother's ancestors had possessed, he would be an excellent sponsor through whom I might obtain rewards, even though before he had insisted that I should be denied them, as I have said. But I had already buried my pretensions and said farewell to my hopes, and it seemed to me safer and more honorable not to come out of my corner, where with divine favor I have spent my time in writing the foregoing, though it may be of no great honor or profit to me. May God be praised for everything.

CHAPTER XVI

The appointment of Don Francisco de Toledo as
viceroy of Peru; the causes of his persecution
of Prince Inca Túpac Amaru, and the
arrest of this poor prince.

LICENTIATE Lope García de Castro, president and governor general of the empire called Peru, was succeeded by Don Francisco de Toledo, the second son of the house of the count of Oropesa. He was appointed by reason of his great virtue and Christian devotion, for he was a gentleman who received the Blessed Sacrament weekly. He went to Peru with the name and title of viceroy, and was received in the city of Lima with the usual solemnities. He governed those kingdoms with mildness and restraint, and had no risings to put down or rebellions to punish.

Two years, more or less, after he assumed power, he decided to bring down from the mountains of Villcapampa Prince Túpac Amaru, the legitimate heir of the empire, the son of Manco Inca and brother of Don Diego Sairi Túpac, of whom we have spoken at length in this eighth book. The inheritance had fallen to him because his brother left no male descent, only a daughter of whom we shall speak presently. The viceroy desired to bring him down by persuasion and kindness (imitating the example of viceroy Don Andrés Hurtado de Mendoza), to add to his own reputation the fame of having performed a great and heroic deed in reducing a fugitive prince who had sought refuge in the mountains to the service of His Catholic Majesty. He therefore tried to follow the former viceroy in his approach, sending messengers to the prince with a request and warning that he was to come down and live among the Spaniards like one of them, since they were now all one: His Majesty would confer honors on him, as he had on his brother, to assist him to maintain his person and house.

But the viceroy's attempted negotiations bore no fruit whatever, for the prince did not respond. The viceroy lacked many of the Indian and Spanish advisers and intermediaries who had served his predecessor in this business, and the Indian prince had difficulty in accepting any kind of arrangement, for his kinsmen and subjects, having learned by experience how little honor his brother had gained by leaving his fastnesses and remembering how short his life had been among the Spaniards, were still as full of grief and resentment as if the Spaniards had caused his death. They therefore advised the Inca not to leave his exile under any circumstances, for it was better to die there than to live among enemies. The viceroy learnt of this decision of the prince from Indians who came and went among the mountains, some being his envoys and others domesticated Indians living with the Spaniards, who spoke to their own masters freely and clearly, and so the news reached the viceroy's ears.

The latter sought the advice of his closest collaborators, who recommended him to bring the prince out by force, since he refused to come down peaceably, and to make war on him until he was arrested and killed. This, they said, would be a great service to His Catholic Majesty and a great benefit to the whole country, for the Inca's fastness was near the royal road from Cuzco to Huamanga and Lima, and his Indian vassals came out and assaulted and robbed Spanish merchants travelling along the road, and committed other acts of aggression, like deadly enemies of the Spaniards. They added that the viceroy should secure the empire against risings which the young prince might provoke whenever he wished, using the help and favor of his relatives the Incas who lived among the Spaniards and the caciques, their subjects, and the mestizos, the children of Spanish fathers and Indian mothers—all of whom, both subjects and kinsfolk, would welcome the opportunity, some to see the Inca restored and the others, the mestizos, in the hope of profiting from the spoils they could seize in the rebellion, for all these people complained of their poverty and lack of the bare necessities for human subsistence.

They also told him that by arresting the Inca he would lay hands on the whole treasure of the Inca kings, which was publicly rumored and reported to have been hidden by the Indians. This treasure was said to include the gold chain made by Huaina Cápac for the solemnities and celebrations to be held when his eldest son Huáscar Inca was named, as we have described. It was said that this piece and the rest of the treasure belonged to His Catholic Majesty, for the empire was his and so was all that belonged to the Incas, since the Spaniards had won it by their arms and might. Many other arguments were brought forward to persuade the viceroy to capture the prince.

With regard to the accusations brought against the prince, it is true that many years before, while his father Manco Inca was alive, there were cases of highway robbery for which his vassals were responsible; but the victims were not Spanish merchants, whose goods they did not need, but such Indians or Spaniards as passed by with Peruvian sheep for sale or barter. The fact that their Inca had no meat to eat drove them out of sheer necessity to steal it, for in those wild forests there are no tame animals, but only tigers, lions, and serpents twenty-five or thirty feet long, as well as other noxious creatures. As we said at length in our history, the whole of that region, like many others, produces nothing more useful to man. For this reason this prince's father ordered several raids to be made on the flocks of Peruvian sheep, saying that the whole empire and everything in it had been his and he intended to enjoy, as far as he could, whatever he required for food. But all this happened during the lifetime of that Inca; and I remember having heard as a child of three or four cases of assault and robbery committed by his subjects. Once the Inca died, these disturbances ceased.

The viceroy, however, was persuaded by the arguments of his advisers to make war on the Inca prince using all the means within his power to capture him. It seemed to him very wrong that the prince should continue on the frontier in enmity with the Spaniards and, as his advisers told him, disturbing the countryside, ravaging the highways, robbing the merchants, and producing general disquiet and insecurity throughout the kingdom, while spies reported that his presence spread unrest among the Indians who knew that he was near, but could not acknowledge or serve him as they would have liked. In this persuasion, the viceroy appointed as captain of the expedition a gentleman called Martín García Loyola, who had performed many great services for His Majesty on notable occasions in the past. He was instructed to raise a force under pretence of going off to succor the kingdom of Chile, where the Araucanians had reduced the Spanish settlers to sore straits. More than 250 men were collected for the expedition, and they soon departed for Villcapampa, with a good supply of offensive and defensive weapons. They were able to penetrate into those wild fastnesses, for since Prince Diego Sairi Túpac had left, the roads had been cleared and opened, and there was no opposition.

Prince Túpac Amaru learnt of the entry of the Spanish force, and be-

ing unable to resist, fell back more than twenty leagues down the valley
of a river. The Spaniards realized that he was in retreat and hastily made
great rafts on which to follow him. Since it was impossible for the prince
to defend himself for lack of men, and also because he felt himself completely blameless and had never even thought of rebellion or any other
criminal offence, he allowed himself to be taken. He preferred to trust
in the generosity of his pursuers than to perish in flight among the forests
and the great rivers that pour into the river called La Plata. He surrendered to Captain Martín García Loyola and his companions, thinking
that they would take pity on him on finding him destitute and give him
the wherewithal to live, as they had his brother Don Diego Sairi Túpac,
but not in the least suspecting that they might seek to kill him or do him
any other harm, since he had committed no crime. He therefore gave in
to the Spaniards. They collected all the Indians who were with him, men
and women, and the princess, his wife, and their two sons and daughter.
With these prisoners the Spanish captain and his men returned to Cuzco
in great triumph. The viceroy was waiting for them there, having gone to
receive them on hearing of the capture of the poor prince.

CHAPTER XVII

The trial of the prince and the Incas of the
royal blood, and of the mestizos, the
children of the conquerors of
the empire by Indian women.

As soon as the prince arrived under arrest, a prosecutor was appointed
to draw up accusations against him. These consisted of the headings
we have just mentioned: that he ordered his subjects and servants to come
down from the mountains to assault and rob travelling merchants, chiefly
Spaniards, all of whom he regarded as his enemies; that he had a pact and
treaty with his kinsfolk, the Incas, who dwelt among the Spaniards, and
planned with them to rebel on an agreed day and kill all the Spaniards
they could, in agreement with the caciques who had been lords of vassals
under his ancestors.

The mestizos, the sons of the conquerors of the empire by Indian

women, were also involved in the charges. They were accused of having
conspired with Prince Túpac Amaru and the other Incas to rise in revolt,
because some of the mestizos were related to the Incas through their
mothers, and they had entered the conspiracy by complaining to the Inca,
that, though they were the sons of the conquerors of the empire and of
Indian mothers, some of whom were of royal blood and many others of
noble families, being daughters, nieces, and grandchildren of *curacas*,
nevertheless they themselves benefited neither from the merits of their
fathers nor from the lawful and natural estates of their mothers and
grandparents; they were the sons of the worthiest gentlemen of the empire, so they said, yet the governors had seen to it that their own relatives
and friends received what their fathers had won and their mothers' people
had owned, leaving them destitute, reduced to begging for their bread or
forced to live by robbing on the highway and die by hanging. According
to the accusation, they had begged the prince to take pity on them, as they
too were natives of his empire, and to receive them into his service and
admit them as soldiers, in which capacity they would serve him loyally
and die if need be. All this was included in the charges against the mestizos. All those in Cuzco of twenty years of age or more and capable of
bearing arms were arrested. Some were condemned to torture, in the hope
of bringing out what the accusers confusedly feared.

In the midst of this fury of arrests, charges and condemnations, an Indian woman went to visit her son in prison, whom she knew to be among
those condemned to torment. She contrived to get to the cell where he
was, and shouted: "I know you have been condemned to torture. Suffer
and bear it like a man, and accuse no one, for God will help you and repay you for the struggle your father and his companions made to win this
land for Christianity and bring its natives into his Church. Shame on
them that all you who are sons of the conquerors should die in return for
your fathers having won them this empire!"

She said a great deal more to the same effect, screaming and shouting
like a raving lunatic, calling on God and man to hear the guilt and crimes
of those sons of Peru and of Peru's conquerors and declaring that if there
was any reason or justice in killing them (as there was said to be), then
let their mothers be killed too, for they deserved the same fate for giving
birth to them and rearing them and helping their fathers, the Spaniards,
to win the empire, against their own race. Pachacámac had permitted all
this because the Indian women were traitors to their Inca, their caciques,
and their lords, for love of the Spaniards. And as she condemned herself
in the name of all the rest, she begged and pleaded that the Spanish cap-

tain and his men would speedily carry out his will and do justice on her, and put her out of her misery, for God would repay him amply in this world and the next. With such and similar discourse and loud cries and screams, she left the prison, and fled through the streets shouting and causing a general uproar.

Her clamor assisted the cause of the mestizos greatly, for the viceroy perceived that she was right and desisted from his design, so as to cause no more disturbance. Thus none of the mestizos was condemned to die, though they were awarded a longer and more painful death by being exiled to various parts of the New World far from their fathers' conquests. Many were sent to the kingdom of Chile. These included a son of Pedro del Barco, of whom we have spoken at some length in our story, for he was my fellow pupil at school and a ward of my father, who was his guardian. Others were sent to the New Kingdom of Granada and various of the Windward Islands and Panama and Nicaragua; and some were sent to Spain, one of whom was Juan Arias Maldonado, a son of Diego de Maldonado the Rich. He remained in exile in Spain, for above ten years. I saw him and twice put him up in my house, in one of the towns in the bishopric of Córdova, where I then lived, and he told me a great deal of the foregoing, though I have not included all he said. After a long period in exile, he was granted a permit by the Supreme Royal Council of the Indies to go back to Peru for three years to recover his property and then return to spend the rest of his life in Spain. On his departure, he passed the place where I was with his wife whom he had married in Madrid, and asked me to assist him with some furniture and utensils for his house, for he was returning to Peru in great need and poverty. I gave him all the linen I had and taffeta sheets I had had made in military fashion, like infantry flags in many colors. A year earlier I had sent to him in Madrid a fine horse he had asked me for. All this would be worth five hundred ducats, and he told me: "Trust in me, brother, for as soon as I reach our native land, I will send you two thousand pesos for the horse and the present you have given me." I think he would have done so, but my fortune prevented it, for on his arrival at Paita, which is where Peru begins, he died within three days of pure joy and pleasure at being back in his own country. I hope I may be forgiven for this digression, which I have taken the liberty of including as it refers to a fellow pupil of mine. All those who were thus banished died in exile, and none of them returned to his native land.

CHAPTER XVIII

The exile of the Indians of the royal blood and
the mestizos; their deaths and end; the sentence
pronounced on the prince, his reply, and
how he receives holy baptism.

T HE INDIANS of the royal blood, thirty-six in number, and including
the most famous worthies and closest relatives of the former rulers
of Peru, were exiled to the city of Lima, being ordered not to leave it
without permission from the Spanish authorities. They were accompanied
by two little boys, the sons of the captive prince, and his daughter, none
of whom was more than ten years old. When the Incas reached Rímac,
otherwise the city of Los Reyes, the archbishop, Don Jerónimo de Loaisa,
took pity on them and received the little girl into his household. The other
exiles were so sick at leaving their own towns, their homes, and their
native haunts, that within just over two years thirty-five of them had
died, including the two little boys. Apart from grief, their end was hastened by the climate of the city, which is in the hot coastal zone called
the llanos, a very different climate from what is called the sierra. The
natives of the sierra, as we explained in the First Part of this history, fall
sick very easily if they come down to the llanos, just as if they were
brought to a plague spot. And so the poor Incas soon met their end.

The three that were left, who included my fellow pupil Don Carlos,
the son of Don Cristóbal Paullu, whom we have repeatedly mentioned,
were sent back to their homes by order of the royal *audiencia,* which took
pity on them, but they were so undermined by their misfortunes that they
all died within a year and a half. The royal line of the empire did not
however fail, for there was still a son of this Don Carlos, of whom we
have spoken in the last chapter of the First Part of the *Commentaries.*
He came to Spain to receive the great rewards he had been promised in
Peru, and died at Alcalá de Henares in 1610 of depression at being confined in a convent after having had a quarrel with another member of the
order of Santiago. He died quite suddenly of melancholy because after
having been kept eight months in a different convent for the same reason

he was now confined again. He left a son, a boy of three or four months, who was legitimized so that he might inherit the grant that His Majesty had assigned to him from the Contratación in Seville. But he died before the end of that year, and on his death the whole of his income was lost: thus the prophecies of the great Huaina Cápac about the royal family and the empire were fulfilled.

In the kingdom of Mexico, where the kings were so mighty in the days of their heathendom (as López de Gómara writes in his *General History of the Indies*), there was no problem about the succession, since the kingdom was not inherited from father to son, but was transmitted by the election of the subjects. When the ruler died, the leading subjects chose whoever seemed most worthy and able to be king. Consequently there has been no pretender and no disturbance arising from this cause to put down since the Spanish conquest. Once the king was dead, there was no one to aspire to the succession except by the grace and election of the electors. But in my native land such scandals have occurred, though they have been due to suspicion of the intentions of the legitimate heirs rather than to blameworthy intentions on their part.

This was the case with the poor prince we have now before us. He was sentenced to death, and beheaded with a proclamation denouncing his rebellion and the treachery he was supposed to have planned with his followers, Indians or mestizos, for the rebellion of the empire against the crown of His Catholic Majesty King Philip II, king of Spain and emperor of the New World. The sentence was announced to him very briefly: he was merely told that instructions had been given for him to be beheaded, without being told why. The poor Inca replied that he had committed no crime that deserved death, and that the viceroy should be content to send him under arrest and well guarded to Spain, where he would be glad to kiss the hand of his lord King Philip; this would assure the viceroy and his advisers that any fears or suspicions they might have had that he meant to start a rebellion were completely foreign to his intentions. The folly of such a purpose was demonstrated by the impossibility of success, for if his father had failed with 200,000 warriors when he had 200 Spaniards surrounded in the city, it was inconceivable that he could think of starting a rebellion when there were now so many more inhabitants in every Christian settlement, apart from the Spaniards scattered up and down the empire. If he had ever contemplated any offence against the Spaniards, he would not have allowed himself to be arrested, but have fled a great distance where he could not be found. But being guiltless and innocent, he had waited for the arrival of his captors, and readily accompanied them, supposing that they were summoning him from his fastnesses to offer him some favor, as they had to his brother Don Diego Sairi Túpac. He appealed to his lord, the king of Castile, and to Pachacámac, since the viceroy was not content to enjoy his empire and rule over it, but now wished even to take his life though he was quite guiltless. He added that he would die gladly and with good cheer, since death was offered him in place of the return of his empire. He said many other pitiful things, and Indians and Spaniards wept bitterly to hear such pathetic words.

The religious of the city of Cuzco came to teach him Christian doctrine and persuade him to be baptized, following the example of his brother Don Diego Sairi Túpac and his uncle Atahuallpa. The prince said that he would be glad to be baptized in order to enjoy the Christian religion, which his grandfather Huaina Cápac had said was better than their own. He wished therefore to become a Christian and to assume the name of Don Felipe, so as to enjoy the name of his Inca and King Philip, since the viceroy would not let him enjoy the sight of him by sending him to Spain. He was thereupon baptized, with as much weeping and grief from those present as there had been joy and merrymaking when his brother Don Diego Sairi Túpac was baptized, as we have said.

The Spaniards who were in the imperial city, both religious and secular, though they had heard the sentence and seen the events we have described, and much more that we omit for the sake of brevity, never thought that the sentence would be carried out, for it seemed contrary to humanity and clemency so to treat a prince bereft of so vast an empire, and it was thought that it would not please King Philip, but on the contrary distress and anger him that the prince had not been allowed to go to Spain. But the viceroy thought otherwise, as we shall see.

CHAPTER XIX

*The execution of the sentence against the prince;
the consultations to prevent it; the viceroy
refuses to heed them; the courageous
death of the Inca.*

HAVING determined to carry through the sentence, the viceroy had a scaffold erected with due solemnity in the main square of the city, and ordered the prince to be executed, as befitting the security and peace of the empire. The news astonished the whole city, and the senior gentlemen and religious discussed the possibility of an assembly to request the viceroy not to commit such a merciless deed, which would be abominated by everyone wherever it was told, and which would anger the king himself. Let him be satisfied to send the prince to Spain in perpetual exile, a longer and more painful torment than death. The inhabitants discussed all this and much more, and resolved to urge the viceroy very strongly and even petition him and protest against the execution of the sentence. But as he had spies posted in the city to inform him how the inhabitants received the sentence and what was the general reaction to it, he learnt about the meeting that was to petition him and ordered the doors of his house to be shut, placing a guard at the gate to prevent anyone from being allowed to enter under pain of death. He also ordered the Inca to be taken out and executed forthwith, so that the disturbance would settle down, for he was afraid that the people might rescue him.

The poor prince was led out on a mule with a rope round his neck and his hands tied together. He was preceded by a crier who announced his death and the reasons for it: he was a rebel and a traitor to the crown of His Catholic Majesty. The prince heard the crier, but not understanding Spanish, asked the religious who accompanied him what the man was saying. They explained that he was being killed because he was an *auca* against his lord, the king. Then he asked them to call the man, and when he approached, said to him: "Don't say what you are saying, for you know it is a lie. I have done no treason and thought no treason, as all the world knows. Say that I am being killed because the viceroy wants to have me killed, and not because of my crimes, for I have committed none against him or against the king of Castile. I call on Pachacámac: he knows that what I say is true." Whereupon the executioners went on.

At the entrance to the square a large band of women of all ages, some of the royal blood, together with the wives and daughters of the caciques of the neighborhood, came out and cried aloud with much weeping and wailing, in which the Spaniards, both religious and secular, joined: "Inca, why are they taking you to execution? What crimes, what treachery have you committed to deserve such a death? Beg your slayer to kill us all, for we are yours by blood and kin, and we shall be happier to go with you than to remain behind as the serfs and slaves of your murderers."

Then it was feared that some disturbance would break out in the city, so great was the hubbub and shouting and crying of those who were watching the execution of a sentence they had never thought possible. More than 300,000 souls were in the two squares and the streets and at the windows and on the roofs to see it. The executioners hastened to the scaffold. The prince mounted, the religious accompanying him, and behind them the executioner, with his scimitar in his hand. When the Indians saw their Inca so near death another great murmur, and a wave of shouting and crying arose from grief and pain, so loud that not a word could be heard.

The priests who were addressing the prince asked him to bid the Indians be silent. The Inca raised his right arm with his hand open, then brought it to his ear, and dropped it gradually to his right thigh. From this the Indians understood that they were being told to be silent, and the shouting and crying ceased, and they became so quiet that it seemed as if there was not a living soul in the whole city, to the great astonishment of the Spaniards, and even of the viceroy, who was watching the execution from a window. They observed with some alarm how implicitly the Indians obeyed their prince, a fact that was demonstrated publicly by this incident. The Inca was then beheaded. He suffered the supreme penalty with the courage and greatness of soul that the Incas and all the Indian nobility usually display in the face of any cruelty or inhumanity practiced on them, as will have been seen from episodes in our history of Florida and the present work, not to mention those which have occurred and still do in the wars in Chile between the Araucanians and the Spaniards, which the writers of those events have described in verse, or the many cruel deeds done in Mexico and Peru by Spaniards of high rank, some of whom were known to me, though I desist from setting them down, lest our history become tinged with hatred.

The courage with which the poor prince—yet rather rich and happy, since he died a Christian—met his end caused great sorrow among the religious who assisted at his execution. They were Franciscans, Mercedarians, Dominicans, and Augustinians as well as many priests, all of whom wept tenderly from pity that so great a prince should come to such an end, and said many masses for his soul. They took comfort from the magnanimity he displayed in his ordeal, and recounted his patience and his Christian actions in adoring the images of our Lord Christ and the Virgin His Mother that the priests carried before him. So ended the Inca, the legitimate heir to the empire by the direct male line from the first Inca Manco Cápac to himself. The line continued, as Padre Blas Valera says, for more than five and nearly six hundred years. There was general sorrow throughout the land, and the tale aroused compassion and pity among Indians and Spaniards alike. It may be that the viceroy had other reasons to justify the deed.

When the good prince had been executed, his sons and relatives were banished to the city of Lima, and the mestizos to various parts of the New and Old Worlds, as we have said, anticipating this part of our story so as to leave till last the saddest event in the whole history of our country, which is indeed a tragedy, as the end of the book of this Second Part of our *Commentaries* proves. May God be praised for all.

CHAPTER XX

The coming of Don Francisco de Toledo to Spain;
he is rebuked by His Catholic Majesty; his
end and death; the death of Governor
Martín García Loyola.

SO THAT the death of the Inca Don Felipe Túpac Amaru shall not go alone and unaccompanied, we may properly give a brief account of the end of the viceroy, Don Francisco de Toledo. At the end of his viceroyalty, which was a lengthy one, extending, it is said, to more than sixteen years, he returned to Spain with great prosperity and wealth, it being publicly reported that he had more than 500,000 pesos of gold and silver. With this wealth and his reputation for it he entered the capital expecting to become one of the great ministers of Spain, on account of the great services he fancied he had rendered His Catholic Majesty by extirpating and extinguishing the royal succession of the Inca kings of Peru, so that no one could any longer claim or suppose that the inheritance and succession of the empire belonged to the Incas and so that the crown of Spain might possess and enjoy it without the shadow of a fear that any pretender should arise to claim it. He also imagined that he would be rewarded for the numerous laws and ordinances he had established in Peru, some designed to increase the royal estates by benefiting the silver mines and the quicksilver mine—where by his orders so many Indians from all the provinces of Peru took turns to labor in return for their daily pay—others calculated to serve and assist the Spanish residents in Peru, imposing obligations on the Indians to pay the value of the articles they were supposed to produce for the Spaniards. But as these are lengthy and complicated matters, we shall not go into them.

Supposing himself to have acquired these considerable merits, the viceroy presented himself to kiss King Philip's hand. His Catholic Majesty, who had a full and detailed report of everything that had happened in Peru and particularly of the death of Túpac Amaru and the exile of his nearest relatives, whereafter they all perished, did not receive the viceroy with the approval the latter expected, but in a completely different manner. He briefly ordered the viceroy to return to his house, remarking that he had not been sent to Peru to kill kings, but to serve them. He thereupon left the royal presence and went to his dwelling, very disconsolate at this unexpected display of royal displeasure. This was redoubled when some of the viceroy's rivals informed the Council of the Royal Treasury that his servants and officials had received their salary in pesos instead of ducats, taking 40,000 pesos instead of 40,000 ducats, and as the viceroy had been so long governing the empire more than 120,000 ducats had been paid out, to the detriment of the royal treasury; for which reason the council ordered all the gold and silver Don Francisco de Toledo had brought from Peru to be apprehended until such time as the sum belonging to the royal treasury had been ascertained and proven. Don Francisco de Toledo, conscious that this second motive for the king's displeasure was no less important than the first, fell into great sorrow and melancholy, and died within a few days.

It remains to tell how Captain Martín García Loyola met his end, which occurred in the following manner. As a reward for having captured the Inca and for many other services he had rendered the Spanish crown, he had received in marriage an Inca princess, the niece of the prince and daughter of his brother Sairi Túpac, with the right to enjoy the allocation of Indians this lady had inherited from her father the Inca. To his own greater honor and content and to His Majesty's service, he was appointed governor and captain general of the kingdom of Chile. He departed for that kingdom attended by a goodly company of Spanish gentlemen and soldiers, and governed it for several months or years with great prudence and discretion and to the satisfaction of his companions, though the period was one of great toil and difficulty for all of them owing to the continuous state of warfare sustained by hostile Indians. This state of affairs still continues in the present year of 1613, and has existed since the rebellion of 1553. During this long period, the Indians have never laid down their arms, as we have observed elsewhere.

While Governor Loyola was serving in these campaigns, it happened one day that he went to visit the Spanish fortified towns on the Indian frontier (as indeed he had often done before). These forts served to contain the enemy and prevent them from raiding the tame Indians in Spanish service. After Loyola had supplied them all with arms, munitions, and supplies, he returned to govern the pacified part of the kingdom, and when it seemed to him that he was out of reach of the enemy, he dismissed two hundred soldiers who formed his guard and sent them back to their strongholds and forts, himself remaining with thirty companions, including several senior captains and experienced soldiers who had seen many years of service. They camped in a splendid plain, where they put up their tents to rest and pass a few nights peacefully recuperating after the sleepless time they had passed on the frontier and in the fortified posts, where the Indian warriors carefully saw to it that they had not an hour's rest to eat or sleep.

The Araucanian Indians and the rebels of the neighboring provinces (who had been subjects of the Incas) came out as spies under cover of night to see what the Spaniards were doing and whether they slept with sentries or without. Finding them as careless and forgetful as an enemy could possibly wish, they made signs, calling to one another with the squawking of birds and barking of nocturnal animals, so as not to reveal their presence. These cries are continually used by them as signs and countersigns for any purpose on similar occasions. Hearing them, a great band of Indians collected at a given point and they entered the camp with all possible stealth, and finding the Spaniards asleep and naked in their shirts, slaughtered them all. The Indians victoriously carried off their horses and arms and other spoils from them.

Such was the end of Governor Martín García Loyola. It caused great regret in the kingdom of Chile and was much commented on by Indians and Spaniards throughout Peru. It was said that fortune had governed his affairs so that the vassals of the prince he captured should slay him in revenge for the death of the Inca; for although they had such savage enemies at their backs and so near at hand, he and his men were caught sleeping and let themselves be killed without making the slightest resistance, though they were practiced and experienced veterans in Chile, both captains and men.

Governor Martín García Loyola left a daughter by his wife, the princess, the daughter of Prince Don Diego Sairi Túpac. This daughter was brought to Spain and married to an eminent gentleman called Don Juan Enrique de Borja. His Catholic Majesty, as I hear in letters from the capital, has conferred on her, in addition to the allocation of Indians which the princess inherited from her father, the title of marquesa de Oropesa, a town founded in Peru by Viceroy Don Francisco de Toledo and called Oropesa to commemorate in Peru the house and estate of his parents and ancestors. In addition to this grant and title, I am told that the illustrious presidents of the Royal Council of Castile and of the Indies, His Majesty's confessor, and two other judges of the Council of the Indies, are considering the question of bestowing other great favors on her in recognition of the many notable services her father the governor rendered His Majesty, and in restitution of her patrimonial inheritance. I am informed that the First Part of our *Commentaries* has been of no little assistance in this, by reason of the account there given of the Inca kings. This news gratifies and rewards me for the labor and care I have taken in the writing of the work, which I undertook, as I have said elsewhere, without any hope of reward.

CHAPTER XXI

End of the Eighth Book, the last of this history.

HAVING begun this history with the commencement and origin of the Inca kings in Peru, and having noticed at length their conquests and generous deeds, their lives, their government in peace and war, and the idolatrous religion they had in heathen times—all of which were performed at length in the first part of these *Commentaries,* with divine aid—we fulfilled the obligation we felt toward our mother country and our maternal stock. In the Second Part, as we have seen, a long account was given of the deeds and heroic actions that the brave and valiant Spaniards performed in conquering that wealthy empire, wherein we have fulfilled, even though not completely, our paternal obligations, which we owe to our father and his illustrious and generous companions. It now seems to me proper to conclude this work, as I now do, at the end of the succession of the Inca kings, who numbered thirteen from their first possession of the empire until the arrival of the Spaniards, until the unfortunate Huáscar Inca. Five others succeeded later, Manco Inca and his two sons, Don Diego and Don Felipe, and his two grandchildren, who never possessed any part of the kingdom except the right to it. There were thus in all eighteen successors in the direct male line from the first Inca Manco Cápac to the last of these children, whose name I do not know. The Inca Atahuallpa is not included by the Indians as one of their kings, for they describe him as *auca.*

With regard to the descendants of these kings not in the direct line, in the last chapter of the First Part of these *Commentaries* we mentioned how many descendants there were of each of the past kings. As I stated there, they themselves sent me a document in the name of all of them with power of attorney in favor of Don Melchor Carlos, Don Alonso de Mesa, and myself, so that any of the three of us could present it on their behalf of His Catholic Majesty and the Supreme Royal Council of the Indies. This document requested that, as descendants of kings, they should be relieved of the vexations they suffered. I sent the petition and the accompanying papers (which were addressed to me) to the capital directed to the said Don Melchor Carlos and Don Alonso de Mesa, but the former, though his own claims were of the same nature and based on the same legal and natural arguments as those of the Incas, was unwilling to present the papers so as not to reveal how many persons there were of the royal blood, thinking that if he did reveal this, he would lose many of the grants and honors he claimed and hoped to receive. He was therefore reluctant to raise his voice on his kinsmen's behalf; and he died, as has been said, without receiving anything for himself or his friends. I have mentioned this in order to clear myself and so that my relatives, wherever they may be, shall know what happened and not accuse me of neglect or ill will in not having done what they bade and requested me. I would indeed have been glad to have devoted my life to the service of people who so greatly deserved it, but I have not been able to do more, as I have been engaged in writing this history, which I hope will have been as great a service to the Spaniards who won the empire as to the Incas who formerly possessed it.

The Divine Majesty, Father, Son, and Holy Ghost, three persons and one single true God, be praised *per omnia saecula saeculorum,* who has granted me the great mercy of allowing me to reach this place. May it be to the glory and honor of His holy name, whose divine mercy, through the blood of our Lord Jesus Christ and the intercession of the ever Virgin Mary, His mother, and of all His heavenly host, be my favor and protection, now and at the hour of my death, amen, Jesus, a hundred thousand times Jesus.

Laus Deo

INDEX

Abáncay River. SEE Amáncay River
Acahuana Inca (mason): 468, 470
Acahuanu Puncu (gate of a fortress): 468
Accha (bridge): 155, 1170, 1171, 1175
accounting (*quipu*): operation of, 124–
125, 258; verse kept by, 127; secular
nature of, 187; taught, 227; of economic
assets, 260, 269–270, 274–275, 326, 330;
in legal system, 262, 265–266; of population, 267, 330; as form of writing, 329–
333; comments on, 397, 823–824; conversations in, 676, 682, 687, 689, 746;
traditions preserved in, 764–765
Acevedo, Arias de: 1045, 1258
Acevedo, Diego de: 1464, 1469
Achanquillo: 595–596
Acllahuaci. SEE Sun, virgins of
Acos, province of: 295
Acosta, José de (Fray): on Columbus, 14;
on name *Peru*, 17–18, 19, 20; on Inca
origin, 93; on landholding, 249–250; on
tributes, 252; on clothing, 257–258; on
Viracocha, 280–282, 304–305; on Cuzco,
464–465, 467; on animals, 514, 516, 517,
518, 519–520; on treasure, 531–532;
536, 539; on cosmetics, 537; on Huaina
Cápac, 543, 565; on giants, 562; on
crops, 603; on Huáscar Inca and Atahuallpa, 724; on *quipu* accounting, 765;
on Potosí, 777; on miscellaneous topics,
116, 129–130, 180, 307–308, 405, 444,
507, 533, 583, 611, 807–808, 847
Acosta, Juan de: in Gonzalo's rebellion,
1029–1030, 1031, 1051, 1077, 1106–
1118 *passim*, 1126–1145 *passim*, 1163,
1176–1187 *passim*; surrender of, 1193;
death of, 1201, 1202
Acuña, Brianda de: 1000
agriculture: pre-Inca lack of, 92; land for,
113, 241–242; as theme for plays, 126
—, crops from: maize, 32, 37, 117, 241–
250 *passim*, 297, 350, 401, 402, 412,
498, 500, 526; of Sun, 75, 248, 249, 250;
worshipped, 83; enumerated, 100; destruction of, 102, 341, 352; storage of,
248–256 *passim*; of Inca, 224, 248, 249,
250; *oca*, 242; *añus*, 242; *quinua*, 242,
250, 401, 402, 499–500; potatoes (*papa*)
242, 246, 250, 401, 480, 500–501;
pimiento (*uchu*) 248, 401, 402; hemp
(*maguey*), 251; cotton, 251, 270; division of, 271–272; collection of, 276;

sugar, 303; poor quality of, 362; beans,
500, 603; calabashes, 501; peanuts, 501;
cuchuchu, 501; sacrificed, 510; coca, 510;
grapes, 595–596, 597, 598; wheat, 596,
602; barley, 596; olives, 596, 598–599;
figs, 598; pomegranates, 598; melons,
598; oranges, 598; limes, 598; *pallares*,
603
—, irrigation for: from mountain rivers,
32; Manco Cápac institutes, 45, 53; on
coast, 162, 247; by Cápac Yupanqui,
176; in Cuzco, 186–187, 811–812; by
Yáhuar Huácac, 230; for maize, 241–
242; water shared for, 248; labor for,
260, 276; in Chinchasuyu and Cuntisuyu,
296–297; in Tucma, 299; in Cajamarca,
346; destroyed, 352; in Ica Valley, 350;
in Chimu, 390; and colonization, 391,
401–402; Inca Yupanqui extends, 430; in
Huacrachucu, 477; in Chachapoyas, 481;
in Huancapampa, 482; by Túpac Yupanqui, 483, 489; in Quito, 493, 547; between Pacasmayu and Túmbez, 546
—, techniques of: Incas teach, 45, 53, 67,
105, 108, 139, 477, 482, 489, 490, 496;
by Spanish, 151; terracing, 191, 241–242,
462, 477, 489; order of tilling in, 243–
244; known to all Incas, 258; communal
nature of, 262–263, 395; for growing
coca, 510; grafting, 600–601
Agüero, Diego de: 816, 818, 906, 908,
962–963
Aguilar, house of: 1154
Aguirre, ———: 1274–1278
Aguirre, ——— (soldier): 1014–1015
Aguirre, Francisco de: 1002, 1112
Aguirre, Juan de: 979
Aguirre, Lope de: 1468
Ailli Panaca (descendents of Yáhuar Hu-
ácac): 626
Aimara, province of: 155, 157, 277
Alarcón, ——— (Captain): 1057, 1058
Alarcón, Alonso de: 743
Alarcón, Martín de: 1018, 1131, 1357, 1369
Alcalá de Henares, Spain: 1477
Alcantará, ——— de: 897
Alcaudete, count of: 1154
Alcobaça, Diego de: 138–139, 261, 460,
683, 982
Alcobaça, Juan de: 261, 982, 983
Alcocer, Gaspar de: 600
Aldana, Lorenzo de: greets Vaca de Castro,

Delgado, Francisco: 424
De libertate Indorum Servanda: 681
Demarcation of Peru: 71, 138, 188, 490, 585
Desaguadero, the (river): 137–138, 139, 143, 168, 1340
Devil, the: Serrano mistaken for, 29; pagan gods as forms of, 33, 91, 680; private dealings with, 39; and pre-Inca Indians, 40, 90; Pachacámac as, 71; uses oracles, 76, 88, 335, 384, 414, 709, 1440; and misionary efforts, 288; vision attributed to, 289; sacrifices to, 317, 509, 951; causes strife, 746–747, 765–766, 789, 933–934, 936, 966, 972, 1169, 1246–1247, 1271, 1335, 1415; and Alvarado, 1376; and Hernández Girón, 1384; mentioned, 81, 291
Dias, João: 743
Díaz, Alonso: 423, 1317, 1323, 1338, 1402, 1425, 1428
Díaz, García: 1007
Díaz, Gonzalo: 985–986, 1019, 1024
Díaz, Ruy: 783, 788, 789–790, 850, 854
Díaz de Arias, Garci
Díaz de los Cameros, Ruy: 638
Díaz de Piñera, Gonzalo: 979, 1023
Diente, Juan: 929
diseases: of Moon, 118, 119; of animals, 122, 513–514, 585, 1153
—, remedies for: bleeding as, 34, 120, 121, 122, 413; plants used in, 114–115, 120–121, 122, 123, 499, 501–511 *passim*, 712, 804, 1373; supplied to craftsmen, 273–274; Pachacútec on, 397; llama meat as, 513; lard as, 514, 585; vicuña as, 517; honey in, 525; lack of, 810; Carvajal gives prisoners, 1148; tallow and llama dung as, 1151
—, of humans: of Inca kings, 87, 121; lawbreaking as cause of, 97; dental, 183; and occupations, 263, 262, 273, 394; convalescence from, 303; charity toward those with, 327; heat causes, 353; prayer to prevent, 414; hospitals for, 430, 431–432, 938, 957, 1169, 1458; coca as cure for, 511; of Huaina Cápac, 576–577; among Pizarro's men, 661–662, 663; mountains cause, 847; Verdugo feigns, 1047; diarrhea, 1360; cancer, 1411; of Garcilaso's father, 1447–1448, 1462
Dolmos, Martín: 427
Drake, Francis: 21, 589
Duarte, Sancho: 1340, 1358, 1360
Dulce, Doña, 638

education, European: Inca education compared to, 31; Pizarro's lack of, 715–716,

893; Almagro's lack of, 893; Gonzalo's lack of, 1074
—, Inca: compared to classical education, 31; schools for, 226–227, 392, 393, 425, 426; Valera on, 262; of military, 366–374, 375–376; in language, 393–394, 403, 404, 405, 406–407, 682–683
Elegies of Illustrious Men of the Indies: 1468
El Gallo, island of: 649, 651
emeralds: Balboa hears of, 20; worship of, 31, 554; adorn buildings, 184, 487; described, 530–531; sewn on clothing, 533; of Catámez, 649; Spaniards break, 661, 664; sent to Panama, 664; sent to Spaniards, 666, 761, 770, 795, 1079; of Carvajal, 1206; adorn Corpus Christi floats, 1415; mentioned, 878, 1442. SEE ALSO jewels
Enciso, Pedro: 1308, 1310
Enrique, ———— (ensign): 930
Enríquez, Alonso: 800, 843
Enríquez, Diego: 1271
Enríquez, Felipe: 1362
Enríquez, Juan, 1217, 1324–1325
Enríquez, María: 983
Enríquez de Orellana, Juan: 1403
Eopuco (a devil): 82
Eraso, Francisco de: 1094
Ercilla y Zúñiga, Alonso de: 64, 457
Ervias, Anselmo de: 1290, 1291–1292
Escalantes, the: 1320, 1326
Escandón, Alonso: 888
Escobar, Diego de: 1122
Escobar, Francisco de: 996
Escobar, Juan de: 983
Escobar, María de: 594
Escobedo, Baltasar de: 1296
Escobedo, Francisco de: 988, 991, 1126
Escobedo, Jerónimo de: 1126
Espinosa, Francisco de: 1136, 1156, 1223, 1234–1235
Espinosa, Gaspar de: 839, 840–841
Esquivel, ———— (licentiate): 1273–1277
Esquivel, Rodrigo de: 430, 583, 1327, 1428
Estacio, Gómez: 986–987, 1030, 1031
Estacio, Manuel: 1104
Estrada, Luis de: 1297
Estruac (a god): 82, 83
Extremadura, Spain: 582, 587, 622, 644, 60, 670, 756, 781, 828, 1012, 1218, 1276, 1406, 1449, 1450

families: cannibalism within, 36–37; incest within, 38–39; language defines, 39, 206; as theme for plays, 126; and punishment of crimes, 199, 201; as wealth, 273, 274; of Chancas, 301; youths' performance reflects on, 366; enslavement

789, 791, 1443; arrest of, 221, 613–623,
700–702, 711, 724, 753, 1444; death of,
287, 318, 591, 616, 622, 701–713 *passim*, 721, 725, 738, 748, 785; naming of,
316, 545, 546, 1472; birth of, 496, 543;
and Huaina Cápac, 567–568; talks with
Soto, 577–578, 700–701; sends ambassador to Pizarro, 665; partisans of, 669;
children of, 1444–1445; Inca line to,
1486; mentioned, 306, 393, 656
Huaura, valley of: 963, 967, 999, 1119
Huayallqui: 1104
Huelva, Spain: 12, 14
Huichu River: 146
hunting: by Spaniards, 27–28, 516, 517,
521, 902, 915, 1272, 1277–1278; by
Incas, 286, 320, 325, 327, 516–517, 518;
by mestizos, 619
Hurin Cuzco (person): 363
Hurin Cuzco (part of Cuzco): 44, 419
Hurin Pacha (the lower world): 84
Hurtado, ———: 1209
Hurtado de Mendoza, Andrés. SEE Cañete,
marqués de
Husando, Francisco: 844

Ica, valley of: 349, 350, 603
Ica River: 1349, 1350
Icona (a god): 82, 83
Idiáquez, Francisco de: 918
Illanes, Juan de: 1043, 1044, 1045, 1046,
1050, 1103, 1129, 1393
Illatopa (Indian): 984
Illescas, Gonzalo de: 969, 1253
Inca Maricanchi: 470
Inca Panaca: 626
Inca Roca: vists realm, 175; conquests by,
176–177, 178, 217–220, 223–225, 234;
succeeds to throne, 179; death of, 226;
Valera on, 226–227, 825; Inca civilization dated from, 261; schools founded by,
392, 393, 425, 426; on social structure,
497; descendents of, 626
Inca Yupanqui: builds Sun temple, 180;
conquests of, 339, 343, 344, 347, 349–
355, 376, 378, 383–384, 385–391, 434–
437, 442–443, 445–450, 546; Spanish
historians on, 392–393; house of, 424;
death of, 462–463; peacetime reign of,
462, 471, 484; travels to coast, 571;
descendants of, 626; mentioned, 862,
863, 1235
Infantado, dukes of: 1450
insects: beetle (*acatanca*), 80; butterflies,
188, 314, 315; lice, 252, 268, 487, 489,
494; flies, 303, 419; mosquitoes, 303,
419, 776, 1452; bees, 525
Inquisition, Council of the. SEE Council
of the Inquisition
Intipampa (a square in Cuzco): 424

Intip Raimi. SEE Raimi
Ipiales: 570
Isabel (beggar): 259
Isabel (servant): 727
Isabella, Queen: 641, 642–643, 961
Isásiga, Francisco de: 1294
Ischen (a goddess): 82

Jalisco: 773
Jara, Gaspar: 423, 869–872, 927, 981
Jauja. SEE Sausa
Jerez de Badajoz, Spain: 15, 1218
Jesuits. SEE Catholic Church
jewels: in legend, 48; adorn buildings, 73,
190, 202, 385; offerred to Sun, 117;
awarded actors, 126; given Inca rulers,
211, 253, 254; lapidaries for, 269; storage of, 275, 318–319, 622; given
Chancas, 295; buried with Inca kings,
322; Incas give conquered peoples, 354,
405; forbidden to commoners, 394;
Cuzco ward named for, 424–425; coca
preferred to, 509; abundance of, 536;
Columbus promises, 643; at Cajamarca,
692; given to Spaniards, 744, 745, 759;
Hernando Pizarro's gifts of, 864; in
Quixos, 880; Contreras' robbery of, 1258
——, particular: pearls, 17, 531–534, 937,
958, 959; diamonds, 184; rubies, 184,
533; turquoises, 184, 487, 530, 531, 649,
661, 666, 761, 770, 795; crystal, 530.
SEE ALSO emeralds
Jiménez, ———: 1150, 1202
Jiménez, ——— (captain): 925
Jiménez, Garci: 1074
Jofré, ——— (captain): 1169
Jofré, Marcos de: 681
John II, King: 639
John of Austria: 1154
Juana, Queen: 639
Juárez, Pedro: 1306

La Canela, province of: 873, 913–915
La Gomera, count of: 988, 1045, 1110,
1280
La Gorgona, island of: 17, 21, 651, 653–
654
Laguna, Paulo de: 647
La Imperial: 459, 460
landholding, Inca system of: 158–159, 205,
209, 242, 245–247, 249–250, 394–395,
396, 481
——, Spanish system of: 734, 1101
language: of Yucatán, 18; Latin, 19, 127–
128, 133, 261, 411, 497, 678, 1102,
1207; of miscellaneous tribes, 36, 39,
206; private Inca, 59, 103, 374, 403,
626; "compound," 69; Aymará, 132,
683; Hebrew, 411; Greek, 411; of monkeys, 520; of Chinchasuyu, 687; of